THE LOEB CLASSICAL LIBRARY

FOUNDED BY JAMES LOEB, LL.D.

JOSEPHUS

V

281

JOSEPHUS

WITH AN ENGLISH TRANSLATION BY

H. ST. J. THACKERAY, M.A.
HON. D.D. OXFORD, HON. D.D. DURHAM

AND

RALPH MARCUS, PH.D.
PROFESSOR OF SEMITIC PHILOLOGY, JEWISH INSTITUTE OF RELIGION
LECTURER IN SEMITIC LANGUAGES, COLUMBIA UNIVERSITY

IN NINE VOLUMES

V

JEWISH ANTIQUITIES, BOOKS V–VIII

CAMBRIDGE, MASSACHUSETTS
HARVARD UNIVERSITY PRESS
LONDON
WILLIAM HEINEMANN LTD
MCMLXXVII

American
ISBN 0-674-99310-1

British
ISBN 0 434 99281 x

First printed 1934
Reprinted 1935, 1950, 1958, 1966, 1977

Printed in Great Britain

CONTENTS OF VOLUME V

PREFACE

When Dr. Thackeray died early in the summer of 1930, he had sent to press the text and translation of *Antiquities* Book V. and a portion of Book VI. (to § 140, with explanatory notes extending to § 60). The present writer has slightly revised this part, and has supplied a text and annotated translation of the rest of Book VI. and of Books VII. and VIII. No one realizes more fully than the writer himself how difficult it is to come up to the standard of excellence set by Dr. Thackeray in his skilful translation of the works of Josephus included in the earlier volumes of this series. An attempt has been made to adhere to the spirit of his rendering, but some changes in style have been made, chiefly in the direction of a less formal and a more modern idiom. In undertaking to continue the edition the writer has greatly profited by being able to consult a roughly drafted translation of Books VI.–VIII., of which Dr. Thackeray's widow has been kind enough to make a fair copy, and by having before him several notebooks containing Dr. Thackeray's studies of Josephus's style, his use of Greek authors and other useful material, which Mrs. Thackeray has generously placed at his disposal. The writer has also had the great advantage of using the ms. of Dr. Thackeray's *Index Verborum*, on the basis of which he was preparing his Greek Lexicon to

Josephus, published under the auspices of the Kohut Foundation of the Jewish Institute of Religion. The first fascicle of this Lexicon appeared some time after Dr. Thackeray's death, and a second fascicle, completed by the writer, is expected to appear shortly.

Beside the earlier versions of the *Antiquities* made by Hudson, Weill and Whiston-Shilleto, two recent works have been consulted in preparing the latter part of this volume; these are *Agada und Exegese bei Flavius Josephus* by Salomo Rappaport, Vienna, 1930, and *Legends of the Jews* by Louis Ginzberg (six volumes), Philadelphia, 1909–1928 (abbr. Ginzberg in the footnotes); the latter is an invaluable collection of rabbinic material illustrating the amplification of scriptural narratives and furnishing many instructive parallels to Josephus's treatment of his biblical text. The writer has, in addition, independently examined the text of the Targum (the Aramaic translation of the Bible, used in the early synagogue) and the mediaeval Hebrew commentaries reprinted in the Rabbinic Bible. For the identification of many of the Biblical place-names the writer is indebted to the researches of Professor W. F. Albright and other scholars, whose results have appeared in the *Bulletin of the American Schools of Oriental Research*.

With regard to the Greek text, the writer, like Dr. Thackeray, has attempted to furnish a critical edition on the basis of the apparatus in Niese's *editio maior*, not (as some reviewers of the earlier volumes by Dr. Thackeray have described it) an edition based solely on Niese's text. Whether the text here given is as satisfactory as the excellent ones furnished by Niese and by Naber in the Teubner series must be left to the critics to decide. The problems of Josephus's text in these books are very complex, partly because of the twofold MS. tradition, partly because of the use made by the author of a Greek version of Scripture, and the corrections made by Christian copyists in the interest of conformity to the biblical text known to them, and partly because of the apparent revisions made by Josephus's Greek assistants. These difficulties are illustrated by the inconsistent spelling of biblical names of persons and places in the same MS. and the variants in the two families of MSS. No editor may reasonably hope to have established, in every case, the forms used by Josephus himself.

The writer has been similarly inconsistent in his rendering of these biblical names. The most commonly known names, such as Hebron, Absalom, etc., are given in the form familiar to English readers, whether or not they accurately reproduce the Greek spelling of Josephus's text; where the name is not quite so well known and where the Greek form differs only slightly from that found in the Authorized Version of Scripture, it is rendered approximately, *e.g.* Abisai (for Abisaios ; bibl. Abishai), Achab (for Achabos ; bibl. Ahab) ; in all other cases the hellenized form is simply transliterated, *e.g.* Jebosthos (bibl. Ish-bosheth), Adrazaros (bibl. Hadadezer).

For a discussion of Josephus's use of the Hebrew original of Scripture and of the Greek version known as the Septuagint (abbr. LXX in the footnotes), the reader may consult Dr. Thackeray's *Josephus, the Man and the Historian* (Stroock Lectures at the Jewish Institute of Religion), N.Y., 1929, Lecture IV. It will be seen from the discussion there and from the explanatory notes in this volume that Josephus's text often agrees with that group of LXX MSS. which represent the so-called Lucianic recension (abbr. Luc. in the footnotes), made at the end of the third century A.D. It is, therefore, evident that this recension is based on a text which existed as early as the time of Josephus. To Dr. Thackeray's comments on Josephus's agreement with the Targum in certain passages against the Hebrew and Greek texts of Scripture, and to the examples of such agreement adduced by Mez (*Die Bibel des Josephus*) and Rappaport, the present writer has added in the footnotes what he ventures to believe are new instances of Josephus's use of an Aramaic translation of Scripture practically identical with the traditional Targum of Jonathan, which has usually been supposed to date from a period almost a century later than Josephus.

R. M.

LIST OF JOSEPHUS' WORKS

SHOWING THEIR DIVISION INTO VOLUMES IN THIS EDITION

JEWISH ANTIQUITIES

ΙΟΥΔΑΪΚΗΣ ΑΡΧΑΙΟΛΟΓΙΑΣ

ΒΙΒΛΙΟΝ Ε

1 (i. 1) Μωυσέος δὲ τὸν προειρημένον τρόπον ἐξ
ἀνθρώπων ἀπογεγονότος Ἰησοῦς, ἁπάντων ἤδη
τῶν ἐπ᾽ αὐτῷ νενομισμένων τέλος ἐχόντων καὶ τοῦ
πένθους λελωφηκότος, παρήγγειλεν ἐπὶ στρατείαν
2 ἕτοιμον εἶναι τὸ πλῆθος, πέμπει τε κατασκόπους
εἰς Ἱεριχοῦντα τήν τε δύναμιν αὐτῶν καὶ τίνα
διάνοιαν ἔχουσιν αὐτοὶ γνωσομένους,[1] αὐτὸς δὲ
ἐξήταζε τὸν στρατὸν ὡς κατὰ καιρὸν διαβησόμενος
3 τὸν Ἰόρδανον. ἀνακαλεσάμενος δὲ τοὺς τῆς Ῥου-
βηλίδος φυλῆς ἄρχοντας καὶ τοὺς τῆς Γάδιδος καὶ
Μανασσήτιδος προεστῶτας, ἐξ ἡμισείας γὰρ καὶ
τῇδε τῇ φυλῇ τὴν Ἀμορίαν κατοικεῖν ἐπετέτραπτο
4 τῆς Χαναναίων γῆς ἕβδομον οὖσαν μέρος, ὑπεμί-
μνησκεν ἃ ὑπέσχοντο Μωυσεῖ, καὶ παρεκάλει
χαριζομένους τῇ τε ἐκείνου προνοίᾳ, μηδ᾽ ὅτε
ἀπέθνησκε περὶ αὐτοὺς καμούσῃ, τῷ τε κοινῇ
συμφέροντι παρέχειν αὐτοὺς εἰς τὰ παραγγελλόμενα
προθύμους. τῶν δ᾽ ἑπομένων ὁπλίταις πεντακισ-

[1] ex Lat.: γνωσόμενος codd.

JEWISH ANTIQUITIES

BOOK V

(i. 1) Moses having in the aforesaid manner been rapt away from men, Joshua, when all the customary rites had now been accomplished in his honour and the mourning had abated, directed the people to make ready for a campaign. He also sent scouts to Jericho to reconnoitre the strength and the disposition of the inhabitants, while he himself reviewed his army, intending at the first opportunity to cross the Jordan. Having, moreover, called up the princes of the tribe of Rubel [a] and the chiefs of the tribes of Gad and of Manasseh—for one half of this tribe too had been permitted to settle in the Amorite country, which forms a seventh part [b] of the land of Canaan —he reminded them of their promises to Moses and exhorted them, out of respect alike for that forethought of his on their behalf which even in his dying moments had never flagged, and for the common weal, to respond to his orders with alacrity. These duly following him, he with fifty thousand [c] men-

Joshua sends spies to Jericho and advances to the Jordan. Jos. i. 10; ii. 1.

i. 12, 13.

[a] Reuben.

[b] The Amorites were one of the "seven nations" that inhabited Canaan (Deut. vii. 1, Jos. iii. 10; *cf.* §§ 88 f. below). From this apparently, as M. Weill suggests, Josephus infers that they occupied a seventh part of the whole country.

[c] 40,000 according to Jos. iv. 13 (Heb. and LXX).

μυρίοις ἀπὸ τῆς Ἀβέλης[1] ἐπὶ τὸν Ἰόρδανον ἐξήει
σταδίους ἑξήκοντα.
5 (2) Καὶ στρατοπεδεύσαντος εὐθὺς οἱ κατάσκοποι
παρῆσαν μηδὲν ἀγνοήσαντες τῶν παρὰ τοῖς
Χαναναίοις· λαθόντες[2] γὰρ τὸ πρῶτον ἅπασαν ἐπ'
ἀδείας αὐτῶν τὴν πόλιν κατενόησαν, τῶν τε τειχῶν
ὅσα καρτερὰ καὶ ὅσα μὴ τοῦτον ἔχει[3] τὸν τρόπον
αὐτοῖς ἀσφαλῶς καὶ τῶν πυλίδων αἳ πρὸς εἴσοδον
6 τῷ στρατοπέδῳ δι' ἀσθένειαν συνέφερον. ἠμέλουν
δὲ θεωμένων οἱ ἐντυγχάνοντες καθ' ἱστορίαν ξένοις
προσήκουσαν ἀκριβῶς ἕκαστα πολυπραγμονεῖν τῶν
ἐν τῇ πόλει νομίζοντες, ἀλλ' οὐχὶ διανοίᾳ πολεμίων.
7 ὡς δὲ γενομένης ὀψίας ὑποχωροῦσιν εἴς τι καταγώγιον τοῦ τείχους πλησίον, εἰς ὃ καὶ προήχθησαν
8 δειπνοποιησόμενοι[4] καὶ περὶ ἀπαλλαγῆς αὐτοῖς τὸ
λοιπὸν ἡ φροντὶς ἦν, μηνύονται τῷ βασιλεῖ περὶ
δεῖπνον ὄντι κατασκεψόμενοί τινες τὴν πόλιν ἀπὸ
τοῦ τῶν Ἑβραίων στρατοπέδου παρεῖναι καὶ
ὄντες ἐν τῷ τῆς Ῥαάβης καταγωγίῳ μετὰ πολλῆς
τῆς τοῦ λανθάνειν προνοίας ὑπάρχειν. ὁ δ' εὐθὺς
πέμψας πρὸς αὐτοὺς[5] ἐκέλευσεν ἀγαγεῖν συλλαβόντας, ἵνα βασανίσας μάθῃ, τί καὶ βουλόμενοι
9 παρεῖεν. ὡς δ' ἔγνω τὴν ἔφοδον αὐτῶν ἡ Ῥαάβη,
λίνου γὰρ ἀγκαλίδας ἐπὶ τοῦ τέγους[6] ἔψυχε, τοὺς
μὲν κατασκόπους εἰς ταύτας ἀποκρύπτει, τοῖς
δὲ πεμφθεῖσιν ὑπὸ τοῦ βασιλέως ἔλεγεν, ὡς ξένοι

[1] RO: Ἀβίλης etc. rell.
[2] codd. Lat.: ἐλθόντες E edd. [3] ἔχοι SP.
[4] ex Lat.: -ποιησάμενοι codd.
[5] fort. αὐτὸν legendum. [6] E: τείχους codd.

[a] Or Abile (bibl. Abel-shittim): *A*. iv. 176 note.

at-arms set out from Abele [a] and advanced sixty stades towards the Jordan.

The spies and Rahab. Jos. ii. 1.

(2) Scarce had he pitched his camp when the scouts reappeared, in nothing ignorant of the condition of the Canaanites. For, undetected at the first, they had surveyed their entire city unmolested, noting where the ramparts were strong and where they offered a less secure protection to the inhabitants, and which of the gates through weakness would facilitate entrance for the army. Those who met them had disregarded their inspection, attributing to a curiosity natural to strangers this busy study of every detail in the city, and in no wise to any hostile intent. But when, at fall of even, they retired to an inn [b] hard by the ramparts, to which they had proceeded [c] for supper, and were now only thinking of departure, word was brought to the king as he supped that certain persons had come from the camp of the Hebrews to spy upon the city and were now in Rahab's inn, mightily anxious to escape detection. And he straightway sent men after them, with orders to arrest and bring them up, that he might discover by torture to what intent they were come. But when Rahab learnt of their approach, being then engaged in drying some bundles of flax upon the roof,[d] she concealed the spies therein, and told the king's messengers that some unknown

[b] The Bible speaks of Rahab the "harlot" (Heb. *zonah*, LXX πόρνη). Josephus follows the Palestinian interpretation found in the Targum on Jos. ii. 1, where the noun is translated *pundeḳita* = Gr. πανδοκεύτρια or πανδόκισσα, "inn-keeper." *Cf. A.* iii. 276 note.

[c] Or "been conducted" or "directed."

[d] Or, according to most MSS., "the wall." Jos. ii. 6 has "the roof" (LXX δῶμα).

τινὲς[1] ἀγνῶτες ὀλίγῳ πρότερον ἢ δῦναι τὸν ἥλιον
παρ' αὐτῇ δειπνήσαντες ἀπαλλαγεῖεν, οὓς εἰ
φοβεροὶ τῇ πόλει δοκοῦσιν, ἢ κίνδυνον τῷ βασιλεῖ
φέροντες ἧκον, ἀπόνως εἶναι λαβεῖν διωχθέντας.
10 οἱ δέ, τῆς γυναικὸς οὕτως αὐτοὺς ὑπελθούσης,
οὐδένα ὑπονοήσαντες δόλον ἀπῆλθον οὐδ' ἐρευνή-
σαντες τὸ καταγώγιον. ἐπεὶ δ' ὁρμήσαντες καθ'
ἃς ἐνόμιζον αὐτοὺς μάλιστα τῶν ὁδῶν ἀπέρχεσθαι
καὶ κατὰ τὰς εἰς τὸν ποταμὸν φερούσας οὐδενὶ
γνωρίσματι περιετύγχανον, παύονται τοῦ πονεῖν.
11 τοῦ δὲ θορύβου σταλέντος ἡ Ῥαάβη καταγαγοῦσα
τοὺς ἄνδρας καὶ τὸν κίνδυνον εἰποῦσα, ὃν ὑπὲρ τῆς
αὐτῶν ὑπέλθοι σωτηρίας, ἁλοῦσαν γὰρ ἀποκρύπ-
τουσαν αὐτοὺς οὐκ ἂν διαφυγεῖν τὴν ἐκ τοῦ βασιλέως
τιμωρίαν, ἀλλὰ πανοικὶ αὐτὴν ἀπολέσθαι κακῶς,
12 παρακαλέσασα διὰ μνήμης ἔχειν, ὅταν ἐγκρατεῖς
τῆς Χαναναίων γῆς καταστάντες ἀμοιβὴν ἐκτῖσαι
δύνωνται τῆς ἄρτι σωτηρίας, χωρεῖν ἐκέλευεν ἐπὶ
τὰ οἰκεῖα ὀμόσαντας ἦ μὴν σώσειν αὐτὴν καὶ τὰ
αὐτῆς, ὅταν τὴν πόλιν ἑλόντες φθείρωσι πάντας
τοὺς ἐν αὐτῇ κατὰ ψήφισμα τὸ παρ' αὐτοῖς γενό-
μενον· ταῦτα γὰρ εἰδέναι σημείοις τοῖς ἐκ τοῦ θεοῦ
13 διδαχθεῖσαν. οἱ δὲ καὶ περὶ[2] τῶν παρόντων αὐτῇ
χάριν ἔχειν ὡμολόγουν καὶ περὶ τῶν αὖθις ὤμνυον
ἔργῳ τὴν ἀμοιβὴν ἀποδώσειν· ἡνίκα δ' ἂν αἴσθηται
μελλούσης ἁλίσκεσθαι τῆς πόλεως, συνεβούλευον
κτῆσίν τε τὴν αὐτῆς καὶ τοὺς οἰκείους ἅπαντας εἰς
τὸ καταγώγιον ἀποθεμένην ἐγκαθεῖρξαι, πρὸ τῶν

[1] P[2] edd.: τινὲς εἶεν rell. codd. [2] om. M.

[a] Jos. ii. 9 f. speaks of Rahab's having heard that the Israelites' God will again aid them as in the past. Perhaps

strangers had shortly before sundown supped with her and gone their way; but, were it thought that the city had cause to fear them or were their coming fraught with peril to the king, they could be caught without difficulty if pursued. The messengers, thus cajoled by the woman and suspecting no guile, departed without even searching the inn; but when, after speeding along the roads by which they thought it most likely that the men had fled, including all those leading to the river, they found no trace of them, they ceased to trouble themselves further. The tumult having subsided, Rahab brought the men down and, having told them of the risk which she had run for their salvation—for, had she been caught concealing them, she would not have escaped the vengeance of the king but she and all her house would have perished miserably—she besought them to bear this in mind when, once masters of the land of the Canaanites, they should be in a position to recompense her for their present salvation; and she bade them depart to their own place, after swearing that they would verily save her and all that was hers when, on taking the city, they should destroy all its inhabitants, a had been decreed by their people, for of this (she said) she knew through certain signs [a] which God had given her. In reply they expressed their gratitude to her for present favours and swore to repay her in future by recompense in act; but they counselled her, when she should see that the city was on the point of being taken, to secure her chattels and all her household within the inn and to shut them in, and to extend

[a] σημεῖα here, as elsewhere in Josephus, means the "miracles" alluded to in the Scriptural passage.

θυρῶν ἀνατείνασαν φοινικίδας, ὅπως εἰδὼς τὴν οἰκίαν ὁ στρατηγὸς φυλάττηται κακῶς ποιεῖν·
14 "μηνύσομεν[1] γὰρ αὐτῷ," ἔφασαν, "διὰ τὸ σὸν σώζεσθαι πρόθυμον. εἰ δέ τις ἐν τῇ μάχῃ πέσοι τῶν σῶν, σύ τε οὐκ ἂν ἡμῖν ἐπενέγκοις αἰτίαν καὶ τὸν θεὸν ὃν ὀμωμόκαμεν παραιτούμεθα μηδὲν ὡς
15 ἐπὶ παραβαίνουσι τοὺς ὅρκους δυσχερᾶναι." καὶ οἱ μὲν ταῦτα συνθέμενοι ἐχώρουν διὰ τοῦ τείχους καθιμήσαντες ἑαυτούς, καὶ διασωθέντες πρὸς τοὺς οἰκείους ἐδήλωσαν ὅσα πράξαντες ἐπὶ τῆς πόλεως ἧκον· Ἰησοῦς δὲ τῷ ἀρχιερεῖ Ἐλεαζάρῳ καὶ τῇ γερουσίᾳ φράζει τὰ τοῖς σκοποῖς ὁμοθέντα πρὸς τὴν Ῥαάβην· οἱ δ' ἐπεκύρουν τὸν ὅρκον.

16 (3) Δεδιότος δὲ τοῦ στρατοῦ[2] τὴν διάβασιν, μέγας γὰρ ἦν ὁ ποταμὸς τῷ ῥεύματι καὶ οὔτε γεφύραις πορευτός, οὐ γὰρ ἔζευκτο τὸ[3] πρότερον, βουλομένους τε γεφυροῦν οὐχ ἕξειν σχολὴν παρὰ τῶν πολεμίων ὑπελάμβανον πορθμείων τε μὴ τυγχανόντων, διαβατὸν αὐτοῖς ὁ θεὸς ἐπαγγέλλεται ποιήσειν τὸν
17 ποταμὸν μειώσας αὐτοῦ τὸ πλῆθος. καὶ δύο ἐπισχὼν ἡμέρας Ἰησοῦς διεβίβαζε τὸν στρατὸν καὶ τὴν πληθὺν ἅπασαν τοιούτῳ τρόπῳ· προῄεσαν μὲν οἱ ἱερεῖς τὴν κιβωτὸν ἔχοντες, ἔπειτα οἱ Λευῖται τήν τε σκηνὴν καὶ τὰ πρὸς ὑπηρεσίαν ταῖς θυσίαις σκεύη κομίζοντες, εἵποντο δὲ τοῖς Λευίταις κατὰ φυλὰς ὁ πᾶς ὅμιλος μέσους ἔχων παῖδας καὶ γυναῖκας, δεδιὼς περὶ αὐτῶν μὴ βιασθεῖεν ὑπὸ τοῦ

[1] RO: μηνύσειν rell.
[2] SP: στρατηγοῦ rell.
[3] RO: πω rell.

[a] Jos. ii. 18, "Thou shalt bind this line of scarlet thread in the window which thou didst let us down by."

[b] Josephus, *more suo*, lessens the supernatural character

red flags before her doors,[a] in order that their general, recognizing the house, might refrain from doing it injury. "For," said they, "we shall report to him that it is to thy zeal that we owe our lives. But, should any of thy kinsmen fall in the battle, thou must not lay that to our charge, and we implore the God by whom we have sworn to be in no wise indignant at us, as though we had transgressed our oaths." So having made this compact, they departed, letting themselves down the wall by a rope and, when safely restored to their friends, they recounted their adventures in the city. Joshua thereupon reported to Eleazar the high priest and to the council of elders what the spies had sworn to Rahab; and they ratified the oath.

(3) Now since the army was afraid to cross the river, which had a strong current and could not be crossed by bridges—for it had not been spanned by any hitherto, and, should they wish to lay them now, the enemy would not, they imagined, afford them the leisure, and they had no ferry-boats—God promised to render the stream passable for them by diminishing its volume.[b] So Joshua, having waited two days,[c] proceeded to transport the army with the whole multitude in the following fashion. At the head went the priests bearing the ark, next the Levites carrying the tabernacle and the vessels for the ministry of the sacrifices, and, after the Levites, followed, tribe by tribe, the whole throng, with the children and women in the centre, for fear of their being swept away by the force of the current.

Crossing of the Jordan.

Jos. iii. 2.

of the miracle: the waters are not "wholly cut off" as in Joshua (iii. 13, 16).

[c] "After three days," Jos. iii. 2.

18 ῥεύματος. ὡς δὲ τοῖς ἱερεῦσι πρώτοις ἐμβᾶσι πορευτὸς ἔδοξεν ὁ ποταμός, τοῦ μὲν βάθους ἐπεσχημένου, τοῦ δὲ κάχληκος, τῷ μὴ πολὺν εἶναι μηδ' ὀξὺν τὸν ῥοῦν ὥσθ' ὑποφέρειν αὐτὸν τῇ βίᾳ, ἀντ' ἐδάφους κειμένου, πάντες ἤδη θαρσαλέως ἐπεραιοῦντο τὸν ποταμόν, οἷον αὐτὸν ὁ θεὸς
19 προεῖπε ποιήσειν τοιοῦτον κατανοοῦντες. ἔστησαν δὲ ἐν μέσῳ οἱ ἱερεῖς ἕως οὗ διαβαίη τὸ πλῆθος καὶ τἀσφαλοῦς ἁψάμενον τύχοι.[1] πάντων δὲ διαβάντων ἐξῄεσαν οἱ ἱερεῖς ἐλεύθερον ἀφέντες ἤδη τὸ ῥεῦμα χωρεῖν κατὰ τὴν συνήθειαν. καὶ ὁ μὲν ποταμὸς εὐθὺς ἐκβάντων αὐτὸν τῶν Ἑβραίων ηὔξετο καὶ τὸ ἴδιον ἀπελάμβανε μέγεθος.

20 (4) Οἱ δὲ πεντήκοντα προελθόντες στάδια βάλλονται στρατόπεδον ἀπὸ δέκα σταδίων τῆς Ἱεριχοῦντος, Ἰησοῦς δὲ τόν τε[2] βωμὸν ἐκ τῶν λίθων ὧν ἕκαστος ἀνείλετο τῶν φυλάρχων ἐκ τοῦ βυθοῦ τοῦ προφήτου κελεύσαντος ἱδρυσάμενος, τεκμήριον γενησόμενον τῆς ἀνακοπῆς τοῦ ῥεύματος, ἔθυεν ἐπ' αὐτοῦ τῷ θεῷ, καὶ τὴν φάσκα ἑώρταζον ἐν
21 ἐκείνῳ τῷ χωρίῳ, πάντων ὧν αὐτοῖς πρότερον συνέβαινε σπανίζειν τότε ῥᾳδίως εὐποροῦντες· τόν τε γὰρ σῖτον ἀκμάζοντα ἤδη τῶν Χαναναίων ἐθέριζον καὶ τὰ λοιπὰ λείαν ἦγον· τότε γὰρ αὐτοὺς καὶ ἡ τῆς μάννας ἐπελελοίπει τροφὴ χρησαμένους ἐπὶ ἔτη τεσσαράκοντα.

22 (5) Ὡς δὲ ταῦτα ποιούντων τῶν Ἰσραηλιτῶν οὐκ ἐπεξῄεσαν οἱ Χαναναῖοι τειχήρεις δ' ἡσύχαζον,

[1] Dindorf: τύχη codd. [2] τε RO: om. τόν τε SPE (Lat.).

[a] Literally " touched safety " : the phrase recalls Thuc. ii. 22 πρὶν . . . τοῦ ἀσφαλοῦς ἀντιλάβοιντο (the escape from Plataea).

When the priests, who were the first to enter, found the river fordable—the depth having diminished and the shingle, which the current was neither full nor rapid enough to force from under their feet, lying as a solid floor—all thereupon confidently traversed the stream, perceiving it to be even as God had foretold that He would make it. But the priests stood still in the midst until the multitude had crossed and reached the firm ground.[a] Then, when all had crossed, the priests emerged, leaving the stream free to resume its accustomed course. And the river, so soon as the Hebrews had quitted it, swelled and recovered its natural magnitude. iii. 17, iv. 17 f.

Erection of an altar and celebration of Passover. Jos. iv. 1.

(4) These, having advanced fifty stades, pitched their camp at a distance of ten stades [b] from Jericho. And Joshua, with the stones which each of the tribal leaders had, by the prophet's orders, taken up from the river-bed, erected that altar that was to serve as a token of the stoppage of the stream, and sacrificed thereon to God.[c] They also kept the feast of the Passover at that spot, being now readily and amply provided with all that they had lacked before; for they reaped the corn of the Canaanites, now at its prime, and took any other booty they could. It was then too that the supply of manna ceased which had served them for forty years. v. 10.

Encompassing of the walls of Jericho. Jos. vi. 1.

(5) Since, notwithstanding these actions of the Israelites, the Canaanites did not sally out against them but remained motionless behind their walls,

[b] These distances are unscriptural. The Gilgal of the camp (Jos. v. 10) is usually identified with a site more than ten stades distant (S.E.) from Jericho.

[c] Josephus here omits the renewal at Gilgal of the rite of circumcision which had been neglected in the wilderness (Jos. v. 2 ff.).

πολιορκεῖν αὐτοὺς Ἰησοῦς ἔγνω. καὶ τῇ πρώτῃ
τῆς ἑορτῆς ἡμέρᾳ τὴν κιβωτὸν οἱ ἱερεῖς φέροντες,
περὶ δ' αὐτὴν ἐν κύκλῳ μέρος τι τῶν ὁπλιτῶν
23 φυλάττον ἦν, ἄλλοι δὲ καὶ[1] προῄεσαν ἑπτὰ κέρασιν
αὐτῶν σαλπίζοντες παρεκάλουν τὸν στρατὸν εἰς
ἀλκήν, περιώδευόν τε τὸ τεῖχος ἑπομένης τῆς
γερουσίας, καὶ σαλπισάντων μόνον τῶν ἱερέων,
τούτου γὰρ οὐδὲν ἐποίησαν περισσότερον, ἀνέζευξαν
24 εἰς τὸ στρατόπεδον. καὶ τοῦτο ἐπὶ ἡμέρας ἓξ
ποιησάντων τῇ ἑβδόμῃ τὸ ὁπλιτικὸν Ἰησοῦς συναγαγὼν καὶ τὸν λαὸν ἅπαντα, τὴν ἅλωσιν αὐτοῖς
τῆς πόλεως εὐηγγελίζετο,[2] ὡς κατ' ἐκείνην τὴν
ἡμέραν αὐτοῖς τοῦ θεοῦ ταύτην παρέξοντος, αὐτομάτως καὶ δίχα τοῦ πόνου τοῦ σφετέρου τῶν τειχῶν
25 κατενεχθησομένων. κτείνειν μέντοι[3] πάνθ' ὁντιν-
οῦν εἰ λάβοιεν παρεκελεύετο καὶ μήτε κάμνοντας
ἀποστῆναι τοῦ φόνου τῶν πολεμίων, μήτ' ἐλέῳ
παραχωρήσαντας φείσασθαι[4] μήτε περὶ ἁρπαγὴν
26 γινομένους περιορᾶν φεύγοντας τοὺς ἐχθρούς· ἀλλὰ
τὰ μὲν ζῷα πάντα διαφθείρειν μηδὲν αὐτοὺς εἰς
ἰδίαν ὠφέλειαν λαμβάνοντας, ὅσα[5] δ' ἂν ἄργυρος ᾖ
καὶ χρυσός, ταῦτα ἐκέλευσε συγκομίζοντας ἀπαρχὴν
ἐξαίρετον τῶν κατωρθωμένων τῷ θεῷ τηρεῖν ἐκ
τῆς πρῶτον ἁλισκομένης πόλεως εἰληφότας· σώζειν
δὲ μόνην Ῥαάβην καὶ τὴν γενεὰν αὐτῆς διὰ τοὺς
γενομένους πρὸς αὐτὴν τοῖς κατασκόποις ὅρκους.

[1] After Lat. (aliique sacerdotes): οἱ καὶ codd.
[2] RO: εὐηγγελίσατο rell. [3] + γε SPL.
[4] SPL: om. rell. [5] ὅσος RO: ὃς M.

[a] *i.e.* of the Passover just mentioned; this date has no support in Scripture or, according to M. Weill, in tradition.

Joshua resolved to besiege them. And, on the first day of the feast,[a] the priests bearing the ark—which was surrounded by a party of armed men to protect it, while seven other priests marched in advance, sounding their horns—exhorted the army to valiance and made the circuit of the walls, followed by the council of elders. After merely those blasts from the priests—for beyond that they did nothing—they returned to the camp. For six days this was repeated, and on the seventh Joshua, having assembled the troops and all the people, announced to them the good news of the impending capture of the city, to wit that on that day God would deliver it to them and that, spontaneously and without effort on their part, the walls would collapse. Howbeit he charged them to slay all, whomsoever they caught, and neither through weariness, nor yielding to pity to desist from the slaughter of their enemies, nor yet while engaged in pillage to suffer the foe to escape. Nay, they were to destroy every living creature without taking aught to themselves for their private profit; but whatsoever there might be of silver or gold,[b] that he commanded them to amass and reserve for God as choice first-fruits of their success, won from the first captured city. They were to spare only Rahab and her family in virtue of the oaths which had been made to her by the spies.

Josephus has traced a connexion between the seven days of blowing of trumpets, mentioned in Scripture, and the duration of the feast. Perhaps, however, he has used a text which, like the LXX Jos. vi. 12, read "on the second day, Joshua rose early, and the priests bore the ark, etc.," and taken it to mean the day after the eve of Passover, or the first full day of the festival.

[b] Jos. vi. 19 adds "or brass or iron"; *cf.* § 32.

27 (6) Ταῦτ' εἰπὼν καὶ διατάξας τὸν στρατὸν προσῆγεν[1] ἐπὶ τὴν πόλιν· περιῄεσαν δὲ πάλιν τὴν πόλιν ἡγουμένης τῆς κιβωτοῦ καὶ τῶν ἱερέων τοῖς κέρασιν ἐξοτρυνόντων τὴν δύναμιν πρὸς τὸ ἔργον. καὶ περιελθόντων ἑπτάκις καὶ πρὸς ὀλίγον ἠρεμησάντων κατέπεσε τὸ τεῖχος μήτε μηχανῆς μήτε ἄλλης βίας αὐτῷ προσενεχθείσης ὑπὸ τῶν Ἑβραίων.

28 (7) Οἱ δ' εἰσελθόντες εἰς Ἱεριχοῦντα πάντας ἔκτεινον, τῶν ἐν αὐτῇ πρὸς τὴν παράδοξον τοῦ τείχους ἀνατροπὴν καταπεπληγότων καὶ τοῦ φρονήματος αὐτοῖς πρὸς ἄμυναν ἀχρείου γεγονότος· ἀνῃροῦντο δ' οὖν ἐν ταῖς ὁδοῖς ἀποσφαττόμενοι
29 καὶ ἐν ταῖς οἰκίαις ἐπικαταλαμβανόμενοι. παρῃτεῖτο δ' οὐδὲν αὐτούς, ἀλλὰ πάντες ἀπώλλυντο ἄχρι γυναικῶν καὶ παιδίων, καὶ νεκρῶν ἡ πόλις ἦν ἀνάπλεως καὶ διέφυγεν οὐδέν. τὴν δὲ πόλιν
30 ἐνέπρησαν ἅπασαν καὶ τὴν χώραν. καὶ τὴν Ῥαάβην σὺν τοῖς οἰκείοις εἰς τὸ καταγώγιον συμφυγοῦσαν ἔσωσαν οἱ κατάσκοποι, καὶ πρὸς αὐτὸν Ἰησοῦς ἀχθείσῃ χάριν ἔχειν ὡμολόγει τῆς σωτηρίας τῶν κατασκόπων καὶ μὴν[2] τῆς εὐεργεσίας ταύτης ἔλεγεν ἐν ταῖς ἀμοιβαῖς οὐχ ἥττονα φανήσεσθαι. δωρεῖται δ' αὐτὴν εὐθὺς ἀγροῖς καὶ διὰ τιμῆς εἶχε τῆς πάσης.

31 (8) Τῆς δὲ πόλεως εἰ καί τι παρέλθοι τὸ πῦρ κατέσκαπτε καὶ κατὰ τῶν οἰκισόντων,[3] εἴ τις πορθηθεῖσαν ἀνεγείρειν ἐθελήσειεν, ἀρὰς ἔθετο, ὅπως θεμελίους μὲν τειχῶν βαλλόμενος[4] στερηθῇ τοῦ πρώτου παιδός, τελειώσας δὲ τὸν νεώτατον τῶν παίδων ἀποβάλῃ. τῆς δὲ ἀρᾶς τὸ θεῖον οὐκ

[1] προσήγαγεν RO.
[2] M: μηδὲν rell.
[3] L: οἰκησόντων rell.
[4] βαλόμενος RO.

(6) Having spoken thus, he marshalled his army and led it towards the city. Again they compassed the city, the ark leading and the priests with the sounding of their horns inciting the troops to action. And when they had compassed it seven times and had halted for a while, the wall fell down, without either engine or force of any other kind having been applied to it by the Hebrews.

Fall of Jericho. Jos. vi. 15.

(7) And they, having entered Jericho, slew every soul, the inhabitants being dumbfounded at the miraculous overthrow of the ramparts and deprived of all effectual spirit for defence. At all events they perished, slaughtered in the streets or surprised in the houses. Nothing could exempt them; all were destroyed down to the women and children, and the city was choked with corpses and nothing escaped. The city itself they burnt entire and the surrounding region. Rahab, who with her kinsfolk had all taken refuge in the inn, was saved by the spies; and Joshua, on her being brought before him, acknowledged his gratitude to her for her protection of the spies and assured her that in recompensing her he would not be found to fall short of such a benefaction. Indeed he presented her with lands forthwith and showed her every consideration.

Massacre of the inhabitants, excepting Rahab. Jos. vi. 21.

(8) As for the city, whatever of it the fire had spared he demolished, and upon those who would settle there should any be fain to re-erect it from its ruins, he pronounced imprecations, that if he laid foundations of walls he should be bereft of his first-born and if he completed the walls he should lose the youngest of his sons. Nor was this curse un-

Destruction of the town and imprecation of Joshua. Jos. vi. 26.

ἠμέλησεν, ἀλλ' ἐν τοῖς ὑστέροις ἀπαγγελοῦμεν τὸ περὶ αὐτὴν πάθος γενόμενον.

32 (9) Ἄπειρον δέ τι πλῆθος ἐκ τῆς ἁλώσεως συναθροίζεται ἀργύρου τε καὶ χρυσοῦ καὶ προσέτι χαλκοῦ, μηδενὸς παραβάντος τὰ δεδογμένα μηδ' εἰς ἰδίαν ὠφέλειαν αὐτὰ διαρπασαμένων, ἀλλ' ἀποσχομένων ὡς ἤδη τῷ θεῷ καθιερωμένων. καὶ ταῦτα μὲν Ἰησοῦς τοῖς ἱερεῦσιν εἰς τοὺς θησαυροὺς παραδίδωσι καταθέσθαι. καὶ Ἱεριχοῦς μὲν τοῦτον ἀπώλετο τὸν τρόπον.

33 (10) Ἄχαρος δέ τις Ζεβεδαίου παῖς ὢν ἐκ τῆς Ἰούδα φυλῆς εὑρὼν χλαμύδα βασίλειον ἐκ χρυσοῦ μὲν πᾶσαν ὑφασμένην, μᾶζαν δὲ χρυσοῦ σταθμὸν ἕλκουσαν σίκλων διακοσίων καὶ δεινὸν ἡγησάμενος ὃ[1] κινδυνεύσας ηὕρατο κέρδος, τοῦτο τῆς ἰδίας χρείας ἀφελόμενος[2] δοῦναι φέρων τῷ θεῷ καὶ μὴ δεομένῳ, ὄρυγμα βαθὺ ποιήσας ἐν τῇ αὐτοῦ σκηνῇ κατώρυξεν εἰς τοῦτο, λήσειν[3] νομίζων ὡς τοὺς συστρατιώτας οὕτως καὶ τὸν θεόν.

34 (11) Ἐκλήθη δὲ ὁ τόπος ἐν ᾧ στρατόπεδον ἐβάλετο Ἰησοῦς Γάλγαλα· σημαίνει δὲ τοῦτο ἐλευθέριον ὄνομα· διαβάντες γὰρ τὸν ποταμὸν ἐλευθέρους ἑαυτοὺς ἤδη ἀπό τε τῶν Αἰγυπτίων καὶ τῆς ἐν τῇ ἐρήμῳ ταλαιπωρίας ἐγίνωσκον.

[1] Ernesti: εἰ ὁ ML: εἰς ὃ RO.
[2] Niese suspects a lacuna after ἀφελόμενος.
[3] ME: λήσεσθαι rell.

---

[a] In the reign of Ahab, 1 Kings xvi. 34. Josephus, however, in the sequel forgets to recount the incident; the verse which records it being apparently absent from the Greek Bible which he was then following (*A.* viii. 318 note).

[b] Heb. "Achan, son of Carmi, son of Zabdi": the form Achar appears here in the LXX, as also in the Heb. in 1 Chron.

regarded by the Deity, but in the sequel we shall recount the calamity which it entailed.[a]

(9) An immense quantity of silver and gold, as also of brass, was amassed from the captured town, none having violated the decrees nor looted these things for his private profit: nay, they abstained therefrom as from objects already consecrated to God. And Joshua delivered them to the priests to lay up in the treasuries. Such, then, was the end of Jericho.

Consecration of the booty to God.

(10) But a certain Achar, son of Zebedee,[b] of the tribe of Judah, having found a royal mantle all woven of gold and a mass of gold of the weight of two hundred shekels,[c] and thinking it cruel that he should deprive himself of the enjoyment of lucre, which he had won at his own peril, and bring and offer it to God, who had no need of it, dug a deep hole in his tent and buried his treasure therein, thinking to elude alike his comrades in arms and withal the eye of God.

The sin of Achar. Jos. vii. 1.

(11) The place where Joshua had established his camp was called Galgala.[d] This name signifies "freedom"[e]; for, having crossed the river, they felt themselves henceforth free both from the Egyptians and from their miseries in the desert.

Joshua at Gilgal. Jos. v. 9.

ii. 7. Moreover the etymological word-play in the Hebrew of Jos. vii. 25 presupposes the form Achar (*'Aḥar*).

[c] Heb. "a mantle of Shinar (*i.e.* Babylonia) and 200 shekels of silver and a wedge of gold of 50 shekels weight" (Jos. vii. 21).

[d] So LXX: Heb. Gilgal.

[e] One of the historian's "free" etymologies, but perhaps taken over from others (Weill quotes the translation ἐλευθερία in Theodoret i. p. 199). Scripture derives the name Gilgal from the verb *galal* ("to roll") and adds the explanation "This day have I rolled away the reproach of Egypt from off you" (by the reinstitution of the practice of circumcision).

35 (12) Μετὰ δ' ὀλίγας ἡμέρας τῆς Ἱεριχοῦντος
συμφορᾶς πέμπει τρισχιλίους ὁπλίτας Ἰησοῦς εἰς[1]
Ναϊὰν[2] πόλιν ὑπὲρ τῆς Ἱεριχοῦντος κειμένην
αἱρήσοντας, οἳ συμβαλόντων αὐτοῖς τῶν Ναϊητῶν
τραπέντες ἀποβάλλουσιν ἄνδρας ἓξ καὶ τριάκοντα.
36 τοῦτ' ἀγγελθὲν τοῖς Ἰσραηλίταις λύπην τε μεγάλην
καὶ δεινὴν ἐποίησεν ἀθυμίαν, οὐ κατὰ τὸ οἰκεῖον
τῶν ἀπολωλότων, καίτοι γε πάντων ἀνδρῶν
ἀγαθῶν καὶ σπουδῆς ἀξίων διεφθαρμένων, ἀλλὰ
37 κατὰ ἀπόγνωσιν· πιστεύοντες γὰρ ἤδη τῆς γῆς
ἐγκρατεῖς εἶναι καὶ σῶον ἕξειν ἐν ταῖς μάχαις τὸν
στρατὸν οὕτως τοῦ θεοῦ προϋπεσχημένου, τε-
θαρρηκότας παραδόξως ἑώρων τοὺς πολεμίους·
καὶ σάκκους ἐπενδύντες ταῖς στολαῖς δι' ὅλης
ἡμέρας ἐν δακρύοις ἦσαν καὶ πένθει, τροφῆς οὐδεμίαν ἐπιζήτησιν ποιούμενοι, μειζόνως δὲ τὸ
συμβεβηκὸς εἶχον ἀχθόμενοι.
38 (13) Βλέπων δὲ οὕτως ὁ Ἰησοῦς τήν τε στρατιὰν
καταπεπληγυῖαν καὶ περὶ τῶν ὅλων πονηρὰν ἤδη
τὴν ἐλπίδα λαμβάνουσαν παρρησίαν λαμβάνει πρὸς
39 τὸν θεόν· "ἡμεῖς" γὰρ εἶπεν "οὐχ ὑπ' αὐθαδείας
προήχθημεν ὥστε ταύτην ὑπάγεσθαι τοῖς ὅπλοις
τὴν γῆν, ἀλλὰ Μωυσέος τοῦ σοῦ δούλου πρὸς τοῦθ'
ἡμᾶς ἐξεγείραντος, ᾧ διὰ πολλῶν τεκμηρίων
ἐπηγγέλλου κτήσασθαι παρέξειν ἡμῖν τήνδε τὴν
γῆν καὶ τὸν στρατὸν ἡμῶν ἀεὶ τῶν πολεμίων
40 ποιήσειν τοῖς ὅπλοις κρείττονα. τινὰ μὲν οὖν κατὰ
τὰς ὑποσχέσεις ἡμῖν ἀπήντησε τὰς σάς, νῦν δὲ
παρὰ δόξαν ἐπταικότες καὶ τῆς δυνάμεώς τινας
ἀποβαλόντες ἐπὶ τούτοις ὡς οὐ βεβαίων τῶν παρὰ

[1] om. Ernesti. [2] Ἀΐαν E Lat.: v.l. Ἄν(ν)αν.

[a] Heb. Ai (*'Ai*), LXX Γαί. The form Ναϊά has arisen out of

A defeat at Naia (Ai). Jos. vii. 2.

(12) A few days after the downfall of Jericho, Joshua sent three thousand men-at-arms to the city of Naia,[a] situated above Jericho, to capture it. These, being opposed by the Naietans, were routed and lost six-and-thirty men. The announcement of this news to the Israelites caused them great grief and dire despondency, not so much because of their kinship to the fallen, albeit they were all valiant and worthy men[b] who had perished, as from utter despair. For, believing themselves already masters of the country and that they would keep their army unscathed in the combats, even as God had promised heretofore, they now beheld their enemies unexpectedly emboldened. And so, putting sackcloth upon their apparel, they passed a whole day in tears and lamentation, without one thought for food, and in their vexation unduly magnified what had befallen.

Joshua's prayer. Jos. vii. 7.

(13) Seeing his army thus cast down and a prey to gloomy forebodings concerning the whole campaign, Joshua frankly appealed to God. "It was," he said, "from no confidence in ourselves that we were induced to subjugate this land by arms: nay, it was Moses, thy servant, who incited us thereto, he to whom by many tokens thou didst promise to vouchsafe to us to win this land, and ever to ensure to our army superiority in battle over our foes. And indeed some things have befallen in accordance with thy promises; but now, having suffered unlooked-for defeat, having lost some of our force, we are distressed at these things, which make thy

[a] 'Aïá—attested by the Latin version and perhaps original—through duplication of the ν in the accusative—τὴν (N)αΐαν; modern Greek supplies many parallels, *e.g.* Νίδα = Ἴδα.

[b] Amplification, for which there is Rabbinical authority (Weill).

σοῦ καὶ ὧν προεῖπε Μωυσῆς ἀχθόμεθα, καὶ χεῖρον ἡ τῶν μελλόντων ἐλπὶς ἡμᾶς ἀνιᾷ τῇ πρώτῃ πείρᾳ
41 τοιαύτῃ συντυχόντας. ἀλλὰ σύ, δέσποτα, δύναμις γάρ σοι τούτων ἴασιν εὑρεῖν, τό τε παρὸν ἡμῶν λυπηρὸν νίκην παρασχόμενος καὶ τὸ περὶ τῶν αὖθις δύσελπι διακείμενον οὕτως τῆς διανοίας ἔξελε."

42 (14) Ταῦτα μὲν Ἰησοῦς ἐπὶ στόμα πεσὼν ἠρώτα τὸν θεόν· χρηματίσαντος δὲ ἀνίστασθαι τοῦ θεοῦ καὶ καθαίρειν τὸν στρατὸν μιάσματος ἐν αὐτῷ γεγονότος κλοπῆς τε τῶν καθιερωμένων αὐτῷ χρημάτων τετολμημένης, διὰ γὰρ ταῦτα τὴν νῦν αὐτοῖς ἧτταν συμπεσεῖν, ἀναζητηθέντος δὲ τοῦ δράσαντος καὶ κολασθέντος νίκην αὐτοῖς ἀεὶ περιέσεσθαι[1] τῶν πολεμίων, φράζει ταῦτα πρὸς τὸν
43 λαὸν Ἰησοῦς, καὶ καλέσας Ἐλεάζαρον τὸν ἀρχιερέα καὶ τοὺς ἐν τέλει κατὰ φυλὴν ἐκλήρου. τούτου δὲ τὸ τετολμημένον ἐκ τῆς Ἰούδα φυλῆς δηλοῦντος κατὰ φατρίας πάλιν ταύτης προτίθησι τὸν κλῆρον. τὸ δ' ἀληθὲς τοῦ κακουργήματος περὶ τὴν Ἀχάρου
44 συγγένειαν ηὑρίσκετο. κατ' ἄνδρα δὲ τῆς ἐξετάσεως γινομένης λαμβάνουσι τὸν Ἄχαρον· ὁ δ' οὐκ ἔχων ἔξαρνος εἶναι, τοῦ θεοῦ δεινῶς αὐτὸν ἐκπεριελθόντος, ὡμολόγει τε τὴν κλοπὴν καὶ τὰ φώρια παρῆγεν εἰς μέσον. καὶ οὗτος μὲν εὐθὺς ἀναιρεθεὶς ἐν νυκτὶ ταφῆς ἀτίμου καὶ καταδίκῳ πρεπούσης τυγχάνει.

[1] conj. Niese: περισώζεσθαι RO: πορίζεσθαι rell.: proveniret Lat.

[a] Jos. vii. 25, "And all Israel stoned him with stones [and they burned them with fire and (Targum 'after that they had') stoned them with stones]." The bracketed words, absent from the LXX, are confused and the addition of later

promises and those predictions of Moses appear unsure; and yet more sorely are we pained at the thought of what the future holds in store, having met with such issue to our first assault. But do thou, Lord, since thou hast power to find healing for these ills, dispel our present affliction by vouchsafing us victory and thus banish from our mind our deep despondency concerning the future."

Discovery and death of the sinner Achar. Jos. vii. 6, 10 ff.

(14) Thus did Joshua, prostrated upon his face, make petition to God. And the response came from God, that he should arise and purge the army of the pollution that had been wrought therein and of a daring theft of objects consecrated to Him, since that was the cause of their recent defeat; but were the culprit sought out and punished, they would for ever be assured of victory over their enemies. All this Joshua repeated to the people and, summoning Eleazar the high priest and the magistrates, he proceeded to draw lots for the several tribes. And when this revealed that the sacrilege issued from the tribe of Judah, he again had lots drawn for its several clans; and the true story of the crime was found to rest with the family of Achar. The inquiry being pursued further man by man, they caught Achar. And he, unable to make denial, being thus shrewdly circumvented by God, avowed his theft and produced the stolen goods before all. He was straightway put to death and at nightfall was given the ignominious burial proper to the condemned.[a]

editors. As M. Weill points out, Josephus doubtless adds the burial, unrecorded in Scripture, to indicate that the Mosaic law on stoning, which he has previously reported (iv. 202), was exactly followed; but he may already have found here some addition in his Biblical text which he interpreted as an allusion to burial.

45 (15) Ἰησοῦς δὲ ἁγνίσας τὸν στρατὸν ἐξῆγεν ἐπὶ
τὴν Ναϊὰν αὐτοὺς[1] καὶ νυκτὸς τὰ περὶ τὴν πόλιν
ἐνέδραις προλοχίσας ὑπὸ τὸν ὄρθρον συμβάλλει
τοῖς πολεμίοις. τῶν δὲ μετὰ θάρσους[2] αὐτοῖς διὰ
τὴν προτέραν νίκην ἐπιόντων ὑποχωρεῖν προσποιη-
σάμενος ἕλκει τῷ τρόπῳ τούτῳ μακρὰν αὐτοὺς τῆς
πόλεως διώκειν οἰομένους καὶ ὡς ἐπὶ νίκῃ κατα-
46 φρονοῦντας. ἔπειτ᾽ ἀναστρέψας τὴν δύναμιν κατὰ
πρόσωπον αὐτοῖς ποιεῖ, σημεῖά τε δοὺς ἃ πρὸς τοὺς
ἐν ταῖς ἐνέδραις συνετέτακτο κἀκείνους ἐπὶ τὴν
μάχην ἐξανίστησιν. οἱ δ᾽ εἰσεπήδων εἰς τὴν πόλιν
τῶν ἔνδον περὶ τοῖς τείχεσιν ὄντων, ἐνίων δὲ καὶ
πρὸς θέαν τῶν ἔξω τὴν γνώμην περισπωμένων.
47 καὶ οἱ μὲν τὴν πόλιν ᾕρουν καὶ πάντας τοὺς ἐντυγ-
χάνοντας ἔκτεινον, Ἰησοῦς δὲ τοὺς προσελθόντας
εἰς χεῖρας βιασάμενος φυγεῖν τρέπεται, συνελαυνό-
μενοι δὲ ὡς εἰς ἀκέραιον τὴν πόλιν ἐπεὶ καὶ ταύτην
ἐχομένην[3] ἑώρων καὶ καταπιμπραμένην ὁμοῦ
γυναιξὶ καὶ τέκνοις κατέλαβον, διὰ τῶν ἀγρῶν
ᾖσαν[4] σκεδασθέντες[5] ἀμύνειν αὐτοῖς ὑπὸ μονώσεως
48 οὐ δυνάμενοι. τοιαύτης δὲ τῆς συμφορᾶς τοὺς
Ναϊτιανοὺς καταλαβούσης, παίδων τε ὄχλος ἑάλω
καὶ γυναικῶν καὶ θεραπείας καὶ τῆς ἄλλης ἀπο-
σκευῆς ἄπειρόν τι πλῆθος, ἀγέλας τε βοσκημάτων
ἔλαβον οἱ Ἑβραῖοι καὶ χρήματα πολλά, καὶ γὰρ
πλούσιον ἦν τὸ χωρίον, καὶ ταῦτα πάντα τοῖς
στρατιώταις Ἰησοῦς διένειμεν ἐν Γαλγάλοις γενόμενος.
49 (16) Γαβαωνῖται δὲ κατοικοῦντες ἔγγιστα τοῖς

[1] ed. pr.: αὐτὸς codd.: om. E Lat. [2] θράσους ME.
[3] οἰχομένην ROE. [4] ᾔεσαν M: ἦσαν SPL: om. rell.
[5] + καὶ ROE.

(15) Joshua, having purified his army, now led them out against Naia, and, after posting ambuscades during the night all about the town,[a] at daybreak joined battle with the enemy. And when these advanced against them with an assurance begotten of their former victory, Joshua, feigning a retreat, drew them in this way to a distance from the town, they imagining themselves in pursuit of a beaten foe and being disdainful of them in anticipation of victory. Then, turning his forces about, he made them face their pursuers and, giving the prearranged signals to those in ambush, roused them also to the fight. These flung themselves into the town, the occupants of which were around the ramparts, some wholly engrossed in watching their friends outside.[b] So while they took the town and slew all whom they encountered, Joshua broke the ranks of his adversaries and forced them to flee. Driven in a body to the town which they supposed to be intact, when they saw that it too was taken and found that it was in flames, along with their wives and children, they scattered throughout the country, incapable through their isolation of offering resistance. Such being the fate that befell the Naietans, a crowd of children, women and slaves was taken, beside an immense mass of material. The Hebrews captured moreover herds of cattle and money in abundance, for the region was rich, and all this Joshua distributed to his soldiers, while he was at Galgala.

Conquest of Naia. Jos. viii. 3.

(16) Now the Gabaonites,[c] who lived quite close

[a] The Greek is modelled on Thuc. ii. 81.
[b] Amplification; according to Jos. viii. 17 not a man had been left in the town.
[c] So LXX (Γαβαών): Heb. "Gibeon."

Ἱεροσολύμοις τά τε τοῖς Ἱεριχουντίοις συμβεβηκότα πάθη καὶ τὰ τοῖς Ναϊτίνοις ὁρῶντες καὶ πρὸς σφᾶς μεταβήσεσθαι τὸ δεινὸν ὑπονοοῦντες, Ἰησοῦν μὲν παρακαλεῖν οὐ διέγνωσαν· οὐδὲ[1] γὰρ τεύξεσθαί τινος τῶν μετρίων ὑπελάμβανον ἐπ' ὀλέθρῳ τοῦ Χαναναίων ἔθνους παντὸς πολεμοῦντος
50 αὐτούς· Κεφηρίτας δὲ καὶ Καριαθιαριμίτας γείτονας ὄντας αὐτοῖς ἐπὶ συμμαχίαν παρεκάλουν, οὐδ' αὐτοὺς διαφεύξεσθαι τὸν κίνδυνον λέγοντες, εἰ φθάσαιεν αὐτοὶ ληφθέντες ὑπὸ τῶν Ἰσραηλιτῶν, συνασπίσαντας δὲ αὐτοῖς διέγνωσαν[2] διαδρᾶναι τὴν
51 δύναμιν αὐτῶν. προσδεξαμένων δὲ τοὺς λόγους αὐτῶν πέμπουσι πρέσβεις πρὸς Ἰησοῦν φιλίαν σπεισομένους οὓς μάλιστα τῶν πολιτῶν ἐδοκίμαζον
52 ἱκανοὺς πρᾶξαι τὰ συμφέροντα τῷ πλήθει. οἱ δὲ ὁμολογεῖν αὐτοὺς Χαναναίους ἐπισφαλὲς ἡγούμενοι, διαφεύξεσθαι τὸν διὰ τοῦτο κίνδυνον ὑπολαμβάνοντες, εἰ λέγοιεν αὐτοὺς μὴ προσήκειν κατὰ μηδὲν Χαναναίοις ἀλλὰ πορρωτάτω τούτων κατοικεῖν, ἥκειν τε κατὰ πύστιν[3] τῆς ἀρετῆς αὐτοῦ πολλὴν ἀνύσαντες ὁδὸν ἔφασκον καὶ τεκμήριον τοῦ λόγου
53 τούτου τὸ σχῆμα ὑπεδείκνυον· τὰς γὰρ ἐσθῆτας καινὰς ὅτε ἐξῄεσαν οὔσας ὑπὸ τοῦ χρόνου τῆς ὁδοιπορίας αὐτοῖς τετρῖφθαι· τρυχίνας γὰρ εἰς τὸ ταῦτα πιστοῦσθαι πρὸς αὐτῶν ἐπίτηδες ἔλαβον.
54 στάντες οὖν εἰς μέσους ἔλεγον, ὡς πεμφθεῖεν ὑπὸ τῶν Γαβαωνιτῶν καὶ τῶν περιοίκων πόλεων πλεῖστον ἀπεχουσῶν τῆσδε τῆς γῆς ποιησόμενοι

[1] Dindorf: οὔτε codd.
[2] possent Lat.: hence I should read ἂν (διέγνωσαν may have come into the text from § 49).
[3] Bekker: πίστιν codd.

to Jerusalem, seeing the disasters that had befallen the inhabitants of Jericho and of Naia and suspecting that they too would be visited by this dire fate, yet resolved not to implore mercy of Joshua; for they did not think to obtain any tolerable terms from a belligerent whose aim was the extermination of the whole race of the Canaanites. But they invited the Kephêrites and the Kariathiarimites,[a] their neighbours, to make alliance with them, telling them that neither would they escape this peril, should they themselves have first been conquered by the Israelites, whereas if they united their arms with theirs they might evade their violence.[b] These overtures being accepted, the Gabaonites sent ambassadors to Joshua to make a league of amity, choosing those of their citizens whom they judged most capable of acting in the interests of the people. And these, deeming it hazardous to avow themselves Canaanites, and thinking to escape the peril of so doing by asserting that they had no connexion whatever with the Canaanites but lived very far away from them, declared that it was the tidings of his valour which had brought them thither, after accomplishing a long journey, and in proof of this statement they pointed to their apparel. Their garments, quite new when they set out, had (they said) been worn out by the length of their journey; for, to get them to believe this story, they had purposely clothed themselves in rags. So, standing amidst the host, they said that they had been sent by the Gabaonites and the neighbouring cities, very remote from that

Ruse of the Gabaonites. Jos. ix. 3.

[a] Chephirah (LXX κεφειρά) and Kiriath-jearim (πόλεις Ἰαρείν) are mentioned in Jos. ix. 18 as allied with Gibeon, along with another city (Beeroth) ignored by Josephus.

[b] Text doubtful.

πρὸς αὐτοὺς φιλίαν ἐφ᾽ αἷς πάτριον αὐτοῖς ἐστι
συνθήκαις· μαθόντες γὰρ ἐκ θεοῦ χάριτος καὶ δωρεᾶς
τὴν Χαναναίων αὐτοῖς γῆν κτήσασθαι δεδόσθαι
τούτοις τ᾽ ἔλεγον ἥδεσθαι καὶ πολίτας ἀξιοῦν
55 αὐτῶν γενέσθαι. καὶ οἱ μὲν ταῦτα λέγοντες καὶ
ἐπιδεικνύντες τὰ τεκμήρια τῆς ὁδοιπορίας παρεκάλουν ἐπὶ συνθήκας καὶ φιλίαν τοὺς Ἑβραίους·
Ἰησοῦς δὲ πιστεύσας οἷς ἔλεγον, ὡς οὐκ εἰσὶ τοῦ
Χαναναίων ἔθνους, ποιεῖται πρὸς αὐτοὺς φιλίαν,
καὶ Ἐλεάζαρος ὁ ἀρχιερεὺς μετὰ τῆς γερουσίας
ὄμνυσιν ἕξειν τε φίλους καὶ συμμάχους καὶ μηδὲν
μοχλεύσεσθαι κατ᾽ αὐτῶν ἄδικον, τοῖς ὅρκοις
56 ἐπισυναινέσαντος τοῦ πλήθους. καὶ οἱ μὲν ὧν
ἤθελον τυχόντες ἐξ ἀπάτης ἀπῄεσαν πρὸς αὐτούς.
Ἰησοῦς δὲ τῆς Χαναναίας στρατεύσας εἰς τὴν
ὑπώρειον καὶ μαθὼν οὐ πόρρω τῶν Ἱεροσολύμων
τοὺς Γαβαωνίτας κατῳκημένους καὶ τοῦ γένους
ὄντας τῶν Χαναναίων, μεταπεμψάμενος αὐτῶν
57 τοὺς ἐν τέλει τῆς ἀπάτης αὐτοῖς ἐνεκάλει. τῶν δ᾽
οὐκ ἄλλην ἀφορμὴν σωτηρίας ἔχειν ἢ ταύτην προ-
φασιζομένων καὶ διὰ τοῦτ᾽ ἐπ᾽ αὐτὴν ἐξ ἀνάγκης
καταφυγεῖν συγκαλεῖ τὸν ἀρχιερέα Ἐλεάζαρον καὶ
τὴν γερουσίαν, καὶ δημοσίους αὐτοὺς δικαιούντων
ποιεῖν ἐπὶ τῷ μὴ παραβῆναι τὸν ὅρκον ἀποδείκνυσιν[1]
εἶναι τοιούτους. καὶ οἱ μὲν τῆς καταλαβούσης
αὐτοὺς συμφοοᾶς τοιαύτην φυλακὴν καὶ ἀσφάλειαν
εὕραντο.
58 (17) Τοῦ δὲ τῶν Ἱεροσολυμιτῶν βασιλέως χαλεπῶς φέροντος ἐπὶ τῷ μετατάξασθαι πρὸς τὸν

[1] ἀποδεικνύουσιν ROML.

[a] Or " engineer," " trump up " (literally " prise up ").

present land, to make alliance with them on such terms as were customary with their fathers; for, having learnt that by the grace and bounty of God the land of the Canaanites had been granted them for their possession, they rejoiced thereat and craved to become their fellow-citizens. With these words, and withal displaying the tokens of their travel, they besought the Hebrews to make a covenant and league of amity with them. Thereupon Joshua, believing what they said, that they were not of the race of the Canaanites, made a league with them; and Eleazar the high priest, along with the council of elders, swore to hold them as friends and allies and to contrive [a] no iniquity against them, and the people ratified the oaths. So the envoys, having attained their end by guile, returned to their own people; but Joshua, having marched into the foothills of Canaan and learnt that the Gabaonites lived not far from Jerusalem and were of the stock of the Canaanites, sent for their magistrates and upbraided them for this fraud. When these alleged that they had no other means of salvation save that, and that they had therefore perforce had recourse to it, Joshua convoked the high priest Eleazar and the council; and, acting upon their judgement that they should be made public slaves,[b] so as to avoid violation of the oath, he appointed them to those functions. Thus did these people, when confronted with calamity, find protection and security for themselves.

(17) But the king of the Jerusalemites,[c] indignant that the Gabaonites should have passed over to the

[b] "Hewers of wood and drawers of water for the congregation," Jos. ix. 27.

[c] Named Adonizedek, Jos. x. 1.

Ἰησοῦν τοὺς Γαβαωνίτας καὶ τοὺς τῶν πλησίον ἐθνῶν παρακαλέσαντος βασιλέας συνάρασθαι τῷ κατ᾽ αὐτῶν πολέμῳ, ὡς τούτους τε εἶδον παρόντας σὺν αὐτῷ, τέσσαρες δὲ ἦσαν, οἱ Γαβαωνῖται καὶ στρατοπεδευσαμένους ἐπί τινι πηγῇ τῆς πόλεως οὐκ ἄπωθεν παρασκευάζεσθαι πρὸς πολιορκίαν,
59 ἐπεκαλοῦντο σύμμαχον Ἰησοῦν· ἐν τούτοις γὰρ ἦν αὐτοῖς τὰ πράγματα, ὡς ὑπὸ μὲν τούτων[1] ἀπολεῖσθαι προσδοκᾶν, ὑπὸ δὲ τῶν ἐπ᾽ ὀλέθρῳ τοῦ Χαναναίων γένους στρατευσάντων σωθήσεσθαι διὰ τὴν
60 γενομένην φιλίαν ὑπολαμβάνειν. καὶ Ἰησοῦς πανστρατιᾷ σπεύσας ἐπὶ τὴν βοήθειαν καὶ δι᾽ ἡμέρας καὶ νυκτὸς ἀνύσας ὄρθριος προσμίγνυσι τοῖς πολεμίοις καὶ τραπεῖσιν εἵπετο διώκων διὰ χωρίων ἐπικλινῶν, Βήθωρα καλεῖται. ἔνθα καὶ τὴν τοῦ θεοῦ συνεργίαν ἔμαθεν ἐπισημήναντος αὐτοῦ βρονταῖς τε καὶ κεραυνῶν ἀφέσει καὶ χαλάζης καταφορᾷ
61 μείζονος τῆς συνήθους· ἔτι γε μὴν καὶ τὴν ἡμέραν αὐξηθῆναι πλέον, ὡς ἂν μὴ καταλαβοῦσα νὺξ ἐπίσχῃ τὸ τῶν Ἑβραίων πρόθυμον, συνέπεσεν, ὥστε καὶ λαμβάνει τοὺς βασιλέας Ἰησοῦς ἔν τινι κρυπτομένους σπηλαίῳ κατὰ Μακχίδα καὶ κολάζει πάντας. ὅτι δὲ τὸ μῆκος τῆς ἡμέρας ἐπέδωκε τότε καὶ τοῦ συνήθους ἐπλεόνασε, δηλοῦται διὰ τῶν ἀνακειμένων ἐν τῷ ἱερῷ γραμμάτων.

62 (18) Κατεστραμμένων δ᾽ οὕτως τῶν περὶ τοὺς βασιλέας, οἳ τοὺς Γαβαωνίτας πολεμήσοντες ἐστράτευσαν, ἐπανῄει πάλιν τῆς Χαναναίας ἐπὶ τὴν

[1] M: τῶν τοιούτων RO: τῶν οἰκείων SPL (Lat. suis).

[a] Bibl. Beth-horon; the pass was the scene of many later

side of Joshua, called upon the kings of the neighbouring nations to join him in a campaign against them; whereat the Gabaonites, having seen these monarchs come with him, four in number, and encamp by a spring not far from their city, preparing to besiege them, appealed to Joshua for aid. For such was their case, that from their countrymen they could await but destruction, while from those who had taken the field for the extermination of the Canaanite race they looked for salvation, thanks to the alliance which had been concluded. Joshua, with his whole army, sped to their assistance and, marching all day and night, at early dawn fell upon the foe, routed them and followed in pursuit down the slopes of the region called Bēthōra.[a] There too he was given to know of God's co-operation, manifested by thunder-claps, the discharge of thunderbolts and the descent of hail of more than ordinary magnitude. Aye and moreover it befell that the day was prolonged, to the end that night should not overtake them and check the Hebrews' ardour; insomuch that Joshua both captured the kings, who were hiding in a cave at Macchida,[b] and punished all their host. That the length of the day was increased on that occasion and surpassed the customary measure, is attested by Scriptures that are laid up in the temple.[c]

Defeat of the league of kings. The lengthened day. Jos. x. 1.

(18) Having thus overthrown that league of kings who had set out to war against the Gabaonites, Joshua remounted into the hill-country of Canaan;

battles, notably of the rout of a Roman legion at the opening of the Jewish War (*B.J.* ii. 546).

[b] Bibl. Makkedah (*Makkedah*), LXX Μαχηδά, Jos. x. 10, 16: perhaps *el-Mughar* ("the cavern") S.W. of Ekron.

[c] *Cf.* iii. 38, iv. 303 with notes.

ὀρεινὴν Ἰησοῦς καὶ πολὺν τῶν ἐν αὐτῇ φόνον ἐργασάμενος καὶ λείαν λαβὼν παρῆν εἰς τὸ ἐν
63 Γαλγάλοις στρατόπεδον. τοῦ δὲ περὶ τῆς τῶν Ἑβραίων ἀρετῆς λόγου πολλοῦ φοιτῶντος εἰς τοὺς περιοίκους κατάπληξις εἶχε τοὺς ἀκούοντας τὸ τῶν ἀπολωλότων πλῆθος, καὶ στρατεύουσιν ἐπ' αὐτοὺς οἱ περὶ Λίβανον ὄρος βασιλεῖς ὄντες Χαναναῖοι καὶ οἱ ἐν τοῖς πεδίοις τῶν Χαναναίων Παλαιστίνους προσλαβόντες στρατοπεδεύουσι[1] πρὸς Βηρώθῃ πόλει Γαλιλαίας τῆς ἄνω Κεδέσης οὐ πόρρω· Γαλιλαίων
64 δ' ἐστὶ καὶ τοῦτο τὸ χωρίον. τοῦ δὲ στρατοῦ παντὸς ὁπλιτῶν μὲν ἦσαν μυριάδες τριάκοντα, μύριοι δ' ἱππεῖς καὶ ἅρματα δισμύρια. καταπλήττει δὲ τὸ πλῆθος τῶν πολεμίων αὐτόν τε Ἰησοῦν καὶ τοὺς Ἰσραηλίτας καὶ πρὸς τὴν ἐλπίδα τοῦ κρείττονος εὐλαβεστέρως εἶχον δι' ὑπερβολὴν
65 τοῦ δέους. τοῦ θεοῦ δ' ἐξονειδίσαντος αὐτοῖς τὸν φόβον καὶ τί[2] πλέον τῆς παρ' αὐτοῦ βοηθείας ποθοῦσιν, ὑποσχομένου τε νικήσειν τοὺς ἐχθροὺς καὶ κελεύσαντος τούς τε ἵππους ἀχρήστους ποιῆσαι καὶ τὰ ἅρματα πυρῶσαι, θαρσαλέος πρὸς τὰς ὑποσχέσεις τοῦ θεοῦ γενόμενος ἐξώρμησεν ἐπὶ τοὺς
66 πολεμίους, καὶ διὰ πέμπτης ἡμέρας ἐπ' αὐτοὺς ἐλθὼν συνάπτει, καὶ καρτερὰ μάχη γίνεται καὶ φόνος κρείττων πίστεως παρὰ τοῖς ἀκροωμένοις. διώκων δ' ἐπὶ πλεῖστον ἐξῆλθε καὶ πᾶν τὸ στρά-

[1] veneruntque Lat. [2] εἰ MSPL Lat.

[a] The Greek, here and throughout, has "Palestinians."
[b] Jos. xi. 5, "at the waters of Merom" (LXX Μαρρών), com-

there he made great carnage of the inhabitants and captured booty, and so returned to the camp at Galgala. The fame of the Hebrews' valour being now mightily noised abroad among the neighbouring peoples, consternation seized them on hearing of those multitudes of slain; and there set off to war against them the kings of the region of Mount Libanus, who were Canaanites, and the Canaanites of the plains, joined by the Philistines,[a] and established their camp at Bērothe,[b] a city of upper Galilee, not far from Kedese,[c] another place within the Galilean area. Their entire army amounted to 300,000 men-at-arms, 10,000 horsemen, and 20,000 chariots.[d] This host of enemies dismayed both Joshua himself and the Israelites, and in the excess of their fear they scarce durst hope for success. But God rebuked them for their terror and for craving aught beyond His aid, promising them victory over their foes and bidding them put their horses out of action and to burn the chariots. Emboldened by these promises of God, Joshua set forth against the enemy, and on the fifth day[e] came upon them and engaged them: a fierce combat ensued and a carnage such that the tale of it would outrun belief. Advancing very far in pursuit, Joshua destroyed the

Defeat of a host of Canaanites and Philistines in Galilee. Jos. x. 43; xi. 1.

xi. 6.

monly but incorrectly (G. A. Smith) identified with the small lake *Huleh*, north of the Lake of Tiberias. The site of the battle is unknown; Josephus seems to identify it with one of the towns which he fortified during the war with Rome and which he calls elsewhere Mero(th) or Ameroth (*B.J.* ii. 573, iii. 39, *Vita* 188).

[c] Kedesh Naphtali, N.W. of the lake *Huleh*.

[d] The numbers are imaginary: Scripture speaks only of "much people, even as the sand that is upon the seashore in multitude, with horses and chariots very many."

[e] Amplification.

τευμα τῶν ἐχθρῶν πλὴν ὀλίγων διέφθειρε, καὶ οἱ
67 βασιλεῖς πάντες ἔπεσον, ὥστε τῶν ἀνθρώπων
ἐπιλελοιπότων πρὸς τὸ κτείνεσθαι τοὺς ἵππους
Ἰησοῦς αὐτῶν ἀνῄρει καὶ τὰ ἅρματα ἐνεπίμπρα,
τήν τε χώραν ἐπ' ἀδείας διεπορεύετο μηδενὸς
τολμῶντος εἰς μάχην ἐπεξελθεῖν, ἀλλὰ πολιορκίᾳ
τὰς πόλεις αἱρῶν καὶ πᾶν ὅ τι λάβοι φονεύων.
68 (19) Ἔτος δὲ πέμπτον ἤδη παρεληλύθει καὶ
Χαναναίων οὐκέτ' οὐδεὶς ὑπολέλειπτο πλὴν εἰ μή
τινες ὀχυρότητι τειχῶν διέφυγον. Ἰησοῦς δ' ἐκ
τῶν Γαλγάλων ἀναστρατοπεδεύσας εἰς τὴν ὄρειον[1]
ἱστᾷ τὴν ἱερὰν σκηνὴν κατὰ Σιλοῦν πόλιν, ἐπιτήδειον γὰρ ἐδόκει τὸ χωρίον διὰ κάλλος, ἕως οἰκο-
69 δομεῖν ναὸν αὐτοῖς τὰ πράγματα παράσχῃ.[2] καὶ
χωρήσας ἐντεῦθεν ἐπὶ Σικίμων σὺν ἅπαντι τῷ λαῷ
βωμόν τε ἵστησιν ὅπου προεῖπε Μωυσῆς καὶ
νείμας τὴν στρατιὰν ἐπὶ μὲν τῷ Γαριζεῖ ὄρει τὴν
ἡμίσειαν ἵστησιν, ἐπὶ δὲ τῷ Ἡβήλῳ[3] τὴν ἡμίσειαν,
ἐν ᾧ καὶ ὁ βωμός,[4] καὶ τὸ Λευιτικὸν καὶ τοὺς
70 ἱερέας. θύσαντες δὲ καὶ ἀρὰς ποιησάμενοι καὶ
ταύτας ἐπὶ τῷ βωμῷ γεγραμμένας καταλιπόντες
εἰς τὴν Σιλοῦν ἀνέζευξαν.

[1] ὀρεινὴν SPE.
[2] παράσχοι Niese. [3] Γηβήλῳ ML.
[4] E: βωμός ἐστι (conj. ἔστη Niese) codd.

---

[a] Scripture makes no such exception: "they smote them until they left them none remaining" (Jos. xi. 8).

[b] A calculation based apparently on Jos. xiv. 7 and 10, where Caleb declares that he was 40 years old when sent out as a spy and that he is now 85. Allowing 40 years for the wanderings, this gives 5 years for the wars of Joshua. Tradition, based on that same passage (together, it would

whole of the enemy's army, save for a few [a]—the kings all fell—in such wise that, when there were no more men to be killed, he slew their horses and burnt the chariots. He then overran the country unmolested, none daring to come out to give him battle; the cities too he captured by siege and massacred every creature that he caught.

Erection of the tabernacle at Shiloh and ceremonies at Shechem Jos. xviii. 1.

(19) A fifth year had now passed away [b] and there was no longer any Canaanite left, save for such as had escaped through the solidity of their walls. So Joshua moved his camp up from Galgala into the hill country and set up the holy tabernacle at the city of Silo,[c] since that spot, by its beauty, seemed meet for it, until circumstances should permit them to build a temple. Proceeding thence to Sikima,[d] with all the people, he erected an altar at the spot fore-ordained by Moses,[e] and, dividing his army, posted one half of it on mount Garizin and the other half on Hēbēl,[f] whereon also stood the altar, along with the Levites and the priests. After sacrificing and pronouncing imprecations,[g] which they also left graven upon the altar, they returned to Silo.

viii. 30 (LXX ix. 3).

seem, with Deut. ii. 14, which restricts the wanderings to 38 years) assigned 7 years to the conquest (Weill).

[c] Greek " Silous ": Heb. Shiloh, LXX Σηλώ.

[d] Bibl. Shechem, LXX Σίκιμα or Σύχεμ, mod. *Nablus.* Scripture places this episode earlier, immediately after the conquest of Ai—unnaturally, because northern Palestine had not then been conquered. Shechem is not mentioned in the Biblical account and there is reason to think that " in order to oppose Samaritan claims, the whole scene of the ceremony has (there) been transported from Shechem to Gilgal " (G. A. Cooke, *Camb. Bible*, on Jos. viii. 30).

[e] *A.* iv. 305.

[f] Bibl. Ebal, LXX Γαιβάλ: in *A.* iv. *l.c.* Βουλή.

[g] Prescribed in Deut. xxvii. ff. (*A.* iv. *l.c.*).

71 (20) Ἰησοῦς δ' ἤδη γηραιὸς ὢν καὶ τὰς τῶν Χαναναίων πόλεις ὁρῶν οὐκ εὐαλώτους ὑπό τε τῆς τῶν χωρίων ἐν οἷς ἦσαν ὀχυρότητος καὶ τῆς τῶν τειχῶν ἰσχύος, ἃ τῇ φυσικῇ τῶν πόλεων πλεονεξίᾳ προσπεριβαλλόμενοι[1] προσεδόκων τοὺς πολεμίους ἀφέξεσθαι πολιορκίας δι' ἀπόγνωσιν τοῦ
72 λαβεῖν, καὶ γὰρ ἐπ' ὀλέθρῳ τῷ ἑαυτῶν οἱ Χαναναῖοι μαθόντες τοὺς Ἰσραηλίτας ποιησαμένους τὴν ἔξοδον τὴν ἀπ' Αἰγύπτου πρὸς τῷ τὰς πόλεις καρτερὰς ποιεῖν ἐκεῖνον ἅπαντ' ἦσαν τὸν χρόνον, συναγαγὼν τὸν λαὸν εἰς τὴν Σιλοῦν ἐκκλησίαν παρήγγειλε.
73 καὶ σπουδῇ συνδραμόντων τά τε ἤδη κατωρθωμένα καὶ τὰς γεγενημένας πράξεις, ὡς εἰσὶν ἄρισται καὶ τοῦ θείου τοῦ παρασχόντος αὐτὰς ἄξιαι καὶ τῆς ἀρετῆς τῶν νόμων οἷς κατακολουθοῦσιν ἔλεγε, βασιλεῖς τε τριάκοντα καὶ ἕνα τολμήσαντας αὐτοῖς εἰς χεῖρας ἐλθεῖν κεκρατῆσθαι δηλῶν, καὶ στρατιὰν ὅση ποτὲ κατελπίσασα τῆς αὐτῶν δυνάμεως εἰς μάχην συνῆψεν ἅπασαν διαφθαρεῖσαν, ὡς μηδὲ
74 γενεὰν αὐτοῖς ὑπολελεῖφθαι. τῶν δὲ πόλεων ἐπειδήπερ αἱ μὲν ἑαλώκεσαν, πρὸς ἃς δὲ δεῖ χρόνου καὶ μεγάλης πολιορκίας διὰ τὴν τῶν τειχῶν ὀχυρότητα καὶ τὴν ἐπὶ ταύτῃ τῶν οἰκητόρων πεποίθησιν, ἠξίου τοὺς ἐκ τῆς περαίας τοῦ Ἰορδάνου συνεξορμήσαντας αὐτοῖς καὶ τῶν κινδύνων συναραμένους ὄντας συγγενεῖς ἀπολύειν ἤδη πρὸς τὰ οἰκεῖα, χάριν αὐτοῖς ὧν συνέκαμον ὁμο-
75 λογοῦντας, ἕνα τε κατὰ φυλὴν ἀρετῇ προύχειν μαρτυρηθέντα πέμπειν, οἳ τὴν γῆν ἐκμετρησάμενοι

[1] προσεπιβαλλόμενοι ROE.

[a] Or perhaps "over-confident of (defeating) their forces."
[b] "Three men for each tribe," Jos. *l.c.*

(20) Joshua, being now old and seeing that the cities of the Canaanites were not lightly to be taken, by reason both of the strength of the sites on which they stood and of the solidity of the walls with which the inhabitants had crowned the natural advantages of their towns, reckoning that their enemies would refrain from besieging what they despaired of capturing—for the Canaanites, since they heard that it was for their destruction that the Israelites had made their exodus from Egypt, had spent all that time in fortifying their cities—Joshua, I say, called his people together to Silo and summoned an assembly. Thither they sped with alacrity, and he spoke to them of the successes already achieved and the exploits accomplished, saying how fine they were and worthy of the Deity who had vouchsafed them and of the excellence of those laws which they were following: he recalled how one and thirty kings who had dared to close with them had been defeated, and how that vast army which once, over-confident in its strength,[a] had joined battle with them, had been entirely destroyed, insomuch that not one family of theirs had survived. Of the cities too some had been taken, but seeing that for the capture of others there was need of time and great siege-works, owing to the strength of their ramparts and the confidence which this inspired in their inhabitants, he deemed it right that those from beyond Jordan who had come to take part in their campaign and had shared their dangers as kinsmen, should now be dismissed to their homes with an expression of thanks for their aid in the task. "Furthermore," said he, "we should send, one from each tribe,[b] men of approved virtue, to measure out the land faith-

Joshua's address to the people at Shiloh. Jos. xiii. 1.

xviii. 1.

xii. 24.

xi. 1 ff.

xxii. 1.

xviii. 4.

πιστῶς καὶ μηδὲν κακουργήσαντες[1] δηλώσουσιν ἡμῖν ἀδόλως αὐτῆς τὸ μέγεθος.

76 (21) Καὶ Ἰησοῦς μὲν τούτους ποιησάμενος τοὺς λόγους συγκάταινον ἔσχε τὸ πλῆθος καὶ ἄνδρας τοὺς ἐκμετρησομένους τὴν χώραν αὐτῶν ἐξέπεμψε παραδοὺς αὐτοῖς τινας γεωμετρίας ἐπιστήμονας, οὓς τἀληθὲς οὐκ ἔμελλε λήσεσθαι διὰ τὴν τέχνην, ἐντολὰς δοὺς ἀποτιμήσασθαι τῆς τε εὐδαίμονος ἰδίᾳ
77 τὸ μέτρον γῆς καὶ τῆς ἧσσον ἀγαθῆς. ἡ γὰρ φύσις τῆς Χαναναίων γῆς τοιαύτη τίς ἐστιν, ὡς ἴδοι τις ἂν πεδία μεγάλα καὶ καρποὺς φέρειν ἱκανώτατα καὶ συγκρινόμενα μὲν ἑτέρᾳ γῇ πανευδαίμονα νομισθησόμενα, τοῖς δ' Ἱεριχουντίων χωρίοις παραβαλλόμενα καὶ τοῖς Ἱεροσολυμιτῶν τὸ μηδὲν
78 ἀναφανησόμενα· καίτοι παντελῶς ὀλίγην αὐτῶν εἶναι τὴν γῆν συμβέβηκε καὶ ταύτης ὀρεινὴν τὴν πολλήν, ἀλλ' ὑπερβολὴν εἰς καρπῶν ἐκτροφήν τε καὶ κάλλος οὐκ ἀπολέλοιπεν ἑτέρᾳ. καὶ διὰ τοῦτο τιμητοὺς μᾶλλον ἢ μετρητοὺς τοὺς κλήρους εἶναι δεῖν ὑπέλαβε, πολλάκις ἑνὸς πλέθρου κἂν χιλίων
79 ἀνταξίου γενομένου. οἱ δὲ ἄνδρες οἱ πεμφθέντες, δέκα δὲ ἦσαν, περιοδεύσαντες καὶ τιμησάμενοι τὴν γῆν ἐν ἑβδόμῳ μηνὶ παρῆσαν πρὸς αὐτὸν εἰς Σιλοῦντα πόλιν, ἔνθα τὴν σκηνὴν ἑστάκεσαν.

[1] Niese: ἐκμετρησόμενοι . . . κακουργήσοντες codd.

[a] The representatives of the tribes (§ 75), excluding the two (Reuben and Gad) for which complete provision had already been made on the east of Jordan. In this account of the division of the land Josephus departs from Scripture and presents a simpler, possibly an older, narrative. In Joshua, after a review of the allotment of land to the 2½ tribes beyond Jordan (chap. xiii.), we are given a preliminary allotment *at Gilgal* (xiv. 6) to Judah, Ephraim and the rest

fully and without fraudulence and honestly to report to us what are its dimensions."

Mission of the measurers of the land. Jos. xviii. 8.

(21) Having delivered this speech and won the assent of the people thereto, Joshua sent out men to measure the country, attaching to them certain expert surveyors, from whom by reason of their skill the truth would not be hid, instructions being given them to assess separately the extent of the favoured land and of that which was less fertile. For the nature of the land of Canaan is such that one may see plains, of great area, fully fitted for bearing crops, and which compared with another district might be deemed altogether blest, yet when set beside the regions of the people of Jericho and Jerusalem would appear as naught. Aye, though the territory of these folk happens to be quite diminutive and for the most part mountainous, yet for its extraordinary productiveness of crops and for beauty it yields to no other. And that was why Joshua held that the allotments should be fixed rather by valuation than by measurement, a single acre being often worth as much as a thousand. So xviii. 9.
the men who had been sent, ten [a] in number, having compassed the land and valued it, in the seventh month [b] returned to him to the city of Silo, where the tabernacle had been set up.

of Manasseh (xv.-xvii.); then from Shiloh emissaries are sent out (3 from each tribe or 21 in all) to measure out the land for the remaining *seven* tribes, and the allotment for these tribes follows (xviii.-xx.). In Josephus there is no preliminary allotment at Gilgal: the apportionment for the 9½ tribes all takes place at Shiloh.

[b] Not in Scripture, which instead has a reference to the "seven portions" into which the land was divided by the emissaries (see last note).

80 (22) Καὶ Ἰησοῦς Ἐλεάζαρόν τε καὶ τὴν γερουσίαν σὺν τοῖς φυλάρχοις παραλαβὼν νέμει ταῖς
ἐννέα φυλαῖς καὶ τῶν Μανασσητῶν τοῖς ἡμίσεσι,
κατὰ μέγεθος ἑκάστης τῶν φυλῶν τὴν μέτρησιν
81 ποιησάμενος. κληρώσαντος δὲ αὐτοῦ, ἡ μὲν Ἰούδα
λαχοῦσα πᾶσαν αἱρεῖται τὴν καθύπερθεν Ἰδουμαίαν
παρατείνουσαν μὲν ἄχρι τῶν Ἱεροσολύμων τὸ δ'
εὖρος ἕως τῆς Σοδομίτιδος λίμνης καθήκουσαν· ἐν
δὲ τῷ κλήρῳ τούτῳ πόλεις ἦσαν Ἀσκάλων καὶ
82 Γάζα. Σεμεωνὶς δέ, δευτέρα γὰρ ἦν, ἔλαχε τῆς
Ἰδουμαίας τὴν Αἰγύπτῳ τε καὶ τῇ Ἀραβίᾳ
πρόσορον οὖσαν. Βενιαμῖται δὲ τὴν ἀπὸ Ἰορδάνου
ποταμοῦ ἔλαχον ἄχρι θαλάσσης μὲν τὸ μῆκος, τὸ
δὲ πλάτος Ἱεροσολύμοις ὁριζομένην καὶ Βεθήλοις·
στενώτατος[1] δὲ ὁ κλῆρος οὗτος ἦν διὰ τὴν τῆς
γῆς ἀρετήν· Ἱεριχοῦντα γὰρ καὶ τὴν Ἱεροσο-
83 λυμιτῶν πόλιν ἔλαβον. ἡ δ' Ἐφραίμου[2] φυλὴ τὴν
ἄχρι Γαζάρων ἀπὸ Ἰορδάνου ποταμοῦ μηκυνο-
μένην ἔλαχεν, εὐρεῖαν δὲ ὅσον ἀπὸ Βεθήλων εἰς
τὸ μέγα τελευτᾷ πεδίον, τῆς τε[3] Μανασσήτιδος οἱ
ἡμίσεις ἀπὸ μὲν Ἰορδάνου μέχρι Δώρων πόλεως,
84 πλάτος δὲ ἐπὶ Βηθησάνων, ἣ νῦν Σκυθόπολις

[1] στενότατος codd. [2] Ἐφρὰν R.
[3] δὲ Bernard (Lat. vers.).

[a] It is difficult to see what part the lot played in the matter beyond determining the order of conferment of territories already allocated in advance proportionate to the size of the various tribes; there can have been no *choice* on the part of the tribes. In rabbinical tradition the Urim and Thummim are said to have been used for the purpose.

[b] "Length" and "breadth" in this description indicate the longer and shorter dimensions of the lots, regardless of their orientation.

[c] The lower end of the Dead Sea.

(22) Then Joshua, taking to him Eleazar and the council of elders, along with the tribal chiefs, distributed all between the nine tribes and the half-tribe of Manasseh, making his measurements proportional to the magnitude of each tribe. When, then, he had cast lots,[a] that of Judah obtained for its lot the whole of upper Idumaea, extending (in length) to Jerusalem and in breadth[b] reaching down to the lake of Sodom[c]; within this allotment were the cities of Ascalon and Gaza. That of Simeon, being the second, obtained the portion of Idumaea bordering on Egypt and Arabia. The Benjamites obtained the region which in length stretches from the river Jordan to the sea[d] and in breadth is bounded by Jerusalem and Bethel. This lot was the narrowest of all by reason of the excellence of the soil, for Jericho and the city of the Jerusalemites fell to their portion. The tribe of Ephraim obtained the land reaching in length from the river Jordan to Gazara[e] and in breadth from Bethel right up to the great plain.[f] The half-tribe of Manasseh had from the Jordan to the city of Dora[g] and in breadth as far as Bēthēsana,[h] now called Scythopolis. After

Allotment of the land between the 9½ tribes. Jos. xviii. 10.

xv. 1.

xix. 1.

xviii. 11.

xvi. 5.

xvii. 1.

xix. 17.

[d] Jos. xviii. 12 "westward" (literally "sea-ward"; LXX ἐπὶ τὴν θάλασσαν); the western border actually lay well inland.

[e] So Jos. xvi. 5 LXX (not in Heb. text). Gazara is the Greek form of the Heb. Gezer (Jos. *ib.* 10), now identified as *Tell Jezar*, some 18 miles N.W. of Jerusalem, on the Philistine border.

[f] The plain of Esdraelon.

[g] Heb. Dor (LXX Δώρ), Jos. xvii. 11; a maritime town 16 miles S. of Carmel (mod. *Tanturah*).

[h] Heb. Beth-shean (LXX Βαιθσάν, mod. *Beisan*, midway between Mt. Gilboa and the Jordan; of the real or supposed Scythian invasion which gave it its other name nothing is known.

καλεῖται, καὶ μετὰ τούτους Ἰσαχαρὶς Κάρμηλόν τε τὸ ὄρος καὶ τὸν ποταμὸν τοῦ μήκους ποιησαμένη τέρμονα,[1] τὸ δὲ Ἰταβύριον ὄρος τοῦ πλάτους. Ζαβουλωνῖται δὲ τὴν μέχρι Γενησαρίδος, καθήκουσαν δὲ περὶ Κάρμηλον καὶ θάλασσαν ἔλαχον.
85 τὴν δὲ ἀπὸ τοῦ Καρμήλου κοιλάδα προσαγορευομένην, διὰ τὸ καὶ τοιαύτην εἶναι, Ἀσηρῖται φέρονται πᾶσαν τὴν ἐπὶ Σιδῶνος τετραμμένην· Ἄρκη δὲ πόλις ὑπῆρχεν αὐτοῖς ἐν τῇ μερίδι ἡ καὶ
86 Ἐκδείπους. τὰ δὲ πρὸς τὰς ἀνατολὰς τετραμμένα μέχρι Δαμασκοῦ πόλεως καὶ τῆς Γαλιλαίας τὰ καθύπερθεν Νεφθαλῖται παρέλαβον ἕως τοῦ Λιβάνου ὄρους καὶ τῶν τοῦ Ἰορδάνου πηγῶν, αἳ τὴν ὁρμὴν ἐκ τοῦ ὄρους ἔχουσιν [ἐκ τοῦ καθήκοντος τοῖς ὅροις κατὰ τὰ βόρεια πόλεως Ἄρκης παροικούσης].[2]
87 Δανῖται δὲ τῆς κοίλης ὅσα πρὸς δυόμενον τέτραπται τὸν ἥλιον λαγχάνουσιν Ἀζώτῳ καὶ Δώροις ὁριζόμενοι, Ἰάμνειάν τε πᾶσαν καὶ Γίτταν ἀπ' Ἀκκαρῶνος ἕως τοῦ ὄρους, ἐξ οὗ ἡ Ἰούδα ἦρκτο φυλή.
88 (23) Καὶ ἓξ μὲν ἔθνη τῶν υἱέων τοῦ Χαναναίου φέροντα τὴν ἐπωνυμίαν διεῖλεν οὕτως Ἰησοῦς καὶ τὴν γῆν ταῖς ἐννέα καὶ τῇ ἡμισείᾳ φυλαῖς ἔδωκε
89 νέμεσθαι· τὴν γὰρ Ἀμορῖτιν καὶ αὐτὴν οὕτως ἀφ' ἑνὸς τῶν Χαναναίου παίδων καλουμένην Μωυσῆς ἤδη προειληφὼς νενεμήκει ταῖς δυσὶ φυλαῖς καὶ τῷ ἡμίσει· τοῦτο δὲ καὶ πρότερον δεδηλώκαμεν.[3]

[1] ML: τέρματα rell. [2] om. Lat.
[3] Niese: δεδηλώκειμεν (-ώκει, -ώκειν) codd.

[a] Mount Tabor; the town of that name is mentioned among the borders of Issachar in Jos. xix. 22.
[b] The sea of Galilee.

these came Issachar, with mount Carmel and the
river for its boundaries in length and mount
Itabyrion [a] as limit of its breadth. They of Zabulon xix. 10
obtained the land which reaches to the (lake of)
Genesar [b] and descends well-nigh to Carmel and the
sea. The region beginning at Carmel, the Vale as xix. 24.
it is called from its nature, was won by the men of
Aser, all of it, that is to say, that faced towards
Sidon; to their portion fell the city of Arce, also
called Ecdipus.[c] The territory to the eastward up xix. 32.
to the city of Damascus, with upper Galilee, was
occupied by the men of Nephthali, as far as mount
Libanus and the sources of the Jordan, which spring
from that mountain.[d] The Danites obtained those xix. 40.
parts of the valley which face the setting sun with
Azotus [e] and Dora for boundaries; they had all
Jamnia,[f] Gitta [g] (and) from Akkaron [h] to the
mountain-range where the tribe of Judah began.

Amoritis and unassigned territory.

(23) Thus did Joshua divide six of the nations that bore the names of the sons of Canaan and gave their land to the nine and a half tribes for their possession; for Amoritis, likewise so called after one of the children of Canaan, had already of yore been taken and apportioned by Moses to the two and a half tribes, as we have previously related.[i] But the

[c] Heb. Achzib (Jos. xix. 29), mod. *ez Zīb*, called Ecdippa, *B.J.* i. 257, on the coast midway between Carmel and Tyre.

[d] The MSS. add some unintelligible words, omitted by the Latin version and perhaps a gloss: (?) "from the part where it descends to the boundary to the north of the adjacent city of Arce."

[e] Heb. Ashdod.

[f] Heb. Jabneel (Jos. xv. 11) or Jabneh, mod. *Yebnah*, another city in the Philistine plain.

[g] Gath. [h] Ekron. [i] iv. 166 ff.

τὰ δὲ περὶ Σιδῶνα καὶ Ἀρουκαίους καὶ Ἀμαθαίους καὶ Ἀριδαίους[1] ἀδιακόσμητα ἦν.

90 (24) Ἰησοῦς δέ, τοῦ γήρως ἐμποδίζοντος ἤδη πράττειν ὅσα καὶ νοήσειε, τῶν τε μετ' αὐτὸν τὴν ἡγεμονίαν παραλαβόντων ἀμελῶς προστάντων τοῦ κοινῇ συμφέροντος, παρήγγειλέ τε[2] φυλῇ ἑκάστῃ τοῦ γένους τῶν Χαναναίων μηδὲν ὑπολιπεῖν ἐν τῇ κατακεκληρωμένῃ γῇ· τὴν γὰρ ἀσφάλειαν αὐτοῖς καὶ τὴν φυλακὴν τῶν πατρίων ἐθῶν ἐν μόνῳ τούτῳ καὶ Μωυσῆν αὐτοῖς εἶναι προειπεῖν καὶ τοῦτ' αὐ-
91 τὸς[3] πεπεῖσθαι· καὶ τοῖς Λευίταις δὲ τὰς ὀκτὼ καὶ τριάκοντα πόλεις ἀποδιδόναι· προειλήφεισαν γὰρ ἤδη κατὰ τὴν Ἀμοραίαν τὰς δέκα. τούτων τρεῖς ἀπονέμει τοῖς φυγάσιν οἰκεῖν ἐν αὐταῖς, πολλὴ γὰρ ἦν πρόνοια τοῦ μηδὲν ὧν Μωυσῆς διέταξε παραλιπεῖν, τῆς μὲν οὖν Ἰούδα φυλῆς Ἕβρωνα, Σίκιμα δὲ τῆς Ἐφραίμ, τῆς Νεφθαλίτιδος δὲ Κεδέσην· ἔστι δὲ τῆς καθύπερθεν Γαλιλαίας τοῦτο
92 τὸ χωρίον. νέμει δὲ καὶ τῆς λείας ὅσα ἦν ἔτι λοιπά, πλείστη δ' ἐγεγόνει, καὶ μεγάλους πλούτους περιεβέβληντο καὶ κοινῇ πάντες καὶ κατ' ἰδίαν ἕκαστος χρυσοῦ τε καὶ ἀργύρου καὶ ἐσθήτων καὶ τῆς ἄλλης ἐπισκευῆς ἕνεκα, τετραπόδων τε πλήθους ὅσον οὐδὲ ἀριθμῷ μαθεῖν ἦν προσγενομένου.

93 (25) Μετὰ δὲ[4] ταῦτα συναγαγὼν εἰς ἐκκλησίαν τὸν στρατὸν τοῖς ὑπὲρ τὸν Ἰόρδανον κατὰ τὴν Ἀμοραίαν ἱδρυμένοις, συνεστράτευον δ' αὐτοῖς

[1] Ἀραδαίους conj. Niese.
[2] om. τε Lat., ed. pr.
[3] Naber: αὐτοὺς codd.
[4] ROE: δὴ rell.

[a] *Cf.* the list of the 11 sons of Canaan (Chananaeus) previously given in *A.* i. 138 f., to which Josephus is here referring. The countries of 7 of these have now been assigned:

regions about Sidon, with those of the Arucaeans, Amathaeans and Aridaeans, remained unassigned.[a]

(24) Joshua, now that age impeded him from carrying out his own designs and also because those who after him took over the command showed themselves careless guardians of the common weal, straitly charged each tribe to leave no remnant of the race of the Canaanites within their allotted territory, since their security and the maintenance of their ancestral institutions hung upon that alone: this Moses had already told them[b] and of this he was himself persuaded. They were also to render up to the Levites those eight and thirty cities—for these had already received the other ten in the Amorite country.[c] Of these cities, he assigned three for fugitives to dwell in—for he took strict care to neglect none of the ordinances of Moses—to wit Hebron belonging to the tribe of Judah, Sikima[d] to Ephraim and Kedese[e] to Nephthali, this last being a place in upper Galilee. He also distributed what yet remained of the spoils, of which there was a vast mass; and all, collectively and individually, found themselves endowed with great riches, gold, silver, apparel and equipment of every kind, over and above such a multitude of cattle[f] as was past numbering.

Cities of Levites and of refuge: division of spoils. Jos. xxiii. 1. xxi. 1. xx. 1. cf. xxii. 8.

(25) Thereafter, having collected his army in assembly, he addressed to those who had their settlement beyond Jordan in Amoraea—of whom 50,000

Joshua's farewell address to the 2½ tribes. Jos. xxii. 1.

the 4 still outstanding are in Biblical nomenclature Zidon, Arkite, Hamathite and Arvadite (Gen. x. 15 ff.). Joshua (xiii. 2-6) also enumerates the unconquered territories, including that of the Philistines, not mentioned by Josephus.

[b] iv. 191 f. [c] iv. 67, 172. [d] Shechem.

[e] Kedesh. [f] lit. "four-footed (beasts)."

πεντακισμύριοι ὁπλῖται, ἔλεξε τάδε· "ἐπεὶ ὁ θεός,[1] πατὴρ καὶ δεσπότης τοῦ Ἑβραίων γένους, γῆν τε κτήσασθαι ταύτην ἔδωκε καὶ κτηθεῖσαν εἰς
94 ἅπαν ἡμετέραν φυλάξειν ὑπέσχηται, συνεργίας δὲ τῆς παρ' ὑμῶν κατ' ἐντολὴν τὴν ἐκείνου δεομένοις ἑαυτοὺς εἰς ἅπαντα προθύμους ἐδώκατε, δίκαιον ὑμᾶς μηδενὸς ἔτι δυσκόλου περιμένοντος ἀναπαύσεως ἤδη τυχεῖν φειδοῖ τῆς προθυμίας ὑμῶν, ἵν' εἰ καὶ πάλιν δεήσειεν ἡμῖν αὐτῆς ἄοκνον ἔχωμεν εἰς τὰ κατεπείξοντα καὶ μὴ τοῖς νῦν καμοῦσαν
95 αὖθις βραδυτέραν. χάριν τε οὖν ὑμῖν ὧν συνήρασθε κινδύνων καὶ οὐχὶ νῦν μόνον ἀλλ' εἰς ἅπαν οὕτως ἕξομεν, ὄντες ἀγαθοὶ μεμνῆσθαι τῶν φίλων καὶ παρὰ τῇ διανοίᾳ κρατεῖν ὅσα παρ' αὐτῶν ἡμῖν ὑπῆρξεν, ὅτι τε τὴν ἀπόλαυσιν τῶν ὑπαρχόντων ὑμῖν ἀγαθῶν δι' ἡμᾶς ἀνεβάλεσθε καὶ πονήσαντες[2] εἰς ἃ νῦν εὐνοίᾳ θεοῦ κατέστημεν ἔπειθ' οὕτως
96 ἐκρίνατε αὐτῶν μεταλαμβάνειν. γέγονε δὲ πρὸς τοῖς ὑπάρχουσιν ἀγαθοῖς ἐκ τῶν σὺν ἡμῖν πόνων πλοῦτος ἄφθονος, λείαν τε πολλὴν ἐπαξομένοις καὶ χρυσὸν καὶ ἄργυρον, καὶ τὸ τούτων ἔτι πλεῖον, ἡ παρ' ἡμῶν[3] εὔνοια καὶ πρὸς ὅ τι βουληθείητε κατ' ἀμοιβὴν πρόθυμον. οὔτε γὰρ ὧν Μωυσῆς προεῖπεν ἀπελείφθητε καταφρονήσαντες ἐξ ἀνθρώπων ἀπελθόντος οὔτ' ἔστιν οὐδὲν ἐφ' ᾧ μὴ χάριν ὑμῖν
97 οἴδαμεν. χαίροντας οὖν ὑμᾶς ἐπὶ τὰς κληρουχίας ἀπολύομεν καὶ παρακαλοῦμεν μηδένα τῆς πρὸς ἡμᾶς συγγενείας ὅρον ὑπολαμβάνειν, μηδ' ὅτι μεταξὺ ποταμὸς οὗτός ἐστιν ἑτέρους ἡμᾶς νομίσητε

[1] θεὸς καὶ MSPL. [2] ROL: συμπονήσαντες SP.
[3] MSPLE: παρ' ἡμῖν RO: vester Lat.

[a] *i.e.* in cattle.

men-at-arms had taken part in their campaign—the following words: "Seeing that God, the Father and Lord of the Hebrew race, has given us to win this land and, being won, has promised to preserve it to us for ever, and seeing that, when at His behest we besought your assistance, ye offered your ready services for all, it is but just, when no further arduous task awaits us, that ye should now obtain repose, husbanding your devotion, to the end that, should we again have need of it, we may find it alert to meet those future emergencies and not so worn by the toils of to-day as to respond more sluggishly hereafter. We therefore tender you our thanks for having shared those perils with us, and not to-day only but for ever shall we be grateful; for we are apt to remember our friends and to keep in mind services which they have rendered to us, even how for our sakes ye deferred the enjoyment of your goodly possessions and resolved that, only after toiling for the end whereto by the grace of God we have now attained, would ye then at last partake of them. Yet, to add to those goods that ye possess, ye have by your labours with us won wealth in abundance: ye will take with you rich booty,[a] gold and silver and, what is more than all, our goodwill and readiness to serve and requite you in whatsoever ye may desire. For ye have in nowise shirked those behests of Moses, nor disdained his authority now that he has passed away, nor is there aught for which we do not accord you gratitude. We therefore let you joyfully depart to your heritages, and we entreat you not to suppose that the kinship which unites us owns any boundary, nor, because this river runs between us, to regard us as strangers and not as

καὶ οὐχὶ Ἑβραίους. Ἀβράμου γὰρ ἅπαντές ἐσμεν οἵ τ᾽ ἐνθάδε κἀκεῖ κατοικοῦντες, θεός τε εἷς, ὃς τούς τε ἡμετέρους προγόνους καὶ τοὺς ὑμῶν αὐτῶν
98 παρήγαγεν εἰς τὸν βίον· οὗ τῆς θρησκείας ἐπιμελεῖσθε καὶ πολιτείας, ἣν αὐτὸς διὰ Μωυσέος διέταξε, φυλακὴν ἔχετε τὴν πᾶσαν, ὡς ἐμμενόντων μὲν τούτοις καὶ τοῦ θεοῦ παρέξοντος εὔνουν εἶναι καὶ σύμμαχον ἑαυτόν, ἐκτραπέντων δὲ εἰς ἑτέρων ἐθνῶν μίμησιν ἀποστραφησομένου τὸ γένος ὑμῶν."
99 ταῦτα εἰπὼν καὶ καθ᾽ ἕνα τοὺς ἐν τέλει καὶ κοινῇ τὸ πλῆθος αὐτῶν ἀσπασάμενος αὐτὸς μὲν ὑπέμεινε, προύπεμπε δ᾽ αὐτοὺς ὁ λαὸς οὐκ ἀδακρυτὶ καὶ μόλις ἀλλήλων ἀπελύθησαν.

100 (26) Διαβᾶσα δὲ τὸν ποταμὸν ἥ τε Ῥουβηλὶς φυλὴ καὶ Γαδὶς καὶ ὅσοι τῶν Μανασσητῶν αὐτοῖς συνείποντο βωμὸν ὑπὲρ τῆς ὄχθης ἱδρύονται τοῦ Ἰορδάνου, μνημεῖον τοῖς ἔπειτα γενησομένοις,[1] σύμβολον[2] τῆς πρὸς τοὺς πέραν κατοικησομένους[3]
101 οἰκειότητος. ἀκούσαντες δὲ οἱ πέραν βωμὸν ἱδρῦσθαι τοὺς ἀπολυθέντας οὐ μεθ᾽ ἧς ἐκεῖνοι γνώμης ἀνέστησαν αὐτόν, ἀλλ᾽ ἐπὶ νεωτερισμῷ καὶ ξενικῶν εἰσαγωγῇ θεῶν, οὐκ ἤθελον ἀπιστεῖν, ἀλλὰ περὶ τὴν θείαν[4] θρησκείαν τὴν διαβολὴν πιθανὴν νομίζοντες ἐν ὅπλοις ἦσαν, ὡς ἐπ᾽ ἀμύνῃ τῶν τὸν βωμὸν ἱδρυσαμένων περαιωσόμενοι τὸν ποταμὸν καὶ κολάσοντες αὐτοὺς τῆς παρατροπῆς τῶν πατρίων
102 ἐθῶν. οὐ γὰρ ἐδόκει τὴν συγγένειαν αὐτοὺς λογίζεσθαι καὶ τὸ ἀξίωμα τῶν τὴν αἰτίαν εἰληφότων,

[1] γενησόμενον Niese.
[2] σύμβολον before τῆς om. E Lat. (probably a gloss, *cf.* § 112).
[3] κατῳκημένους SPE.
[4] θείων RO.

Hebrews. For we are all of Abraham's stock, whether living here or there, and it is one God who brought our forefathers and yours into existence. To the worship of Him pay ye heed, and of that polity, which He Himself has instituted through Moses, observe ye every precept, in the assurance that, while ye remain faithful to these, God also will show Himself your gracious ally, but if ye turn aside to xxii. 6.
imitate other nations He will turn away from your race." Having thus spoken and bidden farewell, to the officers one by one, and to their whole company in general, he himself remained; but the people escorted them on their way not without tears, and hardly were they parted from one another.

They erect an altar beyond Jordan: embassy and expostulation of Phinees.

(26) Having then crossed the river, the tribe of Rubel with that of Gad and all those of Manasseh who accompanied them erected an altar on the bank of the Jordan, as a memorial to future generations of their relationship to the inhabitants on the other side. But those beyond the river,[a] having heard Jos. xxii. 10.
tell that the migrants had erected an altar, not with the purpose which had led them to set it up, but with designs of sedition and the introduction of strange gods, were loth to distrust the report; nay, deeming this calumny concerning divine worship credible, they sprang to arms, with intent to cross the river and be avenged on those that had erected the altar and to punish them for this perversion of the rites of their fathers. For they held that they should take no account of their kinship or of the rank of those thus incriminated, but of the

[a] *i.e.* on the west; "beyond the river" from the point of view of those in trans-Jordania. In Scripture "beyond the river" invariably refers to the eastern side of the Jordan.

ἀλλὰ τὸ τοῦ θεοῦ βουλητὸν καὶ ᾧ τρόπῳ τιμώμενος
103 χαίρει. καὶ οἱ μὲν ἐστράτευσαν ὑπ' ὀργῆς, ἐπέσχε δ' αὐτοὺς Ἰησοῦς καὶ ὁ ἀρχιερεὺς Ἐλεάζαρος καὶ ἡ γερουσία λόγοις συμβουλεύοντες ἀπόπειραν αὐτῶν τῆς γνώμης λαβεῖν πρῶτον, ἔπειτ' ἂν κακοήθη μάθωσι τὴν διάνοιαν αὐτῶν τότε τοῖς
104 ὅπλοις χωρεῖν ἐπ' αὐτούς. πέμπουσιν οὖν πρεσβευτὰς πρὸς αὐτοὺς Φινεέσην τὸν υἱὸν Ἐλεαζάρου καὶ δέκα σὺν αὐτῷ τῶν ἐν τιμῇ παρὰ τοῖς Ἑβραίοις μαθησομένους, τί καὶ φρονήσαντες τὸν βωμὸν ἐπὶ
105 τῆς ὄχθης τοῦ ποταμοῦ διαβάντες ἔστησαν. ὡς δὲ περαιωσαμένων καὶ πρὸς αὐτοὺς ἀφικομένων ἐκκλησία συνελέγη, στὰς Φινεέσης μείζω μὲν αὐτοὺς ἁμαρτεῖν ἔλεγεν ἢ ὥστε λόγοις ἐπιτιμηθέντας νενουθετῆσθαι πρὸς τὰ μέλλοντα· πλὴν οὐ πρὸς τὸ μέγεθος τῆς παρανομίας ἀπιδόντας εὐθὺς ἐφ' ὅπλα καὶ τὴν ἐκ χειρῶν τιμωρίαν ὁρμῆσαι, πρὸς δὲ τὸ συγγενὲς καὶ τὸ τάχα καὶ λόγοις ἂν σωφρονῆσαι σκοπήσαντας οὕτω ποιήσασθαι τὴν
106 πρεσβείαν, "ἵνα τὴν αἰτίαν μαθόντες ὑφ' ἧς προήχθητε τὸν βωμὸν κατασκευάσαι μήτε προπετεῖς δοκῶμεν ὅπλοις μετιόντες ὑμᾶς κατὰ λογισμὸν ὅσιον ποιησαμένους τὸν βωμόν, καὶ[1] δικαίως
107 ἀμυνώμεθα τῆς διαβολῆς ἐλεγχθείσης ἀληθοῦς. οὐ γὰρ ἠξιοῦμεν ὑμᾶς πείρᾳ τῆς τοῦ θεοῦ γνώμης ἐντὸς γεγενημένους καὶ νόμων ὧν αὐτὸς ἡμῖν δέδωκεν ἀκροατὰς ὑπάρχοντας, διαζευχθέντας ἡμῶν καὶ παρόντας εἰς τὸν ἴδιον κλῆρον, ὃν κατὰ χάριν τοῦ θεοῦ καὶ τῆς ἐκείνου περὶ ἡμᾶς[2] προνοίας

[1] ed. pr.: κατι (καὶ ἔτι, etc.) codd.
[2] ὑμᾶς edd.

will of God and the fashion in which He delights to be honoured. So, moved by indignation, they prepared to take the field; but Joshua and Eleazar the high priest and the elders restrained them, counselling them first to test their brethren's mind by a parley, and, should they find their intent mischievous, then and then only to proceed to hostilities. They sent therefore ambassadors to them, Phinees, xxii. 13.
son of Eleazar, and with him ten others highly esteemed among the Hebrews, to discover what they could have meant by erecting that altar on the riverbank after they had passed over. So, the embassy having crossed the river and reached these people, an assembly was convened, and Phinees arose and said that their sin was too grave to be met by a verbal reprimand and an admonition for the future; howbeit, they themselves had not wished to look at the enormity of the crime so as to rush instantly to arms and violent measures, but, looking rather to their kinship and to the possibility that words might suffice to bring them to reason, they had undertaken this embassy. "We are here," said he, "in order that, having learnt what reason induced you to build this altar, we may on the one hand not be deemed precipitate in bearing arms against you, should ye have had some pious motive in erecting it, and on the other that we may take righteous vengeance, should the accusation prove true. For we could not conceive that ye, with your experience of instruction in the will of God, ye who had been hearers of those laws which He Himself has given us, once parted from us and entering on your own heritage, which by the grace of God and His providential care for us has fallen to your lot, could have

ἐλάχετε, λήθην λαβεῖν αὐτοῦ καὶ τὴν σκηνὴν καὶ τὴν κιβωτὸν καταλιπόντας καὶ βωμὸν ὃς ἡμῖν πάτριος ξενικοὺς θεοὺς ἐπιφέρειν τοῖς Χαναναίων
108 κακοῖς προσκεχωρηκότας. ἀλλ' οὐδὲν ἀδικεῖν δόξετε μετανοήσαντες καὶ μὴ περαιτέρω μανέντες, νόμων δὲ πατρίων αἰδῶ καὶ μνήμην λαβόντες. ἂν δ' ἐπιμένητε τοῖς ἡμαρτημένοις, οὐ περιστησόμεθα[1] τὸν ὑπὲρ τῶν νόμων πόνον, ἀλλὰ περαιωσάμενοι τὸν Ἰόρδανον τούτοις βοηθήσομεν καὶ πρὸ αὐτῶν[2] τῷ θεῷ, μηδὲν ὑμᾶς Χαναναίων διαφέρειν ὑπολαμβάνοντες ἀλλ' ὁμοίως ἐκείνοις διαφθείροντες.
109 μὴ γὰρ νομίσητε τῷ διαβεβηκέναι τὸν ποταμὸν καὶ τῆς τοῦ θεοῦ δυνάμεως ἔξω γεγονέναι· πανταχοῦ δ' ἐν τοῖς τούτου ἐστὲ καὶ ἀποδρᾶναι τὴν ἐξουσίαν αὐτοῦ καὶ τὴν ἀπὸ ταύτης δίκην ἀδύνατον. εἰ δ' οἴεσθε τὴν ἐνθάδε παρουσίαν ὑμῖν ἐμπόδιον εἶναι τοῦ σωφρονεῖν, οὐδὲν κωλύει πάλιν τὴν γῆν ἡμᾶς[3]
110 ἀναδάσασθαι καὶ ταύτην ἀνεῖναι μηλόβοτον. ἀλλ' εὖ ποιήσετε σωφρονήσαντες καὶ ἐπὶ νεαροῖς μετατιθέμενοι τοῖς ἁμαρτήμασι. καὶ παρακαλοῦμεν ὑμᾶς πρὸς παίδων καὶ γυναικῶν μὴ παρασχεῖν ἡμῖν ἀνάγκην ἀμύνασθαι. ὡς οὖν τῆς ὑμετέρας αὐτῶν σωτηρίας καὶ τῶν φιλτάτων ὑμῖν ἐν τῇδε τῇ ἐκκλησίᾳ κειμένης οὕτω βουλεύεσθε, λόγοις ἡττηθῆναι συμφέρειν ὑπολαμβάνοντες ἢ πεῖραν ἔργων καὶ πολέμου περιμένειν."
111 (27) Τοσαῦτα τοῦ Φινεέσου διαλεχθέντος οἱ προεστῶτες τῆς ἐκκλησίας καὶ τὸ πλῆθος αὐτὸ πᾶν ἤρξαντο περὶ τῶν ἐγκεκλημένων αὐτοῖς ἀπολογεῖ-

[1] παραιτησόμεθα SPE.
[2] ante omnia Lat.: πρὸς (=προσέτι) αὐτῷ Hudson.
[3] ὑμᾶς codd.

straightway forgotten Him and, abandoning the tabernacle and the ark and the altar of our fathers, introduced some strange gods and gone over to the vices of the Canaanites. Howbeit ye shall be in no wise held guilty, if ye repent and carry this madness no farther, but show that ye revere and are mindful of the laws of your fathers. Should ye, however, persist in your errors, we shall shun no toil in defence of those laws, but, crossing the Jordan, shall rally in support of them, aye and of God on their behalf,[a] deeming you in no wise different from the Canaanites but destroying you in like manner with them. For think not that by crossing the river ye have also passed beyond God's power: nay, everywhere ye are within His domain and escape from His authority and His vengeance is impossible. But if ye regard your coming hither a hindrance to sober living, there is nothing to prevent us[b] from making a redistribution of the land and abandoning this district to the grazing of sheep. Howbeit ye will do well to return to sanity and to change your ways while your sins are fresh. And we entreat you in the name of your children and wives not to constrain us to resort to force. Let, then, the thought that the salvation of your own selves and of them that are dearest to you hangs upon this assembly govern your deliberations, and reckon it more profitable to be defeated by words than to await the trial of deeds and of war."

(27) After this discourse of Phinees, the presidents of the assembly and the whole multitude themselves began to disclaim the crimes wherewith they were

The tribes protest their innocence. Jos. xxii. 21.

[a] Text a little doubtful: perhaps "and, furthermore, of God himself."

[b] The MSS. have "you."

σθαι, καὶ μήτε συγγενείας τῆς πρὸς αὐτοὺς ἀποστήσεσθαι[1] μήτε κατὰ νεωτερισμὸν ἀναστῆσαι τὸν
112 βωμὸν λέγειν, ἀλλὰ θεόν τε ἕνα γινώσκειν τὸν Ἑβραίοις ἅπασι κοινὸν καὶ τὸν πρὸ τῆς σκηνῆς βωμὸν χάλκεον, ᾧ τὰς θυσίας ποιήσειν· τὸν μέντοι γε νῦν ἀνασταθέντα, δι' ὃν καὶ ὕποπτοι γεγόνασιν, οὐ κατὰ θρησκείαν ἱδρῦσθαι, "σύμβολον δὲ ὅπως εἴη καὶ τεκμήριον εἰς τὸν αἰῶνα τῆς πρὸς ὑμᾶς οἰκειότητος καὶ ἀνάγκη τοῦ σωφρονεῖν καὶ τοῖς πατρίοις ἐμμένειν, ἀλλ' οὐχὶ παραβάσεως ἀρχήν,
113 ὡς ὑπονοεῖτε. μάρτυς δ' ἡμῖν τοῦ ἐπὶ τοιαύτῃ τὸν βωμὸν αἰτίᾳ κατασκευάσαι γένοιτο ὁ θεὸς ἀξιόχρεως, ὅθεν ἀμείνονα περὶ ἡμῶν ἔχοντες ὑπόληψιν μηδὲν καταγινώσκετε τούτων, ἐφ' οἷς ἐξώλεις εἶναι δίκαιοι πάντες ὅσοι τοῦ Ἀβράμου γένους ὄντες νεωτέροις ἐπιχειροῦσιν ἔθεσι καὶ τοῦ συνήθους τρόπου παρηλλαγμένοις."

114 (28) Ταῦτα εἰπόντας ἐπαινέσας ὁ Φινεέσης παρῆν πρὸς Ἰησοῦν καὶ τὰ παρ' αὐτῶν ἀνήγγειλε τῷ λαῷ. ὁ δὲ χαίρων, ὅτι μηδεμία στρατολογεῖν αὐτοὺς ἀνάγκη μέλλει μηδ' εἰς αἷμα[2] καὶ πόλεμον ἐξαγαγεῖν κατὰ ἀνδρῶν συγγενῶν, χαριστηρίους
115 ὑπὲρ τούτων τῷ θεῷ θυσίας ἐπιτελεῖ. καὶ διαλύσας μετὰ ταῦτα τὸ πλῆθος εἰς τὰς ἰδίας κληρουχίας Ἰησοῦς αὐτὸς ἐν Σικίμοις διῆγεν. ἔτει δ' ὕστερον εἰκοστῷ ὑπέργηρως ὢν μεταπεμψάμενος τοὺς ἐπ' ἀξιώματος μάλιστα τῶν πόλεων καὶ τὰς ἀρχὰς καὶ τὴν γερουσίαν[3] καὶ τοῦ πλήθους ὅσον ἦν ἐφικτὸν

[1] ἀποστήσασθαι Weill. [2] ὅπλα RO.
[3] τὰς γερουσίας ML.

charged, saying that neither would they renounce[a] their kinship to their brethren, nor had they erected the altar with revolutionary intent: nay, they recognized but the one God, owned by all Hebrews alike, and the brazen altar before the tabernacle whereon the sacrifices should be offered. As for that which they had now set up and which had brought suspicion upon them, they had not erected it for worship: "nay," said they, "but as a symbol and token for eternity of our kinship with you, and an obligation to think soberly and to abide by the laws of our fathers, in no wise as a beginning of transgression, as ye suspect. And that such was our motive in building this altar be God our all-sufficient witness! Wherefore, have a better opinion of us and cease to accuse us of any of those crimes, for which all would justly deserve to be extirpated who, being of the stock of Abraham, embark on new-fangled ways that are perversions of our customary practice."

(28) Phinees, having commended them for this speech, returned to Joshua and reported their answer to the people. And Joshua, rejoicing that there was to be no need to levy troops or to lead them to bloodshed and battle against kinsmen, offered sacrifices of thanksgiving to God for these mercies. Thereafter, having dismissed the multitude to their several provinces, Joshua himself abode at Sikima. Twenty years later,[b] in extreme old age, having sent for the chief notables of the cities, with their magistrates and elders, and assembled as many of the people as could be collected, he,

Jos. xxii 30.

xxiv. 1.

Address of Joshua before his death. Jos. xxiii., xxiv.

[a] Perhaps read, "had they renounced."

[b] Jos. xxiii. 1 "after many days."

αὐτῷ συναγαγών, ἐπεὶ παρῆσαν, τάς τε εὐεργεσίας
τοῦ θεοῦ ἁπάσας ἀνεμίμνησκεν αὐτούς, πολλαὶ δὲ
ἦσαν τοῖς ἐκ ταπεινοῦ σχήματος εἰς τοῦτο δόξης
116 καὶ περιουσίας προελθοῦσι, φυλάττειν τε τὴν τοῦ
θεοῦ προαίρεσιν οὕτως ἔχουσαν πρὸς αὐτοὺς παρεκάλει καὶ τῇ εὐσεβείᾳ[1] γε[2] μόνῃ φίλον αὐτοῖς
διαμενεῖν[3] τὸ θεῖον· αὐτῷ γὰρ καλῶς ἔχειν ἀπιέναι
μέλλοντι τοῦ ζῆν παραίνεσιν αὐτοῖς τοιαύτην καταλιπεῖν κἀκείνους ἠξίου διὰ μνήμης ποιήσασθαι τὴν
παρακέλευσιν.
117 (29) Καὶ ὁ μὲν τοσαῦτα πρὸς τοὺς παρόντας διαλεχθεὶς τελευτᾷ βιοὺς ἑκατὸν ἔτη καὶ δέκα, ὧν
Μωυσεῖ μὲν ἐπὶ διδασκαλίᾳ τῶν χρησίμων συν-
διέτριψε τεσσαράκοντα, στρατηγὸς δὲ μετὰ τὴν
118 ἐκείνου τελευτὴν γίνεται πέντε καὶ εἴκοσιν, ἀνὴρ
μήτε συνέσεως ὢν ἐνδεὴς μήτε τοῦ τὰ νοηθέντα
πρὸς τοὺς πολλοὺς σαφῶς ἐξενεγκεῖν ἄπειρος, ἀλλ'
ἐν ἀμφοτέροις ἄκρος, πρός τε τὰ ἔργα καὶ τοὺς
κινδύνους εὔψυχος καὶ μεγαλότολμος, πρυτανεῦσαί
τε τὰ κατὰ τὴν εἰρήνην δεξιώτατος καὶ πρὸς
119 ἅπαντα καιρὸν τὴν ἀρετὴν ἡρμοσμένος. θάπτεται
δὲ ἐν πόλει Θαμνᾶ τῆς Ἐφραίμου φυλῆς. θνήσκει
δὲ ὑπ' αὐτὸν τὸν καιρὸν καὶ Ἐλεάζαρος ὁ ἀρχιερεὺς
Φινεέσῃ τῷ παιδὶ τὴν ἱερωσύνην καταλιπών, καὶ

[1] Text doubtful: for καὶ τῇ εὐσ. SP read τιμῇ πάσῃ χρωμένους καὶ εὐσεβείᾳ.
[2] L: om. ROSP: ᾗ γε Niese.
[3] Niese: διαμένειν codd.

[a] Or perhaps "to observe God's will, so benevolent towards them."

on their coming, recalled to them all the benefactions of God—and many had they been to folk who from low estate had advanced to that pitch of glory and affluence—and exhorted them to keep God's goodwill unchanged towards them,[a] for by piety[b] alone could they retain the friendship of the Deity. It behoved him, he said, on the eve of departure from life, to leave them such admonition, and he besought them to bear his exhortation in their memory.

(29) And so, after this address to the assembled company, he died, having lived one hundred and ten years; of which he had passed forty in the company of Moses receiving profitable instruction, and after his master's death had been commander-in-chief for five-and-twenty.[c] A man[d] not wanting either in intelligence or in skill to expound his ideas to the multitude with lucidity, nay in both respects supreme, in action and perils he was stout-hearted and greatly daring, in peace-time a most dexterous director of affairs, adapting himself admirably to every occasion. He was buried in the city of Thamna[e] of the tribe of Ephraim. About the same time died also Eleazar the high priest, leaving the priesthood

Death of Joshua and of Eleazar. Jos. xxiv. 29.

xxiv. 33.

[b] Text doubtful. Some MSS. read "by showing Him every honour and that piety," etc.

[c] The duration of Joshua's command is not stated in Scripture. But, according to M. Weill, the figure here given (25 years) is found also in the *Samaritan Chronicle*, while Rabbinical tradition (*Seder Olam Rabba* xii.) extends the period to 28 years.

[d] *Cf.* the previous brief character-sketch in *A.* iii. 49.

[e] Heb. Timnath-serah, identified by tradition with Thamna (mod. *Tibneh*) in mount Ephraim and the seat of a toparchy in Roman times (*B.J.* ii. 567, iii. 55).

μνημεῖον αὐτῷ καὶ τάφος ἐν Γαβαθᾶ πόλει τυγχάνει.

120 (ii. 1) Μετὰ δὲ τὴν τούτων τελευτὴν Φινεέσης
προφητεύει κατὰ τὴν τοῦ θεοῦ βούλησιν ἐπ' ἐξ-
ωλείᾳ τοῦ Χαναναίων γένους τῇ Ἰούδα φυλῇ παρασχεῖν τὴν ἡγεμονίαν· καὶ γὰρ τῷ λαῷ διὰ σπουδῆς
ἦν μαθεῖν τί καὶ τῷ θεῷ δοκεῖ. καὶ προσλαβοῦσα
τὴν Σεμεωνίδα, ἐφ' ᾧτε ἐξαιρεθέντων τῶν ἐκείνης
ὑποτελῶν καὶ τοὺς ἐν αὐτῇ τῇ κληρουχίᾳ τοῦτο
ποιῶσιν * * *[1]
121 (2) Χαναναῖοι δ' ἀκμαζόντων αὐτοῖς κατ' ἐκεῖνον
τὸν καιρὸν τῶν πραγμάτων στρατῷ μεγάλῳ κατὰ
Ζεβέκην αὐτοὺς ὑπέμενον τῷ βασιλεῖ τῶν Ζεβεκηνῶν Ἀδωνιζεβέκῳ τὴν ἡγεμονίαν ἐπιτρέψαντες·
τὸ δὲ ὄνομα τοῦτο σημαίνει Ζεβεκηνῶν κύριος·
ἀδωνὶ γὰρ τῇ Ἑβραίων διαλέκτῳ κύριος γίνεται[2]·
ἤλπιζόν τε κρατήσειν τῶν Ἰσραηλιτῶν διὰ τὸ
122 τεθνάναι Ἰησοῦν. συμμίξαντες δὲ αὐτοῖς Ἰσραηλῖται ταῖς δυσὶ φυλαῖς αἷς προεῖπον ἐμαχέσαντο
λαμπρῶς καὶ κτείνουσι μὲν αὐτῶν ὑπὲρ μυρίους,
τρεψάμενοι δὲ τὸ λοιπὸν καὶ διώκοντες αἱροῦσι
τὸν Ἀδωνιζέβεκον, ὃς ἀκρωτηριασθεὶς ὑπ' αὐτῶν
123 φησιν, " ἀλλ' οὐκ εἰς τὸ πᾶν ἄρα λήσεσθαι θεὸν
ἔμελλον, τάδε πεπονθὼς ἃ κατὰ δυοῖν καὶ ἑβδομή-

[1] Text of clause uncertain. Niese indicates a lacuna: Dindorf instead alters καὶ προσλαβοῦσα above to προσλαβούσῃ.
[2] λέγεται E.

[a] Heb. " in Gibeah (or ' the hill ') of Phinehas his son ": in the MSS. of the LXX the name appears as Γαβαάθ, Γαβάθ, etc.: site unidentified.
[b] Lacuna in the Greek.

to his son Phinees; his monument and tomb are in the city of Gabatha.[a]

(ii. 1) Now after the death of these leaders, Phinees prophetically announced, in accordance with the will of God, that, for the extermination of the Canaanite race, the tribe of Judah should be given the command; for the people were keenly desirous to learn what was God's good pleasure. So this tribe, having enlisted the aid of Simeon, on the condition that, once the Canaanites tributary to Judah had been destroyed, they would do the same to those within the lot of Simeon (advanced to battle).[b]

The tribe of Judah, with Simeon, takes the lead against the Canaanites. Jd. i. 1.

(2) But the Canaanites, who at that time were in a flourishing condition, awaited them with a large army at Zebekē,[c] having entrusted the command to the king of the Zebekēnians, Adonizebek[d]—this name signifies "lord of the Zebekēnians," for *adōni* in the speech of the Hebrews means "lord"—and they were hoping to defeat the Israelites, since Joshua was dead. However the Israelites of the two tribes which I mentioned, having joined battle with them, fought brilliantly, with the result that they slew of the enemy upwards of ten thousand, and having put the rest to rout pursued them and captured Adonizebek, who, with hands and feet mutilated by his captors, exclaimed: "Nay then I was not destined for ever to escape God's eye, having now suffered the fate which I scrupled not of yore

Defeat of Adonizebek and siege of Jerusalem. Jd. i. 4.

[c] Heb. "Bezek": site unidentified.

[d] Heb. Adoni-bezek. The form is suspected and it is thought by some critics that we have in this story in Judges another version of the defeat of Adoni-zedek, King of Jerusalem, narrated in Joshua x., where, however, LXX has Adoni-bezek as here.

κοντα βασιλέων πρᾶξαι πρότερον οὐκ ἐνετράπην."
124 καὶ ζῶντα μὲν κομίζουσιν ἕως Ἱεροσολύμων,
τελευτήσαντα δὲ γῇ θάπτουσι. καὶ διεξῄεσαν
αἱροῦντες τὰς πόλεις, πλείστας τε λαβόντες ἐπο-
λιόρκουν Ἱεροσόλυμα· καὶ τὴν μὲν κάτω λαβόντες
σὺν χρόνῳ πάντας ἔκτεινον τοὺς ἐνοικοῦντας,
χαλεπὴ δ' ἦν ἡ καθύπερθεν αὐτοῖς αἱρεθῆναι τειχῶν
ὀχυρότητι καὶ φύσει τοῦ χωρίου.
125 (3) Ὅθεν μετεστρατοπέδευσαν εἰς Χεβρῶνα[1] καὶ
ταύτην ἑλόντες κτείνουσι πάντας· ὑπελείπετο δὲ
τῶν[2] γιγάντων ἔτι γένος, οἳ διὰ σωμάτων
μεγέθη καὶ μορφὰς οὐδὲν τοῖς ἄλλοις ἀνθρώποις
παραπλησίας παράδοξον ἦσαν θέαμα καὶ δεινὸν
ἄκουσμα. δείκνυται δὲ καὶ νῦν ἔτι τούτων ὀστᾶ
126 μηδὲν τοῖς ὑπὸ πύστιν[3] ἐρχομένοις ἐοικότα. καὶ
τοῦτο μὲν τοῖς Λευίταις ἐξαίρετον γέρας ἔδοσαν
μετὰ καὶ τῶν δισχιλίων πηχῶν, τὴν δὲ γῆν Χαλέβῳ
δωρεὰν ἔδοσαν κατὰ Μωυσέος ἐντολάς· οὗτος δ'
ἦν τῶν κατασκόπων εἷς ὧν ἔπεμψε Μωυσῆς εἰς
127 τὴν Χαναναίαν. διδόασι δὲ καὶ τοῖς Ἰοθόρου τοῦ
Μαδιανίτου ἀπογόνοις, Μωυσέος γὰρ ἦν γαμβρός,
γῆν ἵνα νέμοιντο· τὴν γὰρ πατρίδα καταλιπόντες
ἠκολουθήκεσαν[4] ἐκείνοις καὶ συνῆσαν αὐτοῖς ἐπὶ τῆς
ἐρήμου.
128 (4) Ἡ δὲ Ἰούδα φυλὴ καὶ Σεμεωνὶς τὰς μὲν
κατὰ τὴν ὀρεινὴν τῆς Χαναναίας πόλεις εἷλον, τῶν

[1] Νεβρῶνα RO. [2] RO: τὸ τῶν rell.
[3] Cocceii: πίστιν codd. [4] ML: ἠκολούθησαν rell.

[a] "70" according to Jd. i. 7, but some MSS. of LXX read "72."

[b] The burial is not mentioned in Scripture.

[c] According to Jd. i. 8 the whole city was captured and

to inflict on two and seventy [a] kings." They brought him yet alive to Jerusalem, and at his death gave him sepulture.[b] Then they overran the district, taking the towns, and after capturing very many of them laid siege to Jerusalem. The lower town they mastered in time and slew all the inhabitants; but the upper town proved too difficult to carry through the solidity of its walls and the nature of the site.[c]

(3) So they moved their camp to Hebron, took that town and massacred all therein. Howbeit there remained yet a race of giants,[d] who, by reason of their huge frames and figures in no wise like to the rest of mankind, were an amazing spectacle and a tale of terror to the ear. Their bones are shown to this day, bearing no resemblance to any that have come within men's ken. This town they gave to the Levites as a choice boon, along with the tract of two thousand cubits [e]; but of the rest of the land they made, in accordance with the behests of Moses, a present to Caleb, who was one of the spies whom Moses had sent into Canaan. They gave also to the descendants of Jethro the Madianite, the father-in-law of Moses, territory for habitation; for, quitting their native country, they had followed the Hebrews and companied with them in the wilderness.

Capture of Hebron. Jd. i. 10.

i. 20.

i. 16.

(4) The tribes of Judah and Simeon also captured the cities in the hill-country of Canaan, and among

destroyed—an incorrect statement contradicted by other passages of Scripture. The distinction drawn by Josephus between upper and lower town is an attempt to harmonize Jd. i. 8 with i. 21 and Jos. xv. 63.

[d] The "sons of Anak" driven out by Caleb, Jd. i. 20; for their stature *cf.* the description given by the spies in Numb. xiii. 33 (*A.* iii. 305).

[e] As prescribed by Moses, *A.* iv. 67

δ' ἐν τῷ πεδίῳ καὶ πρὸς θαλάσσῃ Ἀσκάλωνά τε καὶ Ἄζωτον. διαφεύγει δ' αὐτοὺς Γάζα καὶ Ἀκκάρων· πεδίων γὰρ ὄντων καὶ πολλῆς ἁρμάτων εὐπορίας κακῶς ἐποίουν τοὺς ἐπελθόντας. καὶ αἵδε μὲν αἱ φυλαὶ μεγάλως ἐκ τοῦ πολεμεῖν εὐδαιμονήσασαι ἀνεχώρησαν εἰς τὰς ἑαυτῶν πόλεις καὶ κατατίθενται τὰ ὅπλα.

129 (5) Βενιαμῖται δέ, τούτων γὰρ ἦν Ἱεροσόλυμα, τοῖς οἰκήτορσιν αὐτῶν συνεχώρησαν φόρους τελεῖν. καὶ οὕτως παυσάμενοι πάντες οἱ μὲν τοῦ κτείνειν οἱ δὲ κινδυνεύειν ἐργάζεσθαι τὴν γῆν εὐσχόλουν. τὸ δ' αὐτὸ καὶ αἱ λοιπαὶ φυλαὶ τὴν Βενιαμῖτιν μιμησάμεναι ἐποίουν καὶ τοῖς τελουμένοις ἀρκούμενοι φόροις ἐπέτρεπον τοῖς Χαναναίοις ἀπολέμοις εἶναι.

130 (6) Ἡ δ' Ἐφραίμου[1] πολιορκοῦσα Βήθηλα τέλος οὐδὲν ἄξιον τοῦ χρόνου καὶ τῶν πόνων ηὕρισκε τῆς πολιορκίας, οἱ δὲ καίπερ ἀχθόμενοι τῇ καθέδρᾳ
131 προσεκαρτέρουν. ἔπειτα συλλαβόντες τινὰ τῶν ἐν τῇ πόλει προελθόντα[2] ἐπὶ κομιδῇ τῶν ἀναγκαίων πίστεις ἔδοσαν αὐτῷ παραδόντι τὴν πόλιν σώσειν αὐτόν τε καὶ τοὺς συγγενεῖς αὐτοῦ· κἀκεῖνος ἐπὶ τούτοις ὤμνυε τὴν πόλιν αὐτοῖς ἐγχειριεῖν.[3] καὶ ὁ μὲν οὕτως προδοὺς σώζεται μετὰ τῶν οἰκείων, οἱ δὲ ἀποκτείναντες ἅπαντας τοὺς ἐνοικοῦντας εἶχον τὴν πόλιν.

132 (7) Καὶ μετὰ ταῦτα πρὸς μὲν τοὺς πολεμίους μαλακῶς εἶχον οἱ Ἰσραηλῖται, τῆς δὲ γῆς καὶ τῶν

[1] Ἐφρὰν RO.
[2] Niese: προσελθόντα codd.
[3] Dindorf: ἐγχειοεῖν codd.

those in the plain and on the sea-board, Ascalon and Azōtus. But Gaza and Akkarōn escaped them ; for, being situated in the plain and blest with an abundance of chariots, they sorely handled their assailants.[a] So these two tribes, greatly enriched by their warfare, retired to their own cities and laid down their arms.

Further conquests of the two tribes. Jd. i. 9, 17 ff.

(5) The Benjamites, within whose lot lay Jerusalem, permitted its inhabitants to pay them tribute ; and thus all reposing, these from slaughter and those from peril, were at leisure to till the soil. The other tribes, imitating that of Benjamin, did the same and, contenting themselves with the tributes paid to them, suffered the Canaanites to live in peace.

General peace with the Canaanites Jd. i. 21. i. 27 ff.

(6) The tribe of Ephraim, in besieging Bethel, could attain no result proportionate to the time and the toil expended upon the siege ; yet, for all their annoyance, they persevered in the blockade. Afterwards, having caught one of the inhabitants of the town who had gone out in search of provisions, they gave him their word that, if he would betray the city, they would spare the lives of him and his kin ; and he on these terms swore to deliver it into their hands. So he by such treason saved himself with his family, while they, having massacred all the inhabitants, occupied the town.

Capture of Bethel by Ephraim. Jd. i. 22.

(7) Thereafter the Israelites relaxed the struggle against their enemies and devoted themselves to

Peace leads to corruption Jd. ii. 11.

[a] Josephus here differs from both Biblical texts, presenting a sort of compromise between them. According to the Heb. (Jd. i. 18 f.) Judah took Gaza, Ashkelon and Ekron, but failed to drive out the inhabitants of the valley because of their chariots of iron (Ashdod or Azotus is not mentioned) : according to the LXX he could take neither Gaza, Ascalon, Akkaron, nor Azotus.

ταύτης ἔργων ἐπεμελοῦντο. τῶν δὲ κατὰ τὸν πλοῦτον αὐτοῖς ἐπιδιδόντων ὑπὸ τρυφῆς καὶ ἡδονῆς τοῦ κόσμου ὠλιγώρουν τῆς πολιτείας καὶ[1] τῶν
133 νόμων οὐκέτ' ἦσαν ἀκριβεῖς ἀκροαταί. παροξυνθὲν δ' ἐπὶ τούτοις τὸ θεῖον ἀναιρεῖ, πρῶτον μὲν ὡς φείσαιντο παρὰ τὴν αὐτοῦ γνώμην τῶν Χαναναίων, ἔπειθ' ὡς ἐκεῖνοι χρήσοιντο[2] πολλῇ κατ'
134 αὐτῶν ὠμότητι καιροῦ λαβόμενοι. οἱ δὲ καὶ πρὸς τὰ παρὰ τοῦ θεοῦ δυσθύμως εἶχον καὶ πρὸς τὸ πολεμεῖν ἀηδῶς, πολλά τε παρὰ τῶν Χαναναίων λαβόντες καὶ πρὸς τοὺς πόνους ἤδη διὰ τὴν τρυφὴν
135 ἐκλελυμένοι. καὶ συνέβαινεν ἤδη τὴν ἀριστοκρατίαν διεφθάρθαι, καὶ τὰς γερουσίας οὐκ ἀπεδείκνυσαν οὐδ' ἀρχὴν ἄλλην οὐδεμίαν τῶν πρότερον νενομισμένων, ἦσαν δὲ ἐν τοῖς ἀγροῖς ἡδονῇ τοῦ κερδαίνειν προσδεδεμένοι. καὶ διὰ τὴν πολλὴν ἄδειαν στάσις αὐτοὺς πάλιν καταλαμβάνει δεινὴ καὶ προήχθησαν εἰς τὸ πολεμεῖν ἀλλήλοις ἐκ τοιαύτης αἰτίας.

136 (8) Λευίτης ἀνὴρ τῶν δημοτικωτέρων τῆς Ἐφραίμου[3] κληρουχίας ὢν καὶ ἐν ἐκείνῃ κατοικῶν ἄγεται γύναιον ἀπὸ Βηθλέμων, τῆς δὲ Ἰούδα φυλῆς τοῦτ' ἔστι τὸ χωρίον. ἐρῶν δὲ σφόδρα τῆς γυναικὸς καὶ τοῦ κάλλους αὐτῆς ἡττημένος ἠτύχει τῶν παρ' ἐκείνης οὐχ ὁμοίων πειρώμενος.
137 ἀλλοτρίως δ' αὐτῆς ἐχούσης καὶ διὰ τοῦτο μᾶλλον

[1] τῆς πολ. καὶ trs. Niese: καὶ τῆς πολιτείας codd.
[2] Bekker: χρήσαιντο codd. [3] v.ll. Ἐφρὰν, Ἐφράνου.

[a] The remarks on political corruption are an amplification of Scripture.
[b] In Scripture this episode forms an appendix to the book of Judges. Josephus has transposed it (along with another

the soil and to labours thereon. And as their riches increased, under the mastery of luxury and voluptuousness, they recked little of the order of their constitution and no longer hearkened diligently to its laws. Incensed thereat, the Deity warned them by oracle, first that they had acted contrary to His will in sparing the Canaanites, and next that those foes, seizing their occasion, would treat them with great ruthlessness. But the Israelites, while despondent at this message from God, were yet ill-disposed for warfare, for they had won much from the Canaanites and luxury had by now unnerved them for fatigues. Aye, even that aristocracy of theirs was now becoming corrupted: no more did they appoint councils of elders or any other of those magistracies beforetime ordained by law, but lived on their estates, enslaved to the pleasures of lucre.[a] And so, by reason of this gross listlessness, grave discord again assailed them and they were launched into civil war through the following cause.

Jd. ii. 14.

The Levite of Ephraim and the outrage on his wife. Jd. xix. 1.

(8) [b] A Levite of the lower ranks, of the province of Ephraim and residing therein, married a woman of Bethlehem, a place belonging to the tribe of Judah. Being deeply enamoured of his wife and captivated by her beauty, he was unfortunate in meeting with no like return from her. And, whereas she held herself aloof and he thereby only became

appendix) to an earlier date, to the period before the judges: perhaps, as has been suggested, to allow time for the tribe of Benjamin to recover itself before it furnished the nation with its first king. "It is incredible," writes Dr. G. F. Moore (*Int. Crit. Comm.* p. 405), "that the tribe of Benjamin was almost exterminated only a generation or two before the time of Saul; but the events related in these chapters probably fall in a much earlier period . . ."

ἐκκαιομένου τῷ πάθει μέμψεις συνεχεῖς αὐτοῖς ἐγίνοντο, καὶ τέλος ἡ γυνὴ πρὸς αὐτὰς βαρυνομένη καταλιποῦσα τὸν ἄνδρα πρὸς τοὺς γονεῖς παραγίνεται μηνὶ τετάρτῳ. χαλεπῶς δὲ φέρων ὁ ἀνὴρ ἐπὶ τῷ ἔρωτι ἧκε πρὸς τοὺς πενθεροὺς καὶ διαλυσάμενος τὰς μέμψεις καταλλάττεται πρὸς αὐτήν.
138 καὶ τέτταρας μὲν ἡμέρας αὐτόθι[1] διαιτᾶται φιλοφρονουμένων αὐτὸν τῶν γονέων, τῇ δὲ πέμπτῃ δόξαν ἀπιέναι πρὸς αὐτὸν περὶ δείλην ἔξεισι· βράδιον γὰρ ἀπέλυον οἱ γονεῖς τὴν θυγατέρα καὶ τῆς ἡμέρας τριβὴν ἐποιοῦντο. θεράπων δ' αὐτοῖς εἷς εἵπετο καὶ ὄνος ἦν αὐτοῖς, ἐφ' ἧς ὠχεῖτο τὸ
139 γύναιον. γενομένων δ' αὐτῶν κατὰ Ἱεροσόλυμα, σταδίους δ' ἐληλύθεσαν ἤδη τριάκοντα, συνεβούλευεν ὁ θεράπων καταχθῆναί που, μὴ καί τι τῆς νυκτὸς αὐτοὺς ὁδεύοντας καταλάβῃ δύσκολον καὶ ταῦτα οὐδὲ πόρρω πολεμίων ὄντας, τοῦ καιροῦ πολλάκις ἐπισφαλῆ καὶ ὕποπτα ποιοῦντος καὶ τὰ
140 φίλα. τῷ δ' οὐκ ἤρεσεν ἡ γνώμη παρ' ἀλλοφύλοις ἀνδράσι ξενοῦσθαι, Χαναναίων γὰρ ἦν ἡ πόλις, ἀλλὰ προελθόντας εἴκοσι στάδια εἰς οἰκείαν ἠξίου κατάγεσθαι πόλιν, καὶ κρατήσας τῇ γνώμῃ παρῆν εἰς Γάβαν φυλῆς τῆς Βενιαμίτιδος ἤδη[2] ὀψίας
141 οὔσης. καὶ μηδενὸς ἐπὶ ξενίαν τῶν κατὰ τὴν ἀγορὰν αὐτὸν παρακαλοῦντος πρεσβύτης ἐξ ἀγροῦ κατιὼν τῆς μὲν Ἐφραιμίτιδος φυλῆς ὢν ἐν δὲ τῇ Γάβῃ διαιτώμενος συντυγχάνων αὐτῷ, τίς τε ὢν

[1] SPL: πρὸς αὐτόθι ROM: προσαυτόθι Niese.
[2] + δὲ SPE.

[a] A misreading of Scripture. In Jd. xix. 2 the woman returns to her father's house "and was there the space of four months."

the more ardent in his passion, quarrels were continually arising between them, and at last the woman, utterly weary of them, left her husband and in the fourth month [a] rejoined her parents. But her husband, in sore affliction through love of her, visited her parents, redressed her grievances and was reconciled to her. For four days more he abode there, kindly treated by her parents, but on the fifth, having resolved to return to his home, he set off towards evening; for the parents were loth to part with their daughter and let the day slip away. A single servant accompanied them, and they had an ass on which the woman rode. Now when they were come over against Jerusalem, having already gone thirty furlongs,[b] the servant counselled them to lodge somewhere, lest, journeying by night, some misadventure should befall them, above all when they were not far from foes, that hour oft rendering perilous and suspect even the offices of friends. The Levite, however, misliked the thought of seeking shelter with aliens—for the city was in Canaanite hands [c]—preferring rather to proceed twenty furlongs further and to lodge in a town of the Hebrews; and, his counsel prevailing, he arrived at Gaba,[d] in the tribe of Benjamin, when evening had now fallen. No one in the market-place offering him hospitality, an old man returning from the fields, who though of the tribe of Ephraim was residing in Gaba, fell in with him and asked who he was and why he was

[b] Gr. "*stades*" (about $\frac{1}{8}$ mile). Bethlehem is 5 miles S. of Jerusalem: elsewhere the distance is reckoned as only "20 *stades*" (*A.* vii. 312).

[c] *Cf.* § 124 (note).

[d] Heb. Gibeah, usually identified with *Tell el-Ful*, *c.* 4 miles N. of Jerusalem; in *B.J.* v. 51 described as "Gabath Saul . . . about 30 *stades* from Jerusalem."

ἤρετο καὶ δι' ἃς αἰτίας στελλόμενος σκότους ἤδη
142 τὰ πρὸς τὸ δεῖπνον αὐτῷ λαμβάνοι. ὁ δὲ Λευίτης
μὲν ἔφησεν εἶναι, γύναιον δὲ παρὰ τῶν γονέων
ἄγων πρὸς αὐτὸν ἀπιέναι,[1] τὴν δ' οἴκησιν ἐδήλου
τυγχάνειν ἐν τῇ Ἐφραΐμου κληρουχίᾳ. ὁ δὲ
πρεσβύτης καὶ διὰ συγγένειαν καὶ διὰ τὸ τὴν
αὐτὴν φυλὴν νέμειν καὶ διὰ τὴν συντυχίαν παρ'
143 αὐτὸν ξενισθησόμενον ἦγε. νεανίαι δέ τινες τῶν
Γαβαηνῶν ἐπὶ τῆς ἀγορᾶς τὸ γύναιον θεασάμενοι
καὶ τὴν εὐπρέπειαν θαυμάσαντες, ἐπεὶ παρὰ τῷ
πρεσβύτῃ κατηγμένην ἔμαθον καταφρονήσαντες τῆς
ἀσθενείας καὶ τῆς ὀλιγότητος ἧκον ἐπὶ τὰς θύρας.
τοῦ δὲ πρεσβύτου παρακαλοῦντος ἀπαλλάττεσθαι
καὶ μὴ προσφέρειν βίαν μηδὲ ὕβριν, ἠξίουν αὐτὸν
παρασχόντα τὴν ξένην πραγμάτων ἀπηλλάχθαι.
144 συγγενῆ δὲ[2] λέγοντος καὶ Λευίτην[3] τοῦ πρεσβύτου
καὶ δράσειν αὐτοὺς δεινὰ ὑφ' ἡδονῆς εἰς τοὺς νόμους
ἐξαμαρτάνοντας ὠλιγώρουν τοῦ δικαίου καὶ κατεγέλων, ἠπείλουν δὲ ἀποκτείνειν αὐτὸν ἐμποδίζοντα
145 ταῖς ἐπιθυμίαις αὐτῶν. εἰς δ' ἀνάγκην περιηγμένος καὶ μὴ βουλόμενος τοὺς ξένους περιιδεῖν
ὑβρισθέντας, τῆς ἑαυτοῦ θυγατρὸς αὐτοῖς παρεχώρει, πληρώσειν τε τὴν ἐπιθυμίαν αὐτοὺς λέγων
νομιμώτερον δίχα τῆς εἰς τοὺς ξένους ὕβρεως αὐτός
τε[4] μηδὲν ἀδικήσειν οὓς ὑπεδέξατο τούτῳ τῷ
146 τρόπῳ νομίζων. ὡς δ' οὐδὲν τῆς σπουδῆς τῆς
ἐπὶ τὴν ξένην ἐνεδίδοσαν, ἀλλ' ἐνέκειντο ταύτην
παραλαβεῖν ἀξιοῦντες, ὁ μὲν ἱκέτευε μηδὲν τολμᾶν

[1] Dindorf: ἀπεῖναι codd.
[2] ὡς συγγενῆ δὲ RO: ὡς δὲ συγγενῆ τε rell.
[3] Λευῖτιν E.
[4] Dindorf: δὲ codd.

setting off, when it was dark already, taking provisions for his supper. He replied that he was a *cf.* xix. 19.
Levite and that he was escorting his wife from her parents back to his own home, informing him that he had his abode in the province of Ephraim. Thereat the old man, because of their common stock, and because they belonged to the same tribe and because chance had thus brought them together, took him
as his guest to his own home. But some of the young xix. 22.
men of Gaba, who had seen the woman in the market-place and admired her comeliness, when they learnt that she lodged with the old man, scorning the feebleness of these few,[a] came to the doors; and when the old man bade them begone and not to resort to violence and outrage, they required him to hand over his woman guest if he wished to avoid trouble. The old man replying that he[b] was a kinsman and a Levite and that they would be guilty of a dreadful crime in violating the laws at the beck of pleasure, they recked little of righteousness, mocked at it, and threatened to kill him if he thwarted their lusts. Driven to such a pass and unwilling to suffer his guests to be abused, he offered the men his own daughter, declaring that it would be more legitimate for them thus to gratify their lust than by doing violence to his guests, and for his part thinking by this means to avoid wronging those whom he had received. But they in no wise abated their passion for the stranger, being insistent in their demands to have her, and while he was yet imploring them to perpetrate no iniquity,

[a] Gr. "their feebleness and fewness" (*cf. B.J.* iii. 317).

[b] *i.e.* the husband. One MS. reads "that she (the Levite's wife) was a kinswoman" etc.

παράνομον, οἱ δ' ἁρπασάμενοι καὶ προσθέμενοι
μᾶλλον τῷ βιαίῳ τῆς ἡδονῆς ἀπήγαγον πρὸς αὑτοὺς
τὴν γυναῖκα καὶ δι' ὅλης νυκτὸς ἐμπλησθέντες τῆς
147 ὕβρεως ἀπέλυσαν περὶ ἀρχομένην ἡμέραν. ἡ δὲ
τεταλαιπωρημένη τοῖς συμβεβηκόσι παρῆν ἐπὶ τὴν
ξενίαν καὶ ὑπὸ λύπης ὧν ἐπεπόνθει καὶ τοῦ μὴ
τολμᾶν ὑπ' αἰσχύνης εἰς ὄψιν ἐλθεῖν τἀνδρί, τοῦτον
γὰρ μάλιστα τοῖς γεγενημένοις ἔχειν ἀνιάτως
148 ἐλογίζετο, καταπεσοῦσα τὴν ψυχὴν ἀφίησιν. ὁ δὲ
ἀνὴρ αὐτῆς οἰόμενος ὕπνῳ βαθεῖ κατεσχῆσθαι τὴν
γυναῖκα καὶ μηδὲν σκυθρωπὸν ὑφορώμενος ἀνεγείρειν ἐπειρᾶτο παραμυθήσασθαι διεγνωκώς, ὡς
οὐκ ἐξ ἑκουσίου γνώμης αὑτὴν παράσχοι τοῖς
καθυβρίσασιν, ἀλλ' ἁρπασαμένων ἐπὶ τὴν ξενίαν
149 ἐλθόντων αὐτῶν.[1] ὡς δὲ τελευτήσασαν ἔμαθε,
σωφρονισθεὶς[2] πρὸς τὸ μέγεθος τῶν κακῶν ἐπιθέμενος τῷ κτήνει νεκρὰν τὴν γυναῖκα κομίζει
πρὸς αὐτόν, καὶ διελὼν αὐτὴν κατὰ μέλος εἰς μέρη
δώδεκα διέπεμψεν εἰς ἑκάστην φυλήν, ἐντειλάμενος
τοῖς κομίζουσι λέγειν τοὺς αἰτίους τῆς τελευτῆς
τῇ γυναικὶ καὶ τὴν παροινίαν τῆς φυλῆς.[3]

150 (9) Οἱ δ' ὑπό τε τῆς ὄψεως καὶ τῆς ἀκοῆς τῶν
βεβιασμένων κακῶς διατεθέντες, πρότερον οὐδενὸς
τοιούτου πεῖραν εἰληφότες, ὑπ' ὀργῆς ἀκράτου
καὶ δικαίας εἰς τὴν Σιλοῦν συλλεγέντες καὶ πρὸ
τῆς σκηνῆς ἀθροισθέντες εἰς ὅπλα χωρεῖν εὐθὺς
ὥρμηντο καὶ χρήσασθαι τοῖς Γαβαηνοῖς ὡς πολε-
151 μίοις. ἐπέσχε δ' αὐτοὺς ἡ γερουσία πείσασα μὴ

[1] ἀλλ' . . . αὐτῶν om. Lat.

[2] conj. (*cf.* § 256): σωφρόνως (σωφρονῶν SP) codd.

[3] τῆς φυλῆς R: ταῖς φυλαῖς rell.

they seized[a] the woman and, yielding still more to the force of their lust, carried her off to their homes and then, after sating their lewdness all night long, let her go towards the break of day. She, outworn with her woes, repaired to the house of her host, where, out of grief at what she had endured and not daring for shame to face her husband—since he above all, she deemed, would be inconsolable at her fate—she succumbed and gave up the ghost. But her husband, supposing his wife to be buried in deep sleep and suspecting nothing serious, tried to arouse her, with intent to console her by recalling how she had not voluntarily surrendered herself to her abusers, but that they had come to the lodging-house and carried her off. But when he found that she was dead, chastened before the enormity of the wrong, he laid the dead woman upon his beast, bore her to his home and then, dividing her limb by limb into twelve pieces, sent one to each tribe, enjoining the bearers to state who they were who had caused the death of his wife and to recount the debauchery of the tribe.[b]

The Israelites vainly demand the surrender of the culprits. Jd. xx. 1.

(9) The Israelites, sorely moved by the spectacle and the tale of these deeds of violence, the like of which they had never known before, in intense and righteous wrath assembled at Silo[c] and, mustering before the tabernacle, were impatient to rush straight to arms and to treat these people of Gaba as enemies. But they were restrained by the elders, who urged

[a] In Scripture, the Levite himself surrenders the woman.

[b] *Sc.* of Benjamin. "One to each tribe" is not in Scripture ("sent her throughout all the borders of Israel"); were that meant, one might expect the number to be eleven, Benjamin being excluded.

[c] In Scripture, the tribes assemble at Mizpah.

δεῖν ὀξέως οὕτως πρὸς τοὺς ὁμοφύλους ἐκφέρειν πόλεμον πρὶν ἢ λόγοις διαλεχθῆναι περὶ τῶν ἐγκλημάτων, τοῦ νόμου μηδ' ἐπὶ τοὺς ἀλλοτρίους ἐφιέντος δίχα πρεσβείας καὶ τοιαύτης πρὸς τὸ μετανοῆσαι πείρας τοὺς δόξαντας ἀδικεῖν στρατιὰν[1]
152 ἀγαγεῖν· καλῶς οὖν ἔχειν τῷ νόμῳ πειθομένους πρὸς τοὺς Γαβαηνοὺς ἐξαιτοῦντας τοὺς αἰτίους ἐκπέμψαι καὶ παρεχομένων μὲν ἀρκεῖσθαι τῇ τούτων κολάσει, καταφρονησάντων δὲ τότε τοῖς
153 ὅπλοις αὐτοὺς ἀμύνασθαι. πέμπουσιν οὖν πρὸς τοὺς Γαβαηνοὺς κατηγοροῦντες τῶν νεανίσκων τὰ περὶ τὴν γυναῖκα καὶ πρὸς τιμωρίαν αἰτοῦντες τοὺς δράσαντας μὲν οὐ νόμιμα, γενομένους δὲ δικαίους
154 ἀντ' αὐτῶν ἐκείνων ἀποθανεῖν. οἱ δὲ Γαβαηνοὶ οὔτε τοὺς νεανίσκους ἐξέδοσαν καὶ δεινὸν ἀλλοτρίοις ὑπακούειν προστάγμασιν ἡγοῦντο πολέμου φόβῳ, μηδενὸς ἀξιοῦντες εἶναι χείρους ἐν τοῖς ὅπλοις μήτε διὰ πλῆθος μήτε δι' εὐψυχίαν. ἦσαν δὲ ἐν παρασκευῇ μεγάλῃ μετὰ καὶ[2] τῶν ἄλλων φυλετῶν, συναπενοήθησαν γὰρ αὐτοῖς ὡς ἀμυνούμενοι[3] βιαζομένους.

155 (10) Ὡς δὲ τοιαῦτα τοῖς Ἰσραηλίταις τὰ παρὰ τῶν Γαβαηνῶν ἀπηγγέλθη, ὅρκους ποιοῦνται μηδένα σφῶν ἀνδρὶ Βενιαμίτῃ δώσειν πρὸς γάμον θυγατέρα στρατεύσειν τε ἐπ' αὐτούς, μᾶλλον αὐτοῖς δι' ὀργῆς ὄντες ἢ τοῖς Χαναναίοις[4] τοὺς προγόνους

[1] στρατείαν ROSL. [2] μετὰ καὶ Dindorf: καὶ codd.
[3] ex Lat. Niese: ἀμυνόμενοι codd. [4] ed. pr.: +οἷς codd.

[a] Or, with other MSS., "a campaign."

[b] This advice of the elders, not mentioned in Scripture, is added to show that they conformed to the Mosaic law (Deut. xx. 10; *A*. iv. 296).

that they ought not so hurriedly to make war on their brethren, ere they had parleyed with them concerning their grievances, the law not permitting them to lead an army[a] even against aliens without having sent an embassy and made other attempts of this nature to bring the supposed wrongdoers to repentance.[b] It therefore behoved them, in obedience to the law, to send envoys to the Gabaenians to demand the surrender of the culprits and, should they deliver them up, to be content with punishing these individuals; but, should they flout this demand, then to retaliate on them by resort to arms.
So they sent an embassy to Gaba to accuse the xx. 12.
young men of the woman's fate and to require the surrender for punishment of those that had done thus lawlessly and who for those very deeds deserved to die.[c] But the people of Gaba refused to surrender the youths and scorned to bow to the behests of others through fear of war, holding themselves to be inferior in arms to none whether in numbers or valour. So they proceeded to make great preparations along with the rest of their tribe, who joined them in their desperate undertaking in the belief that they were repelling aggressors.

Civil war with the Benjamites defeat of Israel.

(10) Now when word was brought to the Israelites of this response from the men of Gaba, they took an oath that not one among them would give his
daughter to a man of Benjamin and that they would Jd. xxi. 1.
march against them, being more indignant against
them than were our forefathers, as we are told, xx. 17.

[c] Or perhaps (taking αὐτῶν ἐκείνων as masculines) "who deserved to die in lieu of their own people": the balance of clauses (μὲν . . . δὲ . . .) favours this. The lawlessness of the deed warranted wholesale destruction, but at least the culprits should suffer.

156 ἡμῶν παρειλήφαμεν γενομένους. παραχρῆμά τε ἐξῆγον ἐπ' αὐτοὺς τὸ στρατόπεδον μυριάδας τεσσαράκοντα ὁπλιτῶν· καὶ Βενιαμιτῶν τὸ ὁπλιτικὸν ἦν ὑπὸ δισμυρίων καὶ πεντακισχιλίων καὶ ἑξακοσίων, ὧν ἦσαν εἰς πεντακοσίους ταῖς λαιαῖς
157 τῶν χειρῶν σφενδονᾶν ἄριστοι, ὥστε καὶ μάχης πρὸς τῇ Γαβᾷ γενομένης τρέπουσι τοὺς Ἰσραηλίτας οἱ Βενιαμῖται ἄνδρες τε πίπτουσιν ἐξ αὐτῶν εἰς δισμυρίους καὶ δισχιλίους, ἐφθάρησαν δὲ ἴσως ἂν καὶ πλείονες, εἰ μὴ νὺξ αὐτοὺς ἐπέσχε καὶ διέλυσε
158 μαχομένους. καὶ οἱ μὲν Βενιαμῖται χαίροντες ἀνεχώρουν εἰς τὴν πόλιν, οἱ δ' Ἰσραηλῖται καταπεπληγότες ὑπὸ τῆς ἥττης εἰς τὸ στρατόπεδον. τῇ δ' ἐπιούσῃ πάλιν συμβαλόντων οἱ Βενιαμῖται κρατοῦσι καὶ θνήσκουσι τῶν Ἰσραηλιτῶν ὀκτακισχίλιοι καὶ μύριοι, καὶ δείσαντες τὸν φόνον[1]
159 ἐξέλιπον τὸ στρατόπεδον. παραγενόμενοι δὲ εἰς Βέθηλα πόλιν ἔγγιστα κειμένην καὶ νηστεύσαντες κατὰ τὴν ὑστεραίαν τὸν θεὸν ἱκέτευον διὰ Φινεέσου τοῦ ἀρχιερέως παύσασθαι τῆς ὀργῆς τῆς πρὸς αὐτοὺς καὶ ταῖς δυσὶν αὐτῶν ἥτταις ἀρκεσθέντα δοῦναι νίκην καὶ κράτος κατὰ τῶν πολεμίων. ὁ δὲ θεὸς ἐπαγγέλλεται ταῦτα διὰ Φινεέσου προφητεύσαντος.

160 (11) Ποιήσαντες οὖν τὴν στρατιὰν δύο μέρη τὴν μὲν ἡμίσειαν προλοχίζουσι νυκτὸς περὶ τὴν πόλιν, οἱ δ' ἡμίσεις συνέβαλον τοῖς Βενιαμίταις ὑπεχώρουν τε ἐγκειμένων, καὶ ἐδίωκον οἱ Βενιαμῖται ⟨καὶ⟩

[1] om. L Lat.

[a] Heb. 26,000 Benjamites + 700 inhabitants of Gibeah: LXX 25,000 (or 23,000) + 700. In Josephus the preposition

against the Canaanites. And forthwith they led xx. 15 f.
out against them their host of 400,000 men-at-arms; the forces of the Benjamites numbered but some 25,600[a] among whom were 500[b] expert in using the sling with the left hand. And so, a battle ensuing near Gaba, the Benjamites routed the Israelites, and there fell of these 22,000 men; indeed perchance yet more would have perished, had not night checked them and parted the combatants. The Benjamites then withdrew, exultant, to the town, the Israelites, crest-fallen at their defeat, to their camp. On the morrow, when they renewed the attack, the Benjamites were again victorious: 18,000 of the Israelites perished, and daunted by this carnage they abandoned their encampment.
Repairing to Bethel, the city nearest at hand,[c] and xx. 26.
having fasted on the morrow, they besought God, through Phinees the high priest, to abate his anger against them and, content with their two defeats, to vouchsafe them victory and the mastery over their foes. And God promised them their petitions through the mouth of Phinees, His interpreter.

Defeat of the Benjamites: reprisals of the Israelites. Jd. xx. 29.

(11) So, dividing their army in two, they set half in ambush around the town[d] under cover of night; the other half then engaged the Benjamites and before their onset retired. The Benjamites pursued

ὑπό, if genuine, seems to mean "about" and perhaps indicates acquaintance with variant readings in Scripture.

[b] Heb. (with some MSS. of LXX) 700: other MSS. of LXX omit the number.

[c] Bethel is some 8 miles N. of the traditional site of Gibeah (*Tell el-Ful*): Shiloh, the seat of the tabernacle (§ 150), lay considerably farther north.

[d] This battle scene, like others, recalls Thucydides: with προλοχίζειν περὶ τὴν πόλιν *cf.* Thuc. ii. 81, with πασσυδί (§ 161) viii. 1, with περιστάντες κατηκόντισαν (§ 162) vii. 84.

τῶν Ἑβραίων ὑποφευγόντων ἠρέμα καὶ ἐπὶ πολὺ θελόντων εἰς ἅπαν αὐτοὺς ἐξελθεῖν[1] ἀναχωροῦσιν
161 εἵποντο, ὡς καὶ τοὺς ἐν τῇ πόλει πρεσβύτας καὶ νέους ὑπολειφθέντας δι' ἀσθένειαν συνεκδραμεῖν[2] αὐτοῖς πασσυδὶ βουλομένους χειρώσασθαι τοὺς πολεμίους. ὡς δὲ πολὺ τῆς πόλεως ἀπέσχον, ἐπαύσαντο μὲν φεύγοντες οἱ Ἑβραῖοι, ἐπιστραφέντες δ' ἵστανται πρὸς μάχην καὶ τοῖς ἐν ταῖς ἐνέδραις οὖσι τὸ σημεῖον αἴρουσιν ὃ συνέκειτο.
162 οἱ δ' ἐξαναστάντες μετὰ βοῆς ἐπῄεσαν τοῖς πολεμίοις. οἱ δὲ ἅμα τε ἠπατημένους αὐτοὺς ᾔσθοντο καὶ ἐν ἀμηχανίᾳ συνεστήκεσαν, καὶ εἴς τι κοῖλον συνελαθέντας καὶ φαραγγῶδες χωρίον περιστάντες κατηκόντισαν, ὥστε πάντας διαφθαρῆναι πλὴν
163 ἑξακοσίων. οὗτοι δὲ συστραφέντες καὶ πυκνώσαντες ἑαυτοὺς καὶ διὰ μέσων ὠσάμενοι τῶν πολεμίων ἔφυγον ἐπὶ τὰ πλησίον ὄρη, καὶ κατασχόντες ἱδρύθησαν. οἱ δ' ἄλλοι πάντες περὶ δισμυρίους
164 ὄντες καὶ πεντακισχιλίους ἀπέθανον. οἱ δ' Ἰσραηλῖται τήν τε Γάβαν ἐμπιπρᾶσι καὶ τὰς γυναῖκας καὶ τῶν ἀρρένων τοὺς μὴ ἐν ἀκμῇ διεχρήσαντο, τάς τε ἄλλας τῶν Βενιαμιτῶν πόλεις ταὐτὰ δρῶσιν· οὕτως τε ἦσαν παρωξυμμένοι,[3] ὡς καὶ Ἰάβησον τῆς Γαλαδίτιδος οὖσαν, ὅτι μὴ συμμαχήσειεν αὐτοῖς κατὰ τῶν Βενιαμιτῶν, πέμψαντες μυρίους καὶ
165 δισχιλίους ἐκ τῶν τάξεων ἐκέλευσαν ἀνελεῖν. καὶ φονεύουσι τὸ μάχιμον τῆς πόλεως οἱ πεμφθέντες σὺν τέκνοις καὶ γυναιξὶ πλὴν τετρακοσίων παρθένων. ἐπὶ τοσοῦτον ὑπ' ὀργῆς προήχθησαν, τῷ

[1] protrahere (? ἐξελεῖν) Lat., omisso ἐπὶ πολύ aut εἰς ἅπαν.
[2] ed. pr.: διεκδραμεῖν δι' ἀσθένειαν codd.
[3] παρωργισμένοι MSPL.

and, as the Hebrews fell back little by little to a great distance, wishing them to come out[a] to a man, they followed their retreating foe, in such wise that even the old men and lads who had been left in the town as incompetent sallied out also, eager as a united body to crush the enemy. But when they were now remote from the town, the Hebrews stayed their flight and, turning, stood their ground for battle, while they raised the concerted signal for their friends in ambush; and these, emerging with a shout, fell upon the enemy. The Benjamites, from the moment when they saw themselves entrapped, were in a hopeless plight: driven into a rugged hollow, they were there shot down by the darts of the Hebrews who stood around them, with the result that all perished save 600. These, rallying and closing up their ranks, pushed through the enemy's midst, fled for the neighbouring hills, and there, on gaining them, established themselves; all the rest,
in number about 25,000, perished. The Israelites xx. 46.
burnt Gaba and made away with the women and males under age; the other cities of the Benjamites
they treated in like manner. Moreover, so exasper- xxi. 8.
ated were they that, forasmuch as the town of Jabesh in Gilead had not aided them in battle against the Benjamites, they sent thither 12,000 men from their ranks, with orders to destroy it. This detachment massacred all of military age in the town, along with the children and all the women save 400 who were unmarried. To such lengths did their rage carry them,

[a] Or, with the Latin, "wishing to draw them out."

κατὰ τὴν γυναῖκα πάθει προσλαβόντες καὶ τὸ κατὰ τὴν ἀναίρεσιν τῶν ὁπλιτῶν.

166 (12) Μετάνοια δ' αὐτοὺς λαμβάνει τῆς τῶν Βενιαμιτῶν συμφορᾶς καὶ νηστείαν ἐπ' αὐτοῖς προέθεντο, καίτοι δίκαια παθεῖν αὐτοὺς ἀξιοῦντες εἰς τοὺς νόμους ἐξαμαρτάνοντας, καὶ τοὺς διαφυγόντας αὐτῶν ἑξακοσίους διὰ πρεσβευτῶν ἐκάλουν· καθίδρυντο γὰρ ὑπὲρ πέτρας τινὸς Ῥοᾶς καλουμένης
167 κατὰ τὴν ἔρημον. οἱ δὲ πρέσβεις ὡς οὐκ ἐκείνοις τῆς συμφορᾶς μόνοις γεγενημένης ἀλλὰ καὶ αὐτοῖς τῶν συγγενῶν ἀπολωλότων ὀδυρόμενοι πρᾴως ἔπειθον φέρειν καὶ συνελθεῖν εἰς ταὐτὸ καὶ μὴ παντελῆ τῆς Βενιαμίτιδος φυλῆς ὄλεθρον τό γε ἐπ' αὐτοῖς καταψηφίσασθαι. "συγχωροῦμεν δὲ ὑμῖν," ἔλεγον, "τὴν ἁπάσης τῆς φυλῆς γῆν καὶ λείαν
168 ὅσην ἂν ἄγειν δυνηθῆτε[1]"· οἱ δὲ τῶν καθ' ἑαυτοὺς θεοῦ ψήφῳ γεγονότων καὶ κατ' ἀδικίαν τὴν αὐτῶν γνωσιμαχήσαντες κατῄεσαν εἰς τὴν πάτριον φυλὴν πειθόμενοι τοῖς προκαλουμένοις. οἱ δ' Ἰσραηλῖται γυναῖκας αὐτοῖς τὰς τετρακοσίας ἔδοσαν παρθένους τὰς Ἰαβίτιδας, περὶ δὲ τῶν διακοσίων ἐσκόπουν, ὅπως κἀκεῖνοι γυναικῶν εὐπορήσαντες
169 παιδοποιῶνται. γεγενημένων δ' αὐτοῖς ὅρκων ὥστε μηδενὶ Βενιαμίτῃ συνοικίσαι[2] θυγατέρα πρὸ τοῦ πολέμου, οἱ μὲν ὀλιγωρεῖν συνεβούλευον τῶν ὀμωμοσμένων ὡς ὑπ' ὀργῆς ὀμόσαντες οὐ γνώμῃ καὶ κρίσει, τῷ δὲ θεῷ μηδὲν ἐναντίον ποιήσειν εἰ

[1] Niese: δυνηθείητε codd. [2] edd.: συνοικῆσαι codd.

[a] Gr. translation of Heb. Rimmon (="pomegranate"); usually identified as modern *Rammun*, a few miles E. of Bethel, but a more likely site, much nearer to Gibeah, has been proposed (Burney, *Judges*, p. xxi).

because, in addition to what they had suffered on the woman's account, they had further suffered the slaughter of their men-at-arms.

(12) Howbeit they were smitten with remorse for the Benjamites' calamity and they ordained a fast on their behalf, while yet maintaining that they had justly suffered for their sin against the laws; and they summoned by ambassadors those 600 of them who had escaped and established themselves on a rock called Rhoa[a] in the wilderness. These envoys, deploring a calamity which had struck not the Benjamites only but themselves, in that the victims were their kinsmen, urged them to bear it patiently, to come and join them, and not, so far as in them lay, to pronounce sentence of total extinction upon the tribe of Benjamin. "We grant you," said they, "the territory of the whole tribe and of booty[b] as much as ye can carry off." And the Benjamites, recognizing with contrition that their misfortunes were due to God's decree and to their own iniquity, came down again into the tribe of their fathers, in compliance with this invitation. The Israelites gave them for wives those 400 virgins from Jabesh,[c] and then deliberated concerning the remaining 200 men, how they too might be provided with wives and beget children. Now, whereas they had before the war made oath to give no Benjamite a daughter of theirs in wedlock, some were of opinion that they should disregard those oaths as having been sworn under the sway of passion, without reflexion or judgement; that they would be doing nothing in opposition to God, could they so save a

Reconciliation with the Benjamites: how brides were found for them. Jd. xxi. 2, 6. xxi. 13.

xxi. 18.

[b] *i.e.* cattle.

[c] § 165.

φυλὴν ὅλην κινδυνεύουσαν ἀπολέσθαι σῶσαι δυνηθεῖεν, τάς τε ἐπιορκίας οὐχ ὅταν ὑπὸ ἀνάγκης γένωνται χαλεπὰς εἶναι καὶ ἐπισφαλεῖς, ἀλλ' ὅταν
170 ἐν κακουργίᾳ τολμηθῶσι. τῆς δὲ γερουσίας πρὸς τὸ τῆς ἐπιορκίας ὄνομα σχετλιασάσης ἔφη τις τούτοις τε γυναικῶν εὐπορίαν ἔχειν εἰπεῖν καὶ τήρησιν τῶν ὅρκων. ἐρομένων δὲ τὴν ἐπίνοιαν, "ἡμῖν," εἶπεν, "τρὶς τοῦ ἔτους εἰς Σιλὼ συνιοῦσιν ἕπονται
171 κατὰ πανήγυριν αἱ γυναῖκες καὶ αἱ θυγατέρες. τούτων κατὰ ἁρπαγὴν ἐφείσθω γαμεῖν Βενιαμίτας ἃς ἂν[1] δυνηθεῖεν ἡμῶν οὔτε προτρεπομένων οὔτε κωλυόντων. πρὸς δὲ τοὺς πατέρας αὐτῶν δυσχεραίνοντας καὶ τιμωρίαν λαμβάνειν ἀξιοῦντας φήσομεν αὐτοὺς αἰτίους φυλακῆς ἀμελήσαντας τῶν θυγατέρων, ὅτι δὲ δεῖ τῆς ὀργῆς ἐπὶ Βενιαμίτας ὑφεῖναι[2] χρησαμένους αὐτῇ καὶ θᾶττον ἀμέ-
172 τρως." καὶ οἱ μὲν τούτοις πεισθέντες ψηφίζονται τὸν διὰ τῆς ἁρπαγῆς γάμον τοῖς Βενιαμίταις. ἐνστάσης δὲ τῆς ἑορτῆς οἱ μὲν διακόσιοι κατὰ δύο καὶ τρεῖς πρὸ τῆς πόλεως ἐνήδρευον παρεσομένας τὰς παρθένους ἔν τε ἀμπελῶσι καὶ χωρίοις ἐν
173 οἷς λήσειν ἔμελλον, αἱ δὲ μετὰ παιδιᾶς οὐδὲν ὑφορώμεναι τῶν μελλόντων ἀφυλάκτως ὥδευον· οἱ δὲ σκεδασθεισῶν εἵχοντο ἐξαναστάντες. καὶ οὗτοι μὲν οὕτως γαμήσαντες ἐπ' ἔργα τῆς γῆς ἐχώρησαν

[1] ἂν secl. Naber. [2] Bekker: ἀφεῖναι RO, ἐφεῖναι rell.

[a] Jd. xxi. 19 "Behold there is a (or "the") feast (*ḥag*) of the LORD *from year to year* (lit. "from days to days," LXX ἀφ' ἡμερῶν εἰς ἡμέρας) in Shiloh." The *ḥag* here alluded to is the oldest of Jewish festivals, the autumn vintage festival of *Sukkoth* or "Tabernacles"; for its annual observance at Shiloh *cf.* 1 Sam. i. 3. Josephus refers back to those early

whole tribe in danger of extinction ; and that perjuries were not grave or hazardous when they were prompted by necessity, but only when rashly committed with malicious intent. When the elders, however, protested at the mere mention of perjury, someone said that he could suggest how to provide wives for these men and yet to keep their oaths. On being questioned concerning his plan, "When we meet," he replied, "three times a year [a] at Silo, we are accompanied to the festival by our wives and daughters. Let the Benjamites be permitted to capture as their brides such of these maidens as they can, without either encouragement or hindrance on our part. And if their parents make an ado and demand punishment, we will tell them that they have but themselves to blame for neglecting to protect their daughters, and that we must abate that resentment against the Benjamites, in which already in the past [b] we had been immoderate." The assembly assenting thereto decided accordingly to permit the Benjamites this marriage by capture. So, when the festival came round, the 200, in twos and threes, waited in ambush before the city for the coming of the maidens, in the vineyards and other places where they would escape their eye. Meanwhile the damsels, playfully and with no suspicion of what was on foot, came all unguardedly along ; whereat the men sprang out upon them and seized them as they scattered. These Benjamites, thus wedded, then betook themselves to the labours of the soil

days the keeping of the *three* great annual festivals, including Passover and Pentecost.

[b] θᾶττον = πρότερον, as elsewhere (with connotation of precipitancy).

καὶ πρόνοιαν ἐποιήσαντο πάλιν εἰς τὴν προτέραν
174 εὐδαιμονίαν ἐπανελθεῖν. Βενιαμιτῶν μὲν οὖν ἡ φυλὴ κινδυνεύσασα τελέως ἐκφθαρῆναι τῷ προειρημένῳ τρόπῳ κατὰ τὴν Ἰσραηλιτῶν σοφίαν σώζεται, ἤνθησέ τε παραχρῆμα καὶ ταχεῖαν εἴς τε πλῆθος καὶ τὰ ἄλλα πάντα ἐποιήσατο τὴν ἐπίδοσιν. οὗτος μὲν οὖν ὁ πόλεμος οὕτως παύεται.

175 (iii. 1) Ὅμοια δὲ τούτοις παθεῖν καὶ τὴν Δάνιν[1] συνέβη φυλὴν ἐξ αἰτίας τοιαύτης εἰς τοῦτο προ-
176 αχθεῖσαν. τῶν Ἰσραηλιτῶν ἐκλελοιπότων ἤδη τὴν ἐν τοῖς πολέμοις ἄσκησιν καὶ πρὸς τοῖς ἔργοις ὄντων τῆς γῆς Χαναναῖοι καταφρονήσαντες αὐτῶν συνεποιήσαντο δύναμιν, οὐδὲν μὲν αὐτοὶ πείσεσθαι προσδοκῶντες, ὡς δὲ βεβαίαν τὴν τοῦ ποιήσειν κακῶς τοὺς Ἑβραίους ἐλπίδα λαβόντες ἐπ' ἀδείας
177 τὸ λοιπὸν οἰκεῖν τὰς πόλεις ἠξίουν. ἅρματά τε οὖν παρεσκευάζοντο καὶ τὸ ὁπλιτικὸν συνεκρότουν αἵ τε πόλεις αὐτῶν συνεφρόνουν καὶ τῆς Ἰούδα φυλῆς τὴν Ἀσκάλωνα καὶ Ἀκκαρῶνα παρεσπάσαντο ἄλλας τε πολλὰς τῶν ἐν τῷ πεδίῳ καὶ Δανίτας εἰς τὸ ὄρος ἠνάγκασαν συμφυγεῖν οὐδὲ ὀλίγον αὐτοῖς ἐπιβατὸν τοῦ πεδίου καταλιπόντες.
178 οἱ δ' οὔτε πολεμεῖν ὄντες ἱκανοὶ γῆν τε οὐκ ἔχοντες ἀρκοῦσαν πέμπουσιν ἐξ αὐτῶν πέντε ἄνδρας εἰς τὴν μεσόγειον κατοψομένους γῆν, εἰς ἣν μετοικήσαιντο. οἱ δ' οὐ πόρρω τοῦ Λιβάνου ὄρους καὶ ἐλάσσονος Ἰορδάνου τῶν πηγῶν κατὰ τὸ μέγα

[1] Niese: Δάνην (Διανὴν) codd.

[a] Contrast § 128 (note), where we are told that Akkaron

and devoted their efforts to the recovery of their former prosperity. This, then, was the way in which the tribe of Benjamin, when in danger of complete extinction, was saved through the sagacity of the Israelites; and instantly it flourished and made rapid advance both in numbers and in all beside. And thus ended this war. Jd. fin.

(iii. 1) But like sufferings also befell the tribe of Dan, the cause which brought it to this pass being as follows. Now that the Israelites had abandoned the exercise of warfare and were given up to their labours on the land, the Canaanites, holding them in contempt, built up an army, not from expectation of any injury to themselves, but, being now confident of doing mischief to the Hebrews, they counted on henceforth inhabiting their cities in security. So they proceeded to equip chariots and levy troops, their cities unanimously combined, and from the tribe of Judah they wrested Ascalon, Akkarōn[a] and many other cities of the plain, while they forced the Danites to flee in a body to the hills, leaving them not the smallest foothold on the plain. [b]These, incapable of fighting and not having land to suffice them, sent five of their number into the interior to look for a region whither they could migrate. The envoys, having advanced to a spot not far from mount Libanus and the sources of the lesser[c] Jordan, over

The Danites forced to migrate northwards.

Jd. i. 34.

xviii. 1 f.

7-11.

had never been conquered; here Josephus conforms to the Hebrew text of Scripture (Jd. i. 18) which names Ekron among the captured cities.

[b] Here Josephus omits the unedifying story of Micah and his images, which in Scripture is mixed up with this expedition of the Danites (Jd. xvii. f.).

[c] The course of the Jordan north of the modern lake of *Ḥuleh*. *Cf. B.J.* iii. 509 f.

πεδίον Σιδῶνος πόλεως ὁδὸν ἡμέρας μιᾶς[1] προελθόντες καὶ κατασκεψάμενοι γῆν ἀγαθὴν καὶ πάμφορον σημαίνουσι τοῖς αὐτῶν· οἱ δ' ὁρμηθέντες στρατῷ κτίζουσιν αὐτόθι πόλιν Δάνα ὁμώνυμον τῷ Ἰακώβου παιδὶ φυλῆς δ' ἐπώνυμον τῆς αὐτῶν.

179 (2) Τοῖς δ' Ἰσραηλίταις προύβαινεν ὑπό τε ἀπειρίας τοῦ πονεῖν τὰ κακὰ καὶ ὑπὸ[2] τῆς περὶ τὸ θεῖον ὀλιγωρίας· μετακινηθέντες γὰρ ἅπαξ τοῦ κόσμου τῆς πολιτείας ἐφέροντο πρὸς τὸ καθ' ἡδονὴν καὶ βούλησιν ἰδίαν βιοῦν, ὡς καὶ τῶν ἐπιχωριαζόντων παρὰ τοῖς Χαναναίοις ἀναπίμπλασθαι
180 κακῶν. ὀργίζεται τοίνυν αὐτοῖς ὁ θεὸς καὶ ἣν σὺν πόνοις μυρίοις εὐδαιμονίαν ἐκτήσαντο, ταύτην ἀπέβαλον διὰ τρυφήν. στρατεύσαντος γὰρ ἐπ' αὐτοὺς Χουσαρσάθου[3] τοῦ τῶν Ἀσσυρίων βασιλέως, πολλούς τε τῶν παραταξαμένων ἀπώλεσαν καὶ
181 πολιορκούμενοι κατὰ κράτος ᾑρέθησαν, εἰσὶ δ' οἳ διὰ φόβον ἑκουσίως αὐτῷ προσεχώρησαν, φόρους τε τοῦ δυνατοῦ μείζονας ἐπιταγέντες ἐτέλουν καὶ ὕβρεις παντοίας ὑπέμενον ἕως ἐτῶν ὀκτώ, μεθ' ἃ τῶν κακῶν οὕτως ἠλευθερώθησαν.

182 (3) Τῆς Ἰούδα φυλῆς τις Κενίαζος ὄνομα δραστήριος ἀνὴρ καὶ τὸ φρόνημα γενναῖος, χρησθὲν

[1] trium dierum Lat. [2] SP: ἀπὸ rell.
[3] RO: Chusasartho Lat.: Χουσάρθου rell.: similar *v.ll.* in § 183.

---

[a] So we must translate, carrying on the force of the preceding πόρρω. The translation "advanced *in one day's march* to . . . over against the great plain of the city of S." is precluded by distance (upwards of 100 miles); a difficulty which is scarcely met by the reading of the Latin version, "*three* days' march."

[b] Bibl. "Cushan-rishathaim (LXX Χουσαρσαθαίμ) king of

against the great plain, within a day's march of the city of Sidon,[a] and having inspected a land good and wholly fertile, reported this to their brethren ; 29.
and they, setting forth with an army, founded there a city called Dan(a) after the name of the son of Jacob, which was also the name of their own tribe.

(2) But the state of the Israelites went from bad to worse through their loss of aptitude for toil and their neglect of the Divinity. For, having once parted from the ordered course of their constitution, they drifted into living in accordance with their own pleasure and caprice, and thus became contaminated with the vices current among the Canaanites. So God was wroth with them, and all that prosperity which they had won with myriad labours they now through idle luxury cast away. For Chusarsathus, iii. 8.
king of the Assyrians,[b] having marched upon them, they lost multitudes in battle, and were besieged and carried by storm, whilst some in terror voluntarily surrendered to him, paid tribute beyond their means at his behest, and underwent indignities of every kind for eight years, after which they were delivered from their miseries on this wise.

Israel under the Assyrians. Jd. iii. 5.

(3) A man of the tribe of Judah, Keniaz[c] by name, vigorous and noble-hearted, being warned by

Their deliverance by Keniaz. Jd. iii. 9.

Aram-naharaim," *i.e.* "of Aram of the two rivers," *alias* Mesopotamia. The personal name = "Cushan of double-dyed villainy," a Biblical distortion of some older form.

[c] Bibl. "Othniel the son of Kenaz, Caleb's younger brother." Josephus has replaced the son by the father ; similarly in the so-called *Biblical Antiquities of Philo* (*c.* A.D. 100) Cenez figures as the first judge and a person of considerable importance (ed. M. R. James, p. 146 note). The compiler of the Greek summary of the contents of *A.* v. mentions Othniel but reverses the relationship (ἡ διὰ Κενίζου τοῦ Ἀθνιήλου παιδὸς αὐτοῖς ἐλευθερία γενομένη).

αὐτῷ μὴ περιορᾶν ἐν τοιαύτῃ τοὺς Ἰσραηλίτας ἀνάγκῃ κειμένους ἀλλ' εἰς ἐλευθερίαν αὐτοὺς ἐξαιρεῖσθαι τολμᾶν, παρακελευσάμενος[1] συλλαμβάνεσθαι τῶν κινδύνων αὐτῷ τινάς, ὀλίγοι δ' ἦσαν οἷς αἰδὼς ἐπὶ τοῖς τότε παροῦσιν ἐτύγχανε καὶ
183 προθυμία μεταβολῆς, πρῶτον μὲν τὴν παρ' αὐτοῖς οὖσαν φρουρὰν τοῦ Χουσαρσάθου διαφθείρει, προσγενομένων δὲ πλειόνων τῶν συναγωνιζομένων ἐκ τοῦ μὴ διαμαρτεῖν περὶ τὰ πρῶτα τῆς ἐπιχειρήσεως, μάχην τοῖς Ἀσσυρίοις συνάπτουσι καὶ πρὸς τὸ παντελὲς αὐτοὺς ἀπωσάμενοι περαιοῦσθαι τὸν
184 Εὐφράτην ἐβιάζοντο. Κενίαζος δὲ ὡς ἔργῳ πεῖραν αὐτοῦ δεδωκὼς τῆς ἀνδραγαθίας γέρας ὑπὲρ αὐτῆς λαμβάνει παρὰ τοῦ πλήθους ἀρχήν, ὥστε κρίνειν τὸν λαόν. καὶ ἄρξας ἐπ' ἔτη τεσσαράκοντα καταστρέφει τὸν βίον.

185 (iv. 1) Τελευτήσαντος δὲ τούτου πάλιν τὰ τῶν Ἰσραηλιτῶν ὑπὸ ἀναρχίας ἐνόσει πράγματα, καὶ τῷ μὴ διὰ τιμῆς ἄγειν τὸν θεὸν μηδὲ τοῖς νόμοις
186 ὑπακούειν ἔτι μᾶλλον ἐκακοῦντο,[2] ὡς καταφρονήσαντα αὐτῶν τῆς ἀκοσμίας τῆς κατὰ τὴν πολιτείαν Ἐγλῶνα τὸν Μωαβιτῶν βασιλέα πόλεμον πρὸς αὐτοὺς ἐξενεγκεῖν καὶ πολλαῖς μάχαις αὐτῶν κρατήσαντα καὶ τοὺς[3] φρονήμασι τῶν ἄλλων διαφέροντας ὑποτάξαντα πρὸς τὸ παντελὲς αὐτῶν τὴν δύναμιν ταπεινῶσαι καὶ φόρους αὐτοῖς ἐπιτάξαι
187 τελεῖν. καθιδρύσας δ' αὐτῷ ἐν Ἱεριχοῦντι βασίλειον[4] οὐδὲν τῆς εἰς τὸ πλῆθος κακώσεως παρέλιπεν εἴς τε πενίαν αὐτοὺς κατέστησεν ἐπὶ ὀκτωκαίδεκα ἔτη. λαβὼν δ' οἶκτον ὁ θεὸς τῶν Ἰσραηλιτῶν ἐφ'

[1] παρασκευασάμενος ML.
[2] ἐκακοῦτο RO.
[3] τοῖς codd.

an oracle not to leave the Israelites to lie in such deep distress, but to essay to vindicate their liberty, after exhorting some others to share his hazards—and few were they, who were filled with shame at their present state and longed to alter it—began by massacring the garrison of Chusarsathus that was quartered upon them. Then, when larger numbers rallied to his arms, seeing that he had not miscarried at this opening of his enterprise, they joined battle with the Assyrians and, having utterly repulsed them, forced them to recross the Euphrates. Keniaz, having thus given practical proof of his prowess, received as his reward from the people rulership, to act as judge of the nation. And after ruling for forty years he ended his days.

Israel under Eglon, king of Moab. Jd. iii. 12.

(iv. 1) But after his death the affairs of the Israelites again suffered through lack of government, while their failure to render homage to God or to obey the laws aggravated the evil yet more. So, contemptuous of the disorder prevailing in their state, Eglon, king of Moab, made war upon them and, having defeated them in many battles and subjected all who showed more spirit than the rest, utterly humiliated their strength and imposed tribute upon them. Then establishing his capital in Jericho,[a] he ruthlessly molested the people and reduced them to penury for eighteen years. But God, taking pity on the Israelites in their afflictions and moved by

[a] Jd. iii. 13 " he possessed the city of palm-trees," *i.e.* Jericho, as the Targum (like Josephus) interprets the phrase. This implies that Jericho did not remain unbuilt and unfortified between the days of Joshua and of Ahab.

[4] E Lat. ed. pr.: + ταύτην ἀποδείξας rell.

οἷς ἔπασχον καὶ ταῖς ἱκετείαις αὐτῶν ἐπικλασθεὶς ἀπήλλαξε τῆς ὑπὸ τοῖς Μωαβίταις ὕβρεως. ἠλευθερώθησαν δὲ τούτῳ τῷ τρόπῳ.

188 (2) Τῆς Βενιαμίτιδος φυλῆς νεανίας Ἰούδης μὲν τοὔνομα Γήρα δὲ[1] πατρός, τολμῆσαί τε ἀνδρειότατος καὶ τῷ σώματι πρὸς τὰ ἔργα χρῆσθαι δυνατώτατος, τῶν χειρῶν τὴν ἀριστερὰν ἀμείνων κἀπ' ἐκείνης τὴν ἅπασαν ἰσχὺν ἔχων, κατῴκει

189 μὲν ἐν Ἱεριχοῦντι καὶ αὐτός, συνήθης δὲ γίνεται τῷ Ἐγλῶνι δωρεαῖς αὐτὸν θεραπεύων καὶ ὑπερχόμενος, ὡς διὰ τοῦτο καὶ τοῖς περὶ τὸν βασιλέα

190 προσφιλῆ τυγχάνειν αὐτόν. καί ποτε σὺν δυσὶν οἰκέταις δῶρα τῷ βασιλεῖ φέρων ξιφίδιον κρύφα τῷ δεξιῷ σκέλει περιδησάμενος εἰσῄει πρὸς αὐτόν. ὥρα δ' ἦν θέρους καὶ τῆς ἡμέρας ἤδη μεσούσης ἀνεῖντο αἱ φυλακαὶ ὑπό τε τοῦ καύματος καὶ πρὸς

191 ἄριστον τετραμμένων. δοὺς οὖν τὰ δῶρα τῷ Ἐγλῶνι ὁ νεανίσκος, διέτριβε δ' ἔν τινι δωματίῳ δεξιῶς πρὸς θέρος ἔχοντι, πρὸς ὁμιλίαν ἐτράπετο. μόνοι δ' ἦσαν τοῦ βασιλέως καὶ τοὺς ἐπεισιόντας τῶν θεραπόντων ἀπιέναι[2] κελεύσαντος διὰ τὸ πρὸς

192 Ἰούδην ὁμιλεῖν. καθῆστο δ' ἐπὶ θρόνου καὶ δέος εἰσῄει τὸν Ἰούδην, μὴ διαμάρτῃ καὶ οὐ[3] δῷ

193 καιρίαν πληγήν. ἀνίστησιν οὖν αὐτόν, ὄναρ εἰπὼν ἔχειν ἐκ προστάγματος αὐτῷ δηλῶσαι τοῦ θεοῦ. καὶ ὁ μὲν πρὸς τὴν χαρὰν τοῦ ὀνείρατος ἀνεπή-

[1] τε codd.
[2] ed. pr. Lat.: ἀπεῖναι codd. [3] Niese: μὴ codd.

[a] Heb. Ehud: LXX Ἀώδ.

their supplications, rid them of this oppression under the Moabites; and their liberation fell on this wise.

(2) A youth of the tribe of Benjamin, named Judes,[a] son of Gera, of gallant daring and with bodily powers that he was well able to make to serve his ends, being superior with his left hand and therefrom deriving all his strength, was also himself residing in Jericho;[b] there he became familiar with Eglon, courting and cajoling him with presents, whereby moreover he endeared himself to those in waiting on the king.[b] Now one day, when he with two[c] attendants was bringing gifts to the king, he secretly girt a dagger about his right thigh and so went in to him. It was summer-time and, the day being at noon, the guards had been relaxed both by reason of the heat and because they were gone to lunch. So the young man, having presented his gifts to Eglon, who was lodged in a chamber well-adapted for the summer, fell into conversation. They were alone, the king having ordered even such henchmen as intruded to depart because he was conversing with Judes. He was seated upon a chair, and Judes was beset with fear lest he should strike amiss and not deal a mortal blow. So he made him arise by telling him that he had a dream to disclose to him by commandment of God. The king, for joy at news of this dream, leapt up

Judes (Ehud) slays Eglon.
Jd. iii. 15.

[b] Scripture does not mention Ehud's residence in Jericho nor his attentions to Eglon.

[c] Jd. iii. 18 mentions a retinue, "the people that bare the present," who were dismissed after offering it; has the number "two" been extracted, through some misreading, out of the description of the dagger, "and it had two edges," *ib.* 16?

δησεν ἀπὸ τοῦ θρόνου, πλήξας δ' αὐτὸν ὁ Ἰούδης εἰς τὴν καρδίαν καὶ τὸ ξιφίδιον ἐγκαταλιπὼν ἔξεισι προσκλείσας[1] τὴν θύραν. οἵ τε θεράποντες ἠρέμουν, εἰς ὕπνον τετράφθαι νομίζοντες τὸν βασιλέα.

194 (3) Ὁ δ' Ἰούδης τοῖς Ἱεριχουντίοις ἀποσημαίνων κρυπτῶς παρεκάλει τῆς ἐλευθερίας ἀντιλαμβάνεσθαι. οἱ δ' ἀσμένως ἀκούσαντες αὐτοί τε εἰς τὰ ὅπλα ᾔεσαν καὶ διέπεμπον εἰς τὴν χώραν τοὺς ἀποσημαίνοντας κέρασιν οἰῶν· τούτοις γὰρ
195 συγκαλεῖν τὸ πλῆθος πάτριον. οἱ δὲ περὶ τὸν Ἐγλῶνα πολὺν μὲν χρόνον ἠγνόουν τὸ συμβεβηκὸς αὐτῷ πάθος, ἐπεὶ δὲ πρὸς ἑσπέραν ἦν, δείσαντες μή τι νεώτερον εἴη περὶ αὐτὸν γεγονός, εἰσῆλθον εἰς τὸ δωμάτιον καὶ νεκρὸν εὑρόντες ἐν ἀμηχανίᾳ καθειστήκεσαν, καὶ πρὶν τὴν φρουρὰν συστραφῆναι τὸ τῶν Ἰσραηλιτῶν αὐτοῖς ἐπέρχεται
196 πλῆθος. καὶ οἱ μὲν παραχρῆμα ἀναιροῦνται, οἱ δ' εἰς φυγὴν τρέπονται ὡς ἐπὶ τὴν Μωαβῖτιν σωθησόμενοι, ἦσαν δὲ ὑπὲρ μυρίους. καὶ Ἰσραηλῖται προκατειληφότες τοῦ Ἰορδάνου τὴν διάβασιν διώκοντες ἔκτεινον καὶ κατὰ τὴν διάβασιν πολλοὺς αὐτῶν ἀναιροῦσι, διέφυγέ τε οὐδὲ εἷς τὰς χεῖρας
197 αὐτῶν. καὶ οἱ μὲν Ἑβραῖοι τούτῳ τῷ τρόπῳ τῆς ὑπὸ τοῖς Μωαβίταις δουλείας ἀπηλλάγησαν, Ἰούδης δ' ἐκ[2] τῆς αἰτίας ταύτης τιμηθεὶς τῇ τοῦ πλήθους παντὸς ἡγεμονίᾳ τελευτᾷ τὴν ἀρχὴν ἔτεσιν ὀγδοήκοντα κατασχών, ἀνὴρ καὶ δίχα τῆς προειρημένης πράξεως ἐπαίνου δίκαιος τυγχάνειν.

[1] MLE Lat.: προσκλίνας rell.
[2] δ' ἐκ Dindorf ex Lat.: δὲ codd.

from his throne, whereat Judes smote him to the heart and, leaving the dagger in his breast, went forth, locking the door upon him. The henchmen never stirred, supposing that the king had sunk asleep.

(3) Judes meanwhile reported the matter secretly to the men of Jericho [a] and exhorted them to assert their liberty. And they, welcoming his news, themselves rushed to arms and sent heralds throughout the country to give the signal by the sounding of rams' horns, for it was customary to call their people together by these instruments. Eglon's courtiers remained long ignorant of his fate ; but, when evening drew on, fearing that something extraordinary might have befallen him, they entered the chamber and, finding his corpse, stood there in helpless perplexity ; and, before the garrison could be mustered, the host of Israelites was upon them. Some were massacred on the spot ; the rest took flight to seek safety in the land of Moab, in number above ten thousand. But the Israelites, who had betimes occupied the ford of the Jordan, pursued and slew them : at the ford itself multitudes of them were massacred, and not a man escaped their hands. Thus were the Hebrews delivered from their bondage to the Moabites. Judes himself, having for this reason been honoured with the governorship of the whole people, died after holding that office for eighty years [b]—a man, even apart from the aforesaid exploit, deserving of a meed of praise. After

Defeat of Moab and rule of Judes. Jd. iii. 26.

ib. 25.

[a] In Scripture he goes further afield and himself "blew the trumpet in the hill-country of Ephraim."

[b] Jd. iii. 30 "and the land had rest four-score years," to which the LXX adds "and Aod judged them until he died"; in the Heb. there is no mention of his rulership.

καὶ μετὰ τοῦτον Σανάγαρος ὁ Ἀνάθου παῖς αἱρεθεὶς ἄρχειν ἐν τῷ πρώτῳ τῆς ἀρχῆς ἔτει κατέστρεψε τὸν βίον.

198 (v. 1) Ἰσραηλῖται δὲ πάλιν, οὐδὲν γὰρ ἐπὶ διδαχῇ τοῦ κρείττονος ἐλάμβανον τῶν πρότερον ἠτυχημένων ὑπὸ[1] τοῦ μήτε σέβειν τὸν θεὸν μήθ' ὑπακούειν τοῖς νόμοις, πρὶν ἢ καὶ τῆς ὑπὸ Μωαβίταις ἀναπνεῦσαι δουλείας πρὸς ὀλίγον, ὑπὸ Ἀβίτου[2]
199 τοῦ Χαναναίων βασιλέως καταδουλοῦνται. οὗτος γὰρ ἐξ Ἀσώρου πόλεως ὁρμώμενος, αὕτη δ' ὑπέρκειται τῆς Σεμαχωνίτιδος λίμνης, στρατοῦ μὲν ὁπλιτῶν τριάκοντα ἔτρεφε μυριάδας μυρίους δὲ ἱππέας, τρισχιλίων δὲ ἁρμάτων ηὐπόρει. ταύτης οὖν στρατηγῶν τῆς δυνάμεως Σισάρης τιμῆς πρώτης παρὰ τῷ βασιλεῖ τυγχάνων συνελθόντας πρὸς αὐτὸν τοὺς Ἰσραηλίτας ἐκάκωσε δεινῶς, ὥστε αὐτοῖς ἐπιτάξαι τελεῖν φόρους.

200 (2) Εἴκοσι μὲν οὖν ἔτη ταῦτα πάσχοντες ἤνυσαν μήτε αὐτοὶ φρονεῖν ὑπὸ τῆς δυστυχίας ὄντες ἀγαθοὶ καὶ τοῦ θεοῦ πλέον δαμάσαι[3] θέλοντος αὐτῶν τὴν ὕβριν διὰ τὴν περὶ αὐτὸν ἀγνωμοσύνην, ἵνα μεταθέμενοι τοῦ λοιποῦ σωφρονῶσιν· διδαχθέντες δὲ[4] τὰς συμφορὰς αὐτοῖς ἐκ τῆς περιφρονήσεως τῶν νόμων ὑπάρξαι, Δαβώραν τινὰ προφῆτιν, μέλισσαν δὲ σημαίνει τοὔνομα κατὰ τὴν Ἑβραίων γλῶσσαν,
201 ἱκέτευον δεηθῆναι τοῦ θεοῦ λαβεῖν οἶκτον αὐτῶν

[1] + τε codd. [2] Jabid Lat.: Ἰωαβεῖ Niese.
[3] + ἔτι ROE. [4] δὲ ins. Niese.

[a] Heb. Shamgar: LXX Σαμεγάρ (Σεμεγάρ, etc.).
[b] Amplification.
[c] So Heb. and Josephus below (§ 209); here the MSS. have the Latinized form Ἀβίτου (Avitus).

him Sanagar,[a] son of Anath, was elected ruler, but died in the first year of his rule.[b]

Sanagar (Shamgar) succeeds him. ib. 31.

(v. 1) Again, however, the Israelites, who had learnt no lesson of wisdom from their previous misfortunes, since they neither worshipped God nor obeyed the laws, ere they had enjoyed a brief respite from their servitude to the Moabites, fell under the yoke of Jabin,[c] king of the Canaanites. For this monarch, issuing from the city of Asor,[d] situate above the lake Semachōnitis,[e] maintained an army of 300,000 foot and 10,000 horse, and was owner of 3000 chariots.[f] Accordingly the general of these forces, Sisares,[g] who held the first rank in the king's favour, so sorely afflicted the Israelites when they joined battle with him, that he forced them to pay tribute.

Israel oppressed by Jabin, king of Canaan. Jd. iv. 1.

(2) Twenty years, then, did they pass in this miserable plight, themselves incapable of being schooled by adversity, while God willed to tame their insolence yet more by reason of their ingratitude towards Him, to the end that they might change their ways and thenceforward be wise. But when they had learned[h] that their calamities were due to their contempt of the laws, they besought a certain prophetess named Dabora[i]—the name in the Hebrew tongue means "bee"—to pray God

Deborah and Barak lead a revolt. Jd. iv. 3.

[d] Bibl. Hazor; identified by Garstang with *Tell el-Qedah* about 5 miles S.W. of the southern end of the lake mentioned.

[e] The smaller lake N. of the lake of Galilee, *el Ḥuleh*, sometimes called the "waters of Merom."

[f] Imaginary figures (*cf.* § 64): Scripture mentions only "900 chariots of iron."

[g] Bibl. Sisera.

[h] Text and sentence division doubtful.

[i] Bibl. Deborah (= "bee," as correctly stated); Scripture adds that "she was judging Israel at that time."

καὶ μὴ περιιδεῖν ἀπολλυμένους αὐτοὺς ὑπὸ Χαναναίων. ὁ δὲ θεὸς ἐπένευσε σωτηρίαν αὐτοῖς καὶ στρατηγὸν αἱρεῖται Βάρακον τῆς Νεφθαλίτιδος ὄντα φυλῆς· βάρακος δέ ἐστιν ἀστραπὴ κατὰ τὴν Ἑβραίων γλῶσσαν.

202 (3) Μεταπεμψαμένη δ' ἡ Δαβώρα τὸν Βάρακον ἐπιλέξαντα τῶν νέων μυρίους ἐκέλευε χωρεῖν ἐπὶ τοὺς πολεμίους· ἀποχρῆναι γὰρ τοσούτους τοῦ θεοῦ
203 προειρηκότος καὶ νίκην ἀποσημήναντος. Βαράκου δὲ φαμένου οὐ στρατηγήσειν μὴ κἀκείνης αὐτῷ συστρατηγούσης ἀγανακτήσασα, "σὺ μέν," εἶπε, "γυναικὶ παραχωρεῖς ἀξιώματος ὃ σοὶ δέδωκεν ὁ θεός, ἐγὼ δὲ οὐ παραιτοῦμαι." καὶ συναθροίσαντες[1] μυρίους ἐστρατοπεδεύσαντο πρὸς Ἰτα-
204 βυρίῳ ὄρει. ἀπήντα δ' αὐτοῖς ὁ Σισάρης τοῦ βασιλέως κελεύσαντος καὶ στρατοπεδεύονται τῶν πολεμίων οὐκ ἄπωθεν. τοὺς δ' Ἰσραηλίτας καὶ τὸν Βάρακον καταπλαγέντας τὸ πλῆθος τῶν πολεμίων καὶ ἀναχωρεῖν διεγνωκότας ἡ Δαβώρα κατεῖχε τὴν συμβολὴν ποιεῖσθαι κατ' ἐκείνην κελεύουσα τὴν ἡμέραν· νικήσειν γὰρ αὐτοὺς καὶ συλλήψεσθαι τὸν θεόν.

205 (4) Συνῄεσαν οὖν καὶ προσμιγέντων ὄμβρος ἐπιγίνεται μέγας καὶ ὕδωρ πολὺ καὶ χάλαζα, τόν τε ὑετὸν κατὰ πρόσωπον ἤλαυνε τῶν Χαναναίων ἄνεμος ταῖς ὄψεσιν αὐτῶν ἐπισκοτῶν, ὡς τὰς τοξείας ἀχρήστους αὐτοῖς εἶναι καὶ τὰς σφενδόνας· οἵ τε ὁπλῖται διὰ τὸ κρύος χρῆσθαι τοῖς ξίφεσιν

[1] συναριθμήσαντες RO.

[a] Tabor. [b] Amplification.

[c] Not mentioned in the Biblical narrative of the battle, but derived apparently from the verse in the Song of

to take pity on them and not to suffer them to be destroyed by the Canaanites. God thereupon promised them salvation and chose for general Barak of the tribe of Nephthali; *barak* denotes "lightning" in the tongue of the Hebrews.

(3) Dabora then summoned Barak and charged him *ib.* 6. to select ten thousand of the youth and to march against the foe: that number would, she said, suffice, God having prescribed it and betokened victory. But Barak declared that he would not take the command unless she shared it with him; whereto she indignantly replied, "Thou resignest to a woman a rank that God has bestowed on thee! Howbeit I do not decline it." Then, having mustered ten thousand, they pitched their camp on mount Itabyrion.[a] Sisares thereupon went to meet them at the king's orders and his army encamped not far from their foes. The Israelites and Barak were dismayed at the multitude of the enemy and resolved to retire,[b] but were restrained by Dabora, who ordered them to deliver battle that very day, for they would be victorious and God would lend them aid.

Victory of Israel: death of Sisara and Jabin. Jd. iv. 15.

(4) So the forces met, and amidst the clash of arms there came up a great tempest[c] with torrents of rain and hail; and the wind drove the rain in the faces of the Canaanites, obscuring their vision, so that their bows and their slings were of no service to them, and their infantry by reason of the cold could make no use of their swords. But the Israel-

Deborah, "They fought from heaven; the stars in their courses fought against Sisera" (Jd. v. 20). To this there are parallels in rabbinic tradition. For a rather similar scene, when the elements aided the enemy of the Jews, *cf. B.J.* vii. 317 ff.

206 οὐκ εἶχον. τοὺς δ' Ἰσραηλίτας ἧττόν τε ἔβλαπτε κατόπιν γινόμενος ὁ χειμὼν καὶ πρὸς τὴν ἔννοιαν τῆς βοηθείας τοῦ θεοῦ θάρσος ἐλάμβανον, ὥστε εἰς μέσους ὠσάμενοι τοὺς πολεμίους πολλοὺς αὐτῶν ἀπέκτειναν. καὶ οἱ μὲν ὑπὸ τῶν Ἰσραηλιτῶν, οἱ δ' ὑπὸ τῆς οἰκείας ἵππου ταραχθέντες ἔπεσον, ὡς ὑπὸ τῶν ἁρμάτων πολλοὺς αὐτῶν ἀποθανεῖν.
207 Σισάρης δὲ καταπηδήσας τοῦ ἅρματος ὡς εἶδε τὴν τροπὴν γινομένην, φυγὼν ἀφικνεῖται παρά τινα τῶν Κενελίδων[1] γυναῖκα, Ἰάλην ὄνομα, ἣ κρύψαι τε ἀξιώσαντα δέχεται καὶ ποτὸν αἰτήσαντι δίδωσι
208 γάλα διεφθορὸς ἤδη. ὁ δὲ πιὼν τοῦ μέτρου δαψιλέστερον εἰς ὕπνον τρέπεται. ἡ δὲ Ἰάλη κοιμωμένου σιδήρεον ἧλον ἐλάσασα σφύρῃ κατὰ τοῦ στόματος καὶ[2] τοῦ χελυνίου διέπειρε τὸ ἔδαφος καὶ τοῖς περὶ τὸν Βάρακον μικρὸν ὕστερον ἐλθοῦσιν
209 ἐπεδείκνυε τῇ γῇ προσηλωμένον. καὶ οὕτως μὲν ἡ νίκη αὕτη περιέστη κατὰ τὰ ὑπὸ Δαβώρας εἰρημένα εἰς γυναῖκα. Βάρακος δὲ στρατεύσας ἐπ' Ἄσωρον Ἰωαβείν[3] τε ὑπαντιάσαντα κτείνει καὶ τοῦ στρατηγοῦ πεσόντος καθελὼν εἰς ἔδαφος τὴν πόλιν στρατηγεῖ τῶν Ἰσραηλιτῶν ἐπ' ἔτη τεσσαράκοντα.

210 (vi. 1) Τελευτήσαντος δὲ Βαράκου καὶ Δαβώρας κατὰ τὸν αὐτὸν καιρὸν μετὰ ταῦτα Μαδιανῖται παρακαλέσαντες Ἀμαληκίτας τε καὶ Ἄραβας στρατεύουσιν ἐπὶ τοὺς Ἰσραηλίτας καὶ μάχῃ τε νικῶσι τοὺς συμβαλόντας καὶ τὸν καρπὸν δῃώσαν-

[1] Κενετίδων ed. pr.
[2] RO: διὰ τοῦ στόματος κατὰ rell.
[3] Ἰάβ(ε)ινον SP(E): Jabin Lat.

ites were less hampered by the storm, which was at their back, and they took courage at the thought of this succour from God; and so, thrusting into the midst of the foe, they slew multitudes of them. Thus, some beneath the hand of the Israelites, others discomfited by their own cavalry, the enemy fell, many being crushed to death beneath the chariots. But Sisares, having leapt from his chariot when he saw that the rout was come, fled till he reached the abode of a woman of the Kenites [a] named Iale [b]; she, at his request to conceal him, took him in, and, when he asked for drink, gave him milk that had turned sour.[c] And he, having drunk thereof immoderately, fell asleep. Then, as he slumbered, Iale took an iron nail and drove it with a hammer through his mouth and jaw, piercing the ground; and when Barak's company [d] arrived soon after she showed him to them nailed to the earth. Thus did this victory redound, as Dabora had foretold,[e] to a woman's glory. But Barak, marching upon Asor, slew Jabin [f] who encountered him and, the general having fallen, razed the city to the ground; he then held command of the Israelites for forty years.[g] *Cf.* v. 31.

(vi. 1) Barak and Dabora having died simultaneously, thereafter the Madianites, calling the Amalekites and Arabians to their aid, marched against the Israelites, defeated in battle all who opposed them, plundered the crops and carried off the cattle. This

Ravages of the Madianites.
Jd. vi. 1.

[a] Gr. "Kenelides." [b] Bibl. Jael.
[c] "already corrupt," an amplification of the Biblical text.
[d] Barak himself, in Jd. iv. 22.
[e] Jd. iv. 9.
[f] Or, according to some MSS., Joabin.
[g] Scripture says merely "And the land had rest forty years."

211 τες τὴν λείαν ἐπήγοντο.[1] τοῦτο δὲ ποιούντων ἐπ'
ἔτη ἑπτὰ εἰς τὰ ὄρη τῶν Ἰσραηλιτῶν ἀνεστάλη τὸ
πλῆθος καὶ τῶν πεδίων ἐξεχώρουν, ὑπονόμους τε
καὶ σπήλαια ποιησάμενοι πᾶν ὅ τι τοὺς πολεμίους
212 διέφυγεν ἐν τούτοις εἶχον φυλάττοντες. οἱ γὰρ
Μαδιανῖται κατὰ ὥραν θέρους[2] στρατεύοντες τὸν
χειμῶνα γεωργεῖν τοῖς Ἰσραηλίταις ἐπέτρεπον,
ὅπως ἔχωσι πεπονηκότων αὐτῶν εἰς ἃ βλάπτωσι,
λιμὸς δ' ἦν καὶ σπάνις τροφῆς καὶ τρέπονται πρὸς
ἱκετείαν τοῦ θεοῦ σώζειν αὐτοὺς παρακαλοῦντες.
213 (2) Καὶ Γεδεὼν ὁ Ἰάσου παῖς, Μανασσίτιδος
φυλῆς ἐν ὀλίγοις, δράγματα σταχύων φερόμενος
κρυπτῶς εἰς τὴν ληνὸν ἔκοπτε· τοὺς γὰρ πολεμίους
ἐδεδίει φανερῶς τοῦτο ποιεῖν ἐπὶ τῆς ἅλωος.
φαντάσματος δὲ αὐτῷ παραστάντος νεανίσκου
μορφῇ καὶ φήσαντος εὐδαίμονα καὶ φίλον τῷ
θεῷ, ὑποτυχὼν "τοῦτο γοῦν," ἔφη, "τεκμήριον
τῆς εὐμενείας αὐτοῦ μέγιστον τὸ[3] ληνῷ με νῦν
214 ἀντὶ ἅλωος χρῆσθαι." θαρσεῖν δὲ παρακελευσα-
μένου καὶ πειρᾶσθαι τὴν ἐλευθερίαν ἀνασώζειν,
ἀδυνάτως ἔχειν ἔλεγε· τήν τε γὰρ φυλὴν ἐξ ἧς
ὑπῆρχε πλήθους ὑστερεῖν καὶ νέον αὐτὸν εἶναι καὶ
τηλικούτων πραγμάτων[4] ἀσθενέστερον. ὁ δὲ θεὸς
αὐτὸς ἀναπληρώσειν τὸ λεῖπον ἐπηγγέλλετο καὶ
νίκην παρέξειν Ἰσραηλίταις αὐτοῦ στρατηγοῦντος.
215 (3) Τοῦτ' οὖν διηγούμενος ὁ Γεδεὼν τισὶ τῶν

[1] Niese (*cf.* xiii. 101): ὑπήγοντο codd.: ἀπήγοντο ed. pr.
[2] ME Lat.: ἔτους rell.
[3] Zonaras: τῇ codd.
[4] πραγμάτων ἐπινοίας MSPL.

[a] Bibl. Gideon (LXX Γεδεών) son of Joash (Ἰωάς).
[b] Gr. "one of few" (*cf. A.* ii. 78, iv. 329, v. 276); here perhaps with a connotation of the paucity of numbers of the tribe (§ 214).

being repeated for seven years, the more part of the Israelites withdrew to the hills and forsook the plains; and, making for themselves underground passages and caverns, they secured therein all that had escaped the enemy. For the Madianites, making their invasions in the height of summer, permitted the Israelites in winter to till the soil, that through their labours they might have somewhat to ravage. So there was famine and dearth of sustenance, and they turned in supplication to God, imploring Him to save them.

(2) Now Gedeon, son of Jas,[a] one of the foremost[b] among the tribe of Manasseh, used to bring his sheaves of corn and beat them out secretly in the winepress; for, because of the enemy, he feared to do this openly on the threshing-floor. To him there appeared a spectre in the form of a young man, who pronounced him blessed and beloved of God, whereto he made rejoinder: "Indeed, this is a signal proof of his favour that I am now using a winepress instead of a threshing-floor!" But when his visitor bade him take courage and essay to regain liberty, he replied that this was impossible, seeing that the tribe[c] to which he belonged was lacking in numbers and he himself but young and too feeble for exploits so great. Howbeit God promised Himself to supply what he lacked and to grant victory to the Israelites, should he put himself at their head.[d]

The call to Gideon. Jd. vi. 11.

(3) On recounting this matter to some of his

Selection of his army.

[c] Jd. vi. 15 "Behold, my family (Heb. "thousand") is the poorest in Manasseh, and I am the least in my father's house."

[d] Josephus omits Jd. vi. 17-40, comprising (1) the reassuring miracles performed for Gideon, (2) his destruction of the altar of Baal, which earned for him the surname of Jerubbaal.

νέων ἐπιστεύετο, καὶ παραχρῆμα πρὸς τοὺς ἀγῶνας ἕτοιμον ἦν τὸ στρατιωτικὸν[1] μυρίων ἀνδρῶν. ἐπιστὰς δὲ κατὰ τοὺς ὕπνους ὁ θεὸς τῷ Γεδεῶνι τὴν ἀνθρωπίνην φύσιν αὐτῷ φίλαυτον οὖσαν ἐδήλου καὶ πρὸς τοὺς ἀρετῇ διαφέροντας ἀπεχθανομένην, ὅπως τε τὴν νίκην παρέντες τοῦ θεοῦ δοκεῖν νομίσουσιν[2] ἰδίαν ὡς πολὺς στρατὸς ὄντες καὶ πρὸς
216 τοὺς πολεμίους ἀξιόμαχος. ἵνα μάθωσιν οὖν βοηθείας τῆς αὐτοῦ τὸ ἔργον, συνεβούλευε περὶ μεσοῦσαν τὴν ἡμέραν, ἐν ἀκμῇ τοῦ καύματος ὄντος, ἄγειν τὴν στρατιὰν ἐπὶ τὸν ποταμὸν καὶ τοὺς μὲν κατακλιθέντας καὶ οὕτως πίνοντας εὐψύχους ὑπολαμβάνειν, ὅσοι δ' ἐσπευσμένως καὶ μετὰ θορύβου πίνοντες τύχοιεν τούτους[3] δειλοὺς νομίζειν καὶ καταπεπληγότας τοὺς πολεμίους.
217 ποιήσαντος δὲ τοῦ Γεδεῶνος κατὰ τὰς ὑποθήκας τοῦ θεοῦ, τριακόσιοι ἄνδρες εὑρέθησαν ταῖς χερσὶ μετὰ φόβου προσενεγκάμενοι τὸ ὕδωρ τεταραγμένως, ἔφησέ τε ὁ θεὸς τούτους ἐπαγόμενον ἐπιχειρεῖν τοῖς πολεμίοις. ἐστρατοπεδεύοντο δὲ ὑπὲρ τοῦ Ἰορδάνου μέλλοντες εἰς τὴν ἐπιοῦσαν περαιοῦσθαι.
218 (4) Γεδεῶνος δ' ἐν φόβῳ καθεστῶτος, καὶ γὰρ νυκτὸς ἐπιχειρεῖν αὐτῷ ὁ θεὸς προειρήκει, τοῦ

[1] στρατόπεδον ROE. [2] Niese: νομίζουσιν codd.
[3] (after τούτους) δὴ (δὲ M) νομίζειν ὑπὸ δειλίας τοῦτο πάσχειν MSP Suidas Glycas.

[a] In Jd. vii. 3 the army had already been reduced to 10,000, by the dismissal, under divine orders, of 22,000 who were faint-hearted.
[b] Amplification (three words).
[c] Amplification (the hour). [d] Or "lay."

young friends, Gedeon was trusted; and instantly there was an army of 10,000 [a] men ready for the contest. But God, appearing to Gedeon in his sleep,[b] showed to him the proneness of human nature to self-love and the hatred that it bore to those of surpassing merit, and how, far from attributing the victory to God, they would regard it as their own, on the ground that they were a large army and a match for their enemies. In order, therefore, that they might learn that it was His aid that accomplished it, He counselled him towards midday, when the heat was most intense,[c] to march his troops to the river; and then such of them as knelt [d] down to drink, them he should deem the stalwarts, but all who drank hurriedly and with trepidation, these he should rank as cowards [e] and terrified of the foe. Gedeon having then done in accordance with this counsel of God, there were found 300 men who with fear and trembling raised the water in their hands to their lips; and these God bade him take with him to attack the enemy.[f] So they pitched their camp above the Jordan,[g] with intent to cross on the morrow.

Jd. vi. 34; vii. 2 ff.

(4) But Gedeon being terror-struck, having withal been divinely ordered to attack by night, God, with

Dream of a Madianite soldier. Jd. vii. 9.

[e] Some MSS. read "should deem that they had acted this way through cowardice."

[f] The correct interpretation of the confused verses, Jd. vii. 5, 6, is probably that the 300 men who lapped the water with their tongues like dogs were those selected for battle, while those who knelt to drink were rejected. Josephus, taking the lapping to mean drinking "with trepidation," implies that the 300 were chosen "lest Israel vaunt themselves" (Jd. vii. 2), *i.e.* God could give victory even to a cowardly army.

[g] At En Harod (Jd. vii. 1), site uncertain.

δέους αὐτὸν ἀπαγαγεῖν βουλόμενος κελεύει προσλαβόντα ἕνα τῶν στρατιωτῶν πλησίον χωρεῖν ταῖς Μαδιανιτῶν σκηναῖς· παρ' αὐτῶν γὰρ ἐκείνων
219 λήψεσθαι φρόνημα καὶ θάρσος. πεισθεὶς δὲ ᾔει Φρουρὰν τὸν ἑαυτοῦ θεράποντα παραλαβών, καὶ πλησιάσας σκηνῇ τινι καταλαμβάνει τοὺς ἐν αὐτῇ ἐγρηγορότας καὶ τὸν ἕτερον ὄναρ διηγούμενον τῷ συσκηνοῦντι, ὥστε ἀκούειν τὸν Γεδεῶνα. τὸ δὲ τοιοῦτον ἦν· μᾶζαν ἐδόκει κριθίνην ὑπ' εὐτελείας ἀνθρώποις ἄβρωτον διὰ τοῦ στρατοπέδου κυλιομένην τὴν τοῦ βασιλέως σκηνὴν καταβαλεῖν καὶ
220 τὰς τῶν στρατιωτῶν πάντων. ὁ δὲ σημαίνειν ὄλεθρον τοῦ στρατοῦ τὴν ὄψιν ἔκρινε, λέγων ὅθεν τοῦτ' αὐτῷ συνιδεῖν ἐπῆλθε, πάντων τῶν σπερμάτων[1] τὸ καλούμενον κρίθινον εὐτελέστατον ὁμολογεῖσθαι τυγχάνειν, "τοῦ δ' Ἀσιανοῦ παντὸς τὸ Ἰσραηλιτῶν ἔστιν ἰδεῖν ἀτιμότερον νῦν γεγενημένον ὅμοιον δὲ
221 τῷ κατὰ κριθὴν γένει. καὶ τὸ παρὰ τοῖς Ἰσραηλίταις νῦν μεγαλοφρονοῦν τοῦτ' ἂν εἴη Γεδεὼν καὶ τὸ σὺν αὐτῷ στρατιωτικόν. ἐπεὶ οὖν τὴν μᾶζαν φῂς ἰδεῖν τὰς σκηνὰς ἡμῶν ἀνατρέπουσαν, δέδια μὴ ὁ θεὸς Γεδεῶνι τὴν καθ' ἡμῶν νίκην ἐπινένευκε."

222 (5) Γεδεῶνα δ' ἀκούσαντα τὸ ὄναρ ἐλπὶς ἀγαθὴ καὶ θάρσος ἔλαβε, καὶ προσέταξεν ἐν τοῖς ὅπλοις εἶναι τοὺς οἰκείους διηγησάμενος αὐτοῖς καὶ τὴν τῶν πολεμίων ὄψιν, οἱ δ' ἕτοιμοι πρὸς τὰ παραγγελλόμενα φρονηματισθέντες ὑπὸ τῶν δεδηλω-

[1] conj.: πᾶν τὸ σπέρμα codd.

intent to banish his fear, bade him take one of his soldiers and advance close up to the tents of the Madianites, since from the lips of the very foe he would derive courage and confidence. Obediently thereto he went, taking with him his servant Phruras,[a] and, on approaching one of the tents, found that its occupants were awake and that one of them was recounting to his companion a dream, in such fashion that Gedeon could hear it. Now the dream was on this wise: it seemed to him that a barley cake, too vile for man's consumption, came rolling through the camp and struck down the king's tent and those of all his soldiers. His comrade interpreted the vision to betoken the destruction of the army, stating what led him to understand it so: "Of all seeds (he said) that called barley is admitted to be the vilest; and of all Asiatic races that of the Israelites, as may be seen, has now become the most ignominious and like to the nature of barley. And among the Israelites at this moment the high-spirited party can be none but Gedeon and his comrades-in-arms. Since, then, thou sayest that thou sawest that cake overturning our tents, I fear that God has conceded to Gedeon the victory over us."

(5) The hearing of this dream inspired Gedeon with high hopes and confidence, and he commanded his men to be ready in arms, having also recounted to them this vision of the enemy; and they were alert to obey his orders, elated by what they had

Defeat of the Madianites. Jd. vii. 15.

[a] Bibl. Purah, LXX Φαρά (and so the Latin version of Josephus).

223 μένων ἦσαν. καὶ κατὰ τετάρτην μάλιστα φυλακὴν
προσῆγε τὴν αὐτοῦ στρατιὰν Γεδεὼν εἰς τρία μέρη
διελὼν αὐτήν, ἑκατὸν δὲ ἦσαν ἐν ἑκάστῳ. ἐκόμιζον
δὲ πάντες ἀμφορέας κενοὺς καὶ λαμπάδας ἡμμένας
ἐν αὐταῖς, ὅπως μὴ κατάφωρος τοῖς πολεμίοις ἡ
ἔφοδος αὐτῶν γένηται, καὶ ἐν τῇ δεξιᾷ κριοῦ
224 κέρας· ἐχρῶντο δὲ τούτοις ἀντὶ σάλπιγγος. χωρίον
δὲ πολὺ κατεῖχε τὸ τῶν πολεμίων στράτευμα,[1]
πλείστην γὰρ αὐτοῖς εἶναι συνέβαινε κάμηλον, καὶ
κατὰ τὰ[2] ἔθνη νεμηθέντες ὑφ' ἑνὶ κύκλῳ πάντες
225 ἦσαν. οἱ δ' Ἑβραῖοι, προειρημένον[3] αὐτοῖς ὁπόταν
γένωνται πλησίον τῶν πολεμίων ἐκ συνθήματος
σάλπιγξί τε ἠχήσαντας καὶ τοὺς ἀμφορέας κατ-
εάξαντας ὁρμῆσαι μετὰ τῶν λαμπάδων ἀλαλάξαντας[4]
καὶ νικᾶν θεοῦ Γεδεῶνι βοηθήσοντος, τοῦτ' ἐποίη-
226 σαν. ταραχὴ δὲ λαμβάνει τοὺς ἀνθρώπους ἔτι
ὑπνοῦντας καὶ δείματα· νὺξ γὰρ ἦν καὶ ὁ θεὸς
τοῦτο ἤθελεν. ἐκτείνοντο δὲ ὀλίγοι μὲν ὑπὸ τῶν
πολεμίων, οἱ δὲ πλείους ὑπὸ τῶν συμμάχων διὰ
τὸ τῇ γλώσσῃ διαφωνεῖν· ἅπαξ δὲ καταστάντες
εἰς ταραχὴν πᾶν τὸ προστυχὸν ἀνῄρουν νομίζοντες
227 εἶναι πολέμιον, φόνος τε πολὺς ἦν. καὶ φήμης
πρὸς τοὺς Ἰσραηλίτας τῆς Γεδεῶνος νίκης ἀφικο-
μένης ἐν τοῖς ὅπλοις ἦσαν, καὶ διώξαντες λαμβάνουσι τοὺς πολεμίους ἐν κοίλῳ τινὶ χαράδραις
περιειλημμένῳ οὐ δυναμέναις διαπερᾶναι χωρίῳ
καὶ περιστάντες κτείνουσιν ἅπαντας καὶ δύο τῶν
228 βασιλέων Ὥρηβόν τε καὶ Ζῆβον. οἱ δὲ λοιποὶ

[1] ROE: στρατόπεδον rell. [2] τὰ om. SP.
[3] Niese: προειρημένου codd.
[4] Niese: ἠχήσαντες . . . κατεάξαντες . . . ἀλαλάξαντες codd.

been told. Then, at about the fourth watch,[a] Gedeon marched forth his army, which he had divided into three sections, each of an hundred men. They all bore empty pitchers with lighted torches inside them, to prevent the enemy from detecting their approach, and in the right hand a ram's horn, which
served for a trumpet. Their enemy's camp covered 12.
a large area, for they had a vast camel-corps and were divided according to their nationalities, all being enclosed within one ring. The Hebrews had received orders, on approaching the enemy, at a given signal to sound their trumpets, break their pitchers, and rush forward with their torches and with shouts of battle and "Victory, and God will aid Gedeon!" and even so they did. Confusion and panic seized the hapless creatures yet slumbering; for it was night and God willed it so. Thus were they slain, few indeed by their enemies, the more part by the hands of their allies, by reason of their diversity of languages; and, when once confusion reigned, they killed all that they met, taking them for enemies,
and there was a great carnage. A rumour of 28.
Gedeon's victory reaching the Israelites, they too were up in arms, and pursuing caught the enemy in a valley encompassed with impassable ravines,[b] and, having surrounded them, slew them all with two of their kings, Oreb and Zeb. The other chiefs,

[a] In Jd. vii. 19 they reach the outskirts of the enemy's camp at "the beginning of the middle watch" (of three watches of 4 hours each from 6 P.M. to 6 A.M., *i.e.* at about 10 P.M.); Josephus, following the Roman division of the night into four watches of 3 hours each, represents them as leaving their own camp at about 3 A.M.

[b] This death-trap—the "impassable valley" in which the main body of the enemy is cooped up and annihilated—is a familiar feature of these battle-scenes; *cf.* § 162.

τῶν ἡγεμόνων τοὺς περιλειφθέντας τῶν στρατιωτῶν ἐνάγοντες,[1] ἦσαν δὲ ὡς[2] μύριοι καὶ ὀκτακισχίλιοι, στρατοπεδεύονται πολὺ τῶν Ἰσραηλιτῶν ἄπωθεν. Γεδεὼν δὲ οὐκ ἀπηγορεύκει πονῶν, ἀλλὰ διώξας μετὰ παντὸς τοῦ στρατοῦ καὶ συμβαλὼν ἅπαντας διέφθειρε τοὺς πολεμίους καὶ τοὺς λοιποὺς ἡγεμόνας Ζεβὴν καὶ Ζαρμούνην αἰχμα-
229 λώτους λαβὼν ἀνήγαγεν. ἀπέθανον δ' ἐν αὐτῇ τῇ μάχῃ Μαδιανιτῶν τε καὶ τῶν συστρατευσάντων αὐτοῖς Ἀράβων περὶ μυριάδας δώδεκα, λεία τε πολλὴ χρυσὸς καὶ ἄργυρος καὶ ὕφη καὶ κάμηλος καὶ ὑποζύγια λαμβάνεται τοῖς Ἑβραίοις. Γεδεὼν δὲ παραγενόμενος εἰς Ἐφρὰν τὴν ἑαυτοῦ πατρίδα κτείνει τοὺς τῶν Μαδιανιτῶν βασιλέας.

230 (6) Ἡ δ' Ἐφράμιδος φυλὴ τῇ Γεδεῶνος εὐπραγίᾳ δυσχεραίνουσα στρατεύειν ἐπ' αὐτὸν διεγνώκει, τὸ μὴ προαγγεῖλαι[3] τὴν ἐπιχείρησιν αὐτοῖς τὴν κατὰ τῶν πολεμίων ἐγκαλοῦντες. Γεδεὼν δὲ μέτριος ὢν καὶ πᾶσαν ἀρετὴν ἄκρος, οὐκ αὐτὸς ἔλεγεν αὐτοκράτορι χρησάμενος λογισμῷ τοῖς ἐχθροῖς ἐπιθέσθαι χωρὶς αὐτῶν, ἀλλὰ τοῦ θεοῦ κελεύσαντος· τὴν δὲ νίκην οὐχ ἧττον αὐτῶν ἔφασκεν
231 ἰδίαν ἢ τῶν ἐστρατευκότων εἶναι. καὶ τούτοις παρηγορήσας αὐτῶν τὴν ὀργὴν τοῖς λόγοις μᾶλλον τοὺς Ἑβραίους ὠφέλησε τῆς ἐπὶ τῶν πολεμίων εὐπραξίας· ἐμφυλίου γὰρ αὐτοὺς στάσεως ἄρχειν μέλλοντας ἐρρύσατο. τῆς μέντοιγε ὕβρεως ταύτης ἡ φυλὴ δίκην ἐξέτισεν, ἣν δηλώσομεν κατὰ καιρὸν ἴδιον.

[1] colligentes (? συνάγοντες) Lat.: ἄγοντες SPE.
[2] MLE Lat.: om. rell.
[3] Dindorf: προσαγγεῖλαι (παρ.) codd.

urging on their surviving soldiers, numbering some 18,000,[a] encamped when at a great distance from the Israelites. Gedeon, however, had not renounced the viii. 12.
struggle, but, following in pursuit with his whole army, joined battle, annihilated the enemy, and brought back as prisoners the remaining chiefs, Zebes and Zarmunes.[b] In the preceding combat
there had fallen of the Madianites and of their 10.
Arabian comrades-in-arms about 120,000; and abundant booty—gold, silver, woven stuff, camels and
beasts of burden—fell to the Hebrews. Gedeon on 21.
his return to Ephra,[c] his native place, put the kings of the Madianites to death.

The aggrieved tribe of Ephraim. Jd. viii. 1.

(6) But the tribe of Ephraim, aggrieved at Gedeon's success, now resolved to march against him, complaining that he had not informed them of his proposed assault on the enemy. Gedeon, however, being a man of moderation and a model of every virtue, replied that it was not of himself by an arbitrary decision[d] that he had attacked the foe without them, but by divine command; while the victory, he declared, belonged no less to them than to those who had taken the field. And by these words, with which he pacified their wrath, he did the Hebrews a greater service than by his military success; for he rescued them from civil strife when they were on the brink of it. Howbeit for its insolent attitude this tribe paid a penalty, which we shall relate in due season.[e]

[a] "About 15,000," Jd. viii. 10.

[b] Bibl. Zebah (LXX Ζεβεέ) and Zalmunna (Ζαλμανά). The MSS. of Josephus have various spellings.

[c] Bibl. Ophrah (LXX Ἐφραθά or, in some MSS., Ἐφρά); Jd. vi. 11.

[d] αὐτοκράτορι λογισμῷ after Thuc. iv. 108.

[e] *Cf.* § 250.

232 (7) Γεδεὼν δὲ τὴν ἀρχὴν ἀποθέσθαι βουλόμενος
βιασθεὶς ἔσχεν αὐτὴν ἐπ' ἔτη τεσσαράκοντα βραβεύων αὐτοῖς τὰ δίκαια καὶ περὶ τῶν διαφορῶν ἐπ' αὐτὸν βαδιζόντων κύρια[1] πάντα ἦν τὰ ὑπ' αὐτοῦ λεγόμενα. καὶ ὁ μὲν γηραιὸς τελευτήσας ἐν Ἐφρὰν τῇ πατρίδι θάπτεται.

233 (vii. 1) Παῖδες δὲ ἦσαν αὐτῷ γνήσιοι μὲν ἑβδομήκοντα, πολλὰς γὰρ ἔγημε γυναῖκας, νόθος δ' εἷς ἐκ παλλακῆς Δρούμας Ἀβιμέλεχος τοὔνομα, ὃς μετὰ τὴν τοῦ πατρὸς τελευτὴν ἀναχωρήσας ἐπὶ[2] Σίκιμα πρὸς τοὺς ἀπὸ μητρὸς συγγενεῖς, ἐντεῦθεν
234 γὰρ ἦν, καὶ λαβὼν ἀργύριον παρ' αὐτῶν * * *[3] οἳ
διὰ πλῆθος ἀδικημάτων ἦσαν ἐπίσημοι, ἀφικνεῖται σὺν αὐτοῖς εἰς τὸν πατρῷον οἶκον καὶ κτείνει πάντας τοὺς ἀδελφοὺς πλὴν Ἰωθάμου· σώζεται γὰρ οὗτος διαφυγεῖν εὐτυχήσας. Ἀβιμέλεχος δὲ εἰς τυραννίδα τὰ πράγματα μεθίστησι, κύριον αὐτὸν ὅ τι βούλεται ποιεῖν ἀντὶ τῶν νομίμων ἀποδείξας καὶ δεινῶς πρὸς τοὺς τοῦ δικαίου προϊσταμένους ἐκπικραινόμενος.

235 (2) Καί ποτε δημοτελοῦς Σικίμοις οὔσης ἑορτῆς καὶ τοῦ πλήθους παντὸς ἐκεῖ συνειλεγμένου ὁ ἀδελφὸς αὐτοῦ Ἰωθάμης, ὃν καὶ διαφυγεῖν ἔφαμεν, ἀνελθὼν ἐπὶ τὸ ὄρος τὸ Γαριζείν, ὑπέρκειται δὲ τῆς Σικιμίων πόλεως, ἐκβοήσας εἰς ἐπήκοον τοῦ πλήθους ἡσυχίαν αὐτῷ παρασχόντος[4] ἠξίου μαθεῖν
236 τὰ ὑπ' αὐτοῦ λεγόμενα. γενομένης δὲ σιγῆς

[1] Lat.: + τε codd. [2] εἰς RO.
[3] lacuna indicated by Jd. ix. 4.
[4] παρασχόντας Weill.

[a] His making of an ephod, which "became a snare to Gideon and to his house" (Jd. viii. 27), is omitted.

(7) Gedeon then, wishing to resign his command, was constrained to keep it, and continued for forty years to administer justice: men resorted to him concerning their differences, and all his pronouncements had binding weight.[a] He died in ripe old age and was buried at Ephra, his native place.

Gedeon as judge. Jd. viii. 22. 28. 32.

(vii. 1) Now he had seventy sons born in wedlock (for he married many wives) and by a concubine, Druma,[b] one bastard named Abimelech. This last, after his father's death, withdrew to the family of his mother at Shechem,[c] her native place, and, having obtained money from them (hired certain miscreants),[d] who were notorious for a multitude of crimes, and with them repaired to his father's house and slew all his brethren, save Jotham: this one had the good fortune to escape alive. Abimelech then transformed the government into a tyranny, setting himself up to do whatsoever he pleased in defiance of the laws and showing bitter animosity against the champions of justice.

Abimelech the tyrant. Jd. viii. 30. ix. 1.

(2) Now one day when there was a public festival[e] at Shechem and the people were all assembled there, his brother Jotham—the one who, as we said, had escaped—ascended Garizin, the mountain which rises above the city of Shechem, and shouting so as to be heard by the crowd if they would but listen to him quietly, begged them to attend to what he had to say. Silence being established, he told them

Jotham's parable to the Shechemites. Jd. ix. 7.

[b] Name not in Scripture. Perhaps it was taken through error from "Arumah," the name of a town where Abimelech dwelt for a time (Jd. ix. 41).

[c] Gr. Sikima (as in most MSS. of LXX).

[d] Lacuna in Greek, to be supplied from Jd. ix. 4 "Abimelech hired vain and light fellows, which followed him."

[e] The public festival is not mentioned in Scripture.

εἶπεν, ὡς τὰ δένδρα φωνὴν ἀνθρώπειον προϊέμενα συνόδου γενομένης αὐτῶν δεηθείη συκῆς ἄρχειν αὐτῶν. ἀρνησαμένης δ' ἐκείνης διὰ τὸ τιμῆς τῆς ἐπὶ τοῖς καρποῖς οἰκείας οὔσης ἀπολαύειν, οὐχ ὑπ' ἄλλων ἔξωθεν προσγινομένης, τὰ δένδρα τῆς ἐπὶ τῷ ἄρχεσθαι φροντίδος οὐκ ἀπελείπετο, ἐδόκει
237 δ' αὐτοῖς ἀμπέλῳ τὴν τιμὴν παρασχεῖν. καὶ ἡ ἄμπελος χειροτονουμένη τοῖς αὐτοῖς τῇ συκῇ χρησαμένη λόγοις παρῃτεῖτο τὴν ἀρχήν. τὸ δ' αὐτὸ καὶ τῶν ἐλαιῶν ποιησαμένων ῥάμνος, ἐδεήθη γὰρ αὐτῆς ὥστε παραλαβεῖν τὴν βασιλείαν τὰ
238 δένδρα, πυρεῖα[1] δὲ ἀγαθὴ παρασχεῖν τῶν ξύλων ἐστίν, ὑπισχνεῖται τὴν ἀρχὴν ἀναλήψεσθαι καὶ ἀόκνως ἔχειν, δεῖν[2] μέντοι συνιζάνειν αὐτὰ ὑπὸ τὴν σκιάν, εἰ δ' ὄλεθρον ἐπ' αὐτῇ φρονοῖεν,[3] ὑπὸ τοῦ
239 ἐνόντος πυρὸς διαφθαρεῖεν. "ταῦτα δ' οὐ γέλωτος ἕνεκα," φησί, "λέγω," ὅτι δὲ πολλῶν ἀγαθῶν ἐκ Γεδεῶνος πεπειραμένοι περιορῶσιν 'Αβιμέλεχον ἐπὶ τῶν ὅλων ὄντα πραγμάτων σὺν αὐτῷ τοὺς ἀδελφοὺς ἀποκτείναντες, ὃν πυρὸς οὐδὲν διοίσειν. καὶ ὁ μὲν ταῦτα εἰπὼν ὑπεχώρησε καὶ διῃτᾶτο λανθάνων ἐν τοῖς ὄρεσι δεδιὼς ἐπ' ἔτη τρία τὸν 'Αβιμέλεχον.

240 (3) Μετ' οὐ πολὺ δὲ τῆς ἑορτῆς οἱ[4] Σικιμῖται, μετενόησαν γὰρ ἐπὶ τοῖς Γεδεῶνος υἱοῖς πεφονευμένοις, ἐξελαύνουσι τὸν 'Αβιμέλεχον τῆς πόλεως καὶ τῆς φυλῆς· ὁ δὲ κακοῦν τὴν πόλιν ἐφρόντιζε. τῆς δ' ὥρας τῆς τοῦ τρυγᾶν γενομένης ἐδεδίεσαν συλλέγειν τὸν καρπὸν προϊόντες, μή τι δράσῃ κακὸν

[1] πυρία codd.
[2] δεῖ codd.
[3] φρονῶεν codd.
[4] om. RO.

how the trees, once gifted with a human voice, held a meeting and besought a fig-tree [a] to rule over them. And when she refused, because she enjoyed the esteem which her fruits brought her, an esteem that was all her own and not conferred from without by others, the trees did not renounce their intention of having a ruler, but thought good to offer this dignity to the vine. And the vine, when so elected, on the same grounds as those of the fig-tree, declined the sovereignty. The olive-trees having done the like, a bramble—since the trees requested it to accept the kingship, and it is good in giving wood for tinder—promised to undertake the office and to act strenuously. However it behoved them all to sit down beneath her shadow, and should they plot her ruin they would be destroyed by the fire within
her. "I tell this fable," said Jotham, "not for your 16.
merriment, but because notwithstanding the manifold benefits that ye have received from Gedeon ye [b] suffer Abimelech to hold sovereign sway, after aiding him to slay my brethren. Ye will find him in no wise different from a fire." Having spoken thus he
absconded and lived in hiding in the hills for three *Cf.* 22.
years from fear of Abimelech.

Expulsion of Abimelech. Jd. ix. 23.

(3) But not long after the festival [c] the Shechemites, repenting of the murder of the sons of Gedeon, expelled Abimelech from their city and from their tribe; and he laid plans for doing the town an injury. So, when the season of vintage was come, they were afraid to go out and gather the fruit, for

[a] In Judges the olive-tree is approached first, then the fig-tree, then the vine.

[b] In the Greek, the Shechemites are not addressed in the second person.

[c] Not in Scripture.

241 Ἀβιμέλεχος εἰς αὐτούς. ἐπιδημήσαντος δὲ πρὸς
αὐτοὺς τῶν ἀρχόντων τινὸς Γυάλου σὺν ὁπλίταις
καὶ συγγενέσι τοῖς αὐτοῦ, φυλακὴν οἱ Σικιμῖται
δέονται παρασχεῖν αὐτοῖς, ἕως ἂν τρυγήσωσι.
προσδεξαμένου δ' ἐκείνου τὴν ἀξίωσιν προῄεσαν
καὶ Γυάλης σὺν αὐτοῖς τὸ οἰκεῖον ἄγων ὁπλιτικόν.
242 ὅ τε οὖν καρπὸς μετὰ ἀσφαλείας συνάγεται καὶ
δειπνοῦντες κατὰ συμμορίας[1] φανερῶς ἀπετόλμων
ἤδη βλασφημεῖν τὸν Ἀβιμέλεχον, οἵ τε ἄρχοντες
ἐνέδραις καταλαμβανόμενοι τὰ περὶ τὴν πόλιν
πολλοὺς τῶν Ἀβιμελέχου συλλαμβάνοντες ἀνῄρουν.
243 (4) Ζάβουλος δέ τις τῶν Σικιμιτῶν ἄρχων, ξένος
ὢν Ἀβιμελέχου, ὅσα παροξύνειεν Γυάλης τὸν
δῆμον πέμπων ἀγγέλους ἐμήνυεν αὐτῷ καὶ παρῄνει
λοχᾶν πρὸ τῆς πόλεως· πείσειν γὰρ Γυάλην ἐξελθεῖν ἐπ' αὐτόν, καὶ τὸ λοιπὸν ἐπ' ἐκείνῳ τυγχάνειν
ὥστε ἀμύνασθαι· γενομένου γὰρ τούτου διαλλαγὰς
244 αὐτῷ μνηστεύσεσθαι[2] πρὸς τὸν δῆμον. ὅ τε οὖν
Ἀβιμέλεχος ἐκάθισεν ἐνεδρεύων καὶ ὁ Γυάλης
ἀφυλακτοτέρως διέτριβεν ἐπὶ τοῦ προαστείου καὶ
Ζάβουλος σὺν αὐτῷ. ἰδὼν δὲ ὁπλίτας ἐπιφερο-
μένους Γυάλης πρὸς Ζάβουλον ἔλεγεν ἄνδρας
245 αὐτοῖς ἐπιέναι καθωπλισμένους. τοῦ δὲ σκιὰς
εἶναι φαμένου τῶν πετρῶν, πλησίον ἤδη γινομένων
τὸ ἀκριβὲς κατανοῶν οὐ σκιὰς ἔλεγε ταῦτ' εἶναι,
λόχον δ' ἀνδρῶν. καὶ Ζάβουλος "οὐ σὺ μέντοι,"
φησίν, "Ἀβιμελέχῳ κακίαν ἐπεκάλεις; τί οὖν
οὐκ ἐπιδείκνυσαι τὸ τῆς σῆς ἀρετῆς μέγεθος εἰς
246 μάχην αὐτῷ συμβαλών;" Γυάλης δὲ θορυβού-
μενος συνάπτει τοῖς Ἀβιμελέχου καὶ πίπτουσι μέν

[1] ex Lat.: συμμορίαν codd.
[2] Niese: μνηστεύεσθαι codd.

fear that Abimelech would do them some mischief.
But on being visited by Gual,[a] one of their chiefs, 26.
with a retinue of troops and kinsmen, the Shechemites besought him to lend them protection during their vintage. And when he complied with their request, they went forth, accompanied by Gual at the head of his troop. So the fruit was safely gathered in, and while supping in companies they now ventured
openly to revile Abimelech ; and the chiefs, posting 25.
ambuscades about the town, captured and slew many of his followers.

The fate of Shechem. Jd. ix. 30.

(4) But a certain Zabul,[b] a chieftain of the Shechemites and an old friend of Abimelech, sent messengers to report to him how Gual was stirring up the people, and he advised him to lie in wait before the town, since he would induce Gual to sally out against him and it would then rest with Abimelech to avenge himself; that done, he (Zabul) would procure his reconciliation with the townsfolk. So Abimelech sat in ambush, while Gual all too unguardedly tarried in the suburbs, and Zabul with him. Spying some men-at-arms hastening up, Gual said to Zabul that men were upon them in arms. He replied that they were but shadows of the rocks ; but on their nearer approach Gual, perceiving them perfectly, told him that these were no shadows but a company of men. Said Zabul, " But wert thou not accusing Abimelech of cowardice ? Why then displayest thou not that mighty valour of thine by meeting him in combat ? " Thereat Gual, in confusion, closed with Abimelech's men, lost some of his own, and himself

[a] Greek *Guales*, Bibl. Gaal.
[b] Or, with some MSS., " Zebul " (the Biblical name).

τινες τῶν σὺν αὐτῷ, φεύγει δ' αὐτὸς εἰς τὴν πόλιν τοὺς ἄλλους ἀγόμενος. καὶ Ζάβουλος πολιτεύεται Γυάλην ἐκβληθῆναι τῆς πόλεως, κατηγορήσας ὡς μαλακῶς πρὸς τοὺς Ἀβιμελέχου στρατιώτας ἀγωνί-
247 σαιτο. Ἀβιμέλεχος δὲ πυθόμενος ἐξελευσομένους αὖθις κατὰ τρύγητον τοὺς Σικιμίους ἐνέδραις προλοχίζεται τὰ περὶ τὴν πόλιν, καὶ προελθόντων ἡ μὲν τρίτη μοῖρα τῆς στρατιᾶς καταλαμβάνει τὰς πύλας ἀφαιρησομένη τὴν εἴσοδον τοὺς πολίτας, οἱ δ' ἄλλοι σκιδναμένους μεταθέουσι, πανταχοῦ τε
248 φόνος ἦν. καὶ κατασκάψας εἰς ἔδαφος τὴν πόλιν, οὐ γὰρ ἀντέσχε πρὸς[1] πολιορκίαν, ἅλας κατὰ τῶν ἐρειπίων σπείρας προῆγε. καὶ Σικιμῖται πάντες οὕτως ἀπώλοντο· ὅσοι δὲ κατὰ τὴν χώραν σκεδασθέντες διέφυγον τὸν κίνδυνον, οὗτοι συλλεγέντες ἐπί τινα πέτραν ὀχυρὰν[2] ἐπ' αὐτῆς ἱδρύονται
249 τειχίσαι τε ταύτην παρεσκευάζοντο. ἔφθη τε τὴν διάνοιαν αὐτῶν Ἀβιμέλεχος μαθὼν ἐλθεῖν ἐπ' αὐτοὺς μετὰ τῆς δυνάμεως καὶ φακέλους ὕλης ξηρᾶς περιβαλὼν τῷ χωρίῳ δι' αὐτοῦ φέρων ταὐτὰ[3] ποιεῖν τὴν στρατιὰν παρεκελεύσατο. καὶ ταχέως περιληφθείσης ἐν κύκλῳ τῆς πέτρας, τοῖς ξύλοις πῦρ ἐμβάλλουσιν ὅσα τε μᾶλλον ἐξάπτειν φύσιν
250 ἔχει καὶ μεγίστην αἴρουσι φλόγα. καὶ διαφεύγει μὲν ἀπὸ τῆς πέτρας οὐθείς, ἀλλ' ἅμα γυναιξὶ καὶ τέκνοις ἀπώλοντο, ἄνδρες μὲν περὶ πεντακοσίους καὶ χιλίους, τὸ δὲ ἄλλο πλῆθος ἱκανόν. καὶ

[1] + τὴν RO.
[2] συλλεγέντες . . . ὀχυρὰν] πέτραν ὀχυρὰν εὑρόντες RO.
[3] ταὐτὸ MSPL.

fled to the town with the rest at his heels. Zabul 41.
now contrived to secure Gual's expulsion from the town, charging him with feebleness in his encounter with Abimelech's troops.[a] However Abimelech, learning that the Shechemites proposed to come out again for the vintage, posted ambuscades all about the town; then, so soon as they emerged, a third of his force occupied the gates to cut off the citizens from re-entering, the rest chased them as they scattered, and there was carnage on all sides. Then, having razed the city to the ground—for it could not sustain a siege—he sowed salt over the ruins and pushed forward. And so perished all the Shechemites.
As for such as had scattered across country and 46.
escaped that peril, these mustering to a strongly entrenched rock established themselves thereon and were preparing to fortify it with a wall.[b] But they were forestalled by Abimelech, who, hearing of their design, came upon them with his forces and laid faggots of dry wood round the place, carrying them with his own hands and bidding his troops to do the like. The rock being thus quickly encompassed, they set fire to the faggots, flinging in all the most inflammable materials, and raised an immense blaze. From that rock not a soul escaped: they perished with women and children, the men numbering some fifteen hundred,[c] and a great many of the

[a] This charge is not mentioned in Scripture.

[b] The Biblical account is different, mentioning a tower, apparently in an unwalled hamlet of Shechem possessing a temple: Jd. ix. 46 "And when all the men of the tower of Shechem heard thereof, they entered into the hold (or "crypt"—the word is of uncertain meaning) of the temple of El-berith."

[c] "About a thousand men and women," Jd. ix. 49.

Σικιμίταις μὲν τοιαύτη συμφορὰ συνέπεσε μείζων
καὶ τῆς ἐπ' αὐτῇ λύπης γενομένη, πλὴν ὅτι κατὰ
δίκην ἐπ' ἀνδρὸς εὐεργέτου συνθεῖσι κακὸν τηλικοῦτον.
251 (5) Ἀβιμέλεχος δὲ τοῖς Σικιμιτῶν κακοῖς κατα-
πλήξας τοὺς Ἰσραηλίτας, μειζόνων ἐφιέμενος δῆλος
ἦν καὶ μηδαμοῦ περιγράψων τὴν βίαν, εἰ μὴ πάντας
ἀπολέσειεν. ἤλαυνεν οὖν ἐπὶ Θήβας καὶ τὴν μὲν
πόλιν ἐξ ἐπιδρομῆς αἱρεῖ, πύργου δ' ὄντος ἐν αὐτῇ
μεγάλου, εἰς ὃν πᾶν τὸ πλῆθος συνέφυγε, πολι-
252 ορκεῖν τοῦτον παρεσκευάζετο. καὶ αὐτὸν πλησίον
ὁρμῶντα τῶν πυλῶν γυνὴ θραύσματι μύλης βαλοῦσα
κατὰ τῆς κεφαλῆς τυγχάνει, πεσὼν δὲ Ἀβιμέλεχος
τὸν ὑπασπιστὴν παρεκάλει κτείνειν αὐτόν, μὴ τῆς
γυναικὸς ὁ θάνατος αὐτοῦ δόξειεν ἔργον. καὶ ὁ
253 μὲν τὸ προσταχθὲν ἐποίει. ὁ δὲ τοιαύτην ὑπὲρ
τῆς εἰς τοὺς ἀδελφοὺς παρανομίας ποινὴν ἐξέτισε
καὶ τῶν εἰς Σικιμίους αὐτῷ τετολμημένων· τούτοις
δὲ κατὰ τὴν Ἰωθάμου μαντείαν ἡ συμφορὰ συνέπεσε. τὸ μέντοι σὺν Ἀβιμελέχῳ στράτευμα πεσόντος αὐτοῦ σκεδασθὲν ἀνεχώρησεν ἐπὶ τὰ οἰκεῖα.
254 (6) Τῶν δὲ Ἰσραηλιτῶν τὴν ἡγεμονίαν Ἰαείρης
ὁ Γαλαδηνὸς ἐκ τῆς Μανασσίτιδος φυλῆς παραλαμβάνει, ἀνὴρ τά τε ἄλλα εὐδαίμων καὶ παῖδας
ἀγαθοὺς πεποιημένος τριάκοντα μὲν τὸν ἀριθμὸν
ἱππεύειν δὲ ἀρίστους καὶ τῶν κατὰ τὴν Γαλαδηνὴν πόλεων ἀρχὰς ἐγκεχειρισμένους. οὗτος
δύο καὶ εἴκοσι ἔτη τὴν ἀρχὴν κατασχὼν τελευτᾷ

[a] Gideon.

[b] Bibl. Thebez (LXX Θηβής), mod. *Ṭūbās*, some 10 miles N.E. of Shechem.

[c] Gr. "Galadenian." Josephus omits the judge Tola, to

rest. Such was the calamity which befell the Shechemites, a calamity too profound for grief, save that it was a righteous doom for the conspirators of so foul a crime against a benefactor.[a]

(5) Abimelech, having terrorized the Israelites by the miserable fate of the Shechemites, let it be seen that he was aspiring higher and would set no bound to his violence until he had exterminated all. So he marched upon Thebes[b] and carried the city with a rush; but finding there a great tower, wherein all the people had taken refuge, he made preparations to besiege it. And then, as he came rushing close beside the gates, a woman hurled a fragment of a millstone and struck him on the head. Prostrated to earth, Abimelech besought his armour-bearer to slay him, lest his death should be deemed the work of this woman; and he obeyed his behest. Such was the penalty paid by Abimelech for the crime that he perpetrated on his brethren and for his outrageous treatment of the Shechemites; and the fate which befell these last fulfilled the prediction of Jotham. Abimelech's army for their part, on the fall of their chief, dispersed and returned to their homes.

Death of Abimelech. Jd. ix. 50.

(6) The leadership of the Israelites was then taken over by Jair the Gileadite,[c] of the tribe of Manasseh, a man in all ways blessed, and chiefly in his progeny of valiant sons, thirty in number, excellent horsemen, to whom was committed the government of the several cities of Gilead.[d] Their father, after bearing rule for twenty-two years, died in old age

The rule of Jair. Jd. x. 3.

whom Scripture assigns a 23 years' term of office between Abimelech and Jair, Jd. x. 1 f.

[d] Gr. "Galadene."

γηραιὸς καὶ ταφῆς ἐν Καμὼν[1] πόλει τῆς Γαλαδηνῆς ἀξιοῦται.

255 (7) Πάντα δὲ τὰ τῶν Ἑβραίων εἰς ἀκοσμίαν καὶ ὕβριν τοῦ θεοῦ καὶ τῶν νόμων ὑπεφέρετο, καὶ καταφρονήσαντες αὐτῶν Ἀμμανῖται καὶ Παλαιστῖνοι στρατῷ μεγάλῳ διήρπαζον τὴν χώραν καὶ τὴν Περαίαν ἅπασαν κατασχόντες καὶ ἐπὶ τὴν τῶν
256 λοιπῶν ἤδη κτῆσιν διαβαίνειν ἐτόλμων. Ἑβραῖοι δὲ σωφρονισθέντες ὑπὸ τῶν κακῶν, εἰς ἱκετείαν ἐτράποντο τοῦ θεοῦ καὶ θυσίας ἐπέφερον παρακαλοῦντες αὐτὸν μετριάσαντα καὶ πρὸς τὴν δέησιν αὐτῶν ὑπαχθέντα παύσασθαι τῆς ὀργῆς· ὁ δὲ θεὸς μεταβαλόμενος εἰς τὸ ἡμερώτερον ἔμελλεν αὐτοῖς βοηθεῖν.

257 (8) Ἀμμανιτῶν δ' ἐστρατευκότων ἐπὶ τὴν Γαλαδηνὴν ὑπήντων οἱ ἐπιχώριοι πρὸς τὸ ὄρος δεόμενοι τοῦ στρατηγήσοντος. ἦν δέ τις Ἰέφθας ἀνὴρ διὰ τὴν πατρῴαν ἀρετὴν δυνατὸς καὶ δι' οἰκείαν αὐτοῦ
258 στρατιὰν ἣν ἔτρεφεν αὐτὸς μισθοφόρων. πρὸς τοῦτον οὖν πέμψαντες ἠξίουν αὐτὸν συμμαχεῖν ἐπαγγελλόμενοι παρασχεῖν εἰς ἅπαντ' αὐτῷ τὸν χρόνον τὴν ἰδίαν ἡγεμονίαν. ὁ δ' οὐ προσίεται τὴν παράκλησιν αὐτῶν, ἐγκαλῶν ὅτι μὴ βοηθήσειαν
259 αὐτῷ ὑπὸ τῶν ἀδελφῶν ἀδικουμένῳ περιφανῶς· οὐ γὰρ ὄντα ὁμομήτριον αὐτοῖς ἀλλὰ ξένον περὶ τὴν μητέρα δι' ἐρωτικὴν ἐπιθυμίαν ἐπαχθεῖσαν αὐτοῖς ὑπὸ τοῦ πατρός, ἐξέβαλον καταφρονήσαντες τῆς
260 αὐτοῦ ἀσθενείας. καὶ ὁ μὲν διέτριβεν ἐν τῇ Γα-

[1] Καλαμὼν RO.

[a] Perhaps modern *Kumeim*, some 7 miles S.E. of Gadara.

[b] The introduction of the Philistines as invaders (along with the Ammonites) *from the east* is strange and has been

and received honoured burial at Kamon,[a] a city of Gilead.

(7) But everything with the Hebrews was now drifting towards disorder and contempt of God and of the laws; so, holding them in disdain, the Ammanites and Philistines[b] with a large army ravaged their country and, after occupying all Peraea,[c] made bold to cross the river for the further conquest of the rest. But the Hebrews, sobered by their afflictions, turned in supplication to God and offered sacrifices, beseeching Him to be considerate and, yielding to their prayers, to desist from wrath. And God, moved to milder action, was now to succour them.

Israel under the Ammonites and Philistines. Jd. x. 6.

16.

(8) When the Ammanites had invaded Gilead, the people of the country, preparing to meet them, mustered in the hills, lacking a leader to take command. Now there was one Jephthah,[d] a mighty man by reason of the valour of his forefathers as also of his own troop of mercenaries which he maintained himself. To him then they sent, begging him to support them and promising to confer his command upon him for all time. But he declined their request, reproaching them for not having aided him when he was flagrantly wronged by his brethren. For, because he was not their full brother but unconnected on his mother's side, who had been inflicted upon them by their father through his amorous desire, they had cast him out, scorning his helplessness; and so he was living in the region called Galaditis,[e] receiv-

The call to Jephthah. x. 17.

xi. 1.

thought to be due to some confusion in the Biblical text (Jd. x. 7).

[c] Modern Transjordania.

[d] Gr. Jephthas (or Japhthas).

[e] Bibl. (more precisely) "in the land of Tob" (Jd. xi. 3).

λαδίτιδι καλουμένῃ χώρᾳ πάντας τοὺς ὁποθενοῦν παραγινομένους πρὸς αὐτὸν ἐπὶ μισθῷ δεχόμενος· ἐκλιπαρησάντων δ' αὐτῶν καὶ ὀμοσάντων εἰς ἀεὶ παρέξειν αὐτῷ τὴν ἡγεμονίαν ἐστράτευε.

261 (9) Καὶ ποιησάμενος ὀξεῖαν τὴν τῶν πραγμάτων ἐπιμέλειαν ἐν πόλει Μασφαθῇ καθίσας τὸν στρατὸν πρεσβείαν πέμπει παρὰ τὸν Ἀμμανίτην αἰτιώμενος τῆς ἁλώσεως. ὁ δὲ ἀντιπέμψας ᾐτιᾶτο τῶν Ἰσραηλιτῶν τὴν ἔξοδον τὴν ἀπ' Αἰγύπτου καὶ τῆς Ἀμοραίας αὐτοὺς ἠξίου παραχωρεῖν ὡς πατρῴας

262 οὔσης ἀρχῆθεν. ἀποκρινάμενος δὲ ὁ Ἰέφθας, ὡς οὔτε τῆς Ἀμοραίας τοῖς προγόνοις αὐτῶν εὐλόγως ἐγκαλοῦσι χάριν τε μᾶλλον τῆς Ἀμμανίτιδος αὐτοῖς ἔχειν ὀφείλουσι παρεθείσης, δυνατὸν γὰρ Μωυσεῖ καὶ ταύτην λαβεῖν[1]· παραχωρεῖν τε ἰδίας εἰπὼν γῆς, ἣν θεοῦ κατακτησαμένου μετὰ τριακόσια ἔτη νέμονται, μαχεῖσθαι[2] πρὸς αὐτοὺς ἔφησεν.

263 (10) Καὶ τοὺς μὲν πρέσβεις ταῦτ' εἰπὼν ἀπέλυσεν· αὐτὸς δ' εὐξάμενος νίκην καὶ θυσιάσειν ὑποσχόμενος, ἂν σῶος εἰς τὰ οἰκεῖα ὑποστρέψῃ, καὶ πᾶν ὅ τι καὶ πρῶτον αὐτῷ συντύχοι ἱερουργήσειν, συμβαλών τε νικᾷ παρὰ πολὺ καὶ φονεύων ἐδίωκε μέχρι πόλεως Μανιάθης, καὶ διαβὰς εἰς τὴν Ἀμμανῖτιν πόλεις τε ἠφάνισε πολλὰς καὶ λείαν ἤλασε καὶ τοὺς οἰκείους δουλείας ἀπήλλαξεν ἐν

264 ἔτεσιν ὀκτωκαίδεκα ταύτην ὑπομείναντας. ανα-

[1] Niese indicates a lacuna.
[2] ex Lat.: μάχεσθαι codd.

[a] Bibl. Mizpah (LXX Μασσηφά): site uncertain.
[b] "Amoraea" is the country north of the river Arnon. *Cf. A.* iv. 85. The Ammonite country is further north

ing all who resorted to him from whencesoever and paying them wages. However, when the Hebrews made earnest entreaty and swore to confer the command upon him for ever, he took the field.

(9) Having promptly taken charge of affairs and installed the army in the city of Masphath(e),[a] he sent an embassy to the Ammanite to remonstrate with him on his raid. That monarch sent a counter embassy, reproaching the Israelites for their exodus from Egypt and requiring them to quit Amoraea,[b] as the primeval heritage of his forefathers. Whereto Jephthah replied that the enemy had no just grievance against his people's ancestors on the subject of Amoraea and ought rather to be grateful to them for having left them Ammanitis, which Moses might have taken to boot; and, bidding him quit that land[c] of theirs which God had won for them and of which three hundred years later they were in possession, he declared that he would battle with them.

Embassies before battle. Jd. xi. 11.

(10) With these words he dismissed the envoys. Then, after praying[d] for victory and promising to sacrifice, should he return to his home unscathed, and to offer up the first creature that should meet him, he closed with the enemy, defeated them outright, and massacring pursued them up to the city of Maniath(e)[e]; then, crossing into Ammanitis, he destroyed many cities, carried off spoil, and delivered his countrymen from a servitude which they had borne for eighteen years. But on returning

Victory of Jephthah: his daughter's fate. Jd. xi. 30. x. 8.

with its capital at Rabatha (Bibl. Rabbah) on the river Jabbok. *Cf. A.* iv. 98.

[c] Text a little uncertain: possibly "saying that he would (not) quit that land" (Weill).

[d] Or "making vows."

[e] Bibl. Minnith (Jd. xi. 33): site unknown.

στρέφων δὲ συμφορᾷ περιπίπτει κατ' οὐδὲν ὁμοίᾳ τοῖς κατωρθωμένοις αὐτῷ· ὑπήντησε γὰρ ἡ θυγάτηρ αὐτῷ, μονογενὴς δ' ἦν, ἔτι παρθένος. ὁ δὲ ἀνοιμώξας ἐπὶ τῷ μεγέθει τοῦ πάθους, κατεμέμφετο τῆς περὶ τὴν ὑπάντησιν σπουδῆς τὴν θυγατέρα· καθ-
265 ιερῶσαι γὰρ αὐτὴν τῷ θεῷ. τῇ δὲ τὸ συμβησόμενον οὐκ ἀηδῶς προσέπεσεν, ἐπὶ νίκῃ τοῦ πατρὸς καὶ ἐλευθερίᾳ τῶν πολιτῶν τεθνηξομένῃ, παρεκάλεσε δὲ δύο μῆνας αὐτῇ παρασχόντα πρὸς τὸ μετὰ τῶν πολιτῶν ἀποθρηνῆσαι τὴν νεότητα, τότε ποιεῖν
266 τὰ κατὰ τὴν εὐχήν. συγχωρήσας δὲ τὰ κατὰ τὸν προειρημένον χρόνον μετὰ τοῦτον διελθόντα θύσας τὴν παῖδα ὡλοκαύτωσεν, οὔτε νόμιμον οὔτε θεῷ κεχαρισμένην θυσίαν ἐπιτελῶν, μὴ διαβασανίσας τῷ λογισμῷ τὸ γενησόμενον οἷόν τε τὸ[1] πραχθὲν δόξει τοῖς ἀκούσασι.

267 (11) Τῆς δ' Ἐφράνου[2] φυλῆς ἐπ' αὐτὸν στρατευσάσης, ὅτι μὴ κοινώσαιτο τὴν ἐπ' Ἀμμανίτας ἐλασίαν[3] αὐτοῖς, ἀλλὰ μόνος καὶ τὴν λείαν ἔχοι καὶ τὴν ἐπὶ τοῖς πεπραγμένοις δόξαν, πρῶτον μὲν ἔλεγεν, ὡς οὔτε λάθοιεν αὐτοὺς οἱ συγγενεῖς πολεμούμενοι καλούμενοί τε πρὸς συμμαχίαν οὐ παρεγένοντο, δέον καὶ πρὸ δεήσεως ἐγνωκότας ἐπειχθῆ-
268 ναι, ἔπειθ' ὡς ἄδικα πράττειν ἐπιχειροῦσι τοῖς πολεμίοις οὐ τολμήσαντες εἰς χεῖρας ἐλθεῖν, ἐπὶ δὲ τοὺς συγγενεῖς ὡρμηκότες· ἠπείλει τε σὺν τῷ θεῷ λήψεσθαι δίκην παρ' αὐτῶν, ἂν μὴ σωφρονῶσιν.
269 ὡς δ' οὐκ ἔπειθεν, ἀλλὰ συνέβαλεν αὐτοῖς ἐλθοῦσι

[1] τε τὸ] τε or τὸ codd.
[2] R: Ἐφράμου (-αίμου) rell.
[3] ἔλασιν RO.

[a] Phraseology based on Thuc. iii. 113. 3.

he fell foul of a calamity far different from these fair xi. 34.
achievements ; for it was his daughter who met him, his only daughter, a virgin yet. Wailing in anguish at the greatness of the blow,[a] the father chid his daughter for her haste in meeting him, seeing that he had dedicated her to God. But she without displeasure learnt her destiny, to wit that she must die in return for her father's victory and the liberation of her fellow-citizens ; she but asked him to grant her two months wherein to bewail her youth with her fellow-citizens, and thereafter he should do in accordance with his vow. He accorded her the respite aforesaid, and at its close sacrificed his child as a burnt-offering—a sacrifice neither sanctioned by the law nor well-pleasing to God ; for he had not by reflection probed what might befall or in what aspect the deed would appear to them that heard of it.[b]

Jephthah's war with Ephraim. Jd. xii. 1.

(11) The tribe of Ephraim now took arms against him, because he had not imparted the news of his expedition against the Ammanites to them, but had reserved to himself alone the booty and the glory of the achievement. Thereto he replied first that they were not unaware that their kinsfolk were beset and that when called upon for aid they had not come, whereas they ought, even before being asked, to have learnt of the matter and sped to arms ; next that this was an iniquitous enterprise of theirs, after not having dared to face the foe, to rush upon their kinsmen ; and he threatened, God helping, to be avenged on them unless they showed themselves reasonable. Failing, however, to influence them, he met them, when they came, with an army

[b] The rash vow is stigmatized in Rabbinical tradition (Weill, quoting *Genesis Rabba*, lx.).

μετὰ στρατιᾶς, ᾗ μετάπεμπτος ἐκ τῆς Γαλαδηνῆς ἐληλύθει, φόνον τε πολὺν αὐτῶν εἰργάσατο καὶ διώκων τραπέντας προλαβὼν μέρει τινὶ προαπεσταλμένῳ τοῦ Ἰορδάνου τὰς διαβάσεις κτείνει περὶ δισχιλίους καὶ τετρακισμυρίους γεγονότας.

270 (12) Αὐτὸς δὲ ἄρξας ἓξ ἔτη τελευτᾷ καὶ θάπτεται ἐν τῇ αὐτοῦ πατρίδι Σεβέῃ· τῆς Γαλαδηνῆς δ' ἐστὶν αὕτη.

271 (13) Τελευτήσαντος δὲ Ἰάφθα τὴν ἀρχὴν Ἀψάνης παραλαμβάνει φυλῆς ὢν Ἰουδαϊκῆς Βηθλέμων δὲ πόλεως. τούτῳ δὲ παῖδες ἦσαν ἑξήκοντα, τριάκοντα μὲν ἄρρενες αἱ λοιπαὶ δὲ θυγατέρες, οὓς καὶ πάντας ζῶντας κατέλιπε τὰς μὲν ἀνδράσιν ἐκδοὺς τοῖς δὲ γυναῖκας ἠγμένος. πράξας δ' οὐδὲν ἐν τῷ ἑπταετεῖ γενομένῳ χρόνῳ λόγου καὶ μνήμης ἄξιον γηραιὸς ὢν ἀπέθανε καὶ ταφῆς ἐν τῇ πατρίδι τυγχάνει.

272 (14) Ἀψάνους δ' οὕτως ἀποθανόντος οὐδ' ὁ μετ' αὐτὸν παραλαβὼν τὴν ἡγεμονίαν Ἤλων[1] ἐπ' ἔτη δέκα κατασχὼν αὐτὴν φυλῆς ὢν τῆς Ζαβούλης ἔπραξέ τι σπουδῆς ἄξιον.

273 (15) Ἀβδὼν δὲ Ἤλωνος παῖς φυλῆς μὲν τῆς Ἐφραμίτιδος πόλεως δὲ τῆς Φαραθωνιτῶν γεγονώς, αὐτοκράτωρ ἡγεμὼν ἀποδειχθεὶς μετ' Ἤλωνα μόνης ἂν τῆς εὐπαιδίας μνημονευθείη, μηδὲν ἔργον διὰ τὴν εἰρήνην καὶ τὴν ἄδειαν τῶν πραγμάτων λαμπρὸν μηδ' αὐτὸς ἐργασάμενος.[2]
274 υἱεῖς δὲ ἦσαν αὐτῷ τεσσαράκοντα καὶ τούτων

[1] Hilonis Lat. [2] ROML: εἰργασμένος SP.

[a] Josephus omits the details in Jd. xii. 5-6 on the detection of the fleeing Ephraimites by their pronunciation of "shib-

which he had recalled from Gilead, worked great havoc among them, and pursuing the fugitives, having sent a party in advance to occupy the fords of the Jordan, slew in all some two and forty thousand.[a]

(12) After ruling for six years he died and was His death.
buried at his native place of Sebee,[b] in the land of Jd. xii. 7.
Gilead.

(13) Upon the death of Jephthah, the rulership Ibzan. 8.
passed to Apsanes [c] of the tribe of Judah and the city of Bethlehem. He had sixty children, thirty sons and as many daughters, all of whom he left alive at his death,[d] after bestowing wives and husbands upon all. Having achieved in his seven years of office nothing worthy of record and remembrance, he died in old age and was buried at his native place.

(14) Apsanes having thus died, his successor, Elon. 11.
Elon of the tribe of Zabulon, held the leadership for ten years and likewise did nothing of moment.

(15) Abdon, son of Elon,[e] of the tribe of Ephraim Abdon. 13.
and the city of Pharathon,[f] who was appointed sovereign leader after Elon, calls for no mention save for his happy paternity, since, thanks to the prevailing peace and security of the state, he too did no brilliant deed. But he had forty sons and, born

boleth" as "sibboleth," probably because the difference in sound could not have been made clear to Greek readers.

[b] The Heb. of Jd. xii. 7 "in the cities of Gilead" is corrupt: read probably "in his city, in Mizpah of Gilead." The loss of the M in Mizpah produced the reading found in some MSS. of the LXX, ἐν Σεφέ (ἐν Σέφ), and through further corruption the name Sebee in Josephus.

[c] Bibl. Ibzan.

[d] Amplification (as in § 274).

[e] Bibl. "son of Hillel."

[f] Heb. "the Pirathonite": modern *Fer'atha*, 6 miles S.W. of Shechem.

γενεὰς καταλιπόντων[1] τριάκοντα, ἤλαυνέ τε σὺν αὐτοῖς οὖσιν ἑβδομήκοντα πᾶσιν ἱππάζειν ἀρίστοις γεγενημένοις, καὶ πάντας ὑπὲρ γῆς ἀπολιπὼν θνήσκει γηραιὸς καὶ ταφῆς ἐν Φαράθῳ λαμπρᾶς τυγχάνει.

275 (viii. 1) Μετὰ δὲ τοῦτον Παλαιστῖνοι τελευτήσαντα κρατοῦσι τῶν Ἰσραηλιτῶν καὶ φόρους παρ' αὐτῶν ἐλάμβανον ἐπ' ἔτη τεσσαράκοντα. ταύτης δ' ἐλευθεροῦνται τῆς ἀνάγκης τούτῳ τῷ τρόπῳ·

276 (2) Μανώχης τις Δανιτῶν ἐν ὀλίγοις ἄριστος καὶ τῆς πατρίδος ὁμολογουμένως[2] πρῶτος εἶχε γύναιον ἐπ' εὐμορφίᾳ περίβλεπτον καὶ τῶν καθ' αὐτὸ διαφέρον. παίδων δ' οὐ γινομένων αὐτῷ, δυσφορῶν ἐπὶ τῇ ἀπαιδίᾳ τὸν θεὸν ἱκέτευεν ἐπὶ τὸ προάστειον συνεχῶς φοιτῶν μετὰ τῆς γυναικὸς δοῦναι διαδοχὴν αὐτοῖς γνησίαν· μέγα δέ ἐστι

277 τοῦτο τὸ[3] πεδίον. ἦν δὲ καὶ μανιώδης ὑπ' ἔρωτος ἐπὶ τῇ γυναικὶ καὶ διὰ τοῦτο ζηλότυπος ἀκρατῶς. μονωθείσῃ δὲ τῇ γυναικὶ φάντασμα ἐπιφαίνεται, ἄγγελος[4] τοῦ θεοῦ, νεανίᾳ καλῷ παραπλήσιον καὶ μεγάλῳ, εὐαγγελιζόμενον αὐτῇ παιδὸς γονὴν κατὰ θεοῦ πρόνοιαν καλοῦ τε καὶ ῥώμην ἐπιφανοῦς, ὑφ'

278 ᾧ πονήσειν Παλαιστίνους ἀνδρουμένῳ. παρῄνει τε τὰς κόμας αὐτῷ μὴ ἀποκείρειν· ἔσται δ' αὐτῷ

[1] Text doubtful: et alios ex eorum semine descendentes Lat.
[2] ὁμολογούμενος codd.
[3] conj.: om. codd.
[4] MSPLE: τοῦ θεοῦ ἀστέρος RO.

[a] Bibl. "rode on ass colts."
[b] Bibl. "He judged Israel eight years."
[c] Bibl. Manoah (LXX Μανῶε): Josephus indifferently Manoches and Manochos.

of these, thirty grandsons, and was wont to ride with this family of seventy, all excellent horsemen [a]; he left them all in the land of the living when he died in old age [b] and was buried in state at Pharathon.

Israel under the Philistines. Jd. xiii. 1.

(viii. 1) After his death the Philistines conquered the Israelites and exacted tribute from them for forty years. From these straits they were delivered on this wise.

An angel announces the birth of a son to the wife of Manoah. Jd. xiii. 2

(2) A certain Manoch,[c] among the most notable of the Danites and without question the first in his native place, had a wife remarkable for her beauty and pre-eminent among the women of her time. But having no children by her and being distressed at the lack of them, he was wont, on his frequent visits with his wife to the outskirts—where there was a great plain [d]—to entreat God to give them offspring of their wedlock.[e] He was moreover madly enamoured of his wife and hence inordinately jealous.[f] Now once when his wife was alone, a spectre appeared to her from God,[g] in the likeness of a comely and tall youth, bringing her the good news of the approaching birth of a son through God's good providence—a son goodly and illustrious for strength, by whom, on his reaching man's estate, the Philistines would be afflicted. He further charged her not to cut the lad's locks, and that he was to renounce

[d] Unscriptural topographical details.

[e] Gr. " a legitimate succession."

[f] The husband's jealousy and subsequent suspicions are unscriptural. Rabbinical legend attributes his complaints to his wife's barrenness, not to her beauty. For the quarrel between husband and wife *cf.* Ps.-Philo, *Biblical Antiquities*, cap. xlii. (tr. M. R. James).

[g] Or (with most MSS.) " an angel of God."

πρὸς ἄλλο μὲν πᾶν[1] ποτὸν ἀποστροφὴ τοῦ θεοῦ τοῦτο προστάσσοντος, πρὸς ὕδωρ δὲ μόνον οἰκειότης. καὶ ὁ μὲν ταῦτ' εἰπὼν ᾤχετο, κατὰ βούλησιν ἐλθὼν τοῦ θεοῦ.

279 (3) Ἡ δὲ τἀνδρὶ παραγενομένῳ τὰ παρὰ τοῦ ἀγγέλου ἐκδιηγήσατο ἐκθαυμάζουσα τοῦ νεανίσκου τὸ κάλλος καὶ τὸ μέγεθος, ὡς ἐκεῖνον ἐκ τῶν ἐπαίνων εἰς ἔκπληξιν κατὰ ζηλοτυπίαν περιστῆναι καὶ ὑπόνοιαν τὴν ἐκ τοιούτου πάθους κινουμένην.
280 ἡ δὲ βουλομένη τὴν ἄλογον τἀνδρὸς λύπην σταλῆναι τὸν θεὸν ἱκέτευε πάλιν πέμψαι τὸν ἄγγελον, ὡς ἂν καὶ τῷ ἀνδρὶ αὐτῆς ὁραθείη. καὶ παραγίνεται πάλιν κατὰ χάριν τοῦ θεοῦ ὁ ἄγγελος ὄντων ἐν τῷ προαστείῳ καὶ τῇ γυναικὶ φαίνεται τοῦ ἀνδρὸς μεμονωμένῃ. ἡ δ' ἐπιμεῖναι δεηθεῖσα ἕως[2] ἂν ἀγάγῃ[3] τὸν ἄνδρα συγχωρήσαντος μέτεισι τὸν
281 Μάνωχον. ὁ δὲ θεασάμενος οὐδ' οὕτως ἐπαύετο τῆς ὑπονοίας ἠξίου τε καὶ αὐτῷ δηλοῦν ὅσα καὶ τῇ γυναικὶ μηνύσειεν. ἀρκέσειν δὲ φράσαντος ταύτην μόνην εἰδέναι, τίς εἴη λέγειν ἐκέλευεν, ἵνα τοῦ παιδὸς γενομένου χάριν αὐτῷ καὶ δωρεὰν παρά-
282 σχωσι. τοῦ δὲ μηδέ τινων[4] αὐτῷ δεῖσθαι φήσαντος, οὐδὲ γὰρ κατὰ χρείαν ταῦτα εὐαγγελίσασθαι περὶ τῆς τοῦ παιδὸς γονῆς, τοῦ δὲ μεῖναι παρακαλοῦντος καὶ ξενίων μετασχεῖν οὐκ ἐπένευσ', ἐπείσθη[5] δ' ὅμως λιπαροῦντος ἐπιμεῖναι ὡς ἂν ξένιον αὐτῷ τι

[1] πᾶν om. ROE.
[2] Lat. donec: ὡς codd.
[3] L: ἀγάγοι rell.
[4] horum Lat.
[5] Niese ex Lat.: πεισθεὶς codd.

[a] In Jd. xiii. 8 it is Manoah who asks for a further vision of the angel.

all other form of drink (so God commanded) and to accustom himself to water only. And having thus spoken the visitor departed, having come but to execute God's will.

The angel's second visit. Jd. xiii. 6.

(3) The woman, when her husband arrived, reported what she had heard from the angel, extolling the young man's comeliness and stature in such wise that he in his jealousy was driven by these praises to distraction and to conceive the suspicions that such passion arouses. But she,[a] wishing to allay her husband's unreasonable distress, entreated God to send the angel again that her husband also might see him. And again by the grace of God the angel came, while they were in the suburb,[b] and appeared to the woman when parted from her husband. She besought him to stay until she could fetch her husband and, obtaining his assent, went in pursuit of Manoch. But the husband, on beholding the angel, even then did not desist from his suspicion, and he requested him to repeat to him too all that he had revealed to his wife. The angel having declared that it would suffice that it should be made known to her alone, Manoch bade him say who he
was, in order that on the birth of the child they 17.
might tender him their thanks and make him a present. He replied that he had need of naught, for it was not from want that he had announced this good news of the birth of a child; and though Manoch invited him to stay and partake of hospitality, he consented not. Howbeit, at his earnest entreaty, he was persuaded to remain that some token of hospitality might be brought to him. So,

[b] Bibl. "as she sat in the field."

283 κομίσῃ. καὶ θύσαντος ἔριφον τοῦ Μανώχου καὶ τοῦτον ὀπτᾶν τῇ γυναικὶ κελεύσαντος, ἐπεὶ πάντ' ἦν εὐτρεπῆ, προσέταξεν ἐπὶ τῆς πέτρας ἀποθέσθαι τούς τε ἄρτους καὶ τὰ κρέα χωρὶς τῶν ἀγγείων.
284 καὶ ποιησάντων ἅπτεται τῇ ῥάβδῳ ᾗ εἶχε τῶν κρεῶν, τὰ δὲ λάμψαντος πυρὸς ἅμα τοῖς ἄρτοις ἐκαίετο καὶ ὁ ἄγγελος διὰ τοῦ καπνοῦ ὥσπερ ὀχήματος ἀνιὼν εἰς οὐρανὸν αὐτοῖς φανερὸς ἦν. Μανώχην δὲ φοβούμενον, μή τι σφαλερὸν αὐτοῖς ἐκ τῆς ὄψεως τοῦ θεοῦ γενήσοιτο, θαρσεῖν ἡ γυνὴ παρεκελεύετο· ἐπὶ γὰρ συμφέροντι τῷ αὐτῶν τὸν θεὸν αὐτοῖς ὁραθῆναι.

285 (4) Καὶ κύει τε ἐκείνη καὶ φυλακὴν εἶχε τῶν ἐντολῶν καὶ γενόμενον τὸ παιδίον Σαμψῶνα καλοῦσιν, ἰσχυρὸν δ' ἀποσημαίνει τὸ ὄνομα. ηὔξετο δ' ὁ παῖς ῥᾳδίως καὶ δῆλος ἦν προφητεύσων ὑπὸ τῆς περὶ τὴν δίαιταν σωφροσύνης καὶ τῆς τῶν τριχῶν ἀνέσεως.

286 (5) Ἀφικόμενος δὲ μετὰ τῶν γονέων εἰς Θάμνα[1] πόλιν τῶν Παλαιστίνων πανηγύρεως ἀγομένης ἐρᾷ παρθένου τῶν ἐπιχωρίων παρακαλεῖ τε τοὺς γονεῖς ἄγεσθαι πρὸς γάμον αὐτῷ τὴν κόρην. τῶν δὲ ἀρνουμένων διὰ τὸ μὴ ὁμόφυλον εἶναι, τοῦ θεοῦ κατὰ τὸ Ἑβραίων σύμφορον ἐπινοοῦντος τὸν γάμον,

[1] *v.l.* Θαμναθὰ (as also in § 296).

[a] The angel's directions are unscriptural; "apart from (χωρίς) the vessels" possibly has some connexion with the strange reading in some LXX MSS. καὶ διεχώρισεν ποιῆσαι (Jd. xiii. 19).

[b] So Ps.-Philo, *Biblical Antiquities*, xlii. (tr. M. R. James) "the angel put forth (his hand) and touched it with the end of his sceptre."

Manoch having killed a kid and bidden his wife to cook it, when all was ready, the angel ordered them to set out the loaves and the meat upon the rock, without the vessels.[a] That done, he with the rod which he held touched the meat [b] and, a fire blazing out, it was consumed along with the bread, while the angel, borne on the smoke as on a chariot, was plainly seen by them ascending into heaven. Manoch thereat fearing that some mischief might befall them from this vision of God, his wife bade him take heart, since it was for their good that it had been given them to see God.

Birth of Samson. Jd. xiii. 24.

(4) And the woman conceived and paid good heed to the injunctions laid upon her; and when the infant was born they called him Samson, a name which means "strong.[c]" And the child grew apace and it was plain from the frugality of his diet and his loosely flowing locks that he was to be a prophet.

His courtship and encounter with a lion. Jd. xiv. 1.

(5) Now the lad having gone with his parents to Thamna,[d] a town of the Philistines, during the celebration of a festival, became enamoured of a maiden of the country and begged his parents to get the damsel for him to wife. They were for refusing because she was not of their race: God, however, was designing this marriage in the interests of the

[c] One of the author's loose etymological statements. The connexion of the name (Heb. Shimshon: Gr. Σαμψών) with the Hebrew *shemesh* (="sun") "may be considered certain" (Burney). But Josephus may have had in mind biblical passages in which the sun symbolizes strength. The Bab. Talmud (Soṭah 10a) says, "Samson received a name applied to God, for Scripture says (Ps. lxxxiv. 12) 'A sun and shield is the Lord God.'"

[d] Heb. Timnah, LXX Θαμναθά, modern *Tibneh*; a border town in the Shephelah held at various times by Dan, Judah and the Philistines.

287 ἐκνικᾷ μνηστεύσασθαι τὴν παρθένον. συνεχῶς δ' ἀπερχόμενος πρὸς τοὺς γονεῖς αὐτῆς συντυγχάνει λέοντι καὶ γυμνὸς ὢν ἐκδεξάμενος αὐτὸν ἄγχει ταῖς χερσὶ καὶ εἰς τὸ χωρίον τὸ[1] ὑλῶδες ἐνδοτέρω τῆς ὁδοῦ ῥίπτει τὸ θηρίον.

288 (6) Πάλιν τε ἀπιὼν πρὸς τὴν κόρην ἐπιτυγχάνει σμήνει μελιττῶν ἐν τῷ στήθει τοῦ λέοντος ἐκείνου νενοσσευκότων, καὶ ἀνελόμενος τρία μέλιτος κηρία σὺν τοῖς λοιποῖς δώροις οἷς ἐκόμιζε δίδωσι τῇ
289 παιδί. τῶν δὲ Θαμνιτῶν παρὰ τὴν εὐωχίαν τὴν τῶν γάμων, εἱστία γὰρ αὐτοὺς ἅπαντας, διὰ δέος τῆς ἰσχύος τοῦ νεανίσκου τριάκοντα δόντων αὐτῷ τοὺς ἀκμαιοτάτους λόγῳ μὲν ἑταίρους ἐσομένους ἔργῳ δὲ φύλακας, μή τι παρακινεῖν ἐθελήσειεν, τοῦ πότου προβάντος καὶ παιδιᾶς οὔσης, οἷα φιλεῖ παρὰ τοὺς τοιούτους καιρούς, ὁ Σαμψὼν εἶπεν,
290 "ἀλλὰ προβάλλοντος ἐμοῦ λόγον εἰ λύσετε τοῦτον ἐφ' ἡμέρας ἑπτὰ ποιούμενοι τὴν ζήτησιν, ὀθόνας τε καὶ στολὰς γέρας τῆς συνέσεως κατ' ἄνδρα ἕκαστον φέρεσθε παρ' ἐμοῦ." φιλοτιμουμένων δὲ ὁμοῦ τε συνετῶν δόξαν καὶ κέρδος εὕρασθαι καὶ λέγειν ἀξιούντων, φησὶν ὅτι τὸ πάμβορον γεγεννήκοι βορὰν ἡδεῖαν ἐξ αὐτοῦ καὶ πάνυ ἀηδοῦς ὄντος.
291 τῶν δ' ἐπὶ τρεῖς ἡμέρας[2] οὐ δυναμένων ἐξευρεῖν τὸ νοούμενον παρακαλούντων δὲ τὴν κόρην μαθοῦσαν παρὰ τοῦ ἀνδρὸς αὐτοῖς μηνῦσαι, καὶ γὰρ ἠπείλουν πιμρήσειν αὐτὴν τοῦτο μὴ παρασχοῦσαν, ὁ Σαμψὼν δεομένης τῆς κόρης εἰπεῖν αὐτῇ τὸ μὲν πρῶτον

[1] εἴς τι χωρίον SPL.
[2] ἐπὶ τρισὶν ἡμέραις RO.

---

[a] Gr. "within" or "on the inner side of."
[b] Amplification, like other details in this narrative.

Hebrews, and so he won his way to woo the maid. In the course of his constant visits to her parents he encountered a lion and, unarmed as he was, grappled with it, strangled it with his hands, and flung the beast into the coppice on the border of [a] the road.

(6) On another of his journeys to the damsel he came upon a swarm of bees that had hived in that lion's breast, and, taking three [b] honeycombs, he gave them, along with the rest of the gifts which he bore, to the maiden. Now the Thamnites, on the occasion of the wedding feast—for he entertained them all—from fear of this young man's strength, presented him with thirty of their chief stalwarts, ostensibly as companions, in reality as his guardians, lest he should be minded to create any disturbance; and, when the drinking was far gone and joviality prevailed, as is customary on such occasions, Samson said, "Come, I will propound a riddle, and if ye solve it after seven days' search, ye shall receive every man from me fine linen and apparel as a reward for your sagacity." Ambitious to win at once a renown for sagacity and a prize, they begged him to state it, whereupon he said: "The omnivorous eater produced pleasant meat from himself though grossly unpleasant." [c] When the Philistines at the end of three days were unable to discover what it meant, they urged the damsel to find out from her husband and report to them: nay, they threatened to burn her should she fail to do so. Samson, upon the damsel's entreating him to tell her, at

His riddle. Jd. xiv. 8.

[c] Bibl. "Out of the eater came forth meat, and out of the strong came forth sweetness," Jd. xiv. 14. The Peshitto Syriac version, rendering the word "strong" by "bitter," presents, like Josephus, a double antithesis.

292 ἀντεῖχεν,[1] ἐγκειμένης δ' αὐτῆς καὶ εἰς δάκρυα προπιπτούσης καὶ τεκμήριον τιθεμένης τῆς πρὸς αὐτὴν δυσνοίας τὸ μὴ λέγειν αὐτῇ, μηνύει τὰ περὶ τὴν ἀναίρεσιν αὐτῇ τοῦ λέοντος καὶ ὡς τὰ τρία βαστάσας ἐξ αὐτοῦ κηρία μέλιτος γεγονότα κομί-
293 σειεν αὐτῇ. καὶ ὁ μὲν οὐδὲν ὑφορώμενος δολερὸν σημαίνει τὸ πᾶν, ἡ δ' ἐκφέρει τὸν λόγον τοῖς δεηθεῖσι. κατὰ οὖν τὴν ἑβδόμην ἡμέραν, καθ' ἣν ἔδει τὸν προβληθέντα λόγον αὐτῷ διασαφεῖν, πρὶν ἢ δῦναι τὸν ἥλιον συνελθόντες φασίν "οὔτε λέοντος ἀηδέστερόν τι τοῖς ἐντυγχάνουσιν οὔτε ἥδιον
294 μέλιτος χρωμένοις." καὶ ὁ Σαμψὼν εἶπεν οὐδὲ γυναικὸς εἶναί τι δολερώτερον, "ἥτις ὑμῖν ἐκφέρει τὸν ἡμέτερον λόγον." κἀκείνοις μὲν δίδωσιν ἃ ὑπέσχετο λείαν ποιησάμενος Ἀσκαλωνιτῶν τοὺς κατὰ τὴν ὁδὸν αὐτῷ συντυχόντας, Παλαιστῖνοι δ' εἰσὶ καὶ οὗτοι, τὸν δὲ γάμον ἐκεῖνον παραιτεῖται· καὶ ἡ παῖς ἐκφαυλίσασα τῆς ὀργῆς αὐτὸν συνῆν αὐτοῦ φίλῳ νυμφοστόλῳ γεγονότι.

295 (7) Πρὸς δὲ τὴν ὕβριν ταύτην Σαμψὼν παροξυνθεὶς ἅπαντας ἔγνω σὺν αὐτῇ Παλαιστίνους μετέρχεσθαι. θέρους δ' ὄντος καὶ πρὸς ἄμητον ἤδη τῶν καρπῶν ἀκμαζόντων συλλαβὼν τριακοσίας ἀλώπεκας καὶ τῶν οὐρῶν ἐξάψας λαμπάδας ἡμμένας ἐξαφίησιν[2] εἰς τὰς ἀρούρας τῶν Παλαιστίνων.
296 καὶ φθείρεται μὲν οὕτως αὐτοῖς ὁ καρπός, Παλαιστῖνοι δὲ γνόντες Σαμψῶνος εἶναι τὸ ἔργον καὶ τὴν αἰτίαν δι' ἣν ἔπραξε, πέμψαντες τοὺς ἄρχοντας εἰς

[1] ἀντέχειν ἐπειρᾶτο RO.
[2] ἐπαφίησιν E: ἀφίησιν RO.

[a] Bibl. "If ye had not plowed with my heifer, ye had not found out my riddle," Jd. xiv. 18.

first resisted, but, when she pressed him and burst into tears and protested that his refusal to tell her proved his want of affection for her, he revealed the story of the slaying of the lion and how he had carried off the three honeycombs sprung from its carcase and brought them to her. Suspecting no fraud he recounted all, but she betrayed his story to her questioners. So on the seventh day, whereon they were required to give him the answer to the riddle, assembling before sunset they announced, " Nothing is more unpleasant to meet than a lion nor more pleasant to taste than honey." And Samson added, " Nor is ought more deceitful than a woman who betrays our speech to you." [a] And he gave them what he had promised, after despoiling certain Ascalonites who encountered him on the road (these too being Philistines); but he renounced those nuptials, and the girl, scorning him for his wrath, was united to that friend of his who had given her away.[b]

(7) Furious at this affront,[c] Samson resolved to visit it upon all the Philistines along with her. So, summer being come and the crops already ripening for harvest, he caught three hundred foxes and, fastening lighted torches to their tails, let them loose in the fields of the Philistines; and thus their crop was ruined. But the Philistines, on discovering that this was Samson's deed and for what cause he had done it, sent their magistrates to Thamna and burnt

He destroys the crops of the Philistines. Jd. xv. 3.

[b] Or " who had been his best man." The Biblical narrative refers to " the friend of the bridegroom " (John iii. 29).

[c] Josephus omits Samson's interview with his former father-in-law which provoked this outbreak, Jd. xv. 1 f.

Θάμνα, τὴν γενομένην αὐτοῦ γυναῖκα καὶ τοὺς συγγενεῖς ζῶντας κατέπρησαν ὡς αἰτίους τῶν κακῶν γεγονότας.

297 (8) Σαμψὼν δὲ πολλοὺς ἐν τῷ πεδίῳ τῶν Παλαιστίνων ἀποκτείνας Αἰτὰν κατῴκει, πέτρα δ' ἐστὶν ὀχυρὰ τῆς Ἰούδα φυλῆς. Παλαιστῖνοι δ' ἐστράτευον ἐπὶ τὴν φυλήν. τῶν δ' οὐ δικαίως λεγόντων τιμωρίαν αὐτοὺς εἰσπράττεσθαι περὶ τῶν Σαμψῶνος ἁμαρτημάτων φόρους αὐτοῖς[1] τελοῦντας, εἰ βούλονται μὴ ἔχειν αἰτίαν ἔφασαν αὐτοῖς
298 ὑποχείριον Σαμψῶνα δοῦναι. οἱ δὲ ἀνεπίκλητοι βουλόμενοι τυγχάνειν παρῆσαν ἐπὶ τὴν πέτραν τρισχιλίοις ὁπλίταις[2] καὶ καταμεμψάμενοι τῶν εἰς Παλαιστίνους αὐτῷ τετολμημένων ἄνδρας ἅπαντι τῷ γένει τῶν Ἑβραίων συμφορὰν ἐπενεγκεῖν δυναμένους, ἥκειν τε λέγοντες ὅπως αὐτὸν λαβόντες ὑποχείριον δῶσιν αὐτοῖς, ἠξίουν ἑκοντὶ τοῦθ'
299 ὑπομένειν. ὁ δὲ λαβὼν ὅρκους παρ' αὐτῶν μηδὲν τούτων ποιήσειν περισσότερον ἀλλὰ τοῖς ἐχθροῖς ἐγχειριεῖν[3] μόνον, καταβὰς ἐκ τῆς πέτρας αὐτὸν ἐν τῇ τῶν φυλετῶν τίθησιν ἐξουσίᾳ, κἀκεῖνοι δήσαντες αὐτὸν δυσὶ καλωδίοις ἦγον παραδοῦναι
300 τοῖς Παλαιστίνοις. καὶ γενομένων κατά τι χωρίον, ὃ Σιαγὼν καλεῖται νῦν διὰ τὴν Σαμψῶνος ἀνδραγαθίαν ἐπ' αὐτῷ γενομένην, πάλαι δ' ἦν ἀνώνυμον, οὐκ ἄπωθεν ἐστρατοπεδευκότων τῶν Παλαιστίνων, ἀλλ' ὑπαντώντων μετὰ χαρᾶς καὶ βοῆς ὡς ἐπὶ κατωρθωμένοις οἷς ἐβούλοντο, διαρρήξας τὰ δεσμὰ Σαμψὼν ἁρπασάμενος ὄνου σιαγόνα παρὰ ποσὶν

[1] Niese: αὐτοὺς codd. [2] τρισχίλιοι ὁπλῖται RO.
[3] Bekker: ἐγχειρεῖν codd.

[a] Bibl. Etam.

her that had been his wife and her kinsfolk alive, as having been the cause of their disasters.

His exploit with the jawbone. Jd. xv. 8.

(8) Samson, after slaying multitudes of the Philistines in the plain, then settled at Aeta,[a] a rocky stronghold within the tribe of Judah; whereupon the Philistines took the field against that tribe. These pleading that it was unjust to exact punishment for Samson's misdeeds from them that paid them tribute, the Philistines retorted that if they would keep clear of blame they must deliver Samson into their hands. And they, wishing to be above reproach, visited the rock with three thousand men-at-arms, and after roundly rebuking him for his outrageous treatment of the Philistines, people powerful enough to bring ruin upon the whole race of the Hebrews, and telling him that they were come to take and deliver him into their hands, they besought him to submit to this of his own free will. And he, after receiving an oath from them that they would do no more than merely commit him to the hands of the foe, descended from the rock and put himself at the mercy of these representatives of the tribe; and they, having bound him with two cords, led him off to deliver him to the Philistines. Then, when they were come to a spot which to-day is called Jawbone[b] by reason of the exploit there performed by Samson but which of old was nameless, the Philistines being encamped not far off and coming to meet them with exultant cries, thinking to have achieved their end, Samson, bursting his bonds asunder and seizing the

[b] Bibl. Lehi = "Jawbone," as translated here and in the LXX (Σιαγών). "Probably the name was originally given to some hill or ridge on account of its resemblance to a jawbone" (Burney, adducing the similar name Ὄνου γνάθος given to a promontory in Laconia).

οὖσαν εἰς τοὺς πολεμίους ὤσατο καὶ παίων αὐτοὺς
τῇ σιαγόνι[1] κτείνει εἰς χιλίους, τοὺς δὲ ἄλλους
τρέπεται ταραχθέντας.
301 (9) Σαμψὼν δὲ μεῖζον ἢ χρὴ ἐπὶ τούτῳ φρονῶν
οὐ κατὰ θεοῦ συνεργίαν ἔλεγε τοῦτο συμβῆναι, τὴν
δ' ἰδίαν ἀρετὴν ἐπέγραφε τῷ γεγονότι, σιαγόνι[2]
τῶν πολεμίων τοὺς μὲν πεσεῖν τοὺς δ' εἰς φυγὴν
302 τραπῆναι διὰ τοῦ παρ' αὐτοῦ δέους αὐχῶν. δίψους
δ' αὐτὸν ἰσχυροῦ κατασχόντος κατανοῶν ὡς οὐδέν
ἐστιν ἀνθρώπειος ἀρετή, τῷ θεῷ πάντα προσεμαρ-
τύρει καὶ καθικέτευε μηδὲν τῶν εἰρημένων πρὸς
ὀργὴν λαβόντα τοῖς πολεμίοις αὐτὸν ἐγχειρίσαι,
παρασχεῖν δὲ βοήθειαν πρὸς τὸ δεινὸν καὶ ῥύσασθαι
303 τοῦ κακοῦ. καὶ πρὸς τὰς ἱκετείας ἐπικλασθεὶς
ὁ θεὸς πηγὴν κατά τινος πέτρας ἀνίησιν ἡδεῖαν
καὶ πολλήν, ὅθεν καὶ Σαμψὼν ἐκάλει τὸ χωρίον
Σιαγόνα καὶ μέχρι τοῦ δεῦρο τοῦτο λέγεται.
304 (10) Μετὰ δὲ ταύτην τὴν μάχην Σαμψὼν καταφρονῶν τῶν Παλαιστίνων εἰς Γάζαν ἀφικνεῖται
καὶ ἔν τινι τῶν καταγωγίων διέτριβε. μαθόντες
δὲ τῶν Γαζαίων οἱ ἄρχοντες τὴν αὐτόθι παρουσίαν
αὐτοῦ τὰ πρὸ τῶν πυλῶν ἐνέδραις καταλαμβάνου-
305 σιν, ὅπως ἐξιὼν μὴ λάθῃ. Σαμψὼν δέ, οὐ γὰρ
λανθάνουσιν αὐτὸν ταῦτα μηχανησάμενοι, περὶ
μεσοῦσαν ἤδη τὴν νύκτα ἀναστὰς ἐνράσσει ταῖς
πύλαις, αὐταῖς τε φλιαῖς καὶ μοχλοῖς ὅση τε ἄλλη
περὶ αὐταῖς ἦν ξύλωσις ἀράμενος κατωμαδὸν εἰς
τὸ ὑπὲρ Ἑβρῶνος ὄρος φέρων κατατίθησι.

[1] τῇ σιαγόνι om. MSP. [2] om. ROE.

[a] In Judges (xv. 19) En-hakkore ("the spring of him that called"), while Ramath-lehi ("hill of the jawbone") is the

jawbone of an ass that lay at his feet, rushed upon his enemies and smiting them with this weapon slew a thousand of them, routing the rest in dire dismay.

The miraculous spring. Jd. xv. 16.

(9) Yet Samson, unduly proud of this feat, did not say that it was God's assistance that had brought it to pass, but ascribed the issue to his own valour, boasting of having with a jawbone prostrated some of his enemies and put the rest to rout through the terror that he inspired. But, being seized with a mighty thirst and recognizing that human valour is a thing of naught, he acknowledged that all was attributable to God and implored Him not, in anger at any words of his, to deliver him into his enemies' hands, but to lend him aid in his dire need and to rescue him from his distress. And God, moved by his supplications, caused a spring of water to well out of a rock, sweet and abundant; whence it was that Samson called that place Jawbone, a name which it bears to this day.[a]

Samson's escape from Gaza by night. Jd. xvi. 1.

(10) After this combat Samson, scorning the Philistines, came to Gaza and lodged at one of the inns.[b] Thereupon the chiefs of the Gazites, informed of his presence in the town, posted ambuscades before the gates to prevent his leaving it without their knowledge. But Samson, not unaware of these schemes, when midnight was come arose, flung himself against the gates, hoisted them—posts, bolts, woodwork and all—upon his shoulders, bore them to the mountain above Hebron[c] and there deposited them.

name given to the place where he cast his weapon away (17).

[b] Jd. "and saw there an harlot and went in unto her." For the interchange of "harlot" and "innkeeper" see § 8 note.

[c] Nearly 40 miles away!

306 (11) Παρέβαινε δ' ἤδη τὰ πάτρια καὶ τὴν οἰκείαν
δίαιταν παρεχάρασσεν ξενικῶν μιμήσει ἐθισμῶν,
καὶ τοῦτ' ἀρχὴ αὐτῷ κακοῦ γίνεται· γυναικὸς γὰρ
ἑταιριζομένης παρὰ τοῖς Παλαιστίνοις ἐρασθεὶς
307 Δαλάλης[1] τοὔνομα συνῆν αὐτῇ. καὶ τῶν Παλαιστίνων οἱ τοῦ κοινοῦ προεστῶτες ἐλθόντες πρὸς αὐτὴν
πείθουσιν ἐπαγγελίαις μαθεῖν παρὰ τοῦ Σαμψῶνος
τὴν αἰτίαν τῆς ἰσχύος, ὑφ' ἧς ἄληπτός ἐστι τοῖς
ἐχθροῖς. ἡ δὲ παρὰ πότον καὶ τοιαύτην συνουσίαν
θαυμάζουσα τὰς πράξεις αὐτοῦ ἐτεχνίτευε μαθεῖν,
308 τίνι τρόπῳ τοσοῦτον[2] προύχει κατ' ἀρετήν. ὁ
δὲ Σαμψών, ἔτι γὰρ φρονεῖν ἰσχυρὸς ἦν, ἀντ-
ηπάτα τὴν Δαλάλην φάμενος,[3] εἰ κλήμασιν ἑπτὰ
δεθείη ἀμπελίνοις ἔτι καὶ περιειλεῖσθαι δυναμένοις,
309 ἀσθενέστερος ἂν πάντων ἔσοιτο. ἡ δὲ τότε μὲν
ἡσύχασεν, ἀποσημήνασα δὲ τοῖς ἄρχουσι τῶν Παλαιστίνων ἐνήδρευσε τῶν στρατιωτῶν ἔνδον τινὰς
καὶ μεθύοντα[4] κατέδει τοῖς κλήμασι κατὰ τὸ
310 ἰσχυρότατον, ἔπειτ' ἀνεγείρασα ἐδήλου παρεῖναί
τινας ἐπ' αὐτόν. ὁ δὲ ῥήξας τὰ κλήματα βοηθεῖν
ὡς ἐπερχομένων αὐτῷ τινων ἐπειρᾶτο. καὶ ἡ γυνὴ
συνεχῶς ὁμιλοῦντος αὐτῇ τοῦ Σαμψῶνος δεινῶς
ἔχειν ἔλεγεν, εἰ κατ' ἀπιστίαν εὐνοίας τῆς πρὸς
αὐτὸν μὴ λέγει ταῦθ' ἅπερ δεῖται, ὡς οὐ σιγησο-
μένης ὅσα μὴ γινώσκεσθαι συμφέρειν οἶδεν αὐτῷ.
311 τοῦ δὲ πάλιν ἀπατῶντος αὐτὴν καὶ φήσαντος ἑπτὰ

[1] *v.ll.* δαδάλης, δαληδῆς, etc.
[2] M: τοσούτων ROSPE. [3] + ὅτι Dindorf.
[4] dormientem Lat.: pr. καθεύδοντα MSPL.

[a] Bibl. Delilah, LXX Δαλειδά.
[b] Heb. " with seven fresh bowstrings (*or* sinews) which have not been dried " (v. 7).

Delilah delivers him to the Philistines. Jd. xvi. 4.

(11) Howbeit he was already transgressing the laws of his forefathers and debasing his own rule of life by the imitation of foreign usages; and this proved the beginning of his disaster. For, being enamoured of a woman who was a harlot among the Philistines, Dalala [a] by name, he consorted with her; and the presidents of the Philistine confederacy came and induced her by large promises to discover from Samson the secret of that strength which rendered him invulnerable to his foes. So she, over their cups and in like intercourse, by admiration of his exploits would craftily seek to discover by what means he had come by such extraordinary valour. But Samson, whose wits were yet robust, countered Dalala's ruse by another, telling her that were he bound with seven vine-shoots still flexible,[b] he would be the weakest of men. At the moment she held her peace, but, after reporting this to the lords of the Philistines, she posted some soldiers in ambush within and while Samson was drunken [c] bound him with the shoots as firmly as possible, and then awoke him with the announcement that men were upon him. But he burst the shoots asunder and made ready for defence as though his assailants were coming. And then this woman, with whom Samson was continually consorting, would say that she took it ill that he had not confidence enough in her affection for him to tell her just what she desired, as though she would not conceal what she knew must
in his interests not be divulged. But again he de- 11.
luded her, telling her that were he bound with seven [d]

[c] Or, according to another reading, "asleep." Drunkenness, not mentioned in Scripture, indicates violation of his Nazirite vow (*cf.* § 306).

[d] So LXX (many MSS.): the Heb. mentions no number.

κάλοις δεθέντα τὴν ἰσχὺν ἀπολέσειν, ἐπεὶ καὶ τοῦτο ποιήσασα οὐδὲν ἤνυσεν, τρίτον ἐνυφῆναι[1] τὰς κόμας
312 αὐτοῦ ἐμήνυσεν. ὡς δ' οὐδὲ τούτου γενομένου τἀληθὲς[2] ηὑρίσκετο, δεομένης τελευταῖον ὁ Σαμψών, ἔδει γὰρ αὐτὸν συμφορᾷ περιπεσεῖν, χαρίζεσθαι βουλόμενος τῇ Δαλάλῃ "ἐμοῦ," φησίν, "ὁ θεὸς κήδεται καὶ κατὰ τὴν ἐκείνου πρόνοιαν γεννηθεὶς κόμην ταύτην τρέφω παρεγγυήσαντος μὴ ἀποκείρειν τοῦ θεοῦ· τὴν γὰρ ἰσχὺν εἶναί μοι
313 κατὰ τὴν ταύτης αὔξησιν καὶ παραμονήν." ταῦτα μαθοῦσα καὶ στερήσασα τῆς κόμης αὐτὸν παραδιδοῖ τοῖς πολεμίοις οὐκέτ' ὄντα ἰσχυρὸν ἀμύνασθαι τὴν ἔφοδον αὐτῶν. οἱ δ' ἐκκόψαντες αὐτοῦ τοὺς ὀφθαλμοὺς δεδεμένον ἄγειν παρέδοσαν.

314 (12) Προϊόντος δὲ τοῦ χρόνου ηὔξετο ἡ κόμη τῷ Σαμψῶνι, καὶ ἑορτῆς οὔσης τοῖς Παλαιστίνοις δημοτελοῦς καὶ τῶν ἀρχόντων καὶ γνωριμωτάτων ἐν ταὐτῷ εὐωχουμένων, οἶκος δ' ἦν δύο κιόνων στεγόντων αὐτοῦ τὸν ὄροφον, ἄγεται μεταπεμψαμένων ὁ Σαμψὼν εἰς τὸ συμπόσιον, ὅπως ἐν-
315 υβρίσωσιν αὐτῷ παρὰ τὸν πότον. ὁ δὲ δεινότερον τῶν κακῶν ὑπολαμβάνων τὸ μὴ δύνασθαι ὑβριζόμενος ἀμύνασθαι, τὸν χειραγωγοῦντα παῖδα πείθει, προσαναπαύσασθαι χρῄζειν εἰπὼν ὑπὸ κόπου, τοῖς
316 κίοσιν αὐτὸν ἐγγὺς ἀγαγεῖν. ὡς δὲ ἧκεν,[a] ἐνσεισθεὶς αὐτοῖς ἐπικαταβάλλει τὸν οἶκον ἀνατραπέντων τῶν κιόνων τρισχιλίοις ἀνδράσιν, οἳ πάντες ἀπέθανον, ἐν αὐτοῖς δὲ καὶ Σαμψών. καὶ τὸν μὲν

[1] συνυφῆναι RO.
[2] ἀληθὲς codd.: ἀληθὴς (ex Lat. verax) Niese.

[a] Scripture says that "there were upon the roof [apparently overlooking an open courtyard] three thousand men and

cords he would lose his strength; and when she had tried this too with no success, a third time he advised her to weave his locks into a web. But when even by this experiment the truth was not discovered, at last, at her petitions, Samson—since he must needs fall a victim to calamity—wishing to humour Dalala
said: "I am under God's care: and under His 17.
providence since birth, I nurse these locks, God having enjoined upon me not to cut them, for that my strength is measured by their growth and preservation." The secret learnt, she reft him of his locks and delivered him to his enemies, being now powerless to repulse their assault; and they, having put out his eyes, delivered him over to be led away in chains.

Samson's end. Jd. xvi. 22.

(12) But in course of time Samson's locks grew; and once when the Philistines were keeping a public festival and their lords and chief notables were feasting together in one place—a hall with two columns supporting its roof—Samson at their summons was led to the banquet, that they might mock at him over their cups. And he, deeming it direr than all his ills to be unable to be avenged of such insults, induced the boy who led him by the hand—telling him that from weariness he needed a stay whereon to rest—to conduct him close to the columns. And when he was come thither, flinging all his weight upon them, he brought down the hall, overturning the columns, upon three thousand men,[a] who all perished and among them Samson. Such was his

women," in addition to all the lords of the Philistines below, Jd. xvi. 27. Some commentators suspect that these three thousand on the roof "are an addition to the original narrative, exaggerating the catastrophe" (G. F. Moore).

τοιοῦτον κατέσχε τέλος ἄρξαντα τῶν Ἰσραηλιτῶν
317 εἴκοσιν ἔτη. θαυμάζειν δὲ ἄξιον τῆς ἀρετῆς καὶ τῆς ἰσχύος καὶ τοῦ περὶ τὴν τελευτὴν μεγαλόφρονος τὸν ἄνδρα καὶ τῆς ὀργῆς τῆς μέχρι τοῦ τελευτᾶν πρὸς τοὺς πολεμίους. καὶ τὸ μὲν ὑπὸ γυναικὸς ἁλῶναι δεῖ τῇ φύσει τῶν ἀνθρώπων προσάπτειν ἥττονι ἁμαρτημάτων οὔσῃ, μαρτυρεῖν δὲ ἐκείνῳ τὴν εἰς τὰ ἄλλα πάντα τῆς ἀρετῆς περιουσίαν. οἱ δὲ συγγενεῖς ἀράμενοι τὸ σῶμα αὐτοῦ θάπτουσιν ἐν Σαρασᾶ τῇ πατρίδι μετὰ τῶν συγγενῶν.

318 (ix. 1) Μετὰ δὲ τὴν Σαμψῶνος τελευτὴν προέστη τῶν Ἰσραηλιτῶν Ἠλεὶς ὁ ἀρχιερεύς. ἐπὶ τούτου λιμῷ τῆς χώρας κακοπαθούσης αὐτῶν Ἀβιμέλεχος[1] ἐκ Βηθλέμων, ἔστι δὲ ἡ πόλις αὕτη τῆς Ἰούδα φυλῆς, ἀντέχειν τῷ δεινῷ μὴ δυνάμενος τήν τε γυναῖκα Ναάμιν καὶ τοὺς παῖδας τοὺς ἐξ αὐτῆς αὐτῷ γεγεννημένους Χελλιῶνα καὶ Μαλαῶνα ἐπ-
319 αγόμενος εἰς τὴν Μωαβῖτιν μετοικίζεται. καὶ προχωρούντων αὐτῷ κατὰ νοῦν τῶν πραγμάτων ἄγεται τοῖς υἱοῖς γυναῖκας Μωαβίτιδας Χελλιῶνι μὲν Ὀρφὰν Ῥούθην δὲ Μαλαῶνι. διελθόντων δὲ δέκα[2] ἐτῶν ὅ τε Ἀβιμέλεχος καὶ μετ' αὐτὸν οἱ
320 παῖδες δι' ὀλίγου τελευτῶσι, καὶ ἡ Νάαμις πικρῶς ἐπὶ τοῖς συμβεβηκόσι φέρουσα καὶ τὴν ὑπ' ὄψιν[3] τῶν φιλτάτων ἐρημίαν οὐχ ὑπομένουσα, δι' οὓς[4]

[1] Ἐλιμέλεχος L Lat. (*et infra*).
[2] decem et octo Lat. [3] om. Lat.
[4] ed. pr. Lat.: ἣν codd.

[a] Jd. xvi. 31 "between Zorah (LXX Σαραά or in one minuscule, as in Josephus, Σαρασά) and Eshtaol, in the burying-place of Manoah his father"; Zorah is the modern *Ṣurah*, some 14 miles due W. of Jerusalem.

[b] Bibl. simply "in the days when the judges judged";

end, after governing Israel for twenty years. And it is but right to admire the man for his valour, his strength, and the grandeur of his end, as also for the wrath which he cherished to the last against his enemies. That he let himself be ensnared by a woman must be imputed to human nature which succumbs to sins; but testimony is due to him for his surpassing excellence in all the rest. His kinsfolk then took up his body and buried him at Sarasa,[a] his native place, with his forefathers.

The widow Naomi returns to Bethlehem with Ruth. Ruth i. 1.

(ix. 1) After the death of Samson, the leader of the Israelites was Eli the high priest. In his days,[b] their country was afflicted by a famine, and Abimelech[c] of Bethlehem, a city of the tribe of Judah, being unable to withstand this scourge, took with him his wife Naamis[d] and the sons whom he had begotten by her, Chellion[e] and Malaon,[f] and migrated to the land of Moab. His affairs there prospering to his heart's content, he took for his sons[g] wives of the women of Moab, for Chellion Orpha[h] and for Malaon Ruth. Ten years having passed, Abimelech died, and his sons not long after him; and Naamis, sorely disheartened at her misfortunes and unable to bear that bereavement, ever before her eyes, in the loss of her dearest ones, for whose sakes she had

Josephus infers the date of this episode from the number of generations between Boaz and David (Reinach). One rabbinic tradition identifies Boaz with the judge Ibzan, others make him a contemporary of Deborah.

[c] Bibl. Elimelech: the name Abimelech appears also in many MSS. of the LXX.

[d] Bibl. Naomi (or Noomi).

[e] Bibl. Chilion.

[f] Bibl. Mahlon (LXX Μααλών).

[g] In Ruth i. 3 f. the father's death precedes the sons' marriages.

[h] Bibl. Orpah (LXX 'Ορφά).

καὶ τῆς πατρίδος ἐξεληλύθει, πάλιν εἰς αὐτὴν
ἀπηλλάττετο· καὶ γὰρ ἤδη καλῶς τὰ κατ᾽ αὐτὴν
321 ἐπυνθάνετο χωρεῖν. οὐκ ἐκαρτέρουν δὲ διαζευγνύ-
μεναι αὐτῆς αἱ νύμφαι, οὐδὲ παραιτουμένη βου-
λομένας συνεξορμᾶν πείθειν ἐδύνατο, ἀλλ᾽ ἐγκειμένων εὐξαμένη γάμον εὐτυχέστερον αὐταῖς οὗ
διημαρτήκεσαν παισὶ τοῖς αὐτῆς γαμηθεῖσαι καὶ
322 τῶν ἄλλων ἀγαθῶν κτῆσιν, ὅτε τὰ[1] πρὸς αὐτὴν
οὕτως ἐστί, μένειν αὐτόθι παρεκάλει καὶ μὴ συμ-
μεταλαμβάνειν αὐτῇ βούλεσθαι πραγμάτων ἀδήλων
τὴν πάτριον γῆν καταλιπούσας. ἡ μὲν οὖν Ὀρφὰ
μένει, τὴν δὲ Ῥούθην μὴ πεισθεῖσαν ἀπήγαγε
κοινωνὸν παντὸς τοῦ προστυχόντος γενησομένην.
323 (2) Ἐλθοῦσαν δὲ Ῥούθην μετὰ τῆς πενθερᾶς εἰς
τὴν Βηθλεέμων Βόαζος[2] Ἀβιμελέχου συγγενὴς ὢν
δέχεται ξενίᾳ. καὶ ἡ Νάαμις, προσαγορευόντων
αὐτὴν ὀνομαστί,[3] "δικαιότερον" εἶπε "Μαρὰν
ἂν καλοίητέ[4] με"· σημαίνει δὲ καθ᾽ Ἑβραίων
γλῶτταν νάαμις μὲν εὐτυχίαν, μαρὰ δὲ ὀδύνην.
324 ἀμήτου δὲ γενομένου[5] ἐξῄει καλαμησομένη κατὰ
συγχώρησιν τῆς πενθερᾶς ἡ Ῥούθη, ὅπως τροφῆς
εὐποροῖεν, καὶ εἰς τὸ Βοώζου τυχαίως ἀφικνεῖται
χωρίον. παραγενόμενος δὲ Βόαζος μετ᾽ ὀλίγον καὶ
θεασάμενος τὴν κόρην ἀνέκρινε τὸν ἀγροκόμον
περὶ τῆς παιδός. ὁ δὲ μικρὸν ἔμπροσθεν παρ᾽ αὐτῆς ἅπαντα προπεπυσμένος ἐδήλου τῷ δεσπότῃ.

[1] ὅτε (om. τὰ) RO: ὅτι τε τὰ rell.
[2] Ἀλεξῆς M: Ἄλεξις Βόοζος L.
[3] + τῶν πολιτῶν MLE.
[4] ἂν καλοίητε Bekker: καλεῖσθαι RO: vocate Lat.: καλῷ(ι)ητε rell.
[5] RO: ὄντος rell.

[a] In Ruth i. 7 both daughters-in-law actually start with her.

left her country, thought to repair thither again, for she had learnt that all was now going well with it. But her daughters-in-law had not the heart to be parted from her, nor for all her pleading when they were fain to set out with her [a] could she prevail with them; then, as they urged her yet, she prayed that they might find happier wedlock than that whereof they had been disappointed in marrying her sons, and obtain all blessings beside, but, seeing the case in which she lay, she implored them to remain where they were and not to crave to share her uncertain fortunes in quitting their native land. So Orpha stayed, but, since Ruth would not be persuaded, Naamis took her with her, to be her partner in all that should befall.

(2) Now when Ruth was come with her mother- Reception of Ruth by Boaz.
in-law to the town of Bethlehem, Boaz, being a kins-
man of Abimelech, hospitably received them.[b] And Ruth ii. 1.
Naamis, when folk addressed her by that name, i. 19.
said, "More rightly would ye call me Mara"—
Naamis in the Hebrew tongue signifying "felicity"
and Mara "grief."[c] It being now harvest-time, ii. 2.
Ruth by permission of her mother-in-law went out to glean, to provide for their sustenance, and by chance came to the ground of Boaz. Boaz arriving a little later and seeing the young woman, questioned the steward of his estate concerning this child; and he, having just learnt all her story from herself, informed

[b] This statement, which appears inconsistent with the sequel, and is absent from other Biblical texts, recurs in the Armenian version, which appends to Ruth ii. 1 "et dedit Noomin domum viduitatis habitare in ea." We must suppose that Boaz provided a lodging but did not meet his guests.

[c] Naomi = "my delight": Mara = "bitter."

325 ὁ δὲ τῆς περὶ τὴν πενθερὰν εὐνοίας ἅμα καὶ μνήμης τοῦ παιδὸς αὐτῆς ᾧ συνῴκησεν ἀσπασάμενος καὶ εὐξάμενος αὐτῇ πεῖραν ἀγαθῶν, καλαμᾶσθαι μὲν αὐτὴν οὐκ ἠξίωσεν θερίζειν δὲ πᾶν ὅ τι καὶ δύναιτο καὶ λαμβάνειν ἐπιτρέπει προστάξας τῷ ἀγροκόμῳ μηδὲν αὐτὴν διακωλύειν[1] ἄριστόν τε παρέχειν αὐτῇ καὶ ποτόν, ὁπότε σιτίζοι τοὺς
326 θερίζοντας. Ῥούθη δὲ ἄλφιτα λαβοῦσα παρ' αὐτοῦ ἐφύλαξε τῇ ἑκυρᾷ καὶ παρῆν ὀψὲ κομίζουσα μετὰ τῶν σταχύων· ἐτετηρήκει δ' αὐτῇ καὶ ἡ Νάαμις ἀπομοίρας βρωμάτων τινῶν, οἷς αὐτὴν ἐπολυώρουν οἱ γειτονεύοντες· διηγεῖται δὲ αὐτῇ καὶ τὰ παρὰ τοῦ Βοάζου πρὸς αὐτὴν εἰρημένα.
327 δηλωσάσης δ' ἐκείνης ὡς συγγενής ἐστι καὶ τάχα ἂν δι' εὐσέβειαν[2] προνοήσειεν αὐτῶν, ἐξῄει πάλιν ταῖς ἐχομέναις ἡμέραις ἐπὶ καλάμης συλλογὴν σὺν ταῖς Βοάζου θεραπαινίσιν.

328 (3) Ἐλθών τε μετ' οὐ πολλὰς ἡμέρας καὶ Βόαζος ἤδη τῆς κριθῆς λελικμημένης, ἐπὶ τῆς ἅλωος ἐκάθευδε. τοῦτο πυθομένη ἡ Νάαμις τεχνᾶται παρακατακλῖναι τὴν Ῥούθην αὐτῷ· καὶ γὰρ ἔσεσθαι χρηστὸν αὐταῖς ὁμιλήσαντα τῇ παιδί· καὶ πέμπει τὴν κόρην ὑπνωσομένην αὐτοῦ παρὰ τοῖς
329 ποσίν. ἡ δέ, πρὸς οὐδὲν γὰρ ἀντιλέγειν τῶν ὑπὸ τῆς ἑκυρᾶς κελευομένων ὅσιον ἡγεῖτο, παραγίνεται καὶ παραυτίκα μὲν λανθάνει τὸν Βόαζον βαθέως καθυπνωκότα, περιεγερθεὶς δὲ περὶ μέσην νύκτα καὶ αἰσθόμενος τῆς ἀνθρώπου παρακατακει-
330 μένης ἀνέκρινε τίς εἴη. τῆς δ' εἰπούσης τοὔνομα καὶ φαμένης ὡς αὐτῆς[3] δεσπότην συγχωρεῖν, τότε

[1] + λαμβάνειν ROMSP.
[2] εὐλάβειαν ROSP.
[3] ROE: αὐτὸν rell.

his master. And Boaz, alike for her loyalty to her mother-in-law and for her[a] remembrance of that son of hers to whom she had been united, bade her welcome and wished her enjoyment of blessings: he would not have her glean but permitted her to reap and carry away all that she could; while he charged his steward in no wise to hinder her and to provide her with lunch and drink when he fed the reapers.
But Ruth, having received of him barley-meal, kept ii. 14, 18.
thereof for her mother-in-law and brought it to her, on her return at even, along with her sheaves; while Naamis on her side had reserved for her portions of some food with which attentive neighbours had provided her.[b] Ruth also recounted to her mother-in-law what Boaz had said to her. And Naamis having told her that he was a kinsman and might haply for piety's sake take care of them, she went out again on the following days to glean with the handmaids of Boaz.

Boaz and Ruth in the threshing-floor. Ruth iii. 1.

(3) Not many days later Boaz himself came and, when the winnowing of the barley was done, slept on the threshing-floor. On learning of this, Naamis schemed to bring Ruth to his side, deeming that he would be gracious to them after consorting with the child; so she sent the damsel to sleep at his feet. And she, regarding it as a pious duty in nothing to gainsay the behests of her mother-in-law, repaired thither, and at the moment escaped the eye of Boaz, who was fast asleep; but, awaking towards midnight and becoming aware of the woman lying beside him, he inquired who she was. And she having mentioned her name and prayed him, as her master, to pardon

[a] Or perhaps "his"; Naomi's son was Boaz's kinsman as well as Ruth's husband.

[b] Amplification.

μὲν ἡσυχίαν ἄγει, ὄρθριος δὲ πρὶν ἢ τοὺς οἰκέτας ἄρξασθαι κινεῖσθαι πρὸς τὸ ἔργον, περιεγείρας αὐτὴν κελεύει τῶν κριθῶν λαβοῦσαν ὅ τι καὶ δύναιτο πορεύεσθαι πρὸς τὴν ἑκυρὰν πρὶν ὀφθῆναί τισιν αὐτόθι κεκοιμημένην, φυλάττεσθαι[1] σῶφρον ὂν[2] τὴν ἐπὶ τοιούτοις διαβολὴν καὶ μάλιστ' ἐπὶ
331 μὴ γεγονόσι. "περὶ μέντοι τοῦ παντὸς οὕτω," φησίν, "ἔσται, ἐρωτᾶν[3] τὸν ἔγγιστά μου τῷ γένει τυγχάνοντα, εἴ σου χρεία γαμετῆς ἐστιν αὐτῷ, καὶ λέγοντι μὲν ἀκολουθήσεις ἐκείνῳ, παραιτουμένου δὲ νόμῳ σε συνοικήσουσαν ἄξομαι."
332 (4) Ταῦτα τῇ ἑκυρᾷ δηλωσάσης εὐθυμία κατεῖχεν αὐτὰς ἐν ἐλπίδι τοῦ πρόνοιαν ἕξειν αὐτῶν Βόαζον γενομένας. κἀκεῖνος ἤδη μεσούσης τῆς ἡμέρας κατελθὼν εἰς τὴν πόλιν τήν τε γερουσίαν συνῆγε καὶ μεταπεμψάμενος Ῥούθην ἐκάλει καὶ τὸν συγ-
333 γενῆ, καὶ παραγενομένου φησίν· "Ἀβιμελέχου καὶ τῶν υἱῶν αὐτοῦ κλήρων κρατεῖς;" ὁμολογήσαντος δὲ συγχωρούντων τῶν νόμων κατὰ ἀγχιστείαν, "οὐκοῦν," φησὶν ὁ Βόαζος, "οὐκ ἐξ ἡμισείας δεῖ μεμνῆσθαι τῶν νόμων, ἀλλὰ πάντα ποιεῖν κατ' αὐτούς. Μαάλου[4] γὰρ δεῦρ' ἥκει γύναιον, ὅπερ εἰ θέλεις τῶν ἀγρῶν κρατεῖν γαμεῖν σε δεῖ
334 κατὰ τοὺς νόμους." ὁ δὲ Βοάζῳ καὶ τοῦ κλήρου καὶ τῆς γυναικὸς παρεχώρει συγγενεῖ μὲν ὄντι καὶ αὐτῷ τῶν τετελευτηκότων, εἶναι δὲ καὶ γυναῖκα

[1] + γὰρ MSPL. [2] ὂν conj.
[3] om. RO Lat.
[4] v.ll. Μαλλίωνος, Μαλῶνος.

[a] Niese's conjecture, σου for μου, is needless: the superlative in τὸν ἔγγιστά μου includes the comparative.

her, he for the time held his peace; but at daybreak, ere his servants began to move to their work, he roused her and bade her take as much of the barley as she could carry and be off to her mother-in-law, before anyone should see that she had slept there, since it was wise to guard against scandal of that kind, and the more so when nothing had passed. "But as concerning the whole matter," said he, "thus shall it be. He that is nearer of kin (to thee) than I,[a] must be asked whether he would have thee to wife: if he says yea, thou shalt follow him; if he declines, I will take thee for my lawful bride."

Marriage of Boaz and Ruth: their descendants.

(4) Ruth having reported this to her mother-in-law, they were well content, in the expectation that Boaz would take them under his care. And he, having towards midday[b] gone down into the city, Ruth iii. 16
assembled the elders,[b] sent for Ruth and summoned iv. 1.
the kinsman also, upon whose coming he said to him, "Art thou the possessor of the heritage of Abimelech and his sons?" "Yes," he admitted, "the laws cede it to me in virtue of nearness of kin." "Then," said Boaz, "thou oughtest not to remember but one half of those laws, but to do all that they require. Maalon's young wife is come hither: if thou wouldest retain those lands, thou must marry her in accordance with the laws." He, however, renounced both the heritage and the woman to Boaz, who was himself likewise a kinsman of the dead, on the plea that he had a wife and

[b] Amplification, like the question addressed to the kinsman below and other details in this narrative. The reference to the γερουσία, "council of elders" or "senate," has a parallel in the Targum which says that Boaz came before the court of the Sanhedrin. Scripture says merely "he took ten men of the elders of the city" (iv. 2).

335 λέγων αὐτῷ καὶ παῖδας ἤδη. μαρτυράμενος οὖν
ὁ Βόαζος τὴν γερουσίαν ἐκέλευε τῇ γυναικὶ
ὑπολῦσαι αὐτὸν προσελθοῦσαν κατὰ τὸν νόμον καὶ
πτύειν εἰς τὸ πρόσωπον. γενομένου δὲ τούτου
Βόαζος γαμεῖ τὴν Ῥούθην καὶ γίνεται παιδίον
336 αὐτοῖς μετ᾽ ἐνιαυτὸν ἄρρεν. τοῦτο ἡ Ναάμις
τιτθευομένη κατὰ συμβουλίαν τῶν γυναικῶν Ὠβή-
δην ἐκάλεσεν ἐπὶ γηροκομίᾳ τῇ αὐτῆς τραφησό-
μενον· ὠβήδης γὰρ κατὰ διάλεκτον τὴν Ἑβραίων
ἀποσημαίνει δουλεύων. Ὠβήδου δὲ γίνεται[1]
Ἰεσσαῖος, τούτου Δαυίδης ὁ βασιλεύσας καὶ παισὶ
τοῖς αὐτοῦ καταλιπὼν τὴν ἡγεμονίαν ἐπὶ μίαν καὶ
337 εἴκοσι γενεὰς ἀνδρῶν. τὰ μὲν οὖν κατὰ Ῥούθην
ἀναγκαίως διηγησάμην, ἐπιδεῖξαι βουλόμενος τὴν
τοῦ θεοῦ δύναμιν, ὅτι τούτῳ παράγειν ἐφικτόν
ἐστιν εἰς ἀξίωμα λαμπρὸν καὶ τοὺς ἐπιτυχόντας,
εἰς οἷον ἀνήγαγε καὶ Δαυίδην ἐκ τοιούτων γενόμενον.

338 (x. 1) Ἑβραῖοι δὲ τῶν πραγμάτων αὐτοῖς ὑπ-
ενεχθέντων πάλιν πόλεμον ἐκφέρουσι Παλαιστίνοις
διὰ τοιαύτην αἰτίαν· Ἠλεῖ τῷ ἀρχιερεῖ δύο παῖδες
339 ἦσαν Ὀφνίης τε καὶ Φινεέσης. οὗτοι καὶ πρὸς
ἀνθρώπους ὑβρισταὶ γενόμενοι καὶ πρὸς τὸ θεῖον
ἀσεβεῖς οὐδενὸς ἀπείχοντο παρανομήματος, καὶ
τὰ μὲν ἐφέροντο τῶν γερῶν κατὰ τιμήν, ἃ δ᾽
ἐλάμβανον αὐτοῖς[2] ἁρπαγῆς τρόπῳ, γυναῖκάς τε
τὰς ἐπὶ θρησκείᾳ παραγινομένας ὕβριζον φθοραῖς,
ταῖς μὲν βίαν προσφέροντες τὰς δὲ δώροις ὑπαγό-

[1] +παῖς RO. [2] αὐτοῖς codd.

[a] Amplification: there is no mention in Scripture of a previous marriage.

children already.[a] Boaz therefore, having taken the elders to witness, bade the woman loose the man's shoe, approaching him as the law ordained, and to spit in his face.[b] That done, Boaz married Ruth, and a year after a boy was born to them. This infant was nursed by Naamis, who on the counsel of the women called him Obed, because he was to be brought up to be the stay of her old age; for *obed* in the Hebrew tongue signifies "one who serves." Of Obed was born Jesse, and of him David, who became king and bequeathed his dominion to his posterity for one and twenty generations. This story of Ruth I have been constrained to relate, being desirous to show the power of God and how easy it is for Him to promote even ordinary folk to rank so illustrious as that to which he raised David, sprung from such ancestors.

(x. 1) The Hebrews, whose affairs had declined, again made war upon the Philistines, the occasion being on this wise. Eli the high priest had two sons, Hophnies[c] and Phinees.[c] These, grown both insolent to men and impious to the Divinity, abstained from no iniquity: of the offerings some they carried off as the prizes of office, others they seized in robber fashion; they dishonoured the women who came for worship, doing violence to some and seducing

The iniquity of Eli's sons. 1 Sam. ii. 12.

ii. 22.

[b] This last detail is taken from the law (Deut. xxv. 9; *A.* iv. 256), but is not mentioned in Ruth, which describes a different ceremony, the giving of his shoe by the purchaser to the seller, as a symbol of exchange. In this case the kinsman should presumably not have been subjected to the humiliating ceremony prescribed by the law of levirate marriage in Deuteronomy, inasmuch as he was not a brother of Ruth's dead husband.

[c] Bibl. Hophni, and Phinehas.

μενοι· τυραννίδος δ' οὐθὲν ἀπέλειπεν ὁ βίος αὐτῶν.
340 ὅ τε οὖν πατὴρ αὐτὸς[1] ἐπὶ τούτοις χαλεπῶς εἶχεν
ὅσον οὐδέπω προσδοκῶν ἥξειν ἐκ θεοῦ τιμωρίαν
αὐτοῖς ἐπὶ τοῖς πραττομένοις, τό τε πλῆθος ἐδυσ-
φόρει, κἀπειδὴ φράζει τὴν ἐσομένην συμφορὰν ὁ
θεὸς τοῖς παισὶν αὐτοῦ τῷ τε Ἠλεῖ καὶ Σαμουήλῳ
τῷ προφήτῃ παιδὶ τότε[2] ὄντι, τότε φανερὸν ἐπὶ τοῖς
υἱοῖς πένθος ἦγε.
341 (2) Βούλομαι δὲ τὰ περὶ τοῦ προφήτου πρότερον
διεξελθὼν ἔπειθ' οὕτως τὰ περὶ τοὺς Ἠλεῖ παῖδας
εἰπεῖν καὶ τὴν δυστυχίαν τὴν τῷ παντὶ λαῷ
342 Ἑβραίων γενομένην. Ἀλκάνης Λευίτης ἀνὴρ τῶν
ἐν μέσῳ πολιτῶν τῆς Ἐφράμου κληρουχίας Ἀρμαθὰν[3] πόλιν κατοικῶν ἐγάμει δύο γυναῖκας Ἄνναν
τε καὶ Φενάνναν. ἐκ δὴ ταύτης καὶ παῖδες αὐτῷ
γίνονται, τὴν δ' ἑτέραν ἄτεκνον οὖσαν ἀγαπῶν
343 διετέλει. ἀφικομένου δὲ μετὰ τῶν γυναικῶν τοῦ
Ἀλκάνου εἰς Σιλὼ πόλιν θῦσαι, ἐνταῦθα γὰρ ἡ
σκηνὴ τοῦ θεοῦ ἐπεπήγει καθὼς προειρήκαμεν,
καὶ πάλιν κατὰ τὴν εὐωχίαν νέμοντος μοίρας
κρεῶν ταῖς τε γυναιξὶ καὶ τοῖς τέκνοις, ἡ Ἄννα
θεασαμένη τοὺς τῆς ἑτέρας παῖδας τῇ μητρὶ περι-
καθισαμένους, εἰς δάκρυά τε προύπεσε καὶ τῆς
ἀπαιδίας αὑτὴν ὠλοφύρετο καὶ τῆς μονώσεως.

[1] αὐτοῖς M: αὐτῶν LE (quorum Lat.).
[2] MLE: τε rell.: ἔτι Dindorf.
[3] Ῥαμαθὰν ROM: Aramath Lat.: forte l. Ἀραμαθάν.

[a] The order of words is peculiar: the Greek might be rendered "when God announced to his servants, Eli and Samuel . . . the fate that was in store."
[b] For this phrase with regard to the arrangement of the narrative *cf.* iv. 196.
[c] Bibl. Elkanah.
[d] 1 Chron. vi. 27 (not stated in Samuel).

others by presents; in short, their manner of life differed in no whit from a tyranny. And so their father was himself in sore distress thereat, hourly expecting to see them visited by chastisement from God for their misdeeds, and the people were chafing; and when God announced both to Eli and to Samuel the prophet, then but a child, the fate that was in store for his sons,[a] then did Eli openly make mourning over his sons.

(2) But here I would first recount the story of the prophet and then proceed[b] to speak of the fate of Eli's sons and the disaster that befell the whole people of the Hebrews. Alkanes,[c] a Levite[d] of the middle classes, of the tribe of Ephraim and an inhabitant of the city of Armatha,[e] married two wives, Anna and Phenanna.[f] By the latter he had children, but the other, though childless, remained beloved of her husband. Now when Alkanes was come with his wives to the city of Silo to sacrifice—for it was there that the tabernacle of God had been pitched, as we have said before[g]—and when thereafter[h] at the banquet he was distributing portions of meat to his wives and children, Anna, beholding the children of the other wife seated around their mother, burst into tears and bewailed her barrenness and lonesome

Eli announces to Hannah the birth of a son. 1 Sam. i. 1.

[e] Bibl. Ramathaim-zophim (LXX Ἀρμαθαὶμ Σειφά), another name for Ramah and possibly identical with the N.T. Arimathaea: site disputed.

[f] Bibl. Hannah and Peninnah (LXX, like Josephus, Φενάννα).

[g] *A.* v. 68.

[h] πάλιν, probably an Aramaism; Wellhausen notes that in Mark's Gospel "πάλιν, like Aramaic *tub*, means not only 'again,' but also 'further,' 'thereupon'" (*Einleitung in die drei ersten Evangelien*, ed. 2, pp. 21 f.). There are other indications that this Josephan narrative of the birth of Samuel is drawn from an Aramaic source.

344 καὶ τῆς τἀνδρὸς παραμυθίας τῇ λύπῃ κρατήσασα εἰς τὴν σκηνὴν ᾤχετο τὸν θεὸν ἱκετεύουσα δοῦναι γονὴν αὐτῇ καὶ ποιῆσαι μητέρα, ἐπαγγελλομένη τὸ πρῶτον αὐτῇ γενησόμενον καθιερώσειν ἐπὶ διακονίᾳ τοῦ θεοῦ, δίαιταν οὐχ ὁμοίαν τοῖς ἰδιώταις
345 ποιησόμενον. διατριβούσης δ' ἐπὶ ταῖς εὐχαῖς πολὺν χρόνον Ἠλεὶς ὁ ἀρχιερεύς, ἐκαθέζετο γὰρ πρὸ τῆς σκηνῆς, ὡς παροινοῦσαν ἐκέλευεν ἀπιέναι. τῆς δὲ πιεῖν ὕδωρ φαμένης, λυπουμένης δ' ἐπὶ παίδων ἀπορίᾳ τὸν θεὸν ἱκετεύειν, θαρσεῖν παρεκελεύετο, παρέξειν αὐτῇ παῖδας τὸν θεὸν καταγγέλλων.

346 (3) Παραγενομένη δ' εὔελπις πρὸς τὸν ἄνδρα τροφὴν χαίρουσα προσηνέγκατο, καὶ ἀναστρεψάντων εἰς τὴν πατρίδα κύειν ἤρξατο καὶ γίνεται παιδίον αὐτοῖς, ὃν Σαμούηλον προσαγορεύουσι· θεαίτητον ἄν τις εἴποι. παρῆσαν οὖν ὑπὲρ τῆς τοῦ παιδὸς θύσοντες γενέσεως δεκάτας τ' ἔφερον.
347 ἀναμνησθεῖσα δ' ἡ γυνὴ τῆς εὐχῆς τῆς ἐπὶ τῷ παιδὶ γεγενημένης παρεδίδου τῷ Ἠλεῖ ἀνατιθεῖσα τῷ θεῷ προφήτην γενησόμενον· κόμη τε οὖν αὐτῷ ἀνεῖτο καὶ ποτὸν ἦν ὕδωρ. καὶ Σαμούηλος μὲν ἐν τῷ ἱερῷ διῆγε τρεφόμενος, Ἀλκάνῃ δ' ἐκ τῆς Ἄννας υἱεῖς τε ἄλλοι[1] γίνονται καὶ τρεῖς θυγατέρες.

[1] ἄλλοι om. ROM.

[a] A close parallel from a Targum is supplied by Mr. (now Archdeacon) Hunkin, "a woman who begins to bear a first-born," *Journal of Theol. Studies*, xxv. (1924), p. 398, n. 2.

lot. And, her grief proving stronger than her hus- 9.
band's consolation, she went off to the tabernacle,
to beseech God to grant her offspring and to make
her a mother, promising that her first-born should
be consecrated to the service of God and that his
manner of life should be unlike that of ordinary men.
And as she lingered a long time over her prayers, 12.
Eli the high priest, who was seated at the entrance
of the tabernacle, taking her for a drunkard, bade
her begone. But, on her replying that she had
drunk but water and that it was for grief at the lack
of children that she was making supplication to God,
he exhorted her to be of good cheer, announcing that
God would grant her children.

Birth and dedication of Samuel.

(3) Repairing thus in good hope to her husband, she
took her food with gladness, and on their return to
their native place she began to conceive[a]; and an 1 Sam. i. 18.
infant was born to them, whom they called Samuel,
as one might say "asked of God."[b] They came
therefore again to offer sacrifices for the birth of the
child and brought their tithes also.[c] And the woman,
mindful of the vow which she had made concerning
the child, delivered him to Eli, dedicating him to
God to become a prophet; so his locks were left to
grow and his drink was water. Thus Samuel lived ii. 21
and was brought up in the sanctuary, but Alkanes
had by Anna yet other sons and three daughters.[d]

[b] This biblical etymology (1 Sam. i. 20) is now abandoned: "Name of God" is the probable meaning.

[c] The offerings are specified in 1 Sam. i. 24: for the tithes *cf.* the addition in LXX to v. 21, καὶ πάσας τὰς δεκάτας τῆς γῆς αὐτοῦ.

[d] Bibl. "three sons and two daughters": possibly a figure γ′ (=3) has fallen out of the text of Josephus before γίνονται.

348 (4) Σαμούηλος δὲ πεπληρωκὼς ἔτος ἤδη δωδέ-
κατον προεφήτευε. καί ποτε κοιμώμενον ὀνομαστὶ
ἐκάλεσεν ὁ θεός· ὁ δὲ νομίσας ὑπὸ τοῦ ἀρχιερέως
πεφωνῆσθαι παραγίνεται πρὸς αὐτόν. οὐ φαμένου
δὲ καλέσαι τοῦ ἀρχιερέως ὁ θεὸς εἰς τρὶς τοῦτο
349 ποιεῖ. καὶ Ἠλεὶς διαυγασθείς[1] φησι πρὸς αὐτόν,
"ἀλλ' ἐγὼ μέν, Σαμούηλε, σιγὴν ὡς καὶ τὸ πρὶν
ἦγον, θεὸς δ' ἐστὶν ὁ καλῶν, σήμαινέ τε[2] πρὸς
αὐτόν, ὅτι παρατυγχάνω." καὶ τοῦ θεοῦ φθεγ-
ξαμένου πάλιν ἀκούσας ἠξίου λαλεῖν ἐπὶ τοῖς
χρωμένοις· οὐ γὰρ ὑστερήσειν αὐτὸν ἐφ' οἷς ἂν
350 θελήσειε διακονίας. καὶ ὁ θεὸς "ἐπεί," φησί,
"παρατυγχάνεις, μάνθανε συμφορὰν Ἰσραηλίταις
ἐσομένην λόγου μείζονα καὶ πίστεως τοῖς παρα-
τυγχάνουσι, καὶ τοὺς Ἠλεῖ δὲ παῖδας ἡμέρᾳ μιᾷ
τεθνηξομένους καὶ τὴν ἱερωσύνην μετελευσομένην
εἰς τὴν Ἐλεαζάρου οἰκίαν· Ἠλεὶς γὰρ τῆς ἐμῆς
θεραπείας μᾶλλον τοὺς υἱοὺς καὶ παρὰ τὸ συμ-
351 φέρον αὐτοῖς ἠγάπησε." ταῦτα βιασάμενος ὅρκοις
εἰπεῖν αὐτῷ τὸν προφήτην Ἠλείς, οὐ γὰρ ἐβούλετο λυπεῖν αὐτὸν λέγων, ἔτι μᾶλλον βεβαιοτέραν
εἶχε τὴν προσδοκίαν τῆς τῶν τέκνων ἀπωλείας.
Σαμουήλου δὲ ηὔξετο ἐπὶ πλέον ἡ δόξα πάντων ὧν
προεφήτευσεν ἀληθινῶν βλεπομένων.
352 (xi. 1) Κατὰ τοῦτον δὴ τὸν καιρὸν[3] Παλαιστῖνοι

[1] διυπνισθεὶς SPL.
[2] Niese (ex RO ἐσήμαινέ τε): ἀλλὰ σήμαινε rell.
[3] + καὶ ROM.

[a] Age not mentioned in Scripture.
[b] Greek "speak upon (*i.e.* "concerning") His oracles," again suggesting a Semitic original; the Hebrew use of *dibber 'al* is exactly parallel.

(4) Samuel had now completed his twelfth year [a] when he began to act as a prophet. And one night as he slept God called him by name; but he, supposing that he had been summoned by the high priest, went off to him. But the high priest replied that he had not called him, and God did this thing thrice. Then Eli, enlightened, said to him, "Nay, Samuel, *I* held my peace even as before: it is God that calleth thee. Say then to Him, Here am I." So, when God spake again, Samuel hearing Him besought Him to speak [b] His oracles, for he would not fail to serve Him in whatsoever He might desire. And God said, "Since thou art there, learn that a calamity will befall the Israelites passing the speech or belief of them that witness it,[c] aye and that the sons of Eli shall die on the selfsame day and that the priesthood shall pass to the house of Eleazar.[d] For Eli hath loved his sons more dearly than my worship, and not to their welfare." All this Eli constrained the prophet by oath to reveal to him—for Samuel was loth to grieve him by telling it—and he now awaited with yet more certainty than before the loss of his children. But the renown of Samuel increased more and more, since all that he prophesied was seen to come true.

God's revelation to Samuel. 1 Sam. iii. 8.

ii. 29.

iii. 15.

(xi. 1) This then was the time when the Philis-

Victory of the

[c] "Those on the spot" is the usual sense of the verb in Josephus and it has been so used twice just above ("Here am I," "thou art there"); others here render "anyone" ("any chance persons").

[d] *Cf.* 1 Sam. ii. 30 ff.: the prophecy there made to Eli himself was, according to Scripture, fulfilled under king Solomon, when Abiathar of the house of Ithamar was replaced by Zadok of the house of Eleazar (1 Kings ii. 27, 35; *A.* viii. 11).

στρατεύσαντες ἐπὶ τοὺς Ἰσραηλίτας στρατοπεδεύονται κατὰ πόλιν Ἀμφεκᾶν, δεξαμένων δ' ἐξ ὀλίγου τῶν Ἰσραηλιτῶν συνῄεσαν εἰς τὴν ἐχομένην καὶ νικῶσιν οἱ Παλαιστῖνοι καὶ κτείνουσι μὲν τῶν Ἑβραίων εἰς τετρακισχιλίους, τὸ δὲ λοιπὸν πλῆθος συνδιώκουσιν εἰς τὸ στρατόπεδον.

353 (2) Δείσαντες δὲ περὶ τῶν ὅλων Ἑβραῖοι[1] πέμπουσιν ὡς τὴν γερουσίαν καὶ τὸν ἀρχιερέα, τὴν κιβωτὸν τοῦ θεοῦ κελεύοντες κομίζειν, ἵνα παρούσης αὐτῆς παρατασσόμενοι κρατῶσι τῶν πολεμίων, ἀγνοοῦντες ὅτι μείζων ἐστὶν ὁ καταψηφισάμενος αὐτῶν τὴν συμφορὰν τῆς κιβωτοῦ, δι' ὃν καὶ ταύ-
354 την[2] συνέβαινεν εἶναι. παρῆν τε οὖν ἡ κιβωτὸς καὶ οἱ τοῦ ἀρχιερέως υἱεῖς τοῦ πατρὸς αὐτοῖς ἐπιστείλαντος, εἰ ληφθείσης τῆς κιβωτοῦ ζῆν ἐθέλουσιν,[3] εἰς ὄψιν αὐτῷ μὴ παραγίνεσθαι. Φινεέσης δὲ ἤδη καὶ ἱερᾶτο, τοῦ πατρὸς αὐτῷ
355 παρακεχωρηκότος διὰ τὸ γῆρας. θάρσος οὖν ἐπιγίνεται πολὺ τοῖς Ἑβραίοις ὡς διὰ τὴν ἄφιξιν τῆς κιβωτοῦ περιεσομένοις τῶν πολεμίων, κατεπλήττοντο δὲ οἱ πολέμιοι δεδιότες τὴν παρουσίαν τῆς κιβωτοῦ τοῖς Ἰσραηλίταις. ταῖς μέντοι γε ἑκατέρων προσδοκίαις οὐχ ὅμοιον ἀπήντησε τὸ
356 ἔργον, ἀλλὰ συμβολῆς γενομένης ἣν μὲν ἤλπιζον

[1] RO: pr. οἱ rell. [2] + ἐν τιμῇ SP.
[3] ἐθελήσουσιν SP.

[a] Bibl. Aphek: in the plain of Sharon, perhaps the modern *el Mejdel.*

tines, taking the field against the Israelites, pitched their camp over against the city of Amphekas.[a] The Israelites having hastily confronted them, the armies met on the following day, and the Philistines were victorious, slaying some four thousand of the Hebrews and pursuing the remainder of the host to their camp.

Philistines. 1 Sam. iv. 1.

(2) Fearing a complete disaster, the Hebrews sent word to the council of elders[b] and to the high priest to bring the ark of God, in order that, through its presence in their ranks, they might overcome their enemies, ignorant that He who had decreed their discomfiture was mightier than the ark, seeing that it was to Him indeed that it owed its being.[c] And so the ark arrived, and with it the sons of the high priest, having received injunctions from their father, if they wished to survive the capture of the ark, not to venture into his sight. Phinees was already acting as high priest, his father having made way for him by reason of old age.[d] Confidence then mightily revived among the Hebrews, who hoped through the coming of the ark to get the better of their enemies, while the enemy were in consternation, dreading that presence of the ark among the Israelites. Howbeit, the event did not answer to the expectations of either of them, but when the clash

Further defeat of the Hebrews and capture of the ark. 1 Sam. iv. 3.

[b] In scripture the elders at the camp suggest that the ark be brought from Shiloh.

[c] Or, according to another reading, "for His sake that it was held in veneration."

[d] Amplification (along with the father's injunctions to his sons). Rabbinic tradition also states that Phinehas officiated as High Priest in the lifetime of Eli. The latter's blindness (1 Sam. iii. 3) would have disqualified him from office according to Jewish law (Lev. xxi. 18, Josephus, *B.J.* i. 270).

νίκην Ἑβραῖοι τῶν Παλαιστίνων αὕτη γίνεται,
ἣν δ' ἐφοβοῦντο ἧτταν οὗτοι, ταύτην Ἑβραῖοι
παθόντες ἔγνωσαν αὐτοὺς μάτην ἐπὶ τῇ κιβωτῷ
τεθαρσηκότας· ἐτράπησάν τε γὰρ εὐθὺς εἰς χεῖρας
ἐλθόντες τῶν πολεμίων καὶ ἀπέβαλον εἰς τρισμυρίους, ἐν οἷς ἔπεσον καὶ οἱ τοῦ ἀρχιερέως υἱεῖς,
ἥ τε κιβωτὸς ἤγετο πρὸς τῶν πολεμίων.
357 (3) Ἀπαγγελθείσης δὲ τῆς ἥττης εἰς τὴν Σιλὼ
καὶ τῆς αἰχμαλωσίας τῆς κιβωτοῦ, Βενιαμίτης
γάρ τις αὐτοῖς ἄγγελος ἀφικνεῖται νεανίας παρα-
τετευχὼς τῷ γεγονότι, πένθους ἀνεπλήσθη πᾶσα
358 ἡ πόλις. καὶ Ἠλεὶς ὁ ἀρχιερεύς, ἐκαθέζετο γὰρ
καθ' ἑτέρας τῶν πυλῶν ἐφ' ὑψηλοῦ θρόνου, ἀκούσας
οἰμωγῆς καὶ νομίσας νεώτερόν τι πεπρᾶχθαι περὶ
τοὺς οἰκείους καὶ μεταπεμψάμενος τὸν νεανίαν,
ὡς ἔγνω τὰ κατὰ τὴν μάχην, ῥᾴων ἦν ἐπί τε
τοῖς παισὶ καὶ τοῖς συνενηνεγμένοις[1] περὶ τὸ στρατόπεδον ὡς ἂν προεγνωκὼς παρὰ τοῦ θεοῦ τὸ
συμβησόμενον καὶ προαπηγγελκώς· συνέχει[2] γὰρ
ἱκανῶς[3] τὰ παρὰ τὴν[4] προσδοκίαν συντυχόντα τῶν
359 δεινῶν. ὡς δὲ καὶ τὴν κιβωτὸν ἤκουσεν ᾐχμα-
λωτίσθαι πρὸς τῶν πολεμίων, ὑπὸ τοῦ παρ'
ἐλπίδας αὐτῷ τοῦτο προσπεσεῖν περιαλγήσας
ἀποκυλισθεὶς ἀπὸ τοῦ θρόνου τελευτᾷ, ὀκτὼ καὶ
ἐνενήκοντα βιώσας ἔτη τὰ πάντα καὶ τούτων τὰ[5]
τεσσαράκοντα κατασχὼν τὴν ἀρχήν.
360 (4) Θνήσκει δὲ κατ' ἐκείνην τὴν ἡμέραν καὶ ἡ
Φινεέσου τοῦ παιδὸς γυνὴ μὴ καρτερήσασα ζῆν
ἐπὶ τῇ τἀνδρὸς δυστυχίᾳ. κυούσῃ μὲν αὐτῇ

[1] Text doubtful: ἐπὶ τῷ τοῖς παισὶ τοῖς αὐτοῦ συνενηνεγμένῳ Niese.
[2] confundunt Lat.: συγχεῖ Naber.
[3] ἀκριβῶς ROE.
[4] τὰ κατὰ OE: τὰ R.
[5] τὰ om. ROE.

came, that victory for which the Hebrews hoped went to the Philistines, and that defeat which these feared was sustained by the Hebrews, who learnt that their trust in the ark had been in vain. For soon as ever they closed with the enemy they were routed and lost some thirty thousand men, among the fallen being the sons of the high priest; and the ark was carried off by the enemy.

(3) When the defeat and the capture of the ark Death of Eli.
were reported in Silo—the news was brought by a 1 Sam. iv. 12.
young Benjamite who had been present at the action
—the whole city was filled with lamentation. And
Eli the high priest, who was sitting at one of the two
gates on a lofty seat, hearing the wails and surmising
that some grave disaster had befallen his offspring,
sent for the young man; and when he learnt the
issue of the battle, he bore with moderate composure
the fate of his sons and that which had happened to
the army, seeing that he had known beforehand
from God and had forewarned them of that which
was to come, for men are affected most by those
shocks that fall unexpectedly. But when he heard
moreover that the ark had been captured by the
enemy, in an agony of grief at this unlooked for
tidings, he tumbled from his seat and expired,
having lived ninety and eight years in all and for 15.
forty[a] of them held supreme power. 18.

(4) That same day died also the wife of his son Death of
Phinees, having not the strength to survive her the wife of Phinehas.
husband's misfortune. She was indeed with child 1 Sam. iv. 19.

[a] So Heb. and some MSS. of LXX: the majority of the MSS. of the Greek Bible read "twenty."

προσηγγέλη τὸ περὶ τὸν ἄνδρα πάθος, τίκτει δ' ἑπταμηνιαῖον παῖδα, ὃν καὶ ζήσαντα Ἰωχάβην[1] προσηγόρευσαν, σημαίνει δὲ ἀδοξίαν τὸ ὄνομα, διὰ τὴν προσπεσοῦσαν δύσκλειαν τότε τῷ στρατῷ.

361 (5) Ἦρξε δὲ πρῶτος Ἠλεὶς Ἰθαμάρου τῆς ἑτέρου τῶν Ἀαρῶνος υἱῶν οἰκίας· ἡ γὰρ Ἐλεαζάρου οἰκία τὸ πρῶτον ἱερᾶτο παῖς παρὰ πατρὸς ἐπιδεχόμενοι τὴν τιμήν, ἐκεῖνός τε Φινεέσῃ τῷ
362 παιδὶ αὐτοῦ παραδίδωσι, μεθ' ὃν Ἀβιεζέρης υἱὸς ὢν αὐτοῦ τὴν τιμὴν παραλαβὼν παιδὶ αὐτοῦ Βόκκι τοὔνομα αὐτὴν κατέλιπε, παρ' οὗ διεδέξατο Ὄζις υἱὸς ὤν, μεθ' ὃν Ἠλεὶς ἔσχε τὴν ἱερωσύνην, περὶ οὗ νῦν ὁ λόγος, καὶ τὸ γένος τὸ ἀπ' ἐκείνου μέχρι τῶν κατὰ τὴν τοῦ[2] Σολόμωνος βασιλείαν καιρῶν. τότε δὲ οἱ Ἐλεαζάρου πάλιν αὐτὴν ἀπέλαβον.

[1] *v.ll.* Ἰωαχάβην, Ἰαχώβην etc.
[2] τοῦ om. MSPLE.

[a] Unscriptural detail. Rabbinic tradition includes Samuel but not Ichabod, among seven months' children.
[b] Bibl. I-chabod (= " no glory ").

when she was told of his fate, and she gave birth to a seven months'[a] son; and him, since he lived, they called Jochabes[b] (a name signifying "ingloriousness") because of the ignominy that then befell the army.

Succession of the high priests.

(5) Eli was the first to bear rule of the house of Ithamar,[c] the second[d] of Aaron's sons; for the house of Eleazar held the high priesthood at the first, the dignity descending from father to son. Eleazar transmitted it to Phinees his son, after whom Abiezer[e] his son received it, leaving it to his son, named Bokki,[f] from whom Ozis[g] his son inherited it; it was after him that Eli, of whom we have been speaking, held the priesthood, as also his posterity down to the times of the reign of Solomon. Then the descendants of Eleazar once more recovered it.

1 Chron. vi. 4 f.

Cf. 1 Kings ii. 27, 35.

[c] Based not on Scripture, but on tradition (see M. Weill's note).

[d] Gr. "one of two." Of the four sons of Aaron—Nadab, Abihu, Eleazar and Ithamar—the first two died young (1 Chron. xxiv. 1 f.).

[e] Bibl. Abishua (1 Chron. vi. 4).

[f] Bibl. Bukki.

[g] Bibl. Uzzi.

ΒΙΒΛΙΟΝ Ϛ

(i. 1) Λαβόντες δ' οἱ Παλαιστῖνοι τὴν τῶν πολεμίων κιβωτὸν αἰχμάλωτον, ὡς προειρήκαμεν μικρὸν ἔμπροσθεν, εἰς Ἄζωτον ἐκόμισαν πόλιν καὶ παρὰ τὸν αὐτῶν θεὸν ὥσπερ τι λάφυρον, Δαγὼν
2 δ' οὗτος ἐκαλεῖτο, τιθέασι. τῇ δ' ἐπιούσῃ πάντες ὑπὸ τὴν τῆς ἡμέρας ἀρχὴν εἰσιόντες εἰς τὸν ναὸν προσκυνῆσαι τὸν θεὸν ἐπιτυγχάνουσιν αὐτῷ τοῦτο ποιοῦντι τὴν κιβωτόν· ἔκειτο γάρ[1] ἀποπεπτωκὼς τῆς βάσεως, ἐφ' ἧς ἑστὼς διετέλει· καὶ βαστάσαντες πάλιν ἐφιστᾶσιν αὐτὸν ἐπὶ ταύτης, δυσφορήσαντες ἐπὶ τῷ γεγενημένῳ. πολλάκις δὲ φοιτῶντες παρὰ τὸν Δαγὼν καὶ καταλαμβάνοντες ὁμοίως ἐπὶ τοῦ προσκυνοῦντος τὴν κιβωτὸν σχήματος κείμενον, ἐν ἀπορίᾳ δεινῇ καὶ συγχύσει
3 καθίσταντο. καὶ τελευταῖον ἀπέσκηψεν εἰς τὴν τῶν Ἀζωτίων πόλιν καὶ τὴν χώραν αὐτῶν φθορὰν τὸ θεῖον καὶ νόσον· ἀπέθνησκον γὰρ ὑπὸ δυσεντερίας, πάθους χαλεποῦ καὶ τὴν ἀναίρεσιν ὀξυτάτην ἐπιφέροντος πρὶν ἢ τὴν ψυχὴν αὐτοῖς εὐθανάτως ἀπολυθῆναι τοῦ σώματος, τὰ ἐντὸς ἀναφέροντες[2] διαβεβρωμένα καὶ παντοίως ὑπὸ τῆς νόσου διεφθαρμένα· τὰ δ' ἐπὶ τῆς χώρας μυῶν πλῆθος

[1] E: + ἀπ' αὐτῆς SP: + ἐπ' αὐτῆς rell.
[2] + ἐξεμοῦντες codd. (gloss).

BOOK VI

(i. 1) The Philistines, having captured their enemies' ark, as we have said a while ago, carried it to the city of Azotus [a] and placed it as a trophy beside their own god, who was called Dagon. But on the morrow, when all at break of day entered the temple to adore their god, they found him doing the like to the ark; for he lay prostrate, having fallen from the pedestal whereon he had always stood. So they lifted him and set him again thereon, sore distressed at what had passed. But when oft-times [b] visiting Dagon they ever found him in a like posture of prostration before the ark, they were plunged into dire perplexity and dismay. And in the end the Deity launched upon the city of the Azotians and upon their country destruction and disease. For they died of dysentery,[c] a grievous malady and inflicting most rapid dissolution, or ever their soul by blessed death was parted from the body, for they brought up their entrails all consumed and in every way corrupted by the disease. As for what was on the land, a swarm of

The ark in Philistia and the plagues arising therefrom.
1 Sam. v. 1

v. 6 LXX.

[a] The Greek (LXX) name for the Heb. Ashdod.

[b] The Bible mentions only a second visit, adding details on the shattering of the image.

[c] The word used in Scripture probably means "plague boils."

ἀνελθὸν[1] κατέβλαψε μήτε φυτῶν μήτε καρπῶν
4 ἀποσχόμενον. ἐν δὴ τούτοις ὄντες τοῖς κακοῖς
οἱ Ἀζώτιοι καὶ πρὸς τὰς συμφορὰς ἀντέχειν οὐ
δυνάμενοι συνῆκαν ἐκ τῆς κιβωτοῦ ταύτας αὐτοῖς
ἀνασχεῖν, καὶ τὴν νίκην καὶ τὴν ταύτης αἰχμαλω-
σίαν οὐκ ἐπ' ἀγαθῷ γεγενημένην. πέμπουσιν οὖν
πρὸς τοὺς Ἀσκαλωνίτας ἀξιοῦντες τὴν κιβωτὸν
5 αὐτοὺς παρὰ σφᾶς δέχεσθαι. τοῖς δὲ οὐκ ἀηδὴς
ἡ τῶν Ἀζωτίων δέησις προσέπεσεν, ἀλλ' ἐπι-
νεύουσι μὲν αὐτοῖς τὴν χάριν, λαβόντες δὲ τὴν
κιβωτὸν ἐν τοῖς ὁμοίοις δεινοῖς κατέστησαν· συνεξ-
εκόμισε γὰρ αὐτῇ τὰ τῶν Ἀζωτίων ἡ κιβωτὸς
πάθη πρὸς τοὺς ἀπ' ἐκείνων αὐτὴν δεχομένους· καὶ
πρὸς ἄλλους παρ' αὐτῶν ἀποπέμπουσιν Ἀσκαλω-
6 νῖται. μένει δ' οὐδὲ παρ' ἐκείνοις· ὑπὸ γὰρ τῶν
αὐτῶν παθῶν ἐλαυνόμενοι πρὸς τὰς ἐχομένας
ἀπολύουσι πόλεις. καὶ τοῦτον ἐκπεριέρχεται τὸν
τρόπον τὰς πέντε τῶν Παλαιστίνων πόλεις ἡ
κιβωτὸς ὥσπερ δασμὸν ἀπαιτοῦσα παρ' ἑκάστης
τοῦ πρὸς αὐτὰς ἐλθεῖν ἃ δι' αὐτὴν ἔπασχον.
7 (2) Ἀπειρηκότες δὲ τοῖς κακοῖς οἱ πεπειραμένοι καὶ τοῖς ἀκούουσιν αὐτὰ διδασκαλία γινό-
μενοι τοῦ μὴ προσδέξασθαι τὴν κιβωτόν ποτε πρὸς
αὑτοὺς ἐπὶ τοιούτῳ μισθῷ καὶ τέλει, τὸ λοιπὸν
ἐζήτουν μηχανὴν καὶ πόρον ἀπαλλαγῆς αὐτῆς.
8 καὶ συνελθόντες οἱ ἐκ τῶν πέντε πόλεων ἄρχοντες,
Γίττης καὶ Ἀκκάρων καὶ Ἀσκάλωνος ἔτι δὲ

[1] Lat.: + ἐπὶ (τὰ ἐπὶ M, ἀπὸ E, ἐκ SP) τῆς γῆς codd.

mice,[a] coming up from beneath, ravaged it all, sparing neither plant nor fruit. Being, then, in this evil plight and powerless to withstand their calamities, the Azotians understood that it was from the ark that they arose and that their victory and the capture of this trophy had not been for their welfare. They therefore sent to the men of Ascalon[b] and begged them to receive the ark into their keeping. And these, listening not unwillingly to the request of the Azotians, consented to do them this service; but no sooner had they taken the ark than they found themselves in the like woes, for the ark carried along with it the plagues of the Azotians to those who received it from their hands. So the Ascalonites rid themselves of it, sending it off to others. But neither did it abide with these, for, being beset by the same sufferings, they dismissed it to the neighbouring cities. And on this wise the ark went the round of the five cities of the Philistines, exacting from each, as it were toll for its visit to them, the ills which it caused them to suffer.

Deliberation and decision of the Philistines. Cf. 1 Sam. vi. 1.

(2) Exhausted by these miseries, the victims, whose fate was becoming a lesson to all who heard of it never to receive this ark among them at such a meed and price, henceforth sought ways and means to get rid of it. So the lords of the five cities—Gitta, Akkaron, Ascalon, along with Gaza and Azotus—

[a] Josephus agrees with the LXX in mentioning the mice at this point: the Hebrew text only alludes to them later (vi. 4 f.).

[b] In Scripture, after a meeting of the lords of the Philistines, the ark is sent first to Gath and then to Ekron (LXX Ascalon).

Γάζης καὶ Ἀζώτου, ἐσκόπουν τί δεῖ ποιεῖν. καὶ τὸ μὲν πρῶτον ἐδόκει τὴν κιβωτὸν ἀποπέμπειν τοῖς οἰκείοις, ὡς ὑπερεκδικοῦντος αὐτὴν τοῦ θεοῦ καὶ συνεπιδημησάντων αὐτῇ τῶν δεινῶν διὰ τοῦτο καὶ συνεισβαλόντων μετ' ἐκείνης εἰς τὰς πόλεις
9 αὐτῶν· ἦσαν δὲ οἱ λέγοντες τοῦτο μὲν μὴ ποιεῖν μηδ' ἐξαπατᾶσθαι τὴν αἰτίαν τῶν κακῶν εἰς ἐκείνην ἀναφέροντας· οὐ γὰρ ταύτην εἶναι τὴν δύναμιν αὐτῇ[1] καὶ τὴν ἰσχύν· οὐ γὰρ ἄν ποτ' αὐτῆς κηδομένου τοῦ θεοῦ ὑποχείριον ἀνθρώποις γενέσθαι. ἡσυχάζειν δὲ καὶ πρᾴως ἔχειν ἐπὶ τοῖς συμβεβηκόσι παρῄνουν, αἰτίαν τούτων οὐκ ἄλλην ἢ μόνην λογιζομένους τὴν φύσιν, ἣ καὶ σώμασι καὶ γῇ καὶ φυτοῖς καὶ πᾶσι τοῖς ἐξ αὐτῆς συνεστῶσι κατὰ χρόνων περιόδους τίκτει τοιαύτας μεταβολάς.
10 νικᾷ δὲ τὰς προειρημένας γνώμας ἀνδρῶν ἔν τε τοῖς ἐπάνω χρόνοις συνέσει καὶ φρονήσει διαφέρειν[2] πεπιστευμένων συμβουλία καὶ τότε μάλιστα δοξάντων ἁρμοζόντως λέγειν τοῖς παροῦσιν, οἳ μήτ' ἀποπέμπειν ἔφασαν τὴν κιβωτὸν μήτε κατασχεῖν, ἀλλὰ πέντε μὲν ἀνδριάντας ὑπὲρ ἑκάστης πόλεως χρυσοῦς ἀναθεῖναι τῷ θεῷ χαριστήριον, ὅτι προενόησεν αὐτῶν τῆς σωτηρίας καὶ κατέσχεν ἐν τῷ βίῳ διωκομένους ἐξ αὐτοῦ παθήμασιν, οἷς οὐκέτι ἦν ἀντιβλέψαι, τοσούτους δὲ τὸν ἀριθμὸν μύας χρυσοῦς τοῖς κατανεμηθεῖσιν αὐτῶν

[1] ex Lat. Hudson: ὑγιῆ codd. [2] om. ROM.

[a] In Scripture (vi. 2) the Philistines summon "the priests and the diviners," who propose the course which is followed. The meeting described in Josephus, with the views of the three parties, is an invention of the "Sophoclean" assistant: for a similar conflict of opinions *cf. A.* iii. 96 ff., where, as

met to deliberate what they ought to do.[a] Their first resolution was to send the ark back to its own people, inasmuch as God was championing its cause and that was why these horrors had accompanied it and burst along with it into their cities. But there were others who said that they should not do thus nor be deluded into attributing the cause of their misfortunes to the ark: it possessed no such power and might, for, were it under the care of God, it would never have fallen into the hands of men. Their advice was to sit still and to bear these accidents with equanimity, accounting their cause to be no other than nature herself, who periodically produces such changes in men's bodies, in earth, and in plants and all the products of earth. However, both these proposals were defeated by the counsel of men who in times past had obtained credit for superior intelligence and sagacity, and who now above all seemed to say just what befitted the occasion. Their verdict was neither to send back the ark nor to
detain it, but to dedicate to God five images[b] of gold, 4.
one on behalf of each city, as a thank-offering[c] to Him for His care for their salvation and for having kept them in the land of the living when they were like to be harried out of it by plagues which they could no longer face, and withal as many golden mice like to those that had overrun and ruined their

here (§ 9), one party is for retaining composure (πρᾴως ἔχειν). This assistant's love of trichotomy extends to details, *e.g.* the τρίοδος (§ 11) and the division of the 5 cities into 3 + 2 by the insertion of ἔτι δὲ (§ 8).

[b] Statuettes in human form: bibl. "tumours" or rather "boils," LXX ἕδρας (models of the *anus*, as symbols of the plague).

[c] In Scripture as a "guilt-offering" (vi. 3), in compensation for the wrong done to the ark.

11 καὶ διαφθείρασι τὴν χώραν ἐμφερεῖς· ἔπειτα
βαλόντας εἰς γλωσσόκομον αὐτοὺς καὶ θέντας
ἐπὶ τὴν κιβωτόν, ἅμαξαν αὐτῇ καινὴν κατασκευάσαι, καὶ βόας ὑποζεύξαντας ἀρτιτόκους τὰς
μὲν πόρτις ἐγκλεῖσαι καὶ κατασχεῖν, μὴ ταῖς
μητράσιν ἐμποδὼν ἑπόμεναι γένωνται, πόθῳ δ'
αὐτῶν ὀξυτέραν ποιῶνται τὴν πορείαν· ἐκείνας δ'
ἐξελάσαντας τὴν κιβωτὸν φερούσας ἐπὶ τριόδου
καταλιπεῖν αὐταῖς ἐπιτρέψαντας ἣν βούλονται τῶν
12 ὁδῶν ἀπελθεῖν· κἂν μὲν τὴν Ἑβραίων ἀπίωσι καὶ
τὴν τούτων χώραν ἀναβαίνωσιν, ὑπολαμβάνειν τὴν
κιβωτὸν αἰτίαν τῶν κακῶν, "ἂν δὲ ἄλλην τρά-
πωνται, μεταδιώξωμεν αὐτήν," ἔφασαν, "μαθόντες
ὅτι μηδεμίαν ἰσχὺν τοιαύτην ἔχει."
13 (3) Ἔκριναν δ' αὐτὰ καλῶς εἰρῆσθαι καὶ τοῖς
ἔργοις εὐθὺς τὴν γνώμην ἐκύρωσαν. καὶ ποιήσαντες μὲν τὰ προειρημένα προάγουσι τὴν ἅμαξαν
ἐπὶ τὴν τρίοδον καὶ καταλιπόντες ἀνεχώρησαν, τῶν
δὲ βοῶν τὴν ὀρθὴν ὁδὸν ὥσπερ ἡγουμένου τινὸς
αὐταῖς ἀπιουσῶν, ἠκολούθουν οἱ τῶν Παλαιστίνων
ἄρχοντες, ποῦ ποτε στήσονται καὶ πρὸς τίνας
14 ἥξουσι βουλόμενοι μαθεῖν. κώμη δέ τίς ἐστι τῆς
Ἰούδα φυλῆς Βήθης[1] ὄνομα· εἰς ταύτην ἀφικνοῦνται
αἱ βόες, καὶ πεδίου μεγάλου καὶ καλοῦ τὴν
πορείαν αὐτῶν ἐκδεξαμένου παύονται προσωτέρω
χωρεῖν, στήσασαι τὴν ἅμαξαν αὐτόθι. θέα δὲ ἦν
τοῖς ἐν τῇ κώμῃ καὶ περιχαρεῖς ἐγένοντο· θέρους
γὰρ ὥρᾳ πάντες ἐπὶ τὴν συγκομιδὴν τῶν καρπῶν

[1] Βηθσάμη SP, Bethsamis Lat.

[a] Bibl. Beth-shemesh (LXX Βαιθσάμυς), modern *'Ain Shems*, on the border of Judah about 12 miles S.E. of Ekron.

country. Then, having placed these in a coffer and set it upon the ark, they should make for this a new wain, and should yoke thereto kine that had freshly calved, and should shut up and retain the calves, in order that these might not retard their mothers by following them, and they, through yearning for their young, might make the more speed upon their way. Then having driven them, drawing the ark, out to a place where three roads met, they should there leave them, suffering them to take which of the roads they would. Should the kine take the route to the Hebrews 2.
and mount into their country, they must regard the ark as the cause of all these ills; but should they turn elsewhere, "then," said they, "let us pursue after it, having learnt that it possesses no such power."

Return of the ark to Beth-shemesh. 1 Sam. vi. 10.

(3) Judging this to have been well spoken, they straightway ratified the counsel by acting thereon. Having made the objects aforesaid, they conducted the wain to the cross-roads, where they left it and retired. Then, seeing the kine go straight on, as though someone were leading them, the lords of the Philistines followed, fain to find out where they would halt and to whom they would betake themselves. Now there is a village of the tribe of Judah by name Bethes[a]: thither it was that the kine came: a great and beauteous plain awaited their footsteps[b]—they would proceed no further but stayed the wagon there. A sight was this for the villagers and they were overcome with joy; for it being the summer season when all were out in the cornfields to gather

[b] "The cart came into the field of Joshua the Beth-shemite," 1 Sam. vi. 14.

ἐν ταῖς ἀρούραις ὑπάρχοντες, ὡς εἶδον τὴν κιβωτόν, ὑφ' ἡδονῆς ἁρπαγέντες καὶ τὸ ἔργον ἐκ τῶν
χειρῶν ἀφέντες ἔδραμον εὐθὺς ἐπὶ τὴν ἅμαξαν.
15 καὶ καθελόντες τὴν κιβωτὸν καὶ τὸ ἄγγος, ὃ τοὺς
ἀνδριάντας εἶχε καὶ τοὺς μύας, τιθέασιν ἐπί τινος
πέτρας, ἥτις ἦν ἐν τῷ πεδίῳ, καὶ θύσαντες λαμπρῶς
τῷ θεῷ καὶ κατευωχηθέντες τήν τε ἅμαξαν καὶ
τοὺς βόας ὡλοκαύτωσαν. καὶ ταῦτ' ἰδόντες οἱ τῶν
Παλαιστίνων ἄρχοντες ἀνέστρεψαν ὀπίσω.
16 (4) Ὀργὴ δὲ καὶ χόλος τοῦ θεοῦ μέτεισιν ἑβδομήκοντα τῶν ἐκ τῆς Βήθης κώμης, οὓς[1] οὐκ
ὄντας ἀξίους ἅψασθαι τῆς κιβωτοῦ, ἱερεῖς γὰρ οὐκ
ἦσαν, καὶ προσελθόντας αὐτῇ βαλὼν ἀπέκτεινεν.
ἔκλαυσαν δὲ ταῦτα παθόντας αὐτοὺς οἱ κωμῆται,
καὶ πένθος ἐπ' αὐτοῖς[2] ἤγειραν οἷον εἰκὸς ἐπὶ
θεοπέμπτῳ κακῷ καὶ τὸν ἴδιον ἕκαστος ἀπεθρήνει·
17 τοῦ τε μένειν τὴν κιβωτὸν παρ' αὐτοῖς ἀναξίους
ἀποφαίνοντες αὐτοὺς καὶ πρὸς τὸ κοινὸν τῶν
Ἑβραίων πέμψαντες ἐδήλουν ἀποδεδόσθαι τὴν
κιβωτὸν ὑπὸ τῶν Παλαιστίνων. κἀκεῖνοι γνόντες
τοῦτο ἀποκομίζουσιν αὐτὴν εἰς Καριαθιαρεὶμ
18 γείτονα πόλιν τῆς Βήθης κώμης.[3] ἔνθα τινὸς
Λευίτου τὸ γένος Ἀμιναδάβου δόξαν ἔχοντος ἐπὶ
δικαιοσύνῃ καὶ θρησκείᾳ καταβιοῦντος εἰς οἰκίαν

[1] Niese: ὡς codd. [2] edd.: αὐτοὺς codd.
[3] τῆς Β. κώμης] τοῖς Βηθσαμίταις M (Lat.): τοῖς Βηθάμης SP.

---

[a] "To Ekron," *ib.* 16.

[b] Bibl. "seventy men (and) fifty thousand men" (similarly LXX); an impossible reading. The larger figure is commonly rejected as a gloss, from which, it appears, the Biblical text of Josephus was free.

[c] Not in Scripture, which merely says that "they had looked into (or rather "gazed upon") the ark." For the

in the crops, so soon as they saw the ark, they were transported with delight and, dropping their work from their hands, ran straight for the wain. Then, having taken down the ark and the vessel containing the images and the mice, they set them upon a rock which stood in the plain, and, after offering splendid sacrifice to God and keeping merry feast, consumed wagon and kine as a burnt-offering. And, having seen all this, the lords of the Philistines turned back again.[a]

The penalty for touching the ark: its removal to the house of Aminadab. 1 Sam. vi. 19.

(4) Howbeit, the wrath and indignation of God visited seventy[b] of them of the village of Bethes, whom He smote and slew for approaching the ark, which, not being priests,[c] they were not privileged to touch. The villagers bewailed these victims, raising over them lamentation such as was fitting over a God-sent evil, and each man mourned for his own. Then, pronouncing themselves unworthy of retaining the ark among them, they sent word to the general assembly[d] of the Hebrews that the ark had been
restored by the Philistines. And these, on hearing vii. 1.
thereof, conveyed it away to Kariathiareim,[e] a neighbouring city of the village of Bethes; and since there lived there a man of the stock of Levi, Aminadab,[f] reputed for his righteousness and piety,

Rabbinical opinions concerning the nature of their crime see M. Weill's note.

[d] In Scripture (1 Sam. vi. 21) word is sent, not to all the Hebrews, but only to the inhabitants of Kiriath-jearim.

[e] So LXX: Heb. Kiriath-jearim, perhaps the modern *Kuryet el 'Enab*, some 9 miles N.E. of Beth-shemesh. Shiloh, the original home of the ark, was possibly now in Philistine hands.

[f] So LXX: Heb. Abinadab. Scripture does not say that he was a Levite. A Levite Aminadab, contemporary with David, is mentioned in 1 Chr. xv. 11.

τὴν κιβωτὸν ἤγαγον, ὥσπερ εἰς πρέποντα τῷ θεῷ τόπον ἐν ᾧ κατῴκει δίκαιος ἄνθρωπος. ἐθεράπευον δὲ τὴν κιβωτὸν οἱ τούτου παῖδες, καὶ τῆς ἐπιμελείας ταύτης ἕως ἐτῶν εἴκοσι προέστησαν· τοσαῦτα γὰρ ἔμεινεν ἐν τῇ Καριαθιαρεὶμ *ποιήσασα παρὰ τοῖς* Παλαιστίνοις *μῆνας τέσσαρας.*

19 (ii. 1) Τοῦ δὲ *λαοῦ παντὸς ἐκείνῳ τῷ χρόνῳ, καθ' ὃν εἶχεν ἡ τῶν* Καριαθιαριμιτῶν *πόλις τὴν κιβωτόν, ἐπ' εὐχὰς καὶ θυσίας τραπέντος τοῦ θεοῦ καὶ πολλὴν ἐμφανίζοντος τὴν περὶ αὐτὸν θρησκείαν καὶ φιλοτιμίαν, ὁ προφήτης* Σαμουῆλος *ἰδὼν αὐτῶν τὴν προθυμίαν, ὡς εὔκαιρον ὂν*[1] *πρὸς οὕτως ἔχοντας εἰπεῖν περὶ ἐλευθερίας καὶ τῶν ἀγαθῶν τῶν ἐν αὐτῇ, χρῆται λόγοις οἷς ᾤετο μάλιστα τὴν διάνοιαν αὐτῶν προσάξεσθαι καὶ*
20 *πείσειν. "ἄνδρες," γὰρ εἶπεν, "οἷς ἔτι νῦν βαρεῖς μὲν πολέμιοι* Παλαιστῖνοι, *θεὸς δ' εὐμενὴς ἄρχεται γίνεσθαι καὶ φίλος, οὐκ ἐπιθυμεῖν ἐλευθερίας δεῖ μόνον, ἀλλὰ καὶ ποιεῖν δι' ὧν ἂν ἔλθοι πρὸς ὑμᾶς, οὐδὲ βούλεσθαι μὲν ἀπηλλάχθαι δεσποτῶν ἐπιμένειν δὲ πράττοντας ἐξ ὧν οὗτοι διαμενοῦσιν.*
21 *ἀλλὰ γίνεσθε δίκαιοι, καὶ τὴν πονηρίαν ἐκβαλόντες τῶν ψυχῶν καὶ θεραπεύοντες αὐτάς,*[2] *ὅλαις ταῖς διανοίαις προστρέπεσθε*[3] *τὸ θεῖον καὶ τιμῶντες διατελεῖτε· ταῦτα γὰρ ὑμῖν ποιοῦσιν ἥξει τὰ ἀγαθά, δουλείας ἀπαλλαγὴ καὶ νίκη πολεμίων, ἃ λαβεῖν οὔθ' ὅπλοις οὔτε σωμάτων*

[1] conj. Niese.
[2] ex Lat. easque purgantes: *καὶ θεραπεύοντες* (*-σαντες* RO) *αὐτὴν* codd.: *καὶ θ. ἀρετὴν* Weill.
[3] Hudson: *προτρέπεσθε* codd.

[a] Bibl. " Eleazar his son."

they brought the ark into his house, as to a place beseeming God, being the abode of a righteous man. This man's sons [a] tended the ark and had the charge of it for twenty years; for it remained all that time at Kariathiareim, after spending four months [b] among the Philistines.

Samuel exhorts the Hebrews and musters them to Mizpah. 1 Sam. vii. 2.

(ii. 1) Now throughout the time when the city of Kariathiareim had the ark in its keeping, the whole people betook themselves to prayer and the offering of sacrifices to God, and displayed great zeal in serving Him. So the prophet Samuel, seeing their ardour and reckoning the occasion meet, while they were of this mind, to speak to them of liberty and the blessings that it brings, addressed them in words which he deemed most apt to win and to persuade their hearts. "Sirs," said he, "ye who yet to-day have grievous enemies in the Philistines, albeit God is beginning to be gracious to you and a friend, ye ought not to be content to yearn for liberty, but should do also the deeds whereby ye may attain it, nor merely long to be rid of your masters, while continuing so to act that they shall remain so. Nay, be ye righteous and, casting out wickedness [c] from your souls and purging them,[d] turn with all your hearts to the Deity and persevere in honouring Him. Do ye but so and there will come prosperity, deliverance from bondage and victory over your foes, blessings which are to be won neither by arms nor

[b] Bibl. "seven months" (1 Sam. vi. 1).

[c] Bibl. "put away the strange gods and the Ashtaroth from among you" (vii. 3).

[d] Text a little doubtful: it has been proposed, by a slight change, to read "and cultivating virtue" (ἀρετήν in place of αὐτάς).

ἀλκαῖς οὔτε πλήθει συμμάχων δυνατόν ἐστιν· οὐ γὰρ τούτοις ὁ θεὸς ὑπισχνεῖται παρέξειν αὐτά, τῷ δ' ἀγαθοὺς εἶναι καὶ δικαίους· ἐγγυητὴς δὲ
22 αὐτοῦ τῶν ὑποσχέσεων ἐγὼ γίνομαι." ταῦτ' εἰπόντος ἐπευφήμησε τὸ πλῆθος ἡσθὲν τῇ παραινέσει καὶ κατένευσεν αὐτὸ παρέξειν κεχαρισμένον τῷ θεῷ. συνάγει δ' αὐτοὺς ὁ Σαμουῆλος εἴς τινα πόλιν λεγομένην Μασφάτην· κατοπτευόμενον τοῦτο σημαίνει κατὰ τὴν τῶν Ἑβραίων γλῶτταν· ἐντεῦθεν ὑδρευσάμενοί τε σπένδουσι τῷ θεῷ καὶ διανηστεύσαντες ὅλην τὴν ἡμέραν ἐπ' εὐχὰς τρέπονται.
23 (2) Οὐ λανθάνουσι δὲ τοὺς Παλαιστίνους ἐκεῖ συναχθέντες, ἀλλὰ μαθόντες οὗτοι τὴν ἄθροισιν αὐτῶν, μεγάλῃ στρατιᾷ καὶ δυνάμει κατ' ἐλπίδα τοῦ μὴ προσδοκῶσι μηδὲ παρεσκευασμένοις ἐπι-
24 πεσεῖσθαι τοῖς Ἑβραίοις ἐπέρχονται. καταπλήττει δ' αὐτοὺς τοῦτο καὶ εἰς ταραχὴν ἄγει καὶ δέος, καὶ δραμόντες πρὸς Σαμουῆλον, ἀναπεπτωκέναι τὰς ψυχὰς αὐτῶν ὑπὸ φόβου καὶ τῆς προτέρας ἥττης ἔφασκον καὶ διὰ τοῦτ' ἠρεμεῖν, "ἵνα μὴ κινήσωμεν τὴν τῶν πολεμίων δύναμιν, σοῦ δ' ἀναγαγόντος ἡμᾶς ἐπ' εὐχὰς καὶ θυσίας καὶ ὅρκους γυμνοῖς καὶ ἀόπλοις ἐπεστράτευσαν οἱ πολέμιοι· ἐλπὶς οὖν ἡμῖν οὐκ ἄλλη σωτηρίας, ἢ μόνη ἡ παρὰ σοῦ καὶ τοῦ θεοῦ ἱκετευθέντος ὑπὸ

---

[a] Bibl. Mizpah (= "watch-tower," "outlook-point"), LXX Μασ(σ)ηφάθ: identified by some scholars with modern *Neby Samwil*, 5 miles N.W. of Jerusalem, by others with *Tell-en-Naṣbeh*, about 8 miles due N. of Jerusalem.

[b] Or "a conspicuous (place)."

[c] Gr. "with a great army and strength," an instance of hendiadys or the use of two words for one, which from

by personal prowess nor by a host of combatants; for it is not for these that God promises to bestow those blessings, but for lives of virtue and righteousness. And as surety for His promises, here I take my stand." These words were acclaimed by the people, who were delighted with the exhortation and vowed to render themselves acceptable unto God. Samuel then vii. 5.
gathered them to a city called Masphate,[a] which in the Hebrew tongue signifies "espied."[b] There, having drawn water, they made libations to God and, fasting throughout the day, gave themselves unto prayer.

Hebrew victory over the Philistines. 1 Sam. vii. 7.

(2) However their gathering at this spot did not pass unperceived by the Philistines, who, having learnt of their mustering, advanced upon the Hebrews with an army mighty in strength,[c] hoping to surprise them while off their guard and unprepared. Dismayed by this attack and plunged into confusion and alarm, the Hebrews, hastening to Samuel, declared that their courage had flagged through fear and the memory of their former defeat. "That," said they, "was why we sat still, in order not to stir up the enemy's forces. But, when thou hadst brought us up hither for prayers, sacrifices and oaths, now the enemy are upon us while we are naked and unarmed. Other hope of salvation therefore have we none, save from thee alone and from God, should He be entreated

this point onward characterizes this book: *cf.* § 24 *ταραχὴ καὶ δέος, γυμνοῖς καὶ ἀόπλοις*, § 25 *νίκη καὶ κράτος* etc. The preference for the double word distinguishes the writer of this portion—whether Josephus himself or another assistant—from the "Sophoclean" assistant who has a partiality for grouping in threes (*e.g.* § 21 *τὰ ἀγαθά, δουλείας ἀπαλλαγὴ καὶ νίκη . . . οὔθ' ὅπλοις οὔτε σωμάτων ἀλκαῖς οὔτε πλήθει*). See Vol. IV. Introduction.

25 σοῦ παρασχεῖν ἡμῖν διαφυγεῖν Παλαιστίνους." ὁ
δὲ θαρρεῖν τε προτρέπεται καὶ βοηθήσειν αὐτοῖς
τὸν θεὸν ἐπαγγέλλεται, καὶ λαβὼν ἄρνα γαλαθηνὸν
ὑπὲρ τῶν ὄχλων θύει καὶ παρακαλεῖ τὸν θεὸν
ὑπερσχεῖν αὐτῶν τὴν δεξιὰν ἐν τῇ πρὸς Παλαιστίνους μάχῃ καὶ μὴ περιϊδεῖν αὐτοὺς δεύτερον δυσ-
τυχήσαντας. ἐπήκοος δὲ γίνεται τῶν εὐχῶν ὁ
θεὸς καὶ προσδεξάμενος εὐμενεῖ καὶ συμμάχῳ τῇ
διανοίᾳ τὴν θυσίαν ἐπινεύει νίκην αὐτοῖς καὶ
26 κράτος. ἔτι δ' ἐπὶ τοῦ βωμοῦ τὴν θυσίαν ἔχοντος
τοῦ θεοῦ καὶ μήπω πᾶσαν διὰ τῆς ἱερᾶς φλογὸς
ἀπειληφότος, προῆλθεν ἐκ τοῦ στρατοπέδου ἡ τῶν
πολεμίων δύναμις καὶ παρατάσσεται εἰς μάχην,
ἐπ' ἐλπίδι μὲν νίκης, ὡς ἀπειλημμένων ἐν ἀπορίᾳ
τῶν Ἰουδαίων μήτε ὅπλα ἐχόντων μήτε ὡς ἐπὶ
μάχῃ ἐκεῖσε ἀπηντηκότων, περιπίπτουσι δὲ οἷς
27 οὐδ' εἰ προύλεγέ τις ῥᾳδίως ἐπείσθησαν. πρῶτον
μὲν γὰρ αὐτοὺς ὁ θεὸς κλονεῖ σεισμῷ καὶ τὴν
γῆν αὐτοῖς ὑπότρομον καὶ σφαλερὰν κινήσας τίθησιν, ὡς σαλευομένης τε τὰς βάσεις ὑποφέρεσθαι
καὶ διϊσταμένης εἰς ἔνια τῶν χασμάτων καταφέρε-
σθαι, ἔπειτα βρονταῖς καταψοφήσας καὶ διαπύροις
ἀστραπαῖς ὡς καταφλέξων αὐτῶν τὰς ὄψεις
περιλάμψας καὶ τῶν χειρῶν ἐκκροτήσας τὰ ὅπλα,
28 γυμνοὺς εἰς φυγὴν ἀπέστρεψεν. ἐπεξέρχεται δὲ
Σαμουῆλος μετὰ τῆς πληθύος καὶ πολλοὺς κατα-
σφάξας κατακολουθεῖ μέχρι Κορραίων τόπου τινὸς
οὕτω λεγομένου, καὶ καταπήξας ἐκεῖ λίθον ὥσπερ

[a] Gr. "God still had the sacrifice upon the altar" etc.; a Semitic form of expression (sacrifice being conceived as the food of the Deity) here imported into the Biblical text, which has merely "And as Samuel was offering up the burnt-offering."

by thee to afford us escape from the Philistines." But Samuel bade them be of good cheer and promised that God would succour them. Then, taking a sucking lamb, he sacrificed it on behalf of the throng and besought God to extend His right hand over them in the battle with the Philistines and not suffer them to undergo a second reverse. And God hearkened to his prayers and, accepting the sacrifice in gracious and befriending spirit, gave them assurance of victory
and triumph. God's victim was still upon the altar vii. 10
and He had not yet wholly consumed it through the sacred flame,[a] when the enemy's forces issued from their camp and drew up for battle, expectant of victory, thinking to have caught the Jews [b] in a hopeless plight, seeing that they were without arms and had assembled there with no intention of battle. But the Philistines encountered what, had one foretold it, they would scarcely have believed. For, first, God vexed them with earthquake,[c] rocking and making tremulous and treacherous the ground beneath them, so that from its reeling their footsteps staggered and at its parting they were engulfed in sundry of its chasms. Next He deafened them with thunderclaps, made fiery lightning to flash around them as it were to burn out their eyes, struck the arms from their hands, and so turned them weaponless to flight. But Samuel now rushed upon them with his people and, having massacred many, pursued them to a certain place called Korraea [d]; and there he set up

[b] A recurrent anachronism for "Hebrews" or "Israelites" (§§ 30, 40 etc.).

[c] Scripture mentions only "a great thunder."

[d] Bibl. Beth-car, LXX Βαιθχόρ: possibly modern *'Ain Karim*, some 5 miles S. of Mizpah, and due W. of Jerusalem.

ὅρον τῆς νίκης καὶ τῆς φυγῆς τῶν πολεμίων, ἰσχυρὸν αὐτὸν προσαγορεύει, σύμβολον τῆς παρὰ τοῦ θεοῦ γενομένης αὐτοῖς κατὰ τῶν ἐχθρῶν ἰσχύος.

29 (3) Οἱ δὲ μετ' ἐκείνην τὴν πληγὴν οὐκέτ' ἐστράτευσαν[1] ἐπὶ τοὺς Ἰσραηλίτας, ἀλλ' ὑπὸ δέους καὶ μνήμης τῶν συμβεβηκότων ἡσύχαζον· ὃ δ' ἦν πάλαι θάρσος τοῖς Παλαιστίνοις ἐπὶ τοὺς Ἑβραί-
30 ους, τοῦτ' ἐκείνων μετὰ τὴν νίκην ἐγένετο. καὶ Σαμουῆλος στρατεύσας ἐπ' αὐτοὺς ἀναιρεῖ πολλοὺς καὶ τὰ φρονήματ' αὐτῶν εἰς τὸ παντελὲς ταπεινοῖ καὶ τὴν χώραν ἀφαιρεῖται, ἣν τῶν Ἰουδαίων ἀπετέμοντο πρότερον κρατήσαντες τῇ μάχῃ· αὕτη δ' ἦν μέχρι πόλεως Ἀκκάρων ἀπὸ τῶν τῆς Γίττης ὅρων ἐκτεταμένη. ἦν δὲ κατ' ἐκεῖνον τὸν καιρὸν φίλια τοῖς Ἰσραηλίταις τὰ ὑπολειπόμενα τῶν Χαναναίων.

31 (iii. 1) Ὁ δὲ προφήτης Σαμουῆλος διακοσμήσας τὸν λαὸν καὶ πόλιν ἑκάστοις[2] ἀποδοὺς εἰς ταύτην ἐκέλευσε συνερχομένοις περὶ τῶν πρὸς ἀλλήλους κρίνεσθαι διαφορῶν, αὐτὸς δὲ δι' ἔτους[3] ἐπερχόμενος τὰς πόλεις ἐδίκαζεν αὐτοῖς καὶ πολλὴν
32 ἐβράβευεν εὐνομίαν ἐπὶ χρόνον πολύν. (2) ἔπειθ' ὑπὸ γήρως βαρυνόμενος καὶ τὰ συνήθη πράττειν ἐμποδιζόμενος, τοῖς υἱοῖς τὴν ἀρχὴν καὶ τὴν προ-

[1] οὐκέτ' ἐστράτ. Niese: οὐκ ἐπεστράτευσαν codd.
[2] conj.: αὐτοῖς codd.
[3] δι' ἔτους RO: δὶς τοῦ ἔτους rell., Lat., E (vid.).

[a] Bibl. Eben-'ezer (=" stone of help "), LXX Ἀβενέζερ (adding the translation λίθος τοῦ βοηθοῦ, " stone of the helper "); in place of *'ezer* Josephus probably read *'oz* (" strength ").

a stone as landmark of the victory and of the flight of the foe, and called it "Strong (stone)," [a] in token of the strength which God had lent them against their enemies.

Samuel recovers conquered territory. 1 Sam. vii. 13.

(3) Those enemies, after that discomfiture, invaded the Israelites no more, but through fear and a remembrance of what had befallen them remained still; and that confidence which of old had animated the Philistines against the Hebrews passed after this victory to their opponents. And so Samuel, taking the field against them, slew multitudes, utterly humbled their pride, and took from them the country which they had erstwhile torn from the Jews after their victory in battle, to wit the region extending from the borders of Gitta to the city of Akkaron.[b] And at that time there was amity between the Israelites and the remnant of the Canaanites.[c]

Samuel as judge. 1 Sam. vii. 15.

(iii. 1) Moreover, the prophet Samuel, having redivided the people and assigned a city to each group,[d] bade them resort thither for trial of the differences that arose between them. He himself going annually [e] on circuit to these cities judged their causes and so continued for long to administer perfect justice.

Degeneracy of Samuel's sons.

(2) Thereafter, oppressed with age and impeded from following his wonted course, he consigned the

[b] *i.e.* "from Ekron even unto Gath" (1 Sam. vii. 14).

[c] Bibl. "And there was peace between Israel and the Amorites."

[d] With slight emendation of the Greek, which reads "a city to them." Scripture mentions three cities—Bethel, Gilgal, Mizpah—which Samuel annually visited from his home at Ramah.

[e] Another reading is "*twice* a year." M. Weill, adopting this text, suggests that it is "a Haggadic deduction from the repetition of the word *shanah* (year) in the Hebrew (LXX *κατ' ἐνιαυτὸν ἐνιαυτόν*)."

στασίαν τοῦ ἔθνους[1] παραδίδωσιν, ὧν ὁ μὲν πρεσβύτερος Ἰοῦλος[2] προσηγορεύετο, τῷ δὲ νεωτέρῳ Ἀβίρα[3] ὄνομα ἦν. προσέταξε δὲ τὸν μὲν ἐν Βεθήλῳ πόλει καθεζόμενον κρίνειν, τὸν δ᾽ ἕτερον ἐν Βερσουβεὶ[4] μερίσας τὸν ὑπακουσόμενον ἑκατέρῳ
33 λαόν. ἐγένοντο δὲ σαφὲς οὗτοι παράδειγμα καὶ τεκμήριον τοῦ μὴ τὸν τρόπον ὁμοίους τοῖς φύσασι γίνεσθαί τινας, ἀλλὰ τάχα μὲν χρηστοὺς καὶ μετρίους ἐκ πονηρῶν, τότε μέν γε φαύλους ἐξ
34 ἀγαθῶν παρέσχον αὑτοὺς γενομένους· τῶν γὰρ τοῦ πατρὸς ἐπιτηδευμάτων ἐκτραπόμενοι καὶ τὴν ἐναντίαν ὁδὸν ἀπελθόντες δώρων καὶ λημμάτων αἰσχρῶν καθυφίεντο τὸ δίκαιον, καὶ τὰς κρίσεις οὐ πρὸς τὴν ἀλήθειαν ἀλλὰ πρὸς τὸ κέρδος ποιούμενοι καὶ πρὸς τρυφὴν καὶ πρὸς διαίτας πολυτελεῖς ἀπονενευκότες, πρῶτον μὲν ὑπεναντία ταῦτα ἔπρασσον τῷ θεῷ, δεύτερον δὲ τῷ προφήτῃ πατρὶ δ᾽ ἑαυτῶν, ὃς πολλὴν καὶ τοῦ τὸ πλῆθος εἶναι δίκαιον σπουδὴν εἰσεφέρετο καὶ πρόνοιαν.

35 (3) Ὁ δὲ λαὸς ἐξυβριζόντων εἰς τὴν προτέραν κατάστασιν καὶ πολιτείαν τῶν τοῦ προφήτου παίδων, χαλεπῶς τε τοῖς πραττομένοις ἔφερε καὶ πρὸς αὐτὸν συντρέχουσι, διέτριβε δ᾽ ἐν Ἀρμαθᾶ πόλει, καὶ τάς τε τῶν υἱῶν παρανομίας ἔλεγον καὶ ὅτι γηραιὸς ὢν αὐτὸς ἤδη καὶ παρειμένος ὑπὸ τοῦ χρόνου τῶν πραγμάτων οὐκέτι τὸν αὐτὸν προ-
36 εστάναι δύναται τρόπον· ἐδέοντό τε καὶ ἱκέτευον ἀποδεῖξαί τινα αὐτῶν βασιλέα, ὃς ἄρξει τοῦ ἔθνους καὶ τιμωρήσεται Παλαιστίνους ὀφείλοντας ἔτ᾽ αὐ-

[1] RO: πλήθους rell. [2] RO: Οὔηλος vel Ἰώηλος (Ἰωήλ) rell.
[3] M(SP): Ἐβίᾳ RO: Ἀβίας E Lat.: Ἀβία Zon.
[4] Βαρσουβαὶ MSP: Bersabe Lat.

government and direction of the nation to his sons, of whom the elder was called Iulus [a] and the younger bore the name of Abira [b]; and he charged the one to sit in judgement at the city of Bethel and the other at Bersubei,[c] apportioning the people that should come under the jurisdiction of each. Howbeit these youths furnished a signal illustration and proof that sons need not be like in character to their sires, nay, that maybe good, honest folk are sprung from knaves, while the offspring of virtuous parents have proved depraved. For they, turning from their father's ways and taking the contrary road, betrayed justice for bribes and filthy lucre, pronounced judgement with regard not to the truth but to their own profit, and abandoned themselves to luxury and sumptuous fare, thereby acting in defiance first of God and secondly of the prophet, their own father, who was devoting much zeal and care to instilling even into the multitude the idea of righteousness.

1 Sam. viii. 1.

(3) But the people,[d] seeing these outrages upon their former constitution and government committed by the prophet's sons, brooked their proceedings ill and together sped to Samuel, then living in the city of Armatha.[e] They told him of his sons' iniquities and added that, old as he now was and enfeebled by age, he could no longer himself direct affairs as aforetime; they therefore begged and implored him to appoint from among them a king, to rule the nation and to wreak vengeance on the Philistines,

The people's demand for a king. 1 Sam. viii. 4.

[a] Bibl. Joel.

[b] Bibl. Abijah (LXX Ἀβιά, with *v.l.* Ἀβειρά as in Josephus).

[c] Bibl. "They were judges in Beer-sheba" (Bethel not being mentioned).

[d] Bibl. "all the elders of Israel."

[e] Ramah.

τοῖς δίκας τῶν προτέρων ἀδικημάτων. ἐλύπησαν δὲ σφόδρα τὸν Σαμουῆλον οἱ λόγοι διὰ τὴν σύμφυτον δικαιοσύνην καὶ τὸ πρὸς τοὺς βασιλέας μῖσος· ἥττητο γὰρ δεινῶς τῆς ἀριστοκρατίας ὡς θείας καὶ μακαρίους ποιούσης τοὺς χρωμένους αὐτῆς τῇ
37 πολιτείᾳ. ὑπὸ δὲ φροντίδος καὶ βασάνου τῆς ἐπὶ τοῖς εἰρημένοις οὔτε τροφῆς ἐμνημόνευσεν οὔτε ὕπνου, δι' ὅλης δὲ τῆς νυκτὸς στρέφων τὰς περὶ τῶν πραγμάτων ἐννοίας διεκαρτέρει.

38 (4) Ἔχοντι δὲ οὕτως ἐμφανίζεται τὸ θεῖον καὶ παραμυθεῖται μὴ δυσφορεῖν ἐφ' οἷς ἠξίωσε τὸ πλῆθος, ὡς οὐκ ἐκεῖνον ὑπερηφανήσαντας ἀλλ' ἑαυτόν,[1] ἵνα[2] μὴ βασιλεύσῃ[3] μόνος· ταῦτα δὲ ἀφ' ἧς ἡμέρας ἐξήγαγεν αὐτοὺς ἀπ' Αἰγύπτου μηχανᾶσθαι τὰ ἔργα· λήψεσθαι μέντοι γε οὐκ εἰς μακρὰν μετάνοιαν αὐτοὺς ἐπίπονον, "ὑφ' ἧς οὐδὲν μὲν ἀγένητον ἔσται τῶν ἐσομένων, ἐλεγχθήσονται δὲ καταφρονήσαντες καὶ βουλὰς οὐκ εὐχαρίστους πρὸς
39 ἐμὲ καὶ τὴν σὴν προφητείαν λαβόντες. κελεύω δή σε[4] χειροτονεῖν αὐτοῖς ὃν ἂν ἐγὼ[5] προείπω βασιλέα προδηλώσαντα ποταπῶν τε πειραθήσονται βασιλευόμενοι κακῶν καὶ διαμαρτυράμενον ἐφ' οἵαν σπεύδουσι μεταβολήν."

40 (5) Ταῦτ' ἀκούσας Σαμουῆλος ἅμα ἕῳ συγκαλέσας τοὺς Ἰουδαίους ἀποδείξειν αὐτοῖς βασιλέα ὡμολόγησεν, ἔφη δὲ δεῖν πρῶτον μὲν αὐτοῖς ἐκδιηγήσασθαι τὰ παρὰ τῶν βασιλέων ἐσόμενα καὶ ὅσοις συνενεχθήσονται κακοῖς· "γινώσκετε γὰρ

[1] ἢ αὐτὸν SP: εἰς αὐτὸν E: αὐτὸν M.
[2] εἰ RO.
[3] βασιλεύσει R: βασιλεὺς ᾖ SP.
[4] σοι SE.
[5] +σοι SPE.

who yet owed them an accounting for past injuries. These words sorely grieved Samuel by reason of his innate righteousness and his hatred of kings; for he was keenly enamoured of aristocratic government, accounting it divine and productive of bliss to those who adopted it. So, from the anxiety and the torment which these speeches caused him, he had no thought for food or sleep, but passed the whole night turning over these matters in his mind.[a]

God charges Samuel to elect a king. 1 Sam. viii. 7.

(4) Such was his state when the Deity appeared and consoled him, telling him not to take these demands of the multitude amiss, since it was not him whom they had spurned, but God Himself, not wishing Him to reign alone; these deeds, moreover, they had (He said) been devising from the day when He had brought them forth from Egypt; howbeit they would ere long be seized with painful remorse, "a remorse by which nought will be undone of that which is to be, but which will convict them of contempt and of adopting a course ungrateful toward Me and to thy prophetic office. I therefore now charge thee to elect for them whomsoever I shall name as king, after forewarning them what ills they will suffer under kingly rule and solemnly testifying into what a change they are rushing."

Samuel warns the people of the evils of monarchy. 1 Sam. viii. 10.

(5) Having heard these words, Samuel at daybreak called the Jews[b] together and consented to appoint them a king, but he said that he must first set forth to them what would befall them at the hands of their kings and how many ills they would encounter. "For ye must know," said he, "that first they will

[a] Amplification (*cf. A.* ii. 171): Scripture says merely "And Samuel prayed unto the Lord" (1 Sam. viii. 6).

[b] See § 26 note.

ὅτι πρῶτον μὲν ὑμῶν ἀποσπάσουσι τὰ τέκνα καὶ τὰ μὲν αὐτῶν ἁρματηλάτας εἶναι κελεύσουσι, τοὺς δ' ἱππεῖς καὶ σωματοφύλακας, δρομεῖς δὲ ἄλλους καὶ χιλιάρχους καὶ ἑκατοντάρχους, ποιήσουσι δὲ καὶ τεχνίτας ὁπλοποιοὺς καὶ ἁρματοποιοὺς καὶ ὀργάνων τέκτονας γεωργούς τε καὶ τῶν ἰδίων
41 ἀγρῶν ἐπιμελητὰς καὶ σκαπανεῖς ἀμπέλων, καὶ οὐδέν ἐστιν ὃ μὴ κελευόμενοι ποιήσουσιν ἀνδραπόδων ἀργυρωνήτων τρόπον· καὶ τὰς θυγατέρας δ' ὑμῶν μυρεψοὺς ἀποφανοῦσι καὶ ὀψοποιοὺς καὶ σιτοποιούς, καὶ πᾶν ἔργον ὃ θεραπαινίδες ἐξ ἀνάγκης πληγὰς φοβούμεναι καὶ βασάνους ὑπηρετήσουσι. κτῆσιν δὲ τὴν ὑμετέραν ἀφαιρήσονται καὶ ταύτην εὐνούχοις καὶ σωματοφύλαξι δωρήσονται καὶ βοσκημάτων ἀγέλας τοῖς αὐτῶν προσνεμοῦσι.
42 συνελόντι δ' εἰπεῖν, δουλεύσετε μετὰ πάντων τῶν ὑμετέρων τῷ βασιλεῖ σὺν[1] τοῖς αὐτῶν οἰκέταις· ὃς γενόμενος[2] μνήμην ὑμῖν τῶνδε τῶν λόγων γεννήσει καὶ τῷ[3] πάσχειν αὐτὰ μεταγινώσκοντας ἱκετεῦσαι τὸν θεὸν ἐλεῆσαί τε ὑμᾶς καὶ δωρήσασθαι ταχεῖαν ἀπαλλαγὴν τῶν βασιλέων· ὁ δ' οὐ προσδέξεται τὰς δεήσεις, ἀλλὰ παραπέμψας ἐάσει δίκην ὑποσχεῖν ὑμᾶς τῆς αὐτῶν κακοβουλίας."

43 (6) Ἦν δ' ἄρα καὶ πρὸς τὰς προρρήσεις τῶν συμβησομένων ἀνόητον τὸ πλῆθος καὶ δύσκολον ἐξελεῖν τῆς διανοίας κρίσιν ἤδη παρὰ τῷ λογισμῷ καθιδρυμένην· οὐδὲ γὰρ ἐπεστράφησαν οὐδ' ἐμέλη-

[1] καὶ MSP: om. Lat.
[2] ὃς γενόμενος] ἴσοι γενόμενοι M Lat. (+ καὶ Lat. ut vid.).
[3] τὸ ROSP.

[a] "Hundreds" as in LXX (1 Sam. viii. 12), whereas the Heb. has "fifties."

carry off your children and will order some of them to be charioteers, others horsemen and bodyguards, others runners or captains of thousands or of hundreds[a]; they will make of them craftsmen also, makers of armour, of chariots and of instruments; husbandmen too, tillers of their estates, diggers of their vineyards; nay, there is nothing which your sons will not do at their behest, after the manner of slaves bought at a price. Of your daughters also they will make perfumers, cooks and bakers, and subject them to every menial task which handmaids must perforce perform from fear of stripes and tortures. They will moreover rob you of your possessions and bestow them upon eunuchs and bodyguards, and confer your herds of cattle upon their retainers. In a word, ye with all yours will be bondservants to the king along with your own domestics; and he, when he is come,[b] will beget in you a memory of these words of mine and (cause you) through these sufferings to repent and to implore God to take pity on you and to grant you speedy deliverance from your kings. Howbeit He will not hearken to your prayers, but will disregard them and suffer you to pay the penalty for your own perversity."

He yields to their insistence. 1 Sam. viii. 19.

(6) Yet even to these predictions of what was to come the multitude was deaf and obstinately refused[c] to eradicate from their minds a resolution now deep-seated in their calculations. Nay, they would not be turned, nor recked they aught of the words of Samuel,

[b] Text doubtful. According to another reading, ". . . to the king, being made equal to your own domestics; and your suffering will beget, etc., . . . and (cause you) to repent, etc."

[c] Or "and it was difficult."

σεν αὐτοῖς τῶν Σαμουήλου λόγων, ἀλλ' ἐνέκειντο λιπαρῶς καὶ χειροτονεῖν ἠξίουν ἤδη τὸν βασιλέα
44 καὶ μὴ φροντίζειν τῶν ἐσομένων· ἐπὶ γὰρ τιμωρίᾳ τῶν ἐχθρῶν ἀνάγκη τὸν πολεμήσοντα σὺν αὐτοῖς ἔχειν, καὶ οὐδὲν ἄτοπον εἶναι τῶν πλησιοχώρων βασιλευομένων τὴν αὐτὴν ἔχειν αὐτοὺς πολιτείαν. ὁρῶν δ' αὐτοὺς μηδ' ὑπὸ τῶν προειρημένων ἀπεστραμμένους ὁ Σαμουῆλος, ἀλλ' ἐπιμένοντας "νῦν μέν," εἶπεν, "ἄπιτε πρὸς αὐτοὺς ἕκαστος, μεταπέμψομαι δὲ ὑμᾶς εἰς δέον, ὅταν μάθω παρὰ τοῦ θεοῦ τίνα δίδωσιν ὑμῖν βασιλέα."
45 (iv. 1) Ἦν δέ τις ἐκ τῆς Βενιαμίτιδος φυλῆς ἀνὴρ εὖ γεγονὼς καὶ ἀγαθὸς τὸ ἦθος, Κεὶς ὄνομα· τούτῳ παῖς ὑπῆρχεν, ἦν δὲ νεανίας τὴν μορφὴν ἄριστος καὶ τὸ σῶμα μέγας, τό τε φρόνημα καὶ τὴν
46 διάνοιαν ἀμείνων τῶν βλεπομένων· Σαοῦλον αὐτὸν ἐκάλουν. οὗτος ὁ Κείς, ὄνων αὐτῷ ἐκ τῆς νομῆς καλῶν ἀποπλανηθεισῶν, ἥδετο γὰρ αὐταῖς ὡς οὐκ ἄλλῳ τινὶ τῶν κτημάτων, τὸν υἱὸν μεθ' ἑνὸς θεράποντος ἐπὶ ζήτησιν τῶν κτηνῶν ἐξέπεμψεν· ὁ δ' ἐπεὶ τὴν πάτριον περιῆλθε φυλὴν ἐξερευνῶν τὰς ὄνους[1] εἰς τὰς ἄλλας ἀφίκετο, οὐδ' ἐν ταύταις δ' ἐπιτυχὼν ἀπιέναι[2] διεγνώκει, μὴ ποιήσῃ περὶ
47 αὐτοῦ τῷ πατρὶ λοιπὸν φροντίδα. τοῦ δ' ἑπομένου θεράποντος ὡς ἐγένοντο κατὰ τὴν Ἀρμαθὰ πόλιν εἶναι προφήτην ἐν αὐτῇ φήσαντος ἀληθῆ καὶ πρὸς αὐτὸν βαδίζειν συμβουλεύσαντος, γνώσεσθαι γὰρ παρ' αὐτοῦ τὸ περὶ τῶν ὄνων τέλος, οὐθὲν ἔχειν

[1] ἐξερ. τ. ὄνους om. RO. [2] ἀνιέναι conj. Boysen.

[a] Gr. Keis (with LXX): Heb. Kish.

but pressed him importunately and insisted that he should elect their king forthwith, and take no thought for the future; since for the punishment of their foes they must needs have one to fight their battles with them, and there could be nothing strange, when their neighbours were ruled by kings, in their having the same form of government. So Samuel, seeing that even by his predictions they were not turned from their intent but persisted therein, said, "For the present, depart ye each to his home: I will summon you at need, when I shall have learnt from God whom He gives you for your king."

SAUL, in quest of his father's asses, encounters Samuel. 1 Sam. ix. 1.

(iv. 1) Now there was a man of the tribe of Benjamin of good birth and virtuous character, named Kis.[a] He had a son, a youth of a noble presence and tall of stature, and withal gifted with a spirit and mind surpassing these outward advantages; they called him Saul. This Kis, one day when some fine asses of his had strayed from the pastures, in which he took more delight than in all that he possessed, sent off his son with one servant in search of the beasts. And he, after going all over his father's tribe in quest of the asses, passed to the other tribes and failing there also to find them, resolved to return, lest he should now cause his father anxiety concerning himself. But when they were come over against the city of Armatha,[b] the servant who accompanied him told him that there was there a true prophet, and counselled that they should go to him, since they would learn from him what had become of the asses. Whereto

[b] Ramah (v. 342 note, vi. 35): bibl. "when they were come to the land of Zuph" (1 Sam. ix. 5), naming the district in Ephraim wherein Ramah lay, *cf.* 1 Sam. i. 1 "a certain man of Ramathaim-zophim."

πορευθέντας εἶπεν ἀντὶ τῆς προφητείας ὃ παρά-
σχωσιν αὐτῷ· κεκενῶσθαι γὰρ ἤδη τῶν ἐφοδίων.
48 τοῦ δ' οἰκέτου τέταρτον αὐτῷ παρεῖναι σίκλου
φήσαντος καὶ τοῦτο δώσειν, ὑπὸ γὰρ ἀγνοίας τοῦ
μὴ λαμβάνειν τὸν προφήτην μισθὸν ἐπλανῶντο,
παραγίνονται καὶ πρὸς ταῖς πύλαις παρατυγχά-
νοντες παρθένοις ἐφ' ὕδωρ βαδιζούσαις ἐρωτῶσιν
αὐτὰς τοῦ προφήτου τὴν οἰκίαν. αἱ δὲ σημαίνουσι
καὶ σπεύδειν παρεκελεύσαντο πρὶν αὐτὸν εἰς τὸ
δεῖπνον κατακλιθῆναι· πολλοὺς γὰρ ἑστιᾶν καὶ
49 προκατακλίνεσθαι τῶν κεκλημένων. ὁ δὲ Σαμουῆλος διὰ τοῦτο πολλοὺς ἐπὶ τὴν ἑστίαν τότε
συνήγαγε· δεομένῳ γὰρ κατὰ πᾶσαν ἡμέραν αὐτῷ
τοῦ θεοῦ προειπεῖν τίνα ποιήσει βασιλέα τῇ
παρελθούσῃ τοῦτον μηνύσαντος, πέμψειν γὰρ
αὐτός τινα νεανίσκον ἐκ τῆς Βενιαμίτιδος φυλῆς
κατὰ τήνδε τὴν ὥραν, αὐτὸς μὲν ἐπὶ τοῦ δώ-
ματος καθεζόμενος ἐξεδέχετο τὸν καιρὸν γενέσθαι,
πληρωθέντος δ' αὐτοῦ καταβὰς ἐπὶ τὸ δεῖπνον
50 ἐπορεύετο. συναντᾷ δὲ τῷ Σαούλῳ καὶ ὁ θεὸς
αὐτῷ σημαίνει τοῦτον εἶναι τὸν ἄρξειν μέλλοντα.
Σαοῦλος δὲ πρόσεισι τῷ Σαμουήλῳ καὶ προσαγορεύσας ἐδεῖτο μηνύειν τὴν οἰκίαν τοῦ προφήτου·
51 ξένος γὰρ ὢν ἀγνοεῖν ἔφασκε. τοῦ δὲ Σαμουήλου
αὐτὸν εἶναι φράσαντος καὶ ἄγοντος ἐπὶ τὸ δεῖπνον,
ὡς τῶν ὄνων ἐφ' ὧν τὴν ζήτησιν ἐκπεμφθείη
σεσωσμένων τά τε πάντα ἀγαθὰ ἔχειν αὐτῷ
κεκυρωμένα, ὑποτυχών[1] "ἀλλ' ἥττων," εἶπεν,
"ἐγώ, δέσποτα, ταύτης τῆς ἐλπίδος καὶ φυλῆς

[1] Holwerda: προστυχών codd.

[a] Scripture does not say that Samuel accepted no reward.

Saul replied that, if they went to the prophet, they had nothing to offer him in return for his oracle, since their supplies were by now exhausted. However, the servant said that he had a quarter of a shekel and would present that—for their ignorance that the prophet accepted no reward misled them [a]—and so they went and, meeting at the gates maidens going to draw water, they asked them which was the prophet's house. And these pointed it out and bade them make speed ere he sat down to supper, for he was entertaining many and would take his seat before his invited guests.[b] Now the reason why Samuel had at that hour assembled so many to the feast was this: he had been praying daily to God to reveal to him whom He would make king and, on the day before, God had announced him, saying that He would Himself send him a young man of the tribe of Benjamin at that selfsame hour. So, seated upon the housetop, Samuel was awaiting the coming of the time, and when the hour was ripe he descended to go to the supper. And he met Saul, and God revealed to him that this was he that was to rule. But Saul approached Samuel and greeting him prayed him to show him the prophet's house, for he said that as a stranger he was ignorant of it. Samuel then told him that he was the prophet and led him to the supper, assuring him that the asses in quest of which he had been sent were safe and that for him (Saul) were destined all good things [c]; whereat Saul broke in, "Nay, master, I am too lowly to hope for this, I come of a

[b] According to Scripture, Samuel was not the host, but attended the feast as one in charge of public sacrifice.

[c] The text is a little awkward. but the meaning is clear. *Cf.* 1 Sam. ix. 20, "To whom belong all the desirable things of Israel, if not to thee (Saul) and thy father's house?"

μικροτέρας ἢ βασιλέας ποιεῖν καὶ πατριὰς ταπεινοτέρας τῶν ἄλλων πατριῶν. σὺ δὲ παίζεις καὶ γέλωτά με τίθεσαι περὶ μειζόνων ἢ κατὰ τὴν
52 ἐμὴν χώραν[1] διαλεγόμενος." ὁ δὲ προφήτης ἀγαγὼν αὐτὸν ἐπὶ τὴν ἑστίασιν κατακλίνει καὶ τὸν ἀκόλουθον ἐπάνω τῶν κεκλημένων· οὗτοι δ' ἦσαν ἑβδομήκοντα τὸν ἀριθμόν· προστάσσει δὲ τοῖς διακόνοις παραθεῖναι τῷ Σαούλῳ μερίδα βασιλικήν. ἐπεὶ δὲ κοίτης ὥρα προσῆγεν, οἱ μὲν ἀναστάντες ἀνέλυον πρὸς αὑτοὺς ἕκαστοι, ὁ δὲ Σαοῦλος παρὰ τῷ προφήτῃ σὺν τῷ θεράποντι κατεκοιμήθη.

53 (2) Ἅμα δὲ ἡμέρᾳ Σαμουῆλος ἀναστήσας αὐτὸν ἐκ τῆς κοίτης προύπεμπε καὶ γενόμενος ἔξω τῆς πόλεως ἐκέλευσε τὸν μὲν θεράποντα ποιῆσαι προελθεῖν, ὑπολείπεσθαι δὲ αὐτόν· ἔχειν γὰρ αὐτῷ
54 τι φράσαι μηδενὸς ἄλλου παρόντος.[2] καὶ ὁ μὲν Σαοῦλος ἀποπέμπεται τὸν ἀκόλουθον, λαβὼν δ' ὁ προφήτης τὸ ἀγγεῖον,[3] ἔλαιον καταχεῖ τῆς τοῦ νεανίσκου κεφαλῆς καὶ κατασπασάμενος "ἴσθι," φησί, "βασιλεὺς ὑπὸ τοῦ θεοῦ κεχειροτονημένος ἐπί τε Παλαιστίνους καὶ τὴν ὑπὲρ Ἑβραίων ἄμυναν. τούτων δὲ ἔσται σοι σημεῖον ὅ σε
55 βούλομαι προγινώσκειν· ὅταν ἀπέλθῃς ἐντεῦθεν καταλήψῃ τρεῖς ἀνθρώπους ἐν τῇ ὁδῷ προσκυνῆσαι τῷ θεῷ πορευομένους εἰς Βέθηλα, ὧν τὸν μὲν πρῶτον τρεῖς ἄρτους ὄψει κομίζοντα, τὸν δὲ δεύτερον ἔριφον, ὁ τρίτος δὲ ἀσκὸν οἴνου φέρων

[1] χρείαν MSP. [2] μηδενὸς παρόντος om. RO.
[3] ROE Lat. (cf. 1 Sam. x. 1, LXX τὸν φακὸν τοῦ ἐλαίου): ἅγιον rell.

tribe too little to create kings, and of a family of humbler sort than all others. Thou but mockest and makest sport of me in speaking of matters too high for my station." Howbeit the prophet led him to the banquet-chamber, gave him and his attendant places above the invited guests, who were seventy [a] in number, and charged his henchmen to set a royal portion before Saul. Then, when bedtime came, the rest arose and departed each to his own home, but Saul and his servant slept at the prophet's house.[b]

(2) At break of day Samuel roused him from his bed, escorted him on his way, and, when outside the town, bade him cause his servant to go on before and to remain behind himself, for he had somewhat to tell him privately. So Saul dismissed his companion, and the prophet, taking his vial, poured oil upon the young man's head and kissed him and said: "Know that thou art king, elected of God to combat the Philistines and to defend the Hebrews. And of this there shall be unto thee a sign which I would have thee learn beforehand. When thou art departed hence, thou shalt find on thy road three men [c] going to worship God at Bethel; the first thou shalt see carrying three loaves, the second a kid,[d] and the third

Samuel anoints Saul. 1 Sam. ix. 26.

x. 1.

[a] So LXX: Heb. "about thirty," 1 Sam. ix. 22.

[b] After LXX, which here preserves the true text, *καὶ διέστρωσαν τῷ Σαοὺλ ἐπὶ τῷ δώματι καὶ ἐκοιμήθη*, Heb. "he communed with S. upon the housetop," 1 Sam. ix. 25. In the Biblical narrative the sacrifice and subsequent feast are held at "the high place," whence Samuel and Saul descend to the city to the prophet's house.

[c] Josephus reverses the Biblical order of the first two incidents: there the meeting with the messenger at Rachel's tomb comes first.

[d] "One carrying three kids and another carrying three loaves," 1 Sam.

ἀκολουθήσει. ἀσπάσονται δέ σε οὗτοι καὶ φιλο-
φρονήσονται καὶ δώσουσί σοι ἄρτους δύο, σὺ δὲ
56 λήψῃ. κἀκεῖθεν ἥξεις εἰς τὸ Ῥαχήλας καλούμενον μνημεῖον, ὅπου συμβαλεῖς τῷ σεσῶσθαί
σου τὰς ὄνους εὐαγγελιουμένῳ· ἔπειτ' ἐκεῖθεν
ἐλθὼν εἰς Γαβαθὰ[1] προφήταις ἐκκλησιάζουσιν
ἐπιτεύξῃ καὶ γενόμενος ἔνθεος προφητεύσεις σὺν
αὐτοῖς, ὡς πάνθ' ὅντιν'[2] ὁρῶντα ἐκπλήττεσθαί
τε καὶ θαυμάζειν λέγοντα "πόθεν εἰς τοῦτο εὐ-
57 δαιμονίας ὁ Κεισαίου παῖς παρῆλθεν;" ὅταν δέ
σοι ταῦτα γένηται τὰ σημεῖα, τὸν θεὸν ἴσθι μετὰ
σοῦ τυγχάνοντα, ἄσπασαί τε τὸν πατέρα σου καὶ
τοὺς συγγενεῖς. ἥξεις δὲ μετάπεμπτος εἰς Γάλγαλα
ὑπ'[3] ἐμοῦ, ἵνα χαριστήρια τούτων θύσωμεν τῷ
θεῷ." φράσας ταῦτα καὶ προειπὼν ἀποπέμπει
τὸν νεανίσκον· τῷ Σαούλῳ δὲ πάντα κατὰ τὴν
Σαμουήλου προφητείαν ἀπήντησεν.
58 (3) Ὡς δ' ἦλθεν εἰς τὴν οἰκίαν, τοῦ συγγενοῦς
αὐτοῦ Ἀβηνάρου, καὶ γὰρ ἐκεῖνον τῶν ἄλλων
οἰκείων μᾶλλον ἔστεργεν, ἀνερωτῶντος περὶ τῆς
ἀποδημίας καὶ τῶν κατ' αὐτὴν[4] γεγονότων, τῶν
μὲν ἄλλων οὐδὲν ἀπεκρύψατο οὐδ' ὡς ἀφίκοιτο
παρὰ Σαμουῆλον τὸν προφήτην οὐδ' ὡς ἐκεῖνος
αὐτῷ σεσῶσθαι τὰς ὄνους ἔφρασε, περὶ δὲ τῆς
59 βασιλείας καὶ τῶν κατ' αὐτήν, ἃ[5] φθόνον ἀκουό-

[1] Γεβαθὰ RO: Γαιβαθὰ SP. [2] + οὖν MSP.
[3] ἐξ OE. [4] αὐτὸν ROE.
[5] ἃ καὶ MSP Lat.

[a] Bibl. "two men."
[b] Bibl. "to Gibeah (or "the hill," LXX τὸν βουνόν) of God." *Cf.* on § 95.
[c] These last words are amplification. Scripture has "do what thy hand shall find."

will follow bearing a wine-skin. These men will
salute thee, show thee kindness and give thee two
loaves; and thou shalt accept them. And thence 2.
thou shalt come to the place called ‘Rachel's tomb,’
where thou shalt meet one[a] who will bring thee
news that thy asses are safe. Thereafter, on coming
thence to Gabatha,[b] thou shalt light upon an assembly 5.
of prophets and, divinely inspired, thou shalt prophesy
with them, insomuch that whosoever beholdeth thee *Cf.* 11 f.
shall be amazed and marvel, saying, ‘How hath the
son of Kis come to this pitch of felicity?’ And when 7.
these signs are come unto thee, know thou that God
is with thee; and go to salute thy father and thy
kinsfolk.[c] But thou shalt come, when summoned by
me, to Galgala, that we may offer thank-offerings to
God for these mercies.” After these declarations and
predictions he let the young man go; and everything
befell Saul as Samuel had foretold.

Saul's discreet silence. 1 Sam. x. 13.

(3) But when he entered his[d] house and his kinsman Abēnar[e]—for he was of all his relatives the one whom he loved the best—questioned him concerning his journey and the events thereof, Saul concealed from him nothing of all the rest, how he had visited Samuel the prophet and how he had told him that the asses were safe. But concerning the kingdom and all relating thereto, deeming that the recital

[d] Gr. “the”; perhaps render “the house of his kinsman A. . . . and he questioned him.” Josephus appears to have read in 1 Sam. x. 13 “he came to the house” (a reading preferred by modern critics) instead of “he came to the high place.”

[e] Scripture mentions his “uncle,” here unnamed but elsewhere called Ner. Josephus speaks of his cousin Abner, the son of Ner and afterwards captain of Saul's host, 1 Sam. xiv. 50. *Cf.* § 130.

μενα καὶ ἀπιστίαν ἔχειν ᾤετο, σιωπᾷ πρὸς αὐτὸν καὶ οὐδὲ πρὸς εὔνουν σφόδρα δοκοῦντα εἶναι καὶ περισσότερον τῶν ἀφ' αἵματος ὑπ' αὐτοῦ στεργόμενον ἀσφαλὲς ἢ σῶφρον ἔδοξε μηνύειν λογισάμενος, οἶμαι, τὴν ἀνθρωπίνην φύσιν οἵα ταῖς ἀληθείαις ἐστίν, ὅτι βεβαίως οὐδεὶς εὔνους[1] οὔτε φίλων οὔτε συγγενῶν οὐδ' ἄχρι τῶν παρὰ τοῦ θεοῦ λαμπρῶν ἀποσώζει τὴν διάθεσιν, ἀλλὰ πρὸς τὰς ὑπεροχὰς κακοήθεις τυγχάνουσιν ἤδη καὶ βάσκανοι.

60 (4) Σαμουῆλος δὲ συγκαλεῖ[2] τὸν λαὸν εἰς Μασφαθὰ πόλιν καὶ πρὸς αὐτὸν διατίθεται λόγους, οὓς κατ' ἐντολὴν φράζειν ἔλεγε τοῦ θεοῦ, ὅτι τὴν ἐλευθερίαν αὐτοῖς ἐκείνου παρασχόντος καὶ τοὺς πολεμίους δουλώσαντος ἀμνημονήσειαν τῶν εὐεργεσιῶν, καὶ τὸν μὲν θεὸν ἀποχειροτονοῦσι τῆς βασιλείας οὐκ εἰδότες ὡς συμφορώτατον ὑπὸ τοῦ
61 πάντων ἀρίστου προστατεῖσθαι, θεὸς δὲ πάντων ἄριστος, αἱροῦνται δ' ἔχειν ἄνθρωπον βασιλέα, ὃς ὡς κτήματι[3] τοῖς ὑποτεταγμένοις κατὰ βούλησιν καὶ ἐπιθυμίαν καὶ τῶν ἄλλων παθῶν ὁρμὴν χρήσεται τῆς ἐξουσίας ἀφειδῶς ἐμφορούμενος, ἀλλ' οὐχ ὡς ἴδιον ἔργον καὶ κατασκεύασμα τὸ τῶν ἀνθρώπων γένος οὕτως διατηρῆσαι σπουδάσει, ὁ θεὸς δὲ κατὰ ταύτην τὴν αἰτίαν ἂν[4] κήδοιτο. "ἀλλ' ἐπεὶ δέδοκται ταῦτα ὑμῖν καὶ κεκράτηκεν ἡ πρὸς τὸν θεὸν ὕβρις, τάχθητε πάντες κατὰ φυλάς τε καὶ σκῆπτρα καὶ κλήρους βάλετε."

[1] εὔνους om. ROE. [2] καλεῖ RO : ἐκάλει E.
[3] κτήμασι ed. pr. : jumentis Lat. [4] ἂν om. codd.

[a] The renewed strictures of Samuel are an amplification of Scripture. His earlier warning (1 Sam. viii. 10) is given above in § 40.

thereof would excite jealousy and distrust, he held his peace; nay, even to one who seemed most loyal of friends and whom he loved more affectionately than all those of his blood, he judged it neither safe nor prudent to disclose this secret—reflecting, I ween, on what human nature in truth is, and how no one, be he friend or kinsman, shows unwavering loyalty or preserves his affection when brilliant distinctions are bestowed by God, but all men straightway regard these eminences with malice and envy.

(4) Samuel now called the people together to the city of Masphatha and made them an address, which he delivered, as he told them, at the commandment of God. He said that, albeit God had granted them liberty and enslaved their enemies, they had been unmindful of His benefits and rejected His sovereignty, unaware that it was to their highest interest to have the best of all rulers at their head and that the best of all was God; nay, they chose to have a man for their king, who would treat his subjects as chattels at his will and pleasure and at the impulse of his other passions, indulging his power to the full; one who, not being the author and creator of the human race, would not lovingly study to preserve it, while God for that very reason would cherish it with care.[a] "Howbeit," he added, "since it pleases you thus, and this intent to outrage God has prevailed, range yourselves all of you by tribes and families[b] and cast lots."

The assembly at Mizpah. 1 Sam. x. 17.

[b] The Gr. σκῆπτρον, lit. "staff," is the usual LXX rendering of Heb. *shēbeṭ* which means both "staff" and "tribe." Josephus here reverses the order of words in the LXX, 1 Sam. x. 19, where σκῆπτρον = "tribe" and φυλή = "family"; φυλή in the LXX usually = "tribe," less often = "family."

62 (5) Ποιησάντων δὲ τοῦτο τῶν Ἑβραίων ὁ τῆς Βενιαμίτιδος κλῆρος ἐξέπεσε, ταύτης δὲ κληρωθείσης ἔλαχεν ἡ Ματρὶς καλουμένη πατριά, ἧς κατ' ἄνδρα κληρωθείσης λαγχάνει ὁ Κεισαίου
63 βασιλεύειν παῖς Σαοῦλος. γνοὺς δὲ τοῦθ' ὁ νεανίσκος φθάσας ἐκποδὼν αὑτὸν ποιεῖ μὴ βουλόμενος, οἶμαι, δοκεῖν τὴν ἀρχὴν ἑκὼν λαμβάνειν, ἀλλὰ τοσαύτην ἐνεδείξατο ἐγκράτειαν καὶ σωφροσύνην, ὥστε τῶν πλείστων οὐδ' ἐπὶ μικραῖς εὐπραγίαις τὴν χαρὰν κατασχεῖν δυναμένων, ἀλλ' εἰς τὸ πᾶσι γενέσθαι φανεροὺς προπιπτόντων,[1] ὁ δ' οὐ μόνον οὐδὲν ἐνέφηνε τοιοῦτον ἐπὶ βασιλείᾳ καὶ τῷ τοσούτων καὶ τηλικούτων ἐθνῶν ἀποδεδεῖχθαι δεσπότης, ἀλλὰ καὶ τῆς ὄψεως αὑτὸν τῆς τῶν βασιλευθησομένων ἐξέκλεψεν καὶ ζητεῖν αὐτὸν καὶ περὶ
64 τοῦτο πονεῖν παρεσκεύασεν. ὧν ἀμηχανούντων καὶ φροντιζόντων ὅ τι καὶ[2] γένοιτο ἀφανὴς ὁ Σαοῦλος, ὁ προφήτης ἱκέτευε τὸν θεὸν δεῖξαι ποῦ ποτ' εἴη καὶ παρασχεῖν εἰς ἐμφανὲς τὸν νεανίσκον.
65 μαθὼν δὲ παρὰ τοῦ θεοῦ τὸν τόπον ἔνθα κέκρυπται[3] ὁ Σαοῦλος πέμπει τοὺς ἄξοντας αὐτὸν καὶ παραγενόμενον ἵστησι μέσον τοῦ πλήθους. ἐξεῖχε δὲ ἁπάντων καὶ τὸ ὕψος ἦν βασιλικώτατος.
66 (6) Λέγει δὲ ὁ προφήτης· "τοῦτον ὑμῖν ὁ θεὸς ἔδωκε βασιλέα· ὁρᾶτε δὲ ὡς καὶ κρείττων ἐστὶ πάντων καὶ τῆς ἀρχῆς ἄξιος." ὡς δ' ἐπευφήμησε τῷ βασιλεῖ σωτηρίαν ὁ λαός, τὰ μέλλοντα συμβήσεσθαι καταγράψας αὐτοῖς ὁ προφήτης ἀνέγνω τοῦ βασιλέως ἀκροωμένου καὶ τὸ βιβλίον τίθησιν

[1] RE: προσπιπτόντων rell.
[2] καὶ om. MSP: ἔτι μὴ conj. Schmidt.
[3] κρύπτεται ROE.

(5) The Hebrews having so done, the lot fell to the tribe of Benjamin, and when lots had been cast for it the family called Matris [a] was successful; and lots being cast for the individuals of that family Saul son of Kis obtained the kingdom. Learning thereof, the young man promptly took himself away, not wishing, I imagine, to appear eager to take the sovereignty. Nay, such was the restraint and modesty [b] displayed by him that, whereas most persons are unable to contain their joy over the slightest success but rush to display themselves before all the world, he, far from showing any such pride on obtaining a kingdom and being appointed lord of all those mighty peoples, actually stole away from the view of his future subjects and forced them to search for him, not without trouble. These being baffled and perplexed at Saul's disappearance, the prophet besought God to show where the young man was and to bring him before their eyes. And having learnt from God the place where Saul lay in hiding, he sent to fetch him and, when he was come, set him in the midst of the throng. And he overtopped them all and in stature was indeed most kingly.

Saul chosen king. 1 Sam. x. 20

(6) Then said the prophet, "This is he whom God hath given you for king; see how he both excels all and is worthy of sovereignty!" But after the acclamations of the people, "Long live the king!" the prophet, having put in writing for them all that should come to pass, read it in the hearing of the king [c] and then laid up the book in the tabernacle of

Saul is acclaimed and returns home. 1 Sam. x. 24.

[a] Bibl. Matri, LXX Ματταρεί, etc.

[b] Rabbinic tradition (*cf.* Ginzberg, vi. 231) also emphasizes Saul's modesty.

[c] 1 Sam. x. 25 "Then Samuel told the people the manner of the kingdom and wrote it in a book."

ἐν τῇ τοῦ θεοῦ σκηνῇ ταῖς μετέπειτα γενεαῖς
67 μαρτύριον ὧν προείρηκε. ταῦτ' ἐπιτελέσας ὁ Σαμουῆλος ἀπολύει τὴν πληθύν· καὶ αὐτὸς δὲ εἰς Ἀρμαθὰ παραγίνεται πόλιν, πατρὶς γὰρ ἦν αὐτῷ, Σαούλῳ δὲ ἀπερχομένῳ εἰς Γαβαθήν, ἐξ ἧς ὑπῆρχε, συνήρχοντο πολλοὶ μὲν ἀγαθοὶ τὴν προσήκουσαν βασιλεῖ τιμὴν νέμοντες, πονηροὶ δὲ πλείους, οἳ καταφρονοῦντες αὐτοῦ καὶ τοὺς ἄλλους[1] ἐχλεύαζον καὶ οὔτε δῶρα προσέφερον οὔτ' ἐν σπουδῇ καὶ λόγῳ τὸ ἀρέσκεσθαι τὸν Σαοῦλον ἐτίθεντο.

68 (v. 1) Μηνὶ δ' ὕστερον ἄρχει[2] τῆς παρὰ πάντων αὐτῷ τιμῆς ὁ πρὸς Ναάσην πόλεμος τὸν τῶν Ἀμμανιτῶν βασιλέα· οὗτος γὰρ πολλὰ κακὰ τοὺς πέραν τοῦ Ἰορδάνου ποταμοῦ κατῳκημένους τῶν Ἰουδαίων διατίθησι, μετὰ πολλοῦ καὶ μαχίμου
69 στρατεύματος διαβὰς ἐπ' αὐτούς· καὶ τὰς πόλεις αὐτῶν εἰς δουλείαν ὑπάγεται, ἰσχύι μὲν καὶ βίᾳ πρὸς τὸ παρὸν αὐτοὺς χειρωσάμενος, σοφίᾳ δὲ καὶ ἐπινοίᾳ πρὸς τὸ μηδ' αὖθις ἀποστάντας δυνηθῆναι τὴν ὑπ' αὐτῷ δουλείαν διαφυγεῖν ἀσθενεῖς ποιῶν· τῶν γὰρ ἢ κατὰ πίστιν ὡς αὐτὸν ἀφικνουμένων ἢ λαμβανομένων πολέμου νόμῳ τοὺς
70 δεξιοὺς ὀφθαλμοὺς ἐξέκοπτεν. ἐποίει δὲ τοῦθ', ὅπως τῆς ἀριστερᾶς αὐτοῖς ὄψεως ὑπὸ τῶν θυρεῶν
71 καλυπτομένης ἄχρηστοι παντελῶς εἶεν. καὶ ὁ μὲν τῶν Ἀμμανιτῶν βασιλεὺς ταῦτ' ἐργασάμενος τοὺς πέραν τοῦ Ἰορδάνου, ἐπὶ τοὺς Γαλαδηνοὺς λεγο-

[1] πολλοὺς ROE. [2] SP: ἀρχὴ rell.

[a] Josephus follows the LXX, which begins a new chapter (1 Sam. xi.) with the words μετὰ μῆνα, probably reading *mi-hōdesh* "after a month," whereas the Heb. (x. 27 = end of

God, as a testimony to after generations of what he had foretold. That task accomplished, Samuel dismissed the multitude and betook himself to the city of Armatha, his native place. Saul, for his part, departed for Gabatha, whence he was sprung; he was accompanied by many honest folk, tendering him the homage due to a king, but by knaves yet more, who, holding him in contempt, derided the rest and neither offered him presents nor took any pains or care to gain the favour of Saul.

(v. 1) However, a month later,[a] he began to win the esteem of all by the war with Naas,[b] king of the Ammanites. For this monarch had done much harm to the Jews who had settled beyond the river Jordan, having invaded their territory with a large and warlike army. Reducing their cities to servitude, he not only by force and violence secured their subjection in the present, but by cunning and ingenuity weakened them in order that they might never again be able to revolt and escape from servitude to him; for he cut out the right eyes of all who either surrendered to him under oath or were captured by right of war. This he did with intent—since the left eye was covered by the buckler—to render them utterly unserviceable. Having then so dealt with the people beyond Jordan,[c] the Ammanite king carried his arms against those called Galadenians.[d]

War with Nahash the Ammonite.
1 Sam. xi. 1.

preceding chapter) has *maḥarîsh* "was silent," referring to Saul's attitude toward the disaffected elements.

[b] Bibl. Nahash, LXX Ναάς.

[c] These earlier conquests of Nahash are not mentioned in Scripture.

[d] Bibl. Jabesh Gilead, that is the city Jabesh (perhaps modern *Wady Yābis*) in Gilead, the country east of the Jordan, extending north and south of the river Jabbok.

μένους ἐπεστράτευσε καὶ στρατοπεδευσάμενος πρὸς τῇ μητροπόλει τῶν πολεμίων, Ἰαβὶς δ' ἐστὶν αὕτη, πέμπει πρὸς αὐτοὺς πρέσβεις κελεύων ἤδη[1] παραδοῦναι σφᾶς αὐτοὺς ἐπὶ τῷ τοὺς δεξιοὺς αὐτῶν ὀφθαλμοὺς ἐξορύξαι, ἢ πολιορκήσειν[2] ἠπείλει καὶ τὰς πόλεις αὐτῶν ἀναστήσειν· τὴν δ' αἵρεσιν ἐπ' αὐτοῖς εἶναι, πότερόν ποτε βραχύ τι τοῦ σώματος ἀποτεμεῖν θέλουσιν ἢ παντάπασιν[3] ἀπολωλέναι.
72 οἱ δὲ Γαλαδηνοὶ καταπλαγέντες πρὸς οὐδέτερον μὲν ἐτόλμησαν οὐδὲν εἰπεῖν, οὔτ' εἰ παραδιδόασιν αὐτοὺς οὔτ' εἰ πολεμοῦσιν, ἀνοχὴν δ' ἡμερῶν ἑπτὰ λαβεῖν ἠξίωσαν, ἵνα πρεσβευσάμενοι πρὸς τοὺς ὁμοφύλους παρακαλέσωσι συμμαχεῖν αὐτοῖς καὶ εἰ μὲν ἔλθοι βοήθεια πολεμῶσιν, εἰ δ' ἄπορα εἴη τὰ παρ' ἐκείνων, παραδώσειν αὐτοὺς ἔφασκον ἐπὶ τῷ παθεῖν ὅ τι ἂν αὐτῷ δοκῇ.

73 (2) Ὁ δὲ Ναάσης καταφρονήσας τοῦ τῶν Γαλαδηνῶν πλήθους καὶ τῆς ἀποκρίσεως αὐτῶν, δίδωσί τε αὐτοῖς τὴν ἀνοχὴν καὶ πέμπειν πρὸς οὓς ἂν θέλωσι συμμάχους ἐπιτρέπει. πέμψαντες[4] οὖν εὐθὺς κατὰ πόλιν τοῖς Ἰσραηλίταις διήγγελον[5] τὰ παρὰ τοῦ Ναάσου καὶ τὴν ἀμηχανίαν ἐν ᾗ καθειστή-
74 κεσαν. οἱ δ' εἰς δάκρυα καὶ λύπην ὑπὸ τῆς ἀκοῆς τῶν περὶ τοὺς Ἰαβισηνοὺς προήχθησαν καὶ πέρα τούτων οὐδὲν αὐτοῖς ἄλλο πράττειν συνεχώρει τὸ δέος· γενομένων δὲ τῶν ἀγγέλων καὶ ἐν τῇ Σαούλου τοῦ βασιλέως πόλει καὶ τοὺς κινδύνους ἐν οἷς εἶναι συνέβαινε τοὺς Ἰαβισηνοὺς φρασάντων, ὁ μὲν λαὸς ταὐτὰ τοῖς πρώτοις ἔπασχεν· ὠδύρετο γὰρ

[1] RO: ἢ rell. [2] conj. Niese: πολιορκῆσαι codd.
[3] πάντες MSP Lat. [4] πέμπουσιν ROE.
[5] οἳ ἤγγελον RO.

Pitching his camp near the capital of his enemies, to wit Jabis, he sent envoys to them, bidding them instantly to surrender on the understanding that their right eyes would be put out: if not, he threatened to besiege and overthrow their cities: it was for them to choose, whether they preferred the cutting out a small portion of the body or to perish utterly. The Galadenians, terror-struck, durst not reply at all to either proposal, whether they would surrender or whether they would fight; but they asked for a seven days' respite, in order to send envoys to their countrymen and solicit their support: if assistance were forthcoming they would fight, but if there should be no hope from that quarter, they undertook to deliver themselves up to suffer whatsoever should seem good to him. 1 Sam. xi. 2

Saul learns of the Gileadites' plight. 1 Sam. xi. 4.

(2) Naas, contemptuous of these Galadenian people and their answer, gave them their respite and permission to send to whatever allies they would. They therefore straightway sent messengers to each city of the Israelites to report the menaces of Naas and the desperate straits whereto they were reduced. These, on hearing of the plight of the men of Jabis, were moved to tears and grief, but, beyond that, fear permitted them to do no more. When, however, the messengers reached the city of king Saul and recounted the peril wherein they of Jabis lay, the people here too were moved even as were those others,

75 τὴν συμφορὰν τὴν τῶν συγγενῶν· ὁ δὲ Σαοῦλος
ἀπὸ τῶν περὶ τὴν γεωργίαν παραγενόμενος ἔργων
εἰς τὴν πόλιν ἐπιτυγχάνει κλαίουσι τοῖς αὐτοῦ
πολίταις, καὶ πυθόμενος τὴν αἰτίαν τῆς συγχύσεως
καὶ κατηφείας αὐτῶν μανθάνει τὰ παρὰ τῶν
76 ἀγγέλων. καὶ ἔνθεος γενόμενος ἀποπέμπει μὲν
τοὺς Ἰαβισηνούς, ὑποσχόμενος αὐτοῖς ἥξειν βοηθὸς
τῇ τρίτῃ τῶν ἡμερῶν καὶ πρὶν ἥλιον ἀνασχεῖν
κρατήσειν τῶν πολεμίων, ἵνα καὶ νενικηκότας ἤδη
καὶ τῶν φόβων ἀπηλλαγμένους ὁ ἥλιος ἐπιτείλας
ἴδῃ· ὑπομεῖναι δ᾽ ἐκέλευσέ τινας αὐτῶν ἡγησομέ-
νους τῆς ὁδοῦ.

77 (3) Βουλόμενος δὲ φόβῳ ζημίας τὸν λαὸν ἐπὶ
τὸν πρὸς Ἀμμανίτας ἐπιστρέψαι πόλεμον καὶ
συνελθεῖν αὐτοὺς ὀξύτερον, ὑποτεμὼν τῶν αὐτοῦ
βοῶν τὰ νεῦρα ταὐτὰ[1] διαθήσειν ἠπείλησε τοὺς
ἁπάντων, εἰ μὴ πρὸς τὸν Ἰόρδανον ὡπλισμένοι κατὰ
τὴν ἐπιοῦσαν ἀπαντήσουσιν ἡμέραν καὶ ἀκολου-
θήσουσιν αὐτῷ καὶ Σαμουήλῳ τῷ προφήτῃ, ὅπου
78 ποτ᾽ ἂν αὐτοὺς ἀγάγωσι. τῶν δὲ δι᾽ εὐλάβειαν
τῆς κατεπηγγελμένης ζημίας εἰς τὸν ὡρισμένον
καιρὸν συνελθόντων ἐξαριθμεῖται ἐν Βαλᾶ τῇ
πόλει τὸ πλῆθος· εὑρίσκει δὲ τὸν ἀριθμὸν χωρὶς
τῆς Ἰούδα φυλῆς εἰς ἑβδομήκοντα μυριάδας
συνειλεγμένους, τῆς δὲ φυλῆς ἐκείνης ἦσαν μυ-
79 ριάδες ἑπτά. διαβὰς δὲ τὸν Ἰόρδανον καὶ σχοίνων

[1] Niese: ταῦτα RO Lat.: ταὐτὸ SPE: τοῦτο M.

for they bewailed the calamity of their brethren ; but Saul, entering the city from his labours in husbandry, encountered his fellow-citizens in tears and, on asking the reason for their distress and dejection, learnt the messengers' report. Thereon, divinely inspired, he dismissed the men from Jabis with a promise to come to their aid on the third day [a] and ere sunrise to defeat the foe, so that the ascending sun should see them already victors and freed from their fears. Some, however, among them he bade remain with him so that they might guide him on his march.

(3) Then wishing to urge the people, through fear of the penalty, to the war against the Ammanites and that they might come together more quickly he cut the sinews [b] of his own oxen and threatened to do the like to the beasts of all who should fail to appear at the Jordan in arms on the following day and follow him and Samuel the prophet whithersoever they should lead them. But when they, through fear of the threatened penalty, mustered at the appointed hour, he had the host numbered at the 1 Sam xi. 8
city of Bala [c] and found them to have gathered together to the number of 700,000,[d] apart from the tribe of Judah : of that tribe there were 70,000.[e] Then crossing the Jordan and accomplishing in an all-

[a] In Scripture (1 Sam. xi. 9) Saul (or, in the Heb., the Israelites) promises that deliverance will come on the morrow; moreover, the promise is made after the tribes are summoned.

[b] In Scripture (1 Sam. xi. 7) Saul dismembers a team of oxen and sends the pieces throughout the borders of Israel.

[c] Bibl. Bezek, LXX Βέζεκ (Ἀβιέζεκ etc.) ἐν Βαμά, perhaps the modern *Khirbet Ibzīq*, about twelve miles N.E. of Shechem and a little W. of the Jordan, opposite Jabesh Gilead.

[d] Heb. 300,000, LXX 600,000.

[e] Heb. 30,000, LXX 70,000.

δέκα δι' ὅλης τῆς νυκτὸς ἀνύσας ὁδὸν φθάνει μὲν
ἥλιον ἀνίσχοντα, τριχῇ δὲ τὸ στράτευμα διελὼν
ἐπιπίπτει πανταχόθεν αἰφνιδίως οὐ προσδοκῶσι
τοῖς ἐχθροῖς, καὶ συμβαλὼν εἰς μάχην ἄλλους τε
πολλοὺς ἀποκτείνει τῶν Ἀμμανιτῶν καὶ Ναάσην
80 τὸν βασιλέα. τοῦτο λαμπρὸν ἐπράχθη τῷ Σαούλῳ
τὸ ἔργον καὶ πρὸς πάντας αὐτὸν διήγγειλε τοὺς
Ἑβραίους ἐπαινούμενον καὶ θαυμαστῆς ἀπολαύοντα
δόξης ἐπ' ἀνδρείᾳ· καὶ γὰρ εἴ τινες ἦσαν οἱ
πρότερον αὐτοῦ κατεφρόνουν, τότε μετέστησαν ἐπὶ
τὸ τιμᾶν καὶ πάντων ἄριστον νομίζειν· οὐ γὰρ
ἤρκεσεν αὐτῷ τοὺς Ἰαβισηνοὺς σεσωκέναι μόνον,
ἀλλὰ καὶ τῇ τῶν Ἀμμανιτῶν ἐπιστρατεύσας χώρᾳ
πᾶσαν αὐτὴν καταστρέφεται καὶ πολλὴν λαβὼν
81 λείαν λαμπρὸς[1] εἰς τὴν οἰκείαν ὑπέστρεψεν. ὁ δὲ
λαὸς ὑφ' ἡδονῆς τῶν Σαούλῳ κατωρθωμένων
ἔχαιρε μὲν ὅτι τοιοῦτον ἐχειροτόνησε βασιλέα,
πρὸς δὲ τοὺς οὐδὲν ὄφελος αὐτὸν ἔσεσθαι τοῖς
πράγμασι λέγοντας ἐβόων "ποῦ νῦν εἰσιν οὗτοι"
καὶ "δότωσαν δίκην" καὶ πάνθ' ὅσα φιλεῖ λέγειν
ὄχλος ἐπ' εὐπραγίαις ἠρμένος πρὸς τοὺς ἐξευτε-
82 λίζοντας ἔναγχος τοὺς τούτων αἰτίους. Σαοῦλος
δὲ τούτων μὲν ἠσπάζετο τὴν εὔνοιαν καὶ τὴν περὶ
αὐτὸν προθυμίαν, ὤμοσε δὲ μήτινα περιόψεσθαι
τῶν ὁμοφύλων ἀναιρούμενον ἐπ' ἐκείνης τῆς
ἡμέρας· ἄτοπον γὰρ εἶναι τὴν ὑπὸ τοῦ θεοῦ δε-
δομένην νίκην αἵματι φῦραι καὶ φόνῳ τῶν ἐκ

[1] λαμπρῶς ROME.

night march a distance of ten *schoenoi*,[a] he arrived before the sun was up and, dividing his army into three, fell suddenly from all sides upon the foe, who looked for no such thing, and having joined battle he slew multitudes of the Ammanites and king Naas himself.[b] This brilliant exploit achieved by Saul spread his praises throughout all the Hebrews and procured him a marvellous renown for valiance; for if there were some who before despised him, they were now brought round to honour him and to deem him the noblest of all men. For, not content with having rescued the inhabitants of Jabis, he invaded the country of the Ammanites, subdued it all, and, having taken much booty, returned in glory to his own land.[c] The people, in their delight at Saul's achievements, exulted at having elected such a king, and, turning upon those who had declared that he would bring no profit to the state, they cried, "Where now are those men?", "Let them pay for it!"—in short all that a crowd, elated by success, is wont to utter against those who were of late disparaging the authors of it. But Saul, while welcoming their goodwill and devotion to himself, yet swore that he would not suffer one of his countrymen to be put to death that day, for it were monstrous to defile that God-given victory with bloodshed and murder of men of

Saul's victory over Nahash the Ammonite. 1 Sam. xi. 12.

[a] The *schoenos* varied in length between thirty and forty stades, that is, roughly between four and five miles. The length of Saul's march, not given in Scripture, was, therefore, between forty and fifty miles. The distance between the supposed sites of Bezek and Jabesh Gilead is less than twenty miles.

[b] 1 Sam. xi. 1 "not two men were left together."

[c] This conquest of Ammonite territory is not mentioned in Scripture.

ταὐτοῦ γένους αὐτοῖς, πρέπειν δὲ μᾶλλον πρὸς ἀλλήλους εὐμενῶς διακειμένους[1] ἑορτάζειν.

83 (4) Σαμουήλου δὲ φήσαντος καὶ δευτέρᾳ δεῖν χειροτονίᾳ Σαούλῳ τὴν βασιλείαν ἐπικυρῶσαι συνίασι πάντες εἰς Γάλγαλα πόλιν· ἐκεῖ γὰρ αὐτοὺς ἐκέλευσεν ἐλθεῖν. καὶ πάλιν ὁρῶντος τοῦ πλήθους ὁ προφήτης χρίει τὸν Σαοῦλον τῷ ἁγίῳ ἐλαίῳ καὶ δεύτερον ἀναγορεύει βασιλέα. καὶ οὕτως ἡ τῶν Ἑβραίων πολιτεία εἰς βασιλείαν
84 μετέπεσεν. ἐπὶ γὰρ Μωυσέος καὶ τοῦ μαθητοῦ αὐτοῦ Ἰησοῦ, ὃς ἦν στρατηγός, ἀριστοκρατούμενοι διετέλουν· μετὰ δὲ τὴν ἐκείνου[2] τελευτὴν ἔτεσι τοῖς πᾶσι δέκα καὶ πρὸς τούτοις ὀκτὼ τὸ
85 πλῆθος αὐτῶν ἀναρχία κατέσχε. μετὰ ταῦτα δ' εἰς τὴν προτέραν ἐπανῆλθον πολιτείαν τῷ κατὰ πόλεμον ἀρίστῳ δόξαντι γεγενῆσθαι καὶ κατ' ἀνδρείαν περὶ τῶν ὅλων δικάζειν ἐπιτρέποντες· καὶ διὰ τοῦτο τὸν χρόνον τοῦτον τῆς πολιτείας κριτῶν ἐκάλεσαν.

86 (5) Ἐκκλησίαν δὲ Σαμουῆλος ποιήσας ὁ προφήτης τῶν Ἑβραίων "ἐπόμνυμαι,"[3] φησίν, "ὑμῖν τὸν μέγιστον θεόν, ὃς τοὺς ἀδελφοὺς τοὺς ἀγαθοὺς[4] ἐκείνους, λέγω δὴ Μωυσῆν καὶ Ἀαρῶνα, παρήγαγεν εἰς τὸν βίον καὶ τοὺς πατέρας ἡμῶν ἐξήρπασεν Αἰγυπτίων καὶ τῆς ὑπ' αὐτοῖς δουλείας, μηδὲν μήτ' αἰδοῖ χαρισαμένους μήτε ὑποστειλαμένους φόβῳ μήτε ἄλλῳ τινὶ πάθει παραχωρήσαντας εἰπεῖν, εἴ[5] τί μοι πέπρακται σκαιὸν καὶ ἄδικον ἢ κέρδους ἕνεκα ἢ
87 πλεονεξίας ἢ χάριτος τῆς πρὸς ἄλλους· ἐλέγξαι δὲ

[1] τῶν ἐκ ταὐτοῦ . . . διακειμένους SP: τῶν πρὸς ἀλλήλους συγγενῶν RO. [2] ἐκείνων SP Lat. [3] ἐπόμνυμι SPE. [4] τοὺς ἀγαθοὺς om. RO. [5] εἴ om. ROME.

their own race, and it better beseemed them to keep feast in a spirit of mutual goodwill.[a]

Samuel a second time proclaims Saul king. 1 Sam. xi. 14.

(4) Samuel having now declared it necessary to confirm the kingdom to Saul by a second election, all assembled at the city of Galgala,[b] for thither had he bade them come. So yet again, in the sight of all the people, the prophet anointed Saul with the holy oil, and for the second time proclaimed him king. And thus was the government of the Hebrews transformed into a monarchy. For under Moses and his disciple Joshua, who was commander-in-chief, they remained under aristocratic rule: after Joshua's death for full eighteen years[c] the people continued in a state of anarchy: whereafter they returned to their former polity, entrusting supreme judicial authority to him who in battle and in bravery had proved himself the best; and that is why they called this period of their political life the age of Judges.

Samuel's address to the people. 1 Sam. xii. 1

(5) Samuel the prophet now called an assembly of the Hebrews and said: "I adjure you by the most High God, who brought those excellent brothers, I mean Moses and Aaron, into this world, and rescued our fathers from the Egyptians and bondage beneath their yoke, that without showing favour through respect, without suppressing aught through fear, without giving room to any other feeling, ye tell me if I have done anything sinister and unjust through love of lucre or cupidity or out of favour to others.

[a] Variant reading (after "bloodshed"): "and to celebrate it (the victory) with the murder of their kinsmen."

[b] Bibl. Gilgal. Probably the city near Jericho is meant. *Cf. A.* v. 20.

[c] The only basis for this number seems to be the interval of Moabite oppression after the death of Kenaz, the first judge (according to Josephus). *Cf. A.* v. 187.

εἰ καὶ τῶν τοιούτων τι προσηκάμην, μόσχον ἢ πρόβατον, ἃ πρὸς τροφὴν ἀνεμέσητον δοκεῖ λαμβάνειν, ἢ εἴ τινος ὑποζύγιον εἰς ἐμὴν ἀποσπάσας χρείαν ἐλύπησα, τούτων ἕν τι κατειπεῖν παρόντος ὑμῶν τοῦ βασιλέως." οἱ δὲ ἀνέκραγον τούτων οὐδὲν ὑπ' αὐτοῦ γεγονέναι, προστῆναι δὲ ὁσίως αὐτὸν καὶ δικαίως τοῦ ἔθνους.

88 (6) Σαμουῆλος δὲ ταύτης ἐξ ἁπάντων τῆς μαρτυρίας αὐτῷ γενομένης "ἐπεὶ δεδώκατέ μοι," φησί, "τὸ μηδὲν ἄτοπον ἔθ' ὑμᾶς περὶ ἐμοῦ δύνασθαι λέγειν, φέρε νῦν μετὰ παρρησίας ἀκούσατέ μου λέγοντος, ὅτι μεγάλα ἠσεβήσατε εἰς
89 τὸν θεόν, αἰτησάμενοι βασιλέα. διαμνημονεύειν δὲ ὑμᾶς προσῆκεν, ὅτι σὺν ἑβδομήκοντα μόνοις ἐκ τοῦ γένους ἡμῶν ὁ πάππος Ἰάκωβος διὰ λιμὸν εἰς Αἴγυπτον ἦλθε, κἀκεῖ πολλῶν μυριάδων ἐπιτεκνωθεισῶν, ἃς εἰς δουλείας καὶ χαλεπὰς ὕβρεις ἤγαγον οἱ Αἰγύπτιοι, ὁ θεὸς εὐξαμένων τῶν πατέρων χωρὶς βασιλέως παρέσχεν αὐτοῖς ῥύσασθαι τῆς ἀνάγκης τὸ πλῆθος, Μωυσῆν αὐτοῖς καὶ Ἀαρῶνα πέμψας ἀδελφούς, οἳ ἤγαγον ὑμᾶς
90 εἰς τήνδε τὴν γῆν, ἣν νῦν ἔχετε. καὶ τούτων ἀπολαύσαντες ἐκ τοῦ θεοῦ προδεδώκατε τὴν θρησκείαν καὶ τὴν εὐσέβειαν. οὐ μὴν ἀλλὰ καὶ τοῖς πολεμίοις ὑποχειρίους γενομένους ἠλευθέρωσε πρῶτον μὲν Ἀσσυρίων καὶ τῆς ἐκείνων ἰσχύος ὑπερτέρους ἀπεργασάμενος, ἔπειτα Ἀμμανιτῶν κρατῆσαι παρασχὼν καὶ Μωαβιτῶν καὶ τελευταίων[1] Παλαιστίνων. καὶ ταῦτ' οὐ βασιλέως ἡγουμένου διεπράξασθε, ἀλλ' Ἰεφθάου καὶ Γε-

[1] τελευταῖον MSP.

Convict me if I have accepted aught of such things, heifer or sheep, the acceptance of which for food is yet deemed void of offence; or if I have aggrieved any man by purloining his beast of burden for my own use, convict me of any one such crime here in the presence of your king." Thereat all cried out that he had done none of these things, but had governed the nation with holiness and justice.

(6) Then Samuel, having received this testimony from them all, said: "Seeing that ye grant me that ye can lay no crime to my charge to this day, come now and hearken while I tell you with all boldness what great impiety ye have shown towards God in asking for a king. Nay, it behoved you to remember how that with but seventy souls of our race our grandsire Jacob, through stress of famine, came into Egypt; and how there, when his posterity, increased by many myriads, had been subjected to bondage and grievous outrage by the Egyptians, God, at the prayer of our fathers, without any king, brought deliverance to the multitude from their distress by sending to them the brothers Moses and Aaron, who brought you into this land which ye now possess. And yet after enjoying these things from God, ye have been traitors to His worship and His religion. Yet for all that, when ye were fallen under the hand of your enemies, He delivered you, first by causing you to triumph over the Assyrians [a] and their might, then by granting you victory over the Ammanites and Moabites, and last over the Philistines. And all this ye accomplished, not under the leadership of a king, but with Jephthah

Samuel protests against election of a king.
1 Sam. xii. 7.

[a] A reference to the victory over King Cushan of Aram-Naharaim (Jd. iii. 8), whom Josephus, *A.* v. 180, calls "king of the Assyrians."

91 δεῶνος στρατηγούντων. τίς οὖν ἔσχεν ὑμᾶς ἄνοια φυγεῖν μὲν τὸν θεόν, ὑπὸ βασιλέα δὲ εἶναι θέλειν; ἀλλ' ἐγὼ μὲν ἀπέδειξα τοῦτον ὃν αὐτὸς ἐπελέξατο. ἵνα μέντοι γε φανερὸν ὑμῖν[1] ποιήσω τὸν θεὸν ὀργιζόμενον καὶ δυσχεραίνοντα τῇ τῆς βασιλείας ὑμῶν αἱρέσει, δηλῶσαι τοῦθ' ὑμῖν τὸν θεὸν[2] παρασκευάσω διὰ σημείων ἐναργῶς· ὃ γὰρ οὐδέπω πρότερον εἶδεν[3] ὑμῶν οὐδεὶς ἐνταῦθα γεγενημένον, θέρους ἀκμῇ χειμῶνα, αἰτησάμενος τὸν θεὸν
92 παρέξω τοῦτο νῦν ὑμῖν ἐπιγνῶναι.'' καὶ ταῦτα εἰπόντος πρὸς τὸ πλῆθος τοῦ Σαμουήλου, βρονταῖς σημαίνει τὸ θεῖον καὶ ἀστραπαῖς καὶ χαλάζης καταφορᾷ τὴν τοῦ προφήτου περὶ πάντων ἀλήθειαν, ὡς τεθαμβηκότας αὐτοὺς καὶ περιδεεῖς γινομένους ἁμαρτεῖν τε ὁμολογεῖν καὶ κατ' ἄγνοιαν εἰς τοῦτο προπεσεῖν, καὶ ἱκετεύειν τὸν προφήτην ὡς πατέρα χρηστὸν καὶ ἐπιεικῆ, τὸν θεὸν αὐτοῖς εὐμενῆ καταστῆσαι καὶ ταύτην ἀφεῖναι τὴν ἁμαρτίαν, ἣν πρὸς οἷς ἐξύβρισαν ἄλλοις καὶ παρ-
93 ηνόμησαν προσεξειργάσαντο. ὁ δὲ ὑπισχνεῖται καὶ παρακαλέσειν τὸν θεὸν συγγνῶναι περὶ τούτων αὐτοῖς καὶ πείσειν, συνεβούλευε μέντοι δικαίους εἶναι καὶ ἀγαθοὺς καὶ μνημονεύειν ἀεὶ τῶν διὰ τὴν παράβασιν τῆς ἀρετῆς αὐτοῖς κακῶν συμπεσόντων καὶ τῶν σημείων τοῦ θεοῦ καὶ τῆς Μωυσέος νομοθεσίας, εἰ σωτηρίας αὐτοῖς καὶ τῆς μετὰ τοῦ βασιλέως εὐδαιμονίας ἐστὶν ἐπιθυμία.
94 εἰ δὲ τούτων ἀμελήσουσιν, ἔλεγεν ἥξειν αὐτοῖς τε καὶ τῷ βασιλεῖ μεγάλην ἐκ θεοῦ πληγήν. καὶ ὁ[4] Σαμουῆλος μὲν ταῦτα τοῖς Ἑβραίοις προφη-

[1] ὑμῖν om. RO.
[2] τὸν θεὸν om. RO.
[3] οἶδεν conj. Niese.
[4] ὁ om. RO.

and Gedeon for generals. What madness then possessed you to flee your God and to wish to be under a king? Nay, I have appointed him whom He Himself hath chosen. Howbeit, to manifest to you that God is wroth and ill-content at your choice of kingly rule, I will prevail with Him to reveal this to you by signs clearly. For that which not one of you ever saw befall here before—a tempest at midsummer—that through prayer to God I shall cause you now to witness." Scarce had Samuel spoken these words to the people, when the Deity by thunderings, lightning, and a torrent of hail, attested the truth of all that the prophet had said; whereat astounded and terrified they confessed their sin, into which, they said, they had fallen through ignorance, and implored the prophet, as a kind and gentle father, to render God gracious to them that He might forgive this sin which they had committed in addition to all their other insolences and transgressions. And he promised that he would beseech God to pardon them in this thing and would withal move Him thereto; howbeit, he exhorted them to be righteous and good, and ever to remember the ills that their transgression of virtue had brought upon them, the miracles of God and the legislation of Moses, if they had any desire for continued salvation and continued felicity under their king. But should they neglect these things, there would come, said he, both on them and on their king a great visitation from God. And after thus prophesying to the Hebrews, Samuel dismissed them to their

The storm attests God's displeasure. 1 Sam. xii. 18.

τεύσας ἀπέλυσεν αὐτοὺς ἐπὶ τὰ οἰκεῖα βεβαιώσας
ἐκ δευτέρου τῷ Σαούλῳ τὴν βασιλείαν.
95 (vi. 1) Οὗτος δ' ἐπιλέξας ἐκ τοῦ πλήθους ὡς
περὶ[1] τρισχιλίους, τοὺς μὲν δισχιλίους ὥστε
σωματοφυλακεῖν αὐτὸν[2] λαβὼν αὐτὸς διέτριβεν
ἐν πόλει Βεθήβῳ,[3] Ἰωνάθῃ δὲ τῷ παιδὶ τοὺς
λοιποὺς δοὺς ὥστε σωματοφυλακεῖν αὐτὸν εἰς
Γέβαλ'[4] ἔπεμψεν. ὁ δ' ἐκπολιορκεῖ τι φρούριον
96 τῶν Παλαιστίνων οὐ πόρρω Γεβάλων. οἱ γὰρ[5]
Παλαιστῖνοι καταστρεφόμενοι τοὺς Ἰουδαίους τά
τε ὅπλα αὐτοὺς ἀφῃροῦντο καὶ τοὺς ὀχυρωτάτους
τῆς χώρας τόπους φρουραῖς κατελαμβάνοντο καὶ
σιδηροφορεῖν χρῆσθαί[6] τε καθάπαξ ἀπηγόρευον
σιδήρῳ, καὶ διὰ ταύτην τὴν ἀπόρρησιν[7] οἱ γεωργοί,
εἴποτε δεήσει' αὐτοὺς ἐπισκευάσαι τι τῶν ἐργαλείων, ἢ ὕνιν ἢ δίκελλαν[8] ἢ ἄλλο τι τῶν εἰς γεωργίαν
χρησίμων, φοιτῶντες εἰς τοὺς Παλαιστίνους ταῦτα
97 ἔπραττον. ὡς δὲ ἠκούσθη τοῖς Παλαιστίνοις ἡ
τῆς φρουρᾶς ἀναίρεσις ἀγανακτήσαντες καὶ δεινὴν
ὕβριν τὴν καταφρόνησιν ἡγησάμενοι στρατεύουσιν
ἐπὶ τοὺς Ἰουδαίους πεζῶν μὲν τριάκοντα μυριάσιν
ἅρμασι δὲ τρισμυρίοις, ἵππον δὲ ἑξακισχιλίαν
98 ἐπήγοντο· καὶ στρατοπεδευσαμένων[9] πρὸς πόλει
Μαχμά, τοῦτο Σαοῦλος ὁ τῶν Ἑβραίων βασιλεὺς

[1] περὶ om. RO.
[2] ὥστε . . . αὐτὸν om. Lat.
[3] Bethleem Lat.
[4] Γαβὰς MSP: Gabatha Lat.
[5] + τῆς Γαβὰς MSP: Lat.
[6] κεχρῆσθαι Schmidt cum RO.
[7] πρόρρησιν RO: causam Lat.
[8] RO: μάκελλαν (-ην) rell.
[9] στρατοπεδεύονται MSP Lat.

[a] Gr. Bethēbos, bibl. Bethel.
[b] The repetition of the Greek phrase "to guard his body" indicates a text corruption.

homes, having for the second time confirmed the kingdom to Saul.

(vi. 1) But Saul chose out of the multitude some three thousand men, and taking two thousand for his bodyguard abode for his part in the city of Bethēl(os)[a]; the rest he gave as guards[b] to his son Jonathan and sent him to Gebala.[c] And Jonathan besieged and took a fortress of the Philistines not far from Gebala. Saul prepares for war with the Philistines. 1 Sam. xiii. 2.

For the Philistines, in their subjugation of the Jews, 19.
had deprived them of their arms and occupied the strongest positions in the country with garrisons, further forbidding the vanquished to carry any weapon of iron or to make any use at all of iron. In consequence of this interdict, whenever the peasantry needed to repair any of their tools, ploughshare or mattock or other agricultural instrument, they would
go to the Philistines to do this. So when the Philis- 5.
tines heard of the destruction of their garrison, infuriated and deeming such scorn of them a monstrous affront, they marched against the Jews with 300,000 footmen,[d] 30,000 chariots, and 6000 horse to support them, and pitched their camp beside the
city of Machma.[e] On learning of this, Saul, king of 3.

[c] Bibl. Gibeath Benjamin, LXX Γαβεέ (Γαβαὰ etc.) τοῦ Βενιαμείν, perhaps a different site from the Gaba (bibl. Gibeah) mentioned in *A*. v. 140. Gibeah (of which Gibeath is a construct form in Hebrew) and Gaba or Geba are related words meaning "hill," *cf*. LXX βουνός. The relation of various sites by these names in the same territory is uncertain because of their confusion in Scripture.

[d] Scripture gives no number for the foot-soldiers. *Cf*. 1 Sam. xiii. 5 "and people like the sand on the seashore in multitude."

[e] Bibl. Michmash, LXX Μαχεμάς, Μαχμάς, etc., modern *Mukhmās*, about two miles N.W. of the supposed site of Geba, and eight miles N.W. of Jerusalem.

μαθὼν εἰς Γάλγαλα καταβαίνει πόλιν καὶ διὰ πάσης κηρύσσει τῆς χώρας, ἐπ' ἐλευθερίᾳ καλῶν τὸν λαὸν ἐπὶ τὸν πόλεμον τὸν πρὸς Παλαιστίνους, τὴν δύναμιν ἐκφαυλίζων αὐτῶν καὶ διασύρων ὡς οὐκ ἀξιόλογον οὐδ' ὥστε φοβεῖσθαι διακινδυνεύειν πρὸς
99 αὐτούς. κατανοήσαντες δὲ τὸ πλῆθος τῶν Παλαιστίνων οἱ τοῦ Σαούλου κατεπλάγησαν, καὶ οἱ μὲν εἰς τὰ σπήλαια καὶ τοὺς ὑπονόμους ἔκρυψαν αὑτούς, οἱ πλείους δὲ εἰς τὴν πέραν τοῦ Ἰορδάνου γῆν ἔφυγον· αὕτη δ' ἦν Γάδου καὶ Ῥουβήλου.
100 (2) Πέμψας δὲ Σαοῦλος πρὸς τὸν προφήτην ἐκάλει πρὸς αὑτὸν συνδιασκεψόμενον περὶ τοῦ πολέμου καὶ τῶν πραγμάτων. ὁ δὲ περιμένειν αὐτὸν ἐκέλευσεν αὐτόθι καὶ παρασκευάζειν θύματα· μετὰ γὰρ ἡμέρας ἓξ[1] πρὸς αὐτὸν ἥξειν, ὅπως θύσωσι τῇ ἑβδόμῃ τῶν ἡμερῶν, ἔπειθ' οὕτως
101 συμβάλωσι τοῖς πολεμίοις. καὶ περιμένει μὲν ὡς ὁ προφήτης ἐπέστειλεν, οὐκέτι μέντοι γε διατηρεῖ τὴν ἐντολήν, ἀλλ' ὡς ἑώρα βραδύνοντα μὲν τὸν προφήτην, αὑτὸν δὲ ὑπὸ τῶν στρατιωτῶν καταλειπόμενον, λαβὼν τὰ θύματα τὴν θυσίαν ἐπετέλει[2]· ἐπεὶ δὲ τὸν Σαμουῆλον ἤκουσε προσιόντα ὑπ-
102 αντησόμενος ἐξῆλθεν. ὁ δ' οὐκ ὀρθῶς αὐτὸν ἔφη πεποιηκέναι παρακούσαντα ὧν ἐπέστειλεν αὐτὸς καὶ φθάσαντα τὴν παρουσίαν, ἣν κατὰ βούλησιν γινομένην τοῦ θείου πρὸς τὰς εὐχὰς καὶ τὰς θυσίας τὰς ὑπὲρ τοῦ πλήθους προλάβοι, κακῶς
103 ἱερουργήσας καὶ προπετὴς γενόμενος. ἀπολογουμένου δὲ τοῦ Σαούλου καὶ περιμεῖναι μὲν τὰς

[1] om. RO: septem Lat.
[2] προσήγαγεν MSP.

the Hebrews, came down to the city of Galgala and sent heralds throughout all the country to call up the people in the name of liberty to the war against the Philistines, belittling and disparaging their strength as inconsiderable and not such that they need fear to hazard battle with them.[a] But, on perceiving that 6.
host of Philistines, Saul's recruits were in consternation; and while some hid themselves in the caverns and cavities, the more part fled beyond the Jordan into the territory of Gad and Rubel.[b]

(2) Saul then sent word to the prophet, summoning him to his presence to confer with him concerning the war and the situation. Samuel bade him wait where he was and make ready victims for sacrifice, for after six days he would come to him, that so they might sacrifice on the seventh day and, that done, join battle with the enemy. So Saul waited awhile as the prophet had enjoined upon him; then, however, he would observe his command no longer, but when he saw that the prophet tarried and that his own soldiers were deserting him, he took the victims and performed the sacrifice himself. Then, hearing that Samuel was approaching, he went out to meet him. But the prophet told him that he had not done rightly in disobeying his injunctions and anticipating his advent: he was paying that visit in accordance with the will of the Deity to preside at the prayers and the sacrifices on behalf of the people, and now he had forestalled him by having offered sacrifice wrongly and by his precipitate haste. Thereat Saul excused himself, saying that he had waited during those

Saul's premature sacrifice. 1 Sam. xiii. 8. x. 8. xiii. 9.

[a] Saul's disparaging remarks about the Philistines are an addition to Scripture.

[b] 1 Sam. xiii. 7 "and the land of Gad and Gilead."

ἡμέρας ἃς ὥρισε λέγοντος, ὑπὸ δὲ ἀνάγκης καὶ ἀναχωρήσεως μὲν τῶν αὐτοῦ στρατιωτῶν διὰ φόβον, στρατοπεδείας δὲ τῶν ἐχθρῶν ἐν Μαχμᾶ καὶ ἀκοῆς τῆς ἐπ' αὐτὸν εἰς Γάλγαλα καταβάσεως ἐπειχθῆναι πρὸς τὴν θυσίαν, ὑπολαβὼν δὲ ὁ
104 Σαμουῆλος "ἀλλὰ σύγε," φησίν, "εἰ δίκαιος ἦσθα καὶ μὴ παρήκουσας ἐμοῦ μηδ' ὧν ὑπέθετό μοι περὶ τῶν παρόντων ὁ θεὸς ὠλιγώρησας ταχύτερος ἢ συνέφερε τοῖς πράγμασι γεγονώς, σοί τ' αὐτῷ πλεῖστον ἂν βασιλεῦσαι χρόνον ἐξεγένετο
105 καὶ τοῖς σοῖς ἐγγόνοις.[1]" καὶ Σαμουῆλος μὲν ἀχθόμενος ἐπὶ τοῖς γεγενημένοις ἀνεχώρησε παρ' αὐτόν, Σαοῦλος δὲ εἰς Γαβαὼν πόλιν ἔχων ἑξακοσίους[2] μεθ' ἑαυτοῦ μόνον ἧκε σὺν Ἰωνάθῃ τῷ παιδί. τούτων δὲ οἱ πλείους οὐκ εἶχον ὅπλα, τῆς χώρας σπανιζούσης σιδήρου καὶ τῶν ὅπλα χαλκεύειν δυναμένων· οὐ γὰρ εἴων οἱ Παλαιστῖνοι ταῦτα εἶναι, καθὼς[3] μικρὸν ἔμπροσθεν δεδη-
106 λώκαμεν. διελόντες δ' εἰς τρία μέρη τὴν στρατιὰν οἱ Παλαιστῖνοι καὶ κατὰ τοσαύτας ὁδοὺς ἐπερχόμενοι τὴν τῶν Ἑβραίων χώραν ἐπόρθουν, βλεπόντων τε Σαούλου τοῦ βασιλέως αὐτῶν καὶ τοῦ παιδὸς Ἰωνάθου ἀμῦναί τε τῇ γῇ, μεθ' ἑξακο-
107 σίων γὰρ μόνων ἦσαν, οὐ δυναμένων. καθεζόμενοι δ' αὐτός τε καὶ ὁ παῖς αὐτοῦ καὶ ὁ ἀρχιερεὺς Ἀχίας,[4] ἀπόγονος ὢν Ἠλὶ τοῦ ἀρχιερέως, ἐπὶ βουνοῦ ὑψηλοῦ καὶ τὴν γῆν λεηλατουμένην ὁρῶντες ἐν ἀγωνίᾳ δεινῇ καθεστήκεσαν. συντίθεται δὲ ὁ Σαούλου παῖς τῷ ὁπλοφόρῳ, κρύφα πορευθέντες αὐτοὶ εἰς τὴν τῶν πολεμίων παρεμβολὴν ἐκδρα-

[1] ἐκγόνοις MSP.
[2] διακοσίους E.
[3] + καὶ SP: καθὰ καὶ M.
[4] Ἐχίας RO.

days which Samuel had appointed, but that necessity, the desertion of his terrified troops, the enemy's encampment at Machma and a report of their intended descent upon him at Galgala, had impelled him to speed the sacrifice. Then Samuel rejoining, "Nay, but for thy part," said he, "hadst thou been righteous and not disobeyed me nor lightly regarded the counsels which God has given me touching the present matter, by acting more hastily than befitted the matter, then would it have been given thee to reign exceeding long, and to thy posterity as well." So Samuel, vexed at what had befallen, returned to his home, while Saul, with but six hundred followers, came with his son Jonathan to the city of Gabaon.[a] Most of his men had no arms, the country being destitute of iron and of men capable of forging arms; for the Philistines had prohibited this, as we said just now.[b] And now, dividing their army into three companies and advancing by as many routes,[c] the Philistines proceeded to ravage the country of the Hebrews under the eyes of Saul, their king, and of his son Jonathan, who, with but six hundred followers, were powerless to defend their land. Seated on a lofty hill, Saul and his son and the high priest Achias,[d] a descendant of Eli the high priest, as they watched the devastation of the land, were in a state of deepest anguish. Saul's son then proposed to his armour-bearer that they should secretly sally out alone into the enemy's

Saul and Jonathan encamp at Gibeah. 1 Sam. xiii. 16.

Jonathan's exploit. 1 Sam. xiv. 1

[a] Bibl. Gibeath Benjamin. *Cf.* on § 95.

[b] § 96.

[c] 1 Sam. xiii. 17 specifies the roads to Ophrah, Beth Horon and "the way of the border looking toward the valley of Zeboim"—all in the territory N. of Jerusalem.

[d] Bibl. Ahiah. His genealogy is given in 1 Sam. xiv. 3. *Cf.* on § 122.

μεῖν καὶ ταραχὴν ἐμποιῆσαι καὶ θόρυβον αὐτοῖς.[1]
108 τοῦ δὲ ὁπλοφόρου προθύμως ἐφέψεσθαι[2] φήσαντος
ὅποι ποτ' ἂν ἡγῆται, κἂν ἀποθανεῖν δέῃ, προσ-
λαβὼν τὴν τοῦ νεανίσκου συνεργίαν καὶ καταβὰς
ἀπὸ τοῦ βουνοῦ πρὸς τοὺς πολεμίους ἐπορεύετο.
ἦν δὲ τὸ τῶν πολεμίων στρατόπεδον ἐπὶ κρημνοῦ,[3]
τρισὶν ἄκραις εἰς λεπτὸν ἀπηκονημέναις μῆκος
πέτρας ἐν κύκλῳ περιστεφανούσης ὥσπερ προ-
109 βόλοις τὰς ἐπιχειρήσεις ἀπομαχόμενον. ἔνθεν συνέβαινεν ἠμελῆσθαι τὰς φυλακὰς τοῦ στρατοπέδου
διὰ τὸ φύσει περιεῖναι τῷ χωρίῳ τὴν ἀσφάλειαν
καὶ παντὶ[4] νομίζειν ἀμήχανον εἶναι κατ' ἐκείνας
110 οὐκ ἀναβῆναι μόνον ἀλλὰ καὶ προσελθεῖν. ὡς
οὖν ἧκον εἰς τὴν παρεμβολὴν ὁ Ἰωνάθης παρ-
εθάρσυνε τὸν ὁπλοφόρον καὶ "προσβάλωμεν τοῖς
πολεμίοις," ἔλεγε, "κἂν μὲν ἀναβῆναι κελεύσωσι
πρὸς αὐτοὺς ἡμᾶς ἰδόντες, σημεῖον τοῦτο νίκης
ὑπολάμβανε,[5] ἐὰν δὲ φθέγξωνται μηδὲν ὡς οὐ
111 καλοῦντες ἡμᾶς, ὑποστρέψωμεν.[6]" προσιόντων δὲ
αὐτῶν τῷ στρατοπέδῳ τῶν πολεμίων ὑποφαι-
νούσης ἤδη τῆς ἡμέρας ἰδόντες οἱ Παλαιστῖνοι,
πρὸς ἀλλήλους ἔλεγον ἐκ τῶν ὑπονόμων καὶ τῶν[7]
σπηλαίων προϊέναι τοὺς Ἑβραίους, καὶ πρὸς
Ἰωνάθην καὶ τὸν ὁπλοφόρον αὐτοῦ "δεῦτ'," ἔφασαν,
"ἀνέλθετε πρὸς ἡμᾶς, ἵνα ὑμᾶς τιμωρησώμεθα
112 τῶν τετολμημένων ἀξίως." ἀσπασάμενος δὲ τὴν
φωνὴν ὁ τοῦ Σαούλου παῖς ὡς νίκην αὐτῷ ση-
μαίνουσαν, παραυτίκα μὲν ἀνεχώρησαν ἐξ οὗπερ

[1] αὐτοῖς om. RO. [2] SP: ἕπεσθαι rell.
[3] S: κρημνῷ rell. [4] πάντῃ M: valde Lat.
[5] M: ὑπολαμβάνειν SP. [6] ὑποστρέψομεν RO.
[7] τῶν om. RO.

camp and create confusion and panic among them. When the armour-bearer replied that he would gladly follow whithersoever he led, though it were to his death, Jonathan, having gained the young man's support, descended from the hill and set off towards the enemy. Now the enemy's camp lay on a cliff, enclosed in a ring of rocks, with three[a] peaks tapering to a long narrow ridge and serving as a bulwark to beat off all attacks. Consequently it came about that no care had been taken to guard the camp, because nature had given the place security and it was believed to be absolutely impossible for any man not merely to scale those crags but even to approach them. When therefore they were nearing the encampment, Jonathan encouraged his armour-bearer, saying: "Now let us attack the enemy; and if, on seeing us, they bid us mount up to them, take that for a presage of victory, but if they utter not a word, as though they invited us not, let us then return." But, as they drew nigh to the enemy's camp, just at the dawn of day,[b] the Philistines espied them and said one to another, "Here are the Hebrews coming out of their holes and caverns," and then to Jonathan and his armour-bearer, "Come on," they cried, "come up to us, to receive the due punishment for your audacity."[c] But Saul's son welcoming that shout as a token of victory, they straightway withdrew from the spot where they

Jonathan and his armour-bearer rout the

[a] Scripture mentions only two peaks, Bozez and Seneb.

[b] The time of the attack is not given in Scripture.

[c] 1 Sam. xiv. 12, "come up and we will show you a thing."

ὤφθησαν τόπου τοῖς πολεμίοις, παραμειψάμενοι[1] δὲ τοῦτον ἐπὶ τὴν πέτραν ἧκον[2] ἔρημον οὖσαν τῶν
113 φυλαττόντων διὰ τὴν ὀχυρότητα. κἀκεῖθεν ἀνερπύσαντες μετὰ πολλῆς ταλαιπωρίας ἐβιάσαντο τὴν τοῦ χωρίου φύσιν ὡς[3] ἀνελθεῖν ἐπὶ τοὺς πολεμίους, ἐπιπεσόντες δ' αὐτοῖς κοιμωμένοις ἀποκτείνουσι μὲν ὡς εἴκοσι, ταραχῆς δὲ καὶ ἐκπλήξεως αὐτοὺς ἐγέμισαν, ὡς τινὰς μὲν φυγεῖν τὰς παν-
114 οπλίας ἀπορρίψαντας, οἱ δὲ πολλοὶ μὴ γνωρίζοντες ἑαυτοὺς διὰ τὸ ἐκ πολλῶν ἐθνῶν εἶναι, πολεμίους ὑπονοοῦντες ἀλλήλους, καὶ γὰρ[4] εἴκαζον ἀναβῆναι πρὸς αὐτοὺς τῶν Ἑβραίων οὐ[5] δύο μόνους, εἰς μάχην ἐτράποντο. καὶ οἱ μὲν αὐτῶν ἀπέθνησκον κτεινόμενοι, τινὲς δὲ φεύγοντες κατὰ τῶν πετρῶν ὠθούμενοι κατεκρημνίζοντο.

115 (3) Τῶν δὲ τοῦ Σαούλου κατασκόπων τεταράχθαι τὸ στρατόπεδον τῶν Παλαιστίνων φρασάντων τῷ βασιλεῖ, Σαοῦλος ἠρώτα μή τις εἴη τῶν αὐτοῦ κεχωρισμένος. ἀκούσας δὲ τὸν υἱὸν καὶ σὺν αὐτῷ τὸν ὁπλοφόρον ἀπεῖναι, κελεύει τὸν ἀρχιερέα λαβόντα τὴν ἀρχιερατικὴν στολὴν προφητεύειν αὐτῷ περὶ τῶν μελλόντων. τοῦ δὲ νίκην ἔσεσθαι καὶ κράτος κατὰ τῶν πολεμίων φράσαντος ἐπεξέρχεται τοῖς Παλαιστίνοις καὶ τεταραγμένοις

[1] παραμειψάμενος MSP.
[2] conj. Niese: ἧκεν codd. Lat.
[3] ὡς om. RO.
[4] + οὐκ SP.
[5] οὐ om. SP.

[a] Details of the fight are an amplification, in harmony with Josephus's rationalizing tendency.

[b] The unscriptural details about the rocks are perhaps suggested by the LXX rendering, in some MSS. (ἐν πετροβόλοις), of the obscure Hebrew text of 1 Sam. xiv. 14.

had been sighted by the enemy and, turning aside from it, reached the rock which by reason of its strength had been left destitute of guards. Thence, creeping up with great labour, they forced their way over the difficulties of the ground and mounted up to the enemy; falling upon these as they slept, they slew some twenty of them and filled the host with such tumult and alarm, that some flung off all their arms and fled, while the more part, not recognizing their comrades, because of the many nationalities of which their army was composed, and taking each other for enemies—for they did not suppose that there had come up against them two only of the Hebrews—they turned to fight one another.[a] And some of them perished by the sword, others as they fled were driven over the rocks and hurled headlong.[b]

Philistines. 1 Sam. xiv. 12.

(3) Saul's spies having now reported to the king that there was a commotion in the camp of the Philistines, Saul inquired whether any of his men had gone from him. Then, on hearing that his son and, with him, his armour-bearer were absent, he ordered the high priest to don his high-priestly robes[c] and to prophesy to him what would befall. The high priest having declared that it would be victory and triumph over his enemies, the king set off against the Philistines and fell upon them while they were yet panic-

Saul's oath of allegiance. 1 Sam. xiv. 16.

[c] In agreement with the LXX which reads "ephod" against the Heb. which has "ark," although the ark was presumably still at Kirjath Jearim. Josephus may, however, have read *'ephod* for *'aron* (ark) in his Heb. text, in which some scholars suspect a deliberate alteration to obviate the inference that there was more than one ark. (*Cf.* W. R. Arnold, *Ephod and Ark.*) The rabbinic commentaries on this passage explain that the ephod with the Urim and Thummin was in the ark.

116 προσβάλλει καὶ φονεύουσιν ἀλλήλους. προσρέουσι
δ' αὐτῷ καὶ οἱ πρότερον εἴς τε τοὺς ὑπονόμους καὶ
εἰς τὰ σπήλαια συμφυγόντες, ἀκούσαντες ὅτι νικᾷ
Σαοῦλος· γενομένων δὲ ὡς μυρίων ἤδη τῶν
Ἑβραίων διώκει τοὺς πολεμίους κατὰ πᾶσαν
ἐσκορπισμένους τὴν χώραν. εἴτε δὲ ὑπὸ τῆς ἐπὶ
τῇ νίκῃ χαρᾶς οὕτω παραλόγως γενομένῃ (συμ-
βαίνει γὰρ μὴ κρατεῖν τοῦ λογισμοῦ τοὺς οὕτως
εὐτυχήσαντας) εἴθ' ὑπὸ ἀγνοίας, εἰς δεινὸν προ-
117 πίπτει[1] καὶ πολλὴν ἔχον κατάμεμψιν ἔργον· βουλόμενος γὰρ αὑτῷ τε τιμωρῆσαι καὶ δίκην ἀπολαβεῖν
παρὰ τῶν Παλαιστίνων ἐπαρᾶται τοῖς Ἑβραίοις,
ἵν' εἴ τις ἀποσχόμενος τοῦ φονεύειν τοὺς ἐχθροὺς
φάγοι[2] μέχρι[3] νὺξ ἐπελθοῦσα τῆς ἀναιρέσεως
καὶ τῆς διώξεως αὐτοὺς παύσει τῶν πολεμίων,
118 οὗτος ἐπάρατος ᾖ. τοῦ δὲ Σαούλου τοῦτο φήσαντος, ἐπεὶ κατά τινα δρυμὸν ἐγένοντο βαθὺν καὶ
μελισσῶν γέμοντα τῆς Ἐφράμου κληρουχίας, ὁ
τοῦ Σαούλου παῖς οὐκ ἐπακηκοὼς τῆς τοῦ πατρὸς
ἀρᾶς οὐδὲ τῆς ἐπ' αὐτῇ τοῦ πλήθους ὁμολογίας,
119 ἀποθλίψας τι κηρίον τοῦ μέλιτος ἤσθιε. μεταξὺ
δὲ γνοὺς ὅτι μετὰ δεινῆς ἀρᾶς ὁ πατὴρ ἀπεῖπε
μὴ γεύσασθαί τινα πρὸ ἡλίου δυσμῶν, ἐσθίων
μὲν ἐπαύσατο, ἔφη δὲ οὐκ ὀρθῶς[4] κωλῦσαι τὸν
πατέρα· μετὰ μείζονος γὰρ ἰσχύος ἂν καὶ προ-

[1] προσπίπτει MSP.
[2] + καὶ μὴ codd. Glycas: an leg. καὶ δὴ ?
[3] μέχρις οὗ MSP Glycas: ἕως οὗ E: antequam Lat.
[4] + τοῦτο MSP

stricken and massacring one another. Moreover those who earlier had taken refuge in the tunnels and caves, on hearing that Saul was victorious, came streaming toward him; and with now some ten thousand[a] Hebrews at his back, he pursued the enemy scattered over the whole countryside. But, whether through exultation at a victory so unexpected—for men are apt to lose control of reason when thus blest by fortune—or through ignorance,[b] he rushed into a dreadful and very blameworthy deed. For, in his desire to avenge himself and to exact punishment from the Philistines, he invoked a curse upon the Hebrews, that should any man desist from slaughtering the foe and take food, before oncoming night should stay them from carnage and the pursuit of the enemy, he should be accursed. Now after that Saul had so spoken, when they were come to a dense oak-coppice[c] swarming with bees in the portion of Ephraim,[d] Saul's son, not having heard his father's curse nor the people's approbation thereof, broke off[e] a piece of a honeycomb and began to eat it. But learning, as he did so, how his father under a dire curse had forbidden any man to taste aught before sundown, he ceased to eat,[f] but said that his father's interdict was not right, for they would have had more strength and ardour for the pursuit, had they

Jonathan's breach of the oath. 1 Sam. xiv. 25.

[a] So in the LXX; Heb. omits the number.

[b] *Cf.* LXX, 1 Sam. xiv. 24 Σαοὺλ ἠγνόησεν ἄγνοιαν μεγάλην: Heb. has nothing corresponding.

[c] The "oak-coppice" is taken from the LXX; Heb. has *ya'ar* which may mean either forest (so the Targum here) or honeycomb.

[d] So the LXX, 1 Sam. xiv. 23; not mentioned in Heb.

[e] 1 Sam. xiv. 27, "put forth the end of the staff that was in his hand and dipped it in the honeycomb."

[f] Scripture does not say that he ceased to eat.

θυμίας διώκοντας, εἰ τροφῆς μετελάμβανον, πολλῷ πλείονας καὶ λαβεῖν τῶν ἐχθρῶν καὶ φονεῦσαι.

120 (4) Πολλὰς γοῦν[1] κατακόψαντες μυριάδας τῶν Παλαιστίνων, δείλης ὀψίας ἐπὶ διαρπαγὴν τοῦ στρατοπέδου τῶν Παλαιστίνων τρέπονται, καὶ λείαν πολλὴν καὶ βοσκήματα λαβόντες κατασφάζουσι καὶ ταῦτ' ἔναιμα[2] κατήσθιον. ἀπαγγέλλεται δὲ τῷ βασιλεῖ ὑπὸ τῶν γραμματέων ὅτι τὸ πλῆθος εἰς τὸν θεὸν ἐξαμαρτάνει θῦσαν καὶ πρὶν ἢ τὸ αἷμα καλῶς ἀποπλῦναι καὶ τὰς σάρκας ποιῆσαι
121 καθαρὰς ἐσθίον. καὶ ὁ Σαοῦλος κελεύει κυλισθῆναι λίθον μέγαν εἰς μέσον καὶ κηρύσσει θύειν ἐπ' αὐτοῦ τὸν ὄχλον τὰ ἱερεῖα, καὶ τὰ κρέα μὴ σὺν τῷ αἵματι δαίνυσθαι· τοῦτο γὰρ οὐκ εἶναι τῷ θεῷ κεχαρισμένον. τοῦτο δὲ πάντων κατὰ τὴν πρόσταξιν τοῦ βασιλέως ποιησάντων ἵστησιν ἐκεῖ βωμὸν ὁ Σαοῦλος καὶ ὠλοκαύτωσεν ἐπ' αὐτοῦ ἐκεῖ[3] τῷ θεῷ. τοῦτον πρῶτον βωμὸν κατεσκεύασεν.

122 (5) Ἄγειν δ' εὐθὺς τὴν στρατιὰν ἐπὶ τὴν παρεμβολὴν τῶν πολεμίων ἐπὶ τὴν διαρπαγὴν τῶν ἐν αὐτῇ βουλόμενος πρὶν ἡμέρας, καὶ τῶν στρατιωτῶν οὐκ ὀκνούντων ἕπεσθαι, πολλὴν δ' εἰς ἃ προστάττει προθυμίαν ἐνδεικνυμένων, καλέσας ὁ βασιλεὺς Ἀχίτωβον τὸν ἀρχιερέα κελεύει[4] αὐτὸν γνῶναι εἰ δίδωσιν αὐτοῖς ὁ θεὸς καὶ συγχωρεῖ βαδίσασιν ἐπὶ τὸ στρατόπεδον τῶν ἐχθρῶν

[1] RO: δ' οὖν MSP: οὖν E.
[2] SPE: ἐν αἵματι rell.
[3] ἐκεῖ secl. edd.; *cf.* LXX, 1 Sam. xiv. 34.
[4] ἐκέλευσεν MSP.

partaken of food, and would thus have captured and slain many more of the foe.

(4) Many, for all that, were the myriads of Philistines whom they cut down ere at dusk they turned to the pillage of the enemy's camp; where, having taken much booty and cattle, they slaughtered and set to devouring them all reeking with blood. Thereupon it was reported to the king by the scribes,[a] that the host were sinning against God in that, having sacrificed, they were now eating, before they had duly washed away the blood and made the flesh clean.[b] Then Saul ordered a great stone to be rolled into the midst and made proclamation to the throng to sacrifice their victims thereon and not to feast upon the flesh with the blood, since that was not well-pleasing to God. And when all had so done in obedience to the king's command, Saul set up an altar there and offered burnt-offerings[c] thereon to God. This was the first altar that he built.

Plundering of the Philistines' camp. 1 Sam. xiv. 31.

(5) Being now desirous to lead his army forthwith to the enemy's encampment to plunder everything therein before daybreak, and seeing that his soldiers, far from hesitating to follow him, showed great alacrity to obey his orders, the king summoned Achitob[d] the high priest and bade him ascertain whether God would grant and permit them to proceed to the camp of the foe and destroy such as were

Saul's discovery of Jonathan's error. 1 Sam. xiv. 36.

[a] Not mentioned in Scripture.

[b] *Cf. A.* iii. 260 on Lev. xix. 26, Deut. xii. 16.

[c] Scripture does not specify that the sacrifices were burnt-offerings, as do Josephus and the rabbis in their discussion of this passage, Bab. Talmud, Zebaḥim 120 a.

[d] Priest's name not mentioned in Scripture; according to § 107, the high priest at this time was Achias (bibl. Ahiah), the son of Achitob (bibl. Ahitub).

123 διαφθεῖραι τοὺς ἐν αὐτῷ τυγχάνοντας. εἰπόντος
δὲ τοῦ ἱερέως μὴ ἀποκρίνεσθαι τὸν θεόν "ἀλλ' οὐ
δίχα αἰτίας,[1]" εἶπεν ὁ Σαοῦλος, "πυνθανομένοις
ἡμῖν φωνὴν οὐ δίδωσιν ὁ θεός, ὃς πρότερον αὐτὸς
προεμήνυσε πάντα καὶ μηδ' ἐπερωτῶσιν ἔφθασε[2]
λέγων, ἀλλ' ἔστι τι λανθάνον ἐξ ἡμῶν ἁμάρτημα
124 πρὸς αὐτὸν αἴτιον τῆς σιωπῆς. καὶ ὄμνυμί γε
τοῦτον αὐτόν, ἦ μὴν κἂν ὁ παῖς ὁ ἐμὸς Ἰωνάθης ᾖ
τὸ ἁμάρτημα τοῦτο ἐργασάμενος ἀποκτείνειν[3]
αὐτὸν καὶ τὸν θεὸν οὕτως ἱλάσασθαι,[4] ὡς ἂν εἰ καὶ
παρ' ἀλλοτρίου καὶ μηδὲν ἐμοὶ προσήκοντος τὴν
125 ὑπὲρ αὐτοῦ δίκην ἀπελάμβανον." τοῦ δὲ πλήθους
τοῦτο ποιεῖν ἐπιβοήσαντος, παραχρῆμα πάντας
ἵστησιν εἰς ἕνα τόπον, ἵσταται δὲ καὶ αὐτὸς σὺν
τῷ παιδὶ κατ' ἄλλο μέρος καὶ κλήρῳ τὸν ἡμαρτη-
κότα μαθεῖν ἐπεζήτει· καὶ λαγχάνει δοκεῖν οὗτος
126 εἶναι Ἰωνάθης. ἐπερωτώμενος δὲ ὑπὸ τοῦ πατρὸς
τί πεπλημμέληκε καὶ τί[5] παρὰ τὸν βίον οὐκ
ὀρθῶς οὐδὲ ὁσίως αὐτῷ διαπραξαμένῳ συνέγνωκε
"πάτερ," εἶπεν, "ἄλλο μὲν οὐδέν," ὅτι δὲ χθὲς
ἀγνοῶν τὴν ἀρὰν αὐτοῦ καὶ τὸν ὅρκον μεταξὺ
διώκων τοὺς πολεμίους ἐγεύσατο κηρίων. Σαοῦλος
δ' ἀποκτείνειν αὐτὸν ὄμνυσι καὶ τῆς γενέσεως καὶ
127 τῆς φύσεως τῶν φίλτρων ἐτίμησε[6] τὸν ὅρκον. ὁ
δ' οὐ καταπλήττεται τὴν ἀπειλὴν τοῦ θανάτου,
παραστησάμενος δ' εὐγενῶς καὶ μεγαλοφρόνως
"οὐδ' ἐγώ σε," φησίν, "ἱκετεύσω φείσασθαί μου,
πάτερ, ἥδιστος δέ μοι ὁ θάνατος ὑπέρ τε τῆς σῆς

[1] + τινός SP.
[2] edd.: ἔφθανε MSP: φθάσαι RO.
[3] codd.: ἀποκτενεῖν Hudson. [4] ἱλάσεσθαι Naber.
[5] τί περ RO: τί πεποίηκε καὶ τί SP Glycas.
[6] προτιμήσας ed. pr.: praeponeret Lat.

found therein. The priest having reported that there was no response from God, "Nay, but it is not without cause," said Saul, "that God gives no answer to our inquiry, He who ere now forewarned us of all Himself and spoke to us even before we inquired of Him. Nay, it is some secret sin against Him on our part that is the cause of this silence.[a] Aye and I swear by God Himself that verily, be it my own son Jonathan who hath committed this sin, I will slay him and thus propitiate God, even as though it were from a stranger without kinship with me that I was taking vengeance on His behalf." The multitude thereon calling upon him so to do, he forthwith caused them all to stand in one place, and stood himself with his son in another, and sought by the lot to discover the sinner; and the lot indicated Jonathan. Being asked by his father wherein he had gone astray and of what wrong or unholy act in all his life he was conscious, "Of nothing, father," said he, "save that yesterday, all ignorant of that imprecation and oath of thine,[b] while in pursuit of the enemy, I tasted a honeycomb." Saul thereat swore to slay him, respecting his oath more than the tender ties of fatherhood and of nature. Yet Jonathan quailed not before this menace of death, but surrendering himself nobly and magnanimously, "Neither will I," said he, "entreat thee to spare me, father. Very sweet to me were death undergone for thy

[a] First part of Saul's speech is an addition to Scripture.
[b] Here the Gr. changes to indirect speech.

εὐσεβείας γινόμενος καὶ ἐπὶ νίκῃ λαμπρᾷ· μέγιστον γὰρ παραμύθιον τὸ καταλιπεῖν Ἑβραίους Παλαι-
128 στίνων κεκρατηκότας." ἐπὶ τούτοις ὁ λαὸς πᾶς ἤλγησε καὶ συνέπαθεν, ὤμοσέ τε μὴ περιόψεσθαι τὸν αἴτιον τῆς νίκης Ἰωνάθην ἀποθανόντα. καὶ τὸν μὲν οὕτως ἐξαρπάζουσι τῆς τοῦ πατρὸς ἀρᾶς, αὐτοὶ δὲ εὐχὰς ὑπὲρ τοῦ νεανίσκου ποιοῦνται τῷ θεῷ ὥστ' αὐτὸν ἀπολῦσαι τοῦ ἁμαρτήματος.

129 (6) Καὶ ὁ Σαοῦλος εἰς τὴν ἑαυτοῦ πόλιν ὑπέστρεψε διαφθείρας ὡσεὶ μυριάδας ἓξ τῶν πολεμίων. βασιλεύει δὲ εὐτυχῶς, καὶ τὰ πλησιόχωρα τῶν ἐθνῶν πολεμήσας χειροῦται τό τε Ἀμμανιτῶν καὶ Μωαβιτῶν καὶ[1] Παλαιστίνους, Ἰδουμαίους τε καὶ[2] Ἀμαληκίτας[3] καὶ τὸν βασιλέα τῆς Σωβᾶς.[4] ἦσαν δὲ παῖδες αὐτῷ τρεῖς μὲν ἄρσενες Ἰωνάθης καὶ Ἰησοῦς καὶ Μέλχισος, θυγατέρες δὲ Μερόβη καὶ Μιχαάλ.[5] στρατηγὸν δὲ εἶχε τὸν τοῦ θείου
130 παῖδα Ἀβήναρον· Νῆρος δ' ἐκεῖνος ἐκαλεῖτο, Νῆρος δὲ καὶ Κεὶς ὁ Σαούλου πατὴρ ἀδελφοὶ ἦσαν, υἱοὶ δ' Ἀβελίου.[6] ἦν δὲ καὶ πλῆθος ἁρμάτων Σαούλῳ καὶ ἱππέων, οἷς[7] δὲ[8] πολεμήσειε νικήσας ἀπηλλάσσετο, καὶ τοὺς Ἑβραίους εἰς εὐπραγίας καὶ μέγεθος εὐδαιμονίας προηγάγετο καὶ τῶν ἄλλων ἀπέδειξεν ἐθνῶν δυνατωτέρους,[9] καὶ τῶν[10] νέων τοὺς δὴ καὶ μεγέθει καὶ κάλλει διαφέροντας φύλακας τοῦ σώματος ἐποιεῖτο.

[1] καὶ om. RO.
[2] τε καὶ SP: om. rell.
[3] om. Lat.: + τε ROME.
[4] Bosius ex Lat.: ὡβᾶς codd. E: σουβᾶ Zon.
[5] M: μελχαὰ SP: χθαάλ RO.
[6] Abihel Lat.: Ἀβιήλου conj. Hudson ex LXX.
[7] οὓς SE.
[8] RO: δ' ἂν rell.
[9] ROE: δυνατωτάτους rell. Lat.
[10] καὶ τῶν RO: τῶν δὲ MSP.

piety's sake and after brilliant victory; for highest consolation were it to leave Hebrews triumphant over Philistines."[a] Thereupon all the people were moved to grief and sympathy and they swore that they would not suffer Jonathan, the author of that victory, to die. Thus then did they snatch him from his father's curse, and themselves offered prayers[b] for the young man to God, that He would grant him absolution from his sin.

(6) So Saul returned to his own city after destroying some sixty thousand of the enemy. He then reigned happily and, having made war on the neighbouring nations, subdued those of the Ammanites and Moabites, besides Philistines, Idumaeans and Amalekites, and the king of Sōba. He had three sons, Jonathan, Jesus[c] and Melchis,[d] and his daughters were Merobe[e] and Michaal.[f] For commander of his army he had Abēnar,[g] his uncle's son; that uncle was named Ner, and Ner and Kis, the father of Saul, were brothers, sons of Abelios.[h] Saul had, moreover, abundance of chariots and horsemen, and with whomsoever he fought he returned victorious; and he brought the Hebrews to greatness of success and prosperity and rendered them more powerful than the other nations, and of the young men such as excelled in stature and beauty he took for his bodyguards.

Saul's victories. 1 Sam. xiv 46.

[a] Jonathan's speech is unscriptural.

[b] "snatch" and "offered prayers" combine the Heb. "redeemed" (or "rescued") and the LXX "prayed for" of 1 Sam. xiv. 45.

[c] Bibl. Ishui, Heb. *Yishwi*, LXX Ἰεσσιούλ (*v.l.* Ἰσουεί).

[d] Bibl. Melchishua, LXX Μελχεισά.

[e] Bibl. Merab, LXX Μερόβ.

[f] Bibl. Michal, LXX Μελχόλ.

[g] Bibl. Abner, Heb. *Abīner*, LXX Ἀβεννήρ. *Cf.* § 58.

[h] Bibl. Abiel.

131 (vii. 1) Σαμουῆλος δὲ παραγενόμενος πρὸς τὸν Σαοῦλον πεμφθῆναι πρὸς αὐτὸν ἔφασκεν ὑπὸ τοῦ θεοῦ, ὅπως αὐτὸν ὑπομνήσῃ ὅτι βασιλέα προκρίνας αὐτὸν ἁπάντων ὁ θεὸς ἀπέδειξε, καὶ διὰ τοῦτο πείθεσθαι καὶ κατήκοον αὐτῷ γενέσθαι, ὡς αὐτοῦ μὲν ἔχοντος τὴν τῶν ἐθνῶν ἡγεμονίαν, τοῦ δὲ θεοῦ τὴν καὶ[1] ἐκείνου καὶ τῶν ὅλων πραγμά-
132 των. λέγειν τοίνυν ἔφασκε τὸν θεόν· "ἐπεὶ πολλὰ κακὰ τοὺς Ἑβραίους Ἀμαληκῖται διέθηκαν κατὰ τὴν ἔρημον, ὅτε ἐξελθόντες ἀπ' Αἰγύπτου εἰς τὴν νῦν ὑπάρχουσαν αὐτοῖς ἐστέλλοντο χώραν, κελεύω πολέμῳ τιμωρησάμενον τοὺς Ἀμαληκίτας
133 καὶ κρατήσαντα μηδέν'[2] αὐτῶν ὑπολιπεῖν, ἀλλὰ πάσης διεξελθεῖν ἡλικίας, ἀρξαμένους ἀπὸ γυναικῶν κτείνειν καὶ νηπίων καὶ τοιαύτην ὑπὲρ ὧν τοὺς προγόνους ὑμῶν εἰργάσαντο τιμωρίαν ἀπολαβεῖν, φείσασθαι δὲ μήτε ὑποζυγίων μήτε τῶν ἄλλων βοσκημάτων εἰς ὠφέλειαν καὶ κτῆσιν ἰδίαν, ἅπαντα δ' ἀναθεῖναι τῷ θεῷ καὶ τὸ Ἀμαλήκου ὄνομα ταῖς Μωυσέος κατακολουθήσαντ' ἐντολαῖς ἐξαλεῖψαι."

134 (2) Ὁμολογεῖ δὲ ποιήσειν Σαοῦλος τὰ προστασσόμενα, τὴν δὲ πειθαρχίαν τὴν πρὸς τὸν θεὸν οὐκ ἐν τῷ ποιήσασθαι τὴν πρὸς τοὺς Ἀμαληκίτας στρατείαν λογιζόμενος εἶναι μόνον, ἀλλὰ καὶ τῷ τὴν ἑτοιμότητα καὶ τὸ τάχος ἀναβολῆς οὐ προσούσης ἔτι μᾶλλον ἐμφανίζειν,[3] ἀθροίζει τε πᾶσαν τὴν δύναμιν καὶ ταύτην ἐξαριθμήσας ἐν Γαλγάλοις εὑρίσκει τῶν Ἰσραηλιτῶν ἔξω τῆς Ἰούδα φυλῆς περὶ τεσσαράκοντα μυριάδας· ἥδε γὰρ ἡ φυλὴ καθ'

[1] τὴν καὶ conj. Niese: καὶ τὴν κατ' codd.
[2] S: μηδὲν rell.
[3] τῷ τὴν . . . ἐμφανίζειν ex Lat.: τὴν . . . ἐμφανίζει codd.

(vii. 1) Samuel now came to Saul and said that he had been sent to him by God to recall to him that God had preferred him above all others and created him king, and that he ought therefore to obey and give ear to Him, for, while he had dominion over the nations, God had dominion both over him and over the universe. He thereupon announced that God had spoken thus: "Forasmuch as the Amalekites did much evil to the Hebrews in the wilderness, when they were come out of Egypt and on their way to the land that now is theirs, I command thee to take vengeance on the Amalekites in war and, when victorious, to leave not one of them remaining; but you shall deal death to all of every age, beginning with the women and infants, and in this wise take vengeance for what they did to your forefathers; thou art to spare neither beasts of burden nor any cattle at all for private profit or possession, but to devote all to God and, in compliance with the behests of Moses,[a] to blot out the name of Amalek."

Samuel sends Saul to exterminate the Amalekites. 1 Sam. xv. 1.

(2) These injunctions Saul promised to fulfil; and reflecting that obedience to God lay not merely in making this campaign against the Amalekites, but would be displayed yet more by an alacrity and haste that brooked no delay, he mustered all his forces and, having numbered them at Galgala,[b] found that the Israelites, apart from the tribe of Judah, were some 400,000 men; that tribe by itself furnished 30,000

Saul musters his troops at Gilgal. 1 Sam. xv. 4.

[a] *Cf. A.* iii. 60 on Ex. xvii. 14, and *A.* iv. 304 on Deut. xxv. 17. Moses is not mentioned in Scripture at this point.

[b] So the LXX; Heb. has Telaim, a city in southern Judah.

135 αὐτήν ἐστι στρατιῶται τρισμύριοι. Σαοῦλος δ' ἐμβαλὼν εἰς τὴν τῶν Ἀμαληκιτῶν χώραν ἐνέδρας πολλὰς καὶ λόχους περὶ τὸν χειμάρρουν τίθησιν, ὡς μὴ μόνον ἐκ τοῦ φανεροῦ μαχόμενος[1] αὐτοὺς κακῶς ποιεῖν, ἀλλὰ καὶ μὴ προσδοκῶσι κατὰ τὰς ὁδοὺς ἐπιπίπτων καὶ κυκλούμενος[2] ἀναιρεῖν· καὶ δὴ συμβαλὼν αὐτοῖς εἰς μάχην τρέπεται τοὺς πολεμίους καὶ διαφθείρει πάντας, φεύγουσιν ἐπ-
136 ακολουθῶν. ὡς δ' ἐκεῖνο τὸ ἔργον αὐτῷ κατὰ τὴν τοῦ θεοῦ προφητείαν ἐχώρησε, ταῖς πόλεσι τῶν Ἀμαληκιτῶν προσέβαλε καὶ τὰς μὲν μηχανήμασι, τὰς δὲ ὀρύγμασιν ὑπονόμοις καὶ τείχεσιν ἔξωθεν ἀντῳκοδομημένοις, τὰς δὲ λιμῷ καὶ δίψει, τὰς δὲ ἄλλοις τρόποις ἐκπολιορκήσας καὶ λαβὼν κατὰ κράτος, ἐπὶ σφαγὴν γυναικῶν καὶ νηπίων ἐχώρησεν, οὐδὲν ὠμὸν οὐδ' ἀνθρωπίνης σκληρότερον διαπράσσεσθαι φύσεως ἡγούμενος, πρῶτον μὲν πολεμίους ταῦτα δρῶν, ἔπειτα προστάγματι θεοῦ, ᾧ
137 τὸ μὴ πείθεσθαι κίνδυνον ἔφερε. λαμβάνει δὲ καὶ τὸν βασιλέα τῶν ἐχθρῶν Ἄγαγον αἰχμάλωτον, οὗ θαυμάσας τὸ κάλλος καὶ τὸ μέγεθος τοῦ σώματος σωτηρίας ἄξιον ἔκρινεν, οὐκέτι τοῦτο ποιῶν κατὰ βούλησιν τοῦ θεοῦ, πάθει δὲ νικώμενος ἰδίῳ καὶ χαριζόμενος ἀκαίρως περὶ ὧν οὐκ εἶχεν
138 ἀκίνδυνον ἐξουσίαν οἴκτῳ. ὁ μὲν[3] γὰρ θεὸς οὕτως ἐμίσησε τὸ τῶν Ἀμαληκιτῶν ἔθνος, ὡς μηδὲ

[1] conj. Niese ex Lat.: μαχομένους codd.
[2] conj. Niese: ἐπιπίπτειν καὶ κυκλουμένους codd.
[3] μὲν om. MSP.

[a] Both numbers in agreement with most MSS. of the LXX; Heb. has 200,000 and 10,000 respectively.
[b] Josephus here omits Saul's invitation to the Kenites to separate themselves from Amalek (1 Sam. xv. 6), before his

combatants.[a] Having then invaded the country of the Amalekites,[b] Saul posted numerous pickets and ambuscades around the ravine,[c] with intent not only to molest them in open warfare, but also to fall upon them unexpectedly on the roads and envelop and destroy them; and in fact, on joining battle with them he routed the enemy and, pursuing the fugitives, destroyed them all. That task having, in accordance with God's prediction, been successfully achieved, he attacked the cities of the Amalekites; and when, some by engines of war, others by mining operations and exterior opposing walls, others by hunger and thirst, and yet others by other means,[d] he had carried and stormed them all, he then proceeded to the slaughter of women and infants, deeming naught therein cruel or too savage for human nature to perform, first because they were enemies whom he was treating thus, and then because of the commandment of God, whom it was dangerous to disobey. But he also took prisoner the enemy's king, Agag, whom out of admiration for his beauty and his stature[e] he accounted worthy to be saved; herein he was no longer acting in accordance with the will of God, but giving way to feelings of his own, and yielding inopportunely to compassion where it was not permitted to him without peril. For God so hated the race of the Amalekites that He had ordered him to spare not

Saul captures Agag.
1 Sam. xv 8

attack upon the latter. In § 140 he alludes to this scriptural passage in mentioning the Sikimites. *Cf.* note *ad loc.*

[c] Scripture does not tell us what ravine (Heb. *naḥal*, "bed of a stream," *cf.* Arabic *wady*) is meant; the geographical details are vague throughout this account.

[d] Details of the invasion and sieges are an amplification.

[e] Saul's aesthetic motive for sparing Agag is an invention of Josephus.

νηπίων φείσασθαι κελεῦσαι πρὸς ἃ μᾶλλον ἔλεος
γίνεσθαι πέφυκε, Σαοῦλος δὲ αὐτῶν[1] τὸν βασιλέα
καὶ τὸν ἡγεμόνα τῶν εἰς Ἑβραίους κακῶν ἔσωσε,
τῆς μνήμης ὧν ἐπέστειλεν ὁ θεὸς τὸ τοῦ πολεμίου
139 κάλλος ἐπίπροσθεν ποιησάμενος. συνεξήμαρτε δ'
αὐτῷ καὶ τὸ πλῆθος· καὶ γὰρ ἐκεῖνοι τῶν ὑποζυγίων καὶ τῶν βοσκημάτων ἐφείσαντο καὶ διήρπασαν, μὴ τηρεῖν αὐτὰ τοῦ θεοῦ κελεύσαντος, τά τε
ἄλλα χρήματα καὶ τὸν πλοῦτον ἐξεφόρησαν, εἰ δέ τι
μὴ σπουδῆς ἦν ἄξιον ὥστε κεκτῆσθαι διέφθειραν.
140 (3) Νικήσας δὲ Σαοῦλος ἅπαντας τοὺς ἀπὸ Πη-
λουσίου τῆς Αἰγύπτου καθήκοντας ἕως τῆς Ἐρυθρᾶς
θαλάσσης διέφθειρε πολεμίους,[2] παραλιπὼν τὸ τῶν
Σικιμιτῶν ἔθνος· οὗτοι γὰρ ἐν τῇ Μαδιηνῇ χώρᾳ
μέσοι κατῴκηνται. πρὸ δὲ τῆς μάχης πέμψας
παρήγγειλεν αὐτοῖς ἀναχωρεῖν, μὴ τοῖς Ἀμαληκίταις κοινωνήσωσι συμφορᾶς· συγγενεῖς γὰρ αὐτοὺς
ὄντας Ῥαγουήλου τοῦ Μωυσέος πενθεροῦ σώζειν
αἰτίαν ἔχειν.
141 (4) Καὶ Σαοῦλος μὲν ὡς μηδενὸς παρακούσας
ὧν ὁ προφήτης ἐπέστειλε μέλλοντι τὸν πρὸς
Ἀμαληκίτας ἐκφέρειν πόλεμον, ἀλλ' ὡς ἐπὶ πᾶσιν
ἐκείνοις ἀκριβῶς πεφυλαγμένοις νενικηκὼς τοὺς
πολεμίους οἴκαδε πρὸς αὐτὸν ὑπέστρεψε χαίρων

[1] αὐτὸν R[1]S: regem Agag Lat.
[2] RO Lat.: τὴν τῶν πολεμίων M (+ χώραν E): τὰ τῶν πολεμίων SP.

[a] 1 Sam. xv. 7 "from Havilah until thou comest to Shur over against Egypt"; Josephus reverses the directions, assuming that Shur corresponds to Pelusium and that Havilah is somewhere near the Red Sea.

[b] 1 Sam. xv. 6 "Kenites." "Sikimites," which is geographically impossible (=inhabitants of Shechem), may

even the infants, to whom it is more natural that pity should be shown; but Saul saved their king, the author of all the injuries to the Hebrews, having had more regard for the beauty of his enemy than for memory of what God enjoined. The people too were his partners in sin; for they spared the beasts and the cattle and took for their prey what God had forbidden to be preserved, and carried off all the chattels and riches beside; but whatever was not worth coveting as a possession that did they destroy.

Saul's further conquests. 1 Sam. xv. 6, 7.

(3) Conquering the whole district extending from Pelusium in Egypt to the Red Sea,[a] Saul destroyed the inhabitants as enemies, saving only the race of the Sikimites,[b] who had settled in the heart of the country of Madian. To these he had, before the combat, sent messengers admonishing them to withdraw, lest they should share the fate of the Amalekites; for, being kinsmen of Raguel, the father-in-law of Moses, he had, as he said, good reason to spare them.[c]

God's anger at Saul's transgression. 1 Sam. xv. 10.

(4) So Saul, as though he had neglected none of the injunctions which he had received from the prophet when embarking on his campaign against the Amalekites, but had strictly observed them all in having conquered his enemies, returned homeward

be due to corruption in Josephus's text. Rappaport makes the interesting suggestion that either Josephus wrote " Silimites," the Greek form of the Targum's name " Shalma'ah " for the Kenites, and that this was corrupted to " Sikimites," or that he connected Shalma'ah with Shechem on the basis of Gen. xxxiii. 18 " Shalem a city of Shechem."

[c] *Cf. A.* v. 127. The reference to the kinship with Moses is paralleled in rabbinic tradition. Scripture ascribes Saul's consideration to the Israelites' memory of services rendered them by the Kenites in the Exodus.

142 ἐπὶ τοῖς κατωρθωμένοις. ὁ δὲ θεὸς ἄχθεται τῇ τε[1] τοῦ βασιλέως τῶν Ἀμαληκιτῶν σωτηρίᾳ καὶ τῇ τῶν βοσκημάτων διαρπαγῇ τοῦ πλήθους, ὅτι μὴ συγχωρήσαντος αὐτοῦ ταῦτ' ἐπράχθη· δεινὸν γὰρ ἡγεῖτο νικᾶν μὲν καὶ περιγίνεσθαι τῶν ἐχθρῶν ἐκείνου τὴν ἰσχὺν διδόντος αὐτοῖς, καταφρονεῖσθαι δὲ καὶ παρακούεσθαι μηδὲ ὡς ἄνθρωπον βασιλέα.
143 μετανοεῖν οὖν ἔλεγε πρὸς τὸν προφήτην Σαμουῆλον ἐπὶ τῷ χειροτονῆσαι βασιλέα τὸν Σαοῦλον, μηδὲν ὧν αὐτὸς κελεύει πράττοντα, τῇ δ' οἰκείᾳ βουλήσει χρώμενον. σφόδρα ταῦτ' ἀκούσας ὁ Σαμουῆλος συνεχύθη[2] καὶ δι' ὅλης τῆς νυκτὸς παρακαλεῖν ἤρξατο τὸν θεὸν καταλλάττεσθαι τῷ Σαούλῳ καὶ
144 μὴ χαλεπαίνειν. ὁ δὲ τὴν συγγνώμην οὐκ ἐπένευσεν εἰς τὸν Σαοῦλον αἰτουμένῳ τῷ προφήτῃ, λογισάμενος οὐκ εἶναι δίκαιον ἁμαρτήματα[3] χαρίζεσθαι παραιτήσει[4]· οὐ γὰρ ἐξ ἄλλου τινὸς φύεσθαι μᾶλλον ἢ τοῦ καταμαλακίζεσθαι[5] τοὺς ἀδικουμένους· θηρωμένους γὰρ δόξαν ἐπιεικείας καὶ χρηστότητος λανθάνειν αὐτοὺς[6] ταῦτα γεννῶντας.
145 ὡς οὖν ἀπεῖπεν ὁ θεὸς τῇ τοῦ προφήτου δεήσει καὶ δῆλος ἦν[7] μεταμελόμενος, ἅμ' ἡμέρᾳ Σαμουῆλος εἰς Γάλγαλα παραγίνεται πρὸς Σαοῦλον· θεασάμενος δ' αὐτὸν ὁ βασιλεὺς προστρέχει καὶ κατασπασάμενος "τῷ θεῷ," φησίν, "εὐχαριστῶ δόντι μοι τὴν νίκην, ἅπαντα μέντοι γε τὰ κελευσθέντα
146 ὑπ' αὐτοῦ πέπρακται.[8]" Σαμουῆλος δὲ πρὸς τοῦθ' ὑπολαβὼν "πόθεν οὖν ἀκούω θρεμμάτων," εἶπε,

[1] M Suidas: τῇ ROE: ἐπί τε τῇ SP.
[2] διεχύθη RO.
[3] ed. pr.: ἁμαρτήμασι codd.
[4] Niese: παραίτησιν codd. (-τήσεσιν ed. pr.).
[5] μαλακίζεσθαι O.
[6] P²: αὐτοὺς rell.
[7] + μὴ MSP Lat.^vid.
[8] O: πεπρᾶχθαι rell.

exultant at his success. But God was ill pleased at his sparing the life of the king of Amalek and at the people's making plunder of the cattle, because these things had not been permitted by Him; for He deemed it an outrage that when they had conquered and defeated the foe through the might which He had given them, He should meet with such contempt and disobedience as they would show to no human king. He therefore told the prophet Samuel that He repented of having elected Saul as king, since he was in no wise executing His commands, but doing according to his own pleasure. On hearing this Samuel was sore troubled, and all night long set himself to entreat God to be reconciled to Saul and not wroth with him. But God would grant no pardon to Saul at the prophet's request, accounting it not just to condone sins at the intercession of another; for nothing more favoured their growth than laxity on the part of the wronged, who in seeking a reputation for mildness and kindness are unwittingly the begetters of crime. When therefore God had refused the prophet's prayer and showed that He repented Himself,[a] Samuel at break of day repaired to Galgala to meet Saul. At sight of him, the king ran to him and embraced him. "I render thanks," said he, "to God who has given me victory; and moreover, all His commands have been performed." Whereto Samuel replied, "Whence comes it then

Samuel at Gilgal prophesies Saul's doom. 1 Sam. xv. 12.

[a] *i.e.* of having made Saul king, *cf.* 1 Sam. xv. 35. The variant text δῆλος ἦν μὴ μεταμελόμενος "and showed no change of mind" is probably due to scribes who thought that Josephus was referring to God's decision to punish Saul in spite of Samuel's intercession.

"καὶ ὑποζυγίων βοῆς ἐν τῷ στρατοπέδῳ;" ὁ δὲ τὸν λαὸν ταῦτ' εἰς θυσίας ἀπεκρίνατο τετηρηκέναι· τὸ μέντοι γε τῶν Ἀμαληκιτῶν γένος ἅπαν ἐξηφανίσθαι κατὰ τὴν ἐντολὴν καὶ περιλείπεσθαι ἄλλον μηδένα, πρὸς δ' αὐτὸν ἀγαγεῖν μόνον τηρήσαντα αὐτῶν τὸν βασιλέα, περὶ οὗ τί δεῖ ποιεῖν βουλεύσε-
147 σθαι[1] πρὸς ἀλλήλους ἔφασκεν. ὁ δὲ προφήτης οὐχὶ θυσίαις ἔλεγεν ἥδεσθαι τὸ θεῖον, ἀλλὰ τοῖς ἀγαθοῖς καὶ δικαίοις· οὗτοι δέ εἰσιν οἱ τῇ βουλήσει καὶ ταῖς ἐντολαῖς αὐτοῦ κατακολουθοῦντες καὶ μηδὲν ἄλλο πραχθήσεσθαι καλῶς ὑφ' ἑαυτῶν νομίζοντες ἢ ὅ τι ἂν ποιήσωσι τοῦ θεοῦ κεκελευκότος· καταφρονεῖσθαι γὰρ οὐχ ὅταν αὐτῷ μὴ θύῃ τις,
148 ἀλλ' ὅταν ἀπειθεῖν δοκῇ. "παρὰ δὲ τῶν οὐχ ὑποτασσομένων οὐδ' ἀληθῆ καὶ μόνην τῷ θεῷ κεχαρισμένην θρησκευόντων θρησκείαν, οὔτ' ἂν πολλὰ καὶ πιμελῆ καταθύσωσιν ἱερεῖα, οὔτ' ἂν κόσμον ἀναθημάτων ἐξ ἀργύρου καὶ χρυσοῦ πεποιημένων προσφέρωσι, δέχεται ταῦτ' εὐμενῶς, ἀλλ' ἀποστρέφεται καὶ δείγματα τῆς πονηρίας οὐκ
149 εὐσέβειαν ἡγεῖται. τοῖς δ' ἓν καὶ μόνον τοῦθ' ὅ τι περ ἂν φθέγξηται καὶ κελεύσῃ ὁ θεὸς διὰ μνήμης ἔχουσι καὶ τεθνάναι μᾶλλον ἢ παραβῆναί τι τούτων αἱρουμένοις ἐπιτέρπεται, καὶ οὔτε θυσίαν ἐπιζητεῖ παρ' αὐτῶν καὶ παρὰ θυόντων δέ, κἂν ᾖ λιτά, τῆς πενίας ἥδιον τὴν τιμὴν ἢ παρὰ τῶν πλουσιωτάτων
150 δεξιοῦται. σὺ τοίνυν ἴσθι σαυτὸν δι' ὀργῆς ὄντα τῷ θεῷ· κατεφρόνησας γὰρ καὶ κατημέλησας ὧν ἐπέστειλε. πῶς οὖν οἴει τὴν θυσίαν ἂν αὐτὸν προσβλέπειν ἐξ ὧν κατέκρινεν ἀπολέσθαι γινο-

[1] Ernesti ex Lat.: βουλεύεσθαι codd.

that I hear sounds of cattle and beasts of burden in the camp?" The king answered that the people had reserved these for sacrifice, but that the race of the Amalekites had been utterly exterminated in accordance with the divine command, and that not one had been left alive, save only their king, whom he had preserved and brought to Samuel, and concerning whose fate they would, he said, take counsel together. But the prophet answered that the Deity took not delight in sacrifices, but in good and righteous men, namely such as follow His will and His commandments and deem that no act of theirs will have been rightly done save what they do at God's bidding; for contempt of God, he said, is shown not in withholding sacrifice but in appearing to disobey Him. "And from such as submit not nor offer the true worship that alone is acceptable to God, even though they sacrifice many fat victims, even though they present to Him sumptuous offerings wrought of silver and gold, yet does He not receive these gifts graciously, but rejects them and regards them as tokens of iniquity rather than as piety. But they who are mindful of this one thing alone, to wit what God has spoken and commanded, and who choose rather to die than to transgress aught thereof, in them does He rejoice; from them He requires no sacrifice, or, should they offer any, however modest, more gladly does He welcome this homage from poverty than that of the wealthiest. Know, then, that thou thyself hast incurred the wrath of God, for thou hast held lightly and neglected His commandments. How thinkest thou that He could look upon a sacrifice offered from those things which He doomed

μένην; πλὴν εἰ μὴ νομίζεις ὅμοιον ὀλέθρῳ[1] τὸ θύεσθαι ταῦτα τῷ θεῷ. προσδόκα τοίνυν τὴν βασιλείαν ἀφαιρεθησόμενος καὶ τὴν ἐξουσίαν, ἀφ' ἧς ὁρμώμενος τοῦ παρασχόντος σοι θεοῦ ταύτην
151 ἠμέλησας." Σαοῦλος δὲ ἀδικεῖν ὡμολόγει καὶ τὴν ἁμαρτίαν οὐκ ἠρνεῖτο· παραβῆναι γὰρ τὰς ἐντολὰς τοῦ προφήτου· κατὰ μέντοι γε δέος καὶ τὸν ἀπὸ τῶν στρατιωτῶν φόβον μὴ κωλῦσαι διαρπάζοντας αὐτοὺς τὴν λείαν μηδ' ἐπισχεῖν. "ἀλλὰ συγγίνωσκε καὶ πρᾷος ἴσθι·" φυλάξεσθαι γὰρ εἰς τοὐπιὸν ἁμαρτεῖν, παρεκάλει δὲ τὸν προφήτην ὑποστρέψαντα θυσίας χαριστηρίους ἐπιτελέσαι τῷ θεῷ· ὁ δέ, οὐ γὰρ ἑώρα τὸν θεὸν διαλλαττόμενον, ἀπῄει πρὸς ἑαυτόν.

152 (5) Σαοῦλος δὲ κατασχεῖν βουλόμενος τὸν Σαμουῆλον ἐλλαμβάνεται[2] τῆς διπλοΐδος, καὶ βιαίας τῆς ὁλκῆς διὰ τὸ μεθ' ὁρμῆς ἀπιέναι[3] τὸν Σαμου-
153 ῆλον γενομένης διασχίζει τὸ ἱμάτιον. τοῦ δὲ προφήτου τὴν βασιλείαν οὕτως αὐτοῦ διασχισθῆναι φήσαντος καὶ λήψεσθαι ταύτην ἀγαθὸν καὶ δίκαιον, ἐμμένειν γὰρ τὸν θεὸν τοῖς περὶ αὐτοῦ κεκριμένοις, ὡς τοῦ μεταβάλλεσθαι καὶ στρέφειν τὴν γνώμην
154 ἀνθρωπίνου πάθους ὄντος οὐχὶ θείας ἰσχύος, ὁ[4] Σαοῦλος ἀσεβῆσαι μὲν ἔλεγεν, ἀγένητα δὲ ποιῆσαι τὰ πεπραγμένα μὴ δύνασθαι· τιμῆσαί γε μὴν αὐτὸν παρεκάλει, τοῦ πλήθους ὁρῶντος, σὺν αὐτῷ παραγενόμενον τὸν θεὸν προσκυνῆσαι. δίδωσι δὲ τοῦτο Σαμουῆλος αὐτῷ καὶ συνελθὼν προσκυνεῖ τῷ θεῷ.

[1] SPM[1]: ὀλέθρου M[2]: ὄλεθρον O.
[2] ἐπιλαμβάνεται S[2] Zon (*cf.* LXX codd.).
[3] Dindorf: ἀπεῖναι codd.
[4] + δὲ codd.

to destruction? Unless it be that thou regardest the sacrificing of them to God as equivalent to destroying them! Expect, therefore, that thou wilt be deprived of thy kingship and of the power upon which thou hast presumed in neglecting the God who gave it thee." Saul admitted that he had done wrong and did not deny his sin; yes, he said, he had transgressed the prophet's commands; yet indeed it was from fear and dread of his soldiers that he had not prevented them from plundering the spoils nor restrained them. "But," said he, "pardon me and be merciful," and promised to beware of offending in future. Then he besought the prophet to return (with him) and sacrifice thank-offerings[a] to God. But Samuel, seeing that God was not to be reconciled, departed to his home.

(5) Then Saul, seeking to detain Samuel, laid hold upon his mantle and, since Samuel was hastening to be gone, pulled it so violently that he rent the garment in twain. Whereat the prophet said that even so had his kingdom been rent from him, and that one would succeed to it who was virtuous and just, for God would abide by what He had decreed concerning him, as change and reversal of judgement were the part of human frailty and not of divine power. Saul replied that, impious though he had been, he could not undo what had been done; howbeit he besought him at least to do him honour in the eyes of the multitude by coming with him to worship God.[b] Samuel granted him this request and went with him and worshipped God. Then too was

Samuel has Agag put to death.
1 Sam. xv. 26.

[a] 1 Sam. xv. 25 "that I may worship the Lord."
[b] Josephus infers that Samuel also worshipped. Scripture says that Samuel returned with Saul and "Saul worshipped the Lord."

155 ἄγεται δὲ καὶ ὁ τῶν Ἀμαληκιτῶν βασιλεὺς Ἄγαγος
πρὸς αὐτόν· καὶ πυνθανομένου πῶς εἴη πικρὸς ὁ
θάνατος, εἶπεν "ὡς σὺ πολλὰς μητέρας Ἑβραίων
ἐπὶ τέκνοις ὀδύρεσθαι καὶ πένθος ἄγειν ἐποίησας,
οὕτως ὀδυνήσεις ἐπὶ σαυτῷ διαφθαρέντι τὴν μητέρα." καὶ κελεύει παραχρῆμα αὐτὸν ἐν Γαλγάλοις ἀποθανεῖν. καὶ αὐτὸς δὲ εἰς Ἀρμαθὰν πόλιν
ἀπαλλάσσεται.
156 (viii. 1) Σαοῦλος δὲ ὁ βασιλεὺς αἰσθόμενος ὧν
ἂν[1] πειραθείη κακῶν ἐχθρὸν αὐτῷ τὸν θεὸν
κατασκευάσας, εἰς τὸ βασίλειον ἀναβαίνει Γαβᾶ,
σημαίνει[2] βουνὸν ἑρμηνευόμενον τὸ ὄνομα, καὶ μετ'
ἐκείνην οὐκέτι τὴν[a] ἡμέραν εἰς ὄψιν ἔρχεται τῷ
157 προφήτῃ. Σαμουήλῳ δὲ λυπουμένῳ περὶ αὐτοῦ
παύσασθαι μὲν τῆς φροντίδος ἐκέλευσεν ὁ θεός,
λαβόντι δὲ τὸ ἅγιον ἔλαιον[3] εἰς Βηθλέμην ἀπελθεῖν
πόλιν πρὸς Ἰεσσαῖον παῖδα Ὠβήδου καὶ χρῖσαι
τῶν υἱῶν αὐτοῦ ὃν ἂν αὐτὸς ἐπιδείξῃ βασιλέα
γενησόμενον. ὁ δὲ εὐλαβεῖσθαι φήσας, μὴ τοῦτο
μαθὼν Σαοῦλος ἀνέλῃ λοχήσας αὐτὸν ἢ καὶ
φανερῶς, ὑποθεμένου τοῦ θεοῦ καὶ δόντος ἀσφα-
158 λείας ὁδὸν ἧκεν εἰς τὴν προειρημένην πόλιν. καὶ
πάντες αὐτὸν ἠσπάζοντό τε καὶ τὴν αἰτίαν τῆς
ἀφίξεως ἀνηρώτων, ἔλεγε δὲ ἥκειν ἵνα θύσῃ τῷ
θεῷ. ποιήσας οὖν τὴν θυσίαν καλεῖ τὸν Ἰεσσαῖον
μετὰ τῶν τέκνων ἐπὶ τὰ ἱερὰ[4] καὶ θεασάμενος

[1] ἂν ins. Niese. [2] + δὲ MSP.
[3] ἅγιον ἔλαιον] ἀγγεῖον τοῦ ἐλαίου E Lat.
[4] ἱερεῖα MSP.

[a] So, apparently, the LXX and Targum of 1 Sam. xv. 32. The Hebrew is obscure and is variously explained by Jewish interpreters.

brought to him Agag, king of the Amalekites; and when the prisoner asked what manner of bitter death his would be,[a] Samuel said, "As thou hast made many mothers of Hebrews to lament and mourn for their children, so shalt thou cause thy mother to grieve over thine own destruction." He then ordered him instantly to be put to death[b] in Galgala, and he himself departed to the city of Armatha.

(viii. 1) But King Saul, perceiving what ills he had incurred in making God his enemy, went up to his palace at Gaba[c] (a name which is interpreted to mean "hill") and from that day onward came no more into the prophet's sight. As Samuel, however, yet grieved for him, God bade him banish his care and, taking the holy oil, to repair to the city of Bethlehem to Jesse son of Obed,[d] and to anoint from among his sons him whom He Himself should point out as the future king. Samuel replied that he was fearful lest Saul on learning of this should slay him by ambush or even openly; but, God having advised him[e] and provided him a way of safety, he came to the city aforesaid. Here all greeted him and questioned him concerning the cause of his coming, and he said that he was come to sacrifice to God. Having then performed the sacrifice, he called Jesse with his children to the sacred feast, and when

Samuel goes to Bethlehem to anoint a son of Jesse as king. 1 Sam. xv. 34.

[b] Josephus discreetly passes over the details; 1 Sam. xv. 33 "and Samuel hewed Agag in pieces before the Lord." Rabbinic tradition states that the execution was not in accordance with Jewish forms of justice.

[c] So LXX; Heb. Gibeah of Saul. *Cf.* § 95 note.

[d] 1 Sam. xvi. 1 "Jesse the Bethlehemite." His father's name is given earlier, *A.* v. 336 (Ruth iv. 22).

[e] Scripture explains more fully by mentioning, at this point, the pretext of sacrificing.

αὐτοῦ τὸν πρεσβύτατον τῶν υἱῶν εὐμεγέθη καὶ καλόν, εἴκασεν ἐκ τῆς εὐμορφίας τοῦτον εἶναι τὸν
159 μέλλοντα βασιλεύειν. διαμαρτάνει δὲ τῆς τοῦ θεοῦ προνοίας· ἐπερωτήσαντι γὰρ αὐτὸν εἰ χρίσει τῷ ἐλαίῳ τὸν νεανίσκον ὃν αὐτὸς ἐτεθαυμάκει[1] καὶ τῆς βασιλείας ἄξιον ἔκρινεν, οὐ τὰ αὐτὰ βλέπειν
160 ἀνθρώπους εἶπε καὶ θεόν· "ἀλλὰ σὺ μὲν εἰς τὸ κάλλος ἀπιδὼν τοῦ νεανίσκου καὶ δὴ τοῦτον ἡγῇ ἄξιον τοῦ βασιλεύειν εἶναι, ἐγὼ δ' οὐ σωμάτων εὐμορφίας ἔπαθλον ποιοῦμαι τὴν βασιλείαν ἀλλὰ ψυχῶν ἀρετῆς, καὶ ζητῶ ὅστις ταύτης[2] ἐστὶ τελέως εὐπρεπής, εὐσεβείᾳ καὶ δικαιοσύνῃ καὶ ἀνδρείᾳ καὶ πειθοῖ, ἐξ ὧν τὸ τῆς ψυχῆς συνίσταται κάλλος,
161 κατακεκοσμημένος." ταῦτα φράσαντος τοῦ θεοῦ πάντας ἐκέλευσεν αὐτῷ τὸν Ἰεσσαῖον τοὺς υἱοὺς ἐπιδεῖξαι Σαμουῆλος· ὁ δὲ πέντε ἄλλους ἐποίησεν ἐλθεῖν, ὧν ὁ μὲν πρεσβύτερος Ἐλίαβος,[3] ὁ δεύτερος Ἀμινάδαβος, Σάμαλος ὁ τρίτος, ὁ τέταρτος Ναθαναῆλος, καὶ Ῥάηλος ὁ πέμπτος ἐκαλεῖτο, ὁ δὲ
162 ἕκτος Ἄσαμος. ἰδὼν δὲ καὶ τούτους ὁ προφήτης μηδὲν χείρους τοῦ πρεσβυτέρου[4] ταῖς μορφαῖς ἐπηρώτησε τὸν θεὸν τίνα τούτων αἱρεῖται βασιλέα. εἰπόντος δ' οὐδένα, πυνθάνεται τοῦ Ἰεσσαίου, μὴ
163 πρὸς τούτοις αὐτῷ καὶ ἄλλοι παῖδές εἰσι. φήσαντος δὲ εἶναι Δαυίδην[5] τοὔνομα, ποιμαίνειν δὲ καὶ τῆς

[1] αὐτός τε θαυμάζει RO.
[2] ταύτῃ Cocceji: ταύτην Ernesti.
[3] Ταλίαβος RO.
[4] πρεσβυτάτου Niese. [5] Δαβίδην RO et sic infra.

[a] His name, Eliab, is given below, § 161.
[b] These virtues, perhaps intended to correspond to the

he beheld his eldest son,[a] well-grown and fair, he surmised from his comeliness that this was the destined king. But he mistook God's design; for, when he asked Him whether he should anoint with the oil this young man whom he himself had admired and accounted worthy of the kingship, He replied that men and God see not the same things. "Nay, thou, looking upon this young man's beauty, thinkest none other than him worthy to be king; but I make not of the kingdom a prize for comeliness of body, but for virtue of soul, and I seek one who in full measure is distinguished by this, one adorned with piety, justice, fortitude and obedience, qualities[b] whereof beauty of soul consists." When God had thus spoken, Samuel bade Jesse bring all his sons before him, and he caused five[c] others to appear. The eldest was called Eliab, the second Aminadab,[d] the third Samal,[e] the fourth Nathanael, the fifth Rael,[f] and the sixth Asam.[g] The prophet, seeing these to be in no way inferior to the eldest in appearance, asked God which among them He chose for king. When God answered, "None," he inquired of Jesse whether he had yet other children. He said that he had one named David, but that he was a

Platonic-Stoic cardinal virtues, are, of course, not specified in Scripture.

[c] 1 Sam. xvi. 10 (*cf.* xvii. 12) mentions seven sons excluding David, and the chapter gives the names of only the three eldest; the others' names are supplied from 1 Chron. ii. 13 ff. which tells us that there were seven sons altogether.

[d] So LXX; Heb. Abinadab.

[e] Bibl. Shammah (Chron. *Shim'a*), LXX Σαμά (*v.l.* Σαμαά κτλ.).

[f] Bibl. Raddai, LXX Ζαδδαί (*v.l.* Ζαβδαί, Ῥαδδαί), Luc. Ρεηλαί.

[g] Bibl. Ozem (Heb. *'Osem*), LXX Ἄσομ, Luc. Ἄσαμ.

τῶν βοσκημάτων φυλακῆς ἐπιμελεῖσθαι, κελεύει καλεῖν αὐτὸν ἐν τάχει· κατακλιθῆναι γὰρ εἰς εὐωχίαν οὐκ εἶναι δυνατὸν αὐτοῖς ἐκείνου μὴ
164 παρόντος. ὡς δ' ἧκεν ὁ Δαυίδης μεταπεμφθεὶς ὑπὸ τοῦ πατρός, παῖς ξανθὸς μὲν τὴν χρόαν γοργὸς δὲ τὰς ὄψεις καὶ καλὸς ἄλλως "οὗτός ἐστιν," εἰπὼν ἡσυχῇ πρὸς αὐτὸν Σαμουῆλος, "ὁ βασιλεύειν ἀρέσας τῷ θεῷ," κατακλίνεται μὲν αὐτός, κατακλίνει δ' ὑφ' αὐτὸν τὸν νεανίσκον καὶ τὸν Ἰεσσαῖον
165 μετὰ καὶ τῶν παίδων. ἔπειτα λαβὼν ὁρῶντος τοῦ Δαυίδου τὸ ἔλαιον ἀλείφει τ' αὐτὸν καὶ πρὸς τὸ οὖς ἠρέμα λαλεῖ καὶ σημαίνει τοῦθ', ὅτι βασιλεύειν αὐτὸν ὁ θεὸς ᾕρηται. παρῄνει δ' εἶναι δίκαιον καὶ κατήκοον αὐτοῦ τῶν προσταγμάτων· οὕτως γὰρ αὐτῷ παραμενεῖν τὴν βασιλείαν εἰς πολὺν χρόνον καὶ τὸν οἶκον λαμπρὸν καὶ περιβόητον γενήσεσθαι,[1] καταστρέψεσθαι[2] δὲ καὶ Παλαιστίνους, καὶ οἷς ἂν ἔθνεσι πολεμῇ νικῶντα καὶ περιόντα τῇ μάχῃ κλέος ἀοίδιμον ζῶντά τε ἕξειν καὶ τοῖς μετ' αὐτὸν ἀπολείψειν.

166 (2) Καὶ Σαμουῆλος μὲν ἀπαλλάσσεται ταῦτα παραινέσας, πρὸς δὲ τὸν Δαυίδην μεταβαίνει τὸ θεῖον καταλιπὸν Σαοῦλον. καὶ ὁ μὲν προφητεύειν ἤρξατο τοῦ θείου πνεύματος εἰς αὐτὸν μετοικισαμένου· τὸν Σαοῦλον δὲ περιήρχετο πάθη τινὰ καὶ δαιμόνια πνιγμοὺς αὐτῷ καὶ στραγγάλας ἐπιφέροντα, ὡς τοὺς ἰατροὺς ἄλλην μὲν αὐτῷ θεραπείαν μὴ ἐπινοεῖν, εἰ δέ τίς ἐστιν ἐξᾴδειν δυνάμενος καὶ ψάλλειν ἐπὶ κινύρᾳ τοῦτον ἐκέλευσαν ζητή-

[1] Dindorf: παραμένειν . . . γενέσθαι codd.
[2] ed. pr.: καταστρέψασθαι MSP.

[a] 1 Sam. xvi. 12 "with beautiful eyes."

shepherd and busied with keeping the flocks; whereat Samuel bade him call him in haste, for it was not possible for them to sit down to the feast without him. Now so soon as David appeared at his father's summons,—a lad of ruddy colour, with piercing [a] eyes and in other ways handsome,—"This," said Samuel softly to himself,[b] "is he whom it has pleased God to make king"; and he sat himself down and made the youth sit beside him, and then Jesse with his other sons. Then, in the sight of David, he took the oil and anointed him and spoke low into his ear, explaining that God had chosen him to be king. He also exhorted [c] him to be righteous and obedient to His commandments, for so would the kingship long continue to be his, and his house would become splendid and renowned; he would subdue the Philistines and, victorious and triumphant over all nations with whom he might wage war, he would in his lifetime attain glorious fame and bequeath it to his posterity.

Samuel anoints David. 1 Sam. xvi. 12.

(2) So, after these exhortations, Samuel went his way,[d] and the Deity abandoned Saul and passed over to David, who, when the divine spirit had removed to him, began to prophesy.[e] But as for Saul, he was beset by strange disorders and evil spirits which caused him such suffocation [f] and strangling that the physicians [g] could devise no other remedy save to order search to be made for one with power to charm away spirits and to play upon the harp, and, whenso-

Saul takes David as his musician and armour-bearer. 1 Sam. xvi. 13.

[b] In Scripture, God prompts Samuel to recognize David.
[c] The exhortation is unscriptural. [d] To Ramah.
[e] Scripture does not say that David prophesied.
[f] After the LXX of 1 Sam. xvi. 14 ἔπνιγεν; Heb. has simply "troubled."
[g] Bibl. "the servants of Saul."

σαντας, ὁπόταν αὐτῷ προσίῃ[1] τὰ δαιμόνια καὶ ταράττῃ,[2] ποιεῖν ὑπὲρ κεφαλῆς στάντα ψάλλειν τε
167 καὶ τοὺς ὕμνους ἐπιλέγειν. ὁ δὲ οὐκ ἠμέλησεν, ἀλλὰ ζητεῖσθαι προσέταξε τοιοῦτον ἄνθρωπον· φήσαντος δέ τινος αὐτῷ τῶν παρόντων ἐν Βηθλεέμῃ πόλει τεθεᾶσθαι Ἰεσσαίου μὲν υἱὸν ἔτι παῖδα τὴν ἡλικίαν, εὐπρεπῆ δὲ καὶ καλὸν τά τε ἄλλα σπουδῆς ἄξιον καὶ δὴ καὶ ψάλλειν εἰδότα καὶ ᾄδειν ὕμνους καὶ πολεμιστὴν ἄκρον, πέμψας πρὸς τὸν Ἰεσσαῖον ἐκέλευσεν ἀποστέλλειν αὐτῷ τὸν Δαυίδην τῶν ποιμνίων ἀποσπάσαντα· βούλεσθαι γὰρ αὐτὸν ἰδεῖν, περὶ τῆς εὐμορφίας καὶ
168 τῆς ἀνδρείας ἀκούσας τοῦ νεανίσκου. ὁ δὲ Ἰεσσαῖος πέμπει τὸν υἱὸν καὶ ξένια δοὺς κομίσαι τῷ Σαούλῳ. ἐλθόντι δὲ ἥσθη καὶ ποιήσας ὁπλοφόρον διὰ πάσης ἦγε[3] τιμῆς· ἐξῄδετο γὰρ ὑπ' αὐτοῦ καὶ πρὸς τὴν ἀπὸ τῶν δαιμονίων ταραχήν, ὁπότε αὐτῷ ταῦτα προσέλθοι, μόνος ἰατρὸς ἦν λέγων τε τοὺς ὕμνους καὶ ψάλλων ἐν τῇ κινύρᾳ
169 καὶ ποιῶν ἑαυτοῦ γίνεσθαι τὸν Σαοῦλον. πέμπει τοίνυν πρὸς τὸν πατέρα τοῦ παιδὸς Ἰεσσαῖον ἐᾶσαι παρ' αὐτῷ τὸν Δαυίδην κελεύων· ἥδεσθαι γὰρ αὐτῷ βλεπομένῳ καὶ παρόντι· τὸν δ' οὐκ ἀντειπεῖν[4] τῷ Σαούλῳ, συγχωρῆσαι[5] δὲ κατέχειν.

170 (ix. 1) Χρόνοις δ' ὕστερον οὐ πολλοῖς οἱ Παλαιστῖνοι πάλιν συνελθόντες καὶ δύναμιν ἀθροίσαντες μεγάλην ἐπίασι τοῖς Ἰσραηλίταις καὶ μεταξὺ Σωχοῦς καὶ Ἀζηκοῦς[6] καταλαμβανόμενοι στρατο-

[1] προσίοι SPE. [2] ταράττοι codd. E.
[3] εἶχε MSP.
[4] τὸν δ' οὐκ ἀντ.] ὁ δὲ οὐκ ὂν ἀντειπεῖν Holwerda.
[5] RO: συνεχώρησε MSP (+ δὴ Holwerda).
[6] Azeca Lat.

ever the evil spirits should assail and torment Saul, to have him stand over the king and strike the strings and chant his songs. Saul did not neglect this advice, but ordered search to be made for such a man. And when one of those present said that he had seen in the city of Bethlehem a son of Jesse, a mere boy in years, but of pleasing and fair appearance and in other ways worthy of regard, who was, moreover, skilled in playing on the harp and in the singing of songs, and an excellent soldier, Saul sent to Jesse and ordered him to take David from the flocks and send him to him; he wished, he said, to see the young man, having heard of his comeliness and valour. So Jesse sent his son, also giving him presents to carry to Saul. When he came, Saul was delighted with him, made him his armour-bearer and held him in the highest honour, for his illness was charmed away by him; and against that trouble caused by the evil spirits, whensoever they assailed him, he had no other physician than David, who, by singing his songs and playing upon the harp, restored Saul to himself. He accordingly sent to Jesse, the lad's father, desiring him to leave David with him, since the sight of the boy and his presence gave him pleasure. Jesse would not gainsay Saul, but permitted him to keep David.

Goliath challenges the Hebrews to combat. 1 Sam. xvii. 1.

(ix. 1) Not long afterwards the Philistines again assembled and mustered a great force, and marched against the Israelites; occupying the ground between Sochūs [a] and Azēkūs [b] they established their

[a] Bibl. Sochoh (A.V. Shochoh), LXX Σοκχώθ.

[b] Bibl. Azekah. Both places are in the valley of Elah (1 Sam. xvii. 2) on the border of Judah and Philistia, about 15 miles due W. of Bethlehem.

πεδεύονται. ἀντεπεξάγει δ' αὐτοῖς τὴν στρατιὰν καὶ Σαοῦλος καὶ ἐπί τινος ὄρους στρατοπεδευσάμενος ἀναγκάζει τοὺς Παλαιστίνους τὸ μὲν πρῶτον στρατόπεδον καταλιπεῖν, ὁμοίως δ' ἐπί τινος[1] ὄρους ἀντικρὺ τοῦ καταληφθέντος ὑπὸ τοῦ Σαούλου
171 στρατοπεδεύσασθαι. διέστησε[2] δ' ἀπ' ἀλλήλων τὰ στρατόπεδα μέσος αὐλὼν τῶν ὀρῶν ἐφ' ὧν ἦν. καταβὰς οὖν τις τῶν ἐκ τοῦ Παλαιστίνων στρατοπέδου, Γολίαθος[3] ὄνομα πόλεως δὲ Γίττης, ἀνὴρ παμμεγεθέστατος· ἦν γὰρ πηχῶν τεσσάρων καὶ σπιθαμῆς, ὅπλα τῇ φύσει τοῦ σώματος ἀναλογοῦντα περικείμενος· θώρακα μὲν γὰρ ἐνεδέδυτο σταθμὸν ἄγοντα πέντε χιλιάδας σίκλων, κόρυθα δὲ καὶ κνημῖδας χαλκέας ὁποίας εἰκὸς ἦν ἀνδρὸς οὕτω παραδόξου τὸ μέγεθος σκεπάσαι μέλη,[4] δόρυ δὲ ἦν οὐ κοῦφον βάσταγμα δεξιᾶς, ἀλλ' ἐπὶ τῶν ὤμων αὐτὸ αἴρων ἔφερεν, εἶχε δὲ καὶ λόγχην ἑξακοσίων σίκλων, εἵποντο δὲ πολλοὶ βαστάζοντες τὰ ὅπλα·
172 στὰς τοίνυν ὁ Γολίαθος οὗτος μεταξὺ τῶν παρατάξεων βοήν τε ἀφίησι μεγάλην καὶ πρὸς τὸν Σαοῦλον καὶ τοὺς Ἑβραίους λέγει· "μάχης μὲν ὑμᾶς καὶ κινδύνων ἀπαλλάττω· τίς γὰρ ἀνάγκη τὴν στρατιὰν ὑμῶν[5] συμπεσοῦσαν κακοπαθεῖν;
173 δότε δ' ὅστις ἐμοὶ μαχεῖται τῶν ὑμετέρων, καὶ βραβευθήσεται τὰ τοῦ πολέμου[6] ἑνὶ[7] τῷ νενικηκότι·

[1] δ' ἐπί τινος Niese: δέ τινος RO: ἐπὶ ὁμοίου δέ τινος MSP.
[2] διέστη ROE: διίστη Niese.
[3] Γολιάθης codd., sed infra Γολίαθος codd. plur.
[4] Niese ex Lat.: μέρη codd. [5] SP: ἡμῶν rell.
[6] τὸ τοῦ πολέμου τέλος MSP.
[7] ἑνὶ ex Lat.: ἐν codd.

[a] Josephus infers from 1 Sam. xvii. 3, mentioning a moun-

camp there. Saul, on his side, led out his army against them, and, having pitched his camp on a certain mountain, forced the Philistines to abandon their first camp [a] and to take up a similar position on another mountain over against that which he had occupied himself. The two camps were separated by a valley between the hills on which they lay. And now there came down from the camp of the Philistines one by name Goliath, of the city of Gitta, a man of gigantic stature. For he measured four [b] cubits and a span, and was clad in armour proportioned to his frame. He wore a breastplate weighing 5000 shekels, with a helmet and greaves of bronze such as were meet to protect the limbs of a man of such prodigious size. His spear was not light enough to be borne in the right hand, but he carried it elevated on his shoulders; he had also a spear weighing 600 shekels,[c] and many followed him, carrying his armour.[d] Standing, then, between the opposing forces, this Goliath gave a mighty shout and said to Saul and the Hebrews, "I hereby deliver you from battle and its perils. For what need is there for your [e] troops to join arms and to suffer heavy losses? Give me one of your men to fight with me, and the issue of the war shall be decided by the single victor, and to

tain for the first time, that the Philistines had changed their camp.

[b] So most MSS. of the LXX; Heb. and LXX A have "six." The figures here given equal about 6 ft. 8 in.

[c] Or "and it had a head weighing 600 shekels"; whether the whole spear or the spearhead alone weighed 600 shekels is not clear either from the Heb. or LXX of 1 Sam. xvii. 7. The latter, like Josephus, has λόγχη, which means either "spear" or "spearhead."

[d] Bibl. "and his shield-bearer went before him."

[e] Variant "our."

δουλεύσουσι γὰρ ἐκεῖνοι τοῖς ἑτέροις, ὧν ἂν ὁ νικήσας γένηται· πολὺ δὲ κρεῖττον οἶμαι[1] καὶ σωφρονέστατον ἑνὸς κινδύνῳ λαβεῖν ὃ βούλεσθε
174 ἢ τῷ ἁπάντων.[2]" ταῦτ' εἰπὼν ἀνεχώρησεν εἰς τὸ τῶν οἰκείων στρατόπεδον. τῇ δ' ἐχομένῃ πάλιν ἐλθὼν τοὺς αὐτοὺς ἐποιήσατο λόγους καὶ μέχρι τεσσαράκοντα ἡμερῶν οὐ διέλειπε προκαλούμενος ἐπὶ τοῖς προειρημένοις τοὺς πολεμίους, ὡς καταπλαγῆναι αὐτόν τε τὸν Σαοῦλον καὶ τὴν στρατιάν. καὶ παρετάσσοντο μὲν ὡς εἰς μάχην, οὐκ ἤρχοντο δὲ εἰς χεῖρας.

175 (2) Τοῦ δὲ πολέμου συνεστηκότος τοῖς Ἑβραίοις καὶ τοῖς Παλαιστίνοις Σαοῦλος ἀπέλυσε τὸν Δαυίδην πρὸς τὸν πατέρα Ἰεσσαῖον ἀρκούμενος αὐτοῦ τοῖς τρισὶν υἱοῖς, οὓς ἐπὶ συμμαχίαν καὶ
176 τοὺς κινδύνους ἔπεμψεν. ὁ δὲ τὸ μὲν πρῶτον ἐπὶ τὰ ποίμνια πάλιν καὶ τὰς νομὰς τῶν βοσκημάτων παραγίνεται, μετ' οὐ πολὺ δὲ ἔρχεται εἰς τὸ στρατόπεδον τῶν Ἑβραίων πεμφθεὶς ὑπὸ τοῦ πατρὸς κομίσαι τε τοῖς ἀδελφοῖς ἐφόδια καὶ γνῶναι τί
177 πράττουσι. τοῦ δὲ Γολιάθου πάλιν ἐλθόντος καὶ προκαλουμένου καὶ ὀνειδίζοντος ὅτι μηδείς ἐστιν ἀνδρεῖος ἐν αὐτοῖς, ὃς εἰς μάχην αὐτῷ τολμᾷ καταβῆναι, μεταξὺ τοῖς ἀδελφοῖς ὁμιλῶν Δαυίδης περὶ ὧν ἐπέστειλεν ὁ πατήρ, ἀκούσας βλασφημοῦντος τὴν στρατιὰν καὶ κακίζοντος τοῦ Παλαιστίνου ἠγανάκτησε καὶ πρὸς τοὺς ἀδελφοὺς αὐτοῦ εἶπεν
178 ἑτοίμως ἔχειν μονομαχῆσαι τῷ πολεμίῳ. πρὸς τοῦθ' ὁ πρεσβύτατος τῶν ἀδελφῶν Ἐλίαβος[3] ἐπέπληξεν αὐτῷ, τολμηρότερον παρ' ἡλικίαν καὶ ἀμαθῆ τοῦ προσήκοντος εἰπών, ἐκέλευσέ τε πρὸς τὰ ποίμνια καὶ τὸν πατέρα βαδίζειν. κατ-

the people of the victor the other side shall be slaves. It is far better, I think, and more prudent to attain your end by the hazard of one man's life rather than of all." Having so spoken he retired to his own camp. On the morrow he came again and delivered the same speech, and so, for forty days, he did not cease to challenge his enemies in these same terms, to the utter dismay both of Saul and his army. And though they remained drawn up as for battle, they never came to close quarters. xvii. 16.

David asks Saul for permission to fight Goliath. 1 Sam. xvii. 13.

(2) Now, on the outbreak of the war between the Hebrews and the Philistines, Saul had sent David away to his father Jesse, being content with the latter's three sons whom he had sent to share the dangers of the campaign. David then returned at first to his flocks and cattle-pastures, but before long visited the camp of the Hebrews, being sent by his father to carry provisions to his brothers and to learn how they fared. Now when Goliath came again, challenging and taunting the Hebrews with not having among them a man brave enough to venture down to fight with him, David was talking with his brothers about the matters wherewith his father had charged him, and hearing the Philistine reviling and abusing their army, he became indignant and said to his brothers that he was ready to meet this adversary in single combat. Thereat the eldest of his brothers, Eliab, rebuked him, telling him that he was bolder than became his years and ignorant of what was fitting, and bade him be off to the flocks and to his

---

[1] Bekker: εἶναι codd.
[2] Niese: τῶν ἁπάντων RO: τῷ πάντων SP.
[3] MSP: Ἰάναβος RO: Aminadab Lat.

αιδεσθεὶς δὲ τὸν ἀδελφὸν ὑπεχώρησε καὶ πρός
τινας τῶν στρατιωτῶν ἀπελάλησεν ὅτι θέλοι μάχε-
179 σθαι τῷ προκαλουμένῳ. δηλωσάντων δ' εὐθὺς τῷ
Σαούλῳ τὴν τοῦ νεανίσκου προαίρεσιν μεταπέμπεται αὐτὸν ὁ βασιλεύς, καὶ πυθομένου τί βούλεται λέγει[1] "μὴ ταπεινὸν ἔστω τὸ φρόνημα μηδ'
εὐλαβές,[2] ὦ βασιλεῦ· καθαιρήσω γὰρ ἐγὼ τὴν
ἀλαζονείαν τοῦ πολεμίου χωρήσας αὐτῷ διὰ μάχης
καὶ τὸν ὑψηλὸν καὶ μέγαν ὑπ' ἐμαυτῷ βαλών.
180 γένοιτο μὲν ἂν αὐτὸς οὕτως καταγέλαστος, ἔνδοξον
δὲ τὸ σὸν στράτευμα, εἰ μηδ' ὑπ' ἀνδρὸς πολεμεῖν
ἤδη δυναμένου καὶ πιστευομένου παράταξιν καὶ
μάχας, ἀλλ' ὑπὸ παιδὸς ἔτι δοκοῦντος καὶ ταύτην
ἔχοντος τὴν ἡλικίαν ἀποθάνοι."
181 (3) Τοῦ δὲ Σαούλου τὸ μὲν τολμηρὸν αὐτοῦ καὶ
τὴν εὐψυχίαν θαυμάζοντος, οὐ θαρροῦντος δὲ ἐπ'
αὐτῷ διὰ τὴν ἡλικίαν, ἀλλ' ἀσθενέστερον εἶναι διὰ
ταύτην πρὸς εἰδότα πολεμεῖν μάχεσθαι λέγοντος,
"ταῦτ'," εἶπε Δαυίδης, "ἐπαγγέλλομαι τῷ θεῷ
θαρρῶν ὄντι μετ' ἐμοῦ· πεπείραμαι γὰρ αὐτοῦ τῆς
182 βοηθείας. λέοντα γὰρ ἐπελθόντα μού ποτε τοῖς
ποιμνίοις καὶ ἁρπάσαντα ἄρνα διώξας καταλαμ-
βάνω καὶ τὸν μὲν ἄρνα τοῦ[3] στόματος ἐξαρπάζω
τοῦ θηρός, αὐτὸν δ' ὁρμήσαντα ἐπ' ἐμὲ τῆς οὐρᾶς
183 βαστάσας καὶ προσρήξας τῇ γῇ διαφθείρω. ταὐτὸ
δὲ καὶ ἄρκτον ἀμυνόμενος διατίθεμαι. νομιζέσθω
δὴ καὶ ὁ πολέμιος ἐκείνων εἶναι τῶν θηρίων,
ὀνειδίζων ἐκ πολλοῦ τὴν στρατιὰν καὶ βλασφημῶν
ἡμῶν τὸν θεόν, ὃς αὐτὸν ὑποχείριον ἐμοὶ θήσει."

[1] Niese: (καὶ) λέγειν codd. [2] + εἶπεν SP.
[3] ἐκ τοῦ MSPE.

father. Out of respect for his brother David withdrew, but gave out to some of the soldiers that he wished to fight with the challenger. As they straightway reported the lad's resolve to Saul, the king sent for him; and David, when asked by him what he wished, said, "Let not thy spirit be downcast nor fearful, O King, for I will bring down the presumption of the foe by joining battle with him and throwing this mighty [a] giant down before me. Thus would he be made a laughing-stock, and thine army have the more glory, should he be slain, not by a grown man fit for war and entrusted with the command of battles, but by one to all appearance and in truth no older than a boy." [b]

David answers Saul's doubts. 1 Sam. xvii. 33.

(3) Saul admired the lad's daring and courage, but could not place full confidence in him by reason of his years, because of which, he said, he was too feeble to fight with a skilled warrior. "These promises," replied David, "I make in the assurance that God is with me; for I have already had proof of His aid. Once when a lion attacked my flocks and carried off a lamb, I pursued and caught him and snatched the lamb from the beast's jaws, and, when he sprang upon me, lifted him by the tail and killed him by dashing him upon the ground.[c] And I did the very same thing in battle with a bear. Let this enemy then be reckoned even as one of those wild beasts, so long has he insulted our army and blasphemed our God, who will deliver him into my hands."

[a] Or "lofty-vaunting," as Professor Capps suggests.

[b] The last part of David's speech is an amplification of Scripture.

[c] 1 Sam. xvii. 35 "I seized him by the beard (LXX and Targum "throat" or "jaws") and struck him and killed him."

184 (4) Τῇ προθυμίᾳ τοιγαροῦν καὶ τῇ τόλμῃ τοῦ παιδὸς ὅμοιον γενέσθαι τέλος παρὰ τοῦ θεοῦ Σαοῦλος εὐξάμενος "ἄπιθι," φησί, "πρὸς τὴν μάχην." καὶ περιθεὶς αὐτῷ τὸν αὐτοῦ θώρακα καὶ περιζώσας τὸ ξίφος καὶ περικεφαλαίαν ἁρ-
185 μόσας ἐξέπεμψεν.[1] ὁ δὲ Δαυίδης βαρυνόμενος ὑπὸ τῶν ὅπλων, οὐκ ἐγεγύμναστο γὰρ οὐδ' ἐμεμαθήκει φέρειν ὅπλα, "ταῦτα μέν," εἶπεν, "ὦ βασιλεῦ, σὸς ἔστω κόσμος τοῦ καὶ βαστάζειν δυναμένου, συγχώρησον δὲ ὡς δούλῳ σου καὶ ὡς ἐγὼ βούλομαι μαχεσθῆναι." τίθησιν οὖν τὰ ὅπλα καὶ τὴν βακτηρίαν ἀράμενος καὶ πέντε λίθους ἐκ τοῦ χειμάρρου βαλὼν εἰς τὴν πήραν τὴν ποιμενικὴν καὶ σφενδόνην ἐν τῇ δεξιᾷ χειρὶ φέρων ἐπὶ τὸν Γολίαθον
186 ἐπορεύετο. καταφρονεῖ δὲ οὕτως ἰδὼν αὐτὸν ὁ πολέμιος ἐρχόμενον καὶ προσέσκωψεν, ὡς οὐχ οἷα πρὸς ἄνθρωπον[2] ὅπλα νενόμισται ταῦτ' ἔχων μέλλοι μάχεσθαι, οἷς δὲ κύνας ἀπελαύνομεν καὶ φυλασσόμεθα. μὴ αὐτὸν ἀντὶ ἀνθρώπου κύνα εἶναι δοκεῖ; ὁ δ' οὐχὶ τοιοῦτον ἀλλὰ καὶ χείρω κυνὸς αὐτὸν νομίζειν ἀπεκρίνατο. κινεῖ δὲ πρὸς ὀργὴν τὸν Γολίαθον, καὶ ἀρὰς αὐτῷ τίθεται ἐκ τῆς προσηγορίας τοῦ θεοῦ καὶ δώσειν ἠπείλησε τὰς σάρκας αὐτοῦ τοῖς ἐπιγείοις καὶ τοῖς μεταρσίοις
187 διασπάσασθαι· ἀμείβεται δ' αὐτὸν ὁ Δαυίδης· "σὺ μὲν ἐπέρχῃ μοι ἐν ῥομφαίᾳ καὶ δόρατι καὶ θώρακι, ἐγὼ δὲ χωρῶν ἐπὶ σὲ τὸν θεὸν ὥπλισμαι, ὅς σέ τε καὶ τὴν πᾶσαν ὑμῶν στρατιὰν χερσὶ ταῖς ἡμετέραις διολέσει. καρατομήσω μὲν γάρ σε σήμερον καὶ τὸ

[1] SP: ἐξέπεμπεν ME: ἔπεμψεν RO.
[2] ἀνθρώπων Niese (ex Lat. hominum).

David goes forth to meet Goliath. 1 Sam. xvii. 37.

(4) So then Saul, praying that the lad's zeal and hardihood might be rewarded by God with a like success, said, "Go forth to battle."[a] And he clad him in his own breastplate, girt his sword about him, fitted a helmet upon his head and so sent him out. But David was weighed down by this armour, for he had not been trained nor taught to wear armour, and said, "Let this fine apparel be for thee, O King, for thou indeed art able to wear it,[b] but suffer me, as thy servant, to fight just as I will." Accordingly he laid down the armour and, taking up his staff, he put five stones from the brook into his shepherd's wallet, and with a sling in his right hand advanced against Goliath. The enemy, seeing him approaching in this manner, showed his scorn, and derided him for coming to fight, not with such weapons as men are accustomed to use against other men, but with those wherewith we drive away and keep off dogs. Or did he perhaps take him for a dog, and not a man? "No," replied David, "not even for a dog, but something still worse."[c] This roused Goliath's anger, and he called down curses upon him in his god's name and threatened to give his flesh to the beasts of earth and the birds of heaven to rend asunder. But David answered him, "Thou comest against me with sword, spear and breastplate, but I, in coming against thee, have God for my armour, who will destroy both thee and all your host by our hands. For I will this day

[a] 1 Sam. xvii. 37 "Go forth and may the Lord be with thee." Weill's note, "in the Bible this prayer is put in David's mouth," overlooks the fact that David's brief prayer for deliverance is given by Josephus in the preceding sentence. Here he is amplifying Saul's blessing just quoted.

[b] Amplification.

[c] So the LXX; this reply is not found in the Hebrew.

ἄλλο σῶμα τοῖς ὁμοφύλοις κυσὶ παραβαλῶ, μαθήσονται δὲ πάντες ὅτι προέστηκεν Ἑβραίων τὸ θεῖον καὶ ὅπλα ἡμῖν καὶ ἰσχὺς τοῦτ' ἔστι κηδόμενον, ἡ δ' ἄλλη παρασκευὴ καὶ δύναμις ἀνωφελὴς
188 θεοῦ μὴ παρόντος." ὁ δὲ Παλαιστῖνος ὑπὸ βάρους τῶν ὅπλων εἰς ὠκύτητα καὶ δρόμον ἐμποδιζόμενος βάδην ἐπὶ τὸν Δαυίδην παραγίνεται καταφρονῶν καὶ πεποιθὼς γυμνὸν ὁμοῦ καὶ παῖδα ἔτι τὴν ἡλικίαν ἀπόνως ἀναιρήσειν.

189 (5) Ἀπαντᾷ δὲ ὁ νεανίσκος μετὰ συμμάχου μὴ βλεπομένου τῷ πολεμίῳ· θεὸς δ' ἦν οὗτος. καὶ ἀνελόμενος ἐκ τῆς πήρας ὧν εἰς αὐτὴν κατέθηκεν ἐκ τοῦ χειμάρρου λίθον ἕνα καὶ ἁρμόσας τῇ σφενδόνῃ βάλλει ἐπὶ τὸν Γολίαθον εἰς τὸ μέτωπον· καὶ διῆλθεν ἕως τοῦ ἐγκεφάλου τὸ βληθέν, ὡς εὐθὺς καρωθέντα πεσεῖν τὸν Γολίαθον ἐπὶ τὴν
190 ὄψιν. δραμὼν δ' ἐφίσταται τῷ πολεμίῳ κειμένῳ καὶ τῇ ῥομφαίᾳ τῇ ἐκείνου, μάχαιραν οὐκ ἔχων
191 αὐτός, ἀποτέμνει τὴν κεφαλὴν αὐτοῦ. πεσὼν δ' ὁ Γολίαθος ἧττα καὶ φυγὴ γίνεται Παλαιστίνοις· τὸν γὰρ δοκιμώτατον ἰδόντες ἐρριμμένον καὶ περὶ τῶν ὅλων δείσαντες οὐκέτι μένειν διέγνωσαν, ἀλλ' αἰσχρᾷ καὶ ἀκόσμῳ φυγῇ παραδόντες ἑαυτοὺς ἐξαρπάζειν τῶν κινδύνων ἐπειρῶντο. Σαοῦλος δὲ καὶ πᾶς ὁ τῶν Ἑβραίων στρατὸς ἀλαλάξαντες ἐκπηδῶσιν εἰς αὐτοὺς καὶ πολλοὺς ἀποσφάττοντες διώκουσιν ἄχρι τῶν Γίττης ὁρίων καὶ τῶν πυλῶν

[a] 1 Sam. xvii. 46 "I will give the carcase of the camp

cut off thine head and fling thy carcase to the dogs, thy fellows,[a] and all men shall learn that Hebrews have the Deity for their protection, and that He in His care for us is our armour and strength, and that all other armament and force are unavailing where God is not." And now the Philistine, impeded by the weight of his armour from running more swiftly, came on toward David at a slow pace,[b] contemptuous and confident of slaying without any trouble an adversary at once unarmed and of an age so youthful.

David slays Goliath; the Philistines are routed. 1 Sam. xvii. 49.

(5) But the youth advanced to the encounter, accompanied by an ally invisible to the foe, and this was God. Drawing from his wallet one of the stones from the brook which he had put therein, and fitting it to his sling, he shot it at Goliath, catching him in the forehead, and the missile penetrated to the brain, so that Goliath was instantly stunned and fell upon his face. Then, running forward, David stood over his prostrate foe and with the other's broadsword, having no sword of his own, he cut off his head. Goliath's fall caused the defeat and rout of the Philistines; for, seeing their best warrior laid low and fearing a complete disaster, they resolved to remain no longer, but sought to save themselves from danger by ignominious and disorderly flight. But Saul and the whole Hebrew army, with shouts of battle, sprang upon them and with great carnage pursued them to the borders of Gitta [c] and to the gates of Ascalon.[d]

of the Philistines to the birds of heaven, etc." Josephus evidently read "thy carcase to the camp, etc."

[b] Unscriptural details.

[c] Bibl. Gath. *Cf. A.* v. 87.

[d] So the LXX in the first occurrence of the name in 1 Sam. xvii. 52; in the second part of the verse it agrees with the Hebrew in reading Ekron.

192 τῶν Ἀσκάλωνος. καὶ θνήσκουσι μὲν τῶν Παλαιστίνων εἰς τρισμυρίους, δὶς δὲ τοσοῦτοι τραυματίαι γίνονται. Σαοῦλος δὲ ὑποστρέψας εἰς τὸ στρατόπεδον αὐτῶν διαρπάζει τὸ χαράκωμα καὶ ἐνέπρησε· τὴν κεφαλὴν δὲ Γολιάθου[1] Δαυίδης εἰς τὴν ἰδίαν σκηνὴν ἐκόμισε καὶ τὴν ῥομφαίαν ἀνέθηκε τῷ θεῷ.

193 (x. 1) Φθόνον δὲ καὶ μῖσος τοῦ Σαούλου πρὸς αὐτὸν αἱ γυναῖκες ἐρεθίζουσιν· ὑπαντῶσαι γὰρ τῇ στρατιᾷ νικηφόρῳ μετὰ κυμβάλων καὶ τυμπάνων καὶ παντοίας χαρᾶς ᾖδον αἱ μὲν γυναῖκες, ὡς πολλὰς Σαοῦλος ἀπώλεσε Παλαιστίνων χιλιάδας, αἱ παρθένοι δέ, ὡς μυριάδας Δαυίδης ἀφανίσειε.

194 τούτων δὲ ἀκούων ὁ βασιλεύς, ὡς τὸ μὲν ἔλαττον τῆς μαρτυρίας αὐτὸς λάβοι, τὸ δὲ τῶν μυριάδων πλῆθος ἀνατεθείη τῷ νεανίσκῳ, καὶ λογισάμενος μηδὲν οὕτω μετὰ λαμπρὰν εὐφημίαν ἢ τὴν βασιλείαν ὑστερεῖν αὐτῷ, φοβεῖσθαι καὶ ὑποπτεύειν

195 ἤρξατο τὸν Δαυίδην. καὶ τῆς μὲν πρώτης τάξεως, ἐπεὶ τῷ δέει πλησίον αὐτοῦ καὶ λίαν ἐγγὺς ἐδόκει, ἐποίησε γὰρ αὐτὸν ὁπλοφόρον, μεταστήσας ἀποδείκνυσι χιλίαρχον δοὺς αὐτῷ χώραν ἀμείνονα μὲν ἀσφαλεστέραν[2] δὲ ὡς ἐνόμιζεν αὑτῷ[3]· ἐβούλετο

[1] RO: τὴν δὲ κεφαλὴν τοῦ Γ. rell.
[2] σφαλερὰν SP.
[3] Niese: αὐτῷ codd.

[a] Unscriptural numbers.

[b] 1 Sam. xvii. 53 "The Israelites returned from pursuing the Philistines and plundered (LXX κατεπάτουν "trampled down") their camp." Perhaps Josephus took the Heb. root *dlq*, "pursue," in its other sense "burn" (*cf.* Latin version of Scripture, *comburentes*), or possibly read κατέκαιον instead of κατεπάτουν.

[c] The reverse of Scripture, 1 Sam. xvii. 54 which reads "And David took the head of the Philistine and brought it to Jerusalem, but his armour he put in his tent." Later, in

Of the Philistines 30,000 [a] were slain and twice as many wounded. Saul then returning to their camp destroyed the palisade and set fire to it [b]; while David carried the head of Goliath to his own tent and dedicated his sword to God.[c]

Saul is made envious by David's triumph. 1 Sam. xviii. 6.

(x. 1) [d] But envy and hatred of David were now aroused in Saul by the women. For they, coming to meet the victorious army with cymbals, timbrels and every sign of rejoicing, sang, the elder women how Saul had slain many thousands of the Philistines, but the maidens [e] how David had destroyed tens of thousands. The king on hearing this, and how he was given the lesser portion of the credit, while the larger number, the myriads, was ascribed to the youth, thought within himself that after so splendid an acclamation nothing more was lacking to David save the kingship, and now began to fear him and to regard him with suspicion. So he removed him from his former station—for he had made him his armour-bearer—since in his alarm he thought this far too close to his person, and appointed him captain of a thousand,[f] thus giving him a better post, but one, as he thought, safer for himself.[g] For

§ 244, Josephus tells us, in accordance with Scripture, 1 Sam. xxi. 9 (10), that David had dedicated Goliath's sword to God in the temple at Nob.

[d] Josephus, with many MSS. of the LXX, omits the presentation of David by Abner and the covenant with Jonathan which follow immediately upon the close of the battle, 1 Sam. xviii. 1-4.

[e] Scripture does not distinguish the women by age.

[f] Gr. "chiliarch." In the Hebrew this change is made after Saul's attack on David while playing the harp, 1 Sam. xviii. 10-11. Josephus omits the incident, as do many MSS. of the LXX.

[g] Variant "more treacherous for him (David)."

γὰρ εἰς τοὺς πολεμίους αὐτὸν ἐκπέμπειν καὶ τὰς μάχας ὡς ἐν τοῖς κινδύνοις τεθνηξόμενον.

196 (2) Δαυίδης δὲ πανταχοῦ τὸν θεὸν ἐπαγόμενος ὅποι ποτ' ἀφίκοιτο κατώρθου καὶ διευπραγῶν ἐδείκνυτο,[1] ὡς δι' ὑπερβολὴν τῆς ἀνδρείας τόν τε λαὸν αὐτοῦ[2] καὶ τὴν Σαούλου θυγατέρα παρθένον ἔτι οὖσαν λαβεῖν ἔρωτα καὶ τοῦ πάθους ὑπερκρατοῦντος γενέσθαι φανερὰν καὶ διαβληθῆναι πρὸς
197 τὸν πατέρα. ὁ δ' ὡς ἀφορμῇ χρησόμενος[3] τῆς ἐπὶ Δαυίδην ἐπιβουλῆς ἡδέως ἤκουσε καὶ δώσειν προθύμως αὐτῷ τὴν παρθένον πρὸς τοὺς τὸν ἔρωτα μηνύσαντας αὐτῆς ἔφη, γενησόμενον ἀπωλείας καὶ κινδύνων αἴτιον αὐτῷ ληψομένῳ· "κατεγγυῶ γάρ," εἶπεν, "αὐτῷ τὸν τῆς θυγατρός μου γάμον, ἂν
198 ἑξακοσίας μοι κομίσῃ κεφαλὰς τῶν πολεμίων. ὁ δὲ καὶ γέρως οὕτω λαμπροῦ προτεθέντος καὶ βουλόμενος ἐπ' ἔργῳ παραβόλῳ καὶ ἀπίστῳ λαβεῖν κλέος, ὁρμήσει μὲν ἐπὶ τὴν πρᾶξιν, διαφθαρήσεται δὲ ὑπὸ τῶν Παλαιστίνων καὶ χωρήσει μοι τὰ κατ' αὐτὸν εὐπρεπῶς· ἀπαλλαγήσομαι γὰρ αὐτοῦ, δι' ἄλλων αὐτόν, ἀλλ' οὐχὶ δι' ἐμαυτοῦ κτείνας."
199 διάπειραν δὴ τῆς τοῦ Δαυίδου διανοίας κελεύει τοὺς οἰκέτας λαμβάνειν, πῶς ἔχει πρὸς τὸ γῆμαι τὴν κόρην. οἱ δ' ἤρξαντο διαλέγεσθαι πρὸς αὐτόν, ὅτι στέργει μὲν αὐτὸν ὁ βασιλεὺς Σαοῦλος καὶ ὁ λαὸς ἅπας, βούλεται δ' αὐτῷ κηδεῦσαι τὴν
200 θυγατέρα. ὁ δέ "μικρὸν ἄρ' ὑμῖν," εἶπε, "δοκεῖ γαμβρὸν γενέσθαι βασιλέως; ἐμοὶ δ' οὐχὶ τοιοῦτον

[1] RO: ἐβλέπετο rell. (Lat.).
[2] + ἐρᾶν M.
[3] M: χρησάμενος rell.

[a] His younger daughter, Michal, *cf.* § 204 note. Josephus

he proposed to send him out against the enemy and into battle, in the hope that amidst these dangers he would meet his death.

Saul's daughter Michal (Melcha) falls in love with David. 1 Sam. xviii. 20.

(2) But David, being everywhere attended by God whithersoever he went, achieved success and showed himself so fortunate in all things that by his extraordinary valour he won the heart not only of the people but of Saul's daughter,[a] who was still a virgin; and so overmastering was her passion that it betrayed her and was reported to her father. He, thinking to seize this occasion for plotting against David, welcomed the news and told those who had informed him of his daughter's love that he would gladly give David the maiden, since the match, should he accept it, would prove the cause of danger and destruction to him. "For," said he, "I pledge him my daughter in marriage, if he will but bring me the heads of six hundred [b] of the foe. Now, at the offer of a prize so splendid and in his desire to win renown for a hazardous and incredible exploit, he will rush to perform it and be killed by the Philistines; so will my designs against him succeed admirably, for I shall be rid of him, yet cause his death at the hands of others and not my own." He accordingly ordered his men to sound the mind of David touching marriage with the maid; and they began to speak with him, telling him that King Saul felt affection for him, as did all the people, and wished to unite his daughter with him in marriage. Whereto David replied, "Does it then seem to you a small thing to become a king's son-in-law? To me it does not appear so,

Saul treacherously lays down conditions for the marriage. 1 Sam. xviii. 22.

omits the Scriptural reference, 1 Sam. xviii. 17, to Saul's offer of his elder daughter, Merab.

[b] Bibl. "a hundred foreskins of the Philistines."

φαίνεται καὶ μάλιστα ὄντι ταπεινῷ καὶ δόξης καὶ τιμῆς ἀμοίρῳ." Σαοῦλος δὲ ἀγγειλάντων αὐτῷ τῶν οἰκετῶν τὰς τοῦ Δαυίδου ἀποκρίσεις "οὐ χρημάτων," ἔφη, "δεῖσθαί με φράζετε αὐτῷ οὐδὲ ἕδνων, ἀπεμπολᾶν γὰρ ἔστιν οὕτως[1] τὴν θυγατέρα μᾶλλον ἢ συνοικίζειν, γαμβροῦ δὲ ἀνδρείαν ἔχοντος καὶ τὴν ἄλλην ἀρετὴν ἅπασαν, ἣν ὁρᾶν ὑπάρχουσαν
201 αὐτῷ. βούλεσθαι δή με παρ' αὐτοῦ λαβεῖν ἀντὶ τοῦ γάμου τῆς θυγατρὸς οὐ χρυσὸν οὐδ' ἄργυρον οὐδ' ὅπως ταῦτα ἐκ τῶν τοῦ πατρὸς οἰκιῶν[2] κομίσῃ, Παλαιστίνων δὲ τιμωρίαν καὶ κεφαλὰς
202 αὐτῶν ἑξακοσίας. αὐτῷ τε γὰρ ἐμοὶ τούτων οὐδὲν ἂν οὔτε ποθεινότερον οὔτε λαμπρότερον[3] δῶρον γένοιτο, τῇ τε παιδί μου πολὺ τῶν νενομισμένων ἕδνων ζηλωτότερον τὸ συνοικεῖν ἀνδρὶ τοιούτῳ καὶ μαρτυρουμένῳ τὴν τῶν πολεμίων ἧτταν."

203 (3) Κομισθέντων δὲ τούτων πρὸς τὸν Δαυίδην τῶν λόγων ἡσθεὶς τὸν Σαοῦλον ἐσπουδακέναι νομίζων αὐτοῦ περὶ τὴν συγγένειαν, οὐδὲ βουλεύσασθαι περιμείνας οὐδ' εἰ δυνατὸν ἢ δύσκολόν ἐστι τὸ προκείμενον ἔργον τῷ λογισμῷ περινοήσας ὥρμησεν εὐθὺς μετὰ τῆς ἑταιρίας ἐπὶ τοὺς πολεμίους καὶ τὴν ὑπὲρ τοῦ γάμου κατηγγελμένην πρᾶξιν καὶ (θεὸς γὰρ ἦν ὁ πάντα ποιῶν εὐμαρῆ καὶ δυνατὰ τῷ Δαυίδῃ) κτείνας πολλοὺς καὶ κεφαλὰς ἑξακοσίων ἀποτεμὼν ἧκε πρὸς τὸν βασιλέα διὰ τῆς τούτων ἐπιδείξεως τὸν ἀντὶ τούτων γάμον ἀπαιτῶν.
204 Σαοῦλος δὲ οὐκ ἔχων ἀναφυγεῖν[4] ἐκ τῶν ὑπεσχημένων, αἰσχρὸν γὰρ ὑπελάμβανεν ἢ ψεύσασθαι

[1] τοῦτο Ernesti. [2] ME: οἰκείων rell.
[3] + οὔτε προτιμότερον SPE.
[4] ἀναφυγὴν Naber.

especially as I am of such humble rank and with no portion of glory or honour." When Saul was informed by his men of David's response, "Tell him," he said, "that I desire no money nor wedding gifts—that would be to sell my daughter, not to give her in marriage—but a son-in-law possessed of fortitude and all other virtues, such as I see in him. I wish, therefore, to receive of him, in return for his marriage with my daughter, neither gold nor silver—not these would I have him bring from his father's house—but the punishment of the Philistines and six hundred of their heads. For to myself no gift could be more desirable or magnificent [a] than that, and to my child it would be far more pleasing than the customary wedding presents to be united to such a husband who has the credit for defeating our enemies." [b]

David wins Michal by slaying six hundred Philistines. 1 Sam. xviii. 26.

(3) When these words were reported to David, he was delighted at the thought that Saul was eager to be related to him, and without waiting to deliberate, without reasonably considering whether the proposed enterprise was possible or difficult, he straightway, with his companions, set upon the foe to accomplish the task that was appointed him as the condition of the marriage; and, thanks to God, who rendered all things possible and easy to David, he slew many men, cut off the heads of six hundred [c] and returned to the king, displaying these and claiming the bride as his recompense. So Saul, finding no way to evade his promises—since he saw that it would be disgraceful for him either to appear to have lied or to have held

[a] Some MSS. add "nor more precious."

[b] Saul's speech is an amplification of 1 Sam. xviii. 25.

[c] 1 Sam. xviii. 27 "he and his men . . . slew of the Philistines two hundred (LXX "one hundred") and David brought their foreskins."

δοκεῖν ἢ δι' ἐπιβουλὴν ἵν'[1] ἀδυνάτοις ἐπιχειρῶν ὁ Δαυίδης ἀποθάνῃ τὸν γάμον ἐπηγγέλθαι, δίδωσιν αὐτῷ τὴν θυγατέρα Μελχὰν[2] ὀνόματι.

205 (xi. 1) Ἔμελλε δὲ οὐκ ἐπὶ πολὺ τοῖς γεγενημένοις ἐμμένειν Σαοῦλος ἄρα· ὁρῶν γὰρ τὸν Δαυίδην παρὰ τῷ θεῷ καὶ παρὰ τοῖς ὄχλοις εὐδοκιμοῦντα κατέδεισε, καὶ τὸν φόβον οὐκ ἔχων ἀποκρύψασθαι περὶ μεγάλων ὄντα, βασιλείας τε καὶ ζωῆς, ὧν καὶ θατέρου στερηθῆναι συμφορὰ δεινή, κτείνειν τὸν Δαυίδην διεγνώκει καὶ προστάσσει τὴν ἀναίρεσιν αὐτοῦ Ἰωνάθῃ τε τῷ παιδὶ καὶ τοῖς πιστοτάτοις
206 τῶν οἰκετῶν. ὁ δὲ τὸν πατέρα τῆς ἐπὶ τῷ Δαυίδῃ μεταβολῆς θαυμάσας οὐκ ἐπὶ μετρίοις ἀπὸ τῆς πολλῆς εὐνοίας ἀλλ' ἐπὶ θανάτῳ γενομένης, καὶ τὸν νεανίσκον ἀγαπῶν καὶ τὴν ἀρετὴν αὐτοῦ καταιδούμενος λέγει πρὸς αὐτὸν τὸ τοῦ πατρὸς
207 ἀπόρρητον καὶ τὴν προαίρεσιν. συμβουλεύει μέντοι φυλάσσεσθαι γενόμενον ἐκποδὼν τὴν ἐπιοῦσαν ἡμέραν· αὐτὸς γὰρ ἀσπάσεσθαι[3] τὸν πατέρα καὶ καιροῦ παραφανέντος αὐτῷ διαλεχθήσεσθαι περὶ αὐτοῦ καὶ τὴν αἰτίαν μαθήσεσθαι καὶ ταύτην
208 ἐκφαυλίσειν, ὡς οὐ δεῖν ἐπ' αὐτῇ κτείνειν τοσαῦτα μὲν ἀγαθὰ τὸ πλῆθος ἐργασάμενον εὐεργέτην δ' αὐτοῦ γεγενημένον, δι' ἃ καὶ συγγνώμην ἂν ἐπὶ τοῖς μεγίστοις ἁμαρτήμασιν εἰκότως εὕρατο. "δηλώσω δέ σοι τὴν τοῦ πατρὸς γνώμην." Δαυίδης δὲ πεισθεὶς συμβουλίᾳ χρηστῇ ὑπεξίσταται τῆς τοῦ βασιλέως ὄψεως.

209 (2) Τῇ δ' ἐπιούσῃ πρὸς τὸν Σαοῦλον Ἰωνάθης

[1] + ὡς codd.
[2] Μελχώνην SP: Μελχὼ Glycas: Melchon Lat.
[3] ed. pr., Lat.: ἀσπάσασθαι codd.

out this marriage merely in order to bring about David's death on an impossible enterprise[a]—gave him his daughter, Melcha[b] by name.

Jonathan warns David of Saul's plot; David flees. 1 Sam. xix. 1.

(xi. 1) However Saul was not for long to acquiesce in this state of things; for, seeing David in favour both with God and with the multitude, he took alarm and, being unable to conceal his fears—concerning, as they did, such great interests as his kingdom and his life, the loss of either of which would be a dreadful calamity—he resolved to slay David and charged Jonathan his son and the most trusted of his men to make away with him. Jonathan was amazed at this change in his father's feelings toward David from great benevolence to not merely moderate dislike but to the compassing of his death; and, loving the lad and reverencing him for his virtue, he told him of his father's secret plan and intent. He counselled him, moreover, to take heed to himself and to keep out of sight on the morrow, saying that he would himself go to greet his father and, when the opportunity presented itself, would converse with him about David, and discover the reason (of his dislike); he would then make light of this, representing that he ought not on such ground to put to death one who had rendered so many services to the people and proved a benefactor to Saul himself, on account of which he might well have secured pardon for even the gravest crimes. "And I will inform thee," he added, "what is my father's mind." David, in compliance with this excellent counsel, withdrew himself from the king's sight.

(2) The next day Jonathan went to Saul and, find-

[a] No such thoughts are attributed to Saul in Scripture.

[b] Bibl. Michal. LXX Μελχόλ.

ἐλθὼν ὡς ἱλαρόν τε καὶ χαίροντα κατέλαβεν ἤρξατο λόγους αὐτῷ περὶ τοῦ Δαυίδου προσφέρειν· "τί καταγνοὺς αὐτοῦ μικρὸν ἢ μεῖζον ἀδίκημα, πάτερ,[1] προσέταξας ἀνελεῖν ἄνδρα μέγα μὲν αὐτῷ πρὸς σωτηρίαν ὄφελος γεγενημένον, μεῖζον δὲ πρὸς τὴν
210 Παλαιστίνων τιμωρίαν, ὕβρεως δὲ καὶ χλεύης ἀπαλλάξαντα τὸν Ἑβραίων λαὸν ἣν ἐπὶ τεσσαράκοντα ἡμέρας ὑπέμεινεν οὐδενὸς τολμῶντος[2] ὑποστῆναι τὴν τοῦ πολεμίου πρόκλησιν, καὶ μετὰ ταῦτα κομίσαντα μὲν ὅσας ἐπετάχθη κεφαλὰς τῶν ἐχθρῶν, λαβόντα δ' ἐπὶ τούτῳ γέρας τὴν ἐμὴν ἀδελφὴν πρὸς γάμον, ὡς ἂν ἀλγεινὸς[3] αὐτοῦ γένοιθ' ἡμῖν ὁ θάνατος οὐ διὰ τὴν ἀρετὴν μόνον, ἀλλὰ καὶ διὰ τὴν συγγένειαν· συναδικεῖται γὰρ αὐτοῦ τῷ θανάτῳ καὶ ἡ σὴ θυγάτηρ χηρείαν πρὶν ἢ τῆς συμβιώσεως
211 εἰς ὄνησιν ἐλθεῖν μέλλουσα πειράζειν. ταῦτα λογισάμενος μεταβαλοῦ πρὸς τὸ ἡμερώτερον καὶ μηδὲν ποιήσῃς κακὸν ἄνδρα πρῶτον μὲν ἡμᾶς[4] εὐεργεσίαν μεγάλην εὐεργετήσαντα τὴν σὴν σωτηρίαν, ὅτε σοι τοῦ πονηροῦ πνεύματος καὶ τῶν δαιμονίων ἐγκαθεζομένων τὰ μὲν ἐξέβαλεν, εἰρήνην δὲ ἀπ' αὐτῶν τῇ ψυχῇ σου παρέσχεν, δεύτερον δὲ τὴν ἀπὸ τῶν πολεμίων ἐκδικίαν· αἰσχρὸν γὰρ τούτων ἐπιλελῆ-
212 σθαι." τούτοις παρηγορεῖται τοῖς λόγοις Σαοῦλος καὶ μηδὲν ἀδικήσειν τὸν Δαυίδην ὄμνυσι τῷ παιδί· κρείττων γὰρ ὀργῆς καὶ φόβου δίκαιος λόγος. Ἰωνάθης δὲ μεταπεμψάμενος τὸν Δαυίδην σημαίνει τε αὐτῷ χρηστὰ καὶ σωτήρια τὰ παρὰ τοῦ πατρός,

[1] ὦ πάτερ MSP.

Jonathan persuades Saul to take David back. 1 Sam. xix. 4.

ing him cheerful and gay,[a] began to address him concerning David. "What wrongdoing small or great, father, canst thou have found in him that thou hast ordered us to put to death one who has done so much in aiding thine own welfare and yet more in punishing the Philistines, and so has delivered the Hebrew people from the contumely and derision which for forty days they had endured when no one else dared face the enemy's challenge, and who thereafter brought thee the appointed number of enemy heads and received as his recompense my sister in marriage? Thus his death would be grievous to us, not only by reason of his merits, but also of the ties of kinship; for thy daughter will likewise be wronged by his death, destined to experience widowhood before even entering on the joy of wedded life. Let these reflections move thee to greater mildness; do no injury to one who first rendered us that great service of restoring thee to health, when he drove out the evil spirit and the demons that beset thee and brought peace from them to thy soul, and then avenged us upon our enemies. Shameful would it be to forget these things."[b] By these words Saul was won over and he swore to his son that he would do David no wrong; so does a just cause prevail over anger and fear. Jonathan then sent for David and not only informed him of the kindly and reassuring attitude

[a] Unscriptural detail.
[b] The references to Michal and to the healing of Saul are unscriptural.

[2] οὐδενὸς τολμῶντος ex Lat. Niese: μόνος τολμῶν codd.: μόνον τολμῶντα Naber.
[3] ἀλγεινότερος MSP Lat.
[4] ἡμᾶς om. RO.

ἄγει τε πρὸς αὐτόν, καὶ παρέμενε τῷ βασιλεῖ Δαυίδης ὥσπερ ἔμπροσθεν.

213 (3) Κατὰ δὲ τοῦτον τὸν καιρὸν τῶν Παλαιστίνων στρατευσαμένων πάλιν ἐπὶ τοὺς Ἑβραίους πέμπει μετὰ στρατιᾶς τὸν Δαυίδην πολεμήσοντα τοῖς Παλαιστίνοις, καὶ συμβαλὼν πολλοὺς αὐτῶν ἀπέκτεινε καὶ νικήσας ἐπάνεισι πρὸς τὸν βασιλέα. προσδέχεται δ' αὐτὸν ὁ Σαοῦλος οὐχ ὡς ἤλπισεν ἀπὸ τοῦ κατορθώματος, ἀλλ' ὑπὸ τῆς εὐπραγίας αὐτοῦ λυπηθεὶς ὡς ἐπισφαλέστερος αὐτὸς ἐκ τῶν
214 ἐκείνου πράξεων γενόμενος. ἐπεὶ δὲ πάλιν αὐτὸν προσελθὸν τὸ δαιμόνιον ἐθορύβει πνεῦμα καὶ συνετάραττε, καλέσας εἰς τὸ δωμάτιον ἐν ᾧ κατέκειτο, κατέχων τὸ δόρυ προσέταξε τῷ ψαλμῷ καὶ τοῖς ὕμνοις ἐξᾴδειν αὐτόν. ἐκείνου δὲ τὰ κελευσθέντα ποιοῦντος διατεινάμενος ἀκοντίζει τὸ δόρυ· καὶ τὸ μὲν προϊδόμενος ὁ Δαυίδης ἐξέκλινε, φεύγει δὲ εἰς τὸν οἶκον τὸν αὑτοῦ καὶ δι' ὅλης ἔμεινεν ἡμέρας αὐτόθι.

215 (4) Νυκτὸς δὲ πέμψας ὁ βασιλεὺς ἐκέλευσεν αὐτὸν ἄχρι τῆς ἕω φυλάττεσθαι μὴ καὶ λάθῃ παντελῶς ἀφανὴς γενόμενος, ἵνα παραγενόμενος[1] εἰς τὸ δικαστήριον καὶ κρίσει παραδοὺς ἀποκτείνῃ. Μελχὰ δὲ ἡ γυνὴ Δαυίδου θυγάτηρ δὲ τοῦ βασιλέως τὴν τοῦ πατρὸς μαθοῦσα διάνοιαν τῷ ἀνδρὶ παρίσταται δειλὰς ἔχουσα τὰς περὶ αὐτοῦ ἐλπίδας καὶ περὶ τῆς ἰδίας ψυχῆς ἀγωνιῶσα· οὐδὲ γὰρ αὐτὴν
216 ζῆν ὑπομενεῖν[2] ἐκείνου στερηθεῖσαν. καί "μή σε," φησίν, "ὁ ἥλιος ἐνταυθοῖ καταλάβῃ[3]· οὐ γὰρ

[1] παραγόμενος conj. Thackeray.
[2] Dindorf: ὑπομένειν codd.
[3] E: καταλάβοι codd.

of his father, but brought him into his presence ; and David stayed with the king as before.

(3) About this time the Philistines again took the field against the Hebrews, and Saul sent David with an army to fight against them, and he, having joined battle with them, slew many and returned victorious to the king. Saul, however, did not give him the reception which he expected after that achievement, but was aggrieved by his success, believing that David had become more dangerous to him by reason of his exploits. And when the evil spirit again came upon him to trouble and confuse him, he called David to the chamber wherein he lay, and, holding his spear in his hand, bade him charm away the spell with his harp and songs. Then, when David did as he had been commanded, Saul hurled his spear at him with all his might. David, seeing it coming, got out of its way ; then he fled to his own house and remained there all that day.

Saul attacks David on his return from battle with the Philistines. 1 Sam. xix.

(4) But at night the king sent officers with orders to guard him till dawn lest he escape and disappear altogether ; Saul's intent was to come before the court and deliver him to justice to be put to death.[a] But when Melcha, the wife of David and daughter of the king, learned of her father's intent, she came to aid her husband, having faint hope for him and also feeling dreadful anxiety about her own life, for she could not endure to live if bereft of him.[b] " Let not the sun," she said, " find thee here ; else it will never

Michal's stratagem saves David from arrest. 1 Sam. xix. 11.

[a] Scripture says nothing of Saul's intention to have David put on trial ; 1 Sam. xix. 11 " Saul also sent messengers to David's house to watch him and to slay him in the morning."

[b] This motive is supplied by Josephus.

ἔτ' ὄψεταί σε. φεῦγε δ' ἕως[1] τοῦτό σοι δύναται παρασχεῖν ἡ παροῦσα νύξ· καὶ ποιήσειε[2] δέ σοι ταύτην ὁ θεὸς μακροτέραν· ἴσθι γὰρ σαυτὸν ἂν
217 εὑρεθῇς ὑπὸ τοῦ πατρὸς ἀπολούμενον." καὶ καθιμήσασα διὰ θυρίδος αὐτὸν ἐξέσωσεν· ἔπειτα σκευάσασα τὴν κλίνην ὡς ἐπὶ νοσοῦντι καὶ ὑποθεῖσα τοῖς ἐπιβολαίοις ἧπαρ αἰγός, ἅμ' ἡμέρᾳ τοῦ πατρὸς ὡς αὐτὴν[3] πέμψαντος ἐπὶ τὸν Δαυίδην ὠχλῆσθαι διὰ τῆς νυκτὸς εἶπε τοῖς παροῦσιν, ἐπιδείξασα τὴν κλίνην κατακεκαλυμμένην καὶ τῷ πηδήματι τοῦ ἥπατος σαλεύοντι τὴν ἐπιβολὴν πιστωσαμένη
218 τὸ κατακείμενον τὸν Δαυίδην ἀσθμαίνειν.[4] ἀπαγγειλάντων δὲ τῶν πεμφθέντων ὅτι γένοιτο διὰ τῆς νυκτὸς ἀσθενέστερος, ἐκέλευσεν οὕτως ἔχοντα κομισθῆναι· βούλεσθαι γὰρ αὐτὸν ἀνελεῖν. ἐλθόντες δὲ καὶ ἀνακαλύψαντες τὴν κλίνην καὶ τὸ σόφισμα τῆς γυναικὸς εὑρόντες ἀπήγγειλαν τῷ
219 βασιλεῖ. μεμφομένου δὲ τοῦ πατρὸς αὐτὴν ὅτι σώσειε μὲν τὸν ἐχθρὸν αὐτοῦ κατασοφίσαιτο δ'[5] αὐτόν, ἀπολογίαν σκήπτεται πιθανήν· ἀπειλήσαντα γὰρ αὐτὴν ἀποκτείνειν ἔφησε τυχεῖν ἐκ τοῦ δέους τῆς πρὸς τὸ σωθῆναι συνεργίας· ὑπὲρ ἧς συγγνῶναι καλῶς ἔχειν αὐτῇ, κατ' ἀνάγκην ἀλλὰ μὴ κατὰ προαίρεσιν γενομένης· "οὐ γὰρ οὕτως," ἔλεγεν, "οἶμαι τὸν ἐχθρὸν ἐζήτεις ἀποθανεῖν, ὡς

[1] ex Lat. Niese: δὲ ὡς codd.
[2] ποιήσει RO: ποιήσοι MSP: faciat Lat.
[3] ὡς αὐτὴν] αὐτῆς MSP.
[4] M: ἀσθενεῖν rell.: dormire Lat.
[5] ed. pr.: τ' codd.: vero Lat.

[a] 1 Sam. xix. 13 "And Michal took the teraphim (A.V. "an image") and laid them in the bed and placed a goat's skin (?) at its head" (A.V "put a pillow of goats' *hair* for his

look on thee again. Flee while the night which is still upon us permits, and may God prolong its hours for thee; for know that if thou art found by my father, thou art a lost man." And she let him down through a window and got him safely away. Next she made up the bed as for a sick person and put a goat's liver [a] beneath the covers; and when at daybreak her father sent to fetch David, she told those who came for him that he had been attacked by illness during the night, and she showed them the bed all covered up, and by the quivering of the liver which shook the bedclothes convinced them that what lay there was David gasping for breath.[b] When the messengers reported to Saul that David had fallen ill during the night, he ordered him to be brought just as he was, for he wished to kill him. And when they came and uncovered the bed, they discovered the woman's trick, which they reported to the king. But when her father rebuked her for having saved his enemy and tricked himself, she resorted to a plausible defence; her husband, she declared, had threatened to kill her and so, by terrifying her, had secured her aid in his escape, for which she deserved pardon, seeing that she had acted under constraint and not of her own free will. "For," said she, "I cannot think that thou wert as desirous for thy enemy's death as for the safety of my life."

Michal excuses her conduct to Saul. 1 Sam. xix. 17.

bolster"). The teraphim were probably household images in human form. The Heb. *kebîr*, here rendered "skin," is of doubtful meaning, and was read as *kebēd*, "liver," by the LXX, followed by Josephus. The context shows that it must have been something round and hairy to give the appearance of a human head, and so it was understood by the rabbis.

[b] The details of Michal's stratagem are invented by Josephus.

ἐμὲ σώζεσθαι." καὶ συγγινώσκει δὲ τῇ κόρῃ
220 Σαοῦλος. ὁ δὲ Δαυίδης ἐκφυγὼν τὸν κίνδυνον ἧκε πρὸς τὸν προφήτην Σαμουῆλον εἰς Ἀρμαθὰ καὶ τὴν ἐπιβουλὴν αὐτῷ τὴν τοῦ βασιλέως ἐδήλωσε καὶ ὡς παρὰ μικρὸν ὑπ' αὐτοῦ τῷ δόρατι βληθεὶς ἀποθάνοι, μήτ' ἐν τοῖς πρὸς αὐτὸν κακὸς γενόμενος μήτ' ἐν τοῖς πρὸς τοὺς πολεμίους ἀγῶσιν ἄνανδρος, ἀλλ' ἐν ἅπασι μετὰ τοῦ θεοῦ[1] καὶ ἐπιτυχής. τοῦτο δ' ἦν αἴτιον Σαούλῳ τῆς πρὸς Δαυίδην ἀπεχθείας.

221 (5) Μαθὼν δ' ὁ προφήτης τὴν τοῦ βασιλέως ἀδικίαν καταλείπει μὲν τὴν πόλιν Ἀρμαθάν, ἀγαγὼν δὲ τὸν Δαυίδην ἐπί τινα τόπον Γαλβουὰθ[2] ὄνομα ἐκεῖ διέτριβε σὺν αὐτῷ. ὡς δ' ἀπηγγέλη τῷ Σαούλῳ παρὰ τῷ προφήτῃ τυγχάνων ὁ Δαυίδης, πέμψας ὁπλίτας πρὸς αὐτὸν ἄγειν προσέταξε συλ-
222 λαμβάνοντας.[3] οἱ δ' ἐλθόντες πρὸς τὸν Σαμουῆλον καὶ καταλαβόντες προφητῶν ἐκκλησίαν, τοῦ θείου μεταλαμβάνουσι πνεύματος καὶ προφητεύειν ἤρξαντο· Σαοῦλος δ' ἀκούσας ἄλλους ἔπεμψεν ἐπὶ τὸν Δαυίδην· κἀκείνων ταὐτὸ τοῖς πρώτοις παθόντων πάλιν ἀπέστειλεν ἑτέρους· προφητευόντων δὲ καὶ τῶν τρίτων τελευταῖον ὀργισθεὶς αὐτὸς ἐξ-
223 ώρμησεν. ἐπεὶ δ' ἐγγὺς ἦν ἤδη, Σαμουῆλος πρὶν ἰδεῖν αὐτὸν προφητεύειν ἐποίησεν. ἐλθὼν δὲ πρὸς αὐτὸν Σαοῦλος ὑπὸ τοῦ πολλοῦ πνεύματος ἐλαυνόμενος ἔκφρων γίνεται καὶ τὴν ἐσθῆτα περιδύσας ἑαυτὸν καταπεσὼν ἔκειτο δι' ὅλης ἡμέρας τε καὶ νυκτὸς Σαμουήλου τε καὶ Δαυίδου βλεπόντων.

224 (6) Ἰωνάθης δὲ ὁ Σαούλου παῖς, ἀφικομένου πρὸς

[1] (τοῦ) θυμοῦ RO: et pronus Lat.
[2] Βαλγουὰθ SP: Γελβούαθον E.
[3] συλλαβόντας SP.

David finds refuge with Samuel at Ramah (Armatha). 1 Sam. xix. 18.

So Saul pardoned the girl. Meanwhile David, having escaped from danger, repaired to the prophet Samuel at Armatha, and recounted to him the king's plot against him, and how he had wellnigh been struck by his spear and killed, though he had never dealt ill with him nor been cowardly in combating his foes, but had ever with God's aid been indeed fortunate. Now that was the reason for Saul's hatred of David.

Saul and his men, pursuing David, are possessed and prophesy. *Ib.*

(5) On learning of the king's iniquity, the prophet left the city of Armatha and brought David to a place named Galbouath [a] and there abode with him. Now when it was told Saul that David was staying with the prophet, he sent armed men with orders to arrest him and bring him to him. But they, on coming to Samuel and finding there an assembly of prophets, were themselves possessed by the spirit of God and began to prophesy. Saul, hearing thereof, sent others after David, and when these met with the same experience as the first, he dispatched yet more; but this third company prophesied likewise, and finally in a rage he set out himself. But so soon as he came near them, Samuel, even before seeing him, caused him too to prophesy.[b] On reaching him, Saul, losing his reason under the impulse of that mighty spirit, stripped off his clothes and lay prostrate on the ground for a whole day and night in the sight of Samuel and David.

(6) Thence David betook himself to Jonathan, son

[a] Bibl. Naioth (Heb. *Nawath* or *Nayōth*), LXX Αὐὰθ (*v.l.* Ναυιώθ κτλ.) ἐν Ῥαμά; these forms appear to be corrupt. The Targum renders it *Beth 'ulphānā* "house of instruction." The source of Josephus's form is unknown.

[b] Josephus omits to state, as does Scripture, 1 Sam. xix. 24, that this incident explains the saying "Is Saul also among the prophets?"

αὐτὸν ἐκεῖθεν Δαυίδου καὶ περὶ τῆς τοῦ πατρὸς ἀποδυρομένου ἐπιβουλῆς καὶ λέγοντος ὡς οὐδὲν ἀδικήσας οὐδ'[1] ἐξαμαρτὼν σπουδάζοιτο ὑπὸ τοῦ πατρὸς αὐτοῦ φονευθῆναι, μήθ' ἑαυτῷ τοῦθ' ὑπονοοῦντι πιστεύειν παρεκάλει μήτε τοῖς διαβάλλουσιν, εἴ τινες ἄρα εἰσὶν οἱ τοῦτο πράττοντες, ἀλλ' αὐτῷ προσέχειν καὶ θαρρεῖν· μηδὲν γὰρ τοιοῦτον ἐπ' αὐτῷ φρονεῖν τὸν πατέρα· φράσαι γὰρ ἂν αὐτῷ περὶ τούτου καὶ σύμβουλον παραλαβεῖν,
225 τῇ κοινῇ γνώμῃ καὶ τἆλλα πράττοντα. ὁ δὲ Δαυίδης ὤμνυεν ἦ μὴν οὕτως ἔχειν, καὶ πιστεύοντ' ἠξίου προνοεῖν αὐτοῦ μᾶλλον ἢ καταφρονοῦντ' ἐπ' ἀληθέσι τοῖς λόγοις τότε ἀληθὲς ὑπολαβεῖν, ὅταν ἢ θεάσηται πεφονευμένον αὐτὸν[2] ἢ πύθηται· μηδὲν λέγειν δ' αὐτῷ τὸν πατέρα περὶ τούτων ἔφασκεν εἰδότα τὴν πρὸς αὐτὸν φιλίαν καὶ διάθεσιν.

226 (7) Λυπηθεὶς δ' ἐφ' ὅτῳ πιστωσάμενος τὴν τοῦ Σαούλου προαίρεσιν Ἰωνάθης οὐκ ἔπεισεν, ἐπηρώτα τίνος ἐξ αὐτοῦ βούλεται τυχεῖν. ὁ δέ "οἶδα γάρ," ἔφη, "πάντα σε χαρίζεσθαί μοι καὶ παρέχειν ἐθέλοντα· νουμηνία μὲν εἰς τὴν ἐπιοῦσάν ἐστιν, ἔθος
227 δ' ἔχω δειπνεῖν σὺν τῷ βασιλεῖ καθήμενος· εἰ δή σοι δοκεῖ, πορευθεὶς ἔξω τῆς πόλεως ἐν τῷ πεδίῳ λανθάνων διαμενῶ, σὺ δ' ἐπιζητήσαντος αὐτοῦ λέγε πορευθῆναί με εἰς τὴν πατρίδα Βηθλεέμην ἑορτήν μου τῆς φυλῆς ἀγούσης, προστιθεὶς ὅτι σύ μοι συγκεχώρηκας. κἂν μέν, οἷον εἰκὸς καὶ σύνηθές ἐστι λέγειν ἐπὶ φίλοις ἀποδημοῦσιν, 'ἐπ' ἀγαθῷ

[1] Dindorf: οὔτ' codd.
[2] πεφονευμένον αὐτὸν om. RO Lat.

of Saul, and complained to him of his father's designs, saying that though he had been guilty of no iniquity or crime, his father was making every effort to have him murdered. Jonathan entreated him to put no faith either in his own suspicions or in slanderers, if indeed there were any such, but to pay heed to him and take courage; for, he said, his father was meditating nothing of the sort, else he would have told him of it and taken him into his counsel, since in all else he acted in concert with him. But David swore[a] that it was truly so, and he asked Jonathan to believe him and look out for his safety instead of contemptuously questioning the truth of his words and waiting to recognize their truth until he should actually behold or learn of his assassination. His father, he declared, had told him nothing of all this because he knew of his son's friendship and affection for himself.

David complains to Jonathan of Saul's enmity. 1 Sam. xx. 1.

(7) Grieved that his assurance of Saul's disposition failed to convince David, Jonathan asked him what he would have him do. "I know," he replied, "that thou art ready to grant me any favour or do any thing. Now to-morrow is the new moon, when my custom is to dine with the king. If, then, it please thee, I will go forth from the city and remain concealed in the plain; but do thou, if he ask for me, say that I am gone to my native Bethlehem, where my tribe[b] is keeping a feast, adding that thou didst give me leave. Should he then say, as is proper and customary to say about friends going away, 'A good

Jonathan agrees to inform David secretly of Saul's intention. 1 Sam. xx. 4.

[a] So the Hebrew; LXX "answered."

[b] Or "clan"; *cf.* Heb. *mishpāḥāh* (A.V. "family"), which the LXX here renders, like Josephus, by φυλή, but the latter can mean "clan" (subdivision of a tribe) as well as "tribe," *cf.* § 62 note.

βεβάδικεν' εἴπῃ, ἴσθι μηδὲν ὕπουλον παρ' αὐτοῦ εἶναι μηδ' ἐχθρόν· ἂν δ' ὡς ἄλλως ἀποκρίνηται τοῦτ' ἔσται τεκμήριον τῶν κατ' ἐμοῦ βεβουλευ-
228 μένων. μηνύσεις δέ μοι τὴν διάνοιαν τὴν τοῦ πατρός, οἴκτῳ τε νέμων τοῦτο καὶ φιλίᾳ, δι' ἣν πίστεις τε παρ' ἐμοῦ λαβεῖν ἠξίωκας αὐτός τε ἐμοὶ δοῦναι δεσπότης ὢν οἰκέτῃ σῷ.[1] εἰ δ' εὑρίσκεις τι ἐν ἐμοὶ πονηρόν, αὐτὸς ἄνελε καὶ φθάσον τὸν πατέρα."

229 (8) Πρὸς δὲ τὸ τελευταῖον δυσχεράνας τῶν λόγων Ἰωνάθης ποιήσειν ταῦτ' ἐπηγγείλατο κἂν τι σκυθρωπὸν ὁ πατὴρ αὐτοῦ καὶ τὴν ἀπέχθειαν ἐμφανίζον[2] ἀποκρίνηται μηνύσειν.[3] ἵνα δ' αὐτῷ θαρρῇ μᾶλλον, ἐξαγαγὼν αὐτὸν εἰς ὕπαιθρον καὶ καθαρὸν ἀέρα οὐδὲν παρήσειν ὑπὲρ τῆς Δαυίδου
230 σωτηρίας ὤμνυε· "τὸν γὰρ θεόν," εἶπε, "τοῦτον ὃν πολὺν ὁρᾷς καὶ πανταχοῦ κεχυμένον, καὶ πρὶν ἑρμηνεῦσαί με τοῖς λόγοις τὴν διάνοιαν ἤδη μου ταύτην εἰδότα, μάρτυρα ποιοῦμαι τῶν πρὸς σὲ συνθηκῶν, ὡς οὐκ ἀνήσω τὸν πατέρα πολλάκις αὐτοῦ τῆς προαιρέσεως διάπειραν λαμβάνων, πρὶν ἢ καταμαθεῖν ἥτις ἐστὶ καὶ παρὰ τοῖς ἀπορρήτοις
231 αὐτοῦ τῆς ψυχῆς γενέσθαι. καταμαθὼν δ' οὐκ ἀποκρύψομαι, καταμηνύσω δὲ πρὸς σὲ καὶ πρᾷον ὄντα καὶ δυσμενῶς διακείμενον. οἶδε δὲ οὗτος[4] ὁ θεὸς πῶς αὐτὸν εἶναι μετὰ σοῦ διὰ παντὸς εὔχομαι· ἔστι μὲν γὰρ νῦν καὶ οὐκ ἀπολείψει σε, ποιήσει δὲ τῶν ἐχθρῶν ἄντε ὁ πατὴρ ὁ ἐμὸς ᾖ[5] ἄντ' ἐγὼ
232 κρείττονα. σὺ μόνον μνημόνευε τούτων, κἂν ἀπο-

[1] οἰκέτῃ σῷ om. RO. [2] ἐμφανίζων ROMS.
[3] Niese: μηνύειν codd. [4] αὐτὸς Naber.
[5] Niese: εἴη RO: om. MSP: est Lat.

journey to him,'[a] know that he bears no hidden malice nor enmity; but should he answer otherwise, that will be a sign of his designs against me. And thou shalt inform me of thy father's state of mind in token of thy pity and of that friendship for which thou hast seen fit to receive pledges from me and to grant me the like thyself, though thou art the master, and I thy servant. But if thou findest any wickedness in me, slay me thyself and so anticipate thy father."

Jonathan swears an oath of friendship to David. 1 Sam. xx. 9.

(8) Although displeased by these last words, Jonathan promised to do this and said that if his father gave some sullen answer indicative of hate, he would inform David thereof. And, that he might have the more confidence in him, he brought him out into the open and pure air and swore to leave nothing undone for his safety. "This God," said he, "whom thou seest to be so great and everywhere extended, and who, before I have expressed my thought in words, already knows what it is,[b]—Him do I take as witness of my covenant with thee, to wit, that I will not give up my constant endeavour to discover my father's purpose until I have clearly learnt it and come close to the secrets of his soul. And having learnt it, I will not hide it, but will disclose to thee whether he be graciously or evilly disposed. This God of ours knows how I pray that He may always be with thee. Indeed, He is with thee now and will not forsake thee, but will make thee stronger than thy foes, be it my father or be it myself. Do thou but remember this,

[a] A free rendering of 1 Sam. xx. 7 "It is well," perhaps suggested by the customary Hebrew salutation, "Go in peace."

[b] These divine attributes are an amplification of the Scriptural "Lord God of Israel."

θανεῖν μοι γένηται τὰ τέκνα μου σῶζε, καὶ τὴν ὑπὲρ τῶν παρόντων μοι ἀμοιβὴν εἰς ἐκεῖνα κατάθου.'' ταῦτ' ἐπομόσας ἀπολύει τὸν Δαυίδην εἴς τινα τόπον ἀπελθεῖν τοῦ πεδίου φράσας, ἐν ᾧ γυμναζόμενος διετέλει· γνοὺς γὰρ τὰ παρὰ τοῦ πατρὸς ἥξειν πρὸς αὐτὸν ἔφησεν ἐκεῖ μόνον ἐπ-
233 αγόμενος παῖδα. "κἂν[1] τρία ἀκόντια δὲ βαλὼν ἐπὶ τὸν σκοπὸν κομίσαι τῷ παιδὶ προστάσσω τὰ ἀκόντια (κεῖσθαι γὰρ ἔμπροσθεν αὐτοῦ[2]), γίνωσκε μηδὲν εἶναι φαῦλον παρὰ τοῦ πατρός· ἂν δὲ τὰ ἐναντία τούτων ἀκούσῃς μου λέγοντος, καὶ τὰ
234 ἐναντία παρὰ τοῦ βασιλέως προσδόκα. τῆς μέντοι γε ἀσφαλείας τεύξῃ παρ' ἐμοῦ καὶ οὐδὲν μὴ πάθῃς ἄτοπον· ὅπως δὲ μνησθῇς τούτων παρὰ τὸν τῆς εὐπραγίας καιρὸν σκόπει καὶ τοῖς υἱοῖς μου γενοῦ χρήσιμος.'' Δαυίδης μὲν οὖν ταύτας λαβὼν παρὰ Ἰωνάθου τὰς πίστεις εἰς τὸ συγκείμενον ἀπηλλάγη χωρίον.

235 (9) Τῇ δ' ἐχομένῃ, νουμηνία δ' ἦν,[3] ἁγνεύσας, ὡς ἔθος εἶχεν, ὁ βασιλεὺς ἧκεν ἐπὶ τὸ δεῖπνον, καὶ παρακαθεσθέντων αὐτῷ τοῦ μὲν παιδὸς Ἰωνάθου ἐκ δεξιῶν Ἀβεννήρου δὲ τοῦ ἀρχιστρατήγου ἐκ τῶν ἑτέρων, ἰδὼν τὴν τοῦ Δαυίδου καθέδραν κενὴν ἡσύχασεν ὑπονοήσας οὐ καθαρεύσαντα αὐτὸν ἀπὸ
236 συνουσίας ὑστερεῖν. ὡς δὲ καὶ τῇ δευτέρᾳ τῆς νουμηνίας οὐ παρῆν ἐπυνθάνετο παρὰ τοῦ παιδὸς Ἰωνάθου ὅτι καὶ τῇ παρελθούσῃ καὶ ταύτῃ τοῦ

[1] S: καὶ rell. [2] + καὶ ἂν ταῦτα φησὶν ἀκούσῃς RO.
[3] δ' ἦν ed. pr.: δ' ἦν δι' ἦν codd.

[a] Unscriptural detail.
[b] So, apparently, the LXX (σχίζαις ἀκοντίζων); Heb. "arrows."

and, should death befall me, preserve my children's lives and make over to them the recompense that is due me for my present services." After he had taken these oaths, he dismissed David, telling him to go to a certain place in the plain where he (Jonathan) was wont to exercise himself[a]; there, he said, when he had learnt his father's mind, he would rejoin him, accompanied only by a lad. "And if, after throwing three darts[b] at the mark, I order the lad to bring them to me, for they will be found lying in front of it,[c] know that no mischief is to be feared from my father; but if thou hearest me say the contrary, then look thou also for the contrary from the king. Howbeit thou wilt find safety at my hands and thou shalt suffer no harm. But see that thou rememberest this in the time of thy prosperity, and deal kindly with my children." Then David, having received these pledges from Jonathan, departed to the appointed place.

Jonathan excuses David's absence at the feast. 1 Sam. xx. 24.

(9) The next day, which was the new moon, the king, after purifying himself as the custom was, came to the feast; and when his son Jonathan had seated himself on his right side and Abener, the commander of the army, on his left, he marked that David's seat was empty, but held his peace, surmising that he had been delayed by not having finished his purification after sexual intercourse.[d] But when, on the second day of the feast of the new moon, David again did not appear, he asked his son Jonathan why, both on the

[c] *i.e.* the mark, or perhaps "him," *i.e.* the lad; 1 Sam. xx. 21 "the arrows are this side of thee."

[d] This interpretation of 1 Sam. xx. 26 "it is an accident" (A.V. "something hath befallen him") is similar to that of the rabbis, who took *miqreh*, lit. "happening," in its physiological sense of nocturnal emission.

δείπνου καὶ τῆς ἑστιάσεως ὁ τοῦ Ἰεσσαίου παῖς ἀπολέλειπται. ὁ δὲ πεπορεῦσθαι κατὰ τὰς συνθήκας ἔφησεν αὐτὸν εἰς τὴν ἑαυτοῦ πατρίδα, τῆς φυλῆς ἑορτὴν ἀγούσης, ἐπιτρέψαντος αὐτοῦ· παρακαλέσαι μέντοι καὶ αὐτὸν ἐλθεῖν ἐπὶ τὴν θυσίαν καὶ εἰ συγχωρηθείη φησὶν ἀπέρχεσθαι[1]· " τὴν γὰρ
237 εὔνοιάν μου τὴν πρὸς αὐτὸν ἐπίστασαι." τότε τὴν πρὸς Δαυίδην τοῦ πατρὸς Ἰωνάθης ἐπέγνω δυσμένειαν καὶ τρανῶς τὴν ὅλην αὐτοῦ βούλησιν εἶδεν· οὐ γὰρ κατέσχε Σαοῦλος τῆς ὀργῆς, ἀλλὰ βλασφημῶν ἐξ αὐτομόλων γεγενημένον καὶ πολέμιον ἀπεκάλει καὶ κοινωνὸν τοῦ Δαυίδου καὶ συνεργὸν ἔλεγεν καὶ μήτ'[2] αὐτὸν αἰδεῖσθαι μήτε τὴν μητέρα αὐτοῦ ταῦτα φρονοῦντα καὶ μηδὲ βουλόμενον πεισθῆναι τοῦθ', ὅτι μέχρις οὗ περίεστι Δαυίδης ἐπισφαλῶς αὐτοῖς τὰ τῆς βασιλείας ἔχει· " μετάπεμψαι τοιγαροῦν αὐτόν," ἔφησεν, " ἵνα δῷ δίκην."
238 ὑποτυχόντος δ' Ἰωνάθου, " τί δ' ἀδικοῦντα κολάσαι θέλεις;" οὐκέτ' εἰς λόγους καὶ βλασφημίας τὴν ὀργὴν ὁ Σαοῦλος ἐξήνεγκεν, ἀλλ' ἁρπάσας τὸ δόρυ ἀνεπήδησεν ἐπ' αὐτὸν ἀποκτεῖναι θέλων. καὶ τὸ μὲν ἔργον οὐκ ἔδρασε διακωλυθεὶς ὑπὸ τῶν φίλων, φανερὸς δ' ἐγένετο τῷ παιδὶ μισῶν τὸν Δαυίδην καὶ διαχρήσασθαι ποθῶν, ὡς παρὰ μικρὸν δι' ἐκεῖνον αὐτόχειρ καὶ τοῦ παιδὸς γεγονέναι.

239 (10) Καὶ τότε μὲν ὁ τοῦ βασιλέως παῖς ἐκπηδήσας ἀπὸ τοῦ δείπνου καὶ μηδὲν ὑπὸ λύπης προσενέγκασθαι δυνηθείς, κλαίων αὐτὸν μὲν τοῦ παρὰ μικρὸν ἀπολέσθαι τοῦ κατακεκρίσθαι δ' ἀποθανεῖν Δαυίδην

[1] κἂν συγχωρῇς ἀπέρχομαι MSP (Lat. E).
[2] Dindorf: μηδ' codd.

past day and on this, the son of Jesse had been absent from the festive meal. Jonathan replied, as had been agreed, that he had gone to his native place where his tribe was keeping festival, and with his (Jonathan's) permission. "What is more," he added, "he even invited me to attend that sacrifice, and, if leave be given me, I shall go; for thou knowest the affection that I bear to him." [a] Then did Jonathan discover all his father's malevolence toward David and plainly perceive his whole intent. For Saul did not restrain his wrath, but with curses denounced him as the offspring of renegades and an enemy, and accused him of being in league with David and his accomplice, and as having respect neither for himself nor for his mother in taking that attitude and in refusing to believe that, so long as David lived, their hold upon the kingdom was insecure. "Now then, send for him," said he, "that he may be punished." "But," Jonathan objected, "for what crime wouldst thou punish him?" Whereupon the wrath of Saul found vent no more in words and abuse, but, seizing his spear, he leapt toward him with intent to slay him. And although his friends prevented him [b] from perpetrating the deed, he had now made plain to his son how he hated David and craved to make away with him, seeing that on his account he had wellnigh become the slayer even of his own son.

Saul attacks Jonathan as David's accomplice. 1 Sam. xx. 30.

(10) The king's son instantly rushed from the feast and, prevented by grief from tasting a morsel, passed the night in tears at the thought that he himself had narrowly escaped death and that David was doomed

Jonathan secretly meets David in the fields to say farewell.

[a] David's invitation to Jonathan is unscriptural.
[b] Unscriptural detail.

διενυκτέρευσεν. ἅμα δὲ ἡμέρᾳ πρὸ τῆς πόλεως εἰς τὸ πεδίον ὡς γυμνασόμενος μὲν δηλώσων δὲ τῷ φίλῳ τὴν τοῦ πατρὸς διάθεσιν, ὡς συνέθετο,
240 πρόεισι. ποιήσας δὲ ὁ Ἰωνάθης τὰ συγκείμενα τὸν μὲν ἑπόμενον ἀπολύει εἰς τὴν πόλιν παῖδα, ἦν δ' ἠρεμία[1] τῷ Δαυίδῃ παρελθεῖν[2] εἰς ὄψιν αὐτῷ καὶ λόγους. ἀναφανεὶς δ' οὗτος πίπτει πρὸ τῶν Ἰωνάθου ποδῶν καὶ προσκυνῶν σωτῆρα αὐτοῦ τῆς
241 ψυχῆς ἀπεκάλει. ἀνίστησι δ' ἀπὸ τῆς γῆς αὐτόν, καὶ περιπλακέντες ἀλλήλοις μακρά τε ἠσπάζοντο καὶ δεδακρυμένα, τήν τε ἡλικίαν ἀποθρηνοῦντες αὐτῶν καὶ τὴν ἐφθονημένην ἑταιρίαν καὶ τὸν μέλλοντα διαχωρισμόν, ὃς οὐδὲν αὐτοῖς ἐδόκει θανάτου διαφέρειν. μόλις δ' ἐκ τῶν θρήνων ἀνανήψαντες καὶ μεμνῆσθαι τῶν ὅρκων ἀλλήλοις παρακελευσάμενοι διελύθησαν.

242 (xii. 1) Δαυίδης δὲ φεύγων τὸν βασιλέα καὶ τὸν ἐξ αὐτοῦ θάνατον εἰς Ναβὰν παραγίνεται πόλιν πρὸς Ἀβιμέλεχον[3] τὸν ἀρχιερέα,[4] ὃς ἐπὶ τῷ μόνον ἥκοντα ἰδεῖν καὶ μήτε φίλον σὺν αὐτῷ μήτ' οἰκέτην παρόντα ἐθαύμασε καὶ τὴν αἰτίαν τοῦ μηδένα εἶναι
243 σὺν αὐτῷ μαθεῖν ἤθελεν. ὁ δὲ πρᾶξιν ἀπόρρητον ἐπιταγῆναι παρὰ τοῦ βασιλέως ἔφησεν, εἰς ἣν συνοδίας αὐτῷ βουλομένῳ λαθεῖν οὐκ ἔδει· "τοὺς μέντοι θεράποντας εἰς τόνδε μοι τὸν τόπον ἀπαντᾶν

[1] ὁ δ' ἐν ἐρημίᾳ MSP (Lat.).
[2] παρῆλθεν MSP: ἦλθεν E.
[3] ROE Zonaras: Ἀχιμέλεχον MSP (Lat.).
[4] ἱερέα MSP Lat.

[a] Unscriptural detail.
[b] Josephus omits the account, 1 Sam. xx. 36-37, of Jona-

to die. But at daybreak he went out into the plain before the city, seemingly for exercise,[a] in reality to make known to his friend, in accordance with their agreement, the temper of his father. Then, after doing what had been prearranged, Jonathan sent back the boy who attended him to the city,[b] and David was undisturbed in coming out to meet him and to speak with him. Appearing in the open, he fell at Jonathan's feet and did him homage, calling him the preserver of his life. But Jonathan raised him from the ground, and, putting their arms about each other, they took a long and tearful farewell, bewailing their youth, the companionship which was begrudged them and their coming separation,[c] which seemed to them nothing less than death. Then, hardly recovering from their lamentation and exhorting each other to remember their oaths, they parted. 1 Sam. xx. 34.

David receives help from the high priest Ahimelech (Abimelech) at Nob (Naba). 1 Sam. xxi. 1 (2 Heb.).

(xii. 1) But David, fleeing from the king and death at his hands, now came to the city of Naba[d] to Abimelech[e] the high priest, who was astonished to see him arrive alone with neither friend nor servant in attendance, and desired to know the reason why no man accompanied him. He replied that he had been charged by the king with a secret matter for which he required no escort since he wished to remain unknown. "Howbeit," he added, "I have ordered my servants to join me at this place.[f]" He also re-

than's shooting the arrows beyond the lad to indicate Saul's displeasure.

[c] These details of their parting are an amplification.

[d] Bibl. Nob, LXX Νόμβα. The exact site is uncertain, but it was probably a little north of Jerusalem, in the territory of Benjamin, *cf.* Neh. xi. 32.

[e] Variant Achimelech, as in Scripture; the LXX MSS. also vary between the two forms.

[f] Bibl. "at such and such a place."

προσέταξα." ἠξίου δὲ λαβεῖν ἐφόδια· φίλου γὰρ αὐτὸν ποιήσειν ἔργον παρασχόντα καὶ πρὸς τὸ
244 προκείμενον συλλαμβανομένου. τυχὼν δὲ τούτων ᾔτει καὶ ὅπλον τι μετὰ χεῖρας ῥομφαίαν ἢ δοράτιον[1] παρῆν δὲ καὶ Σαούλου δοῦλος γένει μὲν Σύρος Δώηγος[2] δὲ ὄνομα τὰς τοῦ βασιλέως ἡμιόνους νέμων· ὁ δ' ἀρχιερεὺς ἔχειν μὲν αὐτὸς οὐδέν τι εἶπε τοιοῦτον, εἶναι δὲ τὴν Γολιάθου ῥομφαίαν, ἣν ἀποκτείνας τὸν Παλαιστῖνον αὐτὸς ἀναθείη τῷ θεῷ.
245 (2) Λαβὼν δὲ ταύτην ὁ Δαυίδης ἔξω τῆς τῶν Ἑβραίων χώρας εἰς Γίτταν διέφυγε τὴν Παλαιστίνων, ἧς Ἄγχους ἐβασίλευεν.[3] ἐπιγνωσθεὶς δὲ ὑπὸ τῶν τοῦ βασιλέως οἰκετῶν καὶ φανερὸς αὐτῷ γενόμενος, μηνυόντων ἐκείνων ὅτι Δαυίδης ὁ πολλὰς ἀποκτείνας Παλαιστίνων μυριάδας εἴη, δείσας μὴ πρὸς αὐτοῦ θάνῃ καὶ τὸν κίνδυνον ὃν ἐξέφυγε παρὰ Σαούλου παρ' ἐκείνου πειράσῃ προσποιεῖται μανίαν καὶ λύσσαν, ὡς ἀφρὸν κατὰ τοῦ στόματος αὐτοῦ φερόμενον καὶ τὰ ἄλλα[4] ὅσα συνίστησι μανίαν[5] πίστιν παρὰ τῷ Γίττης βασιλεῖ γενέσθαι[6] τῆς νόσου.
246 καὶ τοῖς οἰκέταις ὁ βασιλεὺς προσδυσχεράνας ὡς ἔκφρονα πρὸς αὐτὸν ἀγάγοιεν ἄνθρωπον ἐκέλευσε τὸν Δαυίδην ὡς τάχος ἐκβάλλειν.
247 (3) Διασωθεὶς δὲ οὕτως[7] ἐκ τῆς Γίττης εἰς τὴν Ἰούδα παραγίνεται φυλὴν καὶ ἐν τῷ πρὸς Ἀδουλ-

[1] ῥομφ. ἢ δορ. om. Lat. E.
[2] Δώηκος SPE.
[3] SP: ἐβασίλευσεν rell.
[4] + δὲ MSP.
[5] μανίας MSP.
[6] Niese: γενήσεσθαι ROM: γεγενῆσθαι SP.
[7] οὗτος ROME.

quested him to furnish him with provisions for a journey; in so doing, he would, he said, be acting like a friend and assisting the cause in hand. Having obtained these,[a] he further asked for any weapon in his keeping, sword or spear. Now there was present also a certain slave of Saul, of Syrian[b] race, by name Doeg, keeper of the king's mules.[c] The high priest replied that he himself possessed no such thing, but that he had there that sword of Goliath which David himself, after slaying the Philistine, had dedicated to God.[d]

(2) Taking this weapon, David fled beyond Hebrew territory to Gitta, a city of the Philistines, of which Anchūs[e] was king. Here he was recognized by the king's servants who then made his presence known to the king, reporting that this was that David who had slain many myriads of Philistines. Thereat David, fearing that he would be put to death by him and, after escaping that peril at the hands of Saul, meet the like fate at his hands, feigned raging madness, foaming at the mouth and displaying all the other symptoms of madness, so as to convince the king of Gitta of his malady. The king was exceedingly angry with his servants for having brought him a madman and gave orders for David's instant expulsion.

David flees to Gath (Gitta); feigning madness he is expelled. 1 Sam. xxi. 10 (11 Heb.

(3) Having thus escaped with his life from Gitta, he betook himself to the tribe of Judah[f] and, taking

[a] Josephus omits the Scriptural details about the hallowed bread which was the only food at the priest's disposal.

[b] So the LXX; Heb. "an Edomite."

[c] So the LXX; Heb. "chief of the shepherds" (A.V. "herdsmen").

[d] *Cf.* § 192.

[e] So the LXX (Luc. Ἀκχούς); bibl. Achish.

[f] The reference to Judah is an added detail.

λάμῃ[1] πόλει σπηλαίῳ διατρίβων πέμπει πρὸς τοὺς ἀδελφοὺς δηλῶν αὐτοῖς ἔνθα εἴη. οἱ δὲ μετὰ πάσης συγγενείας ἧκον πρὸς αὐτόν· καὶ τῶν ἄλλων δὲ ὅσοις ἢ χρεία ἦν ἢ φόβος ἐκ Σαούλου τοῦ βασιλέως συνερρύησαν πρὸς αὐτὸν καὶ ποιεῖν τὰ ἐκείνῳ δοκοῦντα ἑτοίμως ἔχειν ἔλεγον. ἐγένοντο δὲ οἱ
248 πάντες ὡσεὶ τετρακόσιοι. θαρρήσας δὲ ὡς καὶ χειρὸς αὐτῷ καὶ συνεργίας ἤδη προσγεγενημένης ἀπάρας ἐκεῖθεν ἀφικνεῖται πρὸς τὸν τῶν Μωαβιτῶν βασιλέα, καὶ τοὺς γονεῖς αὐτοῦ εἰς τὴν ἑαυτοῦ χώραν προσδεξάμενον ἕως ἂν ἐπιγνῷ[2] τὸ καθ' αὑτὸν τέλος ἔχειν παρεκάλει· κατανεύσαντος δ' αὐτοῦ τὴν χάριν καὶ πάσης τοὺς γονεῖς τοῦ Δαυίδου τιμῆς παρ' ὃν ἐτύγχανον παρ' αὐτῷ χρόνον ἀξιώσαντος.
249 (4) Αὐτὸς τοῦ προφήτου κελεύσαντος αὐτὸν τὴν μὲν ἐρημίαν ἐκλιπεῖν, πορευθέντα δ' εἰς τὴν κληρουχίαν τῆς Ἰούδα φυλῆς ἐν αὐτῇ διάγειν πείθεται καὶ παραγενόμενος εἰς Σάριν[3] πόλιν ἐν αὐτῇ
250 κατέμενε. Σαοῦλος δ' ἀκούσας ὅτι μετὰ πλήθους ὀφθείη ὁ Δαυίδης, οὐκ εἰς τυχόντα θόρυβον καὶ ταραχὴν ἐνέπεσεν, ἀλλ' εἰδὼς τὸ φρόνημα τοῦ ἀνδρὸς καὶ τὴν εὐτολμίαν οὐδὲν ἐξ αὐτοῦ μικρὸν ἀνακύψειν ἔργον, ὑφ' οὗ κλαύσεσθαι πάντως καὶ
251 πονήσειν, ὑπενόησε. καὶ συγκαλέσας τοὺς φίλους καὶ τοὺς ἡγεμόνας καὶ τὴν φυλὴν ἐξ ἧς αὐτὸς ἦν

[1] M: Ἀδολλαάμῃ RO: Ἀδυλλάμῃ SP.
[2] ἕως οὗ ἐπὶ RO: ἕως ἂν ἀπογνῷ rell. Lat.
[3] Σάρην SP.

[a] Called Odollam (as in the LXX) in *A*. viii. 246; bibl. "cave of Adullam." It has been identified by some with the modern *Khirbet 'Aid el-Ma*, 12 miles S.W. of Bethlehem, by others with *Khirbet esh-Sheikh Madhkūr* close by. Both

up his abode in a cave close to the city of Adullam,[a] sent word to his brothers where he was to be found. They, with all his kinsfolk, came to him; and besides them, all who were in want or in fear of King Saul streamed to him and declared themselves ready to obey his orders. They were in all about four hundred. Encouraged at now finding himself with a force to assist him, David departed thence and made his way to the Moabite king and besought him to receive his parents into his country and to keep them until he himself should know what was finally to become of him. This favour the king accorded him and showed all honour to David's parents so long as they were with him.

David's rebel camp in the cave of Adullam. 1 Sam. xxii. 1.

(4) David himself was bidden by the prophet[b] to quit the desert and repair to the territory of the tribe of Judah and remain there; so, obedient to this counsel, he came to the city of Saris[c] and there abode. But Saul, on hearing that David had been seen with a large following, was thrown into no ordinary confusion and dismay; for, knowing the mettle and hardihood of the man, he surmised that it would be no small labour that would arise from David's acts, but one that would surely cause him regret and suffering. So summoning to him his friends and chieftains and the tribe from which he himself came, to the hill[d] where

David in Judah; Saul urges his friends to remain loyal. 1 Sam. xxii. 5.

places, incidentally, are at the southern end of the Valley of Elah, *cf.* § 170 note.

[b] The prophet Gad, according to Scripture.

[c] So, nearly, the LXX; Heb. "forest of Hareth"; the site is uncertain but is identified by some with the modern *Kharas*, 7 miles N.W. of Hebron, and a little S.E. of the supposed sites of Adullam.

[d] Josephus, like the LXX, takes Gibeah ("hill") as a common noun.

πρὸς αὐτὸν ἐπὶ τὸν βουνόν, οὗ τὸ βασίλειον εἶχε, καὶ καθίσας ἐπ' Ἀρούρης, τόπος δ' ἦν τις οὕτω προσαγορευόμενος,[1] τιμῆς πολιτικῆς περὶ αὐτὸν οὔσης καὶ[2] τάξεως σωματοφυλάκων λέγει πρὸς αὐτούς· "ἄνδρες ὁμόφυλοι, μέμνησθε μὲν οἶδ' ὅτι τῶν ἐμῶν εὐεργεσιῶν, ὅτι καὶ ἀγρῶν τινας ἐποίησα δεσπότας καὶ τιμῶν τῶν ἐν τῷ πλήθει καὶ τάξεων
252 ἠξίωσα. πυνθάνομαι τοιγαροῦν εἰ μείζονας τούτων δωρεὰς καὶ πλείονας παρὰ τοῦ Ἰεσσαίου παιδὸς προσδοκᾶτε· οἶδα γὰρ ὅτι πάντες ἐκείνῳ προστέθεισθε[3] τοὐμοῦ παιδὸς Ἰωνάθου αὐτοῦ τε
253 οὕτως φρονήσαντος καὶ ὑμᾶς ταὐτὰ[4] πείσαντος· οὐ γὰρ ἀγνοῶ τοὺς ὅρκους καὶ τὰς συνθήκας τὰς πρὸς Δαυίδην αὐτῷ γεγενημένας, οὐδ' ὅτι σύμβουλος μὲν καὶ συνεργὸς Ἰωνάθης ἐστὶ τῶν κατ' ἐμοῦ συντεταγμένων, μέλει δὲ ὑμῶν οὐδενὶ περὶ τούτων, ἀλλὰ τὸ ἀποβησόμενον ἡσυχάζοντες σκοπεῖτε."
254 σιωπήσαντος δὲ τοῦ βασιλέως ἄλλος μὲν οὐδεὶς ἀπεκρίνατο τῶν παρόντων, Δώηγος δ' ὁ Σύρος ὁ τὰς ἡμιόνους αὐτοῦ βόσκων εἶπεν ὡς ἴδοι τὸν Δαυίδην εἰς Ναβὰν πόλιν πρὸς Ἀβιμέλεχον ἐλθόντα τὸν ἀρχιερέα τά τε μέλλοντα παρ' αὐτοῦ προφητεύσαντος μαθεῖν, καὶ λαβόντα ἐφόδια καὶ τὴν ῥομφαίαν τοῦ Γολιάθου πρὸς οὓς ἐβούλετο μετὰ ἀσφαλείας προπεμφθῆναι.

255 (5) Μεταπεμψάμενος οὖν τὸν ἀρχιερέα καὶ πᾶσαν αὐτοῦ τὴν γενεὰν Σαοῦλος "τί παθὼν ἐξ ἐμοῦ," εἶπε, "δεινὸν καὶ ἄχαρι τὸν Ἰεσσαίου παῖδα προσεδέξω καὶ σιτίων μὲν αὐτῷ μετέδωκας καὶ ὅπλων

[1] οὕτω προσ. om. RO.
[2] καὶ om. codd.
[3] (R)ME: προστεθήσεσθε O: προστίθεσθε SP Lat.
[4] Ernesti: ταῦτα codd.

he had his palace, and seating himself at a certain spot called Arūra,[a] with his officers of state [b] and his company of bodyguards [b] around him, he addressed them thus : " Fellow tribesmen, you remember, I doubt not, my benefactions, how I have made some of you owners of estates and to others have granted honours and high positions among the people. I ask you, therefore, if you look for larger and more bounties than these from the son of Jesse ? I know very well that you have all gone over to him, because my own son Jonathan himself has taken this stand and has persuaded you to do the like. Nor am I ignorant of those oaths and covenants that he has made with David, nor that Jonathan is the counsellor and accomplice of those who are arrayed against me ; and not one of you is concerned about these things, but you are quietly waiting to see what will happen." When the king was silent, no other of those present made reply ; only Doeg the Syrian, the keeper of his mules, said that he had seen David when he came to the city of Naba to Abimelech the high priest, where through the priest's prophecies David had learnt what was to come, and, having received provisions and the sword of Goliath, he had safely been sent on his way to those whom he was seeking.

Doeg the informer. 1 Sam. xxii. 9.

(5) Saul, therefore, sent for the high priest and all his family, and said : " What wrong have I done thee or what injury that thou didst receive the son of Jesse and gavest food and arms to him who is a

Saul rebukes Ahimelech, who excuses himself. 1 Sam. xxii. 11.

[a] " Plowland " ; so the LXX translates Heb. *'ēshel*, a kind of tree (A.V. " tamarisk "). *Cf.* § 377

[b] Bibl. "servants."

ὄντι τῆς ἐμῆς βασιλείας ἐπιβούλῳ, τί δὲ δὴ περὶ τῶν μελλόντων ἐχρημάτιζες; οὐ γὰρ δή σε φεύγων
256 ἐμὲ καὶ μισῶν τὸν ἐμὸν οἶκον ἐλάνθανεν." ὁ δ' ἀρχιερεὺς οὐκ ἐπ' ἄρνησιν ἐτράπη τῶν γεγονότων, ἀλλὰ μετὰ παρρησίας ταῦτα παρασχεῖν ὡμολόγει οὐχὶ Δαυίδῃ χαριζόμενος, ἀλλ' αὐτῷ· πολέμιον γὰρ σὸν οὐκ εἰδέναι ἔφασκε, πιστὸν δὲ ἐν τοῖς μάλιστα δοῦλον καὶ χιλίαρχον καὶ τὸ τούτων μεῖζον γαμ-
257 βρόν τε ἤδη καὶ συγγενῆ. ταῦτα δ' οὐκ ἐχθροῖς παρέχειν τοὺς ἀνθρώπους, ἀλλὰ τοῖς εὐνοίᾳ καὶ τιμῇ τῇ πρὸς αὐτοὺς ἀρίστοις. προφητεῦσαι δὲ οὐ νῦν πρῶτον αὐτῷ, πολλάκις δὲ καὶ ἄλλοτε τοῦτο πεποιηκέναι· "φήσαντι δὲ ὑπὸ σοῦ πεμφθῆναι κατὰ πολλὴν σπουδὴν ἐπὶ πρᾶξιν, τὸ[1] μηδὲν παρασχεῖν ὧν ἐπεζήτει, σοὶ μᾶλλον ἀντιλέγειν ἢ
258 ἐκείνῳ περὶ αὐτῶν ἐλογιζόμην. διὸ μηδὲν πονηρὸν κατ' ἐμοῦ φρονήσῃς μηδὲ πρὸς ἃ νῦν ἀκούεις Δαυίδην ἐγχειρεῖν πρὸς ταῦτα τὴν τότε μου δοκοῦσαν φιλανθρωπίαν ὑποπτεύσῃς· φίλῳ γὰρ καὶ γαμβρῷ σῷ καὶ χιλιάρχῳ παρέσχον, οὐ πολεμίῳ."
259 (6) Ταῦτα λέγων ὁ ἀρχιερεὺς οὐκ ἔπεισε τὸν Σαοῦλον (δεινὸς γὰρ ὁ φόβος μηδ' ἀληθεῖ πιστεύειν ἀπολογίᾳ), κελεύει δὲ τοῖς ὁπλίταις περιστᾶσιν[2] αὐτὸν μετὰ τᾶς γενεᾶς[3] ἀποκτεῖναι. μὴ θαρρούντων δ' ἐκείνων ἅψασθαι τοῦ ἀρχιερέως, ἀλλὰ τὸ θεῖον εὐλαβουμένων μᾶλλον ἢ τὸ παρακοῦσαι τοῦ βασιλέως, τῷ Σύρῳ Δωήγῳ προστάσσει τὸν φόνον.
260 καὶ παραλαβὼν ὁμοίως αὑτῷ[4] πονηροὺς ἐκεῖνος ἀποκτείνει τὸν Ἀβιμέλεχον καὶ τὴν γενεὰν αὐτοῦ·

[1] τῷ ex Lat. Niese.
[2] περισταθεῖσιν ROME.
[3] μετὰ τ. γεν. om. RO.
[4] Niese: ὁμοίους αὐτῷ codd.

plotter against my realm? And why, pray, didst thou deliver oracles concerning the future? For assuredly thou wert not ignorant that he was fleeing from me and that he hated my house." The high priest did not resort to a denial of what had taken place, but frankly confessed that he had rendered those services, yet not to gratify David, but Saul. "I knew him not," said he, "for thine enemy, but as one of thy most faithful servants and thy captain, and, what is more, as thy son-in-law now and kinsman. Men bestow such dignities not on their enemies, but on those who show them the greatest goodwill and esteem. Nor was this the first time that I prophesied for him; often have I done so on other occasions as well. And when he told me that he had been sent by thee in great haste on a certain matter, had I refused any of his desires, I should have thought this to be gainsaying thee rather than him.[a] Therefore, think not ill of me, nor, from what thou now hearest of David's designs, regard with suspicion what I then deemed an act of humanity; for it was to thy friend and to thy son-in-law and captain that I rendered it, not to thine enemy."

At Saul's order, Doeg slays Ahimelech and his kin; Nob is destroyed. 1 Sam. xxii. 16.

(6) These words of the high priest did not persuade Saul, for fear is strong enough to disbelieve even a truthful plea; and he ordered his soldiers to surround him and his kin, and slay them. But as they dared not lay hands on the high priest, dreading more to offend the Deity than to disobey the king, he charged Doeg the Syrian to carry out the murder. This fellow, taking to help him others as wicked as himself,[b] slew Abimelech and his kin, who were in all

[a] This last sentence is an addition to Scripture.
[b] In Scripture, Doeg alone slays the priests.

ἦσαν δὲ πάντες ὡσεὶ πέντε καὶ τριακόσιοι.[1] πέμψας δὲ Σαοῦλος καὶ εἰς τὴν πόλιν τῶν ἱερέων Ναβὰν πάντας τε αὐτοὺς ἀπέκτεινεν, οὐ γυναικῶν οὐ νηπίων οὐδ' ἄλλης ἡλικίας φεισάμενος, αὐτὴν
261 δὲ ἐνέπρησε. διασώζεται δὲ παῖς εἷς Ἀβιμελέχου Ἀβιάθαρος ὄνομα. ταῦτα μέντοι γε συνέβη, καθὼς προεφήτευσεν ὁ θεὸς τῷ ἀρχιερεῖ Ἠλί, διὰ τὰς τῶν υἱῶν αὐτοῦ δύο παρανομίας εἰπὼν διαφθαρήσεσθαι τοὺς ἐγγόνους.

262 (7) Σαοῦλος δὲ ὁ βασιλεὺς ὠμὸν οὕτως ἔργον διαπραξάμενος καὶ γενεὰν ὅλην ἀρχιερατικῆς ἀποσφάξας τιμῆς καὶ μήτ' ἐπὶ νηπίοις λαβὼν οἶκτον μήτ' ἐπὶ γέρουσιν αἰδῶ, καταβαλὼν δὲ καὶ τὴν πόλιν, ἣν πατρίδα καὶ τροφὸν τῶν ἱερέων καὶ προφητῶν αὐτὸ[2] τὸ θεῖον ἐπελέξατο καὶ μόνην εἰς τὸ τοιούτους φέρειν ἄνδρας ἀπέδειξε, μαθεῖν ἅπασι παρέσχε καὶ κατανοῆσαι τὸν ἀνθρώπινον τρόπον,
263 ὅτι μέχρις οὗ μέν εἰσιν ἰδιῶταί τινες καὶ ταπεινοί, τῷ μὴ δύνασθαι χρῆσθαι τῇ φύσει μηδὲ τολμᾶν ὅσα θέλουσιν, ἐπιεικεῖς εἰσι καὶ μέτριοι καὶ μόνον διώκουσι τὸ δίκαιον, καὶ πρὸς αὐτὸ[3] τὴν πᾶσαν εὔνοιάν[4] τε καὶ σπουδὴν ἔχουσι, τότε δὲ καὶ περὶ τοῦ θείου πεπιστεύκασιν ὅτι πᾶσι τοῖς γινομένοις ἐν τῷ βίῳ πάρεστι καὶ οὐ τὰ ἔργα μόνον ὁρᾷ τὰ πραττόμενα, ἀλλὰ καὶ τὰς διανοίας ἤδη σαφῶς
264 οἶδεν, ἀφ' ὧν μέλλει ταῦτ' ἔσεσθαι· ὅταν δὲ εἰς ἐξουσίαν παρέλθωσι καὶ δυναστείαν, τότε πάντ' ἐκεῖνα μετεκδυσάμενοι καὶ ὥσπερ ἐπὶ σκηνῆς

[1] ex Lat. Niese (*cf.* LXX): πέντε καὶ ὀγδοήκοντα RO: πέντε καὶ ὀγδοήκοντα καὶ τριακόσιοι MSP: πεντακόσιοι καὶ τριάκοντα E

[2] conj. edd.: αὐτόθι codd.: om. Lat.

[3] αὐτῷ Niese.

[4] ἔννοιαν Dindorf.

some three hundred and five.[a] Moreover Saul sent men to Naba, the city of the priests, and slew all therein, sparing neither women nor infants nor those of any age, and burnt the town. One son of Abimelech alone escaped, Abiathar [b] by name. Now all these things came to pass in full accordance with what God had foretold to Eli the high priest, when He declared that by reason of the iniquities of his two sons his posterity should be destroyed.[c]

Reflections on the changes in character caused by accession to power.

(7) [d] But as for King Saul, by perpetrating a deed so cruel as slaughtering a whole family of high-priestly rank, feeling neither pity for infants nor reverence for age, and then proceeding to demolish the city which the Deity Himself had chosen as the home and nurse of priests and prophets and set apart as the sole place to produce such men—Saul thereby gave all to know and understand the character of men, namely that so long as they are of private and humble station, through inability to indulge their instincts or to dare all that they desire, they are kindly and moderate and pursue only what is right, and turn thereto their every thought and endeavour; then too, concerning the Deity, they are persuaded that He is present in all that happens in life and that He not only sees the acts that are done, but clearly knows even the thoughts whence those acts are to come. But when once they attain to power and sovereignty, then, stripping off all those qualities and laying aside their habits and ways as if they were

[a] Emended text, agreeing with the LXX, 1 Sam. xxii. 18, where the Heb. has 85; the MSS. vary between 85 and 385, while the Epitome has 530. Below, § 268, Josephus has 300.

[b] Heb. *Ebyāthār*.

[c] *Cf. A.* v. 350.

[d] With this digression in criticism of Saul contrast the eulogy below, §§ 343 ff.

προσωπεῖα τὰ ἤθη καὶ τοὺς τρόπους ἀποθέμενοι μεταλαμβάνουσι τόλμαν ἀπόνοιαν καταφρόνησιν ἀν-
265 θρωπίνων τε καὶ θείων, καὶ ὅτε μάλιστα δεῖ τῆς εὐσεβείας αὐτοῖς καὶ τῆς δικαιοσύνης, ἔγγιστα τοῦ φθονεῖσθαι γεγενημένοις καὶ πᾶσι φανεροῖς ἐφ' οἷς ἂν νοήσωσιν ἢ πράξωσι καθεστῶσι, τόθ' ὡς οὐκέτι βλέποντος αὐτοὺς τοῦ θεοῦ ἢ διὰ τὴν ἐξουσίαν δεδιότος οὕτως ἐμπαροινοῦσι τοῖς πράγ-
266 μασιν. ἃ δ' ἂν ἢ φοβηθῶσιν ἀκούσαντες[1] ἢ μισήσωσι * * θελήσαντες[2] ἢ στέρξωσιν ἀλόγως, ταῦτα κύρια καὶ βέβαια καὶ ἀληθῆ καὶ ἀνθρώποις ἀρεστὰ καὶ θεῷ δοκοῦσι, τῶν δὲ μελλόντων λόγος
267 αὐτοῖς οὐδὲ εἷς· ἀλλὰ τιμῶσι μὲν τοὺς πολλὰ ταλαιπωρήσαντας, τιμήσαντες δὲ φθονοῦσι, καὶ παραγαγόντες εἰς ἐπιφάνειαν οὐ ταύτης ἀφαιροῦνται μόνον τοὺς τετυχηκότας, ἀλλὰ διὰ ταύτην καὶ τοῦ ζῆν ἐπὶ πονηραῖς αἰτίαις καὶ δι' ὑπερβολὴν αὐτῶν ἀπιθάνοις· κολάζουσι δ' οὐκ ἐπ' ἔργοις δίκης ἀξίοις, ἀλλ' ἐπὶ διαβολαῖς καὶ κατηγορίαις ἀβασανίστοις, οὐδ' ὅσους[3] ἔδει τοῦτο παθεῖν, ἀλλ'
268 ὅσους ἀποκτεῖναι δύνανται. τοῦτο Σαοῦλος ἡμῖν ὁ Κείσου παῖς, ὁ πρῶτος μετὰ τὴν ἀριστοκρατίαν καὶ[4] τὴν ἐπὶ τοῖς κριταῖς πολιτείαν Ἑβραίων βασιλεύσας, φανερὸν πεποίηκε τριακοσίους ἀποκτείνας ἱερέας καὶ προφήτας ἐκ τῆς πρὸς Ἀβιμέλεχον ὑποψίας, ἐπικαταβαλὼν δὲ αὐτοῖς καὶ τὴν πόλιν, καὶ τὸν[5] τρόπῳ τινὶ ναὸν σπουδάσας ἱερέων καὶ προφητῶν ἔρημον καταστῆσαι, τοσούτους μὲν ἀν-

[1] ἀκούσιοι conj. Thackeray.
[2] ἐθελήσαντες SP : ἐθελοκακήσαντες Naber.
[3] οὓς Niese.
[4] καὶ om. RO.
[5] + ἐν codd.

stage masks, they assume in their place audacity, recklessness, contempt for things human and divine; and at the moment when they most need piety and righteousness, being now within closest reach of envy, with all their thoughts and acts exposed to all men, then, as though God no longer saw them or were overawed by their power, they break out into these riotous acts. Their fear of rumours, their wilful hates,[a] their irrational loves—these they regard as valid, sure and true, acceptable to man and God, but of the future they take not the least account. They first honour those who have toiled in their service, and then envy them the honours which they have conferred; and, after promoting men to high distinction, they deprive them not only of this, but, on its very account, of life itself, on malicious charges which their extravagance renders incredible. Their punishments are inflicted not for acts deserving of chastisement, but on the faith of calumnies and unsifted accusations, nor do they fall on those who ought so to suffer, but on whomsoever they can put to death. Of this we have a signal example in the conduct of Saul, son of Kis, the first to become king of the Hebrews after the period of aristocracy and the government under the judges, for he slew three hundred priests and prophets from suspicion of Abimelech, and further demolished their city and strove to leave what was virtually their temple[b] destitute of priests and prophets,[c] by first slaying so many of

[a] Text uncertain.

[b] The first real temple was, of course, to be built later in Jerusalem by Solomon.

[c] The reference to prophets is unscriptural.

ελών, μεῖναι δ' ἐάσας οὐδὲ τὴν πατρίδα αὐτῶν πρὸς τὸ καὶ μετ' ἐκείνους ἄλλους γενέσθαι.

269 (8) Ὁ δ' Ἀβιάθαρος ὁ τοῦ Ἀβιμελέχου παῖς ὁ μόνος διασωθῆναι[1] δυνηθεὶς ἐκ τοῦ γένους τῶν ὑπὸ Σαούλου φονευθέντων ἱερέων φυγὼν πρὸς Δαυίδην τὴν τῶν οἰκείων αὐτοῦ συμφορὰν ἐδήλωσε καὶ τὴν
270 τοῦ πατρὸς ἀναίρεσιν. ὁ δ' οὐκ ἀγνοεῖν ἔφη ταῦτα περὶ αὐτοὺς ἐσόμενα ἰδὼν τὸν Δώηγον· ὑπονοῆσαι γὰρ διαβληθήσεσθαι πρὸς αὐτοῦ τὸν ἀρχιερέα τῷ βασιλεῖ, καὶ τῆς ἀτυχίας ταύτης αὐτοῖς αὐτὸν ᾐτιᾶτο. μένειν[2] δ' αὐτόθι καὶ σὺν αὐτῷ διατρίβειν ὡς οὐκ ἐν ἄλλῳ τόπῳ λησόμενον οὕτως ἠξίου.

271 (xiii. 1) Κατὰ δὲ τοῦτον τὸν καιρὸν ἀκούσας ὁ Δαυίδης τοὺς Παλαιστίνους ἐμβεβληκότας εἰς τὴν Κιλλανῶν χώραν καὶ ταύτην διαρπάζοντας δίδωσιν ἑαυτὸν στρατεύειν ἐπ' αὐτούς, τοῦ θεοῦ διὰ τοῦ προφήτου πυθόμενος εἰ ἐπιτρέπει νίκην. τοῦ δὲ σημαίνειν φήσαντος ἐξώρμησεν ἐπὶ τοὺς Παλαιστίνους μετὰ τῶν ἑταίρων καὶ φόνον τε αὐτῶν
272 πολὺν ἐξέχεε καὶ λείαν ἤλασεν. καὶ παραμείνας τοῖς Κιλλανοῖς, ἕως οὗ τὰς ἅλως[3] καὶ τὸν καρπὸν συνεῖλον ἀδεῶς, Σαούλῳ τῷ βασιλεῖ μηνύεται παρ' αὐτοῖς ὤν· τὸ γὰρ ἔργον καὶ τὸ κατόρθωμα οὐκ ἔμεινε παρ' οἷς ἐγένετο, φήμη[4] δ' ἐπίπαν εἴς τε τὰς τῶν ἄλλων ἀκοὰς καὶ πρὸς τὰς τοῦ βασιλέως διεκομίσθη αὐτό[5] τε συνιστάνον καὶ τὸν πεποιη-
273 κότα. χαίρει δὲ Σαοῦλος ἀκούσας ἐν Κίλλᾳ τὸν

[1] διασωθ. om. RO.
[2] τὸ μένειν codd.
[3] ἅλω codd.: ἀλώνας ed. pr.
[4] φήμη Ernesti.
[5] αὐτό Dindorf.

[a] *Cf.* below on § 273.
[b] In Scripture no mention is made at this point of a prophet,

them and then not suffering even their native place to remain, that others might come after them.

Abiathar, the high priest's son, flees to David. 1 Sam. xxii. 20.

(8) Now Abiathar, the son of Abimelech, who alone of the family of priests slaughtered by Saul had been able to escape, fled to David and told him of the tragedy of his kin and the slaying of his father. David replied that he had known that this fate would befall them, when he saw Doeg ; he had, he said, suspected that the high priest would be denounced to the king by this man, and he blamed himself as the cause of this misfortune to them. Howbeit he besought Abiathar to abide there and to live with him, since nowhere else would he be so safely hidden.

David saves Keilah (Killa) from the Philistines. 1 Sam. xxiii 1.

(xiii. 1) At this same time David, hearing that the Philistines had invaded the country of the Killanians [a] and were ravaging it, offered to take the field against them, after inquiring of God through the prophet [b] whether He would grant him victory. And when the prophet reported that God had so signified, he threw himself upon the Philistines with his companions, made a great slaughter of them and carried off their spoils. As he then remained with the Kilanians until they had secured their threshing-floors and safely got in their crops,[c] his presence there was reported to King Saul. For this exploit and its success did not remain confined to those who had witnessed them, but the fame of it was carried abroad to the ears of all, the king's included, with praise of the deed and the doer of it. Saul rejoiced to hear

but in 1 Sam. xxiii. 9 we read that David consulted God about leaving Keilah, through the priest Abimelech by means of the ephod—a detail omitted in Josephus's account below, § 274.

[c] The safeguarding of the crops is an amplification of Scripture.

Δαυίδην, καί "θεὸς ἤδη χερσὶ ταῖς ἐμαῖς ὑπέθετο αὐτόν," εἰπών, "ἐπεὶ καὶ συνηνάγκασεν ἐλθεῖν εἰς πόλιν τείχη καὶ πύλας καὶ μοχλοὺς ἔχουσαν," τῷ λαῷ παντὶ προσέταξεν ἐπὶ τὴν Κίλλαν ἐξορμῆσαι καὶ πολιορκήσαντι καὶ ἑλόντι τὸν Δαυίδην
274 ἀποκτεῖναι. ταῦτα δὲ αἰσθόμενος ὁ Δαυίδης καὶ μαθὼν παρὰ τοῦ θεοῦ ὅτι μείναντα παρ' αὐτοῖς οἱ Κιλλῖται ἐκδώσουσι τῷ Σαούλῳ, παραλαβὼν τοὺς τετρακοσίους ἀπῆρεν ἀπὸ τῆς πόλεως εἰς τὴν ἔρημον ἐπάνω τῆς Ἐνγεδὼν[1] λεγομένης. καὶ ὁ μὲν βασιλεὺς ἀκούσας αὐτὸν πεφευγότα παρὰ τῶν Κιλλιτῶν ἐπαύσατο τῆς ἐπ' αὐτὸν στρατείας.

275 (2) Δαυίδης δὲ ἐκεῖθεν ἄρας εἴς τινα τόπον Καινὴν[2] καλουμένην τῆς Ζιφηνῆς παραγίνεται, εἰς ὃν Ἰωνάθης ὁ τοῦ Σαούλου παῖς συμβαλὼν αὐτῷ καὶ κατασπασάμενος θαρρεῖν τε καὶ χρηστὰς περὶ τῶν μελλόντων ἔχειν ἐλπίδας παρεκάλει καὶ μὴ κάμνειν τοῖς παροῦσι· βασιλεύσειν γὰρ αὐτὸν καὶ πᾶσαν τὴν Ἑβραίων δύναμιν ἕξειν ὑφ' ἑαυτῷ, φιλεῖν δὲ τὰ τοιαῦτα σὺν μεγάλοις ἀπαντᾶν πόνοις.
276 πάλιν δ' ὅρκους ποιησάμενος τῆς εἰς ἅπαντα τὸν βίον πρὸς ἀλλήλους εὐνοίας καὶ πίστεως καὶ τὸν θεὸν μάρτυρα καλέσας, ὧν ἐπηράσατο αὐτῷ παρα-

[1] Ἐνγελαΐν MS: Ἐνγαλαΐν P: Ἐνγεδαΐν Naber.
[2] M Lat.: Κενὴν ROSPE.

that David was in Killa.[a] "At last," said he, "God has delivered him into my hands, since He has forced him to enter a city with walls, gates and bars," and he ordered the whole people to march against Killa and, when they had besieged and taken it,[b] to kill David. But when David discovered this and learned from God that if he remained in Killa the inhabitants would give him up to Saul, he took his four hundred[c] men and withdrew from the city into the desert lying above a place called Engedōn.[d] Thereupon the king, hearing that he had fled from the people of Killa, abandoned his campaign against him.

Jonathan renews his pledge to David at Ziph. 1 Sam. xxiii. 16.

(2) David, departing thence, came to a place called Kainē[e] ("New") in the region of Ziphēnē.[f] Here he was met by Jonathan, son of Saul, who, after embracing him, bade him take courage, hope well for the future and not be crushed by his present state, for (he assured him) he would yet be king and would have all the forces of the Hebrews under him, but such things were wont to demand great toil for their attainment. Then, having renewed his oaths of life-long, mutual affection and fidelity, and having called God to witness the curses which he invoked

[a] Bibl. Keilah, LXX Κεειλά, perhaps the modern *Khirbet Qila*, about 2 miles S. of the supposed site of Adullam (*cf.* § 247 note).

[b] Or "besieged it and taken him."

[c] So the LXX; Heb. 600.

[d] Bibl. Engedi; mentioned below, § 282. 1 Sam. xxiii. 13 "and went whithersoever they could go."

[e] So the LXX, reading Heb. *ḥadāshāh* "new" for *ḥōreshāh* "thicket" in 1 Sam. xxiii. 15; the latter is perhaps to be taken as a proper name, and may be the modern *Khirbet Khoreisa*.

[f] Bibl. Ziph, LXX Ζείφ, probably the modern *Tell Zif*, 4 miles S.E. of Hebron.

βάντι τὰ συγκείμενα καὶ μεταβαλλομένῳ[1] πρὸς τἀναντία, τὸν μὲν αὐτόθι καταλείπει μικρὰ τῶν φροντίδων καὶ τοῦ δέους ἐπικουφίσας, αὐτὸς δὲ
277 πρὸς αὐτὸν ἐπανέρχεται. οἱ δὲ Ζιφηνοὶ χαριζόμενοι τῷ Σαούλῳ μηνύουσιν αὐτῷ παρ' αὐτοῖς διατρίβειν τὸν Δαυίδην καὶ παραδώσειν ἔφασαν ἐπ' αὐτὸν ἐλθόντι· καταληφθέντων γὰρ τῶν τῆς Ζιφηνῆς
278 στενῶν οὐκ εἶναι φυγεῖν αὐτὸν[2] πρὸς ἄλλους. ὁ δὲ βασιλεὺς ἐπῄνεσεν αὐτούς, χάριν ἔχειν ὁμολογήσας τὸν ἐχθρὸν αὐτῷ μεμηνυκόσι, καὶ οὐκ εἰς μακρὰν ἀμείψεσθαι[3] τῆς εὐνοίας ὑποσχόμενος αὐτούς, ἔπεμψε τοὺς ζητήσοντας τὸν Δαυίδην καὶ τὴν ἐρημίαν ἐξερευνήσοντας, αὐτὸς δ' ἀκολουθήσειν ἀπεκρίνατο.
279 καὶ οἱ μὲν ἐπὶ τὴν θήραν καὶ τὴν σύλληψιν τοῦ Δαυίδου προῆγον τὸν βασιλέα σπουδάζοντες μὴ μόνον αὐτῷ[4] μηνῦσαι τὸν ἐχθρόν, ἀλλὰ καὶ τῷ παρασχεῖν αὐτὸν εἰς ἐξουσίαν φανερωτέραν καταστῆσαι αὐτῷ τὴν εὔνοιαν[5]· διήμαρτον δὲ τῆς ἀδίκου καὶ πονηρᾶς ἐπιθυμίας, οἳ μηδὲν κινδυνεύειν ἔμελ-
280 λον ἐκ τοῦ μὴ ταῦτ' ἐμφανίσαι τῷ Σαούλῳ, διὰ δὲ κολακείαν καὶ κέρδους προσδοκίαν παρὰ τοῦ βασιλέως ἄνδρα θεοφιλῆ καὶ παρὰ δίκην ζητούμενον ἐπὶ θανάτῳ καὶ λανθάνειν δυνάμενον διέβαλον καὶ παραδώσειν ὑπέσχοντο· γνοὺς γὰρ ὁ Δαυίδης τὴν τῶν Ζιφηνῶν κακοήθειαν καὶ τὴν τοῦ βασιλέως ἔφοδον ἐκλείπει μὲν τὰ στενὰ τῆς ἐκείνων χώρας,

[1] μεταβαλομένῳ Bekker.
[2] φυγὴν αὐτῷ SP: φυγεῖν αὐτῷ M.
[3] Niese: ἀμείψασθαι codd. (Lat. vid.).
[4] αὐτῷ τῷ MSP.
[5] αὐτῷ τὴν εὔνοιαν om. RO: post ἐχθρὸν (supra) rell.

[a] At Gibeah (LXX "the hill," *cf.* § 251 note), 1 Sam. xxiii. 19.

upon himself should he violate their covenant and change to the contrary, he left him there, having a little lightened his cares and fear, and returned to his own home. But the men of Ziph, to win favour with Saul, reported to him [a] that David was sojourning among them, and promised, if he would come after him, to deliver him up; for, if the passes into their country were occupied, it would be impossible for him to escape elsewhere. The king commended them and expressed his thanks for their having given him information of his enemy, and promised that their loyalty should not long await its reward [b]; he then sent a party to search for David and to scour the desert, assuring them that he would himself follow. Thus they spurred the king on to the pursuit and capture of David, because they were anxious not merely to denounce his enemy to him, but to give more palpable proof of their loyalty to him by actually delivering David into his hands. They failed, however, in their iniquitous and base desire, which was the more so in that they would have incurred no risk by not informing Saul of these things; yet, from obsequiousness and in the expectation of receiving gain from the king, they calumniated and promised to deliver up a God-favoured man whose death was being unjustly sought, and who might have remained concealed.[c] For David, learning of the evil designs of the Ziphites and the king's approach, quitted the

The men of Ziph betray David to Saul. 1 Sam. xxiii. 19.

[b] This promise is not mentioned in Scripture.
[c] These reflections on the conduct of the Ziphites are an addition to Scripture.

φεύγει δὲ ἐπὶ τὴν μεγάλην πέτραν τὴν οὖσαν ἐν τῇ Σίμωνος ἐρήμῳ.

281 (3) Ὥρμησεν δὲ ἐπ' ἐκείνην διώκειν Σαοῦλος· κατὰ γὰρ τὴν ὁδὸν ἀναχωρήσαντα ἐκ τῶν στενῶν μαθὼν τὸν Δαυίδην, ἐπὶ τὸ ἕτερον μέρος τῆς πέτρας ἀπῆρεν. ἀντιπεριέσπασαν δὲ τὸν Σαοῦλον ἀπὸ τῆς διώξεως τοῦ Δαυίδου μέλλοντος ἤδη συλλαμβάνεσθαι Παλαιστῖνοι πάλιν ἐπὶ τὴν Ἑβραίων ἐστρατευκέναι χώραν ἀκουσθέντες· ἐπὶ γὰρ τούτους ἀνέστρεψε φύσει πολεμίους ὄντας, αὐτοὺς ἀμύνασθαι κρίνας ἀναγκαιότερον ἢ τὸν ἴδιον σπουδάζοντα λαβεῖν ἐχθρὸν ὑπεριδεῖν τὴν γῆν κακωθεῖσαν.

282 (4) Καὶ Δαυίδης μὲν οὕτως ἐκ παραλόγου τὸν κίνδυνον διαφυγὼν εἰς τὰ στενὰ τῆς Ἐγγεδηνῆς ἀφικνεῖται· Σαούλῳ δὲ ἐκβαλόντι τοὺς Παλαιστίνους ἧκον ἀπαγγέλλοντές τινες τὸν Δαυίδην ἐν
283 τοῖς Ἐγγεδηνῆς διατρίβειν ὅροις. λαβὼν δὲ τρισχιλίους ἐπιλέκτους[1] ὁπλίτας ἐπ' αὐτὸν ἠπείγετο, καὶ γενόμενος οὐ πόρρω τῶν τόπων ὁρᾷ παρὰ τὴν ὁδὸν σπήλαιον βαθὺ καὶ κοῖλον, εἰς πολὺ καὶ μῆκος ἀνεῳγὸς καὶ πλάτος, ἔνθα συνέβαινε τὸν Δαυίδην μετὰ τῶν τετρακοσίων κεκρύφθαι· ἐπειγόμενος οὖν ὑπὸ τῶν κατὰ φύσιν εἴσεισιν εἰς αὐτὸ μόνος θεαθεὶς
284 δ' ὑπό τινος τῶν μετὰ Δαυίδου· καὶ φράσαντος

[1] ἐπιλέκτους post ὁπλίτας MSP: om. E Lat.

[a] 1 Sam. xxiii. 24 "in the wilderness of Maon, in the plain on the south (lit. "right") of Jeshimon," LXX ἐν τῇ ἐρήμῳ τῇ Μαὰν (*v.l.* Μαὼν, Luc. ἐν τῇ ἐπηκόῳ) καθ' ἑσπέραν ἐκ δεξιῶν τοῦ Ἰεσσαιμοῦ. Thackeray, *Josephus the Man*, etc. p. 88, writes "both in Josephus and in Lucian an intrusive initial shin has converted the proper name [Maon] into *Shim'on* . . . Lucian translates it by ἐπήκοος 'into the

defiles of their country and fled to the great rock which is in the wilderness of Simon.[a]

A Philistine invasion diverts Saul from pursuit of David. 1 Sam. xxiii. 26.

(3) Thither Saul hastened to pursue him; for he had learnt on the way that David had withdrawn from the defiles, and so he set off for the other side of the rock. But, just as David was about to be caught, Saul was diverted from the pursuit by the news that the Philistines had made a fresh invasion into Hebrew territory. He accordingly returned to face them as his natural enemies, judging it more imperative to fight against them than, through his zeal to capture his personal enemy, to leave the land to be ravaged.[b]

David spares Saul's life at En-gedi (Engedene). 1 Sam. xxiii. 29 (xxiv. 1 Heb., LXX).

(4) David, after this unexpected escape from danger, repaired to the narrow passes of Engedēnē[c]; but, after Saul had expelled the Philistines, word was brought to him that David was sojourning within the borders of Engedēnē. So, with three thousand picked soldiers, he pressed on after him. And, when he was not far from the region, he saw by the wayside a deep and hollow cave, extending to a great distance both in length and breadth, where, as it chanced, David with his four hundred men lay concealed. Urged then by the needs of nature, Saul entered it alone, and was espied by one of David's companions.

listening wilderness,' as in fact Josephus does elsewhere," and refers to *A.* i. 304 "the name Σεμέων signifies that God listened (ἐπήκοον γεγονέναι)." I think, however, that Josephus's *Simōn* represents the bibl. Jeshimon (Heb. *Yeshīmōn*), which it might easily have done if Josephus had read it in a form like that of the Targum where, with the preposition *l*[e], it is *liyshīmōn* (by a phonetic law, the consonant *y* is assimilated to the preceding vowel), from an apparent root *Shīmōn* = Gr. *Simōn*.

[b] The last sentence is an amplification of Scripture.

[c] Bibl. En-gedi, LXX Ἐνγάδδει, modern *'Ain Jidy*, a rocky height half-way down the west shore of the Dead Sea.

τοῦ θεασαμένου πρὸς τὸν ἐχθρὸν αὐτοῦ παρὰ τοῦ θεοῦ καιρὸν ἔχειν ἀμύνης καὶ συμβουλεύοντος τοῦ Σαούλου ἀποτεμεῖν τὴν κεφαλὴν καὶ τῆς πολλῆς ἄλης αὐτὸν ἀπαλλάξαι καὶ ταλαιπωρίας, ἀναστὰς ἀναίρει μὲν τὴν κροκύδα[1] τοῦ ἱματίου μόνον οὗ Σαοῦλος ἀμπείχετο, μετανοήσας δ' εὐθὺς "οὐ δίκαιον," εἶπε, "φονεύειν τὸν αὐτοῦ δεσπότην, οὐδὲ τὸν ὑπὸ τοῦ θεοῦ βασιλείας ἀξιωθέντα· καὶ γὰρ εἰ πονηρὸς οὗτος εἰς ἡμᾶς, ἀλλ' οὐκ ἐμὲ
285 δεῖ τοιοῦτον εἶναι πρὸς αὐτόν." τοῦ δὲ Σαούλου τὸ σπήλαιον ἐκλιπόντος προελθὼν[2] ὁ Δαυίδης ἔκραγεν, ἀκοῦσαι τὸν Σαοῦλον ἀξιῶν. ἐπιστραφέντος δὲ τοῦ βασιλέως προσκυνεῖ τε αὐτὸν πεσὼν ἐπὶ πρόσωπον, ὡς ἔθος, καί φησιν· "οὐ πονηροῖς, ὦ βασιλεῦ, καὶ ψευδεῖς πλάττουσι διαβολὰς παρέχοντα δεῖ τὰς ἀκοὰς χαρίζεσθαι μὲν ἐκείνοις τὸ πιστεύειν αὐτοῖς, τοὺς δὲ φιλτάτους δι' ὑπονοίας ἔχειν, ἀλλὰ τοῖς ἔργοις σκοπεῖν τὴν ἁπάντων διά-
286 θεσιν. διαβολὴ μὲν γὰρ ἀπατᾷ, σαφὴς δ' ἀπόδειξις εὐνοίας τὰ πραττόμενα· καὶ λόγος μὲν ἐπ' ἀμφότερα πέφυκεν ἀληθής τε καὶ ψευδής, τὰ δὲ
287 ἔργα γυμνὴν ὑπ' ὄψει τὴν διάνοιαν τίθησιν. ἴσθι τοίνυν ἐκ τούτων καλῶς ἔχειν με πρὸς σὲ καὶ τὸν σὸν οἶκον κἀμοὶ[3] πιστεῦσαι δεῖ, καὶ μὴ τοῖς κατηγοροῦσιν ἃ μήτε εἰς νοῦν ἐβαλόμην μήτε δύναται γενέσθαι προσθέμενον μεταδιώκειν τὴν ἐμὴν ψυχήν, καὶ μηδὲν μήθ' ἡμέρας μήτε νυκτὸς ἔχειν διὰ φροντίδος ἢ τὴν ἐμὴν ἀναίρεσιν, ἣν ἀδίκως μετα-

[1] ἀναίρει . . . κροκύδα] ἀποτέμνει . . . πτέρυγα SPE (Lat.).
[2] E: προσελθὼν codd. Lat.
[3] ex Lat. conj. Thackeray: ἐμοὶ codd.

The man who saw him said to David that here was his God-sent opportunity for vengeance on his enemy and counselled him to cut off Saul's head[a] and so deliver himself from his long wandering and misery, whereupon David arose and only pulled off some of the woollen nap[b] of the mantle that Saul was wearing; but, repenting forthwith, said, "It is not right to murder one's own master or one whom God has accounted worthy of kingship. And even though he treats me ill, yet I must not do the like to him." Then, when Saul had left the cave, David came forth and cried aloud, beseeching Saul to hear him. And, as the king turned, he prostrated himself before him with his face to the ground, as the custom was, and said, "Thou oughtest not, O King, to give ear to miscreants and fabricators of lying charges and do them the honour of believing their lies, while holding thy best friends in suspicion; no, but by their actions shouldest thou judge the character of all men. For calumny only deceives, while actions clearly reveal the honest friend; words are of two-fold nature, either true or false, but deeds lay bare to sight the intention.[c] Know then by these tokens that I wish well to thee and to thy house, and thou shouldst trust in me instead of putting faith in those who accuse me of things which I never took into my head to do and which could never even have been done, and constantly seeking my life, with no thought day or night except for my destruction, for which thou

David reproaches Saul. 1 Sam. xxiv. 9 (10).

[a] Bibl. "do to him as it shall seem good unto thee."

[b] Variant (as in Scripture) "cut off the skirt" (πτέρυγα); this latter text is found below, § 289.

[c] The last remark, like some of the other moral reflections in David's speech, is an amplification of Scripture.

288 πορεύῃ· πῶς γὰρ οὐχὶ[1] ψευδῆ περὶ ἐμοῦ δόξαν εἴληφας ὡς ἀποκτεῖναί σε θέλοντος; ἢ πῶς οὐκ ἀσεβεῖς εἰς τὸν θεόν, ἄνθρωπον τήμερον αὐτῷ τιμωρῆσαι δυνάμενον καὶ παρὰ σοῦ λαβεῖν δίκην καὶ μὴ θελήσαντα μηδὲ τῷ καιρῷ χρησάμενον, ὃν εἰ σοὶ κατ' ἐμοῦ περιέπεσεν οὐκ ἂν αὐτὸς[2] παρῆκας,
289 διαχρήσασθαι ποθῶν καὶ νομίζων πολέμιον; ὅτε γάρ σου τὴν πτέρυγα τοῦ ἱματίου ἀπέτεμον, τότε σου καὶ τὴν κεφαλὴν ἠδυνάμην." ἐπιδείξας δὲ τὸ ῥάκος ἰδεῖν πιστεύειν παρεῖχεν. "ἀλλ' ἐγὼ μὲν ἀπεσχόμην δικαίας ἀμύνης," φησί, "σὺ δὲ μῖσος ἄδικον οὐκ αἰδῇ κατ' ἐμοῦ τρέφων.[3] ὁ θεὸς ταῦτα δικάσειε καὶ τὸν ἑκατέρου τρόπον ἡμῶν ἐλέγξειε."
290 Σαοῦλος δὲ ἐπὶ τῷ παραδόξῳ τῆς σωτηρίας θαυμάσας καὶ τὴν τοῦ νεανίσκου μετριότητα καὶ φύσιν ἐκπλαγεὶς ἀνῴμωξε· τὸ δ' αὐτὸ κἀκείνου ποιήσαντος αὐτὸν εἶναι δίκαιον στένειν ἀπεκρίνατο· "σὺ μὲν γάρ," φησίν, "ἀγαθῶν αἴτιος ἐμοὶ γέγονας, ἐγὼ δὲ σοὶ συμφορῶν. ἐπεδείξω δὲ σήμερον τὴν ἀρχαίων ἔχοντα σαυτὸν δικαιοσύνην, οἳ τοὺς ἐχθροὺς ἐν ἐρημίᾳ λαβόντας[4] σώζειν παρ-
291 ήγγελλον. πέπεισμαι δὴ νῦν ὅτι σοὶ τὴν βασιλείαν ὁ θεὸς φυλάττει καὶ περιμένει σε τὸ πάντων τῶν Ἑβραίων κράτος. δὸς δή μοι πίστεις ἐνόρκους μή μου τὸ γένος ἐξαφανίσαι μηδ' ἐμοὶ μνησικακοῦντα τοὺς ἐμοὺς ἐγγόνους ἀπολέσαι, τηρῆσαι δέ μοι καὶ σῶσαι τὸν οἶκον." ὀμόσας δὲ καθὼς ἠξίωκε[5] Δαυίδης Σαοῦλον μὲν εἰς τὴν ἰδίαν ἀπέλυσε βασιλείαν,

[1] οὐχὶ om. MSP.
[2] αὐτὸν RO: οὕτως ex Lat. conj. Naber.
[3] E: φέρων rell.
[4] Hudson: λαβόντες codd.
[5] ἠξίωσε conj. Niese.

strivest so unjustly. How indeed could the opinion not be false which thou didst hold of me, namely that I wished to kill thee, or how canst thou be other than impious toward God when thou art eager to destroy, and accountest as an enemy, a man who this day had it in his power to avenge himself and to punish thee, and yet refused to do so or to avail himself of an opportunity, which, had it been given to thee to use against me, thou wouldst never have let slip? For when I cut off the skirt of thy mantle, I might at the same time have cut off thy head." And here he produced the piece of cloth in token of the truth of his words. "But yet," he continued, "I refrained from righteous vengeance, while thou art not ashamed to nurse unjust hatred against me. May God be judge thereof and examine the motives of us both." Thereupon Saul, in wonder at his extraordinary escape and amazed at the youth's forbearance and nature, wailed aloud. And when David did the like, he replied, "It is for me to moan,[a] since thou hast brought me only good, while I have brought thee affliction. Thou hast shown thyself this day to have the righteousness of the ancients, who bade those who captured their enemies in a lonely place to spare their lives.[b] Now, therefore, I fully believe that God is reserving the kingdom for thee and that dominion over all the Hebrews awaits thee. Give me then assurance on oath that thou wilt not exterminate my race nor, from rancour against me, destroy my posterity, but wilt save and preserve my house." David gave the desired oath and let Saul depart to his kingdom,

Saul is reconciled to David. 1 Sam. xxiv. 16 (17).

[a] Unscriptural detail.

[b] An amplification of 1 Sam. xxiv. 19 (20) (of which, however, the text seems to be defective), "If a man find his enemy will he let him go well away?"

αὐτὸς δὲ μετὰ τῶν σὺν αὐτῷ εἰς τὴν Μασθηρῶν ἀνέβη στενήν.

292 (5) Ἀποθνήσκει δὲ κατὰ τοῦτον τὸν καιρὸν καὶ Σαμουῆλος ὁ προφήτης, ἀνὴρ οὐ τῆς τυχούσης ἀπολαύσας[1] παρὰ τοῖς Ἑβραίοις τιμῆς· ἐνεφάνισε γὰρ τὴν ἀρετὴν αὐτοῦ καὶ τὴν τοῦ πλήθους πρὸς αὐτὸν εὔνοιαν τὸ πένθος, ὃ ἐπὶ πολὺν χρόνον ὁ λαὸς ἤγετο, καὶ ἡ περὶ τὴν ταφὴν αὐτοῦ καὶ τὴν τῶν νομιζομένων ἀναπλήρωσιν φιλοτιμία τε
293 καὶ σπουδή. θάπτουσι γὰρ αὐτὸν ἐν τῇ πατρίδι Ἀρμαθᾳ καὶ ἐπὶ πολλὰς πάνυ ἡμέρας ἔκλαυσαν, οὐ κοινὸν τοῦτο πάσχοντες ὡς ἐπ᾽ ἀλλοτρίου τελευτῇ,
294 ὡς[2] οἰκεῖον δ᾽ ἕκαστος ἴδιον ποθῶν. ἐγένετο δ᾽ ἀνὴρ δίκαιος καὶ χρηστὸς τὴν φύσιν καὶ διὰ τοῦτο μάλιστα φίλος τῷ θεῷ. ἦρξε δὲ καὶ προέστη τοῦ λαοῦ μετὰ τὴν Ἠλεὶ τοῦ ἀρχιερέως τελευτὴν μόνος μὲν ἔτη δώδεκα, μετὰ δὲ Σαούλου τοῦ βασιλέως δέκα πρὸς τοῖς ὀκτώ. καὶ τὰ μὲν περὶ Σαμουῆλον οὕτω πέρας ἔσχεν.

295 (6) Ἦν δέ τις τῶν Ζιφηνῶν ἐκ πόλεως Ἐμμᾶν[3] πλούσιος καὶ πολυθρέμματος· τρισχιλίων μὲν γὰρ αὐτῷ[4] ποίμνη προβάτων ἐνέμετο, χιλίων δ᾽ αἰγῶν. ταῦτα Δαυίδης ἀσινῆ τηρεῖν τε καὶ ἀβλαβῆ παρήγγελλε τοῖς σὺν αὐτῷ καὶ μήτε ὑπὸ ἐπιθυμίας μήτε ὑπὸ ἐνδείας μήτε ὑπὸ τῆς ἐρημίας καὶ τοῦ δύνασθαι

[1] SP: ἀπολάβων RO: ἀπολαύων Niese cum Hudson.
[2] + εἰς MSP.
[3] Ἐμμᾶ MSP Exc.: Ammon Lat.
[4] Cocceji: αὐτοῦ codd. E.

[a] Heb. *'al ha-meṣûdāh* " up to the stronghold " ; Josephus follows the LXX which takes this as a proper name and, in a duplicate rendering, translates it as εἰς τὴν Μεσσαρὰ στενήν.

while he with his men went up to the pass of Masthera.[a]

(5) About this time the prophet Samuel died, a man who had enjoyed no common esteem among the Hebrews. His virtue and the affection of the multitude for him were manifested by the prolonged mourning which the people made, and by the display and zeal given to his burial and to the observance of the customary rites. For they buried him in his native Armatha and wept for him very many days, with no mere public mourning as for the death of a stranger, but each privately grieving as for his own.[b] He was a man of just and kindly nature and for that reason very dear to God. He was ruler and leader of the people after the death of the high priest Eli, for twelve years alone, and together with King Saul for eighteen more.[c] Such then was the end of Samuel.

Death and burial of Samuel. 1 Sam. xxv. 1.

(6) Now there was a certain Ziphite of the city of Emman,[d] who was wealthy and had much cattle; indeed he maintained a flock of three thousand sheep and a thousand goats. Now David had charged his men to see that these flocks should be safe and unharmed, and that neither through greed nor want nor because they were in the wilderness and could escape detection, should they do them any injury,

The wealthy Nabal churlishly refuses presents to David. 1 Sam. xxv. 2.

[b] The details of the burial and mourning are additions to Scripture.

[c] No figures are given in Scripture; the common rabbinic tradition fixes Samuel's term as prophet at 12 years, another. also found in Julius Africanus, makes it 40 years. Ginzberg plausibly suggests that the latter figure was reached by combining Josephus's statement that Samuel began to prophesy at 12 years, *A.* v. 348, with the rabbinic tradition that Samuel was 52 years old when he died.

[d] Bibl. "A man of Maon"; his possessions were in Carmel, just south of Ziph.

λανθάνειν καταβλάπτειν, τούτων δ' ἁπάντων ἐπάνω τίθεσθαι τὸ μηδέν'[1] ἀδικεῖν καὶ τὸ τῶν ἀλλοτρίων ἅπτεσθαι δεινὸν ἡγεῖσθαι καὶ πρόσαντες τῷ θεῷ.
296 ταῦτα δ' ἐδίδασκεν αὐτοὺς οἰόμενος ἀνθρώπῳ χαρίζεσθαι ἀγαθῷ καὶ ταύτης τυγχάνειν ἀξίῳ τῆς προνοίας· ἦν δὲ Νάβαλος, τοῦτο γὰρ εἶχεν ὄνομα, σκληρὸς καὶ πονηρὸς τοῖς ἐπιτηδεύμασιν ἐκ κυνικῆς ἀσκήσεως πεποιημένος τὸν βίον, γυναικὸς δ' ἀγαθῆς καὶ σώφρονος καὶ τὸ εἶδος σπουδαίας λελογχώς.[2]
297 πρὸς οὖν τὸν Νάβαλον τοῦτον καθ' ὃν ἔκειρε τὰ πρόβατα καιρὸν πέμψας ὁ Δαυίδης ἄνδρας δέκα τῶν σὺν αὐτῷ διὰ τούτων αὐτὸν ἀσπάζεται καὶ συνεύχεται τοῦτο ποιεῖν ἐπ' ἔτη πολλά· παρασχεῖν δὲ ἐξ ὧν δυνατός ἐστιν αὐτῷ παρεκάλει μαθόντα[3] παρὰ τῶν ποιμένων ὅτι μηδὲν αὐτοὺς ἠδίκησαν,[4] ἀλλὰ φύλακες αὐτῶν τε καὶ τῶν ποιμνίων γεγόνασι[4] πολὺν ἐν τῇ ἐρήμῳ διατρίβοντες ἤδη χρόνον· μετανοήσει δ' οὐδὲν Δαυίδῃ παρασχόμενος.
298 ταῦτα δὲ τῶν πεμφθέντων διακονησάντων πρὸς τὸν Νάβαλον ἀπανθρώπως σφόδρα καὶ σκληρῶς ἀπήντησεν· ἐρωτήσας γὰρ αὐτούς, τίς ἐστι Δαυίδης, ὡς τὸν υἱὸν ἤκουσεν Ἰεσσαίου, "νῦν ἄρα," εἶπε, "μέγα φρονοῦσιν ἐφ' αὑτοῖς οἱ δραπέται καὶ σεμνύνονται τοὺς δεσπότας καταλιπόντες."
299 ὀργίζεται δ' αὐτῶν φρασάντων ὁ Δαυίδης καὶ τετρακοσίους μὲν ὡπλισμένους αὐτῷ κελεύσας ἕπεσθαι, διακοσίους δὲ φύλακας τῶν σκευῶν καταλιπών, ἤδη γὰρ εἶχεν ἑξακοσίους, ἐπὶ τὸν Νάβαλον ἐβάδιζεν ὀμόσας

[1] μηδένα Exc.: μηδὲν codd. Lat.
[2] ὡραίας λελαχώς RO.
[3] Exc., edd.: μαθόντι codd.
[4] RO Lat.: ἠδικήσαμεν . . . γεγόναμεν rell.

but should hold it more important than all these things to wrong no man and should reckon it a crime and an offence against God to touch what belonged to another. These instructions he gave to his men in the belief that he was obliging a good man and one worthy of such consideration.[a] But Nabal—such was his name—was a hard man and of bad character, who lived according to the practices of the cynics.[b] He had, however, been blessed with a wife who was virtuous, discreet and good to look upon. At the time, then, when this Nabal was shearing his sheep, David sent ten of his men by whom he greeted him and joined him in praying that he might be so employed for many years to come. He then besought him to grant him somewhat from his abundant means ; he would have learnt from his shepherds that David and his men had done them no wrong, but had been the guardians of their persons and of their flocks throughout their long sojourn in the wilderness, nor would he ever repent of having given anything to David. The messengers acquitted themselves of this mission to Nabal, but he gave them a very uncivil and harsh reception. He first asked them who this David was, and, on being told that he was the son of Jesse, said, " So then nowadays fugitives think much of themselves and boast about deserting their masters." These words being reported to David aroused his indignation, and bidding four hundred of his men to follow him in arms and leaving two hundred to guard the baggage—for he had by now six hundred men—he marched against Nabal, having sworn utterly to

[a] David's instructions are an amplification of Scripture.

[b] Bibl. " and he was a Calebite " ; LXX, reading Heb. *keleb* " dog," καὶ ὁ ἄνθρωπος κυνικός, which Josephus takes in its technical philosophical sense.

ἐκείνῃ τῇ νυκτὶ τὸν οἶκον αὐτοῦ καὶ τὴν κτῆσιν ὅλην ἀφανίσειν· οὐ γὰρ ἄχθεσθαι μόνον ὅτι γέγονεν ἀχάριστος εἰς αὐτούς, μηδὲν ἐπιδοὺς πολλῇ φιλανθρωπίᾳ πρὸς αὐτὸν χρησαμένοις, ἀλλ' ὅτι καὶ προσεβλασφήμησε καὶ κακῶς εἶπε μηδὲν ὑπ' αὐτῶν λελυπημένος.

300 (7) Δούλου δέ τινος τῶν τὰ ποίμνια φυλασσόντων τὰ τοῦ Ναβάλου πρὸς τὴν δέσποιναν μὲν ἑαυτοῦ γυναῖκα δ' ἐκείνου κατειπόντος ὅτι πέμψας ὁ Δαυίδης αὐτῆς πρὸς τὸν ἄνδρα μηδενὸς τύχοι τῶν μετρίων, ἀλλὰ καὶ προσυβρισθείη βλασφημίαις δειναῖς πάσῃ περὶ αὐτοὺς προνοίᾳ καὶ φυλακῇ τῶν ποιμνίων χρησάμενος, γέγονε[1] δὲ τοῦτο ἐπὶ κακῷ
301 τῷ τοῦ δεσπότου καὶ αὐτῆς[2]· ταῦτ' ἐκείνου φήσαντος Ἀβιγαία, προσηγορεύετο γὰρ οὕτως, ἐπισάξασα[3] τοὺς ὄνους καὶ πληρώσασα παντοίων ξενίων καὶ μηδὲν εἰποῦσα τἀνδρί, ὑπὸ γὰρ μέθης ἀναίσθητος ἦν, ἐπορεύετο πρὸς Δαυίδην· καταβαινούσῃ δὲ τὰ στενὰ τοῦ ὄρους ἀπήντησε Δαυίδης μετὰ τῶν
302 τετρακοσίων ἐπὶ Νάβαλον ἐρχόμενος. θεασαμένη δ' αὐτὸν ἡ γυνὴ κατεπήδησε καὶ πεσοῦσα ἐπὶ πρόσωπον προσεκύνει[4] καὶ τῶν μὲν Ναβάλου λόγων ἐδεῖτο μὴ μνημονεύειν, οὐ γὰρ ἀγνοεῖν[5] αὐτὸν ὅμοιον ὄντα τῷ ὀνόματι, Νάβαλος γὰρ κατὰ τὴν Ἑβραίων γλῶτταν ἀφροσύνην δηλοῖ, αὐτὴ δ' ἀπελογεῖτο μὴ θεάσασθαι τοὺς πεμφθέντας ὑπ' αὐτοῦ·
303 " διὸ συγγίνωσκέ μοι," φησί, " καὶ τῷ θεῷ χάριν

[1] RO: γεγονέναι rell. [2] αὐτῆς ex Lat. ins. Niese.
[3] εὐθέως ἐπισ. SP. [4] προσεκύνησε ROE.
[5] οὐ γὰρ ἀγν. om. ROE Lat.

[a] The latter motive is not found in Scripture.

destroy his house and all his possessions that selfsame night; for he was angry not merely at his ingratitude in making no return to those who had shown him such great kindness, but also because he had further insulted and abused those from whom he had received no injury.[a]

(7) But one of the slaves[b] that kept the flocks of Nabal brought word to his mistress, Nabal's wife, that David had sent a message to her husband and not only had failed to receive a fair answer but had been further insulted with shocking abuse, although he had shown all consideration to the shepherds and had protected their flocks. Such action, he added, would result in mischief for his master and for herself. At the servant's story, Abigaia[c]—such was her name—saddled her asses, loaded them with all manner of presents[d] and, without a word to her husband, who was insensible from drink,[e] set off to find David. And as she was descending the defiles of the mountain, she was met by David coming against Nabal with his four hundred men. At sight of him the woman leapt to the ground, and falling on her face bowed down before him; she entreated him not to mind the words of Nabal, for he could not be ignorant that the man was like his name (*Nabal* in the Hebrew tongue signifies "folly"),[f] while for herself she pleaded that she had not seen David's messengers. "Wherefore pardon me," she said, "and render thanks to God who has prevented thee

Abigail (Abigaia), Nabal's wife, appeases David by presents.
1 Sam. xxv. 14.

[b] Bibl. "young men."
[c] Bibl. Abigail, LXX Ἀβειγαία.
[d] In the form of provisions, according to Scripture.
[e] Unscriptural detail, anticipating 1 Sam. xxv. 36, *cf.* § 306.
[f] So also the LXX translates.

ἔχε κωλύοντί σε μιανθῆναι ἀνθρωπίνῳ αἵματι· μένοντα γάρ σε καθαρὸν ἐκεῖνος αὐτὸς ἐκδικήσει παρὰ τῶν πονηρῶν· ἃ γὰρ ἐκδέχεται κακὰ Νάβαλον ταῦτα καὶ ταῖς τῶν ἐχθρῶν σου κεφαλαῖς ἐμπέσοι.
304 γενοῦ δὲ εὐμενής μοι κρίνας ἀξίαν τοῦ παρ' ἐμοῦ ταῦτα δέξασθαι, καὶ τὸν θυμὸν καὶ τὴν ὀργὴν τὴν ἐπὶ τὸν ἄνδρα μου καὶ τὸν οἶκον αὐτοῦ εἰς τὴν ἐμὴν τιμὴν ἄφες· πρέπει γὰρ ἡμέρῳ σοι καὶ φιλανθρώπῳ τυγχάνειν, καὶ ταῦτα μέλλοντι βασιλεύειν."
305 ὁ δὲ τὰ δῶρα δεξάμενος "ἀλλά σε," φησίν, "ὦ γύναι, θεὸς εὐμενὴς ἤγαγε πρὸς ἡμᾶς τήμερον· οὐ γὰρ ἂν τὴν ἐπερχομένην ἡμέραν εἶδες, ἐμοῦ τὸν οἶκον τὸν Ναβάλου διὰ τῆσδε τῆς νυκτὸς ὀμόσαντος ἀπολέσειν[1] καὶ μηδένα ὑμῶν ἀπολείψειν ἀπὸ ἀνδρὸς[2] πονηροῦ καὶ ἀχαρίστου πρὸς ἐμὲ καὶ τοὺς ἐμοὺς ἑταίρους γενομένου. νῦν δὲ φθάσασα προέλαβες καταμειλίξασθαί μου τὸν θυμὸν κηδομένου σου τοῦ θεοῦ. ἀλλὰ Νάβαλος μὲν κἂν ἀφεθῇ διὰ σὲ νῦν τῆς τιμωρίας οὐ φεύξεται τὴν δίκην, ἀλλ' ὁ τρόπος αὐτὸν ἀπολεῖ λαβὼν αἰτίαν ἄλλην."

306 (8) Ταῦτ' εἰπὼν ἀπολύει τὴν γυναῖκα· ἡ δ' εἰς τὸν οἶκον ἐλθοῦσα καὶ καταλαβοῦσα τὸν ἄνδρα μετὰ πολλῶν εὐωχούμενον καὶ κεκαρωμένον ἤδη, τότε μὲν οὐδὲν τῶν γεγενημένων διεσάφει, τῇ δὲ ἐπιούσῃ νήφοντι ἅπαντα δηλώσασα παρεθῆναι καὶ πᾶν αὐτῷ νεκρωθῆναι τὸ σῶμα ὑπὸ τῶν λόγων καὶ τῆς ἐπ' αὐτοῖς λύπης ἐποίησε· καὶ δέκα οὐ πλείους ἐπιζήσας ἡμέρας τὸν βίον κατέστρεψεν ὁ Νάβαλος.
307 ἀκούσας δ' αὐτοῦ τὴν τελευτὴν ὁ Δαυίδης ἐκδικηθῆναι μὲν αὐτὸν ὑπὸ τοῦ θεοῦ καλῶς ἔλεγεν· ἀπο-

[1] Niese: ἀπολέσαι codd. [2] + ἕως τετραπόδου RO.

from soiling thy hands with human blood. For if thou remainest clean, He Himself will avenge thee on the wicked; and may the evil that awaits Nabal fall likewise on the heads of thy foes. But be gracious to me in deigning to receive these presents from me, and, out of regard for me, dismiss thy indignation and wrath against my husband and against his house. For it becomes thee to show mildness and humanity, especially as thou art destined to be king." And David accepted the presents and said, "In truth, lady, it was gracious God who led thee to us this day; else thou wouldst not have seen the coming day, for I had sworn to destroy the house of Nabal this very night and to leave not one of you, belonging as you do to a man who has been so mean and ungrateful to me and to my comrades. But now thou hast forestalled me and mollified my wrath, since thou art in God's care. But as for Nabal, though for thy sake to-day he be spared chastisement, yet will he not escape retribution, but his conduct will find another occasion to prove his ruin."[a]

Death of Nabal; David marries Abigail. 1 Sam. xxv. 36.

(8) Having so spoken, he dismissed the woman. And she, returning to her home, found her husband carousing with a large company and already heavy with drink, and so, at the moment, she revealed nothing of what had passed; but on the morrow, when he was sober, she told him all, causing him to collapse and his whole body to become dead through her words and the pain they produced. Ten days and no more did Nabal remain alive and then departed this life. And when David heard of his death, he said that he had been well avenged by God, for Nabal

[a] This prediction is unscriptural.

θανεῖν γὰρ Νάβαλον ὑπὸ τῆς ἰδίας πονηρίας καὶ δοῦναι δίκην αὐτῷ καθαρὰν ἔχοντι τὴν δεξιάν· ἔγνω δὲ καὶ τότε τοὺς πονηροὺς ἐλαυνομένους ὑπὸ τοῦ θεοῦ,[1] μηδενὸς τῶν ἐν ἀνθρώποις ὑπερορῶντος, διδόντος δὲ τοῖς μὲν ἀγαθοῖς τὰ ὅμοια, τοῖς δὲ
308 πονηροῖς ὀξεῖαν[2] ἐπιφέροντος τὴν ποινήν. πέμψας δ' αὐτοῦ πρὸς τὴν γυναῖκα συνοικήσουσαν καὶ γαμηθησομένην ἐκάλει πρὸς αὐτόν· ἡ δὲ ἀναξία μὲν εἶναι καὶ ποδῶν ἅψασθαι τῶν ἐκείνου πρὸς τοὺς παρόντας ἔλεγεν, ὅμως δὲ μετὰ πάσης τῆς[3] θεραπείας ἧκε. καὶ συνῴκησε μὲν αὐτῷ ταύτην λαβοῦσα τὴν τιμὴν καὶ διὰ τὸ τὸν τρόπον σώφρονα εἶναι καὶ δίκαιον, τυχοῦσα δ' αὐτῆς καὶ διὰ τὸ
309 κάλλος. εἶχε δὲ Δαυίδης γυναῖκα πρότερον, ἣν ἐξ Ἀβισάρου πόλεως ἔγημε· Μελχὰν δὲ τὴν Σαούλου τοῦ βασιλέως θυγατέρα τὴν γενομένην τοῦ Δαυίδου γυναῖκα ὁ πατὴρ τῷ Φελτίῳ υἱῷ Λίσου συνέζευξεν ἐκ πόλεως ὄντι Γεθλᾶς.[4]

310 (9) Μετὰ ταῦτά τινες ἐλθόντες τῶν Ζιφηνῶν ἀπήγγειλαν τῷ Σαούλῳ, ὡς εἴη πάλιν ὁ Δαυίδης ἐν τῇ χώρᾳ αὐτῶν καὶ δύνανται συλλαβεῖν αὐτὸν βουλομένῳ συνεργῆσαι. ὁ δὲ μετὰ τρισχιλίων ὁπλιτῶν ἐβάδιζεν ἐπ' αὐτὸν καὶ νυκτὸς ἐπελθούσης ἐστρατοπέδευσεν ἐπί τινι τόπῳ Σικέλλα[5] λεγο-

[1] + καὶ codd.
[2] ROP: ἀξίαν MS Exc. Lat.
[3] + ἰδίας E Lat.
[4] Goliath Lat. (*cf.* LXX[L]).
[5] Σεκέλλα M: Σεκελλὰ (Σεκελᾶ *infra*) SP: Sicela Lat.

[a] Variant "condign."
[b] 1 Sam. xxv. 41 "let thine handmaid be a servant to wash the feet of the servants of my lord."
[c] Called Achima below, § 320; Bibl. Ahinoam, LXX Ἀχεινάαι (*v.l.* Ἀχινάαμ).

had died through his own wickedness and had given him revenge, while he himself still had clean hands. At the same time he learnt that the wicked are pursued by God who overlooks no act of man but repays the good in kind, while He inflicts swift[a] punishment upon the wicked. David then sent to the woman, inviting her to live with him and become his wife. She replied to the messengers that she was unworthy so much as to touch his feet,[b] but came nevertheless with all her servants. And so she lived with him, having attained that honour because of her modest and upright character and also because of her beauty. David already had a wife,[c] whom he had taken from the city of Abisar[d]; as for Melcha, the daughter of Saul and once the wife of David, her father had given her in marriage to Pheltias[e] son of Lisos[f] of the city of Gethla.[g]

David spares Saul's life a second time. 1 Sam. xxvi. 1.

(9) [h] After this certain of the Ziphites came and informed Saul that David was again in their country and that they could catch him, if Saul would lend them aid. So with three thousand soldiers he marched against him and, on the approach of night, encamped at a place called Sikella.[i] David, hearing

[d] Bibl. Jezreel, LXX Ἰεζραέλ (*v.l.* Ἰσραήλ κτλ.).

[e] Bibl. Phalti, LXX Φαλτεί (Φελτεί).

[f] Bibl. Laish, LXX Ἀμείς, Luc. Ἰωάς.

[g] Bibl. Gallim, LXX Ῥομμά, Luc. Γολιάθ.

[h] The following account of David's second encounter with Saul (1 Sam. xxvi.) is obviously a variant of that found in 1 Sam. xxiv., *cf.* §§ 282 ff.

[i] In 1 Sam. xxvi. 1 Heb. has Hachilah, LXX Χελμάθ (*v.l.* Ἀχιλά), Luc. Ἐχελά; in vs. 4 Heb. has "Saul came in readiness" (A.V. "in very deed"), LXX ἕτοιμος εἰς Κεειλά, Luc. Σεκελάγ. Josephus either followed a LXX reading similar to Lucian's, or confused the name here with Σεκέλλα = bibl. Ziklag mentioned below, § 322.

311 μένῳ. Δαυίδης δὲ ἀκούσας τὸν Σαοῦλον ἐπ' αὐτὸν
ἥκοντα πέμψας κατασκόπους ἐκέλευσε δηλοῦν αὐτῷ,
ποῦ τῆς χώρας Σαοῦλος ἤδη προεληλύθοι.[1] τῶν
δ' ἐν Σικέλλᾳ φρασάντων διανυκτερεύειν διαλαθὼν
τοὺς ἰδίους εἰς τὸ τοῦ Σαούλου στρατόπεδον παραγίνεται ἐπαγόμενος τὸν ἐκ τῆς ἀδελφῆς αὐτοῦ
Σαρουίας Ἀβισαῖον καὶ Ἀβιμέλεχον[2] τὸν Χετ-
312 ταῖον. τοῦ δὲ Σαούλου κοιμωμένου καὶ περὶ αὐτὸν ἐν κύκλῳ τῶν ὁπλιτῶν καὶ τοῦ στρατηγοῦ Ἀβεννήρου κειμένων, ὁ Δαυίδης εἰσελθὼν εἰς τὸ στρατόπεδον τὸ τοῦ βασιλέως οὔτ' αὐτὸς ἀναιρεῖ τὸν Σαοῦλον, ἐπιγνοὺς αὐτοῦ τὴν κοίτην ἐκ τοῦ δόρατος, τοῦτο γὰρ αὐτῷ παρεπεπήγει, οὔτε τὸν Ἀβισαῖον βουλόμενον φονεῦσαι καὶ πρὸς τοῦτο ὡρμηκότα εἴασεν, ἀλλὰ τὸν ὑπὸ τοῦ θεοῦ κεχειροτονημένον βασιλέα φήσας εἶναι δεινὸν ἀποκτεῖναι κἂν ᾖ πονηρός, ἥξειν γὰρ αὐτῷ παρὰ τοῦ δόντος τὴν ἀρχὴν σὺν χρόνῳ τὴν δίκην, ἐπέσχε τῆς ὁρμῆς.
313 σύμβολον δὲ τοῦ κτεῖναι δυνηθεὶς ἀποσχέσθαι λαβὼν αὐτοῦ τὸ δόρυ καὶ τὸν φακὸν τοῦ ὕδατος, ὃς ἦν παρ' αὐτῷ κείμενος[3] τῷ Σαούλῳ, μηδενὸς αἰσθομένου τῶν ἐν τῷ στρατοπέδῳ πάντων δὲ κατακοιμωμένων ἐξῆλθεν, ἀδεῶς πάντ' ἐργασάμενος ὅσα καὶ τοῦ καιροῦ δόντος αὐτῷ καὶ τῆς
314 τόλμης διέθηκε τοὺς τοῦ βασιλέως. διαβὰς δὲ τὸν χείμαρρον καὶ ἐπὶ τὴν κορυφὴν ἀνελθὼν τοῦ ὄρους,

[1] Niese: προσεληλύθοι, -ει codd.
[2] Ἀχιμέλεχον MSP Lat.
[3] ὃς . . . κειμ.] + κοιμωμένῳ P(S): ὃς κοιμωμένῳ παρέκειτο M: appositum dormienti Saul Lat.

[a] Bibl. Abishai, LXX Ἀβεσσά (v.l. Ἀβεισά κτλ.).

that Saul was coming against him, sent out scouts with orders to report what part of the country Saul had now reached; and when they told him that he was passing the night at Sikella, he set off, without the knowledge of his men, for Saul's camp, taking with him Abisai,[a] son of his sister Saruia,[b] and Abimelech[c] the Hittite. Saul was sleeping, with his soldiers and their commander Abenner lying in a circle around him, when David penetrated to the king's camp; yet he would not himself slay Saul, whose sleeping-place he recognized from the spear fixed in the ground at his side, nor would he permit Abisai, who wished to kill him and darted forward with that intent, to do so. He objected that it was monstrous to slay the king elected of God, even if he was a wicked man, saying that from Him who had given him the sovereignty punishment would come in due time; and so he stayed Abisai from his purpose. However, in token that he might have slain him and yet had refrained, he took the spear and the flask of water that was placed just beside Saul and, unseen by any in the camp where all lay fast asleep, he passed out, having safely accomplished all the things that the favourable opportunity and his daring had enabled him to inflict on the king's men. Then, after crossing a stream[d] and climbing to the top of

David rebukes Abner

[b] Bibl. Zeruiah (Heb. *Ṣerûyāh*), LXX = Josephus. That she was David's sister is stated in 1 Chron. ii. 16.

[c] Variant (as in Scripture) Achimelech; the LXX MSS. also vary between the two forms. According to Scripture, however, only Abishai accompanied David.

[d] 1 Sam. xxvi. 13 "Then David went over to the other side and stood on the top of a hill afar off; a great space being between them." Josephus naturally thought of the space as being a *wady*, the bed of a winter stream (χειμάρρους), such as are common in Palestine.

ὅθεν ἔμελλεν ἐξάκουστος εἶναι, ἐμβοήσας τοῖς στρατιώταις τοῦ Σαούλου καὶ τῷ στρατηγῷ Ἀβεννήρῳ διανίστησιν αὐτοὺς ἐκ τοῦ ὕπνου τοῦτόν τε ἐφώνει καὶ τὸν λαόν. ἐπακούσαντος δὲ τοῦ στρατηγοῦ καὶ τίς ὁ καλέσας αὐτόν ἐστιν ἐρομένου
315 Δαυίδης εἶπεν· "ἐγώ, παῖς μὲν Ἰεσσαίου, φυγὰς δὲ ὑμέτερος. ἀλλὰ τί δήποτε μέγας τε ὢν καὶ τὴν πρώτην ἔχων παρὰ τῷ βασιλεῖ τιμήν, οὕτως ἀμελῶς τὸ τοῦ δεσπότου φυλάσσεις σῶμα, καὶ ὕπνος ἡδίων ἐστί σοι τῆς τούτου σωτηρίας καὶ προνοίας; θανάτου γὰρ ἄξια ταῦτα καὶ τιμωρίας, οἵ γε μικρὸν ἔμπροσθεν εἰσελθόντας τινὰς ὑμῶν εἰς τὸ στρατόπεδον ἐπὶ τὸν βασιλέα καὶ πάντας τοὺς ἄλλους[1] οὐκ ἐνοήσατε. ζήτησον οὖν τὸ δόρυ τοῦ βασιλέως καὶ τὸν φακὸν τοῦ ὕδατος καὶ μαθήσῃ πηλίκον ὑμᾶς ἔλαθε κακὸν ἐντὸς γενό-
316 μενον." Σαοῦλος δὲ γνωρίσας τὴν τοῦ Δαυίδου φωνὴν καὶ μαθὼν ὅτι λαβὼν αὐτὸν ἔκδοτον ὑπὸ τοῦ ὕπνου καὶ τῆς τῶν φυλασσόντων ἀμελείας οὐκ ἀπέκτεινεν, ἀλλ' ἐφείσατο δικαίως ἂν αὐτὸν ἀνελών, χάριν ἔχειν αὐτῷ τῆς σωτηρίας ἔλεγε καὶ παρεκάλει θαρροῦντα καὶ μηδὲν ἔτι πείσεσθαι δεινὸν ἐξ αὐτοῦ φοβούμενον ἀναχωρεῖν ἐπὶ τὰ οἰκεῖα·
317 πεπεῖσθαι γὰρ ὅτι μηδ' αὐτὸν[2] οὕτως ἀγαπήσειεν, ὡς ὑπ' ἐκείνου στέργεται, ὃς[3] τὸν μὲν φυλάττειν αὐτὸν δυνάμενον καὶ πολλὰ δείγματα τῆς εὐνοίας παρεσχημένον ἐλαύνοι καὶ τοσοῦτον ἐν φυγῇ χρόνον καὶ ταῖς περὶ τὴν ψυχὴν ἀγωνίαις ἠνάγκασε ζῆσαι φίλων καὶ συγγενῶν ἔρημον· αὐτὸς δ' οὐ παύεται

[1] ἐπὶ . . . ἄλλους om. RO: καὶ . . . ἄλλους om. E.
[2] ex Lat. Bekker: αὐτὸν codd.
[3] ὡς RO.

a hill from which his voice could be heard, he shouted to the troops of Saul and to their commander Abenner, and, awaking them from their sleep, addressed him and his people. When the commander heard this and asked who was calling him, David replied, "I, son of Jesse, the fugitive from you.[a] But how comes it that one so great as thou, holding the first rank in the king's service, art so negligent in guarding the person of thy master, and that sleep is more to thy liking than his safety and protection? This conduct indeed merits the punishment of death, for a little while since some men penetrated right through your camp to the king's person and to all the others, and you did not even perceive it. Look now for the king's spear and his flask of water and thou wilt learn what mischief has befallen in your midst without your knowing of it." Then Saul, when he recognized the voice of David and learned that though he had had him at his mercy, being asleep and neglected by his guards, he had yet not slain him but spared the life which he might justly have taken, gave him thanks for his preservation and exhorted him to be of good courage and, without fear of suffering further injury from himself, to return to his home.[b] For, he said, he was now persuaded that he did not love his own self so well as he was loved by David, seeing that he had pursued this man who might have been his safeguard and who had given many proofs of his loyalty, and that he had forced him to live so long in exile, in terror of his life, bereft of friends and of kindred, while he himself had been repeatedly spared by him

for his neglect of Saul. 1 Sam. xxvi. 13.

Saul is again reconciled to David. 1 Sam. xxvi. 17.

[a] This phrase is unscriptural. There is also some amplification in the rest of David's speech.

[b] Josephus omits David's protest against Saul's treatment of him, 1 Sam. xxvi. 18-20.

πολλάκις[1] ὑπ' αὐτοῦ σωζόμενος, οὐδὲ τὴν ψυχὴν
318 φανερῶς ἀπολλυμένην λαμβάνων. ὁ δὲ Δαυίδης πέμψαντα ἀπολαβεῖν ἐκέλευσε τὸ δόρυ καὶ τὸν φακὸν τοῦ ὕδατος, ἐπειπὼν ὡς "ὁ θεὸς ἑκατέρῳ τῆς ἰδίας φύσεως καὶ τῶν κατ' αὐτὴν πεπραγμένων ἔσται δικαστής, ὃς ὅτι καὶ κατὰ τὴν παροῦσαν ἡμέραν ἀποκτεῖναί σε δυνηθεὶς ἀπεσχόμην οἶδε."
319 (10) Καὶ Σαοῦλος μὲν δεύτερον διαφυγὼν τὰς Δαυίδου χεῖρας εἰς τὰ βασίλεια καὶ τὴν οἰκείαν ἀπηλλάσσετο, φοβηθεὶς δὲ Δαυίδης μὴ μένων αὐτόθι συλληφθῇ ὑπὸ τοῦ Σαούλου, συμφέρειν ἔκρινεν εἰς τὴν Παλαιστίνην καταβὰς[2] διατρίβειν ἐν αὐτῇ, καὶ μετὰ τῶν ἑξακοσίων, οἳ περὶ αὐτὸν ἦσαν, παραγίνεται πρὸς Ἀγχοῦν τὸν Γίττης βασι-
320 λέα· μία δ' ἦν αὕτη τῶν πέντε πόλεων. δεξαμένου δ' αὐτὸν τοῦ βασιλέως σὺν τοῖς ἀνδράσι καὶ δόντος οἰκητήριον, ἔχων ἅμα καὶ τὰς δύο γυναῖκας Ἀχιμὰν καὶ Ἀβιγαίαν διῆγεν ἐν τῇ Γίττῃ. Σαούλῳ δὲ ταῦτ' ἀκούσαντι λόγος οὐκέτ' ἦν πέμπειν ἐπ' αὐτὸν ἢ βαδίζειν· δὶς γὰρ ἤδη κινδυνεῦσαι παρὰ μικρὸν ἐπ' ἐκείνῳ γενόμενον, συλλαβεῖν αὐτὸν σπου-
321 δάσαντα. Δαυίδῃ δ' οὐκ ἔδοξεν ἐν τῇ πόλει τῶν Γιττῶν μένειν, ἀλλ' ἐδεήθη τοῦ βασιλέως αὐτῶν, ἵν' ἐπειδὴ φιλανθρώπως αὐτὸν ὑπεδέξατο καὶ τοῦτο χαρίσηται, τόπον τινὰ τῆς χώρας δοὺς αὐτῷ πρὸς κατοίκησιν· αἰδεῖσθαι γὰρ διατρίβων ἐν τῇ πόλει
322 βαρὺς αὐτῷ καὶ φορτικὸς εἶναι. δίδωσι δὲ Ἀγχοῦς

[1] πολλάκις om. RO.
[2] ex Lat. Niese: ἀναβὰς codd.

[a] Saul's speech is greatly amplified by Josephus.

and had received at his hands a life clearly marked for destruction.[a] David then bade him send someone to fetch the spear and the flask of water,[b] adding, "God shall be judge of the character of either of us and of the actions arising therefrom. He knows that when this day I had power to slay thee I refrained."

(10) So Saul, having for the second time escaped from David's hands, returned to his palace and his country; but David, fearful of being captured by Saul if he remained where he was, deemed it wise to go down to the land of the Philistines and abide there. With his band of six hundred followers he betook himself to Anchūs,[c] king of Gitta, which was one of their five cities.[d] The king welcomed him and his men and gave them a habitation; and so, along with his two wives, Achima[e] and Abigaia, he settled in Gitta. Saul, on hearing of this, thought no more of sending or marching against him, for twice already he had been in imminent danger of falling into his hands while striving to catch him.[f] David, however, was not minded to remain in the city of Gitta, but besought its king, since he had given him kindly welcome, to grant one favour more and give him some place in his country to dwell in; he had scruples, he said, about being a burden and encumbrance to him by continuing to live in that city.[g] So Anchūs gave

David is welcomed by Achish (Anchus), king of Gath, and settles in Philistia. 1 Sam xxvii. 1.

[b] The return of the flask of water is not mentioned in Scripture.

[c] Bibl. Achish, *cf.* § 245 note.

[d] The five Philistine cities were Gath (Gitta), Ekron (Akkaron), Ascalon, Gaza, Ashdod (Azotus), *cf. A.* v. 128, vi. 8.

[e] Bibl. Ahinoam, *cf.* § 309 note.

[f] This reason is not mentioned in Scripture.

[g] David's scrupulous request is an amplification of 1 Sam. xxvii. 5.

αὐτῷ κώμην τινὰ Σέκελλαν καλουμένην, ἣν βασιλεύσας ὁ Δαυίδης ἀγαπῶν ἴδιον κτῆμα ἐτίμησεν εἶναι καὶ οἱ παῖδες αὐτοῦ. ἀλλὰ περὶ μὲν τούτων ἐν ἄλλοις δηλώσομεν· ὁ δὲ χρόνος ὃν κατῴκησε Δαυίδης ἐν Σεκέλλᾳ τῆς Παλαιστίνης ἐγένετο
323 μῆνες τέσσαρες πρὸς ταῖς εἴκοσιν ἡμέραις. ἐπερχόμενος δὲ λάθρα τοῖς πλησιοχώροις τῶν Παλαιστίνων Σερρίταις καὶ Ἀμαληκίταις διήρπαζεν αὐτῶν τὴν χώραν καὶ λείαν πολλὴν κτηνῶν καὶ καμήλων λαμβάνων ὑπέστρεφεν· ἀνθρώπων γὰρ ἀπείχετο δεδιὼς μὴ καταμηνύσωσιν αὐτὸν πρὸς Ἀγχοῦν τὸν βασιλέα, τὸ μέντοι γε τῆς λείας μέρος
324 αὐτῷ δωρεὰν ἔπεμπε. τοῦ δὲ βασιλέως πυθομένου τίσιν ἐπιθέμενος τὴν λείαν ἀπήλασε; τοῖς πρὸς τὸν νότον τῶν Ἰουδαίων τετραμμένοις καὶ ἐν τῇ πεδιάδι κατοικοῦσιν εἰπὼν πείθει τὸν Ἀγχοῦν φρονῆσαι οὕτως· ἤλπισε γὰρ οὗτος ὅτι Δαυίδης ἐμίσησε τὸ ἴδιον ἔθνος, καὶ δοῦλον ἕξειν παρ' ὃν ζῇ χρόνον ἐν τοῖς αὐτοῦ καταμένοντα.

325 (xiv. 1) Κατὰ δὲ τὸν αὐτὸν καιρὸν τῶν Παλαιστίνων ἐπὶ τοὺς Ἰσραηλίτας στρατεύειν διεγνωκότων καὶ περιπεμψάντων πρὸς τοὺς συμμάχους ἅπαντας, ἵνα παρῶσιν[1] αὐτοῖς εἰς τὸν πόλεμον εἰς

[1] συμπαρῶσιν MSP.

[a] Bibl. Ziklag (Heb. *Ṣiqlag*), LXX Σεκελάκ. The site is uncertain; it may be the modern *Khirbet Zuḥeiliqah*, about 10 miles S.E. of Gaza.

[b] 1 Sam. xxvii. 6 " Wherefore Ziklag pertaineth to the kings of Judah unto this day."

[c] The only other reference to Ziklag is in §§ 356 ff. where its sack by the Amalekites is described.

[d] Heb. " a year (lit. " days ") and four months," LXX " four months."

him a certain village called Sekella,[a] which David so well liked after becoming king that he regarded it as his private domain, as did his sons after him.[b] But of that we shall speak elsewhere.[c] Now the time during which David dwelt in Sekella in Philistia was four months and twenty days.[d] He made clandestine raids on the neighbours of the Philistines, the Serrites[e] and Amalekites, ravaging their country and returning with abundant booty of cattle and camels; he refrained from (taking captive)[f] any men, for fear that they would denounce him to King Anchūs, to whom, however, he sent a present of a portion of the spoils.[g] And when the king inquired whom he had attacked to have carried off all this booty, he said it was the people lying southward of the Judaeans, inhabiting the plain,[h] and succeeded in making Anchūs believe this. For the king had hopes that David had come to hate[i] his own nation and that he would have him for his servant so long as he lived, settled among his own people.

David makes raids from Ziklag (Sekella) on neighbouring tribes. 1 Sam. xxvii. 8.

(xiv. 1) About the same time the Philistines resolved to take the field against the Israelites and sent word around to all their allies to join them at

Achish enlists David in Philistine

[e] Bibl. the Geshurite and Girzite (Targum Gizrite, A.V. Gezrite), LXX τὸν Γεσειρί, Luc. τὸν Γεσουραῖον καὶ τὸν Ἰεζραῖον.

[f] A euphemism for "killed," *cf.* 1 Sam. xxvii. 9, 11 "and left neither man nor woman alive." Other translators take ἀπείχετο in its usual sense of "spared" and note the contradiction to Scripture.

[g] Scripture does not say that David sent Achish a portion of the spoils.

[h] 1 Sam. xxvii. 10 specifies the peoples involved.

[i] So the Targum of 1 Sam. xxvii. 12; Heb. "is in bad odour among his people" (A.V. "made his people Israel utterly to abhor him"), LXX "is put to shame among his people."

Ῥεγάν,[1] ἔνθεν ἔμελλον ἀθροισθέντες ἐξορμᾶν ἐπὶ τοὺς Ἑβραίους, ὁ τῶν Γιττῶν βασιλεὺς Ἀγχοῦς συμμαχῆσαι τὸν Δαυίδην αὐτῷ μετὰ τῶν ἰδίων
326 ὁπλιτῶν ἐκέλευσε.[2] τοῦ δὲ προθύμως ὑποσχομένου καὶ φήσαντος παραστῆναι καιρόν, ἐν ᾧ τὴν ἀμοιβὴν αὐτῷ τῆς εὐεργεσίας καὶ τῆς ξενίας ἀποδώσει, ποιήσειν αὐτὸν καὶ[3] φύλακα τοῦ σώματος μετὰ τὴν νίκην καὶ τοὺς ἀγῶνας τοὺς πρὸς τοὺς πολεμίους κατὰ νοῦν χωρήσαντας αὐτοῖς ἐπηγγείλατο, τῆς τιμῆς καὶ πίστεως ὑποσχέσει τὸ πρόθυμον αὐτοῦ μᾶλλον αὔξων.

327 (2) Ἔτυχε δὲ Σαοῦλος ὁ τῶν Ἑβραίων βασιλεὺς τοὺς μάντεις καὶ τοὺς ἐγγαστριμύθους καὶ πᾶσαν τὴν τοιαύτην τέχνην ἐκ τῆς χώρας ἐκβεβληκὼς ἔξω τῶν προφητῶν. ἀκούσας δὲ τοὺς Παλαιστίνους ἤδη παρόντας καὶ ἔγγιστα Σούνης πόλεως ἐν τῷ πεδίῳ[4] ἐστρατοπεδευκότας ἐξώρμησεν ἐπ'
328 αὐτοὺς μετὰ τῆς δυνάμεως. καὶ παραγενόμενος πρὸς ὄρει τινὶ Γελβουὲ καλουμένῳ βάλλεται στρατόπεδον ἀντικρὺ τῶν πολεμίων. ταράττει δ' αὐτὸν

[1] Ῥεγγᾶν MS: Ῥέγγαν P: Ῥιγὰν O: Rella Lat.: φάραγγα(ν) conj. Mez.

[2] ἐκέλευε E: ἐπὶ τοὺς Ἑβραίους ἠξίου MSP Lat.

[3] ἀποδώσει . . . καὶ] ex Lat. Niese: ἀποδώσειν αὐτὸν καὶ RO: ἀποδώσειν καὶ ποιήσειν αὐτὸν M: αὐτὸν ἀποδώσειν καὶ ποιήσειν αὐτὸν SP.

[4] +κειμένης SP Exc. Lat. (-η M).

---

[a] No such place is mentioned in Scripture; it is explained by Mez *ap.* Thackeray, *op. cit.* p. 88 n. 39, as a corruption of φάραγγα(ν) "valley," which was, in turn, a mistranslation of the Targum *ḥēlā* meaning both "valley," and "warfare"

Rega[a] whence they would make a combined assault upon the Hebrews. Accordingly Anchūs, king of Gitta, bade David aid him with his own soldiers. David promptly promised to do so, declaring that here was an opportunity for him to repay Anchūs for his good offices and hospitality, whereupon the king undertook to make him his bodyguard[b] after the victory, if the outcome of the struggle against the enemy should be favourable to them.[c] By this promise of honour and confidence he hoped to increase David's ardour still more.

army. 1 Sam. xxviii. 1.

Saul and the witch of Endor. 1 Sam. xxviii. 3.

(2) Now Saul, the king of the Hebrews, had, as it happened, banished from the country the diviners, ventriloquists[d] and all practitioners of such arts, except the prophets.[e] Hearing now that the Philistines were upon him and had encamped quite close to the city of Sūnē[f] in the plain, he went out against them at the head of his forces, and, on reaching a mountain called Gelboue,[g] pitched his camp over against the enemy. But here he was greatly dis-

or "host"—the latter rendering being called for by the Heb. *ṣābā'* "warfare" in 1 Sam. xxviii. 1.

[b] Bibl. "keeper of my head," LXX ἀρχισωματοφύλακα "chief of the bodyguard."

[c] In Scripture, Achish does not make the conferring of the title conditional upon victory in battle.

[d] So the LXX translates Heb. *'ōb* (A.V. "one that had familiar spirits"); the exact meaning is unknown, but its Biblical use and Jewish tradition show that a talisman as an instrument of divination is meant, rather than a person—the latter being called in Hebrew *ba'al 'ōb* "possessor of the *'ōb*."

[e] The prophets are not expressly excepted in Scripture.

[f] Bibl. Shunem, LXX Σωμάν (*v.l.* Σωνάμ); the modern *Solam* in the Plain of Esdraelon, about half-way between Nazareth and Mt. Gilboa in a N.W.-S.E. line.

[g] So the LXX; bibl. Gilboa, modern *Jebel Fuku'a*.

οὐχ ὡς ἔτυχεν ἰδόντα[1] ἡ τῶν ἐχθρῶν δύναμις πολλή τε οὖσα καὶ τῆς οἰκείας κρείττων ὑπονοουμένη, καὶ τὸν θεὸν διὰ τῶν προφητῶν ἠρώτα περὶ τῆς μάχης καὶ τοῦ περὶ ταύτην ἐσομένου τέλους
329 προειπεῖν. οὐκ ἀποκρινομένου δὲ τοῦ θεοῦ ἔτι μᾶλλον ὁ Σαοῦλος κατέδεισε καὶ τὴν ψυχὴν ἀνέπεσε, τὸ κακὸν οἷον εἰκὸς οὐ παρόντος αὐτῷ κατὰ χεῖρα τοῦ θείου προορώμενος. ζητηθῆναι δ' αὐτῷ κελεύει γύναιόν τι τῶν ἐγγαστριμύθων καὶ τὰς τῶν τεθνηκότων ψυχὰς ἐκκαλουμένων ὡς οὕτως γνωσομένῳ ποῖ χωρεῖν αὐτῷ μέλλει τὰ πράγματα·
330 τὸ γὰρ τῶν ἐγγαστριμύθων γένος ἀνάγον τὰς τῶν νεκρῶν ψυχὰς δι' αὐτῶν προλέγει τοῖς δεομένοις τὰ ἀποβησόμενα. μηνυθέντος δ' αὐτῷ παρά τινος τῶν οἰκετῶν εἶναί τι γύναιον τοιοῦτον ἐν πόλει Δώρῳ,[2] λαθὼν πάντας τοὺς ἐν τῷ στρατοπέδῳ καὶ μετεκδὺς τὴν βασιλικὴν ἐσθῆτα δύο παραλαβὼν οἰκέτας, οὓς ᾔδει πιστοτάτους ὄντας,[3] ἧκεν εἰς τὴν Δῶρον πρὸς τὴν γυναῖκα καὶ παρεκάλει μαντεύεσθαι καὶ ἀνάγειν
331 αὐτῷ ψυχὴν οὗπερ ἂν αὐτὸς εἴπῃ. τῆς δὲ γυναικὸς ἀπομαχομένης καὶ λεγούσης οὐ καταφρονήσειν τοῦ βασιλέως, ὃς τοῦτο τὸ γένος τῶν μάντεων ἐξήλασεν, οὐδ' αὐτὸν δὲ ποιεῖν καλῶς ἀδικηθέντα μηδὲν ὑπ' αὐτῆς, ἐνεδρεύοντα δὲ εἰς τὰ κεκωλυμένα λαβεῖν αὐτὴν ἵνα δῷ δίκην, ὤμοσε μηδένα γνώσεσθαι μηδὲ παρ' ἄλλον ἄγειν αὐτῆς τὴν μαντείαν, ἔσεσθαι δ'
332 ἀκίνδυνον. ὡς δὲ τοῖς ὅρκοις αὐτὴν ἔπεισε μὴ δεδιέναι, κελεύει τὴν Σαμουήλου ψυχὴν ἀναγαγεῖν αὐτῷ. ἡ δ' ἀγνοοῦσα τὸν Σαμουῆλον ὅστις ἦν καλεῖ τοῦτον ἐξ ᾅδου· φανέντος δ' αὐτοῦ θεα-

[1] ἰδόντα om. ROE.
[2] Ἀενδώρῳ MSP: Endor Lat.
[3] ἄνδρας RO: om. Lat.

mayed at sight of the hostile force which was very large and, as he surmised, superior to his own; and he asked through the prophets for an oracle from God concerning the battle and its issue. But, as no response came from God, Saul was yet more afraid and his heart failed him, foreseeing inevitable disaster since the Deity was no longer at his side. However, he gave orders to search out for him a woman among the ventriloquists and those who call up the spirits of the dead, that so he might learn how matters would turn out for him. For this sort of ventriloquist raises up the spirits of the dead and through them foretells the future to those who inquire of them. Being informed by one of his servants that there was such a woman in the city of Dor,[a] Saul, without the knowledge of any in the camp, stripped off his royal robes and, accompanied by two servants whom he knew to be quite trustworthy, came to Dor to this woman and besought her to bring up for him by divination the soul of whomever he should name. The woman, however, objected, saying that she would not defy the king, who had expelled that class of diviners; nor was it fair on his part, who had suffered no wrong from her, to lay this snare to catch her in forbidden acts and cause her to be punished. Thereupon Saul swore that none should know of it, that he would tell no one else of her divination and that she should be in no danger. Having by these oaths persuaded her to forget her fears, he bade her bring up for him the soul of Samuel. The woman, ignorant who Samuel was, summoned him from Hades. And when he

The witch raises the spirit of

[a] Bibl. Endor, LXX Ἀελδώρ (*v.l.* Ἀενδώρ, *cf.* *v.l.* in Josephus); modern *'Endor*, about 3 miles N.E. of Shunem, on the slopes of *Jebel Dūhy*.

σάμενον τὸ γύναιον ἄνδρα σεμνὸν καὶ θεοπρεπῆ ταράττεται, καὶ πρὸς τὴν ὄψιν ἐκπλαγέν, "οὐ σύ," φησίν, "ὁ βασιλεὺς εἶ Σαοῦλος;" ἐδήλωσε γὰρ
333 αὐτὸν Σαμουῆλος. ἐπινεύσαντος δ' ἐκείνου καὶ τὴν ταραχὴν αὐτῆς ἐρομένου πόθεν γένοιτο, βλέπειν εἶπεν ἀνελθόντα τῷ θεῷ τινα τὴν μορφὴν ὅμοιον. τοῦ δὲ τὴν εἰκόνα φράζειν[1] καὶ τὸ σχῆμα τοῦ θεαθέντος καὶ τὴν ἡλικίαν κελεύσαντος,[2] γέροντα μὲν ἤδη καὶ ἔνδοξον ἐσήμαινεν, ἱερατικὴν
334 δὲ περικείμενον διπλοΐδα. ἐγνώρισεν ἐκ τούτων ὁ βασιλεὺς τὸν Σαμουῆλον ὄντα καὶ πεσὼν ἐπὶ τὴν γῆν ἠσπάζετο καὶ προσεκύνησε· τῆς δὲ Σαμουήλου ψυχῆς πυθομένης διὰ τί κινήσειεν αὐτὴν καὶ ἀναχθῆναι ποιήσειεν, τὴν[3] ἀνάγκην ἀπωδύρετο· τοὺς πολεμίους γὰρ[4] ἐπικεῖσθαι βαρεῖς αὐτῷ, αὐτὸν δὲ ἀμηχανεῖν τοῖς παροῦσιν ἐγκαταλελειμμένον ὑπὸ τοῦ θεοῦ καὶ μηδὲ[5] προρρήσεως τυγχάνοντα μήτε διὰ προφητῶν μήτε δι' ὀνειράτων, "καὶ διὰ τοῦτο ἐπὶ σὲ τὸν[6] ἐμοῦ προνοησόμενον[7] κατέφυγον."
335 Σαμουῆλος δὲ τέλος αὐτὸν ἔχοντα ἤδη τῆς μεταβολῆς ὁρῶν "περισσὸν μέν," εἶπεν, "ἔτι καὶ παρ' ἐμοῦ βούλεσθαι μαθεῖν τοῦ θεοῦ καταλελοιπότος αὐτόν· ἄκουέ γε μὴν ὅτι βασιλεῦσαι δεῖ Δαυίδην
336 καὶ κατορθῶσαι τὸν πόλεμον, σὲ δὲ καὶ τὴν ἀρχὴν

[1] + εἰπόντος SPE.
[2] κελεύσαντος om. ROE.
[3] τὴν om. ROE.
[4] γὰρ Hudson cum cod. Vat.: om. rell.
[5] Dindorf: μήτε codd.
[6] + ἀεὶ M Lat.
[7] προνοησάμενον ed. pr. Lat.

[a] Scripture does not tell us how the witch recognized Saul; 1 Sam. xxviii. 12 "Why hast thou deceived me? for thou art Saul." Rabbinic tradition accounts for it by the legend

appeared, the woman, beholding a venerable and godlike man, was overcome and, in her terror at the apparition, cried, "Art thou not King Saul?" for Samuel revealed who he was.[a] When Saul indicated that it was so and asked whence came her alarm, she replied that she saw someone arise in form like God. Saul then bade her describe the appearance, the dress and the age of the man she saw, and she represented him as of advanced age, of distinguished aspect and clad in a priestly mantle.[b] By these tokens the king recognized him to be Samuel and, falling to the ground, saluted him and made obeisance. Being asked by the shade of Samuel wherefore he had disturbed him and caused him to be brought up, Saul bewailed his necessity; the enemy, he said, was pressing heavily upon him and he was helpless in his present plight, being abandoned by God and failing to obtain an oracle whether through prophets or through dreams. "That is why I have betaken myself to thee, for thou wilt provide for me." But Samuel, seeing that Saul was now approaching a final change of fortune,[c] said, "It is idle to seek to learn any more from me, since God has abandoned thee. But this much thou mayest hear, that David is destined to be king and to achieve success in this war, while thou must lose both thy sovereignty and thy

Samuel, who foretells Saul's doom. 1 Sam. xxviii. 11.

that spirits appear head downward unless summoned by a king.

[b] Heb. *me'il* "upper garment" (A.V. "mantle"), LXX διπλοΐς. Josephus adds the word "priestly" because *me'il* is the word used regularly in later Hebrew of the priest's robe. Tradition states that this garment worn by Samuel's spirit was the same as that made for him by his mother when he was a child (1 Sam. ii. 19) and that he had been buried in.

[c] Lit. "having already an end of change."

καὶ τὴν ζωὴν ἀπολέσαι, τοῦ θεοῦ παρακούσαντα ἐν τῷ πρὸς Ἀμαληκίτας πολέμῳ καὶ τὰς ἐντολὰς αὐτοῦ μὴ φυλάξαντα, καθὼς προεφήτευσά σοι καὶ ζῶν. ἴσθι τοίνυν καὶ τὸν λαὸν ὑποχείριον τοῖς ἐχθροῖς γενησόμενον καὶ σαυτὸν μετὰ τῶν τέκνων αὔριον πεσόντα ἐπὶ τῆς μάχης μετ' ἐμοῦ γενησόμενον."

337 (3) Ταῦτ' ἀκούσας ὁ Σαοῦλος ἄφωνος ὑπὸ λύπης ἐγένετο καὶ κατενεχθεὶς εἰς τοὔδαφος, εἴτε διὰ τὴν προσπεσοῦσαν ἐκ τῶν δεδηλωμένων ὀδύνην, εἴτε διὰ τὴν ἔνδειαν, οὐ γὰρ προσενήνεκτο τροφὴν τῇ παρελθούσῃ ἡμέρᾳ τε καὶ νυκτί, ῥᾳδίως ἔκειτο
338 νέκυς ὥς τις.[1] μόλις δὲ ἑαυτοῦ γενόμενον συνηνάγκασεν ἡ γυνὴ γεύσασθαι, ταύτην αἰτουμένη παρ' αὐτοῦ τὴν χάριν ἀντὶ τῆς παραβόλου μαντείας, ἣν οὐκ ἐξὸν αὐτῇ ποιήσασθαι διὰ τὸν ἐξ αὐτοῦ φόβον ἀγνοουμένου τίς ἦν, ὅμως ὑπέστη καὶ παρέσχεν. ἀνθ' ὧν παρεκάλει τράπεζάν τε αὐτῷ παραθεῖναι καὶ τροφήν, ὡς ἂν τὴν ἰσχὺν συλλεξάμενος εἰς τὸ τῶν οἰκείων ἀποσωθῇ στρατόπεδον· ἀντέχοντα δὲ καὶ τελέως ἀπεστραμμένον
339 ὑπὸ ἀθυμίας ἐβιάσατο καὶ συνέπεισεν. ἔχουσα δὲ μόσχον ἕνα συνήθη καὶ τῆς κατ' οἶκον ἐπιμελείας καὶ τροφῆς ἀξιούμενον ὑπ' αὐτῆς, ὡς γυνὴ χερνῆτις καὶ τούτῳ μόνῳ προσαναπαυομένη τῷ κτήματι,

[1] Niese: ἔκειτο νέκυς ὅστις RO: κατενήνεκτο MSP (Exc.): non facile valebat exurgere Lat.

---

[a] Text uncertain.

[b] Or "joined (his servants) in constraining"; *cf.* 1 Sam. xxviii. 23 "But his servants, together with the woman, compelled him."

life, because thou disobeyedst God in the war with the Amalekites and didst not observe His commandments, even as I foretold to thee while I was alive. Know then that thy people shall be delivered into the hands of their foes and that thou thyself with thy sons shalt fall to-morrow in the battle, and thou shalt be with me."

(3) On hearing these words, Saul was made speechless by grief and, falling to the ground, whether from the shock inflicted by these revelations or through exhaustion—for he had taken no food during the past day and night—lay inert[a] as a corpse. Then, when with difficulty he had come to himself, the woman constrained[b] him to partake of food, asking this favour of him in return for that hazardous act of divination, which though not lawful for her to perform through fear of him so long as she had not recognized him,[c] she had nevertheless undertaken to carry out. Wherefore she entreated him to let her set a table with food before him, that so having collected his strength he might return safely to his own camp; and, when in his despondency he refused and resolutely turned away, she insisted and helped to persuade him. Though she owned but one calf, which she had brought up[d] and had taken trouble to care for and feed beneath her roof, for she was a labouring woman and had to be content with this as her sole

The witch of Endor succours Saul. 1 Sam. xxviii. 20.

[c] The language of Josephus is ambiguous. It may mean that the witch feared to defy the king, whom she did not recognize in the person of Saul, or that she had been afraid to do Saul's bidding so long as she was ignorant of his identity.

[d] Lit. "familiar" or "tame"; Heb. *marbeq* "tied up" (A.V. "fat," *cf.* Targum "fatted"), LXX δαμαλὶς νομάς "grazing heifer" (Luc. μοσχάριον γαλαθηνόν "sucking calf").

κατασφάξασα τοῦτον καὶ τὰ κρέα παρασκευάσασα τοῖς οἰκέταις αὐτοῦ καὶ αὐτῷ παρατίθησι. καὶ Σαοῦλος μὲν διὰ τῆς νυκτὸς ἦλθεν εἰς τὸ στρατόπεδον.

340 (4) Δίκαιον δὲ ἀποδέξασθαι τῆς φιλοτιμίας τὴν γυναῖκα, ὅτι καίπερ τῇ τέχνῃ κεκωλυμένη χρήσασθαι ὑπὸ τοῦ βασιλέως, παρ' ἧς ἂν αὐτῇ τὰ κατὰ τὸν οἶκον ἦν ἀμείνω καὶ διαρκέστερα, καὶ μηδέποτε αὐτὸν πρότερον τεθεαμένη οὐκ ἐμνησικάκησε τῆς ἐπιστήμης ὑπ' αὐτοῦ καταγνωσθείσης, οὐκ ἀπεστράφη δὲ ὡς ξένον καὶ μηδέποτε ἐν
341 συνηθείᾳ γεγενημένον, ἀλλὰ συνεπάθησέ τε καὶ παρεμυθήσατο καὶ πρὸς ἃ διέκειτο λίαν ἀηδῶς προετρέψατο, καὶ τὸ μόνον αὐτῇ παρὸν ὡς ἐν πενίᾳ τοῦτο παρέσχεν ἐκτενῶς καὶ φιλοφρόνως, οὔθ' ὑπὲρ εὐεργεσίας ἀμειβομένη τινὸς γεγενημένης οὔτε χάριν μέλλουσαν θηρωμένη, τελευτήσοντα γὰρ αὐτὸν ἠπίστατο, φύσει τῶν ἀνθρώπων ἢ πρὸς τοὺς ἀγαθόν τι παρεσχημένους φιλοτιμουμένων, ἢ παρ' ὧν ἄν τι δύνωνται λαβεῖν ὄφελος
342 τούτους προθεραπευόντων. καλὸν οὖν ἐστι μιμεῖσθαι τὴν γυναῖκα καὶ ποιεῖν εὖ πάντας τοὺς ἐν χρείᾳ γενομένους, καὶ μηδὲν ὑπολαμβάνειν ἄμεινον μηδὲ μᾶλλόν τι προσήκειν τῷ τῶν ἀνθρώπων γένει τούτου μηδ' ἐφ' ᾧ[1] τὸν θεὸν εὐμενῆ καὶ χορηγὸν τῶν ἀγαθῶν ἕξομεν.[2] καὶ τὰ μὲν περὶ τῆς γυναικὸς
343 ἐν τοσούτοις ἀρκεῖ δεδηλῶσθαι· τὸν δὲ πόλεσι καὶ δήμοις καὶ ἔθνεσι συμφέροντα λόγον καὶ προσ-

[1] ὅτῳ S[2] Vat. ap. Hudson.
[2] μᾶλλον ἕξομεν conj. Naber.

[a] The following eulogy of the witch of Endor is, of course, an addition to Scripture.

possession, she slaughtered it, prepared the meat and set it before his servants and himself. And Saul that night returned to his camp.

(4) [a] Here it is but right to commend the generosity of this woman who, though she had been prevented by the king from practising an art which would have made it easier and more comfortable for her at home, and though she had never seen Saul before, yet bore him no resentment for having condemned her profession nor turned him away as a stranger and as one with whom she had never been acquainted; but instead she gave him sympathy and consolation, exhorted him to do that which he regarded with great unwillingness,[b] and offered him with open friendliness the one thing which in her poverty she possessed. And this she did, not in return for any benefit received, nor in quest of any favour to come—for she knew that he was about to die—, whereas men are by nature wont either to emulate those who have bestowed some kindness upon them or to be beforehand in flattering those from whom they may possibly receive some benefit. It is well, then, to take this woman for an example and show kindness to all who are in need, and to regard nothing as nobler than this or more befitting the human race or more likely to make God gracious and ready to bestow upon us His blessings. Concerning this woman, then, let these words suffice. [c] But now I shall touch on a subject profitable to states, peoples and nations, and of

Eulogy of the witch of Endor.

Reflections on the heroism of Saul.

[b] That is, to partake of food.

[c] Contrast the eulogy of Saul which follows (and is an addition to Scripture) with the characterization above, §§ 262 ff. So also rabbinic tradition is divided between blame of Saul's pride and praise of his heroism.

ἥκοντα τοῖς ἀγαθοῖς, ὑφ' οὗ προαχθήσονται πάντες ἀρετὴν διώκειν[1] καὶ ζηλοῦν τὰ[2] δόξαν καὶ μνήμην αἰώνιον παρασχεῖν δυνησόμενα,[3] ποιήσομαι, πολλὴν καὶ βασιλεῦσιν ἐθνῶν καὶ ἄρχουσι πόλεων ἐπιθυμίαν καὶ σπουδὴν τῶν καλῶν ἐνθήσοντα, καὶ πρός τε κινδύνους καὶ τὸν ὑπὲρ τῶν πατρίδων θάνατον προτρεψόμενον, καὶ πάντων καταφρονεῖν
344 διδάξοντα τῶν δεινῶν. ἔχω δ' αἰτίαν τοῦ λόγου τούτου Σαοῦλον τὸν τῶν Ἑβραίων βασιλέα· οὗτος γὰρ καίπερ εἰδὼς τὰ συμβησόμενα καὶ τὸν ἐπικείμενον θάνατον τοῦ προφήτου προειρηκότος οὐκ ἔγνω φυγεῖν αὐτὸν οὐδὲ φιλοψυχήσας προδοῦναι μὲν τοὺς οἰκείους τοῖς πολεμίοις καθυβρίσαι δὲ
345 τὸ τῆς βασιλείας ἀξίωμα, ἀλλὰ παραδοὺς αὑτὸν πανοικὶ μετὰ τῶν τέκνων τοῖς κινδύνοις καλὸν ἡγήσατο εἶναι πεσεῖν μετὰ τούτων ὑπὲρ τῶν βασιλευομένων μαχόμενος, καὶ τοὺς παῖδας ἀποθανεῖν μᾶλλον ἀγαθοὺς ὄντας ἢ καταλιπεῖν ἐπ' ἀδήλῳ τῷ ποδαποὶ γενήσονται τὸν τρόπον· διάδοχον[4] γὰρ καὶ γένος τὸν ἔπαινον καὶ τὴν ἀγήρω
346 μνήμην ἕξειν. οὗτος οὖν δίκαιος καὶ ἀνδρεῖος καὶ σώφρων ἔμοι γε δοκεῖ μόνος καὶ[5] εἴ τις γέγονε τοιοῦτος ἢ γενήσεται τὴν μαρτυρίαν ἐπ' ἀρετῇ καρποῦσθαι παρὰ πάντων ἄξιος· τοὺς γὰρ μετ' ἐλπίδων ἐπὶ πόλεμον ἐξελθόντας ὡς καὶ κρατήσοντας καὶ σῶς[6] ὑποστρέψοντας,[7] ἐπειδάν τι διαπράξωνται λαμπρόν, οὔ μοι δοκοῦσι καλῶς ποιεῖν ἀνδρείους

[1] Dindorf: διώξειν codd.
[2] ζηλοῦν τὰ] Bekker: ζηλοῦντα vel δηλοῦντα codd.: ζηλοῦν τὸ Niese.
[3] δυνησόμενον ROS² Exc.
[4] διαδοχὴν MSP Exc.
[5] δοκεῖν καὶ μόνος conj. Niese.
[6] ἴσως RO: σώους MSP Exc.
[7] Bekker: ἐπιστρέψοντας codd.

interest to all good men—one whereby all should be induced to pursue virtue and to aspire to those things which may procure them glory and eternal renown, one, moreover, that should instil into the hearts of kings of nations and rulers of cities a great desire and zeal for noble deeds, should stimulate them to face dangers and death for their country's sake, and teach them to despise all terrors. The occasion for this discourse I find in the person of Saul, king of the Hebrews. For he, although he knew of what was to come and his impending death, which the prophet had foretold, yet determined not to flee from it or, by clinging to life, to betray his people to the enemy and dishonour the dignity of kingship ; instead, he thought it noble to expose himself, his house and his children to these perils and, along with them, to fall fighting for his subjects.[a] He preferred to have his sons meet death as brave men rather than leave them behind, while still uncertain what kind of men they might prove to be ; for thus, as successors and posterity, he would obtain glory and an ageless name.[b] Such a man alone, in my opinion, is just, valiant and wise, and he, if any has been or shall be such, deserves to have all men acknowledge his virtue. For men who have gone forth to war with high hopes, thinking to conquer and return in safety, and have accomplished some brilliant feat are, to my mind, mistakenly de-

[a] The rabbis also emphasize Saul's heroism in exposing himself and his sons to danger in battle.

[b] That is, glory etc. would take the place of physical posterity. The last phrase is perhaps a conscious echo of ἀγήρων ἔπαινον in Pericles' funeral oration, Thucydides ii. 43.

ἀποκαλοῦντες, ὅσοι περὶ τῶν τοιούτων ἐν ταῖς ἱστορίαις καὶ τοῖς ἄλλοις συγγράμμασιν εἰρήκασιν·
347 ἀλλὰ δίκαιοι μέν εἰσι κἀκεῖνοι τυγχάνειν ἀποδοχῆς, εὔψυχοι δὲ καὶ μεγαλότολμοι καὶ τῶν δεινῶν καταφρονηταὶ μόνοι δικαίως ἂν λέγοιντο πάντες οἱ Σαοῦλον μιμησάμενοι. τὸ μὲν γὰρ οὐκ εἰδότας τί μέλλει συμβήσεσθαι κατὰ τὸν πόλεμον αὐτοῖς μὴ μαλακισθῆναι περὶ αὐτόν, ἀλλ' ἀδήλῳ τῷ μέλλοντι παραδόντας αὐτοὺς ἐπ' αὐτοῦ σαλεύειν οὔπω[1] γεν-
348 ναῖον, κἂν ἔργα πολλὰ διαπραξάμενοι τύχωσι· τὸ δὲ μηδὲν τῇ διανοίᾳ χρηστὸν προσδοκῶντας, ἀλλὰ προειδότας ὡς δεῖ θανεῖν καὶ τοῦτο παθεῖν μαχομένους, εἶτα μὴ φοβηθῆναι μηδὲ καταπλαγῆναι τὸ δεινόν, ἀλλ' ἐπ' αὐτὸ χωρῆσαι προγινωσκόμενον, τοῦτ' ἀνδρείου ἀληθῶς τεκμήριον ἐγὼ κρίνω.
349 Σαοῦλος τοίνυν τοῦτο ἐποίησεν ἐπιδείξας ὅτι πάντας μὲν προσήκει τῆς μετὰ τὸν θάνατον εὐφημίας γλιχομένους ταῦτα ποιεῖν, ἐξ ὧν ἂν αὐτοῖς ταύτην καταλείποιεν,[2] μάλιστα δὲ τοὺς βασιλέας, ὡς οὐκ ἐξὸν αὐτοῖς διὰ τὸ μέγεθος τῆς ἀρχῆς οὐ μόνον οὐ κακοῖς εἶναι περὶ τοὺς ἀρχομένους, ἀλλ' οὐδὲ
350 μετρίως χρηστοῖς. ἔτι τούτων πλείω περὶ Σαούλου καὶ τῆς εὐψυχίας λέγειν ἠδυνάμην, ὕλην ἡμῖν χορηγησάσης τῆς ὑποθέσεως, ἀλλ' ἵνα μὴ φανῶμεν ἀπειροκάλως αὐτοῦ χρῆσθαι τοῖς ἐπαίνοις, ἐπάνειμι πάλιν ἀφ' ὧν εἰς τούτους ἐξέβην.
351 (5) Κατεστρατοπεδευκότων γὰρ τῶν Παλαιστίνων, ὡς προεῖπον, καὶ κατὰ ἔθνη καὶ βασιλείας καὶ σατραπείας ἐξαριθμούντων τὴν δύναμιν, τελευ-

[1] οὐδ' οὕτω(ς) M Exc.: οὐχ οὕτως SP: non valde Lat.
[2] καταλίποιεν SP: -λίποιε M.

scribed as valiant by the historians and other writers who have spoken of such persons. Certainly it is just that these too receive approbation; but the terms "stout-hearted," "greatly daring," "contemptuous of danger" can justly be applied only to such as have emulated Saul. That men, not knowing what is to happen to them in war, should not flinch from it, but should commit themselves to an uncertain future and ride the stormy seas of chance—all this still falls short of magnanimity,[a] however many the exploits they may accomplish. On the other hand, to harbour in one's heart no hope of success, but to know beforehand that one must die and die fighting, and then not to fear nor be appalled at this terrible fate, but to meet it with full knowledge of what is coming—that, in my judgement, is proof of true valour. And this Saul did, thereby showing that it behoves all men who aspire to fame after death so to act as to leave such a name after them; especially should kings do so, since the greatness of their power forbids them not merely to be bad to their subjects, but even to be less than wholly good. I might say still more than this about Saul and his courage, for they are subjects which afford us ample material; but, lest we should appear to lack good taste in delivering this panegyric, I will return again to the point from which I made this digression.

(5) The Philistines had pitched their camp, as I said before, and were reviewing their forces by nations, kingdoms and satrapies,[b] when last of all

The Philistines compel Achish

[a] Variant "is not so magnanimous."

[b] Suggested by the LXX σατράπαι τῶν ἀλλοφύλων = Heb. *ṣarne Pelishtīm* (A.V. "lords of the Philistines"); *cf.* 1 Sam. xxix. 2 "And the lords of the Philistines passed on by hundreds and by thousands."

ταῖος βασιλεὺς παρῆλθεν Ἀγχοῦς μετὰ τῆς ἰδίας
στρατιᾶς καὶ[1] Δαυίδης μετὰ τῶν ἑξακοσίων ὁπλιτῶν
352 εἵπετο. θεασάμενοι δὲ αὐτὸν οἱ στρατηγοὶ τῶν
Παλαιστίνων, πόθεν εἴησαν ἥκοντες οἱ Ἑβραῖοι
καὶ τίνων καλεσάντων ἠρώτων τὸν βασιλέα. ὁ δὲ
Δαυίδην ἔλεγεν εἶναι, ὃν[2] φυγόντα Σαοῦλον τὸν
ἑαυτοῦ δεσπότην καὶ πρὸς αὐτὸν ἐλθόντα δέξασθαι,
καὶ νῦν τῆς χάριτος ἀμοιβὴν ἐκτῖσαι βουλόμενον
καὶ τιμωρήσασθαι τὸν Σαοῦλον συμμαχεῖν αὐτοῖς.
353 ἐμέμφθη δὲ ὑπὸ τῶν στρατηγῶν ἄνδρα παρειληφὼς
ἐπὶ συμμαχίᾳ πολέμιον, καὶ ἀποπέμπειν συνεβούλευον, μὴ καὶ λάθῃ μέγα δι᾽ αὐτὸν κακὸν τοὺς
φίλους ἐργασάμενος· καιρὸν[3] γὰρ αὐτῷ[4] παρέξειν
τοῦ καταλλαγῆναι[5] πρὸς τὸν δεσπότην κακώσαντι[6]
354 τὴν ἡμετέραν δύναμιν. ὃ δὴ καὶ προορώμενον εἰς
τὸν τόπον ὃν ἔδωκεν αὐτῷ κατοικεῖν ἐκέλευον
ἀποπέμπειν σὺν τοῖς ἑξακοσίοις ὁπλίταις· τοῦτον
γὰρ εἶναι τὸν[7] Δαυίδην, ὃν ᾄδουσιν αἱ παρθένοι
πολλὰς μυριάδας Παλαιστίνων ἀπολέσαντα. ταῦτ᾽
ἀκούσας ὁ τῶν Γιττῶν βασιλεὺς καὶ καλῶς εἰρῆσθαι
λογισάμενος καλέσας τὸν Δαυίδην "ἐγὼ μέν,"
355 εἶπε, "μαρτυρῶ σοι πολλὴν περὶ ἐμὲ σπουδὴν καὶ
εὔνοιαν καὶ διὰ τοῦτό σε σύμμαχον ἐπηγόμην· οὐ
δοκεῖ δὲ ταὐτὸ τοῖς στρατηγοῖς. ἀλλ᾽ ἄπιθι μεθ᾽
ἡμέραν εἰς ὃν ἔδωκά σοι τόπον μηδὲν ὑπονοῶν
ἄτοπον, κἀκεῖ φύλασσέ μοι τὴν χώραν, μή τινες
εἰς αὐτὴν τῶν πολεμίων ἐμβάλωσιν. ἔστι δὲ καὶ

[1] + μετὰ τοῦτον (αὐτὸν) δ᾽ (δὲ) ὁ MSPE: et post eum Lat.
[2] Niese: τὸν codd. [3] M Lat.: καὶ rell.
[4] οὕτω RO. [5] + πρόφασιν SP.
[6] Naber: κακώσαντα vel κακώσοντα codd.
[7] τὸν om. MSPE.

appeared King Anchūs with his own troops, followed by David with his six hundred soldiers. On seeing him, the Philistine generals asked the king whence these Hebrews[a] had come and who had summoned them. The king replied that this was David who had fled from Saul, his master, and had come to him; he had received him, and now David, wishing to repay that favour and to be avenged on Saul, was fighting in their ranks.[b] The generals, however, reproached him for having taken as an ally one that was their enemy, and they advised him to dismiss him lest on David's account he should unwittingly do grave mischief to his friends; for he would be affording David an opportunity of becoming reconciled to his master by injuring their army. Accordingly they bade him with this in mind to send David with his six hundred soldiers back to the place which he had given him for his habitation; for this was that same David of whom the virgins sang that he had slain many myriads of the Philistines. Having listened to these words and considering them well spoken, the king of Gitta called David and said, "For myself, I can testify to the great zeal and friendliness which thou hast shown to me, and it was for that reason that I brought thee as an ally; but such is not the view of our chiefs. Now then, go within a day's time to the place which I have given thee, and suspect nothing untoward. There keep guard for me over the country, lest any of the enemy invade it. That too

to dismiss David from his army. 1 Sam. xxix. 1.

[a] So the Hebrew, *'Ibrîm*; LXX, reading *'ôbrîm* "passers-by," has διαπορευόμενοι.

[b] This explanation of David's motives is added by Josephus.

356 τοῦτο συμμαχίας μέρος." καὶ Δαυίδης μέν, ὡς ἐκέλευσεν ὁ τῶν Γιττῶν βασιλεύς, ἧκεν εἰς Σέκελλαν. καθ' ὃν δὲ καιρὸν ἐξ αὐτῆς συμμαχήσων τοῖς Παλαιστίνοις ἀπῆλθε τὸ τῶν Ἀμαληκιτῶν ἔθνος ἐπελθὸν αἱρεῖ τὴν Σέκελλαν κατὰ κράτος, καὶ ἐμπρήσαντες καὶ πολλὴν λείαν[1] ἔκ τ' αὐτῆς ἐκείνης καὶ τῆς ἄλλης τῶν Παλαιστίνων χώρας λαβόντες ἀνεχώρησαν.

357 (6) Ἐκπεπορθημένην δὲ τὴν Σέκελλαν καταλαβὼν ὁ Δαυίδης καὶ διηρπαγμένα πάντα καὶ τὰς γυναῖκας τὰς ἑαυτοῦ, δύο γὰρ ἦσαν, καὶ τὰς γυναῖκας τῶν ἑταίρων σὺν τοῖς τέκνοις ᾐχμαλω-
358 τισμένας, περιρρήγνυται εὐθὺς τὴν ἐσθῆτα. κλαίων δὲ καὶ ὀδυρόμενος μετὰ τῶν φίλων ἐπὶ τοσοῦτον παρείθη τοῖς κακοῖς, ὥστε αὐτὸν ἐπιλιπεῖν ἤδη καὶ τὰ δάκρυα· ἐκινδύνευσε[2] δὲ καὶ βληθεὶς ὑπὸ τῶν ἑταίρων ἀλγούντων ἐπὶ ταῖς αἰχμαλωσίαις τῶν γυναικῶν καὶ τῶν τέκνων ἀποθανεῖν· αὐτὸν γὰρ
359 τῶν γεγονότων ᾐτιῶντο. ἀνασχὼν δ' ἐκ τῆς λύπης καὶ τὴν διάνοιαν πρὸς τὸν θεὸν ἀναστήσας παρεκάλεσε τὸν ἀρχιερέα Ἀβιάθαρον ἐνδύσασθαι τὴν ἱερατικὴν στολὴν καὶ ἐπερωτῆσαι τὸν θεὸν καὶ προφητεῦσαι εἰ διώξαντι τοὺς Ἀμαληκίτας δίδωσι καταλαβεῖν καὶ σῶσαι μὲν τὰς γυναῖκας καὶ τὰ
360 τέκνα, τιμωρήσασθαι δὲ τοὺς ἐχθρούς. τοῦ δ' ἀρχιερέως διώκειν κελεύσαντος ἐκπηδήσας μετὰ τῶν ἑξακοσίων ὁπλιτῶν εἵπετο τοῖς πολεμίοις· παραγενόμενος δ' ἐπί τινα χειμάρρουν Βάσελον λεγό-

[1] λείαν ἄλλην codd.: ἄλλην om. Lat.
[2] κινδυνεῦσαι RO.

[a] This last instruction to guard Philistine territory is an amplification of the LXX addition to 1 Sam. xxix. 11, φυ-

is the part of an ally." [a] So David, as the king of Gitta ordered, went to Sekella. But at the very time when he had left there to lend aid to the Philistines, the Amalekite nation had made an invasion and taken Sekella by storm, and, after setting fire to it and capturing much booty both from that town and from the rest of the Philistine territory, had retired.

David finds Ziklag sacked by the Amalekites. 1 Sam. xxx. 1.

(6) Now when David found that Sekella had been sacked and everything therein pillaged and that his two wives and the wives of his comrades along with their children had been taken captive, he straightway rent his clothes,[b] and, wailing and lamenting with his friends, he was so utterly undone by this calamity that at length even tears failed him. Moreover he was not far from being stoned to death by his comrades, who were deeply grieved by the capture of their wives and children, and held him responsible for what had happened. Recovering from his grief, however, and lifting his thoughts to God, he besought the high priest Abiathar to put on his priestly robe [c] and to inquire of God and predict to him whether, if he pursued the Amalekites, He would grant him to overtake them, and to rescue the women and children and avenge himself on his foes. And when the high priest bade him pursue, he rushed off with his six hundred soldiers on the track of the enemy. On reaching a stream called Baselos,[d] he came upon

The Israelites mourn for their captured wives and children. 1 Sam. xxx. 4.

God commands David to pursue the Amalekites 1 Sam. xxx. 8.

λάσσειν τὴν γῆν; the Hebrew says merely "And David and his men rose early in the morning to return to the land of the Philistines."

[b] The rending of the clothes is an unscriptural detail.

[c] 1 Sam. xxx. 7 "bring me hither the ephod."

[d] Bibl. Besor, LXX Βοσόρ; site unknown.

μενον καὶ πλανωμένῳ τινὶ περιπεσὼν Αἰγυπτίῳ μὲν τὸ γένος ὑπ᾽ ἐνδείας δὲ καὶ λιμοῦ παρειμένῳ, τρισὶ γὰρ ἡμέραις ἐν τῇ ἐρημίᾳ πλανώμενος ἄσιτος διεκαρτέρησε, πρῶτον αὐτὸν ποτῷ καὶ τροφῇ παραστησάμενος καὶ ἀναλαβὼν ἐπύθετο
361 τίς[1] τε εἴη καὶ πόθεν. ὁ δὲ γένος μὲν ἐσήμαινεν Αἰγύπτιος ὤν, καταλειφθῆναι δὲ ὑπὸ τοῦ δεσπότου κατ᾽ ἀρρωστίαν ἕπεσθαι μὴ δυνάμενον· ἐδήλου δ᾽ αὐτὸν[2] τῶν καταπρησάντων καὶ διηρπακότων ἄλλα
362 τε τῆς Ἰουδαίας καὶ τὴν Σέκελλαν εἶναι. χρησάμενος οὖν ὁ Δαυίδης τούτῳ ἐπὶ τοὺς Ἀμαληκίτας ὁδηγῷ καὶ καταλαβὼν αὐτοὺς[3] ἐπὶ γῆς ἐρριμμένους, καὶ τοὺς μὲν ἀριστῶντας, τοὺς δὲ καὶ μεθύοντας ἤδη καὶ λελυμένους ὑπὸ τοῦ οἴνου καὶ τῶν λαφύρων καὶ τῆς λείας ἀπολαύοντας, ἐπιπεσὼν αἰφνιδίως πολὺν αὐτῶν φόνον εἰργάσατο· γυμνοὶ γὰρ ὄντες καὶ μηδὲν προσδοκῶντες τοιοῦτον, ἀλλὰ πρὸς τὸ πιεῖν καὶ εὐωχεῖσθαι τετραμμένοι πάντες
363 ἦσαν εὐκατέργαστοι. καὶ οἱ μὲν αὐτῶν ἔτι τῶν τραπεζῶν παρακειμένων ἐπικαταλαμβανόμενοι παρ᾽ αὐταῖς ἀνῃροῦντο καὶ παρέσυρεν αὐτοῖς τὰ σιτία καὶ τὴν τροφὴν τὸ αἷμα, τοὺς δὲ δεξιουμένους ἀλλήλους ταῖς προπόσεσι διέφθειρεν, ἐνίους δὲ καὶ πρὸς ὕπνον ὑπὸ τοῦ ἀκράτου κατενηνεγμένους. ὁπόσοι δ᾽ ἔφθασαν περιθέμενοι τὰς πανοπλίας ἐξ ἐναντίας αὐτῷ[4] στῆναι, τούτους οὐδὲν ἧττον εὐχερῶς
364 τῶν γυμνῶν κατακειμένων ἀπέσφαττε.[5] διέμειναν δὲ οἱ σὺν τῷ Δαυίδῃ καὶ αὐτοὶ[6] ἀναιροῦντες ἀπὸ

[1] τίνος MSP Lat. (*cf.* LXX).
[2] Edd.: αὐτον ROM: αὐτῷ SP.
[3] αὐτοὺς om. RO.
[4] ed. pr.: τε (τ᾽) αὐτῷ codd.
[5] ἀπέσφαττον RO.
[6] αὐτὸς conj. Niese.

a straggler, an Egyptian by race, who was exhausted from want and hunger, having endured three days' wandering in the wilderness without food. After he had first revived him and restored him with food and drink, David asked him who he was [a] and whence he came. He revealed that he was of Egyptian race and had been left behind by his master, being unable to follow because of sickness; he further made known that he was one of those who had burnt and ravaged Sekella as well as parts of Judaea. So David made use of the man to guide him to the Amalekites, and came upon them lying around on the ground, some at their morning meal, others already drunken and relaxed with wine, regaling themselves with their spoils and booty. Falling suddenly upon them, he made a great slaughter of them, for, being unarmed and expecting no such thing but intent upon drinking and revelry, they were all an easy prey. Some, being surprised at the outspread tables, were massacred beside them, and their streaming blood swept victuals and food away; others were drinking each other's health when he slew them; still others, under the influence of strong drink, were plunged in sleep; while those who had been quick enough to put on their armour and make a stand against him—these too he cut to pieces with no less ease than those who lay defenceless on the ground.[b] David's companions too continued the slaughter from the first

David's men surprise the Amalekites and massacre them.
1 Sam. xxx. 15.

[a] Variant (as in Scripture) "to whom he belonged."
[b] The details of the massacre are an amplification of Scripture.

πρώτης ὥρας ἕως ἑσπέρας, ὡς μὴ περιλειφθῆναι τῶν Ἀμαληκιτῶν πλείονας ἢ τετρακοσίους· καὶ οὗτοι δὲ δρομάσι καμήλοις ἐπιβάντες διέφυγον. ἀνέσωσε δὲ τά τ' ἄλλα[1] πάντα ἃ διήρπασαν αὐτῶν οἱ πολέμιοι καὶ τάς τε αὐτοῦ γυναῖκας καὶ τὰς
365 τῶν ἑταίρων. ὡς δὲ ἀναστρέφοντες ἧκον ἐπὶ τὸν τόπον, ἔνθα διακοσίους μὴ δυναμένους αὐτοῖς ἕπεσθαι καταλελοίπεσαν ἐπὶ τῶν σκευῶν, οἱ μὲν τετρακόσιοι τῆς μὲν ἄλλης ὠφελείας τε καὶ λείας οὐκ ἠξίουν αὐτοῖς ἀπομερίζειν· οὐ συνακολουθήσαντας γὰρ ἀλλὰ μαλακισθέντας περὶ τὴν δίωξιν ἀγαπήσειν ἀνασεσωσμένας τὰς γυναῖκας ἀπολαμ-
366 βάνοντας ἔλεγον· Δαυίδης δὲ πονηρὰν καὶ ἄδικον αὐτῶν ταύτην ἀπέφηνε τὴν γνώμην· εἶναι γὰρ ἀξίους, τοῦ θεοῦ παρασχόντος αὐτοῖς ἀμύνασθαι μὲν τοὺς πολεμίους, κομίσασθαι δὲ πάντα τὰ αὑτῶν, πᾶσιν ἐξ ἴσου τοῖς συστρατευσαμένοις μερίζεσθαι τὴν ὠφέλειαν, καὶ ταῦτ' ἐπὶ φυλακῇ τῶν
367 σκευῶν μεμενηκότων. καὶ ἐξ ἐκείνου νόμος οὗτος ἐκράτησε παρ' αὐτοῖς ἵνα ταὐτὰ τοῖς μαχομένοις λαμβάνωσιν οἱ τὰ σκεύη φυλάσσοντες. γενόμενος δ' ἐν Σεκέλλᾳ Δαυίδης διέπεμψε πᾶσι τοῖς ἐν τῇ Ἰούδα φυλῇ συνήθεσι καὶ φίλοις ἀπομοίρας τῶν λαφύρων. καὶ τὰ μὲν περὶ τὴν Σεκέλλων πόρθησιν καὶ Ἀμαληκιτῶν ἀναίρεσιν οὕτως ἐγένετο.

368 (7) Τῶν δὲ Παλαιστίνων συμβαλόντων καὶ καρτερᾶς μάχης γενομένης νικῶσιν[2] οἱ Παλαιστῖνοι καὶ πολλοὺς ἀναιροῦσι τῶν ἐναντίων, Σαοῦλος δὲ ὁ

[1] Niese: τὰ ἄλλα vel τἄλλα codd.
[2] νικῶσι μὲν SP Lat.

hour until evening, so that there were left of the Amalekites no more than four hundred; these, by mounting swift camels, had escaped. So David recovered not only the booty which the enemy had carried off, but also his wives and those of his companions. When, on their return, they arrived at the spot where they had left in charge of the baggage two hundred men who were unable to follow, the other four hundred were unwilling to share with them in their gains and booty, saying that, as they had not gone along but had been unequal to the pursuit, they ought to be content with getting back their wives who had been rescued. But David pronounced this view of theirs wicked and unjust; for, he said, seeing that God had enabled them to avenge themselves on their enemies and to recover all their possessions, they were bound to give an equal share of their gains to all who had taken part in the expedition, especially as they had remained to guard the baggage. And thenceforward this law has prevailed among them, that those who guard the baggage receive the same share as those who do the fighting. Moreover, on his return to Sekella, David sent around portions of the spoils to all his acquaintances and friends in the tribe of Judah.[a] Such, then, was the affair of the sacking of Sekella and the slaughter of the Amalekites.

A dispute about spoils is equitably decided by David.
1 Sam. xxx. 21.

(7) Meanwhile[b] the Philistines had joined battle with the Israelites and, after a sharp contest, the Philistines were victorious and slew multitudes of

The Philistines defeat the Israelites at

[a] Bibl. "to the elders of Judah, to his friends" (LXX "kinsmen"). Josephus omits the names of the favoured cities, 1 Sam. xxx. 27-30.

[b] Continuing the account of the battle near Mt. Gilboa from §§ 327 ff.

τῶν Ἰσραηλιτῶν βασιλεὺς καὶ οἱ παῖδες αὐτοῦ γενναίως ἀγωνιζόμενοι καὶ πάσῃ προθυμίᾳ χρώμενοι, ὡς ἐν μόνῳ τῷ καλῶς ἀποθανεῖν καὶ παραβόλως διακινδυνεῦσαι τοῖς πολεμίοις τῆς ὅλης αὐτοῖς δόξης ἀποκειμένης, οὐδὲν γὰρ τούτου περισσότερον εἶχον,
369 ἐπιστρέφουσι πᾶσαν εἰς αὐτοὺς τὴν τῶν ἐχθρῶν φάλαγγα καὶ περικυκλωθέντες ἀποθνήσκουσι πολλοὺς τῶν Παλαιστίνων καταβαλόντες. ἦσαν δὲ οἱ παῖδες[1] Ἰωνάθης καὶ Ἀμινάδαβος καὶ Μέλχισος. τούτων πεσόντων τρέπεται τὸ τῶν Ἑβραίων πλῆθος καὶ ἀκοσμία καὶ σύγχυσις γίνεται καὶ φόνος ἐπι-
370 κειμένων τῶν πολεμίων. Σαοῦλος δὲ φεύγει τὸ καρτερὸν ἔχων[2] περὶ αὐτόν· καὶ τῶν Παλαιστίνων ἐπιπεμψάντων ἀκοντιστὰς καὶ τοξότας πάντας μὲν ἀποβάλλει πλὴν ὀλίγων, αὐτὸς δὲ λαμπρῶς ἀγωνισάμενος καὶ πολλὰ τραύματα λαβών, ὡς μηκέτι διακαρτερεῖν μηδ' ἀντέχειν ταῖς πληγαῖς, ἀποκτεῖναι μὲν αὐτὸν ἠσθένει, κελεύει δὲ τὸν ὁπλοφόρον σπασάμενον τὴν ῥομφαίαν ταύτην αὐτοῦ διελάσαι, πρὶν
371 ζῶντα συλλαβεῖν αὐτὸν τοὺς πολεμίους. μὴ τολμῶντος δὲ τοῦ ὁπλοφόρου κτεῖναι τὸν δεσπότην, αὐτὸς τὴν ἰδίαν σπασάμενος[3] καὶ στήσας ἐπὶ τὴν ἀκμὴν ῥίπτει κατ' αὐτῆς ἑαυτόν· ἀδυνατῶν δὲ[4] μήτ'[5] ὤσασθαι[6] μήτ' ἐπερείσας διαβαλεῖν αὐτοῦ τὸν σίδηρον ἐπιστρέφεται, καὶ νεανίσκου τινὸς ἑστῶτος πυθόμενος τίς εἴη καὶ μαθὼν ὡς Ἀμαλη-

[1] Σαούλου παῖδες MSP Lat.
[2] καρτερὸν στῖφος ἔχων M: καρτερὸν ἔχων στῖφος SP.
[3] + μάχαιραν SP Lat. Glycas.
[4] δὲ ins. Niese: ἀδυνατῶν RO: καὶ μὴ δυνάμενος MSPE.
[5] μηδ' codd.
[6] ἵστασθαι RO.

[a] So most MSS. of the LXX (*v.l.* Ἰωναδάβ); bibl. Abinadab.
[b] Bibl. Melchishua (Heb. *Malki-shu'a*), LXX Μελχεισά.

their adversaries. Saul, king of Israel, and his sons struggled valiantly and threw all their ardour into the fight, as though their entire glory rested solely on their dying nobly and desperately hazarding all against the enemy, for nothing else was left them. Thus they drew upon themselves the whole line of the foe and, so surrounded, perished, after laying many of the Philistines low. Now his sons were Jonathan, Aminadab[a] and Melchis.[b] When these fell, the Hebrew host took flight, disorder and confusion ensued, and there was a massacre as the enemy fell upon them. But Saul fled, having the ablest men around him; of these, when the Philistines sent javelin-throwers and archers after him, he lost all but a few. He himself, after fighting magnificently and receiving numerous wounds,[c] until he could no longer hold out nor endure under these blows, was too weak to kill himself and bade his armour-bearer draw his sword and thrust it through him before the enemy should take him alive. But, as the armour-bearer did not dare to slay his master, Saul drew his own sword himself and, fixing it with its point toward him, sought to fling himself upon it, but was unable either to push it in or, by leaning upon it, to drive the weapon home. Then he turned[d] and, seeing a youth standing there, asked him who he was, and, on learning that he was an Amalekite,

Mt. Gilboa. Saul's sons are slain. 1 Sam. xxxi. 1.

Saul, too weak to kill himself, bids an Amalekite slay him. 1 Sam. xxxi. 4; 2 Sam. i. 6.

[c] So the LXX ἐτραυματίσθη, 1 Sam. xxxi. 3, translating Heb. *wayyāḥel*, which the Targum and Jewish interpreters render "was afraid." The details of the rout are unscriptural.

[d] Josephus has combined the contradictory accounts of Saul's death given by Scripture in 1 Sam. xxxi. and 2 Sam. i. In the earlier account Saul kills himself after his armour-bearer declines to do so through fear; in the later chapter he is slain, at his own request, by the Amalekite. Josephus repeats the second account below, *A*. vii. 1 ff.

κίτης ἐστὶ παρεκάλεσεν ἐπερείσαντα τὴν ῥομφαίαν, διὰ τὸ μὴ ταῖς χερσὶν αὐτὸν τοῦτο δύνασθαι ποιῆσαι,[1] παρασχεῖν αὐτῷ τελευτὴν ὁποίαν αὐτὸς
372 βούλεται. ποιήσας δὲ τοῦτο καὶ περιελόμενος τὸν περὶ τὸν βραχίονα αὐτοῦ χρυσὸν καὶ τὸν βασιλικὸν στέφανον ἐκποδὼν ἐγένετο. θεασάμενος δ' ὁ ὁπλοφόρος Σαοῦλον ἀνῃρημένον ἀπέκτεινεν ἑαυτόν· διεσώθη δ' οὐδεὶς τῶν σωματοφυλάκων τοῦ βασιλέως, ἀλλὰ πάντες ἔπεσον περὶ τὸ καλούμενον Γελβουὲ
373 ὄρος. ἀκούσαντες δὲ τῶν Ἑβραίων οἱ τὴν κοιλάδα πέραν τοῦ Ἰορδάνου κατοικοῦντες καὶ οἱ ἐν τῷ πεδίῳ τὰς πόλεις ἔχοντες, ὅτι Σαοῦλος πέπτωκε καὶ οἱ παῖδες αὐτοῦ, καὶ τὸ σὺν αὐτῷ πλῆθος ἀπόλωλε, καταλιπόντες τὰς ἑαυτῶν πόλεις εἰς ὀχυρότητας[2] ἔφυγον. οἱ δὲ Παλαιστῖνοι τὰς καταλελειμμένας ἐρήμους εὑρόντες κατῴκησαν.

374 (8) Τῇ δ' ἐπιούσῃ σκυλεύοντες οἱ Παλαιστῖνοι τοὺς τῶν πολεμίων νεκροὺς ἐπιτυγχάνουσι τοῖς τοῦ Σαούλου καὶ τῶν παίδων αὐτοῦ σώμασι καὶ σκυλεύσαντες ἀποτέμνουσιν αὐτῶν τὰς κεφαλάς, καὶ κατὰ πᾶσαν περιήγγειλαν τὴν χώραν πέμψαντες ὅτι πεπτώκασιν οἱ πολέμιοι· καὶ τὰς μὲν πανοπλίας αὐτῶν ἀνέθηκαν εἰς τὸ Ἀστάρτειον ἱερόν, τὰ δὲ σώματα ἀνεσταύρωσαν πρὸς τὰ τείχη τῆς Βηθσὰν[3] πόλεως, ἣ νῦν Σκυθόπολις καλεῖται.
375 ἐπεὶ δὲ ἤκουσαν οἱ ἐν Ἰαβεῖ[4] πόλει τῆς Γαλαδίτιδος κατοικοῦντες, ὅτι λελώβηνται τὸν Σαούλου νεκρὸν

[1] τοῦτο . . ποιῆσαι MSP: δύνασθαι RO: διὰ τὸ . . . ποιῆσαι om. E Lat.

[2] Coccei: ὀχυροτάτας (-ωτάτας) codd.

[3] RO: Βηθσιὼν rell.: Bessam Lat.

[4] E: Ναβεῖ RO: Ἰαβ(ε)ισσῷ SP: Iabes Lat.

begged him to force the sword in, since he could not do this with his own hands, and so procure him such a death as he desired. This he did, and, after stripping off the bracelet of gold on Saul's arm and his royal crown, disappeared. Then the armour-bearer, seeing that Saul was dead, killed himself; and of the king's bodyguard not a man escaped, but all fell on that mountain called Gelboue. And when the Hebrews who inhabited the valley across the Jordan and those who had their cities in the plain[a] heard that Saul and his sons had fallen and that all his host had perished, they forsook their cities and fled to the strongholds[b]; and the Philistines, finding these cities deserted, settled therein.

1 Sam. xxxi. 7.

(8) On the morrow the Philistines, while stripping the corpses of their enemies, came upon the bodies of Saul and his sons; these they stripped and cut off their heads, and then sent tidings throughout all the country round about that their enemies had fallen. Their armour they set up as an offering in the temple of Astarte,[c] and impaled their bodies to the walls of the city of Bethsan,[d] which is now called Scythopolis. But when the inhabitants of Jabis[e] in the region of Galaditis heard that they had mutilated the corpses

The men of Jabesh-Gilead bury the mutilated bodies of Saul and his sons.
1 Sam. xxxi. 11.

[a] Of Esdraelon.

[b] Emended text; MSS. "to the strongest (cities)." Scripture says simply "they fled."

[c] 1 Sam. xxxi. 10 does not make clear where the temple was; 1 Chron. x. 10 reads "And they put his armour in the house of their gods, and fastened his head in the temple of Dagon," that is, in Philistia. Recent excavations have uncovered a Canaanite temple of the fifteenth century B.C. and figures of Astarte (bibl. Ashtoreth) in Beth Shan.

[d] Bibl. Beth-Shan, LXX Βαιθσάν (*v.l.* Βαιθέμ), modern *Beisan*, *cf. A.* v. 83 note.

[e] Bibl. Jabesh-Gilead, *cf.* § 71 note.

καὶ τοὺς τῶν παίδων αὐτοῦ, δεινὸν ἡγησάμενοι περιϊδεῖν ἀκηδεύτους, ἐξελθόντες οἱ ἀνδρειότατοι καὶ τόλμῃ διαφέροντες (ἡ δὲ πόλις αὕτη καὶ σώμασιν ἀλκίμους καὶ ψυχαῖς φέρει) καὶ δι' ὅλης τῆς
376 νυκτὸς ὁδεύσαντες ἦλθον εἰς Βηθσάν· καὶ προσελθόντες τῷ τείχει τῶν πολεμίων καὶ καθελόντες τὸ σῶμα Σαούλου καὶ τὰ τῶν παίδων αὐτοῦ κομίζουσιν εἰς Ἰάβησαν μηδὲ τῶν πολεμίων αὐτοὺς κωλῦσαι δυνηθέντων ἢ[1] τολμησάντων διὰ τὴν ἀν-
377 δρείαν. οἱ δὲ Ἰαβησηνοὶ πανδημεὶ κλαύσαντες[2] θάπτουσι τὰ σώματα ἐν τῷ καλλίστῳ τῆς χώρας τόπῳ Ἀρούρης λεγομένῳ, καὶ πένθος ἐφ' ἡμέρας ἑπτὰ σὺν γυναιξὶ καὶ τέκνοις ἐπ' αὐτοῖς ἦγον κοπτόμενοι καὶ θρηνοῦντες τὸν βασιλέα καὶ τοὺς παῖδας αὐτοῦ μήτε τροφῆς μήτε ποτοῦ γευσάμενοι.
378 (9) Τοῦτο Σαοῦλος τὸ τέλος ἔσχε προφητεύσαντος Σαμουήλου διὰ τὸ παρακοῦσαι τοῦ θεοῦ τῶν ἐπ' Ἀμαληκίταις ἐντολῶν, καὶ ὅτι τὴν Ἀβιμελέχου τοῦ ἀρχιερέως γενεὰν καὶ Ἀβιμέλεχον αὐτὸν καὶ τὴν τῶν ἀρχιερέων πόλιν ἀνεῖλεν. ἐβασίλευσε δὲ Σαμουήλου ζῶντος ἔτη ὀκτὼ πρὸς τοῖς δέκα, τελευτήσαντος δὲ δύο καὶ εἴκοσι.[3] καὶ Σαοῦλος μὲν οὕτω κατέστρεψε τὸν βίον.

[1] δυν. ἢ om. ROE. [2] καύσαντες conj. Niese (*cf.* LXX). [3] δ. καὶ εἴκοσι] duos Lat.

---

[a] Unscriptural detail.

[b] So the MSS., κλαύσαντες; Niese conjectures καύσαντες "having burnt," to make Josephus agree with Scripture, 1 Sam. xxxi. 12.

[c] So the LXX; Heb. *'ēshel*, a kind of tree; *cf.* § 251 note.

[d] *Cf.* § 336.

[e] Josephus agrees with rabbinic tradition in making the

of Saul and his sons, they were horrified at the thought of leaving them unburied, and so the most valiant and hardy among them—and this city breeds men stalwart of body and soul—set forth and, having marched all night, reached Bethsan. Then, having advanced to the enemy's ramparts and taken down the bodies of Saul and his sons, they bore them to Jabēsa, and the enemy was neither able nor dared to hinder them, because of their prowess.[a] The Jabēsēnians with public mourning[b] buried the bodies in the fairest spot in their country, called Aroura[c] (" Plowland "), and, with their wives and children, continued for seven days to mourn for them, beating the breast and bewailing the king and his sons, without touching either meat or drink.

(9) To such an end did Saul come, as Samuel had predicted, because he had disobeyed God's commandments touching the Amalekites,[d] and because he had destroyed the family of Abimelech the high priest and Abimelech himself and the city of the high priests.[e] He reigned eighteen years during the lifetime of Samuel and for twenty-two[f] years more after the latter's death. Thus then did Saul depart this life.

Brief summary of Saul's reign. *Cf.* 1 Chron. x. 13.

slaughter of the priests of Nob one of the reasons for Saul's doom, but omits reference to the sin of consulting the witch, *cf.* 1 Chron. x. 13.

[f] Or (with Lat.) " two," *i.e.* 20 years in all, instead of 40. This would agree with *A.* x. 143 and with later Jewish tradition (*Sepher Yuḥasin*) citing this passage. No figures are given in Scripture, but *cf.* the LXX addition to 1 Sam. xiii. 1 stating that Saul reigned 2 years (Luc. 30 years). On the other hand the tradition in Acts xiii. 21 gives 40 years. Rappaport suggests that a Christian scribe has changed the text of Josephus here to " twenty-two " to make it conform to the New Testament, and that the author of *Sepher Yuḥasin* is indirectly combating this view.

ΒΙΒΛΙΟΝ Ζ

(i. 1) Συνέβη δὲ ταύτην γενέσθαι τὴν μάχην
καθ' ἣν ἡμέραν καὶ Δαυίδης τοὺς Ἀμαληκίτας
νικήσας εἰς Σέκελλαν ὑπέστρεψεν. ἤδη δὲ αὐτοῦ
δύο ἡμέρας ἔχοντος ἐν τῇ Σεκέλλᾳ τῇ τρίτῃ παραγίνεται διασωθεὶς ἐκ τῆς μάχης τῆς πρὸς Παλαιστίνους ὁ τὸν Σαοῦλον ἀνελών, τήν τε ἐσθῆτα
περιερρηγμένος καὶ τῇ κεφαλῇ τέφραν περι-
2 χεάμενος. καὶ προσκυνήσας αὐτὸν πυνθανομένῳ
πόθεν ἥκοι τοιοῦτος, ἀπὸ τῆς τῶν Ἰσραηλιτῶν
μάχης ἔλεγε· γενέσθαι δ' ἀτυχὲς αὐτῆς τὸ τέλος
ἐδήλου πολλῶν μὲν ἀναιρεθεισῶν τοῖς Ἑβραίοις
μυριάδων, πεσόντος δὲ καὶ τοῦ βασιλέως αὐτῶν
3 Σαούλου μετὰ τῶν τέκνων· ταῦτα δὲ σημαίνειν
ἔφασκεν αὐτὸς παρατυχὼν τῇ τροπῇ τῶν Ἑβραίων
καὶ τῷ βασιλεῖ πεφευγότι παρών, ὃν καὶ κτεῖναι
μέλλοντα ὑπὸ τῶν πολεμίων λαμβάνεσθαι παρα-
κληθεὶς αὐτὸς ὡμολόγει· τῇ ῥομφαίᾳ γὰρ αὐτὸν
ἐπιπεσόντα διὰ τὴν τῶν τραυμάτων ὑπερβολὴν
4 αὐτὸν[1] ἀσθενῆσαι κατεργάσασθαι. καὶ σύμβολα[2]
τῆς ἀναιρέσεως ἐπεδείκνυεν τόν τε περὶ τοῖς
βραχίοσι χρυσὸν τοῦ βασιλέως καὶ τὸν στέφανον,

[1] edd.: αὐτὸν codd. [2] + δὲ (δ' P) αὐτοῦ SP Lat.

BOOK VII

(i. 1) Now this battle, as it happened, took place on the same day on which David returned to Sikella after his victory over the Amalekites.[a] And when he had already been two days in Sikella, there came, on the third day, the slayer of Saul, who had escaped from the battle with the Philistines, with his clothes rent and ashes [b] sprinkled on his head. He prostrated himself before David and, to his question whence he had come in such condition, replied, "From the battle of the Israelites." He then went on to tell that its issue had been disastrous to the Hebrews, for many tens of thousands of them had been slain and Saul, their king, had also fallen along with his sons. These things he claimed to report as one who had himself been present at the rout of the Hebrews and had been with the king when he fled, and he further confessed to having killed Saul at his own request when he was about to be taken by the enemy; for, after he had fallen upon his sword, he had been too weak, because of the great number of his wounds, to do away with himself.[c] As token of Saul's having been slain, he showed the gold ornament that had been on the king's arm and his crown, which he had

David learns of Saul's death from the Amalekite. 2 Sam. i. 1.

[a] Scripture says merely that David returned to Ziklag (Sikella) after Saul's death.

[b] Earth, according to Scripture.

[c] *Cf. A.* vi. 371 note.

ἃ περιδύσας τὸν Σαούλου νεκρὸν κομίσειεν αὐτῷ. Δαυίδης δὲ μηκέτ᾿ ἀπιστεῖν ἔχων ἀλλ᾿ ἐναργῆ τεκμήρια τοῦ Σαούλου θανάτου βλέπων καταρρηγνύει μὲν τὴν ἐσθῆτα, κλαίων δὲ καὶ ὀδυρόμενος μετὰ τῶν ἑταίρων ὅλην διεκαρτέρησε τὴν ἡμέραν.
5 ποιεῖ[1] δ᾿ αὐτῷ τὴν λύπην χαλεπωτέραν ὁ Σαούλου παῖς Ἰωνάθης πιστότατός τε ὢν φίλος αὐτῷ καὶ σωτηρίας αἴτιος γεγενημένος. τοσαύτην δ᾿ ἐπεδείξατο τὴν ἀρετὴν καὶ τὴν πρὸς τὸν Σαοῦλον εὔνοιαν, ὡς μὴ μόνον ἐπὶ τεθνηκότι χαλεπῶς ἐνεγκεῖν, πολλάκις ὑπ᾿ αὐτοῦ κινδυνεύσας ἀφαιρεθῆναι τὸν
6 βίον, ἀλλὰ καὶ τὸν ἀποκτείναντα κολάσαι. φήσας γὰρ πρὸς αὐτόν, ὡς αὐτὸς αὐτοῦ[2] γένοιτο κατήγορος ἀνελὼν τὸν βασιλέα, καὶ μαθὼν ὡς εἴη πατρὸς Ἀμαληκίτου γένος, ἐκέλευσεν αὐτὸν ἀπολέσθαι. ἔγραψε δὲ καὶ θρήνους καὶ ἐπιταφίους ἐπαίνους Σαούλου καὶ Ἰωνάθου, οἳ καὶ μέχρις ἐμοῦ διαμένουσιν.

7 (2) Ἐπεὶ δὲ τούτοις ἐξετίμησε τὸν βασιλέα, παυσάμενος τοῦ πένθους ἤρετο τὸν θεὸν διὰ τοῦ προφήτου τίνα δίδωσιν αὐτῷ κατοικῆσαι πόλιν τῆς Ἰούδα καλουμένης φυλῆς. φήσαντος δ᾿ αὐτοῦ διδόναι Χεβρῶνα[3] καταλιπὼν τὴν Σέκελλαν εἰς ἐκείνην παραγίνεται τάς τε γυναῖκας ἐπαγόμενος τὰς αὐτοῦ, δύο δὲ ἦσαν, καὶ τοὺς ὁπλίτας τοὺς
8 σὺν αὐτῷ. συνελθὼν δὲ πρὸς αὐτὸν ἅπας ὁ τῆς φυλῆς τῆς προειρημένης λαὸς ἀποδείκνυσιν αὐτὸν βασιλέα. ἀκούσας δ᾿ ὅτι τὸν Σαοῦλον καὶ τοὺς υἱοὺς αὐτοῦ θάψειαν οἱ ἐν Ἰαβησῷ[4] τῆς Γαλαδίτιδος

[1] ἐποίει SP. [2] ex Lat. Naber: αὑτοῦ ed. pr.: om. codd.
[3] Γιβρῶνα RO hic et infra: Chebron Lat.
[4] Ἰαβείσῳ M: Ἰαβεισῷ S: Ἰαβισῷ PE: Iabes Lat.

stripped from the corpse of Saul and brought to him. David, being no longer able to doubt him with these clear proofs of Saul's death before his eyes, rent his garments and continued all of that day to weep and lament together with his companions. His grief was made heavier by (the thought of) Saul's son Jonathan who had been his most faithful friend and had been responsible for saving his life. And such nobility did David show and such loyalty to Saul that not only was he grieved at his death, although he had several times been in danger of losing his own life at his hands, but he also punished the man who had killed him; he told him that he had accused himself of having slain the king, and when he learned that his father was of the Amalekite race, he ordered him to be put to death. David also composed laments and eulogies for the funeral of Saul and Jonathan, which have survived to my own time.[a]

David's grief at the death of Saul and Jonathan. 2 Sam. i. 11.

(2) After he had duly paid these honours to the king and had ceased to mourn, he inquired of God through the prophet[b] what city He granted him to dwell in among those of the tribe called Judah, and, when God answered that He granted Hebron, he left Sikella and went to that place, taking along his wives, of whom there were two, and the soldiers then with him. There all the people of the aforesaid tribe gathered to him and proclaimed him king. Now when he heard that those who inhabited Jabēsos of

God bids David dwell in Hebron. 2 Sam. ii 1.

[a] A reference to the dirge in 2 Sam. i. 19 ff.
[b] No prophet is mentioned in Scripture.

κατοικοῦντες, ἔπεμψε πρὸς αὐτοὺς ἐπαινῶν καὶ ἀποδεχόμενος αὐτῶν τὸ ἔργον, καὶ χάριτας ἀποδώσειν ἀντὶ τῆς πρὸς τοὺς τεθνηκότας σπουδῆς ὑπισχνούμενος, ἅμα δὲ καὶ δηλῶν ὡς ἡ Ἰούδα φυλὴ κεχειροτόνηκεν αὐτὸν βασιλέα.

9 (3) Ὁ δὲ τοῦ Σαούλου μὲν ἀρχιστράτηγος Ἀβεννῆρος Νήρου δὲ παῖς, ἀνὴρ δραστήριος καὶ ἀγαθὸς τὴν φύσιν, ὡς ἔγνω πεσόντα τὸν βασιλέα καὶ τὸν Ἰωνάθην καὶ τοὺς δύο τοὺς ἄλλους αὐτοῦ παῖδας, ἐπειχθεὶς εἰς τὴν παρεμβολὴν καὶ τὸν περιλειπόμενον ἐξαρπάσας υἱὸν αὐτοῦ, Ἰέβοσθος δ' ἐκαλεῖτο, διαβιβάζει πρὸς τοὺς πέραν τοῦ Ἰορδάνου καὶ παντὸς ἀποδείκνυσι τοῦ πλήθους βασιλέα πάρεξ
10 τῆς Ἰούδα φυλῆς. βασίλειον δ' ἐποίησεν αὐτῷ τὴν κατὰ μὲν τὴν ἐπιχώριον γλῶτταν Μάναλιν, κατὰ δὲ τὴν Ἑλλήνων Παρεμβολὰς λεγομένην· ὥρμησε δ' ἐκεῖθεν Ἀβεννῆρος μετὰ στρατιᾶς ἐπιλέκτου, συμβαλεῖν τοῖς ἐκ τῆς Ἰούδα φυλῆς προαιρούμενος· ὤργιστο γὰρ αὐτοῖς βασιλέα τὸν
11 Δαυίδην κεχειροτονηκόσιν. ἀπήντησε δ' αὐτῷ πεμφθεὶς ὑπὸ Δαυίδου Σαρουίας μὲν παῖς, πατρὸς δὲ Σουρί, ἐκ δὲ τῆς ἀδελφῆς τῆς ἐκείνου γεγονὼς αὐτῷ Ἰώαβος ἀρχιστράτηγος ὢν αὐτοῦ, μετὰ καὶ τῶν ἀδελφῶν Ἀβισαίου καὶ Ἀσαήλου καὶ πάντων τῶν Δαυίδου ὁπλιτῶν καὶ περιτυχὼν ἐπί τινος

[a] Bibl. Jabesh-Gilead, also called Jabis (*A.* vi. 71, 375) and Jabēsa (*A.* vi. 376).

[b] Bibl. Ish-bosheth (a deliberate alteration of the Canaanite name Ish-baal, attested by 1 Chron. viii. 33 and some LXX

Galaditis[a] had buried Saul and his sons, he sent them messages of praise and commendation for their act, and promised that he would repay them for their devotion to the dead ; at the same time he informed them that the tribe of Judah had chosen him king.

(3) When Saul's commander-in-chief Abenner, son of Ner, a man of action and of good character, learned that the king and Jonathan and his two other sons had fallen, he hastened to the camp and, carrying off his surviving son, who was called Jebosthos,[b] brought him over to the people across the Jordan and proclaimed him king of all the multitude except the tribe of Judah, and as his royal residence he appointed the city called Manalis[c] in the native tongue, which in Greek means "Camps" (Parembolai). From there Abenner set out with a picked army, intending to engage the men of the tribe of Judah, for he was angry that they had chosen David king. He was met by Joab, who had been sent by David—Joab was a son of Saruia and of Suri,[d] his mother being a sister of David whose commander-in-chief he was—and along with him were his brothers Abisai and Asaēl[e] and all of David's soldiers. Joab, coming

Abner rescues Saul's son. 2 Sam. ii. 8.

Joab's men meet Abner's in single combat. 2 Sam. ii. 13.

MSS. in this passage; *bosheth* means "shame"), LXX Ἰεβοσθέ, Ἰεβοῦσθε κτλ.

[c] Bibl. Mahanaim, lit. "camps." A corruption of Μανάειμ or the like for Heb. *Maḥanaim.* The Hebrew name is explained by Josephus in the next sentence. Here he is following the LXX, in which the words ἀνεβίβασεν αὐτὸν ἐκ τῆς παρεμβολῆς εἰς Μαναέμ contain a doublet, mistranslating the Hebrew, "and brought him over (the Jordan) to Mahanaim." The site has not been identified. It probably lay near the Jabbok river and the Jordan valley.

[d] Scripture does not give the name of Joab's father. Possibly Josephus thought of Seraiah (LXX Σαραί), the father of a Joab mentioned in 1 Chron. iv. 14.

[e] Bibl. Asahel, LXX Ἀσαήλ, Luc. Ἀσσαήλ.

κρηνίδος ἐν Γαβαὼν πόλει παρατάσσεται πρὸς
12 μάχην. τοῦ δ' Ἀβεννήρου φήσαντος πρὸς αὐτὸν
βούλεσθαι μαθεῖν πότερος αὐτῶν ἀνδρειοτέρους
στρατιώτας ἔχει, συντίθεται παρ' ἀμφοτέρων δυοκαίδεκα μαχησομένους συμβαλεῖν. προελθόντες[1]
τοίνυν εἰς τὸ μεταξὺ τῶν παρατάξεων οἱ πρὸς τὴν
μάχην ὑφ' ἑκατέρων τῶν στρατηγῶν ἐξειλεγμένοι
καὶ τὰς αἰχμὰς ἐπ' ἀλλήλους ἀφέντες σπῶνται τὰς
μαχαίρας καὶ τῶν κεφαλῶν ἐλλαμβανόμενοι κατέχοντες αὐτοὺς ἔπαιον εἰς τὰς πλευρὰς καὶ τὰς
λαγόνας ἀλλήλους ταῖς ῥομφαίαις, ἕως οὗ πάντες
13 ὥσπερ ἐκ συνθήματος ἀπώλοντο. πεσόντων δὲ
τούτων συνέρρηξε καὶ ἡ λοιπὴ στρατιά, καὶ καρτερᾶς τῆς μάχης γενομένης ἡττήθησαν οἱ τοῦ
Ἀβεννήρου· καὶ τραπέντας οὐκ ἀνίει διώκων
Ἰώαβος, ἀλλ' αὐτός τε ἐπέκειτο παρακελευόμενος
τοὺς ὁπλίτας ἐκ ποδὸς ἕπεσθαι καὶ μὴ κάμνειν
14 ἀναιροῦντας, οἵ τε ἀδελφοὶ προθύμως ἠγωνίσαντο,
καὶ διαφανέστερος τῶν ἄλλων μάλιστα ὁ νεώτερος
Ἀσάηλος, ὃς ἐπὶ ποδῶν ὠκύτητι κλέος εἶχεν· οὐ
γὰρ ἀνθρώπους ἐνίκα μόνον, ἀλλὰ καὶ ἵππῳ[2] καταστάντα εἰς ἅμιλλαν λέγουσι παραδραμεῖν, καὶ τὸν
Ἀβεννῆρον ἐδίωκεν ὑπὸ ῥύμης καὶ τῆς ἐπ' ὀρθὸν
15 φορᾶς εἰς οὐδέτερον ἐγκλιθεὶς τῶν μερῶν. ἐπιστραφέντος δὲ τοῦ Ἀβεννήρου καὶ κατασοφίζεσθαι
τὴν ὁρμὴν αὐτοῦ πειρωμένου καὶ ποτὲ μὲν εἰπόντος ἑνὸς τῶν αὐτοῦ στρατιωτῶν ἀφέμενος τῆς
διώξεως ἀφελέσθαι τὴν πανοπλίαν, πάλιν δ' ὡς

[1] ex Lat. Bekker: προσελθόντες codd.
[2] Niese: ἵππων ROM: ἵππον SP: ἵππους E Lat.

[a] Bibl. Gibeon, LXX Γαβαών. Probably the modern *el-Jib*

upon him at a certain spring in the city of Gabaōn,[a] drew up his men for battle. Abenner then said to him that he wished to discover which of them had the braver soldiers, and it was agreed that twelve men from either side should meet in combat. Accordingly there advanced to the space between the opposing lines the men who had been chosen by either of the commanders. They threw their spears[b] and then drew their swords and each, taking hold of his opponent's head and holding him fast, pierced the other's ribs and flanks with his sword until all were killed as though by agreement. And when these had fallen, the rest of the army also went into action and, after a stubborn fight, Abenner's men were defeated. Once they were routed, Joab did not relax the pursuit, but himself pressed after them and gave orders to his soldiers to follow at their heels and not weary in dealing death. His brothers also fought with eagerness, and most conspicuous among them was the youngest, Asaēl, who was famous for his fleetness of foot, for not only could he beat men, but he was said to have outrun a horse with which he had been matched in a race.[c] So he pursued Abenner with a rush, dashing straight ahead, and turning neither to the one side nor to the other. Abenner, however, turned around and attempted to talk him out of his fixed intent, first telling him to stop pursuing and take the armour of one of his own soldiers for

Defeat and pursuit of Abner.
2 Sam. ii. 17.

c. 5 m. N.W. of Jerusalem, is meant. Josephus mentions the spring in *A.* v. 58, vii. 283, where he locates it at 40 stades (*c.* 5 m.) from Jerusalem, and in *B.J.* ii. 516 at 50 stades (*c.* 6 m.).

[b] The spears are not mentioned in Scripture.

[c] Asahel's race with a horse is an invention of Josephus. Scripture says merely, " And Asahel was as light of foot as one of the roes in the field."

οὐκ ἔπειθε τοῦτο ποιεῖν κατασχεῖν αὐτὸν καὶ μὴ διώκειν παραινοῦντος, μὴ κτείνας αὐτὸν ἀπολέσῃ τὴν πρὸς τὸν ἀδελφὸν αὐτοῦ παρρησίαν, οὐ προσέμενον[1] τοὺς λόγους, ἀλλ' ἐπιμείναντα τῇ διώξει[2] φεύγων ὡς εἶχε τὸ δόρυ πλήξας εἰς τοὐπίσω
16 καιρίως παραχρῆμ' ἀπέκτεινεν. οἱ δὲ μετ' αὐτοῦ διώκοντες τὸν Ἀβεννῆρον ὡς ἦλθον ἐπὶ τὸν τόπον οὗ κεῖσθαι συνέβαινε τὸν Ἀσάηλον, περιστάντες τὸν νεκρὸν οὐκέτι τοὺς πολεμίους ἐδίωκον· ὁ δὲ Ἰώαβος αὐτὸς καὶ ὁ ἀδελφὸς αὐτοῦ Ἀβισαῖος παραδραμόντες τὸ πτῶμα καὶ τῆς πλείονος ἐπὶ τὸν Ἀβεννῆρον σπουδῆς αἰτίαν τὴν ὑπὲρ τοῦ τετελευτηκότος ὀργὴν λαβόντες, ἀπίστῳ τάχει καὶ προθυμίᾳ χρώμενοι μέχρι τόπου τινός, Ἀμμάταν[3] καλοῦσιν, ἐδίωξαν τὸν Ἀβεννῆρον, ἤδη περὶ δυσμὰς
17 ὄντος ἡλίου. ἀναβὰς δ' ἐπί τινα βουνόν, ὅς ἐστιν ἐν ἐκείνῳ τῷ τόπῳ μετὰ[4] τῆς Βενιαμίτιδος φυλῆς, αὐτούς τε κατεσκέπτετο καὶ τὸν Ἀβεννῆρον. τούτου δὲ ἀνακεκραγότος καὶ φήσαντος μὴ δεῖν ἄνδρας ὁμοφύλους εἰς ἔριδα καὶ μάχην παροξύνειν, ἁμαρτεῖν δὲ καὶ τὸν ἀδελφὸν αὐτοῦ Ἀσάηλον, ὃς παραινοῦντος μὴ διώκειν οὐκ ἐπείσθη καὶ διὰ τοῦτο βληθεὶς ἀπέθανε, συμφρονήσας καὶ παράκλησιν ἡγησάμενος τούτους τοὺς λόγους ὁ Ἰώαβος ἀνακαλεῖ τῇ σάλπιγγι σημάνας τοὺς στρατιώτας καὶ τῆς ἐπὶ

[1] προσιέμενον RO. [2] ed. pr.: τὴν δίωξιν codd.
[3] Ὀμματὸν M: ὃν Ματὸν RO: (nomine) Maton Lat.
[4] μέγας RO: corruptelam latere statuit Niese.

[a] Bibl. "with the hinder part of the spear."
[b] Bibl. Ammah, LXX Ἀμμάν, Ἀμμά, Luc. Ἐμμάθ. The site is unknown, although Scripture adds, "that lies before Giah (LXX Γαί) on the way to the wilderness of Gibeon."

himself, and then, as he could not persuade him to do this, urging him to restrain himself and give up the pursuit, lest he should kill him and so end his friendly relations with his brother (Joab). But as Asaēl paid no attention to these words and continued in pursuit, Abenner, while still in flight, with a well-aimed blow of his spear hurled backwards,[a] struck him dead on the spot. When the men who were pursuing Abenner with Asaēl came to the place where he lay, they surrounded his dead body and gave up their pursuit of the enemy. But Joab himself and his brother Abisai ran past the corpse and, finding cause for pressing still harder after Abenner in their wrath at the death of Asaēl, with incredible speed and determination pursued Abenner up to a certain place called Ammata[b] it being now about sunset. Climbing a certain hill in that place, Joab caught sight of Abenner and the men of the tribe of Benjamin who were with him.[c] Abenner then cried out and said that it was not right to stir up fellow-countrymen to strife and warfare, and furthermore that Joab's brother Asaēl had been in the wrong in not listening to him when he had urged him to give up the pursuit, for which reason he had been struck and killed. Accepting his view and considering these words as an expression of sympathy, Joab gave a signal on the trumpet and recalled his men, so putting a stop to

Abner slays Joab's brother Asahel. 2 Sam. ii. 23.

Joab makes peace with Abner. 2 Sam. ii. 27.

[c] The text is probably corrupt. Scripture says that the Benjamites were gathered together with Abner on a hill. Perhaps the variant μέγας in Josephus conceals the name Γαί (bibl. Giah), mentioned in the verse quoted in the preceding note. I suspect that the text originally read somewhat as follows: "Climbing a certain hill in Gai (in the territory) of the tribe of Benjamin, Joab caught sight of them (*i.e.* the Benjamites) and Abner."

18 πολὺ διώξεως ἐπέσχε.[1] καὶ οὗτος μὲν ἐπ' ἐκείνου
καταστρατοπεδεύεται τοῦ τόπου τὴν νύκτα ταύτην,
'Αβεννῆρος δὲ δι' ὅλης αὐτῆς ὁδεύσας καὶ περαιω-
σάμενος τὸν 'Ιόρδανον ποταμὸν ἀφικνεῖται πρὸς
τὸν τοῦ Σαούλου παῖδα εἰς τὰς Περαμβολὰς
'Ιέβοσθον. τῇ δ' ἐχομένῃ τοὺς νεκροὺς ὁ 'Ιώαβος
19 ἐξαριθμήσας ἅπαντας ἐκήδευσεν. ἔπεσον δὲ τῶν
μὲν 'Αβεννήρου στρατιωτῶν ὡς τριακόσιοι καὶ
ἑξήκοντα, τῶν δὲ Δαυίδου δέκα πρὸς τοῖς ἐννέα
καὶ 'Ασάηλος, οὗ τὸ σῶμα κομίσαντες ἐκεῖθεν
'Ιώαβος καὶ 'Αβισαῖος εἰς Βηθλεέμην καὶ θάψαντες
ἐν τῷ πατρῴῳ μνήματι πρὸς Δαυίδην εἰς Χεβρῶνα
20 παρεγένοντο. ἤρξατο μὲν οὖν ἐξ ἐκείνου τοῦ
χρόνου τοῖς 'Εβραίοις ἐμφύλιος πόλεμος καὶ διέμεινεν ἄχρι πολλοῦ, τῶν μὲν μετὰ Δαυίδου κρειτ-
τόνων ἀεὶ γινομένων καὶ πλεῖον ἐν τοῖς κινδύνοις
φερομένων, τοῦ δὲ Σαούλου παιδὸς[2] καὶ τῶν
ὑπηκόων αὐτοῦ κατὰ πᾶσαν σχεδὸν ἡμέραν ἐλατ-
τουμένων.

21 (4) 'Εγένοντο δὲ κατὰ τοῦτον τὸν καιρὸν καὶ
παῖδες Δαυίδῃ τὸν ἀριθμὸν ἕξ, ἐκ γυναικῶν
τοσούτων,[3] ὧν ὁ μὲν πρεσβύτατος ἐκ μητρὸς
'Αχίνας γενόμενος 'Αμνὼν ἐκλήθη, ὁ δὲ δεύτερος
ἐκ γυναικὸς 'Αβιγαίας Δανίηλος, τῷ τρίτῳ δ' ἐκ
τῆς Θολομαίου θυγατρὸς Μαχάμης φύντι τοῦ
Γεσσηρῶν βασιλέως 'Αψάλωμος[4] ὄνομα, τὸν δὲ
τέταρτον 'Αδωνίαν ἐκ γυναικὸς 'Αγίθης[5] προσ-

[1] ἐπισχὼν RO.
[2] ex Lat. Niese: τῶν δὲ Σ. παίδων codd. E.
[3] ἐκ . . . τοσούτων om. RO.
[4] RO: 'Αβεσ(σ)άλωμος rell. hic et infra.
[5] 'Αήθης RO.

[a] In Hebron, as Scripture adds. The sons born to David in Jerusalem are enumerated in § 70.

further pursuit. Then, while Joab encamped that night upon the spot, Abenner marched through the whole night and, after crossing the river Jordan, came to Saul's son Jebosthos at "The Camps." On the following day Joab counted the dead and gave them all burial. There had fallen about three hundred and sixty of Abenner's soldiers, and of David's nineteen beside Asaēl, whose body Joab and Abisai brought from there to Bethlehem and buried it in the tomb of their fathers; then they came to David at Hebron. Beginning with this time there was civil war among the Hebrews which lasted for a long while; those on David's side continually became stronger and came off best in the fortunes of war, while Saul's son and his subjects grew weaker almost daily.

(4) About this time also there were born[a] to David six sons by as many wives; the eldest of these, whom he had by Achina,[b] was called Amnōn; the second, by Abigaia, was Daniel[c]; the name of the third, born to Machamē,[d] daughter of Tholomaios,[e] king of the Gesserites, was Absalom[f]; the fourth, by his wife Agithē,[g] he named Adonias[h]; the fifth, son

David's six sons (born in Hebron). 2 Sam. iii. 2; 1 Chron iii. 1.

[b] Bibl. Ahinoam; *cf. A.* vi. 309, 320 notes.

[c] So in 1 Chron.; 2 Sam. Chileab (Heb. *Kileab*), LXX Δαλουιά. According to rabbinic tradition, he was really Nabal's son, born after Abigail's marriage to David; his name was Daniel but he was also called Kileab, because he resembled his father (*kelō 'ab*).

[d] Bibl. Maacah, LXX Μααχά (Chron. Μωχά).

[e] Bibl. Talmai, LXX Θολμεί, Θομμεί (Chron. Θολμεί Θοαμαί, Luc. Θολομί).

[f] Variant Abessalōm, as in LXX; Heb. *'Abshalōm.*

[g] Variant Aēthē; bibl. Haggith, LXX Φεγγείθ, Luc. 'Αγγείθ.

[h] Bibl. Adonijah (Heb. *'Adoniyyāh*); LXX 'Ορνεία, 'Ορνείλ (Chron. 'Αδωνεία, 'Αδωνίας).

ηγόρευσε, τὸν πέμπτον δὲ Σαφατίαν τῆς Ἀβιτάλης καὶ τὸν ἕκτον Ἰεθρόαν[1] τῆς Αἰγλᾶς[2] ἐπωνόμασε.
22 τοῦ δ' ἐμφυλίου πολέμου συνεστῶτος καὶ συμπιπτόντων εἰς ἔργα καὶ μάχην πυκνῶς τῶν μεθ'[3] ἑκατέρου τῶν βασιλέων, Ἀβεννῆρος ὁ τοῦ Σαούλου παιδὸς ἀρχιστράτηγος συνετὸς ὢν καὶ σφόδρα εὔνουν ἔχων τὸ πλῆθος πάντας συμμεῖναι τῷ Ἰεβόσθῳ[4] παρεσκεύασε· καὶ διέμειναν ἱκανὸν
23 χρόνον τὰ ἐκείνου φρονοῦντες. ὕστερον δ' ἐν ἐγκλήματι γενόμενος Ἀβεννῆρος καὶ λαβὼν αἰτίαν ὡς συνέλθοι τῇ Σαούλου παλλακῇ Ῥεσφᾶ μὲν τοὔνομα Σιβάτου δὲ θυγατρί, καὶ καταμεμφθεὶς ὑπὸ Ἰεβόσθου περιαλγήσας καὶ θυμωθείς, ὡς οὐ δικαίων τῶν παρ' αὐτοῦ τυγχάνοι πάσῃ προνοίᾳ περὶ αὐτὸν χρώμενος, ἠπείλησε μὲν τὴν βασιλείαν εἰς Δαυίδην περιστήσειν, ἐπιδείξειν δὲ ὡς οὐχὶ διὰ τὴν ἰδίαν ῥώμην καὶ σύνεσιν ἄρχοι τῶν πέραν Ἰορδάνου, διὰ δὲ τὴν αὐτοῦ στρατηγίαν τε καὶ
24 πίστιν. καὶ πέμψας εἰς Χεβρῶνα παρὰ Δαυίδην λαβεῖν ὅρκους τε καὶ πίστεις ἠξίου, ἦ μὴν ἕξειν αὐτὸν ἑταῖρον καὶ φίλον ἀναπείσαντα τὸν λαὸν τοῦ Σαούλου μὲν ἀποστῆναι παιδός, αὐτὸν δὲ ἀποδεί-

[1] Γεθερσὰν ROM: Γεθραάμην ex cod. Vat. Hudson: Therran Lat.
[2] Γαλαὰς RO: Γάλα M Lat.: Αἴγλης E.
[3] τῶν μεθ' cod. Vat. ap. Hudson: μεθ' rell.: utriusque regis exercitus Lat. [4] τῷ Ἰεβόσθῳ om. RO.

---

[a] Bibl. Abital; LXX Ἀβειτάλ, Ἀβιτάλ, Luc. Ἀβειταάλ (Chron. Σαβειτάλ, Ἀβιτάλ).
[b] So Luc. in Sam. and most MSS. of LXX in Chron.; bibl. Shephetaiah (Heb. *Shephatyāh*), LXX Σαβατεία.
[c] Bibl. Eglah, LXX Αἰγάλ, Ἀγλά κτλ. (Chron. Ἀλά, Ἀγλά).

of Abitalē,[a] he called Saphatias[b]; and the sixth, by Aigla,[c] he named Jethroas.[d] Now when civil war broke out and the followers of each of the two kings had frequent encounters and fights, Abenner, the commander-in-chief of Saul's son, being a clever man and enjoying very great favour with the populace, contrived to keep them on the side of Jebosthos, and for a considerable time they supported him. Later, however, when Abenner was made the object of complaints and accused of intimacy with Saul's concubine, named Respha,[e] the daughter of Sibatos,[f] and was censured by Jebosthos, he was very much hurt and angered at receiving what he thought was unjust treatment from him in spite of all the kindness he had shown Jebosthos. He therefore threatened to transfer the kingship to David and to show that it was not through his own strength and understanding that Jebosthos ruled over the people across the Jordan, but through his generalship and loyalty. Then he sent to David at Hebron[g] and asked for a sworn pledge[h] that he would own him as a comrade and friend when once he had persuaded the people to revolt from Saul's son and caused David to be

Abner transfers allegiance from Ish-bosheth to David.
2 Sam. iii. 7.

[d] Bibl. Ithream (Heb. *Yithre'ām*), LXX Ἰεθεραάμ (Chron. Ιθαράμ, Ἰεθραάμ κτλ.), Luc. Ἰεθράμ.

[e] Bibl. Rizpah (Heb. *Riṣpāh*), LXX Ῥεσφά.

[f] *Cf.* Luc. Σειβά; bibl. Aiah, LXX Ἰάλ, Ἰώλ (but Αἰά 2 Sam. xxi. 8 ff.).

[g] So Luc.; LXX εἰς Θαιλάμ, apparently Telem or Telaim, a city in the south of Judah. The Hebrew "sent messengers to David where he was, saying, 'To whom is the land?'" is corrupt.

[h] This "sworn pledge" is probably derived from the Targum's rendering of the obscure Hebrew verse quoted in the preceding note, "Let us swear by Him who made the earth."

25 ξαντα πάσης τῆς χώρας βασιλέα. τοῦ δὲ Δαυίδου ποιησαμένου τὰς ὁμολογίας, ἥσθη γὰρ ἐφ' οἷς Ἀβεννῆρος διεπρεσβεύσατο πρὸς αὐτόν, καὶ πρῶτον τεκμήριον παρασχεῖν τῶν συνθηκῶν ἀξιώσαντος ἀνασώσαντα πρὸς αὐτὸν τὴν γυναῖκα μεγάλοις ὠνηθεῖσαν ὑπ' αὐτοῦ κινδύνοις καὶ Παλαιστίνων κεφαλαῖς ἑξακοσίαις, ἃς ὑπὲρ αὐτῆς ἐκόμισε τῷ
26 πατρὶ Σαούλῳ, πέμπει μὲν αὐτῷ τὴν Μελχάλην ἀποσπάσας Ὀφελτίου τοῦ τότε συνοικοῦντος αὐτῇ, πρὸς τοῦτο καὶ Ἰεβόσθου συμπράξαντος· ἐγεγράφει γὰρ αὐτῷ Δαυίδης τὴν γυναῖκα δικαίως ἀπολαβεῖν· συγκαλέσας δὲ τοὺς γεγηρακότας τοῦ πλήθους καὶ ταξιάρχους καὶ χιλιάρχους[1] λόγους ἐποιήσατο πρὸς
27 αὐτούς, ὡς ἔχοντας ἑτοίμως ἀποστῆναι μὲν Ἰεβόσθου Δαυίδῃ δὲ προσθέσθαι ταύτης ἀποστρέψειε τῆς ὁρμῆς, νῦν μέντοι γε ἐπιτρέποι χωρεῖν οἷ βούλονται· καὶ γὰρ εἰδέναι τὸν θεὸν διὰ Σαμουήλου τοῦ προφήτου Δαυίδην χειροτονήσαντα πάντων Ἑβραίων βασιλέα, προειπεῖν δ' ὅτι Παλαιστίνους ἐκεῖνος αὐτὸς τιμωρήσεται καὶ ποιήσει κρατήσας
28 ὑποχειρίους. ταῦτ' ἀκούσαντες οἱ πρεσβύτεροι καὶ ἡγεμόνες, ὡς καὶ[2] τὴν Ἀβεννήρου γνώμην ᾗ[3] πρότερον εἶχον αὐτοὶ περὶ τῶν πραγμάτων σύμφωνον προσέλαβον, τὰ Δαυίδου φρονεῖν μετ-
29 εβάλοντο.[4] πεισθέντων δὲ τούτων Ἀβεννῆρος συγκαλεῖ τὴν Βενιαμιτῶν φυλήν· οἱ γὰρ ἐκ ταύτης

[1] καὶ χιλ. om. ROM Zonaras.
[2] καὶ om. RO.
[3] ex Lat. Niese: ἡ RO: ἣν MSP.
[4] μετεβάλλοντο ROS.

[a] *Cf. A.* vi. 203 note.
[b] Bibl. Michal; *cf. A.* vi. 204, where she is called Melcha, and vii. 85, where she is called Michalē.

declared king of the whole country. When David, pleased at the offer which Abenner had made to him through his envoys, accepted these terms, he asked Abenner to furnish a first proof of carrying out their agreement by recovering for him the wife who had been purchased by him with great perils and the heads of six hundred[a] Philistines, which he had brought as payment for her to her father Saul. Accordingly, Abenner took Melchalē[b] away from Opheltias[c] who was then living with her, and sent her to David, Jebosthos also assisting in the matter, for David had written to him that he had a just claim to recover his wife. Then Abenner called together the elders of the people and the lower officers and the captains of a thousand,[d] and addressed them, saying that when they had prepared to revolt from Jebosthos and to join David's side, he had dissuaded them from this attempt, but that now he gave them leave to go where they liked, his reason being that he knew that God, through the prophet Samuel, had chosen David king of all the Hebrews and had foretold that none other than he would chastise the Philistines and, by his victories, make them subject. When the elders and the leaders heard this and perceived that Abenner's view of the situation was in agreement with that which they themselves had previously held, they changed over to David's side; and when they had been won over, Abenner called together the tribe of Benjamin—for it was from this tribe that all the body-

David recovers his wife Michal. 2 Sam. iii. 13.

Abner's address to the Israelites in support of David. 2 Sam. iii. 17.

[c] Bibl. Phaltiel; *cf. A.* vi. 309 note.

[d] Scripture mentions only the elders. The word here translated "lower officers" (Gr. "taxiarchs") corresponded, in Josephus's time, to the Roman "military tribune" as well as "centurion," but is used here, as elsewhere in the *Antiquities*, of subordinate officers generally.

ἅπαντες Ἰεβόσθου σωματοφύλακες ἦσαν· καὶ ταὐτὰ[1] πρὸς αὐτοὺς διαλεχθείς, ἐπεὶ μηδὲν ἀντικρούοντας ἑώρα, προστιθεμένους δ' οἷς ἐβούλετο, παραλαβὼν ὡς εἴκοσι τῶν ἑταίρων ἧκε πρὸς Δαυίδην, τοὺς ὅρκους παρ' αὐτοῦ ληψόμενος αὐτὸς (πιστότερα γὰρ τῶν δι' ἄλλου πραττομένων ὅσα δι' αὑτῶν ἕκαστοι ποιοῦμεν εἶναι δοκεῖ) καὶ προσέτι τοὺς γενομένους αὐτῷ λόγους πρός τε τοὺς ἡγε-
30 μόνας καὶ τὴν φυλὴν ἅπασαν σημανῶν.[2] ὑποδεξαμένου δ' αὐτὸν φιλοφρόνως καὶ λαμπρᾷ καὶ πολυτελεῖ τραπέζῃ ξενίσαντος ἐπὶ πολλὰς[3] ἡμέρας, ἠξίωσεν ἀφεθεὶς ἀγαγεῖν τὸ πλῆθος, ἵνα παρόντι καὶ βλεπομένῳ παραδῶσι[4] τὴν ἀρχήν.

31 (5) Ἐκπέμψαντος δὲ τοῦ Δαυίδου τὸν Ἀβεννῆρον οὐδὲ ὀλίγον διαλιπὼν εἰς Χεβρῶνα ἧκεν Ἰώαβος ὁ ἀρχιστράτηγος[5] αὐτοῦ, καὶ μαθὼν ὡς εἴη παρὼν πρὸς αὐτὸν Ἀβεννῆρος καὶ μικρὸν ἔμπροσθεν ἀπηλλαγμένος ἐπὶ συνθήκαις καὶ ὁμολογίαις τῆς ἡγεμονίας, δείσας μὴ τὸν μὲν ἐν τιμῇ καὶ τῇ πρώτῃ ποιήσειε[6] τάξει συνεργόν τε τῆς βασιλείας ἐσόμενον καὶ τἆλλα δεινὸν ὄντα συνιδεῖν πράγματα καὶ τοὺς καιροὺς ὑποδραμεῖν, αὐτὸς δ' ἐλαττωθείη καὶ τῆς στρατηγίας ἀφαιρεθείη,[7] κακ-
32 οῦργον καὶ πονηρὰν ὁδὸν ἄπεισι. καὶ πρῶτον μὲν ἐπιχειρεῖ διαβαλεῖν αὐτὸν πρὸς τὸν βασιλέα, φυλάττεσθαι παραινῶν καὶ μὴ προσέχειν οἷς Ἀβεννῆρος συντίθεται· πάντα γὰρ ποιεῖν αὐτὸν ἐπὶ τῷ βε-

[1] Ernesti: τὰ αὐτὰ E: ταῦτα codd.: ista Lat.
[2] E: σημαίνων codd. [3] συχνὰς MSPE.
[4] Niese: παραδώσει ROMS^{2}P^2: παραδώσῃ S^{1}P^1: traderet Lat.
[5] ἀντιστράτηγος RO: pro eo militiae princeps Lat.
[6] Niese: ποιήσεται codd.: ποιήσηται ed. pr.
[7] ἀφεθείη RO.

guards of Jebosthos came [a]—and made the same speech to them. As he saw that they made no objection but acceded to his wishes, he took some twenty companions and came to David in order to receive his oath in person—for we all seem to have more faith in what we do ourselves than in what is done through others,—and also to acquaint him with the speech he had made to the leaders and to the whole tribe. David received him in friendly fashion and entertained him with splendid and lavish feasts that lasted many days.[b] Then Abenner asked to be dismissed and given leave to bring the people, in order that they might hand over the royal power to David when present and before their eyes.

Abner visits David at Hebron. 2 Sam. iii. 20.

(5) Hardly had David sent Abenner away when Joab, his commander-in-chief, came to Hebron and, when he learned that Abenner had been there to see David and had departed a little while before, after reaching an understanding and agreement about the sovereignty, he feared that David might give him honours of the first rank as one who would help him in securing the kingdom and who was, besides, apt in understanding matters of state and in seizing opportunities, while he himself might be set down and deprived of his command.[c] He therefore took a dishonest and evil course; first of all he attempted to calumniate Abenner to the king, urging him to be on his guard and not to pay attention to the agreements Abenner had made; for he was doing everything, he said, in order to secure the sovereignty for

Joab's envy of Abner. 2 Sam. iii. 23.

[a] Addition to Scripture.
[b] The "many days" is a detail added by Josephus.
[c] This motive for Joab's hatred of Abner is supplied by Josephus; *cf.* § 36.

βαιώσασθαι τῷ Σαούλου παιδὶ τὴν ἡγεμονίαν, ἐπὶ δὲ ἀπάτῃ καὶ δόλῳ πρὸς αὐτὸν ἐλθόντα μεθ' ἧς ἐβούλετο νῦν ἐλπίδος καὶ οἰκονομίας τῶν κατα-
33 σκευαζομένων ἀπελθεῖν. ὡς δ' οὐκ ἔπειθε τὸν Δαυίδην τούτοις οὐδὲ παροξυνόμενον ἑώρα, τρέπεται ταύτης τολμηροτέραν ὁδὸν καὶ κρίνας Ἀβεννῆρον ἀποκτεῖναι πέμπει τοὺς ἐπιδιώξοντας, οἷς καταλαβοῦσι προσέταξεν αὐτὸν καλεῖν ἐκ τοῦ Δαυίδου ὀνόματος, ὡς ἔχοντος αὐτοῦ τινα περὶ τῶν πραγμάτων πρὸς αὐτόν, ἃ μὴ διεμνημόνευσε
34 παρόντος, εἰπεῖν. Ἀβεννῆρος δ' ὡς ἤκουσε τὰ παρὰ τῶν ἀγγέλων, κατέλαβον γὰρ αὐτὸν ἐν τόπῳ τινὶ Βησηρᾶ καλουμένῳ ἀπέχοντι τῆς Χεβρῶνος σταδίους εἴκοσι, μηδὲν ὑπιδόμενος[1] τῶν συμβησομένων ὑπέστρεψεν. ἀπαντήσας δ' αὐτῷ πρὸς τῇ πύλῃ ὁ Ἰώαβος καὶ δεξιωσάμενος ὡς μάλιστ' εὔνους καὶ φίλος, ὑποκρίνονται γὰρ ἱκανῶς πολλάκις εἰς τὸ ἀνύποπτον τῆς ἐπιβουλῆς τὰ τῶν ἀληθῶς ἀγαθῶν οἱ πράγμασιν ἐγχειροῦντες ἀτόποις,
35 ἀποσπᾷ μὲν τῶν οἰκείων αὐτὸν ὡς ἐν ἀπορρήτῳ διαλεξόμενος, παραγαγὼν δὲ εἰς τὸ ἐρημότερον τῆς πύλης μόνος αὐτὸς ὢν σὺν Ἀβισαίῳ τῷ ἀδελφῷ σπασάμενος τὴν μάχαιραν ὑπὸ τὴν λαγόνα παίει.
36 καὶ τελευτᾷ μὲν Ἀβεννῆρος τοῦτον ἐνεδρευθεὶς τὸν τρόπον ὑπὸ Ἰωάβου, ὡς μὲν αὐτὸς ἔλεγε τιμωρήσαντος Ἀσαήλῳ τῷ ἀδελφῷ, ὃν διώκοντα λαβὼν Ἀβεννῆρος ἀπέκτεινεν ἐν τῇ πρὸς Χεβρῶνι μάχῃ, ὡς δὲ τἀληθὲς εἶχε δείσαντος περὶ τῆς στρατηγίας καὶ τῆς παρὰ τῷ βασιλεῖ τιμῆς, μὴ τούτων μὲν

[1] Bekker: ὑπειδόμενος codd.

[a] Joab's message is an amplification of Scripture.

[b] Bibl. Bor-sirah ("cistern of Sirah"), LXX Φρέατος τοῦ

Saul's son, and, after having come to David with deceit and guile, he had now gone away with the hope of realizing his wish and carrying out his carefully laid plans. But as he could not persuade David by these means and saw that he was not moved to anger, he turned to a course still bolder, and, having decided to kill Abenner, sent men in pursuit of him, to whom he gave orders that when they came up with him they should call to him in David's name and say that he had certain things to discuss with him concerning their affairs, which he had forgotten to mention when Abenner was with him.[a] When Abenner heard this from the messengers—they had come upon him at a certain place called Bēsēra,[b] twenty stades distant from Hebron—he turned back with no suspicion of what was to come. Joab met him at the gate and greeted him with the greatest show of goodwill and friendship—for very often those who undertake disgraceful acts assume the part of truly good men, in order to avert suspicion of their design—and then, having drawn him apart from his attendants, as if to speak with him privately, led him to a more deserted part of the gate, where he was alone with his brother Abisai, drew his sword and struck him under the flank. So died Abenner through this treachery of Joab, who claimed to have done it to avenge his brother Asaēl, for when he had pursued Abenner, the latter had caught and slain him in the fight near Hebron [c]; but in truth it was because he feared for his command of the army and his place of honour with the king, of which he himself might have been

Joab treacherously slays Abner. 2 Sam. iii. 26.

Σεειράμ, Luc. Σεειρά. The site is unidentified. Its distance from Hebron (c. $2\frac{1}{2}$ m.) is a detail added by Josephus.

[c] A slip for "Gibeon," as in Scripture and in the account given earlier by Josephus, § 11.

αὐτὸς ἀφαιρεθείη, λάβοι δὲ παρὰ Δαυίδου τὴν
37 πρώτην τάξιν Ἀβεννῆρος. ἐκ τούτων ἄν τις
κατανοήσειεν, ὅσα καὶ πηλίκα τολμῶσιν ἄνθρωποι
πλεονεξίας ἕνεκα καὶ ἀρχῆς καὶ τοῦ μηδενὶ τούτων παραχωρῆσαι· κτήσασθαι γὰρ αὐτὰ ποθοῦντες
διὰ μυρίων κακῶν λαμβάνουσι, καὶ δείσαντες
ἀποβαλεῖν πολλῷ χείροσι τὸ βέβαιον αὑτοῖς τῆς
38 παραμονῆς περιποιοῦσιν, ὡς οὐχ ὁμοίου δεινοῦ
τυγχάνοντος μὴ[1] πορίσασθαι τηλικοῦτον μέγεθος
ἐξουσίας, καὶ συνήθη τοῖς ἀπ' αὐτῆς ἀγαθοῖς γενόμενον ἔπειτ'[2] αὐτὴν ἀπολέσαι· τούτου δὲ ὑπερβολὴν
ἔχοντος συμφορᾶς, διὰ τοῦτο καὶ χαλεπώτερα μηχανῶνται καὶ τολμῶσιν ἔργα[3] ἐν φόβῳ πάντες
τοῦ ἀποβαλεῖν γενόμενοι. ἀλλὰ περὶ μὲν τούτων
ἐν βραχέσιν ἀρκεῖ δεδηλῶσθαι.

39 (6) Δαυίδης δ' ἀκούσας ἀνῃρημένον τὸν Ἀβεννῆρον ἤλγησε μὲν τὴν ψυχήν, ἐμαρτύρατο δὲ πάντας
ἀνατείνων εἰς τὸν θεὸν τὴν δεξιὰν καὶ βοῶν, ὡς
οὔτε κοινωνὸς εἴη τῆς Ἀβεννήρου σφαγῆς, οὔτε
κατ' ἐντολὴν καὶ βούλησιν ἰδίαν ἀποθάνοι. ἀρὰς
δὲ κατὰ τοῦ πεφονευκότος αὐτὸν δεινὰς ἐτίθετο,
καὶ τὸν οἶκον ὅλον αὐτοῦ καὶ τοὺς συμπράξαντας
ὑπευθύνους ἐποιεῖτο ταῖς ὑπὲρ τοῦ τετελευτηκότος
40 ποιναῖς· ἔμελε γὰρ αὐτῷ μὴ δόξαι παρὰ τὰς πίστεις
καὶ τοὺς ὅρκους οὓς ἔδωκεν Ἀβεννήρῳ τοῦτο εἰργάσθαι. προσέταξε μέντοι γε παντὶ τῷ λαῷ κλαίειν
καὶ πενθεῖν τὸν ἄνδρα καὶ τοῖς νομιζομένοις τιμᾶν
αὐτοῦ τὸ σῶμα περιρρηξαμένῳ μὲν τὰς ἐσθῆτας

[1] μὴ ins. Cocceji.
[2] Holwerda: ἔτι codd.
[3] ἔργα post φόβῳ hab. codd.: del. Holwerda.

deprived while Abenner received the foremost place from David. From this one may perceive to what lengths of recklessness men will go for the sake of ambition and power, and in order not to let these go to another; for, in their desire to acquire them, they obtain them through innumerable acts of wrongdoing and, in their fear of losing them, they ensure the continuance of their possession by much worse acts, their belief being that it is not so great an evil to fail to obtain a very great degree of authority as to lose it after having become accustomed to the benefits derived therefrom. Since this last would be a surpassing misfortune, they accordingly contrive and attempt even more ruthless deeds, always in fear of losing what they have.[a] But concerning such matters it is enough to have discoursed thus briefly.

Reflections on unbridled ambition.

(6) When David heard that Abenner had been slain, he was grieved in spirit and, with his right hand upraised to God and in a loud voice, called upon all to bear witness that he had had no share in Abenner's murder and that it was not by his command or at his own wish that Abenner had died. He also called down terrible curses[b] upon the man who had murdered him and declared his whole house and his accomplices liable to the penalties for having caused his death; for he was concerned that he himself should not seem to have brought this about in violation of the sworn pledges which he had given Abenner. Furthermore, he commanded all the people to weep and mourn for the man and to honour his body with the customary rites by rending their gar-

David protests innocence of Abner's murder, and mourns for him. 2 Sam. iii. 28.

[a] Lit. "all in fear of losing." The text is doubtful.

[b] 2 Sam. iii. 29 "Let there not fail from the house of Joab one that has an issue or is a leper or leans on a staff or falls by the sword or lacks bread."

ἐνδύντι δὲ σάκκους, ταῦτα δὲ ποιεῖν προάγοντας
41 τὴν κλίνην. αὐτὸς δ' ἐφείπετο μετὰ τῶν γεγη-
ρακότων καὶ τῶν ἐν ἡγεμονίαις ὄντων κοπτόμενός
τε καὶ τοῖς δακρύοις ἐνδεικνύμενος τό τε εὔνουν τὸ
πρὸς τὸν ζῶντα καὶ τὴν ἐπὶ τεθνηκότι λύπην, καὶ
42 ὅτι μὴ κατὰ τὴν αὐτοῦ γνώμην ἀνῄρηται. θάψας
δ' αὐτὸν ἐν Χεβρῶνι μεγαλοπρεπῶς ἐπιταφίους τε
συγγραψάμενος θρήνους αὐτὸς ἐπὶ τοῦ τάφου στὰς
πρῶτος ἀνεκλαύσατο καὶ παρέδωκε τοῖς ἄλλοις.
οὕτως δ' αὐτὸν ὁ Ἀβεννήρου συνέσχε θάνατος ὡς
μηδὲ τροφὴν ἀναγκαζόντων αὐτὸν τῶν ἑταίρων
λαβεῖν, ἀλλ' ὤμοσε γεύσεσθαι[1] μηδενὸς ἄχρι ἡλίου
43 δυσμῶν. ταῦτ' εὔνοιαν αὐτῷ παρὰ τοῦ πλήθους
ἐγέννησεν· οἵ τε γὰρ πρὸς τὸν Ἀβεννῆρον φιλο-
στόργως διακείμενοι σφόδρ' αὐτοῦ τὴν πρὸς αὐτὸν
τιμὴν ἀποθανόντα καὶ φυλακὴν τῆς πίστεως ἠγά-
πησαν, ὅτι[2] πάντων αὐτὸν ἀξιώσειεν τῶν νομιζομένων ὡς συγγενῆ καὶ φίλον, ἀλλ' οὐχ ὡς ἐχθρὸν
γενόμενον ὑβρίσειεν ἀκόσμῳ ταφῇ καὶ ἠμελημένῃ·
τό τε ἄλλο πᾶν ὡς ἐπὶ χρηστῷ καὶ ἡμέρῳ τὴν
φύσιν ἔχαιρε, τὴν αὐτὴν ἑκάστου λογιζομένου
πρόνοιαν εἰς αὐτὸν τοῦ βασιλέως ἐν τοῖς ὁμοίοις
ἧς[3] τυγχάνοντα τὸν Ἀβεννήρου νεκρὸν ἑώρα.
44 πρὸς τούτοις[4] οὖν μάλιστα Δαυίδην γλίχεσθαι
δόξης ἀγαθῆς ποιούμενον πρόνοιαν εἰκὸς μὲν ἦν,
ὡς[5] οὐθεὶς ὑπενόησεν ὑπ' αὐτοῦ φονευθῆναι τὸν
Ἀβεννῆρον· ἔλεξε δὲ καὶ πρὸς τὸ πλῆθος ὡς αὐτῷ

[1] ex Lat. Niese: γεύσασθαι codd.
[2] ἔτι RO: ἔτι δὲ ὅτι conj. Thackeray (vid.).
[3] Niese: ὁποίοις codd.: ὁποίων ed. pr.: ὁποίας Naber.
[4] πρὸς τούτοις κτλ. corrupta esse susp. Niese.
[5] εἰκὸς μὲν ἦν ὡς conj.: ὡς εἰκὸς μὲν ἦν ὡς M: ἦν εἰκὸς μὲν ἦν ὡς SP: ὡς εἰκὸς ἦν RO.

ments and putting on sackcloth, and in this fashion to escort the bier. He himself followed with the elders and those in office, beating his breast and showing by his tears both his affection [a] for him when alive and his grief for him in death, and also that the slaying had not been in accordance with his will. He then gave him a magnificent burial in Hebron and composed laments for the dead [b]; standing by his grave, he himself first began the wailing which was taken up by the others. So greatly did Abenner's death affect him that he did not take the food which his comrades forced upon him, but swore that he would taste nothing until the setting of the sun. This conduct procured for him the favour of the people, for those who held Abenner in affection were greatly pleased with him for honouring the dead man and keeping faith with him, in that he had seen fit to pay him all the customary tributes as if he had been a kinsman and friend, and had not treated him shamefully, as if an enemy, by giving him a bare and neglectful funeral; and all the others rejoiced that he was of so kind and gentle a nature, for each thought he himself would in like circumstances receive from the king the same care that he saw the corpse of Abenner receive.[c] Moreover it was quite natural [d] that David should desire to merit a good opinion by showing care (for the dead), so that [d] no one suspected that Abenner had been murdered by him. He also said to the people that he himself felt more

David's grief impresses the people favourably
2 Sam. iii. 36.

[a] There are reminiscences of Thucydides in this sentence (ἐν ἡγεμονίαις . . . τὸ εὔνουν).

[b] A reference to the brief lament in 2 Sam. iii. 33, 34.

[c] The last remarks are an addition to Scripture.

[d] Text doubtful.

μὲν οὐχ ἡ τυχοῦσα λύπη γένοιτ' ἀνδρὸς ἀγαθοῦ τετελευτηκότος, οὐ μικρὰ δὲ τοῖς Ἑβραίων πράγμασι βλάβη στερηθέντων τοῦ[1] καὶ συνέχειν αὐτὰ[2] καὶ σώζειν βουλαῖς τε ἀρίσταις καὶ ῥώμῃ χειρῶν
45 ἐν τοῖς πολεμικοῖς ἔργοις δυναμένου. "ἀλλὰ θεὸς μέν," εἶπεν, "ᾧ μέλει πάντων, οὐκ ἐάσει τοῦτον ἡμῖν[3] ἀνεκδίκητον· ἐγὼ δ' ἐπίστασθε ὡς οὐδὲν Ἰώαβον καὶ Ἀβισαῖον τοὺς Σαρουίας παῖδας ποιεῖν ἱκανός εἰμι πλέον ἐμοῦ δυναμένους, ἀλλ' ἀποδώσει τὴν ὑπὲρ τῶν τετολμημένων αὐτοῖς ἀμοιβὴν τὸ θεῖον." καὶ Ἀβεννῆρος μὲν εἰς τοιοῦτο κατέστρεψε τέλος τὸν βίον.
46 (ii. 1) Ἀκούσας δὲ τὴν τελευτὴν αὐτοῦ ὁ Σαούλου παῖς Ἰέβοσθος οὐ πρᾴως ἤνεγκεν ἀνδρὸς ἐστερημένος συγγενοῦς καὶ τὴν βασιλείαν αὐτῷ παρασχόντος, ἀλλ' ὑπερεπάθησε καὶ λίαν αὐτὸν ὠδύνησεν ὁ Ἀβεννήρου θάνατος. ἐπεβίω δ' οὐδ' αὐτὸς πολὺν χρόνον, ἀλλ' ὑπὸ τῶν Ἐρέμμωνος[4] υἱῶν Βανά,[5] ἑτέρῳ δὲ Θαηνὸς[6] ὄνομα ἦν, ἐπιβουλευ-
47 θεὶς ἀπέθανεν. οὗτοι γὰρ ὄντες τὸ μὲν γένος Βενιαμῖται τοῦ δὲ πρώτου τάγματος, λογισάμενοι δ' ὡς ἂν ἀποκτείνωσι τὸν Ἰέβοσθον μεγάλων παρὰ Δαυίδου τεύξονται δωρεῶν, καὶ στρατηγίας ἤ τινος

[1] Niese: αὐτοῦ codd.
[2] καὶ συνέχειν αὐτὰ om. MSP Lat.
[3] ὑμῖν MSP.
[4] Ἱερέμμωνος MSP: Ἐρεμμῶτος E: Remnon Lat.
[5] Βαναόθα (-ᾶ P) MSP: Βανασθάνου E: Bana (sive Bena) Lat.
[6] Θαῦνος SP: Θάννος M: Βαήβου E: Ratha Lat.

[a] Josephus properly omits the reference at this point in Scripture (2 Sam. iv. 4) to the laming of Jonathan's son Mephibosheth, with whom Saul's son Ishbosheth is confused.

than passing grief at the death of so good a man, while the fortunes of the Hebrews had suffered a great blow when they were deprived of one who could have held them together and preserved them, both by his excellent counsels and by his bodily strength in time of war. "But God," he said, "who has all things in His care will not let us see this deed go unavenged. As for me, you know that I can do nothing to Joab and Abisai, the sons of Saruia, who are more powerful than I, but the Deity will inflict upon them just punishment for their lawless deed." In such manner, then, did Abenner meet his end.

Assassination of Saul's son Ishbosheth (Jebosthos) 2 Sam. iv. 1

(ii. 1) When Saul's son Jebosthos heard of Abenner's passing, he took it not lightly to heart, for he was deprived of a kinsman and one who had procured him the kingship; indeed he suffered exceedingly and was sorely afflicted by Abenner's death. He himself did not long survive,[a] but died the victim of a plot by the sons of Eremmōn,[b] whose names were Bana[c] and Thaēnos.[d] These men, who were Benjamites[e] by birth and of the foremost rank, reckoned that if they killed Jebosthos they would receive great gifts from David and that their deed would bring them a military command or some other mark of

Josephus follows the Hebrew in making Ishbosheth, not Mephibosheth (as in the LXX), the victim of the plot narrated in the following lines.

[b] Bibl. Rimmon, LXX Ῥεμμών.

[c] Bibl. Baanah, LXX Βαανά, Luc. Βαναία.

[d] Bibl. Rechab (Heb. *Rēkāb*), LXX Ῥηχάβ. Josephus's form Thaēnos (var. Thaunos, Thannos) is puzzling. I suspect that it has arisen from a careless reading of the Targum, which translates "the name of the second (son was) Rechab" by *shum tinyānā* etc.; *tinyānā*, "second," was taken as a proper name and corrupted to Thaēnos etc. in the Greek.

[e] From Beeroth (2 Sam. iv. 5).

ἄλλης πίστεως τὸ ἔργον αὐτοῖς ἔσται παρ' αὐτῷ
48 αἴτιον, μόνον εὑρόντες μεσημβρίζοντα καὶ κοιμώμενον τὸν Ἰέβοσθον καὶ μήτε τοὺς φύλακας παρόντας μήτε τὴν θυρωρὸν ἐγρηγορυῖαν, ἀλλὰ καὶ αὐτὴν ὑπό τε τοῦ κόπου καὶ τῆς ἐργασίας, ἣν μετεχειρίζετο, καὶ τοῦ καύματος εἰς ὕπνον καταπεσοῦσαν, παρελθόντες εἰς τὸ δωμάτιον, ἐν ᾧ συνέβαινε κατακεκοιμῆσθαι τὸν Σαούλου παῖδα, κτείνουσιν αὐτόν.
49 καὶ τὴν κεφαλὴν ἀποτεμόντες καὶ δι' ὅλης νυκτὸς καὶ ἡμέρας ποιησάμενοι τὴν πορείαν, ὡς ἂν φεύγοντες ἐκ τῶν ἠδικημένων πρὸς τὸν ληψόμενόν τε τὴν χάριν καὶ παρέξοντα τὴν ἀσφάλειαν, εἰς Χεβρῶνα παρεγένοντο· καὶ τὴν κεφαλὴν ἐπιδείξαντες τῷ Δαυίδῃ τὴν Ἰεβόσθου συνίστων αὐτοὺς ὡς εὔνους καὶ τὸν ἐχθρὸν αὐτοῦ καὶ τῆς βασιλείας
50 ἀνταγωνιστὴν ἀνῃρηκότας. ὁ δ' οὐχ ὡς ἤλπιζον οὕτως αὐτῶν προσεδέξατο τὸ ἔργον, ἀλλ' εἰπών· "ὦ κάκιστοι καὶ παραχρῆμα δίκην ὑφέξοντες, οὐκ ἔγνωτε πῶς ἐγὼ τὸν Σαούλου φονέα καὶ τὸν κομίσαντά μοι τὸν χρυσοῦν αὐτοῦ στέφανον ἠμυνάμην, καὶ ταῦτα ἐκείνῳ χαριζόμενον τὴν ἀναίρεσιν, ἵνα
51 μὴ συλλάβωσιν αὐτὸν οἱ πολέμιοι; ἢ μεταβεβλῆσθαί με καὶ μηκέτ' εἶναι τὸν αὐτὸν ὑπωπτεύσατε, ὡς χαίρειν κακούργοις ἀνδράσι καὶ χάριτας ἡγήσασθαι τὰς κυριοκτόνους ὑμῶν πράξεις, ἀνῃρηκότων ἐπὶ τῆς αὐτοῦ κοίτης ἄνδρα δίκαιον καὶ μηδένα μηδὲν κακὸν εἰργασμένον, ὑμᾶς δὲ καὶ διὰ
52 πολλῆς εὐνοίας καὶ τιμῆς ἐσχηκότα; διὸ δώσετε ποινὴν μὲν αὐτῷ κολασθέντες, δίκην δ' ἐμοὶ τοῦ νομίσαντας ἡδέως ἕξειν με τὴν Ἰεβόσθου τελευτὴν[1]

[1] τῇ . . . τελευτῇ SPE.

confidence from him. So, when they found Jebosthos alone, taking his noonday rest and lying asleep with no guards present and not even the portress awake—she too had fallen asleep as a result of fatigue from the labour she had performed and the heat [a]—they made their way into the particular room where Saul's son lay asleep, and killed him. Then they cut off his head and, travelling a whole night and day [b] with the thought of fleeing from those whom they had wronged to one who would accept their deed as a kindness and offer them security, they came to Hebron. Here they showed the head of Jebosthos to David and presented themselves as his well-wishers, who had removed his enemy and rival for the kingdom. He did not, however, receive their deed in the manner which they had expected, but cried, "Vile wretches, you shall suffer instant punishment! Did you not know how I requited the murderer of Saul who brought me his gold crown,[c] and that too although he slew him as a kindness in order that the enemy might not capture him? Or perhaps you suspected that I have changed and am no longer the same man, so that I take pleasure in evil-doers and consider your regicidal deed a favour—when you slay in his own bed a righteous man who has done no one a single wrong and even showed you great friendliness and honour. You shall, therefore, make amends to him by being punished and shall give satisfaction to me for having slain Jebosthos in

David punishes Ishbosheth's murderers. 2 Sam. iv. 8

[a] In 2 Sam. iv. 6 the Hebrew reads, "And they (feminine!) came into the midst of the house, taking (or "buying") wheat,"—obviously corrupt. Josephus follows the LXX which reads, "and the portress was cleansing wheat and she became drowsy and slept."

[b] Scripture says merely "all night."

[c] *Cf.* § 5.

τοῦτον ἀνελεῖν· οὐ γὰρ ἐδύνασθε μᾶλλον ἀδικῆσαι τὴν ἐμὴν δόξαν ἢ τοῦθ' ὑπολαβόντες." ταῦτ' εἰπὼν πᾶσαν αἰκίαν αὐτοὺς αἰκισάμενος διεχρήσατο καὶ τὴν Ἰεβόσθου κεφαλὴν ἐν τῷ Ἀβεννήρου τάφῳ πάντων ἀξιώσας ἐκήδευσε.

53 (2) Τούτων δὲ τοιοῦτον λαβόντων τέλος ἧκον ἅπαντες οἱ τοῦ λαοῦ τῶν Ἑβραίων πρῶτοι πρὸς Δαυίδην εἰς Χεβρῶνα οἵ τε χιλίαρχοι καὶ ἡγεμόνες αὐτῶν, καὶ παρεδίδοσαν αὐτούς, τήν τε εὔνοιαν, ἣν ἔτι καὶ Σαούλου ζῶντος εἶχον πρὸς αὐτόν, ὑπομιμνήσκοντες καὶ τὴν τιμήν, ἣν γενόμενον τότε χιλίαρχον τιμῶντες οὐ διέλιπον, ὅτι τε βασιλεὺς ὑπὸ τοῦ θεοῦ διὰ Σαμουήλου τοῦ προφήτου χειροτονηθείη καὶ παῖδες αὐτοῦ, καὶ ὡς τὴν Ἑβραίων χώραν αὐτῷ σῶσαι καταγωνισαμένῳ Παλαιστίνους
54 δέδωκεν ὁ θεὸς ἐμφανίζοντες. ὁ δὲ ταύτης τε ἀποδέχεται τῆς προθυμίας αὐτοὺς καὶ παρακαλέσας διαμένειν, οὐ γὰρ ἔσεσθαι μετάνοιαν αὐτοῖς ἐκ τοῦ τοιούτου, καὶ κατευωχήσας καὶ φιλοφρονησάμενος ἔπεμψε τὸν λαὸν παρ' αὐτὸν ἄξοντας
55 ἅπαντα. καὶ συνῆλθον ἐκ μὲν τῆς Ἰούδα φυλῆς ὁπλιτῶν ὡς ὀκτακόσιοι καὶ ἑξακισχίλιοι φοροῦντες ὅπλα θυρεὸν καὶ σιρομάστην· οὗτοι δὲ τῷ Σαούλου παιδὶ παρέμενον· τούτων γὰρ χωρὶς ἡ Ἰούδα φυλὴ
56 τὸν Δαυίδην ἀπέδειξε βασιλέα. ἐκ δὲ τῆς Σεμεωνίδος φυλῆς ἑπτακισχίλιοι καὶ ἑκατόν. ἐκ δὲ τῆς

[a] Or, less probably, "my thoughts (or "intentions")." The last sentence is an amplification of Scripture.

[b] 2 Sam. iv. 12 "And David commanded his servants and

the belief that I should be glad of his death, for you could not have done my reputation [a] a greater wrong than by supposing such a thing." When he had so spoken, he inflicted every kind of torture [b] on them and put them to death. The head of Jebosthos he buried in Abenner's grave with every honour.

(2) When these matters had thus been brought to an end, there came to David at Hebron all the principal men of the Hebrew people, the captains of thousands and their leaders,[c] and offered themselves to him while reminding him of the loyalty they had shown him when Saul was still alive, and the honour which they had not ceased to pay him since he had become captain of a thousand; they also declared that he had been chosen king by God through the prophet Samuel, together with his sons, and that God had given him power to save the Hebrews' country by conquering the Philistines. David commended them for their devotion and urged them to continue in it, for, he said, they would have no regrets for so doing. Then, after entertaining them and treating them hospitably, he sent them to bring all the people to him.[d] Thereupon there came to him from the tribe of Judah about six thousand eight hundred armed men carrying as weapons long shields and barbed lances, who had remained loyal to the son of Saul and had not joined the tribe of Judah in proclaiming David king.[e] From the tribe of Simeon came seven thousand one hundred. From the tribe of Levi came

The tribal leaders pay homage to David at Hebron. 2 Sam. v. 1; 1 Chron. xi. 1.

The tribal forces. 1 Chron. xii. 25.

they slew them and cut off their hands and feet and hanged them beside the pool in Hebron."

[c] Scripture says merely "all the tribes of Israel."

[d] David's reply and the entertainment are not mentioned in Scripture.

[e] The last clause is a detail added by Josephus.

Ληουίτιδος τετρακισχίλιοι καὶ ἑπτακόσιοι ἔχοντες ἄρχοντα Ἰώδαμον· μετὰ τούτοις ἦν ὁ ἀρχιερεὺς Σάδωκος σὺν εἴκοσι δύο συγγενέσιν ἡγεμόσιν. ἐκ δὲ τῆς Βενιαμίτιδος φυλῆς ὁπλῖται τετρακισχίλιοι· ἡ γὰρ φυλὴ περιέμενεν ἔτι τῶν τοῦ γένους Σαούλου
57 τινὰ βασιλεύσειν[1] προσδοκῶσα. ἐκ δὲ τῆς Ἐφραΐμου φυλῆς δισμύριοι καὶ ὀκτακόσιοι τῶν δυνατωτάτων καὶ κατ' ἰσχὺν διαφερόντων. ἐκ δὲ τῆς Μανασσήτιδος φυλῆς τοῦ ἡμίσους μύριοι ὀκτακισχίλιοι.[2] ἐκ δὲ τῆς Ἰσαχάρου φυλῆς διακόσιοι μὲν οἱ προγινώσκοντες τὰ μέλλοντα, ὁπλῖται δὲ
58 δισμύριοι. ἐκ δὲ τῆς Ζαβουλωνίτιδος φυλῆς ὁπλιτῶν ἐπιλέκτων πέντε μυριάδες· αὕτη γὰρ ἡ φυλὴ μόνη πᾶσα πρὸς Δαυίδην συνῆλθεν· οὗτοι πάντες τὸν αὐτὸν ὁπλισμὸν εἶχον τοῖς τῆς Ἰούδα[3] φυλῆς. ἐκ δὲ τῆς Νεφθαλίδος φυλῆς ἐπίσημοι καὶ ἡγεμόνες χίλιοι ὅπλοις χρώμενοι θυρεῷ καὶ δόρατι, ἠκο-
59 λούθει δ' ἡ φυλὴ ἀναρίθμητος οὖσα. ἐκ δὲ τῆς Δανίτιδος φυλῆς ἐκλεκτοὶ δισμύριοι ἑπτακισχίλιοι ἑξακόσιοι. ἐκ δὲ τῆς Ἀσήρου φυλῆς μυριάδες τέσσαρες. ἐκ δὲ τῶν δύο φυλῶν τῶν πέραν τοῦ Ἰορδάνου καὶ τοῦ λοιποῦ τῆς Μανασσήτιδός φυλῆς

[1] ex Lat. Niese: βασιλεῦσαι codd.
[2] + τῶν δυνατωτάτων ROSPE.
[3] Reinach: Γαλάδου O: Γάδου rell.: Gath Lat.

[a] 4600 according to Scripture. Josephus omits the 3700 of the house of Aaron under Jehoiada (*cf.* next note).
[b] Bibl. Jehoiada (Heb. *Yehôyādā'*), LXX Ἰωαδός, Ἰωδαέ κτλ.
[c] 3000 according to Scripture.
[d] 2 Chron. xii. 33 "men that had understanding of the times, to know what Israel should do."
[e] Heb. "their leaders were two hundred and all their

four thousand seven hundred[a] with Jōdamos[b] commanding; among them were the high priest Sadok and twenty-two kinsmen as leaders. From the tribe of Benjamin came four[c] thousand armed men; for (the rest of) the tribe hesitated in the expectation that someone of the family of Saul would still be king. From the tribe of Ephraim came twenty thousand eight hundred of the ablest and exceptionally powerful men. From the half tribe of Manasseh came eighteen thousand. From the tribe of Isachar came two hundred who could foretell the future,[d] and twenty thousand[e] armed men. From the tribe of Zabulon came fifty thousand picked men, for this tribe was the only one which joined David as a whole.[f] All these had the same armour as the tribe of Judah.[g] From the tribe of Nephthali came a thousand eminent men and leaders whose weapons were shield and spear, and (the rest of) the tribe which followed was innumerable.[h] From the tribe of Dan came twenty-seven thousand six hundred[i] picked men. From the tribe of Asher came forty thousand. From the two tribes across the Jordan[k] and the rest of the tribe of Manasseh came a hundred

brothers were at their commandment" (?*'al pîhem*). Possibly Josephus has taken the words *'al pîhem* to mean "in proportion to them" and assumed that the proportion is 100 to 1. Weill suggests that Josephus read *'esrîm 'āleph*, "20,000," instead of *'al pîhem*. The LXX has merely "200, and all their brothers were with them."

[f] Apparently an interpretation of the obscure Heb. text of 1 Chron. xii. 34 "to fight without heart and heart," which some rabbinic commentators explain as "with singleness of mind."

[g] Reinach's plausible emendation for "Gad," which has not yet been mentioned.

[h] 37,000 according to Scripture.

[i] Heb. 28,600, LXX 28,800.

[k] Reuben and Gad.

ὡπλισμένων θυρεὸν καὶ δόρυ καὶ περικεφαλαίαν καὶ ῥομφαίαν μυριάδες δώδεκα· καὶ αἱ λοιπαὶ δὲ[1]
60 φυλαὶ ῥομφαίαις ἐχρῶντο. τοῦτο δὴ πᾶν τὸ πλῆθος εἰς Χεβρῶνα πρὸς Δαυίδην συνῆλθε μετὰ πολλῆς παρασκευῆς σιτίων καὶ οἴνου καὶ τῶν πρὸς τροφὴν πάντων, καὶ μιᾷ γνώμῃ βασιλεύειν τὸν Δαυίδην ἐκύρωσαν. ἐπὶ δὲ τρεῖς ἡμέρας ἑορτάσαντος τοῦ λαοῦ καὶ κατευωχηθέντος ἐν Χεβρῶνι, ὁ Δαυίδης μετὰ πάντων ἐκεῖθεν ἄρας ἧκεν εἰς Ἱεροσόλυμα.
61 (iii. 1) Τῶν δὲ κατοικούντων τὴν πόλιν Ἰεβουσαίων, γένος δ' εἰσὶν οὗτοι Χαναναίων, ἀποκλεισάντων αὐτῷ τὰς πύλας καὶ τοὺς πεπηρωμένους τὰς ὄψεις καὶ τὰς βάσεις καὶ πᾶν τὸ λελωβημένον στησάντων ἐπὶ χλεύῃ τοῦ βασιλέως ἐπὶ τοῦ τείχους καὶ λεγόντων κωλύσειν[2] αὐτὸν εἰσελθεῖν τοὺς ἀναπήρους, ταῦτα δ' ἔπραττον καταφρονοῦντες τῇ τῶν τειχῶν ὀχυρότητι, ὀργισθεὶς πολιορκεῖν ἤρξατο τὰ
62 Ἱεροσόλυμα. καὶ πολλῇ σπουδῇ καὶ προθυμίᾳ χρησάμενος ὡς διὰ τοῦ ταύτην ἑλεῖν εὐθὺς ἐμφανίσων[3] τὴν ἰσχὺν καὶ καταπληξόμενος εἴ τινες ἄρα καὶ ἄλλοι τὸν αὐτὸν ἐκείνοις τρόπον διέκειντο πρὸς αὐτόν, λαμβάνει κατὰ κράτος τὴν κάτω πόλιν.
63 ἔτι δὲ τῆς ἄκρας λειπομένης ἔγνω τιμῆς ὑποσχέσει καὶ γερῶν ὁ βασιλεὺς προθυμοτέρους ἐπὶ τὰ ἔργα τοὺς στρατιώτας παρασκευάσαι, καὶ τῷ διὰ τῶν ὑποκειμένων φαράγγων ἐπὶ τὴν ἄκραν ἀναβάντι

[1] δὲ ex Lat. ins. Niese. [2] Niese: κωλύειν codd.
[3] Ernesti: ἐμφανίζων codd.

[a] 1 Chron. xii. 37 " with all weapons of an army in war."
[b] καταφρονεῖν with the dat. has this peculiar force in Josephus. The details about the cripples on the wall are added by Josephus, who takes literally the Jebusites' state-

and twenty thousand, armed with shield, spear, helmet and sword.[a] The other tribes also used swords. All this multitude, then, assembled before David at Hebron, with a great supply of grain, wine and all sorts of food, and with one voice confirmed David as king. For three days the people feasted and made good cheer at Hebron, and then David with all of them departed from there and came to Jerusalem.

David captures Jerusalem from the Jebusites. 2 Sam. v. 6; 1 Chron. xi. 4.

(iii. 1) But the Jebusites who inhabited the city and were of the Canaanite race shut their gates against him and placed on the wall those who had lost an eye or a leg or were crippled in any way, to mock at the king; these cripples, they said, would prevent him from entering, and they so acted because of their sublime confidence[b] in the strength of their walls. David's wrath, however, was aroused and he began to besiege Jerusalem. By displaying great zeal and ardour in order to show his strength at once by the capture of the city, and to strike terror into any others who might treat him in the same manner as the Jebusites had done, he took the lower[c] city by force. As the citadel[d] still remained, the king decided to increase his soldiers' ardour for their task by the promise of honour and rewards, and offered to give to any man who should climb up to the citadel

ment in 2 Sam. v. 6, " thou shalt not come in hither unless thou remove the blind and the lame, thinking ' David shall not come in hither '."

[c] Probably the southern part of the eastern hill of Jerusalem. The topography of ancient Jerusalem is still uncertain. This " lower city " is not mentioned in Scripture.

[d] The LXX, like Josephus, has ἄκρα for Heb. *meṣûdāh* (A.V. " stronghold "), called " the City of David." This was probably north of the lower city, mentioned above, although Josephus, *B.J.* v. 137, identifies it with the S.W. hill, the upper agora, as did early Christian tradition.

καὶ ταύτην ἑλόντι στρατηγίαν ἅπαντος τοῦ λαοῦ
64 δώσειν ἐπηγγείλατο. πάντων δὲ φιλοτιμουμένων
ἀναβῆναι καὶ μηδένα πόνον ὀκνούντων ὑφίστασθαι
δι' ἐπιθυμίαν τῆς στρατηγίας, ὁ Σαρουίας παῖς
Ἰώαβος ἔφθη τοὺς ἄλλους, καὶ ἀναβὰς ἐβόησε
πρὸς τὸν βασιλέα, τὴν στρατηγίαν ἀπαιτῶν.
65 (2) Ἐκβαλὼν δὲ τοὺς Ἰεβουσαίους ἐκ τῆς ἄκρας
καὶ αὐτὸς ἀνοικοδομήσας τὰ Ἱεροσόλυμα, πόλιν
αὐτὴν Δαυίδου προσηγόρευσε, καὶ τὸν ἅπαντα
χρόνον ἐν αὐτῇ διέτριβε βασιλεύων. ὁ δὲ χρόνος
ὃν τῆς Ἰούδα φυλῆς ἦρξε μόνης ἐν Χεβρῶνι
ἐγένετο ἔτη ἑπτὰ καὶ μῆνες ἕξ. ἀποδείξας δὲ
βασίλειον τὰ Ἱεροσόλυμα λαμπροτέροις αἰεὶ καὶ
μᾶλλον ἐχρῆτο τοῖς πράγμασι, τοῦ θεοῦ προνοου-
μένου κρείττω ποιεῖν αὐτὰ καὶ λαμβάνειν ἐπίδοσιν.
66 πέμψας δὲ πρὸς αὐτὸν καὶ Εἴρωμος[1] ὁ Τυρίων
βασιλεὺς φιλίαν καὶ συμμαχίαν συνέθετο· ἔπεμψε
δ' αὐτῷ καὶ δωρεὰς ξύλα κέδρινα καὶ τεχνίτας
ἄνδρας τέκτονας καὶ οἰκοδόμους, οἳ κατασκευά-
σειαν[2] βασίλειον ἐν Ἱεροσολύμοις. Δαυίδης δὲ τήν
τε κάτω[3] πόλιν περιλαβὼν[4] καὶ τὴν ἄκραν συνάψας
αὐτῇ ἐποίησεν ἓν σῶμα, καὶ περιτειχίσας ἐπιμελη-
67 τὴν τῶν τειχῶν κατέστησεν Ἰώαβον. πρῶτος οὖν
Δαυίδης τοὺς Ἰεβουσαίους ἐξ Ἱεροσολύμων ἐκβαλὼν ἀφ' ἑαυτοῦ προσηγόρευσε τὴν πόλιν· ἐπὶ
γὰρ Ἁβράμου τοῦ προγόνου ἡμῶν Σόλυμα ἐκα-

[1] VE: Ἱέρωμος (Ἱ. R) RO: Χείραμος SP: Εἴραμος M: Chiram Lat.
[2] κατεσκεύασαν RO Lat.
[3] SP: ἄνω rell. E Lat.
[4] παραλαβὼν E: muniens Lat.

[a] Bibl. Hiram or Huram (Chron.), LXX Χειράμ.

from the valley that lay beneath it and capture it, the command of all the people in war. They all vied with each other to make the climb and, in their desire for the post of commander, did not draw back from facing any difficulty, but Joab, the son of Saruia, outdistanced the others and, when he had reached the top, shouted to the king, claiming the office of commander. 1 Chron xi. 6.

(2) When David had driven the Jebusites out of the citadel and had himself rebuilt Jerusalem, he called it the City of David and continued to dwell in it for the whole length of time that he reigned. Now the time that he ruled over the tribe of Judah alone at Hebron was seven years and six months. But after he had chosen Jerusalem for his royal residence, he enjoyed ever more brilliant fortune because of God's provident care in enhancing it and causing it to increase. Eirōmos [a] also, the king of Tyre, wrote to him, proposing friendship and alliance, and sent him gifts of cedar wood and skilled men as carpenters and builders to construct a palace in Jerusalem. And David enclosed the lower city [b] and joined it to the citadel so as to form one whole,[c] and, having put a wall around this, appointed Joab keeper of the walls. Thus David, who was the first to drive the Jebusites out of Jerusalem, named the city after himself [d]; for in the time of our forefather Abraham it was called

Jerusalem fortified by David. 2 Sam. v. 9

[b] Variant "upper city." In view of the uncertainty as to the ancient topography, it is difficult to establish Josephus's text on the basis of 2 Sam. v. 9, "And David built around from Millo and inwards." The meaning and location of "Millo" are not certain. Probably Scripture means that David joined the northern part of the E. hill (the citadel) to the southern spur, the Ophel (the lower city).

[c] Lit. "body."

[d] *i.e.* "the city of David" (1 Kings iii. 1 *et al.*).

λεῖτο, μετὰ ταῦτα δὲ αὐτὴν[1] ὠνόμασεν Ἱεροσόλυμα· τὸ γὰρ ἱερὸν[2] κατὰ τὴν Ἑβραίων γλῶτταν ὠνόμασε
68 τὰ Σόλυμα[3] ὅ ἐστιν ἀσφάλεια. ἦν δὲ πᾶς ὁ χρόνος ἀπὸ τῆς Ἰησοῦ τοῦ στρατηγοῦ ἐπὶ Χαναναίους στρατείας καὶ τοῦ πολέμου, καθ' ὃν κρατήσας αὐτῶν κατένειμε ταύτην τοῖς Ἑβραίοις καὶ οὐκέτι τοὺς Χαναναίους ἐκβαλεῖν ἐξ Ἱεροσολύμων ἐδυνήθησαν οἱ Ἰσραηλῖται, μέχρις ὁ Δαυίδης αὐτοὺς ἐξεπολιόρκησεν, ἔτη πεντακόσια καὶ δέκα καὶ πέντε.

69 (3) Ποιήσομαι δὲ καὶ μνήμην Ὀρόννα[4] πλουσίου μὲν ἀνδρὸς τῶν Ἰεβουσαίων, οὐκ ἀναιρεθέντος δὲ ἐν τῇ Ἱεροσολύμων πολιορκίᾳ ὑπὸ Δαυίδου διὰ τὴν πρὸς τοὺς Ἑβραίους εὔνοιαν αὐτοῦ καί τινα καὶ χάριν καὶ σπουδὴν πρὸς αὐτὸν γενομένην τὸν

[1] post αὐτήν] φασί τινες ὅτι καὶ Ὅμηρος ταῦτ' add. codd.
[2] ἱεροῦ RO: ἱερὸν (τὰ) Σόλυμα MSP.
[3] τὰ Σόλυμα om. MSP.
[4] Hudson (*cf.* § 329): Ὀρφόνα M: Ὀρφνᾶ ROSPLV: Orfin Lat.

---

[a] "But afterwards" etc.: text doubtful. The MSS. read "but some say that afterwards Homer called it Hierosolyma"; these words are probably a gloss, although in *Ap.* i. 172 f. Josephus, quoting from the Greek poet Choerilus (a contemporary of Herodotus), who alludes to the "Solymian hills" after Homer (*Od.* v. 283), identifies them with Jerusalem. In view of the reference in *B.J.* vi. 438 f. (*cf.* also *A.* i. 180) to Melchizedek, who "gave the city, previously called Solyma, the name of Jerusalem," Niese (*Praef.* vol. i. p. xxxii) has reconstructed the present passage as follows: μετὰ ταῦτα δ' αὐτὴν Μελχισεδέκης ὁ τῶν Χαναναιων δυνάστης τειχίσας καὶ ἀσφαλισάμενος Ἱεροσόλυμα ὠνόμασε· τὸ γὰρ ἱεροῦ κατὰ τὴν Ἑβραίων γλῶττάν ἐστιν ἀσφάλεια, "afterwards Melchisedekēs, the ruler of the Canaanites, built walls around it and made it secure, and called it Hierosolyma, for *hierou* in Hebrew means 'security.'" Niese questions

Solyma, but afterwards they named it Hierosolyma, calling the temple (*hieron*) Solyma, which, in the Hebrew tongue, means " security." [a] Now the whole period from the time of Joshua, the commander of the expedition and war against the Canaanites in which he conquered them and apportioned this (city) to the Hebrews [b]—although the Israelites were not able to drive the Canaanites out of Jerusalem—until David took it from them by siege, was five hundred and fifteen years.[c]

(3) I shall also make mention here of Oronnas,[d] who was a wealthy Jebusite but was not slain by David in the siege of Jerusalem because of his friendliness to the Hebrews and also because of a certain kindness and devotion to the king himself which I shall

the genuineness of the reference to the temple (ἱερόν) in our text, but it is difficult to believe that Josephus connected *hierou* (as Niese gives it), rather than Solyma, with the Hebrew word for " security," *i.e. shālôm*.

[b] Jos. x. 5 ff.

[c] This figure agrees with that in *A*. viii. 61, where Josephus reckons 592 years from the Exodus to the building of the temple in Solomon's fourth year (Scripture gives 480 years for this period, 1 Kings vi. 1); if we subtract from 592 the sum of 77 years (40 years for the activity of Moses + 33 years for David's reign in Jerusalem + 4 years for the reign of Solomon before the building of the temple), we get the above figure of 515 years for the period between the conquest of Canaan by Joshua and the conquest of Jerusalem by David. But Josephus has no consistent scheme of Biblical chronology, for in *A*. xx. 230 and *Ap*. ii. 19 he gives 612 instead of 592 years for the interval between the Exodus and the building of the temple. Moreover, Weill finds that the figures given in *A*. bks. v.-vii. for the various judges and rulers between Joshua and Solomon add up to only 504½ years.

[d] Bibl. Arauna (Chron. Ornan), LXX Ὀρνά. Scripture first mentions him in 2 Sam. xxiv. 16.

βασιλέα, ἣν μικρὸν ὕστερον εὐκαιρότερον σημανῶ
70 ἔγημε δὲ καὶ ἄλλας γυναῖκας πρὸς ταῖς οὔσαις
αὐτῷ Δαυίδης καὶ παλλακὰς ἔσχεν. ἐποιήσατο δὲ
καὶ παῖδας ἕνδεκα[1] τὸν ἀριθμόν, οὓς προσηγόρευσεν
Ἀμασέ, Ἀμνοῦ, Σεβάν, Νάθαν, Σολομῶνα, Ἰεβαρῆ,
Ἐλιήν, Φαλναγέην, Ναφήν, Ἰεναέ, Ἐλιφαλέ,[2] ἔτι
δὲ καὶ θυγατέρα Θαμάραν. τούτων οἱ μὲν ἐννέα
ἐξ εὐγενίδων ἦσαν γεγονότες, οὓς δὲ τελευταίους
εἰρήκαμεν δύο ἐκ τῶν παλλακίδων. Θαμάρα δὲ
ὁμομήτριος Ἀψαλώμῳ ἦν.
71 (iv. 1) Γνόντες δ' οἱ Παλαιστῖνοι τὸν Δαυίδην
βασιλέα ὑπὸ τῶν Ἑβραίων ἀποδεδειγμένον στρατεύουσιν ἐπ' αὐτὸν εἰς Ἱεροσόλυμα· καὶ καταλαβόμενοι τὴν κοιλάδα τῶν Γιγάντων[3] καλουμένην, τόπος δέ ἐστιν οὐ πόρρω τῆς πόλεως, ἐν αὐτῇ
72 στρατοπεδεύονται. ὁ δὲ τῶν Ἰουδαίων βασιλεὺς
(οὐδὲν γὰρ ἄνευ προφητείας καὶ τοῦ κελεῦσαι τὸν θεὸν καὶ περὶ τῶν ἐσομένων λαβεῖν ἐγγυητὴν ἐκεῖνον ἑαυτῷ ποιεῖν ἐπέτρεπεν) ἐκέλευσε τὸν ἀρχιερέα τί δοκεῖ τῷ θεῷ καὶ ποδαπὸν ἔσται τὸ
73 τέλος τῆς μάχης προλέγειν αὐτῷ. προφητεύσαντος
δὲ νίκην καὶ κράτος ἐξάγει τὴν δύναμιν ἐπὶ τοὺς

[1] ed. pr.: ἐννέα codd.
[2] Ἀμασέ . . . Ἐλιφαλέ] cf. Hudson ad loc.: "innumeras et monstrosas illorum varietates . . . referre piget."
[3] Τιτάνων SP.

[a] §§ 329 ff.
[b] It is impossible to restore the correct forms of these names in Josephus's text, except those of Nathan and Solomon. Moreover, three separate lists are found in Scripture and neither in the Hebrew nor in the Greek do the various lists exactly agree. It may suffice to give the Biblical forms found in the first passage, 2 Sam. v. 14: Shammua, Shobab, Nathan, Solomon, Ibhar, Elishua, Nepheg, Japhia, Elishama,

point out a little later in a more suitable place.[a] Now David married still other wives in addition to those he had, and took concubines and begot eleven sons whom he named Amase, Amnū, Seba, Nathan, Solomon, Jebarē, Eliēs, Phalnageēs, Naphēs, Jenaë, Eliphale,[b] and also a daughter, Thamara.[c] Of these nine were the offspring of well-born mothers, but the two last mentioned, of concubines.[d] Thamara had the same mother as Absalom.

David's children. 2 Sam. v. 13; 1 Chron. iii. 5, xiv. 4.

(iv. 1) When the Philistines learned that David had been chosen by the Hebrews as their king, they marched against him to Jerusalem and, when they had taken the so-called Valley of the Giants[e]—this is a place not far from the city,—they encamped there. But the king of the Jews, who permitted himself to do nothing without an oracle and a command from God and without having Him as surety for the future, ordered the high priest[f] to foretell to him what was God's pleasure and what the outcome of the battle would be; and when he prophesied a decisive victory,[g] David led his force out against the

The Philistines are defeated by David. 2 Sam. v. 17; 1 Chron. xiv. 8.

Eliada, Eliphelet. The two lists in Chron. repeat Eliphelet and add Nogah, giving 13 names.

[c] Bibl. Tamar, LXX Θαμάρ, Θημάρ.

[d] Scripture implies that none of the eleven were sons of concubines, 1 Chron. iii. 9 "all these were the sons of David beside the sons of the concubines." The preceding verse, however, ends with the word "nine" (wrongly reckoning the number of sons), and Josephus apparently took it to refer to the number of well-born sons.

[e] So the LXX in Chronicles; in Samuel the LXX has Τιτάνων (*cf.* the variant in Josephus); bibl. Valley of Rephaim. Rephaim was traditionally taken to mean "giants." The site is probably the modern *el Buqei'a*, the plain S.W. of Jerusalem.

[f] In Scripture David consults God directly.

[g] Lit. "victory and mastery." This phrase occurs several times in the early books of the *Antiquities*.

Παλαιστίνους· καὶ γενομένης συμβολῆς αὐτὸς κατόπιν αἰφνιδίως ἐπιπεσὼν τοῖς πολεμίοις τοὺς μὲν αὐτῶν ἀπέκτεινε, τοὺς δὲ εἰς φυγὴν ἐτρέψατο.
74 ὑπολάβῃ δὲ μηδεὶς ὀλίγην τὴν τῶν Παλαιστίνων στρατιὰν ἐλθεῖν ἐπὶ τοὺς Ἑβραίους τῷ τάχει τῆς ἥττης καὶ τῷ μηδὲν ἔργον ἐπιδείξασθαι γενναῖον μηδὲ μαρτυρίας ἄξιον στοχαζόμενος αὐτῶν τὴν βραδυτῆτα καὶ τὴν ἀγένειαν, ἀλλὰ γινωσκέτω Συρίαν τε ἅπασαν καὶ Φοινίκην καὶ πρὸς τούτοις ἄλλα ἔθνη πολλὰ καὶ μάχιμα συστρατεῦσαι αὐτοῖς
75 καὶ τοῦ πολέμου κοινωνῆσαι· ὃ καὶ μόνον ἦν αἴτιον τοσαυτάκις αὐτοῖς νικωμένοις καὶ πολλὰς ἀποβαλοῦσι μυριάδας μετὰ μείζονος ἐπιέναι τοῖς Ἑβραίοις δυνάμεως. ἀμέλει καὶ ταύταις πταίσαντες ταῖς μάχαις τριπλάσιος στρατὸς ἐπῆλθε τῷ Δαυίδῃ καὶ εἰς ταὐτὸ χωρίον ἐστρατοπεδεύσατο.
76 πάλιν δὲ τοῦ βασιλέως τῶν Ἰσραηλιτῶν ἐρομένου τὸν θεὸν περὶ τῆς περὶ τὴν μάχην ἐξόδου, προφητεύει ὁ ἀρχιερεὺς ἐν τοῖς ἄλσεσι τοῖς καλουμένοις Κλαυθμῶσι κατέχειν τὴν στρατιὰν οὐκ ἄπωθεν[1] τοῦ τῶν πολεμίων στρατοπέδου, κινεῖν δ' αὐτὸν μὴ πρότερον μηδ' ἄρχεσθαι τῆς μάχης, πρὶν ἢ τὰ
77 ἄλση σαλεύεσθαι μὴ πνέοντος ἀνέμου. ὡς δ' ἐσαλεύθη τὰ ἄλση καὶ ὁ καιρὸς ὃν αὐτῷ προεῖπεν ὁ θεὸς παρῆν, οὐδὲν ἐπισχὼν ἐφ' ἑτοίμην ἤδη καὶ φανερὰν ἐξῆλθε τὴν νίκην· οὐ γὰρ ὑπέμειναν αὐτὸν

[1] + *μὲν οὖσι* MSP Lat.: + *οὖσι* E.

[a] According to Scripture, it was in the second battle with the Philistines (described below) that David took them by surprise in the rear.

[b] The participation of other nations in the war is an invention of Josephus.

[c] Unscriptural detail.

[d] *Cf.* § 72 note.

Philistines. At the first encounter he fell suddenly upon the enemy's rear,[a] slew part of them and put the rest to flight. Let no one, however, suppose that it was a small army of Philistines that came against the Hebrews, or infer from the swiftness of their defeat or from their failure to perform any courageous or noteworthy act that there was any reluctance or cowardice on their part; on the contrary, it should be known that all Syria and Phoenicia and beside them many other warlike nations fought along with them and took part in the war.[b] It was for this reason alone that, after having been defeated so often and lost so many tens of thousands, they attacked the Hebrews with a larger force. In fact, after their discomfiture in these battles, they came against David with an army three times as large,[c] and encamped on the same site. Again the Israelites' king inquired of God concerning the issue of the battle, and the high priest[d] gave the prophetic warning to hold his army in the so-called Weeping Groves[e] not far from the enemy's camp, and not to move nor begin battle until the grove should be agitated with no wind blowing. And, when the grove was agitated and the moment came which God had foretold to him,[f] he delayed no longer but went out to seize the victory which he saw awaiting him. The enemy's

David's second victory over the Philistines. 2 Sam. v. 22; 1 Chron. xiv. 13.

[e] So the LXX, ἀπὸ τοῦ ἄλσους τοῦ κλαυθμῶνος, translating Heb. *mimmûl bekā'îm* "opposite the balsam(?)-trees" (A.V. "mulberry-trees") as if *bekā'îm* were from the root *bkh* "to weep." The Targum and other versions correctly take *bekā'îm* as a kind of tree, as does the LXX in Chronicles, πλησίον τῶν ἀπίων "near the pear-trees."

[f] 2 Sam. v. 24 "when thou hearest the sound of marching in the tops of the balsam-trees, then thou shalt bestir thyself, for then is the Lord gone out before thee to smite the camp of the Philistines."

αἱ τῶν πολεμίων φάλαγγες, ἀλλ' εὐθὺς ἀπὸ τῆς πρώτης συμβολῆς τραπέντας ἐνέκειτο κτείνων· καὶ διώκει μὲν αὐτοὺς ἄχρι πόλεως Γαζάρων, ἥ δ' ἐστὶν ὅρος αὐτῶν τῆς χώρας, διαρπάζει δ'[1] αὐτῶν τὴν παρεμβολὴν καὶ πολὺν εὑρὼν ἐν αὐτῇ πλοῦτον, καὶ τοὺς θεοὺς αὐτῶν διέφθειρε.

78 (2) Τοιαύτης δ' ἀποβάσης καὶ ταύτης τῆς μάχης[2] ἔδοξε Δαυίδῃ συμβουλευσαμένῳ μετὰ τῶν γερόντων καὶ ἡγεμόνων καὶ χιλιάρχων μεταπέμψασθαι τῶν ὁμοφύλων ἐξ ἁπάσης τῆς χώρας πρὸς αὐτὸν τοὺς ἐν ἀκμῇ τῆς ἡλικίας, ἔπειτα τοὺς ἱερεῖς καὶ Ληουίτας[3] πορευθέντας εἰς Καριαθιάριμα μετακομίσαι τὴν τοῦ θεοῦ κιβωτὸν ἐξ αὐτῆς εἰς Ἱεροσόλυμα καὶ θρησκεύειν ἐν αὐτῇ λοιπὸν ἔχοντας αὐτὴν θυσίαις
79 καὶ ταῖς ἄλλαις τιμαῖς, αἷς χαίρει τὸ θεῖον· εἰ γὰρ ἔτι Σαούλου βασιλεύοντος τοῦτ' ἔπραξαν, οὐκ ἂν δεινὸν οὐδὲν ἔπαθον. συνελθόντος οὖν τοῦ λαοῦ παντός, καθὼς ἐβουλεύσαντο, παραγίνεται ὁ βασιλεὺς ἐπὶ τὴν κιβωτόν, ἣν βαστάσαντες[4] ἐκ τῆς Ἀμιναδάβου οἰκίας οἱ ἱερεῖς καὶ ἐπιθέντες ἐφ' ἅμαξαν καινὴν ἕλκειν ἀδελφοῖς τε καὶ παισὶν ἐπ-
80 έτρεψαν μετὰ τῶν βοῶν. προῆγε δ' ὁ βασιλεὺς καὶ

[1] διαρπάσας M: εἶτα διαρπάσας SP: διαρπάσας δὲ E.
[2] τοιαύτης . . . μάχης] τοιούτου δ' ἀποβάντος καὶ ταύτης τῆς μάχης τέλους MSP.
[3] + καὶ codd.
[4] E Suidas: βαστάζοντες RO: βαστάξαντες MSP.

[a] Bibl. Gezer, *cf. A.* v. 83 note.

[b] The plundering of the camp is a detail added by Josephus. Moreover, Scripture mentions the Philistine gods (Heb. " idols ") only in connexion with the first battle. According to 1 Chron. xiv. 12 (*cf.* the Targum on 2 Sam. v. 21) David burnt them.

[c] In mentioning the council of elders, etc., Josephus follows Chronicles. 2 Samuel merely says that he collected 30,000 (LXX 70,000) chosen men.

lines did not stand up under his attack but from the very first encounter were routed, with David close behind, slaughtering them. He pursued them as far as the city of Gazara,[a] which is the border of their country, and, when he plundered their camp, found in it great wealth ; he also destroyed their gods.[b]

(2) But when this battle also had come to such an end, David, after consulting with the elders, leaders and captains of thousands, decided to summon to him those of his countrymen throughout the entire land who were in the prime of life,[c] and then have the priests and Levites proceed to Kariathjarim [d] to take the ark of God from there and bring it to Jerusalem ; there they should in future keep it and worship the Deity with such sacrifices and other forms of homage as are pleasing to Him, for, he believed, if they had done this while Saul was still reigning, they would not have suffered any misfortune.[e] So then, when all the people had assembled in accordance with this plan, the king came to the ark, and the priests carried it out of the house of Aminadab [f] and placed it upon a new wagon which they permitted his brothers and sons [g] to draw with the help of oxen. Before it went

The ark is brought to Jerusalem. 2 Sam. vi. 1; 1 Chron. xiii. 1.

[d] Bibl. Kirjath Jearim, *cf. A.* vi. 17.

[e] The thought here attributed to David is an amplification of 1 Chron. xiii. 3.

[f] Bibl. Abinadab, *cf. A.* vi. 18 note.

[g] 2 Sam. vi. 3 "and Uzzah and Ahio, the sons of Abinadab, drove the new cart." Josephus follows the LXX in reading *'eḥaw* " his brothers " for *'Aḥyô* "Ahio " (the two forms are identical in the consonantal text). The LXX also repeats the phrase *οἱ ἀδελφοὶ αὐτοῦ* " his brothers," meaning Uzzah's, but Josephus takes the *αὐτοῦ* to refer to Abinadab, Uzzah's father. Finally, the omission of Uzzah's name at this point in Josephus's text may be due to a lacuna, as Niese suspects.

πᾶν σὺν αὐτῷ τὸ πλῆθος ὑμνοῦντες τὸν θεὸν καὶ ᾄδοντες πᾶν εἶδος μέλους ἐπιχώριον σύν τε ἤχῳ ποικίλῳ κρουσμάτων τε καὶ ὀρχήσεων καὶ ψαλμῶν ἔτι δὲ σάλπιγγος καὶ κυμβάλων κατάγοντες τὴν
81 κιβωτὸν εἰς Ἱεροσόλυμα. ὡς δ' ἄχρι τῆς Χειδῶνος[1] ἅλωνος, τόπου τινὸς οὕτω καλουμένου, προῆλθον, τελευτᾷ Ὀζᾶς κατ' ὀργὴν τοῦ θεοῦ· τῶν βοῶν γὰρ ἐπινευσάντων τὴν κιβωτὸν ἐκτείναντα τὴν χεῖρα καὶ κατασχεῖν ἐθελήσαντα, ὅτι μὴ ὢν ἱερεὺς ἥψατο
82 ταύτης, ἀποθανεῖν ἐποίησε. καὶ ὁ μὲν βασιλεὺς καὶ ὁ λαὸς ἐδυσφόρησαν ἐπὶ τῷ θανάτῳ τοῦ Ὀζᾶ, ὁ δὲ τόπος ἐν ᾧ ἐτελεύτησεν Ὀζᾶ[2] διακοπὴ καλεῖται. δείσας δ' ὁ Δαυίδης καὶ λογισάμενος μὴ ταὐτὸ πάθῃ τῷ Ὀζᾶ δεξάμενος τὴν κιβωτὸν παρ' αὑτὸν ἐν τῇ πόλει, ἐκείνου διότι μόνον ἐξέτεινε τὴν
83 χεῖρα πρὸς αὐτὴν οὕτως ἀποθανόντος, οὐκ εἰσδέχεται μὲν αὐτὴν πρὸς αὑτὸν εἰς τὴν πόλιν, ἀλλ' ἐκνεύσας εἴς τι χωρίον ἀνδρὸς δικαίου, Ὠβαδάρου[3] ὄνομα Ληουίτου τὸ γένος, παρ' αὐτῷ τὴν κιβωτὸν τίθησιν· ἔμεινε δ' ἐπὶ τρεῖς ὅλους μῆνας αὐτόθι καὶ τὸν οἶκον τὸν Ὠβαδάρου ηὔξησέ τε καὶ πολλῶν
84 αὐτῷ μετέδωκεν ἀγαθῶν. ἀκούσας δὲ ὁ βασιλεὺς ὅτι ταῦτα συμβέβηκεν Ὠβαδάρῳ καὶ ἐκ τῆς προ-

[1] Χείλωνος RO: Χήλωνος E: Χείδονος S Exc. Suidas: Χείδανος P: Chedon Lat.

[2] ἔτι νῦν Ὀζᾶ MSP Lat.

[3] Βαδάρου SP[1]: Ὠβαδάμου ME: Ὠβεδάμου Exc.: Obidam Lat.

---

[a] So the Hebrew in 1 Chron. xiii. 9 (some LXX MSS. have Χειλών; *cf.* the variant in Josephus). In 2 Sam. vi. 6 the Hebrew has Nachon; LXX Νωδάβ, Ναχώρ. It is probable that Nachon (*Nākôn*) is not a proper name but a passive (niphal) ptc. of the verb *kûn* and means "prepared" or the like, as the Targum renders it.

the king and all the people with him, chanting in praise of God and singing all manner of native melodies; thus, with the mingled sounds of stringed instruments and with dancing and singing to the harp, as well as with trumpets and cymbals, they escorted the ark to Jerusalem. When they had come as far as the threshing-floor of Cheidōn[a]—so the place was called,—Ozas[b] met his death through the wrath of God, for, when the oxen tilted the ark forward, he stretched out his hand in an attempt to hold it in place and, because he had touched it though not a priest, God caused his death.[c] Both the king and his people were displeased at the death of Ozas, and the place where he died is called Breach of Ozas.[d] David, therefore, fearful at the thought that he might suffer the same fate as Ozas if he received the ark into his house in the city, since the former had perished in this way merely because he had stretched out his hand toward it, did not bring it into his house in the city; instead he brought it elsewhere to a certain place belonging to a righteous man named Obadaros,[e] a Levite[f] by descent, and deposited the ark with him. It remained there for three whole months and brought increase to Obadaros's house, and for himself procured great good. But when the king heard what had befallen Obadaros, and that from his former poverty and

Death of Uzzah (Ozas). 2 Sam. vi. 6; 1 Chron. xiii. 9.

The ark is left with Obed-Edom (Obadaros) for three months. 2 Sam. vi. 10; 1 Chron. xiii. 13.

[b] Bibl. Uzzah, LXX Ὀζά.

[c] This explanation of Uzzah's death is not given in Scripture, but is derived by Josephus, as by the rabbis, from the Mosaic prescriptions, Num. iv. 5 ff., concerning the duties of priests and Levites in transporting the ark.

[d] Bibl. Perez-Uzzah. Josephus follows the LXX in translating Perez (*Pereṣ*) "breach" by διακοπή.

[e] Bibl. Obed-Edom, LXX Ἀβεδδαρά, Luc. Ἀβεδδαδάν.

[f] According to 1 Chron. xv. 18. In 2 Sam. vi. 10 he is called a Gittite, *i.e.* a native of Gath.

τέρας[1] πενίας καὶ ταπεινότητος ἀθρόως εὐδαίμων
καὶ ζηλωτὸς γέγονε παρὰ πᾶσι τοῖς ὁρῶσι καὶ
πυνθανομένοις τὴν οἰκίαν αὐτοῦ, θαρσήσας ὡς
οὐδενὸς κακοῦ πειρασόμενος τὴν κιβωτὸν πρὸς
85 αὑτὸν μετακομίζει, τῶν μὲν ἱερέων βασταζόντων
αὐτήν, ἑπτὰ δὲ χορῶν οὓς διεκόσμησεν ὁ βασιλεὺς
προαγόντων, αὐτοῦ δ' ἐν κινύρᾳ παίζοντος καὶ κρο-
τοῦντος, ὥστε καὶ τὴν γυναῖκα Μιχάλην[2] Σαούλου
δὲ θυγατέρα τοῦ πρώτου βασιλέως ἰδοῦσαν αὐτὸν
86 τοῦτο ποιοῦντα χλευάσαι. εἰσκομίσαντες δὲ τὴν
κιβωτὸν τιθέασιν ὑπὸ τὴν σκηνήν, ἣν Δαυίδης
ἔπηξεν αὐτῇ,[3] καὶ θυσίας τελείας[4] καὶ εἰρηνικὰς
ἀνήνεγκε, καὶ τὸν ὄχλον εἱστίασε πάντα καὶ γυναιξὶ καὶ ἀνδράσι καὶ νηπίοις διαδοὺς κολλυρίδα
ἄρτου καὶ ἐσχαρίτην καὶ λάγανον τηγανιστὸν καὶ
μερίδα θύματος. καὶ τὸν μὲν λαὸν οὕτως κατευωχήσας ἀπέπεμψεν, αὐτὸς δ' εἰς τὸν οἶκον τὸν
αὑτοῦ παραγίνεται.
87 (3) Παραστᾶσα δὲ αὐτῷ Μιχάλη ἡ γυνὴ Σαούλου
δὲ θυγάτηρ τά τε ἄλλα αὐτῷ κατηύχετο καὶ παρὰ
τοῦ θεοῦ γενέσθαι ᾔτει πάνθ' ὅσα παρασχεῖν αὐτῷ
δυνατὸν εὐμενεῖ τυγχάνοντι, καὶ δὴ κατεμέμψατο
ὡς ἀκοσμήσειεν ὀρχούμενος ὁ τηλικοῦτος βασιλεὺς

[1] τῆς προτέρας om. ROM Exc.
[2] Μελχάλην RE: Μελχόλην SP Lat. hic et infra.
[3] post αὐτῇ lacunam statuit Niese haud recte.
[4] τελείας] τε ἐπετέλεσε πολυτελεῖς (om. τε Exc.) MSP Exc.: πολυτελῶς E: copiosas Lat.

---

[a] An amplification of 2 Sam. vi. 11 "and the Lord blessed Obed-Edom and all his house."

[b] Josephus here follows the order of 2 Sam.; in 1 Chron. the narrative of the ark's entry is preceded by an account of

humble station he had all at once risen to prosperity and become an object of envy to all those who saw his house or heard about it,[a] he was encouraged in the belief that he would suffer no harm, and removed the ark to his own house.[b] It was carried by the priests and these were preceded by seven choirs [c] whom the king had marshalled, while he himself played the harp and loudly plucked its strings,[d] so that Michalē,[e] the daughter of Saul the first king, laughed mockingly to see him act in this way. Then they brought the ark into the city and placed it under a tent which David had set up for it, and he sacrificed whole burnt-offerings and peace-offerings, and feasted the people, distributing among men, women and children twists of bread, ash-baked bread, fried mealcakes and a portion of the sacrifice.[f] Having thus entertained the people, he dismissed them, while he himself went to his own home.

David dances before the ark. 2 Sam. vi. 14

(3) Then Michalē his wife, the daughter of Saul, came to his side and invoked blessings upon him and also asked of God that all those things should be granted him which He in His graciousness might bestow.[g] None the less, she reproached him for his unseemly behaviour in dancing—so great a king as

Michal rebukes David. 2 Sam. vi. 20

Hiram's embassy, David's family, and the preparation of the Levites (1 Chron. xiv.–xv. 24).

[c] So the LXX, 2 Sam. vi. 13; the Heb. has something quite different, "And when those who bore the ark had gone six paces, they sacrificed an ox and a fatling"; 1 Chron. xv. 26 "those who bore the ark sacrificed seven bullocks and seven rams."

[d] Or perhaps "stamped his feet."

[e] Bibl. Michal, *cf.* § 25 note.

[f] The last is a detail added by Josephus.

[g] Scripture says nothing of Michal's blessing, but merely that she came to meet David and reproached him for his unseemly conduct.

καὶ γυμνούμενος ὑπὸ τῆς ὀρχήσεως καὶ ἐν δούλοις
88 καὶ ἐν θεραπαινίσιν. ὁ δ' οὐκ αἰδεῖσθαι ταῦτα
ποιήσας εἰς τὸ τῷ θεῷ κεχαρισμένον ἔφασκεν,
ὃς αὐτὸν καὶ τοῦ πατρὸς αὐτῆς καὶ τῶν ἄλλων
ἁπάντων προετίμησε· παίξειν τε πολλάκις καὶ χορεύ-
σειν,[1] μηδένα τοῦ δόξαι ταῖς θεραπαινίσιν αἰσχρὸν
89 καὶ αὐτῇ τὸ γινόμενον ποιησάμενος λόγον. ἡ δὲ
Μιχάλη αὕτη Δαυίδῃ μὲν συνοικοῦσα παῖδας οὐκ
ἐποιήσατο, γαμηθεῖσα δὲ ὕστερον ᾧ παρέδωκεν
αὐτὴν ὁ πατὴρ Σαοῦλος, τότε δὲ ἀποσπάσας αὐτὸς
εἶχε, πέντε παῖδας ἔτεκε. καὶ περὶ μὲν τούτων
κατὰ χώραν δηλώσομεν.
90 (4) Ὁρῶν δ' ὁ βασιλεὺς κατὰ πᾶσαν αὐτῷ τὰ
πράγματα σχεδὸν ἡμέραν ἀμείνω γινόμενα ἐκ τῆς
τοῦ θεοῦ βουλήσεως ἐνόμιζεν ἐξαμαρτάνειν αὐτόν
εἰ μένων αὐτὸς ἐν οἴκοις ἐκ κέδρου πεποιημένοις
ὑψηλοῖς τε καὶ καλλίστην τὴν ἄλλην κατασκευὴν
ἔχουσι περιορᾷ τὴν κιβωτὸν ἐν σκηνῇ κειμένην·
91 ἐβούλετο δὲ τῷ θεῷ κατασκευάσαι ναόν, ὡς
Μωυσῆς προεῖπε,[2] καὶ περὶ τούτων Νάθᾳ[3] τῷ
προφήτῃ διαλεχθείς, ἐπεὶ ποιεῖν ὅ τι περ ὥρμηται
προσέταξεν αὐτὸν ὡς τοῦ θεοῦ πρὸς ἅπαντ' αὐτῷ
συνεργοῦ παρόντος, εἶχεν ἤδη περὶ τὴν τοῦ ναοῦ
92 κατασκευὴν προθυμότερον. τοῦ θεοῦ δὲ κατ'

[1] παίξειν . . . χορεύσειν] Niese: παίζειν . . . χορεῦσαι codd.
[2] εἶπε RO.
[3] Νάθαν O: Ναθάνᾳ MSP Exc.: Nathan Lat. hic et infra.

[a] Similar to the LXX, 2 Sam. vi. 22 ἔσομαι ἀχρεῖος ἐν ὀφθαλμοῖς σου καὶ μετὰ τῶν παιδισκῶν ὧν εἶπάς με μὴ δοξασθῆναι (v.l. om. μή): Heb. " I shall be base in mine own eyes, and

he was—and in uncovering himself, as he danced, in the presence of slaves and maid-servants. He replied, however, that he was not ashamed of having done what was pleasing to God, who had honoured him above her father and all other men, and that he would often play and dance without caring whether his actions seemed disgraceful to her maid-servants[a] or herself. Now this Michalē, while she lived with David, bore no children, but, after her later marriage to the man[b] on whom her father Saul bestowed her—at this particular time David, who had taken her away from him was again her husband—she bore five children.[c] But of this we shall treat in its proper place.[d]

David plans to build a temple, but God disapproves. 2 Sam. vii. 1; 1 Chron. xvii. 1.

(4) When the king saw that almost from day to day his affairs prospered more and more by the will of God, he thought that he should be guilty of sin if, while he himself lodged in a lofty dwelling made of cedar wood and beautifully appointed in other ways, he allowed the ark to lie in a tent. He wished, therefore, to build such a temple to God as Moses had formerly spoken of, and after discussing this with the prophet Nathan, when he bade him do as he was minded, seeing that God was with him to help him in all things, he became still more eager to build the temple. But God appeared to Nathan that very

with the handmaids of whom thou hast spoken, with them I shall have honour."

[b] Adriel, the son of Barzillai, 2 Sam. xxi. 8.

[c] Josephus harmonizes the contradictions in Scripture. According to 2 Sam. vi. 23 Michal had no children as long as she lived, but 2 Sam. xxi. 8 states that she bore five children to Adriel. Rabbinic tradition following the Targum holds that the five children were Merab's but were brought up by Michal (*cf.* Luc. which has Merab for Michal in 2 Sam. xxi. 8).

[d] Michal is not mentioned again in our text of Josephus.

ἐκείνην τὴν νύκτα τῷ Νάθᾳ φανέντος καὶ φράσαι κελεύσαντος τῷ Δαυίδῃ ὡς τὴν μὲν προαίρεσιν αὐτοῦ καὶ τὴν ἐπιθυμίαν[1] ἀποδέχεται, μηδενὸς μὲν πρότερον εἰς νοῦν βαλομένου ναὸν αὐτῷ κατασκευάσαι, τούτου δὲ ταύτην τὴν διάνοιαν λαβόντος· οὐκ ἐπιτρέπειν δὲ πολλοὺς πολέμους ἠγωνισμένῳ καὶ φόνῳ τῶν ἐχθρῶν μεμιασμένῳ ποιῆσαι ναὸν
93 αὐτῷ. μετὰ μέντοι γε τὸν θάνατον αὐτοῦ, γηράσαντος καὶ μακρὸν ἀνύσαντος βίον, γενήσεσθαι[2] τὸν ναὸν ὑπὸ τοῦ παιδὸς τοῦ μετ᾽ αὐτὸν τὴν βασιλείαν παραληψομένου κληθησομένου δὲ Σολομῶνος, οὗ προστήσεσθαι καὶ προνοήσειν ὡς πατὴρ υἱοῦ κατεπηγγέλλετο, τὴν μὲν βασιλείαν τέκνων ἐγγόνοις φυλάξων καὶ παραδώσων, αὐτὸν δὲ τιμωρήσων,
94 ἂν ἁμαρτὼν τύχῃ, νόσῳ καὶ γῆς ἀφορίᾳ. μαθὼν ταῦτα παρὰ τοῦ προφήτου Δαυίδης καὶ περιχαρὴς γενόμενος ἐπὶ τῷ τοῖς ἐγγόνοις αὐτοῦ τὴν ἀρχὴν διαμένουσαν ἐγνωκέναι βεβαίως, καὶ τὸν οἶκον αὐτοῦ λαμπρὸν ἐσόμενον καὶ περιβόητον πρὸς τὴν
95 κιβωτὸν παραγίνεται· καὶ πεσὼν ἐπὶ πρόσωπον ἤρξατο προσκυνεῖν καὶ περὶ πάντων εὐχαριστεῖν τῷ θεῷ, ὧν τε αὐτῷ παρέσχηκεν ἤδη ἐκ ταπεινοῦ καὶ ποιμένος εἰς τηλικοῦτο μέγεθος ἡγεμονίας τε καὶ δόξης ἀναγαγών, ὧν τε τοῖς ἐγγόνοις αὐτοῦ καθυπέσχετο, ἔτι δὲ περὶ[3] τῆς προνοίας, ἣν

[1] + λίαν ROS.
[2] Niese: γενέσθαι RO: ἔσεσθαι rell.: faciendum Lat.
[3] ἔτι δὲ περὶ ex Lat. add. Niese: καὶ Naber cum Hudson.

[a] This expression of God's approval is unscriptural.
[b] 1 Chron. xxviii. 3.
[c] 2 Sam. vii. 14 " with the rod of men and with the stripes of the children of men," which some rabbinic authorities take to mean evil spirits.

night and bade him tell David that while He approved of his purpose and desire—for no one before him had taken it into his mind to build Him a temple, as David had thought to do—,[a] still He could not permit him to construct a temple for Him, because he had fought in many wars and was stained with the blood of his enemies[b]; but in any case, He said, after David's death at an advanced age and at the end of a long life, the temple should be brought into being by his son and successor to the kingdom, whose name would be Solomon, and whom He promised to watch over and care for as a father for his son, and to preserve the kingdom for his children's children and transmit it to them, but He would punish him, if he sinned, with sickness and barrenness of the soil.[c] When David heard this from the prophet, he rejoiced greatly to know assuredly that the royal power would remain with his descendants and that his house would become glorious and renowned. Then he went to the ark and, falling on his face,[d] began to worship God and render thanks to Him for all that He had already done for him in raising him from the humble station of a shepherd to so great a height of power and glory,[e] and for His promise to his descendants, and

God's promise concerning Solomon. 2 Sam. vii. 12; 1 Chron. xvii. 11.

[d] 2 Sam. vii. 18 "and he sat before the Lord (*i.e.* the ark)." Rappaport suggests that Josephus's paraphrase ("falling on his face" instead of "sat") may have some connexion with the controversy in the Hasmonean period between the partisans of the king and those of the high priests as to whether kings of Davidic lineage had the right to sit in the temple court or not, and that the controversy centred about the interpretation of the verb "sat" in this verse of Scripture.

[e] In Scripture the reference to David's humble origin is found earlier (2 Sam. vii. 8) in God's charge to David by Nathan, and not in David's prayer, as in Josephus.

Ἑβραίων καὶ τῆς τούτων ἐλευθερίας ἐποιήσατο.
ταῦτ᾽ εἰπὼν καὶ τὸν θεὸν ὑμνήσας ἀπαλλάσσεται.
96 (v. 1) Διαλιπὼν δὲ ὀλίγον χρόνον ἔγνω δεῖν ἐπὶ
τοὺς Παλαιστίνους ἐκστρατεύειν, καὶ μηδὲν ἀργὸν
μηδὲ ῥᾴθυμον ἐν τοῖς πράγμασιν περιορᾶν[1] γινόμενον, ἵν᾽ ὡς τὸ θεῖον αὐτῷ προεῖπε καταστρε-
ψάμενος τοὺς πολεμίους ἐν εἰρήνῃ τὸ λοιπὸν τοὺς
97 ἐκγόνους αὐτοῦ βασιλεύοντας καταλείποι. καὶ συγκαλέσας πάλιν τὴν στρατιὰν καὶ παραγγείλας αὐτῇ
πρὸς πόλεμον ἑτοίμην καὶ παρεσκευασμένην τυγχάνειν, ὅτ᾽ ἔδοξεν αὐτῷ καλῶς ἔχειν τὰ παρ᾽
αὐτῆς, ἄρας ἐκ τῶν Ἱεροσολύμων ἐπὶ τοὺς Παλαι-
98 στίνους ἧκε. κρατήσας δ᾽ αὐτῶν τῇ μάχῃ καὶ
πολλὴν τῆς χώρας ἀποτεμόμενος καὶ προσορίσας
τῇ τῶν Ἑβραίων, ἐπὶ τοὺς Μωαβίτας τὸν πόλεμον
μετήγαγε, καὶ τὰ μὲν δύο μέρη τῆς στρατιᾶς
αὐτῶν τῇ μάχῃ νικήσας διέφθειρε, τὸ δὲ λειπόμενον
99 αἰχμάλωτον ἔλαβε. φόρους δὲ αὐτοῖς ἐπιτάξας
κατ᾽ ἔτος τελεῖν ἐπὶ Ἀδράζαρον[2] τὸν Ἀραοῦ μὲν
υἱὸν βασιλέα δὲ τῆς Σωφηνῆς ἐστράτευσε, καὶ συμβαλὼν αὐτῷ παρὰ τὸν Εὐφράτην ποταμὸν τῶν μὲν
πεζῶν αὐτοῦ διέφθειρεν ὡσεὶ δισμυρίους, τῶν δ᾽

[1] Naber: ὁρᾶν codd.
[2] Ἀρτάζαρον ROE.

[a] The account of the preparations is an amplification of Scripture, which merely says, "And after this David smote the Philistines."

[b] 1 Chron. xviii. 1 "and took Gath and its villages out of the hand of the Philistines"; the parallel verse 2 Sam. viii. 1, "and David took Metheg-ha-ammah, etc.," is obscure

also for His care of the Hebrews and their liberty. When he had so spoken and recited the praises of God, he departed.

(v. 1) After a short interval of time, he decided that he ought to march against the Philistines, and not permit any idleness or slackness in his conduct of affairs, in order that he might, as God had foretold to him, overthrow his enemies and leave behind descendants who would reign thereafter in peace. So once again he assembled his army and gave them orders to be in readiness and equipped for war, and, when they seemed to him to be in good condition, he left Jerusalem and advanced upon the Philistines.[a] Having overcome them in battle, he cut off much of their territory and annexed it to the country of the Hebrews.[b] Then he carried the war over to the Moabites, and, upon defeating them in battle, destroyed two-thirds of their army and took the rest captive[c]; he also ordered them to pay a yearly tribute. He next marched against Adrazaros,[d] the son of Araos,[e] king of Sophéné,[f] and encountered him beside the Euphrates river, where he slew some twenty thousand of his infantry and about five

David's victories over Philistines, Moabites, etc. 2 Sam. viii. 1; 1 Chron. xviii. 1.

and probably corrupt; the LXX has καὶ ἔλαβεν Δαυεὶδ τὴν ἀφωρισμένην ἐκ χειρὸς τῶν ἀλλοφύλων.

[c] 2 Sam. viii. 2 "And he smote Moab and measured them with the line, making them lie down on the ground, and he measured two lines to put to death, and one full line to keep alive." Josephus follows the LXX, which has ἐζώγρησεν "took captive" for the Heb. "keep alive."

[d] Variant Artazaros; bibl. Hadadezer, LXX Ἀδραάζαρ.

[e] Bibl. Rehob, LXX Ῥαάβ, Luc. Ῥαάφ.

[f] Bibl. Zobah (*Ṣôbāh*), LXX Σουβά: an Aramaean state N.W. of Damascus in the valley between Lebanon and Anti-Lebanon, according to Kraeling, *Aram and Israel*, p. 40. Josephus's "Sophene" is misleading, as this is the Greek name of a district in Armenia.

ἱπποτῶν ὡς πεντακισχιλίους.[1] ἔλαβε δὲ καὶ αὐτοῦ ἅρματα χίλια, καὶ τὰ πλείω μὲν αὐτῶν ἠφάνισεν, ἑκατὸν δὲ μόνα προσέταξεν αὑτῷ[2] φυλαχθῆναι.

100 (2) Ἀκούσας δὲ ὁ Δαμασκοῦ καὶ Σύρων βασιλεὺς Ἄδαδος ὅτι πολεμεῖ Δαυίδης τὸν Ἀδράζαρον, φίλος ὢν αὐτῷ μετὰ δυνάμεως ἧκεν ἰσχυρᾶς συμμαχήσων· ἀπήλλαξε δ' οὐχ ὡς[3] προσεδόκα συμβαλὼν πρὸς τῷ Εὐφράτῃ ποταμῷ, πταίσας δὲ τῇ μάχῃ πολλοὺς ἀπέβαλε τῶν στρατιωτῶν· ἔπεσον γὰρ ὑπὸ τῶν Ἑβραίων ἀναιρούμενοι τῆς Ἀδάδου δυνάμεως δισμύριοι,[4] οἱ δὲ λοιποὶ πάντες ἔφυγον.
101 μέμνηται δὲ τούτου τοῦ βασιλέως καὶ Νικόλαος ἐν τῇ τετάρτῃ τῶν ἱστοριῶν λέγων οὕτως· "μετὰ δὲ ταῦτα πολλῷ χρόνῳ ὕστερον τῶν ἐγχωρίων τις Ἄδαδος ὄνομα πλεῖον ἰσχύσας Δαμασκοῦ τε καὶ τῆς ἄλλης Συρίας ἔξω Φοινίκης ἐβασίλευσε. πόλεμον δ' ἐξενέγκας πρὸς Δαυίδην βασιλέα τῆς Ἰουδαίας καὶ πολλαῖς μάχαις κριθείς, ὑστάτῃ δὲ παρὰ τὸν Εὐφράτην, ἐν ᾗ ἡττᾶτο, ἄριστος ἔδοξεν
102 εἶναι βασιλέων ῥώμῃ καὶ ἀνδρείᾳ." πρὸς τούτοις δὲ καὶ περὶ τῶν ἀπογόνων αὐτοῦ φησιν, ὡς μετὰ τὴν ἐκείνου τελευτὴν ἐξεδέχοντο παρ' ἀλλήλων καὶ τὴν βασιλείαν καὶ τὸ ὄνομα, λέγων οὕτως· "τελευτήσαντος δὲ ἐκείνου ἀπόγονοι ἐπὶ δέκα γενεὰς ἐβασίλευον ἑκάστου παρὰ τοῦ πατρὸς ἅμα καὶ τὴν ἀρχὴν[5] καὶ τοὔνομ' ἐκδεχομένου, ὥσπερ οἱ Πτολε-

[1] ἑπτακισχιλίους MSP. [2] edd.: αὐτῷ codd.
[3] οὐχ ὡς] Niese: ὡς ROM: ὡς οὐ P.
[4] ὡς δισμύριοι E Lat.
[5] κ. τ. ἀρχὴν] τῇ ἀρχῇ MSP Lat.

[a] 7000 according to 1 Chron. and the LXX in 2 Sam., cf. variant in Josephus; 1700 according to the Heb. of 2 Sam.

thousand[a] of his cavalry. He also seized a thousand of his chariots, most of which he destroyed, and ordered that only one hundred be kept for himself.

(2) Now when Adados,[b] king of Damascus and Syria,[b] heard that David was warring with Adrazaros, whose friend he was, he went to his aid with a powerful force, but came off otherwise than he had expected when he encountered David at the Euphrates river, and, as a result of his defeat in the battle, lost many of his men. For there fell at the hands of the Hebrews twenty thousand[c] of Adados's force, and all the rest fled. This king is also mentioned by Nicolas[d] in the fourth book of his History, who writes as follows: "A long while after this, one of the natives, Adados by name, attained to great power and became ruler of Damascus and the rest of Syria excepting Phoenicia. He waged war against David, king of Judaea, and, after trial of many battles, the last of which was fought beside the Euphrates, where he was defeated, he gained the reputation of being the most vigorous and courageous of kings." In addition, he speaks also of his descendants and tells how, after his death, they succeeded one another in his kingdom and his name. This is what he says: "Upon his death, his posterity reigned for ten generations, each receiving from his father both his authority and his name, as did the Ptolemies in

David's victory over the king of Damascus. 2 Sam. viii. 5; 1 Chron. xviii. 5.

[b] The king's name is not given in Scripture, which has "Aram of Damascus," *i.e.* the Aramaeans of Damascus, LXX Συρία Δαμασκοῦ (Chron. Σύρος ἐκ Δαμασκοῦ). Syria is the Greek name for the Heb. Aram. As Weill suggests, Josephus probably took the name Adados from Nicolas's account, which follows.

[c] Bibl. 22,000.

[d] On the historian Nicolas of Damascus, a contemporary of Herod the Great, *cf. A.* i. 94 note.

103 μαῖοι ἐν Αἰγύπτῳ. μέγιστον δὲ ἁπάντων δυνηθεὶς ὁ τρίτος ἀναμαχέσασθαι βουλόμενος τὴν τοῦ προπάτορος ἧτταν στρατεύσας ἐπὶ τοὺς Ἰουδαίους ἐπόρθησε τὴν νῦν Σαμαρεῖτιν καλουμένην γῆν." οὐ διήμαρτε δὲ τῆς ἀληθείας· οὗτος γάρ ἐστιν Ἄδαδος ὁ στρατευσάμενος ἐπὶ Σαμάρειαν Ἀχάβου βασιλεύοντος τῶν Ἰσραηλιτῶν, περὶ οὗ κατὰ χώραν[1] ἐροῦμεν.

104 (3) Δαυίδης δὲ στρατευσάμενος ἐπὶ Δαμασκὸν καὶ τὴν ἄλλην Συρίαν, πᾶσαν αὐτὴν ὑπήκοον ἐποιήσατο, καὶ φρουρὰς ἐν τῇ χώρᾳ καταστήσας καὶ φόρους αὐτοῖς τελεῖν ὁρίσας ὑπέστρεψε· καὶ τάς τε χρυσᾶς φαρέτρας καὶ τὰς πανοπλίας, ἃς οἱ τοῦ Ἀδάδου σωματοφύλακες ἐφόρουν, ἀνέθηκε τῷ
105 θεῷ εἰς Ἱεροσόλυμα· ἃς ὕστερον ὁ τῶν Αἰγυπτίων βασιλεὺς Σούσακος στρατεύσας ἐπὶ τὸν υἱωνὸν αὐτοῦ Ῥοβόαμον ἔλαβε καὶ πολὺν ἄλλον ἐκ τῶν Ἱεροσολύμων ἐξεφόρησε πλοῦτον· ταῦτα μὲν ὅταν ἔλθωμεν ἐπὶ τὸν οἰκεῖον αὐτῶν τόπον δηλώσομεν. ὁ δὲ τῶν Ἑβραίων βασιλεὺς τοῦ θεοῦ συμπνέοντος αὐτῷ καὶ τοὺς πολέμους συγκατορθοῦντος καὶ ταῖς καλλίσταις τῶν Ἀδραζάρου πόλεων ἐπεστράτευσε

[1] + ὕστερον MSP Lat.

---

[a] *Ant.* viii. 363 ff.

[b] In 2 Sam. viii. 7 the Heb. has *shilṭê*, here meaning "shields" according to Jewish tradition; the LXX has χλίδωνας "bracelets" or "anklets," and in 1 Chron. κλοιούς "collars." In Ezek. xxvii. 11 the LXX translates *shilṭê* by φαρέτρας "quivers," as does Josephus here.

Egypt. The most powerful of all these kings was the third, who, in his desire to make good his grandfather's defeat, marched against the Jews and sacked the country now called Samaritis." And in so writing he has not departed from the truth, for this is the Adados who invaded Samaria when Ahab reigned over the Israelites. About this we shall speak in the proper place.[a]

(3) David then led his army against Damascus and the rest of Syria, and made all of it subject to him; and, after stationing garrisons in their country and fixing the amount of tribute they must pay, he returned home. The gold quivers[b] and the suits of armour[c] which the bodyguards of Adados[d] wore, he dedicated to God in Jerusalem. These were afterwards taken by the Egyptian king Susakos,[e] who marched against David's grandson Roboamos[f] and carried off much other wealth from Jerusalem. But these things we shall narrate when we come to their proper place.[g] Now the king of the Hebrews, with the encouragement of God who gave him success in war, attacked the fairest of Adrazaros's cities, Battaia[h]

Tribute and spoil taken from the Syrians. 2 Sam. viii. 6; 1 Chron. xviii. 6.

[c] Not mentioned in Scripture.

[d] Bibl. "the servants of Hadadezer."

[e] Bibl. Shishak, LXX Σουσακείμ. Josephus here follows the LXX, which anticipates the invasion of Shishak (described later in 1 Kings xiv. 25 ff.), while the Heb. omits it at this point. In the later passage the Heb. mentions only Shishak's taking the gold shields which Solomon had made, while the LXX adds a reference to the spears taken by David from the servants of Hadadezer.

[f] Bibl. Rehoboam, *cf.* § 190 note.

[g] *A.* viii. 253 ff.

[h] 2 Sam. Betah, LXX Μετεβάκ, Μασβάκ κτλ.; 1 Chron. Tibhath, LXX Μεταβηχάς, Ματεβέθ κτλ., Luc. Ταβάθ. (The syllable μα- or με in the LXX forms has arisen from the Heb. preposition *mi* "from" before the name Tibhath.)

Βατταίᾳ καὶ Μάχωνι, καὶ λαβὼν αὐτὰς κατὰ
106 κράτος διήρπασε. χρυσὸς δ' ἐν αὐταῖς εὑρέθη
πάμπολυς καὶ ἄργυρος ἔτι δὲ καὶ χαλκός, ὃν τοῦ
χρυσοῦ κρείττον' ἔλεγον, ἐξ οὗ καὶ Σολομὼν τὸ
μέγα σκεῦος θάλασσαν δὲ καλούμενον ἐποίησε καὶ
τοὺς καλλίστους ἐκείνους λουτῆρας, ὅτε τῷ θεῷ
τὸν ναὸν κατεσκεύασεν.

107 (4) Ὡς δὲ ὁ τῆς Ἀμάθης βασιλεὺς τὰ περὶ τὸν
Ἀδράζαρον ἐπύθετο καὶ τὴν δύναμιν αὐτοῦ διεφθαρ-
μένην ἤκουσε, δείσας περὶ αὑτῷ καὶ τὸν Δαυίδην
πρὶν ἐπ' αὐτὸν ἔλθοι[1] φιλίᾳ καὶ πίστει γνοὺς
ἐνδήσασθαι, πέμπει πρὸς αὐτὸν Ἀδώραμον υἱὸν
αὐτοῦ καὶ περὶ τοῦ τὸν Ἀδράζαρον ἐχθρὸν ὄντ'
αὐτῷ πολεμῆσαι χάριν ἔχειν ὁμολογῶν, καὶ συμ-
108 μαχίαν πρὸς αὐτὸν καὶ φιλίαν ποιούμενος. ἔπεμψε
δ' αὐτῷ καὶ δῶρα σκεύη τῆς ἀρχαίας κατασκευῆς
χρύσεα καὶ ἀργύρεα καὶ χάλκεα. Δαυίδης δὲ
ποιησάμενος τὴν συμμαχίαν πρὸς τὸν Θαῖνον, τοῦτο
γὰρ ἦν ὄνομα τῷ βασιλεῖ τῆς Ἀμάθης, καὶ τὰ
δῶρα δεξάμενος ἀπέλυσεν αὐτοῦ τὸν υἱὸν μετὰ
τιμῆς τῆς πρεπούσης ἑκατέροις. τὰ δὲ πεμφθέντα
ὑπ' αὐτοῦ καὶ τὸν ἄλλον χρυσὸν καὶ ἄργυρον, ὃν ἐκ
τῶν πόλεων εἰλήφει καὶ τῶν κεχειρωμένων ἐθνῶν,
109 φέρων ἀνατίθησι τῷ θεῷ. οὐκ αὐτῷ δὲ πολεμοῦντι

[1] Niese: ἔλθῃ codd.

[a] *Cf.* 1 Chron. Heb. *ûmikkûn* "and from Kun (?)"; 2 Sam. Berothai. In both places the LXX has "from the chosen cities," probably reading *beḥûrôth* "chosen" (pass. ptc. fem. pl.) instead of *Berôthai*.

[b] Scripture does not mention gold or silver at this point (2 Sam. viii. 8), but in vs. 11 speaks of the silver and gold

and Machōn,[a] took them by storm and plundered them. There was found in them a great amount of gold and silver [b] and that kind of bronze,[c] said to be finer than gold, out of which Solomon made the great vessel called "sea," and those very beautiful lavers, when he built the temple to God.[d]

Alliance with the king of Hamath (Amathē). 2 Sam. viii. 9; 1 Chron. xviii. 9.

(4) When the king of Amathē [e] learned of Adrazaros's fate and heard that his army had been destroyed, he became alarmed for himself and decided, before David should come against him, to bind him by a sworn agreement of friendship. He therefore sent his son Adōramos [f] to him, expressing his thanks to him for having made war on Adrazaros who was his enemy, and offering to make an alliance of friendship with him. He also sent him presents of gold, silver and bronze vessels of ancient workmanship.[g] David thereupon made an alliance with Thainos [h]—that was the name of the king of Amathē—and, having accepted the gifts, sent away his son with the honours befitting both sides. The objects sent by Thainos and the rest of the gold and silver which he had taken from the conquered cities and nations, he carried away and dedicated to God. Now it was not

"that he had dedicated of all nations that he had subdued."

[c] A.V. translates Heb. *neḥōsheth* (LXX χαλκός) by "brass."

[d] These details about Solomon's vessels are found in 1 Chron. and in the LXX of 2 Sam., but are omitted in the Heb. of the latter book.

[e] Bibl. Hamath, LXX 'Ημάθ, Luc. (Chron.) Αἰμάθ: an important Hittite city on the river Orontes in N. Syria. On the king's name *cf.* § 108 note.

[f] So Luc. in 1 Chron. where the LXX has 'Ιδουραάμ and the Heb. Hadoram; 2 Sam. Joram (*Yôrâm*), LXX 'Ιεδδουράν.

[g] "Ancient workmanship" is a detail added by Josephus.

[h] 2 Sam. Toi (*Ṭō'î*), LXX Θούου, Θόου, Θάει; 1 Chron. Tou (*Ṭō'û*), LXX Θῶα, Θόου.

μόνον καὶ τῆς στρατιᾶς ἡγουμένῳ τὸ νικᾶν καὶ κατορθοῦν παρεῖχεν ὁ θεός, ἀλλὰ καὶ πέμψαντος αὐτοῦ μετὰ δυνάμεως εἰς τὴν Ἰδουμαίαν Ἀβισαῖον τὸν Ἰωάβου τοῦ ἀρχιστρατήγου[1] ἀδελφόν, δι' ἐκείνου τὴν τῶν Ἰδουμαίων νίκην ἔδωκε· μυρίους γὰρ αὐτῶν καὶ ὀκτακισχιλίους Ἀβισαῖος διέφθειρε τῇ μάχῃ. καὶ τὴν Ἰδουμαίαν ἅπασαν φρουραῖς διαλαβὼν ὁ βασιλεὺς φόρους ὑπέρ τε τῆς χώρας καὶ
110 τῆς ἑκάστου κεφαλῆς παρ' αὐτῶν ἐδέχετο. ἦν δὲ καὶ δίκαιος τὴν φύσιν καὶ τὰς κρίσεις πρὸς τὴν ἀλήθειαν ἀφορῶν ἐποιεῖτο. στρατηγὸν δὲ ἁπάσης εἶχε τῆς στρατιᾶς τὸν Ἰώαβον· ἐπὶ δὲ τῶν ὑπομνημάτων Ἰωσάφατον υἱὸν Ἀχίλου κατέστησεν· ἀπέδειξε δ' ἐκ τῆς Φινεέσου οἰκίας τὸν Σάδωκον ἀρχιερέα μετ' Ἀβιαθάρου, φίλος γὰρ ἦν αὐτῷ· γραμματέα δὲ Σεισὰν[2] ἐποίησε· Βαναίᾳ δὲ τῷ Ἰωάδου τὴν τῶν σωματοφυλάκων ἀρχὴν παρα-

[1] ἀντιστρ. ROM hic et infra.
[2] Εἰσὰν RO: Isan Lat.

---

[a] So 1 Chron.; in 2 Sam. the victory over Edom (Idumaea) is attributed to David himself, but here the Heb. has Aram (A.V. "Syrians"), a corruption of Edom. *Cf.* also the superscription of Ps. lx., where the victory seems to be attributed to Joab.

[b] An amplification of 2 Sam. viii. 14 (1 Chron. xviii. 13), "and he put governors (*neṣîbîm*: A.V. "garrisons") in Edom, throughout all Edom he put governors." Rabbinic commentators explain *neṣîbîm* as officers to collect taxes.

[c] Bibl. Ahilud, LXX Ἀχειά, Ἀχιλούδ κτλ., Luc. Ἀχειναάβ.

only when he himself fought and led the army that God granted him victory and success, but even when he sent Abisai, the brother of Joab the commander-in-chief, with a force into Idumaea, God gave David, through him, victory over the Idumaeans, of whom Abisai slew eighteen thousand in battle.[a] The king then occupied the whole of Idumaea with garrisons and collected tribute both from the country (as a whole) and from the separate individuals therein.[b] He was of a just nature and, when he gave judgement, considered only the truth. As general of his entire army he had Joab; as keeper of the records he appointed Josaphat the son of Achilos [c]; from the house of Phinees [d] he chose Sadok as high priest together with Abiathar, who was his friend [e]; he made Seisa [f] scribe; and to Banaia,[g] son of Jōados,[h] he entrusted the command of the bodyguards,[i] while

Subjection of Edom (Idumaea). 2 Sam. viii. 14; 1 Chron. xviii. 12.

David's officers. 2 Sam. viii. 16; 1 Chron. xviii. 15.

[d] That is, a descendant of Aaron's third son Eleazar, father of Phinehas, whereas Abiathar was supposedly a descendant of Aaron's youngest son Ithamar, *cf. A.* v. 361 note, viii. 12 note.

[e] Many Biblical critics recognize that 2 Sam. viii. 17, "And Zadok the son of Ahitub, and Ahimelech the son of Abiathar, were the priests," should be corrected to read, "And Zadok and Abiathar the son of Ahimelech the son of Ahitub were the priests." Ahimelech, the father of Abiathar, had been killed earlier by Saul (*cf. A.* vi. 260 = 1 Sam. xxii. 16 ff.), whereas Abiathar continued to be the chief priest (together with Zadok) until he was removed by Solomon (*cf. A.* viii. 10 ff. = 1 Kings ii. 26 ff.). Josephus is, therefore, correct in omitting his name here.

[f] Called Sūsa in § 292; 2 Sam. Seraiah, LXX Ἀσά, Σασά κτλ.; 1 Chron. Shavsha, LXX Ἰησοῦς, Σουσά.

[g] So most MSS. of the LXX; bibl. Benaiah (*Benāyāhû*).

[h] So Luc.; bibl. Jehoiada (*Yehôyādā*), LXX Ἰωδαέ.

[i] Bibl. "Cherethites and Pelethites," probably Philistine mercenaries.

δίδωσιν· οἱ δὲ πρεσβύτεροι παῖδες αὐτοῦ περὶ τὸ σῶμα καὶ τὴν τούτου φυλακὴν ἦσαν.

111 (5) Ἐμνήσθη δὲ καὶ τῶν πρὸς Ἰωνάθην τὸν Σαούλου παῖδα συνθηκῶν καὶ ὅρκων καὶ τῆς ἐκείνου πρὸς αὐτὸν φιλίας τε καὶ σπουδῆς· πρὸς γὰρ τοῖς ἄλλοις ἅπασιν ἀγαθοῖς οἷς εἶχεν ἔτι καὶ μνημονικώτατος τῶν εὖ ποιησάντων παρὰ τὸν
112 ἄλλον[1] χρόνον ὑπῆρχε. προσέταξεν οὖν ἀναζητεῖν εἴ τις ἐκ τοῦ γένους αὐτοῦ σώζεται, ᾧ τὰς ἀμοιβὰς ἃς ὤφειλεν Ἰωνάθῃ τῆς ἑταιρίας ἀποδώσει· ἀχθέντος οὖν τινος ἠλευθερωμένου μὲν ὑπὸ Σαούλου δυναμένου δὲ γινώσκειν τοὺς ἐκ τοῦ γένους αὐτοῦ περιόντας, ἀνέκρινεν εἴ τινα ἔχοι λέγειν τῶν Ἰωνάθῃ προσηκόντων ζῶντα καὶ κομίσασθαι τὰς τῶν εὐεργεσιῶν χάριτας δυνάμενον, ὧν καὶ αὐτὸς
113 ἔτυχε παρὰ Ἰωνάθου. φήσαντος δ' υἱὸν αὐτοῦ περιλείπεσθαι Μεμφίβοσθον ὄνομα πεπηρωμένον τὰς βάσεις· τῆς γὰρ τροφοῦ μετὰ τὸ προσαγγελθῆναι τὸν πατέρα τοῦ παιδίου καὶ τὸν πάππον ἐν τῇ μάχῃ πεσόντας ἁρπασαμένης καὶ φευγούσης, ἀπὸ τῶν ὤμων αὐτὸ[2] κατενεχθῆναι καὶ βλαβῆναι τὰς βάσεις· μαθὼν ὅπου τε καὶ παρὰ τίνι τρέφεται πέμψας πρὸς τὸν Μάχειρον εἰς Λάβαθα πόλιν, παρὰ τούτῳ γὰρ ὁ Ἰωνάθου παῖς ἐτρέφετο, μετα-

[1] ὅλον RO. [2] αὐτὸν MSP.

[a] "Elder sons," etc.: so Josephus understands 2 Chron. xviii. 17, "and the sons of David were first next (lit. "to the hand of") the king," taking "first" as an attributive adj. with "sons" in the sense of "elder"; *cf.* LXX υἱοὶ Δαυεὶδ οἱ πρῶτοι διάδοχοι τοῦ βασιλέως. 2 Sam. viii. 18 reads, "and the sons of David were priests" (A.V. "chief rulers"); for "priests" the LXX has "princes of the court," Targum "nobles."

his elder sons were in attendance on him and guarded his person.[a]

(5) He also remembered his sworn covenant with Jonathan, the son of Saul, and Jonathan's friendship and devotion to him, for, beside all the other good qualities he possessed, was also that of being ever mindful of those who had benefited him at any time. Accordingly, he gave orders to inquire whether any of his family survived, to whom he might repay the debt he owed Jonathan for his comradeship. Thereupon there was brought to him one of Saul's freedmen [b] who would know whether any of his family remained alive, and David asked him whether he could name any kinsman of Jonathan who was alive and might be the recipient of kindness in return for the benefits which he himself had received from Jonathan. The man replied that a son was left to him, named Memphibosthos,[c] who was crippled in his feet, for, after the news came that the child's father and grandfather had fallen in battle, his nurse had snatched him up and fled, and he had slipped from her shoulder, thereby sustaining an injury to his feet. When David learned where and by whom he was being brought up, he sent to the city of Labatha [d] to Macheiros [e]—this was the person by whom Jonathan's

David's kindness to Jonathan's son.
2 Sam. ix. 1.

2 Sam. iv. 4.

2 Sam. ix. 4.

[b] Bibl. "servant." His name, Siba (bibl. Ziba), is given below, § 115.

[c] Bibl. Mephibosheth, LXX Μεμφιβόσθε, Luc. Μεμφειβάαλ. His real name was probably Meribbaal (*cf.* 1 Chron. viii. 34, ix. 40), but was altered by Hebrew scribes who disapproved of the Canaanite Baal-name. For a similar alteration *cf.* § 9 note on Ish-bosheth (Jebosthos).

[d] Bibl. Lo-debar, LXX Λαδαβάρ, Λωδαβάρ; site unidentified but probably near Mahanaim in Gilead.

[e] Bibl. Machir, LXX Μαχείρ.

114 πέμπεται πρὸς αὐτόν. ἐλθὼν δ' ὁ Μεμφίβοσθὸς
πρὸς τὸν βασιλέα πεσὼν ἐπὶ πρόσωπον προσεκύνησεν αὐτόν. ὁ δὲ Δαυίδης θαρρεῖν τε πρου-
τρέπετο καὶ τὰ βελτίω προσδοκᾶν· δίδωσι δ' αὐτῷ
καὶ τὸν πατρῷον οἶκον καὶ πᾶσαν τὴν οὐσίαν, ἣν ὁ
πάππος αὐτοῦ Σαοῦλος ἐκτήσατο, σύσσιτόν τε καὶ
ὁμοτράπεζον ἐκέλευσεν εἶναι καὶ μηδεμίαν ἡμέραν
115 ἀπολείπεσθαι τῆς σὺν αὐτῷ διαίτης.[1] τοῦ δὲ
παιδὸς προσκυνήσαντος ἐπί τε τοῖς λόγοις καὶ ταῖς
δωρεαῖς, καλέσας τὸν Σιβὰν τὸν πατρῷον οἶκον
ἔλεγε δεδωρῆσθαι τῷ παιδὶ καὶ πᾶσαν τὴν Σαούλου
κτῆσιν, αὐτόν τε ἐκέλευσεν ἐργαζόμενον αὐτοῦ τὴν
γῆν καὶ προνοούμενον, ἁπάντων τὴν πρόσοδον εἰς
Ἱεροσόλυμα κομίζειν, ἄγειν τε αὐτὸν καθ' ἑκάστην
ἡμέραν ἐπὶ τὴν αὐτοῦ τράπεζαν αὐτόν τε τὸν Σιβὰν
καὶ τοὺς υἱοὺς αὐτοῦ, ἦσαν δ' οὗτοι πεντεκαίδεκα,
καὶ τοὺς οἰκέτας αὐτοῦ τὸν ἀριθμὸν ὄντας εἴκοσι
116 τῷ παιδὶ χαρίζεται Μεμφιβόσθῳ. ταῦτα διαταξα-
μένου τοῦ βασιλέως ὁ μὲν Σιβὰς προσκυνήσας καὶ
πάντα ποιήσειν εἰπὼν ἀνεχώρησεν, ὁ δὲ Ἰωνάθου
παῖς ἐν Ἱεροσολύμοις κατῴκει συνεστιώμενος τῷ
βασιλεῖ καὶ πάσης ὡς υἱὸς αὐτοῦ θεραπείας τυγ-
χάνων· ἐγένετο δ' αὐτῷ καὶ παῖς, ὃν Μίχανον[2]
προσηγόρευσε.
117 (vi. 1) Καὶ οἱ μὲν περιλειφθέντες ἐκ τοῦ Σαούλου
γένους καὶ Ἰωνάθου τούτων ἔτυχον παρὰ Δαυίδου
τῶν τιμῶν. τελευτήσαντος δὲ κατ' ἐκεῖνον τὸν
χρόνον[3] τοῦ τῶν Ἀμμανιτῶν βασιλέως Ναάσου
(φίλος δ' ἦν οὗτος αὐτῷ) καὶ διαδεξαμένου τὴν
βασιλείαν Ἀννὼν τοῦ παιδός, πέμψας Δαυίδης

[1] τραπέζης MSP Lat.
[2] Μιχὰν Hudson, Naber cum Cod. Vat. Lat. [3] καιρὸν SPE.

son was being brought up—and summoned him to his presence. Memphibosthos came before the king and, falling on his face, did obeisance to him, but David bade him take heart and look forward to a better lot. He then gave him his father's house and all the substance which his grandfather Saul had acquired, and gave orders that he should share his own food at his table and not let a day pass without eating with him. In acknowledgement of these words and gifts, the lad did obeisance to him. Then David called Siba [a] and told him that he had made the lad a present of his father's house and all of Saul's possessions, and he ordered Siba to work his land and take care of it, to send all the yield to Jerusalem and to bring the lad to his table every day. David also presented Memphibosthos with Siba himself, his sons, of whom there were fifteen, and his servants, twenty in number. When the king had given these instructions, Siba did obeisance to him, saying that he would do all these things, and withdrew. So Jonathan's son dwelt in Jerusalem, sharing the king's hospitality and receiving every attention as though he were his own son. There was also born to him a son, whom he called Michanos.[b]

(vi. 1) Such, then, were the honours which those who were left of the family of Saul and Jonathan received from David. Now there died at this time the Ammanite king Naasēs,[c] who was a friend of David, and his son Annōn [d] succeeded to his throne.

The Ammonites mistreat David's envoys. 2 Sam. x. 1; 1 Chron. xix. 1

[a] Bibl. Ziba (Ṣîbâ'), LXX Σειβά.
[b] Bibl. Micha, LXX Μειχά.
[c] Bibl. Nahash, *cf.* *A.* vi. 68 note.
[d] So LXX; bibl. Hanun, Luc. Ἀννάν.

πρὸς αὐτὸν παρεμυθήσατο, πρᾴως τε φέρειν ἐπὶ τῷ θανάτῳ τοῦ πατρὸς παραινῶν καὶ τὴν αὐτὴν φιλίαν διαμενεῖν,[1] ἣ πρὸς ἐκεῖνον ἦν, τούτῳ προσδοκᾶν.
118 οἱ δὲ τῶν Ἀμμανιτῶν ἄρχοντες κακοήθως ἀλλ' οὐ κατὰ τὸν Δαυίδου τρόπον ταῦτ' ἐδέξαντο, καὶ παρώτρυναν τὸν βασιλέα λέγοντες κατασκόπους πεπομφέναι τῆς χώρας Δαυίδην καὶ τῆς αὐτῶν δυνάμεως ἐπὶ προφάσει φιλανθρωπίας, φυλάττεσθαί τε συνεβούλευον καὶ μὴ προσέχειν τοῖς λόγοις αὐτοῦ, μὴ καὶ σφαλεὶς ἀπαρηγορήτῳ
119 συμφορᾷ περιπέσῃ. ταῦτ' οὖν δόξας πιθανώτερα λέγειν τοὺς ἄρχοντας ἢ τἀληθὲς εἶχεν, ὁ τῶν Ἀμμανιτῶν βασιλεὺς Ἀννὼν τοὺς παρὰ τοῦ Δαυίδου πεμφθέντας πρέσβεις χαλεπῶς περιύβρισε· ξυρήσας γὰρ αὐτῶν τὰ ἡμίση τῶν γενείων καὶ τὰ ἡμίση τῶν ἱματίων περιτεμών, ἔργοις ἀπέλυσε
120 κομίζοντας οὐ λόγοις τὰς ἀποκρίσεις. ἰδὼν δὲ ταῦθ' ὁ τῶν Ἰσραηλιτῶν βασιλεὺς ἠγανάκτησε καὶ δῆλος ἦν οὐ περιοψόμενος τὴν ὕβριν καὶ τὸν προπηλακισμόν, ἀλλὰ πολεμήσων τοῖς Ἀμμανίταις καὶ τιμωρίαν αὐτῶν τῆς παρανομίας τῆς πρὸς[2] τοὺς
121 πρεσβευτὰς εἰσπραξόμενος τὸν βασιλέα. συνέντες δὲ οἵ τε ἀναγκαῖοι καὶ οἱ ἡγεμόνες ὅτι παρεσπονδήκασι καὶ δίκην ὑπὲρ τούτων ὀφείλουσι, προπαρασκευάζονται εἰς τὸν πόλεμον· καὶ πέμψαντες πρὸς Σύρον τὸν τῶν Μεσοποταμιτῶν βασιλέα χίλια τάλαντα σύμμαχον αὐτὸν ἐπὶ τούτῳ γενέσθαι τῷ

[1] Niese: διαμένειν ROE: μένειν MSP. [2] εἰς MSP.

---

[a] Josephus omits the Scriptural detail "to their buttocks" or (Chron.) "hips," LXX "cloak."

[b] According to Scripture David was told of the insult and

David thereupon sent and comforted him, exhorting him to bear his father's death with resignation, and bidding him to look for the continuance of the same friendship that had been with his father. The Ammanite princes, however, received this message in an ugly spirit and not as David had intended it, and incited the king against him by saying that David had sent men to spy on their country and their forces, on the pretext of friendly offices ; they advised him to be on his guard and pay no attention to David's words, lest he be tricked and meet with irremediable disaster. To these words of the princes Annōn, the king of the Ammanites, gave more credence than they actually deserved, and grievously misused the envoys sent by David by shaving off a half of their beards and cutting off a half of their garments,[a] and then dismissed them to bring back his answer in the form of acts instead of words. At sight of them [b] the king of the Israelites was indignant and made it plain that he would not overlook this insult and outrage, but would make war on the Ammanites and exact satisfaction from their king for their lawless treatment of his envoys. Then the relatives and chiefs (of the Ammanite king), realizing that they had violated the treaty and were liable to punishment for this offence, sent a thousand talents [c] to Syros,[d] the king of the Mesopotamians, and invited him to become their ally

War with Ammon and its Syrian allies.
2 Sam. x. 5 ; 1 Chron. xix. 5.

ordered the envoys to remain in Jericho until their beards should have grown.

[c] Of silver according to 1 Chron. ; the sum is not mentioned in 2 Sam.

[d] 2 Sam. Aram Beth-Rehob = the Aramaeans (A.V. "Syrians") of Beth-Rehob, LXX τὴν Συρίαν (Luc. τὸν Σύρον, as in Josephus) Βαιθραάβ κτλ.; 1 Chron. Aram Naharaim = the Aramaeans of Mesopotamia, LXX Συρίας Μεσοποταμίας. Josephus has mistaken an ethnic for a personal name.

μισθῷ παρεκάλεσαν καὶ Σουβάν· ἦσαν δὲ τοῖς βασιλεῦσι τούτοις πεζοῦ[1] δύο μυριάδες. προσεμισθώσαντο δὲ καὶ τὸν[2] ἐκ τῆς Μιχᾶς καλουμένης χώρας βασιλέα καὶ τέταρτον Ἴστοβον ὄνομα, καὶ τούτους ἔχοντας μυρίους καὶ δισχιλίους ὁπλίτας.

122 (2) Οὐ κατεπλάγη δὲ τὴν συμμαχίαν καὶ τὴν τῶν Ἀμμανιτῶν δύναμιν ὁ Δαυίδης, τῷ δὲ θεῷ πεποιθὼς καὶ τῷ[3] δικαίως αὐτοῖς ἀνθ' ὧν ὑβρίσθη πολεμεῖν μέλλειν, Ἰώαβον τὸν ἀρχιστράτηγον δοὺς αὐτῷ τῆς στρατιᾶς τὸ ἀκμαιότατον, ἐξ αὐτῆς ἔπεμψεν
123 ἐπ' αὐτούς. ὁ δὲ πρὸς τῇ μητροπόλει τῶν Ἀμμανιτῶν Ῥαβαθᾷ[4] κατεστρατοπεδεύσατο. τῶν δὲ πολεμίων ἐξελθόντων καὶ παραταξαμένων οὐχ ὁμοῦ, διχῇ δέ, τὸ μὲν γὰρ ἐπικουρικὸν ἐν τῷ πεδίῳ καθ' αὑτὸ ἐτάχθη, τὸ δὲ τῶν Ἀμμανιτῶν στράτευμα πρὸς ταῖς πύλαις ἀντικρὺ τῶν Ἑβραίων,
124 ἰδὼν τοῦτο Ἰώαβος ἀντιμηχανᾶται· καὶ τοὺς μὲν ἀνδρειοτάτους ἐπιλεξάμενος ἀντιπαρατάσσεται τῷ Σύρῳ καὶ τοῖς μετ' αὐτοῦ βασιλεῦσι, τὸ δ' ἄλλο παραδοὺς Ἀβισαίῳ τῷ ἀδελφῷ τοῖς Ἀμμανίταις ἐκέλευσεν ἀντιπαρατάξασθαι, εἰπών, ἂν τοὺς Σύρους ἴδῃ βιαζομένους αὐτὸν καὶ πλέον δυναμένους, μεταγαγόντα τὴν φάλαγγα βοηθεῖν αὐτῷ· τὸ δ'

[1] πεζῶν MSP.
[2] + τῶν Ἀμαληκιτῶν βασιλέα καὶ τὸν SP.
[3] καὶ τῷ] Niese: καὶ RO: τῷ M: ἐν τῷ SP.
[4] Hudson: Ἀραβαθὰ P: Ἀραμαθᾶ rell. Lat.

[a] 2 Sam. Aram-Zoba = the Aramaeans of Zoba, LXX τὴν Συρίαν Σουβά; 1 Chron. "and from Zoba," LXX παρὰ Σωβάλ. Here Josephus has apparently mistaken a place-name for a personal name. On the location of Zoba *cf.* § 99 note.

for this payment, and they also invited Sūba.[a] These kings had twenty thousand infantry. In addition they engaged the king of the country called Micha,[b] and a fourth named Istobos,[c] these latter having twelve thousand[d] armed men.

(2) Undismayed either by this confederacy or by the Ammanite force, David put his trust in God and in the justice of his cause in going to war to avenge the insult he had suffered, and, giving Joab, his commander-in-chief, the flower of his army, at once sent him against them. Joab pitched his camp close to the Ammanite capital Rabatha.[e] Then the enemy issued forth with their men drawn up not in one body but in two, for the auxiliary force was stationed by itself in the plain, and the Ammanite army at the gates, opposite the Hebrews. When Joab saw this, he contrived counter-measures; he selected the bravest of his men and drew them up over against Syros and the kings with him; the rest he turned over to his brother Abisai, with orders to draw them up over against the Ammanites, and, if he saw the Syrians pressing him hard and getting the better of him, to bring over his division and assist him; he

[b] Bibl. Maacah, LXX Ἀμαλήκ (Chron. Μωχά), Luc. Μααχά; the region N.E. of the lake of Huleh.

[c] Bibl. Ish-tob, LXX Εἰστώβ, Ἰστώβ. Ish-tob may have meant "the men of Tob," a region probably in the neighbourhood of these Aramaean states.

[d] 13,000 according to 2 Sam. (1000 with the king of Maacah + 12,000 with Ish-tob).

[e] Variant Aramatha; Bibl Rabbah, LXX Ῥαββάθ. The name of the city is not given in Scripture, which says that the Ammonites were drawn up for battle "at the entrance of the gate" (Chron. "entrance of the city"). The city is located *c.* 25 m. E. of the Jordan on the upper waters of the river Jabbok; in Hellenistic times it was called Philadelphia, and as the modern *'Ammān* is the capital of Transjordania.

αὐτὸ τοῦτο ποιήσειν καὶ αὐτός, ἂν ὑπὸ τῶν Ἀμ-
125 μανιτῶν αὐτὸν καταπονούμενον θεάσηται. προτρεψάμενος οὖν τὸν ἀδελφὸν καὶ παρακαλέσας εὐψύχως καὶ μετὰ προθυμίας ἀνδράσιν αἰσχύνην φοβουμένοις πρεπούσης ἀγωνίσασθαι, τὸν μὲν ἀπέλυσε τοῖς Ἀμμανίταις μαχησόμενον, αὐτὸς δὲ τοῖς Σύροις
126 συνέβαλε. καὶ πρὸς ὀλίγον ἀντισχόντων αὐτῶν καρτερῶς, πολλοὺς μὲν αὐτῶν ἀπέκτεινεν Ἰώαβος, ἅπαντας δ' ἠνάγκασεν εἰς φυγὴν τραπῆναι. τοῦτο ἰδόντες οἱ Ἀμμανῖται καὶ δείσαντες τὸν Ἀβισαῖον καὶ τὴν μετ' αὐτοῦ στρατιὰν οὐκ ἔμειναν, ἀλλὰ μιμησάμενοι τοὺς συμμάχους εἰς τὴν πόλιν ἔφυγον. κρατήσας οὖν τῶν πολεμίων Ἰώαβος εἰς Ἱεροσόλυμα πρὸς τὸν βασιλέα λαμπρῶς ὑπέστρεψε.

127 (3) Τοῦτο τὸ πταῖσμα τοὺς Ἀμμανίτας οὐκ ἔπεισεν ἠρεμεῖν οὐδὲ μαθόντας τοὺς κρείττονας ἡσυχίαν ἄγειν, ἀλλὰ πέμψαντες πρὸς Χαλαμὰν τὸν τῶν πέραν Εὐφράτου Σύρων βασιλέα μισθοῦνται τοῦτον ἐπὶ συμμαχίᾳ,[1] ἔχοντα μὲν ἀρχιστράτηγον[2] Σέβεκον, πεζῶν δὲ μυριάδας ὀκτὼ καὶ ἱππέων
128 μυρίους. γνοὺς δ' ὁ τῶν Ἑβραίων βασιλεὺς πάλιν ἐπ' αὐτὸν τοὺς Ἀμμανίτας τοσαύτην δύναμιν συνηθροικότας, οὐκέτι διὰ στρατηγῶν αὐτοῖς πολεμεῖν ἔκρινεν, ἀλλ' αὐτὸς σὺν ἁπάσῃ τῇ δυνάμει διαβὰς τὸν Ἰόρδανον ποταμὸν καὶ ὑπαντήσας αὐτοῖς

[1] συμμαχίαν MSP.
[2] ex Lat. Niese: ἀντιστράτηγον codd.

---

[a] Again Josephus has mistaken a place-name for a personal name; in 2 Sam. x. 16 it is Helam, LXX Χαλαμάκ (with doublet Αἰλάμ), Luc. Χαλααμά; in the following verse it appears as

himself would do the same if he saw Abisai being worn down by the Ammanites. Then, after encouraging his brother and exhorting him to fight bravely and with an ardour expected of men who fear disgrace, he sent him off to face the Ammanites in battle, while he himself engaged the Syrians. Although the latter resisted stoutly for a short time, Joab slew many of them and compelled all the rest to turn and flee. At this sight the Ammanites, who were afraid of Abisai and his army, waited no longer, but followed the example of their allies and fled to their city. Having thus overcome the enemy, Joab returned in triumph to the king at Jerusalem.

(3) This defeat did not persuade the Ammanites to remain quiet or to keep the peace in the knowledge that their enemy was superior. Instead they sent to Chalamas,[a] the king of the Syrians across the Euphrates, and hired him as an ally with his commander-in-chief Sebekos[b] and eighty thousand infantry and ten thousand cavalry.[c] When the king of the Hebrews learned that the Ammanites had again assembled a very large force against him, he decided not to conduct the war through generals any longer, but himself crossed the river Jordan with his entire force and, when he met them, engaged them in a

Helama, LXX Αἰλάμ; the name is missing in 1 Chron. Some scholars think that Helam is the modern Aleppo, but Kraeling, *Aram and Israel*, p. 43, holds that this is too far north, and identifies it with Alema of 1 Macc. v. 26, apparently near the head-waters of the river Jarmuk.

[b] 2 Sam. Shobach, LXX Σωβάκ, Luc. (with doublet) Σωβὰ καὶ Σαβεαί; 1 Chron. Shophach, LXX Σωφάρ, Σωφάχ κτλ. In Scripture he is called the commander of the army (A.V. "captain of the host") of Hadarezer (Hadadezer), who brought the auxiliary force from Helam.

[c] These numbers are invented by Josephus.

συνάψας εἰς μάχην ἐνίκησε· καὶ ἀναιρεῖ μὲν αὐτῶν πεζῶν μὲν εἰς τέσσαρας μυριάδας ἱππέων δὲ εἰς ἑπτακισχιλίους, ἔτρωσε δὲ καὶ τὸν στρατηγὸν τοῦ
129 Χαλαμᾶ Σέβεκον, ὃς ἐκ τῆς πληγῆς ἀπέθανεν. οἱ δὲ Μεσοποταμῖται τοιούτου γενομένου τοῦ τέλους τῆς μάχης αὑτοὺς Δαυίδῃ παρέδοσαν καὶ δῶρα ἔπεμψαν αὐτῷ. καὶ ὁ μὲν ὥρᾳ χειμῶνος ἀνέστρεψεν εἰς Ἱεροσόλυμα, ἀρχομένου δὲ τοῦ ἔαρος ἔπεμψε τὸν ἀρχιστράτηγον Ἰώαβον πολεμήσοντα τοῖς Ἀμμανίταις. ὁ δὲ τήν τε γῆν αὐτῶν ἅπασαν ἐπερχόμενος διέφθειρε καὶ αὐτοὺς εἰς τὴν μητρόπολιν συγκλείσας Ῥαβαθὰν[1] ἐπολιόρκει.
130 (vii. 1) Συνέπεσε δὲ καὶ Δαυίδῃ πταῖσμα δεινὸν ὄντι φύσει δικαίῳ καὶ θεοσεβεῖ καὶ τοὺς πατρίους νόμους ἰσχυρῶς φυλάσσοντι· θεασάμενος γὰρ δείλης ὀψίας ἀπὸ τοῦ στέγους[2] τῶν βασιλείων, ἐν ᾧ περιπατεῖν κατ᾽ ἐκεῖνο τῆς ὥρας ἦν ἔθος, γυναῖκα λουομένην ἐν τῇ αὑτῆς οἰκίᾳ ψυχρῷ ὕδατι καλλίστην τὸ εἶδος καὶ πασῶν διαφέρουσαν, ὄνομα αὐτῇ ἦν Βεεθσαβή,[3] ἡττᾶται τοῦ κάλλους τῆς γυναικός· καὶ τῆς ἐπιθυμίας κατασχεῖν[4] οὐ δυνά-
131 μενος μεταπεμψάμενος αὐτὴν[5] συνέρχεται. γενομένης δ᾽ ἐγκύου τῆς γυναικὸς καὶ πεμψάσης πρὸς τὸν βασιλέα, ὅπως τῷ ἁμαρτήματι σκέψηταί τινα τοῦ λαθεῖν ὁδόν, ἀποθανεῖν γὰρ αὐτὴν κατὰ τοὺς πατρίους καθήκειν[6] νόμους μεμοιχευμένην, μετα-

[1] Hudson: Ἀραβαθὰ (-ᾶ R) RMSP Lat.: Ἀραβᾶ O: Ἀραμαθὰν E.
[2] τέγους SP.
[3] Βεερσάβη SP hic et infra; cf. ad § 348.
[4] κρατεῖν Naber.
[5] μεταπεμ. αὐτὴν] αὐτῇ RO.
[6] Niese: καθήκει M: προσήκει rell.

battle in which he was victorious and slew some forty thousand of their infantry and seven thousand of their cavalry,[a] while he also wounded Sebekos, Chalamas's commander, who afterwards died of the wound. Upon the conclusion of the battle in this manner, the Mesopotamians surrendered to David and sent him gifts. Then, as it was the winter season, he returned to Jerusalem; but, at the beginning of spring, he sent his commander-in-chief Joab to make war on the Ammanites. Joab, after overrunning all their country and ravaging it, shut them up in their capital Rabatha and laid siege to it.

David sins with Bath-sheba (Beethsabe). 2 Sam. xi. 2.

(vii. 1) Now David, although he was by nature a righteous and godfearing man, and one who strictly observed the laws of his fathers, nevertheless fell into grave error; for late one evening he saw from the roof of his palace, where he was accustomed to walk at that hour, a woman bathing in her house with cold[b] water. She was very beautiful to look upon and surpassed all other women; her name was Beethsabē.[c] He was captivated by the beauty of the woman and, as he was unable to restrain his desire, he sent for her and lay with her. And when she became pregnant and sent to the king, asking him to contrive some way of concealing her sin—for, according to the laws of the fathers, she was deserving of death as an adulteress[d]—he summoned the

[a] So 1 Chron.; 2 Sam. "Seven hundred chariots and forty thousand horsemen."

[b] Detail added by Josephus.

[c] Variant Beersabē, *cf.* § 348; bibl. Bath-sheba, LXX Βηρσάβεε (cod. A Βηθσάβεε), Luc. Βηρσάβεαι (-αιε).

[d] Bath-sheba's request and the comment on the penalty are an amplification of Scripture, which says, "the woman conceived and she sent and told David, and said, I am with child."

καλεῖται τὸν Ἰωάβου μὲν ὁπλοφόρον ἐκ τῆς πολιορκίας ἄνδρα δὲ τῆς γυναικὸς Οὐρίαν ὄνομα, καὶ παραγενόμενον περί τε τῆς στρατιᾶς καὶ τῆς
132 πολιορκίας ἀνέκρινε. λέγοντος δὲ πάντα κατὰ νοῦν αὐτοῖς κεχωρηκέναι τὰ πράγματα βαστάσας ἐκ τοῦ δείπνου μέρη προσδίδωσιν αὐτῷ καὶ κελεύει πρὸς τὴν γυναῖκα ἀπελθόντα ἀναπαύσασθαι σὺν αὐτῇ. ὁ δὲ Οὐρίας τοῦτο μὲν οὐκ ἐποίησε, παρεκοιμήθη δὲ τῷ βασιλεῖ σὺν τοῖς ἄλλοις ὁπλοφόροις.
133 ὡς δὲ γνοὺς τοῦθ' ὁ βασιλεὺς ἀνέκρινεν αὐτὸν ὅτι μὴ πρὸς[1] τὴν οἰκίαν ἔλθοι μηδὲ πρὸς τὴν γυναῖκα διὰ τοσούτου χρόνου, πάντων ἀνθρώπων ταύτην ἐχόντων τὴν φύσιν ὅταν ἔλθωσιν ἐξ ἀποδημίας, οὐκ εἶναι δίκαιον ἔφη τῶν συστρατιωτῶν αὐτοῦ καὶ τοῦ στρατηγοῦ χαμαὶ κοιμωμένων ἐν τῇ παρεμβολῇ καὶ τῇ τῶν πολεμίων χώρᾳ, μετὰ τῆς
134 γυναικὸς αὐτὸν ἀναπαύεσθαι καὶ τρυφᾶν. ταῦτ' εἰπόντα μεῖναι τὴν ἡμέραν ἐκείνην ἐκέλευσεν[2] αὐτόθι ὡς εἰς τὴν ἐπιοῦσαν ἀπολύσων αὐτὸν πρὸς τὸν ἀρχιστράτηγον. κληθεὶς δ' ἐπὶ δεῖπνον ὑπὸ τοῦ βασιλέως Οὐρίας καὶ μέχρι μέθης προελθὼν ἐν τῷ πότῳ, δεξιουμένου τοῦ βασιλέως αὐτὸν ἐπίτηδες ταῖς προπόσεσιν, οὐδὲν ἧττον πάλιν πρὸ τῶν τοῦ βασιλέως θυρῶν ἐκοιμήθη μηδεμίαν λαβὼν
135 τῆς γυναικὸς ἐπιθυμίαν. ἐπὶ τούτοις δὲ δυσανασχετήσας ὁ βασιλεὺς ἔγραψε τῷ Ἰωάβῳ κολάσαι προστάττων τὸν Οὐρίαν· ἁμαρτεῖν γὰρ αὐτὸν ἐδήλου· καὶ τὸν τρόπον τῆς τιμωρίας ἵνα μὴ γένηται φανερὸς αὐτὸς τοῦτο βουληθεὶς ὑπέθετο·
136 κατὰ γὰρ τὸ δυσμαχώτατον αὐτὸν ἐκέλευσε μέρος

[1] + αὐτὸν εἰς MSP Lat.
[2] προσέταξεν MSPE.

woman's husband, whose name was Uriah and who was also Joab's armour-bearer,[a] from the siege, and, when he appeared, questioned him about the army and the siege. When the man told him that everything had gone as they wished, he took some portions of his supper and gave them to him with the command to go home to his wife and rest with her. Uriah, however, did not do so but slept near the king with the other armour-bearers. And, when the king learned of this, he inquired of him why he had not gone to his house after so long a period of absence, saying that this was the natural thing for men to do when they return from abroad. To this he replied that it was not right for him to enjoy luxurious rest in the company of his wife, while his fellow-soldiers and his commander were sleeping on the ground in their camp in enemy territory. When he had so spoken, the king ordered him to remain there that day, saying that he would send him back to the commander-in-chief on the morrow. So Uriah was invited to supper by the king and continued drinking until he was intoxicated, as the king deliberately pledged his health in cup after cup. Nevertheless he again slept before the king's door and felt no desire for his wife. In great displeasure at this, the king wrote to Joab, ordering him to punish Uriah, whom he made out to be a guilty man[b]; and, in order that he himself should not appear to have willed his punishment, he suggested the manner of it, which was to order Uriah to be stationed opposite the most

David plans Uriah's death.
2 Sam. xi. 14.

[a] Unscriptural detail.

[b] Scripture says nothing of any accusation made by David in the letter to Joab. Some of the rabbis, however, held that Uriah deserved death for disobeying David's order to go home to his wife.

τῶν πολεμίων τάξαι καὶ καθ' ὃ κινδυνεύσει[1] μαχόμενος[2] ἀπολειφθεὶς μόνος· τοὺς γὰρ συμπαραστάτας ἀναχωρῆσαι ἐκ τῆς μάχης γινομένης ἐκέλευσε. ταῦτα γράψας καὶ σημηνάμενος τῇ αὐτοῦ σφραγῖδι τὴν ἐπιστολὴν ἔδωκεν Οὐρίᾳ κομίσαι πρὸς Ἰώαβον.
137 δεξάμενος δὲ Ἰώαβος τὰ γράμματα καὶ τὴν τοῦ βασιλέως προαίρεσιν ἀναγνούς, καθ' ὃν ᾔδει τόπον τοὺς πολεμίους χαλεποὺς αὐτῷ[3] γενομένους κατὰ τοῦτον ἔστησε τὸν Οὐρίαν δοὺς αὐτῷ τινας τῶν ἀρίστων τῆς στρατιᾶς· αὐτὸς δ' ἁπάσῃ τῇ δυνάμει προσεπιβοηθήσειν ἔφησεν, εἰ δυνηθεῖεν ἀνατρέψαντές τι τοῦ τείχους εἰσελθεῖν εἰς τὴν πόλιν·
138 ὄντα δ' αὐτὸν γενναῖον στρατιώτην καὶ δόξαν ἔχοντα παρά τε τῷ βασιλεῖ καὶ πᾶσι τοῖς ὁμοφύλοις ἐπ' ἀνδρείᾳ, χαίρειν τοῖς μεγάλοις πόνοις ἀλλὰ μὴ προσαγανακτεῖν ἠξίου. τοῦ δ' Οὐρία προθύμως ὑποστάντος τὸ ἔργον, τοῖς μετ' αὐτοῦ παρατασσομένοις ἰδίᾳ καταλιπεῖν ὅταν ἐξορμήσαν-
139 τας ἴδωσι τοὺς πολεμίους ἐδήλωσε. προσβαλόντων οὖν τῇ πόλει τῶν Ἑβραίων δείσαντες οἱ Ἀμμανῖται, μὴ κατ' ἐκεῖνον τὸν τόπον, καθ' ὃν Οὐρίαν συνέβαινε τετάχθαι, φθάσαντες ἀναβῶσιν οἱ πολέμιοι, προστησάμενοι τοὺς ἀνδρειοτάτους αὐτῶν καὶ τὴν πύλην ἀνοίξαντες αἰφνιδίως καὶ μετὰ ῥύμης καὶ δρόμου πολλοῦ τοῖς ἐχθροῖς
140 ἐπεξῆλθον. ἰδόντες δὲ αὐτοὺς οἱ σὺν τῷ Οὐρίᾳ πάντες ἀνεχώρησαν ὀπίσω, καθὼς Ἰώαβος αὐτοῖς προεῖπεν· αἰσχυνθεὶς δ' Οὐρίας φυγεῖν καὶ τὴν τάξιν καταλιπεῖν ὑπέμεινε τοὺς πολεμίους· καὶ τὴν ὁρμὴν αὐτῶν ἐκδεξάμενος ἀναιρεῖ μὲν οὐκ ὀλίγους,

formidable part of the enemy, where, if left to fight alone, he would be in greatest danger; he also ordered his comrades in arms to retire when the battle began. When he had written this letter and stamped it with his own seal, he gave it to Uriah to carry to Joab. On receiving the letter and learning from it the king's intention, Joab stationed Uriah at the place where he knew the enemy had been most troublesome to himself, and gave him some of the bravest men in the army. He also said that he would come to his assistance with his whole force if they could throw down part of the wall and enter the city. He therefore asked Uriah, as a good soldier and as one who was esteemed by the king and by all his countrymen for his bravery, to welcome his difficult task rather than object to it. And when Uriah eagerly undertook the work, Joab privately instructed the men who were stationed with him to desert him when they saw the enemy charge. Now when the Hebrews attacked the city, the Ammanites, in their fear that the enemy might surprise them by climbing up at the point where Uriah happened to be posted, put their bravest men in front and, suddenly opening the gates, rushed out upon the enemy with great violence and speed. At sight of them, the men with Uriah all retreated, as Joab had instructed them. But Uriah, who was ashamed to flee and abandon his post, remained to face the foe, and met their charge, slaying not a few; but finally, being surrounded on

---

[1] Niese: *κινδυνεύει* ROM: *κινδυνεύσειε* SP.
[2] post *μαχόμενος* lacunam statuit Niese.
[3] Naber: *αὐτῷ* codd.

κυκλωθεὶς δὲ καὶ ληφθεὶς ἐν μέσῳ τελευτᾷ[1] ἅμα δ' αὐτῷ τινες καὶ ἄλλοι συγκατέπεσον τῶν ἑταίρων.[2]

141 (2) Τούτων οὕτως γενομένων ἔπεμψεν ἀγγέλους Ἰώαβος πρὸς τὸν βασιλέα λέγειν ἐντειλάμενος αὐτοῖς ὡς σπουδάσειε[3] μὲν ταχέως ἑλεῖν τὴν πόλιν, προσβαλὼν δὲ τῷ τείχει καὶ πολλοὺς ἀπολέσας ἀναχωρῆσαι βιασθείη. προστιθέναι δὲ τούτοις ἂν ὀργιζόμενον ἐπ' αὐτοῖς βλέπωσι καὶ τὸν Οὐρία

142 θάνατον. τοῦ δὲ βασιλέως ἀκούσαντος παρὰ τῶν ἀγγέλων ταῦτα καὶ δυσφοροῦντος φάσκοντος ἁμαρτεῖν αὐτοὺς τῷ τείχει προσβαλόντας, δέον ὑπονόμοις καὶ μηχανήμασιν ἑλεῖν πειρᾶσθαι τὴν πόλιν, καὶ ταῦτ' ἔχοντας παράδειγμα τὸν Γεδεῶνος υἱὸν Ἀβιμέλεχον, ὃς ἐπεὶ τὸν ἐν Θήβαις πύργον ἑλεῖν ἐβούλετο βίᾳ, βληθεὶς ὑπὸ πρεσβύτιδος πέτρῳ κατέπεσε καὶ ἀνδρειότατος ὢν διὰ τὸ δυσχερὲς

143 τῆς ἐπιβολῆς[4] αἰσχρῶς ἀπέθανεν· οὗ μνημονεύοντας ἔδει μὴ προσιέναι τῷ τείχει τῶν πολεμίων· ἄριστον γὰρ ἁπάντων τῶν ἐν πολέμῳ πραχθέντων καὶ καλῶς καὶ ὡς ἑτέρως ἐν τοῖς αὐτοῖς κινδύνοις μνήμην ἔχειν, ὡς τὰ μὲν μιμεῖσθαι τὰ δὲ φυλάτ-

[1] τελευτᾷ post μέσῳ tr. Hudson: post ἄλλοι codd.

[2] συγκατ. . . . ἑταίρων Hudson: συγκαταπεσόντων (καὶ) ἑτέρων codd.

[3] Niese: σπουδάσει RO: σπουδάσαι MSP.

[4] Hudson: ἐπιβουλῆς codd.

[a] The account of Uriah's death is greatly amplified. *Cf.* 2 Sam. xi. 16, 17 "And it came to pass, when Joab kept watch upon (or "invested") the city, that he assigned Uriah unto the place where he knew that valiant men were. And the men of the city went out and fought with Joab, and there fell some of the people of the servants of David, and Uriah the Hittite died also."

[b] According to the Heb. text of Scripture, David does not,

all sides, he was caught and killed, and along with him there fell a few others from among his comrades.[a]

(2) After this had taken place Joab sent messengers to the king, instructing them to tell him that he had made every effort to take the city quickly, but that, after an assault on the wall, he had lost many men and had been forced to retire; they were, he said, to add to this, if they saw that the king was wrathful, the news of Uriah's death. But when the king heard the messengers' report, he was greatly displeased and said that the army had blundered in assaulting the wall,[b] whereas they ought to have tried to take the city with mines and engines, especially as they had before them the example of Abimelech, the son of Gedeon,[c] who, in his attempt to take the town of Thebae[d] by force, had been struck down by a rock hurled by an old woman and, in spite of being so very brave, had ignominiously perished because of his unfortunate method of attack.[e] And with this in mind they ought not to have approached the enemy's wall, for it was best to have in mind all things that had been tried in war, whether successfully or otherwise, under the same conditions of danger, in order to imitate the one and avoid the other. But when,

Joab informs David of Uriah's death. 2 Sam. xi. 18.

on hearing the messenger's report, show displeasure at Joab's conduct of the siege, but it is Joab himself who anticipates David's displeasure and his reference to the incident of Abimelech. The LXX has an additional verse, in which David repeats almost verbatim the criticism anticipated by Joab. Josephus simplifies matters by attributing the speech to David after the messenger's report.

[c] Bibl. Jerubbesheth (for original Jerubbaal), LXX Ἰεροβοάμ, Luc. Ἰεροβάαλ; this was another name for Gideon, *cf.* Jd. vi. 32, *A.* v. 214 note.

[d] Bibl. Thebez, LXX Θαμασί (in Jd. Θηβής).

[e] *Cf. A.* v. 251 ff.

144 τεσθαι. ἐπεὶ δὲ οὕτως ἔχοντι[1] καὶ τὸν Οὐρία θάνατον ἐδήλωσεν ὁ ἄγγελος, παύεται μὲν τῆς ὀργῆς, Ἰωάβῳ δ' ἐκέλευσεν ἀπελθόντα λέγειν ἀνθρώπινον εἶναι τὸ συμβεβηκὸς καὶ τὰ τοῦ πολέμου φύσιν ἔχειν τοιαύτην, ὥστε ποτὲ μὲν τοῖς ἐναντίοις εὖ πράττειν συμβαίνειν κατ' αὐτόν, ποτὲ
145 δὲ τοῖς ἑτέροις· τοῦ λοιποῦ μέντοι γε προνοεῖν τῆς πολιορκίας, ὅπως μηδὲν ἔτι πταίσωσι κατ' αὐτήν, ἀλλὰ χώμασι καὶ μηχαναῖς ἐκπολιορκήσαντας καὶ παραστησαμένους τὴν μὲν πόλιν κατασκάψαι, ἅπαντας δ' ἀπολέσαι τοὺς ἐν αὐτῇ. καὶ ὁ μὲν ἄγγελος τὰ ὑπὸ τοῦ βασιλέως ἐντεταλμένα κομίζων
146 πρὸς Ἰώαβον ἠπείγετο. ἡ δὲ τοῦ Οὐρία γυνὴ Βεεθσαβὴ τὸν θάνατον τἀνδρὸς πυθομένη ἐπὶ συχνὰς αὐτὸν ἡμέρας ἐπένθησεν, παυσαμένην δὲ τῆς λύπης καὶ τῶν ἐπ' Οὐρίᾳ δακρύων ὁ βασιλεὺς εὐθὺς ἄγεται γυναῖκα, καὶ παῖς ἄρρην ἐξ αὐτῆς γίνεται αὐτῷ.

147 (3) Τοῦτον οὐχ ἡδέως ἐπεῖδεν ὁ θεὸς τὸν γάμον, ἀλλὰ δι' ὀργῆς ἔχων τὸν Δαυίδην, τῷ προφήτῃ Νάθᾳ φανεὶς κατὰ τοὺς ὕπνους ἐμέμφετο τὸν βασιλέα. ὁ δὲ Νάθας ἀστεῖος καὶ συνετὸς ὢν ἀνήρ, λογισάμενος ὡς οἱ βασιλεῖς ὅταν εἰς ὀργὴν ἐμπέσωσι ταύτῃ πλέον ἢ τῷ δικαίῳ νέμουσι, τὰς μὲν παρὰ τοῦ θεοῦ γεγενημένας ἀπειλὰς ἡσυχάζειν ἔκρινεν, ἄλλους δὲ λόγους χρηστοὺς πρὸς αὐτὸν
148 διεξῆλθε, καὶ δὴ τοιοῦτόν τινα τρόπον περὶ οὗ καὶ τί φρονεῖ ποιῆσαι σαφὲς αὐτῷ παρεκάλει· "δύο γάρ," φησίν, "ἄνδρες τὴν αὐτὴν κατῴκουν πόλιν,

[1] M: ἔχοντα RO: ἔχοντα ἔγνω SP.

[a] David's instructions to Joab are an amplification of Scripture.
[b] Detail added by Josephus.

while he was in this humour, he was further informed by the messenger of Uriah's death, he ceased being angry and ordered him to go back and tell Joab that what had happened was human destiny, and such was the nature of war that now one of the opposing sides happened to be successful therein, and now the other; for the future, however, they should look to the siege and avoid meeting with another reverse in the course of it. They should rather besiege the city with mounds and engines and, after forcing it to surrender, raze it to the ground and destroy all those within it.[a] So the messenger hastened to carry back to Joab the commands of the king, while Beethsabē, the wife of Uriah, learning of her husband's death, mourned for him many days. But, as soon as she had ceased grieving and weeping for Uriah, the king took her to wife, and had by her a son.

(3) God, however, did not look upon this marriage with favour, but was angry with David, and, appearing to the prophet Nathan in a dream,[b] He found fault with the king. Thereupon Nathan, being a man of tact and understanding, and reflecting that when kings fall into a passion they are more influenced by this than by a sense of justice, decided to keep silence about the threats that had been made by God, and instead addressed him in mild terms, and somewhat in the following manner asked him to give him his opinion of a like case[c]: "There were," he said, "two men living in the same city, one of

Nathan's parable of the poor man's lamb. 2 Sam. xii. 1.

[c] With the foregoing contrast the brevity of Scripture: "And the Lord sent Nathan unto David, and he came unto him, and said unto him, there were two men," etc. The last introductory phrase in Josephus's text ("give him his opinion") may have been suggested by Luc.'s addition to 2 Sam. xii. 1, ἀπάγγειλον δή μοι τὴν κρίσιν ταύτην.

ὧν ὁ μὲν πλούσιος ἦν καὶ πολλὰς εἶχεν ἀγέλας ὑποζυγίων τε καὶ θρεμμάτων καὶ βοῶν, τῷ πένητι
149 δ' ἀμνὰς ὑπῆρχε μία. ταύτην μετὰ τῶν τέκνων αὐτοῦ[1] ἀνέτρεφε συνδιαιρούμενος[2] αὐτῇ τὰ σιτία καὶ φιλοστοργίᾳ πρὸς αὐτὴν χρώμενος, ᾗ τις ἂν χρήσαιτο καὶ πρὸς θυγατέρα. ξένου δ' ἐπελθόντος τῷ πλουσίῳ τῶν μὲν ἰδίων οὐδὲν ἠξίωσεν ἐκεῖνος βοσκημάτων καταθύσας εὐωχῆσαι τὸν φίλον, πέμψας δὲ τὴν ἀμνάδα τοῦ πένητος ἀπέσπασε, καὶ ταύτην παρασκευάσας εἱστίασε τὸν ξένον."
150 σφόδρα δ' ἐλύπησεν ὁ λόγος οὗτος τὸν βασιλέα καὶ πονηρὸν πρὸς τὸν Νάθαν τὸν ἄνθρωπον ἐκεῖνον, ὃς δὴ τοῦτο τὸ ἔργον ἐτόλμησεν, ἀπεφήνατο καὶ τετραπλὴν ἀποτῖσαι τὴν ἀμνάδα δίκαιον εἶναι καὶ πρὸς τούτῳ θανάτῳ κολασθῆναι. Νάθας δ' ὑποτυχὼν αὐτὸν ἔλεγεν ἐκεῖνον εἶναι τὸν ἄξιον ταῦτα παθεῖν ὑφ' ἑαυτοῦ κεκριμένον τολμήσαντα μέγα
151 καὶ δεινὸν ἔργον. ἀνεκάλυπτε δ' αὐτῷ καὶ παρεγύμνου τὴν ὀργὴν τοῦ θεοῦ ποιήσαντος μὲν αὐτὸν βασιλέα πάσης[3] τῆς Ἑβραίων δυνάμεως καὶ τῶν ἐν κύκλῳ πάντων ἐθνῶν πολλῶν καὶ μεγάλων κύριον, ῥυσαμένου δ' ἔτι πρὸ τούτων ἐκ τῶν Σαούλου χειρῶν, δόντος δ' αὐτῷ καὶ γυναῖκας ἃς δικαίως καὶ νομίμως ἠγάγετο, καταφρονηθέντος δ' ὑπ' αὐτοῦ καὶ ἀσεβηθέντος, ὃς ἀλλοτρίαν τε γήμας ἔχοι[4] γυναῖκα καὶ τὸν ἄνδρα αὐτῆς ἀποκτείνειεν
152 ἐκδοὺς τοῖς πολεμίοις· δώσειν οὖν αὐτὸν ἀντὶ τούτων δίκας τῷ θεῷ καὶ βιασθήσεσθαι μὲν αὐτοῦ τὰς γυναῖκας ὑφ' ἑνὸς τῶν παίδων, ἐπιβουλευθή-

[1] αὐτὸς MSP. [2] συνδιαιτώμενος M: συνδατούμενος Naber. [3] πάσης om. MSP. [4] Hudson: ἔχει RMSP: ἔχειν O.

whom was wealthy and possessed many herds of beasts of burden, sheep and cattle, while the other had only one ewe lamb. This he brought up with his own children, sharing his food with it and giving it the same affection that one would give one's own daughter. Now once, when the wealthy man was visited by a guest, he did not see fit to slaughter one of his own animals for the feasting of his friend, but he sent men to take away the ewe lamb from the poor man, and prepared it for the delectation of his guest." This story greatly distressed the king and he declared to Nathan that the man who had had the heart to do this thing was a villain, and that it was just that he repay the lamb fourfold [a] and in addition be punished with death. Nathan thereupon rejoined that David himself was the one who deserved this punishment, having been condemned by himself of perpetrating a great and terrible crime. He also revealed to him in the plainest fashion the wrath of God, for though He had made him king of all the Hebrew host and lord of all the many great nations around them, and had, even before that, delivered him from Saul's hands, and had given him wives to take in rightful and lawful marriage, yet He had been disregarded and impiously treated by him when he took another's wife in marriage and caused his death by giving him up to the enemy. For this, he said, he should make amends to God, and his wives should be violated by one of his sons,[b] and he too

Nathan accuses David and reveals his punishment. 2 Sam. xii. 7.

[a] So Heb. and Luc.; LXX "sevenfold." *Cf.* Ex. xxii. 1 (Heb. xxi. 37) on the fourfold penalty for the theft of a sheep.

[b] *i.e.* Absalom, *cf.* § 213 (=2 Sam. xvi. 21 f.). At this point, Scripture merely says, "I will take thine wives before thine eyes, and give them unto thy neighbour."

σεσθαι δὲ καὶ αὐτὸν ὑπ' ἐκείνου, καὶ τὸ ἁμάρτημα τοῦτο κρύφα δράσαντα φανερὰν τὴν ἐπ' αὐτῷ δίκην ὑφέξειν· τεθνήξεσθαι δὲ καὶ τὸν παῖδά σοι παρα-
153 χρῆμα τὸν ἐξ αὐτῆς γεγενημένον. ταραχθέντος δ' ἐπὶ τούτοις τοῦ βασιλέως καὶ συσχεθέντος[1] ἱκανῶς καὶ μετὰ δακρύων καὶ λύπης ἀσεβῆσαι λέγοντος, ἦν γὰρ ὁμολογουμένως θεοσεβὴς καὶ μηδὲν ἁμαρτὼν ὅλως περὶ τὸν βίον ἢ τὰ περὶ τὴν Οὐρία γυναῖκα, ᾤκτειρεν ὁ θεὸς καὶ διαλλάττεται, φυλάξειν αὐτῷ καὶ τὴν ζωὴν καὶ τὴν βασιλείαν ἐπαγγειλάμενος· μετανοοῦντι γὰρ περὶ τῶν γεγενημένων οὐκέτι χαλεπῶς ἔχειν ἔφασκε. καὶ Νάθας μὲν ταῦτα τῷ βασιλεῖ προφητεύσας οἴκαδε ἐπανῆλθε.

154 (4) Τῷ δ' ἐκ τῆς Οὐρία γυναικὸς γενομένῳ παιδὶ Δαυίδῃ νόσον ἐνσκήπτει χαλεπὴν τὸ θεῖον, ἐφ' ᾗ δυσφορῶν ὁ βασιλεὺς τροφὴν μὲν ἐφ' ἡμέρας ἑπτὰ καίτοι γε ἀναγκαζόντων τῶν οἰκείων οὐ προσηνέγκατο, μέλαιναν δὲ περιθέμενος ἐσθῆτα πεσὼν ἐπὶ σάκκου κατὰ γῆς ἔκειτο τὸν θεὸν ἱκετεύων ὑπὲρ τῆς τοῦ παιδὸς σωτηρίας· σφόδρα
155 γὰρ ἔστεργεν αὐτοῦ τὴν μητέρα. τῇ δ' ἑβδόμῃ τῶν ἡμερῶν τελευτήσαντος τοῦ παιδὸς οὐκ ἐτόλμων τῷ βασιλεῖ τοῦτο μηνύειν οἱ θεράποντες λογιζόμενοι μὴ γνοὺς ἔτι μᾶλλον ἀπόσχηται καὶ τροφῆς καὶ τῆς ἄλλης ἐπιμελείας ὡς ἂν ἐπὶ ποθεινοῦ[2] τέκνου τετελευτηκότος, ὅτε καὶ νοσοῦντος οὕτως

[1] συγχυθέντος MSPE: confuso Lat.
[2] Niese: ποθηνοῦ RO: πένθει SP Lat.: πόθῳ (post τέκνου) M.

[a] In Scripture, Nathan's prophecy of the child's death is made after David's confession of sin.
[b] The black garment is not mentioned in Scripture, which

should be plotted against by this same son; and for this sin, which he had committed secretly, he should suffer the penalty in the sight of all. Furthermore the son whom she would bear him would die soon after birth.[a] At these words the king was dismayed and greatly troubled, and with tears of grief admitted his impiety—for he was, as all agreed, a god-fearing man and never sinned in his life except in the matter of Uriah's wife—, whereupon God took pity on him and was reconciled to him. And He promised to preserve both his life and his kingdom, for, He said, now that he repented of his deeds, He was no longer displeased with him. Then Nathan, after prophesying these things to the king, returned to his home.

David's grief at death of Bathsheba's child. 2 Sam. xii. 15.

(4) Now upon the child whom Uriah's wife bore to David the Deity caused a grave illness to fall, and the king, in his unhappiness over this, did not partake of food for seven days, although his servants tried to force him to do so. Instead he put on a black garment and, throwing himself upon sackcloth, lay on the ground, beseeching God to spare the life of the child,[b] whose mother he so deeply loved. But on the seventh day the child died, and the servants dared not inform the king, for they feared that when he learned of it he might even more completely refuse food and other necessary care, in his desolation at the death of his son, seeing that even during the child's illness he had, in his grief, so greatly afflicted

says, "David therefore besought God for the child, and David fasted and went in and lay all night upon the earth," but Luc. and some LXX codd. add (after "went in") "and he slept in sackcloth." On the black garments worn by accused persons on appearing before the judge *cf. A.* xiv. 172 (Herod before the Synhedrion), *B.J.* i. 506 (Pheroras before Herod).

156 ὑπὸ τῆς λύπης ἑαυτὸν ἐκάκου. ταραττομένων δ'
αἰσθόμενος τῶν οἰκετῶν ὁ βασιλεὺς καὶ ταῦτα
πασχόντων, ἃ μάλιστα συγκρύψαι τι θέλουσι συμ-
βαίνει, συνεὶς ὅτι τέθνηκεν ὁ παῖς προσφωνήσας
ἕνα τῶν οἰκετῶν καὶ μαθὼν τἀληθὲς ἀνίσταται,
καὶ λουσάμενος καὶ λαβὼν ἐσθῆτα λευκὴν εἰς τὴν
157 σκηνὴν τοῦ θεοῦ παραγίνεται, καὶ κελεύσας δεῖπνον
αὐτῷ παραθεῖναι πολλὴν ἐπὶ τῷ παραλόγῳ τοῖς
τε συγγενέσι καὶ τοῖς οἰκέταις ἔκπληξιν παρεῖχεν,
ὅτι μηδὲν τούτων ἐπὶ νοσοῦντι τῷ παιδὶ ποιήσας πάνθ' ὁμοῦ τετελευτηκότος ἔπραττε. τήν τε
αἰτίαν, δεηθέντες ἐπιτρέψαι πρῶτον αὐτοῖς πυθέ-
158 σθαι, παρεκάλουν εἰπεῖν τῶν γεγενημένων. ὁ δὲ
ἀμαθεῖς εἰπὼν αὐτοὺς ἐδίδασκεν ὡς ἔτι μὲν ζῶντος
τοῦ παιδὸς ἔχων ἐλπίδα σωτηρίας αὐτοῦ δεόντως
πάντ' ἐποίει, τὸν θεὸν ἡγούμενος τούτοις εὐμενῆ
καταστήσειν, ἀποθανόντος δ' οὐκέτι χρείαν εἶναι
λύπης ματαίας. ταῦτ' εἰπόντος ἐπῄνεσαν τὴν
σοφίαν καὶ τὴν διάνοιαν τοῦ βασιλέως. συνελθὼν
δὲ τῇ γυναικὶ Βεεθσαβῇ ἔγκυον αὐτὴν ἐποίησε,
καὶ γενόμενον[1] ἄρρεν παιδίον Σολομῶνα[2] προσηγόρευσεν, οὕτως Νάθα τοῦ προφήτου κελεύσαντος.
159 (5) Ἰώαβος δὲ τῇ πολιορκίᾳ τοὺς Ἀμμανίτας
ἰσχυρῶς ἐκάκου τῶν τε ὑδάτων αὐτοὺς ἀποτεμνό-
μενος καὶ τῆς τῶν ἄλλων εὐπορίας, ὡς πάνυ ταλαι-
πωρεῖν ἐνδείᾳ ποτοῦ καὶ τροφῆς. ἐξ ὀλίγου γὰρ

[1] γεννησαμένην R: γεννησαμένη O: procreavit Lat.
[2] + τοῦτον RO.

[a] Scripture says merely that "he changed his apparel." Weill and Rappaport find here an allusion to customs followed in Josephus's own time. But in the literature cited by

himself. The king, however, perceived that they were disturbed and were acting in such a manner as is usual with those who wish to conceal something, and so he realized that the child had died. Then he called to him one of his servants and, when he learned the truth, he arose, bathed, put on a white [a] garment and went to the tent of God; and when he ordered a meal to be prepared for him, he caused great astonishment at his strange conduct among his relatives and servants, because he had done none of these things during the child's illness, and was suddenly doing them now that he was dead. So, having first requested permission to inquire, they asked him to tell them the reason for these acts. Thereupon he called them dullards, and explained that while the child was still alive, he had hoped for its recovery and had therefore done everything proper, with the thought of rendering God gracious to him by such means; but now that it was dead, he no longer had any need of vain grief. At these words they praised the king's wisdom and understanding.[b] Then David lay with his wife Beethsabē, and she conceived and bore a son, whom he named Solomon, at the bidding of the prophet Nathan.[c]

Birth of Solomon. 2 Sam. xii. 24.

(5) Now Joab in besieging the Ammanites was inflicting great damage on them by cutting off their water and other supplies, so that they were in a very pitiable condition for lack of food and drink, for they

Joab invites David to sack Rabbah (Rabatha). 2 Sam. xii. 26; 1 Chron. xx. 1.

the latter we have references only to the wearing of white garments on solemn holy days such as New Year, the Fast of Ab and the Day of Atonement.

[b] The approval of the people is a detail added by Josephus.

[c] Scripture adds that the child was also called Jedidiah ("beloved of Yah"), "for the Lord's sake," who "had sent by the hand of Nathan."

φρέατος ἤρτηντο[1] καὶ τούτου τεταμιευμένου,[2] ὡς μὴ τελέως αὐτοὺς ἐπιλιπεῖν τὴν πηγὴν δαψιλέ-
160 στερον χρωμένους. γράφει δὴ τῷ βασιλεῖ ταῦτα δηλῶν καὶ παρακαλῶν αὐτὸν ἐπὶ τὴν αἵρεσιν τῆς πόλεως ἐλθεῖν, ἵνα τὴν νίκην αὐτὸς ἐπιγραφῇ.[3] ταῦτα Ἰωάβου γράψαντος ἀποδεξάμενος αὐτὸν τῆς εὐνοίας καὶ τῆς πίστεως ὁ βασιλεὺς παραλαβὼν τὴν σὺν αὐτῷ δύναμιν ἧκεν ἐπὶ τὴν τῆς Ῥαβαθᾶς πόρθησιν, καὶ κατὰ κράτος ἑλὼν διαρπάσαι τοῖς
161 στρατιώταις ἐφῆκεν. αὐτὸς δὲ τὸν τοῦ βασιλέως τῶν Ἀμμανιτῶν λαμβάνει στέφανον ἕλκοντα χρυσοῦ τάλαντον καὶ πολυτελῆ λίθον ἔχοντα ἐν μέσῳ σαρδόνυχα· ἐφόρει δ' αὐτὸν ἐπὶ τῆς κεφαλῆς διαπαντὸς Δαυίδης. πολλὰ δὲ καὶ ἄλλα σκῦλα λαμπρὰ καὶ πολύτιμα εὗρεν ἐν τῇ πόλει· τοὺς δ' ἄνδρας αἰκισάμενος διέφθειρε. ταὐτὰ δὲ καὶ τὰς ἄλλας τῶν Ἀμμανιτῶν πόλεις διέθηκεν ἑλὼν αὐτὰς κατὰ κράτος.

162 (viii. 1) Ἀναστρέψαντος δ' εἰς Ἱεροσόλυμα τοῦ βασιλέως πταῖσμα αὐτοῦ τὴν οἰκίαν ἐξ αἰτίας τοιαύτης καταλαμβάνει· θυγάτηρ ἦν[4] αὐτῷ παρ-

[1] ἠρύτοντο Naber.
[2] τούτου τεταμ. cod. Vat. ap. Hudson: τοῦτο τεταμιευμένον SP: ταμείας RO(M).
[3] Niese: ἐπιγράφη R: ἐπιγράφει O: ἐπιγραφείη MSP.
[4] γὰρ ἦν RO.

[a] The details of the siege are an amplification of 2 Sam. xii. 27, "And Joab sent messengers to David, and said, I have fought against Rabbah, and I have taken the city of waters."

[b] So the Heb. *malkâm* "their king"; but the LXX reading Μελχὸμ τοῦ βασιλέως indicates that the Ammonite god Milcom (*cf.* 1 Kings xi. 5) was originally meant.

[c] Scripture speaks only of a "precious stone," LXX λίθου

were dependent on a small well and this had to be carefully controlled in order that the spring might not fail them altogether because of too frequent use.[a] Accordingly, he wrote to the king, informing him of this and inviting him to come to the capture of the city in order that he might have the victory ascribed to himself. Upon receiving Joab's letter, the king commended his loyalty and faithfulness; then he took along the force that was with him and came for the sacking of Rabatha, which he took by force and allowed his soldiers to plunder. He himself took the crown of the Ammanite king,[b] which weighed a talent of gold and had in its centre a precious stone, a sardonyx[c]; and thereafter David always wore it on his own head.[d] He also found much other splendid and valuable spoil in the city. As for the inhabitants, he tortured them and put them to death.[e] And the other Ammanite cities, which he took by force, he treated in the same way.

(viii. 1) But when the king returned to Jerusalem, a great misfortune overtook his household, arising from the following cause. He had a daughter who

The story of Amnon and Tamar (Thamara). 2 Sam. xiii. 1

τιμίου. It may be noted that in *A.* iii. 165 Josephus uses σαρδόνυξ to translate Heb. *eben šōhām* "onyx" (?), LXX σμάραγδος "emerald" (?) of Ex. xxviii. 9, while in *A.* iii. 168 he uses the same word to translate Heb. *'ōdem* "sardius" (A.V. "carnelian"), LXX σάρδιον of Ex. xxviii. 17. Evidently Josephus, like the LXX translators, was not sure of the meaning of some Heb. names of precious stones; the same uncertainty marks our renderings to-day.

[d] It is not clear from Scripture whether David thereafter wore the crown or only the jewel in it.

[e] The Heb. text of 2 Sam. xii. 31 is obscure and probably corrupt, leaving it uncertain whether the Ammonites were tortured or merely put to forced labour. It is probable that Josephus omits the Scriptural details because of the difficulty of the text.

θένος μὲν ἔτι τὸ δὲ κάλλος εὐπρεπής, ὡς ἁπάσας ὑπερβάλλειν τὰς εὐμορφοτάτας γυναῖκας, Θαμάρα ὄνομα, τῆς δ᾽ αὐτῆς Ἀψαλώμῳ μητρὸς κεκοινω-
163 νηκυῖα. ταύτης ὁ πρεσβύτατος[1] τῶν Δαυίδου παίδων Ἀμνὼν ἐρασθείς, ὡς οὔτε διὰ τὴν παρθενίαν αὐτῆς οὔτε διὰ τὴν φυλακὴν τυχεῖν τῆς ἐπιθυμίας ἐδύνατο, χαλεπῶς διέκειτο, καὶ τό τε σῶμα τῆς ὀδύνης αὐτὸν κατεσθιούσης κατισχναί-
164 νετο καὶ τὴν χρόαν μετέβαλλε. δῆλος δὲ γίνεται ταῦτα πάσχων Ἰωνάθῃ τινὶ συγγενεῖ καὶ φίλῳ. συνετὸς δ᾽ ἦν οὗτος ἐν τοῖς μάλιστα καὶ τὴν διάνοιαν ὀξύς. ὁρῶν οὖν καθ᾽ ἑκάστην πρωίαν τὸν Ἀμνῶνα μὴ κατὰ φύσιν ἔχοντα τῷ σώματι προσελθὼν ἠρώτα φράσαι τὴν αἰτίαν αὐτῷ, εἰκάζειν μέντοι γε αὐτὸς ἔλεγεν ἐξ ἐρωτικῆς οὕτως
165 ἔχειν αὐτὸν ἐπιθυμίας. τοῦ δὲ Ἀμνῶνος ὁμολογήσαντος τὸ πάθος, ὅτι τῆς ἀδελφῆς ἐρᾷ τυγχανούσης ὁμοπατρίας, ὁδὸν αὐτῷ καὶ μηχανὴν εἰς τὸ περιγενέσθαι τῶν εὐκταίων ὑπέθετο· νόσον γὰρ ὑποκρίνασθαι παρῄνεσεν, ἐλθόντα δὲ πρὸς αὐτὸν τὸν πατέρα πέμψαι τὴν ἀδελφὴν αὐτῷ διακονησομένην ἐκέλευσε παρακαλέσαι· ῥᾴω[2] γὰρ ἔσεσθαι καὶ ταχέως ἀπαλλαγήσεσθαι τῆς νόσου τούτου γενο-
166 μένου. πεσὼν οὖν ὁ Ἀμνὼν ἐπὶ τὴν κλίνην νοσεῖν προσεποιεῖτο κατὰ τὰς Ἰωνάθου ὑποθήκας. παραγενομένου δὲ τοῦ πατρὸς καὶ σκεπτομένου πῶς ἔχοι, τὴν ἀδελφὴν ἐδεῖτο πέμψαι πρὸς αὐτόν· ὁ δ᾽ εὐθὺς ἐκέλευσεν ἀχθῆναι. ἡκούσῃ δὲ προσ-

[1] E Glycas: πρεσβύτερος codd.
[2] Ernesti: ῥάων, ῥᾷον codd.

---

[a] Bibl. Tamar, LXX Θημάρ, Cod. A and Luc. Θαμάρ.
[b] An added detail, suggested, I suspect, by the Targum's

was still a virgin and of such striking beauty that she surpassed all the fairest women; her name was Thamara[a] and she had the same mother as Absalom. Now the eldest of David's sons, Amnon, fell in love with her but, since he could not obtain his desire because of her virginity and because she was closely guarded,[b] he became very ill and, as the pain consumed his body, he wasted away and lost his colour. His unhappy state then became apparent to a certain Jonathes,[c] a relative and friend and a man who was exceedingly clever and sharp-witted. So when he saw Amnon every morning in a bodily state that was not natural, he went up to him and asked him to tell him the reason, but, he said, he himself guessed that he was in this state as a result of love-sickness.[d] And Amnon confessed his passion, saying that he was in love with his sister on the father's side, whereupon the other suggested to him an ingenious way of obtaining his wishes. He advised him to feign illness and, when his father came to him, to request him to send his sister to wait on him. If he did this, he said, he would get better and would soon be rid of his illness. Accordingly, Amnon took to his bed and, following Jonathes' suggestion, pretended to be ill. Then, when his father came and inquired how he felt, he begged him to send his sister to him; thereupon the king immediately ordered her to be brought

rendering of 2 Sam. xiii. 2, where the Heb. has "it was difficult in the eyes of Amnon (A.V. "and it seemed hard to Amnon") to do anything to her"; for "it was difficult" Targum has *hawâ mekassâ* "it was concealed," but Josephus apparently took the ptc. *mekassâ* as feminine and as referring to Tamar.

[c] Bibl. Jonadab, LXX Ἰωναδάβ, Luc. Ἰωναθάν. Scripture adds that he was a son of Shimeah, David's brother, *cf.* § 178.

[d] Detail added by Josephus.

ἔταξεν ἄρτους αὐτῷ ποιῆσαι τηγανιστοὺς αὐτουργῷ
167 γενομένῃ· προσοίσεσθαι γὰρ ἥδιον ἐκ τῶν ἐκείνης χειρῶν. ἡ δ' ἐμβλέποντος τἀδελφοῦ φυράσασα τὸ ἄλευρον καὶ πλάσασα κολλυρίδας καὶ τηγανίσασα προσήνεγκεν αὐτῷ· ὁ δὲ τότε μὲν οὐκ ἐγεύσατο, προσέταξε δὲ τοῖς οἰκέταις παραιτήσασθαι πάντας πρὸ τοῦ δωματίου· βούλεσθαι γὰρ ἀναπαύσασθαι,
168 θορύβου καὶ ταραχῆς ἀπηλλαγμένος. ὡς δὲ τὸ κελευσθὲν ἐγένετο, τὴν ἀδελφὴν ἠξίωσεν εἰς τὸν ἐνδοτέρω οἶκον τὸ δεῖπνον αὐτῷ παρενεγκεῖν· ποιησάσης δὲ τοῦτο τῆς κόρης λαβόμενος αὐτῆς συνελθεῖν αὐτῷ πείθειν ἐπειρᾶτο. ἀνακραγοῦσα δ' ἡ παῖς "ἀλλὰ μὴ σύ γε τοῦτο βιάσῃ με μηδὲ ἀσεβήσῃς," εἶπεν, "ἀδελφέ, τοὺς νόμους παραβὰς καὶ δεινῇ περιβαλὼν σαυτὸν αἰσχύνῃ· παῦσαι δ' οὕτως ἀδίκου καὶ μιαρᾶς ἐπιθυμίας, ἐξ ἧς ὀνείδη
169 καὶ κακοδοξίαν ὁ οἶκος ἡμῶν κερδανεῖ." συνεβούλευέ τε περὶ τούτου διαλεχθῆναι τῷ πατρί· συγχωρήσειν γὰρ ἐκεῖνον. ταῦτα δ' ἔλεγε βουλομένη τὴν ὁρμὴν αὐτοῦ τῆς ὀρέξεως πρὸς τὸ παρὸν διαφυγεῖν. ὁ δ' οὐ πείθεται, τῷ δὲ ἔρωτι καιόμενος καὶ τοῖς τοῦ πάθους κέντροις μυωπιζόμενος
170 βιάζεται τὴν ἀδελφήν. μῖσος δ' εὐθέως μετὰ τὴν διακόρησιν[1] εἰσέρχεται τὸν Ἀμνῶνα καὶ προσ-

[1] κορείαν (-ίαν) ROE: διακορίαν S: διακορήσας Zonaras.

[a] Heb. *štê lebîbôth* "two heart-shaped (or "round") cakes," Targum *tartên ḥalîṭâthâ* "two dumplings" (dough stirred and boiled in water, sometimes fried after boiling), LXX δύο κολλύρας (*v.l.* -ίδας) "two rolls." The LXX word is used by Josephus in § 167.

[b] According to Scripture (Heb., Targum and LXX) they were boiled.

[c] Marriage with a half-sister on the father's side was thus

and, when she arrived, instructed her to make some fried[a] cakes for Amnon with her own hands, for, David said, he would eat more readily from her hands. And so, while her brother looked on, she kneaded the flour and formed it into rolls which she fried[b] and brought to him. He, however, did not immediately taste them, but ordered his servants to send away all who stood at the door of his chamber, as he wished to rest and be free from noise and disturbance. When they had done as he ordered, he asked his sister to serve the meal to him in his inner chamber, and the maid did so, whereupon he took hold of her and attempted to persuade her to lie with him. But the girl cried out and said, "Oh no, do not force me to this nor be so impious, my brother, as to transgress the law and bring upon yourself dreadful shame. Give up this unrighteous and unholy desire, from which our house will reap only disgrace and ill fame." She further counselled him to speak of the matter with his father, for he would consent to their marriage.[c] Thus she spoke in order to escape for the moment from the violence of his lust. He, however, did not listen to her, but, burning with desire and goaded by the spur of passion, violated his sister. But no sooner had Amnon ravished[d] her than he was filled with loathing of her,

Tamar waits on Amnon and is violated. 2 Sam. xiii. 8.

evidently permitted in David's time, although prohibited in the law ascribed to Moses, Lev. xviii. 6 ff. (which scholars generally regard as actually much later than Moses). The rabbis, attempting to reconcile this early practice with the Mosaic law, explained that Tamar's mother had given birth to her before being converted to Judaism, and that therefore Tamar was not strictly a blood-relative of Amnon according to Jewish law.

[d] T. Reinach, hesitating to accept the reading *διακόρησιν*, suggests *μετὰ κόρον* "after surfeit."

λοιδορησάμενος ἐκέλευσεν ἀναστᾶσαν ἀπιέναι.[1] τῆς δὲ χείρω τὴν ὕβριν καὶ διὰ τοῦτο ἀποκαλούσης, εἰ βιασάμενος αὐτὸς μηδ' ἄχρι νυκτὸς ἐπιτρέπει μεῖναι παραχρῆμα δ' ἀπαλλάττεσθαι κελεύει ἐν ἡμέρᾳ καὶ φωτί, ἵνα καὶ μάρτυσι τῆς αἰσχύνης περιπέσοι, προσέταξεν αὐτὴν ἐκβαλεῖν τῷ οἰκέτῃ.
171 ἡ δὲ περιαλγὴς ἐπὶ τῇ ὕβρει καὶ τῇ βίᾳ γενομένη περιρρήξασα τὸν χιτωνίσκον, ἐφόρουν γὰρ αἱ τῶν ἀρχαίων παρθένοι χειριδωτοὺς ἄχρι τῶν σφυρῶν πρὸς τὸ μὴ βλέπεσθαι χιτῶνας, καὶ σποδὸν καταχεαμένη τῆς κεφαλῆς ἀπῄει διὰ τῆς πόλεως μέσης
172 βοῶσα καὶ ὀδυρομένη τὴν βίαν. περιτυχὼν δ' αὐτῇ ὁ ἀδελφὸς Ἀψάλωμος ἀνέκρινε τίνος αὐτῇ δεινοῦ συμβάντος οὕτως ἔχει· κατειπούσης δ' αὐτῆς πρὸς αὐτὸν τὴν ὕβριν, ἡσυχάζειν καὶ μετρίως φέρειν παρηγόρει καὶ μὴ νομίζειν ὑβρίσθαι φθαρεῖσαν ὑπ' ἀδελφοῦ. πεισθεῖσα οὖν παύεται τῆς βοῆς καὶ τοῦ πρὸς πολλοὺς τὴν βίαν ἐκφέρειν, καὶ πολὺν χρόνον χηρεύουσα παρὰ Ἀψαλώμῳ τῷ ἀδελφῷ διεκαρτέρησε.
173 (2) Γνοὺς δὲ τοῦθ' ὁ πατὴρ Δαυίδης τοῖς μὲν πεπραγμένοις ἤχθετο, φιλῶν δὲ τὸν Ἀμνῶνα σφόδρα, πρεσβύτατος γὰρ ἦν αὐτῷ υἱός, μὴ λυπεῖν αὐτὸν ἠναγκάζετο. ὁ δὲ Ἀψάλωμος ἐμίσει[2] χαλεπῶς αὐτὸν καὶ λανθάνων καιρὸν εἰς ἄμυναν αὐτοῦ
174 τῆς ἁμαρτίας ἐπιτήδειον παρεφύλαττεν. ἔτος δ' ἤδη τοῖς περὶ τὴν ἀδελφὴν αὐτοῦ πταίσμασι

[1] Zonaras: ἀπεῖναι codd. E.
[2] + γε MSP: + γὰρ Naber: + τε Ernesti.

[a] Josephus, in translating Heb. *ketōneth passîm* " tunic with sleeves "(?) (A.V. " garment of many colours "), com-

and, heaping abuse upon her head, he ordered her to rise and be gone. And when she denounced it as a still worse outrage that, after himself violating her, he did not allow her to remain until night but ordered her to depart immediately in broad daylight that she might encounter witnesses of her shame, he told his servant to throw her out. Then, in her distress at the outrage and the violence done her, she rent her tunic—in ancient times virgins wore long-sleeved tunics reaching to the ankle,[a] in order not to be exposed—and poured ashes on her head and went away through the midst [b] of the city, crying aloud and bewailing the violence she had suffered. Her brother Absalom meeting her inquired what misfortune had befallen her that she acted in this way. And when she told him of the outrage, he exhorted her to be quiet and to take it calmly and not consider herself outraged in having been ravished by her brother. So she obeyed him and ceased crying and publishing the violation abroad, and remained desolate [c] in the house of her brother Absalom.

Absalom slays Amnon for the wrong done Tamar, his sister. 2 Sam. xiii. 21.

(2) Now when her father David learned of this, he was grieved by what had happened, but, as he loved Amnon greatly,—for he was his eldest son—he was compelled not to make him suffer.[d] Absalom, however, hated him fiercely, and in secret waited for a favourable opportunity to take vengeance for his crime. When the second year had already passed since his

bines the LXX καρπωτός "long-sleeved" and Luc. ἀστραγαλωτός "reaching to the ankle."

[b] Detail added by Josephus.

[c] So the LXX, lit. "widowed"; Heb. *šômēmāh* "desolate" (A.V.).

[d] Josephus's explanation of David's concern for Amnon is taken from the LXX addition to 2 Sam. xiii. 21.

διεληλύθει δεύτερον, καὶ μέλλων ἐπὶ τὴν τῶν ἰδίων
κουρὰν ἐξιέναι θρεμμάτων εἰς Βελσεφών, πόλις δ'
ἐστὶν αὕτη τῆς Ἐφραΐμου κληρουχίας, παρακαλεῖ
τὸν πατέρα σὺν καὶ τοῖς ἀδελφοῖς ἐλθεῖν πρὸς
175 αὐτὸν ἐφ' ἑστίασιν. παραιτησαμένου δ' ὡς μὴ
βαρὺς αὐτῷ γένοιτο, τοὺς ἀδελφοὺς ἀποστεῖλαι
παρεκάλεσε. πέμψαντος δὲ τοῖς ἰδίοις ἐκέλευσεν,
ὁπηνίκ' ἂν[1] ἴδωσι τὸν Ἀμνῶνα μέθῃ παρειμένον
καὶ κάρῳ, νεύσαντος αὐτοῦ φονεύσωσι μηδένα
φοβηθέντες.
176 (3) Ὡς δ' ἐποίησαν τὸ προσταχθὲν ἔκπληξις
καὶ ταραχὴ τοὺς ἀδελφοὺς λαμβάνει, καὶ δείσαντες
περὶ ἑαυτῶν ἐμπηδήσαντες τοῖς ἵπποις ἐφέροντο
πρὸς τὸν πατέρα. φθάσας δέ τις αὐτοὺς ἅπαντας
ὑπὸ Ἀψαλώμου πεφονεῦσθαι τῷ πατρὶ προσήγ-
177 γειλεν. ὁ δ' ὡς ἐπὶ παισὶν ὁμοῦ τοσούτοις ἀπο-
λωλόσι καὶ τοῦθ' ὑπ' ἀδελφοῦ, τῆς λύπης κἀπὶ
τῷ κτεῖναι[2] δοκοῦντι γινομένης πικρότερον, συναρ-
παγεὶς ὑπὸ τοῦ πάθους οὔτε τὴν αἰτίαν ἀνέκρινεν
οὔτ' ἄλλο τι μαθεῖν, οἷον εἰκὸς τηλικούτου προσηγ-
γελμένου κακοῦ καὶ δι' ὑπερβολὴν ἀπιστίαν ἔχοντος,
περιέμεινεν, ἀλλὰ καταρρηξάμενος τὴν ἐσθῆτα καὶ
ῥίψας ἑαυτὸν ἐπὶ τὴν γῆν ἔκειτο πενθῶν τοὺς υἱοὺς
ἅπαντας καὶ τοὺς ἀποθανεῖν δεδηλωμένους καὶ τὸν
178 ἀνῃρηκότα. ὁ δὲ Σαμᾶ τοῦ ἀδελφοῦ αὐτοῦ παῖς

[1] Niese: ὁπηνίκα codd. E: ὅπως ἡνίκα Holwerda: ὅπως ἡνίκ' ἂν Hudson.

[2] + δυναμένης, -οις codd.

---

[a] Bibl. " Baal-hazor, which is beside (lit. " with ") Ephraim," LXX ἐν Βαιλασὼρ τῇ ἐχόμενα Ἐφράϊμ, Luc. Βασελλασὼρ παρὰ Γοφράϊμ. The Γοφράϊμ of Luc. is apparently Ophrah, a city in the territory of Benjamin, not of Ephraim, *cf.* Joshua xviii. 23 ; if this is so, it confirms the theory that Baal-hazor

sister's misfortune, and as he was about to depart for Belsephōn[a]—this is a city in the territory of Ephraim[a]—to shear his sheep, he invited his father, along with his brothers, to come to his home for a feast. But David declined on the ground that he would be a burden to him, whereupon he urged him to send his brothers. Then Absalom sent a message to his men, giving orders that when they saw Amnon overcome by drink and in a daze, they should, at a signal from himself, murder him without fear of anyone.

(3) And when they carried out these commands, dismay and confusion seized his other brothers, and in fear for their lives they leaped on their horses[b] and rode away to their father. But someone reached there before them and reported to the king that they had all been murdered by Absalom. At the loss of so many sons at once and especially at the hands of a brother—his grief being more bitter when he thought who the supposed murderer was[c]—he was overcome by his trouble and did not inquire the reason nor take time to learn anything else,—as might have been expected in view of the greatness of the reported tragedy and its unbelievable atrociousness[d]—but rent his garments and threw himself on the ground to lie there mourning for all his sons, both those whose deaths had been announced and him who had slain them. Then Jonathes, a son of his brother Sama,[e]

Amnon's brothers escape death at Absalom's hands. 2 Sam. xiii. 29.

is the modern *Tell 'Aṣur*, about 5 miles N.E. of *Beitin* (bibl. Bethel).

[b] Bibl. "mules."

[c] The text appears to be corrupt, but no plausible emendation suggests itself.

[d] These reflections are, of course, unscriptural.

[e] So the LXX; bibl. Shimeah. *Cf.* § 164 note.

Ἰωνάθης ἀνεῖναί τι τῆς λύπης παρεκάλει καὶ περὶ μὲν τῶν ἄλλων μὴ πιστεύειν ὡς τεθνᾶσιν, οὐδὲ γὰρ αἰτίαν εὑρίσκειν ὑπολαμβάνειν, περὶ δ' Ἀμνῶνος ἐξετάζειν ἔφη δεῖν· εἰκὸς γὰρ διὰ τὴν Θαμάρας ὕβριν ἀποτολμῆσαι τὸν Ἀψάλωμον τὴν ἀναίρεσιν
179 τὴν ἐκείνου. μεταξὺ δὲ κτύπος ἵππων καὶ θόρυβος προσιόντων τινῶν αὐτοὺς ἐπέστρεψεν· ἦσαν δ' οἱ τοῦ βασιλέως παῖδες οἱ διαδράντες ἀπὸ τῆς ἑστιάσεως. ὑπαντᾷ δ' αὐτοῖς ὁ πατὴρ θρηνοῦσι λυπούμενος καὶ παρ' ἐλπίδας ὁρῶν οὓς ἀκηκόει
180 μικρὸν ἔμπροσθεν ἀπολωλότας. ἦν δὲ παρὰ πάντων δάκρυα καὶ στόνος, τῶν μὲν ὡς ἐπ' ἀδελφῷ τετελευτηκότι, τοῦ δὲ βασιλέως ὡς ἐπὶ παιδὶ κατεσφαγμένῳ. φεύγει δ' Ἀψάλωμος εἰς Γεσσοῦραν[1] πρὸς τὸν πάππον τὸν πρὸς μητρὸς δυναστεύοντα τῆς ἐκεῖ χώρας, καὶ τρισὶν ὅλοις ἔτεσι παρ' αὐτῷ καταμένει.

181 (4) Τοῦ δὲ Δαυίδου προαίρεσιν ἔχοντος ἐπὶ τὸν υἱὸν Ἀψάλωμον πέμπειν, οὐκ ἐπὶ τιμωρίᾳ κατελευσόμενον, ἀλλ' ὅπως εἴη σὺν αὐτῷ, καὶ γὰρ τὰ τῆς ὀργῆς ὑπὸ τοῦ χρόνου λελωφήκει, πρὸς τοῦτο μᾶλλον αὐτὸν Ἰώαβος ὁ ἀρχιστράτηγος παρώρ-
182 μησε· γύναιον γάρ τι τὴν ἡλικίαν ἤδη προβεβηκὸς ἐποίησεν αὐτῷ προσελθεῖν ἐν σχήματι πενθίμῳ, ὡς[2] παίδων ἐπὶ τῆς ἀγροικίας αὐτῇ διενεχθέντων καὶ πρὸς φιλονεικίαν τραπέντων, οὐδενὸς τοῦ καταπαῦσαι δυναμένου παραφανέντος ἔλεγεν ὑπὸ θατέρου
183 τὸν ἕτερον πληγέντα ἀποθανεῖν· ἠξίου τε τῶν συγγενῶν ἐπὶ τὸν ἀνῃρηκότα ὡρμηκότων καὶ ζητούν-

[1] Γεσούρα M: Γεθσοῦραν SP: Gessyr Lat.

[2] ὡς om. M: ἡ ex Lat. Dindorf: post ὡς lacunam statuit Niese.

urged him to moderate his grief somewhat and not believe that his other sons were dead, as he found no reason for supposing such a thing; but, as for Amnon, he ought to make inquiries, for it was likely that, because of the outrage to Thamara, Absalom had been reckless enough to slay him. Meanwhile the clatter of horses and the noise of approaching men caused them to look around [a]; and there were the king's sons who had escaped from the feast. When their father greeted them, they were in tears, and he himself was grief-stricken because it was more than he had hoped for when he beheld those of whose death he had heard but a little while before. So there were tears and laments on both sides, on theirs for their dead brother, and on the king's for his slaughtered son. But Absalom fled to Gessūra [b] to his maternal grandfather,[c] who ruled over that country, and remained with him three whole years.

(4) Now David had the intention of sending for his son Absalom, not that he might be punished on his return, but in order that he might be with him, for in the course of time his anger had abated; to this decision his commander-in-chief Joab strongly urged him on by causing a certain woman, well advanced in years, to come to him in mourner's garb with a story that her sons, having a dispute in the field, had come to an open quarrel and, as no one appeared who could have stopped it, one of them was struck by the other and killed; she had asked her relatives who had set out to hunt the slayer and slay

Joab's stratagem to reconcile David to Absalom. 2 Sam. xiii. 39. 2 Sam. xiv. 1.

[a] Unscriptural details.

[b] Bibl. Geshur, LXX Γεδσούρ (*v.l.* Γεσσείρ); an Aramaic kingdom lying east of the Sea of Galilee.

[c] His name, Talmai (*cf.* § 21 note), is given, at this point, in Scripture.

των αὐτὸν ἀνελεῖν, χαρίσασθαι τὴν σωτηρίαν αὐτῇ τοῦ παιδὸς καὶ μὴ τὰς ἐπιλοίπους[1] τῆς γηροκομίας αὐτὴν ἐλπίδας προσαφαιρεθῆναι· τοῦτο δ' αὐτῇ κωλύσαντα τοὺς βουλομένους ἀποκτεῖναι τὸν υἱὸν αὐτῆς παρέξειν· οὐ γὰρ ἐφέξειν ἐκείνους ἄλλῳ τινὶ
184 τῆς σπουδῆς ἢ τῷ παρ' αὐτοῦ φόβῳ. τοῦ δὲ συγκατανεύσαντος[2] οἷς τὸ γύναιον ἱκέτευσεν, ὑπολαβὸν πάλιν πρὸς τὸν βασιλέα "χάρις μέν," εἶπεν, "ἤδη σου τῇ χρηστότητι κατοικτείραντός μου τὸ γῆρας καὶ τὴν παρὰ μικρὸν ἀπαιδίαν, ἀλλ' ἵνα βέβαια τὰ παρὰ τῆς σῆς μοι ᾖ[3] φιλανθρωπίας, τῷ σαυτοῦ παιδὶ πρῶτον καταλλάγηθι καὶ τὴν πρὸς
185 αὐτὸν ὀργὴν ἄφες· πῶς γὰρ ἂν πεισθείην ἐμοί σε ταύτην ἀληθῶς[4] δεδωκέναι τὴν χάριν αὐτοῦ σοῦ μέχρι νῦν ἐφ' ὁμοίοις ἀπεχθανομένου τῷ παιδί;" τελέως δ' ἀνόητον[5] εἶναι προσθεῖναι τῷ παρὰ
186 γνώμην ἀποθανόντι υἱῷ[6] ἄλλον ἑκουσίως. συνίησι δὲ ὁ βασιλεὺς ὑπόβλητον οὖσαν τὴν σκῆψιν ἐξ Ἰωάβου καὶ τῆς τούτου σπουδῆς· καὶ ἐπειδὴ παρὰ τῆς πρεσβύτιδος πυθόμενος οὕτως ἔχον τἀληθὲς ἔμαθε, προσκαλεσάμενος τὸν Ἰώαβον ἐπιτυχεῖν τε τοῦ προκειμένου κατὰ νοῦν ἔφασκε καὶ τὸν Ἀψάλωμον ἄγειν ἐκέλευσεν· οὐ γὰρ ἔτι χαλεπῶς ἔχειν πρὸς αὐτόν, ἀλλ' ἤδη τὴν ὀργὴν καὶ τὸν θυμὸν
187 ἀφεικέναι. ὁ δὲ προσκυνήσας τὸν βασιλέα καὶ τοὺς λόγους ἀσπασάμενος ἐξώρμησεν εἰς τὴν Γεσσούραν παραυτίκα καὶ τὸν Ἀψάλωμον παραλαβὼν ἧκεν εἰς Ἱεροσόλυμα.

[1] ἔτι λοιπὰς (-ὸν E) ROE.
[2] συγκαταινέσαντος MSE: adnuente Lat.
[3] M: εἴη rell. E.
[4] ἀληθῶς om. RO.
[5] δ' ἀνόητον] δ' ἂν ἀνόητον SP: δ' ἂν M: ἀνόητον δ' E.
[6] ἀποθαν. υἱῷ] ἀποθανόντος τοῦ υἱοῦ MSP: ἀποθανόντι καὶ E.

him in turn, to spare her son's life for her sake and not further deprive her of her last remaining hope of support in her old age. This, she said, the king would secure to her by preventing those who wished to kill her son from so doing, for nothing would restrain them from their purpose except their fear of him. And when he acceded to the woman's petition, she again addressed him with these words, " I do indeed thank you for your kindness in taking pity on my old age and on my near-childlessness, but, in order that I may have full assurance of your humane treatment of me, be first reconciled to your own son and let your anger toward him cease. For how should I be persuaded that you have truly granted me this kindness if you yourself still feel hate toward your son for a like reason? It would be utterly unreasonable if, after one son has perished against your will, you were willingly to cause the death of another." [a] Then the king perceived that this pretended case was an invention of Joab and due to his zeal for Absalom's cause. And when, by questioning the old woman, he learned that it was so in truth, he summoned Joab to tell him that he had gained his end, and he bade him bring Absalom, for he was no longer hostile to him but had already got over his anger and displeasure. Thereupon Joab did obeisance to the king, receiving his words with joy, and at once set out for Gessūra, from which place he brought Absalom back with him to Jerusalem.

[a] The woman's second speech is considerably amplified by Josephus.

188 (5) Προέπεμψε δ' ἔμπροσθεν ὁ βασιλεὺς πρὸς
τὸν υἱὸν ὡς ἤκουσε παραγενόμενον καὶ πρὸς
ἑαυτὸν ἐκέλευσε χωρεῖν· οὔπω γὰρ οὕτως ἔχειν
ὥστ' εὐθὺς ἰδεῖν κατελθόντα. καὶ ὁ μὲν τοῦτο τοῦ
πατρὸς κελεύσαντος ἐξέκλινε τὴν ὄψιν αὐτοῦ καὶ
διετέλει τῆς παρὰ τῶν οἰκείων θεραπείας τυγχάνων.
189 οὐκ ἐπεβέβλαπτο δ' εἰς τὸ κάλλος ὑπό τε τῆς
λύπης καὶ τοῦ μὴ τυγχάνειν τῆς προσηκούσης
ἐπιμελείας υἱῷ βασιλέως, ἀλλ' ἔτι γὰρ ἐξεῖχε καὶ
διέπρεπε πάντων[1] τῷ τε εἴδει καὶ τῷ μεγέθει τοῦ
σώματος καὶ τοὺς ἐν πολλῇ τρυφῇ διαιτωμένους
ὑπερέβαλλε. τοσοῦτον μέντοι γε ἦν τὸ βάθος τῆς
κόμης, ὡς μόλις αὐτὴν ἡμέραις ἀποκείρειν ὀκτώ,
σταθμὸν ἕλκουσαν σίκλους διακοσίους· οὗτοι δ' εἰσὶ
190 πέντε μναῖ. διέτριψε μέντοι γε ἐν Ἱεροσολύμοις
ἔτη δύο, τριῶν μὲν ἀρρένων πατὴρ γενόμενος
μιᾶς δὲ θυγατρὸς τὴν μορφὴν ἀρίστης, ἣν ὁ
Σολομῶνος υἱὸς Ῥοβόαμος ὕστερον λαμβάνει, καὶ
191 γίνεται παιδίον ἐξ αὐτῆς Ἀβίας ὄνομα. πέμψας

[1] Niese: πᾶν ROM: πάντας SP: om. E.

---

[a] Bibl. "it was at every year's end that he polled it," Heb. *miqqēṣ yāmîm leyāmîm*, lit. "from the end (or "period") of days to days," LXX ἀπ' ἀρχῆς ἡμερῶν εἰς ἡμέρας. The Targum and Jewish tradition recognize that the expression *miqqēṣ yāmîm leyāmîm* generally means "from year to year," but some rabbis took it here, as did Josephus, to mean "from week to week," explaining that Absalom was permitted, though a Nazirite, to clip it slightly every week because his hair was particularly heavy (Ginzberg v. 105).

[b] Bibl. "two hundred (Luc. "one hundred") shekels after the king's weight." Reinach's note that the shekel was one fiftieth of a mina and that Josephus should therefore have

Absalom's return; his great beauty. 2 Sam. xiv. 24.

(5) When the king heard of his son's arrival, he sent to him beforehand, ordering him to retire to his own house, for he was not yet in a mood to see him immediately upon his return. So Absalom, in accordance with this command of his father, avoided his presence and continued at the same time to be waited on by his servants. Now he had not suffered any loss of beauty through sorrow or the lack of care proper to a king's son, but was still remarkable and distinguished among all for his looks and bodily stature, and surpassed even those who lived in great luxury. Furthermore, so great was the thickness of his hair that he could scarcely cut it within a week,[a] its weight being two hundred shekels, which equal five minae.[b] He dwelt, however, in Jerusalem two years and became the father of three sons and of one very beautiful daughter, whom Solomon's son Roboamos [c] married later and by whom he had a son named Abias.[d] Then Absalom himself sent to

written "four minae" instead of "five minae" overlooks the fact that in Josephus's time there was a mina of forty shekels as well as one of fifty (*cf.* S. Krauss, *Talmudische Archäologie*, ii. 406). But it must be admitted that Josephus is as inconsistent in metrology as in chronology, *cf. A.* xiv. 106 note.

[c] Bibl. Rehoboam, LXX Ῥοβοάμ. The Heb. at this point mentions Absalom's daughter Tamar (whom Josephus calls Thamara in § 244), but not her subsequent marriage to Rehoboam; this detail is found in the LXX addition to this verse, 2 Sam. xiv. 27. Rehoboam's wife is called Maacah (1 Kings xv. 2; 2 Chron. xi. 20) or Micaiah, the daughter of Uriel (2 Chron. xiii. 2); Luc. removes the difficulty by reading Maacah for Tamar in 2 Sam., but that Josephus here evades it, as Weill supposes, is doubtful in view of § 244. Moreover, instead of evading the difficulty, Josephus resolves it, in *A.* viii. 249, by making Rehoboam's wife Maacah, a daughter of Absalom's daughter Tamar.

[d] Bibl. Abijah, LXX (2 Sam.) Ἀβιαθάρ (*v.l.* Ἀβία).

δ' αὐτὸς Ἀψάλωμος πρὸς Ἰώαβον ἐδεῖτ' αὐτοῦ τελέως καταπραῦναι τὸν πατέρα καὶ δεηθῆναι ὅπως αὐτῷ συγχωρήσῃ πρὸς αὐτὸν ἐλθόντι θεάσασθαί τε καὶ προσειπεῖν. καταμελήσαντος δὲ Ἰωάβου, τῶν ἰδίων τινὰς ἀποστείλας τὴν ὁμοροῦσαν αὐτῷ χώραν ἐπυρπόλησεν. ὁ δὲ τὸ πραχθὲν μαθὼν ἧκε πρὸς τὸν Ἀψάλωμον ἐγκαλῶν τε αὐτῷ
192 καὶ τὴν αἰτίαν πυνθανόμενος. ὁ δὲ "στρατήγημα τοῦτ'," εἶπεν, "εὗρον ἀγαγεῖν σε πρὸς ἡμᾶς δυνάμενον ἀμελοῦντα τῶν ἐντολῶν, ἃς ἵνα μοι τὸν πατέρα διαλλάξῃς ἐποιούμην. καὶ δὴ δέομαί σου παρόντος ἡμερῶσαί μοι τὸν γεγεννηκότα· ὡς ἔγωγε δεινοτέραν τῆς φυγῆς κρίνω τὴν κάθοδον ἔτι τοῦ πατρὸς
193 ἐν ὀργῇ μένοντος." πεισθεὶς δ' ὁ Ἰώαβος καὶ τὴν ἀνάγκην αὐτοῦ κατοικτείρας ἐμεσίτευσε πρὸς τὸν βασιλέα καὶ διαλεχθεὶς περὶ τοῦ παιδὸς οὕτως αὐτὸν ἡδέως διατίθησιν, ὡς εὐθέως καλέσαι πρὸς αὐτόν. τοῦ δὲ ῥίψαντος αὐτὸν ἐπὶ τοὔδαφος καὶ συγγνώμην αἰτουμένου τῶν ἡμαρτημένων ἀνίστησί τε καὶ τῶν γεγονότων ἀμνηστίαν ἐπαγγέλλεται.

194 (ix. 1) Ὁ δὲ Ἀψάλωμος τοιούτων αὐτῷ τῶν παρὰ τοῦ πατρὸς[1] ἀποβάντων πολλοὺς μὲν ἵππους ἐν ὀλίγῳ πάνυ χρόνῳ πολλὰ δ' ἅρματα ἐκέκτητο,
195 καὶ ὁπλοφόροι περὶ αὐτὸν ἦσαν πεντήκοντα· καθ' ἑκάστην δ' ἡμέραν ὄρθριος πρὸς τὰ βασίλεια παρεγίνετο καὶ τοῖς ἐπὶ τὰς κρίσεις ἥκουσι καὶ ἐλαττουμένοις πρὸς ἡδονὴν ὁμιλῶν, ὡς παρὰ τὸ μὴ συμβούλους ἀγαθοὺς εἶναι τῷ πατρὶ τάχ' αὐτῶν[2] καὶ ἀδίκως ἐπταικότων τῶν περὶ τὴν κρίσιν,

[1] + καὶ βασιλέως SP: βασιλέως (om. πατρὸς) M. [2] αὐτῷ ROM.

[a] The first part of Absalom's request is a detail added by Josephus.

Joab, asking him to appease his father [a] and request that he allow him to come to see him and speak with him. But as Joab paid no attention to this,[b] he sent some of his men to set fire to a field adjacent to him.[c] When Joab heard what had been done, he came to Absalom to complain of it to him and to learn the reason for it, whereupon the other said, "I hit upon this scheme as something which might bring you to me, since you have disregarded the injunctions which I laid upon you to reconcile my father to me. Now indeed, that you are before me, I request you to soften my parent toward me, for I hold my return to be a greater misfortune than exile while my father still persists in his anger." Joab was persuaded to do so and, having pity on his need, interceded for him with the king, to whom he spoke about his son and disposed him so favourably toward him that he straightway summoned him into his presence. Then Absalom threw himself upon the ground and asked pardon for his sins, whereupon David raised him up [d] and promised forgetfulness of what had happened.

Absalom persuades Joab to intercede for him with David. 2 Sam. xiv. 29.

(ix. 1) After this experience with his father, Absalom in a very short time acquired a great number of horses and chariots, and had fifty armed men [e] about him. And every day, early in the morning, he went to the palace and spoke ingratiatingly to those who had come for judgement and had lost their suit, suggesting that they had lost the case because his father had not had good counsellors or because

Absalom recruits an armed force for a rebellion. 2 Sam. xv. 1.

[b] Absalom sends twice to Joab in Scripture.

[c] *i.e.* Joab. Scripture says that the field belonged to Joab and was adjacent to Absalom.

[d] Bibl. "and the king kissed Absalom."

[e] Bibl. "fifty men to run before him."

εὔνοιαν αὐτῷ παρὰ πάντων κατεσκεύαζε λέγων ὡς αὐτὸς ἂν εἰ ταύτην εἶχε τὴν ἐξουσίαν πολλὴν
196 αὐτοῖς ἐβράβευσεν εὐνομίαν. τούτοις δημαγωγῶν τὸ πλῆθος ὡς βεβαίαν ἔχειν[1] ἤδη τὴν παρὰ τῶν ὄχλων εὔνοιαν ἐνόμιζε, μετὰ δὲ τὴν τοῦ πατρὸς αὐτῷ[2] καταλλαγὴν τεσσάρων ἐτῶν ἤδη διεληλυθότων, ἐδεῖτο προσελθὼν εἰς Χεβρῶνα συγχωρῆσαι πορευθέντι θυσίαν ἀποδοῦναι τῷ θεῷ· φεύγοντα γὰρ αὐτὸν εὔξασθαι. τοῦ δὲ Δαυίδου τὴν ἀξίωσιν ἐφέντος[3] πορεύεται, καὶ πολὺς ἐπισυνέρρευσεν ὄχλος ἐπὶ πολλοὺς αὐτοῦ διαπέμψαντος.
197 (2) Παρῆν δὲ καὶ ὁ Δαυίδου σύμβουλος ὁ Γελμωναῖος Ἀχιτόφελος καὶ διακόσιοί τινες ἐξ αὐτῶν Ἱεροσολύμων οὐκ εἰδότες μὲν τὴν ἐπιχείρησιν, ὡς δ' ἐπὶ θυσίαν μετεσταλμένοι· καὶ βασιλεὺς ὑπὸ πάντων ἀποδείκνυται, τοῦτο γενέσθαι στρατηγήσας.
198 ὡς δ' ἀπηγγέλη ταῦτα Δαυίδῃ καὶ παρ' ἐλπίδας αὐτῷ τὰ παρὰ τοῦ παιδὸς ἠκούσθη, δείσας ἅμα καὶ τῆς ἀσεβείας καὶ τῆς τόλμης αὐτὸν θαυμάσας, ὅτι μηδὲ τῆς ἐπὶ τοῖς ἡμαρτημένοις συγγνώμης ἐμνημόνευσεν, ἀλλ' ἐκείνων πολὺ χείροσι καὶ παρανομωτέροις ἐπεβάλετο βασιλείᾳ πρῶτον μὲν ὑπὸ θεοῦ οὐ δεδομένῃ, δεύτερον δὲ ἐπ' ἀφαιρέσει τοῦ γεγεννηκότος, ἔγνω φεύγειν εἰς τὰ πέραν τοῦ
199 Ἰορδάνου. καὶ συγκαλέσας τῶν φίλων τοὺς ἐπιτηδειοτάτους καὶ περὶ τῆς τοῦ παιδὸς ἀπονοίας

[1] ἔχειν om. RO. [2] Niese: αὐτοῦ codd.
[3] Niese: ἀφέντος codd. E fort. recte.

[a] So Luc.; Heb. and LXX "forty" ("and it came to pass at the end of forty years," etc.). The rabbis, who realized the difficulty of reading "forty years," which apparently means from the time of David and Absalom's reconciliation, reckoned it from the time when Saul was chosen king.

of an injustice; and he won the goodwill of all by saying that if he himself had had this power he would have dispensed full and equal justice to them. By these means he curried favour with the multitude, and, when he thought that the loyalty of the populace was secured to him,—four [a] years having now passed since his father's reconciliation with him—he went to him and asked for permission to go to Hebron and offer sacrifice to God seeing that he had so vowed when in exile. And, when David granted his request, he departed, and a great multitude streamed to him, for he had sent out messages to many.

David learns of Absalom's plot and flees from Jerusalem. 2 Sam. xv. 12.

(2) There were with him also David's counsellor Achitophel the Gelmonite [b] and two hundred men from Jerusalem itself, who knew nothing of the business in hand, but thought themselves summoned to a sacrifice; and he was chosen by them all as king, as he had contrived should be done. When these things were reported to David and he heard of these unexpected acts of his son, he was both alarmed and surprised at his impiety and audacity, for Absalom was not even mindful of having been pardoned for his sins, but was guilty of much greater acts of lawlessness in having designs upon the kingship, which, in the first place, had not been given him by God and, in the second place, involved the removal of his parent.[c] He therefore decided to flee to the country across the Jordan. And he called together his closest friends and, having taken counsel with them concerning his son's madness, committed

[b] So Luc.; bibl. Gilonite (Heb. *Gîlônî*, *i.e.* from Giloh), LXX cod. B θεκωνεί, cod. A Γιλωναίῳ, al. Γολαμωναῖον. The site of Giloh is uncertain; it is identified by some with *Khirbet Jālā*, 6 miles N. of Hebron.

[c] David's reflections are an amplification of Scripture.

κοινολογησάμενος αὐτοῖς καὶ περὶ πάντων ἐπιτρέψας κριτῇ τῷ θεῷ, καταλιπὼν τὰ βασίλεια φυλάσσειν δέκα παλλακίσιν ἀπῆρεν ἐκ τῶν Ἱεροσολύμων, τοῦ τε ἄλλου πλήθους προθύμως[1] αὐτῷ συνεξορμήσαντος καὶ τῶν ἑξακοσίων ὁπλιτῶν, οἳ καὶ τῆς πρώτης αὐτῷ[2] φυγῆς ἐκοινώνουν, ὅτ' ἔζη
200 Σαοῦλος. τὸν δὲ Ἀβιάθαρον καὶ Σάδωκον τοὺς ἀρχιερεῖς συναπαίρειν αὐτῷ[2] διεγνωκότας καὶ Ληουίτας ἅπαντας μετὰ τῆς κιβωτοῦ μένειν ἔπεισεν, ὡς[3] τοῦ θεοῦ καὶ μὴ μετακομιζομένης
201 αὐτῆς ῥυσομένου. ἐνετείλατο δ' ἕκαστα τῶν γινομένων λάθρα διαγγέλλειν αὐτῷ· πιστοὺς δ' ἔσχε πρὸς πάντα διακόνους παῖδας Ἀχίμαν μὲν Σαδώκου Ἰωνάθην δὲ Ἀβιαθάρου. Ἔθις δ' ὁ Γιτταῖος[4] συνεξώρμησεν αὐτῷ βιασάμενος τὴν Δαυίδου βούλησιν (μένειν γὰρ αὐτὸν ἀνέπειθε) καὶ διὰ τοῦτο
202 μᾶλλον εὔνους αὐτῷ κατεφάνη. ἀναβαίνοντος δ' αὐτοῦ διὰ τοῦ Ἐλαιῶνος ὄρους γυμνοῖς τοῖς ποσὶ καὶ πάντων σὺν αὐτῷ δακρυόντων, ἀγγέλλεται καὶ ὁ Ἀχιτόφελος συνὼν τῷ Ἀψαλώμῳ καὶ τὰ τούτου φρονῶν. ἐπέτεινε δ' αὐτῷ τὸ λυπηρὸν τοῦτ' ἀκουσθέν, καὶ τὸν θεὸν ἐπεκαλεῖτο δεόμενος ἀπαλλοτριῶσαι τὴν Ἀψαλώμου διάνοιαν πρὸς τὸν Ἀχιτόφελον. ἐδεδίει γὰρ μὴ τἀναντία συμβουλεύων πείσειεν αὐτόν, ἀνὴρ ὢν φρενήρης καὶ συν-
203 ιδεῖν τὸ λυσιτελὲς ὀξύτατος. γενόμενος δ' ἐπὶ τῆς κορυφῆς τοῦ ὄρους ἀπεσκόπει τὴν πόλιν καὶ μετὰ

[1] προθύμως om. RO. [2] αὐτῷ om. RO.
[3] ed. pr.: ὅπως codd.
[4] O: Γιτθαῖος rell.: Iettheus Lat.

[a] *v.l.* Achimanos; bibl. Ahimaaz (Heb. *Aḥîma'aṣ*), LXX Ἀχειμαίας, Luc. Ἀχειμάας.
[b] Called Ethaios in § 233; bibl. Ittai, LXX Σεθθεί, Luc.

the entire matter into the hands of God as judge. Then, having left the palace in the keeping of his ten concubines, he departed from Jerusalem with a large number who were eager to accompany him, and also the six hundred armed men who had taken part in his former flight in the lifetime of Saul. But Abiathar and Sadok, the high priests, who had intended to depart with him, and all the Levites he persuaded to remain behind with the ark, for God, he said, would deliver him even if it were not brought along. He also instructed them to report to him secretly everything that happened. In all these matters he had as his faithful aids Achimas,[a] the son of Sadok, and Jonathan, the son of Abiathar. Ethis [b] the Gittite also set out with him, having overcome the objections of David who had tried to persuade him to stay, and in this way he showed his loyalty even more clearly. Now as David was ascending the Mount of Olives with bare feet and with all his company in tears, news was brought to him that Achitophel was with Absalom and now belonged to his party. And when David heard this, his grief was intensified and he called upon God, beseeching Him to alienate Absalom's feeling from Achitophel, for he feared that his hostile counsels might prove persuasive to him, as those of a man of ready wit and quick to see an advantage.[c] And when he reached the crest [d] of the mountain, he gazed

The high priests remain in Jerusalem 2 Sam. xv. 24.

'Ηθεί. In Scripture Ittai is mentioned before the high priests' sons.

[c] The preceding sentence is an amplification of David's prayer in 2 Sam. xv. 31, "O Lord, I pray thee, make foolish the counsel of Ahitophel."

[d] So the Heb., which has *rôš* "head"; LXX transliterates this as a proper name 'Ρωώς.

πολλῶν δακρύων ὡς ἂν βασιλείας ἐκπεσὼν ηὔχετο τῷ θεῷ· συνήντησε δ' αὐτῷ φίλος ἀνὴρ καὶ βέβαιος
204 Χουσὶς ὄνομα. τοῦτον ὁρῶν τὴν ἐσθῆτα κατερρηγμένον καὶ τὴν κεφαλὴν σποδοῦ πλήρη καὶ θρηνοῦντα τὴν μεταβολὴν παρηγόρει καὶ παύσασθαι τῆς λύπης παρεκάλει καὶ τέλος ἱκέτευσεν ἀπελθόντα πρὸς Ἀψάλωμον ὡς τὰ ἐκείνου φρονοῦντα τά τε ἀπόρρητα τῆς διανοίας αὐτοῦ κατανοεῖν καὶ ταῖς Ἀχιτοφέλου συμβουλίαις ἀντιπράττειν· οὐ γὰρ τοσοῦτον ὠφελήσειν αὐτῷ συνερχόμενον, ὅσον παρ' ἐκείνῳ γενόμενον. καὶ ὁ μὲν πεισθεὶς τῷ Δαυίδῃ καταλιπὼν αὐτὸν ἧκεν εἰς Ἱεροσόλυμα· ἀφικνεῖται δ' εἰς αὐτὰ μετ' οὐ πολὺ καὶ Ἀψάλωμος.

205 (3) Ὀλίγον δὲ τῷ Δαυίδῃ προελθόντι[1] Σιβᾶς ὁ τοῦ Μεμφιβόσθου δοῦλος συνήντησεν, ὃν προνοησόμενον ἀπεστάλκει τῶν κτήσεων ἃς δεδώρητο τῷ Ἰωνάθου τοῦ Σαούλου παιδὸς υἱῷ, μετὰ ζεύγους ὄνων καταπεφορτισμένων τοῖς ἐπιτηδείοις, ἐξ ὧν ἐκέλευσε λαμβάνειν ὧν αὐτός τε καὶ οἱ σὺν αὐτῷ
206 δέοιντο. πυνθανομένου δὲ ποῦ καταλέλοιπε τὸν Μεμφίβοσθον, ἐν Ἱεροσολύμοις ἔλεγε προσδοκῶντα χειροτονηθήσεσθαι βασιλέα διὰ τὴν ὑπάρχουσαν ταραχὴν εἰς μνήμην ὧν εὐεργέτησεν αὐτοὺς Σαοῦλος. ἀγανακτήσας δ' ἐπὶ τούτῳ πάνθ' ὅσα τῷ Μεμφιβόσθῳ παρεχώρησε Σιβᾷ χαρίζεται· πολὺ γὰρ δικαιότερον αὐτὸν ἐκείνου ταῦτ' ἔχειν ἐπεγνωκέναι· καὶ ὁ μὲν Σιβᾶς περιχαρὴς ἦν.

[1] ed. pr. Lat.: προσελθόντι codd.

[a] Bibl. Hushai the Arcite, LXX Χουσεὶ ὁ Ἀρχί; some LXX MSS., followed by the ancient versions, mistakenly took Ἀρχί

upon the city and with many tears, as if already fallen from royal power, prayed to God. Then there met him a man who was a firm friend of his, named Chūsis,[a] and when David saw him with his garments torn and his head covered with ashes,[b] weeping over the change of fortune, he comforted him and exhorted him to cease grieving, and finally implored him to go back to Absalom under pretence of being on his side, in order to discover his secret plans and oppose the counsels of Achitophel. He would not, said David, be of as great help to him by coming along as he might be by staying with Absalom. And so, at David's persuasion, he left him and came to Jerusalem, where, not long after, Absalom also arrived.

Hushai (Chusis) returns to Jerusalem as David's agent. 2 Sam. xv. 32.

(3) Now David had gone on a little further when he was met by Siba, the servant of Memphibosthos, whom David had sent to take charge of the property which he had presented to the son of Jonathan, the son of Saul[c]; Siba had with him a couple of asses laden with provisions, from which he bade David take whatever he himself and his men might need. And, when he was asked where he had left Memphibosthos, he said, "In Jerusalem," where he was waiting to be chosen king in the midst of the prevailing confusion, in recognition of the benefits which Saul had conferred on the people. In his indignation at this, David made a present to Siba of all that he had granted to Memphibosthos, for, he said, he recognized that he had a far juster claim to possess them than had the other. And so Siba was greatly pleased.

Ziba (Siba) meets David with provisions. 2 Sam. xvi. 1.

as an adjective compound with the following noun ἑταῖρος, reading ἀρχιέταιρος "chief friend"; *cf.* § 216 note.

[b] Bibl. "earth."

[c] *Cf.* §§ 114 f.

207 (4) Δαυίδῃ δὲ γενομένῳ κατὰ Χώρανον[1] τόπον οὕτως καλούμενον ἐπέρχεται τοῦ Σαούλου συγγενὴς Σαμούις[2] μὲν ὄνομα υἱὸς δὲ Γηρᾶ, καὶ λίθοις τε ἔβαλλεν αὐτὸν καὶ ἐκακηγόρει. περιστάντων δὲ τῶν φίλων καὶ σκεπόντων ἔτι μᾶλλον ὁ Σαμούις βλασφημῶν διετέλει, μιαιφόνον καὶ πολλῶν ἀρχη-
208 γὸν κακῶν ἀποκαλῶν. ἐκέλευε δὲ καὶ τῆς γῆς ὡς ἐναγῆ καὶ ἐπάρατον ἐξιέναι, καὶ τῷ θεῷ χάριν ὡμολόγει τῆς βασιλείας αὐτὸν ἀφελομένῳ καὶ διὰ παιδὸς ἰδίου τὴν ὑπὲρ ὧν ἥμαρτεν εἰς τὸν αὐτοῦ[3] δεσπότην δίκην αὐτὸν εἰσπραξαμένῳ. πάντων δ' ἐπ' αὐτὸν ἠρεθισμένων ὑπ' ὀργῆς καὶ μάλιστα Ἀβισαίου διαχρήσασθαι βουλομένου τὸν Σαμούιν
209 Δαυίδης αὐτὸν τῆς ὀργῆς ἐπέσχε, "μὴ τοῖς παροῦσι κακοῖς ἑτέραν προσεξεργασώμεθα," φησί, "καινοτέραν ἀφορμήν· οὐ γὰρ δὴ τοῦ προσλυσσῶντός μοι τούτου κυνὸς αἰδώς τις ἢ φροντὶς ὑπέρχεται,[4] τῷ θεῷ δὲ εἴκω, δι' ὃν οὗτος ἐφ' ἡμᾶς ἀπενοήθη. θαυμαστὸν δ' οὐδὲν ὑπὸ τούτου με ταῦτα πάσχειν, ὅπου γε καὶ παιδὸς ἀσεβοῦς πεπείραμαι. ἀλλ' ἔσται τις ἴσως[5] οἶκτος ἡμῖν ἐκ θεοῦ καὶ κρατήσομεν τῶν ἐχθρῶν τούτου θελή-
210 σαντος." ἤνυεν οὖν τὴν ὁδὸν οὐ φροντίζων τοῦ Σαμούι παρὰ τὸ ἕτερον μέρος τοῦ ὄρους διατρέχοντος καὶ πολλὰ κακηγοροῦντος· παραγενόμενος δ'

[1] Χώραμον M: Βαουρὶ P: Χώραν ὂν RO: Choran Lat. (cf. infra ad § 225).
[2] Σεμεΐ, -εεὶ (M)SPE: Sumas Lat. (sed infra, § 208, Σουμᾶν MSP).
[3] Niese: αὐτοῦ codd.: ἑαυτοῦ Hudson cum cod. Vat.
[4] ἐπέρχεται RO. [5] ἴσως om. RO.

[a] Bibl. Bahurim, LXX Βουρείμ, Luc. Χορράμ. The variant in Josephus is probably due to scribal correction from the

(4) When David came to Chōranos,[a] as the place was called, there came out a relative of Saul, named Samūis,[b] the son of Gera, who threw stones at him and abused him. And although the king's friends stood around him and protected him, Samūis only continued the more to curse him and denounce him as one stained with blood and as the author of many crimes. He also bade him leave the country as one under a ban and accursed ; and he gave thanks to God for having deprived David of his kingdom and for having exacted punishment of him, through his own son, for the crimes which he had committed against his master.[c] Though they were all provoked to anger at him, especially Abisai, who wished to make an end of him, David restrained his anger, saying, " Let us not add to our present ills by causing new ones to arise, for certainly no feeling of shame or concern touches me on account of this cur's[d] raving against me ; but I submit to God, by whom this fellow has been moved to frenzy against us. Nor is there anything strange in my being so treated by him, when I have experienced the impiety of a son. Nevertheless, God's compassion will rest on us, and we shall overcome our enemies by His will." And so he continued on his way, taking no notice of Samūis, who ran along with him on the other side of the mountain, abusing him freely. And, when

Shimei (Samuis) stones David. 2 Sam. xvi. 5.

LXX. In § 225 the name is written Bocchores. The village lay on the road from Jerusalem to Jericho, but the exact site has not been identified.

[b] Bibl. Shimei, LXX Σεμεεί. The name appears as Sūmūis in § 388.

[c] *i.e.* Saul.

[d] According to Scripture, it is Abishai who calls Shimei " a dead dog."

ἐπὶ τὸν Ἰόρδανον ἀνελάμβανε τοὺς ἰδίους ἐνταῦθα κεκοπωμένους.

211 (5) Ἀψαλώμου δὲ καὶ Ἀχιτοφέλου τοῦ συμβούλου παραγενομένων εἰς Ἱεροσόλυμα σὺν ἅπαντι τῷ λαῷ, καὶ ὁ Δαυίδου φίλος ἧκε πρὸς αὐτοὺς καὶ προσκυνήσας αὐτὸν συνηύχετο τὴν βασιλείαν εἰς αἰῶνα καὶ τὸν πάντα παραμεῖναι χρόνον. φήσαντος δ' ἐκείνου πρὸς αὐτόν, τί δήποτε φίλος ἐν τοῖς μάλιστα τοῦ πατρὸς αὐτοῦ γεγενημένος καὶ πρὸς ἅπαντα πιστὸς εἶναι δόξας οὐ σὺν αὐτῷ νῦν ἐστιν, ἀλλὰ καταλιπὼν ἐκεῖνον μεταβαίη πρὸς αὐτόν,
212 δεξιῶς ἀποκρίνεται καὶ σωφρόνως· εἶπε γὰρ ἕπεσθαι δεῖν[1] τῷ θεῷ καὶ τῷ παντὶ πλήθει. "τούτων οὖν μετὰ σοῦ, ὦ δέσποτα, γεγενημένων εἰκότως ἕπομαι κἀγώ· τὴν γὰρ βασιλείαν ἔλαβες παρὰ τοῦ θεοῦ. τὴν αὐτὴν μέντοι γε πίστιν καὶ εὔνοιαν ἐνδείξομαι πιστευόμενος εἶναι φίλος, ἣν οἶσθά με τῷ πατρί σου παρεσχημένον. ἀγανακτεῖν δ' οὐδὲν προσῆκε τοῖς παροῦσιν· οὐ γὰρ εἰς ἄλλην οἰκίαν ἡ βασιλεία μεταβέβηκε, μεμένηκε δ' ἐπὶ τῆς αὐτῆς,
213 υἱοῦ παραλαβόντος." ταῦτα λέγων ἔπειθεν· ὕποπτον γὰρ αὐτὸν εἶχε. καὶ καλέσας τὸν Ἀχιτόφελον συνεβουλεύετο αὐτῷ τί δεῖ ποιεῖν· ὁ δὲ παρῄνεσε ταῖς τοῦ πατρὸς αὐτὸν παλλακαῖς συνελθεῖν· ἐκ τούτου γὰρ εἴσεσθαι τὸν λαὸν ἔλεγε πιστεύσαντα, ὡς ἀδιάλλακτά σοι τὰ πρὸς αὐτόν ἐστι, καὶ μετὰ πολλῆς συστρατεύσεσθαι[2] προθυμίας ἐπὶ τὸν πατέρα· μέχρι δεῦρο γὰρ φανερὰν ἔχθραν ἀναλαμβάνειν δεδιέναι προσδοκῶντας ὑμᾶς ὁμονοήσειν.

[1] + αὐτὸν codd.

[2] ed. pr.: -ασθαι codd.

he reached the Jordan, he allowed his weary men to rest there.

Absalom consults Hushai and Ahitophel. 2 Sam. xvi. 15.

(5) As soon as Absalom and Achitophel, his adviser, arrived at Jerusalem with all the people, David's friend [a] came to them and did obeisance to him, praying for him that his kingship should continue always and for all time. And when Absalom asked him just why he, who was one of his father's best friends and supposed to be altogether faithful to him, was not now with him, but had deserted him and had gone over to himself, he made a skilful and prudent reply, saying that one ought to follow God and the entire people. "Now, my lord, since they are with you, it is fitting that I too should follow, for you have received the kingdom from God. Furthermore, I shall show the same faithfulness and loyalty to you, if I am accounted a friend, as you know I gave to your father. There is no good reason," he added, "to be dissatisfied with the present state of things, for the kingship has not passed to another house, but remains in the same one, since the king's son has succeeded to it." These words of his won over Absalom, who had before suspected him, and he called Achitophel to deliberate with him about what should be done. The latter advised him to lie with his father's concubines, for, he said, by this act the people would know with certainty that Absalom could not be reconciled to him, and they would join with great eagerness in the fight against his father; up to that time they had been afraid to proceed to open hostility because of their expectation that the two would reach an understanding.[b] Taking this

[a] *i.e.* Hushai.

[b] The last sentence is an amplification of Scripture.

214 πεισθεὶς δὲ τῇ συμβουλίᾳ κελεύει σκηνὴν αὐτῷ[1] πῆξαι τοὺς οἰκέτας ἐπὶ τοῦ βασιλείου καὶ[2] τοῦ πλήθους ὁρῶντος παρελθὼν συνέρχεται ταῖς τοῦ πατρὸς παλλακαῖς. ταῦτα δ' ἐγένετο κατὰ τὴν Νάθα προφητείαν, ἣν τῷ Δαυίδῃ σημαίνων τὴν ἐκ τοῦ παιδὸς ἐσομένην ἐπίθεσιν προεφήτευσε.[a]

215 (6) Ποιήσας δ' Ἀψάλωμος τὰ παραινεθέντα αὐτῷ ὑπὸ τοῦ Ἀχιτοφέλου δεύτερον αὐτὸν ἠξίου συμβουλεύειν περὶ τοῦ πολέμου τοῦ πρὸς τὸν πατέρα. μυρίους[b] δ' αὐτὸν ἐπιλέκτους αἰτήσαντος ἐκείνου καὶ τόν τε πατέρα κτενεῖν[3] αὐτοῦ καὶ τοὺς σὺν αὐτῷ ζωοὺς[4] ἀνάξειν ὑποσχομένου καὶ βεβαίαν τότε τὴν βασιλείαν ἔσεσθαι φήσαντος, Δαυίδου

216 μηκέτι ζῶντος, ἀρεσθεὶς τῇ γνώμῃ μετακαλεῖται καὶ τὸν Χουσὶν τὸν Δαυίδου ἀρχίφιλον[5]· οὕτως γὰρ αὐτὸν ἐκεῖνος ἐκάλει· καὶ τὴν Ἀχιτοφέλου γνώμην αὐτῷ δηλώσας, τί καὶ αὐτῷ δοκεῖ περὶ αὐτῆς ἐπυνθάνετο. συνιδὼν ὅτι γενομένων ὧν Ἀχιτόφελος συνεβούλευσε κινδυνεύσει Δαυίδης συλληφθεὶς ἀποθανεῖν, ἐναντίαν ἐπειρᾶτο γνώμην εἰσφέρειν·

217 "οὐ γὰρ ἀγνοεῖς" εἶπεν, "ὦ βασιλεῦ, τὴν τοῦ πατρὸς καὶ τὴν τῶν συνόντων αὐτῷ ἀνδρείαν, ὅτι καὶ πολλοὺς πολέμους πεπολέμηκε καὶ πάντοτε κρατῶν τῶν ἐχθρῶν ἀπήλλακται. νῦν δὲ εἰκὸς αὐτὸν ἐπὶ στρατοπέδου μένειν· στρατηγῆσαι γὰρ ἱκανώτατος καὶ προϊδεῖν ἀπάτην ἐπερχομένων

[1] Niese: αὐτῷ codd. E.
[2] καὶ ante τοῦ πλήθους ex Lat. Niese: post ὁρῶντος hab. codd.
[3] Niese: κτείνειν codd. [4] σώους RMSP Lat.
[5] φίλον SP: amicum antiquum Lat.

[a] *Cf.* § 152. Scripture does not allude at this point to the prophecy of Nathan.
[b] So Luc.; Heb. and LXX "twelve thousand."

advice, Absalom ordered his servants to pitch a tent for him on the roof of the palace, and, in the sight of the people, went in and lay with his father's concubines. And this came about in accordance with the prophecy which Nathan had made when he revealed to David that his son would one day rise up against him.[a]

(6) After Absalom had acted on the advice given him by Achitophel, he requested him to give him further counsel, this time concerning the war against his father. Thereupon he asked him for ten thousand[b] picked men, and promised to kill his father and bring back his men alive[c]; then, he said, with David no longer alive, his throne would be secure. Absalom was pleased with this proposal, but also summoned Chūsis, David's chief friend[d]—so David called him—and, after informing him of Achitophel's proposal, inquired what he too thought of it. But Chūsis, perceiving that, if Achitophel's advice were acted on, David would be in danger of being captured and put to death,[e] attempted to introduce a counter-proposal. "You are not ignorant, O King," he said, "of the bravery of your father and the men with him, or that he has fought many wars and in every case has come off victorious against the enemy. Just now it is likely that he is remaining within the camp, for he is a very able general and can foresee the ruse of an

Hushai persuades Absalom to reject Ahitophel's advice. 2 Sam. xvii. 1.

[c] Variant "safe"; *cf.* 2 Sam. xvii. 3 "all the people shall be in peace."

[d] The variant φίλον "friend" in MSS. SP is probably due to the copyists taking ἀρχι in ἀρχίφιλον "chief friend" as a proper name, as does the LXX, translating Heb. "Hushai the Arcite," *cf.* § 203 note. A parallel to Josephus's term is afforded by the LXX of 1 Chron. xxvii. 33, where Hushai is called πρῶτος φίλος τοῦ βασιλέως "first friend of the king."

[e] This reflection of Hushai is an amplification of Scripture.

218 πολεμίων· ἀλλὰ κατὰ τὴν ἑσπέραν ἀπολιπὼν τοὺς ἰδίους ἢ εἴς τινα τῶν αὐλώνων ἑαυτὸν ἀποκρύψει ἢ πρὸς πέτρᾳ τινὶ λοχήσει· συμβαλόντων δὲ τῶν ἡμετέρων οἱ μὲν ἐκείνου πρὸς μικρὸν ὑποχωρήσουσιν αὖθις δὲ θαρσήσαντες[1] ὡς τοῦ βασιλέως αὐτοῖς ἐγγὺς ὄντος ἀντιστήσονται, καὶ μεταξὺ τούτων μαχομένων ὁ πατὴρ ἐπιφανεὶς ἐξαίφνης τοῖς μὲν εὐψυχίαν πρὸς τοὺς κινδύνους παρα-
219 σκευάσει τοὺς δὲ σοὺς καταπλήξεται. παράθου δὴ τοίνυν καὶ τὴν ἐμὴν συμβουλίαν τῷ λογισμῷ καὶ ταῦτ᾿ ἐπιγνοὺς ἄριστα τὴν μὲν Ἀχιτοφέλου γνώμην παραίτησαι, πέμψας δ᾿ εἰς πᾶσαν τὴν χώραν τῶν Ἑβραίων παράγγειλον αὐτοῖς τὴν ἐπὶ τὸν πατέρα σου στρατείαν καὶ παραλαβὼν αὐτὸς τὴν δύναμιν τοῦ πολέμου γίνου στρατηγὸς καὶ μὴ πιστεύσῃς
220 τοῦτον ἑτέρῳ. νικήσειν γὰρ προσδόκα ῥᾳδίως αὐτόν, ἂν ἐν φανερῷ καταλάβῃς ὄντα μετ᾿ ὀλίγων, αὐτὸς πολλὰς ἔχων μυριάδας βουλομένων τὴν περὶ σὲ σπουδὴν ἐπιδείξασθαι καὶ προθυμίαν. ἂν δ᾿ ὁ πατὴρ αὐτὸν εἰς πολιορκίαν περικλείσῃ, μηχανήμασι καὶ ὀρύγμασιν ὑπονόμοις καθαιρήσομεν ἐκεί-
221 νην τὴν πόλιν.'' ταῦτ᾿ εἰπὼν εὐδοκίμησε μᾶλλον Ἀχιτοφέλου· τῆς γὰρ ἐκείνου γνώμης ἡ τούτου προεκρίθη παρ᾿ Ἀψαλώμου. θεὸς μέντοι γε ἦν ὁ τούτου τῇ διανοίᾳ τὴν τοῦ Χουσὶ συμβουλίαν συστήσας ἀμείνω εἶναι δοκεῖν.

222 (7) Σπεύσας δὲ πρὸς τοὺς ἀρχιερέας Σάδωκον καὶ Ἀβιάθαρον καὶ τήν τε Ἀχιτοφέλου γνώμην

[1] αὖθις δὲ θαρσ. conj. Niese: αὐτοὶ δὲ θαρσ. O: θαρσήσαντες δ᾿ MSP Lat. (vid.).

[a] Unscriptural detail, and apparently a misunderstanding

attacking enemy; but toward evening [a] he will leave his men and will hide himself in some hollow, or will wait in ambush behind some rock. And when our force attacks, his men will give way for a little, but then they will take heart at the thought that the king is beside them, and will make a stand against us; in the meantime, while the fight is going on, your father will suddenly appear and will inspire them to face danger valiantly, but into your men he will strike terror. Therefore weigh well my counsel also in your mind and, recognizing that it is the best, reject the proposal of Achitophel. And send throughout the entire land of the Hebrews, summoning them to the campaign against your father; then lead out your force and take personal command of the war, and do not entrust it to another. For you may look to defeat him easily if you take him in the open with few men about him, while you yourself have many tens of thousands ready to show their zeal and ardour on your behalf. But if your father shuts himself up to stand a siege, we shall destroy that city by means of engines and mines.[b]" This speech of Chūsis met with more favour than Achitophel's, for his proposal was preferred by Absalom to the other's. It was God, however, who contrived that Chūsis's counsel should seem better to his way of thinking.

(7) Then Chūsis hastened to the high priests Sadok and Abiathar, and, having told them all about

Absalom's plans are reported

of 2 Sam. xvii. 12 "and we will camp (A.V. "light") upon him as the dew falleth on the ground."

[b] The "engines and mines" are an anachronism, not uncommon in Josephus's amplified descriptions of biblical battles. The whole of Hushai's speech, moreover, is an amplification of 2 Sam. xvii. 8-13.

ἐξειπὼν αὐτοῖς καὶ τὴν ἑαυτοῦ καὶ ὅτι δέδοκται τὰ ὑπ' αὐτοῦ παραινεθέντα πράττειν, ἐκέλευσε μηνύειν πέμψαντας Δαυίδῃ καὶ φανερὰ ποιεῖν τὰ συμβεβουλευμένα καὶ προσπαρακελεύσασθαι ταχέως διαβῆναι τὸν Ἰόρδανον, μὴ μεταγνοὺς ὁ παῖς αὐτοῦ διώκειν ὁρμήσῃ καὶ πρὶν ἐν ἀσφαλείᾳ γένηται φθάσας
223 καταλάβῃ. οἱ δὲ ἀρχιερεῖς ἐξεπίτηδες τοὺς υἱοὺς ἔξω τῆς πόλεως κεκρυμμένους εἶχον, ὅπως διακομίσωσι πρὸς τὸν Δαυίδην τὰ πραττόμενα· πέμψαντες οὖν πιστὴν θεραπαινίδα πρὸς αὐτοὺς φέρουσαν τὰ βεβουλευμένα ὑπὸ τοῦ Ἀψαλώμου προσέταξαν μετὰ σπουδῆς ταῦτα Δαυίδῃ σημαίνειν.
224 οἱ δ' οὐδὲν εἰς ἀναβολὰς καὶ μέλλησιν ὑπερέθεντο, λαβόντες δὲ τὰς τῶν πατέρων ἐντολὰς εὐσεβεῖς ἅμα καὶ πιστοὶ γίνονται διάκονοι· καὶ τῆς ὑπηρεσίας τὸ τάχος καὶ τὴν ὀξύτητα κρίναντες ἄριστα εἶναι
225 ἠπείγοντο συμβαλεῖν Δαυίδῃ. γενομένους δ' αὐτοὺς ἀπὸ σταδίων τῆς πόλεως δύο θεῶνταί τινες ἱππεῖς καὶ διαβάλλουσι πρὸς τὸν Ἀψάλωμον· ὁ δ' εὐθὺς ἔπεμψε τοὺς συλληψομένους. νοήσαντες δὲ τοῦτο οἱ τῶν ἀρχιερέων παῖδες ἐκτραπέντες τῆς ὁδοῦ παραχρῆμα εἰς κώμην τινὰ τῶν Ἱεροσολύμων οὐκ ἄπωθεν αὐτοὺς ἔδωκαν, Βοκχόρης[1] ἦν ὄνομα τῇ κώμῃ,[2] καὶ γυναικὸς ἐδεήθησάν τινος κρύψαι καὶ
226 παρασχεῖν αὐτοῖς τὴν ἀσφάλειαν. ἡ δὲ καθιμήσασα τοὺς νεανίσκους εἰς φρέαρ καὶ πλάκας ἄνωθεν

[1] O: Βοκχούρης rell.: Bachor Lat. [2] πόλει O.

[a] At En-rogel, according to Scripture; it was a spring in the valley of Kidron S.E. of the city.
[b] οὐδὲν εἰς ἀναβολάς is a Thucydidean phrase recurring in *A*. xvii.-xix. [c] The distance is not given in Scripture
[d] Bibl. "a lad." [e] Bibl. Bahurim, *cf*. § 207 note.
[f] Their appeal for refuge is an unscriptural detail.

Achitophel's proposal and his own, and also that it had been decided to act upon his advice, he bade them send information of this to David and make plain to him what counsel had been given, and exhort him further to cross the Jordan as quickly as possible lest his son change his mind, set out in pursuit of him, and take him by surprise before he could reach a place of safety. Now the high priests had purposely kept their sons in hiding outside the city [a] in order that they might bring David word of what occurred. So they sent a faithful maidservant to bring them news of Absalom's plans, and instructed them to make haste and report these to David. And they, without any delay [b] or hesitation, set off with their fathers' instructions, like obedient and loyal helpers. And, deciding that speed and dispatch were the best form of service, they made all haste to meet David. Now, when they were two stades [c] from the city, they were seen by some horsemen,[d] who informed against them to Absalom; and he immediately sent men to arrest them. But the high priests' sons, becoming aware of this, at once turned aside from the road and betook themselves to a certain village not far from Jerusalem—the name of the village was Bocchores [e]—and begged one of the women to hide them and afford them safety.[f] So she let the youths down into a well and spread layers of wool [g] over it,

to David. 2 Sam. xvii. 15.

The high priests' sons elude pursuit by Absalom's men. 2 Sam. xvii. 18.

[g] Bibl. "and the woman took and spread the covering over the well's mouth and strewed groats thereon"; "groats" is the A.V.'s rendering of Heb. *riphôth*, a word of uncertain meaning, Targum *diqîlân* "dates" (?) (perhaps a variant of *deqîqân* "grits"), LXX (transliterating) ἀραφώθ, Luc. παλάθας "fruit-cakes." The Jewish commentators explain *riphôth* as "crushed wheat." It is just possible that the LXX ἀραφώθ was vaguely connected by Josephus with ἔριφοι "kids," which he supposed equivalent to ἐρίων "wool."

ἐρίων ἐπιβαλοῦσα, ὡς ἧκον οἱ διώκοντες αὐτοὺς καὶ περὶ αὐτῶν ἀνέκριναν εἰ θεάσαιτο, ἰδεῖν μὲν[1] οὐκ ἠρνήσατο· πιόντας γὰρ παρ' αὐτῇ πάλιν ἀπελθεῖν· εἰ μέντοι γε συντόνως διώξουσι καταλήψεσθαι προύλεγεν. ὡς δ' ἐπὶ πολὺ διώξαντες οὐ
227 κατέλαβον, ἀνέστρεψαν εἰς τοὐπίσω. θεασαμένη δ' αὐτοὺς ἀναζεύξαντας ἡ γυνὴ καὶ μηδένα φόβον τοῖς νεανίσκοις ἀπ' αὐτῶν ἔτι συλλήψεως εἶναι, ἀνιμήσασα τὴν προκειμένην ὁδὸν ἀνύειν παρεκελεύσατο· καὶ πολλῇ σπουδῇ καὶ τάχει χρησάμενοι περὶ τὴν ὁδοιπορίαν ἧκον πρὸς Δαυίδην καὶ πάντ' ἀκριβῶς ἐδήλωσαν αὐτῷ[2] τὰ παρ' Ἀψαλώμου βεβουλευμένα. ὁ δὲ διαβῆναι τὸν Ἰόρδανον τοὺς μεθ' ἑαυτοῦ προσέταξεν ἤδη νυκτὸς οὔσης καὶ μηδὲν ὀκνεῖν δι' αὐτήν.

228 (8) Ἀχιτόφελος δὲ τῆς γνώμης αὐτοῦ παρευδοκιμηθείσης ἐπιβὰς τοῦ κτήνους ἐξώρμησεν εἰς Γελμῶνα[3] τὴν πατρίδα· καὶ συγκαλέσας τοὺς οἰκείους ἅπαντας ἃ συνεβούλευσεν Ἀψαλώμῳ ταῦτ' αὐτοῖς διεξῆλθε, καὶ ὡς οὐ πεισθεὶς φανερός ἐστιν οὐκ εἰς μακρὰν ἀπολούμενος· Δαυίδην δὲ κρατήσειν[4] ἔλεγεν καὶ ἐπανήξειν ἐπὶ τὴν βασιλείαν.
229 ἄμεινον οὖν ἔφησεν εἶναι τοῦ ζῆν αὐτὸν ἐξαγαγεῖν ἐλευθέρως καὶ μεγαλοφρόνως ἢ παρασχεῖν αὐτὸν

[1] μὲν om. OME.
[2] αὐτῷ om. O.
[3] Hudson: Γελμῶν O: Γελμωγάλην M: Γελμῶν γαλὶν SP: Galin Lat.
[4] + μέλλειν MSP: κρατήσαντ' (om. καὶ post ἔλεγεν cum O) Niese.

[a] Amplification. The woman's answer in the Heb. of 2 Sam. xvii. 20 is not wholly intelligible: A.V. "they be gone over the brook of water." The word *mîkal* here trans-

and, when those in pursuit of them came and inquired about them, asking whether she had caught sight of them, she did not deny having seen them; they had, she said, drunk at her house and then had gone away. If, however, they pursued them hotly, they would, she predicted, overtake them.[a] But, though they did pursue for a considerable distance, they did not overtake them, and so they turned back. And, when the woman saw them ride away, and that there was no longer any fear of the youths being captured by them, she drew them up out of the well and urged them to continue on their appointed way.[b] So, after travelling with great haste and speed, they came to David and informed him in detail[c] of all Absalom's plans; and he thereupon commanded his men to cross the Jordan, although it was already night, and permitted no delay on that account.

(8) Now Achitophel, when his proposal failed of acceptance, mounted his beast and set off for Gelmōn,[d] his native city. And, having called together all his people, he recounted to them the advice he had given Absalom, saying that, as Absalom had not followed it, he was clearly destined to perish before very long, for David would conquer him and be restored to his throne. Therefore, he said, it was better for him to remove himself from the world in a free and noble

Ahitophel's humiliation and suicide. 2 Sam. xvii. 23.

lated "brook" is obscure and probably corrupt, as the different versions indicate: Targum "they have already crossed the Jordan," LXX παρῆλθαν μικρὸν τοῦ ὕδατος "they passed a little distance from the water" (?), Luc. διεληλύθασιν σπεύδοντες "they have gone by in haste."

[b] Unscriptural detail. Bibl. "they came up out of the well and went."

[c] Or "accurately."

[d] The Biblical name, which is not mentioned at this point in Scripture, is Giloh, *cf.* § 197 note.

εἰς κόλασιν Δαυίδῃ, καθ' οὗ πάντα συνέπραττεν Ἀψαλώμῳ. ταῦτα διαλεχθεὶς καὶ παρελθὼν εἰς τὸ μυχαίτατον τῆς οἰκίας ἀνήρτησεν ἑαυτόν. καὶ τὸν μὲν Ἀχιτόφελον τοιούτου θανάτου δικαστὴν αὑτῷ γενόμενον καθελόντες ἐκ τῆς ἀγχόνης ἐκήδευσαν οἱ
230 προσήκοντες. ὁ δὲ Δαυίδης διαβὰς τὸν Ἰόρδανον, καθὼς προειρήκαμεν, εἰς Παρεμβολὰς καλλίστην καὶ ὀχυρωτάτην πόλιν παραγίνεται· δέχονται δ' αὐτὸν ἀσμενέστατα πάντες οἱ πρῶτοι τῆς χώρας κατά τε αἰδῶ τῆς τότε φυγῆς καὶ κατὰ τιμὴν τῆς προτέρας εὐπραγίας. ἦσαν δὲ οὗτοι Βερζελαῖος ὁ Γαλαδίτης καὶ Σειφὰρ ὁ τῆς Ἀμμανίτιδος δυνάστης καὶ Μάχειρος ὁ τῆς Γαλαδίτιδος χώρας
231 πρῶτος. οὗτοι πᾶσαν αὐτῷ καὶ τοῖς ἐκείνου τῶν ἐπιτηδείων ἐκτένειαν[1] παρέσχον, ὡς μήτε κλίνας ἐπιλιπεῖν ἐστρωμένας μήτε ἄρτους καὶ οἶνον, ἀλλὰ καὶ θυμάτων ἀφθονίαν χορηγῆσαι καὶ τῶν εἰς ἀνάπαυσιν ἤδη[2] κεκοπωμένοις καὶ τροφὴν χρησίμων εὐπορίαν διαρκῆ παρασχεῖν.

232 (x. 1) Καὶ οἱ μὲν ἐν τούτοις ἦσαν· Ἀψάλωμος δ' ἀθροίσας μεγάλην στρατιὰν τῶν Ἑβραίων[3] ἐπὶ τὸν πατέρα καὶ διαβὰς τὸν Ἰόρδανον ποταμὸν οὐ πόρρω κατέζευξε τῶν Παρεμβολῶν ἐν τῇ Γαλαδιτῶν χώρᾳ, καταστήσας στρατηγὸν πάσης τῆς δυνάμεως Ἀμασᾶν[4] εἰς τὴν Ἰωάβου τάξιν τοῦ

[1] εὐθηνίαν SP: copiam Lat.
[2] ἅμα MSP.
[3] + ἦγεν SPE.
[4] Ἀβασᾶν O: Ἀβεσσὰν ME: Ἀμεσσὰν SP: Amessam Lat.

[a] Ahitophel's speech is an amplification of the brief Scriptural phrase " and he put his household in order."
[b] Unscriptural detail.
[c] Bibl. Mahanaim, *cf.* § 9 note.

spirit than surrender himself to David to be punished for having in all ways helped Absalom against him.[a] After this speech he went into the innermost part[b] of the house and hanged himself. Such was the death to which Achitophel, as his own judge, sentenced himself, and his relatives cut him down from the rope and gave him burial. But David, having, as we said before, crossed the Jordan, came to The Camps,[c] a very fine and well-fortified city. There he was most cordially received by the leading men of the region, both out of regard for his feelings as an exile and in honour of his former greatness. These were Berzelaios[d] the Galadite,[e] Seiphar,[f] the ruler of Ammanitis, and Macheiros,[g] the chief man[h] of the country of Galaditis. They supplied him and his men liberally with everything needed, so that beds with covering were not lacking, nor bread and wine; moreover, they provided an abundance of slaughtered animals and furnished a plentiful supply of all things necessary for the refreshment and nourishment of exhausted men.

David is welcomed at Mahanaim (The Camps). 2 Sam. xvii. 24, 27.

(x. 1) Such, then, was their position. As for Absalom, having collected a great army of Hebrews he led them against his father, and crossing the river Jordan, halted not far from The Camps in the country of Galaditis. He had appointed as commander of his entire force, in Joab's place, Amasa,

The armies of Absalom and David prepare for battle. 2 Sam. xvii. 24.

[d] Called Beerzelos in §§ 272 ff.; bibl. Barzillai, LXX Βερζελλεί.

[e] Bibl. Gileadite, LXX Γαλααδείτης.

[f] Bibl. Shobi ben Nahash, LXX Οὐεσβεὶ (Luc. Σειφεὶ) υἱὸς Ναάς.

[g] Bibl. Machir ben Ammiel, LXX Μαχεὶρ υἱὸς Ἀμειήλ.

[h] This unscriptural detail about Machir is perhaps derived from 2 Sam. ix. 4, *cf.* § 113, where Machir is represented as the protector of Jonathan's son.

συγγενοῦς αὐτοῦ· πατρὸς μὲν γὰρ ἦν Ἰεθράου
μητρὸς δὲ Ἀβιγαίας, αὕτη δὲ καὶ Σαρουία ἡ
233 Ἰωάβου μήτηρ ἀδελφαὶ ἦσαν Δαυίδου. ὡς δ'
ἐξαριθμήσας τοὺς σὺν αὐτῷ Δαυίδης περὶ τετρακισχιλίους εὗρεν ὄντας, οὐκ ἔγνω μένειν πότ'
ἐπ' αὐτὸν Ἀψάλωμος ἔλθῃ, προσθεὶς δὲ τοῖς οὖσι
χιλιάρχους καὶ ἑκατοντάρχους καὶ διελὼν εἰς τρία
μέρη τὴν στρατιὰν[1] τὸ μὲν τῷ στρατηγῷ παρέδωκεν
Ἰωάβῳ, τὸ δὲ τῷ ἀδελφῷ αὐτοῦ Ἀβισαίῳ, τὴν
δὲ τρίτην μοῖραν ἐνεχείρισεν Ἐθαίῳ[2] συνήθει μὲν
ὄντι καὶ φίλῳ ἐκ δὲ τῆς Γιττῶν πόλεως ὑπάρχοντι.
234 βουλόμενον δὲ συνεκστρατεύειν αὐτὸν οὐκ εἴασαν
οἱ φίλοι γνώμῃ κατασχόντες σοφωτάτῃ· νικηθέντες
μὲν γὰρ σὺν αὐτῷ πᾶσαν ἀποβαλεῖν ἐλπίδα χρηστὴν
ἔφασκον, ἂν δὲ ἡττηθέντες ἑνὶ μέρει τῆς δυνάμεως
τῷ λοιπῷ πρὸς αὐτὸν φύγωσιν ἀμείνονα παρα-
σκευάσειν[3] αὐτὸν ἰσχύν· ὑπονοήσειν δὲ καὶ τοὺς
πολεμίους εἰκός ἐστιν ἄλλο μετ' αὐτοῦ στράτευμα
235 εἶναι. πεισθεὶς[4] δὲ τῇ συμβουλίᾳ ταύτῃ μένειν μὲν
αὐτὸς ἐν ταῖς Παρεμβολαῖς ἔκρινεν, ἐκπέμπων δὲ
τοὺς φίλους καὶ τοὺς στρατηγοὺς ἐπὶ τὸν πόλεμον
παρεκάλει προθυμίαν ἐναποδείξασθαι καὶ πίστιν
καὶ μνήμην, εἴ τινος τῶν μετρίως ἐχόντων παρ'
αὐτοῦ ἔτυχον· φείσασθαι δὲ καὶ τοῦ παιδὸς Ἀψαλώμου κρατήσαντας ἠντιβόλει, μὴ κακὸν αὐτὸν

[1] τὴν στρατιὰν om. RO.
[2] Dindorf: Ἐσθάῳ RO: Ἐσθαίῳ rell.: Estheo Lat.
[3] Hudson: παρασκευάζειν codd. E.
[4] E: ἠσθεὶς codd. Lat.

[a] Bibl. Ithra (Heb. *Yithrâ*), LXX Ἰοθόρ.
[b] No number is given in Scripture. Josephus apparently

a relative of the latter, for his father was Jethraos [a] and his mother was Abigaia, and she and Sarūia, the mother of Joab, were both sisters of David. Now when David numbered his men and found that they were some four thousand,[b] he decided not to wait for Absalom to attack him, but appointed captains of thousands and captains of hundreds to the men he had with him, and divided the army into three parts; one division he entrusted to Joab, another to the latter's brother Abisai, while the third part he turned over to Ethaios,[c] who was his comrade and friend although he came from the city of Gitta. He himself wished to go out with them to battle, but his friends would not allow it and kept him back by a very wise decision; for they said that if they were defeated with him present, they would lose every fair hope, but if, on the other hand, one part of their force were beaten and they fell back upon David with the remainder, he would bring them renewed strength, and the enemy would probably suspect that there was still another army with him.[d] So David took this advice [e] and decided to remain at The Camps himself while he sent out his friends and generals to war, exhorting them to show themselves eager and faithful and mindful of whatever fair treatment they might have received from him.[f] He also implored them to spare his son Absalom, if they were victorious,

2 Sam. xviii. 1.

assumes that each of the three generals had more than a thousand men.

[c] Called Ethis in § 201; bibl. Ittai.

[d] This argument is an amplification or an interpretation of the obscure text in 2 Sam. xviii. 3, which seems to mean simply that even if David's men were routed, the enemy would consider it less important than David's capture.

[e] Variant "was pleased with this advice."

[f] This exhortation is an addition to Scripture.

ἐργάσηταί τι τελευτήσαντος αὐτοῦ. καὶ ὁ μὲν νίκην αὐτοῖς ἐπευξάμενος ἐκπέμπει τὴν στρατιάν.

236 (2) Ἰωάβου δὲ παρατάξαντος τὴν δύναμιν ἀντικρὺ τῶν πολεμίων ἐν πεδίῳ μεγάλῳ ἐξόπισθεν περιβεβλημένῳ δρυμὸν ἀντεξάγει τὴν στρατιὰν καὶ Ἀψάλωμος. καὶ συμβολῆς γενομένης ἔργα μεγάλα χειρῶν τε καὶ τόλμης παρ᾽ ἀμφοτέρων ἐπεδείκνυτο, τῶν μὲν ὑπὲρ τοῦ τὴν βασιλείαν ἀπολαβεῖν Δαυίδην παρακινδυνευόντων καὶ πάσῃ προθυμίᾳ χρωμένων, τῶν δ᾽, ἵνα μὴ ταύτην Ἀψάλωμος ἀφαιρεθῇ καὶ δῷ τῷ πατρὶ δίκας κολασθεὶς ἀνθ᾽ ὧν ἐτόλμησεν,
237 οὐδὲν ὀκνούντων οὔτε ποιεῖν οὔτε πάσχειν, ἔτι δὲ τῶν μὲν πλειόνων ἵνα μὴ κρατηθῶσιν ὑπὸ τῶν σὺν Ἰωάβῳ καὶ τοῖς σὺν αὐτῷ στρατηγοῖς ὄντων ὀλίγων, αἰσχύνην γὰρ αὐτοῖς τοῦτ᾽ εἶναι μεγίστην, τῶν δὲ Δαυίδου στρατιωτῶν ἵνα τοσούτων μυριάδων κρατήσωσι φιλοτιμουμένων, ἔρις ἐγένετο καρτερά, καὶ νικῶσιν οἱ Δαυίδου ῥώμῃ τε προύχοντες καὶ
238 τῇ τῶν πολεμικῶν ἐπιστήμῃ. φεύγοντας δὲ διὰ δρυμῶν καὶ φαράγγων ἑπόμενοι τοὺς μὲν ἐλάμβανον πολλοὺς δὲ ἀνῄρουν, ὡς φεύγοντας πεσεῖν πλείονας ἢ μαχομένους· ἔπεσον γὰρ ὡς δισμύριοι ἐπ᾽ ἐκείνης τῆς ἡμέρας. οἱ δὲ τοῦ Δαυίδου πάντες ὥρμησαν ἐπὶ τὸν Ἀψάλωμον· φανερὸς γὰρ αὐτοῖς ὑπό τε τοῦ κάλλους καὶ τοῦ μεγέθους ἐγένετο.
239 δείσας δὲ μὴ καταλάβωσιν αὐτὸν οἱ πολέμιοι,

---

[a] David's threat to harm himself and the prayer for victory are also unscriptural details.

[b] This account of the battle, which as usual is greatly amplified, has Thucydidean echoes in πάσῃ προθυμίᾳ χρωμένων "making every effort" and προύχοντες . . . ἐπιστήμῃ "because of their greater . . . knowledge of war."

threatening to do himself some injury if Absalom met his death. And so, with a prayer for their victory, he sent his army out.[a]

Absalom's force is routed. 2 Sam. xviii. 6.

(2) Then Joab drew up his force opposite the enemy in a great plain bordered by a wood in the rear, and Absalom led out his troops against him. In the ensuing engagement great deeds of strength and daring were performed on both sides, the one scorning danger and making every effort that David might recover his kingdom, while the other did not shrink from doing or suffering anything to prevent Absalom from being deprived of it and being punished by his father for his rash attempt; moreover, the larger force did its best not to be conquered by Joab's men and generals, who were few in number, for that would have brought upon them the greatest disgrace, while, on the other hand, David's soldiers were ambitious to conquer so many tens of thousands, and for these reasons the battle was a fierce one. Finally David's men were victorious because of their greater vigour and knowledge of war. And they pursued the fleeing enemy through woods and ravines, capturing some, but slaying so many that more fell in flight than on the field of battle; for there fell on that day some twenty thousand.[b] Then all of David's men went after Absalom, who was plainly visible to them because of his beauty and great stature,[c] and he, in fear of being captured by his enemies, mounted his

Absalom in flight, is entangled by his hair 2 Sam. xviii. 9.

[c] A detail apparently derived from the Luc. reading in 2 Sam. xviii. 9 ἦν μέγας Ἀβεσσαλὼμ ἐνώπιον τῶν παίδων Δαυείδ "and Absalom was great in the sight of David's servants," where most LXX MSS. have συνήντησεν Ἀβεσσαλὼμ κτλ. which agrees with the Heb. "and Absalom met the servants of David."

ἐπιβὰς τῆς ἡμιόνου τῆς βασιλικῆς ἔφευγε· φερόμενος δὲ μετὰ ῥύμης καὶ ὑπὸ τοῦ σάλου καὶ τῆς κινήσεως κοῦφος ὤν, ἐμπλακείσης αὐτῷ τῆς κόμης τραχεῖ δένδρῳ μεγάλοις ἐπὶ πολὺ κλάδοις ἐκτεταμένῳ παραδόξως ἀνακρεμνᾶται. καὶ τὸ μὲν κτῆνος ὑπ' ὀξύτητος ὡς ἐπικείμενον τὸν δεσπότην ἔτι φέρον ἐχώρει προσωτέρω, ὁ δ' ἐκ τῶν κλάδων
240 αἰωρούμενος ἐκρατεῖτο.[1] τοῦτό τις ἰδὼν τῶν Δαυίδου στρατιωτῶν ἐδήλωσεν Ἰωάβῳ, καὶ πεντήκοντα σίκλους ἂν αὐτῷ δεδωκέναι τοῦ στρατηγοῦ φήσαντος, εἰ βαλὼν ἀπέκτεινε τὸν Ἀψάλωμον, "οὐδ' εἰ χιλίους," εἶπεν, "ἔμελλές μοι παρέξειν, τοῦτ' ἂν διέθηκά μου τὸν τοῦ δεσπότου παῖδα, καὶ ταῦτ' ἐκείνου πάντων ἡμῶν ἀκουόντων φείσασθαι[2]
241 τοῦ νεανίσκου δεηθέντος." ὁ δὲ κελεύσας αὐτῷ δεῖξαι ποῦ κρεμάμενον ἴδοι τὸν Ἀψάλωμον τοξεύσας κατὰ τῆς καρδίας ἀπέκτεινεν· οἱ δὲ τὰ τοῦ Ἰωάβου κομίζοντες ὅπλα περιστάντες ἐν κύκλῳ τὸ
242 δένδρον κατασπῶσι τὸν νεκρόν· καὶ τὸν μὲν εἰς χάσμα βαθὺ καὶ ἀχανὲς ῥίψαντες ἐπιβάλλουσιν αὐτῷ λίθους, ὥστε ἀναπληρωθῆναι καὶ τὸ σχῆμα τάφου καὶ μέγεθος λαβεῖν, σημήνας δὲ ἀνακλητικὸν ὁ Ἰώαβος ἐπέσχε[3] τοῦ διώκειν τοὺς οἰκείους στρατιώτας τὴν τῶν πολεμίων δύναμιν, φειδόμενος τῶν ὁμοφύλων.
243 (3) Ἔστησε δ' Ἀψάλωμος ἐν τῇ κοιλάδι τῇ

[1] + τοῖς πολεμίοις codd.: secl. Niese.
[2] cod. Vat. apud Hudson: + τε RO: + σε MSP.
[3] Cocceji: ἀπέσχετο codd.: revocavit Lat.

[a] Variant "was seized by the enemy."
[b] So some LXX MSS. and Luc.; Heb. and most LXX MSS.

royal mule and fled. As he rode along at full speed, he was lifted up by the unsteady motion, and his hair became entangled in a rugged tree with great branches extending far out, and in this strange fashion he remained suspended. But his swiftly moving beast went on further as though still carrying his master on his back, while Absalom swung from the branches, which held him up.[a] This was seen by one of David's soldiers, who informed Joab of it, and, when the commander said he would have given him fifty [b] shekels if he had struck Absalom and killed him, he replied, "Not if you had been ready to give me a thousand, would I have treated my master's son in that way, especially as we all heard him plead that the youth's life be spared." Joab thereupon ordered him to show him where he had seen Absalom hanging, and shot an arrow [c] into his heart and killed him. Then Joab's armour-bearers surrounded the tree and pulled down the corpse,[d] and, casting it into a deep yawning pit, they threw stones into this until it filled up and took on the form and size of a tomb.[e] Meanwhile Joab sounded the retreat and kept his own soldiers from pursuing the enemy force, and so spared his countrymen.

Joab kills Absalom. 2 Sam. xviii. 14.

(3) Now Absalom had set up in the Valley of Kings

have "ten (shekels) of silver," while all texts add "and a girdle."

[c] Bibl. "took three darts and thrust them"; the Heb. *šebāṭîm* "darts" is translated by βέλη in the LXX, and by κίδας in Luc., either of which may mean "arrows" as well.

[d] According to Scripture Joab's ten armour-bearers completed his work by striking Absalom until he was dead.

[e] An interpretation of bibl. "and placed (A.V. "laid up") a very great heap of stones upon him," probably suggested by the fact that the Heb. *yaṣṣîbû* "placed" also has the technical meaning of "erect" a monument, grave-stele, etc.

βασιλικῇ στήλην λίθου μαρμαρινου δύο σταδίους ἀπέχουσαν Ἱεροσολύμων, ἣν προσηγόρευσεν ἰδίαν χεῖρα, λέγων ὡς καὶ τῶν τέκνων αὐτοῦ διαφθαρέντων ἐν τῇ στήλῃ μενεῖ τὸ ὄνομα· τέκνα γὰρ ἦν αὐτῷ τρία μὲν ἄρρενα, θυγάτηρ δὲ μία Θαμάρα[1]
244 τοὔνομα, ὡς προειρήκαμεν. συνοικησάσης δ' αὐτῆς τῷ Σολομῶνος υἱῷ[2] Ῥοβοάμῳ γίνεται παῖς ὁ διαδεξάμενος τὴν βασιλείαν Ἀβίας. καὶ περὶ μὲν τούτων ἐν ὑστέροις οἰκειότερον τῇ ἱστορίᾳ δηλώσομεν. μετὰ δὲ τὴν Ἀψαλώμου τελευτὴν ὁ μὲν λαὸς εἰς τὰ οἰκεῖα διεσπάρη.
245 (4) Ἀχίμας δὲ ὁ Σαδώκου τοῦ ἀρχιερέως υἱὸς Ἰωάβῳ προσελθὼν ἐδεῖτο αὐτοῦ τὴν νίκην ἐπιτρέψαι πορευθέντι Δαυίδῃ μηνῦσαι, καὶ ὅτι τῆς παρὰ τοῦ θεοῦ βοηθείας ἔτυχε καὶ προνοίας εὐαγγελίσα-
246 σθαι. καὶ τὸν μέν, οὐ προσήκειν εἰπὼν αὐτῷ καλῶν ἄγγελον ἀεὶ γεγενημένον νῦν ἀπιέναι[3] δηλώσοντα θάνατον τῷ βασιλεῖ τοῦ παιδὸς αὐτοῦ, μένειν ἠξίου, καλέσας δὲ τὸν Χουσὶν ἐκείνῳ προσέταξε τὸ ἔργον ἵν' ὅπερ αὐτὸς εἶδε τοῦτο μηνύσειε τῷ βασιλεῖ.
247 τοῦ δ' Ἀχίμα πάλιν δεηθέντος αὐτῷ τὴν ἀγγελίαν ἐφεῖναι, περὶ μόνης γὰρ αὐτὴν ποιήσεσθαι[4] τῇ

[1] O: Θωμάρα rell.: Thamar Lat.
[2] Σολομῶνος υἱῷ R Lat.: Δαυίδου Σολομῶνος υἱῷ O: Δαυίδου υἱωνῷ MSP.
[3] Cocceji: ἀπεῖναι codd.
[4] Hudson: ποιήσασθαι codd.

---

[a] Unscriptural detail.
[b] The distance is not given in Scripture.
[c] So the LXX; Heb. *yad*, lit. "hand" (A.V. "place," agreeing with the Targum), here has the meaning of "monument" or "stele."
[d] § 190 (*cf.* note *ad loc.*). Josephus, in attributing

a marble[a] column, two stades distant from Jerusalem,[b] which he named Absalom's Hand,[c] saying that if his children should perish, his name would remain in connexion with the column. He had, in fact, three sons and one daughter, named Thamara, as we have said before.[d] And from her marriage to Solomon's son Roboamos, there was born a son, Abias, who succeeded to his throne. But of this we shall speak later, in a more suitable part of our history.[e] And so, after the death of Absalom, the people dispersed to their homes.

Absalom's monument; his children. 2 Sam. xviii. 18.

2 Sam. xiv. 27.

(4) Then Achimas, the son of the high priest Sadok, went to Joab and asked him for permission to go and announce the victory to David and bring him the good news that he had obtained help and guidance from God. Joab replied that it was not fitting that he who had always been a messenger of good tidings should now go and inform the king of his son's death, and so asked him to stay, while he called Chūsis[f] and charged him with the task of reporting to the king what he had himself seen. But when Achimas again requested him to entrust the message to him, saying that he would mention only the victory and

Ahimaaz (Achimas) brings David news of Joab's victory. 2 Sam. xviii. 19.

Absalom the fear that his children might die before him, disposes of the difficulty caused by the contradiction between 2 Sam. xiv. 27, referred to in § 190, and the present verse, 2 Sam. xviii. 18, which reads, "for he said, I have no son to keep my name in remembrance." A rabbinic tradition has it that Absalom's sons died before him as a punishment for having set fire to Joab's field; another tradition states that Absalom left sons "but they were so insignificant that Scripture speaks of them as though he died childless" (Ginzberg, *op. cit.* vi. 268).

[e] *A.* viii. 249 f.

[f] Josephus, like the LXX, confuses *kûšî* "Cushite" (or "Ethiopian," *i.e.* a negro slave) with *Ḥûšai*, the name of David's counsellor.

νίκης ἡσυχάσειν δὲ περὶ τῆς Ἀψαλώμου τελευτῆς,
ἐπέτρεψεν αὐτῷ τὴν πρὸς τὸν Δαυίδην ἄφιξιν. καὶ
τὴν ἐπιτομωτέραν ἐκβαλὼν[1] τῶν ὁδῶν, καὶ γὰρ
248 μόνος αὐτὴν ἐγίνωσκε, τὸν Χουσὶν φθάνει. καθ-
εζομένῳ δὲ Δαυίδῃ μεταξὺ τῶν πυλῶν καὶ περι-
μένοντι πότ' αὐτῷ τις ἐλθὼν ἀπὸ τῆς μάχης ἀπαγ-
γείλῃ[2] τὰ κατ' αὐτήν, τῶν σκοπῶν τις ἰδὼν τὸν
Ἀχίμαν τρέχοντα καὶ μήπω τίς ἐστι γνωρίσαι
δυνάμενος εἶπε[3] βλέπειν τινὰ παραγινόμενον πρὸς
249 αὐτόν. τοῦ δ' ἄγγελον εἶναι φήσαντος ἀγαθῶν,[4]
μετ' ὀλίγον ἔπεσθαί τινα καὶ ἕτερον ἐδήλωσεν αὐτῷ.
κἀκεῖνον δὲ ἄγγελον εἰπόντος, ἰδὼν τὸν Ἀχίμαν
ὁ σκοπὸς ἤδη ἐγγὺς γεγενημένον τὸν Σαδώκου
παῖδα τοῦ ἀρχιερέως προστρέχειν ἐσήμαινεν. ὁ
δὲ Δαυίδης περιχαρὴς γενόμενος ἀγαθῶν ἄγγελον
τοῦτον ἔφησεν εἶναι καί τι τῶν εὐκταίων αὐτῷ
φέρειν ἀπὸ τῆς μάχης.
250 (5) Καὶ μεταξὺ ταῦτα λέγοντος τοῦ βασιλέως
φανεὶς ὁ Ἀχίμας προσκυνεῖ τὸν βασιλέα καὶ
πυθομένῳ περὶ τῆς μάχης νίκην εὐαγγελίζεται καὶ
κράτος. ἐρομένου δ' εἴ τι καὶ περὶ τοῦ παιδὸς
ἔχοι λέγειν αὐτὸς μὲν ἔφασκεν εὐθὺς ὁρμῆσαι πρὸς
αὐτὸν τῆς τροπῆς τῶν πολεμίων γενομένης, ἀκοῦσαι
δὲ μεγάλης φωνῆς[5] διωκόντων τὸν Ἀψάλωμον καὶ
πλεῖον τούτου μηδὲν δεδυνῆσθαι[6] μαθεῖν διὰ τὸ
πεμφθέντα ὑπὸ Ἰωάβου δηλῶσαι τὴν νίκην ἐπεί-

[1] ἐκλαβὼν SP: tenens Lat.
[2] ἀγγείλει O: ἀπαγγείλει M: ἀγγελεῖ Niese.
[3] + πρὸς τὸν Δαυίδην codd.: secl. Niese.
[4] Niese: ἀγαθὸν codd. Lat.
[5] βοῆς MSPE: voces Lat.
[6] μὴ δύνασθαι SP: μὴ M.

would keep silence about the death of Absalom, Joab granted him permission to make the journey to David. And so, by striking off into a shorter road, which he alone knew,[a] he arrived before Chūsis. Now as David sat between the gates, waiting until someone should come from the scene of battle and report how it had gone, one of the look-outs saw Achimas running along, and, though he could not yet recognize who it was, told David that he saw someone coming toward him. The latter replied that it was a messenger of good tidings, and when, a moment later, the man informed him that still another was following, David said that he too was a messenger. Then the lookout recognized Achimas, who was now very close, and announced that the man running toward them was the son of the high priest Sadok. At that, David was overjoyed and said that he was a messenger of good tidings and was bringing from the field of battle news of something such as they had prayed for.

Hushai announces to David the death of Absalom. 2 Sam. xviii. 28.

(5) While the king was saying this, Achimas appeared and did obeisance to the king, and, in answer to his inquiry about the battle, announced the welcome news of a decisive victory.[b] But when David asked whether he could also tell him something about his son, he said that he had hastened to him immediately upon the rout of the enemy, and, though he had heard a great shouting of those who were pursuing Absalom, he had been unable to learn anything more than this because he had been sent off in haste by Joab to report the victory. Then,

[a] Details added by Josephus. According to Scripture Ahimaaz ran by way of "the (Jordan) valley" (A.V. "the plain").

[b] On the hendiadys *cf.* § 73 note.

251 γεσθαι. παραγενομένου δὲ τοῦ Χουσὶ καὶ προσκυνήσαντος καὶ τὴν νίκην σημήναντος, περὶ τοῦ παιδὸς αὐτὸν ἀνέκρινεν. ὁ δ' "ἐχθροῖς," εἶπε, "τοῖς σοῖς οἷα συμβέβηκεν Ἀψαλώμῳ γένοιτο."
252 οὗτος ὁ λόγος οὐδὲ τὴν ἐπὶ τῇ νίκῃ χαρὰν εἴασεν οὔτ' αὐτῷ μεῖναι μεγίστην οὖσαν οὔτε τοῖς στρατιώταις· αὐτὸς μὲν γὰρ ἀναβὰς ἐπὶ τὸ ὑψηλότατον τῆς πόλεως ἀπεκλαίετο[1] τὸν υἱὸν τυπτόμενος τὰ στέρνα καὶ τὴν κεφαλὴν σπαραττόμενος καὶ παντοίως αὑτὸν αἰκιζόμενος καὶ "τέκνον," ἐκβοῶν, "εἴθε μοι τὸν θάνατον ἐπελθεῖν ἐγένετο καὶ ἅμα σοι τελευτῆσαι"· φύσει γὰρ ὢν φιλόστοργος, πρὸς
253 ἐκεῖνον μᾶλλον συμπαθῶς εἶχεν. ἡ στρατιὰ δὲ καὶ Ἰώαβος ἀκούσαντες ὅτι πενθεῖ τὸν υἱὸν οὕτως ὁ βασιλεύς, ᾐσχύνθησαν μετὰ τοῦ τῶν νενικηκότων σχήματος εἰσελθεῖν εἰς τὴν πόλιν, κατηφεῖς δὲ καὶ δεδακρυμένοι πάντες ὡς ἀφ' ἥττης παρῆλθον.
254 κατακαλυψαμένου δὲ τοῦ βασιλέως καὶ στένοντος τὸν υἱὸν εἴσεισι πρὸς αὐτὸν Ἰώαβος καὶ παρηγορῶν "ὦ δέσποτα," φησί, "λανθάνεις διαβάλλων σαυτὸν οἷς ποιεῖς, ὅτι τοὺς μὲν ἀγαπῶντάς σε καὶ περὶ σοῦ κινδυνεύοντας καὶ σαυτὸν καὶ τὴν σὴν γενεὰν δοκεῖς μισεῖν, στέργειν δὲ τοὺς ἐχθροτάτους καὶ
255 ποθεῖν οὐκέτ' ὄντας, οἳ δίκῃ τεθνήκασιν· εἰ γὰρ Ἀψάλωμος ἐκράτησε καὶ τὴν βασιλείαν βεβαίως κατέσχεν, οὐδενὸς ἂν ἡμῶν ὑπελείφθη λείψανον, ἀλλὰ πάντες ἂν ἀπὸ σοῦ καὶ τῶν σῶν ἀρξάμενοι

[1] ἀνεκλαίετο M : ἀνεκαλεῖτο SPE.

[a] Bibl. "to the chamber over the gate." It is possible, as Reinach suggests, that πόλεως "city" in Josephus's text is a scribal error for πύλης "gate."

[b] Details added by Josephus, amplifying the biblical phrase "the king weeps and mourns."

when Chūsis arrived and, with an obeisance, announced the victory, David questioned him about his son. "May your enemies," he replied, "suffer the same fate as Absalom." These words took away from both him and his soldiers all their joy over the victory, great as that was. As for David, he went up to the highest part of the city [a] and bewailed his son, beating his breast, tearing his hair and doing himself every kind of injury,[b] and crying out "O my son, would that death had come to me and that I had died with you!" [c] for he was by nature affectionate, and was especially attached to Absalom. And, when the army and Joab heard how deeply the king mourned for his son, they were ashamed to enter the city with the appearance of victors, and, instead, they all came in, as if from a defeat, with bowed heads and tearful faces. Then, while the king with veiled head was moaning for his son, Joab went into him and consoled him, saying, "My lord, you are unwittingly slandering yourself by this conduct,[d] for you seem to hate those who love you and are risking their lives both for you yourself and for your family, while you hold dear those who are most hostile to you, and long for them when they are no longer alive, although they have justly died. For, if Absalom had conquered and had firmly secured the kingdom, not one of us would have been left to survive, but all of us, beginning with you and your children, would

David's lament for Absalom. 2 Sam. xviii. 33. (Heb. xix. 1.)

Joab compels David to cease mourning. 2 Sam. xix. 5 (6).

[c] Bibl. "would God I had died in thy place" (A.V. "for thee"); the Targum adds, "and that thou wert alive this day."

[d] "Consoled him," etc. Joab's language is less respectful in Scripture, "Thou hast shamed this day the faces of all thy servants."

τέκνων ἀπωλώλειμεν οἰκτρῶς, οὐ κλαιόντων ἡμᾶς τῶν πολεμίων ἀλλὰ καὶ χαιρόντων καὶ τοὺς ἐλεοῦντας ἐπὶ τοῖς κακοῖς κολαζόντων. σὺ δ' οὐκ αἰσχύνῃ ταῦτα ποιῶν ἐπὶ μᾶλλον ἐχθρῷ, ὅτι σὸς
256 υἱὸς ὢν ἀσεβὴς οὕτως ἐγένετο. παυσάμενος οὖν τῆς ἀδίκου λύπης προελθὼν ὄφθητι τοῖς σαυτοῦ στρατιώταις καὶ τῆς νίκης αὐτοῖς καὶ τῆς περὶ τοὺς ἀγῶνας προθυμίας εὐχαρίστησον. ὡς ἐγὼ τήμερον, ἂν ἐπιμένῃς τοῖς ἄρτι πραττομένοις, ἀναπείσας ἀποστῆναί σου τὸν λαὸν καὶ τὴν βασιλείαν ἑτέρῳ παραδοῦναι, τότε σοι πικρότερον καὶ ἀληθὲς
257 ποιήσω τὸ πένθος." ταῦτ' εἰπὼν Ἰώαβος ἀπέστρεψεν ἀπὸ τῆς λύπης καὶ ἤγαγεν εἰς τὸν περὶ τῶν πραγμάτων λογισμὸν τὸν βασιλέα· μετασχηματίσας γὰρ ἑαυτὸν Δαυίδης καὶ ποιήσας ἐπιτήδειον εἰς τὴν τοῦ πλήθους θέαν πρὸς ταῖς πύλαις ἐκάθισεν, ὡς ἅπαντα τὸν λαὸν ἀκούσαντα συνδραμεῖν πρὸς αὐτὸν καὶ κατασπάσασθαι. καὶ ταῦτα μὲν τοῦτον ἔσχε τὸν τρόπον.

258 (xi. 1) Οἱ δ' ἐκ τῆς μάχης ἀναχωρήσαντες τῶν Ἑβραίων τῶν μετ' Ἀψαλώμου γενόμενοι παρ' αὐτοῖς ἕκαστοι διεπέμποντο κατὰ πόλεις ὑπομιμνήσκοντες αὐτοὺς ὧν εὐεργέτησεν αὐτοὺς[1] Δαυίδης καὶ τῆς ἐλευθερίας, ἣν ἐκ πολλῶν καὶ μεγάλων
259 ῥυσάμενος αὐτοὺς πολέμων παρέσχε, μεμφόμενοι δ' ὅτι τῆς βασιλείας αὐτὸν ἐκβαλόντες ἄλλῳ ταύτην ἐνεχείρισαν καὶ νῦν τεθνηκότος τοῦ κατασταθέντος ὑπ' αὐτῶν ἡγεμόνος οὐ παρακαλοῦσι Δαυίδην παύσασθαι μὲν τῆς ὀργῆς, εὐνοϊκῶς δὲ πρὸς αὐτοὺς ἔχειν, τῶν δὲ πραγμάτων καθὼς ἤδη καὶ πρότερον

[1] αὐτοὺς om. ROE.

have perished miserably, and the enemy, instead of weeping for us, would have rejoiced and punished any who pitied our misfortunes. And yet you are not ashamed to behave in this way about a man who is the more hateful for having been so impious, though your own son. Cease, therefore, from your unjustified grief and go out and show yourself to your soldiers and thank them for the victory and for their ardour in the fight. For, if you persist in doing as you have just been doing, I will this very day persuade the people to revolt from you and give the kingdom over to another, and then I shall make your sorrow more bitter and real." [a] By these words Joab diverted the king from his grief, and brought him to taking thought about the matter. So David, changing his appearance,[b] made himself presentable to the people,[c] and sat by the gates, until all the people heard of it and ran to greet him. And this was how these matters were.

(xi. 1) Now when those Hebrews on Absalom's side who had escaped from the battlefield returned to their several homes, they sent round to their cities, reminding them how David had benefited them and had procured their freedom by delivering them in many great wars; and they blamed themselves for having driven him from the throne and given it over to another, and because now, when the leader appointed by them was dead, they had not appealed to David to abate his anger, show himself friendly toward them, and resume his throne to take up the

The rebels make peace with David. 2 Sam. xix. 9 (10).

[a] Joab's speech is considerably amplified.
[b] Or "his dress."
[c] Unscriptural detail.

ποιεῖσθαι πρόνοιαν, τὴν βασιλείαν ἀπολαβόντα.
260 ταῦτα μὲν οὖν συνεχέστερον ἀπηγγέλλετο Δαυίδῃ· κἀκεῖνος οὐδὲν ἧττον ἔπεμψε πρὸς Σάδωκον καὶ Ἀβιάθαρον τοὺς ἀρχιερέας, ἵνα τοῖς ἄρχουσι τῆς Ἰούδα φυλῆς διαλεχθῶσιν, ὡς αἰσχρόν ἐστιν[1] αὐτοῖς ἄλλας φυλὰς πρὸ ἐκείνης Δαυίδην χειροτονῆσαι βασιλέα, "καὶ ταῦθ' ὑμῶν συγγενῶν ὄντων καὶ
261 κοινὸν αἷμα πρὸς αὐτὸν κεκληρωμένων." τὰ δ' αὐτὰ καὶ Ἀμασᾷ τῷ στρατηγῷ προσέταξεν αὐτοὺς λέγειν, ὅτι τῆς ἀδελφῆς υἱὸς ὢν αὐτοῦ μὴ πείθει τὸ πλῆθος Δαυίδῃ τὴν βασιλείαν ἀποδοῦναι· προσδοκᾶν δὲ παρ' αὐτοῦ μὴ διαλλαγὴν μόνον, τοῦτο γὰρ ἤδη γέγονεν, ἀλλὰ καὶ τὴν ἅπαντος τοῦ λαοῦ στρατηγίαν, ἣν αὐτῷ καὶ Ἀψάλωμος παρέσχε.
262 καὶ οἱ μὲν ἀρχιερεῖς ἃ μὲν τοῖς τῆς φυλῆς ἄρχουσι διελέχθησαν ἃ δὲ τὸν Ἀμασᾶν ἔπεισαν, τὰ παρὰ τοῦ βασιλέως πρὸς αὐτὸν εἰπόντες, ἐγχειρεῖν ταῖς ὑπὲρ αὐτοῦ φροντίσι. καὶ πείθει γε τὴν φυλὴν παραχρῆμα πέμψαι πρὸς Δαυίδην πρέσβεις παρακαλοῦντας εἰς τὴν ἰδίαν αὐτὸν ἐπανελθεῖν βασιλείαν. τὸ δ' αὐτὸ καὶ πάντες ἐποίουν οἱ Ἰσραηλῖται προτρεψαμένου τοῦ Ἀμασᾶ.
263 (2) Τῶν δὲ πρέσβεων ἀφικομένων πρὸς αὐτὸν εἰς Ἱεροσόλυμα παρεγένετο. πάντας δὲ τοὺς ἄλλους ἔφθασεν ἡ Ἰούδα φυλὴ πρὸς τὸν Ἰόρδανον ποταμὸν ἀπαντῆσαι τῷ βασιλεῖ καὶ ὁ Γήρα παῖς Σαμούις[2] μετὰ χιλίων ἀνδρῶν, οὓς ἐκ τῆς Βενιαμίτιδος φυλῆς

[1] ἐστιν om. RO.
[2] Σουμούϊς R: Σεμεΐας MS(P): Σεμεεὶς E: Semei Lat.

[a] "They had not appealed," etc. is an amplification of 2 Sam. xix. 10 (Heb. 11) "Now therefore why speak ye not a word of bringing the king back?"

direction of affairs just as before.[a] Such were the reports that were continually brought to David, but he none the less sent a message to the high priests Sadok and Abiathar that they should tell the chiefs of the tribe of Judah what a disgrace it was for them that the other tribes had chosen David king before they did, "especially," they were to add, "as you are his kin and have common blood with him." And he instructed them to speak to Amasa, the commander, in the same vein and ask why, although he was a son of David's sister,[b] he had not persuaded the people to restore the kingdom to David; and they were to say that he might expect not only a reconciliation with him,—which had already taken place—but also the chief command of the entire people, like that which Absalom had given him. So the high priests gave the one message to the chiefs of the tribe (of Judah), and the other message of the king they gave to Amasa, whom they persuaded to undertake measures on his behalf. He, in turn, persuaded the tribe immediately to send envoys to David, inviting him to return to his own kingdom.[c] And all the Israelites, at the suggestion of Amasa, did the same thing.

(2) After the envoys came to him, David went on to Jerusalem. And first of all the tribes to meet the king at the river Jordan was Judah; also Samūis, the son of Gera, with a thousand men whom he had brought from the tribe of Benjamin, and Siba, the

The tribes assemble at the Jordan to welcome David. 2 Sam xix. 15 (16).

[b] In Scripture David does not mention the exact relation, but merely says "art thou not of my bone (Targum "my kinsman") and flesh?"

[c] The reconciliation with Amasa and the latter's action in persuading the Israelites to send envoys are unscriptural details.

ἐπήγετο, καὶ Σιβᾶς δὲ ὁ ἀπελεύθερος Σαούλου καὶ οἱ παῖδες αὐτοῦ πεντεκαίδεκα τὸν ἀριθμὸν ὄντες
264 μετὰ οἰκετῶν εἴκοσιν. οὗτοι σὺν τῇ Ἰούδα φυλῇ τὸν ποταμὸν ἐγεφύρωσαν, ἵνα ῥᾷστα διαβῇ μετὰ τῶν ἰδίων ὁ βασιλεύς. ὡς δὲ ἧκεν ἐπὶ τὸν Ἰόρδανον ἠσπάσατο μὲν αὐτὸν ἡ Ἰούδα φυλή, προσπεσὼν δ' ἀναβάντι ἐπὶ τὴν γέφυραν Σαμούις καὶ κατασχὼν αὐτοῦ τοὺς πόδας ἐδεῖτο συγγνῶναι περὶ τῶν εἰς αὐτὸν ἡμαρτημένων καὶ μὴ γενέσθαι πικρὸν αὐτῷ μηδὲ τοῦτο πρῶτον ἡγήσασθαι τὴν τιμωρίαν ἐν ἐξουσίᾳ γενόμενον, λογίσασθαι δ' ὅτι καὶ μετανοήσας ἐφ' οἷς ἐσφάλη πρῶτος ἐλθεῖν πρὸς αὐ-
265 τὸν ἔσπευσε.[1] ταῦτα δ' ἀντιβολοῦντος αὐτοῦ καὶ οἰκτιζομένου Ἀβισαῖος ὁ Ἰωάβου ἀδελφός, "διὰ τοῦτο οὖν," εἶπεν, "οὐ τεθνήξῃ βλασφημήσας τὸν ὑπὸ τοῦ θεοῦ κατασταθέντα βασιλεύειν;" Δαυίδης δ' ἐπιστραφεὶς πρὸς αὐτόν, "οὐ παύσεσθ'," εἶπεν, "ὦ Σαρουίας παῖδες; μὴ κινήσητε πάλιν ἡμῖν
266 καινὰς ἐπὶ ταῖς πρώταις ταραχὰς καὶ στάσεις· οὐ γὰρ ἀγνοεῖν ὑμᾶς προσῆκεν ὅτι σήμερον ἄρχομαι τῆς βασιλείας. διὸ πᾶσιν ἀφιέναι τὰς κολάσεις τοῖς ἀσεβήσασιν ὄμνυμι καὶ μηδενὶ τῶν ἁμαρτόντων ἐπεξελθεῖν. σύ τε," εἶπεν, "ὦ Σαμούι, θάρρει καὶ δείσῃς μηδὲν ὡς τεθνηξόμενος." ὁ δὲ προσκυνήσας αὐτὸν προῆγεν.

267 (3) Ἀπήντησε δ' αὐτῷ καὶ ὁ Σαούλου υἱωνὸς Μεμφίβοσθος ῥυπαράν τε τὴν ἐσθῆτα περικείμενος καὶ τὴν κόμην βαθεῖαν καὶ κατημελημένην ἔχων· μετὰ γὰρ τὴν Δαυίδου φυγὴν οὔτ' ἀπεκείρατο λυπούμενος οὔτ' ἐκάθηρε τὴν ἐσθῆτα κατακρίνας

[1] ἐσπούδασε MSP.

freedman of Saul, and his sons, who were fifteen in number, together with twenty servants. These latter with the tribe of Judah made a bridge [a] over the river, in order that the king and his men might cross the more easily. And, when he came to the Jordan, he was welcomed by the tribe of Judah; then, as he mounted the bridge,[b] Samūis fell down before him and clasped his feet, asking pardon for the wrongs he had done him, and that he should not be harsh with him nor let his first thought, on coming into power, be one of vengeance; he should, Samūis said, take into account that he had repented of his errors and had hastened to be the first to come to him. While he thus made supplication and begged for mercy, Abisai, the brother of Joab, said to him, "Shall you, then, not die for having cursed the one appointed by God to reign?" But David turned to him and said, "Will you not be quiet, sons of Saruia? Do not stir up for us new disorders and dissensions to follow the first. You must not fail to realize that with to-day I begin my reign. I have, therefore, sworn to forgo punishment for acts of rebellion, and not to prosecute any offender. And you, Samūis," he said, "take courage and have no fear that you will be put to death." The other then did obeisance to him and went on before him.

David forgives Shimei. 2 Sam. xix. 18 (19).

(3) And there also met him Saul's grandson Memphibosthos, wearing a soiled garment and with his hair long and unkempt, for, after David's flight, he had not, because of his grief, either cut his hair or washed his garment, but had condemned himself to

Mephibosheth excuses his conduct toward David. 2 Sam. xix. 24 (25).

[a] Heb. *'āberāh* (for *'aberû*?) *hā-'abārāh* seems to mean "they ferried across," as the Targum translates; LXX διέβη ἡ διάβασις, lit. "the crossing went over," is more obscure than the Heb.

[b] Bibl. "as he was crossing the Jordan."

αὐτοῦ συμφορὰν ταύτην ἐπὶ τῇ τοῦ βασιλέως μεταβολῇ· διεβέβλητο δὲ καὶ ὑπὸ τοῦ ἐπιτρόπου Σιβᾶ
268 πρὸς αὐτὸν ἀδίκως. ἀσπασαμένου δ' αὐτοῦ καὶ προσκυνήσαντος ἤρξατο πυνθάνεσθαι τί δήποτ' οὐ συνεξῆλθεν αὐτῷ καὶ κοινωνὸς ἦν τῆς φυγῆς; ὁ δ' ἀδίκημα τοῦτ' ἔλεγεν εἶναι Σιβᾶ· κελευσθεὶς γὰρ παρασκευάσαι τὰ πρὸς τὴν ἔξοδον οὐκ ἐφρόντισεν, ἀλλ' ὥσπερ ἀνδραπόδου τινὸς οὕτως παρήκουσεν.
269 "εἰ μέντοι γε τὰς βάσεις εἶχον ἐρρωμένας, οὐκ ἂν ἀπελείφθην σου, χρῆσθαι πρὸς τὴν φυγὴν ταύταις δυνάμενος. οὐ τοῦτο δὲ μόνον ἠδίκησέ μου τὴν πρὸς σέ, δέσποτα, εὐσέβειαν, ἀλλὰ καὶ προσδιέβαλε καὶ κατεψεύσατο κακουργῶν. ἀλλ' οἶδα γὰρ ὅτι τούτων οὐδὲν ἡ σὴ διάνοια προσίεται δικαία τε
270 οὖσα καὶ τὴν ἀλήθειαν, ἣν ἰσχύειν τε βούλεται[1] καὶ τὸ θεῖον, ἀγαπῶσα· μείζονα γὰρ κινδυνεύσας παθεῖν ὑπὸ τοῦ πάππου τοὐμοῦ καὶ τῆς ὅλης ἡμῶν γενεᾶς ὀφειλούσης εἰς ἐκεῖνα ἀπολωλέναι, σύ γε[2] μέτριος καὶ χρηστὸς ἐγένου, τότε μάλιστα πάντων ἐκείνων λήθην ποιησάμενος, ὅτ' ἐξουσίαν τῆς ὑπὲρ αὐτῶν τιμωρίας εἶχεν ἡ μνήμη. φίλον δὲ σὸν ἔκρινας ἐμὲ καὶ ἐπὶ τῆς τραπέζης εἶχες ὁσημέραι, καὶ οὐδὲν ἀπέλειπον τῶν συγγενῶν τοῦ μάλιστα
271 τιμωμένου." ταῦτ' εἰπόντος οὔτε τὸν Μεμφίβοσθον ἔγνω κολάζειν οὔθ' ὡς καταψευσαμένου τοῦ Σιβᾶ καταδικάζειν, ἀλλ' ὑπὲρ μὲν τοῦ μὴ μετὰ Σιβᾶ πρὸς αὐτὸν[3] ἐλθεῖν ἐκείνῳ πάντα χαρίσασθαι φήσας

[1] ἣν . . . βούλεται] ἐνισχύειν βουλομένη RO.
[2] σύ γε] Niese: σύ τε RO: σὺ MSP.
[3] πρὸς αὐτὸν post Σιβᾶ 1° RO.

[a] Variant "for it is just and wishes the truth to prevail and loves the Deity."

this unhappy state on the king's fall from power. He had, moreover, been unjustly accused before David by his steward Siba. And so, when he greeted David and did obeisance to him, the latter inquired just why he had not gone out with him and shared his exile, whereupon he replied that this was Siba's fault, for, although he had been ordered to prepare for the departure, he had paid no attention, but had disregarded him quite as if he had been a mere slave. " If, indeed," he added, " I had sound feet and had been able to use them in flight, I should not have been far behind you. But this is not the only way, my lord, in which he has wrongfully hindered my obedience to you, for he has also slandered me and has maliciously lied about me. I know very well, however, that none of these calumnies finds admittance into your mind, for it is just and loves the truth, which the Deity also wishes to prevail [a] ; and, though you were exposed to great hardships at the hands of my grandfather, on which account our whole family was deserving of extinction, you were, none the less, forbearing and kind in making yourself forget all these things at the very time when you might have remembered them and also had the power to take vengeance.[b] But you considered me your friend and had me daily at your table, and in no way was I less well treated than the most honoured of your relatives." After this speech of his, David decided neither to punish Memphibosthos nor to condemn Siba for having made false charges, but he told Memphibosthos that, because he had not come to him with Siba, he had presented all his substance to the latter ; however,

[b] Text obscure, lit. " when your memory had power to take vengeance upon them."

αὐτῷ συγγινώσκειν ὑπέσχετο, τὰ ἡμίση τῆς οὐσίας αὐτῷ κελεύσας ἀποδοθῆναι. ὁ δὲ Μεμφίβοσθος "πάντ' ἐχέτω μέν," εἶπε, "Σιβᾶς, ἐμοὶ δ' ἀπόχρη τὸ σὲ τὴν βασιλείαν ἀπολαβεῖν."

272 (4) Βεέρζελον δὲ τὸν Γαλαδίτην ἄνδρα μέγαν καὶ καλὸν καὶ πολλὰ παρεσχημένον ἐν ταῖς Παρεμβολαῖς αὐτῷ Δαυίδην τε[1] προπέμψαντα μέχρι τοῦ Ἰορδάνου παρεκάλει συνελθεῖν ἕως τῶν Ἱεροσολύμων· γηροκομήσειν γὰρ αὐτὸν ἐν πάσῃ τιμῇ καὶ ὡς πατρὸς ἐπιμεληθήσεσθαι καὶ προνοήσειν ἐπηγ-
273 γέλλετο. ὁ δὲ πόθῳ τῶν οἴκοι παρῃτεῖτο τὴν μετ' αὐτοῦ διατριβήν· καὶ τὸ γῆρας λέγων τοιοῦτον[2] αὐτῷ τυγχάνειν, ὥστε μὴ[3] ἀπολαύειν τῶν ἡδέων εἰς ὀγδοήκοντα ἔτη προβεβηκότος, ἀλλ' ὥστε καταλύσεως ἤδη καὶ ταφῆς προνοεῖν, ἐπὶ ταύτην ἠξίου βουλόμενον αὐτῷ χαρίζεσθαι τὰ κατ' ἐπι-
274 θυμίαν αὐτὸν ἀπολῦσαι· οὔτε γὰρ τροφῆς οὔτε ποτοῦ συνιέναι διὰ τὸν χρόνον, ἀποκεκλεῖσθαι δ' αὐτῷ καὶ τὰς ἀκοὰς ἤδη πρὸς αὐλῶν ἤχους καὶ μέλη τῶν ἄλλων ὀργάνων, ὅσα παρὰ βασιλεῦσι τέρπει τοὺς συνδιαιτωμένους. οὕτως δὲ λιπαρῶς δεομένου, "σὲ μέν," εἶπεν, "ἀπολύω, τὸν δ' υἱὸν Ἀχίμανον ἄφες μοι· πάντων γὰρ αὐτῷ μεταδώσω
275 τῶν ἀγαθῶν." καὶ Βεέρζελος μὲν καταλιπὼν τὸν υἱὸν καὶ προσκυνήσας τὸν βασιλέα καὶ πάντων ἐπευξάμενος αὐτῷ τέλος ὧν ἔχει κατὰ ψυχὴν

[1] Δαυίδην τε] Δαυίδῃ RO: Δαυίδης ex E Niese.
[2] οὐ τοιοῦτον MSP.
[3] μὴ om. MSP.

[a] David's reply to Mephibosheth is an amplification of 2 Sam. xix. 29 "and the king said, why speakest thou any

he promised to forgive him and ordered that half the property be restored to him.[a] Thereupon Memphibosthos exclaimed, " Let Siba have it all! As for me, it is enough that you have recovered your kingdom."

(4) Now Beerzelos[b] the Galadite, a great and noble man, who had furnished David many supplies at The Camps, and had escorted him as far as the Jordan, was invited by him to come with him to Jerusalem; for, he said, he would cherish him in his old age with every honour, and he promised to take care of him and provide for him as for a father. But Beerzelos, who longed to be home, declined to stay with him, saying that his age was such that he could not enjoy pleasures,—he was now eighty years old—but must think of his end and burial, and he asked David, if he wished to gratify his desires, to release him for this purpose. He had, he said, no taste for food and drink because of his age, and his ears were deaf to the sound of flutes and the music of other instruments[c] which delight those who live with kings.[d] To this earnest entreaty David replied, " I do release you, but leave me your son Achimanos,[e] for I shall give him of all good things." So Beerzelos left his son behind and, after doing obeisance to the king and praying for the fulfilment of his heart's desire, re-

Barzillai (Beerzelos) declines to live with David. 2 Sam. xix. 31 (32).

more of thy matters? I have said, thou and Ziba divide the land."

[b] Called Berzelaios in § 230, *cf.* note.

[c] *Cf.* Targum " harps and songs of praise "; Heb. and LXX " singing men and women."

[d] Josephus, contrary to his usual procedure, abridges Barzillai's speech.

[e] *Cf.* Luc. Ἀχιμαάν (*v.l.* Ἀχειναάμ κτλ.); bibl. Chimham, LXX Χαμαάμ. In Scripture it is Barzillai who proposes that his son remain with David.

οἴκαδ' ὑπέστρεψε. παραγίνεται δ' εἰς Γάλγαλα Δαυίδης τοῦ λαοῦ παντὸς ἤδη τὸ ἥμισυ περὶ αὐτὸν ἔχων καὶ τὴν Ἰούδα φυλήν.

276 (5) Ἀφικνοῦνται δ' εἰς Γάλγαλα πρὸς αὐτὸν οἱ πάσης φυλῆς[1] πρῶτοι μετὰ πολλοῦ πλήθους[2] καὶ τὴν Ἰούδα φυλὴν κατεμέμφοντο λάθρα πρὸς αὐτὸν ἐλθοῦσαν, ὡς δεῖν ὁμοῦ πάντας μιᾷ γνώμῃ ποιεῖσθαι τὴν ἀπάντησιν. οἱ δ' ἄρχοντες τῆς Ἰούδα φυλῆς μὴ δυσχεραίνειν αὐτοὺς ἠξίουν προληφθέντας· καὶ γὰρ συγγενεῖς ὄντες αὐτοῦ καὶ διὰ τοῦτο μᾶλλον προνοούμενοι καὶ στέργοντες φθάσαι, οὐ μέντοι γε διὰ τὸ προελθεῖν δῶρα λαβεῖν αὐτούς, ἵν' ἔχωσιν ἐπὶ τούτῳ δυσφορεῖν ὕστεροι πρὸς αὐτὸν ἐλθόντες.
277 ταῦτα τῶν τῆς Ἰούδα φυλῆς ἡγεμόνων εἰπόντων οἱ τῶν ἄλλων ἄρχοντες οὐχ ἡσύχασαν, ἀλλ' "ἡμεῖς μέν," ἔφασαν, "ὦ ἀδελφοί, θαυμάζομεν ὑμᾶς αὐτῶν ἀποκαλοῦντας μόνων συγγενῆ τὸν βασιλέα· ὁ γὰρ τὴν ἁπάντων ἐξουσίαν παρὰ τοῦ θεοῦ λαβὼν πάντων ἡμῶν εἶναι συγγενὴς κρίνεται. καὶ διὰ τοῦθ' ὁ μὲν λαὸς ἅπας[3] ἕνδεκα μοίρας ἔχει, μίαν δ' ὑμεῖς, καὶ πρεσβύτεροι ἐσμέν, καὶ οὐκ ἐποιήσατε δίκαια κρύφα καὶ[4] λεληθότως ἐλθόντες πρὸς τὸν βασιλέα."

278 (6) Τοιαῦτα τῶν ἡγεμόνων πρὸς ἀλλήλους διαλεχθέντων ἀνήρ τις πονηρὸς καὶ στάσει χαίρων, ὄνομα Σαβαῖος υἱὸς δὲ Βοχορίου[5] τῆς Βενιαμίτιδος φυλῆς, στὰς ἐν μέσῳ πρὸς τὸ πλῆθος μέγα βοήσας εἶπεν· "οὔτ' ἔχει τις ἡμῶν[6] παρὰ Δαυίδου μοίρας

[1] πάσης φυλῆς] τῆς χώρας MSPE: provinciae Lat.
[2] πολλοῦ πλήθους] πολλῆς πληθύος MSPE.
[3] ἅπας om. RO.
[4] κρύφα καὶ om. RO.
[5] Beddadi Lat.
[6] E Lat.: ὑμῶν codd.

turned to his home. And David came to Galgala, having with him now half of all the people, and the tribe of Judah.

(5) Then there came to him at Galgala the leading men of every tribe [a] with a great multitude, and they reproached the tribe of Judah for having come to him secretly, saying that they should all have met him together at one time. But the chiefs of the tribe of Judah begged them not to be annoyed at having been anticipated, for, they said, they were David's relatives and, being for that reason more thoughtful for him and fonder of him, they had come there first; but they had not indeed, by coming first, received any gifts of which the others, who came to him later, could have reason to complain. The chiefs of the other tribes were not silenced by these words of the leaders of the tribe of Judah, but said, "We are amazed, brothers, that you call the king a relative only of yourselves, for he who receives from God authority over all must be considered a relative of us all. And for this reason the entire people has eleven [b] parts (in him), while you have but one, and we are older [c]; and so you have not done right in coming to the king in secrecy and by stealth."

Rivalry between Israel and Judah for David's favour. 2 Sam. xix. 41 (42).

(6) While the leaders were thus arguing with each other, there stood up among them a certain man of evil character and a lover of dissension, named Sabaios,[d] the son of Bochorios,[e] of the tribe of Benjamin, who addressed the multitude in a loud voice, saying, "None of us [f] has any portion of David or any

Sheba (Sabaios) incites the Israelites against David. 2 Sam. xx. 1

[a] Variant "of the country."
[b] Bibl. "ten."
[c] Or "have a prior claim."
[d] Bibl. Sheba, LXX Σαβεέ.
[e] Bibl. Bichri, LXX Βοχορεί, Luc. Βεδδαδί (*cf.* Latin trans. of Josephus).
[f] Variant "you."

279 οὔτε κλῆρον παρὰ τῷ Ἰεσσαίου παιδί." καὶ μετὰ τοὺς λόγους σαλπίσας κέρατι σημαίνει πόλεμον πρὸς τὸν βασιλέα, καὶ πάντες ἠκολούθησαν ἐκείνῳ Δαυίδην καταλιπόντες· μόνη δ' αὐτῷ παρέμεινεν ἡ Ἰούδα φυλὴ καὶ κατέστησεν αὐτὸν εἰς τὸ ἐν Ἱεροσολύμοις βασίλειον. καὶ τὰς μὲν παλλακάς, αἷς ὁ υἱὸς αὐτοῦ συνῆλθεν Ἀψάλωμος, εἰς ἄλλην μετήγαγεν οἰκίαν, πάντα προστάξας αὐταῖς χορηγεῖν τὰ ἐπιτήδεια τοὺς ἐπιμελομένους, αὐτὸς δ' οὐκέτ'
280 ἐπλησίαζεν αὐταῖς. ἀποδείκνυσι δὲ καὶ τὸν Ἀμασᾶν στρατηγὸν καὶ τὴν τάξιν αὐτῷ ἐφ' ἧς Ἰώαβος ἦν δίδωσιν ἐκέλευσέ τε στρατιὰν ὅσην δύναται συναγαγόντ' ἐκ τῆς Ἰούδα φυλῆς μεθ' ἡμέρας τρεῖς ὡς[1] αὐτὸν ἐλθεῖν, ἵνα παραδοὺς αὐτῷ πᾶσαν τὴν δύναμιν ἐκπέμψῃ πολεμήσοντα τὸν υἱὸν τοῦ Βοχο-
281 ρίου. ἐξελθόντος δὲ τοῦ Ἀμασᾶ καὶ περὶ τὴν ἄθροισιν τῆς στρατιᾶς βραδύνοντος, ὡς οὐκ ἐπανῄει τῇ τρίτῃ τῶν ἡμερῶν ὁ βασιλεὺς πρὸς τὸν Ἰώαβον ἔλεγεν οὐκ εἶναι σύμφορον ἀνοχὴν τῷ Σαβαίῳ διδόναι, μὴ γενόμενος ἐν πλείονι παρασκευῇ, μειζόνων κακῶν καὶ πραγμάτων αἴτιος, ἢ Ἀψάλω-
282 μος αὐτοῖς κατέστη, γένηται. "μὴ περίμενε τοίνυν μηδένα,[2] ἀλλὰ τὴν οὖσαν παραλαβὼν δύναμιν καὶ τοὺς ἑξακοσίους μετὰ Ἀβισαίου τοῦ ἀδελφοῦ σου δίωκε τὸν πολέμιον. καὶ ὅπου ποτ' ἂν αὐτὸν καταλάβῃς ὄντα πειράθητι συμβαλεῖν· σπούδασον δ' αὐτὸν φθάσαι, μὴ πόλεις ὀχυρὰς καταλαβόμενος ἀγῶνας ἡμῖν καὶ πολλοὺς ἱδρῶτας παρασκευάσῃ."
283 (7) Ἰώαβος δ' οὐκέτι μέλλειν ἔκρινεν, ἀλλὰ τόν

[1] πρὸς ROE. [2] ἔτι μηδὲν MSP.

[a] It is not clear from Scripture, 2 Sam. xx. 4, whether David appointed Amasa commander in Joab's place, or simply

lot with the son of Jesse." And with these words he blew his horn and declared war on the king, and they all deserted David to follow him; only the tribe of Judah stood by him, and brought him back to his palace in Jerusalem. And the concubines, with whom his son Absalom had lain, he transferred to another dwelling, instructing their attendants to provide them with all things necessary, but he himself never again came near them. Then he appointed Amasa commander, giving him the office which Joab had held,[a] and ordered him to collect as large an army as possible from the tribe of Judah and to come to him after three days, in order that he might give the entire force over to him and send him out to make war on the son of Bochorios. So Amasa went out, but he was slow in assembling an army, and, as he did not return on the third day, the king said to Joab[b] that it was not a good thing to grant Sabaios a breathing-space, lest he prepare a greater force and cause them more harm and trouble than Absalom had done. "Do not, therefore, wait for anyone, but take the force now here and the six hundred men[c] and, with your brother Abisai, pursue the enemy. And wherever you may come upon them, try to engage them. And now hasten to prevent them from seizing fortified cities and so causing us great exertion and sweat."

David appoints Amasa commander of the army. 2 Sam. xx. 4.

(7) So Joab decided not to wait any longer and,

as a commander of equal rank. Josephus adopts the latter view in § 284.

[b] To Abishai, in Scripture, although it is there implied (vs. 7) that Joab is with Abishai.

[c] Bibl. "thy lord's servants," that is, the bodyguard of Cherethites, Pelethites and "mighty men" mentioned in the next verse, 2 Sam. xx. 7.

τε ἀδελφὸν καὶ τοὺς ἑξακοσίους παραλαβὼν καὶ ὅση λοιπὴ δύναμις ἦν ἐν τοῖς Ἱεροσολύμοις ἕπεσθαι κελεύσας ἐξώρμησεν ἐπὶ τὸν Σαβαῖον. ἤδη δ' ἐν Γαβαὼν (κώμη δ' ἐστὶν αὕτη σταδίους ἀπέχουσα τεσσαράκοντα τῶν Ἱεροσολύμων) γεγενημένος πολλὴν Ἀμασᾶ δύναμιν ἀγαγόντος,[1] ἀπήντησεν αὐτῷ διεζωσμένος μάχαιραν καὶ θώρακα ἐνδεδυμένος ὁ
284 Ἰώαβος· προσιόντος δὲ ἀσπάσασθαι τοῦ Ἀμασᾶ φιλοτεχνεῖ[2] τὴν μάχαιραν αὐτομάτως ἐκ τῆς θήκης ἐκπεσεῖν,[3] βαστάσας δ' αὐτὴν ἀπὸ τῆς γῆς καὶ τῇ ἑτέρᾳ τὸν Ἀμασᾶν ἐγγὺς γενόμενον ὡς καταφιλήσων τοῦ γενείου λαβόμενος, οὐ προϊδόμενον[4] εἰς τὴν γαστέρα πλήξας ἀπέκτεινεν, ἀσεβὲς ἔργον διαπραξάμενος καὶ παντελῶς ἀνόσιον, ἀγαθὸν νεανίαν καὶ συγγενῆ καὶ μηδὲν ἀδικήσαντα ζηλοτυπήσας τῆς στρατηγίας καὶ τῆς παρὰ τῷ βασιλεῖ πρὸς αὐτὸν
285 ἰσοτιμίας. διὰ ταύτην γὰρ τὴν αἰτίαν καὶ τὸν Ἀβεννῆρον ἐφόνευσεν. ἀλλ' ἐκεῖνο μὲν αὐτοῦ τὸ παρανόμημα πρόφασις εὐπρεπὴς συγγνωστὸν ἐδόκει ποιεῖν ὁ ἀδελφὸς Ἀσάηλος ἐκδεδικῆσθαι νομιζόμενος, τοῦ δ' Ἀμασᾶ φόνου οὐδὲν τοιοῦτον ἔσχε
286 παρακάλυμμα. ἀποκτείνας δὲ τὸν συστράτηγον ἐδίωκε τὸν Σαβαῖον καταλιπὼν ἕνα πρὸς τῷ νεκρῷ, βοᾶν ἐντειλάμενος πρὸς τὴν στρατιὰν ὅτι τέθνηκεν Ἀμασᾶς δικαίως καὶ μετ' αἰτίας κολαζούσης· "εἰ δὲ φρονεῖτε τὰ τοῦ βασιλέως, ἕπεσθε τῷ στρατηγῷ αὐτοῦ Ἰωάβῳ καὶ Ἀβισαίῳ τῷ τούτου ἀδελφῷ."
287 κειμένου δὲ τοῦ σώματος ἐπὶ τῆς ὁδοῦ καὶ παντὸς τοῦ πλήθους ἐπ' αὐτῷ συρρέοντος καὶ οἷον ὄχλος

[1] post ἀγαγόντος lacunam statuit Niese.
[2] φιλοτέχνως MSP: om. E.
[3] ἐποίησεν ἐκπεσεῖν MSPE et fort. Zonaras.
[4] Bekker: προειδόμενον codd.

taking with him his brother and the six hundred men and ordering the rest of the force in Jerusalem to follow, he set out to attack Sabaios. But when he reached Gabaon,—this is a village forty stades distant from Jerusalem [a]—he found Amasa there at the head of a large force, and Joab went to meet him with his sword girded on and wearing a breastplate. Then, as Amasa approached to greet him, he artfully contrived to have his sword fall, as if by itself, out of its sheath.[b] And he picked it up from the ground, and with his other hand seized Amasa, who was now near him, by the beard as if to kiss him, and with an unforeseen thrust in the belly killed him. This impious and most unholy deed he committed against a brave youth, who was, moreover, his relative, and had done him no wrong, because he envied him his office of commander and his being honoured by the king with a rank equal to his own. It was for this same reason that he had murdered Abenner also, except that the former crime seemed to have a decent pretext to make it pardonable, that is, when considered as an act of vengeance for his brother Asael; but for the murder of Amasa he had no such excuse. And, when he had killed his fellow-commander, he started in pursuit of Sabaios, leaving behind one man with the corpse, whom he instructed to call out to the army that Amasa had been justly put to death and punished deservedly, and to say, "If you are for the king, follow his commander Joab and his brother Abisai." So the dead body lay in the road, and all the people swarmed around it and, as is the way of crowds,[c] pressed for-

Joab pursues Sheba, and slays Amasa on the way. 2 Sam. xx. 7.

Reflections on Joab's conduct.

[a] On the distance of the bibl. Gibeon from Jerusalem, not given in Scripture, *cf.* § 11 note.

[b] Bibl. "and as he went forth, it fell out."

[c] A Thucydidean phrase.

φιλεῖ ἐθαύμαζον ἠλέουν[1] προϊστάμενοι[2]· βαστάσας δ' ἐκεῖθεν ὁ φύλαξ καὶ κομίσας εἴς τι χωρίον ἀπωτάτω τῆς ὁδοῦ τίθησιν αὐτόθι καὶ καλύπτει ἱματίῳ. τούτου γενομένου πᾶς ὁ λαὸς ἠκολού-
288 θησε τῷ Ἰωάβῳ. διώξαντι δ' αὐτῷ διὰ πάσης τῆς Ἰσραηλιτῶν χώρας τὸν Σαβαῖον δηλοῖ τις ἐν ὀχυρᾷ πόλει τυγχάνειν Ἀβελωχέᾳ[3] λεγομένῃ. παραγενόμενος δ' ἐκεῖ καὶ τῇ στρατιᾷ περικαθίσας τὴν πόλιν καὶ χαράκωμα περὶ αὐτὴν πηξάμενος ὑπορύσσειν ἐκέλευσε τοῖς στρατιώταις τὰ τείχη καὶ καταβάλλειν αὐτά· μὴ δεξαμένων γὰρ αὐτὸν τῶν ἐν τῇ πόλει χαλεπῶς πρὸς αὐτοὺς διετέθη.

289 (8) Γύναιον δέ τι σῶφρον καὶ συνετὸν ἐν ἐσχάτοις ἤδη τὴν πατρίδα κειμένην θεασάμενον ἀναβὰν ἐπὶ τὸ τεῖχος προσκαλεῖται διὰ τῶν ὁπλιτῶν τὸν Ἰώαβον. προσελθόντος δ' ἤρξατο λέγειν ὡς ὁ θεὸς τοὺς βασιλεῖς καὶ τοὺς στρατηγοὺς ἀποδείξειεν, ἵνα τοὺς πολεμίους τοὺς Ἑβραίων ἐξαιρῶσι καὶ παρέχωσιν αὐτοῖς εἰρήνην ἀπ' αὐτῶν[4]· "σὺ δὲ σπουδάζεις μητρόπολιν Ἰσραηλιτῶν καταβαλεῖν καὶ
290 πορθῆσαι μηδὲν ἐξαμαρτοῦσαν." ὁ δὲ ἵλεων μὲν

[1] πλέον MSP: post ἐθαύμαζον lacunam statuit Niese.
[2] προσιστάμενοι SP: ἱστάμενοι M.
[3] Ἀβελμαχέα MSP Lat.: Ἀβελμακᾶ E.
[4] ἀπ' αὐτῶν] ἀπάντων MSP.

[a] Text doubtful; the variant seems to mean "standing beside it, they wondered (or "stared") at it a great while."

[b] Bibl. Abel Beth-maachah, LXX Ἀβὲλ Βαιθμαχά. It has been tentatively identified with the modern *'Abl* in the upper Jordan valley, about 10 miles N. of Lake Huleh.

[c] With Josephus's χαράκωμα *cf.* Luc. χάρακα; LXX has πρόσχωμα.

[d] Bibl. "all the people with Joab were devising (so LXX

ward to wonder at it and pity it,[a] until the guard lifted it up and carried it away from there to a place far from the road, where he laid it down and covered it with a cloak. After this was done, all the people followed Joab. And, after he had pursued Sabaios through the entire Israelite country, someone informed him that he was in a fortified city called Abelōchea.[b] So he went there, and invested the city with his army, and set up a palisade [c] around it; then he ordered his soldiers to undermine the walls and overthrow them,[d] for, as those within the city refused to admit him, he felt very bitter toward them.

Joab besieges Sheba in Abel Beth-Maacah (Abelochea) 2 Sam. xx. 14.

(8) But a certain wise and intelligent old woman, seeing that her native place was now in its last extremity, went up on the wall and summoned Joab through his soldiers. And, when he came near, she began by saying that God had chosen kings and commanders to drive out the enemies of the Hebrews and to secure them peace from these.[e] "But you," she said, "are bent on destroying and sacking a mother-city of the Israelites, which has done no wrong."

An old woman saves the besieged city. 2 Sam. xx. 16.

and Targum translate Heb. *mashḥîthîm*) to throw the wall down." Josephus evidently takes *mashḥîthîm* (a ptc. masc. pl.) as a denominative verb from the root *shaḥath* "pit," hence his rendering "undermine," a meaning proposed in modern times by Ewald. The usual meaning of the verbal root is "destroy" (A.V. here has "battered").

[e] The corrupt and therefore obscure Heb. of 2 Sam. xx. 18, 19a reads lit., "And she spoke, saying, 'In former times they would ask of Abel and so they concluded. I—the peaceful (?) and faithful of Israel, etc.'" Josephus's interpretation seems to be based in part on the Targum, which renders, "And she spoke, saying, 'Let me mention what is written in the Book of the Law, that one should first ask of a city; thus you should have asked Abel whether it wished to make peace. We are making peace with Israel in good faith, etc.'"

εὔχεται τὸν θεὸν αὐτῷ διαμένειν, αὐτὸς δ' οὕτως ἔχειν εἶπεν, ὡς μηδένα τοῦ λαοῦ φονεῦσαι οὐχ ὅτι πόλιν ἐξελεῖν βούλεσθαι τηλικαύτην· λαβὼν μέντοι παρ' αὐτῶν τὸν ἀντάραντα τῷ βασιλεῖ πρὸς τιμωρίαν Σαβαῖον υἱὸν δὲ Βοχορίου, παύσεσθαι[1]
291 τῆς πολιορκίας καὶ τὴν στρατιὰν ἀπάξειν. ὡς δ' ἤκουσεν ἡ γυνὴ τὰ παρὰ τοῦ Ἰωάβου μικρὸν ἐπισχεῖν δεηθεῖσα, τὴν γὰρ κεφαλὴν εὐθέως αὐτῷ ῥιφήσεσθαι τὴν τοῦ πολεμίου, καταβαίνει πρὸς τοὺς πολίτας καὶ "βούλεσθ'," εἰποῦσα, "κακοὶ κακῶς ἀπολέσθαι μετὰ τέκνων καὶ γυναικῶν ὑπὲρ ἀνθρώπου πονηροῦ καὶ μηδὲ τίς ἐστι γνωριζομένου καὶ τοῦτον ἔχειν ἀντὶ Δαυίδου τοῦ τοσαῦτ' εὐεργετήσαντος ὑμᾶς[2] βασιλέα, καὶ πρὸς δύναμιν τοσαύτην
292 καὶ τηλικαύτην ἀνταίρειν μίαν πόλιν;" πείθει τὴν κεφαλὴν ἀποτεμόντας τοῦ Σαβαίου ῥῖψαι ταύτην εἰς τὸ τοῦ Ἰωάβου στράτευμα. τούτου γενομένου σημήνας ἀνακλητικὸν ὁ τοῦ βασιλέως στρατηγὸς ἔλυσε τὴν πολιορκίαν καὶ παραγενόμενος εἰς Ἱεροσόλυμα παντὸς ἀποδείκνυται πάλιν τοῦ λαοῦ
293 στρατηγός. καθίστησι δὲ καὶ Βαναίαν ὁ βασιλεὺς ἐπὶ τῶν σωματοφυλάκων καὶ τῶν ἑξακοσίων, Ἀδώραμον δ' ἐποίησεν ἐπὶ τῶν φόρων καὶ Ἰωσάφατον υἱὸν Ἀχίλου ἐπὶ τῶν ὑπομνημάτων, Σουσὰν δὲ γραμματέα, Σάδωκον δὲ καὶ Ἀβιάθαρον ἀπέφηνεν ἱερεῖς.
294 (xii. 1) Μετὰ δὲ ταῦτα τῆς χώρας λιμῷ φθειρομένης ἱκέτευε[3] Δαυίδης τὸν θεὸν ἐλεῆσαι τὸν λαὸν

[1] Dindorf: παύσασθαι codd. E.
[2] ἡμᾶς OP. [3] ἱκέτευσε MSP Lat.

[a] "To be gracious to him" is derived from LXX ἵλεώς μοι (*sc.* ὁ θεός), a free translation of Heb. *hālîlāh lî* "far be it from me."

Thereupon he prayed that God might continue to be gracious to him,[a] and said that for his part he had no wish to slay any of its people, much less destroy so great a city; furthermore, if he could get them to deliver up for punishment Sabaios, the son of Bochorios, who had rebelled against the king, he would give up the siege and withdraw his army. When the woman heard Joab's words, she asked him to wait a little while, and his enemy's head would very soon be thrown to him; then she went down to the inhabitants of the city and cried, "Do you wish to perish most miserably with your children and wives for the sake of a worthless fellow whom no one even knows, or have him for a king in place of David, who has been your [b] benefactor in so many ways, and set yourselves up, as a single city, against so great and so mighty a power?" [c] And so she persuaded them to cut off Sabaios's head and throw it to Joab's army. When this was done, the king's commander sounded the retreat and raised the siege. Then he came to Jerusalem and was again appointed commander of all the people. The king also put Banaias over the bodyguard and the six hundred, and gave Adoramos [d] charge of the tribute, and Josaphat, the son of Achilos,[e] the records, and designated Sūsa [f] as scribe, and Sadok and Abiathar as priests.

(xii. 1) After these events, the country was ravaged by a famine, and David supplicated God to

God sends a famine to avenge the

[b] Variant "our."

[c] The woman's speech is unscriptural.

[d] Bibl. Adoram, LXX Ἀδωνειράμ.

[e] Bibl. Ahilud, *cf.* § 110 note. All these officers, with the exception of Adoram, are mentioned in the former passage.

[f] So most MSS. of the LXX here (*v.l.* Ἰησοῦς); bibl. Sheva (Heb. *Sheyā*). He is called Seisa in § 110 (bibl. Seraiah).

καὶ τὴν αἰτίαν αὐτῷ καὶ τὴν ἴασιν φανερὰν ποιῆσαι τῆς νόσου. τῶν δὲ προφητῶν εἰπόντων βούλεσθαι τὸν θεὸν ἐκδικίας τυχεῖν τοὺς Γαβαωνίτας, οὓς Σαοῦλος ὁ βασιλεὺς ἀποκτείνας ἠσέβησεν ἐξαπατήσας καὶ τοὺς ὅρκους αὐτοῖς, οὓς ὁ στρατηγὸς
295 Ἰησοῦς ὤμοσε καὶ ἡ γερουσία, μὴ φυλάξας· ἐὰν τοίνυν δίκην ἣν αὐτοὶ θέλουσιν οἱ Γαβαωνῖται λαβεῖν ὑπὲρ τῶν ἀνῃρημένων ταύτην αὐτοῖς παράσχῃ, διαλλαγήσεσθαι καὶ τὸν ὄχλον ἀπαλλάξειν
296 τῶν κακῶν ἐπηγγέλλετο. ὡς οὖν ταῦτα παρὰ τῶν προφητῶν ἔμαθεν ἐπιζητεῖν τὸν θεόν, μεταπέμπεται τοὺς Γαβαωνίτας καὶ τίνος βούλονται τυχεῖν ἐπηρώτα. τῶν δ' ἐκ τοῦ γένους τοῦ Σαούλου παραλαβεῖν ἑπτὰ παῖδας ἀξιωσάντων πρὸς τιμωρίαν, ὁ βασιλεὺς ἀναζητήσας παρέδωκεν αὐτοῖς,
297 Ἰεβόσθου[1] φεισάμενος τοῦ Ἰωνάθου παιδός. παραλαβόντες δ' οἱ Γαβαωνῖται τοὺς ἄνδρας ὡς ἐβούλοντο ἐκόλασαν. ἤρξατο δ' ὕειν παραχρῆμα ὁ θεὸς καὶ τὴν γῆν πρὸς γονὴν καρπῶν ἀνακαλεῖν, ἀπολύσας τοῦ πρότερον αὐχμοῦ· καὶ πάλιν εὐθήνησεν ἡ τῶν Ἑβραίων χώρα.

298 Στρατεύεται δὲ μετ' οὐ[2] πολὺν χρόνον ὁ βασιλεὺς ἐπὶ Παλαιστίνους, καὶ συνάψας μάχην αὐτοῖς καὶ

[1] Memphiuos Lat.: Μεμφιβόσθου ed. pr.
[2] μετ' οὐ ed. pr. Lat.: μετὰ codd.

---

[a] Here, as elsewhere (*e.g.* § 72), Josephus makes the prophets God's interpreters where Scripture has merely "And the Lord answered."

[b] *Cf. A.* v. 55 (Jos. ix. 15).

[c] The last part of God's reply is an amplification of Scripture.

have pity on the people and reveal to him the cause of the affliction, and the remedy. Then the prophets[a] declared that God wished the Gabaonites to be avenged, whom King Saul had wickedly killed and with whom he had dealt treacherously, in violation of the oaths which the commander Joshua and the elders had sworn to them.[b] If, then, he would permit the Gabaonites to exact such satisfaction as they might desire for those who had been slain, God would, He promised, be reconciled to them and would free the multitude from its affliction.[c] Accordingly, after learning from the prophets that this was God's desire, he sent for the Gabaonites and inquired what satisfaction they wanted. And, when they asked that seven sons[d] of Saul's family be given up to them for punishment, the king had a search made for them and surrendered them to the Gabaonites, but he spared Jebosthos,[e] the son of Jonathan. Then the Gabaonites took them and punished them as they saw fit.[f] And God at once began to send rain and to restore the land to its fruitfulness, by delivering it from drought. And once more the country of the Hebrews flourished.

Gibeonites slain by Saul. 2 Sam. xxi. 1.

Not long after this,[g] the king took the field against the Philistines and, after joining battle with them,

Abishai rescues David from

[d] An allusion to the two sons of Saul and Rizpah and the five sons of Saul and Michal, 2 Sam. xxi. 8.

[e] A slip for Memphibosthos (Mephibosheth), corrected in the first printed edition of Josephus.

[f] Josephus omits the Scriptural detail that they were hanged, 2 Sam. xxi. 9, and also passes over the following verses, which tell of Rizpah's mourning and David's removal of the bones of Saul and Jonathan from Jabesh-gilead for burial in the sepulchre of Kish in Benjamin.

[g] Variant "after a long time." In Scripture no interval of time is mentioned.

τρεψάμενος ἐμονώθη διώκων καὶ γενόμενος ἔκλυτος ὤφθη ὑπό τινος τῶν πολεμίων Ἄκμονος μὲν
299 τοὔνομα Ἀράφου δὲ παιδός· οὗτος ἦν μὲν καὶ ἀπόγονος τῶν Γιγάντων, ἔχων δὲ καὶ ξυστόν, οὗ τὴν λαβήν φασιν ἕλκειν[1] σταθμὸν σίκλους τριακοσίους, καὶ θώρακα ἁλυσιδωτὸν καὶ ῥομφαίαν ὥρμησεν ἐπιστραφεὶς ὡς ἀποκτενῶν[2] τὸν τῶν πολεμίων βασιλέα· παρεῖτο γὰρ ὑπὸ τοῦ κόπου. ἐπιφανεὶς δ' ἐξαίφνης Ἀβισαῖος ὁ Ἰωάβου ἀδελφὸς τὸν βασιλέα μὲν ὑπερήσπισε περιβὰς κείμενον,
300 ἀπέκτεινε δὲ τὸν πολέμιον. ἤνεγκε δ' ἐπὶ τῷ παρ' ὀλίγον κινδυνεῦσαι τὸν βασιλέα χαλεπῶς τὸ πλῆθος· καὶ οἱ ἡγεμόνες ὥρκωσαν αὐτὸν μηκέτι εἰς μάχην ἀπαντῆσαι σὺν αὐτοῖς, μὴ δι' ἀνδρείαν καὶ προθυμίαν παθών τι τῶν δεινῶν στερήσῃ τὸν λαὸν τῶν δι' αὐτὸν ἀγαθῶν, ὅσα τε ἤδη παρέσχηκε καὶ ὅσων ἔτι μεθέξουσι πολὺν βιώσαντος χρόνον.
301 (2) Συνελθόντων δὲ τῶν Παλαιστίνων εἰς Γάζαρα πόλιν ἀκούσας ὁ βασιλεὺς ἔπεμψεν ἐπ' αὐτοὺς στρατιάν. ἠρίστευσε δὲ τότε καὶ σφόδρ' ηὐδο-

[1] φασιν ἕλκειν] Naber: συνέλκειν codd.: συνέβη ἕλκειν Niese.
[2] ex Lat. Niese: ἀποκτείνων codd.

[a] Bibl. Ishbi-benob, LXX Ἰεσβί. The Heb. consonantal text, meaning "they dwelled in Nob," is corrupt and conceals a proper name rather different from Ishbi-benob. Weill rightly supposes that Josephus's Akmōn represents Heb. *Ḥakmôn*, but, like others, has failed to see that it is identical with Jashobeam the Hachmonite, 1 Chron. xi. 11 (*cf.* § 308 note). The latter is, to be sure, one of David's warriors, and not his enemy, as here, but whether Scripture or Josephus is responsible for this confusion, there can be no doubt of this identity of names. It may also be noted that rabbinic tradition makes Ishbi a brother of Goliath and describes at length

put them to flight; but in pursuing, he found himself alone, and in this weary state he was seen by one of the enemy, whose name was Akmōn,[a] the son of Araphos,[b] and who was, at the same time, a descendant of the Giants.[b] He had a spear, the haft of which was said to weigh three hundred shekels, a breastplate of chainmail,[c] and a sword, and he turned about and rushed forward with the intention of killing the enemy's king, who was exhausted by his exertions. But suddenly there appeared Abisai, the brother of Joab, who protected the king by standing astride over him[d] as he lay there, and killed his enemy. But the people were distressed by the king's narrow escape from death, and the leaders made him swear that he would never again go out with them to battle, lest, through his bravery and zeal, he should suffer some injury and so deprive the people of the benefits he brought them, both those that he had already conferred, and those that they might still enjoy if he lived for a long time.

a Philistine giant. 2 Sam. xxi. 15.

(2) Then the Philistines assembled at the city of Gazara,[e] and, when the king heard of it, he sent an army against them. On that occasion mighty deeds

Prowess of David's warriors against the Philistines.

Abishai's miraculous rescue of David from his hands, *cf.* Ginzberg iv. 107.

[b] In "Araphos" and "Giants" Josephus combines the bibl. proper name Raphah (*cf.* pl. Rephaim) and its rendering by Targum and some LXX MSS. as "giants" (so A.V.).

[c] Bibl. "was girded with a new —" (A.V. "new *sword*"; the noun is missing); LXX supplies *κορύνην* "club," Luc. *παραζώνην* "girdle," Targum *Ispanîqî* (=Ἰσπανική?) which means either "sword" or "girdle" according to Jewish tradition.

[d] Unscriptural detail.

[e] 1 Chron. Gezer, LXX Γάζερ; 2 Sam. Gob, LXX Γέθ (*v.l.* Γαρζέλ κτλ.), Luc. Γαζέθ. It is uncertain what the name was in the original text of Scripture.

κίμησε Σαβρήχης[1] ὁ Χετταῖος εἷς τῶν περὶ Δαυίδην
ἀνδρειοτάτων· ἀπέκτεινε γὰρ πολλοὺς τῶν αὐχούν-
των προγόνους τοὺς Γίγαντας καὶ μέγα ἐπ' ἀνδρείᾳ
φρονούντων, αἴτιός τε τῆς νίκης τοῖς Ἑβραίοις
302 ἐγένετο. καὶ μετ' ἐκείνην τὴν ἧτταν πάλιν ἐπολέμησαν οἱ Παλαιστῖνοι· καὶ στρατιὰν ἐπ' αὐτοὺς
Δαυίδου πέμψαντος ἠρίστευσεν Ἐφὰν ὁ συγγενὴς
αὐτοῦ· μονομαχήσας γὰρ τῷ πάντων ἀνδρειοτάτῳ
Παλαιστίνων ἀπέκτεινεν αὐτὸν καὶ τοὺς ἄλλους εἰς
φυγὴν ἔτρεψε, πολλοί τε αὐτῶν ἀπέθανον μαχό-
303 μενοι. διαλιπόντες δ' ὀλίγον χρόνον ἐστρατοπεδεύσαντο[2] πρὸς Γίττῃ[3] πόλει τῶν ὅρων τῆς Ἑβραίων
χώρας οὐκ ἄπωθεν. ἦν δ' αὐτοῖς ἀνὴρ τὸ μὲν ὕψος
ἓξ πηχῶν, δακτύλους δ' ἐν ἑκατέρῳ τῶν βάσεων
καὶ τῶν χειρῶν ἑνὶ περισσοτέρους εἶχε τῶν κατὰ
304 φύσιν. ἐκ τῆς οὖν πεμφθείσης ἐπ' αὐτοὺς ὑπὸ
Δαυίδου στρατιᾶς τούτῳ μονομαχήσας Ἰωνάθης ὁ
Σαμᾶ[4] υἱὸς ἀνεῖλέ τε αὐτὸν καὶ τῆς ὅλης νίκης ῥοπὴ

[1] Σαβρήχεις R: Σοβάκχης SP(M): Ἀβάκχης E: Sabuch Lat.
[2] Niese cum cod. Vat. apud Hudson: ἐστρατεύσαντο RO: ἐστρατοπέδευσαν MSP: ἐστράτευσαν E.
[3] Niese: τῇ codd.: τῇ Γίττᾳ Hudson (*cf.* LXX).
[4] ed. pr.: Σουμᾶ codd. Lat.

---

[a] Bibl. Sibbechai, LXX Σοβοχαί, Luc. Σοβεκχί.
[b] So Luc.; bibl. the Hushathite, LXX ὁ Ἀστατωθεί.
[c] Scripture mentions only one victim, Saph (1 Chron. Sippai) "that was of the giants (Heb. *Râphâh*)."
[d] Bibl. Elhanan the son of Jaare-oregim (read Jair as in 1 Chron.) a Bethlehemite, LXX Ἐλεανὰν υἱὸς Ἀριωγεὶμ ὁ Βαιθλεεμείτης, Luc. Ἐλλανὰν υἱὸς Ἰαδδείν; in 1 Chron. LXX has Ἐλλὰν υἱὸς Ἰαείρ.
[e] This was Goliath according to 2 Sam., but as Goliath was supposedly slain by David (*cf.* 1 Sam. xvii. 23 ff., *Ant.* vi. 171 ff.), 1 Chron. harmonistically makes Elhanan's victim

were performed and great glory was won by Sabrĕchēs[a] the Hittite,[b] one of David's bravest men, for he killed many of those who boasted of having the Giants for ancestors,[c] and thought much of their own courage; and so he was responsible for the victory of the Hebrews. After this defeat the Philistines made war a second time, and David sent an army against them, of whom the most valiant was his relative Ephan,[d] for, in single combat with the bravest of all the Philistines,[e] he killed him and put the rest to flight, many of them being slain in battle. But after a brief interval of time they encamped near Gitta,[f] a city not far from the border of the Hebrews' country, and there was among them a man six cubits[g] in height, who had, on both of his feet and hands, one more toe and finger than nature usually provides. Now, of the army sent against them by David, Jonathan, the son of Sama,[h] fought against this man in single combat, and by slaying him, turned the battle

2 Sam. xxi. 18; 1 Chron. xx. 4.

a brother of Goliath, and the epithet *Beth ha-laḥmî* "Bethlehemite" applied to Elhanan in 2 Sam. is converted to a personal name Lahmi, giving the reading, 1 Chron. xx. 5, "And Elhanan the son of Jair slew Lahmi the brother of Goliath the Gittite." Josephus evades the difficulty more simply by omitting the name of Goliath.

[f] Name restored in Josephus's text from the LXX.

[g] Unscriptural detail. In 2 Sam. Heb. has *îsh mādôn* "man of strife," LXX ἀνὴρ Μαδών; in 1 Chron. *îsh middah* "man of stature," LXX ἀνὴρ ὑπερμεγέθης. Possibly Josephus was careless in taking "six," occurring twice in Scripture of the giant's fingers and toes, to apply to his height. It is unlikely that, as Weill suggests, he was thinking of Goliath's height, "six cubits and a span," 1 Sam. xvii. 4, for he follows the LXX in reading "four cubits and a span" in that passage (*A.* vi. 171).

[h] So Luc. and LXX in 1 Chron.; bibl. Shimeah, LXX (2 Sam.) Σεμεέ. He was a nephew of David.

γενόμενος δόξαν ἀριστείας ἀπηνέγκατο· καὶ γὰρ οὗτος ὁ Παλαιστῖνος ηὔχει τῶν Γιγάντων ἀπόγονος εἶναι. μετὰ δὲ ταύτην τὴν μάχην οὐκέτι τοῖς Ἰσραηλίταις ἐπολέμησαν.

305 (3) Ἀπηλλαγμένος δ' ἤδη πολέμων ὁ Δαυίδης καὶ κινδύνων καὶ βαθείας ἀπολαύων τὸ λοιπὸν εἰρήνης, ᾠδὰς εἰς τὸν θεὸν καὶ ὕμνους συνετάξατο μέτρου ποικίλου· τοὺς μὲν γὰρ τριμέτρους, τοὺς δὲ πενταμέτρους ἐποίησεν. ὄργανά τε κατασκευάσας ἐδίδαξε πρὸς αὐτὰ τοὺς Ληουίτας ὑμνεῖν τὸν θεὸν κατά τε τὴν τῶν καλουμένων σαββάτων

306 ἡμέραν καὶ κατὰ τὰς ἄλλας ἑορτάς. ἡ δὲ τῶν ὀργάνων ἐστὶν ἰδέα τοιαύτη τις τὸν τρόπον· ἡ μὲν κινύρα δέκα χορδαῖς ἐξημμένη τύπτεται πλήκτρῳ, ἡ δὲ νάβλα δώδεκα φθόγγους ἔχουσα τοῖς δακτύλοις κρούεται, κύμβαλά τε ἦν πλατέα καὶ μεγάλα χάλκεα. καὶ περὶ μὲν τούτων ἐπὶ τοσοῦτον ἡμῖν, ὥστε μὴ τελέως ἀγνοεῖν τὴν τῶν προειρημένων ὀργάνων φύσιν, ἀρκείσθω λελέχθαι.

307 (4) Τῷ δὲ βασιλεῖ πάντες ἦσαν οἱ περὶ αὐτὸν ἀνδρεῖοι· τούτων δ' οἱ διασημότατοι καὶ λαμπροὶ τὰς πράξεις ὀκτὼ καὶ τριάκοντα, ὧν πέντε μόνων διηγήσομαι τὰ ἔργα· φανερὰς γὰρ καὶ τὰς τῶν ἄλλων ἀρετὰς ἀρκέσουσιν οὗτοι ποιῆσαι· δυνατοὶ γὰρ ἦσαν οὗτοι καὶ χώραν ὑπάγεσθαι καὶ μεγάλων

---

[a] Josephus, in characterizing Hebrew poetry, which is accentual, uses terms familiar to Greek readers, who knew only quantitative poetry. These terms may stand if taken to mean lines of three beats (trimeters) or three plus two beats (pentameters).

[b] The following names are taken by Josephus from the LXX, 1 Chron. xxv. 1 *et al.*, *cf. A.* viii. 94.

[c] Bibl. "harp," Heb. *kinnôr*, elsewhere in the LXX trans-

into a complete victory, and carried off the first prize for valour; this Philistine had also boasted of being a descendant of the Giants. But after this battle they did not again make war on the Israelites.

David's hymns and musical instruments for divine service. 1 Chron. xvi. 7, xxv. 1.

(3) David, being now free from wars and dangers, and enjoying profound peace from this time on, composed songs and hymns to God in varied meters—some he made in trimeters, and others in pentameters.[a] He also made musical instruments, and instructed the Levites how to use them in praising God on the so-called Sabbath day and on the other festivals. Now the forms of these instruments were somewhat as follows[b]: the *kinyra*[c] had ten strings stretched on it, which were struck with a plectrum; the *nabla*,[d] which had twelve notes, was plucked with the fingers; and the *kymbala*[e] were large, broad plates of brass. But now that our readers are not altogether unacquainted with the nature of the afore-mentioned instruments, let this much about them suffice.

David's chief warriors and their exploits. 2 Sam. xxiii. 8; 1 Chron. xi. 10.

(4) As for the men about the king, all of them were brave, but the most distinguished among them and famous for their deeds were thirty-eight[f] in number; of these I shall relate the exploits of only five, for they will serve to make clear the heroic virtues of the rest, being powerful enough to subdue countries and

lated κιθάρα "lyre." Josephus apparently takes the "ten strings" from Ps. xxxiii. 2 and cxliv. 9, taking *nēbel* there (A.V. "instrument") as in apposition with *kinnôr*. On Jewish coins the *kinnôr* has three, five or six strings, while in the Talmud it is said to have seven strings, *cf.* Krauss, *Talmudische Archäologie*, iii. 85.

[d] Bibl. psaltery, Heb. *nēbel*; probably a kind of harp. According to some authorities in the Talmud it had more strings than the *kinnôr*, *cf.* Krauss, *op. cit.* 86 f.

[e] Bibl. cymbals, Heb. *meṣiltayim*.

[f] Thirty-seven, according to Scripture, 2 Sam. xxiii. 39.

308 ἐθνῶν κρατῆσαι. πρῶτος μὲν οὖν Ἴσεβος[1] υἱὸς
Ἀχεμαίου, ὃς πολλάκις εἰς τὴν παράταξιν ἐμπηδῶν
τῶν πολεμίων οὐ πρὶν ἀνεπαύετο μαχόμενος πρὶν
ἐνακοσίους αὐτῶν καταβαλεῖν. μετ' αὐτὸν ἦν
Ἐλεάζαρος υἱὸς Δωδείου, ὃς ἦν μετὰ τοῦ βασιλέως
309 ἐν Ἐρασαμῷ[2]· οὗτός ποτε τῶν Ἰσραηλιτῶν κατα-
πλαγέντων τὸ πλῆθος τῶν Παλαιστίνων καὶ φευ-
γόντων μόνος ἔμεινε καὶ συμπεσὼν τοῖς πολεμίοις
ἀπέκτεινεν αὐτῶν πολλούς, ὡς ὑπὸ τοῦ αἵματος
προσκολληθῆναι τὴν ῥομφαίαν αὐτοῦ τῇ δεξιᾷ καὶ
τοὺς Ἰσραηλίτας ἰδόντας τετραμμένους ὑπ' αὐτοῦ
τοὺς Παλαιστίνους καταβάντας[3] διώκειν καὶ θαυμαστὴν καὶ διαβόητον τότε νίκην ἄρασθαι, τοῦ μὲν
Ἐλεαζάρου κτείνοντος ἑπομένου δὲ τοῦ πλήθους
καὶ σκυλεύοντος τοὺς ἀνῃρημένους. τρίτος δὲ ἦν

[1] Ἴσσαιμος MSP: Ἴσαμος E: Iesebus Lat.
[2] Ἀρασάμῳ M: Ἀρασαμῷ SP: Respha Lat.
[3] + ἀπὸ τῶν ὀρέων P Lat.

---

[a] The Heb. text in 2 Sam. *yôshēb ba-shebeth* "sitting in the seat" is probably a corruption of the name Ishbaal, as indicated by Luc. Ἰεσβαάλ; LXX has Ἰεβοσθέ; in 1 Chron. Heb. has Jashobeam, LXX Ἰεσεβαδά (*v.l.* Ἰσβαάμ κτλ.).

[b] 2 Sam. "the Tachmonite" (omitting "the son of"), LXX ὁ Χαναναῖος, Luc. υἱὸς Θεκεμανεί; 1 Chron. "the son of the Hachmonite," LXX υἱὸς Ἀχαμανεί. On the confusion of the latter name with that of a Philistine *cf.* § 299 note.

[c] "Sprang repeatedly" is not found in Scripture, which says that he slew all his victims "at one time." Possibly it is derived from the Targum's rendering "weaving back

conquer great nations. Now the first was Isebos,[a] the son of Achemaios,[b] who sprang repeatedly[c] upon the enemy's ranks and did not cease fighting until he had felled nine hundred[d] of them. After him was Eleazar, the son of Dōdeios,[e] who was with the king in Erasamos,[f] and who on one occasion, when the Israelites fled in terror before the host of the Philistines, alone held his ground and, falling on the enemy, killed so many of them that his sword stuck to his right hand with their blood, and the Israelites, seeing that the Philistines had been routed by him, returned to the contest[g] and pursued them and thereupon gained a wonderful and celebrated victory, with Eleazar dealing death, and the host following him and despoiling the slain. The third was a son of

Jashobeam (Isebos).

Eleazar.

and forth (?) with his spear" of the unintelligible Heb. in 2 Sam., where the LXX has "drew his sword," Luc. "marshalled his lines"; 1 Chron. "lifted his spear," LXX, as in 2 Sam., "drew his sword."

[d] So Luc.; Heb. and LXX "eight hundred" in 2 Sam., "three hundred" in 1 Chron.

[e] *Cf.* Luc. υἱὸς Δουδεί; in 2 Sam. the consonantal Heb. has "the son of *Dôdî* the son of *Aḥōḥî*" (*i.e.* "the Ahohite" as in A.V.), while the vocalized Heb. has "the son of his uncle (*Dôdô*) the Ahohite," LXX υἱὸς πατραδελφοῦ αὐτοῦ, υἱὸς Σουσεί; 1 Chron. "the son of his uncle the Ahohite," LXX υἱὸς Δωδαὶ ὁ Ἀρχωνεί (*v.l.* Ἀχοχί).

[f] 1 Chron. Pas-dammim (for Ephes-dammim), LXX Ἀφασοδομή; the text in 2 Sam. is quite different, *behârephām ba-Pilishtîm* "in their reviling the Philistines," LXX ἐν τῷ ὀνειδίσαι αὐτὸν ἐν τοῖς ἀλλοφύλοις, while Luc. has a place-name ἐν Σερράν (*cf.* Lat. in Resfam). Josephus's form appears to be a corruption of the latter.

[g] καταβάντας, here in its military sense "return to the contest," was misunderstood by a scribe as "come down," its usual meaning, and, thinking that a phrase was missing, he added the words ἀπὸ τῶν ὀρέων "from the mountains"—hence the variant in MS. P and the Lat. trans.

310 Ἠλοῦ μὲν υἱὸς Σαβαίας[1] δὲ ὄνομα. καὶ οὗτος ἐν
τοῖς πρὸς Παλαιστίνους ἀγῶσιν εἰς τόπον Σιαγόνα
λεγόμενον αὐτῶν παραταξαμένων, ὡς οἱ Ἑβραῖοι
πάλιν τὴν δύναμιν φοβηθέντες οὐχ ὑπέμειναν,
ὑπέστη μόνος ὡς στράτευμα καὶ τάξις, καὶ τοὺς
μὲν αὐτῶν κατέβαλε τοὺς δ' οὐ καρτερήσαντας
αὐτοῦ τὴν ἰσχὺν καὶ τὴν βίαν ἀλλ' εἰς φυγὴν ἀπο-
311 στραφέντας ἐδίωκε.[2] ταῦτα μὲν ἔργα χειρῶν καὶ
μάχης οἱ τρεῖς ἐπεδείξαντο. καθ' ὃν δὲ καιρὸν ἐν
Ἱεροσολύμοις ὄντος τοῦ βασιλέως ἐπῆλθεν ἡ τῶν
Παλαιστίνων δύναμις πολεμῆσαι, Δαυίδης μὲν ἐπὶ
τὴν ἀκρόπολιν ἀνῆλθεν, ὡς προειρήκαμεν, πευ-
312 σόμενος τοῦ θεοῦ περὶ τοῦ πολέμου, τῆς δὲ τῶν
ἐχθρῶν παρεμβολῆς ἐν τῇ κοιλάδι κειμένης, ἣ μέχρι
Βηθλεέμης πόλεως διατείνει σταδίους Ἱεροσολύμων
ἀπεχούσης εἴκοσιν, ὁ Δαυίδης τοῖς ἑταίροις "καλὸν
ὕδωρ," εἶπεν, "ἔχομεν ἐν τῇ πατρίδι μου," καὶ
μάλιστα τὸ ἐν τῷ λάκκῳ τῷ πρὸς τῇ πύλῃ θαυ-
μάζων, εἴ τις ἐξ αὐτοῦ πιεῖν αὐτῷ κομίσειε μᾶλλον
313 ἐθελήσειν ἢ εἰ πολλὰ χρήματα διδοῖ.[3] ταῦτ' ἀκού-

[1] Κησαβαῖος SP. [2] ἐδίωξε MSP.
[3] διδοίη M : δοίη SP.

[a] *Cf.* Luc. Ἠλά; bibl. Agee (Heb. *'Agê'*), LXX Ἀσά. It is difficult to see any connexion between Luc. Ela and *'Agê'*, unless, as a modern scholar, Klostermann, suggests, Agee is to be identified with Elah the father of Shimei, Solomon's governor in Benjamin, 1 Kings iv. 18.

[b] Variant Kēsabaios; bibl. Shammah, LXX Σαμαία. Weill calls attention to the resemblance of Kēsabaios son of Elos to Kabzeel (LXX Καβεσεήλ), 2 Sam. xxiii. 20.

[c] So Luc., reading *leḥî* "jawbone" for Heb. *la-ḥayyâh* "by clans" (A.V. "in a troop"); LXX, taking *ḥayyâh* in its usual sense of "beast," has εἰς θηρία. Lehi is a site well known from the Samson story, *cf.* *A.* v. 297 (Judges xv. 9 ff.).

Ēlos,[a] named Sabaias[b]; in a battle with the Philistines, who were drawn up at a place called Siagon (Jawbone),[c] the Hebrews were again afraid of their force and failed to stand their ground, but this man withstood them alone, being an army and battle-line in himself; some of them he felled, while the rest, who could not face his powerful attack, turned to flee, and he pursued them. These, then, were the mighty deeds of war which the three performed. And once, when the king was at Jerusalem[d] and the Philistine force came to fight against him, David went up to the citadel, as we have said before,[e] to inquire of God concerning the war; and, while the enemy lay encamped in the plain which extends as far as the city of Bethlehem, twenty stades[f] distant from Jerusalem, he said to his companions, "We have good water in my native place," praising especially that in the cistern near the gate, and added that he would be better pleased if someone brought him a drink from it than if he gave him a great deal of money.[g] As

Shammah (Sabaias).

Three men risk their lives for David.

[d] He was in the cave of Adullam according to Scripture, but Josephus might naturally have been confused by the Biblical account, which reads "And three of the thirty chief went down and came to David in the harvest time (Luc., Heb. 1 Chron. "to the rock") in the cave of Adullam; and the troop of the Philistines pitched in the valley of Rephaim. And David was then in the stronghold (A.V. "an hold") and the garrison (1 Chron. "commander") of the Philistines was in Bethlehem." If he was at Adullam, his men need not have run through the enemy's camp to get to Bethlehem, whereas his being at Jerusalem makes the incident understandable. The valley of Rephaim lay south of Jerusalem on the way to Bethlehem.

[e] §§ 71 ff.

[f] *c.* 2½ miles. The actual distance is *c.* 5 miles.

[g] This last (about money) is a detail added by Josephus.

σαντες οἱ τρεῖς ἄνδρες οὗτοι παραχρῆμα ἐκδραμόντες καὶ διὰ μέσου τοῦ τῶν πολεμίων ὁρμήσαντες στρατοπέδου ἧκον εἰς Βηθλεέμην, καὶ τοῦ ὕδατος ἀρυσάμενοι πάλιν διὰ τῆς παρεμβολῆς ὑπέστρεψαν πρὸς τὸν βασιλέα, ὡς τοὺς Παλαιστίνους καταπλαγέντας αὐτῶν τὸ θράσος καὶ τὴν εὐψυχίαν ἠρεμῆσαι καὶ μηδὲν ἐπ' αὐτοὺς τολμῆσαι[1] καταφρονήσαντας
314 τῆς ὀλιγότητος. κομισθέντος δὲ τοῦ ὕδατος οὐκ ἔπιεν ὁ βασιλεύς, κινδύνῳ καὶ αἵματι φήσας ἀνθρώπων αὐτὸ κεκομίσθαι καὶ διὰ τοῦτο μὴ προσήκειν αὐτῷ πιεῖν, ἔσπεισε δὲ ἀπ' αὐτοῦ τῷ θεῷ καὶ περὶ τῆς σωτηρίας τῶν ἀνδρῶν εὐχαρίστησεν αὐτῷ.
315 μετὰ τούτους ἦν ὁ Ἰωάβου ἀδελφὸς Ἀβισαῖος· καὶ γὰρ οὗτος μιᾷ ἡμέρᾳ τῶν πολεμίων ἑξακοσίους ἀπέκτεινε. πέμπτος Βαναίας ὁ ἱερεὺς τῷ γένει· προκληθεὶς γὰρ ὑπ' ἀδελφῶν διασήμων ἐν τῇ Μωαβίτιδι χώρᾳ κατ' ἀρετὴν ἐκράτησεν αὐτῶν. καὶ πάλιν αὐτὸν ἀνδρὸς Αἰγυπτίου τὸ γένος θαυμαστοῦ τὸ μέγεθος προκαλεσαμένου, γυμνὸς ὡπλισμένον, τῷ δόρατι τῷ ἐκείνου βαλὼν ἀπέκτεινε· περιελόμενος γὰρ αὐτοῦ τὸν ἄκοντα καὶ ζῶντα ἔτι καὶ μαχόμενον σκυλεύσας τοῖς ἰδίοις αὐτὸν ὅπλοις
316 διεχρήσατο. προσαριθμήσειε δ' ἄν τις αὐτοῦ καὶ τοῦτο ταῖς προειρημέναις πράξεσιν ἢ ὡς πρῶτον αὐτῶν κατ' εὐψυχίαν ἢ ὡς οὐ μεῖον[2]· νίφοντος γὰρ τοῦ θεοῦ λέων εἴς τινα λάκκον ὀλισθὼν ἐνέπεσε·

[1] καὶ μηδὲν . . . τολμῆσαι om. RO.
[2] οὐ μεῖον ex Lat. Niese: ἀλλοῖον RO: ὁμοῖον rell.

[a] So Luc. and some LXX MSS. (in 1 Chron.); Heb. "three hundred."
[b] Cf. 1 Chron. xxvii. 5.
[c] Cf. LXX (2 Sam.) τοὺς δύο υἱοὺς Ἀριὴλ τοῦ Μωάβ; Heb. "two Ariels of Moab" (A.V. "two lionlike men of Moab,"

soon as they heard this, the three men immediately ran out and dashed through the midst of the enemy's camp, until they came to Bethlehem, and, when they had drawn the water, came back again through the enemy's camp to the king; so amazed were the Philistines at their audacity and courage, that they remained motionless and did not venture to attack them, although they were contemptuous of their fewness. But, when the water was brought to him, the king did not drink it, saying that it had been brought at the risk of men's lives and that therefore it would not be right for him to drink it; then he poured some of it out as a libation to God, and gave Him thanks for the safety of his men. After these three men was Joab's brother Abisai, who in a single day slew six hundred [a] of the enemy. The fifth was Banaias, of priestly descent,[b] who was challenged by famous brothers in the Moabite country,[c] and defeated them by his prowess. And, on another occasion, when a native Egyptian of extraordinary size [d] challenged him, though he was unarmed against an armed foe, he struck him with his own spear and killed him, that is, he wrested the other's lance from him and, while he was still alive and fighting, stripped him of his armour and dispatched him with his own weapons. To the foregoing account of his deeds, one might add another which shows greater, or not less,[e] valour than these: once, when God sent down snow, a lion slipped and fell into a pit, and, as the mouth

Abishai.

Benaiah (Banaias).

based on the etymology *'arî* " lion "), Targum " two nobles of Moab."

[d] Of five cubits, according to 1 Chron.; in 2 Sam. Heb. " a man of appearance " (A.V. " a goodly man "), LXX ἄνδρα ὁρατόν.

[e] Emended text; MSS. " similar," " a different kind of."

στενοῦ δ' ὄντος τοῦ στομίου δῆλος ἦν ἀφανὴς
ἐσόμενος ἐμφραγέντος αὐτοῦ τῇ χιόνι· πόρον οὖν
οὐδένα βλέπων ἐξόδου καὶ σωτηρίας ἐβρυχᾶτο.
317 τοῦ δὲ θηρὸς ἀκούσας ὁ Βαναίας, ὥδευε γὰρ τότε,
καὶ πρὸς τὴν βοὴν ἐλθών, καταβὰς εἰς τὸ στόμιον
πλήξας αὐτὸν μαχόμενον τῷ μετὰ χεῖρας ξύλῳ
παραχρῆμα ἀπέκτεινε. καὶ οἱ λοιποὶ δὲ[1] τοιοῦτοι
τὰς ἀρετὰς ὑπῆρχον.
318 (xiii. 1) Ὁ δὲ βασιλεὺς Δαυίδης βουλόμενος
γνῶναι πόσαι μυριάδες εἰσὶ τοῦ λαοῦ, τῶν Μωυσέος
ἐντολῶν ἐκλαθόμενος, ὃς προεῖπεν ἐὰν ἐξαριθμηθῇ
τὸ πλῆθος ὑπὲρ ἑκάστης κεφαλῆς αὐτοῦ τῷ θεῷ
τελεῖν[2] ἡμίσικλον, προσέταξεν Ἰωάβῳ τῷ στρατηγῷ
319 πορευθέντι πάντα τὸν ὄχλον ἐξαριθμῆσαι. τοῦ δ'
οὐκ ἀναγκαῖον εἶναι φήσαντος τοῦτο ποιεῖν οὐκ
ἐπείσθη, προσέταξε δὲ μηδὲν μελλήσαντα βαδίζειν
ἐπὶ τὴν ἐξαρίθμησιν τῶν Ἑβραίων. Ἰώαβος δὲ
τοὺς ἄρχοντας τῶν φυλῶν παραλαβὼν καὶ γραμματεῖς, ἐπιὼν τὴν τῶν Ἰσραηλιτῶν χώραν καὶ
τὸ πλῆθος ὅσον ἐστὶ κατανοήσας ὑπέστρεψεν εἰς
Ἱεροσόλυμα πρὸς τὸν βασιλέα μετὰ μῆνας ἐννέα
καὶ ἡμέρας εἴκοσι καὶ τὸν ἀριθμὸν ἐπέδωκε[3] τῷ
βασιλεῖ τοῦ λαοῦ χωρὶς τῆς Βενιαμίτιδος φυλῆς
320 ἐξαριθμῆσαι γὰρ αὐτὴν οὐκ ἔφθασεν ἀλλ' οὐδὲ τὴν
Ληουιτῶν φυλήν· μετενόησε γὰρ ὁ βασιλεὺς ὢν εἰς

[1] δὲ τρεῖς M: δὲ λ' S: δὲ τριάκοντα P: numero triginta et tres Lat.
[2] Niese: τελέσειν MSPE: τελέσειεν RO. [3] ἀπέδωκε M.

[a] Josephus considerably amplifies the bibl. sentence, "He went down also and slew a lion in the midst of a pit in time of snow."

[b] *Cf.* Ex. xxx. 12 f. This explanation of David's sin in numbering the people is also found in rabbinic tradition.

of the pit was narrow, the beast was clearly destined to perish when it should have been blocked up by the snow, and so, seeing no way of getting out or of being saved, he began to roar. But Banaias, who was just then passing by, heard the beast's noise and, going in the direction of the sound, went down into the mouth of the pit and struck the beast, as it fought with him, with the staff which he held in his hand, and immediately killed it.[a] And as for the rest (of the warriors), they were just as valiant.

(xiii. 1) Then King David, desiring to know how many tens of thousands there were of the people, forgot the injunctions of Moses[b] who had prescribed that, when the populace was numbered, half a shekel should be paid to God for every person[b]; and he ordered Joab, his commander, to go out and take a census of the entire population. And, though Joab told him that there was no need to do this, he did not listen to him, but ordered him to proceed without delay to the numbering of the Hebrews. Joab, therefore, taking along the chiefs of the tribes and scribes,[c] went through the Israelite country and noted down the extent of the population; then, after nine months and twenty days, he returned to the king at Jerusalem and reported to him the number of people, excepting the tribe of Benjamin and the tribe of Levites, which he did not have time to count,[d] for

David's sin in numbering the people. 2 Sam. xxiv. 1; 1 Chron. xxi. 1.

Scripture, while not explaining why the census was sinful, gives two different accounts of its origin, 2 Sam. " And again the anger of the Lord was kindled against Israel and he incited David against them, saying, Go, number Israel and Judah "; 1 Chron. " And Satan stood up against Israel and incited David to number Israel."

[c] Scribes are not mentioned in Scripture.

[d] *Cf.* Luc. 1 Chron. ὅτι κατετάχυνεν λόγος τοῦ βασιλέως τὸν Ἰωάβ; Heb. "for the king's word was abominable to Joab."

τὸν θεὸν ἥμαρτεν. ἦν δὲ τῶν ἄλλων Ἰσραηλιτῶν ἀριθμὸς ἐνενήκοντα μυριάδες ὅπλα βαστάζειν καὶ στρατεύεσθαι δυναμένων, ἡ δὲ Ἰούδα φυλὴ καθ' ἑαυτὴν τεσσαράκοντα μυριάδες ἦσαν.

321 (2) Τῶν δὲ προφητῶν δηλωσάντων τῷ Δαυίδῃ ὅτι δι' ὀργῆς ἐστιν ὁ θεὸς αὐτῷ, ἱκετεύειν ἤρξατο καὶ παρακαλεῖν εὐμενῆ γενέσθαι καὶ συγγινώσκειν ἡμαρτηκότι. Γάδον δὲ τὸν προφήτην ἔπεμψεν ὁ θεὸς πρὸς αὐτὸν τρεῖς αἱρέσεις κομίζοντα, ὅπως ἐκλέξηται τούτων ἣν ἂν δοκιμάσῃ· πότερον θέλει λιμὸν γενέσθαι κατὰ τὴν χώραν ἐπὶ ἔτη ἑπτά, ἢ τρεῖς μῆνας πολεμήσας ὑπὸ τῶν ἐχθρῶν ἡττηθῆναι, ἢ λοιμὸν ἐνσκῆψαι καὶ νόσον ἐπὶ τρεῖς ἡμέρας τοῖς
322 Ἑβραίοις. ὁ δ' εἰς ἀμήχανον ἐκλογὴν μεγάλων κακῶν ἐμπεσὼν ἐλυπεῖτο καὶ σφόδρ' ἦν συγκεχυμένος. τοῦ δὲ προφήτου τοῦτο δεῖν ἐξ ἀνάγκης γενέσθαι φήσαντος καὶ κελεύοντος ἀποκρίνασθαι ταχέως, ἵνα ἀναγγείλῃ τὴν αἵρεσιν αὐτοῦ τῷ θεῷ, λογισάμενος ὁ βασιλεὺς ὡς εἰ λιμὸν αἰτήσει, δόξει τοῦτο πεποιηκέναι τοῖς ἄλλοις αὐτῷ μὲν ἀφόβως, ὅτι πολὺν αὐτὸς ἐγκεκλεισμένον ἔχοι σῖτον, ἐκείνοις
323 δὲ βλαβερῶς· ἂν δέ[1] γε ἕληται[2] τοὺς τρεῖς μῆνας νικωμένους αὐτούς,[3] ὅτι τοὺς ἀνδρειοτάτους ἔχων περὶ αὐτὸν καὶ φρούρια καὶ διὰ τοῦτο μηδὲν φοβού-

[1] ἂν δέ] κἂν RO.
[2] γε ἕληται M Lat.: γένηται rell.
[3] post αὐτούς lacunam statuit Niese; fort. ἐροῦσιν vel sim. desideratur.

---

[a] So Luc.; Heb. and LXX 800,000 in 2 Sam., 1,100,000 in 1 Chron.
[b] So Luc.; Heb. and LXX 500,000 in 2 Sam., 470,000 in 1 Chron.

the king repented of his sin against God. Now the number of the rest of the Israelites, capable of bearing arms and taking the field, was nine hundred thousand,[a] while the tribe of Judah by itself was four hundred thousand.[b]

(2) When the prophets informed David that God was angry with him,[c] he began to supplicate and entreat Him to be gracious and forgive his sin. Then God sent the prophet Gad to offer him a choice of three things from which to choose that which seemed best to him: he might either have a famine come upon the land for seven years,[d] or face his enemies in battle for three months and suffer defeat, or have pestilence and disease visited upon the Hebrews for three days. Then David, finding himself in the difficult position of having to choose among great evils, was distressed and greatly perturbed. And when the prophet said that this must inevitably come to pass, and bade him give his answer quickly, in order that he might report his choice to God, the king reflected that if he asked for the famine, it would seem to the others that he had done this without risk to himself, as he had plenty of grain stored up, but with great harm to them; if, moreover, he chose to have them suffer three months of defeat, they would say[e] that he had chosen the war because he had the bravest men about him as well as fortresses, and therefore had nothing to fear; so he asked for

David's choice of punishment for his sin. 2 Sam. xxiv. 11; 1 Chron. xxi. 7.

David chooses the pestilence. 2 Sam. xxiv. 14; 1 Chron. xxi. 13.

[c] No prophets are mentioned at this point in Scripture, which says, "And David said unto God, I have sinned greatly."

[d] So Heb. in 2 Sam.; Heb. in 1 Chron. and LXX in both places have "three years."

[e] Text uncertain.

μενος εἵλετο τὸν πόλεμον, ᾐτήσατο πάθος κοινὸν καὶ βασιλεῦσι καὶ τοῖς ἀρχομένοις, ἐν ᾧ τὸ δέος ἴσον ἁπάντων γίνεται, προειπὼν[1] ὅτι πολὺ κρεῖττον εἰς τὰς τοῦ θεοῦ χεῖρας ἐμπεσεῖν ἢ τὰς τῶν πολεμίων.

324 (3) Ταῦτ' ἀκούσας ὁ προφήτης ἀπήγγειλε τῷ θεῷ· ὁ δὲ τὸν λοιμὸν καὶ τὴν φθορὰν ἔπεμψε τοῖς Ἑβραίοις. ἀπέθνησκον δ' οὐ μονοτρόπως οὐδ' ὥστε ῥᾴδιον κατανοῆσαι γενέσθαι τὴν νόσον, ἀλλὰ τὸ μὲν κακὸν ἓν ἦν, μυρίαις δ' αὐτοὺς αἰτίαις καὶ προφάσεσιν οὐδ' ἐπινοῆσαι δυναμένους ἀνήρπαζεν.
325 ἄλλος γὰρ ἐπ' ἄλλῳ διεφθείρετο, καὶ λανθάνον ἐπερχόμενον τὸ δεινὸν ὀξεῖαν τὴν τελευτὴν ἐπέφερεν τῶν μὲν αἰφνιδίως μετ' ἀλγημάτων σφοδρῶν καὶ πικρᾶς ὀδύνης τὴν ψυχὴν ἀφιέντων, ἐνίων δὲ καὶ μαραινομένων τοῖς παθήμασι καὶ μηδ' εἰς κηδείαν ὑπολειπομένων, ἀλλ' ἐν αὐτῷ τῷ κάμνειν εἰς τὸ
326 παντελὲς δαπανωμένων· οἱ δ' αἰφνίδιον σκότους αὐτοῖς τὰς ὄψεις ὑποδραμόντος περιπνιγεῖς ἀπῴμωζον, ἔνιοι δὲ τῶν οἰκείων τινὰ κηδεύοντες ἐναπέθνησκον ἀτελέσι ταῖς ταφαῖς. ἀπώλοντο δ' ἀρξαμένης ἕωθεν τῆς λοιμικῆς νόσου φθείρειν αὐ-
327 τοὺς ἕως ὥρας ἀρίστου μυριάδες ἑπτά. ἐξέτεινε δ' ὁ ἄγγελος τὴν χεῖρα καὶ ἐπὶ τὰ Ἱεροσόλυμα, τὸ δεινὸν κἀκεῖσε πέμπων. ὁ δὲ βασιλεὺς σάκκον

[1] προσειπὼν Niese: dicens Lat.

[a] These reflections of David are an amplification of Scripture, which says merely, "And David said unto God, I am in a great strait; let me fall now into the hand of the Lord, for very great are his mercies, but let me not fall into the hand of man." Similar to Josephus's expansion are the explanations given in rabbinic tradition, *cf.* Ginzberg, iv. 112.

[b] This amplification of the brief Scriptural statement, "So

such an affliction as is common to kings and subjects alike, and one in which all have equal reason for fear, —first saying that it was much better to fall into the hands of God than into those of the enemy.[a]

(3) When the prophet heard this answer, he reported it to God, who thereupon sent pestilence and destruction upon the Hebrews. And they did not all die in the same manner so that the disease could be easily recognized, but, while there was only one (source of) evil, it carried them off for innumerable real or apparent causes, which they could not distinguish. One after the other, they perished, and the dread sickness, coming on them unperceived, brought swift death; some, in the midst of terrible suffering and acute pain, suddenly breathed their last; some were so wasted by their malady that there was nothing of them left for burial, and, in the course of their illness itself, they were completely consumed; others, with sudden darkness falling on their eyes, were suffocated as they groaned; still others died in the act of burying one of their household, and the interment was left unfinished.[b] And, in the destructive pestilence, which lasted from early morning until the hour of the noon meal,[c] there perished seventy thousand souls. Now the angel stretched out his hand against Jerusalem also and sent the plague upon it as well. And the king put on sack-

Description of the plague.

2 Sam. xxiv. 15; 1 Chron. xxi. 14.

the Lord sent pestilence upon Israel," is probably an imitation of the famous description of the plague in Thucydides ii. 47 ff., which also furnished the model for similar passages in later books of the *Antiquities*.

[c] So LXX in 2 Sam. (1 Chron. omits); Heb. "unto the time appointed (*mô'ed*)," Targum "unto the time of burning (the burnt-offering)"; rabbinic tradition, like the LXX, takes the Heb. "time appointed" to mean "midday," as if *mô'ed* here meant "the time appointed for the day's greatest heat."

ἐνδεδυμένος ἔκειτο κατὰ τῆς γῆς ἱκετεύων τὸν θεὸν
καὶ δεόμενος ἤδη λωφῆσαι καὶ τοῖς ἀπολωλόσιν
ἀρκεσθέντα παύσασθαι· ἀναβλέψας δ' εἰς τὸν ἀέρα
ὁ βασιλεὺς καὶ θεασάμενος τὸν ἄγγελον δι' αὐτοῦ
φερόμενον ἐπὶ τὰ Ἱεροσόλυμα καὶ μάχαιραν ἐσπασ-
328 μένον εἶπε πρὸς τὸν θεὸν ὡς αὐτὸς εἴη κολασθῆναι
δίκαιος ὁ ποιμήν, τὰ δὲ ποίμνια σώζεσθαι μηδὲν
ἐξαμαρτόντα, καὶ ἠντιβόλει τὴν ὀργὴν εἰς αὐτὸν καὶ
τὴν γενεὰν αὐτοῦ πᾶσαν ἀποσκήπτειν, φείδεσθαι δὲ
τοῦ λαοῦ.

329 (4) Κατακούσας δὲ ὁ θεὸς τῆς ἱκεσίας ἔπαυσε
τὸν λοιμόν, καὶ πέμψας Γάδον τὸν προφήτην ἐκέλευσεν αὐτὸν ἀναβῆναι παραχρῆμα εἰς τὴν ἅλω
τοῦ Ἰεβουσαίου Ὀρόννα καὶ οἰκοδομήσαντα βωμὸν ἐκεῖ τῷ θεῷ θυσίαν ἐπιτελέσαι. Δαυίδης δ'
ἀκούσας οὐκ ἠμέλησεν, ἀλλ' εὐθὺς ἔσπευσεν ἐπὶ
330 τὸν παρηγγελμένον αὐτῷ τόπον. Ὀρόννας δὲ τὸν
σῖτον ἀλοῶν ἐπεὶ τὸν βασιλέα προσιόντα καὶ τοὺς
παῖδας αὐτοῦ πάντας ἐθεάσατο, προσέδραμεν αὐτῷ
καὶ προσεκύνησεν. ἦν δὲ τὸ μὲν γένος Ἰεβουσαῖος,
φίλος δ' ἐν τοῖς μάλιστα Δαυίδου· καὶ διὰ τοῦτ'
αὐτὸν οὐδὲν εἰργάσατο δεινόν, ὅτε τὴν πόλιν κατε-
331 στρέψατο, ὡς μικρὸν ἔμπροσθεν ἐδηλώσαμεν. τοῦ
δὲ Ὀρόννα πυθομένου τί παρείη πρὸς τὸν δοῦλον ὁ

---

[a] The word "shepherd" is found in the Targum and some LXX MSS. in 2 Sam.; Heb. "I have sinned and I have done wickedly, but these sheep, what have they done?"

[b] According to 2 Sam. xxiv. 16 (1 Chron. xxi. 15) God caused the angel of pestilence to stay his hand as he stood by Araunah's threshing-floor, before David pleaded that the people be spared, while in verses 21-25 (1 Chron. verses 22-27) we read that the plague did not cease until the altar had been built. Josephus ignores this inconsistency here and in § 332.

cloth and lay on the ground, supplicating God and entreating Him at last to be appeased and to rest content with those who had already perished. Then, looking up into the air and beholding the angel being borne through it toward Jerusalem, with his sword drawn, the king said to God that it was he, the shepherd [a] who was rightly to be punished, but the flock, which had committed no sin, should be saved [a]; and he entreated Him to cause His anger to fall upon him and all his line, but to spare the people.

End of the plague. David and Araunah (Oronnas) the Jebusite. 2 Sam. xxiv. 18; 1 Chron. xxi. 18.

(4) And God hearkened to his supplication, and caused the pestilence to cease,[b] and, sending the prophet Gad, He commanded David to go up at once to the threshing-floor of Oronnas [c] the Jebusite, and there build an altar to God and offer sacrifice. When David heard these commands he did not neglect them, but immediately hastened to the place indicated to him. Now Oronnas was threshing his grain and, when he saw the king approaching with all his servants,[d] he ran to him and did obeisance; he was, to be sure, of Jebusite descent, but he was one of David's best friends, and for this reason, the latter did him no harm when he overthrew the city, as we related a little while ago.[e] And when Oronnas inquired why his lord had come to his servant, David

[c] Bibl. Araunah, 1 Chron. Ornan, *cf.* § 69 note.

[d] Hardly "children" as Weill translates; *cf.* bibl. "And Araunah looked and saw the king (*melek*) and his servants crossing over to him," LXX *καὶ διέκυψεν Ὀρνὰ καὶ εἶδεν τὸν βασιλέα καὶ τοὺς παῖδας αὐτοῦ παραπορευομένους ἐπάνω αὐτοῦ.* Weill may have been thinking of the corrupt Heb. in 1 Chron., "and Ornan returned and saw the angel (*mal'âk*), and his four sons with him hid themselves," but here it is Araunah's sons who are spoken of.

[e] § 69.

δεσπότης, εἶπεν ὠνήσεσθαι[1] παρ' αὐτοῦ τὴν ἅλω, ὅπως βωμὸν ἐν αὐτῇ κατασκευάσῃ τῷ θεῷ καὶ ποιήσῃ θυσίαν. ὁ δὲ καὶ τὴν ἅλω εἶπε καὶ τὰ ἄροτρα καὶ τοὺς βόας εἰς ὁλοκαύτωσιν χαρίζεσθαι καὶ τὸν θεὸν ἡδέως εὔχεσθαι τὴν θυσίαν προσέσθαι.
332 ὁ δὲ βασιλεὺς ἀγαπᾶν μὲν αὐτὸν τῆς ἁπλότητος καὶ τῆς μεγαλοψυχίας ἔλεγε καὶ δέχεσθαι τὴν χάριν, τιμὴν δ' αὐτὸν ἠξίου λαμβάνειν πάντων· οὐ γὰρ εἶναι δίκαιον προῖκα θυσίαν ἐπιτελεῖν. τοῦ δὲ Ὀρόννα φήσαντος ποιεῖν ὅ τι βούλεται πεντήκοντα
333 σίκλων ὠνεῖται παρ' αὐτοῦ τὴν ἅλω. καὶ οἰκοδομήσας τὸν βωμὸν ἱερούργησε καὶ ὡλοκαύτωσε καὶ θυσίας ἀνήνεγκεν εἰρηνικάς. καταπραΰνεται δὲ τούτοις τὸ θεῖον καὶ πάλιν εὐμενὲς γίνεται. συνέβη δ' εἰς ἐκεῖνον ἀγαγεῖν τὸν τόπον Ἅβραμον τὸν υἱὸν αὐτοῦ Ἴσακον ὥστε ὁλοκαυτῶσαι, καὶ μέλλοντος ἀποσφάττεσθαι τοῦ παιδὸς κριὸν ἐξαίφνης ἀναφανῆναι παρεστῶτα τῷ βωμῷ, ὃν καὶ κατέθυσεν
334 Ἅβραμος ἀντὶ τοῦ παιδός, ὡς προειρήκαμεν. ὁρῶν δ' ὁ βασιλεὺς Δαυίδης τῆς εὐχῆς αὐτοῦ τὸν θεὸν ἐπήκοον γεγενημένον καὶ τὴν θυσίαν ἡδέως προσδεξάμενον ἔκρινε τὸν τόπον ἐκεῖνον ὅλον βωμὸν[2] προσαγορεῦσαι τοῦ λαοῦ παντὸς καὶ οἰκοδομῆσαι ναὸν τῷ θεῷ, καὶ ταύτην εὐστόχως ἀφῆκεν εἰς τὸ

[1] Naber: ὠνήσασθαι codd.

[2] ὅλον βωμὸν] ἅλων ex Lat. Niese: ὁλοκαυτωμάτων βωμὸν vel sim. conj.

---

[a] *Cf.* Luc. 2 Sam. τὰ ξύλα καὶ τὰ ἄροτρα and LXX 1 Chron. τὸ ἄροτρον εἰς ξύλα; Heb. 2 Sam. "threshing instruments and instruments of the oxen," LXX οἱ τροχοὶ καὶ τὰ σκεύη τῶν βοῶν; Heb. 1 Chron. "threshing instruments for wood and wheat for the meat-offering," Luc. τὰς ἁμάξας εἰς ξύλα καὶ τὸν πυρὸν εἰς θυσίαν.

said that it was to buy the threshing-floor from him, in which to build an altar to God and perform sacrifice. Thereupon he replied that he would present the threshing-floor, as well as the plough [a] and oxen, as a burnt-offering, and prayed that God would graciously accept the sacrifice. The king then said that he admired him for his liberality and greatness of soul, and accepted his kind gifts, but requested him to take payment for them all, for it was not right for anyone to offer a sacrifice that cost him nothing. And when Oronnas said he might do as he pleased, he bought the threshing-floor from him for fifty shekels,[b] and, having built the altar, he consecrated it [c] and offered burnt-offerings and peace-offerings. By these means the Deity was appeased and once more became gracious. As it happened, it was to this very place that Abraham brought his son Isaac, to sacrifice him as a burnt-offering, and, as he was about to slaughter him, there suddenly appeared beside the altar a ram, which Abraham sacrificed in place of his son, as we related earlier.[d] Then, when David saw that God had hearkened to his prayer and had accepted the sacrifice with favour, he resolved to call that entire place the altar [e] of all the people, and to build a temple to God; and, in uttering this

David buys Arauna's threshing-floor as a site for the temple. 2 Sam. xxiv. 24; 1 Chron. xxi. 25.

[b] So 2 Sam.; 1 Chron. "600 shekels of gold by weight."

[c] Or "performed the sacred rites," bibl. (1 Chron.) "and called upon the Lord."

[d] *A.* i. 222 f., 226. *Cf.* notes *ad loc.*

[e] Text doubtful. For ὅλον βωμόν Niese, following the Latin, would read ἅλων "threshing-floor." But it is likely that ὅλον βωμόν is a corruption of (an abbreviated?) ὁλοκαυτωμάτων βωμόν "altar of burnt offerings"; *cf.* 1 Chron. xxii. 1, "And David said, This is the house of the Lord God, and this is the altar of the burnt offering for Israel (LXX θυσιαστήριον εἰς ὁλοκαύτωσιν τῷ Ἰσραήλ)."

γενησόμενον τὴν φωνήν· ὁ γὰρ θεὸς τὸν προφήτην ἀποστείλας πρὸς αὐτὸν ἐκεῖ ναὸν ἔλεγεν οἰκοδομήσειν αὐτοῦ τὸν υἱὸν τὸν μέλλοντα μετ' αὐτὸν τὴν βασιλείαν διαδέχεσθαι.

335 (xiv. 1) Μετὰ δὴ ταύτην τὴν προφητείαν ἐκέλευσεν ὁ βασιλεὺς τοὺς παροίκους ἐξαριθμηθῆναι καὶ εὑρέθησαν εἰς ὀκτὼ μυριάδας καὶ δέκα. ἐκ τούτων ἀπέδειξε λατόμους μὲν τοὺς ὀκτακισμυρίους, τὸ δ' ἄλλο πλῆθος παραφέρειν τοὺς λίθους, τρισχιλίους δὲ καὶ πεντακοσίους τοῖς ἐργαζομένοις ἐξ αὐτῶν ἐπέστησεν. ἡτοίμασε δὲ καὶ πολὺν σίδηρον καὶ χαλκὸν εἰς τὰ ἔργα καὶ ξύλα κέδρινα πολλὰ καὶ παμμεγεθέστατα, Τυρίων αὐτῷ ταῦτα πεμπόντων καὶ Σιδωνίων· ἐπεστάλκει γὰρ αὐτοῖς τὴν τῶν
336 ξύλων χορηγίαν. πρός τε τοὺς φίλους ἔλεγε ταῦτα παρασκευάζεσθαι νῦν, ἵνα τῷ μέλλοντι παιδὶ βασιλεύειν μετ' αὐτὸν ἑτοίμην τὴν ὕλην τῆς οἰκοδομίας τοῦ ναοῦ[1] καταλείπῃ καὶ μὴ τότε συμπορίζῃ νέος ὢν καὶ τῶν τοιούτων ἄπειρος διὰ τὴν ἡλικίαν, ἀλλ' ἔχων παρακειμένην ἐπιτελῇ τὸ ἔργον.

337 (2) Καλέσας δὲ τὸν παῖδα Σολομῶνα κατασκευάσαι τῷ θεῷ ναὸν αὐτὸν ἐκέλευσε διαδεξάμενον τὴν βασιλείαν, λέγων ὡς αὐτὸν βουλόμενον κωλύσειεν ὁ θεὸς αἵματι καὶ πολέμοις πεφυρμένον,

[1] τοῦ ναοῦ om. RO Lat.

[a] This last detail ("and, in uttering this word," etc.) was suggested by the LXX addition to 2 Sam. xxiv. 25 καὶ προσέθηκεν Σαλωμὼν ἐπὶ τὸ θυσιαστήριον ἐπ' ἐσχάτῳ ὅτι μικρὸν ἦν ἐν πρώτοις "and Solomon added to the altar at a later time because it was small at first."

[b] In 1 Chron. xxii. 2 there is mention of a census of aliens taken by David, but no figures are given; in 2 Chron. ii. 17 the figure given for the census taken by Solomon "after the numbering wherewith David his father had numbered

word, he came close to foretelling what was later to happen, for God sent a prophet to say that in this place a temple would be built by the son who was destined to succeed him on the throne.[a]

(xiv. 1) After receiving this prophecy, the king ordered the aliens to be numbered, and there were found to be one hundred and eighty thousand.[b] Of these, he designated eighty thousand to be stone-cutters, and the rest of their number to carry the stones; and three thousand five hundred [c] of them he set over the workmen. He also collected a great quantity of iron and bronze for the work, and many cedar-trees of very great size, sent to him by the Tyrians and Sidonians, from whom he had ordered a supply of the wood. And he told his friends that he was preparing these things now, in order that he might leave the materials for the building of the temple ready for the son who was destined to reign after him, who would thus not have to procure them when he would still be a youth and inexperienced because of his age, but would have them at hand to complete the work.

David collects men and material for building the temple. 1 Kings v. 15-16 (29-30); 2 Chron. ii. 2, 17; 1 Chron. xxii. 2.

(2) Then he called his son Solomon and bade him build the temple to God after he should have succeeded to the throne, telling him that he himself had wished to do so, but God had prevented him because of his being stained with blood shed in war [d]; He had

David's instructions to Solomon concerning the temple. 1 Chron. xxii. 6.

them" is 153,600. This figure corresponds to the total of the classes enumerated in 1 Kings v. 15-16 (Heb. 29-30), 70,000 carriers, 80,000 stone-cutters, 3600 (LXX) overseers = 153,600. Josephus's figure of 180,000 mistakenly includes a levy of 30,000 Israelites (therefore not aliens), and omits the 3600 overseers, whom he counts separately, *cf.* following note.

[c] So LXX cod. A; Heb. 3300, LXX cod. B 3600, Luc. 3700. In *A.* viii. 59 Josephus, in agreement with Heb., has 3300.

[d] *Cf.* §§ 90 ff.

προείποι δ' ὅτι Σολομὼν οἰκοδομήσει τὸν ναὸν[1] αὐτῷ παῖς νεώτατος[2] καὶ τοῦτο κληθησόμενος τοὔνομα, οὗ προνοήσειν μὲν αὐτὸς ὡς πατὴρ ἐπηγγέλλετο, τὴν δ' Ἑβραίων χώραν εὐδαίμονα καταστήσειν ἐπ' αὐτοῦ τοῖς τε ἄλλοις ἀγαθοῖς καὶ δὴ καὶ τῷ μεγίστῳ πάντων εἰρήνῃ καὶ πολέμων ἀπ-
338 αλλαγῇ καὶ στάσεων ἐμφυλίων. "σὺ τοίνυν ἐπεὶ καὶ πρὸ τῆς γενέσεως ἀπεδείχθης βασιλεὺς ὑπὸ τοῦ θεοῦ πειρῶ τά τε ἄλλα γίνεσθαι τῆς τούτου προνοίας ἄξιος, εὐσεβὴς ὢν καὶ δίκαιος καὶ ἀνδρεῖος, καὶ τὰς ἐντολὰς αὐτοῦ καὶ τοὺς νόμους οὓς διὰ Μωυσέος ἔδωκεν ἡμῖν φύλαττε καὶ τοῖς ἄλλοις
339 μὴ παραβαίνειν ἐπίτρεπε. τὸν δὲ ναόν, ὃν ὑπὸ σοῦ βασιλεύοντος εἵλετο αὐτῷ γενέσθαι, σπούδασον ἀποδοῦναι τῷ θεῷ μὴ καταπλαγεὶς τὸ μέγεθος τοῦ ἔργου μηδ' ἀποδειλιάσας πρὸς αὐτό· πάντα γάρ σοι πρὸ τῆς ἐμαυτοῦ τελευτῆς ἕτοιμα ποιήσω.
340 γίνωσκε δὴ[3] χρυσοῦ μὲν ἤδη τάλαντα συνειλεγμένα μύρια, δέκα δ' ἀργύρου μυριάδας ταλάντων, χαλκόν τε καὶ σίδηρον ἀριθμοῦ πλείονα συντέθεικα καὶ ξύλων δὲ καὶ λίθων ὕλην ἄφθονον, ἔχεις δὲ καὶ λατόμων πολλὰς μυριάδας καὶ τεκτόνων· ἂν δέ τι τούτοις προσδέῃ, σὺ προσθήσεις. γίνου τοίνυν
341 ἄριστος[4] τὸν θεὸν ἔχων προστάτην." προσπαρεκελεύσατο δὲ καὶ τοὺς ἄρχοντας τοῦ λαοῦ τῆς οἰκο-

[1] τὸν ναὸν om. RO.
[2] συνετώτατος Naber.
[3] δὲ E: om. RO: siquidem Lat.
[4] γίνου . . . ἄριστος] γινομένου τοίνυν τούτου ἄριστος (ἄρεστος M) ἔσῃ MSP: esto igitur optimus guvernator Lat.

[a] For νεώτατος Naber conjectures συνετώτατος "most intelligent." Reinach, adopting the latter reading, supposes

also foretold that his youngest [a] son Solomon would build Him a temple, and should be called by this name,[a] and promised to watch over him like a father, and bring prosperity to the country of the Hebrews in his reign, with, among other things, the greatest of all blessings, namely peace and freedom from war and civil dissension. "Therefore," he said, "since, even before your birth, you were chosen by God to be king, endeavour to be worthy of His providence by being pious, just and brave; keep the commandments and the laws which He gave us through Moses, and do not permit others to transgress them; as for the temple which He has decreed shall be made for Him in your reign, take pains to complete [b] it for God, and do not be dismayed at the magnitude of the labour, nor shrink from it, for I shall make everything ready for you before my death. You should, indeed, know that ten thousand [c] talents of gold and one hundred thousand [d] talents of silver have already been collected, and that I have brought together more bronze and iron than can be reckoned, and a limitless quantity of wood and stone. You also have many tens of thousands of stone-cutters and carpenters, and whatever else is needed you yourself will add. Be, then, most brave, for you have God as your protector." He further exhorted the chiefs of the people to assist his son in the building, and,

that there was originally in the text an allusion to Solomon's surname of the Wise. There is, however, no reason to suspect the present text, *cf.* 1 Chron. xxii. 9 where the Heb. plays upon the resemblance of Solomon's name (*Shelômôh*) to *shālôm* "peace"—a word-play that could not be conveyed to Josephus's Greek readers.

[b] Lit. "render it as due."

[c] Bibl. 100,000.

[d] Bibl. 1,000,000.

δομίας συλλαβέσθαι τῷ παιδὶ καὶ πάντων ἀδεεῖς ὄντας τῶν κακῶν, περὶ τὴν τοῦ θεοῦ θρησκείαν ἀσχολεῖν[1]· καρπώσεσθαι[2] γὰρ αὐτοὺς ἀντὶ τούτων εἰρήνην καὶ εὐνομίαν, οἷς ἀμείβεται τοὺς εὐσεβεῖς
342 καὶ δικαίους ὁ θεὸς ἀνθρώπους. οἰκοδομηθέντος δὲ τοῦ ναοῦ τὴν κιβωτὸν αὐτὸν ἀποθέσθαι προσέταξε καὶ τὰ ἅγια σκεύη πρὸ πολλοῦ ναὸν ὀφείλοντα ἔχειν, εἰ τῶν ἐντολῶν τοῦ θεοῦ μὴ παρήκουσαν ἡμῶν οἱ πατέρες ἐντειλαμένου μετὰ τὸ τὴν γῆν ταύτην κατασχεῖν οἰκοδομῆσαι ναὸν αὐτῷ. ταῦτα μὲν πρὸς τοὺς ἡγεμόνας ὁ Δαυίδης καὶ τὸν υἱὸν αὐτοῦ διελέχθη.

343 (3) Πρεσβύτερος δὲ ὢν ἤδη καὶ τοῦ σώματος αὐτῷ ψυχομένου διὰ τὸν χρόνον δύσριγος ὑπῆρχεν, ὡς μηδ' ὑπὸ τῆς ἐπιβολῆς ἐκ πολλῶν ἱματίων γινομένης ἀναθερμαίνεσθαι. συνελθόντων δὲ τῶν ἰατρῶν καὶ συμβουλευσάντων ὅπως ἐξ ἁπάσης τῆς χώρας εὐειδὴς ἐπιλεχθεῖσα παρθένος συγκαθεύδῃ τῷ βασιλεῖ, τοῦτο γὰρ αὐτῷ πρὸς τὸ ῥῖγος ἔσεσθαι
344 βοήθημα θαλπούσης αὐτὸν τῆς κόρης, εὑρίσκετ' ἐν πόλει[3] γυνὴ μία πασῶν τὸ εἶδος ἀρίστη γυναικῶν Ἀβισάκη τοὔνομα, ἣ συγκοιμωμένη μόνον τῷ βασιλεῖ συνεθέρμαινεν αὐτόν· ὑπὸ γὰρ γήρως ἦν πρὸς τἀφροδίσια καὶ γυναικὸς ὁμιλίαν ἀσθενής. ἀλλὰ περὶ μὲν ταύτης τῆς παρθένου μετ' ὀλίγον δηλώσομεν.

345 (4) Ὁ δὲ τέταρτος υἱὸς Δαυίδου νεανίας εὐειδὴς καὶ μέγας, ἐκ γυναικὸς αὐτῷ Ἀγίθης[4] γεγονὼς

[1] ed. pr. Lat.: εὐσχολεῖν codd.
[2] ed. pr. Lat.: καρπώσασθαι codd.
[3] post πόλει desideratur nomen oppidi, quod in γυνὴ latere conj. Boysen.
[4] Niese: Αἰγίσθης codd.: Aegeth Lat.

without fear of any evil, to devote themselves wholly to the worship of God, saying that as a reward for this they would enjoy peace and order, with which God repays pious and just men. And he gave orders that, when the temple was built, Solomon should deposit in it the ark and the holy vessels, which should long since have had a temple, if our fathers had not disobeyed God's command to build a temple to Him after they had taken possession of this land.[a] Such, then, were the words which David addressed to the leaders and to his son.

Abishag (Abisake) comforts David's old age. 1 Kings i. 1

(3) Now as David was already very old, and, because of his age, his body felt cold and numb so that not even by the heaping on of many garments could he be kept warm, his physicians [b] came together and advised that a beautiful virgin be chosen out of the whole country to sleep with the king, as it would help him against the cold to have the maid warm him; and there was found, in the city of . . .,[c] a woman who surpassed all others in beauty, Abisakē [d] by name, but she merely slept in the same bed with him and kept him warm, for at his age he was too feeble to have sexual pleasure or intercourse with her. Of this virgin, however, we shall speak a little later.[e]

Adonijah (Adōnias) plots to succeed David. 1 Kings i. 5.

(4) Now the fourth son of David, a tall and handsome youth borne to him by his wife Agithē [f] and

[a] The reference to the disobedience of the fathers is added by Josephus.

[b] Bibl. "his servants."

[c] Shunem, the name of the city, has dropped out of Josephus's text, or has, perhaps, been corrupted to γυνή "woman," as Boysen conjectures; the Greek form of the name was probably Συνήμ, *cf.* Luc. in Jos. xix. 18.

[d] Bibl. Abishag, LXX Ἀβεισά.

[e] *A.* viii. 5 ff.

[f] Bibl. Haggith, *cf.* § 21 note.

Ἀδωνίας δὲ προσαγορευόμενος, ἐμφερὴς ὢν Ἀψαλώμῳ τὴν[1] διάνοιαν αὐτὸς ὡς βασιλεύσων ἐπῆρτο καὶ πρὸς τοὺς φίλους ἔλεγεν ὡς τὴν ἀρχὴν αὐτὸν δεῖ παραλαβεῖν· κατεσκεύασε δὲ ἅρματα πολλὰ καὶ ἵππους καὶ πεντήκοντα ἄνδρας τοὺς προδρόμους.
346 ταῦθ' ὁρῶν ὁ πατὴρ οὐκ ἐπέπληττεν οὐδ' ἐπεῖχεν αὐτὸν τῆς προαιρέσεως οὐδὲ μέχρι τοῦ πυθέσθαι διὰ τί ταῦτα πράττει προήχθη. συνεργοὺς δ' εἶχεν Ἀδωνίας τὸν στρατηγὸν Ἰώαβον καὶ τὸν ἀρχιερέα Ἀβιάθαρον, μόνοι δ' ἀντέπραττον ὁ ἀρχιερεὺς Σάδωκος καὶ ὁ προφήτης Νάθας καὶ Βαναίας ὁ ἐπὶ τῶν σωματοφυλάκων καὶ Σιμούεις[2] ὁ Δαυίδου φίλος
347 καὶ πάντες οἱ ἀνδρειότατοι. τοῦ δὲ Ἀδωνία παρασκευασαμένου δεῖπνον ἔξω τῆς πόλεως παρὰ τὴν πηγὴν[3] τὴν ἐν τῷ βασιλικῷ παραδείσῳ καὶ πάντας καλέσαντος τοὺς ἀδελφοὺς χωρὶς Σολομῶνος, παραλαβόντος δὲ καὶ τὸν στρατηγὸν Ἰώαβον καὶ Ἀβιάθαρον καὶ τοὺς ἄρχοντας τῆς Ἰούδα φυλῆς, οὔτε δὲ Σάδωκον τὸν ἀρχιερέα[4] καὶ Νάθαν τὸν προφήτην καὶ τὸν ἐπὶ τῶν σωματοφυλάκων Βαναίαν καὶ πάντας τοὺς ἐκ τῆς ἐναντίας αἱρέσεως καλέ-
348 σαντος[5] ἐπὶ τὴν ἑστίασιν, τοῦτο πρὸς τὴν Σολομῶνος κατεμήνυσε μητέρα Βερσάβην Νάθας ὁ προφήτης ὡς Ἀδωνίας βασιλεύς ἐστι καὶ τοῦτ' ἀγνοεῖ Δαυίδης[6] συνεβούλευέ τε σώζειν αὐτὴν καὶ τὸν παῖδα Σολομῶνα καὶ πρὸς Δαυίδην προσελθοῦσαν μόνην αὐτὴν λέγειν ὡς αὐτὸς μὲν ὀμόσειε μετ'

[1] + τε RO. [2] Σεμεῖς M: Σουμούεις E: Simus Lat.
[3] πύλην RO: γῆν M.
[4] οὔτε δὲ . . . ἀρχιερέα] τοὺς δὲ περὶ τὸν ἀρχιερέα M: οὗτοι μὲν πάντες παρῆσαν τοὺς δὲ περὶ τὸν ἀρχιερέα SP.
[5] οὐκ ἐκάλεσεν MSP Lat.
[6] βασιλεύς ἐστι . . . Δαυίδης] βασιλεῦσαι βούλεται RO.

named Adōnias,[a] had thoughts similar to those of Absalom and, aspiring to be king himself, told his friends that he ought to succeed to the royal power. So he provided himself with many chariots and horses and fifty men to run before him. When his father saw this, he did not rebuke him nor restrain him from his purpose, nor even go so far as to ask him why he did these things. And Adōnias had as accomplices the commander Joab and the high priest Abiathar; the only ones opposed to him were the high priest Sadok, the prophet Nathan, Banaias, the chief of the bodyguards, David's friend Simūeis[b] and all the foremost warriors. And Adōnias prepared a dinner outside the city beside the spring in the royal garden,[c] and invited all his brothers except Solomon; he also brought with him the commander Joab and Abiathar and the chiefs of the tribe of Judah, but he did not invite to the feast either the high priest Sadok[d] or the prophet Nathan or Banaias, the chief of the bodyguard, or any of the opposing party. These things the prophet Nathan reported to Solomon's mother Bersabē, saying that Adōnias was king and David did not know it[e]; at the same time he advised her to save herself and her son Solomon, and to go alone to David and tell him that, although he had sworn

Nathan advises Bath-sheba to warn David of Adonijah's plot 1 Kings i. 11.

[a] Bibl. Adonijah, *cf. ibid.*

[b] *Cf.* Luc. Σαμαίας καὶ οἱ ἑταῖροι αὐτοῦ, reading *rē'âw* "his friends" for the personal name Rei; bibl. Shimei and Rei, LXX Σεμεεὶ καὶ Ῥησεί. Josephus read *rē'a* "friend" or *rē'ô* "his (David's) friend."

[c] Bibl. "by the stone of Zoheleth which is by En-rogel" (*En* = "spring"); on the latter *cf.* § 223 and § 355 notes. The "royal garden" seems to be an invention of Josephus.

[d] Variant "the high priest Sadok and his followers."

[e] Variant (after "Adonias") "wished to be king."

αὐτὸν Σολομῶνα βασιλεύειν μεταξὺ δ'[1] Ἀδωνίας
349 τὴν ἀρχὴν ἤδη παραλάβοι.[2] ταῦτα δὲ τῷ βασιλεῖ
διαλεγομένης ὁ προφήτης εἰσελεύσεσθαι καὶ αὐτὸς
ἔφησε καὶ τοῖς λόγοις αὐτῆς ἐπιμαρτυρήσειν. ἡ
δὲ Βερσάβη πεισθεῖσα τῷ Νάθᾳ πάρεισι πρὸς τὸν
βασιλέα καὶ προσκυνήσασα καὶ λόγον αἰτησαμένη
350 πάντ' αὐτῇ καθὼς ὁ προφήτης ὑπέθετο καὶ διεξ-
έρχεται τό τε δεῖπνον τὸ Ἀδωνία καὶ τοὺς ὑπ'
αὐτοῦ κεκλημένους Ἀβιάθαρον τὸν ἀρχιερέα καὶ
Ἰώαβον τὸν ἄρχοντα καὶ τοὺς υἱοὺς αὐτοῦ χωρὶς
Σολομῶνος καὶ τῶν ἀναγκαίων αὐτοῦ φίλων
μηνύσασα· ἔλεγέ τε πάντα τὸν λαὸν ἀφορᾶν τίνα
χειροτονήσει βασιλέα, παρεκάλει τε κατὰ νοῦν
ἔχειν, ὡς μετὰ τὴν ἀπαλλαγὴν αὐτοῦ βασιλεύσας
αὐτήν τε καὶ Σολομῶνα τὸν υἱὸν αὐτῆς ἀναιρήσει.
351 (5) Διαλεγομένης δὲ ἔτι τῆς γυναικὸς ἤγγειλαν οἱ
τοῦ δωματίου προεστῶτες ὅτι βούλεται Νάθας
ἰδεῖν αὐτόν. τοῦ δὲ βασιλέως ἐκδέξασθαι[3] κελεύσαντος εἰσελθών, εἰ τήμερον ἀποδείξειε τὸν Ἀδωνίαν βασιλέα καὶ παραδοίη τὴν ἀρχὴν ἐπυνθάνετο·
352 λαμπρὸν γὰρ αὐτὸν ποιήσαντα δεῖπνον κεκληκέναι
τοὺς υἱοὺς αὐτοῦ πάντας χωρὶς Σολομῶνος καὶ τὸν
στρατηγὸν Ἰώαβον, οἳ μετὰ κρότου καὶ παιδιᾶς
εὐωχούμενοι πολλῆς αἰώνιον αὐτῷ συνεύχονται τὴν
ἡγεμονίαν· "ἐκάλεσε δὲ οὔτε ἐμὲ οὔτε τὸν ἀρχιερέα Σάδωκον οὔτε Βαναίαν τὸν ἐπὶ τῶν σωματο-
φυλάκων· δίκαιον δ' εἶναι ταῦτα γινώσκειν ἅπαντας,

[1] καὶ πρὸς Δαυίδην . . . μεταξὺ δ'] εἴπερ RO: βασιλεύειν μεταξὺ δ' M: καὶ πρὸς Δαυίδην ἐλθοῦσαν ταῦτα λέγειν E.

[2] post παραλάβοι add. καὶ περὶ τούτου πυθέσθαι τοῦ βασιλέως RO.

[3] μὴ ἐκδέξασθαι MSP: εἰσδέξασθαι Cocceji.

that Solomon should be king after his death, Adōnias had meanwhile taken over the royal power.[a] And the prophet said that while she was telling this to the king, he himself would enter and confirm her words. So Bersabē took Nathan's advice and went to the king; then, after doing obeisance and asking for permission to speak, she recounted to him all that the prophet had suggested, telling him of Adōnias's dinner and the guests who had been invited by him, and mentioning Abiathar, the high priest, and Joab, the commander, and the king's sons except Solomon and the latter's closest friends. She added that all the people were waiting to see whom he would choose king, and urged him to bear in mind that, if, after his death, Adōnias became king, he would put her and her son Solomon to death.

David reassures Bath-sheba. 1 Kings i. 22

(5) While his wife was still speaking, the keepers of the chamber announced that Nathan wished to see him, and, when the king bade them admit him, he entered and inquired whether David had that day declared Adōnias king and given over the royal power to him, for, he said, he had prepared a splendid dinner and had invited all the king's sons, except Solomon, and the commander Joab, and these were feasting to the accompaniment of clapping of hands and much jesting,[b] and were wishing Adōnias lasting sovereignty. "But," he added, "he invited neither me nor the high priest Sadok nor Banaias, the chief of the bodyguard, and it is right that all should know

[a] Variant (after "her son Solomon") "if, indeed, Adonias had already taken over the royal power, and to inquire of the king concerning this matter."

[b] Details added by Josephus; bibl. "they eat and drink before him."

353 εἰ κατὰ τὴν σὴν γνώμην ἐγένετο." ταῦτα τοῦ
Νάθα φήσαντος ὁ βασιλεὺς ἐκέλευσε καλέσαι τὴν
Βερσάβην πρὸς αὑτόν· ἐκπεπηδήκει γὰρ ἐκ τοῦ
δωματίου τοῦ προφήτου παραγενομένου. τῆς δὲ
γυναικὸς ἐλθούσης "ὄμνυμί σοι," φησί, "τὸν
μέγιστον θεόν, ἦ μὴν τὸν υἱόν σου Σολομῶνα
βασιλεύσειν, ὡς καὶ πρότερον ὤμοσα, καὶ τοῦτον
ἐπὶ τοὐμοῦ καθιεῖσθαι[1] θρόνου· καὶ τοῦτο ἔσται
354 τήμερον." προσκυνησάσης δ' αὐτὸν τῆς γυναικὸς
καὶ μακρὸν εὐξαμένης αὐτῷ βίον, Σάδωκον μεταπέμπεται τὸν ἀρχιερέα καὶ Βαναίαν τὸν ἐπὶ τῶν
σωματοφυλάκων, καὶ παραγενομένοις κελεύει παραλαβεῖν Νάθαν τόν τε προφήτην καὶ τοὺς περὶ τὴν
355 αὐλὴν ὁπλίτας,[2] καὶ ἀναβιβάσαντας τὸν υἱὸν αὐτοῦ
Σολόμωνα ἐπὶ τὴν βασιλικὴν ἡμίονον ἔξω τῆς
πόλεως ἀγαγεῖν ἐπὶ τὴν πηγὴν τὴν λεγομένην
Γειὼν καὶ περιχρίσαντας τὸ ἅγιον ἔλαιον ἀποδεῖξαι
βασιλέα· τοῦτο δὲ ποιῆσαι προσέταξε Σάδωκον τὸν
356 ἀρχιερέα καὶ Νάθαν τὸν προφήτην. ἀκολουθοῦντάς
τε προσέταξε διὰ μέσης τῆς πόλεως τοῖς κέρασιν
ἐπισαλπίζοντας βοᾶν εἰς αἰῶνα Σολομῶνα τὸν
βασιλέα καθίσαι ἐπὶ τοῦ βασιλικοῦ θρόνου, ἵνα γνῷ
πᾶς ὁ λαὸς ἀποδεδειγμένον αὐτὸν ὑπὸ τοῦ πατρὸς

[1] καθεδεῖσθαι SP: καθῆσθαι M.
[2] + ἅπαντας MSPE.

whether this was done with your approval." When Nathan had thus spoken, the king ordered Bersabē to be summoned to him,—for she had hurried from the room when the prophet arrived [a]—and, when his wife came, he said, " I swear to you by Almighty God that your son Solomon shall assuredly be king, as I have sworn before, and he shall sit upon my throne ; and it shall be this very day." Thereupon she did obeisance to him and wished him long life. The king then sent for Sadok, the high priest, and Banaias, the chief of the bodyguard, and, when they came, he ordered them to take with them the prophet Nathan and the soldiers about the court, and, after mounting his son Solomon upon the royal mule, to lead him outside the city to the spring called Geiōn,[b] anoint him with the holy oil, and proclaim him king. This he commanded the high priest Sadok and the prophet Nathan to do. And he ordered them to accompany him through the midst of the city, blowing horns and shouting, " May King Solomon sit upon the royal throne for ever ! " [c] in order that all the people might know that he had been declared

David orders Zadok and Nathan to anoint Solomon.
1 Kings i. 32.

[a] Scripture merely says that, after Nathan's speech, David summoned Bath-sheba, and does not indicate at precisely what moment she had left his presence. Her leaving upon Nathan's entrance was probably in accord with oriental etiquette. One medieval Jewish commentator explains that Bath-sheba had left in order to avoid any appearance of collusion with Nathan.

[b] The LXX form of bibl. Gihon (Heb. *Giḥôn*), by some scholars identified with *'Ain Sitti Maryam* " Fountain of the Virgin Mary " in the valley of Kidron, S.E. of Jerusalem, *c.* ½ mile N. of *Bir 'Ayyûb* the supposed site of En-rogel mentioned above in § 347 note.

[c] Bibl. " (Long) live king Solomon " (A.V. " God save king Solomon ").

βασιλέα, Σολομῶνι δ' ἐντετάλθαι περὶ τῆς ἀρχῆς, ἵνα εὐσεβῶς καὶ δικαίως προστῇ τοῦ τε Ἑβραίων
357 ἔθνους παντὸς καὶ τῆς Ἰούδα φυλῆς. Βαναία δὲ εὐξαμένου τὸν θεὸν Σολομῶνι εὐμενῆ γενέσθαι μηδὲ μικρὸν διαλιπόντες ἀναβιβάζουσιν ἐπὶ τὴν ἡμίονον τὸν Σολομῶνα, καὶ προαγαγόντες ἔξω τῆς πόλεως ἐπὶ τὴν πηγὴν καὶ τῷ ἐλαίῳ χρίσαντες εἰσήγαγον εἰς τὴν πόλιν ἐπευφημοῦντες καὶ τὴν βασιλείαν
358 αὐτῷ γενέσθαι πολυχρόνιον εὐχόμενοι, καὶ παραγαγόντες εἰς τὸν οἶκον τὸν βασιλικὸν καθίζουσιν αὐτὸν ἐπὶ τοῦ θρόνου, καὶ πᾶς ὁ λαὸς ἐπ' εὐωχίαν εὐθὺς ἐτράπη καὶ ἑορτὴν χορεύων καὶ αὐλοῖς τερπόμενος, ὡς ὑπὸ τοῦ πλήθους τῶν ὀργάνων ἅπασαν περιηχεῖσθαι τὴν γῆν καὶ τὸν ἀέρα.
359 (6) Ὡς δ' ᾔσθοντο τῆς βοῆς Ἀδωνίας τε καὶ οἱ παρόντες ἐπὶ τὸ δεῖπνον ἐταράχθησαν, ὅ τε στρατηγὸς Ἰώαβος ἔλεγεν οὐκ ἀρέσκεσθαι τοῖς ἤχοις οὐδὲ τῇ σάλπιγγι· παρακειμένου δὲ τοῦ δείπνου καὶ μηδενὸς γευομένου πάντων δ' ἐπ' ἐννοίας ὑπαρχόντων, εἰστρέχει πρὸς αὐτοὺς ὁ τοῦ ἀρχιερέως
360 Ἀβιαθάρου παῖς Ἰωνάθης. τοῦ δ' Ἀδωνία θεασαμένου τὸν νεανίαν ἡδέως καὶ προσειπόντος ἀγαθῶν[1] ἄγγελον, ἐδήλου πάντ' αὐτοῖς τὰ περὶ τὸν Σολομῶνα

[1] ex Lat. Niese: ἀγαθὸν codd.

[a] These instructions are an amplification of 1 Kings i. 35. The infinitive ἐντετάλθαι is here to be taken, as elsewhere in Josephus, as a finite verb, the indirect discourse after προσέταξε "ordered" being carelessly continued, *cf.* LXX ἐγὼ ἐνετειλάμην (Luc. αὐτῷ ἐντελοῦμαι) τοῦ εἶναι εἰς ἡγούμενον ἐπὶ Ἰσραὴλ καὶ Ἰουδά; Heb. "I have appointed him to be ruler over Israel and Judah." Weill, taking ἐντετάλθαι as a continuation of David's order to Zadok and Nathan, understands it to mean that they were to give the instructions about the kingdom to Solomon; he remarks "this last

king by his father. He then gave instructions to Solomon,[a] concerning the kingdom, in order that he might rule with piety and justice over all the Hebrew nation and the tribe of Judah. Then, after Banaias prayed that God might be gracious to Solomon, without delaying a moment they mounted Solomon upon the mule, escorted him to the spring outside the city, and anointed him with the oil; then they brought him into the city with acclamations, praying that his reign would be a long one, and, having conducted him to the royal dwelling, they seated him upon the throne.[b] And all the people gave themselves over to feasting and merrymaking with dancing and joyful playing of pipes, so that the multitude of their instruments caused the whole earth and the air to resound.

Solomon is acclaimed by the people. 1 Kings i. 36.

(6) When Adōnias and those present at the dinner heard this noise, they were thrown into confusion, and the commander Joab said that he was uneasy about the shouting and the trumpet blast; and, with the dinner before them, which no one tasted,[c] all being occupied with their thoughts, there came running to them the high priest Abiathar's son Jonathan. Adōnias was very glad to see the youth and called him a messenger of good tidings, but, when he told them all about Solomon and the decision

Adonijah, deserted by his friends, asks forgiveness of Solomon. 1 Kings i. 41.

detail is added by Josephus and has often been misunderstood." It appears that Weill himself has misunderstood the construction and has overlooked the reference to 1 Kings i. 35; *cf.* also § 384.

[b] A detail added from Jonathan's report to Adonijah, 1 Kings i. 46.

[c] According to Scripture they had finished eating when they heard the shouting, but perhaps Josephus understood the Heb. *killû le'ekōl* "they had finished eating" differently, *cf.* Targum *sappiqû* "they had enough."

καὶ τὴν Δαυίδου τοῦ βασιλέως γνώμην· ἀναπηδήσαντες δ' ἐκ τοῦ συμποσίου ὅ τε Ἀδωνίας καὶ οἱ κεκλημένοι πάντες ἔφυγον πρὸς ἑαυτοὺς ἕκαστοι.
361 φοβηθεὶς δ' Ἀδωνίας τὸν βασιλέα περὶ τῶν γεγονότων ἱκέτης γίνεται τοῦ θεοῦ καὶ τῶν τοῦ θυσιαστηρίου κεράτων ἃ δὴ προεῖχεν ἐλλαβόμενος δηλοῦται τοῦτο Σολομῶνι πεποιηκὼς καὶ πίστεις ἀξιῶν παρ' αὐτοῦ λαβεῖν, ὥστε μὴ μνησικακῆσαι μηδ'
362 ἐργάσασθαι δεινὸν αὐτὸν μηδέν. ὁ δὲ ἡμέρως πάνυ καὶ σωφρόνως τῆς μὲν τότε ἁμαρτίας αὐτὸν ἀφῆκεν ἀθῷον, εἰπὼν δέ, εἰ ληφθείη τι πάλιν καινοποιῶν, ἑαυτῷ αἴτιον τῆς τιμωρίας ἔσεσθαι, πέμψας ἀνίστησιν αὐτὸν ἀπὸ τῆς ἱκεσίας· ἐλθόντα δὲ πρὸς αὐτὸν[1] καὶ προσκυνήσαντα εἰς τὴν ἰδίαν οἰκίαν ἀπελθεῖν ἐκέλευσε μηδὲν ὑφορώμενον καὶ τοῦ λοιποῦ παρέχειν αὑτὸν ἀγαθὸν ὡς αὐτῷ τοῦτο συμφέρον ἠξίου.

363 (7) Βουλόμενος δὲ Δαυίδης ἐπὶ παντὸς τοῦ λαοῦ ἀποδεῖξαι τὸν υἱὸν βασιλέα συγκαλεῖ τοὺς ἄρχοντας εἰς Ἱεροσόλυμα καὶ τοὺς ἱερεῖς καὶ τοὺς Ληουίτας. ἐξαριθμήσας δὲ τούτους πρῶτον εὑρίσκει τῶν ἀπὸ τριάκοντα ἐτῶν ἕως πεντήκοντα τρισμυρίους ὀκτα-
364 κισχιλίους. ἐξ ὧν ἀπέδειξεν ἐπιμελητὰς μὲν τῆς οἰκοδομίας τοῦ ναοῦ δισμυρίους τετρακισχιλίους,[2] κριτὰς δὲ τοῦ λαοῦ καὶ γραμματεῖς τούτων ἑξακισχιλίους, πυλωροὺς δὲ τετρακισχιλίους[3] καὶ τοσούτους ὑμνῳδοὺς τοῦ θεοῦ ᾄδοντας τοῖς ὀργάνοις οἷς
365 Δαυίδης κατεσκεύασε, καθὼς προειρήκαμεν. δι-

[1] πρὸς αὐτὸν om. RO. [2] τρισχιλίους MSP Lat.
[3] + τοῦ οἴκου τοῦ θεοῦ MSP Lat.

[a] Lit. " from his supplication " ; bibl. " from the altar," LXX ἀπάνωθεν (Luc. ἀπὸ) τοῦ θυσιαστηρίου. [b] The Levites.

of King David, Adōnias and all the guests sprang up from the banquet table and fled, each to his own home. And Adōnias, being afraid of the king because of what he had done, became a suppliant to God and grasped the horns of the altar,—that is, its projections; and this act of his was reported to Solomon, and also that he had asked to have a pledge from him that he would bear him no malice and do him no harm. Solomon with great mildness and moderation let him off this time without punishment for his offence, but said that if he were ever again caught in an attempt at revolution, he would have himself to blame for his punishment; then he sent men to remove him from his place of sanctuary,[a] and, when he came before him and did obeisance, Solomon ordered him to go back to his own house without any fear, and requested him to conduct himself well in future, as this would be to his own advantage.

(7) Then David, wishing to appoint his son king over all the people, summoned to Jerusalem the chiefs and the priests and Levites, and, having first numbered these,[b] he found that there were thirty-eight thousand of them between the ages of thirty and fifty[c] years. Twenty-four thousand of them he appointed as overseers of the building of the temple, six thousand as judges of the people and as scribes,[d] four thousand as gatekeepers, and an equal number to sing the praises of God to the accompaniment of the instruments which David had made, as we said

David divides priests and Levites into courses. 1 Chron. xxiii. 1.

[c] 1 Chron. xxiii. 3 " from the age of thirty years and upward "; verses 24, 27 " from the age of twenty years and upward." The upper limit of 50 years is derived from Num. iv. 3 f., viii. 25.

[d] So LXX; bibl. " officers "; the Heb. *shôterîm* probably included scribes.

εμέρισε δ' αὐτοὺς καὶ κατὰ πατριὰς καὶ χωρίσας ἐκ τῆς φυλῆς τοὺς ἱερεῖς εὗρε τούτων εἴκοσι τέσσαρας πατριάς, ἐκ μὲν τῆς Ἐλεαζάρου οἰκίας ἑκκαίδεκα, ἐκ δὲ τῆς Ἰθαμάρου ὀκτώ, διέταξέ τε μίαν πατριὰν διακονεῖσθαι τῷ θεῷ ἐπὶ ἡμέρας ὀκτὼ ἀπὸ σαβ-
366 βάτου ἐπὶ σάββατον. καὶ οὕτως αἱ πατριαὶ πᾶσαι διεκληρώσαντο Δαυίδου παρόντος καὶ Σαδώκου καὶ Ἀβιαθάρου τῶν ἀρχιερέων καὶ πάντων τῶν ἀρχόντων· καὶ ἡ πρώτη μὲν ἀναβᾶσα πατριὰ ἐγράφη πρώτη, ἡ δὲ δευτέρα ἀκολούθως ἄχρι τῶν εἴκοσι τεσσάρων· καὶ διέμεινεν οὗτος ὁ μερισμὸς ἄχρι τῆς
367 σήμερον ἡμέρας. ἐποίησε δὲ καὶ τῆς Ληουίτιδος φυλῆς εἴκοσι μέρη καὶ τέσσαρα καὶ κληρωσαμένων κατὰ τὸν αὐτὸν ἀνέβησαν τρόπον ταῖς τῶν ἱερέων ἐφημερίσιν ἐπὶ ἡμέρας ὀκτώ. τοὺς δ' ἀπογόνους τοὺς Μωυσέος ἐτίμησεν· ἐποίησε γὰρ αὐτοὺς φύλακας τῶν θησαυρῶν τοῦ θεοῦ καὶ τῶν ἀναθημάτων, ἃ συνέβη τοὺς βασιλεῖς ἀναθεῖναι· διέταξε δὲ πᾶσι τοῖς ἐκ τῆς Ληουίτιδος φυλῆς καὶ τοῖς ἱερεῦσι δουλεύειν κατὰ νύκτα καὶ ἡμέραν τῷ θεῷ, καθὼς αὐτοῖς ἐπέστειλε Μωυσῆς.

368 (8) Μετὰ ταῦτα διεμέρισε πᾶσαν[1] τὴν στρατιὰν εἰς δώδεκα μοίρας σὺν ἡγεμόσι καὶ ἑκατοντάρχοις καὶ ταξιάρχοις. εἶχεν δ' ἑκάστη τῶν μοιρῶν δισμυρίους καὶ τετρακισχιλίους, ὧν ἐκέλευσε προσεδρεύειν κατὰ τριάκονθ' ἡμέρας ἀπὸ τῆς πρώτης ἕως τῆς ὑστάτης Σολομῶνι τῷ βασιλεῖ σὺν τοῖς

[1] πᾶσαν om. RO.

[a] § 306.

[b] Of Levi.

[c] These are grouped by Josephus, in *Ap.* ii. 108, into fou

before.[a] He then divided them into families, and, after separating the priests from the rest of the tribe,[b] he found that of these there were twenty-four families,[c] sixteen of the house of Eleazar and eight of the house of Ithamar; he further arranged that one family should minister to God each week from Sabbath to Sabbath.[d] Now this is the way in which all the families drew lots in the presence of David and the high priests Sadok and Abiathar and all the chiefs: the family which came out first in the drawing was inscribed as the first to serve, and the second similarly, and so with all twenty-four. And this apportionment has lasted down to this day. He also divided the tribe of Levites into twenty-four parts, and, according to the order in which the lots were drawn, they were chosen for a week, in the same manner as the priestly courses. And he honoured the descendants of Moses by making them keepers of the treasury of God and of such offerings as the kings had made.[e] He also ordained that all those of the tribe of Levites and the priests should serve God night and day, as Moses had enjoined them.

1 Chron. xxiv. 3.

1 Chron. xxvi. 24.

(8) After this, he divided the army into twelve divisions with their leaders, captains of hundreds and lower officers,[f] each division having twenty-four thousand men, whom he ordered to be in attendance on Solomon for thirty days at a time, from the first day of the month until the last, together with their

Regulation of the army and treasury. 1 Chron. xxvii. 1.

priestly classes (Schürer suspects a corruption of 24 to 4); in *Vita* 2 he mentions only the 24 courses (ἐφημερίδες), as here.

[d] This weekly alternation, not mentioned in Scripture, is found in the Mishnah and represents the arrangement in use in Josephus's time.

[e] *Cf.* § 379 note.

[f] Lit. "taxiarchs," *cf.* § 26 note; bibl. "captains of thousands and of hundreds and their officers (LXX γραμματεῖς)."

369 χιλιάρχοις καὶ ἑκατοντάρχοις. κατέστησε δὲ καὶ ἄρχοντα ἑκάστης μοίρας ὃν ἀγαθὸν ᾔδει καὶ δίκαιον, ἐπιτρόπους τε τῶν θησαυρῶν καὶ κωμῶν καὶ ἀγρῶν ἄλλους καὶ κτηνῶν, ὧν οὐκ ἀναγκαῖον ἡγησάμην μνησθῆναι τῶν ὀνομάτων.

370 (9) Ὡς δ᾿ ἕκαστα τούτων κατὰ τὸν προειρημένον διέταξε τρόπον, εἰς ἐκκλησίαν συγκαλέσας τοὺς ἄρχοντας τῶν Ἑβραίων καὶ τοὺς φυλάρχους καὶ τοὺς ἡγεμόνας τῶν διαιρέσεων καὶ τοὺς ἐπὶ πάσης πράξεως ἢ κτήσεως τοῦ βασιλέως τεταγμένους, στὰς ἐφ᾿ ὑψηλοτάτου βήματος ὁ βασιλεὺς ἔλεξε

371 πρὸς τὸ πλῆθος· "ἀδελφοὶ καὶ ὁμοεθνεῖς, γινώσκειν ὑμᾶς βούλομαι ὅτι ναὸν οἰκοδομῆσαι τῷ θεῷ διανοηθεὶς χρυσόν τε πολὺν παρεσκευασάμην καὶ ἀργύρου ταλάντων μυριάδας δέκα, ὁ δὲ θεὸς ἐκώλυσέ με διὰ τοῦ προφήτου Νάθα διά τε τοὺς ὑπὲρ ὑμῶν πολέμους καὶ τὸ[1] φόνῳ τῶν ἐχθρῶν μεμιάνθαι τὴν δεξιάν, τὸν δὲ υἱὸν ἐκέλευσε τὸν διαδεξόμενον

372 τὴν βασιλείαν κατασκευάσαι τὸν ναὸν αὐτῷ. νῦν οὖν ἐπεὶ καὶ τῷ προγόνῳ ἡμῶν Ἰακώβῳ δυοκαίδεκα παίδων γενομένων ἴστε τὸν Ἰούδαν ἀποδειχθέντα βασιλέα, καὶ ἐμὲ τῶν ἀδελφῶν ἓξ ὄντων προκριθέντα καὶ τὴν ἡγεμονίαν λαβόντα παρὰ τοῦ θεοῦ καὶ μηδένα τούτων[2] δυσχεράναντα, οὕτως ἀξιῶ κἀγὼ τοὺς ἐμαυτοῦ παῖδας μὴ στασιάζειν πρὸς ἀλλήλους Σολομῶνος τὴν βασιλείαν παρειληφότος, ἀλλ᾿ ἐπισταμένους ὡς ὁ θεὸς αὐτὸν ἐξελέξατο

373 φέρειν ἡδέως αὐτὸν δεσπότην. οὐ δεινὸν γὰρ θεοῦ

[1] τῷ MS[1]. [2] τούτῳ Bekker.

[a] Their names are given in 1 Chron. xxvii. 25 ff.

[b] Heb. "and David the king stood upon his feet," LXX καὶ ἔστη Δαυίδης ἐν μέσῳ τῆς ἐκκλησίας.

captains of thousands and captains of hundreds. He also appointed as chief of each division a man whom he knew to be brave and just; others he made custodians of the treasuries and of the villages, fields and cattle, but I have not thought it necessary to mention their names.[a]

(9) When he had arranged each of these matters in the above manner, the king convoked an assembly of the heads of the Hebrews and the tribal chiefs and the leaders of the (military) divisions and those in charge of any of the king's affairs or property, and, standing upon a very high tribune,[b] he addressed the gathering as follows: "Brothers and fellow-countrymen, I wish you to know that with the intention of building a temple to God I collected a great quantity of gold and one hundred thousand talents of silver[c]; but God, through the prophet Nathan,[d] has kept me from doing so, because of the wars I have fought on your behalf and because my hand is stained with the blood of the enemy, and He has commanded my son, who will succeed to my throne, to build the temple to Him. Now since, of our forefather Jacob's twelve sons, it was Judah, as you know, who was appointed king, and since I was preferred to my six brothers and received the sovereignty from God without complaint from any of them, I, in turn, ask that my sons similarly refrain from civil dissension, now that Solomon has received the kingship, and, in recognition of the fact that God has chosen him, cheerfully accept him as their lord. For it is not such a terrible thing to serve

David commends Solomon to the people. 1 Chron. xxviii. 1.

[c] Bibl. "and had made ready for the building"; no amount of money is specified at this point in Scripture.

[d] Nathan is not mentioned at this point in Scripture, 1 Chron. xxviii. 3, which has, "But God said unto me, Thou shalt not build," etc.

θέλοντος οὐδ' ἀλλοτρίῳ κρατοῦντι δουλεύειν, χαίρειν δ' ἐπ' ἀδελφῷ ταύτης τυχόντι τῆς τιμῆς προσῆκεν ὡς κοινωνοῦντας αὐτῆς. εὔχομαι δὴ τὰς ὑποσχέσεις τοῦ θεοῦ παρελθεῖν εἰς τέλος καὶ τὴν εὐδαιμονίαν ταύτην ἀνὰ πᾶσαν τὴν χώραν σπαρῆναι καὶ τὸν ἅπαντα ταύτῃ παραμεῖναι χρόνον, ἣν αὐτὸς ἐπηγγείλατο παρέξειν ἐπὶ Σολομῶνος βασιλέως.
374 ἔσται δὲ ταῦτα βέβαια καὶ καλὸν ἕξει πέρας, ἂν εὐσεβῆ καὶ δίκαιον σαυτὸν[1] καὶ φύλακα τῶν πατρίων παρέχῃς[2] νόμων, ὦ τέκνον· εἰ δὲ μή, τὰ χείρω προσδόκα[3] ταῦτα παραβαίνων."

375 (10) Ὁ μὲν οὖν βασιλεὺς τούτους ποιησάμενος τοὺς λόγους ἐπαύσατο, τὴν δὲ[4] διαγραφὴν καὶ διάταξιν τῆς οἰκοδομίας τοῦ ναοῦ πάντων ὁρώντων ἔδωκε Σολομῶνι θεμελίων καὶ οἴκων καὶ ὑπερῴων, ὅσοι τε τὸ πλῆθος καὶ πηλίκοι τὸ ὕψος καὶ τὸ εὖρος γένοιντο, ὅσα τε σκεύη χρυσᾶ καὶ ἀργυρᾶ
376 τούτων τὸν σταθμὸν ὥρισε. προσπαρώρμησε δὲ καὶ λόγοις αὐτόν τε πάσῃ χρήσασθαι προθυμίᾳ περὶ τὸ ἔργον καὶ τοὺς ἄρχοντας καὶ τὴν Ληουιτῶν φυλὴν συναγωνίσασθαι διά τε τὴν ἡλικίαν καὶ διὰ τὸ τὸν θεὸν ἐκεῖνον ἑλέσθαι καὶ τῆς οἰκοδομίας τοῦ
377 ναοῦ καὶ τῆς βασιλείας προστάτην. εὐμαρῆ δ' αὐτοῖς καὶ οὐ σφόδρα ἐπίπονον τὴν οἰκοδομίαν ἀπέφαινεν αὐτοῦ πολλὰ μὲν τάλαντα χρυσοῦ πλείω δ' ἀργύρου καὶ ξύλα καὶ τεκτόνων πλῆθος καὶ λατόμων ἤδη παρεσκευασμένου σμαράγδου τε καὶ
378 πάσης ἰδέας λίθου πολυτελοῦς· καὶ νῦν δ' ἔτι τῆς ἰδίας ἀπαρχὴν[5] διακονίας ἄλλα τρισχίλια τάλαντα

[1] αὐτὸν RO: αὑτὸν Niese.
[2] παρέχῃ RO. [3] προσδοκάτω RO. [4] τε RO.
[5] Niese: ἀπαρχῆς ROSP: ἀρχῆς M: primitias Lat. (unde ἀπαρχὰς conj. Niese).

even a foreign master, if God so wills, and, when it is one's brother to whom this honour has fallen, one should rejoice at having a share in it.[a] I pray, then, that the promises of God will be fulfilled and that the prosperity which He Himself has declared He will send during Solomon's reign will be diffused throughout the entire land and continue with it for all time. These things will be assured and will come to a happy issue, if you show yourself to be pious and just, my son, and an observer of our country's laws. Otherwise, if you transgress them, you must expect a worse fate."

David gives Solomon the plans of the temple. 1 Chron. xxviii. 11.

(10) Such, then, was the address which the king made, and, when he had finished, he gave to Solomon, in the sight of all, the plan and arrangement of the building of the temple, the foundations, chambers and upper rooms, showing how many there were to be and of what height and breadth, and also fixing the weight of the gold and silver vessels. Then he spoke again, further exhorting him to show the utmost zeal in the work, and also the chiefs and the tribe of Levites to assist Solomon in the labour, because of his youth and because God had chosen him to preside over the building of the temple and over the kingdom. He also made clear to them that the building would be easy for them and not very difficult, because he had already secured many talents of gold and more of silver, and wood and a host of carpenters and stonecutters, as well as emeralds[b] and precious stones of every kind. Moreover he said that he would give as his private offering[c] for the service an additional

1 Chron. xxix. 1.

[a] This part of David's speech is amplified by Josephus.

[b] Heb. *shōham* (A.V. "onyx"), LXX *σόομ*, Luc. (λίθους) ὄνυχος.

[c] Text doubtful.

χρυσοῦ καθαροῦ παρέξειν ἔλεγεν εἰς τὸ ἄδυτον καὶ εἰς τὸ ἅρμα τοῦ θεοῦ τοὺς Χερουβεῖς, οὓς ἐφεστάναι δεήσει τὴν κιβωτὸν καλύπτοντας. σιωπήσαντος δὲ τοῦ Δαυίδου πολλὴ καὶ τῶν ἀρχόντων καὶ τῶν ἱερέων καὶ τῆς Ληουίτιδος φυλῆς προθυμία συμβαλλομένων καὶ ποιουμένων ἐπαγγελίας λαμπρὰς καὶ
379 μεγαλοπρεπεῖς ἐγένετο· χρυσοῦ μὲν γὰρ ὑπέστησαν εἰσοίσειν τάλαντα πεντακισχίλια καὶ στατῆρας μυρίους, ἀργύρου δὲ μύρια τάλαντα, καὶ σιδήρου μυριάδας ταλάντων πολλάς· καὶ εἴ τινι λίθος ἦν πολυτελὴς ἐκόμισε καὶ παρέδωκεν εἰς τοὺς θησαυρούς, ὧν ἐπετρόπευεν[1] ὁ Μωυσέος ἔκγονος Ἴαλος.

380 (11) Ἐπὶ τούτοις ἥσθη τε ὁ λαὸς ἅπας, καὶ Δαυίδης τὴν σπουδὴν καὶ τὴν φιλοτιμίαν τῶν ἀρχόντων καὶ ἱερέων καὶ τῶν ἄλλων ἁπάντων ὁρῶν, τὸν θεὸν εὐλογεῖν ἤρξατο, μεγάλῃ βοῇ πατέρα τε καὶ γένεσιν τῶν ὅλων ἀποκαλῶν καὶ δημιουργὸν ἀνθρωπίνων καὶ θείων, οἷς αὐτὸν ἐκόσμησε, προστάτην τε καὶ κηδεμόνα γένους τῶν Ἑβραίων καὶ τῆς τούτων εὐδαιμονίας ἧς τε αὐτῷ βασιλείας ἔδωκεν.
381 ἐπὶ τούτοις εὐξάμενος τῷ τε παντὶ λαῷ τὰ ἀγαθὰ καὶ τῷ παιδὶ Σολομῶνι διάνοιαν ὑγιῆ καὶ δικαίαν καὶ πᾶσι τοῖς τῆς ἀρετῆς μέρεσιν ἐρρωμένην, ἐκέλευσε καὶ τὸ πλῆθος εὐλογεῖν τὸν θεόν. καὶ οἱ μὲν πεσόντες ἐπὶ τὴν γῆν προσεκύνησαν, εὐχαρίστησαν δὲ καὶ Δαυίδῃ περὶ πάντων ὧν αὐτοῦ τὴν βασιλείαν

[1] Niese: ἐπετρόπευσεν codd.

---

[a] Scripture adds, "and seven thousand talents of refined silver."

[b] The priests and Levites are not included among the contributors in Scripture.

[c] Heb. *'adarkônîm* (A.V. "drams"), LXX χρυσοῦς. The *'adarkôn* was the Persian daric, which the Greeks called

three thousand talents of pure gold [a] for the shrine and for the chariot of God, the Cherubim, which were to be placed upon the ark as a covering. And, when David had done, the chiefs and priests and the tribe of Levites [b] showed great eagerness in contributing and making offers of splendid and magnificent gifts; they undertook to bring in five thousand talents and ten thousand staters [c] of gold, ten thousand talents of silver, and many tens of thousands of talents of iron [d]; and whoever had a precious stone brought it and gave it to the treasury, of which Ialos,[e] the descendant of Moses, had charge.

1 Chron. xxviii. 18.

David's prayer for Solomon. 1 Chron. xxix. 9.

(11) At this all the people rejoiced, and David, seeing the zeal and rivalry in giving of the chiefs and priests and all the others, began to bless God in a loud voice, addressing Him as father and source of the universe, as creator of things human and divine, with which He had adorned Himself, and as the protector and guardian of the Hebrew race and of its prosperity and of the kingdom which He had given him. Thereupon he prayed for the happiness of all the people and that his son Solomon might have a sound and just mind, strengthened by all virtuous qualities [f]; and then he commanded the multitude also to bless God. And so they fell upon the ground and prostrated themselves; and they also gave thanks to David for all the blessings they had en-

στατὴρ δαρεικός—hence Josephus's στατῆρας. This Persian coin was, of course, not in use until long after the time of David, and the passage in 1 Chron. is therefore a late addition.

[d] Bibl. "of bronze (A.V. "brass") eighteen thousand talents and one hundred thousand talents of iron."

[e] Bibl. Jehiel (Heb. *Yeḥî'ēl*), LXX Ἰειήλ; he is called a Gershonite, 1 Chron. xxix. 8.

[f] Josephus briefly summarizes David's prayer, 1 Chron. xxix. 11-19.

382 παραλαβόντος ἀπέλαυσαν. τῇ δ' ἐπιούσῃ θυσίας τῷ θεῷ παρέστησαν μόσχους χιλίους καὶ κριοὺς τοσούτους καὶ χιλίους ἀμνούς, οὓς ὡλοκαύτωσαν· ἔθυσαν δὲ καὶ τὰς εἰρηνικὰς θυσίας, πολλὰς μυριάδας ἱερείων κατασφάξαντες. καὶ δι' ὅλης τῆς ἡμέρας ἑώρτασεν ὁ βασιλεὺς σὺν παντὶ τῷ λαῷ, καὶ Σολομῶνα δεύτερον ἔχρισαν τῷ ἐλαίῳ καὶ ἀπέδειξαν αὐτὸν βασιλέα καὶ Σάδωκον ἀρχιερέα τῆς πληθύος ἁπάσης. εἴς τε τὸ βασίλειον ἀγαγόντες Σολομῶνα καὶ καθίσαντες αὐτὸν ἐπὶ θρόνου τοῦ πατρῴου ἀπ' ἐκείνης τῆς ἡμέρας ὑπήκουον αὐτῷ.

383 (xv. 1) Μετ' ὀλίγον δὲ χρόνον ὁ Δαυίδης καταπεσὼν εἰς νόσον ὑπὸ γήρως καὶ συνειδὼς ὅτι μέλλει τελευτᾶν καλέσας τὸν υἱὸν Σολομῶνα διελέχθη πρὸς αὐτὸν τοιάδε· "ἐγὼ μέν, ὦ τέκνον, εἰς τὸ χρεὼν ἤδη καὶ πατέρας τοὺς ἐμοὺς ἀπαλλάσσομαι κοινὴν ὁδὸν ἁπάντων τῶν τε νῦν ὄντων καὶ τῶν ἐσομένων πορευόμενος, ἐξ ἧς οὐκέτι οἷόν τε ἐπανελ-
384 θόντα γνῶναι τί κατὰ τὸν βίον πράττεται. διὸ ζῶν ἔτι καὶ πρὸς αὐτῷ γεγονὼς[1] τῷ τελευτᾶν παραινῶ σοι ταῦθ' ἃ καὶ πρότερον ἔφθην συμβουλεύσας, δικαίῳ μὲν εἶναι πρὸς τοὺς ἀρχομένους, εὐσεβεῖ δὲ πρὸς τὸν τὴν βασιλείαν δεδωκότα θεόν, φυλάττειν δ' αὐτοῦ τὰς ἐντολὰς καὶ τοὺς νόμους, οὓς αὐτὸς διὰ Μωυσέος κατέπεμψεν ἡμῖν, καὶ μήτε χάριτι μήτε θωπείᾳ μήτ' ἐπιθυμίᾳ μήτε ἄλλῳ πάθει προσ-
385 τιθέμενον τούτων ἀμελῆσαι· τὴν γὰρ τοῦ θείου πρὸς σαυτὸν[2] εὔνοιαν ἀπολεῖς παραβάς τι τῶν νομίμων[3]

[1] + ὄντως M: + ἄρτι SP: iam constitutus Lat.
[2] ed. pr.: αὐτὸν ROMP: αὑτὸν S.
[3] τι τῶν νομίμων] τὰ νόμιμα MSP Lat.

joyed since he had succeeded to the throne. And, on the following day, they presented to God as sacrifices a thousand calves and as many rams and a thousand lambs, which they gave as burnt-offerings; they also sacrificed many peace-offerings, and slaughtered many tens of thousands of victims.[a] And throughout the whole day the king feasted with all the people, and they anointed Solomon with oil a second time and proclaimed him king, with Sadok as high priest of the entire nation. And they led Solomon to the palace and seated him upon his father's throne, and from that day forth they were obedient to him.

Feast in honour of Solomon's accession. 1 Chron. xxix. 21.

(xv. 1) Now a little while after this, David fell ill by reason of old age, and, realizing that he was about to die, he called his son Solomon and spoke to him as follows: "I am now, my son, going to my destiny and must depart to my fathers and travel the common road of all men now alive or yet to be, from which no one can ever return to learn what is happening among the living. Therefore, while I am still alive, though very close to death, I exhort you, in the same manner as when I counselled you once before,[b] to be just toward your subjects and pious toward God, who has given you the kingship, and to keep His commandments and laws, which He Himself sent down to us by Moses; do not neglect them by yielding either to favour or flattery or lust or any other passion, for you will lose the goodwill of the Deity toward you, if you transgress any of His ordinances, and you will

David's dying charge to Solomon. 1 Kings ii. 1

[a] In addition to these burnt-offerings with their drink-offerings, Scripture mentions only "sacrifices in abundance"; these sacrifices would naturally be peace-offerings, as Josephus supposes.

[b] *Cf.* § 356 note.

καὶ πρὸς τἀναντί'[1] αὐτοῦ τὴν ἀγαθὴν ἀποστρέψεις πρόνοιαν· τοιοῦτον δὲ σαυτὸν παρέχων, ὁποῖον εἶναί τε δεῖ κἀγὼ δὲ παρακαλῶ, καθέξεις ἡμῶν τὴν βασιλείαν τῷ γένει καὶ οἶκος ἄλλος Ἑβραίων οὐκ ἂν δεσπόσειεν, ἀλλ' ἡμεῖς αὐτοὶ διὰ τοῦ παντὸς
386 αἰῶνος. μέμνησο δὲ καὶ τῆς Ἰωάβου τοῦ στρατηγοῦ παρανομίας ἀποκτείναντος διὰ ζηλοτυπίαν δύο στρατηγοὺς δικαίους καὶ ἀγαθούς, Ἀβεννῆρόν τε τὸν Νήρου παῖδα καὶ τὸν Ἀμασᾶν υἱὸν Ἰέθρα· ὧν[2] ὅπως ἄν σοι δόξῃ τὸν θάνατον ἐκδίκησον, ἐπεὶ καὶ κρείττων ἐμοῦ καὶ δυνατώτερος ὁ Ἰώαβος ὢν μέχρι
387 νῦν τὴν δίκην διέφυγε. παρατίθεμαι δέ σοι καὶ τοὺς Βερζέλου τοῦ Γαλαδίτου παῖδας, οὓς ἐν τιμῇ πάσῃ καὶ προνοίᾳ τοῦτ' ἐμοὶ χαριζόμενος ἕξεις· οὐ προκατάρχομεν γὰρ εὐποιίας, ἀλλ' ἀμοιβὴν ὧν ὁ πατὴρ αὐτῶν παρὰ τὴν φυγὴν ὑπῆρξέ μοι χρεο-
388 λυτοῦμεν. καὶ τὸν Γήρα δὲ υἱὸν Σουμούιν τὸν ἐκ τῆς Βενιαμίτιδος φυλῆς, ὃς πολλὰ βλασφημήσας με παρὰ τὴν φυγήν, ὅτ' εἰς Παρεμβολὰς ἐπορευόμην, ἀπήντησεν ἐπὶ τὸν Ἰόρδανον καὶ πίστεις ἔλαβεν ὡς μηδὲν αὐτὸν παθεῖν τότε, νῦν ἐπιζητήσας αἰτίαν εὔλογον ἄμυνα.[3]"

389 (2) Ταῦτα παραινέσας τῷ παιδὶ περί τε τῶν ὅλων πραγμάτων καὶ περὶ τῶν φίλων καὶ οὓς ᾔδει τιμωρίας ἀξίους γεγενημένους ἀπέθανεν ἔτη μὲν βιώσας ἑβδομήκοντα, βασιλεύσας δὲ ἑπτὰ μὲν ἐν Χεβρῶνι τῆς Ἰούδα φυλῆς καὶ μῆνας ἕξ, ἐν Ἱεροσολύμοις δὲ ἁπάσης τῆς χώρας τρία καὶ τριάκοντα
390 οὗτος ἄριστος ἀνὴρ ἐγένετο καὶ πᾶσαν ἀρετὴν ἔχων

[1] Niese: ἅπαντ' codd.
[2] Ἰέθρα· ὧν ex Lat. Niese: Ἰεθράων RO: Ἰεθράνου MSP.
[3] ἄμυνε ROSP[1].

turn His kind watchfulness into a hostile attitude.[a] But, if you show yourself to be such as you should be and as I urge you to be, you will secure the kingdom to our line, and no other house than we shall be lords over the Hebrews for all time. Remember also the crime of Joab, the commander, who, because of envy, killed two just and brave generals, Abenner, the son of Ner, and Amasa, the son of Jethras, and, in whatever way you may think best, avenge their deaths; for Joab, being stronger and more powerful than I, has until now escaped punishment. But I commend to you the sons of Berzelos the Galadite, whom you shall hold in all honour and care for, and thus gratify me; for in this matter we are not the first to show kindness, but are repaying the debt owed them for their father's service to me during my exile. And as for Sūmūis,[b] the son of Gēra, of the tribe of Benjamin, who cursed me repeatedly during my flight, on the way to The Camps, and, when he met me at the Jordan, received a pledge that he would suffer no harm for the time being,—look now for a reasonable pretext to punish him."

David's instructions concerning his enemies and friends. 1 Kings ii. 5.

(2) With these recommendations to his son concerning the state and his friends and those whom he knew to be deserving of punishment, David died at the age of seventy, having reigned seven years and six months[c] in Hebron, over the tribe of Judah, and thirty-three years in Jerusalem, over the entire country. He was a most excellent[d] man and pos-

Death of David. 1 Kings ii. 10.

[a] Emended text; MSS. "you will altogether alienate His kind watchfulness."

[b] Called Samuis in § 207; bibl. Shimei.

[c] 1 Kings has only 7 years for David's reign in Hebron; the figure given by Josephus is found in 2 Sam. v. 5.

[d] Or "very brave."

ἣν ἔδει τῷ βασιλεῖ καὶ τοσούτων ἐθνῶν σωτηρίαν
ἐγκεχειρισμένῳ προσεῖναι·[1] ἀνδρεῖος γὰρ ἦν ὡς οὐκ
ἄλλος τις, ἐν δὲ τοῖς ὑπὲρ τῶν ὑπηκόων ἀγῶσι
πρῶτος ἐπὶ τοὺς κινδύνους ὥρμα τῷ πονεῖν καὶ
μάχεσθαι παρακελευόμενος τοὺς στρατιώτας ἐπὶ
τὰς παρατάξεις[2] ἀλλ' οὐχὶ τῷ προστάττειν ὡς
391 δεσπότης, νοῆσαί τε καὶ συνιδεῖν καὶ περὶ τῶν
μελλόντων καὶ τῆς τῶν ἐνεστηκότων οἰκονομίας
ἱκανώτατος, σώφρων ἐπιεικὴς χρηστὸς πρὸς τοὺς
ἐν συμφοραῖς ὑπάρχοντας, δίκαιος φιλάνθρωπος, ἃ
μόνοις ἐξαίρετα τοῖς[3] βασιλεῦσιν εἶναι προσῆκε,
μηδὲν ὅλως παρὰ τοσοῦτο μέγεθος ἐξουσίας ἁμαρτὼν ἢ τὸ περὶ τὴν Οὐρία γυναῖκα. κατέλιπε δὲ καὶ
πλοῦτον ὅσον οὐκ ἄλλος βασιλεὺς οὔθ' Ἑβραίων
οὔτ' ἄλλων ἐθνῶν.
392 (3) Ἔθαψε δὲ αὐτὸν ὁ παῖς Σολομὼν ἐν Ἱεροσολύμοις διαπρεπῶς τοῖς τε ἄλλοις οἷς περὶ κηδείαν
νομίζεται βασιλικὴν ἅπασι καὶ δὴ καὶ πλοῦτον
αὐτῷ πολὺν καὶ ἄφθονον συνεκήδευσεν, ὧν τὴν
ὑπερβολὴν τεκμήραιτ'[4] ἄν τις ῥᾳδίως ἐκ τοῦ λεχθη-
393 σομένου· μετὰ γὰρ χρόνον ἐτῶν χιλίων καὶ τριακοσίων Ὑρκανὸς ὁ ἀρχιερεὺς πολιορκούμενος ὑπ'
Ἀντιόχου τοῦ Εὐσεβοῦς ἐπικληθέντος υἱοῦ δὲ

[1] οὗτος ἄριστος . . . προσεῖναι haud dubie corrupta: οὕτως ἀρίστῳ ἀνδρὶ γεγενημένῳ καὶ πᾶσαν ἀρετὴν ἔχοντι καὶ τοσούτων ἐθνῶν σωτηρίαν ἐγκεχειρισμένῳ βασιλεῖ ἔδει προσεπαινέσαι καὶ τό τε τῆς δυνάμεως αὐτοῦ εὐσθενὲς καὶ τὸ τῆς σωφροσύνης συνετόν RO.

[2] πράξεις MSP Exc. Suidas.

[3] ἐξαίρετα τοῖς] δικαιότατα RO.

sessed of every virtue which should be found in a king entrusted with the safety of so many nations;[a] there was no one like him for bravery, and, in the contests fought on behalf of his subjects, he was the first to rush into danger, encouraging his soldiers against the opposing lines by his labours in the fight, and not by commanding them like a master. He was also most apt in perceiving and understanding the course of future events and in dealing with the immediate situation, prudent, mild, kind to those in trouble, just and humane,—qualities which only the greatest kings are expected to have; and, with so great a measure of authority, never once did he do wrong, except in the matter of Uriah's wife. Moreover he left behind such wealth as no other king, whether of the Hebrews or other nations, ever did.

His character.

(3) Then his son Solomon interred him in Jerusalem with all the splendour customary at royal funerals, and also buried with him a great abundance of wealth, the vastness of which one may easily gather from what is now to be related: after a period of thirteen hundred years,[b] when Hyrcanus, the high priest, was besieged by Antiochus, surnamed the

David's burial. 1 Kings ii. 10.

Later history of David's tomb.

[a] The text (from "He was a most excellent man") is probably corrupt. The variant reads "In addition to his having been so excellent a man, possessed of every virtue and entrusted with the safety of so many nations, one must praise him for the vigour of his (bodily) strength and his prudence and intelligence."

[b] The siege of Jerusalem, here referred to, took place in 135/134 B.C. Josephus thus places David's death in 1435 B.C., which is almost 500 years earlier than the generally accepted date (*c.* 970 B.C.).

[4] ex E Niese: τεκμήρετ' R: τεκμαίρετ' OS[1]P: τεκμαίροιτ' MS[2].

Δημητρίου, βουλόμενος χρήματ' αὐτῷ δοῦναι ὑπὲρ τοῦ λῦσαι τὴν πολιορκίαν καὶ τὴν στρατιὰν ἀπαγαγεῖν, καὶ ἀλλαχόθεν οὐκ εὐπορῶν, ἀνοίξας ἕνα οἶκον τῶν ἐν τῷ Δαυίδου μνήματι καὶ βαστάσας τρισχίλια τάλαντα μέρος ἔδωκεν Ἀντιόχῳ καὶ διέλυσεν οὕτως τὴν πολιορκίαν, καθὼς καὶ ἐν
394 ἄλλοις δεδηλώκαμεν. μετὰ δὲ τοῦτο ἐτῶν πολλῶν διαγενομένων πάλιν ὁ βασιλεὺς Ἡρώδης ἕτερον ἀνοίξας οἶκον ἀνείλετο χρήματα πολλά. ταῖς μέντοι γε θήκαις τῶν βασιλέων οὐδεὶς αὐτῶν ἐπέτυχεν· ἦσαν γὰρ ὑπὸ τὴν γῆν μηχανικῶς κεκηδευμέναι πρὸς τὸ μὴ φανεραὶ εἶναι τοῖς εἰς τὸ μνῆμα εἰσιοῦσιν. ἀλλὰ περὶ μὲν τούτων ἡμῖν τοσοῦτον ἀπόχρη δεδηλῶσθαι.

---

[a] This was Antiochus VII. Euergetes, surnamed Sidetes, a son of Demetrius I. Soter. Josephus calls him Antiochus Soter in *A*. xiii. 271. In the same book, § 244, his surname

Pious (*Eusebēs*),[a] the son of Demetrius, he wished to give the latter money to raise the siege and withdraw his army, and, as he had no other resource, he opened one of the chambers in David's tomb and carried off three thousand talents, part of which he gave to Antiochus and so put an end to the siege, as we have elsewhere related.[b] And again, after an interval of many years, King Herod opened another chamber and took away a large sum of money.[c] Neither of them, however, came upon the coffins of the kings, for these had been artfully buried under the earth so that they could not be seen by anyone entering the tomb. But concerning these matters let it suffice us to have related this much.

of Pious is said to have been given him because of his "extraordinary piety." These surnames, Soter and Eusebes, applied to Antiochus Sidetes by Josephus, are not found elsewhere in ancient sources.

[b] *B.J.* i. 61 (‖ *A.* xiii. 249). Weill has overlooked this earlier passage in his note.

[c] *Cf. A.* xvi. 179.

ΒΙΒΛΙΟΝ Η

(i. 1) Περὶ μὲν οὖν Δαυίδου καὶ τῆς ἀρετῆς
αὐτοῦ καὶ ὅσων ἀγαθῶν αἴτιος γενόμενος τοῖς
ὁμοφύλοις πολέμους τε καὶ μάχας ὅσας κατορ-
θώσας γηραιὸς ἐτελεύτησεν, ἐν τῇ πρὸ ταύτης
2 βίβλῳ δεδηλώκαμεν. Σολομῶνος δὲ τοῦ παιδὸς
αὐτοῦ νέου τὴν ἡλικίαν ἔτι ὄντος τὴν βασιλείαν
παραλαβόντος, ὃν ἔτι ζῶν ἀπέφηνε τοῦ λαοῦ δεσπότην κατὰ τὴν τοῦ θεοῦ βούλησιν, καθίσαντος ἐπὶ
τὸν θρόνον ὁ μὲν πᾶς ὄχλος ἐπευφήμησεν, οἷον
εἰκὸς ἐπ' ἀρχομένῳ βασιλεῖ, τελευτῆσαι καλῶς
αὐτῷ τὰ πράγματα καὶ πρὸς γῆρας ἀφικέσθαι
λιπαρὸν καὶ πανεύδαιμον τὴν ἡγεμονίαν.

3 (2) Ἀδωνίας δέ, ὃς καὶ τοῦ πατρὸς ἔτι ζῶντος
ἐπεχείρησε τὴν ἀρχὴν κατασχεῖν, παρελθὼν πρὸς
τὴν τοῦ βασιλέως μητέρα Βερσάβην καὶ φιλοφρόνως αὐτὴν ἀσπασάμενος, πυθομένης εἰ καὶ διὰ
χρείαν τινὰ πρὸς αὐτὴν ἀφῖκται καὶ δηλοῦν κε-
4 λευούσης ὡς ἡδέως παρεξομένης ἤρξατο λέγειν ὅτι
γινώσκει μὲν τὴν βασιλείαν καὶ αὐτὴ καὶ διὰ τὴν
ἡλικίαν καὶ διὰ τὴν τοῦ πλήθους προαίρεσιν οὖσαν
αὐτοῦ, μεταβάσης δὲ πρὸς Σολομῶνα τὸν υἱὸν
αὐτῆς κατὰ τὴν τοῦ θεοῦ γνώμην στέργει καὶ

[a] In § 211 Josephus makes Solomon fourteen years old at his accession, while some of the LXX MSS. here add that he was twelve, with which figure rabbinic tradition agrees.

BOOK VIII

(i. 1) CONCERNING David and his prowess and the many benefits which he conferred upon his countrymen and how, after successfully conducting many wars and battles, he died at an advanced age, we have written in the preceding book. Now when his son Solomon, whom he had while yet alive, in accordance with the will of God, proclaimed sole ruler of the people, took over the kingship, being still a mere youth,[a] and sat upon the throne, the entire multitude, as is usual at the beginning of a king's reign, greeted him joyfully with the prayer that his affairs might have a fortunate issue and that he might end his rule in a rich and happy old age.[b]

Solomon's accession. 1 Kings ii. 12.

(2) But Adōnias, who even in his father's lifetime had attempted to seize the royal power, went to the king's mother Bersabē [c] and greeted her in a friendly manner, and, when she inquired whether he had come to her with any request and bade him make it known, as she would gladly grant it, he began by saying that she herself knew that the kingship belonged to him both by reason of his age and the people's preference, but since, in accordance with the wish of God, it had gone to her son Solomon, he was willing and happy

Adonijah (Adonias) asks for Abishag (Abisake) as wife. 1 Kings ii. 13.

[b] "end . . . in a rich . . . old age" is an Homeric phrase, *cf. Od.* xi. 136 γήρῳ ὕπο λιπαρῷ ἀρημένον.

[c] Bibl. Bath-sheba, *cf. A.* vii. 130 note.

ἀγαπᾷ τὴν ὑπ' αὐτῷ δουλείαν καὶ τοῖς παροῦσιν
5 ἥδεται πράγμασιν.[1] ἐδεῖτο δ' οὖν διακονῆσαι πρὸς
τὸν ἀδελφὸν αὐτῷ καὶ πεῖσαι δοῦναι τὴν τῷ πατρὶ
συγκοιμωμένην πρὸς γάμον αὐτῷ Ἀβισάκην· οὐ
γὰρ πλησιάσαι τὸν πατέρα διὰ τὸ γῆρας αὐτῇ,
6 μένειν δ' ἔτι παρθένον. ἡ δὲ Βερσάβη καὶ δια-
κονήσειν σπουδαίως ὑπέσχετο καὶ καταπράξεσθαι[2]
τὸν γάμον δι' ἀμφότερα, τοῦ τε βασιλέως αὐτῷ
χαρίσασθαί τι βουλησομένου καὶ δεησομένης αὐτῆς
λιπαρῶς. καὶ ὁ μὲν εὔελπις ἀπαλλάττεται περὶ
τοῦ γάμου, ἡ δὲ τοῦ Σολομῶνος μήτηρ εὐθὺς
ὥρμησεν ἐπὶ τὸν υἱὸν διαλεξομένη περὶ ὧν Ἀδωνίᾳ
7 δεηθέντι κατεπηγγείλατο. καὶ προϋπαντήσαντος
αὐτῇ τοῦ παιδὸς καὶ περιπλακέντος, ἐπεὶ παρήγαγεν
αὐτὴν εἰς τὸν οἶκον οὗ συνέβαινεν αὐτῷ κεῖσθαι τὸν
βασιλικὸν θρόνον, καθίσας ἐκέλευσεν ἕτερον ἐκ
δεξιῶν τεθῆναι τῇ μητρί. καθεσθεῖσα δ' ἡ Βερσάβη
"μίαν," εἶπεν, "ὦ παῖ, χάριν αἰτουμένῃ μοι
κατάνευσον καὶ μηδὲν ἐξ ἀρνήσεως δύσκολον μηδὲ
8 σκυθρωπὸν ἀπεργάσῃ." τοῦ δὲ Σολομῶνος προστάττειν κελεύοντος (πάντα γὰρ ὅσιον εἶναι μητρὶ
παρέχειν) καί τι προσμεμψαμένου τὴν ἀρχὴν ὅτι
μὴ μετ' ἐλπίδος ἤδη βεβαίας τοῦ τυχεῖν ὧν ἀξιοῖ
ποιεῖται τοὺς λόγους ἀλλ' ἄρνησιν ὑφορωμένη,
δοῦναι τὴν παρθένον αὐτὸν Ἀβισάκην Ἀδωνίᾳ
τἀδελφῷ πρὸς γάμον παρεκάλει.
9 (3) Λαβὼν δὲ πρὸς ὀργὴν ὁ βασιλεὺς τὸν λόγον
ἀποπέμπεται μὲν τὴν μητέρα μειζόνων ὀρέγεσθαι

[1] ἥδεται πράγμασιν om. RO.

[2] Bekker: καταπράξασθαι codd. E Zonaras.

---

[a] The last is an unscriptural detail.

[b] Bibl. Abishag, *cf. A.* vii. 344 note.

to serve under him and was satisfied with the present state of affairs.[a] He requested her, however, to intercede for him with his brother and persuade him to give him in marriage Abisakē,[b] who had lain with his father; for, he said, his father by reason of his age had not had intercourse with her, and she still remained a virgin. And Bersabē promised to intercede for him zealously and to bring the marriage about, both because the king would wish to do him a favour and because she would earnestly entreat him.[c] And so he departed with high hopes of the marriage, while Solomon's mother straightway hastened to her son to tell him of the promise she had made Adōnias upon his request. And her son came forward to meet her and embraced her, and when he had led her to the chamber where, at that time, his royal throne was, and had taken his seat upon it, he ordered another throne to be placed for his mother at his right hand. When Bersabē was seated she said, "I have, my son, one favour to ask; grant me this and do not act disagreeably or angrily by denying it." And, as Solomon bade her command him, for, he said, it is a sacred duty to do everything for a mother, and added a word of reproach for the way she had begun, in that she had not spoken with a sure hope of obtaining what she requested but had been fearful of being denied,[d] she asked him to give the virgin Abisakē to his brother Adōnias in marriage.

(3) But the king took offence at her words and sent his mother away, saying that Adōnias was aiming at

Solomon orders Benaiah (Ban-

[c] Bath-sheba's reply is an amplification of 1 Kings ii. 18, "Well; I will speak for thee to the king."

[d] The foregoing is an amplification of 1 Kings ii. 20, "Ask on, my mother, for I will not say thee nay."

πραγμάτων εἰπὼν Ἀδωνίαν καὶ θαυμάζειν πῶς οὐ
παραχωρῆσαι καὶ τῆς βασιλείας ὡς πρεσβυτέρῳ
παρακαλεῖ, τὸν γάμον αὐτῷ τὸν Ἀβισάκης αἰτουμένη φίλους ἔχοντι δυνατοὺς Ἰώαβον τὸν στρατηγὸν
καὶ Ἀβιάθαρον τὸν ἱερέα, μεταπεμψάμενος δὲ
Βαναίαν τὸν ἐπὶ τῶν σωματοφυλάκων ἀποκτεῖναι
10 προσέταξεν αὐτῷ τὸν ἀδελφὸν Ἀδωνίαν. καλέσας
δὲ τὸν Ἀβιάθαρον τὸν ἱερέα "θανάτου μέν," εἶπε,
"ῥύεταί σε τά τε ἄλλα ὅσα τῷ πατρί μου συνέκαμες
καὶ ἡ κιβωτός, ἣν σὺν αὐτῷ μετήνεγκας. ταύτην
δέ σοι τὴν τιμωρίαν ἐπιτίθημι ταξαμένῳ μετὰ
Ἀδωνία καὶ τὰ ἐκείνου φρονήσαντι· μήτε ἐνθάδε
ἴσθι μήτε εἰς ὄψιν ἀπάντα τὴν ἐμήν, ἀλλ' εἰς τὴν
πατρίδα πορευθεὶς ἐν τοῖς ἀγροῖς ζῆθι καὶ τοῦτον
ἄχρι τελευτῆς ἔχε τὸν βίον ἁμαρτὼν τοῦ μηκέτ'
11 εἶναι δικαίως ἐν ἀξίᾳ." καταλύεται μὲν οὖν ἀπὸ
τῆς ἱερατικῆς τιμῆς ὁ Ἰθαμάρου οἶκος διὰ τὴν
προειρημένην αἰτίαν, καθὼς καὶ τῷ Ἀβιαθάρου
πάππῳ προεῖπεν ὁ θεὸς Ἠλεί, μετέβη δ' εἰς τὸ
12 Φινεέσου γένος πρὸς Σάδωκον. οἱ δὲ ἰδιωτεύ-
σαντες ἐκ τοῦ Φινεέσου γένους μεθ' ὃν καιρὸν εἰς
τὸν Ἰθαμάρου οἶκον ἡ ἀρχιερωσύνη μετῆλθεν,
Ἠλεὶ πρώτου ταύτην παραλαβόντος, ἦσαν οὗτοι·
ὁ τοῦ ἀρχιερέως Ἰησοῦ[1] υἱὸς Βοκκίας, τούτου δὲ
Ἰώθαμος, Ἰωθάμου δὲ Μαραίωθος, Μαραιώθου

[1] Ἰωσήπου MSP Lat.

---

[a] Anathoth.

[b] *Cf. A.* v. 338 ff. = 1 Sam. ii. 12 ff.

[c] *Cf. A.* v. 361-362 notes, vii. 110 note.

[d] With the following genealogy contrast that given in *A.* v. 361.

greater things, and that he wondered she did not ask him, when seeking the marriage with Abisakē for Adōnias, to yield up the kingdom also to him, on the ground that he was his elder brother and had powerful friends in Joab the commander and Abiathar the priest. Then, having sent for Banaias, who was in charge of the bodyguard, he ordered him to kill his brother Adōnias. And he called Abiathar the priest and said, "You owe your life to the hardships you shared with my father and to the ark which you brought over with him; but I impose the following punishment upon you for having gone over to Adōnias's side and sympathized with him: you shall not remain here nor ever come into my presence, but go to your native place [a] and live in the fields and continue so to live until your death, for you have sinned too greatly to remain justly in office any longer." And so the house of Ithamar was deprived of the priestly privilege for the afore-mentioned reason, just as God had foretold to Eli the grandfather of Abiathar,[b] and it was transferred to the family of Phinees, to Sadok.[c] Now the members of the family of Phinees who lived as private persons after the time when the high-priesthood passed over to the house of Ithamar—of whom Eli was the first to receive it—were as follows:[d] Bokkias[e] the son of the high priest Jesus,[f] Jōthamos[g] the son of Bokkias, Maraiōthos[h] the son of Jōthamos, Arophaios[i] the

(Banaias) to execute Adonijah. 1 Kings ii. 22.

Abiathar is deposed from the high priesthood. 1 Kings ii. 27.

Genealogy of Zadok, the new high priest. 1 Chron. vi. 5 (Heb. v. 81).

[e] Bibl. Bukki, LXX Βωέ, Βωκαί.
[f] Var. Josephos; bibl. Abishua, LXX Ἀβεισού. He is called Abiezer in *A.* v. 362.
[g] Bibl. Uzzi (as Josephus writes in *A.* v. 362), LXX Ὀζεί. Josephus here omits Zerahiah the son of Uzzi.
[h] Bibl. Meraioth, LXX Μαρειήλ, Μαραιώθ, Luc. Μαρεώθ.
[i] Bibl. Amariah, LXX Ἀμαρειά.

δὲ Ἀροφαῖος, Ἀροφαίου δὲ Ἀχίτωβος, Ἀχιτώβου
δὲ Σάδωκος, ὃς πρῶτος ἐπὶ Δαυίδου τοῦ βασιλέως
ἀρχιερεὺς ἐγένετο.
13 (4) Ἰώαβος δὲ ὁ στρατηγὸς τὴν ἀναίρεσιν ἀκούσας τὴν Ἀδωνία περιδεὴς ἐγένετο, φίλος γὰρ ἦν
αὐτῷ μᾶλλον ἢ τῷ βασιλεῖ Σολομῶνι, καὶ κίνδυνον
ἐκ τούτου διὰ τὴν πρὸς ἐκεῖνον εὔνοιαν οὐκ ἀ-
λόγως ὑποπτεύων καταφεύγει μὲν ἐπὶ τὸ θυσιαστήριον, ἀσφάλειαν δὲ ἐνόμιζεν αὐτῷ ποριεῖν ἐκ τῆς
14 πρὸς τὸν θεὸν εὐσεβείας τοῦ βασιλέως. ὁ δὲ ἀπαγγειλάντων αὐτῷ τὴν Ἰωάβου γνώμην πέμψας
Βαναίαν ἐκέλευσεν · ἀναστήσαντα αὐτὸν ἐπὶ τὸ
δικαστήριον ἄγειν ὡς ἀπολογησόμενον. Ἰώαβος δὲ
οὐκ ἔφη καταλείψειν τὸ ἱερόν, ἀλλ' αὐτοῦ τεθνήξε-
15 σθαι μᾶλλον ἢ ἐν ἑτέρῳ χωρίῳ. Βαναίου δὲ τὴν
ἀπόκρισιν αὐτοῦ τῷ βασιλεῖ δηλώσαντος προσέταξεν ὁ Σολομὼν ἐκεῖ τὴν κεφαλὴν αὐτοῦ ἀποτεμεῖν, καθὼς βούλεται, καὶ ταύτην λαβεῖν τὴν
δίκην ὑπὲρ τῶν δύο στρατηγῶν, οὓς ὁ Ἰώαβος
ἀνοσίως ἀπέκτεινε, θάψαι δ' αὐτοῦ τὸ σῶμα, ὅπως
τὰ μὲν ἁμαρτήματα μηδέποτε καταλείπῃ τὸ γένος
τὸ ἐκείνου, τῆς δὲ Ἰωάβου τελευτῆς αὐτός τε καὶ
16 ὁ πατὴρ ἀθῷοι τυγχάνωσι. καὶ Βαναίας μὲν τὰ
κελευσθέντα ποιήσας αὐτὸς ἀποδείκνυται στρατηγὸς πάσης τῆς δυνάμεως, Σάδωκον δὲ ποιεῖ μόνον
ἀρχιερέα ὁ βασιλεὺς εἰς τὸν Ἀβιαθάρου τόπον, ὃν
μετεστήσατο.

[a] Bibl. Ahitub, LXX Ἀχειτώβ.

[b] Josephus, like some LXX MSS. and Luc., read "Solomon" for "Absalom" in 1 Kings ii. 28, "for Joab had turned after Adonijah, though he turned not after Absalom."

[c] ἀνιστάναι has the technical meaning "make a suppliant leave a sanctuary."

son of Maraiōthos, Achitōb[a] the son of Arophaios, and Sadok the son of Achitōb, who was the first to become high priest in the reign of David.

(4) Now when Joab the commander heard that Adōnias had been put to death, he was greatly afraid, for he was more friendly to him than to King Solomon,[b] and, as he not unreasonably expected that danger threatened him because of his goodwill to Adōnias, he fled for refuge to the altar, where he imagined he would secure safety for himself because of the king's piety toward God. But when the king was told of Joab's plan, he sent Banaias with orders to remove him[c] and bring him to the judgement-hall to make his defence.[d] Joab, however, said that he would not leave the temple but would die there rather than in any other place. When Banaias reported his answer to the king, Solomon ordered his head to be cut off there, as Joab wished it,—this being the penalty exacted for the two generals whom he had impiously slain—and his body to be buried, in order that his sins might never leave his family (in peace), while Solomon himself and his father should be blameless for Joab's death.[e] And so Banaias, after having carried out these orders, was himself appointed commander of the entire army, and the king made Sadok sole high priest in place of Abiathar, whom he had removed.

Joab is also executed by Benaiah. 1 Kings ii. 28.

[d] This detail is unscriptural (*cf.* a similar addition in *A.* v. 215). Scripture says, "Solomon sent Benaiah . . . saying, Go, fall upon him." Rabbinic tradition gives a long account of Joab's trial before Solomon, *cf.* Ginzberg, iv. 126.

[e] According to Scripture, Solomon, while explicitly holding his father and himself guiltless of the blood of those whom Joab had slain, only implies that he is also blameless for Joab's death, 1 Kings ii. 32, "And the Lord shall return his blood upon his own head, who fell upon two men," etc.

17 (5) Σουμουίσῳ δὲ προσέταξεν οἰκίαν οἰκοδομήσαντι μένειν ἐν Ἱεροσολύμοις αὐτῷ προσεδρεύοντι καὶ μὴ διαβαίνειν τὸν χειμάρρουν Κεδρῶνα ἔχειν ἐξουσίαν, παρακούσαντι δὲ τούτων[1] θάνατον ἔσεσθαι τὸ πρόστιμον. τῷ δὲ μεγέθει τῆς ἀπειλῆς καὶ
18 ὅρκους αὐτῷ προσηνάγκασε ποιήσασθαι. Σουμούισος δὲ χαίρειν οἷς προσέταξεν αὐτῷ Σολομὼν φήσας καὶ ταῦτα ποιήσειν προσομόσας καταλιπὼν τὴν πατρίδα τὴν διατριβὴν ἐν τοῖς Ἱεροσολύμοις ἐποιεῖτο. διελθόντων δὲ τριῶν ἐτῶν ἀκούσας δύο δούλους ἀποδράντας αὐτὸν ἐν Γίττῃ τυγχάνοντας
19 ὥρμησεν ἐπὶ τοὺς οἰκέτας. ἐπανελθόντος δὲ μετ' αὐτῶν ὁ βασιλεὺς αἰσθόμενος, ὡς καὶ τῶν ἐντολῶν αὐτοῦ καταφρονήσαντος καὶ τὸ μεῖζον τῶν ὅρκων τοῦ θεοῦ μηδεμίαν ποιησαμένου φροντίδα, χαλεπῶς εἶχε καὶ καλέσας αὐτόν "οὐ σύ," φησίν, "ὤμοσας μὴ καταλείψειν ἐμὲ μηδ' ἐξελεύσεσθαί ποτ' ἐκ
20 ταύτης τῆς πόλεως εἰς ἄλλην; οὔκουν ἀποδράσῃ τὴν τῆς ἐπιορκίας δίκην, ἀλλὰ καὶ ταύτης καὶ ὧν τὸν πατέρα μου παρὰ τὴν φυγὴν[2] ὕβρισας τιμωρήσομαί σε πονηρὸν γενόμενον, ἵνα γνῷς ὅτι κερδαίνουσιν οὐδὲν οἱ κακοὶ μὴ παρ' αὐτὰ τἀδικήματα κολασθέντες, ἀλλὰ παντὶ τῷ χρόνῳ[3] ᾧ νομίζουσιν ἀδεεῖς εἶναι μηδὲν πεπονθότες αὔξεται καὶ γίνεται μείζων ἡ κόλασις αὐτοῖς ἧς ἂν παραυτίκα

[1] Niese: τούτῳ codd.: τούτου Exc.
[2] φύσιν RO.
[3] ἀλλ' ἀντὶ τοῦ χρόνου Niese.

[a] Josephus follows the Heb. in making Shimei's story come directly after the appointment of Benaiah and Zadok.

(5) [a]As for Sūmūisos,[b] he ordered him to build a house and remain in Jerusalem in attendance upon him, and did not give him permission to cross the brook Kedron, saying that if he disobeyed the commands, death would be the penalty. To the severity of this threat he added the obligation of taking an oath.[c] So Sūmūisos, saying that he was pleased with Solomon's commands, and also swearing to observe them, left his native place and made his home in Jerusalem. But after three years had passed, upon hearing that two of his slaves who had escaped from him were in Gitta,[d] he set out after the men. And when he returned with them, the king heard of it and, holding that he had made light of his commands and—what was worse—had shown no regard for the oaths sworn to God, he was angered and having called him, said, "Did you not swear not to leave me nor ever go out from this city to another? You shall not, therefore, escape the penalty for your perjury, but I shall punish you as a miscreant both for this crime and for your insolence to my father at the time of his flight, in order that you may know that evildoers gain nothing by not being punished at the time of their crimes, but during the whole time in which they think themselves secure because they have suffered nothing, their punishment increases and becomes more severe than that which they would have paid at

Shimei (Sumuisos) is executed for leaving Jerusalem. 1 Kings ii. 36.

[a] The LXX inserts, between vss. 35 and 36 of 1 Kings ii., a long passage concerning Solomon's marriage to Pharaoh's daughter (*cf.* Heb. iii. 1), his buildings and officers.

[b] Bibl. Shimei; for variants in Josephus *cf. A.* vii. 207, 388.

[c] The oath is mentioned at this point, 1 Kings ii. 37, in the LXX, but in the Heb. not until vs. 42.

[d] Bibl. Gath.

πλημμελήσαντες ἔδοσαν.” καὶ Σουμούισον μὲν κελευσθεὶς Βαναίας ἀπέκτεινεν.

21 (ii. 1) Ἤδη δὲ τὴν βασιλείαν βεβαίως ἔχων Σολομὼν καὶ τῶν ἐχθρῶν κεκολασμένων ἄγεται τὴν Φαραώθου τοῦ τῶν Αἰγυπτίων βασιλέως θυγατέρα· καὶ κατασκευάσας τὰ τείχη τῶν Ἱεροσολύμων πολλῷ μείζω καὶ ὀχυρώτερα τῶν πρόσθεν ὄντων διεῖπε τὰ πράγματα λοιπὸν ἐπὶ πολλῆς εἰρήνης μηδ' ὑπὸ τῆς νεότητος πρός τε δικαιοσύνην καὶ φυλακὴν τῶν νόμων καὶ μνήμην ὧν ὁ πατὴρ τελευτῶν ἐπέστειλε βλαπτόμενος, ἀλλὰ πάνθ' ὅσα οἱ τοῖς χρόνοις προβεβηκότες καὶ πρὸς τὸ φρονεῖν ἀκμάζοντες μετὰ πολλῆς ἀκριβείας ἐπιτελῶν.
22 ἔγνω δ' εἰς Γιβρῶνα[1] παραγενόμενος ἐπὶ τοῦ χαλκοῦ θυσιαστηρίου τοῦ κατασκευασθέντος ὑπὸ Μωυσέος θῦσαι τῷ θεῷ καὶ χίλια τὸν ἀριθμὸν ὡλοκαύτωσεν ἱερεῖα. τοῦτο δὲ ποιήσας μεγάλως ἔδοξε τὸν θεὸν τετιμηκέναι· φανεὶς γὰρ αὐτῷ κατὰ τοὺς ὕπνους ἐκείνης τῆς νυκτὸς ἐκέλευσεν αἱρεῖσθαι τίνας ἀντὶ τῆς εὐσεβείας παράσχῃ δωρεὰς αὐτῷ.
23 Σολομὼν δὲ τὰ κάλλιστα καὶ μέγιστα καὶ θεῷ παρασχεῖν ἥδιστα καὶ λαβεῖν ἀνθρώπῳ συμφορώτατα τὸν θεὸν ᾔτησεν· οὐ γὰρ χρυσὸν οὐδ' ἄργυρον οὐδὲ τὸν ἄλλον πλοῦτον ὡς ἄνθρωπος καὶ νέος ἠξίωσεν αὑτῷ προσγενέσθαι (ταῦτα γὰρ σχεδὸν νενόμισται παρὰ τοῖς πλείστοις μόνα σπουδῆς ἄξια καὶ θεοῦ δῶρα εἶναι) ἀλλά “ δός μοι,” φησί,

[1] Γαβαῶνα ex LXX conj. edd.

---

[a] The latter part of Solomon's speech is an amplification.
[b] Here again Josephus follows the Heb. order, *cf.* 1 Kings iii. 1 ff.; in the LXX the execution of Shimei is followed by

the very moment of their wrongdoing.[a]" Then Banaias at the king's command put Sūmūisos to death.

(ii. 1) [b] Solomon, having now firm possession of the kingdom, and his enemies having been chastised, married the daughter of Pharaōthēs the king of the Egyptians. He also made the walls of Jerusalem much greater and stronger than they had been before, and thereafter governed the state in perfect peace, nor was he hindered by his youth from dealing justice and observing the laws and remembering the injunctions of his dying father, but performed all tasks with as great scrupulousness as do those of advanced age and mature wisdom. And he decided to go to Gibron [c] and sacrifice to God upon the bronze altar built by Moses,[d] and he offered whole burnt-offerings of a thousand victims. By having done this he seemed greatly to have honoured God, for He appeared to him that night in his sleep and bade him choose what gifts He should confer upon him in return for his piety. And Solomon asked for the most excellent and greatest gifts, most pleasing to God to confer and most beneficial for man to receive, for it was not gold or silver or other form of wealth that he asked to be bestowed upon him, as a man and a young one might have done—such are considered by most men as almost the only things worthy of regard and as gifts of God—but he said, "Give me, O

Solomon's good government. 1 Kings iii. 1.

2 Chron. i. 3, 5.

Solomon at Gibron (Hebron) asks God for wisdom. 1 Kings iii. 6.

an account of Solomon's revenues and officers, corresponding in part to the Heb. of iv. 20 ff.

[c] (=Bibl. Hebron), either a slip for, or a corruption of, Γαβαῶνα, bibl. Gibeon.

[d] The bronze altar, made by Bezalel, is mentioned in connexion with the tabernacle of Moses at Gibeon in 2 Chron. i. 3 ff.

"δέσποτα, νοῦν ὑγιῆ καὶ φρόνησιν ἀγαθήν, οἷς ἂν τὸν λαὸν τἀληθῆ καὶ τὰ δίκαια λαβὼν[1] κρίνοιμι."
24 τούτοις ἥσθη τοῖς αἰτήμασιν ὁ θεὸς καὶ τά τε ἄλλα πάνθ' ὧν οὐκ ἐμνήσθη παρὰ τὴν ἐκλογὴν δώσειν ἐπηγγείλατο, πλοῦτον δόξαν νίκην πολεμίων, καὶ πρὸ πάντων σύνεσιν καὶ σοφίαν οἵαν οὐκ ἄλλος τις ἀνθρώπων ἔσχεν οὔτε βασιλέων οὔτ' ἰδιωτῶν· φυλάξειν δὲ καὶ τοῖς ἐκγόνοις αὐτοῦ τὴν βασιλείαν ἐπὶ πλεῖστον ὑπισχνεῖτο χρόνον, ἂν δίκαιός τε ὢν διαμένῃ καὶ πειθόμενος αὐτῷ καὶ τὸν πατέρα
25 μιμούμενος ἐν οἷς ἦν ἄριστος. ταῦτα τοῦ θεοῦ Σολομὼν ἀκούσας ἀνεπήδησεν εὐθὺς ἐκ τῆς κοίτης καὶ προσκυνήσας αὐτὸν ὑπέστρεψεν εἰς Ἱεροσόλυμα, καὶ πρὸ τῆς σκηνῆς μεγάλας ἐπιτελέσας θυσίας κατευώχει τοὺς ἰδίους[2] ἅπαντας.

26 (2) Ταύταις δὲ ταῖς ἡμέραις κρίσις ἐπ' αὐτὸν ἤχθη δυσχερής, ἧς τὸ τέλος εὑρεῖν ἦν ἐπίπονον· τὸ δὲ πρᾶγμα περὶ οὗ συνέβαινεν εἶναι τὴν δίκην ἀναγκαῖον ἡγησάμην δηλῶσαι, ἵνα τοῖς ἐντυγχάνουσι τό τε δύσκολον τῆς κρίσεως γνώριμον ὑπάρξῃ, καὶ τοιούτων μεταξὺ πραγμάτων γενόμενοι λάβωσιν ὥσπερ ἐξ εἰκόνος τῆς τοῦ βασιλέως ἀγχινοίας τὸ ῥᾳδίως ἀποφαίνεσθαι περὶ τῶν ζητου-
27 μένων δυνηθῆναι. δύο γυναῖκες ἑταῖραι τὸν βίον ἧκον ἐπ' αὐτόν, ὧν ἡ ἀδικεῖσθαι δοκοῦσα πρώτη λέγειν ἤρξατο· "οἰκῶ μέν," εἶπεν, "ὦ βασιλεῦ, μετὰ ταύτης ἐν ἑνὶ δωματίῳ, συνέβη δ' ἀμφοτέραις ἡμῖν ἐπὶ μιᾶς ἡμέρας ἀποτεκεῖν κατὰ τὴν αὐτὴν
28 ὥραν ἄρρενα παιδία. τρίτης δὲ ἡμέρας διελθούσης

[1] λαλῶν cod. Vat. ap. Hudson.
[2] Ἰουδαίους RO: om. Lat.

[a] Var. "the Jews"; bibl. "his servants."

Lord, a sound mind and good understanding wherewith I may judge the people, having truth and justice in me." With this prayer God was pleased, and promised to give him, in addition to what he had chosen, also the other things he had not mentioned, wealth, honour and victory over his enemies and, above all, intelligence and wisdom such as no other man whether king or commoner had ever had. And He also promised to preserve the kingdom for his descendants a very long time, if he continued to be righteous and to imitate his father in those things wherein he was excellent. When Solomon heard these words of God he at once leaped from his bed and did obeisance to Him; then he returned to Jerusalem and, after offering great sacrifices before the tabernacle, feasted all his household.[a]

God's promises to bless Solomon. 1 Kings iii. 10.

(2) Now in these days a difficult case was brought before him, for which it was troublesome to find a solution. I have thought it necessary to explain the matter about which the suit happened to be, in order that my readers may have an idea of the difficulty of the case and that those who are involved in such matters may take example from the king's sagacity so as to be able to give a ready opinion on questions at issue. Two women who lived as harlots came before him and she who seemed to be the injured one first began to speak, saying, "I, O King, live with this woman in the same room,[b] and it so happened that we both gave birth on the same day and at the same hour [b] to male children. But on the

The dispute of two harlots about their infants. 1 Kings iii. 16.

[b] According to Scripture, the plaintiff's child was born three days before the other woman's. Probably, as Rappaport suggests, Josephus was confused by a phrase in the preceding verse (1 Kings iii. 17), "And I was delivered of a child with her in the house."

ἐπικοιμηθεῖσα τῷ αὐτῆς παιδίῳ αὕτη τοῦτο μὲν ἀποκτείνει, βαστάσασα δὲ τοὐμὸν ἐκ τῶν γονάτων πρὸς αὐτὴν μεταφέρει καὶ τὸ νεκρὸν ἐμοῦ κοιμω-
29 μένης εἰς τὰς ἀγκάλας μου τίθησι. πρωῒ δὲ θηλὴν ὀρέξαι βουλομένη τῷ παιδίῳ τὸ μὲν ἐμὸν οὐχ εὗρον, τὸ δὲ ταύτης νεκρὸν ὁρῶ μοι παρακείμενον· ἀκριβῶς γὰρ κατανοήσασα τοῦτο ἐπέγνων· ὅθεν ἀπαιτῶ τὸν ἐμὸν υἱὸν καὶ οὐκ ἀπολαμβάνουσα καταπέφευγα, δέσποτα, ἐπὶ τὴν παρὰ σοῦ βοήθειαν· τῷ[1] γὰρ εἶναι μόνας ἡμᾶς καὶ μηδένα τὸν ἐλέγξαι δυνάμενον φοβεῖσθαι καταφρονοῦσα ἰσχυ-
30 ρῶς ἀρνουμένη παραμένει." ταῦτ' εἰπούσης ὁ βασιλεὺς ἀνέκρινε τὴν ἑτέραν τί τοῖς εἰρημένοις ἀντιλέγειν ἔχει. τῆς δὲ ἀρνουμένης τοῦτο πεποιηκέναι, τὸ δὲ παιδίον τὸ αὐτῆς ζῆν λεγούσης, τὸ δὲ τῆς ἀντιδίκου τεθνηκέναι, μηδενὸς ἐπινοοῦντος τὴν κρίσιν ἀλλ' ὥσπερ ἐπ' αἰνίγματι περὶ τὴν εὕρεσιν αὐτοῦ πάντων τῇ διανοίᾳ τετυφλωμένων μόνος ὁ
31 βασιλεὺς ἐπενόησέ τι τοιοῦτον· κελεύσας κομισθῆναι καὶ τὸ νεκρὸν καὶ τὸ ζῶν παιδίον μεταπέμπεταί τινα τῶν σωματοφυλάκων καὶ σπασάμενον ἐκέλευσε[2] τὴν μάχαιραν ἀμφότερα διχοτομῆσαι τὰ παιδία, ὅπως ἑκάτεραι λάβωσιν ἀνὰ ἥμισυ τοῦ τε
32 ζῶντος καὶ τοῦ τετελευτηκότος. ἐπὶ τούτῳ πᾶς μὲν ὁ λαὸς λανθάνων ἐχλεύαζεν ὡς μειράκιον τὸν βασιλέα, μεταξὺ δὲ τῆς μὲν ἀπαιτούσης καὶ ἀληθοῦς μητρὸς ἀνακραγούσης τοῦτο μὴ ποιεῖν ἀλλὰ παραδιδόναι τῇ ἑτέρᾳ τὸ παιδίον ὡς ἐκείνης, ἀρ-

[1] Hudson: τὸ RMSP: τοῦ O. [2] προσέταξε MSPE.

[a] Scripture does not imply, as does Josephus, that Solomon waited for the others to find a solution.

[b] Josephus follows Luc. in saying that both the living

third day this woman by sleeping on her child caused its death, and she took my child from my lap and carried it over to her side and then laid the dead child in my arms as I slept. And in the morning when I wished to give the breast to the child, I did not find my son but I saw this woman's dead child lying beside me, for I looked at it carefully and recognized whose it was. I therefore demanded my son back, and, as I have not obtained him, I have come to appeal to you, my lord, for help ; for, contemptuously relying on the fact that we were alone and that she has no one to fear who can convict her, she stubbornly persists in her denial." After she had spoken the king asked the other woman what she had to say in contradiction to these statements. And she denied having done this thing, saying that it was her child that was alive, while her adversary's was the dead one. And when no one could see what judgement to give, but all were mentally blinded, as by a riddle, in finding a solution, the king alone devised the following plan :[a] he ordered both the dead and the living child to be brought, and then sent for one of the bodyguard and ordered him to draw his sword and cut both children in half, in order that either woman might take half of the dead child and half of the living child.[b] Thereupon all the people secretly made fun of the king as of a boy.[c] But meanwhile the woman who had demanded the child and was its true mother cried out that they should not do this but should give the child over to the other woman as if

Solomon as a sagacious judge discovers the real mother 1 Kings iii. 24.

and the dead child were to be divided ; the Heb. and LXX mention only the division of the living child. Perhaps the Luc. addition is, as Weill suggests, a reminiscence of the procedure followed in another case, *cf.* Ex. xxi. 35.

[c] Unscriptural detail.

κεῖσθαι γὰρ τῷ ζῆν αὐτὸ καὶ βλέπειν μόνον κἂν ἀλλότριον δοκῇ, τῆς δ' ἑτέρας ἑτοίμως ἐχούσης διαιρούμενον ἰδεῖν τὸ παιδίον καὶ προσέτι βασανι-
33 σθῆναι καὶ αὐτὴν ἀξιούσης, ὁ βασιλεὺς ἐπιγνοὺς τὰς ἑκατέρων φωνὰς ἀπὸ τῆς ἀληθείας γεγενημένας τῇ μὲν ἀνακραγούσῃ τὸ παιδίον προσέκρινε, μητέρα γὰρ αὐτὴν ἀληθῶς εἶναι, τῆς δὲ ἄλλης κατέγνω πονηρίαν τό τε ἴδιον ἀποκτεινάσης καὶ τὸ τῆς φίλης σπουδαζούσης ἀπολλύμενον θεάσασθαι.
34 τοῦτο μέγα δεῖγμα καὶ τεκμήριον τῆς τοῦ βασιλέως φρονήσεως καὶ σοφίας ἐνόμιζε τὸ πλῆθος, κἀξ ἐκείνης τὸ λοιπὸν τῆς ἡμέρας ὡς θείαν ἔχοντι διάνοιαν αὐτῷ προσεῖχον.

35 (3) Στρατηγοὶ δ' αὐτῷ καὶ ἡγεμόνες ἦσαν τῆς χώρας ἁπάσης οἵδε· τῆς μὲν Ἐφραίμου κληρουχίας Οὔρης· ἐπὶ δὲ τῆς Βιθιέμες[1] τοπαρχίας ἦν Διόκληρος· τὴν δὲ τῶν Δώρων καὶ τὴν παραλίαν Ἀβινάδαβος εἶχεν ὑφ' αὐτῷ[2] γεγαμηκὼς τὴν
36 Σολομῶνος θυγατέρα· τὸ δὲ μέγα πεδίον ἦν ὑπὸ Βαναίᾳ τῷ Ἀχίλου παιδί, προσεπῆρχε[3] δὲ καὶ τῆς ἄχρι Ἰορδάνου πάσης· τὴν δὲ Γαλαδῖτιν καὶ Γαυλανῖτιν ἕως τοῦ Λιβάνου ὄρους καὶ πόλεις ἑξήκοντα

[1] Βηθλεέμης SP: Bethlem Lat.: Βηθσέμες Bosius: Βαιθσέμες Schotanus.
[2] Dindorf: ὑπ' αὐτῷ codd.
[3] Hudson: προσυπῆρχε codd.

---

[a] That is, to prove her veracity; the text may, however, mean that she wished her opponent to be tortured. The phrase is an unscriptural detail.

[b] Josephus here omits the list of Solomon's court officers, given in 1 Kings iv. 2 ff.

[c] Heb. *Ben Ḥûr* (A.V. son of Hur), LXX Βαιώρ, *v.l.* Βὲν υἱὸς Ὥρ.

it were hers, for she would be content to have it alive and only look at it, even if it should seem to be another's, while the other woman was prepared to see it divided and even asked that she herself[a] be put to torture. Thereupon the king, recognizing that the words of either were prompted by her true sentiments, adjudged the child to the one who cried out, holding that she was really its mother, and condemned the other for her wickedness both in having killed her own son and in being anxious to see her friend's child destroyed. This the multitude considered a great sign and proof of the king's prudence and wisdom, and from that day on hearkened to him as to one possessed of a godlike understanding.

Solomon's provincial governors. 1 Kings iv. 7.

(3) [b] Now his generals and governors of the whole country were as follows: over the territory of Ephraim was Urēs[c]; and over the toparchy of Bithiemes[d] was Dioklēros[e]; the district of Dor and the coast were under Abinadab,[f] who had married Solomon's daughter[g]; the great plain[h] was under Banaias[i] the son of Achilos,[j] who also governed all the country as far as the Jordan; all of Galaditis and Gaulanitis[k] up to Mount Lebanon was governed by

[d] Bibl. Beth-shemesh, LXX Βαιθσάμυς. Scripture adds three other cities as belonging to this district.

[e] Heb. *Ben Deqer* (A.V. son of Dekar), LXX υἱὸς Δακάρ, cod. B Ῥῆχας, Luc. Ῥῆχαβ. Josephus's form, if not a corruption of the first LXX form, may be a deliberate Hellenization of the name.

[f] So the Heb. and some LXX MSS.; other LXX MSS. Ἀμιναδάβ. Josephus omits Hesed, the governor of Aruboth, Sochoh and Hepher, vs. 10.

[g] Called Taphath in Scripture.

[h] Including Taanach, Megiddo and Beth-shean.

[i] Bibl. Baana, LXX Βαανά, cod. B Βακχά, Luc. Βαχά.

[j] Bibl. Ahilud, LXX Ἀχιλούθ, cod. B Ἀχειμάχ, Luc. Ἀχιάβ.

[k] Bibl. Gilead and Argob in Bashan.

μεγάλας καὶ ὀχυρωτάτας ἔχων ὑφ᾽ αὑτὸν Γαβάρης διεῖπεν· Ἀχινάδαβος δὲ τῆς Γαλιλαίας ὅλης ἄχρι Σιδῶνος ἐπετρόπευε συνοικῶν καὶ αὐτὸς θυγατρὶ
37 Σολομῶνος Βασίμα τοὔνομα· τὴν δὲ περὶ Ἀκὴν[1] παραλίαν εἶχε Βανακάτης· Σαφάτης δὲ τὸ Ἰταβύριον ὄρος καὶ Καρμήλιον καὶ τὴν κάτω Γαλιλαίαν ἄχρι τοῦ ποταμοῦ Ἰορδάνου χώραν[2] πᾶσαν ἐπετέτραπτο· Σουμούις δὲ τὴν Βενιαμίτιδος κληρουχίαν ἐγκεχείριστο· Γαβάρης δὲ εἶχε τὴν πέραν τοῦ Ἰορδάνου χώραν· ἐπὶ δὲ τούτων εἷς πάλιν ἄρχων
38 ἀποδέδεικτο. θαυμαστὴν δ᾽ ἐπίδοσιν ἔλαβεν ὅ τε τῶν Ἑβραίων λαὸς καὶ ἡ Ἰούδα φυλὴ πρὸς γεωργίαν τραπέντων καὶ τὴν τῆς γῆς ἐπιμέλειαν· εἰρήνης γὰρ ἀπολαύοντες καὶ πολέμοις καὶ ταραχαῖς μὴ περισπώμενοι καὶ προσέτι τῆς ποθεινοτάτης ἐλευθερίας ἀκρατῶς ἐμφορούμενοι πρὸς τὸ[3] συναύξειν ἕκαστος τὰ οἰκεῖα καὶ ποιεῖν ἄξια πλείονος ὑπῆρχεν.
39 (4) Ἦσαν δὲ καὶ ἕτεροι τῷ βασιλεῖ ἡγεμόνες, οἳ τῆς τε Σύρων γῆς καὶ τῶν ἀλλοφύλων, ἥτις ἦν ἀπ᾽ Εὐφράτου ποταμοῦ διήκουσα μέχρι τῆς

[1] περὶ Ἀκὴν M: Περιαλκῆ RO: Πετριακὴν SP: circa arcae civitatem Lat.: περὶ Ἀρκὴν Naber.
[2] + ἐπὶ (δὲ) τούτων (τούτῳ) codd. [3] τῷ Niese.

[a] Heb. *Ben Geber* (A.V. son of Geber), LXX υἱὸς Γάβερ, Luc. Γάμερ.
[b] Josephus here combines two verses, 1 Kings iv. 14, 15, which mention two separate governors, "14. Ahinadab, the son of Iddo, had Mahanaim. 15. Ahimaaz was in Naphtali; he also took Basmath (LXX Βασεμμάθ), the daughter of Solomon, to wife."
[c] Bibl. Asher and Aloth; this was west of Naphtali, in the neighbourhood of Tyre.
[d] Bibl. Baanah, LXX Βαανά, *v.l.* Βαναίας.
[e] Bibl. Jehoshaphat, LXX Ἰωσαφάτ. Josephus follows the

Gabarēs,[a] who had under him sixty great and strongly fortified cities; Achinadab administered all of Galilee as far as Sidon, and he was also married to a daughter of Solomon, named Basima[b]; the coast about Akē[c] was under Banakatēs[d]; to Saphatēs[e] was entrusted Mount Itabyrion[f] and Mount Carmel and all of lower Galilee as far as the river Jordan[g]; Sūmūis[h] was given the territory of Benjamin to rule; Gabarēs[i] had the country across the Jordan. And one more was appointed as ruler over these.[j] Now a wonderful increase was obtained by the people of the Hebrews and the tribe of Judah when they turned to husbandry and the cultivation of the soil, for, as they enjoyed peace and were undistracted by wars and disturbances and also enjoyed to the fullest most desirable freedom, they devoted themselves, each one to increasing his holdings and making them more valuable.

The requisitions for Solomon's table.

(4) The king also had other governors, who ruled the land of the Syrians and the non-Israelites, extending from the Euphrates[k] river to Egypt, and col-

Heb. in mentioning Jehoshaphat directly after Baanah, while the LXX inserts two verses mentioning Shimei in Benjamin and Geber in Gilead.

[f] Bibl. Tabor.

[g] Scripture does not specify, saying only "in Issachar."

[h] Bibl. Shimei, LXX Σεμεεί, Luc. Σαμαά.

[i] Bibl. Geber, LXX Γάβερ.

[j] Heb. (vs. 19 end), "and one governor (*neṣîb*) was in the land" (A.V. "and he <*i.e.* Geber> was the only officer which was in the land"), LXX καὶ Νασὲφ εἷς ἐν γῇ Ἰούδᾳ (Luc. ἐν τῇ γῇ). The Biblical text is obscure and probably corrupt. Josephus's "appointed" seems to be based on the Targum.

[k] Heb. "from the river of the land of the Philistines," which must be corrected, as is done in 2 Chron. ix. 26, to "from the river (*i.e.* the Euphrates, the river *par excellence*) to the land of the Philistines," etc.

Αἰγυπτίων, ἐπῆρχον ἐκλέγοντες αὐτῷ φόρους παρὰ
40 τῶν ἐθνῶν. συνετέλουν δὲ καὶ τῇ τραπέζῃ καθ' ἡμέραν καὶ τῷ δείπνῳ τοῦ βασιλέως σεμιδάλεως μὲν κόρους τριάκοντα, ἀλεύρου δ' ἑξήκοντα, σιτιστοὺς δὲ βόας δέκα καὶ νομάδας βόας εἴκοσι, σιτιστοὺς δὲ ἄρνας ἑκατόν. ταῦτα πάντα πάρεξ τῶν ἀπ' ἄγρας, ἐλάφων λέγω καὶ βουβάλων καὶ τῶν πετεινῶν καὶ ἰχθύων, ἐκομίζετο καθ' ἡμέραν τῷ
41 βασιλεῖ παρὰ τῶν ἀλλοφύλων. τοσοῦτον δὲ πλῆθος ἦν ἁρμάτων Σολομῶνι, ὡς τέσσαρας εἶναι μυριάδας φατνῶν τῶν ὑποζευγνυμένων ἵππων· χωρὶς δὲ τούτων ἦσαν ἱππεῖς δισχίλιοι καὶ μύριοι, ὧν οἱ μὲν ἡμίσεις τῷ βασιλεῖ προσήδρευον ἐν Ἱεροσολύμοις, οἱ δὲ λοιποὶ κατὰ τὰς βασιλικὰς διεσπαρμένοι κώμας ἐν αὐταῖς κατέμενον. ὁ δ' αὐτὸς ἡγεμὼν ὁ τὴν τοῦ βασιλέως δαπάνην πεπιστευμένος καὶ τοῖς ἵπποις ἐχορήγει τὰ ἐπιτήδεια συγκομίζων εἰς ὃν ὁ βασιλεὺς διέτριβε τόπον.

42 (5) Τοσαύτη δ' ἦν ἣν ὁ θεὸς παρέσχε Σολομῶνι φρόνησιν καὶ σοφίαν, ὡς τούς τε ἀρχαίους ὑπερβάλλειν ἀνθρώπους καὶ μηδὲ τοὺς Αἰγυπτίους, οἳ πάντων συνέσει διενεγκεῖν λέγονται, συγκρινομένους λείπεσθαι παρ' ὀλίγον, ἀλλὰ καὶ πλεῖστον ἀφεστηκότας τῆς τοῦ βασιλέως φρονήσεως ἐλέγ-
43 χεσθαι. ὑπερῆρε δὲ καὶ διήνεγκε σοφίᾳ καὶ τῶν κατὰ τὸν αὐτὸν καιρὸν δόξαν ἐχόντων παρὰ τοῖς Ἑβραίοις ἐπὶ δεινότητι, ὧν οὐ παρελεύσομαι τὰ

[a] The *kor*, also called *homer*, was equivalent to about 370 litres or 11 bushels.

lected tribute for him from the nations. They also contributed daily to the king's table for his dinner thirty *kors* [a] of fine flour, sixty of meal, ten fatted oxen and twenty pastured oxen and a hundred fatted [b] lambs,—all these, in addition to wild game, that is, deer and antelopes and birds and fish, were daily brought to the king by the foreigners. And Solomon had so great a number of chariots that there were forty thousand stalls for the yoked horses.[c] Beside these he had twelve thousand horsemen, half of whom attended the king in Jerusalem, while the rest were scattered about the royal villages and dwelt in them. And the same officer who was entrusted with the king's expenses also furnished supplies for the horses, bringing them to the place where the king resided.[d]

1 Kings iv. 21 (Heb. v. 1).

(5) Now so great was the prudence and wisdom which God granted Solomon that he surpassed the ancients,[e] and even the Egyptians, who are said to excel all men in understanding, were not only, when compared with him, a little inferior but proved to fall far short of the king in sagacity. He also surpassed and excelled in wisdom those who in his own time had a reputation for cleverness among the Hebrews, and whose names I shall not omit; they were Athanos [f]

Solomon's great wisdom. 1 Kings iv. 39 (Heb. v. 9).

[b] Unscriptural detail.

[c] Recent excavations at Megiddo have uncovered stables of the Solomonic period, built to accommodate some 300 horses, *cf.* Olmstead, *History of Palestine and Syria*, pp. 344 f.

[d] Scripture, 1 Kings iv. 28 (Heb. v. 8), does not make clear whether these provisions were brought to the place where the king resided or where the various officers were.

[e] So the LXX, translating Heb. *benê qedem* "sons of the east"; the variant is readily understandable since the root *qdm* also means "ancient."

[f] Bibl. Ethan, LXX Γαιθάν, Luc. Αἰθάμ.

ὀνόματα· ἦσαν δὲ Ἄθανος καὶ Αἱμανὸς καὶ Χάλ-
44 κεος καὶ Δάρδανος υἱοὶ Ἡμάωνος. συνετάξατο δὲ καὶ βιβλία περὶ ᾠδῶν καὶ μελῶν πέντε πρὸς τοῖς χιλίοις καὶ παραβολῶν καὶ εἰκόνων βίβλους τρισχιλίας· καθ' ἕκαστον γὰρ εἶδος δένδρου παραβολὴν εἶπεν ἀπὸ ὑσσώπου ἕως κέδρου, τὸν αὐτὸν δὲ τρόπον καὶ περὶ κτηνῶν καὶ τῶν ἐπιγείων ἁπάντων ζῴων καὶ τῶν νηκτῶν καὶ τῶν ἀερίων· οὐδεμίαν γὰρ[1] φύσιν ἠγνόησεν οὐδὲ παρῆλθεν ἀνεξέταστον, ἀλλ' ἐν πάσαις ἐφιλοσόφησε καὶ τὴν ἐπιστήμην τῶν ἐν αὐταῖς ἰδιωμάτων ἄκραν ἐπεδεί-
45 ξατο. παρέσχε δ' αὐτῷ μαθεῖν ὁ θεὸς καὶ τὴν κατὰ τῶν δαιμόνων τέχνην εἰς ὠφέλειαν καὶ θεραπείαν τοῖς ἀνθρώποις· ἐπῳδάς τε συνταξάμενος αἷς παρηγορεῖται τὰ νοσήματα καὶ τρόπους ἐξορκώσεων κατέλιπεν, οἷς οἱ ἐνδούμενοι[2] τὰ δαι-
46 μόνια ὡς μηκέτ' ἐπανελθεῖν ἐκδιώκουσι.[3] καὶ αὕτη μέχρι νῦν παρ' ἡμῖν ἡ θεραπεία πλεῖστον ἰσχύει· ἱστόρησα γάρ τινα Ἐλεάζαρον τῶν ὁμοφύλων Οὐεσπασιανοῦ παρόντος καὶ τῶν υἱῶν αὐτοῦ καὶ χιλιάρχων καὶ ἄλλου στρατιωτικοῦ πλήθους τοὺς ὑπὸ τῶν δαιμονίων λαμβανομένους ἀπολύοντα τούτων. ὁ δὲ τρόπος τῆς θεραπείας τοιοῦτος ἦν·

[1] + τούτων MSP.
[2] οἱ ἐνδούμενοι RO: ἐνδούμενοι MP: ἐνδούμενα E Lat.: ἐναδόμενα S.
[3] ἐκδιώξουσι ROE.

---

[a] Bibl. Heman, LXX Αἰνάν, Ἡμάν, Luc. Αἱμάν.
[b] Bibl. Chalcol, LXX Χαλκάδ, Χαλκάλ, Luc. Χαλκάχ.
[c] Bibl. Darda, LXX Δαραλά, Δαρδά, Luc. Δαρδαέ. Reitzenstein, *Poimandres*, p. 163, sees here a reference to the Dardanos often mentioned in Graeco-Egyptian magical texts as the founder of the mysteries of the Mother Goddess.

and Haimanos [a] and Chalkeos [b] and Dardanos,[c] sons of Hĕmaŏn.[d] He also composed a thousand and five books of odes and songs,[e] and three thousand books of parables and similitudes,[f] for he spoke a parable about every kind of tree from the hyssop to the cedar, and in like manner about birds and all kinds of terrestrial creatures and those that swim and those that fly. There was no form of nature with which he was not acquainted or which he passed over without examining, but he studied them all philosophically and revealed the most complete knowledge of their several properties. And God granted him knowledge of the art used against demons for the benefit and healing of men. He also composed incantations by which illnesses are relieved, and left behind forms of exorcisms with which those possessed by demons drive them out, never to return.[g] And this kind of cure is of very great power among us to this day, for I have seen a certain Eleazar,[h] a countryman of mine, in the presence of Vespasian, his sons, tribunes and a number of other soldiers, free men possessed by demons, and this was the manner of the cure: he

His proverbs. 1 Kings iv. 32 (LXX iv. 28; Heb. v. 12).

His charms against demons.

[d] Bibl. Mahol, LXX Μαούλ, Μάλ.

[e] So the Heb.; LXX 5000. Both texts, however, refer to the number of songs, not the number of books of songs.

[f] Here too Scripture gives the number of parables, not the number of books of parables.

[g] Though Scripture says nothing of Solomon's power over demons and skill in healing, both Jewish and Christian as well as Muslim tradition contain many legends on these subjects, some of them to be found in the *Arabian Nights*.

[h] Perhaps, as Weill suggests, he was an Essene, for this sect possessed books of medicine attributed to Solomon. *Cf.* Ginzberg vi. 291 note 48, "the recognized authorities of rabbinic Judaism condemn the use of the conjuring books ascribed to Solomon, whereas the early Church held them in high esteem."

47 προσφέρων ταῖς ῥισὶ τοῦ δαιμονιζομένου τὸν δακτύλιον ἔχοντα ὑπὸ τῇ σφραγῖδι ῥίζαν ἐξ ὧν ὑπέδειξε Σολομὼν ἔπειτα ἐξεῖλκεν ὀσφρομένῳ διὰ τῶν μυκτήρων τὸ δαιμόνιον, καὶ πεσόντος εὐθὺς τἀνθρώπου μηκέτ' εἰς αὐτὸν ἐπανήξειν[1] ὥρκου Σολομῶνός τε μεμνημένος καὶ τὰς ἐπῳδὰς ἃς
48 συνέθηκεν ἐκεῖνος ἐπιλέγων. βουλόμενος δὲ πεῖσαι καὶ παραστῆσαι τοῖς παρατυγχάνουσιν ὁ Ἐλεάζαρος ὅτι ταύτην ἔχει τὴν ἰσχύν, ἐτίθει μικρὸν ἔμπροσθεν ἤτοι ποτήριον πλῆρες ὕδατος ἢ ποδόνιπτρον καὶ τῷ δαιμονίῳ προσέταττεν ἐξιόντι τἀνθρώπου ταῦτ' ἀνατρέψαι καὶ παρασχεῖν ἐπιγνῶναι τοῖς ὁρῶσιν ὅτι καταλέλοιπε τὸν ἄνθρωπον.
49 γενομένου[2] δὲ τούτου σαφὴς ἡ Σολομῶνος καθίστατο σύνεσις καὶ σοφία δι' ἥν, ἵνα γνῶσιν ἅπαντες αὐτοῦ τὸ μεγαλεῖον τῆς φύσεως καὶ τὸ θεοφιλὲς καὶ λάθῃ μηδένα τῶν ὑπὸ τὸν ἥλιον ἡ τοῦ βασιλέως περὶ πᾶν εἶδος ἀρετῆς ὑπερβολή, περὶ τούτων εἰπεῖν προήχθημεν.

50 (6) Ὁ δὲ τῶν Τυρίων βασιλεὺς Εἴρωμος ἀκούσας ὅτι Σολομὼν τὴν τοῦ πατρὸς διεδέξατο βασιλείαν ὑπερήσθη (φίλος γὰρ ἐτύγχανε τῷ Δαυίδῃ) καὶ πέμψας πρὸς αὐτὸν ἠσπάζετό τε καὶ συνέχαιρεν ἐπὶ τοῖς παροῦσιν ἀγαθοῖς. ἀποστέλλει δὲ πρὸς αὐτὸν Σολομὼν γράμματα δηλοῦντα τάδε·
51 "βασιλεὺς Σολομὼν Εἰρώμῳ βασιλεῖ. ἴσθι μου τὸν πατέρα βουληθέντα κατασκευάσαι τῷ θεῷ ναὸν ὑπὸ τῶν πολέμων καὶ τῶν συνεχῶν στρατειῶν κεκωλυμένον· οὐ γὰρ ἐπαύσατο πρότερον τοὺς ἐχθροὺς καταστρεφόμενος πρὶν ἢ πάντας αὐτοὺς

[1] ἐπανελθεῖν MSPE.
[2] Niese: γινομένου codd.

put to the nose of the possessed man a ring which had under its seal one of the roots[a] prescribed by Solomon, and then, as the man smelled it, drew out the demon through his nostrils, and, when the man at once fell down, adjured the demon never to come back into him, speaking Solomon's name and reciting the incantations which he had composed. Then, wishing to convince the bystanders and prove to them that he had this power, Eleazar placed a cup or foot-basin full of water a little way off and commanded the demon, as it went out of the man, to overturn it and make known to the spectators that he had left the man. And when this was done, the understanding and wisdom of Solomon were clearly revealed, on account of which we have been induced to speak of these things, in order that all men may know the greatness of his nature and how God favoured him, and that no one under the sun may be ignorant of the king's surpassing virtue of every kind.

Hiram (Eirōmos), King of Tyre, sends greetings to Solomon.
1 Kings v. 1 (Heb. v. 15).

(6) Now when Eirōmos,[b] the king of the Tyrians, heard that Solomon had succeeded to his father's kingdom, he was overjoyed, for he was a friend of David, and sent him greetings and congratulations on his present good fortune. Then Solomon wrote a letter in return, the contents of which were as follows:[c] "King Solomon to King Eirōmos. Know that my father wished to build a temple to God but was prevented by wars and continual expeditions, for he did not leave off subduing his enemies until he

[a] T. Reinach plausibly conjectures that this was the *baaras* plant described in *B.J.* vii. 180 ff.

[b] Bibl. Hiram, *cf. A.* vii. 66 note.

[c] *Cf. Ap.* i. 111 note and the text of the letters, given by the Jewish Alexandrian writer Eupolemos *ap.* Eusebius, *Praep. Evang.* ix. 33 ff.

52 φόρων ὑποτελεῖς πεποιηκέναι.[1] ἐγὼ δὲ χάριν οἶδα τῷ θεῷ τῆς παρούσης εἰρήνης καὶ διὰ ταύτην εὐσχολῶν οἰκοδομῆσαι τῷ θεῷ βούλομαι τὸν οἶκον· καὶ γὰρ ὑπ' ἐμοῦ τοῦτον ἔσεσθαι τῷ πατρί μου προεῖπεν ὁ θεός. διὸ παρακαλῶ σε συμπέμψαι τινὰς τοῖς ἐμοῖς εἰς Λίβανον τὸ ὄρος κόψοντας ξύλα· πρὸς γὰρ τομὴν ὕλης ἐπιστημονέστερον ἔχουσι τῶν ἡμετέρων οἱ Σιδώνιοι. μισθὸν δ' ὃν ἂν ὁρίσῃς ἐγὼ τοῖς ὑλουργοῖς παρέξω."

53 (7) Ἀναγνοὺς δὲ τὴν ἐπιστολὴν Εἴρωμος καὶ τοῖς ἐπεσταλμένοις ἡσθεὶς ἀντιγράφει τῷ Σολομῶνι· "βασιλεὺς Εἴρωμος βασιλεῖ Σολομῶνι. τὸν μὲν θεὸν εὐλογεῖν ἄξιον ὅτι σοι τὴν πατρῴαν παρέδωκεν ἡγεμονίαν ἀνδρὶ σοφῷ καὶ πᾶσαν ἀρετὴν ἔχοντι, ἐγὼ δὲ τούτοις ἡδόμενος ἅπαντα ὑπουργήσω τὰ
54 ἐπεσταλμένα· τεμὼν γὰρ ξύλα πολλὰ καὶ μεγάλα κέδρου τε καὶ κυπαρίσσου διὰ τῶν ἐμῶν καταπέμψω ἐπὶ θάλασσαν καὶ κελεύσω τοὺς ἐμοὺς σχεδίαν πηξαμένους εἰς ὃν ἂν βουληθῇς τόπον τῆς σαυτοῦ χώρας πλεύσαντας ἀποθέσθαι· ἔπειθ' οἱ σοὶ διακομίσουσιν εἰς Ἱεροσόλυμα. ὅπως δὲ καὶ σὺ παράσχῃς ἡμῖν ἀντὶ τούτων σῖτον, οὗ διὰ τὸ νῆσον οἰκεῖν δεόμεθα, φρόντισον."

55 (8) Διαμένει δὲ ἄχρι τῆς τήμερον τὰ τῶν ἐπιστολῶν τούτων ἀντίγραφα οὐκ ἐν τοῖς ἡμετέροις μόνον σωζόμενα βιβλίοις ἀλλὰ καὶ παρὰ Τυρίοις, ὥστ' εἴ τις ἐθελήσειε τὸ ἀκριβὲς μαθεῖν, δεηθεὶς τῶν ἐπὶ τοῦ[2] Τυρίων γραμματοφυλακείου δημοσίων εὕροι συμφωνοῦντ' ἂν[3] τοῖς εἰρημένοις ὑφ' ἡμῶν
56 τὰ παρ' ἐκείνοις. ταῦτα μὲν οὖν διεξῆλθον βου-

[1] ἐποίησεν MSP.
[2] Niese: τῶν codd.
[3] ἂν add. Niese.

had forced all of them to pay tribute. But I give thanks to God for the peace I now enjoy, and as on that account I am at leisure, I wish to build a house to God, for He indeed foretold to my father that this would be made by me. I therefore request you to send some men along with mine to Mount Lebanon to cut timber, for the Sidonians are more skilful in cutting timber than are our men. And whatever wage you may fix, I will give it to the woodcutters."

(7) When Eirōmos read this letter, he was pleased with the request contained in it, and wrote back to Solomon, "King Eirōmos to King Solomon. It is proper to praise God for having given to you, who are a wise man endowed with every virtue, your father's royal power. As for me, I am very glad of this and I will assist you in all the things mentioned in your letter. I will have my men cut down many great cedars and cypresses [a] and send them down to the sea, and will order my servants to put together a raft and sail and deliver them at whatever place in your country you may choose, and then your men shall carry them to Jerusalem. And take care, on your part, to furnish us in return for them with grain, of which we are in need because we live on an island." [b]

Hiram agrees to help Solomon build the temple. 1 Kings v. 7 (Heb. v. 21).

(8) To this day there remain copies of these letters, preserved not only in our books but also by the Tyrians, so that if anyone wished to learn the exact truth, he would, by inquiring of the public officials in charge of the Tyrian archives, find that their records are in agreement with what we have said. [c] These things I have given in detail because I wish

Preservation of the correspondence of Hiram and Solomon.

[a] LXX πεύκινα "pines"; Heb. *berôš*, which is elsewhere in the LXX translated as κυπάρισσος "cypress."

[b] Or "peninsula" (νῆσος means both), which Tyre really was. The detail is unscriptural.

[c] *Cf. Ap.* i. 106 ff.

λόμενος γνῶναι τοὺς ἐντευξομένους ὅτι μηδὲν μᾶλλον ἔξω τῆς ἀληθείας λέγομεν, μηδὲ πιθανοῖς τισι καὶ πρὸς ἀπάτην καὶ τέρψιν ἐπαγωγοῖς τὴν ἱστορίαν διαλαμβάνοντες τὴν μὲν ἐξέτασιν φεύγειν πειρώμεθα, πιστεύεσθαι δ' εὐθὺς ἀξιοῦμεν, οὐδὲ[1] συγκεχωρημένον ἡμῖν κατεξανισταμένοις τοῦ πρέποντος τῇ πραγματείᾳ[2] ἀθῴοις ὑπάρχειν, ἀλλὰ μηδεμιᾶς ἀποδοχῆς τυγχάνειν παρακαλοῦντες, ἂν μὴ μετὰ ἀποδείξεως καὶ τεκμηρίων ἰσχυρῶν ἐμφανίζειν δυνώμεθα τὴν ἀλήθειαν.

57 (9) Ὁ δὲ βασιλεὺς Σολομὼν ὡς ἐκομίσθη τὰ παρὰ τοῦ Τυρίων βασιλέως γράμματα τήν τε προθυμίαν αὐτοῦ καὶ τὴν εὔνοιαν ἐπῄνεσε καὶ οἷς ἠξίωσε τούτοις αὐτὸν ἠμείψατο, σίτου μὲν αὐτῷ κατ' ἔτος πέμψας δισμυρίους κόρους καὶ τοσούτους ἐλαίου βάτους[3]· ὁ δὲ βάτος δύναται[4] ξέστας ἑβδομήκοντα δύο· τὸ δ' αὐτὸ μέτρον καὶ οἴνου παρ-
58 εἶχεν. ἡ μὲν οὖν Εἰρώμου φιλία καὶ Σολομῶνος ἀπὸ τούτων ἔτι μᾶλλον ηὔξησε καὶ διαμενεῖν[5] ὤμοσαν εἰς ἅπαν. ὁ δὲ βασιλεὺς ἐπέταξε παντὶ τῷ λαῷ φόρον ἐργάτας τρισμυρίους, οἷς ἄπονον τὴν ἐργασίαν κατέστησε μερίσας αὐτὴν συνετῶς· μυρίους γὰρ ἐποίησε κόπτοντας ἐπὶ μῆνα ἕνα ἐν τῷ Λιβάνῳ ὄρει δύο δὲ μῆνας ἀναπαύεσθαι παραγενομένους ἐπὶ τὰ οἰκεῖα, μέχρις οὗ[6] πάλιν οἱ δισμύριοι τὴν ἐργασίαν ἀναπληρώσωσι[7] κατὰ τὸν
59 ὡρισμένον χρόνον· ἔπειθ' οὕτως συνέβαινε τοῖς πρώτοις μυρίοις διὰ τετάρτου μηνὸς ἀπαντᾶν ἐπὶ

[1] ὡς οὐδὲ Naber. [2] Niese: τῆς πραγματείας codd.
[3] βάδους MSPE.
[4] + χωρῆσαι MSP Theodoretus (vid.).
[5] Niese: διαμένειν codd. [6] ἂν Naber.
[7] ἀναπληρώσουσι conj. Niese.

my readers to know that we have said nothing more than what is true, and have not, by inserting into the history various plausible and seductive passages meant to deceive and entertain, attempted to evade critical inquiry, asking to be instantly believed; nor should we be indulgently held blameless if we depart from what is proper to a historical narrative; on the contrary, we ask that no hearing be given us unless we are able to establish the truth with demonstrations and convincing evidence.

(9) Now King Solomon, on receiving the letter from the king of the Tyrians, commended his zeal and goodwill, and gave him in return the supplies he had requested, sending him yearly twenty thousand *kors* [a] of grain and as many [b] *baths* of oil—the *bath* containing seventy-two *sextarii* (*xestai*).[c] He also furnished the same measure of wine. And so the friendship of Eirōmos and Solomon increased through these things, and they swore that it should continue for ever. And the king imposed on all the people a levy of thirty thousand workmen, whose labour he made less difficult by dividing it wisely among them, for he had ten thousand cut timber for a month on Mount Lebanon and then return to their homes and rest for two months until the other twenty thousand had finished their work in the appointed time. Thus it would then be the turn of the first ten thousand to return to their work in the fourth month. The

Solomon's gifts to Hiram. 1 Kings v. 11 (Heb. v. 25).

Division of the labour. 1 Kings v. 13 (Heb. v. 27).

[a] *Cf.* § 40 note.

[b] So LXX; Heb. has "20 *baths*" instead of 20,000; both texts in the parallel passage, 2 Chron. ii. 10, add "20,000 *kors* of barley."

[c] The *bath* was equivalent to about 36 litres or 9 gallons; it contained 72 *logs*, which are thus equated by Josephus with *sextarii*.

τὸ ἔργον. ἐγεγόνει δ' ἐπίτροπος τοῦ φόρου τούτου Ἀδώραμος.[a] ἦσαν δ' ἐκ τῶν παροίκων οὓς Δαυίδης καταλελοίπει τῶν μὲν παρακομιζόντων τὴν λιθίαν καὶ τὴν ἄλλην ὕλην ἑπτὰ μυριάδες, τῶν δὲ λατομούντων ὀκτάκις μύριοι, τούτων δ' ἐπι-
60 στάται τρισχίλιοι καὶ τριακόσιοι.[b] προστετάχει δὲ λίθους μὲν αὐτοῖς τέμνειν μεγάλους εἰς τοὺς τοῦ ναοῦ θεμελίους, ἁρμόσαντας δὲ πρῶτον καὶ συνδήσαντας ἐν τῷ ὄρει κατακομίζειν οὕτως εἰς τὴν πόλιν. ἐγίνετο δὲ ταῦτ' οὐ παρὰ τῶν οἰκοδόμων τῶν ἐγχωρίων μόνον, ἀλλὰ καὶ ὧν ὁ Εἴρωμος ἔπεμψε τεχνιτῶν.
61 (iii. 1) Τῆς δ' οἰκοδομίας τοῦ ναοῦ Σολομὼν ἤρξατο τέταρτον ἔτος ἤδη τῆς βασιλείας ἔχων μηνὶ δευτέρῳ, ὃν Μακεδόνες μὲν Ἀρτεμίσιον καλοῦσιν Ἑβραῖοι δὲ Ἰάρ,[c] μετὰ ἔτη πεντακόσια καὶ ἐνενήκοντα καὶ δύο τῆς ἀπ' Αἰγύπτου τῶν Ἰσραηλιτῶν ἐξόδου,[d] μετὰ δὲ χίλια καὶ εἴκοσι ἔτη τῆς Ἁβράμου εἰς τὴν Χαναναίαν ἐκ τῆς Μεσοποταμίας ἀφίξεως, ἀπὸ δὲ τῆς ἐπομβρίας μετὰ
62 χίλια καὶ τετρακόσια καὶ τεσσαράκοντα· ἀπὸ δὲ τοῦ πρώτου γεννηθέντος Ἀδάμου ἕως οὗ τὸν ναὸν ᾠκοδόμησε Σολομών, διεληλύθει τὰ πάντα ἔτη τρισχίλια καὶ ἑκατὸν καὶ δύο. καθ' ὃν δὲ ὁ ναὸς

---

[a] Bibl. Adoniram, *cf. A.* vii. 293 note.

[b] So Heb.; LXX 3600, *v.l.* 3500, Luc. 3700. Both Heb. and LXX have 3600 in 2 Chron. ii. 18. *Cf. A.* vii. 335 note.

[c] Josephus gives the later Hebrew name (Iyyar) of the month = April-May. Scripture here uses the old Canaanite name, *Ziw* (A.V. Zif).

[d] Heb. and Luc. 480, LXX 440. Josephus's figure agrees with that given in *A.* vii. 68 (*cf.* note *ad loc.*), but differs from his chronology in *A.* xx. 230 and *Ap.* ii. 19.

officer in charge of this levy was Adōramos.[a] And of the aliens whom David had left, there were seventy thousand to carry stone and other material, and eighty thousand stone-cutters, and over them were three thousand three hundred[b] overseers. Now he had ordered them to hew large stones for the foundations of the temple and, after fitting them and binding them together on the mountain, to bring them down in this way to the city. And this was done not only by the native builders but also by the artisans whom Eirōmos had sent.

(iii. 1) Solomon began the building of the temple in the fourth year of his reign, in the second month, which the Macedonians call Artemisios and the Hebrews Iar,[c] five hundred and ninety-two years after the Israelites' exodus from Egypt,[d] one thousand and twenty years after the coming of Abraham to Canaan from Mesopotamia,[e] one thousand four hundred and forty years after the deluge[f]; and from the creation of Adam the first man to the time when Solomon built the temple there elapsed altogether three thousand one hundred and two years.[g] And

Chronology of the temple.
1 Kings vi. 1.

[e] In *A.* ii. 318 (=Ex. xii. 40) Josephus dates Abraham's coming to Canaan 430 years before the exodus, *i.e.* 1022 years before the building of the temple.

[f] According to this reckoning, 420 years (1440–1020) elapsed between the deluge and Abraham's coming to Canaan, but in *Ant.* i. 148 ff. the interval is to be reckoned as 1067 years.

[g] According to *Ant.* i. 82 the deluge came 2262 years after Adam's creation; if to this we add 1440 years, given above as the interval between the deluge and the building of the temple, we get 3702 instead of 3102 years between Adam's creation and the building of the temple. For an explanation of these chronological discrepancies *cf. Ant.* i. 82 note.

ἤρξατο οἰκοδομεῖσθαι χρόνον, κατ' ἐκεῖνον ἔτος ἤδη τῆς ἐν Τύρῳ βασιλείας ἑνδέκατον ἐνειστήκει Εἰρώμῳ, ἀπὸ δὲ τῆς[1] οἰκίσεως[2] εἰς τὴν οἰκοδομίαν τοῦ ναοῦ διεγεγόνει χρόνος ἐτῶν τεσσαράκοντα καὶ διακοσίων.

63 (2) Βάλλεται μὲν οὖν τῷ ναῷ θεμελίους ὁ βασιλεὺς ἐπὶ μήκιστον τῆς γῆς βάθος ὕλης λίθων ἰσχυρᾶς καὶ πρὸς χρόνον ἀντέχειν δυναμένης, οἳ τῇ τε γῇ συμφυέντες ἔμελλον ἔδαφος καὶ ἔρεισμα τῆς ἐποικοδομηθησομένης[3] κατασκευῆς ἔσεσθαι καὶ διὰ τὴν κάτωθεν ἰσχὺν οἴσειν ἀπόνως μέγεθός τε τῶν ἐπικεισομένων καὶ κάλλους πολυτέλειαν, ᾗ βάρος ἔμελλεν οὐχ ἧττον εἶναι τῶν ἄλλων ὅσα πρὸς ὕψος καὶ πρὸς ὄγκον κόσμου τε χάριν καὶ
64 μεγαλουργίας ἐπενοεῖτο. ἀνήγαγε δ' αὐτὸν ἄχρι τῆς ὀροφῆς ἐκ λευκοῦ λίθου πεποιημένον. τὸ μὲν οὖν ὕψος ἦν ἑξήκοντα πηχῶν, τῶν δ' αὐτῶν καὶ τὸ μῆκος, εὖρος δ' εἴκοσι. κατὰ τούτου δὲ ἄλλος ἦν ἐγηγερμένος ἴσος τοῖς μέτροις, ὥστε εἶναι τὸ πᾶν ὕψος τῷ ναῷ πηχῶν ἑκατὸν καὶ εἴκοσι· τέτραπτο
65 δὲ πρὸς τὴν ἀνατολήν. τὸ δὲ προνάιον αὐτοῦ προύστησαν[4] ἐπὶ πήχεις μὲν εἴκοσι τὸ μῆκος πρὸς τὸ εὖρος τοῦ οἴκου τεταμένον,[5] ἔχον δὲ πλάτος πήχεις δέκα εἰς ὕψος δὲ ἀνεγηγερμένον πηχῶν

[1] ἀπὸ δὲ τῆς ed. pr. Lat.: τῆς δὲ codd.
[2] ex Lat. Bekker: οἰκήσεως codd.
[3] ἐποικοδομησομένης ROM.
[4] προύστησεν Naber. [5] τεταγμένον MSP.

[a] Twelfth, according to *Ap.* i. 126.
[b] Justinus, in his Epitome of Trogus Pompeius, xviii. 3. 5, says that Tyre was founded a year before the fall of Troy. This, in turn, is dated by the Parian marble (*cf. Cambridge*

at the time when the temple began to be built—in that same year, Eirōmos was already in the eleventh [a] year of his reign at Tyre; from the founding (of this city) to the building of the temple there was an interval of two hundred and forty years.[b]

(2) And so the king had the foundations for the temple laid very very deep in the ground, the material being strong stones capable of resisting the wear of time, which would grow to the soil and be a base and support for the structure to be erected upon them, and which, because of their strength from below, would without difficulty bear the great mass resting on them and the precious ornaments, the weight of which would be no less than that of the other parts designed for height and massiveness and for graceful beauty and magnificence as well.[c] He built it up to the roof of white marble;[d] its height was sixty [e] cubits, its length was the same,[f] and its breadth was twenty cubits. Upon it was erected another story of equal proportions, so that the total height of the temple was a hundred and twenty cubits;[g] it faced toward the east. Then they placed a porch in front of it, twenty cubits in length, extending the width of the building, and ten cubits wide, and rising to a

Foundations of the temple. 1 Kings v. 17 (LXX vi. 2; Heb. v. 31).

Dimensions of the temple. 1 Kings vi. 2 (LXX vi. 6).

Ancient History, i. 178) in the year corresponding to 1209–1208 B.C.

[c] In the foregoing description Josephus has greatly amplified Scripture.

[d] Unscriptural detail.

[e] Heb. thirty, LXX twenty-five (*v.l.* = Heb.).

[f] So Heb.; LXX forty (*v.l.* = Heb.).

[g] This detail shows a confused understanding of 1 Kings vi. 3 and the parallel passage, 2 Chron. iii. 4, which speak of the porch before the temple, 120 cubits high according to 2 Chron. Josephus proceeds, in the next sentence, to describe this same porch.

ἑκατὸν καὶ εἴκοσι. περιῳκοδόμησε δὲ τὸν ναὸν
ἐν κύκλῳ τριάκοντα βραχέσιν οἴκοις, οἳ συνοχή
τε τοῦ παντὸς ἔμελλον ἔσεσθαι διὰ πυκνότητα καὶ
πλῆθος ἔξωθεν περικείμενοι, καὶ δὴ καὶ τὰς
66 εἰσόδους αὐτοῖς δι' ἀλλήλων κατεσκεύασεν. ἕκαστος δὲ τῶν οἴκων τούτων εὖρος μὲν εἶχε πέντε
πήχεις, μῆκος[1] δὲ τοὺς αὐτούς, ὕψος δὲ εἴκοσιν.
ἐπῳκοδόμηντο δὲ τούτοις ἄνωθεν ἕτεροι οἶκοι καὶ
πάλιν ἄλλοι κατ' αὐτῶν ἴσοι καὶ τοῖς μέτροις καὶ
τῷ ἀριθμῷ, ὡς τὸ πᾶν ὕψος αὐτοὺς λαβεῖν τῷ
κάτωθεν οἴκῳ παραπλήσιον· ὁ γὰρ ὑπερῷος οὐκ ἦν
67 περιῳκοδομημένος. ὄροφος δὲ αὐτοῖς ἐπεβέβλητο
κέδρου· καὶ τοῖς μὲν οἴκοις ἴδιος ἦν οὗτος ἑκάστῳ
πρὸς τοὺς πλησίον οὐ συνάπτων, τοῖς δ' ἄλλοις
ὑπῆρχεν ἡ στέγη κοινὴ δι' ἀλλήλων δεδομημένη
μηκίσταις δοκοῖς καὶ διηκούσαις ἁπάντων, ὡς τοὺς
μέσους τοίχους ὑπὸ τῶν αὐτῶν συγκρατουμένους
68 ξύλων ἐρρωμενεστέρους διὰ τοῦτο γίνεσθαι. τὴν
δὲ ὑπὸ τὰς δοκοὺς στέγην τῆς αὐτῆς ὕλης ἐβάλετο
πᾶσαν ἐξεσμένην εἰς φατνώματα καὶ προσκόλλησιν
χρυσοῦ. τοὺς δὲ τοίχους κεδρίναις διαλαβὼν
σανίσι χρυσὸν αὐταῖς ἐνετόρευσεν, ὥστε στίλβειν

[1] Niese: μήκους codd. E Lat.

---

[a] Scripture does not state how many chambers there were. This number may be derived from the description of Ezekiel's temple, Ezek. xl. 17, or, as Weill thinks, may have been reckoned by Josephus on the basis of the length of three sides of the temple (140 cubits), divided by the width of each chamber (5 cubits); this gives 28 chambers, and with the addition of 2 chambers at the corners 30 chambers altogether.

[b] Unscriptural detail.

[c] The height of the chambers is not given in Scripture.

height of a hundred and twenty cubits. And all around the temple he built thirty [a] small chambers which, surrounding it on the outside, were to hold it together by their compactness and number. He also made entrances in them, leading from one to the other.[b] Each of these chambers was five cubits in breadth, the same in length, and twenty cubits in height.[c] And above these were built other chambers and again still others above them, equal in proportion and number,[d] so that they reached a combined height equivalent to that of the lower building, the upper story not having chambers built around it. And a roof of cedar was put over the edifice. But the chambers each had a separate roof not joined to the next, while the rest of the building had a common roof constructed of very long beams crossing one another and reaching all sides,[e] so that the middle walls,[f] being held together by the same pieces of timber, were thereby made stronger. And under the beams he laid a ceiling of the same material, which was all smoothly divided into panels and overlaid with gold. The walls he covered at intervals with cedar boards, which he embossed with gold, so that the

The side-chambers. 1 Kings vi. 5 (LXX vi. 10).

Josephus apparently divides 60 cubits, the height of the temple, by 3 (the number of stories of chambers).

[d] Josephus omits to state that these rows of side chambers projected from the temple wall in step fashion, each story extending one cubit beyond the story below, *cf.* 1 Kings vi. 5.

[e] The text is difficult; in part it seems to refer to brackets running diagonally from the horizontal ceiling timbers to the vertical timbers of the walls. Josephus apparently takes Heb. *yaṣīʿa* (A.V. "chambers") in 1 Kings vi. 10 in the sense of "bracing timbers," *cf.* LXX ἐνδέσμους "bondings."

[f] Which middle walls are meant is far from clear. Possibly Josephus means the walls as they were before being covered with cedar and gold.

ἅπαντα τὸν ναὸν καὶ περιλάμπεσθαι τὰς ὄψεις τῶν εἰσιόντων ὑπὸ τῆς αὐγῆς τοῦ χρυσοῦ παν-
69 ταχόθεν φερομένης.[1] ἡ δ' ὅλη τοῦ ναοῦ οἰκοδομία κατὰ πολλὴν τέχνην ἐκ λίθων ἀκροτόμων ἐγένετο συντεθέντων ἁρμονίως πάνυ καὶ λείως, ὡς μήτε σφύρας μήτε ἄλλου τινὸς ἐργαλείου τεκτονικοῦ τοῖς κατανοοῦσιν ἐργασίαν δηλοῦσθαι, ἀλλὰ δίχα τῆς τούτων χρήσεως πᾶσαν ἡρμόσθαι τὴν ὕλην προσφυῶς, ὡς ἑκούσιον τὴν ἁρμονίαν αὐτῆς δοκεῖν
70 μᾶλλον ἢ τῆς τῶν ἐργαλείων ἀνάγκης. ἐφιλοτέχνησε δὲ ὁ βασιλεὺς ἄνοδον εἰς τὸν ὑπερῷον οἶκον διὰ τοῦ εὔρους τοῦ τοίχου· οὐ γὰρ εἶχε θύραν μεγάλην κατὰ τῆς ἀνατολῆς ὡς εἶχεν ὁ κάτωθεν οἶκος, ἀλλ' ἐκ τῶν πλευρῶν ἦσαν εἴσοδοι διὰ μικρῶν πάνυ θυρῶν. διέλαβε δὲ τὸν ναὸν καὶ ἔνδοθεν καὶ ἔξωθεν ξύλοις κεδρίνοις ἁλύσεσι παχείαις συνδεδεμένοις, ὥστε ἀντ' ὀχυρωμάτων καὶ ῥώμης τοῦτο[2] εἶναι.

71 (3) Διελὼν δὲ τὸν ναὸν εἰς δύο τὸν μὲν ἔνδοθεν οἶκον εἴκοσι πηχῶν ἐποίησεν ἄδυτον,[3] τὸν δὲ τεσσαράκοντα πηχῶν ἅγιον ναὸν ἀπέδειξεν. ἐκτεμὼν δὲ τὸν μέσον τοῖχον θύρας ἐπέστησε κεδρίνας χρυσὸν αὐταῖς πολὺν ἐνεργασάμενος καὶ τορείαν
72 ποικίλην. κατεπέτασε δὲ ταύτας ὕφεσιν εὐανθεστάτοις ἐξ ὑακίνθου καὶ πορφύρας καὶ κόκκου πεποιημένοις, οὐ μὴν ἀλλὰ καὶ βύσσου λαμπρο-

[1] φαινομένης Naber.
[2] τοῦτ' αὐτοῖς Naber.
[3] + εἶναι SP.

whole temple gleamed and dazzled the eyes of those who entered by the radiance of the gold which met them on every side. And the whole construction of the temple was carried out with great skill by means of stones cut fine and laid together so neatly and smoothly that to the beholder there appeared no sign of the use of mallets or other work-tools, but all the material seemed to have fitted itself together naturally without the use of these things, so that their fitting together seemed to have come about of itself rather than through the force of tools.[a] And the king contrived a stairway to the upper story through the thickness of the wall, for it had no great door on the east as the lower building had, but it had entrances through very small doors on the sides. He also overlaid the temple both inside and outside with cedar boards fastened together with thick chains, so as to serve as support and strength.

The masonry. 1 Kings vi. 7 (LXX vi. 12).

The stairway. 1 Kings vi. 8 (LXX vi. 13)

2 Chron. iii. 5.

(3) And he divided the temple into two parts, and made the inner space [b] of twenty cubits an adytum,[c] while the rest, forty cubits long, he designated as the Holy Temple.[d] Then he cut through the middle wall [e] and set doors of cedar in it, working into them much gold and intricate carving. And he curtained these with a cloth brightly coloured in hyacinth blue and purple and scarlet, which was, moreover, made

The Holy of Holies (Adytum). 1 Kings vi. 16 (LXX vi. 17).

2 Chron. iii 14.

[a] A very free paraphrase of 1 Kings vi. 7 "And the house, when it was in building, was built of stone made ready before it was brought thither, so that there was neither hammer nor axe nor any tool of iron heard in the house while it was in building."

[b] At the western end of the temple.

[c] Heb. *debîr* or *qōdeš qodāšîm* (A.V. "oracle" or "most holy place"), LXX δαβείρ or ἅγιον τῶν ἁγίων.

[d] Heb. *hēkāl* (A.V. "temple"), LXX ναός.

[e] The wall dividing the adytum from the temple.

τάτης καὶ μαλακωτάτης. ἀνέθηκε δ' εἰς τὸ ἄδυτον εἴκοσι πηχῶν τὸ εὖρος τῶν δ' αὐτῶν καὶ τὸ μῆκος δύο Χερουβεῖς ὁλοχρύσους πηχῶν ἑκατέραν τὸ ὕψος πέντε, δύο δ' ἦσαν ἑκατέρᾳ πτέρυγες ἐπὶ
73 πέντε πήχεις ἐκτεταμέναι. διὸ καὶ οὐ μακρὰν[1] ἀπ' ἀλλήλων αὐτὰς ἀνέστησεν, ἵνα τῶν πτερύγων τῇ μὲν ἅπτωνται τοῦ κατὰ νότον κειμένου τοίχου τοῦ ἀδύτου, τῇ δὲ κατὰ βορέαν, αἱ δ' ἄλλαι πτέρυγες αὑταῖς συνάπτουσαι τεθείσῃ μεταξὺ αὐτῶν τῇ κιβωτῷ σκέπη τυγχάνωσι. τὰς δὲ Χερουβεῖς οὐδεὶς ὁποῖαί τινες ἦσαν[2] εἰπεῖν οὐδ'
74 εἰκάσαι δύναται. κατέστρωσε δὲ καὶ τοῦ ναοῦ τὸ ἔδαφος ἐλάσμασι χρυσοῦ, ἐπέθηκε δὲ καὶ τῷ πυλῶνι τοῦ ναοῦ θύρας πρὸς τὸ ὕψος τοῦ τοίχου συμμεμετρημένας εὖρος ἐχούσας πηχῶν εἴκοσι,
75 καὶ ταύτας κατεκόλλησε χρυσῷ. συνελόντι δ' εἰπεῖν, οὐδὲν εἴασε τοῦ ναοῦ μέρος οὔτε ἔξωθεν οὔτε ἔνδοθεν, ὃ μὴ χρυσὸς ἦν. κατεπέτασε δὲ καὶ ταύτας τὰς θύρας ὁμοίως ταῖς[3] ἐνδοτέρω καταπετάσμασιν. ἡ δὲ τοῦ προναΐου πύλη τούτων οὐδὲν εἶχε.
76 (4) Μεταπέμπεται δ' ἐκ Τύρου Σολομὼν παρὰ Εἰρώμου τεχνίτην Χείρωμον[4] ὄνομα μητρὸς μὲν ὄντα Νεφθαλίτιδος τὸ γένος (ἐκ γὰρ ταύτης

[1] οὐ μακρὰν ed. pr.: μακρὰν οὐκ codd. E.
[2] εἰσιν RO.
[3] Dindorf: τοῖς codd.
[4] Χείραμον MSP: Chirom Lat.

[a] Josephus closely follows the wording of the LXX in 2 Chron. (1 Kings omits the curtain) but fails to mention the figures of cherubim woven in the curtain. On this reluctance to dwell on them *cf.* next note but one.

of the most gleaming and softest linen.[a] In the adytum, which was twenty cubits in length and the same in breadth, he set up two cherubim of solid gold, each five[b] cubits in height and each having two wings with a spread of five cubits; for that reason he set them up not far from each other, in order that they might with one of their wings touch the southern wall of the adytum, and with the other the northern wall, while their inner wings joined each other so as to form a covering for the ark, which was placed between them. As for the cherubim themselves, no one can say or imagine what they looked like.[c] And he also paved the floor of the temple with plates of gold, and to the gate of the temple set doors in proportion to the height of the walls, in breadth twenty cubits,[d] and these he inlaid with gold. In a word, he left no part of the temple, whether on the outside or on the inside, which was not gold. These doors he also overhung with curtains in the same way as those within.[e] But the entrance of the porch had none of these.

The cherubim. 1 Kings vi. 23 (LXX vi. 22).

(4) [f] And Solomon summoned from Tyre, from Eirōmos's court, a craftsman named Cheirōmos,[g] who was of Naphthalite descent on his mother's side—for

The Tyrian craftsman, Hiram (Cheirōmos).

[b] Bibl. ten.

[c] In this statement Rappaport sees an attempt to smooth over the theological difficulties involved in Solomon's apparent disregard of the prohibition in the decalogue against the making of images.

[d] Unscriptural detail. Reinach compares Ezek. xli. 2.

[e] According to Scripture they were carved and embossed with gold, but had no curtain.

[f] Heb. here, 1 Kings vii. 1 ff., gives a description of Solomon's palace, which Josephus, like the LXX, postpones, *cf.* §§ 130 ff.

[g] Bibl. Hiram (Heb. *Ḥîrām*), LXX Χειράμ.

ὑπῆρχε τῆς φυλῆς) πατρὸς δὲ Οὐρίου γένος Ἰσραηλίτου. οὗτος ἅπαντος μὲν ἐπιστημόνως εἶχεν ἔργου, μάλιστα δὲ τεχνίτης ἦν χρυσὸν ἐργάζεσθαι καὶ ἄργυρον καὶ χαλκόν, ὑφ' οὗ δὴ καὶ πάντα κατὰ τὴν τοῦ βασιλέως βούλησιν τὰ περὶ τὸν ναὸν
77 ἐμηχανήθη.[1] κατεσκεύασε δὲ ὁ Χείρωμος οὗτος καὶ στύλους δύο χαλκοῦς ἔσωθεν τὸ πάχος[2] τεσσάρων δακτύλων. ἦν δὲ τὸ μὲν ὕψος τοῖς κίοσιν ὀκτωκαίδεκα πήχεων, ἡ δὲ περίμετρος δέκα καὶ δύο πηχῶν· χωνευτὸν δ' ἐφ' ἑκατέρᾳ κεφαλῇ κρίνον ἐφειστήκει τὸ ὕψος ἐπὶ πέντε πήχεις ἐγηγερμένον, ᾧ περιέκειτο δίκτυον ἐλάτῃ χαλκέᾳ
78 περιπεπλεγμένον καλύπτον τὰ κρίνα. τούτου δὲ ἀπήρτηντο κατὰ διστιχίαν καὶ ῥοιαὶ διακόσιαι. τούτων τῶν κιόνων τὸν μὲν ἕτερον κατὰ τὴν δεξιὰν ἔστησε τοῦ προπυλαίου παραστάδα καλέσας αὐτὸν Ἰαχείν, τὸν δ' ἕτερον κατὰ τὸ ἀριστερὸν ὀνομάσας αὐτὸν Ἀβαίζ.[3]

79 (5) Ἐχώνευσε δὲ καὶ θάλασσαν χαλκῆν εἰς ἡμισφαίριον ἐσχηματισμένην· ἐκλήθη δὲ τὸ χαλκούργημα θάλασσα διὰ τὸ μέγεθος· ἦν γὰρ ὁ

[1] ἐξεμηχανήθη MSP.
[2] + cum canalibus cavatione Lat.
[3] Βαΐζ MS: Βαΐς P: Baez Lat.

[a] Bibl. "his father was a man of Tyre"; Josephus's "Urias" is generally explained as a corruption of the LXX Τύριος; possibly it is due to confusion with Uri, LXX Οὐρείας, the father of Bezaleel the artificer of the bronze altar mentioned in 2 Chron. ii. 5, *cf.* § 22 note.

[b] Josephus is evidently harmonizing the contradiction between this passage in 2 Kings and 2 Chron. ii. 14, where Hiram's mother is said to be "of the daughters of Dan," by making Hiram's father an Israelite, presumably a Danite; while rabbinic tradition assumes that Hiram was a Naphthalite

she was of that tribe—and whose father was Ūrias,[a] an Israelite by race.[b] This man was skilled in all kinds of work, but was especially expert in working gold, silver and bronze,[c] and it was he who constructed all the things about the temple, in accordance with the king's will. This Cheirōmos also made two pillars of bronze which was four fingers in thickness,[d] the height of the columns being eighteen cubits and their circumference twelve[e] cubits; and on the capital of each rested a lily formed of cast metal, rising to a height of five cubits, about which was a network intertwined with bronze palm-buds, which covered the lilies. And from this depended two hundred pomegranates in two rows. One of these columns he placed as a doorpost[f] on the right of the gateway, calling it Jachein,[g] while the other, on the left, he named Abaiz.[h]

1 Kings vii. 13 (LXX vii. 1).

The pillars Jachin and Boaz. 1 Kings vii. 15 (LXX vii. 3).

(5) He also cast a bronze "sea" in the shape of a hemisphere; this bronze vessel was called a sea because of its size,[i] for the laver was ten cubits in

The bronze "Sea." 1 Kings vii. 23 (LXX vii. 10).

on his father's side and a Danite on his mother's side, *cf.* Ginzberg vi. 295 note 61.

[c] Gold and silver, as well as other materials, are mentioned in 2 Chron.; 1 Kings speaks only of bronze (A.V. "brass").

[d] So LXX; Heb. omits. The thickness refers to the shell of the hollow columns.

[e] So Heb.; LXX fourteen.

[f] Or perhaps "in the vestibule." παραστάς signifies the square pillar or pilaster in the front wall of a temple and, by extension, the vestibule or entrance to the temple.

[g] Bibl. Jachin (Heb. *Yākîn*), LXX Ἰαχούμ, *v.l.* Ἰαχούν, Luc. Ἰακούμ.

[h] Bibl. Boaz, LXX Βάλαζ, *v.l.* Βοώζ, Luc. Βαάζ. In 2 Chron. iii. 17 LXX translates the Heb. names (lit. "he sets up" and "in him is strength") by κατόρθωσις "setting up" and ἰσχύς "strength."

[i] The real reason for this peculiar name is unknown to us.

λουτὴρ τὴν διάμετρον πηχῶν δέκα καὶ ἐπὶ παλαι-
στιαῖον πάχος κεχωνευμένος. ὑπερήρειστο[1] δὲ
κατὰ τὸ μεσαίτατον τοῦ κύτους σπείρᾳ περι-
80 αγομένῃ εἰς ἕλικας δέκα· ἦν δὲ τὴν διάμετρον
πήχεως, περιειστήκεσαν δὲ περὶ αὐτὴν μόσχοι
δώδεκα πρὸς τὰ κλίματα τῶν τεσσάρων ἀνέμων
ἀποβλέποντες καθ' ἕκαστον αὐτῶν τρεῖς εἰς[2] τὰ
ὀπίσθια νενευκότες, ὥστ' αὐτοῖς ἐπικαθέζεσθαι
τὸ ἡμισφαίριον κατὰ περιαγωγὴν ἔνδον ἀπονεῦον.[3]
ἐδέχετο δὲ ἡ θάλασσα βάτους τρισχιλίους.

81 (6) Ἐποίησε δὲ καὶ λουτήρων δέκα βάσεις
χαλκᾶς τετραγώνους.[4] τούτων ἑκάστη μῆκος γε-
γόνει πηχῶν πέντε πλάτος τεσσάρων ὕψος ἕξ.
συνεκέκλειστο[5] δὲ τὸ ἔργον κατὰ μέρος τετορευ-
μένον οὕτως· τέσσαρες ἦσαν κιονίσκοι κατὰ γωνίαν
ἑστῶτες τετράγωνοι, τὰ πλευρὰ τῆς βάσεως ἐξ
ἑκατέρου μέρους ἐν αὐτοῖς ἔχοντες ἐξηρμοσμένα.
82 ἦν δὲ ταῦτα τριχῇ διῃρημένα· ἑκάστην δὲ χώραν
ὅρος[6] ἐπεῖχεν εἰς ὑπόβασιν κατεσκευασμένος,[7]
ἐφ' ἧς[8] ἐτετόρευτο πῇ μὲν λέων πῇ δὲ ταῦρος καὶ
ἀετός, ἐπὶ δὲ τῶν κιονίσκων ὁμοίως ἐξείργαστο
83 τοῖς κατὰ τὰ πλευρὰ τετορευμένοις. τὸ δὲ πᾶν
ἔργον ἐπὶ τεσσάρων αἰωρούμενον τροχῶν εἱστήκει.

[1] Dindorf: ὑπήρειστο RO: ὑπηρεῖτο P: ὑπήρητο S: ὑπήρει M.
[2] ἔσω MSP.
[3] ἐπινεῦον MSP.
[4] ex Lat. Ernesti: τετραγώνων codd.
[5] S: συνεκέκλειτο MP: συνεκέκλιτο RO.
[6] M: ὅρος rell. [7] κατεσκευασμένον MSP.
[8] Niese: οἷς codd.: αἷς Hudson.

[a] *Cf.* 1 Kings vii. 24, "and under the brim of it round about there were colocynths" (Heb. *peqā'īm*, A.V. "knops," LXX ὑποστηρίγματα "props," Targum "egg-shapes") "compassing it, ten cubits" (A.V., like the LXX, "ten in a cubit").

diameter and was cast to the thickness of a palm's breadth. The vessel was supported underneath at its centre by a rounded base which curved around in ten volutes and was one cubit in diameter.[a] And round about the sea there stood twelve calves facing the four quarters of the winds, three in each direction, and with their hinder parts sloping down so that the hemisphere might rest upon them, narrowing inwards all around. The sea could hold three thousand *baths*.[b]

(6) He also made ten square bronze bases for lavers, each of which was five [c] cubits in length, four cubits in breadth and six [d] in height. And the work, which in every part was carved in relief, was enclosed [e] as follows : there were four square little columns at each corner, each of which held two intersecting sides of the base fitted into it ; these sides were divided into three fields,[f] and in each of these spaces was a dividing strip extending to the sub-base [g] ; in the space itself was carved in relief here a lion, there a bull and an eagle,[h] while the little columns were worked in relief in the same way as the sides of the base. And so the whole thing stood, raised upon four wheels.

The lavers and their bases. 1 Kings vii. 27 (LXX vii. 14).

[b] So 2 Chron. iv. 5 ; 1 Kings, 2000. On the *bath cf.* § 57 note.

[c] So LXX ; Heb. four.

[d] So LXX ; Heb. three.

[e] *Cf.* LXX συγκλειστὸν αὐτοῖς translating Heb. *misgerôth lāhem* " they had bands " (? A.V. " borders ").

[f] Apparently, horizontal fields.

[g] Josephus's text and the Scriptural text, 1 Kings vii. 28, are both rather difficult to understand.

[h] Bibl. cherubim. Possibly, as Rappaport suggests, Josephus is influenced by the description, in Ezekiel's vision, Ezek. i. 10, of the angelic beings with the faces of an eagle, lion and ox.

χωνευτοὶ δ' ἦσαν οὗτοι, πλήμνας καὶ ἄντυγας πήχεως καὶ ἡμίσους ἔχοντες τὴν διάμετρον. ἐθαύμασεν ἄν τις τὰς ἀψῖδας τῶν τροχῶν θεασάμενος, ὅπως συντετορευμέναι καὶ τοῖς πλευροῖς τῶν βάσεων προσηνωμέναι ἁρμονίως ταῖς ἄντυξιν
84 ἐνέκειντο· ἦσαν δ' ὅμως οὕτως ἔχουσαι. τὰς δὲ γωνίας ἄνωθεν συνέκλειον ὦμοι χειρῶν ἀνατεταμένων, οἷς ἐπεκάθητο σπεῖρα κατὰ κοῖλον ἐπικειμένη τὸν λουτῆρα ταῖς χερσὶν ἐπαναπαυόμενον ἀετοῦ καὶ λέοντος αὐτοῖς ἐφηρμοσμένων, ὡς σύμφυτα ταῦτ' εἶναι δοκεῖν τοῖς ὁρῶσι. μεταξὺ δὲ τούτων φοίνικες ἦσαν τετορευμένοι. τοιαύτη
85 μὲν ἡ κατασκευὴ τῶν δέκα[1] βάσεων ὑπῆρχε. προσεξείργαστο δὲ καὶ χυτρογαύλους[2] δέκα λουτῆρας στρογγύλους χαλκοῦς, ὧν ἕκαστος ἐχώρει τεσσαράκοντα χόας· τὸ γὰρ ὕψος εἶχε τεσσάρων πηχῶν καὶ τοσούτοις ἀπ' ἀλλήλων αὐτοῖς διειστήκει τὰ χείλη. τίθησι δὲ τοὺς λουτῆρας τούτους ἐπὶ τῶν δέκα βάσεων τῶν κληθεισῶν Με-
86 χωνώθ.[3] πέντε δὲ λουτῆρας ἵστησιν ἐξ ἀριστεροῦ μέρους τοῦ ναοῦ, τέτραπτο δὲ τοῦτο κατὰ βορέαν ἄνεμον, καὶ τοσούτους ἐκ τοῦ δεξιοῦ πρὸς νότον ἀφορῶντας εἰς τὴν ἀνατολήν· κατὰ δ' αὐτὸ καὶ
87 τὴν θάλασσαν ἔθηκε. πληρώσας δὲ ὕδατος τὴν

[1] δώδεκα SP hic et mox infra.
[2] Theodoretus: κυθρογαύλους MSP: κυτροκαύλους RO.
[3] Μεχενώθ RO: Moecenoth Lat.

---

[a] ἀψίς usually means the felly or rim of a wheel, but sometimes the wheel itself. Here Josephus is evidently describing a solid wheel with sides or plates of bronze, and not one with spokes as is usually understood of the bibl. text.

[b] Meaning of the Greek doubtful. Scripture says that the

These also were cast in metal, and had hubs and rims a cubit and a half in diameter. One would marvel to see how cunningly the drums [a] of the wheels, which were carved in relief of the same design,[b] and united with the sides of the bases, were fitted into the rims. But none the less they did so. And to the upper part of the corners were attached projections [c] in the form of outstretched hands, on which was supported a spiral moulding [d] placed around the bottom of the laver, and the laver rested on the paws of an eagle [e] and a lion which were so well fitted together that to one looking at them they seemed to be one natural growth. Between these were palm-trees carved in relief. Such, then, was the construction of the ten bases. And in addition he also wrought ten round basins [f] or lavers of bronze, each of which held forty *choeis*,[g] for they were four cubits in height and the diameter of their rims was the same distance.[h] And he placed these lavers on the ten bases called *Mechōnōth*.[i] Five of the lavers he placed on the left side of the temple, which was the side toward the north, and the same number on the south-east. In the same part he also placed the Sea. And, having 2 Chron. iv. 6.

were carved in the same way as a chariot (A.V. " chariot wheel ").

[c] Lit. " shoulders " ; so also the LXX literally translates Heb. *ketēphôth* (A.V. " undersetters ").

[d] Bibl. " round compass."

[e] Bibl. cherubim, *cf.* § 82 note.

[f] Josephus uses the LXX word for Heb. *kiyyôrôth*.

[g] So the LXX ; Heb. *bath*. The Attic *chous* is equal to about ¾ gallon, whereas the *bath* is equal to about 9 gallons. Josephus himself tells us, in *A.* iii. 197, that the *hin* (⅙ *bath*) is equal to 2 Attic *choeis*, *i.e.* one *bath* is equal to 12 *choeis*, which is correct.

[h] This last is an unscriptural detail.

[i] Here Josephus uses the LXX transliteration.

μὲν θάλασσαν ἀπέδειξεν εἰς τὸ νίπτειν τοὺς εἰς τὸν ναὸν εἰσιόντας ἱερεῖς ἐν αὐτῇ τὰς χεῖρας καὶ τοὺς πόδας μέλλοντας ἀναβαίνειν ἐπὶ τὸν βωμόν, τοὺς δὲ λουτῆρας εἰς τὸ καθαίρειν τὰ ἐντὸς τῶν ὁλοκαυτουμένων ζῴων καὶ τοὺς πόδας αὐτῶν.

88 (7) Κατεσκεύασε δὲ καὶ θυσιαστήριον χάλκεον
εἴκοσι πηχῶν τὸ μῆκος καὶ τοσούτων τὸ εὖρος τὸ
δὲ ὕψος δέκα πρὸς τὰς ὁλοκαυτώσεις. ἐποίησε
δὲ αὐτοῦ καὶ τὰ σκεύη πάντα χάλκεα ποδιστῆρας
καὶ ἀναλημπτῆρας· οὐ μὴν ἀλλὰ πρὸς τούτοις
Χείρωμος καὶ λέβητας καὶ ἅρπαγας καὶ πᾶν σκεῦος
ἐδημιούργησεν ἐκ χαλκοῦ τὴν αὐγὴν ὁμοίου χρυσῷ
89 καὶ τὸ κάλλος· τραπεζῶν τε πλῆθος ἀνέθηκεν ὁ
βασιλεύς, καὶ μίαν μὲν μεγάλην χρυσέαν, ἐφ' ἧς
ἐτίθεσαν τοὺς ἄρτους τοῦ θεοῦ, καὶ ταύτῃ παραπλησίας μυρίας πρὸς αὐταῖς ἑτέρῳ τρόπῳ γεγενημένας, ἐφ' ὧν ἐπέκειτο τὰ σκεύη φιάλαι τε καὶ
σπονδεῖα χρύσεα μὲν δισμύρια ἀργύρεα δὲ τετρα-
90 κισμύρια. καὶ λυχνίας δὲ μυρίας ἐποίησε κατὰ
τὴν Μωυσέος προσταγήν, ἐξ ὧν μίαν ἀνέθηκεν εἰς
τὸν ναόν, ἵνα καίηται καθ' ἡμέραν ἀκολούθως τῷ
νόμῳ, καὶ τράπεζαν μίαν ἐπικειμένην ἄρτους πρὸς
τὸ βόρειον τοῦ ναοῦ μέρος ἀντικρὺ τῆς λυχνίας·
ταύτην γὰρ κατὰ νότον ἔστησεν, ὁ δὲ χρύσεος

---

[a] Scripture does not state for what offerings the altar was made.

[b] Hiram.

[c] The Greek word is the same as that used in LXX 2 Chron.; Heb. *sîrôth* (A.V. "pots"). In 1 Kings LXX has λέβητας.

[d] Here too Josephus uses the same word as in LXX 2 Chron.; Heb. *yā'îm* (A.V. "shovels"). In 1 Kings LXX has θερμάστρεις "tongs."

[e] Again the Greek word is the same as in LXX 2 Chron.;

filled the Sea with water, he set it apart for the priests to wash their hands and feet in when they entered the temple and were about to go up to the altar, while the lavers were for cleansing the entrails and feet of the animals used as whole burnt-offerings.

(7) He also made a bronze altar, twenty cubits in length and the same in breadth and ten cubits in height, for the whole burnt-offerings.[a] And he[b] made the vessels for it, tripods[c] and ladles,[d] all of bronze. Moreover, beside these, Cheiromos fashioned basins[e] and hooks and all other vessels of bronze, in brightness and beauty like gold.[f] The king also set up a great number of tables,[g] including one large one of gold on which they placed the loaves[h] of God, and countless others besides, very much like this one but made in a different style, upon which were placed the vessels, shallow bowls and libation-cups, twenty thousand of gold and forty thousand of silver.[i] He also made ten thousand lampstands,[j] in accordance with the commandment of Moses, one of which he set up in the temple to burn all day in obedience to the law, and placed one table, with loaves laid on it, on the north side of the temple over against the lampstand, for this he set on the south side, while the

The bronze altar. 2 Chron. iv. 1.

The table of shewbread. 1 Kings vii. 48 (LXX vii. 34); 2 Chron. iv. 8.

The lampstands. 1 Kings vii. 49 (LXX vii. 35); 2 Chron. iv. 7.

Heb. has *mizlāgôth* "forks," a corruption of *mizrāqôth* (A.V. "basons") which is rendered φιάλας by LXX in 1 Kings.

[f] Bibl. "of polished (LXX "pure") bronze" (A.V. "of bright brass").

[g] There were ten, according to 2 Chron.; 1 Kings mentions only one table of gold.

[h] Bibl. shewbread.

[i] These numbers are invented by Josephus. Scripture speaks of "exceeding many."

[j] There were only ten, according to Scripture, 1 Kings vii. 49, "five on the right side and five on the left, before the oracle."

βωμὸς μέσος αὐτῶν ἔκειτο. ταῦτα πάντα εἶχεν ὁ τῶν τεσσαράκοντα πηχῶν οἶκος πρὸ τοῦ καταπετάσματος τοῦ ἀδύτου· ἐν τούτῳ δὲ ἡ κιβωτὸς ἔμελλε κεῖσθαι.

91 (8) Οἰνοχόας δ' ὁ βασιλεὺς μυριάδας ὀκτὼ κατεσκεύασε καὶ φιαλῶν χρυσέων δέκα ἀργυρέας δὲ διπλασίονας. πινάκων δὲ χρυσέων εἰς τὸ προσφέρειν ἐν αὐτοῖς πεφυραμένην σεμίδαλιν τῷ βωμῷ μυριάδας ὀκτώ, τούτων δ' ἀργυροῦς διπλασίονας. κρατῆρας δ' οἷς ἐνεφύρων τὴν σεμίδαλιν μετ' ἐλαίου χρυσέους μὲν ἑξακισμυρίους,
92 ἀργυρέους δὲ δὶς τοσούτους. τὰ μέτρα δὲ τοῖς Μωυσείοις[1] λεγομένοις δὲ εἶν καὶ ἀσσαρῶνες[2] παραπλήσια, χρυσᾶ μὲν δισμύρια ἀργύρεα δὲ διπλασίονα. θυμιατήρια δὲ χρυσᾶ ἐν οἷς ἐκομίζετο τὸ θυμίαμα εἰς τὸν ναὸν δισμύρια· ὁμοίως ἄλλα θυμιατήρια οἷς ἐκόμιζον ἀπὸ τοῦ μεγάλου βωμοῦ πῦρ ἐπὶ τὸν μικρὸν βωμὸν τὸν ἐν τῷ ναῷ πεν-
93 τακισμύρια. στολὰς δὲ ἱερατικὰς τοῖς ἀρχιερεῦσι σὺν ποδήρεσιν ἐπωμίσι καὶ λογίῳ καὶ λίθοις χιλίας· ἡ δὲ στεφάνη, εἰς ἣν τὸν θεὸν Μωυσῆς ἔγραψε, μία ἦν καὶ διέμεινεν ἄχρι τῆσδε τῆς ἡμέρας· τὰς δὲ ἱερατικὰς στολὰς ἐκ βύσσου κατεσκεύασε καὶ
94 ζώνας πορφυρᾶς εἰς ἕκαστον μυρίας. καὶ σαλπίγγων κατὰ Μωυσέος ἐντολὴν μυριάδας εἴκοσι, καὶ στολῶν τοῖς ὑμνῳδοῖς Ληουιτῶν ἐκ βύσσου μυριάδας εἴκοσι· καὶ τὰ ὄργανα τὰ μουσικὰ καὶ πρὸς τὴν ὑμνῳδίαν ἐξηυρημένα, ἃ καλεῖται νάβλας

[1] ex Lat. Niese: Μωυσήου RO(M): Μωυσέως SP.

[2] cod. Vat. ap. Hudson Lat.: ἐσσάρωνες R: ἐσσαρῶνες O: ἐσσαρώναις SP.

golden altar stood between them. All these things were contained in the hall of forty cubits before the curtain of the adytum; and in that the ark was to rest.

(8) [a] The king also made eighty thousand pitchers and a hundred thousand shallow bowls of gold and a double number of silver; eighty thousand golden platters on which to carry the mixed fine flour for the altar, and a double number of silver; sixty thousand golden bowls in which they mixed the fine flour with oil, and twice as many of silver; of the measures which resembled those of Moses, called *hin* [b] and *assarōn*,[c] there were twenty thousand of gold, and a double number of silver; of golden censers in which they carried the incense into the temple there were twenty thousand. Similarly, of other censers in which they carried fire from the great altar to the small altar in the temple there were fifty thousand. Of the priestly vestments for the high priests, including long robes, upper garments, oracle [d] and precious stones, he made a thousand; but the crown on which Moses had inscribed God's name was unique and has remained to this day; of the (simple) priests' vestments he made ten thousand of linen and purple girdles for each. And he made two hundred thousand trumpets, in accordance with the commandment of Moses, and two hundred thousand robes of linen for the Levite singers; and of the musical instruments devised for singing psalms, which

The pitchers and bowls.

The censers.

The priestly vestments.

The musical instruments.

[a] All the numbers given in the following account of the temple vessels are invented by Josephus.

[b] *Cf. A.* iii. 197.

[c] *Cf. A.* iii. 29 note, 142 note.

[d] *Cf. A.* iii. 163 notes.

καὶ κινύρας, ἐξ ἠλέκτρου κατεσκεύασε τετρακισμύρια.

95 (9) Ταῦτα πάντα ὁ Σολομὼν εἰς τὴν τοῦ θεοῦ τιμὴν πολυτελῶς καὶ μεγαλοπρεπῶς κατεσκεύασε μηδενὸς φεισάμενος ἀλλὰ πάσῃ φιλοτιμίᾳ περὶ τὸν τοῦ ναοῦ κόσμον χρησάμενος, ἃ καὶ κατέθηκεν ἐν τοῖς θησαυροῖς τοῦ θεοῦ. περιέβαλε δὲ τοῦ ναοῦ κύκλῳ γείσιον[1] μὲν κατὰ τὴν ἐπιχώριον γλῶτταν θριγκὸν[2] δὲ παρ' Ἕλλησι λεγόμενον εἰς τρεῖς πήχεις ἀναγαγὼν τὸ ὕψος, εἴρξοντα μὲν τοὺς πολλοὺς τῆς εἰς τὸ ἱερὸν εἰσόδου, μόνοις δὲ ἀνειμένην

96 αὐτὴν τοῖς ἱερεῦσι σημανοῦντα. τούτου δ' ἔξωθεν ἱερὸν ᾠκοδόμησεν ἐν τετραγώνου[3] σχήματι στοὰς ἐγείρας μεγάλας καὶ πλατείας καὶ πύλαις ὑψηλαῖς ἀνεῳγμένας, ὧν ἑκάστη πρὸς ἕκαστον τῶν ἀνέμων ἐτέτραπτο χρυσέαις κλειομένη θύραις. εἰς τοῦτο τοῦ λαοῦ πάντες οἱ διαφέροντες ἁγνείᾳ καὶ παρα-

97 τηρήσει τῶν νομίμων εἰσῄεσαν. θαυμαστὸν δὲ καὶ λόγου παντὸς ἀπέφηνε μεῖζον, ὡς[4] δὲ εἰπεῖν καὶ τῆς ὄψεως, τὸ τούτων ἔξωθεν ἱερόν· μεγάλας γὰρ ἐγχώσας φάραγγας, ἃς διὰ βάθος ἄπειρον οὐδὲ

[1] γεῖσον MSP: γεισὸν E: gison Lat.
[2] τριγχὸν RO: θριγγὸν E.
[3] ex Lat. Niese: τετραγώνῳ codd. E.
[4] μεῖζον ὡς Hudson: μειζόνως codd.: μεῖζον E.

[a] *Cf. A.* vii. 306 notes.

[b] A compound of gold and silver.

[c] The following unscriptural account of the temple courts etc. is probably based on Josephus's knowledge of the temple of Herod, *cf. A.* xv. 398 ff., *B.J.* v. 184 ff.

[d] Apparently this corresponds to the γείσιον separating the Priests' Court from the Israelites' Court in Herod's temple, *B.J.* v. 226; this latter wall, however, was only one cubit high. Perhaps the height of the imagined wall in

are called *nablai* and *kinyrai*,[a] he made forty thousand of electrum.[b]

The temple courts ("sacred precincts"). 1 Kings vii. 51 (LXX vii. 37); 2 Chron. v. 1. *Cf.* 1 Kings vii. 9 (LXX vii. 46).

(9) [c] All these things Solomon prepared with great expense and magnificence to the glory of God, sparing no cost, but acting with the utmost munificence in adorning the temple, and he deposited them in the treasuries of God. He also surrounded the temple with a parapet called *geision* [d] in the native tongue [e] and *thrinkos* [f] by the Greeks, which he raised to a height of three cubits; it was to keep the multitude from entering the sacred precinct [g] and to signify that entry was permitted only to the priests. Outside of this he built another sacred precinct [h] in the form of a quadrangle and erected great and wide porticoes which were entered by high gates, each of which faced one of the four quarters and was closed by golden doors. Into this precinct all the people who were distinguished by purity and their observance of the laws might enter. But wonderful and surpassing all description, and even, one might say, all sight, was the (third) sacred precinct [i] which he made outside of these, for he filled up with earth great valleys, into which because of their immense depth

Solomon's temple has some connexion with the stone barrier (δρύφακτος λίθινος) of three cubits high separating the outer court from the inner court, mentioned in *B.J.* v. 193. This is called *sôrēg* in the Mishnah, *Middoth* ii. 3.

[e] That γείσιον is a Syriac word, as Weill explains, seems to me very doubtful. It looks like a diminutive of γεῖσον "coping."

[f] "Coping."

[g] This corresponds to the Priests' Court in Herod's temple.

[h] Corresponding to the Israelites' Court in Herod's temple.

[i] This corresponds to the Women's Court in Herod's temple. With the following account of the filling in of the site *cf.* *B.J.* v. 184 ff.

ἀπόνως ἐννεύσαντας ἣν ἰδεῖν, καὶ ἀναβιβάσας εἰς τετρακοσίους πήχεις τὸ ὕψος ἰσοπέδους τῇ κορυφῇ τοῦ ὄρους ἐφ' ἧς ὁ ναὸς ᾠκοδόμητο κατεσκεύασε· καὶ διὰ τοῦτο ὕπαιθρον ὂν τὸ ἔξωθεν ἱερὸν ἴσον
98 ὑπῆρχε τῷ ναῷ. περιλαμβάνει δ' αὐτὸ καὶ στοαῖς διπλαῖς μὲν τὴν κατασκευήν, λίθου δ' αὐτοφυοῦς τὸ ὕψος κίοσιν ἐπερηρεισμέναις· ὀροφαὶ δ' αὐταῖς ἦσαν ἐκ κέδρου φατνώμασιν ἀνεξεσμέναι. τὰς δὲ θύρας τῷ ἱερῷ τούτῳ πάσας ἐπέστησεν ἐξ ἀργύρου.

99 (iv. 1) Τὰ μὲν οὖν ἔργα ταῦτα καὶ τὰ μεγέθη καὶ κάλλη τῶν τε οἰκοδομημάτων καὶ τῶν εἰς τὸν ναὸν ἀναθημάτων Σολομὼν ὁ βασιλεὺς ἐν ἔτεσιν ἑπτὰ συντελέσας καὶ πλούτου καὶ προθυμίας ἐπίδειξιν ποιησάμενος, ὥστε ἃ ἄν[1] τις ἰδὼν ἐνόμισε μόλις ἐν[2] τῷ παντὶ κατασκευασθῆναι χρόνῳ, ταῦτα ἐν οὕτως ὀλίγῳ πρὸς τὸ μέγεθος συγκρινομένῳ[3] τοῦ ναοῦ συμπερανθῆναι, γράψας τοῖς ἡγεμόσι καὶ τοῖς πρεσβυτέροις τῶν Ἑβραίων ἐκέλευσεν ἅπαντα τὸν λαὸν συναγαγεῖν εἰς Ἱεροσόλυμα ὀψόμενόν τε τὸν ναὸν καὶ μετακομιοῦντα τὴν
100 τοῦ θεοῦ κιβωτὸν εἰς αὐτόν. καὶ περιαγγελθείσης τῆς εἰς τὰ Ἱεροσόλυμα πᾶσιν ἀφίξεως ἑβδόμῳ μηνὶ μόλις συνίασιν, ὑπὸ μὲν τῶν ἐπιχωρίων Θισρί,[4] ὑπὸ δὲ τῶν Μακεδόνων Ὑπερβερεταίῳ λεγομένῳ.

[1] ὥστε ἃ ἂν Bekker: ὡς ἂν codd.
[2] μόλις ἐν conj. Niese (μόλις ἂν in edit.): ὡς ἐν RO: ἐν MSP.
[3] Cocceji: συγκρινόμενα codd.
[4] ex Lat. Hudson: Ἀθύρει RO: Θοίρι M: Θοιρί SP: Θυρί E.

[a] Josephus follows the order of 2 Chron. and Heb. 1 Kings which mention the assembly right after the account of the temple vessels (on Josephus's omission at this point of the

one could not without difficulty look down, and bringing them up to a height of four hundred cubits he made them level with the top of the mountain on which the temple was built; in this way the outer precinct, which was open to the sky, was on a level with the temple. And he surrounded it with double porticoes supported by high columns of native stone, and they had roofs of cedar which were smoothly finished in panels. And all the doors which he made for this sacred precinct were of silver.

The people assemble at Jerusalem to view the temple.

(iv. 1) These works, then, and these great and beautiful buildings and offerings for the temple King Solomon completed in seven years, making such display both of wealth and zeal that the work which any beholder would think could hardly have been constructed in the whole course of time was finished in a space of time that was very short when compared with the magnitude of the temple. He then wrote [a] to the leaders and elders of the Hebrews and ordered them to assemble all the people at Jerusalem in order to see the temple and join in bringing the ark into it. And although the summons to Jerusalem was sent around to all, it was hardly by the seventh month that they came together, which month is called Thisri [b] by the natives and Hyperberetaios by the

1 Kings viii. 1; 2 Chron. v. 2.

building of Solomon's palace *cf.* § 76 note), while LXX 1 Kings introduces the passage on the assembly by the words, "And it came to pass that after Solomon had finished building the house of the Lord and his own house, after twenty years (7 years for the temple + 13 years for the palace), that King Solomon assembled, etc."

[b] Conj. from Latin: MSS. *Athyri*, *Thoire*—forms which are corruptions probably arising from confusion of *Thisri* with the Greco-Egyptian month *Athyris*. Josephus gives the later Heb. name Tishri, while Scripture uses the old Canaanite name Ethanim, LXX Ἀθαμείν, *v.l.* Ἀθανείμ.

συνέδραμε δ' εἰς τὸν αὐτὸν χρόνον καὶ ὁ τῆς σκηνοπηγίας καιρὸς ἑορτῆς σφόδρα παρὰ τοῖς Ἑβραίοις
101 ἁγιωτάτης καὶ μεγίστης. βαστάσαντες οὖν τὴν κιβωτὸν καὶ τὴν σκηνήν, ἣν Μωυσῆς ἐπήξατο, καὶ πάντα τὰ πρὸς τὴν διακονίαν τῶν θυσιῶν τοῦ θεοῦ σκεύη μετεκόμιζον εἰς τὸν ναόν. προῆγον δὲ μετὰ θυσιῶν αὐτός τε ὁ βασιλεὺς καὶ ὁ λαὸς ἅπας καὶ οἱ Ληουῖται σπονδαῖς τε καὶ πολλῶν ἱερείων αἵματι τὴν ὁδὸν καταντλοῦντες καὶ θυμιῶντες
102 ἄπειρόν τι θυμιαμάτων πλῆθος, ὡς ἅπαντα τὸν πέριξ ἀέρα πεπληρωμένον καὶ τοῖς πορρωτάτω τυγχάνουσιν ἡδὺν ἀπαντᾶν, καὶ γνωρίζειν ἐπιδημίαν θεοῦ καὶ κατοικισμὸν κατ' ἀνθρωπίνην δόξαν εἰς νεοδόμητον αὐτῷ καὶ καθιερωμένον χωρίον· καὶ γὰρ οὐδ' ὑμνοῦντες οὐδὲ χορεύοντες
103 ἕως οὗ πρὸς τὸν ναὸν ἦλθον ἔκαμον. τούτῳ μὲν οὖν τῷ τρόπῳ τὴν κιβωτὸν μετήνεγκαν. ὡς δ' εἰς τὸ ἄδυτον αὐτὴν εἰσενεγκεῖν ἔδει, τὸ μὲν ἄλλο πλῆθος μετέστη, μόνοι δὲ κομίσαντες οἱ ἱερεῖς μεταξὺ τῶν δύο Χερουβεῖν κατέθεσαν· αἱ δὲ τοὺς ταρσοὺς συμπλέξασαι (καὶ γὰρ οὕτως ἦσαν ὑπὸ τοῦ τεχνίτου κατεσκευασμέναι), τὴν κιβωτὸν ὡς
104 ὑπὸ σκηνῇ τινι καὶ θόλῳ κατεσκέπασαν. εἶχε δὲ ἡ κιβωτὸς οὐδὲν ἕτερον ἢ δύο λιθίνας πλάκας, αἳ τοὺς δέκα λόγους τοὺς ὑπὸ τοῦ θεοῦ Μωυσεῖ[1] λαληθέντας ἐν Σιναίῳ ὄρει ἐγγεγραμμένους αὐταῖς ἔσωζον. τὴν δὲ λυχνίαν καὶ τὴν τράπεζαν καὶ τὸν βωμὸν τὸν χρύσεον ἔστησαν ἐν τῷ ναῷ πρὸ

[1] Niese: Μωυσῇ codd.: Mose Lat.

[a] Which falls on the fifteenth of Tishri. Scripture speaks only of "the festival," Heb. *ḥag* (A.V. "feast"), but this

Macedonians. At this same time happened to fall the festival of Tabernacles,[a] which is considered especially sacred and important by the Hebrews. So, then, they lifted up the ark and the tabernacle which Moses had set up, and all the vessels for the service of the sacrifices to God, and carried them into the temple. And before it went the king himself and all the people and the Levites, with sacrifices, drenching the ground with libations and the blood of numerous victims, and burning so vast a quantity of incense that all the air around was filled with it and carried its sweetness to those who were at a great distance; this was a sign of God's being present and dwelling—according to human belief—in the place which had been newly built and consecrated to Him. And indeed they did not weary of singing hymns or dancing until they reached the temple.[b] This, then, was the way in which they conveyed the ark. But when it was time to bring it into the adytum, the rest of the people went away, and only the priests carried it and set it down between the two cherubim. These, which were interlocked by the tips of their wings—so they had been made by the craftsman—covered the ark as under a kind of tent or dome. And the ark held nothing but the two stone tablets which preserved the ten commandments spoken by God to Moses on Mount Sinai inscribed upon them. But the lampstand and the table and the golden altar they placed in the temple before the adytum in the

The ark is brought into the temple. 1 Kings vi. 3.

word in Josephus's time was used particularly of the festival of Tabernacles.

[b] Scripture does not mention incense. The singing (but not dancing) is mentioned only in 2 Chron. and seems to have followed the deposition of the ark in the sanctuary.

τοῦ ἀδύτου κατὰ τοὺς αὐτοὺς τόπους, οὓς καὶ τότε ἐν τῇ σκηνῇ κείμενοι κατεῖχον, καὶ τὰς καθ-
105 ημερινὰς θυσίας ἀνέφερον. τὸ δὲ θυσιαστήριον τὸ χάλκεον ἵστησι πρὸ τοῦ ναοῦ ἀντικρὺ τῆς θύρας, ὡς ἀνοιχθείσης αὐτὸ κατὰ πρόσωπον εἶναι καὶ βλέπεσθαι τὰς ἱερουργίας καὶ τὴν τῶν θυσιῶν πολυτέλειαν. τὰ δὲ λοιπὰ σκεύη πάντα συναλίσας ἔνδον εἰς τὸν ναὸν κατέθετο.

106 (2) Ἐπεὶ δὲ πάντα διακοσμήσαντες οἱ ἱερεῖς τὰ περὶ τὴν κιβωτὸν ἐξῆλθον, ἄφνω πίλημα νεφέλης οὐ σκληρὸν οὐδ' οἷον ὥρᾳ χειμῶνος ὑετοῦ γέμον ἵσταται κεχυμένον δὲ καὶ κεκραμένον εἰς τὸν ναὸν εἰσερρύη, καὶ ταῖς μὲν ὄψεσι τῶν ἱερέων ὡς μηδὲ καθορᾶν ἀλλήλους ἐπεσκότει, ταῖς δὲ διανοίαις ταῖς ἁπάντων φαντασίαν καὶ δόξαν παρεῖχεν ὡς τοῦ θεοῦ κατεληλυθότος εἰς τὸ ἱερὸν καὶ κατεσκηνωκό-
107 τος ἡδέως ἐν αὐτῷ. καὶ οἱ μὲν ἐπὶ ταύτης εἶχον αὐτοὺς τῆς ἐννοίας· ὁ δὲ βασιλεὺς Σολομὼν ἐξ-εγερθείς (ἔτυχε γὰρ καθεζόμενος) ἐποιήσατο λόγους πρὸς τὸν θεόν, οὓς τῇ θείᾳ φύσει πρέποντας ὑπ-ελάμβανε καὶ καλῶς ἔχειν[1] αὐτῷ λέγειν· "σοὶ γάρ," εἶπεν, "οἶκον μὲν αἰώνιον, ὦ δέσποτα, κἀξ ὧν σαυτῷ εἰργάσω γεγονότα τὸν οὐρανὸν οἴδαμεν καὶ ἀέρα καὶ γῆν καὶ θάλασσαν, δι' ὧν ἁπάντων
108 οὐδὲ τούτοις ἀρκούμενος κεχώρηκας, τοῦτον δὲ σοι κατεσκεύακα τὸν ναὸν ἐπώνυμον, ὡς ἂν ἀπ' αὐτοῦ σοι τὰς εὐχὰς θύοντες καὶ καλλιεροῦντες ἀναπέμπωμεν εἰς τὸν ἀέρα καὶ πεπεισμένοι δια-

[1] Cod. Vat. ap. Hudson: εἶχεν rell.

same positions which they had formerly occupied when standing in the tabernacle, and then they offered up the daily sacrifices. And the bronze altar he set up before the temple opposite the door, so that when this was opened the altar was before the eyes (of those within the temple), and the sacred ministrations and the splendour of the sacrifices might be seen.[a] And all the other vessels he collected and deposited within the temple.

(2) And when the priests had set in order all that concerned the ark, and had gone out, there suddenly appeared a thick cloud, not threatening nor like a swollen rain-cloud in the winter season, but diffused and temperate,[b] which streamed into the temple and so darkened the sight of the priests that they could not see one another; and it produced in the minds of all of them an impression and belief that God had descended into the temple and had gladly made His abode there. And while they were occupied with this thought, Solomon arose—for he chanced to be seated—and addressed God in words which he considered suitable to the divine nature and fitting for him to speak. "That Thou, O Lord," he said, "hast an eternal dwelling in those things which Thou didst create for Thyself we know—in the heaven and air and earth and sea, through all of which Thou movest and yet art not contained by them. But I have built this temple to Thy name so that from it we may, when sacrificing and seeking good omens, send up our prayers into the air to Thee, and may ever be per-

The divine manifestation in the adytum; Solomon's prayer. 1 Kings viii. 10.

Cf. 23, 27.

[a] The foregoing details concerning the arrangement of the temple furniture are added by Josephus.

[b] An amplification of the brief scriptural phrase "and a (lit. "the") cloud filled the house."

τελοίημεν ὅτι πάρει καὶ μακρὰν οὐκ ἀφέστηκας[1]· τῷ μὲν γὰρ πάντ' ἐφορᾶν καὶ πάντ' ἀκούειν οὐδὲ νῦν ὅπου σοι θέμις οἰκῶν[2] ἀπολείπεις τοῦ πᾶσιν ἔγγιστα εἶναι, μᾶλλον δ' ἑκάστῳ καὶ βουλευομένῳ
109 καὶ διὰ νυκτὸς καὶ ἡμέρας συμπάρει." ταῦτ' ἐπιθειάσας πρὸς τὸν θεὸν ἀπέστρεψεν εἰς τὸ πλῆθος τοὺς λόγους, ἐμφανίζων τοῦ θεοῦ τὴν δύναμιν αὐτοῖς καὶ τὴν πρόνοιαν, ὅτι Δαυίδῃ τῷ πατρὶ περὶ τῶν μελλόντων ἅπαντα καθὼς ἀποβέβηκεν ἤδη τὰ πολλὰ καὶ γενήσεται τὰ λείποντα δηλώσειε,
110 καὶ ὡς αὐτὸς ἐπιθείη τὸ ὄνομ' αὐτῷ μήπω γεγεννημένῳ καὶ τίς μέλλοι καλεῖσθαι προείποι καὶ ὅτι τὸν ναὸν οὗτος οἰκοδομήσει[3] αὐτῷ, βασιλεὺς μετὰ τὴν τοῦ πατρὸς τελευτὴν γενόμενος· ἃ βλέποντας κατὰ τὴν ἐκείνου προφητείαν ἐπιτελῆ τὸν θεὸν εὐλογεῖν ἠξίου καὶ περὶ μηδενὸς ἀπογινώσκειν ὧν ὑπέσχηται πρὸς εὐδαιμονίαν ὡς οὐκ ἐσομένου, πιστεύοντας ἐκ τῶν ἤδη βλεπομένων.

111 (3) Ταῦτα διαλεχθεὶς πρὸς τὸν ὄχλον ὁ βασιλεὺς ἀφορᾷ πάλιν εἰς τὸν ναὸν καὶ τὴν δεξιὰν εἰς τὸν οὐρανὸν[4] ἀνασχών "ἔργοις μέν," εἶπεν, "οὐ δυνατὸν ἀνθρώποις ἀποδοῦναι θεῷ χάριν ὑπὲρ ὧν εὖ πεπόνθασιν· ἀπροσδεὲς γὰρ τὸ θεῖον ἁπάντων καὶ κρεῖττον τοιαύτης ἀμοιβῆς· ᾧ δὲ τῶν ἄλλων

[1] + οὐ δὲ σαυτῷ ROM: + a tuis sedibus Lat.: τῶν σεαυτοῦ conj. Cocceji. [2] Ernesti: οἰκεῖν codd. Lat.
[3] ex Lat. Ernesti: ᾠκοδομήσειεν ROM: οἰκοδομήσειεν SP.
[4] ex LXX Niese: ὄχλον codd.

[a] Eduard Norden, *Agnostos Theos*, p. 19 note 2, comments on the Stoic colouring of the last phrase. Josephus does, indeed, often use Stoic terminology in describing the divine attributes, and the present text of Scripture is well suited for such amplification. For a special treatment of this

suaded that Thou art present and not far removed.[a] For, as Thou seest all things and hearest all things, Thou dost not, even when dwelling here where is Thy rightful place, leave off being very near to all men, but rather art present with everyone who asks for guidance, both by night and by day." After this solemn appeal to God he turned to address the multitude and made clear to them the power and providence of God in that most of the future events which He had revealed to David, his father, had actually come to pass, and the rest would also come about, and how God Himself had given him his name even before he was born, and had foretold what he was to be called and that none but he should build Him a temple, on becoming king after his father's death. And now that they saw the fulfilment of these things in accordance with David's prophecies, he asked them to praise God and not despair of anything He had promised for their happiness, as if it were not to be, but to have faith because of what they had already seen.

Solomon blesses the people. 1 Kings viii. 14.

(3) When the king had thus spoken to the crowd, he looked again toward the temple and, raising his right hand [b] up to heaven,[c] said, "Not by deeds is it possible for men to return thanks to God for the benefits they have received, for the Deity stands in need of nothing [d] and is above any such recompense.

Solomon's prayer. 1 Kings viii. 22; 2 Chron. vi. 12.

subject *cf.* A. Schlatter, "Wie sprach Josefus von Gott?" in *Beiträge zur Förderung christlicher Theologie*, xv. 1, 1910.

[b] Bibl. "spread his hands."

[c] Emended text; MSS. "to the multitude."

[d] ἀπροσδεής is a Stoic attribute of God. For instances of similar borrowings in Jewish Greek writings see R. Marcus, "Divine Names and Attributes in Hellenistic Jewish Literature" in *Proceedings of the American Academy for Jewish Research*, 1931–1932.

ζῴων ὑπὸ σοῦ, δέσποτα, κρείττονες γεγόναμεν, τούτῳ τὴν σὴν εὐλογεῖν μεγαλειότητα καὶ περὶ τῶν ὑπηργμένων εἰς τὸν ἡμέτερον οἶκον καὶ τὸν
112 Ἑβραίων λαὸν εὐχαριστεῖν ἀνάγκη. τίνι γὰρ ἄλλῳ μᾶλλον ἱλάσασθαι μηνίοντα καὶ δυσμεναίνοντα εὐμενῆ δεξιοῦσθαι ἀξιώτερον[1] ἐστιν ἡμῖν ἢ φωνῇ, ἣν ἐξ ἀέρος τε ἔχομεν καὶ δι' αὐτοῦ πάλιν ἀνιοῦσαν οἴδαμεν; χάριν οὖν ἔχειν δι' αὐτῆς ὁμολογῶ σοι περί τε τοῦ πατρὸς πρῶτον, ὃν ἐξ
113 ἀφανοῦς εἰς τοσαύτην ἀνήγαγες δόξαν, ἔπειθ' ὑπὲρ ἐμαυτοῦ πάντα μέχρι τῆς παρούσης ἡμέρας ἃ προεῖπας πεποιηκότι, δέομαί τε τοῦ λοιποῦ χορηγεῖν ὅσα θεῷ δύναμις ἀνθρώποις ὑπὸ σοῦ τετιμημένοις, καὶ τὸν οἶκον τὸν ἡμέτερον αὔξειν εἰς ἅπαν, ὡς καθωμολόγησας Δαυίδῃ τῷ πατρί μου καὶ ζῶντι καὶ παρὰ τὴν τελευτήν, ὅτι παρ' ἡμῖν ἡ βασιλεία μενεῖ καὶ τὸ ἐκείνου γένος αὐτὴν διαδοχαῖς ἀμείψει μυρίαις. ταῦτ' οὖν ἡμῖν ἐπάρκεσον καὶ παισί[2] τοῖς ἐμοῖς ἀρετὴν ᾗ σὺ χαίρεις παράσχου.
114 πρὸς δὲ[3] τούτοις ἱκετεύω καὶ μοῖράν τινα τοῦ σοῦ πνεύματος εἰς τὸν ναὸν ἀποικίσαι, ὡς ἂν καὶ ἐπὶ γῆς ἡμῖν εἶναι δοκῇς. σοὶ μὲν γὰρ μικρὸν οἰκητήριον καὶ τὸ πᾶν οὐρανοῦ καὶ τῶν κατὰ τοῦτον ὄντων κύτος, οὐχ ὅτι γε οὗτος ὁ τυχὼν ναός, ἀλλὰ φυλάσσειν τε ἀπόρθητον ἐκ πολεμίων ὡς ἴδιον εἰς ἅπαν καὶ προνοεῖν ὡς οἰκείου κτήματος παρακαλῶ.
115 κἂν ἁμαρτών ποτε ὁ λαὸς ἔπειτα πληγῇ τινι

[1] δεξιοῦσθαι ἀξιώτερον Cocceji: δεξιώτερον codd.
[2] πᾶσι ROM.
[3] Bekker: δὴ codd.

But with that (gift of speech), O Lord, through which we have been made by Thee superior to other creatures, we cannot but praise Thy greatness and give thanks for Thy kindnesses to our house and the Hebrew people, for with what other thing is it more fitting for us to appease Thee when wrathful, and, when ill disposed, to make Thee gracious than with our voice, which we have from the air, and know to ascend again through this element? [a] And so, with my voice I render thanks to Thee, first for my father's sake, whom Thou didst raise from obscurity to such great glory, and next on my own behalf, for whom unto the present day Thou hast done all that Thou didst foretell. And I beseech Thee henceforth to grant whatever God has power to bestow on men esteemed by Thee, and to increase our house for ever, as Thou didst promise David, my father, both in his lifetime and when he was near death, saying that the kingship should remain among us and that his descendants should transmit it to numberless successors. These things, therefore, do Thou grant us, and to my sons give that virtue in which Thou delightest. Beside these things I entreat Thee also to send some portion of Thy spirit to dwell in the temple, that Thou mayest seem to us to be on earth as well. For to Thee even the whole vault of heaven and all its host is but a small habitation—how much less this poor temple! Nonetheless I pray Thee to guard it for ever from sacking by our enemies, as Thine own temple, and to watch over it as Thine own possession. And if ever the people sin and then because of their

[a] This portion of Solomon's prayer is amplified by Josephus, while in the following he condenses the scriptural text.

κακῶται[1] διὰ τὴν ἁμαρτίαν ἐκ σοῦ, γῆς ἀκαρπίᾳ καὶ φθορᾷ λοιμικῇ ἤ τινι τούτων τῶν παθημάτων, οἷς σὺ τοὺς παραβάντας τι τῶν ὁσίων μετέρχῃ, καὶ καταφεύγῃ πᾶς ἀθροισθεὶς ἐπὶ τὸν ναὸν ἱκετεύων σε καὶ σωθῆναι δεόμενος, ἐπήκοος αὐτοῦ γενόμενος ὡς ἔνδον ὢν ἐλεήσῃς καὶ τῶν συμφορῶν
116 ἀπαλλάξῃς. ταύτην δὲ οὐχ Ἑβραίοις μόνον δέομαι παρὰ σοῦ τὴν βοήθειαν εἶναι σφαλεῖσιν, ἀλλὰ κἂν ἀπὸ περάτων τῆς οἰκουμένης τινὲς ἀφίκωνται κἂν ὁποθενδηποτοῦν προστρεπόμενοι καὶ τυχεῖν τινος ἀγαθοῦ λιπαροῦντες, δὸς αὐτοῖς ἐκήκοος γενόμενος.
117 οὕτως γὰρ ἂν μάθοιεν πάντες ὅτι σὺ μὲν αὐτὸς ἐβουλήθης παρ' ἡμῖν κατασκευασθῆναί σοι τὸν οἶκον, ἡμεῖς δ' οὐκ ἀπάνθρωποι τὴν φύσιν ἐσμὲν οὐδ' ἀλλοτρίως πρὸς τοὺς οὐχ[2] ὁμοφύλους ἔχομεν, ἀλλὰ πᾶσι κοινὴν τὴν ἀπὸ σοῦ βοήθειαν καὶ τὴν τῶν ἀγαθῶν ὄνησιν ὑπάρχειν ἠθελήσαμεν."
118 (4) Εἰπὼν ταῦτα καὶ ῥίψας αὑτὸν ἐπὶ τὴν γῆν καὶ ἐπὶ πολλὴν ὥραν προσκυνήσας, ἀναστὰς θυσίας τῷ βωμῷ προσῆγε[3] καὶ γεμίσας τῶν ὁλοκλήρων ἱερείων ἐναργέστατα τὸν θεὸν ἡδέως ἔγνω τὴν θυσίαν προσδεχόμενον· πῦρ γὰρ ἐξ ἀέρος διαδραμὸν καὶ πάντων ὁρώντων ἐπὶ τὸν βωμὸν ᾆξαν ἅπασαν τὴν θυσίαν ἀνήρπασε καὶ κατεδαίσατο.
119 ταύτης δὲ τῆς ἐπιφανείας γενομένης ὁ μὲν λαὸς δήλωσιν εἶναι τοῦτ' εἰκάσας τῆς ἐν τῷ ναῷ τοῦ θεοῦ διατριβῆς ἐσομένης καὶ ἡσθεὶς προσεκύνει

[1] Conj. Thackeray: κακῷ codd.: pessima Lat.
[2] Cocceji: οὐκ M: om. rell.
[3] βωμῷ προσῆγε MSE (Zonaras): θεῷ προσῆγε P: θεῷ προσήνεγκε RO: in templo obtulit Lat.

[a] Emended text.
[b] This last is an apologetic variation of Scripture, 1 Kings

sin are smitten [a] by some evil from Thee, by unfruitfulness of the soil or a destructive pestilence or any such affliction with which Thou visitest those who transgress any of the sacred laws, and if they all gather to take refuge in the temple, entreating Thee and praying to be saved, then do Thou hearken to them as though Thou wert within, and pity them and deliver them from their misfortunes. And this help I ask of Thee not alone for the Hebrews who may fall into error, but also if any come even from the ends of the earth or from wherever it may be and turn to Thee, imploring to receive some kindness, do Thou hearken and give it them. For so would all men know that Thou Thyself didst desire that this house should be built for Thee in our land, and also that we are not inhumane by nature nor unfriendly to those who are not of our country, but wish that all men equally should receive aid from Thee and enjoy Thy blessings." [b]

The sacrifices are miraculously consumed. 2 Chron. vii 1.

(4) Having spoken in these words, he threw himself upon the ground and did obeisance for a long time; then he arose and brought sacrifices to the altar,[c] and, when he had heaped it with whole victims, he knew that God was gladly accepting the sacrifice, for a fire darted out of the air and, in the sight of all the people, leaped upon the altar and, seizing on the sacrifice, consumed it all. When this divine manifestation occurred, all the people supposed it to be a sign that God would thereafter dwell in the temple, and with joy they fell upon the ground

viii. 43 b, " that all people of the earth may know thy name to reverence thee as do thy people Israel."

[c] Josephus here follows the order in 2 Chron.; in 1 Kings (viii. 54-61) Solomon blesses the people before offering sacrifice.

πεσὼν ἐπὶ τοὔδαφος, ὁ δὲ βασιλεὺς εὐλογεῖν τε ἤρξατο καὶ τὸ πλῆθος ταὐτὸ ποιεῖν[1] παρώρμα δείγματα μὲν ἔχοντας ἤδη τῆς τοῦ θεοῦ πρὸς αὐτοὺς
120 εὐμενείας, εὐχομένους δὲ τοιαῦτα ἀποβαίνειν ἀεὶ τὰ παρ᾽ ἐκείνου, καὶ τὴν διάνοιαν αὐτοῖς καθαρὰν ἀπὸ πάσης φυλάττεσθαι κακίας ἐν δικαιοσύνῃ καὶ θρησκείᾳ καὶ τῷ τὰς ἐντολὰς τηρεῖν ἃς διὰ Μωυσέος αὐτοῖς ἔδωκεν ὁ θεὸς διαμένουσιν[2]· ἔσεσθαι γὰρ οὕτως εὔδαιμον τὸ Ἑβραίων ἔθνος
121 καὶ παντὸς ἀνθρώπων γένους μακαριώτερον. παρεκάλει τε μνημονεύειν ὡς οἷς ἐκτήσατο τὰ παρόντα ἀγαθὰ τούτοις αὐτὰ καὶ βέβαια ἕξειν[3] καὶ μείζω καὶ πλείω καταστήσειν[4]· οὐ γὰρ λαβεῖν αὐτὰ μόνον δι᾽ εὐσέβειαν καὶ δικαιοσύνην, ἀλλὰ καὶ καθέξειν διὰ ταῦτα προσῆκεν ὑπολαμβάνειν· εἶναι δὲ τοῖς ἀνθρώποις οὐχ οὕτως μέγα τὸ κτήσασθαί τι τῶν οὐχ ὑπαρχόντων, ὡς τὸ σῶσαι τὰ πορισθέντα καὶ μηδὲν ἁμαρτεῖν εἰς βλάβην αὐτῶν.

122 (5) Ὁ μὲν οὖν βασιλεὺς διαλεχθεὶς ταῦτα πρὸς τὸ πλῆθος διαλύει τὴν ἐκκλησίαν τελέσας θυσίας ὑπέρ τε αὐτοῦ καὶ πάντων Ἑβραίων, ὡς μόσχους μὲν καταθῦσαι μυρίους καὶ δισχιλίους, προβάτων
123 δὲ μυριάδας δώδεκα. τὸν γὰρ ναὸν τότε πρῶτον ἔγευσεν ἱερουργημάτων καὶ κατευωχήθησαν ἐν αὐτῷ πάντες σὺν γυναιξὶν Ἑβραῖοι καὶ τέκνοις, ἔτι δὲ καὶ τὴν σκηνοπηγίαν καλουμένην ἑορτὴν πρὸ τοῦ ναοῦ λαμπρῶς καὶ μεγαλοπρεπῶς ἐπὶ δὶς

[1] E Lat.: εἰπεῖν codd.
[2] Dindorf: διαμενούσης P: διαμενούσας rell.
[3] ἕξουσι ed. pr.
[4] καταστήσουσιν MSP.

and did obeisance. But the king began to bless God and urged the multitude to do the like, seeing that they now had tokens of God's goodwill toward them, and to pray that such would be His treatment of them always and that their minds might be kept pure from all evil as they continued in righteousness and worship and in observance of the commandments which God had given them through Moses; for thus would the Hebrew nation be happy and the most blessed of all the races of men. And he exhorted them to remember that in the same way in which they had acquired their present blessings they would also preserve them surely and would make them greater and more numerous. For, he said, they ought to realize that not only had they received them because of their piety and righteousness, but that they would also maintain them through these same qualities, and that it is not so great a thing for men to acquire something which they have not had before as to preserve what is given them and be guilty of nothing which may harm it.[a] 1 Kings viii. 54.

(5) And so, when the king had thus addressed the multitude, he dismissed the assembly after offering sacrifices both for himself and for the Hebrews with the slaughter of twelve thousand[b] calves and one hundred and twenty thousand sheep, for this was the first time that he gave the temple a portion[c] of victims, and all the Hebrews with their women and children feasted therein. Moreover the festival called the Setting up of Booths (Tabernacles) was splendidly and magnificently celebrated before the

The sacrifices and celebration of Tabernacles. 1 Kings viii. 62.

[a] Solomon's speech is somewhat amplified.
[b] Bibl. 22,000.
[c] Lit. "gave the temple a taste."

ἑπτὰ ἡμέρας ἤγαγεν ὁ βασιλεὺς σὺν ἅπαντι τῷ λαῷ κατευωχούμενος.

124 (6) Ἐπεὶ δ᾿ εἶχεν αὐτοῖς ἀποχρώντως ταῦτα καὶ μηδὲν ἐνέδει τῇ περὶ τὸν θεὸν εὐσεβείᾳ, πρὸς αὐτοὺς ἕκαστοι τοῦ βασιλέως ἀπολύσαντος ἀπῄεσαν εὐχαριστήσαντες τῷ βασιλεῖ τῆς τε περὶ αὐτοὺς προνοίας καὶ ὧν ἐπεδείξατο ἔργων, καὶ εὐξάμενοι τῷ θεῷ παρασχεῖν αὐτοῖς εἰς πολὺν χρόνον Σολομῶνα βασιλέα, τὴν πορείαν ἐποιοῦντο μετὰ χαρᾶς καὶ παιδιᾶς ὕμνους εἰς τὸν θεὸν ᾄδοντες, ὡς ὑπὸ τῆς ἡδονῆς ἀπόνως τὴν ὁδὸν τὴν ἐπὶ τὰ οἰκεῖα
125 πάντας ἀνύσαι. καὶ οἱ μὲν τὴν κιβωτὸν εἰς τὸν ναὸν εἰσαγαγόντες καὶ τὸ μέγεθος καὶ τὸ κάλλος ἱστορήσαντες αὐτοῦ, καὶ θυσιῶν ἐπ᾿ αὐτῷ μεγάλων καὶ ἑορτῶν μεταλαβόντες, εἰς τὰς αὐτῶν[1] ἕκαστοι πόλεις ὑπέστρεψαν. ὄναρ δ᾿ ἐπιφανὲν τῷ βασιλεῖ κατὰ τοὺς ὕπνους ἐσήμαινεν αὐτῷ τῆς εὐχῆς
126 ἐπήκοον τὸν θεὸν γεγονέναι, καὶ ὅτι φυλάξει τε τὸν ναὸν καὶ διὰ παντὸς ἐν αὐτῷ μενεῖ[2] τῶν ἐκγόνων αὐτοῦ[3] καὶ τῆς ἁπάσης πληθύος τὰ δίκαια ποιούσης, αὐτὸν δὲ πρῶτον ἐμμένοντα ταῖς τοῦ πατρὸς ὑποθήκαις ἔλεγεν εἰς ὕψος καὶ μέγεθος εὐδαιμονίας ἀνοίσειν ἄπειρον καὶ βασιλεύσειν ἀεὶ τῆς χώρας τοὺς ἐκ τοῦ γένους αὐτοῦ καὶ τῆς Ἰούδα
127 φυλῆς· προδόντα μέντοι τὰ ἐπιτηδεύματα καὶ λήθην αὐτῶν ποιησάμενον καὶ ξενικοὺς θεοὺς θρησκεύειν μεταβαλόμενον[4] πρόρριζον ἐκκόψειν καὶ μήτε τοῦ γένους τι λείψανον αὐτῶν[5] ἐάσειν μήτε τὸν τῶν

[1] Hudson: αὐτῶν codd.
[2] Ernesti: μένοι codd. [3] + καὶ αὐτοῦ E.
[4] Bekker: μεταβαλλόμενον codd.
[5] αὐτοῦ Zonaras Lat.: αὐτὸν conj. Niese (αὐτῶν in edit.).

temple for twice seven days [a] by the king, who feasted together with all the people.

(6) And when they had had enough of these things and had omitted nothing that was required by piety toward God, the king dismissed them and they went away, each to his home; and, giving thanks to the king for his care of them and for the display he had made, and praying to God to grant them Solomon as king for a long time, they set out on their way with joyfulness and mirth and singing hymns to God, so that by reason of their delight they all accomplished the journey homeward without fatigue. And those who had brought the ark into the temple and beheld its size and beauty and partaken of the great sacrifices and the feasts there, returned, each to his own city. But to the king a dream appeared in his sleep, which revealed to him that God had hearkened to his prayer [b] and that He would preserve the temple and would abide in it for ever, if his descendants and all the people acted righteously; as for the king himself, God said that if he abided by his father's counsels, He would first raise him to a height and greatness of happiness beyond measure, and that those of his own line should for ever rule the country and the tribe of Judah. If, however, he should be faithless to his task and forget it and turn to the worship of foreign gods, He would cut him off root and branch and would not suffer any of their line to survive nor

God again appears to Solomon in a dream. 1 Kings viii 66.

[a] So Heb. and several LXX MSS.; Cod. B of LXX has "seven days." The festival of Tabernacles lasted only seven days and was followed by a "closing festival" (*'asereth*), *cf. A.* iii. 244 ff.

[b] Bibl. "the Lord appeared to Solomon a second time."

Ἰσραηλιτῶν λαὸν ἀπαθῆ παρόψεσθαι, πολέμοις δ' αὐτοὺς καὶ κακοῖς ἐξαφανίσειν μυρίοις, κἀκ τῆς γῆς ἣν τοῖς πατράσιν αὐτῶν ἔδωκεν ἐκβαλὼν ἐπή-
128 λυδας ἀλλοτρίας καταστήσειν, τὸν δὲ ναὸν τὸν νῦν οἰκοδομηθέντα καταπρησθησόμενον τοῖς ἐχθροῖς παραδώσειν καὶ διαρπαγησόμενον, κατασκάψειν δὲ καὶ τὴν πόλιν χερσὶ τῶν πολεμίων καὶ ποιήσειν μύθων ἄξια τὰ παρ' αὐτοῖς κακὰ καὶ πολλῆς δι'
129 ὑπερβολὴν μεγέθους ἀπιστίας, ὡς τοὺς προσοίκους ἀκούοντας τὴν συμφορὰν θαυμάζειν καὶ τὴν αἰτίαν πολυπραγμονεῖν, δι' ἣν οὕτως ἐμισήθησαν Ἑβραῖοι τῷ θεῷ, πρότερον εἰς δόξαν καὶ πλοῦτον ὑπ' αὐτοῦ παραχθέντες, καὶ παρὰ τῶν ὑπολειπομένων ἀκούειν ἐξομολογουμένων τὰς ἁμαρτίας αὐτῶν καὶ τὰς τῶν πατρίων νομίμων παραβάσεις. ταῦτα μὲν οὖν αὐτῷ τὸν θεὸν εἰπεῖν κατὰ τοὺς ὕπνους ἀναγέγραπται.

130 (v. 1) Μετὰ δὲ τὴν τοῦ ναοῦ κατασκευὴν ἐν ἔτεσιν ἑπτὰ καθὼς προειρήκαμεν γενομένην τὴν τῶν βασιλείων οἰκοδομὴν[1] κατεβάλετο, ἣν ἔτεσι τρισὶ καὶ δέκα μόγις ἀπήρτισεν· οὐ γὰρ τὸν αὐτὸν ἐσπουδάζετο τρόπον ὅνπερ καὶ τὸ ἱερόν, ἀλλὰ τὸ μὲν καίπερ ὂν μέγα καὶ θαυμαστῆς ἐργασίας καὶ παραδόξου τετυχηκός, ἔτι καὶ θεοῦ συνεργοῦντος, εἰς ὃν ἐγίνετο, τοῖς προειρημένοις ἔτεσιν ἔλαβε
131 πέρας· τὰ δὲ βασίλεια πολὺ[2] τῆς ἀξίας τοῦ ναοῦ καταδεέστερα τυγχάνοντα τῷ μήτε τὴν ὕλην ἐκ

[1] οἰκοδομίαν MSPE. [2] πολύ τε RO: πολύ τι Niese.

[a] Bibl. "this house . . . will I cast out of my sight."

[b] In Scripture the building of the palace is described directly after that of the temple, and the second appearance of God follows upon the completion of both buildings.

allow the people of Israel to go unharmed, but would utterly destroy them with wars and countless afflictions and, after driving them out of the land which He had given to their fathers, would make them aliens in a strange land, and the temple, which had only now been built, He would give over to their enemies to burn down and sack,[a] and would also raze their city to the ground by the hand of their enemies, and would make the evils that should fall on them like stories which men tell, beyond belief because of their surpassing magnitude, so that when their neighbours heard of their misfortune they would wonder at it and would curiously inquire why the Hebrews were now so hated by God by whom they had formerly been raised to glory and wealth, and from the survivors they would hear the reason as these confessed their sins and their transgressions against the laws of their fathers. These things, then, it is written in Scripture, God spoke to him in his sleep.

The building of Solomon's palace. 1 Kings vii. 1 (LXX vii. 38).

(v. 1) [b] After the building of the temple, which, as we have said before,[c] took seven years, he laid the foundations of the palace buildings, which he hardly completed in thirteen years, for it was not built with the same industry as the temple had been; the latter, though it was so great and of a workmanship so wonderful and surpassing belief, was nevertheless finished in the fore-mentioned number of years, since God, for whom it was built, also assisted in the work.[d] But the palace, which was much inferior in dignity to the temple because the materials had not been pre-

[c] § 99.

[d] For rabbinic legends about the miraculous building of the temple see Ginzberg iv. 155.

τοσούτου χρόνου καὶ τῆς αὐτῆς ἡτοιμάσθαι φιλοτιμίας καὶ βασιλεῦσιν οἰκητήριον ἀλλὰ μὴ θεῷ
132 γίνεσθαι, βράδιον ἠνύσθη. καὶ αὐτὰ μὲν οὖν ἄξια λόγου καὶ κατὰ τὴν εὐδαιμονίαν τῆς Ἑβραίων χώρας καὶ τοῦ βασιλέως ᾠκοδομήθη, τὴν δὲ ὅλην αὐτῶν διάταξιν καὶ τὴν διάθεσιν εἰπεῖν ἀναγκαῖον, ἵν' οὕτως ἐκ τούτου στοχάζεσθαι καὶ συνορᾶν ἔχωσι τὸ μέγεθος οἱ τῇ γραφῇ μέλλοντες ἐντυγχάνειν.

133 (2) Οἶκος ἦν μέγας καὶ καλὸς πολλοῖς στύλοις ἐρηρεισμένος, ὃν εἰς τὰς κρίσεις καὶ τὴν τῶν πραγμάτων διάγνωσιν πλῆθος ὑποδέξασθαι καὶ χωρῆσαι σύνοδον ἀνθρώπων ἐπὶ δίκας συνεληλυθότων κατεσκεύασεν, ἑκατὸν μὲν πηχῶν τὸ μῆκος εὖρος δὲ πεντήκοντα τὸ δ' ὕψος τριάκοντα, κίοσι μὲν τετραγώνοις ἀνειλημμένον ἐκ κέδρου πᾶσιν, ἐστεγασμένον δὲ Κορινθίως, ἰσομέτροις δὲ φλιαῖς καὶ θυρώμασι τριγλύφοις ἀσφαλῆ τε ὁμοῦ καὶ
134 κεκαλλωπισμένον. ἕτερος δὲ οἶκος ἦν ἐν μέσῳ κατὰ ὅλου τοῦ πλάτους τεταγμένος τετράγωνος[1] εὖρος πηχῶν τριάκοντα, ἄντικρυς ἔχων ναὸν[2] παχέσι στύλοις ἀνατεταμένον· ἦν δὲ ἐν αὐτῷ

[1] τετράγωνος om. RO Lat. [2] στοὰν Weill.

---

[a] Unscriptural details.

[b] Called, in Scripture, "the house of the forest of Lebanon."

[c] This unscriptural detail is, of course, an anachronism.

[d] Both the Heb. and LXX of 1 Kings vii. 5 are obscure, partly because Heb. *šāqēph* may mean either "beam" (so the Targum translates) or "window" (lit. "transparency"). The word θυρώματα used by Josephus is found in the LXX, where it translates Heb. *meḥezāh* which seems to mean "window," but θυρώματα may also mean "door." It seems

pared so long before nor with the same expense,[a] and because it was a dwelling for kings and not for God, was more slowly completed. Yet it too was worthy of note, and was built in a manner suitable to the prosperity of the Hebrews' country and their king; but we must describe its whole plan and arrangement, in order that those who will read this work may from this description form an idea and have some notion of its size.

Description of the palace buildings. 1 Kings vii. 2 (LXX vii. 39).

(2) There was a great and beautiful hall,[b] supported by many pillars, which he built to admit a great number of people to judgements and decisions of state cases and to provide room for gatherings of men who opposed each other in trials[a]; it was a hundred cubits in length, fifty in breadth and thirty in height, and was held up by square columns all of cedar; it was roofed in Corinthian[c] style and was at the same time strengthened and ornamented with pilasters of the same size and three-grooved panels.[d] And there was another hall[e] in the middle of the group of buildings, extending along the whole width of the first building, which was quadrangular and thirty cubits in breadth,[f] and was opposite a temple[g] raised on massive pillars. In this was a magnificent

useless to render here the difficult Heb. and LXX texts, which were probably as unintelligible to Josephus as to modern scholars.

[e] Called, in Scripture, "the hall (A.V. "porch") of pillars."

[f] Bibl. "the length thereof was fifty cubits and the breadth thereof thirty cubits."

[g] Bibl. "a hall (A.V. "porch") was before them" (*i.e.* the pillars). For *ναόν* "temple" Weill suggests reading *στοάν*, "porch," which, he holds, corresponds to Heb. *'ûlām*. But *'ûlām* here seems to mean "hall," and Josephus's *ναόν* is probably an interpretation of this too general term.

ἐξέδρα διαπρεπής, ἐν ᾗ καθεζόμενος ὁ βασιλεὺς ἔκρινεν, ᾗ παρέζευκτο κατεσκευασμένος ἄλλος οἶκος τῇ βασιλίσσῃ καὶ τὰ λοιπὰ τὰ πρὸς τὴν δίαιταν καὶ τὰς ἀναπαύσεις οἰκήματα μετὰ τὴν τῶν πραγμάτων ἀπόλυσιν, ἐστρωμένα πάντα σανίσι
135 τετμημέναις ἐκ κέδρου. καὶ τὰ μὲν ᾠκοδομήσατο λίθοις δεκαπήχεσιν, ἑτέρῳ δὲ πριστῷ τοὺς τοίχους καὶ πολυτελεῖ κατημφίεσεν, ὃς[1] εἰς κόσμον ἱερῶν καὶ βασιλείων οἴκων θεωρίαν[2] γῇ μεταλλεύεται τοῖς φέρουσιν αὐτὸν τόποις ἐπαινουμένῃ.[3]
136 καὶ τὸ μὲν ἀπ' αὐτοῦ κάλλος ἐπὶ τριστιχίαν ἦν ἐνυφασμένον, τετάρτη δὲ μοῖρα γλυφέων παρεῖχε θαυμάζειν ἐπιστήμην, ὑφ' ὧν πεποίητο δένδρα καὶ φυτὰ παντοῖα σύσκια τοῖς κλάδοις καὶ τοῖς ἐκκρεμαμένοις αὐτῶν πετάλοις, ὡς ὑπονοεῖν αὐτὰ καὶ σαλεύεσθαι δι' ὑπερβολὴν λεπτότητος καλύπ-
137 τοντα τὸν ὑπ' αὐτοῖς λίθον. τὸ δὲ ἄλλο μέχρι τῆς στέγης χριστὸν ἦν καὶ καταπεποικιλμένον χρώμασι καὶ βαφαῖς.[4] προσκατεσκεύασε δὲ τούτοις ἄλλα τε πρὸς τρυφὴν οἰκήματα καὶ δὴ καὶ στοὰς μηκίστας καὶ ἐν καλῷ τῶν βασιλείων κειμένας, ἐν αἷς λαμπρότατον οἶκον εἰς ἑστίασιν καὶ συμπόσια χρυσοῦ περίπλεων[5]· καὶ τἆλλα δὲ ὅσα τοῦτον ἔχειν ἔδει πρὸς τὴν τῶν ἑστιωμένων ὑπηρεσίαν σκεύη
138 πάντ' ἐκ χρυσοῦ κατεσκεύαστο. δύσκολον δ' ἐστὶν καταριθμήσασθαι[6] τὸ μέγεθος καὶ τὴν

[1] κατημφίεσεν ὃς Hudson: κατημφίασεν ὃν RO: κατημφιεσμένον MSP Lat.

[2] Hudson: θεωρίων RO: θεωρία MSP: Τυρίων Ernesti: Βαιθώρων T, Reinach.

[3] γῇ . . . ἐπαινουμένῃ Hudson: γῆ . . . ἐπαινουμένη (ἀπαρνουμένη RO) codd.

[4] γραφαῖς MSP.

[5] Cocceji: περίπλεω codd.

[6] + καὶ διηγήσασθαι SP.

hall[a] where the king sat to give judgement, and to it was joined another hall built for the queen, and the remaining chambers for eating and for resting after the discharge of public business, all of them floored with boards cut out of cedar. Some of these he built with stones of ten cubits,[b] and he covered the walls with another kind of sawn stone of great value, which is mined for the adornment of temples and enhancing the appearance of royal palaces, in a region celebrated for the places that produce it.[c] And the beauty of this stone was displayed in a pattern of three rows, while the fourth row made one admire the skill of the sculptors who had fashioned trees and plants of all kinds, giving shade with their branches and the leaves hanging down from them, and so exceedingly delicate that one would have imagined they actually moved and were covering the stone under them. The rest of the wall, up to the roof, was painted and enlivened with various colours and tints. And in addition to these, he built other chambers for pleasure, among them very long colonnades, situated in a beautiful part of the palace, in which was a very splendid hall for feasts and banquets, filled with gold. And the other vessels such as were needed in the hall for the service of guests at the feasts were all made of gold. But it is difficult to describe in detail the size and variety of the palace

[a] Bibl. "hall (A.V. "porch") of judgement."
[b] Bibl. "and the foundation was of costly stones, . . . stones of ten cubits and stones of eight cubits."
[c] Emended text.

ποικιλίαν τῶν βασιλείων, ὅσα μὲν ἦν αὐτοῖς τὰ μέγιστα οἰκήματα, πόσα δὲ τὰ τούτων ὑποδεέστερα καὶ πόσα ὑπόγεια καὶ ἀφανῆ, τό τε τῶν ἀνειμένων εἰς ἀέρα κάλλος καὶ τὰ ἄλση πρὸς θεωρίαν ἐπιτερπεστάτην καὶ θέρους ὑποφυγὴν καὶ σκέπην
139 εἶναι τοῖς σώμασιν. ἐν κεφαλαίῳ δ' εἰπεῖν, τὴν ὅλην οἰκοδομίαν ἐκ λίθου λευκοῦ καὶ κέδρου καὶ χρυσοῦ καὶ ἀργύρου πᾶσαν ἐποιήσατο, τοὺς ὀρόφους καὶ τοὺς τοίχους τοῖς ἐγκλειομένοις χρυσῷ λίθοις διανθίσας τὸν αὐτὸν τρόπον, ὡς καὶ τὸν τοῦ
140 θεοῦ ναὸν τούτοις κατηγλάισεν. εἰργάσατο δὲ καὶ ἐξ ἐλέφαντος θρόνον παμμεγεθέστατον ἐν κατασκευῇ βήματος ἔχοντα μὲν ἓξ ἀναβαθμούς,[1] ἑκάστῳ δὲ τούτων ἐξ ἑκατέρου μέρους δύο λέοντες ἐφειστήκεσαν τοσούτων ἄνωθεν ἄλλων παρεστώτων. τὸ δ' ἐνήλατον τοῦ θρόνου χεῖρες ἦσαν δεχόμεναι τὸν βασιλέα, ἀνακέκλιτο δ' εἰς μόσχου προτομὴν τὰ κατόπιν αὐτοῦ βλέποντος, χρυσῷ δὲ ἅπας ἦν δεδεμένος.

141 (3) Ταῦτα Σολομὼν εἰκοσαετίᾳ κατασκευάσας, ἐπεὶ πολὺν μὲν αὐτῷ χρυσὸν πλείω δ' ἄργυρον ὁ τῶν Τυρίων βασιλεὺς Εἴρωμος εἰς τὴν οἰκοδομίαν συνήνεγκεν ἔτι δὲ καὶ ξύλα κέδρου καὶ πίτυος, ἀντεδωρήσατο καὶ αὐτὸς μεγάλαις δωρεαῖς τὸν Εἴρωμον σῖτόν τε κατ' ἔτος πέμπων αὐτῷ καὶ οἶνον καὶ ἔλαιον, ὧν μάλιστα διὰ τὸ νῆσον οἰκεῖν,
142 ὡς καὶ προειρήκαμεν ἤδη, χρῄζων διετέλει. πρὸς τούτοις δὲ καὶ πόλεις αὐτῷ τῆς Γαλιλαίας εἴκοσι μὲν τὸν ἀριθμόν, οὐ πόρρω δὲ τῆς Τύρου κειμένας

[1] βαθμούς RO.

[a] These details are invented by Josephus; they are

buildings, how many larger chambers there were, how many smaller ones and how many were underground and not visible, and the beauty of those parts open to the air, and the groves which gave a most delightful view and served as a refuge and shelter to the body from the heat of summer.[a] To sum it up, he made the whole building of white marble, cedar, gold and silver, and decorated the roofs and walls with stones set in gold in the same manner as he had beautified the temple of God with them. He also had them make an immense throne of ivory in the form of a dais with six steps leading up to it, and on each of these on either side stood two lions, and there were two others at the top, standing on either side; the seat of the throne had arms to receive the king, and it rested on the head of a calf[b] which faced toward the back of the throne; and the entire throne was plated[c] with gold.

Solomon's throne. 1 Kings x. 18.

(3) These works Solomon completed in twenty years, and, since Eirōmos, the king of Tyre, had contributed much gold and more silver[d] to their building, as well as wood of cedar and pine[e] trees, he too presented Eirōmos in return with great gifts, sending him every year grain and wine and oil, of which, because, as we have already said before,[f] he inhabited an island, he was always particularly in need. Beside these he made him a present of some cities in Galilee, twenty in number, which lay not far from Tyre[g];

Solomon and Hiram, king of Tyre. 1 Kings ix. 10.

probably based, as Weill suggests, on the arrangements of Herod's buildings.

[b] So the LXX, *προτομαὶ μόσχων*, reading in the Heb. text *râšê 'ēgel* "heads of calves" instead of *rôš 'āgôl* "a rounded top."

[c] Lit. "fastened."

[d] Silver is not mentioned in Scripture.

[e] *Cf.* § 54 note.

[f] § 54.

[g] Bibl. "in the land of Galilee."

ἐχαρίσατο, ἃς ἐπελθὼν καὶ κατανοήσας Εἴρωμος καὶ δυσαρεστήσας τῇ δωρεᾷ πέμψας πρὸς Σολομῶνα μὴ δεῖσθαι τῶν πόλεων ἔλεγε· κἄκτοτε προσηγορεύθησαν Χαβαλὼν γῆ· μεθερμηνευόμενον γὰρ τὸ χάβαλον κατὰ Φοινίκων γλῶτταν οὐκ
143 ἀρέσκον σημαίνει. καὶ σοφίσματα δὲ καὶ λόγους αἰνιγματώδεις διεπέμψατο πρὸς Σολομῶνα ὁ τῶν Τυρίων βασιλεὺς παρακαλῶν ὅπως αὐτῷ σαφηνίσῃ τούτους καὶ τῆς ἀπορίας τῶν ἐν αὐτοῖς ζητουμένων ἀπαλλάξῃ. τὸν δὲ δεινὸν ὄντα καὶ συνετὸν οὐδὲν τούτων παρῆλθεν, ἀλλὰ πάντα νικήσας τῷ λογισμῷ καὶ μαθὼν αὐτῶν τὴν διάνοιαν ἐφώτισε.
144 Μέμνηται δὲ τούτων τῶν δύο βασιλέων καὶ Μένανδρος ὁ μεταφράσας ἀπὸ τῆς Φοινίκων διαλέκτου τὰ Τυρίων ἀρχεῖα εἰς τὴν Ἑλληνικὴν φωνὴν λέγων οὕτως· "τελευτήσαντος δὲ Ἀβιβάλου διεδέξατο τὴν βασιλείαν παρ' αὐτοῦ υἱὸς Εἴρωμος, ὃς βιώσας ἔτη πεντήκοντα τρία ἐβασίλευσε
145 τριάκοντα καὶ τέσσαρα. οὗτος ἔχωσε τὸ Εὐρύχωρον τόν τε χρυσοῦν κίονα τὸν ἐν τοῖς τοῦ Διὸς ἀνέθηκεν· ἔτι τε ὕλην ξύλων ἀπελθὼν ἔκοψεν ἀπὸ τοῦ ὄρους τοῦ λεγομένου Λιβάνου εἰς τὰς τῶν
146 ἱερῶν στέγας· καθελών τε τὰ ἀρχαῖα ἱερὰ καινὰ ἀνῳκοδόμησε[1] τοῦ Ἡρακλέους καὶ τῆς Ἀστάρ-

[1] καινὰ ἀνῳκοδόμησε Niese: καὶ ναὸν ᾠκοδόμησε codd.

[a] Bibl. Cabul; LXX (reading *gebûl*) ὅριον "boundary."

[b] The only Semitic etymology which seems to fit this interpretation is the Aramaic root *kbl*, one meaning of which is "be barren." Josephus's explanation "not pleasing" is

but when Eirōmos went to them and looked them over, he was ill pleased with the gift and sent word to Solomon that he had no use for the cities. And from that time on they were called the Land of Chabalōn,[a] for Chabalōn in the Phoenician tongue is interpreted to mean "not pleasing.[b]" And the king of Tyre also sent Solomon tricky problems and enigmatic sayings, requesting him to clear them up for him and relieve his difficulties concerning the questions propounded. But, as Solomon was clever and keen-witted, none of these proved too hard for him and he successfully solved them all by the force of reason, and having discovered their meaning, brought it to light.

Phoenician writers on Hiram's reign.

These two kings are also mentioned by Menander,[c] who translated the Tyrian records from the Phoenician language into Greek speech, in these words: "And on the death of Abibalos, his son Eirōmos succeeded to his kingdom, who lived to the age of fifty-three and reigned thirty-four years. He it was who made the Eurychōros (Broad Place) embankment and set up the golden column in the temple of Zeus.[d] Moreover he went off and cut timber from the mountain called Libanos for the roofs of the temples, and pulled down the ancient temples and erected new ones to Heracles[e]

apparently based on the Scriptural phrase "and they (*i.e.* the cities) pleased him not." One rabbinic tradition explains the name from the usual meaning of *kābûl* which is "chained down"; other Jewish commentaries give an explanation which is closer to that of Josephus.

[c] *Cf. Ap.* i. 116 ff. where the following excerpt is given in identical words.

[d] Zeus was the Greek equivalent of the native Tyrian Baal, as Josephus calls him in *A.* ix. 138.

[e] Heracles was the Greek equivalent of the Tyrian Melkart.

της, πρῶτός τε τοῦ Ἡρακλέους ἔγερσιν ἐποιήσατο ἐν τῷ Περιτίῳ μηνί· τοῖς τε Ἰτυκαίοις[1] ἐπεστρατεύσατο μὴ ἀποδιδοῦσι τοὺς φόρους καὶ ὑποτάξας πάλιν αὐτῷ ἀνέστρεψεν. ἐπὶ τούτου ἦν Ἀβδήμονος παῖς νεώτερος, ὃς ἀεὶ ἐνίκα[2] τὰ προβλήματα, ἃ ἐπέτασσε Σολομὼν ὁ Ἱεροσολύμων βασιλεύς."

147 μνημονεύει δὲ καὶ Δῖος[3] λέγων οὕτως· " Ἀβιβάλου τελευτήσαντος ὁ υἱὸς αὐτοῦ Εἴρωμος ἐβασίλευσεν. οὗτος τὰ πρὸς ἀνατολὰς μέρη τῆς πόλεως προσέχωσε καὶ μεῖζον τὸ ἄστυ ἐποίησε καὶ τοῦ Ὀλυμπίου Διὸς τὸ ἱερὸν καθ' ἑαυτὸ ὂν[4] ἐγχώσας τὸν μεταξὺ τόπον συνῆψε τῇ πόλει καὶ χρυσοῖς ἀναθήμασιν ἐκόσμησεν· ἀναβὰς δὲ εἰς τὸν Λίβανον

148 ὑλοτόμησε πρὸς τὴν τῶν ἱερῶν κατασκευήν. τὸν δὲ τυραννοῦντα Ἱεροσολύμων Σολομῶνα πέμψαι φασὶ[5] πρὸς Εἴρωμον αἰνίγματα καὶ[6] παρ' αὐτοῦ λαβεῖν ἀξιοῦντα, τὸν δὲ μὴ δυνηθέντα διακρῖναι

149 τῷ λύσαντι χρήματα ἀποτίνειν. ὁμολογήσαντα δὲ τὸν Εἴρωμον καὶ μὴ δυνηθέντα λῦσαι τὰ αἰνίγματα πολλὰ τῶν χρημάτων εἰς τὸ ἐπιζήμιον ἀναλῶσαι· εἶτα δι'[7] Ἀβδήμονά τινα Τύριον ἄνδρα τὰ προτεθέντα λῦσαι καὶ αὐτὸν ἄλλα προβαλεῖν, ἃ μὴ

[1] Gutschmid: Ἡυκαίοις RO: Ἰυκέοις SP: Ἡϋκέοις M Lat.: Τιτυαίοις Eusebius ap. Syncellum.
[2] + λύων Eusebius.
[3] Niese: Δίος vel Διὸς codd.: Δίων Syncellus Lat.
[4] ὂν ex contra Apion. add. Niese.
[5] O codd. contra Apion.: φησὶ rell.
[6] + λύσιν RO Lat.
[7] δὲ RO: δὴ LV codd. contra Apion.

and Astarte; and he was the first to celebrate the awakening[a] of Heracles in the month of Peritius. And he undertook a campaign against the Itykaians (Uticans), who had not paid their tribute, and, when he had again made them subject to him, returned home. In his reign lived Abdēmonos, a young lad who always successfully solved the problems which were submitted to him by Solomon, the king of Jerusalem." They are also mentioned by Diŏs[b] in these words: "On the death of Abibalos, his son Eirōmos became king. He it was who added embankments to the eastern parts of the city and made the town larger; and the temple of Zeus Olympios, which stood apart by itself, he joined to the city by filling up the space between them, and adorned it with dedicatory offerings of gold. He also went up to Libanos and cut timber for the building of temples. And they say that Solomon, who was tyrant of Jerusalem, sent riddles to Eirōmos and asked to receive others from him as well, proposing that he who was unable to interpret them should pay a fine to the one who did solve them. But Eirōmos, having agreed to this, was unable to solve the riddles and paid out large sums of money as a fine. Afterwards through a certain Abdēmon, a Tyrian citizen, he solved[c] the riddles proposed and himself offered

[a] I follow Weill in taking ἔγερσιν in this sense rather than in that of "erection" (of a temple) as Hudson, Whiston and Thackeray (in *Ap.* i. 119) do. Menander is probably referring to the celebration of a festival in honour of Melkart-Heracles as a fertility-god, *cf.* S. A. Cook, *The Religion of Ancient Palestine*, etc. (Schweich Lectures), 1930, pp. 135 ff.

[b] *Cf. Ap.* i. 113 ff. where the following extract is given in identical words.

[c] Variant "Abdemon . . . solved."

λύσαντα τὸν Σολομῶνα πολλὰ τῷ Εἰρώμῳ προσ-
αποτῖσαι χρήματα." καὶ Δῖος μὲν οὕτως εἴρηκεν.
150 (vi. 1) Ἐπεὶ δ' ἑώρα τὰ τῶν Ἱεροσολύμων
τείχη ὁ βασιλεὺς πύργων πρὸς ἀσφάλειαν δεόμενα
καὶ τῆς ἄλλης ὀχυρότητος (πρὸς γὰρ τἀξίωμα τῆς
πόλεως ἡγεῖτο δεῖν καὶ τοὺς περιβόλους εἶναι)
ταῦτά τε προσεπεσκεύασε καὶ πύργοις αὐτὰ
151 μεγάλοις προσεξῆρεν. ᾠκοδόμησε δὲ καὶ πόλεις
ταῖς βαρυτάταις ἐναρίθμους Ἄσωρόν τε καὶ Μα-
γέδω,[1] τρίτην[2] δὲ Γάζαρα, τὴν[3] τῆς Παλαιστίνων
χώρας ὑπάρχουσαν ἣν Φαραὼ[4] ὁ τῶν Αἰγυπτίων
βασιλεὺς στρατευσάμενος καὶ πολιορκήσας αἱρεῖ
κατὰ κράτος· ἀποκτείνας δὲ πάντας τοὺς ἐνοικοῦντας αὐτὴν κατέσκαψεν, εἶτα δωρεὰν ἔδωκε τῇ
152 αὐτοῦ θυγατρὶ Σολομῶνι γεγαμημένῃ. διὸ καὶ
ἀνήγειρεν αὐτὴν ὁ βασιλεὺς οὖσαν ὀχυρὰν φύσει
καὶ πρὸς πολέμους καὶ τὰς τῶν καιρῶν μεταβολὰς
χρησίμην εἶναι δυναμένην. οὐ πόρρω δ' αὐτῆς
ἄλλας ᾠκοδόμησε δύο πόλεις· Βητχώρα τῇ ἑτέρᾳ
153 ὄνομα ἦν, ἡ δ' ἑτέρα Βαλὲθ[5] ἐκαλεῖτο. προσκατεσκεύασε δὲ ταύταις καὶ ἄλλας εἰς ἀπόλαυσιν
καὶ τρυφὴν ἐπιτηδείως ἐχούσας, τῇ τε τῶν ἀέρων
εὐκρασίᾳ καὶ τοῖς ὡραίοις εὐφυεῖς καὶ νάμασιν
ὑδάτων ἐνδρόσους. ἐμβαλὼν δὲ καὶ εἰς τὴν ἔρημον
τῆς[6] ἐπάνω Συρίας καὶ κατασχὼν αὐτὴν ἔκτισεν

[1] Μαγεδών MSP Lat. [2] Niese: τὴν τρίτην codd.
[3] ἣν RO. [4] ἣν Φαραὼν M: Φαραώνης RO: Φαραώθης Niese.
[5] Βελὲθ RO. [6] τὴν MSP.

[a] Or (as Thackeray renders in *Ap.* i. 115) "paid back to Hirom more than he had received."

[b] Bibl. Hazor, LXX Ἀσσούρ; *cf. A.* v. 199 note.

[c] Bibl. Megiddo, LXX Μαγεδδώ, the modern *Tell el-Mutesellim* on the southern edge of the Great Plain of Esdraelon,

others, which Solomon was unable to solve and paid large sums to Eirōmos in return.[a] " Such are the words of Dios.

(vi. 1) Now when the king saw that the walls of Jerusalem needed towers and other defences for security—for he thought that even the surrounding walls should be in keeping with the dignity of the city—he repaired them and raised them higher with great towers. He also built cities which are counted among the most powerful, Asōr [b] and Magedō,[c] and a third, Gazara,[d] which had belonged to the country of the Philistines and against which Pharaō had marched, and after a siege had taken it by storm and after killing all its inhabitants had razed it to the ground and then had given it as a gift to his daughter, who had been married to Solomon. The king, therefore, rebuilt it also, for it was naturally strong and could be useful in war or in times of sudden change.[e] And not far from it he built two other cities, the name of one being Bētchōra,[f] while the other was called Baleth.[g] In addition to these he built still others, which were conveniently placed for enjoyment and pleasure and were naturally favoured with a mild temperature and seasonable fruits and irrigated with streams of water. He also advanced into the desert of Upper Syria [h] and, having taken possession of it,

Solomon's fortifications. 1 Kings ix. 15; 2 Chron. viii. 1.

where excavations have yielded important finds dating from Solomon's times, as well as from other periods.

[d] Bibl. Gezer, *cf. A.* v. 83 note.

[e] Or perhaps " revolution."

[f] Bibl. Beth-horon, LXX Βαιθωρών. Scripture calls it " Beth-horon the nether," which is the modern *Beit 'Ur et-taḥtā* about 10 miles N.W. of Jerusalem.

[g] Bibl. Baalath, LXX Βααλάθ (*v.l.* Βαλαάθ κτλ.), possibly the modern *Belain* about 2 miles N. of *Beit 'Ur et-taḥtā*.

[h] Variant " the desert above Syria."

ἐκεῖ πόλιν μεγίστην δύο μὲν ἡμερῶν ὁδὸν ἀπὸ τῆς ἄνω Συρίας διεστῶσαν, ἀπὸ δ' Εὐφράτου μιᾶς, ἀπὸ δὲ τῆς μεγάλης Βαβυλῶνος ἓξ ἡμερῶν ἦν τὸ
154 μῆκος. αἴτιον δὲ τοῦ τὴν πόλιν οὕτως ἀπὸ τῶν οἰκουμένων μερῶν τῆς Συρίας ἀπῳκίσθαι τὸ κατωτέρω μὲν οὐδαμοῦ τῆς γῆς ὕδωρ εἶναι, πηγὰς δ' ἐν ἐκείνῳ τῷ τόπῳ μόνον εὑρεθῆναι καὶ φρέατα. ταύτην οὖν τὴν πόλιν οἰκοδομήσας καὶ τείχεσιν ὀχυρωτάτοις περιβαλὼν Θαδάμοραν[1] ὠνόμασε καὶ τοῦτ' ἔτι νῦν καλεῖται παρὰ τοῖς Σύροις, οἱ δ' Ἕλληνες αὐτὴν προσαγορεύουσι Πάλμυραν.[2][a]

155 (2) Σολομὼν μὲν οὖν ὁ βασιλεὺς ταῦτα κατ' ἐκεῖνον τὸν καιρὸν πράττων διετέλει. πρὸς δὲ τοὺς ἐπιζητήσαντας ὅτι πάντες οἱ Αἰγυπτίων βασιλεῖς ἀπὸ Μιναίου τοῦ Μέμφιν οἰκοδομήσαντος, ὃς ἔτεσι πολλοῖς ἔμπροσθεν ἐγένετο τοῦ πάππου ἡμῶν Ἁβράμου, μέχρι Σολομῶνος πλειόνων ἐτῶν ἢ τριακοσίων καὶ χιλίων μεταξὺ διεληλυθότων Φαραῶθαι ἐκλήθησαν, ἀπὸ τοῦ μετὰ τοὺς[3] ἐν τῷ μεταξὺ χρόνους[4] ἄρξαντος βασιλέως Φαραώθου τὴν προσηγορίαν λαβόντες, ἀναγκαῖον ἡγησάμην εἰπεῖν, ἵνα τὴν ἄγνοιαν αὐτῶν ἀφέλω καὶ ποιήσω τοῦ ὀνόματος φανερὰν τὴν αἰτίαν, ὅτι[5] Φαραὼ κατ'
156 Αἰγυπτίους βασιλέα σημαίνει. οἶμαι δ' αὐτοὺς

[1] Θαδάμορα SP[1]LV: Thadamor Lat.
[2] ex Lat. ed. pr. Niese: Παράμαλλαν ROSPLV: Παραμάλχαν M.
[3] μετὰ τοὺς MSPV: μετ' αὐτοὺς RO: μετὰ τοῖς L: κατ' αὐτοὺς Gutschmid.
[4] τῷ μεταξὺ χρόνους SP: τοῖς μεταξὺ χρόνοις rell.
[5] Gutschmid: ὁ codd.

[a] Bibl. Tadmor, LXX (2 Chron.) Θεδμόρ (*v.l.* Θοδμόρ), is about 100 miles E. of Homs on the Orontes and about 160

founded there a very great city at a distance of two days' journey from Upper Syria and one day's journey from the Euphrates, while from the great Babylon the distance was a journey of six days.[a] Now the reason for founding the city so far from the inhabited parts of Syria was that further down there was no water anywhere in the land and that only in this place were springs and wells to be found. And so, when he had built this city and surrounded it with very strong walls, he named it Thadamora,[a] as it is still called by the Syrians, while the Greeks call it Palmyra.

(2) Such, then, were the activities which King Solomon at that time was carrying on. Now to those who ask why all the Egyptian kings from Minaias, the builder of Memphis, who lived many years before our forefather Abraham, down to Solomon—an interval of more than one thousand three hundred years[b]—were called Pharaōthai, taking this name from Pharaōthēs, the first king to reign after the period intervening,[c] I have thought it necessary to explain—in order to dispel their ignorance and make clear the reason for the name—that *Pharaō* in Egyptian signifies "king."[d] But I believe that

The name "Pharaoh."

miles W. of Werdi on the Euphrates; from here it is a distance of more than 200 miles down the river to Babylon.

[b] On the interval of time between Abraham and Solomon *cf.* § 61 note.

[c] Apparently the period before Minaias (Menes), reputed founder of the United Kingdom, is meant, but the text is uncertain. Weill thinks the last phrase is an interpolation.

[d] According to F. Ll. Griffith in Hastings' *Dictionary of the Bible*, iii. 819, the Egyptian word *pr'o*, meaning "great house," was originally applied to the royal estate rather than to the person of the king and only came into common use as a title at the time of the New Kingdom (*c.* 1600 B.C.).

ἐκ παίδων ἄλλοις χρωμένους ὀνόμασιν, ἐπειδὰν βασιλεῖς γένωνται τὸ σημαῖνον αὐτῶν τὴν ἐξουσίαν κατὰ τὴν πάτριον γλῶτταν μετονομάζεσθαι· καὶ γὰρ οἱ τῆς Ἀλεξανδρείας βασιλεῖς ἄλλοις ὀνόμασι καλούμενοι πρότερον, ὅτε τὴν βασιλείαν ἔλαβον, Πτολεμαῖοι προσηγορεύθησαν ἀπὸ τοῦ πρώτου
157 βασιλέως. καὶ οἱ Ῥωμαίων δὲ αὐτοκράτορες ἐκ γενετῆς ἀπ' ἄλλων χρηματίσαντες ὀνομάτων Καίσαρες καλοῦνται, τῆς ἡγεμονίας καὶ τῆς τιμῆς τὴν προσηγορίαν αὐτοῖς θεμένης, ἀλλ' οὐχ οἷς ὑπὸ τῶν πατέρων ἐκλήθησαν τούτοις ἐπιμένοντες. νομίζω δὲ καὶ Ἡρόδοτον τὸν Ἁλικαρνασέα διὰ τοῦτο μετὰ Μιναίαν τὸν οἰκοδομήσαντα Μέμφιν τριάκοντα καὶ τριακοσίους βασιλεῖς Αἰγυπτίων γενέσθαι λέγοντα μὴ δηλῶσαι αὐτῶν τὰ ὀνόματα, ὅτι
158 κοινῶς Φαραῶθαι ἐκαλοῦντο· καὶ γὰρ μετὰ τὴν τούτων τελευτὴν γυναικὸς βασιλευσάσης λέγει τοὔνομα Νικαύλην καλῶν, δηλῶν ὡς τῶν μὲν ἀρρένων βασιλέων τὴν αὐτὴν προσηγορίαν ἔχειν δυναμένων, τῆς δὲ γυναικὸς οὐκέτι κοινωνεῖν ἐκείνης, καὶ διὰ τοῦτ' εἶπεν αὐτῆς τὸ φύσει δεῆσαν
159 ὄνομα. ἐγὼ δὲ καὶ ἐν τοῖς ἐπιχωρίοις ἡμῶν βιβλίοις εὗρον ὅτι μετὰ Φαραώθην τὸν Σολομῶνος πενθερὸν οὐκέτ' οὐδεὶς τοῦτο τοὔνομα βασιλεὺς Αἰγυπτίων ἐκλήθη, καὶ ὅτι ὕστερον ἧκε πρὸς Σολομῶνα ἡ προειρημένη γυνὴ βασιλεύουσα τῆς Αἰγύπτου καὶ τῆς Αἰθιοπίας. περὶ μὲν οὖν ταύτης μετ' οὐ πολὺ δηλώσομεν·· νῦν δὲ τούτων ἐπεμνήσθην, ἵνα παραστήσω τὰ ἡμέτερα βιβλία καὶ τὰ παρ' Αἰγυπτίοις περὶ πολλῶν ὁμολογοῦντα.[1]

[1] ὁμοφωνοῦντα SPLV.

from childhood they had other names, and that when they became kings they changed them for that name which in their ancestral tongue signifies their royal authority. For so also the kings of Alexandria were first called by other names, but, when they assumed the kingship, were named Ptolemies after the first king. And the Roman emperors also, who from their birth are known by other names, are called Caesars, receiving this title from their princely office and rank, and do not keep the names by which their fathers called them. And I think it was for this reason that Herodotus of Halicarnassus, when he says [a] that there were three hundred and thirty kings of Egypt after Minaias, who built Memphis, did not mention their names, because they were all in common called Pharaōthai. For, after the death of these kings, a woman ruled as queen, and he gives her name as Nikaulē,[b] making it clear that while the male kings could all have the same name, the woman could not share this, and for that reason he mentioned her by the name that naturally belonged to her. And I myself have discovered in the books of our own country that after the Pharaōthēs who was Solomon's father-in-law no king of Egypt was ever again called by this name,[c] and that later the afore-mentioned woman as queen of Egypt and Ethiopia came to Solomon. Now about her we shall write very shortly.[d] But I have mentioned these matters at this point in order to make plain that our books in many things agree with those of the Egyptians.

[a] Apparently a reference to the sketch of Egyptian history in Herod. ii. 99 ff.

[b] The name is given as Nitocris in our texts of Herodotus.

[c] Josephus overlooks the Scriptural reference to Pharaoh Necho, 2 Kings xxiii. 29 and elsewhere.

[d] In § 165.

160 (3) Ὁ δὲ βασιλεὺς Σολομὼν τοὺς ἔτι τῶν Χαναναίων οὐχ ὑπακούοντας, οἳ ἐν τῷ Λιβάνῳ διέτριβον ὄρει καὶ μέχρι πόλεως Ἀμάθης,[1] ὑποχειρίους ποιησάμενος φόρον αὐτοῖς προσέταξε, καὶ πρὸς τὸ θητεύειν αὐτῷ καὶ τὰς οἰκετικὰς χρείας ἐκτελεῖν καὶ πρὸς γεωργίαν κατ' ἔτος ἐξ αὐτῶν
161 ἐπελέγετο. τῶν γὰρ Ἑβραίων οὐδεὶς ἐδούλευεν (οὐδ' ἦν εὔλογον ἔθνη πολλὰ τοῦ θεοῦ δεδωκότος αὐτοῖς ὑποχείρια, δέον ἐκ τούτων ποιεῖσθαι τὸ θητικόν, αὐτοὺς κατάγειν εἰς τοῦτο τὸ σχῆμα), ἀλλὰ πάντες ἐν ὅπλοις ἐφ' ἁρμάτων καὶ ἵππων
162 στρατευόμενοι μᾶλλον ἢ δουλεύοντες διῆγον. τῶν δὲ Χαναναίων, οὓς εἰς τὴν οἰκετείαν ἀπήγαγεν, ἄρχοντας ἀπέδειξε πεντακοσίους καὶ πεντήκοντα τὸν ἀριθμόν, οἳ τὴν ὅλην αὐτῶν ἐπιτροπὴν εἰλήφεσαν παρὰ τοῦ βασιλέως, ὥστε διδάσκειν αὐτοὺς τὰ ἔργα καὶ τὰς πραγματείας, ἐφ' ἃς[2] αὐτῶν ἔχρῃζεν.

163 (4) Ἐναυπηγήσατο δὲ ὁ βασιλεὺς ἐν τῷ Αἰγυπτιακῷ κόλπῳ σκάφη πολλὰ τῆς Ἐρυθρᾶς θαλάσσης ἔν τινι τόπῳ λεγομένῳ Γασιωνγάβελ οὐ πόρρω Αἰλανῆς[3] πόλεως, ἣ νῦν Βερενίκη καλεῖται· αὕτη γὰρ ἡ χώρα τὸ πρὶν Ἰουδαίων ἦν. ἔτυχε δὲ καὶ τῆς ἁρμοζούσης εἰς τὰς ναῦς δωρεᾶς παρ' Εἰρώμου
164 τοῦ Τυρίων βασιλέως· ἄνδρας γὰρ αὐτῷ κυβερνήτας καὶ τῶν θαλασσίων ἐπιστήμονας ἔπεμψεν ἱκανούς, οἷς ἐκέλευσε πλεύσαντας μετὰ καὶ τῶν ἰδίων

[1] EV: Ἀμαθῆς L: Ἀμμάθης (-ῆς SP) rell.: Amathi Lat.
[2] Niese: ἃς ἂν codd.
[3] Hudson: Ἰλάνεως RO: Ἰλανῆς MS(P)V: Ἐλάνης E: Hilana Lat.

(3) King Solomon also reduced to subjection those of the Canaanites who were still unsubmissive, that is, those who lived on Mt. Libanos and as far as Amathē,[a] and imposed a tribute upon them and raised a yearly levy from them to be his serfs and perform menial tasks and till the soil. But of the Hebrews no one was a slave—nor was it reasonable, when God had made so many nations subject to them, from among whom they ought to raise their force of serfs, that they themselves should be reduced to that condition—but they all bore arms and served in the field on chariots and horses rather than lead the lives of slaves. And over the Canaanites, whom he had reduced to domestic slavery, he appointed five hundred and fifty[b] officers, who received full charge of them from the king, so as to instruct them in those tasks and activities for which he needed them.

Solomon's military exploits. 1 Kings ix. 20; 2 Chron. viii. 7.

(4) The king also built many ships in the Egyptian gulf[c] of the Red Sea at a certain place called Gasiōngabel[d] not far from the city of Ailanē,[e] which is now called Berenikē. For this territory formerly belonged to the Jews. Moreover he obtained a present suitable to the needs of his ships from Eirōmos, the king of Tyre, who sent him pilots and a goodly number of men skilled in seamanship, and these Solomon ordered to sail along with his own stewards to the

Solomon's fleet. 1 Kings ix. 26; 2 Chron. viii. 17.

[a] Bibl. Hamath, *cf. A.* i. 138 note. Scripture enumerates "all the people who were left of the Amorites, Hittites, Perizzites, Hivites and Jebusites."

[b] So 1 Kings; 2 Chron. 250.

[c] The modern Gulf of Akabah.

[d] Bibl. Ezion-geber (*'Eṣyôn geber*), LXX cod. B Ἐμαεσειὼν Γάβερ, cod. A Γασιὼν Γάβερ.

[e] Bibl. Eloth, LXX 1 Kings Αἰλάθ, 2 Chron. Αἰλάμ.

οἰκονόμων εἰς τὴν πάλαι μὲν Σώφειραν νῦν δὲ χρυσῆν γῆν καλουμένην (τῆς Ἰνδικῆς ἐστιν αὕτη) χρυσὸν αὐτῷ κομίσαι. καὶ συναθροίσαντες ὡς τετρακόσια τάλαντα πάλιν ἀνεχώρησαν πρὸς τὸν βασιλέα.

165 (5) Τὴν δὲ τῆς Αἰγύπτου καὶ τῆς Αἰθιοπίας τότε βασιλεύουσαν γυναῖκα σοφίᾳ διαπεπονημένην καὶ τἆλλα θαυμαστὴν ἀκούουσαν τὴν Σολομῶνος ἀρετὴν καὶ φρόνησιν ἐπιθυμία τῆς ὄψεως αὐτοῦ ἐκ[1] τῶν ὁσημέραι περὶ τῶν ἐκεῖ λεγομένων πρὸς
166 αὐτὸν ἤγαγε· πεισθῆναι γὰρ ὑπὸ τῆς πείρας ἀλλ' οὐχ ὑπὸ τῆς ἀκοῆς (ἣν εἰκός ἐστι καὶ ψευδεῖ δόξῃ συγκατατίθεσθαι καὶ μεταπεῖσαι πάλιν, ὅλη γὰρ ἐπὶ τοῖς ἀπαγγέλλουσι κεῖται) θέλουσα πρὸς αὐτὸν ἐλθεῖν διέγνω, καὶ μάλιστα[2] τῆς σοφίας αὐτοῦ βουλομένη λαβεῖν πεῖραν αὐτή,[3] προτείνασα καὶ λῦσαι τὸ ἄπορον τῆς διανοίας δεηθεῖσα, ἧκεν[4] εἰς Ἱεροσόλυμα μετὰ πολλῆς δόξης καὶ πλούτου παρα-
167 σκευῆς· ἐπηγάγετο γὰρ καμήλους χρυσίου μεστὰς καὶ ἀρωμάτων ποικίλων καὶ λίθων πολυτελῶν. ὡς δ' ἀφικομένην αὐτὴν ἡδέως ὁ βασιλεὺς προσ-

[1] Niese: καὶ codd. Lat.
[2] καὶ μάλιστα Niese: μάλιστα καὶ ROM: μάλιστα SP.
[3] Exc. Bekker: αὕτη ROSP: αὐτὴν M.
[4] ἧκεν οὖν M Lat.: ἧκε δ' Exc. Bekker.

[a] So Luc. and LXX 2 Chron.; bibl. Ophir, LXX 1 Kings Σωφηρά.
[b] *Cf.* Isa. xiii. 12, Ps. xlv. 9, Job xxii. 24 *et al.*
[c] The actual location of Ophir is a matter of speculation. Some modern scholars agree with Josephus in locating it in or near India.
[d] 1 Kings Heb. and Luc. 420, LXX 120; 2 Chron. Heb. and LXX 450.
[e] Scripture calls her "Queen of Sheba." Sheba was a

land anciently called Sōpheir,[a] but now the Land of Gold[b]; it belongs to India.[c] And when they had amassed a sum of four hundred[d] talents they returned again to the king.

The Queen of Sheba visits Solomon. 1 Kings x. 1; 2 Chron. ix. 1.

(5) Now the woman who at that time ruled as queen of Egypt and Ethiopia[e] was thoroughly trained in wisdom and remarkable in other ways, and, when she heard of Solomon's virtue and understanding, was led to him by a strong desire to see him which arose from the things told daily about his country. For, wishing to be convinced by experience and not merely by hearsay—which is likely to give assent to a false belief and then convince one of the opposite, since it depends wholly on those who bring reports—she decided to go to him; and being very desirous of herself making trial of his wisdom by propounding questions and asking him to solve their difficult meaning, she came to Jerusalem with great splendour and show of wealth. For she brought with her camels laden with gold and various spices and precious stones. And the king received her gladly on her

kingdom in S.W. Arabia, *cf.* Gen. x. 28, Job vi. 19 and Mt. xii. 42 ("the Queen of the South"). Rabbinic tradition describes Sheba as a land of sorcerers somewhere in the East, and Ginzberg vi. 292 thinks it "possible that the substitution of Egypt for Sheba by Josephus . . . is to be ascribed to the fact that in the Haggadah Egypt is the land of magic and witchcraft *par excellence.*" But Josephus probably knew of some native Egyptian or Ethiopic tradition which connected the queen of the Arabian kingdom with Egypt and Ethiopia (*cf.* Isa. xliii. 3). This tradition which he got from Herodotus or some other Greek source (*cf.* §§ 158 f.) is found in Ethiopic literature and states that Menelik, the first king of Abyssinia, was a son of Solomon and Makkeda, whom they identify with the Queen of Sheba. For a discussion of this subject see J. B. Coulbeaux, *Histoire de l'Abyssinie*, i. 108 ff.

εδέξατο, τά τε ἄλλα περὶ αὐτὴν φιλότιμος ἦν καὶ τὰ προβαλλόμενα σοφίσματα ῥᾳδίως τῇ συνέσει καταλαμβανόμενος θᾶττον ἢ προσεδόκα τις ἐπ-
168 ελύετο. ἡ δ' ἐξεπλήσσετο μὲν καὶ τὴν σοφίαν τοῦ Σολομῶνος, οὕτως ὑπερβάλλουσαν αὐτὴν καὶ τῆς ἀκουομένης τῇ πείρᾳ κρείττω καταμαθοῦσα, μάλιστα δ' ἐθαύμαζε τὰ βασίλεια τοῦ τε κάλλους καὶ τοῦ μεγέθους οὐχ ἧττον δὲ τῆς διατάξεως τῶν οἰκοδομημάτων· καὶ γὰρ ἐν ταύτῃ πολλὴν τοῦ
169 βασιλέως καθεώρα φρόνησιν. ὑπερεξέπληττε δ' αὐτὴν ὅ τε οἶκος ὁ δρυμὼν ἐπικαλούμενος Λιβάνου καὶ ἡ τῶν καθ' ἡμέραν δείπνων πολυτέλεια καὶ τὰ τῆς παρασκευῆς αὐτοῦ καὶ διακονίας ἥ τε τῶν ὑπηρετούντων ἐσθὴς καὶ τὸ μετ' ἐπιστήμης αὐτῶν περὶ τὴν διακονίαν εὐπρεπές, οὐχ ἥκιστα δὲ καὶ αἱ καθ' ἡμέραν ἐπιτελούμεναι τῷ θεῷ θυσίαι καὶ τὸ τῶν ἱερέων καὶ Ληουιτῶν περὶ αὐτὰς ἐπιμελές.
170 ταῦθ' ὁρῶσα καθ' ἡμέραν ὑπερεθαύμαζε, καὶ κατασχεῖν οὐ δυνηθεῖσα τὴν ἔκπληξιν τῶν βλεπομένων, φανερὰν ἐποίησεν αὑτὴν θαυμαστικῶς διακειμένην· πρὸς γὰρ τὸν βασιλέα προήχθη λόγους εἰπεῖν, ὑφ' ὧν ἠλέγχθη σφόδρα τὴν διάνοιαν ἐπὶ τοῖς προ-
171 ειρημένοις ἡττημένη· "πάντα μὲν γάρ," εἶπεν, "ὦ βασιλεῦ, τὰ δι' ἀκοῆς εἰς γνῶσιν ἐρχόμενα μετ' ἀπιστίας παραγίνεται, τῶν δὲ σῶν ἀγαθῶν, ὧν αὐτός τε ἔχεις ἐν σαυτῷ, λέγω δὲ τὴν σοφίαν καὶ τὴν φρόνησιν, καὶ ὧν ἡ βασιλεία σοι δίδωσιν, οὐ ψευδὴς ἄρα ἡ φήμη πρὸς ἡμᾶς διῆλθεν, ἀλλ' οὖσα ἀληθὴς πολὺ καταδεεστέραν τὴν εὐδαιμονίαν ἀπ-
172 έφηνεν ἧς ὁρῶ νῦν παροῦσα· τὰς μὲν γὰρ ἀκοὰς πείθειν ἐπεχείρει μόνον, τὸ δὲ ἀξίωμα τῶν πραγμάτων οὐχ οὕτως ἐποίει γνώριμον, ὡς ἡ ὄψις αὐτὸ

arrival and was studious to please her in all ways, in particular by mentally grasping with ease the ingenious problems she set him and solving them more quickly than anyone could have expected. But she was amazed at Solomon's wisdom when she realized how extraordinary it was and how much more excellent upon trial than what she had heard about it. She especially admired the palace for its beauty and size and, no less, for the arrangement of the buildings, for in this she saw the great wisdom of the king. But she was more than amazed at the hall called the Forest of Libanos and the lavishness of the daily meals and his table-ware and service and the apparel of his attendants, as well as the decorum, combined with skill, of their serving; and not least the sacrifices daily offered to God and the care bestowed on them by the priests and Levites. Seeing these things day by day she admired them beyond measure, and was not able to contain her amazement at what she saw, but showed clearly how much admiration she felt, for she was moved to address the king in words which revealed how greatly overcome were her feelings by the things we have described. "All things indeed, O King," she said, "that come to our knowledge through hearsay are received with mistrust, but concerning the good things that are yours, both those which you possess in your own person, I mean your wisdom and prudence, and those which the kingship gives you, it was by no means a false report that reached us; on the contrary, though it was true, it indicated a prosperity far below that which I see, now being here. For the report attempted only to persuade our ears but did not make known the dignity of your state as fully as seeing it and being in

The Queen of Sheba praises Solomon. 1 Kings x. 6; 2 Chron. ix. 7.

καὶ τὸ παρ' αὐτοῖς εἶναι συνίστησιν. ἐγὼ γοῦν[1] οὐδὲ τοῖς ἀπαγγελλομένοις διὰ πλῆθος καὶ μέγεθος ὧν ἐπυνθανόμην πιστεύουσα, πολλῷ πλείω τούτων
173 ἱστόρηκα. καὶ μακάριόν τε τὸν Ἑβραίων λαὸν εἶναι κρίνω δούλους τε τοὺς σοὺς καὶ φίλους, οἳ καθ' ἡμέραν τῆς σῆς ἀπολαύουσιν ὄψεως καὶ τῆς σῆς σοφίας ἀκροώμενοι διατελοῦσιν. εὐλογήσειεν ἄν τις τὸν θεὸν ἀγαπήσαντα τήνδε τὴν χώραν καὶ τοὺς ἐν αὐτῇ κατοικοῦντας οὕτως, ὥστε σὲ ποιῆσαι βασιλέα."

174 (6) Παραστήσασα δὲ καὶ διὰ τῶν λόγων πῶς αὐτὴν διέθηκεν ὁ βασιλεύς, ἔτι καὶ ταῖς δωρεαῖς τὴν διάνοιαν αὐτῆς ἐποίησε φανεράν· εἴκοσι μὲν γὰρ αὐτῷ τάλαντα ἔδωκε χρυσίου ἀρωμάτων τε πλῆθος ἀσυλλόγιστον καὶ λίθων πολυτελῶν[2]· λέγουσι δ' ὅτι καὶ τὴν τοῦ ὀποβαλσάμου ῥίζαν, ἣν ἔτι[3] νῦν ἡμῶν ἡ χώρα φέρει, δούσης ταύτης τῆς
175 γυναικὸς ἔχομεν. ἀντεδωρήσατο δ' αὐτὴν πολλοῖς καὶ Σολομὼν ἀγαθοῖς καὶ μάλισθ' ὧν κατ' ἐπιθυμίαν ἐξελέξατο· οὐδὲν γὰρ ἦν ὅ τι δεηθείσῃ λαβεῖν οὐ παρέσχεν, ἀλλ' ἑτοιμότερον ὧν αὐτὸς κατὰ τὴν οἰκείαν ἐχαρίζετο προαίρεσιν ἅπερ ἐκείνη τυχεῖν ἠξίου προϊέμενος, τὴν μεγαλοφροσύνην ἐπεδείκνυτο. καὶ ἡ μὲν τῶν Αἰγυπτίων καὶ τῆς Αἰθιοπίας βασίλισσα ὧν προειρήκαμεν τυχοῦσα καὶ μεταδοῦσα πάλιν τῷ βασιλεῖ τῶν παρ' αὐτῆς, εἰς τὴν οἰκείαν ὑπέστρεψε.

176 (vii. 1) Κατὰ δὲ τὸν αὐτὸν καιρὸν κομισθέντων

[1] ἐγὼ γοῦν O: ἔγωγ' οὖν rell.
[2] λίθων πολυτελῶν Niese: λίθον πολυτελῆ codd.: λίθους πολυτελεῖς ex Lat. Hudson.
[3] + καὶ SP.

its presence showed it to be. I, for my part, did not believe the things reported because of the multitude and greatness of what I heard about them, and yet I have witnessed here things far greater than these. Fortunate do I hold the Hebrew people to be, and your servants and friends as well, who daily enjoy the sight of you and continually listen to your wisdom. Let us bless God who has so well loved this country and its inhabitants as to make you their king."

(6) And, after she had shown by her words how she felt toward the king, she revealed her feelings still more clearly by her gifts, for she gave him twenty [a] talents of gold and an incalculable quantity of spices and precious stones; and they say that we have the root of the opobalsamon, which our country still bears,[b] as a result of this woman's gift. In return Solomon also presented her with many fine gifts, in particular with those which she selected as most desirable, for there was nothing which he did not give when she asked to have it; on the contrary, he showed his magnanimity by giving up whatever she asked for more readily than he presented gifts to her of his own choice. And so the queen of Egypt and Ethiopia, having obtained the gifts we have mentioned and given others to the king from among her possessions, returned to her own country.

Solomon and the Queen of Sheba exchange gifts. 1 Kings x. 10; 2 Chron. ix. 9.

(vii. 1) [c] About that same time there were brought

[a] Bibl. 120.

[b] *Cf. B.J.* iv. 469 on the balsam of Jericho, and *A.* ix. 7 on the balsam of Engedi on the Dead Sea.

[c] Scripture introduces the following passage before completing the account of the queen's visit with her departure. Josephus changes the order by completing her story before turning to the subject of Solomon's imports.

ἀπὸ τῆς χρυσῆς καλουμένης γῆς λίθου πολυτελοῦς[1] τῷ βασιλεῖ καὶ ξύλων πευκίνων, τοῖς ξύλοις εἰς ὑποστήριγμα τοῦ τε ναοῦ καὶ τῶν βασιλείων κατεχρήσατο καὶ πρὸς τὴν τῶν μουσικῶν ὀργάνων κατασκευὴν κινύρας τε καὶ νάβλας, ὅπως ὑμνῶσιν οἱ Ληουῖται τὸν θεόν· πάντων δὲ τῶν πώποτε κομισθέντων αὐτῷ τὰ κατ' ἐκείνην τὴν ἡμέραν
177 ἐνεχθέντα καὶ μεγέθει καὶ κάλλει διέφερεν. ὑπολάβῃ δὲ μηδεὶς ὅτι τὰ τῆς πεύκης ξύλα τοῖς νῦν εἶναι λεγομένοις καὶ ταύτην ὑπὸ τῶν πιπρασκόντων τὴν προσηγορίαν ἐπὶ καταπλήξει τῶν ὠνουμένων λαμβάνουσίν ἐστι παραπλήσια. ἐκεῖνα γὰρ τὴν μὲν ἰδέαν ἐμφερῆ τοῖς συκίνοις γίνεται, λευκότερα
178 δέ ἐστι καὶ στίλβει πλέον. τοῦτο μὲν οὖν[2] πρὸς τὸ μηδένα τὴν διαφορὰν ἀγνοῆσαι μηδὲ τὴν φύσιν τῆς ἀληθοῦς πεύκης, ἐπεὶ διὰ τὴν τοῦ βασιλέως χρείαν ἐμνήσθημεν αὐτῆς, εὔκαιρον εἶναι καὶ φιλάνθρωπον δηλῶσαι νομίσαντες εἰρήκαμεν.

179 (2) Ὁ δὲ τοῦ χρυσοῦ σταθμὸς τοῦ κομισθέντος αὐτῷ τάλαντα ἑξακόσια καὶ ἑξήκοντα καὶ ἕξ, μὴ συγκαταριθμουμένου καὶ τοῦ ὑπὸ τῶν ἐμπόρων ὠνηθέντος μηδ' ὧν οἱ τῆς Ἀραβίας τοπάρχαι καὶ βασιλεῖς ἔπεμπον αὐτῷ δωρεῶν.[3] ἐχώνευσε

[1] λίθων πολυτελῶν SP Lat.
[2] οὖν om. ROM.
[3] δῶρον RO: δώρων Niese.

[a] Bibl. Ophir, *cf.* § 114.

[b] So LXX in 2 Chron., 1 Kings Heb. *'almuggim* (A.V. "almug"), LXX πελεκητά "hewn," 2 Chron. Heb.

to the king from the country called the Land of Gold[a] precious stones and pine[b] wood, which wood he used as supports[c] for the temple and the palace and for the construction of musical instruments, *kinyrai* and *nablai*,[d] with which the Levites might sing hymns to God. And the wood that was delivered on that day far surpassed in size and beauty any that had ever been brought to him before. But let no one suppose that the pine wood was like that which is now called pine and which receives this name from men who sell it as such in order to dazzle purchasers, for that we speak of was similar in appearance to the wood of fig-trees, but was whiter and more gleaming.[e] This much, then, we have said in order that no one may remain ignorant of the nature of genuine pine and its difference from other kinds ; and, as we have spoken of the use which the king made of it, it seemed in place and an act of kindness to explain more fully.

The products of Ophir. 1 Kings x. 11; 2 Chron. ix. 10.

(2) The weight of the gold that was brought to him was six hundred and sixty-six talents, not including what was brought by the merchants or the gifts which the governors and the kings of Arabia[f] sent to him.[g] And this gold he melted down to make

Solomon's wealth. 1 Kings x. 14; 2 Chron. ix. 13.

'algummim. It is not known what kind of tree the almug was, but many scholars identify it with red sandal-wood, which comes from the islands near India.

[c] So LXX translates Heb. *mis'ad* (A.V. "pillars") in 1 Kings; in 2 Chron. LXX has ἀναβάσεις "steps" for Heb. *mesillôth* "paths" (?) (A.V. "terraces").

[d] On these instruments *cf. A.* vii. 306 notes.

[e] These details about the rare wood are, of course, unscriptural.

[f] So 2 Chron.; in 1 Kings Heb. has *'ereb*, a word of doubtful meaning here, which Targum translates by "allies," and LXX, reading *'ēber*, has τοῦ πέραν "of the (country) beyond."

[g] Every year, according to Scripture.

δὲ τὸν χρυσὸν εἰς διακοσίων κατασκευὴν θυρεῶν
180 ἀνὰ σίκλους ἀγόντων ἑξακοσίους. ἐποίησε δὲ καὶ
ἀσπίδας τριακοσίας ἀγούσης ἑκάστης χρυσίου μνᾶς
τρεῖς· ἀνέθηκε δὲ ταύτας φέρων εἰς τὸν οἶκον τὸν
δρυμῶνα Λιβάνου καλούμενον. οὐ μὴν ἀλλὰ καὶ
τὰ ἐκπώματα διὰ χρυσοῦ καὶ λίθου τὰ πρὸς τὴν
ἑστίασιν ὡς ἔνι μάλιστα φιλοτεχνῶν[1] κατεσκεύασε
καὶ τὴν ἄλλην τῶν σκευῶν δαψίλειαν χρυσέαν
181 ἅπασαν ἐμηχανήσατο· οὐδὲν γὰρ ἦν ὅ τις ἀργύρῳ
ἐπίπρασκεν ἢ πάλιν ἐωνεῖτο· πολλαὶ[2] γὰρ ἦσαν
νῆες,[3] ἃς ὁ βασιλεὺς ἐν τῇ Ταρσικῇ λεγομένῃ
θαλάττῃ καταστήσας παραγαγεῖν[4] εἰς τὰ ἐνδοτέρω
τῶν ἐθνῶν παντοίαν ἐμπορίαν προσέταξεν, ὧν
ἐξεμπολουμένων ἄργυρός τε καὶ χρυσὸς ἐκομίζετο
τῷ βασιλεῖ καὶ πολὺς ἐλέφας Αἰθίοπές τε καὶ
πίθηκοι. τὸν δὲ πλοῦν ἀπιοῦσαί τε καὶ ἐπαν-
ερχόμεναι τρισὶν ἔτεσιν ἤνυον.
182 (3) Φήμη δὲ λαμπρὰ πᾶσαν ἐν κύκλῳ τὴν χώραν
περιήρχετο διαβοῶσα τὴν Σολομῶνος ἀρετὴν καὶ
σοφίαν, ὡς τούς τε πανταχοῦ βασιλεῖς ἐπιθυμεῖν
εἰς ὄψιν αὐτῷ παραγενέσθαι, τοῖς λεγομένοις δι'
ὑπερβολὴν ἀπιστοῦντας, καὶ δωρεαῖς μεγάλαις
183 προσεμφανίζειν τὴν περὶ αὐτὸν σπουδήν· ἔπεμπον
γὰρ αὐτῷ σκεύη χρυσᾶ καὶ ἀργυρᾶ καὶ ἁλουργεῖς
ἐσθῆτας καὶ ἀρωμάτων γένη πολλὰ καὶ ἵππους

[1] Niese: φιλοτέχνων RO Lat. (vid.): φιλοτέχνως MSP.
[2] ἀλλὰ πολλαὶ RO Lat. [3] Dindorf: ναῦς codd.
[4] ἀπάγειν MSP.

[a] So Heb. and LXX 2 Chron.; LXX 1 Kings has ὅπλα "weapons." [b] LXX 1 Kings 300.
[c] So 1 Kings; 2 Chron. 300 (shekels). The mina (Heb. *mānēh*) was equal to 60 shekels.

two hundred shields[a] weighing six hundred[b] shekels apiece. He also made three hundred bucklers, each weighing three minae.[c] And he brought them to be set up in the hall called the Forest of Libanos. Furthermore he made drinking-cups of gold and precious stone[d] for the use of guests with the greatest art and fashioned an abundance of other vessels all of gold, as no one sold or bought anything for silver.[e] For the king had many ships stationed in the Sea of Tarsus,[f] as it was called, which he ordered to carry all sorts of merchandise to the inland nations, and from the sale of these there was brought to the king silver and gold and much ivory and Ethiopians[g] and apes. The sea voyage, going and returning, took three years.

Gifts sent to Solomon; his horses and chariots. 1 Kings x. 23 (LXX x. 26); 2 Chron. ix. 22.

(3) [h] And so glowing a report was circulated through the whole country round about, proclaiming Solomon's virtue and wisdom, that everywhere the kings desired to see him with their own eyes, not crediting what had been told them because of its extravagance, and to give further evidence of their regard for him by their costly presents. Accordingly, they sent him vessels of gold and silver and sea-purple[d] garments and many kinds of spices and

[d] Unscriptural detail.

[e] Scripture says, "there was no silver (in the vessels), for it was accounted as nothing in the days of Solomon."

[f] Bibl. Tarshish, LXX Θαρσεῖς, Targum "Africa." Most modern scholars identify Tarshish with Tartessos in Spain, not with Tarsus in Cilicia as does Josephus.

[g] Heb. *tukkîyîm*, LXX ταώνων, both meaning "peacocks"; *tukkîyîm* may, as Weill suggests, have been misread by Josephus as *kuššîyîm* "Ethiopians."

[h] LXX at this point (after 1 Kings x. 22) has a passage on Solomon's fortifications and conquests, which is given earlier in the Heb. (1 Kings ix. 15 ff.), *cf.* § 150.

καὶ ἅρματα καὶ τῶν ἀχθοφόρων ἡμιόνων ὅσους καὶ ῥώμῃ καὶ κάλλει τὴν τοῦ βασιλέως ὄψιν εὖ διαθήσειν ἐπελέγοντο, ὥστε τοῖς οὖσιν αὐτῷ πρότερον ἅρμασι καὶ ἵπποις ἐκ τῶν πεμπομένων προσθέντα ποιῆσαι τὸν μὲν τῶν ἁρμάτων ἀριθμὸν τετρακοσίοις περισσότερον (ἦν γὰρ αὐτῷ πρότερον χίλια), τὸν δὲ τῶν ἵππων δισχιλίοις (ὑπῆρχον γὰρ
184 αὐτῷ δισμύριοι ἵπποι). ἤσκηντο δ' οὗτοι πρὸς εὐμορφίαν καὶ τάχος, ὡς μήτ' εὐπρεπεστέρους ἄλλους εἶναι συμβαλεῖν αὐτοῖς μήτε ὠκυτέρους, ἀλλὰ καλλίστους τε πάντων ὁρᾶσθαι καὶ ἀπαρ-
185 αμίλλητον αὐτῶν εἶναι τὴν ὀξύτητα. ἐπεκόσμουν δὲ αὐτοὺς καὶ οἱ ἀναβαίνοντες νεότητι μὲν πρῶτον ἀνθοῦντες ἐπιτερπεστάτῃ, τὸ δὲ ὕψος ὄντες περίοπτοι καὶ πολὺ τῶν ἄλλων ὑπερέχοντες, μηκίστας μὲν καθειμένοι χαίτας ἐνδεδυμένοι δὲ χιτῶνας τῆς Τυρίας πορφύρας. ψῆγμα δὲ χρυσοῦ καθ' ἡμέραν αὐτῶν ἐπέσηθον ταῖς κόμαις, ὡς στίλβειν αὐτῶν τὰς κεφαλὰς τῆς αὐγῆς τοῦ χρυσοῦ πρὸς τὸν ἥλιον
186 ἀντανακλωμένης. τούτων περὶ αὐτὸν ὄντων ὁ βασιλεὺς καθωπλισμένων καὶ τόξα ἐξηρτημένων ἐφ' ἅρματος αὐτὸς ὀχούμενος καὶ λευκὴν ἠμφιεσμένος ἐσθῆτα πρὸς αἰώραν ἔθος εἶχεν ἐξορμᾶν. ἦν δέ τι χωρίον ἀπὸ δύο σχοίνων Ἱεροσολύμων, ὃ καλεῖται μὲν Ἠτάν, παραδείσοις δὲ καὶ ναμάτων

[a] Heb. has merely 1400, without indicating how many he had formerly; LXX cod. B "four thousand horses for chariots," cod. A and Luc. (2 Chron.) "forty thousand horses for chariots."

horses and chariots and as many mules for carrying burdens as could be counted on to please the king's eye by their strength and beauty, so that, with the addition of these that were sent to the chariots and horses he formerly had, he increased the number of his chariots by four hundred—previously he had a thousand [a]—and the number of his horses by two thousand—he already had twenty thousand [b] horses. These were trained for beauty of form and for speed, so that there were none more handsome or swifter to compare with them, but they were most beautiful of all in appearance and were also unrivalled in swiftness. A further adornment to them were their riders, who, in the first flower of a youth that was most delightful to see, and of a conspicuous height, were much taller than other men; they let their hair hang down to a very great length and were dressed in tunics of Tyrian purple. And every day they sprinkled their hair with gold dust so that their heads sparkled as the gleam of the gold was reflected by the sun. With these men about him dressed in armour and equipped with bows, the king himself was accustomed to mount his chariot, clothed in a white garment, and go out for a ride.[c] Now there was a certain spot two *schoinoi* [d] distant from Jerusalem, which is called Étan,[e] delightful for, and

[b] Bibl. 12,000 horsemen; Heb. *pārāšîm*, however, may mean "horses" as well as "horsemen."

[c] This peculiar meaning of *αἰώρα* is established by the use of *αἰωρούμενος* below and the same verb in *A.* xviii. 185 *αἰωρεῖτο μὲν Τιβέριος ἐπὶ φορείου κείμενος.*

[d] Between 8 and 10 miles.

[e] Probably the same place as Etam (Etamē in § 246), LXX *Αἰτάμ*, *Αἰτάν*, the modern *'Ain 'Aṭān* about 5 miles S.W. of Bethlehem; it is mentioned in the list of Rehoboam's fortified cities.

ἐπιρροαῖς ἐπιτερπὲς ὁμοῦ καὶ πλούσιον· εἰς τοῦτο τὰς ἐξόδους αἰωρούμενος ἐποιεῖτο.

187 (4) Θείᾳ δὲ περὶ πάντα χρώμενος ἐπινοίᾳ τε καὶ σπουδῇ καὶ λίαν ὢν φιλόκαλος οὐδὲ τῶν ὁδῶν ἠμέλησεν, ἀλλὰ καὶ τούτων τὰς ἀγούσας εἰς Ἱεροσόλυμα βασίλειον οὖσαν λίθῳ κατέστρωσε μέλανι, πρός τε τὸ ῥᾳστώνην[1] εἶναι τοῖς βαδίζουσι, καὶ πρὸς τὸ δηλοῦν τὸ ἀξίωμα τοῦ πλούτου καὶ τῆς
188 ἡγεμονίας. διαμερίσας δὲ τὰ ἅρματα καὶ διατάξας, ὥστε ἐν ἑκάστῃ πόλει τούτων ἀριθμὸν ὡρισμένον ὑπάρχειν, αὐτὸς μὲν περὶ αὐτὸν ἐτήρησεν ὀλίγα, τὰς δὲ πόλεις ταύτας ἁρμάτων προσηγόρευσε. τοῦ δ' ἀργυρίου τοσοῦτον ἐποίησε[2] πλῆθος ἐν Ἱεροσολύμοις ὁ βασιλεύς, ὅσον ἦν καὶ τῶν λίθων, καὶ τῶν κεδρίνων ξύλων οὐ πρότερον ὄντων, ὥσπερ καὶ τῶν δένδρων τῶν συκαμινίνων, ὧν[3] πληθύει
189 τὰ τῆς Ἰουδαίας πεδία. προσέταξε δὲ καὶ τοῖς ἐμπόροις Αἰγύπτου κομίζουσιν αὐτῷ πιπράσκειν τὸ μὲν ἅρμα σὺν ἵπποις δυσὶν ἑξακοσίων δραχμῶν ἀργυρίου, αὐτὸς δὲ τοῖς τῆς Συρίας βασιλεῦσι καὶ τοῖς πέραν Εὐφράτου διέπεμπεν αὐτούς.
190 (5) Γενόμενος δὲ πάντων βασιλέων ἐνδοξότατος

[1] Niese: ῥάστην codd.
[2] ἐποιήσατο RO.
[3] ὧν add. Niese.

[a] This whole passage (§§ 184-187) is an addition to Scripture.

[b] So Heb.; LXX "gold and silver."

[c] Heb. "a chariot came up and went out of Egypt for six hundred (shekels) of silver, and a horse for a hundred and fifty"; LXX "and the export went up from Egypt, a chariot for a hundred (shekels) of silver, and a horse for fifty (shekels) of silver." Josephus takes a shekel as equal to four Attic drachmas (*A*. iii. 194), so that the price of 150 shekels given in the LXX for a chariot with *one* horse

abounding in, parks and flowing streams, and to this place he would make excursions, mounted high on his chariot.

Solomon's chariot cities and horse trading.

(4) Exercising a divine thoughtfulness and zeal in all things and being an ardent lover of beauty, he did not neglect the roads either, but those leading to Jerusalem, which was the royal city, he paved with black stone, both for the convenience of wayfarers and in order to show the greatness of his wealth and power.[a] And he divided the chariots and disposed them in such a way that there was a definite number of them in every city, while he himself kept only a few about him; and these cities he called Cities of Chariots. As for silver,[b] the king made it as plentiful in Jerusalem as were stones, and cedar-wood, which had not been found there before, he made as plentiful as the sycamore-trees with which the plains of Judea abound. He also gave orders to the merchants of Egypt to bring and sell him a chariot with two horses for six hundred drachmas [c] of silver, which he himself sent [d] to the kings of Syria and those beyond the Euphrates.[e]

1 Kings x. 26 (LXX x. 29); 2 Chron. ix. 25.

(5) But though he had been the most illustrious of

would be equal to 600 drachmas. In making 600 drachmas the price of a chariot with *two* horses, Josephus combines the Heb. and LXX texts, as Weill has noted.

[d] The bibl. text (1 Kings x. 29) is obscure and does not make clear who exported the horses to the east. Heb. has *beyādām hôṣî'û* "by their hand they sent them out," apparently referring to "the king's merchants" mentioned in vs. 28; LXX, reading *beyādām* as *bayyām* "by sea," has κατὰ θάλασσαν ἐξεπορεύοντο. With the other textual difficulties in the bibl. verse we need not deal, as they do not bear on Josephus's text.

[e] Bibl. "for all the kings of the Hittites and the kings of Syria (Heb. Aram)."

καὶ θεοφιλέστατος καὶ φρονήσει καὶ πλούτῳ διενεγκὼν τῶν πρὸ αὐτοῦ τὴν Ἑβραίων ἀρχὴν ἐσχηκότων, οὐκ ἐπέμεινε τούτοις ἄχρι τελευτῆς, ἀλλὰ καταλιπὼν τὴν τῶν πατρίων ἐθισμῶν φυλακὴν οὐκ εἰς ὅμοιον οἷς προειρήκαμεν αὐτοῦ
191 τέλος κατέστρεψεν, εἰς δὲ γυναῖκας ἐκμανεὶς καὶ τὴν τῶν ἀφροδισίων ἀκρασίαν, οὐ ταῖς ἐπιχωρίοις μόνον ἠρέσκετο, πολλὰς δὲ καὶ ἐκ τῶν ἀλλοτρίων ἐθνῶν γήμας Σιδωνίας καὶ Τυρίας καὶ Ἀμμανίτιδας καὶ Ἰδουμαίας παρέβη μὲν τοὺς Μωυσέος νόμους, ὃς ἀπηγόρευσε συνοικεῖν ταῖς οὐχ ὁμο-
192 φύλοις, τοὺς δ᾽ ἐκείνων ἤρξατο θρησκεύειν θεούς, ταῖς γυναιξὶ καὶ τῷ πρὸς αὐτὰς ἔρωτι χαριζόμενος, τοῦτ᾽ αὐτὸ ὑπιδομένου[1] τοῦ νομοθέτου καὶ[2] προειπόντος μὴ γαμεῖν τὰς ἀλλοτριοχώρους, ἵνα μὴ τοῖς ξένοις ἐπιπλακέντες ἔθεσι τῶν πατρίων ἀποστῶσι, μηδὲ τοὺς ἐκείνων σέβωνται[3] θεοὺς παρέντες
193 τιμᾶν τὸν ἴδιον. ἀλλὰ τούτων μὲν κατημέλησεν ὑπενεχθεὶς εἰς ἡδονὴν ἀλόγιστον Σολομών, ἀγαγόμενος δὲ γυναῖκας ἀρχόντων καὶ διασήμων θυγατέρας ἑπτακοσίας τὸν ἀριθμὸν καὶ παλλακὰς τριακοσίας, πρὸς δὲ ταύταις καὶ τὴν τοῦ βασιλέως τῶν Αἰγυπτίων θυγατέρα, εὐθὺς μὲν ἐκρατεῖτο πρὸς αὐτῶν, ὥστε μιμεῖσθαι τὰ παρ᾽ ἐκείναις, καὶ τῆς εὐνοίας καὶ φιλοστοργίας ἠναγκάζετο παρέχειν αὐταῖς δεῖγμα τὸ βιοῦν ὡς αὐταῖς πάτριον ἦν,
194 προβαινούσης δὲ τῆς ἡλικίας καὶ τοῦ λογισμοῦ διὰ τὸν χρόνον ἀσθενοῦντος ἀντέχειν πρὸς τὴν μνήμην τῶν ἐπιχωρίων ἐπιτηδευμάτων, ἔτι μᾶλλον

[1] Dindorf: ὑπειδομένου codd. [2] καὶ om. ROM.
[3] σέβωσι RSP Exc.

all kings and most beloved by God, and in understanding and wealth surpassed those who had ruled over the Hebrews before him, he did not persevere in this way until his death, but abandoned the observance of his fathers' customs and came to an end not at all like what we have already said about him, for he became madly enamoured of women and indulged in excesses of passion ; not satisfied with the women of his own country alone, he married many from foreign nations as well, Sidonians,[a] Tyrians,[b] Ammanites and Idumaeans,[c] thereby transgressing the laws of Moses who forbade marriage with persons of other races,[d] and he began to worship their gods to gratify his wives and his passion for them—which is the very thing the lawgiver foresaw when he warned the Hebrews against marrying women of other countries lest they might be entangled with foreign customs and fall away from those of their fathers, and worship the gods of these women while neglecting to honour their own God. But Solomon, carried away by thoughtless pleasure, disregarded these warnings and took as wives seven hundred women, the daughters of princes and nobles, and three hundred concubines, and beside these the daughter of the king of Egypt ; and he was very soon prevailed upon by them to the extent of imitating their ways, and was forced to give a sign of his favour and affection for them by living in accordance with their ancestral customs. As he advanced in age, and his reason became in time too feeble to oppose to these the memory of his

Solomon's foreign wives.

1 Kings xi. 1.

[a] So Heb. ; LXX omits.

[b] Not mentioned in Scripture, but perhaps a corruption of LXX Σύρας.

[c] Scripture adds Moabites and Hittites.

[d] *Cf.* Ex. xxxiv 16, Deut. vii. 3, xxiii. 3.

τοῦ μὲν ἰδίου θεοῦ κατωλιγώρησε, τοὺς δὲ τῶν
195 γάμων τῶν ἐπεισάκτων τιμῶν διετέλει. καὶ πρὸ
τούτων δὲ ἁμαρτεῖν αὐτὸν ἔτυχε καὶ σφαλῆναι
περὶ τὴν φυλακὴν τῶν νομίμων, ὅτε τὰ τῶν χαλκῶν
βοῶν ὁμοιώματα κατεσκεύασε τῶν ὑπὸ τῇ θαλάττῃ
τῷ ἀναθήματι καὶ τῶν λεόντων τῶν περὶ τὸν
θρόνον τὸν ἴδιον· οὐδὲ γὰρ ταῦτα ποιεῖν ὅσιον
196 εἰργάσατο. κάλλιστον δ' ἔχων καὶ οἰκεῖον παράδειγμα τῆς ἀρετῆς τὸν πατέρα καὶ τὴν ἐκείνου
δόξαν, ἣν αὐτῷ συνέβη καταλιπεῖν διὰ τὴν πρὸς
τὸν θεὸν εὐσέβειαν, οὐ μιμησάμενος αὐτὸν καὶ
ταῦτα δὶς αὐτῷ τοῦ θεοῦ κατὰ τοὺς ὕπνους φανέντος καὶ τὸν πατέρα μιμεῖσθαι παραινέσαντος
197 ἀκλεῶς ἀπέθανεν. ἧκεν οὖν εὐθὺς ὁ προφήτης
ὑπὸ τοῦ θεοῦ πεμφθείς, οὔτε λανθάνειν αὐτὸν ἐπὶ
τοῖς παρανομήμασι λέγων οὔτ' ἐπὶ πολὺ χαιρήσειν
τοῖς πραττομένοις ἀπειλῶν, ἀλλὰ ζῶντος μὲν οὐκ
ἀφαιρεθήσεσθαι τὴν βασιλείαν ἐπεὶ τῷ πατρὶ
Δαυίδῃ τὸ θεῖον ὑπέσχετο διάδοχον αὐτὸν ποιήσειν
198 ἐκείνου, τελευτήσαντος δὲ τὸν υἱὸν αὐτοῦ ταῦτα
διαθήσειν, οὐχ ἅπαντα μὲν τὸν λαὸν ἀποστήσας
αὐτοῦ, δέκα δὲ φυλὰς παραδοὺς αὐτοῦ τῷ δούλῳ,
δύο δὲ μόνας καταλιπὼν τῷ υἱωνῷ τῷ Δαυίδου
δι' αὐτὸν ἐκεῖνον, ὅτι τὸν θεὸν ἠγάπησε, καὶ διὰ
τὴν πόλιν Ἱεροσόλυμα, ἐν ᾗ ναὸν ἔχειν ἐβουλήθη.

---

[a] Neither Scripture nor rabbinic tradition imputes any sin to Solomon in making these vessels and images. Tradition does, however, find fault with his amassing of gold and silver, *cf.* Ginzberg iv. 129. Perhaps Josephus has chosen these two examples of wrongdoing in preference to mentioning the altars which Solomon built in Jerusalem to Ammonite and Moabite gods, 1 Kings xi. 7.

own country's practices, he showed still greater disrespect for his own God and continued to honour those whom his wives had introduced. But even before this there had been an occasion on which he sinned and went astray in respect of the observance of the laws, namely when he made the images of the bronze bulls underneath the sea which he had set up as an offering, and those of the lions around his own throne, for in making them he committed an impious act.[a] And though he had a most excellent and near example of virtue in his father and in the glory which his father was able to leave behind him because of his piety toward God, he did not imitate him—not even after God had twice appeared to him in his sleep and exhorted him to imitate his father,—and so he died ingloriously. For at once there came a prophet [b] sent by God, who told him that his unlawful acts had not escaped Him, and threatened that he should not long continue in his course with impunity but that, while in his lifetime he should not be deprived of his kingdom since the Deity had promised his father David to make him his successor, on his death He would cause this to befall Solomon's son and, while not taking all the people away from him, would deliver ten tribes to his servant [c] and leave only two [d] to David's grandson for the sake of David himself, because he had loved God, and for the sake of Jerusalem, in which He wished to have a temple.

Solomon is warned of God's displeasure. 1 Kings xi. 11.

[b] Here, as elsewhere (*cf. A.* vii. 72, 294), Josephus introduces a prophet where Scripture represents God as speaking to a certain person directly; a rabbinic tradition agrees with Josephus in mentioning the prophet Ahijah as God's spokesman on this occasion.

[c] Jeroboam, *cf.* § 205.

[d] Bibl. " one tribe " (Judah), but *cf.* § 207 note.

199 (6) Ταῦτ' ἀκούσας Σολομὼν ἤλγησε καὶ σφο-
δρῶς συνεχύθη πάντων αὐτῷ σχεδὸν τῶν ἀγαθῶν
ἐφ' οἷς ζηλωτὸς ἦν εἰς μεταβολὴν ἐρχομένων
πονηράν. οὐ πολὺς δὲ διῆλθε χρόνος ἀφ' οὗ
κατήγγειλεν ὁ προφήτης αὐτῷ τὰ συμβησόμενα
καὶ πολέμιον εὐθὺς ἐπ' αὐτὸν ἤγειρεν ὁ θεὸς
Ἄδερον[1] μὲν ὄνομα τὴν δ' αἰτίαν τῆς ἔχθρας
200 λαβόντα τοιαύτην· παῖς οὗτος ἦν, Ἰδουμαῖος γένος
ἐκ βασιλικῶν σπερμάτων. καταστρεψαμένου δὲ
τὴν Ἰδουμαίαν Ἰωάβου τοῦ Δαυίδου στρατηγοῦ
καὶ πάντας τοὺς ἐν ἀκμῇ καὶ φέρειν ὅπλα δυναμένους διαφθείραντος μησὶν ἕξ,[2] φυγὼν ἧκε πρὸς
201 Φαραῶνα τὸν Αἰγυπτίων βασιλέα. ὁ δὲ φιλοφρόνως αὐτὸν ὑποδεξάμενος[3] οἶκόν τε αὐτῷ δίδωσι
καὶ χώραν εἰς διατροφήν, καὶ γενόμενον ἐν ἡλικίᾳ
λίαν ἠγάπα, ὡς καὶ τῆς αὑτοῦ γυναικὸς αὐτῷ
δοῦναι πρὸς γάμον τὴν ἀδελφὴν ὄνομα Θαφίνην,
ἐξ ἧς αὐτῷ υἱὸς γενόμενος τοῖς τοῦ βασιλέως παισὶ
202 συνανετράφη.[4] ἀκούσας οὖν τὸν Δαυίδου θάνατον
ἐν Αἰγύπτῳ καὶ τὸν Ἰωάβου προσελθὼν ἐδεῖτο
τοῦ Φαραῶνος ἐπιτρέπειν αὐτῷ βαδίζειν εἰς τὴν
πατρίδα. τοῦ δὲ βασιλέως ἀνακρίνοντος τίνος
ἐνδεὴς ὢν ἢ τί παθὼν ἐσπούδακε καταλιπεῖν αὐτόν,
ἐνοχλῶν πολλάκις καὶ παρακαλῶν τότε μὲν οὐκ
203 ἀφείθη· κατ' ἐκεῖνον δὲ τὸν καιρόν, καθ' ὃν ἤδη
Σολομῶνι τὰ πράγματα κακῶς ἔχειν ἤρχετο διὰ
τὰς προειρημένας παρανομίας καὶ τὴν ὀργὴν τὴν
ἐπ' αὐτοῖς τοῦ θεοῦ, συγχωρήσαντος τοῦ Φαραῶνος

[1] ed. pr.: Ἀδέραν R: Ἄδεραν OM (Exc.): Ἄδερ SPE: Adher Lat.

[2] μησὶν ἕξ ROM: μόνος οὗτος SP: μησὶν ἕξ, μόνος οὗτος Naber.
[3] δεξάμενος RO.
[4] συνετράφη RO.

Hadad (Adados) the Edomite rebels against Solomon. 1 Kings xi. 14.

(6) When Solomon heard this, he was grieved and sorely troubled at the thought that almost all the good things for which he was envied were changing for the worse. Nor did a long time elapse after the prophet's announcement to him of what was coming, but immediately God set up an enemy against him, named Aderos,[a] who had the following reason for his enmity. He was a child of royal lineage of Idumean race when Joab, David's commander, subdued Idumea[b] and within six months destroyed all those who were of fighting age and able to bear arms; and he fled and came to Pharaō, king of Egypt, who received him kindly and gave him a dwelling and land to sustain him. And when he grew up, Pharaō loved him so much that he gave him in marriage his own wife's sister, named Thaphinē,[c] and by her he had a son, who was brought up together with the children of the king. Now when Aderos heard in Egypt of the death of both David and Joab, he went to Pharaō and asked him for permission to go to his native country. But the king inquired what he lacked or what had befallen him that he was anxious to leave him, and, although Aderos frequently pressed him and pleaded with him, he did not at that time obtain his release.[d] But at the time when things were already beginning to go ill for Solomon because of the unlawful acts we have mentioned and God's anger on their account, Pharaō gave his consent

[a] *Cf.* LXX Ἀδέρ: bibl. Hadad.
[b] *Cf. A.* vii. 109 note.
[c] Bibl. Tahpenes, LXX Θεκεμείνας: this was the name of the queen, not her sister's name.
[d] Amplification.

ὁ Ἄδερος ἧκεν εἰς τὴν Ἰδουμαίαν· καὶ μὴ δυνηθεὶς αὐτὴν ἀποστῆσαι τοῦ Σολομῶνος, κατείχετο
γὰρ φρουραῖς πολλαῖς καὶ οὐκ ἦν ἐλεύθερος δι'
αὐτὰς οὐδ' ἐπ' ἀδείας ὁ νεωτερισμός, ἄρας ἐκεῖθεν
204 εἰς τὴν Συρίαν ἀφίκετο. συμβαλὼν δ' ἐκεῖ τινι
Ῥάζῳ[1] μὲν τοὔνομα τὸν δὲ τῆς Σωφηνῆς ἀπο-
δεδρακότι βασιλέα Ἀδραάζαρον δεσπότην ὄντα καὶ
λῃστεύοντι τὴν χώραν, εἰς φιλίαν αὐτῷ συνάψας
ἔχων τε[2] περὶ αὐτὸν στῖφος λῃστρικὸν ἀναβαίνει,
καὶ κατασχὼν τὴν ἐκεῖ Συρίαν βασιλεὺς αὐτῆς ἀποδείκνυται καὶ κατατρέχων τὴν τῶν Ἰσραηλιτῶν
γῆν ἐποίει κακῶς καὶ διήρπαζε Σολομῶνος ζῶντος
ἔτι. καὶ ταῦτα μὲν ἐκ τοῦ Ἀδέρου συνέβαινε
πάσχειν τοὺς Ἑβραίους.
205 (7) Ἐπιτίθεται δὲ Σολομῶνι καὶ τῶν ὁμοφύλων
τις Ἱεροβόαμος υἱὸς Ναβαταίου, κατὰ προφητείαν
πάλαι γενομένην αὐτῷ τοῖς πράγμασιν ἐπελπίσας·
παῖδα γὰρ αὐτὸν ὑπὸ τοῦ πατρὸς καταλειφθέντα
καὶ ὑπὸ τῇ μητρὶ παιδευόμενον ὡς εἶδε γενναῖον
καὶ τολμηρὸν Σολομὼν ὄντα τὸ φρόνημα, τῆς τῶν
τειχῶν οἰκοδομίας ἐπιμελητὴν κατέστησεν, ὅτε
206 τοῖς Ἱεροσολύμοις τὸν κύκλον περιέβαλεν. οὕτως
δὲ τῶν ἔργων προενόησεν, ὥστε ὁ βασιλεὺς αὐτὸν ἀπεδέξατο καὶ γέρας αὐτῷ στρατηγίαν ἐπὶ

[1] Ῥααζάρῳ MSP.
[2] ἔχων τε Niese: ἔχοντι codd.: ἔχων τι Naber.

---

[a] So LXX; Heb. omits Hadad's return.
[b] So cod. A of the LXX, and certain ancient versions; Heb. abruptly turns from the subject of Hadad, after telling of his appeal to Pharaoh, and proceeds with the story of Rezon, 1 Kings xi. 23.
[c] Bibl. Rezon, LXX Ἐσρώμ (*v.ll.* Ναζρών, Ῥαζρών κτλ.), Luc Ἐσρών.

and Aderos came to Idumea.[a] And not being able to cause it to revolt from Solomon—for it was occupied by many garrisons and because of them a revolution was not a matter of free choice nor without peril,—he removed from there and went to Syria.[b] There falling in with a certain person named Razos,[c] who had run away from his master Adraazaros,[d] the king of Sophēnē,[e] and was pillaging the country, he joined forces with this man and with a band of robbers under him went up country and, taking possession of that part of Syria,[f] was proclaimed king thereof[g]; and he overran the country of the Israelites, damaging it and plundering it while Solomon was still alive. Such, then, were the injuries which the Hebrews were fated to suffer at the hands of Aderos.

(7) There also rose up against Solomon one of his own countrymen, Jeroboam the son of Nabataios,[h] who had faith in his chances of success because of a prophecy that had been made to him long before. For he had been bereaved of his father when still a child and was brought up by his mother, and Solomon, seeing that he was of a noble and daring spirit, appointed him overseer of the building of the walls when he surrounded Jerusalem with defences. And so well did he supervise the work that the king marked him with his approval and as a reward gave him the

The rise of Jeroboam. 1 Kings xi. 26.

[d] *Cf.* Luc. Ἀδραάζαρ; bibl. Hadadezer, LXX Ἀδράζαρ (*v.l.* Ἀδαδέζερ).

[e] Bibl. Zobah (*Ṣôbāh*), LXX Σουβά; on Sophene *cf. A.* vii. 99 note.

[f] Damascus, in Scripture.

[g] According to Scripture, it was Rezon who became king of Damascus, while Hadad became king of Edom.

[h] Bibl. Nebat, LXX Ναβάτ (*v.l.* Ναβάθ).

τῆς Ἰωσήπου φυλῆς ἔδωκεν. ἀπερχομένῳ δὲ τῷ Ἱεροβοάμῳ κατ᾽ ἐκεῖνον τὸν καιρὸν ἐκ τῶν Ἱεροσολύμων συνεβόλησε[1] προφήτης ἐκ πόλεως μὲν Σιλὼ Ἀχίας[2] δὲ ὄνομα. καὶ προσαγορεύσας αὐτὸν ἀπήγαγεν ἐκ τῆς ὁδοῦ μικρὸν ἀπονεύσας εἴς τι
207 χωρίον, εἰς ὃ[3] παρῆν μηδὲ εἷς ἄλλος. σχίσας δὲ εἰς δώδεκα φάρση τὸ ἱμάτιον, ὅπερ ἦν αὐτὸς περιβεβλημένος, ἐκέλευσε τὸν Ἱεροβόαμον λαβεῖν τὰ δέκα, προειπὼν[4] ὅτι ταῦτα ὁ θεὸς βούλεται καὶ σχίσας τὴν Σολομῶνος ἀρχὴν τῷ παιδὶ μὲν τῷ τούτου διὰ τὴν πρὸς Δαυίδην γεγενημένην ὁμολογίαν αὐτῷ μίαν φυλὴν καὶ τὴν ἑξῆς αὐτῇ[5] δίδωσι, "σοὶ δὲ τὰς δέκα Σολομῶνος εἰς αὐτὸν ἐξαμαρτόντος καὶ ταῖς γυναιξὶ καὶ τοῖς ἐκείνων θεοῖς
208 αὐτὸν ἐκδεδωκότος. εἰδὼς οὖν τὴν αἰτίαν δι᾽ ἣν μετατίθησι τὴν αὐτοῦ γνώμην ἀπὸ Σολομῶνος ὁ θεὸς δίκαιος εἶναι πειρῶ καὶ φύλαττε τὰ νόμιμα, προκειμένου σοι τῆς εὐσεβείας καὶ τῆς πρὸς τὸν θεὸν τιμῆς ἄθλου μεγίστου τῶν ἁπάντων, γενήσεσθαι τηλικούτῳ ἡλίκον οἶσθα Δαυίδην γενόμενον."
209 (8) Ἐπαρθεὶς οὖν τοῖς τοῦ προφήτου λόγοις Ἱεροβόαμος φύσει θερμὸς ὢν νεανίας καὶ μεγάλων ἐπιθυμητὴς πραγμάτων οὐκ ἠρέμει. γενόμενος δ᾽ ἐν τῇ στρατηγίᾳ καὶ μεμνημένος τῶν ὑπὸ Ἀχία δεδηλωμένων εὐθὺς ἀναπείθειν ἐπεχείρει τὸν λαὸν ἀφίστασθαι Σολομῶνος καὶ κινεῖν καὶ παράγειν[6]

[1] συνήντησε M²SPE Zonaras.
[2] E: Ἀχία (-ᾶ SP Zonaras) codd. Lat.
[3] ὁ μὴ SP.
[4] προσειπὼν SP.
[5] ed. pr.: αὐτῆς MSP: ἣν αὐτὸς RO.
[6] Niese: ταράττειν ROS²P: παράττειν M: παραττάτειν S¹: contraderet Lat.: περιάγειν Naber.

command over the tribe of Joseph.[a] Now, as Jeroboam on that occasion was going out of Jerusalem, there met him a prophet from the city of Silō, named Achias,[b] and, having greeted Jeroboam, he led him away from the road and went aside a little distance to a spot where there was no one else.[c] Then, tearing the cloak which covered him into twelve pieces, he bade Jeroboam take ten of them, announcing that such was God's will and that He had torn apart the kingdom of Solomon, giving one tribe and that adjoining it to his son[d] because of the promise He had made to David, " while to you He has given ten tribes, since Solomon has sinned against Him and gone over wholly to his wives and their gods. Now that you know the reason why God has changed and has set His mind against Solomon, try to be righteous and observe the laws, for there awaits you the greatest of all rewards for piety and honour shown to God, which is to become as great as you know David to have been."

(8) Elated, therefore, by the prophet's words, Jeroboam, who was a youth of ardent nature and ambitious of great things, did not remain idle. And when he entered upon his command and called to mind what had been revealed by Achias, he at once attempted to persuade the people to turn away from Solomon and to start a revolt and transfer the supreme

Jeroboam's revolt and flight.

[a] Bibl. " appointed him in charge of all the forced labour (A.V. " charge " ; LXX ἄρσεις " burdens ") of the house of Joseph."

[b] Bibl. Ahijah (*'Ahîyāh*), LXX Ἀχείας (*v.l.* Ἀχία).

[c] Amplification of 1 Kings xi. 29.

[d] *Cf.* LXX " two tribes shall be for him " ; Heb. " one tribe shall be for him " ; *cf.* § 197 note, 221 note.

210 εἰς αὐτὸν τὴν ἡγεμονίαν. μαθὼν δὲ τὴν διάνοιαν αὐτοῦ καὶ τὴν ἐπιβουλὴν[1] Σολομὼν ἐζήτει συλλαβὼν αὐτὸν ἀνελεῖν. φθάσας δὲ γνῶναι τοῦτο Ἱεροβόαμος πρὸς Ἴσακον φεύγει τὸν Αἰγυπτίων βασιλέα, καὶ μέχρι τῆς Σολομῶνος τελευτῆς ἐκεῖ μείνας τό τε μηδὲν ὑπ' αὐτοῦ παθεῖν ἐκέρδησε καὶ
211 τὸ τῇ βασιλείᾳ φυλαχθῆναι. ἀποθνήσκει δὲ Σολομὼν ἤδη γηραιὸς ὢν βασιλεύσας μὲν ὀγδοήκοντα ἔτη, ζήσας δὲ ἐνενήκοντα καὶ τέσσαρα· θάπτεται δὲ ἐν Ἱεροσολύμοις ἅπαντας ὑπερβαλὼν εὐδαιμονίᾳ τε καὶ πλούτῳ καὶ φρονήσει τοὺς βασιλεύσαντας, εἰ μὴ ὅσα γε πρὸς τὸ γῆρας ὑπὸ τῶν γυναικῶν ἀπατηθεὶς παρηνόμησε· περὶ ὧν καὶ τῶν δι' αὐτὰς κακῶν συμπεσόντων Ἑβραίοις εὐκαιρότερον ἕξομεν[2] διασαφῆσαι.

212 (viii. 1) Μετὰ δὲ τὴν Σολομῶνος τελευτὴν διαδεξαμένου τοῦ παιδὸς αὐτοῦ τὴν βασιλείαν Ῥοβοάμου, ὃς ἐκ γυναικὸς Ἀμμανίτιδος ὑπῆρχεν αὐτῷ γεγονὼς Νοομᾶς τοὔνομα, πέμψαντες εὐθὺς εἰς τὴν Αἴγυπτον οἱ τῶν ὄχλων ἄρχοντες ἐκάλουν τὸν Ἱεροβόαμον. ἀφικομένου δὲ πρὸς αὐτοὺς εἰς Σίκιμα πόλιν καὶ Ῥοβόαμος εἰς αὐτὴν παραγίνεται· δέδοκτο γὰρ αὐτὸν ἐκεῖσε συνελθοῦσι τοῖς Ἰσραη-
213 λίταις ἀποδεῖξαι βασιλέα. προσελθόντες οὖν οἵ τε ἄρχοντες αὐτῷ τοῦ λαοῦ καὶ Ἱεροβόαμος παρ-

[1] ἐπιβολὴν Niese, Naber.

[2] εὐκαιρ. ἕξομεν RO: εἰς καιρὸν ἕτερον ἔδοξέ μοι MSP.

[a] These details are not found in the Heb., in which Ahijah's message is immediately followed by Solomon's attempt to kill Jeroboam; they are based on the LXX addition, 1 Kings xii. 24 b.

[b] Bibl. Shishak, LXX Σουσακείμ; the name appears as Isōkos in § 253, and as Sūsakos in *A*. vii. 105.

power to him.[a] But when Solomon learned of his intention and his plot, he sought to arrest him and execute him. Jeroboam, however, hearing of this in time, fled to Isakos,[b] the king of Egypt, and remained with him until Solomon's death, thereby gaining the two-fold advantage of escaping harm from Solomon and being preserved for the kingship.[c] Then Solomon died at a good old age, having reigned for eighty [d] years and lived for ninety-four,[e] and was buried in Jerusalem. He surpassed all other kings in good fortune, wealth and wisdom, except that as he approached old age he was beguiled by his wives into committing unlawful acts. Concerning these acts and the misfortunes which befell the Hebrews on their account we shall find a more convenient occasion to write fully.[f]

1 Kings xi. 40.

Solomon's death. 1 Kings xi. 42.

(viii. 1) After the death of Solomon, his son Roboamos,[g] who was borne to him by an Ammanite woman named Nooma,[h] succeeded to his kingdom, and the leaders of the common people immediately sent to Egypt to summon Jeroboam. But when he came to them at the city of Sikima,[i] Roboamos also arrived there, for it had been decided by the Israelites to assemble there and proclaim him king. So the leaders of the people and Jeroboam went to him and

Rehoboam (Roboamos) succeeds Solomon as king. 1 Kings xi. 43.

[c] These last remarks are an addition to Scripture.

[d] Bibl. 40. As Weill notes, Josephus's figure is more consistent with the Scriptural statement, 1 Kings xi. 4, about Solomon's old age.

[e] *Cf.* § 2 note.

[f] Apparently a reference to §§ 253 ff. on Shishak's invasion of Palestine.

[g] *Cf.* LXX Ῥοβοάμ : bibl. Rehoboam.

[h] So LXX in 2 Chron. xii. 13 ; bibl. Naamah, LXX 1 Kings Μααχάμ (*v.l.* Νααμά).

[i] Bibl. Shechem, *cf. A.* v. 69 note.

εκάλουν λέγοντες ἀνεῖναί τι τῆς δουλείας αὐτοῖς καὶ γενέσθαι χρηστότερον τοῦ πατρός· βαρὺν γὰρ ὑπ' ἐκείνῳ ζυγὸν αὐτοὺς ὑπενεγκεῖν· εὐνούστεροι δὲ ἔσεσθαι πρὸς αὐτὸν καὶ ἀγαπήσειν τὴν δουλείαν
214 διὰ τὴν ἐπιείκειαν ἢ διὰ τὸν φόβον. ὁ δὲ μετὰ τρεῖς ἡμέρας εἰπὼν αὐτοῖς ἀποκρινεῖσθαι[1] περὶ ὧν ἀξιοῦσιν ὕποπτος μὲν εὐθὺς γίνεται μὴ παραχρῆμα ἐπινεύσας αὐτοῖς τὰ πρὸς ἡδονήν, πρόχειρον γὰρ ἠξίουν εἶναι τὸ χρηστὸν καὶ φιλάνθρωπον καὶ ταῦτ' ἐν νέῳ, ἐδόκει δ' ὅμως καὶ τὸ βουλεύσασθαι τῷ[2] μὴ παραυτίκα ἀπειπεῖν ἀγαθῆς ἐλπίδος ἔχεσθαι.
215 (2) Συγκαλέσας δὲ τοὺς πατρῴους φίλους ἐσκοπεῖτο μετ' αὐτῶν ποδαπὴν δεῖ ποιήσασθαι τὴν ἀπόκρισιν πρὸς τὸ πλῆθος. οἱ δ', ἅπερ εἰκὸς τοὺς εὔνους καὶ φύσιν ὄχλων εἰδότας, παρῄνουν αὐτῷ φιλοφρόνως ὁμιλῆσαι τῷ λαῷ καὶ δημοτικώτερον ἢ κατὰ βασιλείας ὄγκον· χειρώσεσθαι[3] γὰρ οὕτως εἰς εὔνοιαν αὐτόν, φύσει τῶν ὑπηκόων ἀγαπώντων τὸ προσηνὲς καὶ παρὰ μικρὸν ἰσότιμον τῶν βασι-
216 λέων. ὁ δ' ἀγαθὴν οὕτως καὶ συμφέρουσαν ἴσως πρὸς τὸ πᾶν, εἰ δὲ μή, πρός γε[4] τὸν τότε καιρὸν ὅτ' ἔδει γενέσθαι βασιλέα γνώμην ἀπεστράφη τοῦ θεοῦ ποιήσαντος, οἶμαι, κατακριθῆναι τὸ συμφέρον ὑπ' αὐτοῦ· καλέσας δὲ μειράκια τὰ συντεθραμμένα καὶ τὴν τῶν πρεσβυτέρων αὐτοῖς συμβουλίαν εἰπών,
217 τί δοκεῖ ποιεῖν αὐτοῖς ἐκέλευσε λέγειν. τὰ δέ,

[1] ex Lat. Niese: ἀποκρίνασθαι ROE: ἀποκρίνεσθαι MSP.
[2] Niese: τοῦ codd.
[3] ed. pr.: χειρώσασθαι codd.
[4] ed. pr.: τε codd.

---

[a] These remarks on the people's response are an addition to Scripture.

urged him to lighten their bondage somewhat and to be more lenient than his father, for, they said, the yoke they had borne under him had been heavy indeed, and they would be better disposed toward him and accept servitude more willingly if treated with kindness than if made to fear him. But when he said that in three days he would give them an answer to their request, he immediately roused their suspicions by not assenting to their wishes on the spot, for they held kindness and friendliness to be an easy matter, especially for a young man. Nevertheless the fact of his deliberating and not refusing them on the instant seemed to offer some ground for good hope.[a]

Rehoboam's harsh answer to the people. 1 Kings xii. 6; 2 Chron. x. 6.

(2) He then called together his father's friends and considered with them what kind of answer he should give the multitude. And they, as was to be expected of men of kindly disposition and acquainted with the nature of crowds, advised him to speak to the people in a friendly spirit and in more popular style than was usual for the royal dignity, for in this way he would secure their goodwill, since subjects naturally liked affability in their kings and to be treated by them almost as equals.[b] But this advice, which was so good and beneficial, perhaps for all occasions, or, if not for all, at any rate for that particular occasion, he rejected; and it was God, I believe, who caused him to condemn what should have been of benefit to him. He then called together the young men who had been brought up with him and, after telling them what the advice of the elders had been, bade them say what they thought he should do. So

[b] In Scripture the elders advise Rehoboam to be the people's servant.

οὔτε γὰρ ἡ νεότης οὔτε ὁ θεὸς ἠφίει νοεῖν τὰ κρείττω, παρῄνεσαν ἀποκρίνασθαι τῷ λαῷ τὸν βραχύτατον[1] αὐτοῦ δάκτυλον τῆς τοῦ πατρὸς ὀσφύος εἶναι παχύτερον καί, εἰ σκληροῦ λίαν ἐπειράθησαν ἐκείνου, πολὺ μᾶλλον αὐτοῦ λήψεσθαι πεῖραν δυσκόλου· καὶ εἰ μάστιξιν αὐτοὺς ἐκεῖνος ἐνουθέτει, σκορπίοις τοῦτο ποιήσειν αὐτὸν προσ-
218 δοκᾶν. τούτοις ἡσθεὶς[2] ὁ βασιλεὺς καὶ δόξας προσήκειν τῷ τῆς ἀρχῆς ἀξιώματι τὴν ἀπόκρισιν, ὡς συνῆλθεν ἀκουσόμενον τὸ πλῆθος τῇ τρίτῃ τῶν ἡμερῶν, μετεώρου τοῦ λαοῦ παντὸς ὄντος καὶ λέγοντος ἀκοῦσαί τι τοῦ βασιλέως ἐσπουδακότος, οἰομένου δέ τι καὶ φιλάνθρωπον, τὴν τῶν μειρακίων αὐτοῖς συμβουλίαν, παρεὶς τὴν τῶν φίλων, ἀπεκρίνατο. ταῦτα δ' ἐπράττετο κατὰ τὴν τοῦ θεοῦ βούλησιν, ἵνα λάβῃ τέλος ἃ προεφήτευσεν Ἀχίας.

219 (3) Πληγέντες δ' ὑπὸ τῶν λόγων[3] καὶ ἀλγήσαντες ὡς ἐπὶ πείρᾳ τοῖς εἰρημένοις ἠγανάκτησαν καὶ μέγα πάντες ἐκβοήσαντες οὐκέτι οὐδὲν αὐτοῖς εἶναι συγγενὲς πρὸς Δαυίδην καὶ τοὺς ἀπ' αὐτοῦ μετ' ἐκείνην ἔφασαν τὴν ἡμέραν· παραχωρεῖν δ' αὐτῷ μόνον[4] τὸν ναὸν ὃν ὁ πάππος αὐτοῦ κατ-

[1] Theodoretus: βραχύτερον codd. E Lat.
[2] πεισθεὶς Naber.
[3] + ὡς ὑπὸ σιδήρου MSP: + velut opere Lat.
[4] ed. pr.: μόνῳ codd. E.

[a] Josephus, like the LXX in 2 Chron. and some LXX MSS.

they, whom neither their youth nor God permitted to discern a better course, advised him to reply to the people that his little finger [a] was thicker than his father's loins and, if they had found his father excessively harsh, they would experience much more unpleasant treatment from himself; if his father had chastised them with whips, they should expect him to do the same with scorpions.[b] With this advice the king was pleased, thinking such an answer proper to the royal dignity; and, when the multitude assembled on the third day to hear him speak, all the people were excited and anxious to hear what the king might say, supposing that it would be something friendly.[c] But, ignoring the counsel of his (older) friends, he answered them as the young men had advised. This came about in accordance with the will of God, in order that what Achias had prophesied might be accomplished.[d]

(3) Struck a cruel blow by these words [e] and hurt as though actually experiencing what he had spoken of doing, they became indignant and all cried out in a loud voice to say that they no longer had any common tie with David and his descendants from that day on; and, declaring that they would leave to Roboamos only the temple which his grandfather

The northern tribes revolt from Rehoboam. 1 Kings xii. 16; 2 Chron. x. 16.

in 1 Kings, supplies δάκτυλος in rendering the Heb. which has *qoṭonnî*, " my little " (*sc.* part, *i.e.* finger).

[b] Josephus uses the LXX word translating Heb. *'aqrabbîm*, here probably meaning some sort of club with barbed points. J. Strachan in Hastings' *Dictionary of the Bible*, iv. 419, compares the Roman *scorpio* " described by Isidore as *virga nodosa et aculeata*."

[c] This last sentence, describing the people's attitude, is an addition to Scripture.

[d] *Cf.* §§ 206 ff.

[e] Variant adds " as if by a sword."

220 εσκεύασεν εἰπόντες καταλείψειν ἠπείλησαν. οὕτως δ' ἔσχον πικρῶς καὶ τὴν ὀργὴν ἐτήρησαν, ὡς πέμψαντος αὐτοῦ τὸν ἐπὶ τῶν φόρων Ἀδώραμον, ἵνα καταπραΰνῃ καὶ συγγνόντας τοῖς εἰρημένοις, εἴ τι προπετὲς ὑπὸ νεότητος[1] καὶ δύσκολον ἦν ἐν αὐτοῖς, ποιήσῃ[2] μαλακωτέρους, οὐχ ὑπέμειναν,
221 ἀλλὰ βάλλοντες αὐτὸν λίθοις ἀπέκτειναν. τοῦτ' ἰδὼν Ῥοβόαμος καὶ νομίσας αὐτὸν βεβλῆσθαι τοῖς λίθοις, οἷς τὸν ὑπηρέτην ἀπέκτεινεν αὐτοῦ τὸ πλῆθος, δείσας μὴ καὶ ἔργῳ πάθῃ τὸ δεινὸν ἐπιβὰς εὐθὺς ἐπὶ ἅρματος ἔφυγεν εἰς Ἱεροσόλυμα. καὶ ἡ μὲν Ἰούδα φυλὴ καὶ ἡ Βενιαμῖτις χειροτονοῦσιν αὐτὸν βασιλέα, τὸ δὲ ἄλλο πλῆθος ἀπ' ἐκείνης τῆς ἡμέρας τῶν Δαυίδου παίδων ἀποστὰν τὸν Ἱεροβόαμον ἀπέδειξε τῶν πραγμάτων κύριον.
222 Ῥοβόαμος δὲ ὁ Σολομῶνος παῖς ἐκκλησίαν ποιήσας τῶν δύο φυλῶν, ἃς εἶχεν ὑπηκόους, οἷός τε ἦν λαβὼν ὀκτωκαίδεκα παρ' αὐτῶν στρατοῦ μυριάδας ἐπιλέκτους ἐξελθεῖν ἐπὶ τὸν Ἱεροβόαμον καὶ τὸν λαόν, ὅπως πολεμήσας ἀναγκάσῃ δουλεύειν αὐτῷ.
223 κωλυθεὶς δ' ὑπὸ τοῦ θεοῦ διὰ τοῦ προφήτου[3]

[1] ὑπὸ νεότητος om. RO.
[2] Niese: ποιήσειν codd.
[3] + Σαμαία Zonaras Lat.

[a] This is based on 1 Kings xii. 16, "Now see to thine own house, David," LXX νῦν βόσκε (2 Chron. βλέπε) τὸν οἶκόν σου, Δαυείδ. Josephus apparently takes οἶκον in the sense of "temple," a meaning which is common in 1 Kings and elsewhere. The Targum translates "Now rule over the men of thy house, David."

[b] Bibl. Adoram, LXX 1 Kings Ἀδωνιράμ, 2 Chron. Ἀδωράμ; *cf. A.* vii. 293.

[c] Scripture says nothing of any speech made by Adoram: *cf.* 1 Kings xii. 18 (2 Chron. x. 18), "Then King Rehoboam

had built,[a] they threatened to desert him. So bitter did they feel toward him and so great was the anger they nourished that, when he sent Adōramos,[b] who was in charge of the levies, to appease them and soften their mood by persuading them to forgive what he had said if there had been in it anything rash or ill-tempered owing to his youth, they did not let him speak but threw stones at him and killed him.[c] Roboamos, seeing this and imagining himself the target of the stones with which the crowd had killed his minister, was afraid that he might actually suffer this dreadful fate [d] and immediately mounted his chariot and fled to Jerusalem. Although the tribes of Judah and Benjamin elected him king,[e] the rest of the populace from that day revolted from the sons of David and proclaimed Jeroboam head of the state. Then Roboamos, the son of Solomon, held an assembly of the two tribes which remained subject to him, and was prepared to take from their number an army of a hundred and eighty thousand [f] chosen men and march out against Jeroboam and his people in order to force him by war to be his servant; but he was prevented by God through the prophet [g] from

sent Adoram, who was over the tribute; and all Israel stoned him with stones, that he died."

[d] This explanation of Rehoboam's flight is an amplification of Scripture.

[e] Josephus consistently ignores (*cf.* §§ 197, 207) the contradiction in Scripture, 1 Kings xii., between vs. 20 (omitted in 2 Chron.) which says that only the tribe of Judah followed Rehoboam, and vs. 21 in which Judah and Benjamin are both said to be under his rule.

[f] So 2 Chron. and Heb. 1 Kings; LXX 1 Kings 120,000.

[g] Scripture, 1 Kings xii. 22 (2 Chron. xi. 2), gives his name as Shemaiah, LXX Σαμαίας. This name is found in the Lat. translation of Josephus and in Zonaras's excerpt.

ποιήσασθαι τὴν στρατείαν, οὐ γὰρ εἶναι δίκαιον τοὺς ὁμοφύλους πολεμεῖν οὗτος ἔλεγε καὶ ταῦτα κατὰ τὴν τοῦ θεοῦ προαίρεσιν τῆς τοῦ πλήθους
224 ἀποστάσεως γεγενημένης, οὐκέτ' ἐξῆλθε.[1] διηγήσομαι[2] δὲ πρῶτον, ὅσα Ἱεροβόαμος ὁ τῶν Ἰσραηλιτῶν βασιλεὺς ἔπραξεν, εἶτα δὲ τούτων ἐχόμενα τὰ ὑπὸ Ῥοβοάμου τοῦ τῶν δύο φυλῶν βασιλέως γεγενημένα δηλώσομεν· φυλαχθείη γὰρ ἂν οὕτως ἄχρι παντὸς τῆς ἱστορίας τὸ εὔτακτον.

225 (4) Ὁ τοίνυν Ἱεροβόαμος οἰκοδομήσας βασίλειον ἐν Σικίμῃ πόλει ἐν ταύτῃ τὴν δίαιταν εἶχε, κατεσκεύασε δὲ καὶ ἐν Φανουὴλ πόλει λεγομένῃ. μετ' οὐ πολὺ δὲ τῆς σκηνοπηγίας ἑορτῆς ἐνίστασθαι μελλούσης λογισάμενος ὡς ἐὰν ἐπιτρέψῃ τῷ πλήθει προσκυνῆσαι τὸν θεὸν εἰς Ἱεροσόλυμα πορευθέντι καὶ ἐκεῖ τὴν ἑορτὴν διαγαγεῖν, μετανοῆσαν ἴσως καὶ δελεασθὲν ὑπὸ τοῦ ναοῦ καὶ τῆς θρησκείας τῆς ἐν αὐτῷ τοῦ θεοῦ καταλείψει μὲν αὐτόν, προσχωρήσει δὲ τῷ πρώτῳ βασιλεῖ, καὶ κινδυνεύσει τούτου γενομένου τὴν ψυχὴν ἀποβαλεῖν, ἐπιτεχνᾶταί τι
226 τοιοῦτον· δύο ποιήσας δαμάλεις χρυσᾶς καὶ οἰκοδομήσας ναΐσκους τοσούτους ἕνα μὲν ἐν Βηθήλῃ πόλει, τὸν ἕτερον δὲ ἐν Δάνῃ, ἣ δ' ἐστὶ πρὸς ταῖς πηγαῖς τοῦ μικροῦ Ἰορδάνου, τίθησι τὰς δαμάλεις

[1] οὐ κατεξῆλθε M : οὐκ ἐπεξῆλθε Naber.
[2] ante διηγήσομαι lacunam statuit Niese.

[a] Nevertheless we read in 1 Kings xv. 6 "and there was war between Rehoboam and Jeroboam all the days of his life," a discrepancy which Josephus ignores. Some LXX MSS. also omit the latter verse.

[b] Bibl. Shechem, *cf.* *A.* v. 69 note.

[c] So LXX; bibl. Penuel. Scripture says that he "built

undertaking the campaign—for he said that it was not right to make war on one's countrymen, especially as the revolt of the multitude had taken place in accordance with the purpose of God,—and so he did not march out.[a] I shall now relate, first the acts of Jeroboam, the king of Israel, and then in what follows we shall tell what happened in the reign of Roboamos, the king of the two tribes. For in this way an orderly arrangement can be preserved throughout the history.

(4) Jeroboam, then, built a palace in Sikima[b] and made his dwelling there ; he also constructed a palace in a city called Phanūēl.[c] But not long after, when the festival of Tabernacles was about to take place,[d] he reflected that, if he permitted the people to go to Jerusalem to worship God and to celebrate the festival there, they might perhaps repent and be captivated by the temple[e] and the ceremonies performed in it and so desert him and go over to their former king ; and that, if this happened, he would be in danger of losing his life. He therefore devised the following plan. Making two golden heifers[f] and building shrines for both, one in the city of Bethel and the other in Dan—this being near the sources of the Little Jordan,[g]—he

Jeroboam builds a sanctuary at Bethel. 1 Kings xii. 25.

Shechem . . . and built Penuel," which Jewish commentators take to mean "repaired" or "fortified." Josephus avoids the difficulty of referring to the building of already existing sites by inserting the word "palace" in each case.

[d] The festival is not mentioned at this point in Scripture, *cf.* § 230 note.

[e] δελεάζειν, lit. "ensnare," usually has the meaning "seduce"; bibl. "their hearts shall be turned again to their Lord."

[f] Josephus, like the LXX, uses δαμάλεις which is feminine ; Heb. *'eglê* "calves."

[g] Unscriptural detail ; for the site *cf. A.* v. 178 note.

ἐν ἑκατέρῳ τῶν ἐν ταῖς προειρημέναις πόλεσι ναΐσκων, καὶ συγκαλέσας τὰς δέκα φυλὰς ὧν αὐτὸς ἦρχεν ἐδημηγόρησε τούτους ποιησάμενος
227 τοὺς λόγους· "ἄνδρες ὁμόφυλοι, γινώσκειν ὑμᾶς νομίζω τοῦτο, ὅτι πᾶς τόπος ἔχει τὸν θεὸν καὶ οὐκ ἔστιν ἓν ἀποδεδειγμένον χωρίον ἐν ᾧ πάρεστιν, ἀλλὰ πανταχοῦ τε ἀκούει καὶ τοὺς θρησκεύοντας ἐφορᾷ. ὅθεν οὔ μοι δοκεῖ νῦν ἐπείγειν ὑμᾶς εἰς Ἱεροσόλυμα πορευθέντας εἰς τὴν τῶν ἐχθρῶν
228 πόλιν μακρὰν οὕτως ὁδὸν προσκυνεῖν· ἄνθρωπος γὰρ κατεσκεύακε τὸν ναόν, πεποίηκα δὲ κἀγὼ δύο χρυσᾶς δαμάλεις ἐπωνύμους τῷ θεῷ καὶ τὴν μὲν ἐν Βηθήλῃ πόλει καθιέρωσα τὴν δ' ἐν Δάνῃ, ὅπως ὑμῶν οἱ τούτων ἔγγιστα τῶν πόλεων κατῳκημένοι προσκυνῶσιν[1] εἰς αὐτὰς ἀπερχόμενοι τὸν θεόν. ἀποδείξω δέ τινας ὑμῖν καὶ ἱερεῖς ἐξ ὑμῶν αὐτῶν καὶ Ληουίτας, ἵνα μὴ χρείαν ἔχητε τῆς Ληουίτιδος φυλῆς καὶ τῶν υἱῶν Ἀαρῶνος, ἀλλ' ὁ βουλόμενος ὑμῶν ἱερεὺς εἶναι προσενεγκάτω μόσχον τῷ θεῷ καὶ κριόν, ὃ καὶ τὸν πρῶτον ἱερέα
229 φασὶν Ἀαρῶνα πεποιηκέναι." ταῦτ' εἰπὼν ἐξηπάτησε τὸν λαὸν καὶ τῆς πατρίου θρησκείας ἀποστάντας ἐποίησε παραβῆναι τοὺς νόμους. ἀρχὴ κακῶν ἐγένετο τοῦτο τοῖς Ἑβραίοις καὶ τοῦ πολέμῳ κρατηθέντας ὑπὸ τῶν ἀλλοφύλων αἰχμαλωσίᾳ περιπεσεῖν. ἀλλὰ ταῦτα μὲν κατὰ χώραν δηλώσομεν.

[1] προσκυνήσωσιν MSP.

---

[a] Jeroboam's speech down to "worship God" is an

placed the heifers in either of the shrines in the cities mentioned and, having called together the ten tribes over which he ruled, harangued them in the following words [a]: "Fellow-countrymen, I think you know that every place has God in it and that there is no one spot set apart for His presence, but everywhere He hears and watches over His worshippers.[b] Therefore I do not think I should now urge you to go so long a journey to Jerusalem, the city of our enemies, in order to worship. For it was a man that built that temple; and I too have made two golden heifers bearing the name of God and I have consecrated them, one in the city of Bethel and the other in Dan, in order that those of you who live nearest either of these cities may go to them and worship God. I shall appoint for you priests and Levites [c] from your own number, in order that you may have no need of the tribe of Levi and the sons of Aaron, but let him among you who wishes to be a priest offer up to God a calf and a ram, as Aaron, the first priest, is said to have done.[d]" By these words he misled the people and caused them to abandon the worship of their fathers and transgress the laws. This was the beginning of the Hebrews' misfortunes and led to their being defeated in war by other races and to their falling captive. But of these things we shall write in the proper place.[e]

amplification of 1 Kings xii. 28, "It is too much for you to go up to Jerusalem; behold thy gods, O Israel, which brought thee up out of the land of Egypt."

[b] *Cf.* §§ 107 ff.

[c] The Levites are not mentioned in Scripture.

[d] *Cf.* Lev. xvi. 3. In Scripture Jeroboam makes no reference to this priestly ceremony.

[e] *A.* ix. 277 ff.

230 (5) Ἐνστάσης δὲ τῆς ἑορτῆς ἑβδόμῳ μηνὶ βουλόμενος καὶ αὐτὸς ἐν Βηθήλῃ ταύτην ἀγαγεῖν,
ὥσπερ ἑώρταζον καὶ αἱ δύο φυλαὶ ἐν Ἱεροσολύμοις,
οἰκοδομεῖ μὲν θυσιαστήριον πρὸ τῆς δαμάλεως,
γενόμενος δὲ αὐτὸς ἀρχιερεὺς ἐπὶ τὸν βωμὸν ἀνα-
231 βαίνει σὺν τοῖς ἰδίοις ἱερεῦσι. μέλλοντος δ' ἐπιφέρειν τὰς θυσίας καὶ τὰς ὁλοκαυτώσεις ἐν ὄψει
τοῦ λαοῦ παντὸς παραγίνεται πρὸς αὐτὸν ἐξ Ἱεροσολύμων προφήτης Ἰάδων ὄνομα τοῦ θεοῦ πέμψαντος, ὃς σταθεὶς ἐν μέσῳ τῷ πλήθει τοῦ βασιλέως
ἀκούοντος εἶπε τάδε πρὸς τὸ θυσιαστήριον ποιού-
232 μενος τοὺς λόγους· "ὁ θεὸς ἔσεσθαί τινα προλέγει
ἐκ τοῦ Δαυίδου γένους Ἰωσίαν ὄνομα, ὃς ἐπὶ σοῦ
θύσει τοὺς ψευδιερεῖς τοὺς κατ' ἐκεῖνον τὸν καιρὸν γενησομένους καὶ τὰ ὀστᾶ τῶν λαοπλάνων
τούτων καὶ ἀπατεώνων καὶ ἀσεβῶν ἐπὶ σοῦ καύσει.
ἵνα μέντοι γε πιστεύσωσιν οὗτοι τοῦθ' οὕτως ἕξειν,
σημεῖον αὐτοῖς προερῶ γενησόμενον· ῥαγήσεται τὸ
θυσιαστήριον παραχρῆμα καὶ πᾶσα ἡ ἐπ' αὐτοῦ
233 πιμελὴ τῶν ἱερείων ἐπὶ γῆν χυθήσεται." ταῦτ'
εἰπόντος τοῦ προφήτου παροξυνθεὶς ὁ Ἱεροβόαμος
ἐξέτεινε τὴν χεῖρα κελεύων συλλαβεῖν αὐτόν. ἐκ-

---

[a] Scripture dates Jeroboam's festival on the 15th of the eighth month, which would be exactly a month after the traditional celebration of the festival of Tabernacles. Josephus is, perhaps, more logical in making Jeroboam's celebration coincide with that in Jerusalem, but Jewish commentators justify the Biblical text (*cf.* 1 Kings xii. 33, "in the month which he had devised of his own heart") by explaining that Jeroboam wished either deliberately to alter the older custom or to avoid entirely alienating the Judaeans, by giving them an opportunity of visiting his sanctuary after they had observed the festival at Jerusalem in the seventh month.

(5) When the festival came round in the seventh [a] month, Jeroboam, wishing to observe it himself in Bethel just as the two tribes were celebrating it in Jerusalem, built an altar before the heifer and, having made himself high priest,[b] went up to the altar with his own priests. But as he was about to offer the sacrifices and the whole burnt-offerings [c] in the sight of all the people, there came to him from Jerusalem a prophet named Jadōn,[d] whom God had sent, and, standing in the midst of the multitude and in the hearing of the king, addressed the altar in these words: "God has foretold that there shall be one of the line of David, named Josias, who will sacrifice upon you the false priests living in his time and will burn upon you the bones of these misleaders of the people, these impostors and unbelievers. Furthermore, that these people may believe that so it will be, I shall foretell to them a sign that will be given. The altar shall be broken in an instant and all the fat of the victims on it shall be spilled upon the ground." Roused to fury by these words of the prophet, Jeroboam stretched out his hand to order his arrest. But

A prophet rebukes Jeroboam at Bethel. 1 Kings xii. 32.

[b] Scripture says merely that he himself made the offering.

[c] Apparently Josephus takes Heb. *ya'al* as a *hiph'îl* (causative) form meaning "offered the burnt-offering (*'ôlāh*)," while LXX, taking it as a *qal* (intransitive) form meaning "went up," has ἀνέβη. Or possibly the "whole burnt-offerings" in Josephus's text may be an interpretation of Heb. *haqṭîr* (LXX ἐπιθῦσαι; A.V. wrongly "burn incense") which implies the offering of various kinds of sacrifice including the burnt-offering.

[d] The name is not found in 1 Kings, but *cf.* 2 Chron. ix. 29 which mentions "the visions of Iddo (LXX Ἰωήλ) the seer against Jeroboam the son of Nebat"; rabbinic tradition also identifies the unnamed prophet of 1 Kings with Iddo (*Ye'dî, v.l. Ye'dô*).

τεταμένη δ' ἡ χεὶρ εὐθέως παρείθη καὶ οὐκέτ' ἴσχυε ταύτην[1] πρὸς αὑτὸν ἀναγαγεῖν, ἀλλὰ νεναρκηκυῖαν καὶ νεκρὰν εἶχεν ἀπηρτημένην. ἐρράγη δὲ καὶ τὸ θυσιαστήριον καὶ κατηνέχθη πάντα ἀπ' αὐτοῦ,
234 καθὼς προεῖπεν ὁ προφήτης. μαθὼν δὲ ἀληθῆ τὸν ἄνθρωπον καὶ θείαν ἔχοντα πρόγνωσιν παρεκάλεσεν αὐτὸν δεηθῆναι τοῦ θεοῦ ἀναζωπυρῆσαι τὴν δεξιὰν αὐτῷ. καὶ ὁ μὲν ἱκέτευσε τὸν θεὸν τοῦτ' αὐτῷ παρασχεῖν, ὁ δὲ τῆς χειρὸς τὸ κατὰ φύσιν ἀπολαβούσης χαίρων ἐπ' αὐτῇ τὸν προφήτην παρεκάλει δειπνῆσαι
235 παρ' αὐτῷ. Ἰάδων δ' ἔφησεν οὐχ ὑπομένειν εἰσελθεῖν πρὸς αὐτὸν οὐδὲ γεύσασθαι ἄρτου καὶ ὕδατος ἐν ταύτῃ τῇ πόλει· τοῦτο γὰρ αὐτῷ τὸν θεὸν ἀπειρηκέναι καὶ τὴν ὁδὸν ἣν ἦλθεν ὅπως μὴ δι' αὐτῆς ποιήσηται τὴν ἐπιστροφήν, ἀλλὰ δι' ἄλλης ἔφασκεν· τοῦτον μὲν οὖν ἐθαύμαζεν ὁ βασιλεὺς τῆς ἐγκρατείας, αὐτὸς δ' ἦν ἐν φόβῳ, μεταβολὴν αὐτοῦ τῶν πραγμάτων ἐκ τῶν προειρημένων οὐκ ἀγαθὴν ὑπονοῶν.
236 (ix.) Ἦν δέ τις ἐν τῇ πόλει πρεσβύτης πονηρὸς ψευδοπροφήτης, ὃν εἶχεν ἐν τιμῇ Ἱεροβόαμος ἀπατώμενος ὑπ' αὐτοῦ τὰ πρὸς ἡδονὴν λέγοντος. οὗτος τότε μὲν κλινήρης ἦν διὰ τὴν ἀπὸ τοῦ γήρως ἀσθένειαν, τῶν δὲ παίδων αὐτῷ δηλωσάντων τὰ περὶ τοῦ παρόντος ἐξ Ἱεροσολύμων προφήτου καὶ
237 τῶν σημείων τῶν γενομένων, καὶ ὡς παρεθεῖσαν αὐτῷ τὴν δεξιὰν Ἱεροβόαμος εὐξαμένου πάλιν ἐκείνου ζῶσαν ἀπολάβοι, δείσας μὴ παρευδοκιμήσειεν αὐτὸν ὁ ξένος παρὰ τῷ βασιλεῖ καὶ πλείονος

[1] ἴσχυεν αὐτὴν M : ἴσχυσεν αὐτὴν SP.

[a] The last sentence is an addition to Scripture.

[b] Targum and Old Latin version of Scripture also have "false prophet"; Heb. and LXX "a certain old prophet."

no sooner was his hand stretched out than it was paralysed and he no longer had the power to draw it back to himself but found it hanging numb and lifeless. And the altar was broken and everything on it was swept to the ground, as the prophet had foretold. Then, having learnt that the man was telling the truth and possessed divine foreknowledge, he begged him to pray that God bring back life to his right hand. So the prophet entreated God to grant him this prayer, and Jeroboam, overjoyed when his hand regained its natural use, asked the prophet to dine with him. But Jadōn said that he dare not enter his house nor taste bread or water in that city, for God had forbidden this to him as well as to return by the road on which he had come, saying he must go by another. The king admired him for his self-control but was himself in a state of fear, suspecting from what had been foretold to him a change in his fortunes that would not be for his good.[a]

The false prophet of Bethel deceives Jadon. 1 Kings xiii 11.

(ix.) Now there was in that city a wicked old man, a false prophet[b] whom Jeroboam held in honour, being deceived by the things he said to please him. At that time the man was bed-ridden through the infirmity of old age,[c] but his sons told him about the prophet who had come from Jerusalem and the signs that had been given, and how, when Jeroboam's right hand had been paralysed, he had it restored to life through the prophet's prayer. Then the old man, fearing that the stranger might find more favour with the king than himself and enjoy greater honour,[d]

[c] These details about the old prophet's infirmity and Jeroboam's favour are unscriptural.

[d] This explanation of the old prophet's motives is an addition to Scripture.

ἀπολαύοι τιμῆς, προσέταξε τοῖς παισὶν εὐθὺς ἐπι-
στρώσασι τὸν ὄνον ἕτοιμον πρὸς ἔξοδον αὐτῷ παρα-
238 σκευάσαι. τῶν δὲ σπευσάντων ὃ προσετάγησαν
ἐπιβὰς ἐδίωξε τὸν προφήτην καὶ καταλαβὼν ἀνα-
παυόμενον ὑπὸ δένδρῳ δασεῖ[1] καὶ σκιὰν ἔχοντι
δρυὸς εὐμεγέθους ἠσπάσατο πρῶτον, εἶτ' ἐμέμφετο
μὴ παρ' αὐτὸν εἰσελθόντα καὶ ξενίων μεταλαβόντα.
239 τοῦ δὲ φήσαντος κεκωλῦσθαι πρὸς τοῦ θεοῦ γεύσασθαι παρά τινι τῶν ἐν ἐκείνῃ τῇ πόλει, "ἀλλ'
οὐχὶ παρ' ἐμοὶ πάντως," εἶπεν, "ἀπηγόρευκέ σοι
τὸ θεῖον παραθέσθαι τράπεζαν· προφήτης γάρ εἰμι
κἀγὼ καὶ τῆς αὐτῆς σοι κοινωνὸς πρὸς αὐτὸν
θρησκείας, καὶ πάρειμι νῦν ὑπ' αὐτοῦ πεμφθεὶς
240 ὅπως ἀγάγω σε πρὸς ἐμαυτὸν ἑστιασόμενον." ὁ
δὲ ψευσαμένῳ πεισθεὶς ἀνέστρεψεν· ἀριστώντων δ'
ἔτι καὶ φιλοφρονουμένων ὁ θεὸς ἐπιφαίνεται τῷ
Ἰάδωνι καὶ παραβάντα τὰς ἐντολὰς αὐτοῦ τιμωρίαν ὑφέξειν ἔλεγεν καὶ ποδαπὴν ἐδήλου· λέοντα
γὰρ αὐτῷ κατὰ τὴν ὁδὸν ἀπερχομένῳ συμβαλεῖν
ἔφραζεν, ὑφ' οὗ διαφθαρήσεσθαι καὶ τῆς ἐν τοῖς
241 πατρῴοις μνήμασι ταφῆς ἀμοιρήσειν. ταῦτα δ'
ἐγένετο οἶμαι κατὰ τὴν τοῦ θεοῦ βούλησιν, ὅπως
μὴ προσέχοι τοῖς τοῦ Ἰάδωνος λόγοις Ἱεροβόαμος
ἐληλεγμένῳ ψεύδει.[2] πορευομένῳ τοίνυν τῷ Ἰάδωνι
πάλιν εἰς Ἱεροσόλυμα συμβάλλει λέων καὶ κατα-

[1] βαθεῖ MSP Lat.

[2] M: ψευδῆ O: ψευδεῖ rell.: ἐληλεγμένου ψεῦδος ed. pr.: ὡς ἐληλεγμένου ψευδοῦς ex Lat. conj. Niese.

[a] Unscriptural details; bibl. "under a terebinth" (or "oak").

[b] Unscriptural detail.

[c] In Scripture, God does not reveal the manner of his death nor mention the lion.

ordered his sons to saddle his ass at once and make it ready for his departure. So they made haste to do as they were ordered, and he mounted it to ride in pursuit of the prophet; when he came upon him resting under a tree that was thick with leaves and gave as much shade as a huge oak,[a] he first greeted him and then proceeded to blame him for not entering his house and partaking of his hospitality. But the other said that he had been forbidden by God to taste food in the house of anyone in that city, whereupon he replied, "But not in my house, at least, did the Deity forbid you to have food served to you. For I too am a prophet, sharing with you in the same worship of Him, and I am now here having been sent by Him to bring you to my house as my guest." Thereupon the prophet, believing his lies, returned. But, as they were eating the midday[b] meal and conversing in a friendly manner, God appeared to Jadōn and said that he should suffer punishment for transgressing His commands; and He revealed what the punishment would be, saying that as he went on his way a lion would meet him and destroy him[c] and that he should be deprived of burial[d] in the tombs of his fathers. This came about, I think, in accordance with the will of God, in order that Jeroboam might not give heed to the words of Jadōn, who had been convicted of lying.[e] And so, as Jadōn was journeying back to Jerusalem,[f] a lion did meet him and pulled

The prophet Jadon disobeys God and is punished. 1 Kings xiii. 19.

[d] With ταφῆς ἀμοιρήσειν *cf.* the Sophoclean phrase ταφῆς ἄμοιρον, *Ajax* 1326.

[e] This explanation of God's motive in causing the prophet's death is an addition to Scripture.

[f] Scripture does not mention Jerusalem, *cf.* 1 Kings xiii. 24 "and he went away."

σπάσας αὐτὸν ἀπὸ τοῦ κτήνους ἀπέκτεινε, καὶ τὸν μὲν ὄνον οὐδὲν ὅλως ἔβλαψε, παρακαθεζόμενος δ' ἐφύλασσε κἀκεῖνον καὶ τὸ τοῦ προφήτου σῶμα, μέχρις οὗ τινες τῶν ὁδοιπόρων ἰδόντες ἀπήγγειλαν
242 ἐλθόντες εἰς τὴν πόλιν τῷ ψευδοπροφήτῃ. ὁ δὲ τοὺς υἱοὺς πέμψας ἐκόμισε τὸ σῶμα εἰς τὴν πόλιν καὶ πολυτελοῦς κηδείας ἠξίωσεν ἐντειλάμενος τοῖς παισὶ καὶ αὐτὸν ἀποθανόντα σὺν ἐκείνῳ θάψαι, λέγων ἀληθῆ μὲν εἶναι πάνθ' ὅσα προεφήτευσε κατὰ τῆς πόλεως ἐκείνης καὶ τοῦ θυσιαστηρίου καὶ τῶν ἱερέων καὶ τῶν ψευδοπροφητῶν, ὑβρισθήσεσθαι δ' αὐτὸς μετὰ τὴν τελευτὴν οὐδὲν σὺν ἐκείνῳ ταφείς, τῶν ὀστῶν οὐ γνωρισθησομένων.[1]
243 κηδεύσας οὖν τὸν προφήτην καὶ ταῦτα τοῖς υἱοῖς ἐντειλάμενος πονηρὸς ὢν καὶ ἀσεβὴς πρόσεισι τῷ Ἱεροβοάμῳ καὶ "τί δήποτ' ἐταράχθης," εἰπών, "ὑπὸ τῶν τοῦ ἀνοήτου λόγων;" ὡς τὰ περὶ τὸ θυσιαστήριον αὐτῷ καὶ τὴν αὐτοῦ χεῖρα διηγήσαθ' ὁ βασιλεύς, θεῖον ἀληθῶς καὶ προφήτην ἄριστον ἀποκαλῶν, ἤρξατο ταύτην αὐτοῦ τὴν δόξαν ἀναλύειν κακουργῶν[2] καὶ πιθανοῖς περὶ τῶν γεγενημένων χρώμενος λόγοις βλάπτειν αὐτῶν τὴν
244 ἀλήθειαν. ἐπεχείρει γὰρ πείθειν αὐτὸν ὡς ὑπὸ κόπου μὲν ἡ χεὶρ αὐτῷ ναρκήσειε βαστάζουσα τὰς θυσίας, εἶτ' ἀνεθεῖσα πάλιν εἰς τὴν αὐτῆς ἐπανέλθοι φύσιν, τὸ δὲ θυσιαστήριον καινὸν ὂν καὶ δεξάμενον θυσίας πολλὰς καὶ μεγάλας ῥαγείη

[1] R: γνωσθησομένων OMSP.
[2] κακουργῶν om. Lat., secl. Niese.

[a] Bibl. "and the ass stood by it (*i.e.* the corpse) and the lion stood by the corpse."

him off his beast and killed him ; to the ass he did no harm at all but lay down beside him and guarded him as well as the prophet's corpse,[a] until some wayfarers saw them and came to the city to tell the false prophet. Thereupon he sent his sons and brought the body into the city and, having honoured it with a costly funeral,[b] instructed his sons to bury him also, when he was dead, with the prophet, saying that everything was true which he had prophesied against that city and the altar and the priests and the false prophets, but that he himself would suffer no mutilation after death if he were buried together with the prophet, as their bones could not be told apart. And so, after burying the prophet and giving his sons these instructions, being a wicked and impious man he went to Jeroboam and said,[c] " Why, I should like to know, were you disturbed by that foolish fellow's words ? " And, when the king told him what had happened to the altar and his own hand, and spoke of him as a truly divine and excellent prophet, the old man began to weaken this opinion of him with cunning and, by giving a plausible explanation of the things that had happened, to impair their true significance ; for he attempted to persuade him that his hand had been numbed by the fatigue of carrying the sacrifices and then, after being rested, had again returned to its natural condition, and that the altar, being new and having received a great many large victims, had fallen

The false prophet reassures Jeroboam.

[b] The " costly " funeral is an unscriptural detail.

[c] The whole of the following speech (§§ 243-245) is an addition to Scripture, probably put in by Josephus, as Weill suggests, to explain why Jeroboam continued in his evil course, *cf.* 1 Kings xiii. 33 " After this thing Jeroboam turned not from his evil way."

καὶ πέσοι διὰ βάρος τῶν ἐπενηνεγμένων. ἐδήλου δ' αὐτῷ καὶ τὸν θάνατον τοῦ τὰ σημεῖα ταῦτα προειρηκότος ὡς ὑπὸ λέοντος ἀπώλετο· "οὕτως οὐδὲ ἓν οὔτ' εἶχεν οὔτ' ἐφθέγξατο προφήτου."

245 ταῦτ' εἰπὼν πείθει τὸν βασιλέα, καὶ τὴν διάνοιαν αὐτοῦ τελέως ἀποστρέψας ἀπὸ τοῦ θεοῦ καὶ τῶν ὁσίων ἔργων καὶ δικαίων ἐπὶ τὰς ἀσεβεῖς πράξεις παρώρμησεν. οὕτως δ' ἐξύβρισεν εἰς τὸ θεῖον καὶ παρηνόμησεν ὡς οὐδὲν ἄλλο καθ' ἡμέραν ζητεῖν ἢ τί καινὸν καὶ μιαρώτερον τῶν ἤδη τετολμημένων ἐργάσηται. καὶ τὰ μὲν περὶ Ἱεροβόαμον ἐπὶ τοῦ παρόντος ἐν τούτοις ἡμῖν δεδηλώσθω.

246 (x. 1) Ὁ δὲ Σολομῶνος υἱὸς Ῥοβόαμος ὁ τῶν δύο φυλῶν βασιλεύς, ὡς προειρήκαμεν, ᾠκοδόμησε πόλεις ὀχυράς τε καὶ μεγάλας Βηθλεὲμ καὶ Ἠταμὲ καὶ Θεκωὲ καὶ Βηθσοὺρ καὶ Σωχὼ καὶ Ὀδολλὰμ καὶ Εἰπὰν καὶ Μάρισαν[1] καὶ τὴν Ζιφὰ καὶ Ἀδωραὶμ καὶ Λάχεις καὶ Ἀζηκὰ[2] καὶ

[1] Niese: Μάρησαν RO(M)SP[1]: Μάρισσαν P[2]: Marisam Lat.
[2] Hudson: Ζηκὰ codd.

[a] Josephus here departs from the order of events found in Scripture, which continues, xiv. 1 ff., with the story of Jeroboam, and does not mention Rehoboam until vs. 21. The account given in §§ 246 ff. follows 2 Chron.

[b] Some LXX MSS. have Βαιθσεέμ = Beth-shemesh.

[c] Bibl. Etam, LXX Αἰτάμ (*v.l.* Ἀπάν, *cf.* note *h* below); *cf.* § 186 note.

[d] So LXX; bibl. Tekoa.

[e] Bibl. Beth-zur (*Bêth-Ṣûr*), LXX Βαιθσουρά; formerly thought to be the modern *Burj eṣ-Ṣur*, it has recently been identified by Père Abel and Albright with *Khirbet eṭ-Ṭubeiqah*, *c.* 7 miles N. by W. of Hebron.

[f] Bibl. Soco (A.V. Shoco), LXX Σοκχώθ (*v.l.* Σοκχώ); *cf.* *A.* vi. 170 note.

[g] Bibl. Adullam; *cf.* *A.* vi. 247 note.

[h] Bibl. Gath, LXX Γέθ. Eipan in Josephus's text seems to be a corrupt form of a doublet of Etam mentioned above (*cf.*

down from the weight of the things laid upon it. He then told him of the death of the man who had given these prophetic signs and how he had lost his life when attacked by a lion. Thus, he said, there was nothing of a prophet either in his person or in what he had spoken. By these words he convinced the king, and, having wholly turned his thoughts away from God and from holy and righteous deeds, he urged him on to impious acts. And so greatly did he outrage the Deity and transgress His laws that every day he sought to commit some new act more heinous than the reckless acts he was already guilty of. So much concerning Jeroboam it may suffice us, for the present, to have written.

(x. 1) [a] Now Solomon's son Roboamos, who was, as we have said before, king of the two tribes, built the strong and large cities of Bethlehem,[b] Ētame,[c] Thekōe,[d] Bethsur,[e] Sōchō,[f] Odollam,[g] Eipan,[h] Marisa,[i] Zipha,[j] Adoraim,[k] Lacheis,[l] Azēka,[m] Saram,[n] Ēlōm,[o] and

Rehoboam fortifies his kingdom. 2 Chron. xi. 5.

LXX *v.l.* Ἀπάν). Weill rightly remarks that it is strange to find a Philistine city among the cities fortified by Rehoboam.

[i] Bibl. Mareshah, LXX Μαρεισά; it is identified by Albright with the modern *Tell Sandaḥanna*, *c.* a mile S. of *Beit Jibrîn* (Eleutheropolis), in the low hill country near the Philistine border.

[j] Bibl. Ziph, LXX Ζείφ; *cf. A.* vi. 275 note.

[k] The modern *Dûra*, 6 miles W.S.W. of Hebron.

[l] Bibl. Lachish, usually identified with the modern *Tell el-Ḥesy*, 18 miles from the sea in the latitude of Hebron, but now thought to be *Tell ed-Duweir*, several miles further east.

[m] Usually identified with the modern *Tell Zakarîyeh*, *c.* 15 miles due W. of Bethlehem (on the map); *cf. A.* vi. 170 note.

[n] Bibl. Zorah (*Ṣor'āh*), LXX Σαραά, the modern *Ṣarah*, 15 miles due W. of Jerusalem on the map.

[o] Bibl. Aijalon (*'Ayyālôn*), LXX Αἰαλών (*v.l.* Ἀλδών), the modern *Yalō*, 15 miles N.W. of Jerusalem.

247 Σαρὰμ καὶ Ἠλὼμ καὶ Χεβρῶνα. ταύτας μὲν ἐν
τῇ Ἰουδαίᾳ φυλῇ καὶ κληρουχίᾳ[1] πρώτας ᾠκοδόμησε, κατεσκεύασε δὲ καὶ ἄλλας μεγάλας ἐν τῇ
Βενιαμίτιδι κληρουχίᾳ, καὶ τειχίσας φρουράς τε
κατέστησεν ἐν ἁπάσαις καὶ ἡγεμόνας, σῖτόν τε
πολὺν καὶ οἶνον καὶ ἔλαιον τά τε ἄλλα τὰ πρὸς[2]
διατροφὴν ἐν ἑκάστῃ τῶν πόλεων δαψιλῶς ἀπέθετο,
πρὸς δὲ τούτοις θυρεοὺς καὶ σιρομάστας εἰς πολλὰς
248 μυριάδας. συνῆλθον δὲ οἱ παρὰ πᾶσι τοῖς Ἰσραηλίταις ἱερεῖς πρὸς αὐτὸν εἰς Ἱεροσόλυμα καὶ
Ληουῖται καὶ εἴ τινες ἄλλοι τοῦ πλήθους ἦσαν
ἀγαθοὶ καὶ δίκαιοι, καταλιπόντες αὐτῶν τὰς
πόλεις, ἵνα θρησκεύσωσιν ἐν Ἱεροσολύμοις τὸν
θεόν· οὐ γὰρ ἡδέως εἶχον προσκυνεῖν ἀναγκαζό-
μενοι τὰς δαμάλεις ἃς Ἱεροβόαμος κατεσκεύασε·
καὶ ηὔξησαν τὴν Ῥοβοάμου βασιλείαν ἐπ' ἔτη
249 τρία. γήμας δὲ συγγενῆ τινα καὶ τρεῖς ποιησάμενος ἐξ αὐτῆς παῖδας ἤγετο ὕστερον καὶ τὴν ἐκ
τῆς Ἀψαλώμου θυγατρὸς Θαμάρης Μαχάνην
ὄνομα καὶ αὐτὴν οὖσαν συγγενῆ· καὶ παῖς ἐξ
αὐτῆς ἄρρην αὐτῷ γίνεται, ὃν Ἀβίαν προσηγόρευσεν. τέκνα δὲ εἶχεν[3] καὶ ἐξ ἄλλων γυναικῶν
πλειόνων, ἁπασῶν δὲ μᾶλλον ἔστερξε τὴν Μαχάνην.
250 εἶχε δὲ τὰς μὲν νόμῳ συνοικούσας αὐτῷ γυναῖκας
ὀκτωκαίδεκα παλλακὰς δὲ τριάκοντα, καὶ υἱοὶ μὲν
αὐτῷ γεγόνεισαν ὀκτὼ καὶ εἴκοσι θυγατέρες δ'
ἑξήκοντα. διάδοχον δὲ ἀπέδειξε τῆς βασιλείας τὸν

[1] Ἰουδαίᾳ . . . κληρουχίᾳ RO: Ἰούδα κληρουχίᾳ rell. Lat.: καὶ κληρουχίᾳ secl. Niese.
[2] τὰ πρὸς Niese: πρὸς codd.
[3] τέκνα δὲ εἶχεν ed. pr.: τέκνα δὲ codd.: τεκνοῖ δὲ Niese.

[a] Bibl. "very many."

Hebron. These, which were in the tribe and territory of Judah, he built first; and he also constructed other large cities in the territory of Benjamin, and, having walled them about, set garrisons and captains in all of them and in each of the cities stored much grain, wine and oil and an abundance of other things needed for sustenance, and, in addition to these, shields and barbed lances amounting to many tens of thousands.[a] Then there came to him at Jerusalem priests from among all the Israelites, and Levites and any others of the people who were good and righteous men and had left their own cities to worship God in Jerusalem, for they would not submit to being forced to worship the heifers which Jeroboam had made. And they added strength to Jeroboam's kingdom for three years. Now he had married a kinswoman,[b] by whom he had three children, and later took another wife named Machanē,[c] whose mother was Absalom's daughter Thamarē[d] and who was also related to him. By her he had a son, whom he named Abias.[e] He also had children by many other wives, but he loved Machanē best of all. He had eighteen lawful wives and thirty[f] concubines, and there were born to him twenty-eight sons and sixty daughters. As his successor to the kingdom he appointed Abias, his son

Rehoboam's wives. 2 Chron. xi. 18.

[b] Named Mahalath, 2 Chron. xi. 18; her father was a son of David.

[c] Bibl. Maachah, LXX Μααχά.

[d] *Cf. A.* vii. 190 note, 243 note.

[e] Bibl. Abijah (*'Abîyāh*), LXX 'Αβιά.

[f] So cod. B LXX; Heb. and most LXX MSS. have 60.

ἐκ τῆς Μαχάνης Ἀβίαν καὶ τοὺς θησαυροὺς αὐτῷ καὶ τὰς ὀχυρωτάτας πόλεις ἐπίστευσεν.

251 (2) Αἴτιον δ' οἶμαι πολλάκις γίνεται κακῶν καὶ παρανομίας τοῖς ἀνθρώποις τὸ τῶν πραγμάτων μέγεθος καὶ ἡ πρὸς τὸ βέλτιον αὐτῶν τροπή[1]· τὴν γὰρ βασιλείαν αὐξανομένην οὕτω βλέπων Ῥοβόαμος εἰς ἀδίκους καὶ ἀσεβεῖς ἐξετράπη πράξεις, καὶ τῆς τοῦ θεοῦ θρησκείας κατεφρόνησεν, ὡς καὶ τὸν ὑπ' αὐτῷ λαὸν μιμητὴν γενέσθαι τῶν ἀνομημάτων.
252 συνδιαφθείρεται γὰρ τὰ τῶν ἀρχομένων ἤθη τοῖς τῶν ἡγεμόνων τρόποις, καὶ ὡς ἔλεγχον τῆς ἐκείνων ἀσελγείας τὴν αὐτῶν σωφροσύνην παραπέμποντες ὡς ἀρετῇ ταῖς κακίαις αὐτῶν ἕπονται· οὐ γὰρ ἔνεστιν ἀποδέχεσθαι δοκεῖν τὰ τῶν βασιλέων ἔργα
253 μὴ ταὐτὰ πράττοντας. τοῦτο τοίνυν συνέβαινε καὶ τοῖς ὑπὸ Ῥοβοάμῳ τεταγμένοις ἀσεβοῦντος αὐτοῦ καὶ παρανομοῦντος σπουδάζειν μὴ προσκρούσωσι τῷ βασιλεῖ θέλοντες εἶναι δίκαιοι. τιμωρὸν δὲ τῶν εἰς αὐτὸν ὕβρεων ὁ θεὸς ἐπιπέμπει τὸν Αἰγυπτίων βασιλέα Ἴσωκον,[2] περὶ οὗ πλανηθεὶς Ἡρόδοτος τὰς πράξεις αὐτοῦ Σεσώστρει
254 προσάπτει. οὗτος γὰρ ὁ Ἴσωκος πέμπτῳ ἔτει τῆς Ῥοβοάμου βασιλείας ἐπιστρατεύεται μετὰ πολλῶν αὐτῷ μυριάδων· ἅρματα μὲν γὰρ αὐτῷ χίλια καὶ διακόσια τὸν ἀριθμὸν ἠκολούθει, ἱππέων δὲ μυριάδες ἕξ, πεζῶν δὲ μυριάδες τεσσαράκοντα. τούτων τοὺς πλείστους Λίβυας ἐπήγετο καὶ

[1] ῥοπή conj. Niese.
[2] Σούσακον MSPE: Sisoch Lat.

[a] According to Scripture, Rehoboam placed his other sons in charge of the fortified cities.

by Machanē, and entrusted to him his treasures and his strongest cities.[a]

(2) But often, I think, a cause of men's falling into evil ways and lawlessness lies in the greatness of their affairs and in the improvement of their position. So, for example, Roboamos, seeing how greatly his kingdom had increased in strength, was misled into unjust and impious acts and showed disrespect for the worship of God, so that even the people under his rule began to imitate his unlawful deeds. For the morals of subjects are corrupted simultaneously with the characters of their rulers, and they do not allow their own moderation to remain a reproach to their rulers' intemperance but follow their evil ways as if they were virtues, since it is impossible to show approval of the acts of kings except by doing as they do.[b] This, then, was the case with the people governed by Roboamos, who, when he acted impiously and in violation of the laws, were careful not to give offence to the king by wishing to be righteous. But, as an avenger of the outrage to Him, God sent the Egyptian king Isōkos,[c] about whom Herodotus was in error in attributing his acts to Sesōstris.[d] For it was this Isōkos who in the fifth year of Roboamos's reign marched against him with many tens of thousands, and there followed him one thousand two hundred chariots, sixty thousand horsemen and four hundred thousand foot-soldiers.[e] Most of these men whom he brought were Libyans and

Rehoboam's degeneracy. 2 Chron. xii. 1; 1 Kings xiv. 22.

Shishak (Isokos) invades Palestine. 2 Chron. xii. 2; 1 Kings xiv. 25.

[b] These reflections are, of course, an amplification of Scripture.

[c] Bibl. Shishak; *cf.* § 210 note.

[d] *Cf.* § 260 note.

[e] The number of foot-soldiers is not given in Scripture, which says merely "people without number."

255 Αἰθίοπας. ἐμβαλὼν οὖν εἰς τὴν χώραν τῶν
Ἑβραίων καταλαμβάνεται[1] τὰς ὀχυρωτάτας τῆς
Ῥοβοάμου βασιλείας πόλεις ἀμαχητὶ καὶ ταύτας
ἀσφαλισάμενος ἔσχατον ἐπῆλθε τοῖς Ἱεροσολύμοις.
(3) Ἐγκεκλεισμένου τοῦ Ῥοβοάμου καὶ τοῦ
πλήθους ἐν αὐτοῖς διὰ τὴν Ἰσώκου στρατείαν καὶ
τὸν θεὸν ἱκετευόντων δοῦναι νίκην καὶ σωτηρίαν,
256 οὐκ[2] ἔπεισαν τὸν θεὸν ταχθῆναι μετ' αὐτῶν· ὁ δὲ
προφήτης Σαμαίας ἔφησεν αὐτοῖς τὸν θεὸν ἀπειλεῖν
ἐγκαταλείψειν αὐτούς, ὡς καὶ αὐτοὶ τὴν θρησκείαν
αὐτοῦ κατέλιπον. ταῦτ' ἀκούσαντες εὐθὺς ταῖς
ψυχαῖς ἀνέπεσον καὶ μηδὲν ἔτι σωτήριον ὁρῶντες
ἐξομολογεῖσθαι πάντες ὥρμησαν ὅτι δικαίως αὐτοὺς
ὁ θεὸς ὑπερόψεται γενομένους περὶ αὐτὸν ἀσεβεῖς
257 καὶ συγχέοντας τὰ νόμιμα. κατιδὼν δ' αὐτοὺς
ὁ θεὸς οὕτω διακειμένους καὶ τὰς ἁμαρτίας ἀνθ-
ομολογουμένους οὐκ ἀπολέσειν αὐτοὺς εἶπε πρὸς
τὸν προφήτην, ποιήσειν μέντοι γε τοῖς Αἰγυπτίοις
ὑποχειρίους, ἵνα μάθωσι πότερον ἀνθρώπῳ δου-
258 λεύειν ἐστὶν ἀπονώτερον ἢ θεῷ. παραλαβὼν δὲ
Ἴσωκος ἀμαχητὶ τὴν πόλιν, δεξαμένου Ῥοβοάμου
διὰ τὸν φόβον, οὐκ ἐνέμεινε ταῖς γενομέναις συνθήκαις, ἀλλ' ἐσύλησε τὸ ἱερὸν καὶ τοὺς θησαυροὺς
ἐξεκένωσε τοῦ θεοῦ καὶ τοὺς βασιλικούς, χρυσοῦ
καὶ ἀργύρου μυριάδας ἀναριθμήτους βαστάσας
259 καὶ μηδὲν ὅλως ὑπολιπών. περιεῖλε δὲ καὶ τοὺς
χρυσοῦς θυρεοὺς καὶ τὰς ἀσπίδας, ἃς κατεσκεύασε

[1] καταλαμβάνει τε RO. [2] ἀλλ' οὐκ ROM.

[a] Scripture adds the Sukkiim, LXX Τρωγλοδύται. Margoliouth in Hastings' *Dictionary of the Bible*, iv. 627, suggests that the LXX rendering "Troglodytes" was due to the fact that a place called Sūchē was one of the cities in the country

Ethiopians.[a] So then, after invading the country of the Hebrews, he seized the strongest cities of Roboamos's kingdom without a battle and, having secured them with garrisons, at last advanced upon Jerusalem.

(3) Although Roboamos and the multitude, who were shut up in the city by the advance of Isōkos's army, entreated God to grant them victory and deliverance,[b] they did not prevail upon God to side with them. Then the prophet Samaias[c] told them that God threatened to abandon them just as they had abandoned their worship of Him. When they heard this, their spirits at once fell and, no longer seeing any hope of deliverance, they all hastened to acknowledge that God might justly turn away from them since they had acted impiously toward Him and had violated His ordinances. But when God saw them in this state of mind and confessing their sins, He said to the prophet that He would not destroy them but would, nevertheless, make them subject to the Egyptians, in order that they might learn which was the easier task, whether to serve man or God. And when Isōkos took the city without a battle, Roboamos admitting him because he feared him, he did not abide by the terms of the agreement they had made,[d] but sacked the temple, emptied the treasuries of God and the king, and carried off untold amounts of gold and silver, leaving not a single thing behind. He also removed the golden shields and bucklers,

Shishak sacks Jerusalem. 2 Chron. xii. 5.

of the Troglodytes, and cites Pliny, *Hist. Nat.* vi. 172 and Strabo xvi. 3. 8.

[b] Amplification of Scripture, which says merely "Rehoboam and the princes of Judah . . . were gathered together in Jerusalem because of Shishak."

[c] So most LXX MSS. (cod. B Σαμμαίας); bibl. Shemaiah.

[d] No agreement is mentioned in Scripture.

Σολομὼν ὁ βασιλεύς, οὐκ εἴασε δὲ οὐδὲ τὰς χρυσᾶς φαρέτρας, ἃς ἀνέθηκε Δαυίδης τῷ θεῷ λαβὼν παρὰ τοῦ τῆς Σωφηνῆς βασιλέως, καὶ τοῦτο ποιήσας
260 ἀνέστρεψεν εἰς τὰ οἰκεῖα. μέμνηται δὲ ταύτης τῆς στρατείας καὶ ὁ Ἁλικαρνασεὺς Ἡρόδοτος περὶ μόνον τὸ τοῦ βασιλέως πλανηθεὶς ὄνομα, καὶ ὅτι ἄλλοις τε πολλοῖς ἐπῆλθεν ἔθνεσι καὶ τὴν Παλαιστίνην Συρίαν ἐδουλώσατο λαβὼν ἀμαχητὶ
261 τοὺς ἀνθρώπους τοὺς ἐν αὐτῇ. φανερὸν δ' ἐστὶν ὅτι τὸ ἡμέτερον ἔθνος βούλεται δηλοῦν κεχειρωμένον ὑπὸ τοῦ Αἰγυπτίου· ἐπάγει γὰρ ὅτι στήλας κατέλιπεν ἐν τῇ τῶν ἀμαχητὶ παραδόντων ἑαυτοὺς αἰδοῖα γυναικῶν ἐγγράψας· Ῥοβόαμος δ' αὐτῷ παρέδωκεν ὁ ἡμέτερος βασιλεὺς ἀμαχητὶ
262 τὴν πόλιν. φησὶ δὲ καὶ Αἰθίοπας παρ' Αἰγυπτίων μεμαθηκέναι τὴν τῶν αἰδοίων περιτομήν· "Φοίνικες γὰρ καὶ Σύροι οἱ ἐν τῇ Παλαιστίνῃ ὁμολογοῦσι παρ' Αἰγυπτίων μεμαθηκέναι." δῆλον οὖν ἐστιν ὅτι μηδένες ἄλλοι περιτέμνονται τῶν ἐν τῇ Παλαιστίνῃ Σύρων ἢ μόνοι ἡμεῖς. ἀλλὰ περὶ μὲν τούτων ἕκαστοι λεγέτωσαν ὅ τι ἂν αὐτοῖς δοκῇ.

263 (4) Ἀναχωρήσαντος δὲ Ἰσώκου Ῥοβόαμος ὁ βασιλεὺς ἀντὶ μὲν τῶν χρυσέων θυρεῶν καὶ τῶν ἀσπίδων χάλκεα ποιήσας τὸν αὐτὸν ἀριθμὸν παρέδωκε τοῖς τῶν βασιλείων φύλαξιν. ἀντὶ δὲ τοῦ μετὰ στρατηγίας ἐπιφανοῦς καὶ τῆς ἐν τοῖς πράγμασι λαμπρότητος διάγειν ἐβασίλευσεν ἐν ἡσυχίᾳ πολλῇ καὶ δέει πάντα τὸν χρόνον ἐχθρὸς ὢν Ἱερο-

[a] This detail is based on the LXX addition to 1 Kings xiv. 26; this, however, has δόρατα "spears" instead of φαρέτρας "quivers." *Cf. A.* vii. 104 note.

which King Solomon had made, nor did he overlook the golden quivers which David had set up as an offering to God after taking them from the King of Sophēnē.[a] This done, he returned to his own country. This expedition is also mentioned by Herodotus of Halicarnassus, who was in error only about the king's name and in saying that he marched against many other nations and reduced Palestinian Syria to slavery after capturing the inhabitants without a battle.[b] Now it is evident that it is our nation which he means to refer to as subdued by the Egyptians, for he adds that their king left behind, in the country of those who had surrendered without a battle, pillars on which he had female sex-organs engraved.[c] But it was Roboamos, our king, who surrendered the city without a battle. Herodotus also says that the Ethiopians had learned the practice of circumcision from the Egyptians, " for the Phoenicians and the Syrians in Palestine admit that they learned it from the Egyptians." Now it is clear that no others of the Syrians in Palestine practise circumcision beside ourselves. But concerning these matters everyone may speak as he sees fit.

(4) Now when Isōkos had withdrawn, King Roboamos, in place of the golden shields and bucklers, made an equal number of bronze and delivered them to the guards of the palace. And instead of leading the life of an illustrious commander and a brilliant statesman, he reigned in great quiet and fear, being all his days an enemy of Jeroboam. He

The end of Rehoboam. 2 Chron. xii. 10; 1 Kings xiv. 27.

[b] Herod. ii. 102 ff. The latter part of the citation from Herodotus appears also in *Ap*. i. 168.

[c] Indicating, according to Herod., that his enemies were as weak as women.

264 βοάμῳ. ἐτελεύτησε δὲ βιώσας ἔτη πεντήκοντα καὶ ἑπτά, βασιλεύσας δ' αὐτῶν ἑπτακαίδεκα, τὸν τρόπον ἀλαζὼν ἀνὴρ καὶ ἀνόητος καὶ διὰ τὸ μὴ προσέχειν τοῖς πατρῴοις φίλοις τὴν ἀρχὴν ἀπολέσας· ἐτάφη δ' ἐν Ἱεροσολύμοις ἐν ταῖς θήκαις τῶν βασιλέων. διεδέξατο δ' αὐτοῦ τὴν βασιλείαν ὁ υἱὸς Ἀβίας, ὄγδοον ἤδη καὶ δέκατον ἔτος Ἱερο-
265 βοάμου τῶν δέκα φυλῶν βασιλεύοντος. καὶ ταῦτα μὲν τοιοῦτον ἔσχε τὸ τέλος· τὰ δὲ περὶ Ἱεροβόαμον ἀκόλουθα τούτων ἔχομεν πῶς κατέστρεψε τὸν βίον διεξελθεῖν· οὗτος γὰρ οὐ διέλιπεν οὐδ' ἠρέμησεν εἰς τὸν θεὸν ἐξυβρίζων, ἀλλὰ καθ' ἑκάστην ἡμέραν ἐπὶ τῶν ὑψηλῶν ὀρῶν βωμοὺς ἀνιστὰς καὶ ἱερεῖς ἐκ τοῦ πλήθους ἀποδεικνὺς διετέλει.

266 (xi. 1) Ταῦτα δ' ἔμελλεν οὐκ εἰς μακρὰν τἀσεβήματα καὶ τὴν ὑπὲρ αὐτῶν δίκην εἰς τὴν αὐτοῦ κεφαλὴν καὶ πάσης αὐτοῦ τῆς γενεᾶς τρέψειν τὸ θεῖον. κάμνοντος δ' αὐτῷ κατ' ἐκεῖνον τὸν καιρὸν τοῦ παιδός, ὃν Ὀβίμην ἐκάλουν, τὴν γυναῖκα αὐτοῦ προσέταξε τὴν στολὴν ἀποθεμένην καὶ σχῆμα λαβοῦσαν ἰδιωτικὸν πορευθῆναι πρὸς Ἀχίαν
267 τὸν προφήτην· εἶναι γὰρ θαυμαστὸν ἄνδρα περὶ τῶν μελλόντων προειπεῖν· καὶ γὰρ περὶ τῆς βασιλείας αὐτῷ τοῦτον δεδηλωκέναι· παραγενομένην δ' ἐκέλευσε περὶ τοῦ παιδὸς ἀνακρίνειν ὡς ξένην, εἰ διαφεύξεται τὴν νόσον. ἡ δὲ μετασχηματισαμένη, καθὼς αὐτῇ προσέταξεν ὁ ἀνήρ, ἧκεν εἰς
268 Σιλὼ πόλιν· ἐκεῖ γὰρ διέτριβεν ὁ Ἀχίας. καὶ μελλούσης εἰς τὴν οἰκίαν αὐτοῦ εἰσιέναι τὰς ὄψεις ἠμαυρωμένου διὰ τὸ γῆρας, ἐπιφανεὶς ὁ θεὸς ἀμφό-

[a] According to Scripture, he began to reign at the age of

died at the age of fifty-seven, after a reign of seventeen years [a]; he was a man of boastful and foolish nature, who, by not heeding his father's friends, lost his royal power. He was buried in Jerusalem in the tombs of the kings and was succeeded on the throne by his son Abias in the eighteenth year of Jeroboam's reign over the ten tribes. This, then, is the end of Roboamos's history. But now in what follows we have to relate the events of Jeroboam's reign and how he ended his life. For he did not cease nor desist from outraging God, but all the time continued to erect altars on the high mountains and to appoint priests from among the common people.

Jeroboam sends his wife to consult the prophet Ahijah about their son's illness. 1 Kings xiv. 1.

(xi. 1) These impieties, however, and the punishment attendant on them, the Deity was at no far distant time to visit upon both his own head and the heads of all his line. For when, at that time, his son, whom they called Obimē,[b] was ill, he ordered his wife to remove her robe and put on the dress of a simple woman and go to the prophet Achias,[c] who was, he said, a man with a wonderful power of foretelling the future and who had indeed revealed to him that he would be king. He bade her go and inquire, as if she were a stranger, whether the child would survive his illness. So she changed her dress, as her husband had ordered her,[d] and came to the city of Silō, where Achias was living. And as she was about to enter the house of the prophet, whose eyes were dim from age, God appeared to him and

forty-one; thus he would have been fifty-eight years old at his death.

[b] Bibl. Abijah (*'Abîyāh*), LXX 'Αβιά.

[c] Bibl. Ahijah; *cf.* § 206 note.

[d] Josephus omits the Scriptural details of the gifts she brought the prophet.

τερα αὐτῷ μηνύει τήν τε Ἱεροβοάμου γυναῖκα πρὸς αὐτὸν ἀφιγμένην καὶ τί δεῖ περὶ ὧν πάρεστιν
269 ἀποκρίνασθαι. παριούσης δὲ τῆς γυναικὸς εἰς τὴν οἰκίαν ὡς ἰδιώτιδος καὶ ξένης ἀνεβόησεν "εἴσελθε, ὦ γύναι Ἱεροβοάμου· τί κρύπτεις σαυτήν; τὸν γὰρ θεὸν οὐ λανθάνεις, ὃς ἀφιξομένην τέ μοι φανεὶς ἐδήλωσε καὶ προσέταξε τίνας ποιήσομαι τοὺς λόγους. ἀπελθοῦσα οὖν πρὸς τὸν ἄνδρα φράζε
270 αὐτὸν[1] ταῦτα λέγειν· 'ἐπεί σε μέγαν ἐκ μικροῦ καὶ μηδενὸς ὄντος ἐποίησα καὶ ἀποσχίσας τὴν βασιλείαν ἀπὸ τοῦ Δαυίδου γένους σοὶ ταύτην ἔδωκα, σὺ δὲ τούτων ἠμνημόνησας καὶ τὴν ἐμὴν θρησκείαν καταλιπὼν χωνευτοὺς θεοὺς κατασκευάσας ἐκείνους ἐτίμας,[2] οὕτω σε πάλιν καθαιρήσω καὶ πᾶν ἐξολέσω σου τὸ γένος καὶ κυσὶ καὶ ὄρνισι
271 βορὰν ποιήσω γενέσθαι. βασιλεὺς γὰρ ἐξεγείρεταί τις ὑπ' ἐμοῦ τοῦ λαοῦ παντός, ὃς οὐδένα ὑπολείψει τοῦ Ἱεροβοάμου γένους· μεθέξει[3] δὲ τῆς τιμωρίας καὶ τὸ πλῆθος ἐκπεσὸν τῆς ἀγαθῆς γῆς καὶ διασπαρὲν εἰς τοὺς πέραν Εὐφράτου τόπους, ὅτι τοῖς τοῦ βασιλέως ἀσεβήμασι κατηκολούθησε καὶ τοὺς ὑπ' αὐτοῦ γενομένους προσκυνεῖ θεοὺς τὴν ἐμὴν
272 θυσίαν ἐγκαταλιπόν.' σὺ δέ, ὦ γύναι, ταῦτ' ἀπαγγελλοῦσα[4] σπεῦδε πρὸς τὸν ἄνδρα. τὸν δὲ υἱὸν καταλήψῃ τεθνηκότα· σοῦ γὰρ εἰσιούσης εἰς τὴν πόλιν ἀπολείψει τὸ ζῆν αὐτόν. ταφήσεται δὲ κλαυσθεὶς ὑπὸ τοῦ πλήθους παντὸς κοινῷ τιμηθεὶς πένθει· καὶ γὰρ μόνος τῶν ἐκ τοῦ Ἱεροβοάμου

[1] ex Lat. conj. Niese: αὐτῷ codd.
[2] M Exc.: τιμήσας RO: ἐτίμησας SPE: τιμᾷς Suidas.
[3] E Lat.: μεθέξειν codd. Exc.
[4] Niese: ἀπαγγέλλουσα ROSP: παραγγέλλουσα M Exc.

told him both that Jeroboam's wife had come to him and how he was to answer what she had come there to ask. So, when the woman entered the house in the guise of a commoner and a stranger, he cried out, "Come in, wife of Jeroboam! Why do you disguise yourself? For your coming here is not unknown to God, who has appeared to me and revealed your coming, and has instructed me in the things I am to say. Return, therefore, to your husband and tell him that God has spoken as follows. 'Just as I made you great when you were a little man, indeed were nothing, and took the kingdom away from David's line to give it to you—of which things you have been unmindful and have given up worshipping me, to make gods of molten metal, and have honoured them,—so too I will again put you down and will utterly destroy all your line and will make them the prey of dogs and birds. For a certain one will be set up by me as king over all this people, and not one of Jeroboam's line will he leave alive. The people too shall share this punishment by being driven from their good land and scattered over the country beyond the Euphrates,[a] because they have followed the impious ways of the king and worship the gods made by him, abandoning their sacrifices to me.' And you, woman, hasten to your husband and tell him these things. But your son you will find dead, for, as you enter the city, his life will leave him. And, when he is buried, he shall be wept for by all the people and honoured with general mourning, for of all of Jeroboam's line

Ahijah foretells the doom of Jeroboam's line. 1 Kings xiv. 7.

[a] Bibl. "the river." Josephus, like the Targum, takes this to mean, as it frequently does in Scripture, the Euphrates river.

273 γένους ἀγαθὸς οὗτος ἦν." ταῦτ' αὐτοῦ προφητεύσαντος ἐκπηδήσασα ἡ γυνὴ τεταραγμένη καὶ τῷ τοῦ προειρημένου παιδὸς θανάτῳ περιαλγής, θρηνοῦσα διὰ τῆς ὁδοῦ καὶ τὴν μέλλουσαν τοῦ τέκνου κοπτομένη τελευτὴν ἀθλία τοῦ πάθους ἠπείγετο κακοῖς ἀμηχάνοις καὶ σπουδῇ μὲν ἀτυχεῖ χρωμένη διὰ τὸν υἱὸν αὐτῆς (ἔμελλε γὰρ αὐτὸν ἐπειχθεῖσα θᾶττον ὄψεσθαι νεκρόν), ἀναγκαίᾳ δὲ διὰ τὸν ἄνδρα. καὶ παραγενομένη τὸν μὲν ἐκπεπνευκότα καθὼς εἶπεν ὁ προφήτης εὗρε, τῷ δὲ βασιλεῖ πάντα ἀπήγγειλεν.

274 (2) Ἱεροβόαμος δ' οὐδενὸς τούτων φροντίσας πολλὴν ἀθροίσας στρατιὰν ἐπὶ τὸν Ῥοβοάμου παῖδα τῶν δύο φυλῶν τὴν βασιλείαν τοῦ πατρὸς διαδεξάμενον Ἀβίαν ἐξεστράτευσε πολεμήσων· κατεφρόνει γὰρ αὐτοῦ διὰ τὴν ἡλικίαν. ὁ δὲ ἀκούσας τὴν ἔφοδον τὴν Ἱεροβοάμου πρὸς αὐτὴν οὐ κατεπλάγη, γενόμενος δ' ἐπάνω καὶ τῆς νεότητος τῷ φρονήματι καὶ τῆς ἐλπίδος τοῦ πολεμίου, στρατιὰν ἐπιλέξας ἐκ τῶν δύο φυλῶν ἀπήντησε τῷ Ἱεροβοάμῳ εἰς τόπον τινὰ καλούμενον ὄρος Σαμαρῶν καὶ στρατοπεδευσάμενος ἐγγὺς αὐτοῦ
275 τὰ πρὸς τὴν μάχην εὐτρέπιζεν. ἦν δ' ἡ δύναμις αὐτοῦ μυριάδες τεσσαράκοντα, ἡ δὲ τοῦ Ἱεροβοάμου στρατιὰ διπλασίων ἐκείνης. ὡς δὲ τὰ στρατεύματα πρὸς τὰ ἔργα καὶ τοὺς κινδύνους ἀντιπαρετάσσετο καὶ συμβαλεῖν ἔμελλε, στὰς ἐφ' ὑψηλοῦ τινος Ἀβίας τόπου καὶ τῇ χειρὶ κατασείσας, τὸ πλῆθος καὶ τὸν Ἱεροβόαμον ἀκοῦσαι
276 πρῶτον αὐτοῦ μεθ' ἡσυχίας ἠξίωσε. γενομένης δὲ

he alone was good." When he had prophesied these things, the woman rushed out, thrown into confusion and deeply grieved at the death of the son spoken of; along the way she lamented and beat her breast at the thought of the child's approaching end, and wretched over her misfortune and beset by irremediable woe, she pressed on with a haste that meant ill luck for her son—for the more she hurried, the sooner she was destined to see him dead—but was necessary on her husband's account.[a] And, when she arrived, she found the child breathing his last, as the prophet had said; and she told the king everything.

Jeroboam prepares for war with Abijah of Judah. 2 Chron. xiii. 2.

(2) But Jeroboam took no thought of these things, and, collecting a large army, led it out to make war on Abias, the son of Roboamos, who had succeeded his father as king of the two tribes and whom Jeroboam despised on account of his youth. And, when the other heard of Jeroboam's approach, he was not dismayed, but, with a spirit rising above his youth and the hopes of the enemy, raised an army from among the two tribes and confronted Jeroboam at a place called Mount Samarōn,[b] near which he encamped and prepared for battle. His force amounted to four hundred thousand, while Jeroboam's army was twice as large. Now, as the armies were drawn up against each other, ready for action and the hazards of war, and were about to engage, Abias, who stood on an elevated spot, motioned with his hand and asked the people and Jeroboam first to hear him in quiet; and,

[a] Amplification of the brief Scriptural statement, "And Jeroboam's wife arose and departed and came to Tirzah."

[b] Bibl. Zemaraim (*Ṣemārayim*), LXX Σομορών; its site is unidentified.

σιωπῆς ἤρξατο λέγειν· “ ὅτι μὲν τὴν ἡγεμονίαν ὁ θεὸς Δαυίδῃ καὶ τοῖς ἐκγόνοις αὐτοῦ κατένευσεν εἰς ἅπαντα χρόνον, οὐδ' ὑμεῖς ἀγνοεῖτε· θαυμάζω δὲ πῶς ἀποστάντες τοὐμοῦ πατρὸς τῷ δούλῳ Ἱεροβοάμῳ προσέθεσθε καὶ μετ' ἐκείνου πάρεστε νῦν ἐπὶ τοὺς ὑπὸ τοῦ θεοῦ βασιλεύειν κεκριμένους πολεμήσοντες καὶ τὴν ἀρχὴν ἀφαιρησόμενοι τὴν ὑπάρχουσαν· τὴν μὲν γὰρ πλείω μέχρι νῦν Ἱερο-
277 βόαμος ἀδίκως ἔχει. ἀλλ' οὐκ οἶμαι ταύτης[1] αὐτὸν ἀπολαύσειν ἐπὶ πλείονα χρόνον, ἀλλὰ δοὺς καὶ τοῦ παρεληλυθότος δίκην τῷ θεῷ παύσεται τῆς παρανομίας καὶ τῶν ὕβρεων, ἃς οὐ διαλέλοιπεν εἰς αὐτὸν ὑβρίζων καὶ ταὐτὰ ποιεῖν ὑμᾶς ἀναπεπεικώς, οἳ μηδὲν ἀδικηθέντες ὑπὸ τοὐμοῦ πατρός, ἀλλ' ὅτι μὴ πρὸς ἡδονὴν ἐκκλησιάζων ὡμίλησεν, ἀνθρώπων πονηρῶν συμβουλίᾳ πεισθείς, ἐγκατελίπετε τῷ μὲν δοκεῖν ὑπ' ὀργῆς ἐκεῖνον, ταῖς δ' ἀληθείαις αὑτοὺς ἀπὸ τοῦ θεοῦ καὶ τῶν ἐκείνου
278 νόμων ἀπεσπάσατε. καίτοι συνεγνωκέναι καλῶς εἶχεν ὑμᾶς οὐ λόγων μόνον δυσκόλων ἀνδρὶ νέῳ καὶ δημαγωγίας ἀπείρῳ, ἀλλ' εἰ καὶ πρός τι δυσχερὲς ἡ νεότης αὐτὸν καὶ ἡ ἀμαθία τῶν πραττομένων ἐξῆγεν ἔργον, διά τε Σολομῶνα τὸν πατέρα καὶ τὰς εὐεργεσίας τὰς ἐκείνου· παραίτησιν γὰρ εἶναι δεῖ τῆς τῶν ἐκγόνων ἁμαρτίας τὰς τῶν
279 πατέρων εὐποιίας. ὑμεῖς δ' οὐδὲν τούτων ἐλογίσασθε οὔτε τότε οὔτε νῦν, ἀλλ' ἧκε[2] στρατὸς ἐφ' ἡμᾶς τοσοῦτος· τίνι καὶ πεπιστευκὼς περὶ τῆς

[1] καὶ ταύτης RO. [2] ἥκετε MSP.

when silence was obtained, he began to speak, saying, "That God has granted the sovereignty to David and his descendants for all time, not even you are unaware. I wonder, therefore, how you could revolt from my father and go over to his servant Jeroboam, and have now come here with him to make war on those who were chosen by God to reign, and to deprive them of the royal power which still remains to them, for the larger part of the realm Jeroboam has until now been unjustly holding. But I do not believe that he will enjoy possession of this for very long, but, when he has paid God the penalty for what he has done in the past, he will end his transgressions and the insults which he has never ceased to offer Him, persuading you to do the same. As for you who were never wronged in any way by my father, but because, following the advice of wicked men, in a public assembly he spoke in a manner that displeased you,—you deserted him, as it seemed, but in reality you have separated yourselves from God and His laws. And yet it would have been fair for you to forgive not only the unpleasant words of a man so young and inexperienced in governing people, but also any further disagreeable act to which his youth and his ignorance of public affairs might have led him, for the sake of his father Solomon and the benefits you have received from him. For the merits of the fathers should be a palliation of the sins of their children.[a] You, however, took no account of these things either then or now, but have brought this great army of yours against us ; and in what does

Abijah's protest against Jeroboam's invasion. 2 Chron. xiii. 4.

[a] This argument is not found in Scripture. On the late biblical doctrine of the "merits of the fathers" *cf.* R. Marcus, *Law in the Apocrypha*, p. 14.

νίκης; ἢ[1] ταῖς χρυσαῖς δαμάλεσι καὶ τοῖς ἐπὶ τῶν ὀρῶν βωμοῖς, ἃ δείγματα τῆς ἀσεβείας ἐστὶν ὑμῶν ἀλλ' οὐχὶ τῆς θρησκείας; ἢ τὸ πλῆθος ὑμᾶς εὐέλπιδας ἀπεργάζεται τὴν ἡμετέραν στρατιὰν
280 ὑπερβάλλον; ἀλλ' οὐδ' ἡτισοῦν[2] ἰσχὺς μυριάδων στρατοῦ μετ' ἀδικημάτων πολεμοῦντος· ἐν γὰρ μόνῳ τῷ δικαίῳ καὶ πρὸς τὸ θεῖον εὐσεβεῖ τὴν βεβαιοτάτην ἐλπίδα τοῦ κρατεῖν τῶν ἐναντίων ἀποκεῖσθαι συμβέβηκεν, ἥτις ἐστὶ παρ' ἡμῖν τετηρηκόσιν ἀπ' ἀρχῆς τὰ νόμιμα καὶ τὸν ἴδιον θεὸν σεβομένοις, ὃν οὐ χεῖρες ἐποίησαν ἐξ ὕλης φθαρτῆς οὐδ' ἐπίνοια πονηροῦ βασιλέως ἐπὶ τῇ τῶν ὄχλων ἀπάτῃ κατεσκεύασεν, ἀλλ' ὃς ἔργον ἐστὶν αὐτοῦ
281 καὶ ἀρχὴ καὶ τέλος τῶν ἁπάντων. συμβουλεύω τοιγαροῦν ὑμῖν ἔτι καὶ νῦν μεταγνῶναι καὶ λαβόντας ἀμείνω λογισμὸν παύσασθαι τοῦ πολεμεῖν καὶ τὰ πάτρια καὶ τὸ προαγαγὸν ὑμᾶς ἐπὶ τοσοῦτον μέγεθος εὐδαιμονίας γνωρίσαι."

282 (3) Ταῦτα μὲν Ἀβίας διελέχθη πρὸς τὸ πλῆθος· ἔτι δὲ αὐτοῦ λέγοντος λάθρα τινὰς τῶν στρατιωτῶν Ἱεροβόαμος ἔπεμψε περικυκλωσομένους τὸν Ἀβίαν ἔκ τινων οὐ φανερῶν τοῦ στρατοπέδου μερῶν. μέσου δ' αὐτοῦ περιληφθέντος τῶν πολεμίων ἡ μὲν στρατιὰ κατέδεισε καὶ ταῖς ψυχαῖς ἀνέπεσεν, ὁ δ' Ἀβίας παρεθάρρυνε καὶ τὰς ἐλπίδας ἔχειν ἐν τῷ θεῷ παρεκάλει· τοῦτον γὰρ οὐ κε-
283 κυκλῶσθαι πρὸς τῶν πολεμίων. οἱ δὲ ὁμοῦ πάντες ἐπικαλεσάμενοι τὴν παρὰ τοῦ θεοῦ συμμαχίαν τῶν ἱερέων τῇ σάλπιγγι σημανάντων ἀλαλάξαντες
284 ἐχώρησαν ἐπὶ τοὺς πολεμίους· καὶ τῶν μὲν ἔθραυσε

[1] ex Lat. Niese: ἡ codd. E.

[2] Naber: οὐδ' ἥτις οὖν SP: οὐ δή τις RO: οὐ δή τις οὖν M.

it place its hope of victory? Is it, perhaps, in the golden heifers and the altars on the mountains, which are proofs of your impiety and not by any means of your devoutness? Or is it your numbers, which far exceed those of our army, that make you confident? But there is no strength whatever in many tens of thousands when an army fights in an unjust cause. For it is only in justice and piety toward God that the surest hope of conquering one's adversaries is bound to lie, and this belongs to us who have from the beginning observed the laws and worshipped our own God, whom no hands have formed out of perishable matter and no wicked king has cunningly made to deceive the populace, but who is His own work and the beginning and end of all things. I advise you, therefore, even now to repent and adopt the better plan of ceasing from warfare and to respect the rights of your country and the power which has led you on to so great a height of prosperity."[a]

Abijah's victory over Jeroboam. 2 Chron. xiii. 13.

(3) Such was the speech which Abias made to the people. But, while he was still speaking, Jeroboam secretly sent some of his soldiers to surround Abias from certain parts of the camp that were not observed. And, when he was caught in the enemy's midst, his army was alarmed and their spirits sank, but Abias encouraged them and urged them to put their hope in God, saying that He was not encircled by the enemy.[b] And all of them together called upon God to be their ally and, when the priests had sounded the trumpets, they rushed upon the enemy with an exultant shout.

[a] Josephus greatly amplifies the speech of Abijah.

[b] The Judaeans' discouragement and Abijah's exhortation are unscriptural details.

τὰ φρονήματα καὶ τὰς ἀκμὰς αὐτῶν ἐξέλυσεν ὁ θεός, τὴν δὲ Ἀβία στρατιὰν ὑπερτέραν ἐποίησεν· ὅσος γὰρ οὐδέποτ' ἐμνημονεύθη φόνος ἐν πολέμῳ γεγονέναι οὔθ' Ἑλλήνων οὔτε βαρβάρων, τοσούτους ἀποκτείναντες τῆς Ἱεροβοάμου δυνάμεως θαυμαστὴν καὶ διαβόητον νίκην παρὰ τοῦ θεοῦ λαβεῖν ἠξιώθησαν· πεντήκοντα γὰρ μυριάδας τῶν ἐχθρῶν κατέβαλον καὶ τὰς πόλεις αὐτῶν διήρπασαν τὰς ὀχυρωτάτας ἑλόντες κατὰ κράτος, τήν τε Βηθήλην καὶ τὴν τοπαρχίαν αὐτῆς καὶ τὴν Ἰσανὰν καὶ τὴν
285 τοπαρχίαν αὐτῆς.[1] καὶ Ἱεροβόαμος μὲν οὐκέτι μετὰ ταύτην τὴν ἧτταν ἴσχυσεν ἐφ' ὅσον Ἀβίας περιῆν χρόνον. τελευτᾷ δ' οὗτος ὀλίγον τῇ νίκῃ χρόνον ἐπιζήσας ἔτη βασιλεύσας τρία, καὶ θάπτεται μὲν ἐν Ἱεροσολύμοις ἐν ταῖς προγονικαῖς θήκαις, ἀπολείπει δὲ υἱοὺς μὲν δύο καὶ εἴκοσι θυγατέρας δὲ ἑκκαίδεκα. πάντας τούτους ἐκ γυναικῶν δεκα-
286 τεσσάρων ἐτεκνώσατο. διεδέξατο δ' αὐτοῦ τὴν βασιλείαν ὁ υἱὸς[2] Ἄσανος· καὶ ἡ μήτηρ τοῦ νεανίσκου Μαχαία τοὔνομα. τούτου κρατοῦντος εἰρήνης ἀπέλαυεν ἡ χώρα τῶν Ἰσραηλιτῶν ἐπὶ ἔτη δέκα.

287 (4) Καὶ τὰ μὲν περὶ Ἀβίαν τὸν Ῥοβοάμου τοῦ Σολομῶνος οὕτως παρειλήφαμεν. ἐτελεύτησε δὲ καὶ Ἱεροβόαμος ὁ τῶν δέκα φυλῶν βασιλεύς, ἄρξας ἔτη δύο καὶ εἴκοσι. διαδέχεται δ' αὐτὸν ὁ

[1] καὶ . . . αὐτῆς om. RO Lat. [2] + αὐτοῦ RO.

[a] The phrase " such . . . was never recorded to have been made " is reminiscent of Thucydides ii. 47.
[b] On this phrase *cf. A.* vii. 309.
[c] Bibl. Jeshanah (*Yešānāh*), LXX Κανά, Luc. Ἰεσανά.

Then God crushed the spirit of the enemy and broke their strength, while He made Abias's army stronger. Such a slaughter was never recorded to have been made[a] in any war of Greeks or barbarians as they made in slaying the soldiers of Jeroboam when they were permitted by God to win so wonderful and celebrated a victory,[b] for they struck down five hundred thousand of their foes and plundered their strongest cities after taking them by storm ; these were Bethel and its province and Isana[c] and its province.[d] And Jeroboam, after this defeat, was never again powerful so long as Abias lived. The latter, however, lived only a short time beyond his victory, dying after a reign of three years, and was buried in Jerusalem in the tomb of his forefathers ; he left behind twenty-two sons and sixteen daughters. All these children he had by fourteen wives.[e] And he was succeeded on the throne by his son Asanos,[f] this youth's mother being named Machaia.[g] During his government the land of the Israelites[h] enjoyed peace for ten years.

Abijah's death. 2 Chron. xiv. 1 (Heb. xiii. 23).

1 Kings xv. 10.

(4) Such, then, is the account we have received concerning Abias, the son of Roboamos the son of Solomon. Now Jeroboam, the king of the ten tribes, also died, after ruling twenty-two years.[i] He was

Jeroboam is succeeded by Nadab (Nabados). 1 Kings xv. 25.

[d] Scripture adds the city of Ephraim, LXX 'Εφρών. On the variant account (2 Chron. xvii. 2) that Asa, the son of Abijah, captured these cities *cf.* § 393 note.

[e] In Scripture, Abijah's wives and children are mentioned before his death.

[f] Bibl. Asa, LXX 'Ασά.

[g] Bibl. Maachah, LXX Μααχά. Weill understands Josephus's text to mean that Asa's mother was associated with him on the throne.

[h] A slip for " the two tribes " or " Jerusalem " ; Asa was king of Judah.

[i] 1 Kings xiv. 20.

παῖς Νάβαδος[1] δευτέρου ἔτους ἤδη τῆς βασιλείας Ἀσάνου διεληλυθότος. ἦρξε δὲ[2] ὁ τοῦ Ἱεροβοάμου παῖς ἔτη δύο, τῷ πατρὶ τὴν ἀσέβειαν καὶ
288 τὴν πονηρίαν ἐμφερὴς ὤν. ἐν δὲ τούτοις τοῖς δυσὶν ἔτεσι στρατευσάμενος ἐπὶ Γαβαθῶνα πόλιν Παλαιστίνων οὖσαν πολιορκίᾳ λαβεῖν αὐτὴν προσέμενεν· ἐπιβουλευθεὶς δ' ἐκεῖ ὑπὸ φίλου τινὸς Βασάνου[3] ὄνομα Σειδοῦ[4] δὲ παιδὸς ἀποθνήσκει, ὃς μετὰ τὴν τελευτὴν αὐτοῦ τὴν βασιλείαν παρα-
289 λαβὼν ἅπαν τὸ Ἱεροβοάμου γένος διέφθειρε. καὶ συνέβη κατὰ τὴν τοῦ θεοῦ προφητείαν τοὺς μὲν ἐν τῇ πόλει τῶν Ἱεροβοάμου συγγενῶν ἀποθανόντας ὑπὸ κυνῶν σπαραχθῆναι καὶ δαπανηθῆναι, τοὺς δ' ἐν τοῖς ἀγροῖς ὑπ' ὀρνίθων. ὁ μὲν οὖν Ἱεροβοάμου οἶκος τῆς ἀσεβείας αὐτοῦ καὶ τῶν ἀνομημάτων ἀξίαν ὑπέσχε δίκην.

290 (xii. 1) Ὁ δὲ τῶν Ἱεροσολύμων βασιλεὺς Ἄσανος ἦν τὸν τρόπον ἄριστος καὶ πρὸς τὸ θεῖον ἀφορῶν καὶ μηδὲν μήτε πράττων μήτ' ἐννοούμενος ὃ μὴ πρὸς τὴν εὐσέβειαν εἶχε καὶ τὴν τῶν νομίμων φυλακὴν τὴν ἀναφοράν. κατώρθωσε δὲ τὴν αὑτοῦ[5] βασιλείαν ἐκκόψας εἴ τι πονηρὸν ἦν ἐν αὐτῇ καὶ
291 καθαρεύσας ἁπάσης κηλῖδος. στρατοῦ δ' εἶχεν ἐπιλέκτων ἀνδρῶν ὡπλισμένων θυρεὸν καὶ σιρο-

[1] Νάδαβος S: Nadab Lat.
[2] δὴ ROSP.
[3] O: Βασσάμου R: Βοασάμου MSP.
[4] Εἴδου M: Εἴλου S: Ἴλου PE: Μαχείλου ed. pr. (Lat. ?).
[5] Niese: αὐτοῦ codd. E.

[a] Variant Nadabos; bibl. Nadab, LXX Ναδάβ (*v.l.* Ναβάτ).
[b] So LXX; bibl. Gibbethon, perhaps to be identified with

succeeded by his son Nabados [a] in the second year of the reign of Asanos. And the son of Jeroboam, who ruled two years, resembled his father in impiety and wickedness. In the course of these two years he led an army against Gabathōn,[b] a city belonging to the Philistines, and undertook a long siege to capture it. But he was killed as the victim of a plot formed by one of his friends named Basanēs,[c] the son of Seidos,[d] who took over the royal power after Asanos's death and destroyed the entire family of Jeroboam. And so it came about, in accordance with the prophecy of God, that some of Jeroboam's kin met death in the city and were torn to pieces and devoured by dogs, while others died in the fields and were eaten by birds.[e] Thus did the house of Jeroboam suffer fitting punishment for his impiety and lawlessness.

(xii. 1) But Asanos, the king of Jerusalem, was of an excellent character, looking to the Deity for guidance and neither doing nor thinking anything that did not show due regard for piety and the observance of the laws. He put his kingdom in order by cutting away whatever evil growths were found in it and cleansing it from every impurity.[f] And he had an army of picked men, three hundred thousand from

The king of Ethiopia attacks Asa. 2 Chron. xiv. 2 (Heb. xiv. 1).

the modern *Qibbia*, *c.* 5 miles N. of Modin, in the low hill country W. of Ephraim.

[c] Bibl. Baasha, LXX Βαασά. Scripture does not call him a friend of Nadab.

[d] The variants Eilos, Macheilos are possibly corruptions of LXX Βελαάν, the name of his father's family, not given in the Heb.; bibl. Ahijah, LXX Ἀχεία.

[e] These details (*cf.* § 270) are not referred to in Scripture at this point, 1 Kings xv. 29.

[f] Josephus passes over the Scriptural statement about the idols and altars of strange gods removed by Asa (*cf.* § 297 note).

μάστην[1] ἐκ μὲν τῆς Ἰούδα φυλῆς μυριάδας τριάκοντα, ἐκ δὲ τῆς Βενιαμίτιδος ἀσπίδας φορούντων
292 καὶ τοξοτῶν μυριάδας πέντε καὶ εἴκοσι. ἤδη δὲ
αὐτοῦ δέκα ἔτη βασιλεύοντος στρατεύει μεγάλῃ
δυνάμει Ζαραῖος ἐπ' αὐτὸν ὁ τῆς Αἰθιοπίας βασιλεὺς ἐνενήκοντα μὲν πεζῶν μυριάσιν ἱππέων δὲ
δέκα τριακοσίοις δ' ἅρμασι. καὶ μέχρι πόλεως
Μαρίσας, ἔστι δ' αὕτη τῆς Ἰούδα φυλῆς, ἐλάσαντος
αὐτοῦ μετὰ τῆς οἰκείας δυνάμεως ἀπήντησεν
293 Ἄσανος, καὶ ἀντιπαρατάξας αὐτῷ τὴν στρατιὰν
ἔν τινι φάραγγι Σαφαθὰ[2] λεγομένῃ τῆς πόλεως
οὐκ ἄπωθεν, ὡς κατεῖδε τὸ τῶν Αἰθιόπων πλῆθος,
ἀναβοήσας νίκην ᾔτει παρὰ τοῦ θεοῦ καὶ τὰς
πολλὰς ἑλεῖν μυριάδας τῶν πολεμίων· οὐδὲ γὰρ
ἄλλῳ τινὶ θαρσήσας ἔλεγεν ἢ τῇ παρ' αὐτοῦ βοη-
θείᾳ δυναμένῃ καὶ τοὺς ὀλίγους ἀπεργάσασθαι
κρείττους τῶν πλειόνων καὶ τοὺς ἀσθενεῖς τῶν
ὑπερεχόντων ἀπαντῆσαι πρὸς μάχην τῷ Ζαραίῳ.
294 (2) Ταῦτα λέγοντος Ἀσάνου νίκην ἐσήμαινεν ὁ
θεός, καὶ συμβαλὼν μετὰ χαρᾶς τῶν προδεδη-
λωμένων ὑπὸ τοῦ θεοῦ πολλοὺς ἀποκτείνει τῶν
Αἰθιόπων καὶ τραπέντας εἰς φυγὴν ἐδίωξεν ἄχρι
τῆς Γεραρίτιδος χώρας. ἀφέμενοι δὲ τῆς ἀναιρέσεως ἐπὶ τὴν διαρπαγὴν τῶν πόλεων[3] (ἥλω
γὰρ ἡ Γεράρων) ἐχώρησαν καὶ τῆς παρεμβολῆς

[1] θυρεῷ καὶ σειρομάστῃ Naber cum cod. Vat. ap. Hudson.
[2] M Lat.: Σαβαθὰ RO: Σαφθὰ SP.
[3] πολεμίων M: τῆς πόλεως Bekker.

[a] So LXX; Heb. and Luc. 280,000.
[b] Scripture does not explicitly state at what period of Asa's reign the Ethiopian invasion occurred, but in 2 Chron. xiv. 1 it is said that "in his days the land had rest for ten years."
[c] *Cf.* Luc. Ζαραί; bibl. Zerah (*Zeraḥ*), LXX Ζάρε.

the tribe of Judah armed with shields and barbed lances, and two hundred and fifty thousand [a] from the tribe of Benjamin carrying round shields and bows. Now he had been reigning for ten years [b] when Zaraios,[c] the king of Ethiopia, marched against him with a large force consisting of nine hundred thousand foot-soldiers, one hundred thousand horsemen [d] and three hundred chariots. And when he had marched as far as the city of Marisa[e]—this being in the tribe of Judah—, Asanos met him with his own force and drew up his army over against him in a certain valley called Saphatha,[f] not far from the city. But on seeing the Ethiopian host he cried aloud and prayed to God for victory and the destruction of many myriads of the enemy, for, he said, in nothing else than His help,[g] which can make the few triumph over the many, and the weak over the strong, would he put his trust when going out to meet Zaraios in battle.

(2) While Asanos spoke these words, God gave a sign that he would be victorious, and so, with joy at what had been foretold by God,[h] he encountered the foe and slew many of the Ethiopians; and those who turned to flee he pursued as far as the territory of Gerar.[i] Then they left off slaughtering and proceeded to plunder the cities—Gerar had already been taken—and the camp of the enemy, so that they

Asa's victory over the Ethiopians. 2 Chron. xiv. 12 (Heb. 11).

[d] Bibl. "with a host of a thousand thousand"; the separate numbers of infantry and cavalry are not given.

[e] Bibl. Mareshah, *cf.* § 246 note.

[f] Bibl. Zephathah (*Ṣephāthāh*); LXX, reading *ṣāphônāh*, "to the north," has κατὰ βορρᾶν.

[g] This seems to be a misunderstanding of Heb., "it is nothing for thee (God) to help"; LXX οὐκ ἀδυνατεῖ παρά σοι σώζειν.

[h] Scripture does not mention any sign given by God.

[i] So Heb. and Luc.; LXX Γεδώρ; it lay in the south of Philistia, not far from the sea.

αὐτῶν,[1] ὡς πολὺν μὲν ἐκφορῆσαι χρυσὸν πολὺν δὲ ἄργυρον λείαν τε πολλὴν ἀπαγαγεῖν καμήλους τε
295 καὶ ὑποζύγια καὶ βοσκημάτων ἀγέλας. Ἄσανος μὲν οὖν καὶ ἡ σὺν αὐτῷ στρατιὰ τοιαύτην παρὰ τοῦ θεοῦ νίκην λαβόντες καὶ ὠφέλειαν ἀνέστρεφον εἰς Ἱεροσόλυμα, παραγενομένοις δὲ αὐτοῖς ἀπήντησε κατὰ τὴν ὁδὸν προφήτης Ἀζαρίας ὄνομα. οὗτος ἐπισχεῖν κελεύσας τῆς ὁδοιπορίας ἤρξατο λέγειν πρὸς αὐτοὺς ὅτι ταύτης εἶεν τῆς νίκης παρὰ τοῦ θεοῦ τετυχηκότες, ὅτι δικαίους καὶ ὁσίους ἑαυτοὺς παρέσχον καὶ πάντα κατὰ βούλησιν θεοῦ
296 πεποιηκότας. ἐπιμένουσι μὲν οὖν ἔφασκεν ἀεὶ κρατεῖν αὐτοὺς τῶν ἐχθρῶν καὶ τὸ ζῆν μετ' εὐδαιμονίας παρέξειν τὸν θεόν, ἀπολιποῦσι δὲ τὴν θρησκείαν ἅπαντα τούτων ἐναντία συμβήσεσθαι καὶ γενήσεσθαι χρόνον ἐκεῖνον, "ἐν ᾧ μηδεὶς ἀληθὴς εὑρεθήσεται προφήτης ἐν τῷ ὑμετέρῳ
297 ὄχλῳ οὐδὲ ἱερεὺς τὰ δίκαια χρηματίζων, ἀλλὰ καὶ αἱ πόλεις ἀνάστατοι γενήσονται καὶ τὸ ἔθνος κατὰ πάσης σπαρήσεται γῆς, ἔπηλυν βίον καὶ ἀλήτην βιωσόμενον." καιρὸν δ' αὐτοῖς ἔχουσι συνεβούλευεν ἀγαθοῖς γίνεσθαι καὶ μὴ φθονῆσαι τῆς εὐμενείας αὐτοῖς[2] τοῦ θεοῦ. ταῦτ' ἀκούσας ὁ βασιλεὺς καὶ ὁ λαὸς ἐχάρησαν καὶ πολλὴν πρόνοιαν ἐποιοῦντο κοινῇ τε πάντες καὶ κατ' ἰδίαν τοῦ δικαίου· διέπεμψε δ' ὁ βασιλεὺς καὶ τοὺς ἐν τῇ χώρᾳ τῶν νομίμων ἐπιμελησομένους.

[1] ἐπὶ τὴν διαρπαγὴν . . . αὐτῶν corrupta esse putat Niese.
[2] Niese: αὐτοῖς codd. E.

[a] Gold and silver are not mentioned in Scripture.

carried off much gold and silver[a] and brought away a great deal of spoil and camels, beasts of burden and flocks of sheep. And so, when Asanos and the army with him had received from God this great victory and gain, they turned back to Jerusalem. As they were approaching it, there met them on the road a prophet named Azarias.[b] He bade them halt their journey, and began to speak to them, saying that they had obtained this victory from God because they had shown themselves righteous and pure and had always acted in accordance with the will of God. If, then, he said, they so continued, God would grant them always to overcome their foes and live happily, but, if they abandoned His worship, everything would turn out to the contrary and the time would come "when no true prophet will be found among your people nor any priest to give righteous judgement, but your cities shall be laid waste and the nation scattered over all the earth to lead the life of aliens and wanderers."[c] He therefore advised them to be virtuous while they still had time, and not ungraciously refuse to accept the benevolence of God. When the king and the people heard these words, they rejoiced, and all together and each privately took thought for what was right. The king also sent men throughout the country to watch over the enforcement of the laws.[d]

The admonition of the prophet Azariah. 2 Chron. xv. 1.

[b] So LXX; bibl. Azariah (*'Azaryāhû*); Scripture adds that he was the son of Oded.

[c] This unscriptural reference to the future exile is perhaps an interpretation of 2 Chron. xv. 5, "In those days (there will be) no peace to him that goes out nor to him that comes in."

[d] Here again (*cf.* § 290 note) Josephus passes over the Scriptural details of Asa's removal of idols and unlawful shrines.

298 (3) Καὶ τὰ μὲν Ἀσάνου τοῦ βασιλέως τῶν δύο
φυλῶν ἐν τούτοις ὑπῆρχεν. ἐπάνειμι δ' ἐπὶ τὸ
πλῆθος τῶν Ἰσραηλιτῶν καὶ τὸν βασιλέα αὐτῶν
Βασάνην[1] τὸν ἀποκτείναντα τὸν Ἱεροβοάμου υἱὸν
299 Νάβαδον καὶ κατασχόντα τὴν ἀρχήν. οὗτος γὰρ
ἐν Θαρσῇ[2] πόλει διατρίβων καὶ ταύτην οἰκητήριον
πεποιημένος[3] εἴκοσι μὲν ἐβασίλευσεν ἔτη καὶ τέσσαρα, πονηρὸς δὲ καὶ ἀσεβὴς ὑπὲρ Ἱεροβόαμον
καὶ τὸν υἱὸν αὐτοῦ γενόμενος, πολλὰ καὶ τὸ
πλῆθος κακὰ διέθηκε καὶ τὸν θεὸν ἐξύβρισεν· ὃς
αὐτῷ πέμψας Ἰηοῦν[4] τὸν προφήτην προεῖπε δια-
φθερεῖν αὐτοῦ πᾶν τὸ γένος καὶ τοῖς αὐτοῖς οἷς καὶ
τὸν Ἱεροβοάμου κακοῖς περιέβαλεν οἶκον ἐξολέσειν,
300 ὅτι βασιλεὺς ὑπ' αὐτοῦ γενόμενος οὐκ ἠμείψατο
τὴν εὐεργεσίαν τῷ δικαίως προστῆναι τοῦ πλήθους
καὶ εὐσεβῶς, ἅπερ αὐτοῖς πρῶτον τοῖς οὖσι τοιούτοις ἀγαθά, ἔπειτα τῷ θεῷ φίλα, τὸν δὲ κάκιστον
Ἱεροβόαμον ἐμιμήσατο καὶ τῆς ψυχῆς ἀπολομένης
τῆς ἐκείνου ζῶσαν αὐτοῦ τὴν πονηρίαν ἐνεδείξατο·
πεῖραν οὖν ἕξειν εἰκότως τῆς ὁμοίας συμφορᾶς
301 αὐτὸν ἔλεγεν ὅμοιον αὐτῷ γενόμενον. Βασάνης
δὲ προακηκοὼς τὰ μέλλοντα αὐτῷ συμβήσεσθαι
κακὰ μεθ' ὅλης τῆς γενεᾶς ἐπὶ τοῖς τετολμημένοις
οὐ πρὸς τὸ λοιπὸν ἡσύχασεν, ἵνα μὴ μᾶλλον
πονηρὸς δόξας ἀποθάνῃ καὶ περὶ τῶν παρῳχη-
μένων ἔκτοτε γοῦν μετανοήσας συγγνώμης παρὰ
302 τοῦ θεοῦ[5] τύχῃ, ἀλλ' ὥσπερ οἱ προκειμένων αὐτοῖς

[1] τὸ πλῆθος . . . Βασάνην] τὸν τοῦ πλήθους τῶν Ἰσραηλιτῶν βασιλέα Βασάνην MSP Lat.

[2] Hudson: Θαρσάλῃ codd.: Tersalin Lat.

[3] πεποιηκὼς RO.

[4] Schotanus: Ἰησοῦν RO: Ἰοῦν MSP: Γιμοῦ E: Gimun Lat.

[5] παρὰ τοῦ θεοῦ om. RO.

(3) Such was the state of things under Asanos, the king of the two tribes. I shall now return to the people of Israel and their king Basanēs, who killed Jeroboam's son Nabados and seized the royal power. Now he lived in the city of Tharsē,[a] which he had made his residence, and reigned there twenty-four years. But being more wicked and impious than Jeroboam and his son, he brought many evils upon the people and gravely outraged God, who sent to him the prophet Jēūs[b] and warned him that He would destroy all his line and would utterly crush them under the same calamities as He had brought upon the house of Jeroboam, because, after having been made king by Him, he had not requited His kindness by justly and piously governing the people—a course which would, in the first place, be of benefit to those who followed it, and then pleasing to God as well—but had imitated Jeroboam, the vilest of men, and, although Jeroboam himself was dead, had revealed his wickedness as still living. Therefore, He said, Basanēs should justly experience a like ill fate since he had acted in a like manner.[c] But Basanēs, although he heard beforehand what evils were destined to befall him together with his whole family because of his reckless conduct, did not restrain himself thereafter in order to avoid being thought still more wicked and so meeting death, nor seek, by repenting thenceforth at least of his past misdeeds, to obtain pardon from God; on the contrary, like those

The reign of Baasha of Israel. 1 Kings xv. 33.

Baasha's wickedness.

[a] Emended text; MSS. Tharsalē; bibl. Tirzah (*Tirṣāh*), LXX Θερσά, tentatively identified by Albright with the modern *Tell el-Far'ah*, *c.* 7 miles N.E. of Nablus.

[b] Variant Jesūs; bibl. Jehu (*Yehû*), LXX Εἰού, Luc. Ἰού (?); Scripture adds that he was the son of Hanani.

[c] Josephus greatly amplifies Jehu's speech.

ἄθλων ἐπὰν περί τι σπουδάσωσιν οὐ διαλείπουσι περὶ τοῦτο ἐνεργοῦντες, οὕτω καὶ Βασάνης προειρηκότος αὐτῷ τοῦ προφήτου τὰ μέλλοντα ὡς ἐπ᾽ ἀγαθοῖς τοῖς μεγίστοις κακοῖς ὀλέθρῳ γένους καὶ οἰκίας ἀπωλείᾳ χείρων ἐγένετο, καὶ καθ᾽ ἑκάστην ἡμέραν ὥσπερ ἀθλητὴς κακίας τοῖς περὶ ταύτην
303 πόνοις προσετίθει. καὶ τελευταῖον τὴν στρατιὰν παραλαβὼν πάλιν ἐπῆλθε πόλει τινὶ τῶν οὐκ ἀφανῶν Ἀραμαθῶνι τοὔνομα σταδίους ἀπεχούσῃ Ἱεροσολύμων τεσσαράκοντα, καὶ καταλαβόμενος αὐτὴν ὠχύρου προδιεγνωκὼς καταλιπεῖν ἐν αὐτῇ δύναμιν, ἵν᾽ ἐκεῖθεν ὡρμημένοι τὴν Ἀσάνου βασιλείαν κακώσωσι.

304 (4) Φοβηθεὶς δὲ Ἄσανος τὴν ἐπιχείρησιν τοῦ πολεμίου καὶ λογισάμενος ὡς πολλὰ διαθήσει κακὰ τὴν ὑπ᾽ αὐτῷ βασιλευομένην ἅπασαν ὁ καταλειφθεὶς ἐν Ἀραμαθῶνι στρατός, ἔπεμψε πρὸς τὸν Δαμασκηνῶν βασιλέα πρέσβεις καὶ χρυσὸν καὶ ἄργυρον, παρακαλῶν συμμαχεῖν[1] καὶ ὑπομιμνήσκων ὅτι καὶ πατρῴα φιλία πρὸς ἀλλήλους ἐστὶν
305 αὐτοῖς. ὁ δὲ τῶν χρημάτων τὸ πλῆθος ἀσμένως ἐδέξατο καὶ συμμαχίαν ἐποιήσατο πρὸς αὐτόν, διαλύσας τὴν πρὸς τὸν Βασάνην φιλίαν, καὶ πέμψας εἰς τὰς ὑπ᾽ αὐτοῦ βασιλευομένας πόλεις τοὺς ἡγεμόνας τῆς ἰδίας δυνάμεως ἐκέλευσε κακοῦν

[1] Niese: συμμαχίαν codd.

who have a prize held out before them and, in their earnest effort to obtain it, do not leave off striving toward it, so too Basanēs, after the prophet had foretold what was to come, acted as if these greatest of misfortunes, the death of his family and the destruction of his house, were blessings instead, and became still worse; every day, like a champion of wickedness, he increased his labours on its behalf.[a] And finally he took his army and again attacked a certain city of no little importance, named Aramathōn,[b] which was forty stades from Jerusalem,[b] and, after taking it, fortified it, for he had previously determined to leave a force in it in order that they might use it as a base from which to set out and ravage the kingdom of Asanos.

1 Kings xv. 17; 2 Chron. xvi. 1.

(4) But Asanos, who feared the enemy's attack and thought that the army left in Aramathōn might inflict great damage upon the entire country ruled by him, sent envoys to the king of Damascus[c] with gold and silver, requesting him to become his ally, and reminding him that there had been friendship between them since their fathers' time. This king gladly accepted the large sum of money and formed an alliance with him after breaking off friendly relations with Basanēs; and he sent the commanders of his own force to the cities of Basanēs' realm with

Asa allies himself with the Syrians against Baasha. 1 Kings xv. 18; 2 Chron. xvi. 2.

[a] These reflections on Baasha's conduct are, of course, an addition to Scripture.

[b] Bibl. Ramah, LXX Ῥααμά (*v.l.* Ῥαμά); elsewhere in Josephus (*e.g.* *A.* vi. 220) it is called Armatha; it is the modern *er-Rām*, *c.* 5 miles N. of Jerusalem. Josephus's reckoning of its distance from Jerusalem (an unscriptural detail) is therefore correct.

[c] Scripture gives his name, Ben-hadad (LXX υἱὸν Ἀδέρ), son of Tabrimmon.

αὐτάς. οἱ δὲ τὰς μὲν ἐνεπίμπρασαν τὰς δὲ διήρπασαν πορευθέντες, τήν τε Αἰῶνα[1] λεγομένην
306 καὶ Δάνα καὶ Ἀβελλάνην καὶ ἄλλας πολλάς. ταῦτ' ἀκούσας ὁ τῶν Ἰσραηλιτῶν βασιλεὺς τοῦ μὲν οἰκοδομεῖν καὶ ὀχυροῦν τὴν Ἀραμαθῶνα ἐπαύσατο, μετὰ δὲ[2] σπουδῆς ὡς βοηθήσων τοῖς οἰκείοις κακουμένοις ἀνέστρεψεν, ὁ δ' Ἄσανος ἐκ τῆς παρεσκευασμένης ὑπ' αὐτοῦ πρὸς οἰκοδομίαν ὕλης πόλεις ἀνήγειρεν ἐν αὐτῷ τῷ τόπῳ δύο καρτεράς,
307 ἡ μὲν Γαβαὰ[3] ἐκαλεῖτο, ἡ δὲ Μασφά.[4] καὶ μετὰ ταῦτα καιρὸν οὐκ ἔσχεν ὁ Βασάνης τῆς ἐπὶ τὸν Ἄσανον στρατείας· ἐφθάσθη γὰρ ὑπὸ τοῦ χρεών, καὶ θάπτεται μὲν ἐν Θαρσῇ[5] πόλει, παραλαμβάνει δ' αὐτοῦ τὴν ἀρχὴν παῖς Ἤλανος. οὗτος ἄρξας ἐπ' ἔτη δύο τελευτᾷ φονεύσαντος αὐτὸν ἐξ ἐπιβουλῆς Ζαμβρίου[6] τοῦ ἱππάρχου τῆς ἡμι-
308 σείας τάξεως· κατευωχηθέντα γὰρ αὐτὸν παρὰ τῷ οἰκονόμῳ αὐτοῦ Ὠσᾶ[7] τοὔνομα πείσας ἐπιδραμεῖν τῶν ὑφ' αὐτὸν ἱππέων τινὰς ἀπέκτεινε δι' αὐτῶν μεμονωμένον τῶν περὶ αὐτὸν ὁπλιτῶν καὶ ἡγε-

[1] Hudson: Ἰωάνου M: Ἰωάννου ROSP: Helon Lat.
[2] καὶ μετὰ RO.
[3] ex Lat. Niese: Γαβὰ MSP: Χαβαᾶ RO.
[4] ex Lat. Hudson: Μασταφάς RO: Μεσταφάς MSP.
[5] Hudson: Ἀρσῇ RO: Ἀρσάνῃ MSP: Thersa Lat.
[6] Ζαμαρίου MSPE Lat.
[7] Ὀλσᾶ SPE: Ὀρσᾶ Hudson.

[a] Emended text, *cf.* LXX 2 Chron. Αἰών; MSS. Joannū, etc.; bibl. Ijon (*'Iyyôn*), LXX 1 Kings Ἀίν (*v.l.* Ναίν); its site is unidentified.

[b] Bibl. 1 Kings Abel-beth-maachah, LXX Ἀβὲλ οἴκου Μααχά—*bêth* means "house"—(*v.l.* Ἀδελμάθ), Luc. Ἀβελμαά; 2 Chron. Abel-maim, LXX Ἀβελμαίν. Josephus's form seems to be a corruption of that in LXX 2 Chron.

orders to ravage them. So they set out and burnt some of the cities and sacked others, including Aiōn,[a] as it was called, Dan, Abellanē [b] and many others.[c] When the king of Israel heard of this, he left off building and fortifying Aramathōn and returned in haste to bring help to his injured subjects. Then Asanos took the materials prepared by Basanēs for building Aramathōn, and with them erected two strong cities in the same region, one of which was called Gabaa [d] and the other, Maspha.[e] And after this Basanēs had no further opportunity to march against Asanos, for he was very soon overtaken by Fate and was buried in the city of Tharsē,[f] whereupon his son Ēlanos [g] took over his kingdom. He, 1 Kings xvi. 8.
in turn, died after a reign of two years, being treacherously slain by Zambrias,[h] the commander of half of his body of horsemen,[i] in this way: as he was being entertained at table by his steward, whose name was Ōsa,[j] Zambrias persuaded some of the horsemen under his command to rush upon him, and had him killed [k] while he was quite alone, without his

[c] Located, according to Scripture, in the territory of Naphtali, N.W. of the lake of Chinnereth.

[d] So LXX 2 Chron. (*v.l.* Γαβαέ); bibl. Geba (of Benjamin); LXX 1 Kings, taking the name Geba as a common noun meaning "hill," has βουνὸν (Βενιαμεὶν).

[e] So LXX 2 Chron.; bibl. Mizpah (*Miṣpāh*); LXX 1 Kings, taking the name Mizpah as a common noun meaning "lookout," has σκοπιάν.

[f] Bibl. Tirzah, *cf.* § 299 note.

[g] Bibl. Elah, LXX Ἠλά.

[h] Bibl. Zimri, LXX Ζαμβρεί.

[i] Heb. and Luc. "commander of half of his chariots," LXX "commander of half of his horses."

[j] This form and the variant Olsa are both found in the LXX; bibl. Arza (*'Arṣā'*).

[k] According to Scripture, Zimri himself killed Elah.

μόνων· οὗτοι γὰρ ἅπαντες περὶ τὴν πολιορκίαν τῆς Γαβαθώνης ἐγίνοντο τῆς Παλαιστίνων.

309 (5) Φονεύσας δὲ τὸν Ἤλανον ὁ ἵππαρχος Ζαμβρίας αὐτὸς βασιλεύει καὶ πᾶσαν τὴν Βασάνου γενεὰν κατὰ τὴν Ἰηοῦ[1] προφητείαν διαφθείρει· τῷ γὰρ αὐτῷ τρόπῳ συνέβη τὸν οἶκον αὐτοῦ πρόρριζον ἀπολέσθαι διὰ τὴν ἀσέβειαν, ὡς καὶ τὸν
310 Ἱεροβοάμου διαφθαρέντα γεγράφαμεν. ἡ δὲ πολιορκοῦσα τὴν Γαβαθώνην στρατιὰ πυθομένη τὰ περὶ τὸν βασιλέα καὶ ὅτι Ζαμβρίας ἀποκτείνας αὐτὸν ἔχει τὴν βασιλείαν καὶ αὐτὴ τὸν ἡγούμενον αὐτῆς Ἀμαρῖνον ἀπέδειξε βασιλέα, ὃς ἀπὸ τῆς Γαβαθώνης ἀναστήσας τὸν στρατὸν εἰς Θαρσὴν παραγίνεται τὸ βασίλειον καὶ προσβαλὼν τῇ πόλει
311 κατὰ κράτος αἱρεῖ. Ζαμβρίας δὲ τὴν πόλιν ἰδὼν ᾑρημένην[2] συνέφυγεν εἰς τὸ μυχαίτατον τῶν βασιλείων καὶ ὑποπρήσας αὐτὰ[3] συγκατέκαυσεν ἑαυτὸν βασιλεύσας ἡμέρας ἑπτά. διέστη δ' εὐθὺς ὁ τῶν Ἰσραηλιτῶν λαὸς καὶ οἱ μὲν αὐτῶν Θαμαναῖον[4] βασιλεύειν ἤθελον, οἱ δὲ τὸν Ἀμαρῖνον. νικήσαντες δ' οἱ τοῦτον ἄρχειν ἀξιοῦντες ἀποκτείνουσι τὸν Θαμαναῖον, καὶ παντὸς βασιλεύει ὁ Ἀμαρῖνος τοῦ
312 ὄχλου. τριακοστῷ δὲ ἔτει τῆς Ἀσάνου βασιλείας ἦρξεν ὁ Ἀμαρῖνος ἔτη δώδεκα· τούτων τὰ μὲν ἓξ ἐν Θάρσῳ πόλει, τὰ δὲ λοιπὰ ἐν Σωμαρεῶνι[5] λεγομένῃ πόλει ὑπὸ δὲ Ἑλλήνων Σαμαρείᾳ καλου-

[1] Hudson: Ἰηοῦς RO: Ἰοῦς MSP.
[2] ex Lat. Bekker: ἡρημωμένην (ἐρημ. RO) codd.
[3] Niese: αὐτὸ codd.
[4] Θαμναῖον OP: Θάμανον M: Θάναιον S: Thaman Lat.
[5] Niese (duce Hudson): Μαρεώνῃ codd. E Zonaras.

soldiers and commanders, who were all occupied in the siege of Gabathōn [a] in the Philistine country.

(5) After slaying Ēlanos, Zambrias, the commander of the horse, made himself king and destroyed the entire family of Basanēs in accordance with the prophecy of Jēūs. For it came about that, because of his impiety, his house perished root and branch in the same way as the house of Jeroboam was destroyed, as we have narrated.[b] Now, when the army besieging Gabathōn learned what had befallen the king and that Zambrias had killed him and was ruling the kingdom, they, in turn, chose their commander Amarinos [c] as king, whereupon he withdrew his army from Gabathōn and came to Tharsē, the royal city, attacked it and took it by storm. Zambrias, seeing the city's fall,[d] fled into the inmost part of the palace and, setting it on fire, allowed himself to be consumed with it, after a reign of only seven days. Immediately thereafter the people of Israel were divided into two parties, some wishing Thamanaios [e] to be their king, others, Amarinos. And, as those who wanted Amarinos to rule were victorious, they killed Thamanaios,[f] and Amarinos became king of all the people in the thirtieth [g] year of the reign of Asanos; he reigned twelve years, six of them in the city of Tharsē and the rest in a city called Sōmareōn,[h] known to the Greeks as Samaria. So it was called

The end of Zimri of Israel. 1 Kings xvi. 11.

The reign of Omri of Israel. 1 Kings xvi. 22.

[a] Bibl. Gibbethon, *cf.* § 288 note.

[b] § 289.

[c] Bibl. Omri, LXX Ζαμβρεί, Luc. Ἀμβρί.

[d] Emended text.

[e] Bibl. Tibni, LXX Θαμνεί, Luc. Θαβεννεί.

[f] Scripture says merely that Tibni died.

[g] Bibl. "thirty-first."

[h] Emended text; Heb. *Šōmerôn* (A.V. Samaria), LXX Σεμερών, Luc. Σομορών.

μένῃ. προσηγόρευσε δ' αὐτὴν οὕτως Ἀμαρῖνος[1] ἀπὸ τοῦ τὸ ὄρος ἀποδομένου αὐτῷ ἐφ' ᾧ κατ-
313 εσκεύασε τὴν πόλιν Σωμάρου. διέφερε δ' οὐδὲν τῶν πρὸ αὐτοῦ βασιλευσάντων ἢ τῷ χείρων αὐτῶν εἶναι· ἅπαντες γὰρ ἐζήτουν πῶς ἀποστήσωσιν ἀπὸ τοῦ θεοῦ τὸν λαὸν τοῖς καθ' ἡμέραν ἀσεβήμασι καὶ διὰ τοῦτο δι' ἀλλήλων αὐτοὺς ὁ θεὸς ἐποίησεν ἐλθεῖν καὶ μηδένα τοῦ γένους ὑπολιπεῖν. ἐτελεύτησε δὲ καὶ οὗτος ἐν Σαμαρείᾳ, διαδέχεται δ' αὐτὸν ὁ παῖς Ἄχαβος.

314 (6) Μαθεῖν δ' ἔστιν ἐκ τούτων ὅσην τὸ θεῖον ἐπιστροφὴν ἔχει τῶν ἀνθρωπίνων πραγμάτων, καὶ πῶς μὲν ἀγαπᾷ τοὺς ἀγαθούς, μισεῖ δὲ τοὺς πονηρούς[2] καὶ προρρίζους ἀπόλλυσιν· οἱ μὲν γὰρ τῶν Ἰσραηλιτῶν βασιλεῖς ἄλλος ἐπ' ἄλλῳ διὰ τὴν παρανομίαν καὶ τὰς ἀδικίας ἐν ὀλίγῳ χρόνῳ πολλοὶ κακῶς διαφθαρέντες ἐγνώσθησαν[3] καὶ τὸ γένος αὐτῶν, ὁ δὲ τῶν Ἱεροσολύμων καὶ τῶν δύο φυλῶν βασιλεὺς Ἄσανος δι' εὐσέβειαν καὶ δικαιοσύνην εἰς μακρὸν καὶ εὔδαιμον ὑπὸ τοῦ θεοῦ προήχθη γῆρας καὶ τεσσαράκοντα καὶ ἓν ἄρξας ἔτος
315 εὐμοίρως ἀπέθανε. τελευτήσαντος δ' αὐτοῦ διεδέξατο τὴν ἡγεμονίαν ὁ υἱὸς Ἰωσαφάτης ἐκ γυναικὸς Ἀβιδᾶς τοὔνομα γεγενημένος. τοῦτον μιμητὴν Δαυίδου τοῦ προπάππου κατά τε ἀνδρείαν καὶ εὐσέβειαν ἅπαντες ἐν τοῖς ἔργοις ὑπέλαβον. ἀλλὰ περὶ μὲν τούτου τοῦ βασιλέως οὐ κατεπείγει νῦν λέγειν.

[1] οὕτως Ἀμαρῖνος conj.: αὐτὸς Σωμαραῖος RO: αὐτὸς Σαμάραιος MSP: αὐτὸς Σεμαρεῶνα Hudson.
[2] μοχθηρούς MSP.
[3] εὑρέθησαν MSP: ᾑρέθησαν Hudson.

by Amarinos [a] after Sōmaros,[b] the man who had sold him the mountain on which he built the city. Now he was in no way different from those who had reigned before him except in being worse than they, for they all sought to turn the people away from God by daily impieties, and therefore God caused them to destroy one another and leave no one of their family alive. Amarinos also died in Samaria and was succeeded by his son Achab.[c]

(6) From these events one may learn how close a watch the Deity keeps over human affairs and how He loves good men but hates the wicked, whom He destroys root and branch. For many of the kings of Israel, because of their lawlessness and iniquity, one after the other in a short space of time were marked for destruction together with their families, while Asanos, the king of Jerusalem and the two tribes, because of his piety and righteousness was brought by God to a long and blessed old age and, after a reign of forty-one years, died in a happy state.[d] Upon his death he was succeeded in the kingship by Josaphat,[e] his son by a wife named Abida.[f] That Asanos imitated his great-grandfather David in courage and piety, all men have recognized from his deeds. But there is no great necessity to speak of this king just now.

The end of Asa of Judah.

1 Kings xv. 24; 2 Chron xvi. 13.

1 Kings xxii 42 (*cf.* LXX xvi. 28 b).

[a] Text emended, following a hint of Niese that the reading Sōmaraios, etc., of the MSS. concealed the name of King Amarinos (Omri). [b] Bibl. Shemer, LXX Σαμήρ (*v.l.* Σεμήρ).

[c] Gr. Achabos; bibl. Ahab (*'Aḥāb*), LXX 'Αχαάβ.

[d] Josephus omits the disease of the feet with which Asa was afflicted in his old age.

[e] Gr. Jōsaphatēs; bibl. Jehoshaphat, LXX 'Ιωσαφάθ (*v.l.* 'Ιωσαφάτ).

[f] Bibl. Azubah (*'Azûbāh*), LXX 'Αζαεβά (*v.ll.* 'Αζουβά, 'Αζουβά).

316 (xiii. 1) Ὁ δὲ Ἄχαβος ὁ τῶν Ἰσραηλιτῶν βασιλεὺς κατῴκει μὲν ἐν Σαμαρείᾳ, τὴν δ' ἀρχὴν κατέσχεν ἕως ἐτῶν εἴκοσι καὶ δύο, μηδὲν καινίσας
τῶν πρὸ αὐτοῦ βασιλέων, εἰ μὴ ὅσα γε πρὸς τὸ
χεῖρον καθ' ὑπερβολὴν πονηρίας ἐπενόησεν, ἅπαντα
δ' αὐτῶν τὰ κακουργήματα καὶ τὴν πρὸς τὸ θεῖον
ὕβριν ἐκμιμησάμενος καὶ μάλιστα τὴν Ἱεροβοάμου
317 ζηλώσας παρανομίαν· καὶ γὰρ οὗτος τὰς δαμάλεις
τὰς ὑπ' ἐκείνου κατασκευασθείσας προσεκύνησε
καὶ τούτοις ἄλλα παράδοξα προσεμηχανήσατο.
ἔγημε δὲ γυναῖκα θυγατέρα μὲν Ἰθωβάλου τοῦ
Τυρίων καὶ Σιδωνίων βασιλέως Ἰεζαβέλην δὲ
ὄνομα, ἀφ' ἧς τοὺς ἰδίους αὐτῆς θεοὺς προσκυνεῖν
318 ἔμαθεν. ἦν δὲ τὸ γύναιον δραστήριόν τε καὶ τολ-
μηρόν, εἰς τοσαύτην δ' ἀσέλγειαν καὶ μανίαν
προύπεσεν, ὥστε καὶ ναὸν τῷ Τυρίων θεῷ ὃν
Βελίαν[1] προσαγορεύουσιν ᾠκοδόμησε καὶ ἄλσος
παντοίων δένδρων κατεφύτευσε· κατέστησε δὲ καὶ
ἱερεῖς καὶ ψευδοπροφήτας τούτῳ τῷ θεῷ· καὶ
αὐτὸς δ' ὁ βασιλεὺς πολλοὺς τοιούτους περὶ αὐτὸν
εἶχεν ἀνοίᾳ καὶ πονηρίᾳ πάντας ὑπερβεβληκὼς
τοὺς πρὸ αὐτοῦ.
319 (2) Προφήτης δέ τις τοῦ μεγίστου[2] θεοῦ ἐκ
πόλεως Θεσβώνης[3] τῆς Γαλαδίτιδος χώρας προσελθὼν Ἀχάβῳ προλέγειν αὐτῷ τὸν θεὸν ἔφασκεν

[1] Βὲλ (in marg. Βελεὶ) M: Βῆλαν P: Βῆλα S: Βὴλ Zonaras: Bahel Lat.
[2] μεγάλου RO.
[3] Θεσσεβώνης RO.

[a] Bibl. "And Ahab made an *'ašērāh*" (A.V. "grove"); the *'ašērāh* was a tree trunk representing the Canaanite g[oddess] of fertility.

(xiii. 1) Now Achab, the king of Israel, dwelt in Samaria and exercised the royal power for twenty-two years; in no way did he make a new departure from the kings before him except, indeed, to invent even worse courses in his surpassing wickedness, while closely imitating all their misdeeds and their outrageous behaviour to God and, in particular, emulating the lawlessness of Jeroboam. For he too worshipped the heifers which Jeroboam had made and, in addition, constructed other unheard of objects of worship.[a] And he took to wife the daughter of Ithōbalos,[b] the king of Tyre and Sidon, whose name was Jezabelē,[c] and from her learned to worship her native gods. Now this woman, who was a creature both forceful and bold, went to such lengths of licentiousness and madness that she built a temple to the Tyrian god whom they call Belias,[d] and planted a grove of all sorts of trees; she also appointed priests and false prophets to this god. And the king himself had many such men about him, and in folly and wickedness surpassed all the kings before him.[e]

Ahab of Israel marries Jezebel of Tyre. 1 Kings xvi. 29.

(2) Now there was a certain prophet[f] of the most high God, from the city of Thesbōnē[g] in the country of Galaditis, who came to Achab and said that God

Elijah prophesies a drought. 1 Kings xvii. 1.

[b] Bibl. Ethbaal, LXX Ἰεθεβαάλ.

[c] Bibl. Jezebel (*'Îzebel*), LXX Ἰεζάβελ.

[d] Bibl. Baal, LXX Βάαλ; *cf.* § 145 note.

[e] Josephus, like Luc., omits the reference to the building of Jericho by Hiel, 1 Kings xvi. 34.

[f] Elijah, the prophet meant, is named at this point in Scripture. Weill raises the question whether the name may not have fallen out of Josephus's text here.

[g] *Cf.* LXX Θεσσβών reading, in the Heb., *mittišbî* "from Tishbi," instead of *mittôšābê* "of the inhabitants of" (Gilead).

μήθ' ὕσειν αὐτὸν ἐν ἐκείνοις τοῖς ἔτεσι μήτε δρόσον καταπέμψειν εἰς τὴν χώραν, εἰ μὴ φανέντος[1] αὐτοῦ. καὶ τούτοις ἐπομόσας ἀνεχώρησεν εἰς τὰ πρὸς νότον μέρη, ποιούμενος παρὰ χειμάρρῳ τινὶ τὴν διατριβήν, ἐξ οὗ καὶ τὸ ποτὸν εἶχε· τὴν γὰρ τροφὴν αὐτῷ καθ' ἡμέραν κόρακες προσέφερον.
320 ἀναξηρανθέντος δὲ τοῦ ποταμοῦ δι' ἀνομβρίαν εἰς Σαρεφθὰ[2] πόλιν οὐκ ἄπωθεν τῆς Σιδῶνος καὶ Τύρου (μεταξὺ γὰρ κεῖται) παραγίνεται τοῦ θεοῦ κελεύσαντος· εὑρήσειν γὰρ ἐκεῖ γυναῖκα χήραν,
321 ἥτις αὐτῷ παρέξει τροφάς. ὢν δ' οὐ πόρρω τῆς πύλης ὁρᾷ γυναῖκα χερνῆτιν ξυλιζομένην· τοῦ δὲ θεοῦ δηλώσαντος ταύτην εἶναι τὴν μέλλουσαν αὐτὸν διατρέφειν, προσελθὼν ἠσπάσατο καὶ κομίσαι ὕδωρ παρεκάλεσεν, ὅπως πίῃ, καὶ πορευομένης μετακαλεσάμενος καὶ ἄρτον ἐνεγκεῖν ἐκέλευσε.
322 τῆς δ' ὀμοσάσης μηδὲν ἔχειν ἔνδον ἢ μίαν ἀλεύρου δράκα καὶ ὀλίγον ἔλαιον, πορεύεσθαι δὲ συνειλοχυῖαν τὰ ξύλα, ἵνα φυράσασα ποιήσῃ αὑτῇ καὶ τῷ τέκνῳ ἄρτον, μεθ' ὃν ἀπολεῖσθαι λιμῷ δαπανηθέντα[3] μηκέτι μηδενὸς ὄντος ἔλεγεν, "ἀλλὰ θαρσοῦσα," εἶπεν, "ἄπιθι καὶ τὰ κρείττω προσδοκῶσα, καὶ ποιήσασα πρῶτον ἐμοὶ βραχὺ κόμισον· προλέγω γάρ σοι μηδέποτ' ἐπιλείψειν ἀλεύρων

[1] φάναντος RO: φήσαντος conj. Weill.
[2] Σαριφθὰν R: Σαριφθὰ O: Ἀρεφθὰν E.
[3] δαπανηθέντας RO.

[a] That is, until Elijah should appear to Ahab. Weill, on the basis of the Scriptural phrase, spoken by Elijah, "but according to my word," conjectures that Josephus's text may originally have read "until he himself should say so."
[b] Bibl. "eastward."

had foretold to him that He would not give rain in those years nor send down dew upon the land until he himself should appear.[a] And, having sworn to these things, he withdrew into the south country[b] and made his home beside a stream[c] which also gave him water to drink; as for his food, the ravens brought it to him every day. But, when the river dried up for want of rain, he came to the city of Sarephtha,[d] not far from Sidon and Tyre—it lies between them—at the command of God, for He said that he would there find a widow who would provide him with food. Now when he was a little way from the city gate, he saw a labouring woman who was gathering wood. Thereupon, as God revealed to him that this was she who was to give him food,[e] he went up to her and, after greeting her, asked her to fetch him some water to drink, but, when she started out, he called her back and bade her bring some bread as well. But she swore that she had nothing in the house except a handful of meal and a little oil, and said that she was setting out for home, after gathering the wood, to knead the meal and make bread for herself and her child[f]; after this was eaten they must perish, consumed by hunger, for there was no longer anything left. Whereupon he said, "Even so, be of good courage and go your way in hope of better things; but first prepare a little food and bring it to me, for I prophesy to you that neither the bowl of meal

Elijah and the widow. 1 Kings xvii. 10.

[c] Bibl. "the brook Cherith, that is before Jordan."
[d] Bibl. Zarephath (*Ṣārephāth*), LXX Σαρεπτά (*v.l.* as in Josephus).
[e] This detail of God's prompting Elijah is unscriptural.
[f] So Heb.; LXX τέκνοις "children."

ἐκεῖνο τὸ ἄγγος μηδ᾿ ἐλαίου τὸ κεράμιον, μέχρις
323 οὗ ἂν ὕσῃ ὁ θεός." ταῦτ᾿ εἰπόντος τοῦ προφήτου
παραγενομένη πρὸς αὑτὴν ἐποίησε τὰ εἰρημένα
καὶ αὐτῇ τε ἔσχε καὶ τῷ τέκνῳ χορηγεῖν τὴν
διατροφὴν καὶ τῷ προφήτῃ, ἐπέλιπε δ᾿ οὐδὲν
αὐτοὺς τούτων, ἄχρις οὗ καὶ ὁ αὐχμὸς ἐπαύσατο.
324 μέμνηται δὲ τῆς ἀνομβρίας ταύτης καὶ Μένανδρος
ἐν ταῖς Ἰθωβάλου τοῦ Τυρίων βασιλέως πράξεσι
λέγων οὕτως· "ἀβροχία τ᾿ ἐπ᾿ αὐτοῦ ἐγένετο ἀπὸ
τοῦ Ὑπερβερεταίου μηνὸς ἕως τοῦ ἐχομένου ἔτους
Ὑπερβερεταίου, ἱκετείαν[1] δ᾿ αὐτοῦ ποιησαμένου
κεραυνοὺς ἱκανοὺς βεβληκέναι. οὗτος πόλιν Βότρυν
ἔκτισε τὴν ἐπὶ Φοινίκῃ καὶ Αὖζαν τὴν ἐν Λιβύῃ."
καὶ ταῦτα μὲν δηλῶν τὴν ἐπ᾿ Ἀχάβου γενομένην
ἀνομβρίαν (κατὰ γὰρ τοῦτον καὶ Ἰθώβαλος ἐβα-
σίλευε Τυρίων) ὁ Μένανδρος ἀναγέγραφεν.
325 (3) Ἡ δὲ γυνὴ περὶ ἧς πρὸ τούτων εἴπομεν,
ἡ τὸν προφήτην διατρέφουσα, τοῦ παιδὸς αὐτῇ
καταπεσόντος εἰς νόσον, ὡς καὶ τὴν ψυχὴν ἀφεῖναι
καὶ δόξαι νεκρόν, ἀνακλαιομένη καὶ ταῖς τε χερσὶν
αὑτὴν αἰκιζομένη καὶ φωνὰς οἵας ὑπηγόρευε τὸ
πάθος ἀφιεῖσα κατῃτιᾶτο τῆς παρ᾿ αὐτῇ παρουσίας
τὸν προφήτην ὡς ἐλέγξαντα τὰς ἁμαρτίας αὐ-
326 τῆς καὶ διὰ τοῦτο τοῦ παιδὸς τετελευτηκότος. ὁ
δὲ παρεκελεύετο θαρρεῖν καὶ παραδοῦναι τὸν υἱὸν
αὐτῷ· ζῶντα γὰρ αὐτὸν ἀποδώσειν. παραδούσης
οὖν βαστάσας εἰς τὸ δωμάτιον, ἐν ᾧ διέτριβεν
αὐτός, καὶ καταθεὶς ἐπὶ τῆς κλίνης ἀνεβόησε πρὸς
τὸν θεὸν οὐ καλῶς ἀμείψεσθαι[2] τὴν ὑποδεξαμένην
καὶ θρέψασαν, τὸν υἱὸν αὐτῆς ἀφαιρησόμενον,

[1] ante ἱκετείαν lacunam statuit Niese.
[2] Niese: ἀμείψασθαι codd.

nor the jar of oil shall be empty until God sends rain." When the prophet had said these things, she went to her home and did as he had told her; and she had enough food for herself and her child as well as for the prophet, nor did they lack anything to eat until the drought finally ended. This rainless time is also mentioned by Menander [a] in his account of the acts of Ithōbalos, the king of Tyre, in these words: "There was a drought in his reign, which lasted from the month of Hyperberetaios until the month of Hyperberetaios in the following year. But he made supplication to the gods, whereupon a heavy thunderstorm broke out. He it was who founded the city of Botrys in Phoenicia, and Auza in Libya." This, then, is what Menander wrote, referring to the drought which came in Achab's reign, for it was in his time that Ithōbalos was king of Tyre.

Elijah revives the widow's son. 1 Kings xvii. 17.

(3) Now the woman of whom we spoke above, who gave food to the prophet—her son fell ill so seriously that he ceased to breathe and seemed to be dead, whereupon she wept bitterly, injuring herself with her hands and uttering such cries as her grief prompted [b]; and she reproached the prophet for having come to her to convict her of sin and on that account causing the death of her son. But he urged her to take heart and give her son over to him, for he would, he said, restore him to her alive. So she gave him over, and he carried him into the chamber in which he himself lived, and placed him on the bed; then he cried aloud to God, saying that He would ill requite the woman who had received him and nourished him, if He took her son from her, and he

[a] *Cf. Ap.* i. 116 note.
[b] These details of the woman's grief are unscriptural.

ἐδεῖτό τε τὴν ψυχὴν εἰσπέμψαι πάλιν τῷ παιδὶ
327 καὶ παρασχεῖν αὐτῷ τὸν βίον. τοῦ δὲ θεοῦ κατ-
οικτείραντος μὲν τὴν μητέρα, βουληθέντος δὲ καὶ
τῷ προφήτῃ χαρίσασθαι τὸ μὴ δόξαι πρὸς αὐτὴν ἐπὶ
κακῷ παρεῖναι, παρὰ πᾶσαν προσδοκίαν ἀνεβίωσεν.
ἡ δ' εὐχαρίστει τῷ προφήτῃ καὶ τότε σαφῶς ἔλεγε
μεμαθηκέναι ὅτι τὸ θεῖον αὐτῷ διαλέγεται.

328 (4) Χρόνου δ' ὀλίγου διελθόντος παραγίνεται πρὸς
Ἄχαβον τὸν βασιλέα κατὰ βούλησιν τοῦ θεοῦ,
δηλώσων αὐτῷ τὸν γενησόμενον ὑετόν. λιμὸς δὲ
τότε κατεῖχε τὴν χώραν ἅπασαν καὶ πολλὴ τῶν
ἀναγκαίων ἀπορία, ὡς μὴ μόνον ἀνθρώπους ἄρτων[1]
σπανίζειν, ἀλλὰ καὶ τὴν γῆν μηδ' ὅσα τοῖς ἵπποις
καὶ τοῖς ἄλλοις κτήνεσι πρὸς νομήν ἐστι χρήσιμα
329 διὰ τὴν ἀνομβρίαν ἀναδιδόναι. τὸν οὖν ἐπιμελό-
μενον αὐτοῦ τῶν κτημάτων ὁ βασιλεὺς καλέσας
Ὠβεδίαν, ἀπιέναι[2] βούλεσθαι πρὸς αὐτὸν εἶπεν ἐπὶ
τὰς πηγὰς τῶν ὑδάτων καὶ τοὺς χειμάρρους, ἵν' εἴ
που παρ' αὐτοῖς εὑρεθείη πόα ταύτην εἰς τροφὴν
ἀμησάμενοι τοῖς κτήνεσιν ἔχωσι. καὶ[3] περιπέμ-
ψαντα κατὰ πᾶσαν τὴν οἰκουμένην τοὺς ζητήσοντας
τὸν προφήτην Ἠλίαν οὐχ εὑρηκέναι· συνέπεσθαι
330 δ' ἐκέλευσε κἀκεῖνον αὐτῷ. δόξαν οὖν ἐξορμᾶν
αὐτοῖς, μερισάμενοι τὰς ὁδοὺς ὅ τε Ὠβεδίας καὶ
ὁ βασιλεὺς ἀπῄεσαν ἕτερος ἑτέραν τῶν ὁδῶν.
συνεβεβήκει δὲ καθ' ὃν Ἰεζαβέλη ἡ βασίλισσα
καιρὸν τοὺς προφήτας ἀπέκτεινε τοῦτον ἑκατὸν
ἐν τοῖς ὑπογείοις[4] σπηλαίοις κρύψαι προφήτας καὶ

[1] αὐτῶν SP.
[2] Hudson: ἀπεῖναι codd.
[3] ante καὶ lacunam statuit Niese.
[4] ὑπὸ Γάρις R: ὑπὸ γάροις O: om. Lat.

prayed God to send the breath into the child again and give him life. Thereupon God, because He took pity on the mother and also because He wished graciously to spare the prophet from seeming to have come to her for the purpose of harming her,[a] beyond all expectation brought the child back to life. Then the mother thanked the prophet and said that now she clearly realized that the Deity spoke with him.

Ahab sends men to find Elijah. 1 Kings xviii. 1.

(4) After a little time[b] had passed, the prophet, in accordance with the will of God, went to King Achab to inform him that rain was coming. Now at that time a famine held the whole country in its power, and there was a lack of necessary provisions so that not only did men have a scarcity of bread but, because of the drought, the earth did not yield even the grass necessary for the pasturing of horses and other beasts. So the king called Obedias,[c] who was in charge of his estate, and told him that he wished him to go out to the springs of water and winter streams in order to cut any grass that they might find near them and give it to the beasts for fodder; he also said that he had sent men throughout the entire earth to look for the prophet Elijah, but they had not found him; and he commanded Obedias to accompany him. So, when they had decided to set out, Obedias and the king, dividing the roads, went each by a different road. Now it had happened at the time when Queen Jezabelē killed the prophets that Obedias hid a hundred prophets in underground

[a] This explanation of God's motive is an addition to Scripture.

[b] Bibl. " after many days . . . in the third year."

[c] Bibl. Obadiah (*'Ōbadyāhû*), LXX 'Αβδιού (*v.l.* 'Αβδειού).

τρέφειν αὐτοὺς ἄρτον χορηγοῦντα μόνον καὶ
331 ὕδωρ. μονωθέντι δ'[1] ἀπὸ τοῦ βασιλέως Ὠβεδίᾳ συνήντησεν ὁ προφήτης Ἠλίας· καὶ πυθόμενος παρ'
αὐτοῦ τίς εἴη καὶ μαθὼν προσεκύνησεν αὐτόν· ὁ
δὲ πρὸς τὸν βασιλέα βαδίζειν ἐκέλευσε καὶ λέγειν
332 ὅτι παρείη πρὸς αὐτόν. ὁ δὲ τί κακὸν ὑπ' αὐτοῦ
πεπονθότα πρὸς τὸν ἀποκτεῖναι ζητοῦντα καὶ
πᾶσαν ἐρευνήσαντα γῆν πέμπειν αὐτὸν ἔλεγεν·
ἢ τοῦτ' ἀγνοεῖν αὐτὸν ὅτι μηδένα τόπον κατέλιπεν,
εἰς ὃν οὐκ ἀπέστειλε τοὺς ἀνάξοντας εἰ λάβοιεν
333 ἐπὶ θανάτῳ; καὶ γὰρ εὐλαβεῖσθαι πρὸς αὐτὸν
ἔφασκε, μὴ τοῦ θεοῦ φανέντος αὐτῷ πάλιν εἰς
ἄλλον ἀπέλθῃ τόπον, εἶτα διαμαρτὼν αὐτοῦ,
πέμψαντος τοῦ βασιλέως, μὴ δυνάμενος[2] εὑρεῖν
334 ὅπου ποτ' εἴη γῆς ἀποθάνῃ. προνοεῖν οὖν αὐτοῦ
τῆς σωτηρίας παρεκάλει τὴν περὶ τοὺς ὁμοτέχνους
αὐτοῦ σπουδὴν λέγων, ὅτι σώσειεν ἑκατὸν προφήτας Ἰεζαβέλης πάντας τοὺς ἄλλους ἀνῃρηκυίας,
καὶ ἔχοι κεκρυμμένους αὐτοὺς καὶ τρεφομένους
ὑπ' αὐτοῦ. ὁ δὲ μηδὲν δεδιότα βαδίζειν ἐκέλευε
πρὸς τὸν βασιλέα δοὺς αὐτῷ πίστεις ἐνόρκους ὅτι
πάντως κατ' ἐκείνην Ἀχάβῳ φανήσεται τὴν
ἡμέραν.
335 (5) Μηνύσαντος δὲ τῷ βασιλεῖ Ὠβεδίου τὸν
Ἠλίαν ὑπήντησεν ὁ Ἄχαβος καὶ ἤρετο μετ'

[1] δ' αὖ MSP. [2] καὶ μὴ δυναμένου MSP.

[a] The word "underground," adopted as the correct reading, is an unscriptural detail; the variant "in caves under Garis" is unintelligible. It is just possible, however, that ὑπὸ Γάρις arises from a careless reading of Heb. *mĕ'ārāh* (or Targum *mĕ'arthā*) "cave"; the syllable *me* may have been taken as the Heb. prep. "from," and *'ārāh* transliterated (as normally) as Γαρά, thus giving ἀπὸ Γαρά (or Γαρθά),

caves [a] and fed them, though giving them only bread and water. As Obedias, therefore, was separated from the king and was alone, the prophet Elijah [b] met him. Obedias inquired of him who he was,[c] and, when he found out, did obeisance to him. Thereupon the prophet bade him go to the king and tell him that Elijah was coming to him. The other then asked him what harm he himself had done him that he was sending him to one who was seeking to kill the prophet and had searched every land for him; did he perhaps not know that the king had not overlooked a single place to which he might send men who were to lead Elijah to his death if they caught him? Indeed, he said, he was afraid that if God appeared to Elijah a second time, the prophet might go away to another place and then, when the king sent for him, he would not be able to find him in whatever part of the world he might be, and so he himself would be put to death. He therefore urged him to look out for his safety, telling him of his zeal on behalf of Elijah's fellows in the prophetic art,[d] for he had saved a hundred prophets after Jezabelē had destroyed all the others, and had kept them hidden and fed them. But Elijah bade him go without any fear to the king, first giving him sworn assurances that he would positively appear before Achab that very day.

(5) When Obedias informed the king of Elijah's appearance, Achab went to meet him and asked him

which was further corrupted to ὑπὸ Γάρις. This suggestion is advanced with great hesitancy.

[b] Gr. Ēlias as in Luc.; Heb. *'Ēlîyāhû*, LXX Ἠλειού.

[c] In Scripture Obadiah recognizes Elijah immediately, but asks, for certainty (or in astonishment), " Is it thou, my master, Elijah ? " (A.V. " Art thou that my lord Elijah ? ").

[d] Lit. " fellow-craftsmen."

ὀργῆς εἰ αὐτὸς εἴη ὁ τὸν Ἑβραίων λαὸν κακώσας καὶ τῆς ἀκαρπίας αἴτιος γεγενημένος. ὁ δ' οὐδὲν ὑποθωπεύσας αὐτὸν εἶπεν ἅπαντα τὰ δεινὰ πεποιηκέναι καὶ τὸ γένος αὐτοῦ, ξενικοὺς ἐπεισενηνοχότας[1] τῇ χώρᾳ θεοὺς καὶ τούτους σέβοντας,[2] τὸν δ' ἴδιον αὐτῶν, ὃς μόνος ἐστὶ θεός, ἀπολελοιπότας καὶ
336 μηδεμίαν ἔτι πρόνοιαν αὐτοῦ ποιουμένους. νῦν μέντοι γε ἀπελθόντα[3] ἐκέλευε πάντα τὸν λαὸν εἰς τὸ Καρμήλιον ὄρος ἀθροῖσαι πρὸς αὐτὸν καὶ τοὺς προφήτας αὐτοῦ καὶ τῆς γυναικός, εἰπὼν ὅσοι τὸν ἀριθμὸν εἴησαν, καὶ τοὺς τῶν ἀλσῶν προφήτας ὡς
337 τετρακοσίους τὸ πλῆθος ὄντας. ὡς δὲ συνέδραμον πάντες εἰς τὸ προειρημένον ὄρος Ἀχάβου διαπέμψαντος, σταθεὶς αὐτῶν ὁ προφήτης Ἠλίας μεταξύ, μέχρι πότε διῃρημένους αὐτοὺς τῇ διανοίᾳ καὶ ταῖς δόξαις οὕτως βιώσειν ἔφασκε· νομίσαντας μὲν γὰρ τὸν ἐγχώριον θεὸν ἀληθῆ καὶ μόνον, ἕπεσθαι τούτῳ καὶ ταῖς ἐντολαῖς αὐτοῦ παρῄνει, μηδὲν δὲ τοῦτον ἡγουμένους ἀλλὰ περὶ τῶν ξενικῶν ὑπειληφότας ὡς ἐκείνους δεῖ θρησκεύειν αὐτοῖς
338 συνεβούλευε κατακολουθεῖν. τοῦ δὲ πλήθους μηδὲν πρὸς ταῦτ' ἀποκριναμένου ἠξίωσεν Ἠλίας πρὸς διάπειραν τῆς τε τῶν ξενικῶν θεῶν ἰσχύος καὶ τῆς τοῦ ἰδίου, μόνος ὢν αὐτοῦ προφήτης ἐκείνων δὲ τετρακοσίους ἐχόντων, λαβεῖν αὐτός τε βοῦν καὶ ταύτην θύσας ἐπιθεῖναι ξύλοις πυρὸς οὐχ ὑφαφθέντος, κἀκείνους ταὐτὸ ποιήσαντας ἐπικαλέσασθαι τοὺς ἰδίους θεοὺς ἀνακαῦσαι τὰ ξύλα· γενομένου

[1] ἐνηνοχότας RO: ἐπεισενηνοχότα S²P: εἰσενηνοχότα E.
[2] σέβοντα SP².
[3] ἀνελθόντα R(O).

[a] 450, according to Scripture.

in anger whether it was he who had brought evil upon the Hebrew people and had caused the barrenness of the soil. Thereupon the prophet, without flattering him in the least, said that it was Achab himself and his family who had brought on all these misfortunes by introducing foreign gods into the country and worshipping them, while their own God, who was the only true one, they had abandoned and no longer gave Him any thought. Now, however, he bade him go off and gather all the people to him on Mount Carmel as well as his prophets and those of his wife—telling him how many there were[a]—and also the prophets of the groves, some four hundred in number. And, when at Achab's summons they had all gathered together on the afore-mentioned mountain, the prophet Elijah stood up in their midst and asked how long they would go on living in that way, divided in thought and opinion. If they believed the native God to be the only true God, he urged them to follow Him and His commandments, but if they thought nothing of Him and, instead, considered that they ought to serve the foreign gods, he advised them to go with these. Then, as the people made no answer to these words, Elijah asked that a test be made of the respective powers of the foreign gods and his own and that he, being His only prophet, while their gods had four hundred,[b] be allowed to take an ox and, after slaughtering it, place it on a pile of wood without kindling a fire, and that they do the same; then they should call upon their gods and he upon his to set the wood on fire, for if this happened,

Elijah's contest with the prophets of Baal on Mt. Carmel. 1 Kings xviii. 16.

[b] Josephus here seems to be referring to the 400 prophets of the asherah (A.V. "groves"), who are mentioned with the 450 prophets of Baal in the LXX 1 Kings xviii. 22.

γὰρ τούτου μαθήσεσθαι αὐτοὺς[1] τὴν ἀληθῆ φύσιν
339 τοῦ θεοῦ. ἀρεσάσης δὲ τῆς γνώμης ἐκέλευσεν
Ἠλίας τοὺς προφήτας ἐκλεξαμένους βοῦν πρώτους
τε θῦσαι καὶ τοὺς αὐτῶν[2] ἐπικαλέσασθαι θεούς.
ἐπεὶ δ' οὐδὲν ἀπήντα παρὰ τῆς εὐχῆς[3] καὶ τῆς
ἐπικλήσεως θύσασι τοῖς προφήταις, σκώπτων ὁ
Ἠλίας μεγάλῃ βοῇ καλεῖν αὐτοὺς ἐκέλευε τοὺς
340 θεούς· ἢ γὰρ ἀποδημεῖν αὐτοὺς ἢ καθεύδειν. τῶν
δ' ἀπ' ὄρθρου τοῦτο ποιούντων μέχρι μέσης ἡμέρας
καὶ τεμνόντων αὑτοὺς μαχαίραις καὶ σιρομάσταις
κατὰ τὸ πάτριον ἔθος, μέλλων αὐτὸς ἐπιτελεῖν τὴν
θυσίαν ἐκέλευσε τοὺς μὲν ἀναχωρῆσαι, τοὺς δ'
ἐγγὺς προσελθόντας τηρεῖν αὐτόν, μὴ πῦρ λάθρα
341 τοῖς ξύλοις ἐμβάλῃ. τοῦ δὲ ὄχλου προσελθόντος
λαβὼν δώδεκα λίθους κατὰ φυλὴν τοῦ λαοῦ τῶν
Ἑβραίων ἀνέστησεν ἐξ αὐτῶν θυσιαστήριον καὶ
περὶ αὐτὸ δεξαμενὴν ὤρυξε βαθυτάτην, καὶ συνθεὶς
τὰς σχίζας ἐπὶ τοῦ βωμοῦ καὶ κατ' αὐτῶν ἐπι-
θεὶς τὰ ἱερεῖα, τέσσαρας ἀπὸ τῆς κρήνης ὑδρίας
προσέταξε πληρωθείσας[4] ὕδατος κατασκεδάσαι τοῦ
θυσιαστηρίου, ὡς ὑπερβαλεῖν αὐτὸ καὶ τὴν δεξαμενὴν ἅπασαν γεμισθῆναι ὕδατος ὡς πηγῆς[5] ἀνα-
342 δοθείσης. ταῦτα δὲ ποιήσας ἤρξατο εὔχεσθαι τῷ
θεῷ καὶ παρακαλεῖν αὐτὸν[6] ποιεῖν τῷ πεπλανημένῳ

[1] τότε MSP.
[2] Niese: αὐτῶν codd. E.
[3] + αὐτοῖς MSPE.
[4] ὑδρίας . . . πληρ.] ἐκέλευσεν ὑδρίας RO.
[5] ὡς πηγῆς Niese: πηγῆς codd.
[6] παρακαλεῖν αὐτὸν ex Lat. conj. Niese (aliter in ed.): καλεῖν αὐτὸν καὶ codd.

[a] In Scripture Elijah speaks of one god.
[b] So Heb.; LXX omits. Josephus, however, omits

they would learn the true nature of God. When this proposal was accepted, Elijah bade the prophets select an ox and sacrifice first and call upon their own gods. But, since nothing came of the prophets' prayers and appeals after they had sacrificed, Elijah mocked them and told them to call their gods [a] in a loud voice, for either they were on a journey [b] or were asleep. So they did this from dawn to midday [c] and cut themselves with knives and barbed lances after the custom of their country, until, when about to offer his sacrifice, he bade them retire and the others draw near to watch that he should not secretly apply fire to the wood.[d] Then, when the crowd had come near, he took twelve stones, one for each tribe of the Hebrew people, and with them erected an altar, around which he dug a very deep trench ; next he placed the faggots on the altar and upon them laid the victims, after which he ordered the people to take four jars filled with water from the fountain and pour them over the altar so that the water overflowed and the whole trench was filled as though from a welling spring. Having done these things,[e] he began to pray to God and entreat Him to make His power manifest

Elijah's taunt about their god being busied with " thinking or conversation," if that is what the Heb. means (A.V. "either he is talking, or he is pursuing"; Targum "eases himself," which interpretation Josephus may have followed and therefore omitted the unseemly detail).

[c] Bibl. " until the offering of the evening (or " late afternoon ") sacrifice."

[d] This explanation of Elijah's invitation to the people to draw near is an addition to Scripture. A rabbinic tradition speaks of Elijah's precautions against the tampering with the kindling wood by the prophets of Baal, *cf.* Ginzberg, iv. 198.

[e] According to Scripture, the jars of water were filled and poured three times.

πολὺν ἤδη χρόνον λαῷ φανερὰν τὴν αὑτοῦ[1] δύναμιν. καὶ ταῦτα λέγοντος ἄφνω πῦρ ἐξ οὐρανοῦ, τοῦ πλήθους ὁρῶντος, ἐπὶ τὸν βωμὸν ἔπεσε καὶ τὴν θυσίαν ἐδαπάνησεν, ὡς ἀνακαῆναι καὶ τὸ ὕδωρ καὶ ψαφαρὸν γενέσθαι τὸν τόπον.

343 (6) Οἱ δ' Ἰσραηλῖται τοῦτ' ἰδόντες ἔπεσον ἐπὶ τὴν γῆν καὶ προσεκύνουν ἕνα θεὸν καὶ μέγιστον καὶ ἀληθῆ μόνον ἀποκαλοῦντες, τοὺς δ' ἄλλους ὀνόματα ὑπὸ φαύλης καὶ ἀνοήτου δόξης πεποιημένα[2]· συλλαβόντες δ' αὐτῶν καὶ τοὺς προφήτας ἀπέκτειναν, Ἠλία τοῦτο παραινέσαντος. ἔφη δὲ καὶ τῷ βασιλεῖ πορεύεσθαι πρὸς ἄριστον μηδὲν ἔτι φροντίσαντα· μετ' ὀλίγον γὰρ ὄψεσθαι τὸν θεὸν
344 ὕοντα. καὶ ὁ μὲν Ἄχαβος ἀπηλλάγη, Ἠλίας δ' ἐπὶ τὸ ἀκρωτήριον τοῦ Καρμηλίου ἀναβὰς ὄρους καὶ καθίσας ἐπὶ τῆς γῆς προσηρείσατο τοῖς γόνασι τὴν κεφαλήν, τὸν δὲ θεράποντα ἐκέλευσεν ἀνελθόντα ἐπί τινα σκοπὴν εἰς τὴν θάλασσαν ἀποβλέπειν, κἂν ἴδῃ νεφέλην ἐγειρομένην ποθέν, φράζειν αὐτῷ· μέχρι γὰρ τότε καθαρῷ συνέβαινε τῷ ἀέρι εἶναι.
345 τοῦ δὲ ἀναβάντος καὶ μηδὲν πολλάκις ὁρᾶν φήσαντος, ἕβδομον ἤδη βαδίσας ἑωρακέναι μελαινόμενον εἶπέ τι τοῦ ἀέρος οὐ πλέον ἴχνους ἀνθρωπίνου. ὁ δὲ Ἠλίας ταῦτ' ἀκούσας πέμπει πρὸς τὸν Ἄχαβον κελεύων αὐτὸν εἰς τὴν πόλιν ἀπέρχεσθαι πρὶν ἢ
346 καταρραγῆναι τὸν ὄμβρον. καὶ ὁ μὲν εἰς Ἰεζά-

[1] Niese: αὐτοῦ codd.

[2] ὀνόματα . . . πεποιημένα] ὀνόματι . . . πεποιημένους RO.

to the people which had now for so long a time been in error. And, as he said this, suddenly, in the sight of the multitude, fire fell from heaven and consumed the altar, so that even the water went up in steam,[a] and the ground became completely dry.

(6) When the Israelites saw this, they fell upon the earth and worshipped the one God, whom they acknowledged as the Almighty and only true God, while the others were mere names invented by unworthy and senseless opinion.[b] Then they seized their prophets and killed them at Elijah's behest.[c] He also told the king to go to his midday [d] meal without further care, for in a little while he should see the rain sent by God. And so Achab departed, while Elijah went up to the summit of Mount Carmel and, sitting [e] on the ground, leaned his head upon his knees; and he ordered his servant to go up to a certain look-out and gaze at the sea and if he saw a cloud rising in any direction to tell him of it, for until then the sky had been clear. The servant, therefore, went up and several times informed him that he saw nothing, but after the seventh time he came and told him that he had seen a spot of blackness in the sky no larger than a man's footprint.[f] When Elijah heard this, he sent to Achab, bidding him go back to the city before the rain should pour down in torrents. So the king went to the city of

Elijah's triumph over the prophets of Baal. 1 Kings xviii. 39.

[a] Lit. "was kindled" or "burnt up."

[b] In Scripture no reference is made to the false gods.

[c] It was Elijah himself who slew them, according to Scripture.

[d] Unscriptural detail.

[e] Or "supporting himself"; bibl. "bowed himself" (A.V. "cast himself").

[f] So LXX, translating Heb. *kaph*, which may mean either "sole of the foot" or "palm of the hand" (so Targum here).

ρηλαν[1] πόλιν παραγίνεται· μετ᾽ οὐ πολὺ δὲ τοῦ
ἀέρος ἀχλύσαντος καὶ νέφεσι καλυφθέντος πνεῦμά
τε λάβρον ἐπιγίνεται καὶ πολὺς ὄμβρος. ὁ δὲ προφήτης ἔνθεος γενόμενος τῷ τοῦ βασιλέως ἅρματι
μέχρι τῆς Ἰεζαρήλας[2] πόλεως συνέδραμε.
347 (7) Μαθοῦσα δὲ ἡ τοῦ Ἀχάβου γυνὴ Ἰεζαβέλη
τά τε σημεῖα τὰ ὑπὸ Ἡλία γενόμενα καὶ ὅτι τοὺς
προφήτας αὐτῶν ἀπέκτεινεν, ὀργισθεῖσα πέμπει
πρὸς αὐτὸν ἀγγέλους ἀπειλοῦσα δι᾽ αὐτῶν ἀποκτείνειν αὐτόν, ὡς κἀκεῖνος τοὺς προφήτας αὐτῆς
348 ἀπολέσειε. φοβηθεὶς δ᾽ ὁ Ἡλίας φεύγει εἰς πόλιν
Βερσουβεὲ λεγομένην (ἐπ᾽ ἐσχάτης δ᾽ ἐστὶν αὕτη
τῆς χώρας τῶν τῆς Ἰούδα φυλῆς ἐχόντων τὰ κατὰ
τὴν Ἰδουμαίων γῆν) καταλιπὼν δ᾽ ἐκεῖ τὸν θεράποντα εἰς τὴν ἔρημον ἀνεχώρησεν· εὐξάμενος δ᾽
ἀποθανεῖν, οὐ γὰρ δὴ κρείττων εἶναι τῶν πατέρων,
349 ἵνα ἐκείνων ἀπολωλότων αὐτὸς ζῆν γλίχηται,
κατεκοιμήθη πρός τινι δένδρῳ· διεγείραντος δ᾽
αὐτόν τινος ἀναστὰς εὑρίσκει παρακειμένην αὐτῷ
τροφὴν καὶ ὕδωρ· φαγὼν δὲ καὶ συλλεξάμενος ἐκ
τῆς τροφῆς ἐκείνης τὴν δύναμιν εἰς τὸ Σιναῖον
καλούμενον ὄρος παραγίνεται, οὗ Μωυσῆς τοὺς
350 νόμους παρὰ τοῦ θεοῦ λέγεται λαβεῖν. εὑρὼν δ᾽
ἐν αὐτῷ σπήλαιόν τι κοῖλον εἴσεισι καὶ διετέλει

[1] conj.: Ἰερέζηλα RO: Ἰεσράηλ MSP: Ἰεσράηλαν Hudson.
[2] + Ἀζάρου MSP: + Ἰσαχάρου Cocceji.

---

[a] Emended form (*cf.* §§ 355 ff.), MSS. Jerezēla, Jezraēl; bibl. Jezreel (*Yizre'ēl*), LXX Ἰσραήλ (*v.l.* Ἰεζραέλ), Luc. Ἰεζραήλ.

[b] Bibl. "ran before."

[c] Bibl. "a messenger"; the Armenian version of Scripture agrees with Josephus in using the plural.

[d] "By their hands" is an unscriptural detail. The Greek

Jezarēla,[a] and not long after the sky was darkened and overcast with clouds, a violent wind came up and a heavy rain fell. And the prophet, who was filled with the spirit of God, ran beside [b] the king's chariot as far as the city of Jezarēla.

Elijah flees from Jezebel to the wilderness. 1 Kings xix. 1.

(7) When Achab's wife Jezabelē learned of the prophetic signs given by Elijah and that he had killed their prophets, she was filled with anger and sent messengers [c] to him, threatening to kill him by their hands [d] just as he had destroyed her own prophets. In fear of this Elijah fled to the city called Bersūbee [e] —it is the furthest city in that part of the territory of the tribe of Judah which borders on the country of the Idumaeans—and, after leaving his servant there, withdrew into the wilderness. Then he prayed that he might die, saying he was no better than his fathers that he should long for life when they were gone, and lay down to sleep under a tree.[f] But he was wakened by someone and, when he arose, found food and water laid before him.[g] So he ate it and, after gathering strength from the food, went to the mountain called Sinai,[h] where Moses is said to have received the laws from God. And he found in it a certain hollow cave, which he entered, and there

may, however, mean "threatening through them to kill him."

[e] Bibl. Beersheba, LXX Βηρσάβεε. Variant forms are found in earlier books of the *Antiquities*.

[f] A juniper-tree (Heb. *rôtem*, LXX, transliterating, ῥαθμέν).

[g] Josephus paraphrases the LXX text, "and someone touched him and said, Arise and eat"; Heb. "an angel touched him and said, etc." Both Heb. and LXX speak of a second appearance of the angel.

[h] Bibl. Horeb (elsewhere in Scripture identified with Sinai). Scripture adds that Elijah reached it after a journey of forty days and forty nights.

ποιούμενος ἐν αὐτῷ τὴν μονήν. ἐρομένης δέ τινος αὐτὸν φωνῆς ἐξ ἀδήλου τί παρείη καταλελοιπὼς τὴν πόλιν ἐκεῖσε, διὰ τὸ κτεῖναι μὲν τοὺς προφήτας τῶν ξενικῶν θεῶν, πεῖσαι δὲ τὸν λαὸν ὅτι μόνος εἴη θεὸς ὁ ὤν,[1] ὃν ἀπ' ἀρχῆς ἐθρήσκευσαν, ἔφησε· ζητεῖσθαι γὰρ ἐπὶ τούτῳ πρὸς τιμωρίαν
351 ὑπὸ τῆς γυναικὸς τοῦ βασιλέως. πάλιν δὲ ἀκούσας προελθεῖν[2] εἰς τὸ ὕπαιθρον τῇ ἐπιούσῃ (γνώσεσθαι γὰρ οὕτως τί δεῖ ποιεῖν), προῆλθεν ἐκ τοῦ σπηλαίου μεθ' ἡμέραν καὶ σεισμοῦ τε ἐπακούει καὶ λαμ-
352 πρὰν πυρὸς αὐγὴν ὁρᾷ. καὶ γενομένης ἡσυχίας φωνὴ θεία μὴ ταράττεσθαι τοῖς γινομένοις αὐτὸν παρακελεύεται, κρατήσειν γὰρ οὐδένα τῶν ἐχθρῶν αὐτοῦ, προσέταξέ τε ὑποστρέψαντα εἰς τὴν οἰκείαν ἀποδεῖξαι τοῦ πλήθους βασιλέα Ἰηοῦν τὸν Νεμεσαίου παῖδα, Δαμασκοῦ[3] δὲ τῶν Σύρων Ἀζάηλον· ἀντ' αὐτοῦ δὲ προφήτην Ἐλισσαῖον ὑπ' αὐτοῦ γενήσεσθαι ἐκ πόλεως Ἀβέλας· "διαφθερεῖ δὲ τοῦ ἀσεβοῦς ὄχλου τοὺς μὲν Ἀζάηλος τοὺς δὲ Ἰηοῦς."

[1] ὁ ὤν om. MSPE Lat. [2] προσελθεῖν ROMSE.
[3] Niese: ἐκ Δαμασκοῦ codd.

[a] Bibl. "and behold, the word of the Lord (came) to him." The following verses in both texts, moreover, show that Elijah knew that it was God who spoke to him.

[b] Lit. "the existing one"—a common Hellenistic Jewish rendering of the tetragram YHWH. It is found in the LXX Ex. iii. 14 where Heb. has, "I am who I am." In this passage (1 Kings xix. 10), however, Heb. has "the Lord God of hosts," LXX τῷ κυρίῳ παντοκράτορι.

[c] So LXX; Heb. does not specify the time.

[d] Weill justly complains of Josephus's colourless rationalizing of Scripture's finely poetic account of the divine manifestation.

[e] Josephus omits the Scriptural repetition (1 Kings xix. 13 b, 14) of Elijah's explanation to God of his reasons for

made his abode for some time. But a voice which came from someone, he knew not whom,[a] asked him why he had left the city to come to that spot, whereupon he said that it was because he had killed the prophets of the strange gods and had convinced the people that the only true God was the Eternal,[b] whom they had worshipped from the beginning ; it was for this reason that he was being sought for punishment by the wife of the king. And again he heard a voice telling him to come out into the open air on the morrow,[c] for so he should learn what he must do. The next day, therefore, he came out of the cave and heard the earth rumble and saw a brilliant fiery light.[d] And, when all became quiet, a divine voice exhorted him not to be alarmed by what was happening, for none of his enemies should have him in their power[e] ; and it commanded him to return to his own land and appoint Jehu,[f] the son of Nemesaios,[g] to be king of the people,[h] and Azaēlos[i] to be king of Damascus in Syria,[j] while he should make Elisha,[k] of the city of Abela,[l] prophet in his place. "But," said the voice, "of the impious people Azaēlos shall destroy some, and Jehu others.[m]"

fleeing to the wilderness, and substitutes for it this statement of God that Elijah's enemies should not harm him.

[f] Gr. Jēūs ; Heb. *Yēhû*, LXX Εἰούς (*v.l.* Ἰηού).

[g] Bibl. Nimshi, LXX Ναμεσσεί (*v.l.* Ναμεσθεί).

[h] That is, of Israel.

[i] Bibl. Hazael, LXX Ἀζαήλ.

[j] Emended text ; MSS. "Azaēlos of Damascus to be king of Syria."

[k] Gr. Ἐλισσαῖος, *cf.* LXX Ἐλισσαιέ (*v.l.* Ἐλεισαιέ) ; Heb. *'Elîšā'*.

[l] Bibl. Abel-meholah, LXX Ἀβελμαουλά, tentatively identified by Albright with the modern *Tell Abū Sifri* near *'Ain Ḥelweh*, a little W. of the Jordan in the latitude of Samaria.

[m] Scripture adds, "and him that escapes the sword of Jehu, shall Elisha slay."

353 ὁ δ' Ἠλίας ὑποστρέφει ταῦτ' ἀκούσας εἰς τὴν Ἑβραίων χώραν καὶ τὸν Σαφάτου παῖδα Ἐλισσαῖον καταλαβὼν ἀροῦντα καὶ μετ' αὐτοῦ τινας ἄλλους ἐλαύνοντας ζεύγη δώδεκα προσελθὼν ἐπ-
354 έρριψεν αὐτῷ τὸ ἴδιον ἱμάτιον. ὁ δ' Ἐλισσαῖος εὐθέως προφητεύειν ἤρξατο καὶ καταλιπὼν τοὺς βόας ἠκολούθησεν Ἠλίᾳ. δεηθεὶς δὲ συγχωρῆσαι αὐτῷ τοὺς γονεῖς ἀσπάσασθαι, κελεύοντος τοῦτο ποιεῖν, ἀποταξάμενος αὐτοῖς εἵπετο καὶ ἦν Ἠλίου τὸν ἅπαντα χρόνον τοῦ ζῆν καὶ μαθητὴς καὶ διάκονος. καὶ τὰ μὲν περὶ τοῦ προφήτου τούτου τοιαῦτα ἦν.

355 (8) Νάβωθος[1] δέ τις ἐξ Ἰεζαρήλου πόλεως ἀγρογείτων ὢν τοῦ βασιλέως παρακαλοῦντος αὐτὸν ἀποδόσθαι τιμῆς ὅσης βούλεται τὸν πλησίον αὐτοῦ τῶν ἰδίων ἀγρόν, ἵνα συνάψας ἓν αὐτὸ ποιήσῃ κτῆμα, εἰ δὲ μὴ βούλοιτο χρήματα λαβεῖν ἐπιτρέποντος ἐκλέξασθαι τῶν ἀγρῶν τινα τῶν ἐκείνου, τοῦτο μὲν οὔ φησι ποιήσειν, αὐτὸς δὲ τὴν ἰδίαν καρπώσεσθαι[2] γῆν, ἣν ἐκληρονόμησε τοῦ πατρός.
356 λυπηθεὶς δ' ὡς ἐφ' ὕβρει τῷ μὴ τἀλλότρια λαβεῖν ὁ βασιλεὺς οὔτε λουτρὸν προσηνέγκατο οὔτε τροφήν, τῆς δ' Ἰεζαβέλης τῆς γυναικὸς αὐτοῦ πυνθανομένης ὅ τι λυπεῖται καὶ μήτε λούεται μήτε ἄριστον αὐτῷ παρατίθεται μήτε δεῖπνον, διηγήσατο αὐτῇ τὴν Ναβώθου σκαιότητα καὶ ὡς χρησάμενος

[1] Niese: Ναβώθης RO: Νάβουθος MSP Exc.: Ναβουθαῖος E: Naboth Lat.
[2] Exc. Suidas: καρπώσασθαι codd.

[a] Bibl. Shaphat, LXX Σαφάθ (*v.l.* Σαφάτ).
[b] Elisha's prophesying is an unscriptural detail.
[c] Josephus adds the detail about Elisha's leave-taking but

When Elijah heard these words, he returned to the country of the Hebrews and came upon Elisha, the son of Saphatēs,[a] as he was ploughing and some others with him, who were driving twelve yoke of oxen, and, going up to him, he threw his own mantle over him. Thereupon Elisha immediately began to prophesy,[b] and, leaving his oxen, followed Elijah. But he asked to be allowed to take leave of his parents, and, when Elijah bade him do so, he parted from them and then went with the prophet [c]; and so long as Elijah was alive he was his disciple and attendant. Such, then, is the history of this prophet.

Ahab and Naboth's vineyard. 1 Kings xxi. 1 (LXX xx. 1).

(8) [d] Now a certain Naboth,[e] from the city of Jezarēl,[f] had a field adjoining those of the king, who asked him to sell this field next to his own lands at any price, in order that he might join it to them and make them one property; or, if he did not wish to take money for it, he would permit him to select any one of his own fields. But the other refused to do this, saying that he would himself enjoy the fruits of his own land, which he had inherited from his father. Then the king, who was aggrieved, as if at an insult, at not getting the other's property, would neither bathe [g] nor take food; and, when his wife Jezabelē inquired why he grieved and would neither bathe nor have his midday meal or supper served to him, he told her of Naboth's contrariness and how, in spite of

omits the Scriptural statement (1 Kings xix. 21) that Elisha slaughtered a yoke of oxen to feed his people.

[d] Josephus follows the LXX in narrating the story of Naboth (Heb. ch. xxi) before the war of Ahab and Benhadad (Heb. ch. xx.), *cf.* §§ 363 ff.

[e] Gr. Nabōthos; LXX Ναβουθαί.

[f] Bibl. Jezreel, *cf.* § 346 note.

[g] Unscriptural detail. Josephus, however, omits the Scriptural detail that Ahab took to his bed.

ἐπιεικέσι πρὸς αὐτὸν λόγοις καὶ βασιλικῆς ἐξουσίας
357 ὑποδεεστέροις ὑβρισθείη μὴ τυχὼν ὧν ἠξίου. ἡ
δὲ μὴ μικροψυχεῖν ἐπὶ τούτοις παρεκάλει, παυσάμενον δὲ τῆς λύπης ἐπὶ τὴν συνήθη τρέπεσθαι[1] τοῦ σώματος πρόνοιαν· μελήσειν γὰρ αὐτῇ περὶ
358 τῆς Ναβώθου τιμωρίας. καὶ παραχρῆμα πέμπει
γράμματα πρὸς τοὺς ὑπερέχοντας τῶν Ἰεζαρηλιτῶν[2] ἐκ τοῦ Ἀχάβου ὀνόματος νηστεῦσαί τε κελεύουσα καὶ ποιησαμένους ἐκκλησίαν προκαθίσαι μὲν αὐτῶν Νάβωθον (εἶναι γὰρ αὐτὸν γένους ἐπιφανοῦς), παρασκευασαμένους δὲ τρεῖς τολμηρούς τινας τοὺς καταμαρτυρήσοντας αὐτοῦ, ὡς τὸν θεόν τε εἴη βλασφημήσας καὶ τὸν βασιλέα, καταλεῦσαι
359 καὶ τούτῳ διαχρήσασθαι τῷ τρόπῳ. καὶ Νάβωθος
μέν, ὡς ἔγραψεν ἡ βασίλισσα, οὕτως καταμαρτυρηθεὶς βλασφημῆσαι τὸν θεόν τε καὶ Ἄχαβον βαλλόμενος ὑπὸ τοῦ πλήθους ἀπέθανεν, ἀκούσασα δὲ ταῦτα Ἰεζαβέλη εἴσεισι πρὸς τὸν βασιλέα καὶ κληρονομεῖν τὸν Ναβώθου ἀμπελῶνα προῖκα
360 ἐκέλευσεν. ὁ δὲ Ἄχαβος ἥσθη τοῖς γεγενημένοις
καὶ ἀναπηδήσας ἀπὸ τῆς κλίνης ὀψόμενος ἧκε τὸν ἀμπελῶνα τὸν Ναβώθου. ἀγανακτήσας δ' ὁ θεὸς πέμπει τὸν προφήτην Ἠλίαν εἰς τὸ Ναβώθου χωρίον Ἀχάβῳ συμβαλοῦντα καὶ περὶ τῶν πεπραγμένων ἐρησόμενον ὅτι κτείνας τὸν ἀληθῆ δεσπότην τοῦ χωρίου κληρονομήσειεν αὐτὸς ἀδίκως.

[1] τραπέσθαι (M)SP Exc. Suidas.
[2] Niese (duce Hudson): Ἰσραηλιτῶν codd.

---

[a] Amplification.
[b] Unscriptural detail, but according to rabbinic tradition he was a cousin of Ahab.

his having used mild words toward him, hardly in keeping with the royal authority,[a] he had been insulted by being refused what he had asked for. She, however, urged him not to be dispirited over these things but to cease grieving and turn to caring for his body as usual, for she would attend to Naboth's punishment. And she at once sent letters in Achab's name to the chief men among the Jezarēlites, ordering them to keep a fast and hold an assembly over which Naboth, since he came of an illustrious family,[b] was to preside; and, after they should have brought three[c] unscrupulous men to bear witness against him to the effect that he had blasphemed both God and the king,[d] they were to stone him to death and so make an end of him. Thus, as a result of the queen's letter, Naboth was accused of having blasphemed both God and Achab, and was stoned to death by the people. When Jezabelē heard of this, she went in to the king and bade him take possession of Naboth's vineyard without paying for it. Thereupon Achab, who was pleased[e] at what had happened, leaped from his bed and went to see Naboth's vineyard. But God was angry and sent the prophet Elijah to Naboth's field to meet Achab and ask him about what he had done and why, after killing the real owner of the field, he had himself unjustly taken

Naboth is killed through Jezebel's plot. 1 Kings xxi. (LXX xx.) 13.

[c] Bibl. "two." Ginzberg writes, vi. 312, that Josephus's reference to *three* witnesses "presupposes the older Halakah [law], according to which, in cases involving capital punishment, three witnesses (or to be more accurate, one accuser and two witnesses) are necessary."

[d] Crimes forbidden by the Mosaic law, Ex. xxii. 28.

[e] LXX 1 Kings xxi. 16, "and he tore his clothes and put on sackcloth"; Heb. omits the sentence at this point, but has it further on (vs. 27), after the warning sent to Ahab by God.

361 ὡς δ' ἧκε πρὸς αὐτόν, εἰπόντος τοῦ βασιλέως ὅ τι
βούλεται χρήσασθαι αὐτῷ (αἰσχρὸν γὰρ ὄντα ἐπὶ
ἁμαρτήματι ληφθῆναι ὑπ' αὐτοῦ), κατ' ἐκεῖνον
ἔφη τὸν τόπον ἐν ᾧ τὸν Ναβώθου νεκρὸν ὑπὸ
κυνῶν δαπανηθῆναι συνέβη, τό τε αὐτοῦ καὶ τὸ
τῆς γυναικὸς χυθήσεσθαι αἷμα καὶ πᾶν αὐτοῦ τὸ
γένος ἀπολεῖσθαι, τοιαῦτα ἀσεβῆσαι τετολμηκότος
καὶ παρὰ τοὺς πατρίους νόμους πολίτην ἀδίκως
362 ἀνῃρηκότος. Ἀχάβῳ δὲ λύπη τῶν πεπραγμένων
εἰσῆλθε καὶ μετάμελος, καὶ σακκίον ἐνδυσάμενος
γυμνοῖς τοῖς ποσὶ διῆγεν οὐχ ἁπτόμενος τροφῆς
ἀνθομολογούμενός τε τὰ ἡμαρτημένα καὶ[1] τὸν θεὸν
οὕτως ἐξευμενίζων. ὁ δὲ ζῶντος μὲν αὐτοῦ πρὸς
τὸν προφήτην εἶπεν[2] ὑπερβαλεῖσθαι τὴν τοῦ γένους
τιμωρίαν ἐπεὶ ἐπὶ[3] τοῖς τετολμημένοις μετανοεῖ,
τελέσειν δὲ τὴν ἀπειλὴν ἐπὶ τῷ υἱῷ τοῦ Ἀχάβου.
καὶ ὁ μὲν προφήτης ταῦτ' ἐδήλωσε τῷ βασιλεῖ.
363 (xiv. 1) Τῶν δὲ περὶ τὸν Ἄχαβον ὄντων τοιούτων
κατὰ τὸν αὐτὸν καιρὸν ὁ τοῦ Ἀδάδου υἱὸς βασιλεύων τῶν Σύρων καὶ Δαμασκοῦ δύναμιν ἐξ
ἁπάσης τῆς χώρας συναγαγὼν καὶ συμμάχους
τοὺς πέραν Εὐφράτου βασιλέας ποιησάμενος τριά-
364 κοντα καὶ δύο, ἐστράτευσεν ἐπὶ τὸν Ἄχαβον. ὁ δ'
οὐκ ὢν ὅμοιος αὐτῷ τῇ στρατιᾷ πρὸς μάχην μὲν
οὐ παρετάξατο, πάντα δ' εἰς τὰς ὀχυρωτάτας

[1] ὡς Naber.
[2] εἶπεν om. RO.
[3] ἐπεὶ ἐπὶ conj.: εἶπεν ἐφ' οἷς ἐπὶ RO: ἐπὶ M: ἐπεὶ SPE Exc.

[a] This confession of sin by Ahab is an unscriptural detail.
[b] Dr. Thackeray, *Josephus, the Man*, etc., p. 82, has pointed out Josephus's dependence here on the Targum, which has

possession of it. And when he came to him, the king said that the prophet might do with him as he wished, for he had acted shamefully and had been taken by him in sin,[a] whereupon the other said that in that very place where Naboth's body had been devoured by dogs, his own blood and his wife's should be shed and all his family should perish because he had unscrupulously committed these so impious deeds, and, in violation of his country's laws, had unjustly slain a citizen. Then Achab began to feel grief and remorse for what he had done; putting on sackcloth, he went with bare feet[b] and touched no food and confessed his sins, seeking in this way to propitiate God. And God said to the prophet that while Achab lived, He would put off punishing his family, since he repented of[c] his violent deeds, but He would carry out His threat on Achab's son. And so the prophet revealed these things to the king.

Ben-hadad (Adados) of Syria besieges Ahab in Samaria. 1 Kings xx. (LXX xxi.) 1

(xiv. 1) [d] At the same time that this state of affairs existed for Achab, the son of Adados,[e] who was king of Syria and Damascus, collected a force from all parts of his country and, after making allies of the thirty-two kings beyond the Euphrates,[f] marched against Achab. The latter, not having an army equal to his, did not draw up his men for battle, but shut up all the wealth of the country in the most strongly

"barefoot," while Heb. has *'aṭ* "quietly" (A.V. "softly") and LXX MSS. omit or render "bowed down."

[c] Emended text.

[d] *Cf.* § 355 note.

[e] Bibl. Ben-hadad (lit. "the son of Hadad"), LXX υἱὸς Ἀδέρ; it has been conjectured that the king's full name was Ben-hadad bir-adri.

[f] Scripture does not say that the kings came from beyond the Euphrates.

πόλεις ἐγκλείσας τὰ ἐν τῇ χώρᾳ αὐτὸς μὲν ἔμεινεν ἐν Σαμαρείᾳ· τείχη γὰρ αὕτη[1] λίαν ἰσχυρὰ περιεβέβλητο καὶ τὰ ἄλλα δυσάλωτος ἐδόκει· ὁ δὲ Σύρος ἀναλαβὼν τὴν δύναμιν ἧκεν ἐπὶ τὴν Σαμάρειαν καὶ περικαθίσας αὐτῇ τὸν στρατὸν ἐπολιόρκει.
365 πέμψας δὲ κήρυκα πρὸς Ἄχαβον ἠξίου πρεσβευτὰς δέξασθαι παρ' αὐτοῦ, δι' ὧν αὐτῷ δηλώσει τί βούλεται. τοῦ δὲ τῶν Ἰσραηλιτῶν βασιλέως πέμπειν ἐπιτρέψαντος ἐλθόντες οἱ πρέσβεις ἔλεγον κατ' ἐντολὴν τοῦ βασιλέως τὸν Ἀχάβου πλοῦτον καὶ τὰ τέκνα αὐτοῦ καὶ τὰς γυναῖκας Ἀδάδου τυγχάνειν· ἂν δ' ὁμολογήσῃ καὶ λαβεῖν αὐτὸν τούτων ὅσα βούλεται συγχωρήσῃ, τὴν στρατιὰν ἀπάξει
366 καὶ παύσεται πολιορκῶν αὐτόν. ὁ δ' Ἄχαβος τοῖς πρέσβεσιν ἐκέλευσε πορευθεῖσι λέγειν τῷ βασιλεῖ αὐτῶν ὅτι καὶ αὐτὸς καὶ οἱ ἐκείνου πάντες κτήματά
367 εἰσιν αὐτοῦ. ταῦτα δ' ἀπαγγειλάντων πέμπει πάλιν πρὸς αὐτὸν ἀξιῶν ἀνωμολογηκότα πάντα εἶναι ἐκείνου δέξασθαι τοὺς πεμφθησομένους εἰς τὴν ἐπιοῦσαν ὑπ' αὐτοῦ δούλους, οἷς ἐρευνήσασι τά τε βασίλεια καὶ τοὺς τῶν φίλων καὶ συγγενῶν οἴκους ἐκέλευε διδόναι πᾶν ὅ τι ἂν ἐν αὐτοῖς εὕρωσι κάλλιστον, "τὰ δ' ἀπαρέσαντα σοὶ καταλείψου-
368 σιν." Ἄχαβος δ' ἀγασθεὶς ἐπὶ τῇ δευτέρᾳ πρεσβείᾳ τοῦ τῶν Σύρων βασιλέως, συναγαγὼν εἰς ἐκκλησίαν τὸ πλῆθος ἔλεγεν ὡς αὐτὸς μὲν ἑτοίμως εἶχεν ὑπὲρ σωτηρίας αὐτοῦ καὶ εἰρήνης καὶ γυναῖκας τὰς ἰδίας προέσθαι τῷ πολεμίῳ καὶ τὰ τέκνα καὶ πάσης παραχωρῆσαι κτήσεως· ταῦτα γὰρ ἐπιζητῶν ἐπρεσβεύσατο πρῶτον ὁ Σύρος.

[1] αὐτῇ RO.

fortified cities, while he himself remained in Samaria, for this city was surrounded by exceedingly strong walls and seemed in all ways difficult to take. But the Syrian with his force came to Samaria, placed his army around it and besieged it. Then he sent a herald to Achab, asking that his envoys be received by him, that through them he might inform him of his wishes.[a] And, when the Israelite king gave him leave to send them, the envoys came and, at their king's command, said that Achab's wealth, children and wives belonged to Adados; if Achab came to terms and allowed him to take of these what he pleased, he would withdraw his army and raise the siege. Thereupon Achab bade the envoys go and tell their king that both he and all those belonging to him were the possessions of Adados. When they reported these words to him, he again sent to Achab and demanded, since he admitted that all his belongings were Adados's, that he receive the servants who were to be sent to him the next day to search the palace and the houses of his friends and relatives, and give them whatever they might find there that was most desirable, adding, "What doesn't please them, they will leave for you."[b] But Achab, who was indignant at the second message of the Syrian king, brought the people together in assembly and told them that he himself was ready, in the interests of their safety and peace, to give up his own wives and children to the enemy and yield all his possessions, for this was what the Syrian had demanded when he sent his envoys the first time. "But now

[a] This description of Samaria and Ben-hadad's request that his envoys be received are additions to Scripture.

[b] This last sentence is an addition to Scripture.

369 " νῦν δ' ἠξίωκε δούλους πέμψαι τάς τε πάντων οἰκίας ἐρευνῆσαι καὶ μηδὲν ἐν αὐταῖς καταλιπεῖν τῶν καλλίστων κτημάτων, πρόφασιν βουλόμενος πολέμου λαβεῖν, εἰδὼς ὅτι τῶν μὲν ἐμαυτοῦ δι' ὑμᾶς οὐκ ἂν φεισαίμην, ἀφορμὴν δ' ἐκ τοῦ περὶ τῶν ὑμετέρων ἀηδοῦς[1] πραγματευόμενος εἰς τὸ
370 πολεμεῖν· ποιήσω γε μὴν τὰ ὑμῖν δοκοῦντα." τὸ δὲ πλῆθος μὴ δεῖν ἀκούειν τῶν κατ' αὐτὸν ἔλεγεν, ἀλλὰ καταφρονεῖν καὶ πρὸς τὸ πολεμεῖν ἑτοίμως ἔχειν. τοῖς οὖν πρεσβευταῖς ἀποκρινάμενος λέγειν ἀπελθοῦσιν ὅτι τοῖς τὸ πρῶτον ἀξιωθεῖσιν ὑπ' αὐτοῦ καὶ νῦν ἐμμένει τῆς τῶν πολιτῶν ἀσφαλείας ἕνεκα πρὸς δὲ τὴν δευτέραν ἀξίωσιν οὐχ ὑπακούει, ἀπέλυσεν αὐτούς.

371 (2) Ὁ δ' Ἄδαδος ἀκούσας ταῦτα καὶ δυσχεράνας τρίτον ἔπεμψε πρὸς Ἄχαβον τοὺς πρέσβεις ἀπειλῶν ὑψηλότερον τῶν τειχῶν οἷς καταφρονεῖ χῶμα τούτοις ἐπεγείρειν αὐτοῦ τὴν στρατιὰν κατὰ δράκα γῆς λαμβάνουσαν, ἐμφανίζων αὐτῷ τῆς δυνάμεως τὸ
372 πλῆθος καὶ καταπληττόμενος. τοῦ δ' Ἀχάβου μὴ καυχᾶσθαι δεῖν ἀποκριναμένου καθωπλισμένον ἀλλὰ τῇ μάχῃ κρείττω γενόμενον, ἐλθόντες οἱ πρέσβεις καὶ δειπνοῦντα καταλαβόντες τὸν βασιλέα μετὰ τριάκοντα καὶ δύο βασιλέων συμμάχων ἐδήλωσαν αὐτῷ τὴν ἀπόκρισιν· ὁ δ' εὐθέως τοῦτο[2]

[1] αἰδοῦς RO.

[2] post τοῦτο lacunam statuit Niese, recte videtur.

[a] Josephus greatly amplifies Ahab's speech.

[b] Josephus seems to have misunderstood the Heb. (and Luc.) text of 1 Kings xx. 10, which reads " the dust of Samaria will not be enough for handfuls (*še'ālîm*) for all the people at my feet (*i.e.* " following me ")," that is, there were more men in Ben-hadad's army than there were handfuls of dust in

he insists on sending his servants to search all houses and leave none of the most desirable possessions in them, for he wishes to find a pretext for making war, and though he knows that on your account I would not spare what belongs to me, he is trying hard to make this disagreeable treatment of you an occasion for war. Nevertheless, I shall do what you think best."[a] Then the people said that he ought not to listen to Adados's terms but should treat him scornfully and prepare for war. Accordingly, in reply to the envoys he told them to go back and say that for the sake of the citizens' safety he still agreed to the demands first made by Adados, but would not submit to the second demand. He then dismissed them.

Ahab is encouraged by a prophecy of victory over the Syrians. 1 Kings xx. (LXX xxi.) 10.

(2) When Adados heard these words, he was greatly vexed and sent envoys to Achab a third time, threatening that his army would take each man a handful of earth and erect earthworks higher than the walls[b] in which he had such sublime confidence,[c] in this way displaying to him the great number of his force and seeking to strike terror into him. But Achab replied that the time to boast was not when arming oneself but after coming off victorious in battle.[d] And, when the envoys came to the king, they found him dining with the thirty-two kings who were his allies, and reported this answer to him.

Samaria. The LXX, reading *šûʿālîm* "foxes" instead of *šeʿālîm* "handfuls," has εἰ ἐκποιήσει ὁ χοῦς Σαμαρείας ταῖς ἀλώπεξιν παντὶ τῷ λαῷ τοῖς πεζοῖς μοῦ, which makes no sense.

[c] On this meaning of καταφρονεῖν with the dative *cf.* *A.* vii. 61 note.

[d] So Targum ; Heb. "Let not the one who girds on (his sword) boast like the one who takes it off," LXX μὴ καυχάσθω ὁ κυρτὸς ὡς ὁ ὀρθός "let not the crooked man boast like the erect man."

προσέταξε καὶ περιχαρακοῦν τὴν πόλιν καὶ χώματα βάλλεσθαι καὶ μηδένα τρόπον ἀπολιπεῖν πολιορκίας.
373 ἦν δ' Ἄχαβος τούτων πραττομένων ἐν ἀγωνίᾳ δεινῇ σὺν παντὶ τῷ λαῷ· θαρρεῖ δὲ καὶ τῶν φόβων ἀπολύεται προφήτου τινὸς αὐτῷ προσελθόντος καὶ φήσαντος αὐτῷ τὸν θεὸν ὑπισχνεῖσθαι ποιήσειν τὰς τοσαύτας τῶν πολεμίων μυριάδας ὑποχειρίους.
374 πυθομένῳ δὲ διὰ τίνων ἂν ἡ νίκη γένοιτο, "διὰ τῶν παίδων," εἶπε, "τῶν ἡγεμόνων, ἡγουμένου σοῦ διὰ τὴν ἀπειρίαν ἐκείνων." καλέσας δὲ τοὺς τῶν ἡγεμόνων υἱούς, εὑρέθησαν δ' ὡς διακόσιοι καὶ τριακονταδύο, μαθὼν τὸν Σύρον πρὸς εὐωχίαν καὶ ἄνεσιν τετραμμένον, ἀνοίξας τὰς πύλας ἐξ-
375 έπεμψε τοὺς παῖδας. τῶν δὲ σκοπῶν δηλωσάντων τοῦτο τῷ Ἀδάδῳ πέμπει τινὰς ὑπαντησομένους, ἐντειλάμενος, ἂν μὲν εἰς μάχην ὦσι προεληλυθότες, ἵνα δήσαντες ἀγάγωσι πρὸς αὐτόν, ἂν δ' εἰρηνικῶς,
376 ὅπως ταὐτὸ ποιῶσιν. εἶχε δ' ἑτοίμην Ἄχαβος καὶ τὴν ἄλλην στρατιὰν ἐντὸς τῶν τειχῶν. οἱ δὲ τῶν ἀρχόντων παῖδες συμβαλόντες τοῖς φύλαξι πολλοὺς αὐτῶν ἀποκτείνουσι καὶ τοὺς ἄλλους ἄχρι τοῦ στρατοπέδου διώκουσιν. ἰδὼν δὲ τούτους νικῶντας ὁ τῶν Ἰσραηλιτῶν βασιλεὺς ἐξαφίησι
377 καὶ τὴν ἄλλην στρατιὰν ἅπασαν. ἡ δ' αἰφνιδίως ἐπιπεσοῦσα τοῖς Σύροις ἐκράτησεν αὐτῶν, οὐ γὰρ προσεδόκων αὐτοὺς ἐπεξελεύσεσθαι, καὶ διὰ τοῦτο

---

[a] The text is uncertain; there is probably a lacuna in the MSS.

[b] So LXX; Heb. "place yourselves (in position), and they placed themselves against the city," Targum "prepare yourselves, and they lay in ambush against the city."

[c] Ahab's anxiety is an unscriptural detail.

He at once gave orders [a] to build a stockade around the city and throw up earthworks [b] and not leave any way of besieging it untried. While these things were being done, Achab was in a terrible state of anxiety together with all his people.[c] But he took heart and was relieved of his fears when a certain prophet came to him and told him that God promised to deliver these many myriads of the enemy into his hand. And, when he asked through whom the victory would be won, the prophet said, "Through the sons of the governors,[d] with you to lead them because of their inexperience." [e] So he summoned the sons of the governors, who were found to number some two hundred and thirty-two,[f] and, when he learned that the Syrian was giving himself up to feasting and taking his ease, he opened the gates and sent the youths out. And when the look-outs reported this to Adados, he sent out some of his men to meet them, with instructions that, if the others came out to battle, they should bind them and bring them to him; and even if the enemy came out peaceably, they should do the same thing. But Achab had still another army waiting within the walls. Then the sons of the nobles engaged the guards and killed many of them, while the rest they pursued as far as their camp. And when the Israelite king saw his men winning the victory, he released all of his second army as well. Thereupon they suddenly fell upon the Syrians and defeated them, for these had not expected them to come out against them, and for

Ahab's victory over Ben-hadad. 1 Kings xx. (LXX xxi.) 19.

[d] Bibl. "the young men of the rulers of the provinces."

[e] "Because of their inexperience" is an addition to Scripture.

[f] Josephus omits the numbering of the Israelite army.

γυμνοῖς καὶ μεθύουσι προσέβαλλον, ὥστε τὰς
πανοπλίας ἐκ τῶν στρατοπέδων φεύγοντας καταλιπεῖν καὶ τὸν βασιλέα διασωθῆναι μόλις ἐφ'
378 ἵππου ποιησάμενον τὴν φυγήν. Ἄχαβος δὲ πολλὴν ὁδὸν διώκων τοὺς Σύρους ἤνυσεν ἀναιρῶν
αὐτούς, διαρπάσας δὲ τὰ ἐν τῇ παρεμβολῇ (πλοῦτος
δ' ἦν οὐκ ὀλίγος, ἀλλὰ καὶ χρυσοῦ πλῆθος καὶ
ἀργύρου), τά τε ἅρματα τοῦ Ἀδάδου καὶ τοὺς
ἵππους λαβὼν ἀνέστρεψεν εἰς τὴν πόλιν. τοῦ δὲ
προφήτου παρασκευάζεσθαι φήσαντος καὶ τὴν δύναμιν ἑτοίμην ἔχειν, ὡς τῷ ἐπιόντι πάλιν ἔτει
στρατεύσοντος ἐπ' αὐτὸν τοῦ Σύρου, ὁ μὲν Ἄχαβος
πρὸς τούτοις ἦν.
379 (3) Ὁ δὲ Ἄδαδος διασωθεὶς ἐκ τῆς μάχης μεθ'
ὅσης ἠδυνήθη στρατιᾶς συνεβουλεύσατο τοῖς αὐτοῦ
φίλοις, πῶς[1] ἐπιστρατεύσηται τοῖς Ἰσραηλίταις.
οἱ δ' ἐν μὲν τοῖς ὄρεσιν οὐκ ἐδίδοσαν γνώμην συμβαλεῖν αὐτοῖς· τὸν γὰρ θεὸν αὐτῶν ἐν τοῖς τοιούτοις
δύνασθαι τόποις καὶ διὰ τοῦτο νῦν ὑπ' αὐτῶν νε-
νικῆσθαι· κρατήσειν δὲ ἔλεγον ἐν πεδίῳ ποιησα-
380 μένους τὴν μάχην. συνεβούλευον δὲ πρὸς τούτῳ
τοὺς μὲν βασιλέας οὓς ἐπηγάγετο συμμάχους ἀπολῦσαι πρὸς τὰ οἰκεῖα, τὴν δὲ στρατιὰν αὐτῶν
κατασχεῖν, ἀντ' ἐκείνων σατράπας καταστήσαντα·
εἰς δὲ τὴν τῶν ἀπολωλότων τάξιν στρατολογῆσαι
δύναμιν ἐκ τῆς χώρας τῆς αὐτῶν καὶ ἵππους καὶ
ἅρματα. δοκιμάσας οὖν ταῦτα εἰρῆσθαι καλῶς
οὕτως διεκόσμησε τὴν δύναμιν.

[1] Naber: πῶς ἂν codd.

[a] "A long way" is an unscriptural detail.
[b] This spoil is not mentioned in Scripture.

that reason were unarmed and drunk when they were attacked, so that they fled from the camp, leaving all their armour behind, and the king barely saved himself by making his escape on horseback. Achab went a long way [a] in pursuit of the Syrians, and slew them. Then, after plundering their camp, in which there was no little sum of wealth and also a large quantity of gold and silver,[b] and taking the chariots and horses of Adados, he returned to the city. But the prophet told him to prepare himself and hold his force in readiness, for the Syrian would again attack him in the following year; and so Achab attended to these things.

Ben-hadad again prepares for war with Ahab. 1 Kings xx. (LXX xxi.) 23.

(3) Now Adados, after escaping from the scene of battle with as much of his force as he could save, took counsel with his friends concerning how he should again take the field against the Israelites. And they were of the opinion that he should not engage them in the hills, on the ground that their god had most power in such places, and for that reason they had recently been defeated. But, they said, they would conquer them if they fought the battle in the plain. They also advised him further to send back to their homes the kings whom he had brought along as allies, but to retain their armies and appoint satraps [c] in their places, while, to fill the ranks of those who had been killed, he should levy a force from their own country, as well as horses and chariots. Thereupon he approved of these words as well spoken, and arranged his force accordingly.

[c] σατράπαι is the LXX word translating Heb. *pahôth* " provincial governors " or " commanders " (A.V. " captains "); *pahôth* is an Assyrian loan-word, while σατράπης is a Persian loan-word.

381 (4) Ἀρξαμένου δὲ ἔαρος ἀναλαβὼν τὴν στρατιὰν ἦγεν ἐπὶ τοὺς Ἑβραίους, καὶ γενόμενος πρὸς πόλει τινί, Ἀφεκὰ δ' αὐτὴν καλοῦσιν, ἐν μεγάλῳ στρατοπεδεύεται πεδίῳ. Ἄχαβος δ' ἀπαντήσας αὐτῷ μετὰ τῆς δυνάμεως ἀντεστρατοπεδεύσατο· σφόδρα δ' ἦν ὀλίγον αὐτοῦ τὸ στράτευμα πρὸς τοὺς πο-
382 λεμίους ἀντιπαραβαλλόμενον. τοῦ δὲ προφήτου προσελθόντος αὐτῷ πάλιν καὶ νίκην τὸν θεὸν αὐτῷ διδόναι φήσαντος, ἵνα τὴν ἰδίαν ἰσχὺν ἐπιδείξηται μὴ μόνον ἐν τοῖς ὄρεσιν ἀλλὰ κἂν τοῖς πεδίοις ὑπάρχουσαν, ὅπερ οὐκ εἶναι δοκεῖ τοῖς Σύροις, ἑπτὰ μὲν ἡμέρας[1] ἀντεστρατοπεδευκότες ἡσύχαζον, τῇ δὲ ὑστάτῃ τούτων ὑπὸ τὸν ὄρθρον προελθόντων ἐκ τοῦ στρατοπέδου τῶν πολεμίων καὶ παραταξαμένων εἰς μάχην ἀντεπεξῆγε καὶ Ἄχαβος τὴν
383 οἰκείαν δύναμιν. καὶ συμβαλὼν καρτερᾶς τῆς μάχης γενομένης τρέπεται τοὺς πολεμίους εἰς φυγὴν καὶ διώκων ἐπέκειτο.[2] οἱ δὲ καὶ ὑπὸ τῶν ἁρμάτων καὶ ὑπ' ἀλλήλων ἀπώλοντο, ἴσχυσαν δ' ὀλίγοι διαφυγεῖν εἰς τὴν Ἀφεκὰ πόλιν αὐτῶν.
384 ἀπέθανον δὲ καὶ αὐτοὶ τῶν τειχῶν αὐτοῖς ἐπιπεσόντων ὄντες δισμύριοι ἑπτακισχίλιοι. διεφθάρησαν δ' ἐν ἐκείνῃ τῇ μάχῃ ἄλλαι μυριάδες δέκα. ὁ δὲ βασιλεὺς τῶν Σύρων Ἄδαδος φεύγων μετά τινων πιστοτάτων οἰκετῶν εἰς ὑπόγειον οἶκον
385 ἐκρύβη. τούτων δὲ φιλανθρώπους καὶ ἐλεήμονας εἶναι φησάντων τοὺς τῶν Ἰσραηλιτῶν βασιλέας

[1] Niese: ἡμέραις codd.
[2] + κτείνων MSPE Zonaras.

[a] Bibl. Aphek. There were several Palestinian cities of this name ; the location of the city here mentioned is uncer-

(4) At the beginning of spring Adados marched with his army against the Hebrews and, after coming to a certain city which is called Apheka,[a] encamped in a great plain. And Achab met him with his force and encamped over against him, although his army was a very small one in comparison with the enemy.[b] But the prophet came to him again and said that God would give him victory in order that He might show His power to exist not only in the hills but also in the plains, which was what the Syrians did not believe. And for seven days both armies remained quiet in their camps, facing each other, but, when on the last day the enemy came out of their camp at dawn and drew themselves up for battle, Achab also led his force out against them. Then, after engaging them in a battle which was stubbornly fought, he put the enemy to flight and followed hard in pursuit. And they were killed by their own chariots and by one another,[c] although a few succeeded in escaping to their city Apheka. But these too perished when the walls fell upon them—twenty-seven thousand of them. And in that battle another hundred thousand were slain. Adados, the Syrian king, fled with some of his most faithful servants and hid in an underground chamber.[d] But when these told him that the Israelite kings were humane and merciful and that

Ben-hadad encounters Ahab's force at Aphek. 1 Kings xx. (LXX xxi.) 26.

tain; it is thought by some scholars to have been in the Plain of Esdraelon, by others it is identified with the modern *Fīq*, *c.* 5 miles E. of the lake of Galilee, on the road to Damascus.

[b] Scripture puts it much more picturesquely, "and the Israelites pitched before them like two little flocks of kids, and the Syrians filled the country."

[c] Unscriptural details.

[d] Heb. "chamber in chamber," *i.e.* into an inner chamber or hiding-place, LXX εἰς τὸ ταμεῖον.

καὶ δυνήσεσθαι τῷ συνήθει τρόπῳ τῆς ἱκετείας χρησαμένους τὴν σωτηρίαν αὐτῷ[1] παρ' Ἀχάβου λαβεῖν, εἰ συγχωρήσειεν αὐτοῖς πρὸς αὐτὸν ἀπελθεῖν, ἀφῆκεν· οἱ δὲ σάκκους ἐνδυσάμενοι καὶ σχοινία ταῖς κεφαλαῖς περιθέμενοι (οὕτως γὰρ τὸ παλαιὸν ἱκέτευον οἱ Σύροι), πρὸς Ἄχαβον παρεγένοντο καὶ δεῖσθαι τὸν Ἄδαδον σώζειν αὐτὸν ἔλεγον, εἰς ἀεὶ δοῦλον αὐτοῦ τῆς χάριτος γενησό-
386 μενον. ὁ δὲ συνήδεσθαι φήσας αὐτῷ περιόντι καὶ μηδὲν ἐν τῇ μάχῃ πεπονθότι, τιμὴν καὶ εὔνοιαν ἣν ἄν τις ἀδελφῷ παράσχοι κατεπηγγείλατο. λαβόντες δὲ ὅρκους παρ' αὐτοῦ μηδὲν ἀδικήσειν φανέντα προάγουσι πορευθέντες ἐκ τοῦ οἴκου ἐν ᾧ ἐκέκρυπτο καὶ προσάγουσι τῷ Ἀχάβῳ ἐφ' ἅρματος καθεζομένῳ· ὁ δὲ προσεκύνησεν αὐτόν.
387 Ἄχαβος δὲ διδοὺς[2] αὐτῷ τὴν δεξιὰν ἀναβιβάζει ἐπὶ τὸ ἅρμα καὶ καταφιλήσας θαρρεῖν ἐκέλευε καὶ μηδὲν τῶν ἀτόπων προσδοκᾶν, Ἄδαδος δ' εὐχαρίστει καὶ παρ' ὅλον τὸν τοῦ ζῆν χρόνον ἀπομνημονεύσειν τῆς εὐεργεσίας ὡμολόγει καὶ τὰς πόλεις τῶν Ἰσραηλιτῶν, ἃς ἀπήνεγκαν οἱ πρὸ αὐτοῦ βασιλεῖς, ἀποδώσειν ἐπηγγείλατο καὶ Δαμασκὸν ὥστε ἐξελαύνειν εἰς αὐτήν, καθὼς καὶ οἱ πατέρες αὐτοῦ εἰς Σαμάρειαν εἶχον τοῦτο ποιεῖν, ἀνήσειν.
388 γενομένων δ' αὐτοῖς ὅρκων καὶ συνθηκῶν πολλὰ δωρησάμενος αὐτῷ Ἄχαβος ἀπέπεμψεν εἰς τὴν ἰδίαν βασιλείαν. καὶ τὰ μὲν περὶ τῆς Ἀδάδου τοῦ

[1] αὐτῶν MSP.

[2] δὲ διδοὺς Niese: δ' ἐπιδοὺς codd.: δὲ δοὺς E.

[a] Bibl. "thy servant Ben-hadad says, may my life be spared."

[b] Scripture says nothing of an oath given by Ahab; Josephus also omits the difficult phrase (1 Kings xx. 32) which

by using the customary form of supplication they could obtain his life from Achab, if he would allow them to go to him, he let them go. So they dressed in sackcloth and put ropes around their necks—this was the manner in which the ancient Syrians appeared as suppliants—and, going to Achab, told him that Adados begged him to spare his life and would always be his servant in return for his kindness.[a] And the king, after saying that he rejoiced at Adados's surviving and not having suffered any harm in the battle, promised that he would show him the same honour and goodwill that one would accord a brother. So, when they had received his oath not to do Adados any wrong when he appeared,[b] they departed and brought him forth from the chamber in which he had hidden and brought him to Achab, who was seated in a chariot. He then did obeisance to him, but Achab gave him his right hand and let him come up into the chariot and, after embracing him, bade him take heart and not be apprehensive of any outrage, whereupon Adados thanked him and promised to show himself mindful of his beneficence all the days of his life,[c] and offered to give back the Israelite cities which the kings before him had taken away, and to throw Damascus open to them so that they might travel there, just as his fathers had been able to go to Samaria. Then, after they had made sworn covenants, Achab presented him with many gifts[d] and sent him away to his own kingdom. So ended

seems to mean that Ben-hadad's servants seized upon Ahab's words, "he is my brother" as a good omen. Possibly, however, Josephus takes this expression as an oath.

[c] The preceding is an amplification of Scripture, which says merely that Ahab brought Ben-hadad up into his chariot.

[d] The gifts are an unscriptural detail.

Σύρων βασιλέως στρατείας ἐπὶ Ἄχαβον καὶ τοὺς Ἰσραηλίτας τοιοῦτον ἔσχε τὸ τέλος.

389 (5) Προφήτης δέ τις τοὔνομα Μιχαίας προσελθών τινι τῶν Ἰσραηλιτῶν ἐκέλευεν αὐτὸν εἰς τὴν κεφαλὴν πλῆξαι· τοῦτο γὰρ ποιήσειν κατὰ βούλησιν τοῦ θεοῦ. τοῦ δὲ μὴ πεισθέντος προεῖπεν αὐτῷ παρακούσαντι τῶν τοῦ θεοῦ προσταγμάτων λέοντι περιτυχόντα διαφθαρήσεσθαι. συμβάντος τούτου τἀνθρώπῳ, πρόσεισιν ἑτέρῳ πάλιν ὁ προ-
390 φήτης ταὐτὸ προστάσσων. πλήξαντος δ' ἐκείνου καὶ θραύσαντος αὐτοῦ τὸ κρανίον, καταδησάμενος τὴν κεφαλὴν προσῆλθε τῷ βασιλεῖ λέγων αὐτῷ συνεστρατεῦσθαι καὶ παραλαβεῖν ἐπὶ φυλακῇ τινα τῶν αἰχμαλώτων παρὰ τοῦ ταξιάρχου, φυγόντος δ' αὐτοῦ κινδυνεύειν ὑπὸ τοῦ παραδεδωκότος ἀποθανεῖν· ἀπειλῆσαι γὰρ αὐτόν, εἰ διαφύγοι ὁ
391 αἰχμάλωτος, ἀποκτείνειν. δίκαιον δὲ φήσαντος Ἀχάβου τὸν θάνατον εἶναι, λύσας τὴν κεφαλὴν ἐπιγινώσκεται ὑπ' αὐτοῦ Μιχαίας ὁ προφήτης ὤν. ἐκέχρητο δὲ σοφίσματι πρὸς αὐτὸν τῷ γενομένῳ
392 πρὸς τοὺς μέλλοντας λόγους· εἶπε γὰρ ὡς ὁ θεὸς ἀφέντ' αὐτὸν διαδράναι τὴν τιμωρίαν Ἄδαδον τὸν βλασφημήσαντα εἰς αὐτὸν μετελεύσεται καὶ ποιήσει αὐτὸν μὲν ἀποθανεῖν ὑπ' ἐκείνου, τὸν δὲ λαὸν ὑπὸ τῆς στρατιᾶς αὐτοῦ. παροξυνθεὶς δ' Ἄχαβος πρὸς τὸν προφήτην τὸν μὲν ἐγκλεισθέντα φυλάττεσθαι

the expedition of Adados, the king of Syria, against Achab and the Israelites.

A prophet rebukes Ahab for releasing Ben-hadad. 1 Kings xx. (LXX xxi.) 35.

(5) Now a certain prophet, whose name was Michaias,[a] came to an Israelite and bade him strike him on the head, for it was in accordance with the will of God that he should do so. And, when he refused, the prophet warned him that for disobeying the commands of God he should meet a lion and be killed. This was what happened to the man. So the prophet went to another and gave him the same order and, when the man struck him and cracked his skull, he bound up his head[b] and, going to the king, told him that he had served in his army and had had one of the captives turned over to him by his officer[c] for guarding but the prisoner had escaped, and he was in danger of being put to death by the officer who had turned the man over to him and had threatened to kill him if the prisoner escaped. Achab then said that the punishment of death was a just one, whereupon he unbound his head and was recognized by the king as the prophet Michaias.[d] He had employed this trick, in dealing with him, as a way of introducing what he was going to say, which was that God would punish him for having allowed Adados, who had blasphemed Him, to escape punishment, and would cause him to die at Adados's hands, and Achab's people to die at the hands of his army. Incensed at the prophet, Achab ordered him to be locked up and

[a] The prophet is not named in Scripture, but Josephus, like the rabbis, very reasonably supposes it is Micaiah, mentioned as Ahab's adversary in 1 Kings xxii. 8, *cf.* § 403.

[b] Heb. "disguised himself with a bandage (A.V. "ashes"!) on his eyes," LXX κατεδήσατο τελαμῶνι τοὺς ὀφθαλμοὺς αὐτοῦ "bound a bandage around his eyes."

[c] Bibl. "a man."

[d] See p. 782 note *a*.

ἐκέλευσε, συγκεχυμένος δ' αὐτὸς ἐπὶ τοῖς Μιχαίου λόγοις ἀνεχώρησεν εἰς τὴν οἰκίαν.[1]

393 (xv. 1) Καὶ Ἄχαβος μὲν ἐν τούτοις ἦν· ἐπάνειμι δὲ ἐπὶ τὸν Ἱεροσολύμων βασιλέα Ἰωσάφατον, ὃς αὐξήσας τὴν βασιλείαν καὶ δυνάμεις ἐν ταῖς πόλεσι ταῖς ἐν τῇ τῶν ὑπηκόων χώρᾳ καταστήσας οὐδὲν ἧττον ταῖς ὑπὸ Ἀβία[2] τοῦ πάππου καταληφθείσαις[3] τῆς Ἐφραΐμου κληρουχίας Ἱεροβοάμου βασι-
394 λεύοντος τῶν δέκα φυλῶν, φρουρὰς ἐγκαθίδρυσεν ἀλλ' εἶχεν εὐμενές τε καὶ συνεργὸν τὸ θεῖον, δίκαιος ὢν καὶ εὐσεβὴς καὶ τί καθ' ἑκάστην ἡμέραν ἡδὺ ποιήσει καὶ προσηνὲς τῷ θεῷ ζητῶν. ἐτίμων δ' αὐτὸν οἱ πέριξ βασιλικαῖς[4] δωρεαῖς, ὡς πλοῦτόν τε ποιῆσαι βαθύτατον καὶ δόξαν ἄρασθαι μεγίστην.

395 (2) Τρίτῳ δ' ἔτει τῆς βασιλείας συγκαλέσας τοὺς ἡγεμόνας τῆς χώρας καὶ τοὺς ἱερεῖς ἐκέλευε τὴν γῆν περιελθόντας ἅπαντα τὸν λαὸν τὸν ἐπ' αὐτῆς[5] διδάξαι κατὰ πόλιν τοὺς Μωυσέος νόμους καὶ φυλάσσειν τούτους καὶ σπουδάζειν περὶ τὴν θρησκείαν τοῦ θεοῦ. καὶ ἥσθη πᾶν τὸ πλῆθος οὕτως, ὡς μηδὲν ἄλλο φιλοτιμεῖσθαι μηδὲ ἀγαπᾶν ὡς τὸ
396 τηρεῖν τὰ νόμιμα. οἵ τε προσχώριοι διετέλουν στέργοντες τὸν Ἰωσάφατον καὶ πρὸς αὐτὸν εἰρήνην

[1] οἰκείαν Bekker.

[2] ταῖς ὑπὸ Ἀβία conj.: Ἀβία RO: ὑπὸ Ἀβία MSP: quam Abia Lat.: ταῖς ἐπὶ Ἀβία Naber.

[3] P: καταλειφθείσαις MS: καταλειφθείσης RO.

[4] βασιλεῖς MSPE Lat.

[5] ἐπ' αὐτῆς Niese: ἐπ' αὐτῇ R: περὶ αὐτὸν M: ὑπ' αὐτὸν SPE Lat.

---

[a] Josephus here anticipates the later account of Ahab's treatment of Micaiah, 1 Kings xxii. 26. Scripture does not tell what became of the unnamed prophet mentioned in ch. xx.

kept under guard [a]; he himself, greatly troubled by Michaias's words, returned to his house.

(xv. 1) Such, then, was the condition of Achab. But I shall now return to Josaphat, the king of Jerusalem, who increased his kingdom and stationed forces in the cities of the country inhabited by his subjects; no less did he establish garrisons in those cities of the territory of Ephraim which had been taken [b] by his grandfather Abias [c] when Jeroboam reigned over the ten tribes. Moreover he had the favour and assistance of the Deity since he was upright and pious and daily sought to do something pleasing and acceptable to God. And those around him honoured him with kingly presents,[d] so that he amassed very considerable wealth and acquired the greatest glory.

The reign of Jehoshaphat (Josaphat) of Judah. 2 Chron. xvii. 1.

(2) Now in the third year of his reign he summoned the governors of the country and the priests,[e] and ordered them to go throughout the land and teach all the people therein, city by city, the laws of Moses, both to keep them and to be diligent in worshipping God. And so much were all the people pleased with this that there was nothing for which they were so ambitious or so much loved as the observance of the laws.[f] The neighbouring peoples also continued to cherish Josaphat and remained at peace with him.

Jehoshaphat's administration and army. 2 Chron. xvii. 7.

[b] Emended text.

[c] Bibl. "Asa, his father." Josephus consistently (*cf.* § 284) follows the variant account, 2 Chron. xiii. 19, according to which it was Abijah who captured the Ephraimite cities from Jeroboam.

[d] Variant "the kings around him honoured him with presents"; bibl. "all Judah brought presents."

[e] Scripture also mentions Levites.

[f] The remarks on the people's observance of the laws are an addition to Scripture.

ἄγοντες· οἱ δὲ Παλαιστῖνοι τακτοὺς ἐτέλουν αὐτῷ φόρους καὶ Ἄραβες ἐχορήγουν κατ' ἔτος ἄρνας ἑξήκοντα καὶ τριακοσίους καὶ ἐρίφους τοσούτους. πόλεις τε ὠχύρωσε μεγάλας ἄλλας τε καὶ βάρεις[1] καὶ δύναμιν στρατιωτικὴν καὶ ὅπλα πρὸς τοὺς
397 πολεμίους[2] ηὐτρέπιστο. ἦν δὲ ἐκ μὲν τῆς Ἰούδα φυλῆς στρατὸς ὁπλιτῶν μυριάδες τριάκοντα, ὧν Ἐδναῖος τὴν ἡγεμονίαν εἶχεν, Ἰωάννης δὲ μυριάδων εἴκοσι. ὁ δ' αὐτὸς οὗτος ἡγεμὼν κἀκ τῆς Βενιαμίτιδος φυλῆς εἶχε τοξοτῶν πεζῶν μυριάδας εἴκοσι, ἄλλος δ' ἡγεμὼν Ὀχόβατος[3] ὄνομα μυριάδας ὁπλιτῶν ὀκτωκαίδεκα τὸ πλῆθος τῷ βασιλεῖ προσένειμε πάρεξ ὧν εἰς τὰς ὀχυρωτάτας διέπεμψε πόλεις.
398 (3) Ἠγάγετο δὲ τῷ παιδὶ Ἰωράμῳ τὴν Ἀχάβου θυγατέρα τοῦ τῶν δέκα φυλῶν βασιλέως Ὀθλίαν[4] ὄνομα. πορευθέντα δ' αὐτὸν μετὰ χρόνον τινὰ εἰς Σαμάρειαν φιλοφρόνως Ἄχαβος ὑπεδέξατο καὶ τὸν ἀκολουθήσαντα στρατὸν ἐξένισε λαμπρῶς σίτου τε καὶ οἴνου καὶ θυμάτων ἀφθονίᾳ, παρεκάλεσέ τε συμμαχῆσαι κατὰ τοῦ Σύρων βασιλέως, ἵνα τὴν ἐν
399 τῇ Γαλαδηνῇ πόλιν Ἀραμαθὰν ἀφέληται· τοῦ γὰρ

[1] βαρεῖς ROM.
[2] καὶ ὅπλα . . . πολεμίους] πρὸς πολέμους RO.
[3] ᾧ Χάβαθος RO.
[4] Γοθολίαν SP Lat.

[a] Bibl. 7700 rams and 7700 he-goats.
[b] βάρεις is the Luc. rendering of Heb. *bîrānîyôth* "strongholds"; LXX οἰκήσεις "dwellings." Scripture adds "store-cities."
[c] Bibl. Adnah, LXX Ἐδναάς, Luc. Αἰδηάς.
[d] Bibl. 280,000.
[e] Bibl. Jehohanan (*Yehôḥānān*), LXX Ἰωανάν (*v.l.* Ἰωνάν).
[f] According to Scripture, Eliada was commander of the 200,000 archers from Benjamin. Josephus also omits the 200,000 men under Amasiah.

And the Philistines paid him the appointed tribute, while the Arabs every year supplied him with three hundred and sixty lambs and as many kids.[a] He also fortified large cities, among which were strongholds,[b] and prepared a force of soldiers and weapons against his enemies. From the tribe of Judah there was an army of three hundred thousand heavy-armed soldiers, of which Ednaios[c] had command, and two hundred thousand[d] under Joannēs,[e] who was at the same time[f] commander of two hundred thousand archers on foot from the tribe of Benjamin. Another commander named Ochobatos[g] put at the king's disposal a host of a hundred and eighty thousand heavy-armed soldiers. These did not include the men whom the king had sent to the several best fortified cities.

(3) Now Josaphat married his son Joram[h] to the daughter of Achab, the king of the ten tribes, her name being Othlia.[i] And, when some time afterward he went to Samaria, Achab gave him a friendly welcome and, after splendidly entertaining the army which had accompanied him, with an abundance of grain and wine[j] and meat, invited[k] him to become his ally in a war against the king of Syria in order to recover the city of Aramatha in Galadēnē,[l] for it had

Jehoshaphat's alliance with Ahab against the Syrians. 1 Kings xxii. 2; 2 Chron. xviii. 1.

[g] Bibl. Jehozabad (*Yehôzābād*), LXX Ἰωζαβάδ.

[h] *Cf. A.* ix. 27. He is not named at this point in Scripture.

[i] Variant Gotholiah; bibl. Athaliah, *cf. A.* ix. 140 note. She is not named at this point in Scripture.

[j] Unscriptural details.

[k] Heb. "persuaded by guile," LXX ἠγάπα, a corruption of ἠπάτα "deceived," Luc. ἔπεισε "persuaded."

[l] Called Aramathē in § 411; bibl. Ramoth in Gilead, LXX 1 Kings Ῥεμμὰθ Γαλαάδ, 2 Chron. Ῥαμὼθ τῆς Γαλααδείτιδος, identified by Dalman with the modern *Tell el-Ḥusn*, *c.* 20 miles E. of the Jordan in the latitude of Beth-shean (*Beisān*), on the Roman road leading to Bozrah.

πατρὸς αὐτὴν τοῦ αὐτοῦ πρῶτον τυγχάνουσαν ἀφῃρῆσθαι τὸν ἐκείνου πατέρα. τοῦ δὲ Ἰωσαφάτου τὴν βοήθειαν ἐπαγγειλαμένου (καὶ γὰρ εἶναι δύναμιν αὐτῷ μὴ ἐλάττω τῆς ἐκείνου) καὶ μεταπεμψαμένου τὴν δύναμιν ἐξ Ἱεροσολύμων εἰς Σαμάρειαν, προεξελθόντες ἔξω τῆς πόλεως οἱ δύο βασιλεῖς καὶ καθίσαντες ἐπὶ τοῦ ἰδίου θρόνου ἑκάτερος τοῖς οἰκείοις στρατιώταις τὸ στρατιωτικὸν διένεμον.
400 Ἰωσάφατος δ' ἐκέλευσεν εἴ τινές εἰσι προφῆται καλέσαντ' αὐτοὺς ἀνακρῖναι περὶ τῆς ἐπὶ τὸν Σύρον ἐξόδου, εἰ συμβουλεύουσι κατ' ἐκεῖνον τὸν καιρὸν αὐτῷ ποιήσασθαι τὴν στρατείαν· καὶ γὰρ εἰρήνη τε καὶ φιλία τότε τῷ Ἀχάβῳ πρὸς τὸν Σύρον ὑπῆρχεν ἐπὶ τρία ἔτη διαμείνασα, ἀφ' οὗ λαβὼν αὐτὸν αἰχμάλωτον ἀπέλυσεν ἄχρις ἐκείνης τῆς ἡμέρας.

401 (4) Καλέσας δὲ Ἄχαβος τοὺς αὑτοῦ προφήτας ὡσεὶ τετρακοσίους τὸν ἀριθμὸν ὄντας ἐκέλευσεν ἔρεσθαι τὸν θεόν,[1] εἰ δίδωσιν αὐτῷ στρατευσαμένῳ ἐπὶ Ἄδαδον νίκην καὶ καθαίρεσιν τῆς πόλεως, δι'
402 ἣν ἐκφέρειν μέλλει τὸν πόλεμον. τῶν δὲ προφητῶν συμβουλευσάντων ἐκστρατεῦσαι, κρατήσειν γὰρ τοῦ Σύρου καὶ λήψεσθαι ὑποχείριον αὐτὸν ὡς καὶ τὸ πρῶτον, συνεὶς ἐκ τῶν λόγων Ἰωσάφατος ὅτι ψευδοπροφῆται τυγχάνουσιν, ἐπύθετο τοῦ Ἀχάβου εἰ καὶ ἕτερός τίς ἐστι προφήτης τοῦ θεοῦ, "ἵνα ἀκριβέστερον μάθωμεν περὶ τῶν μελλόντων."
403 ὁ δ' Ἄχαβος εἶναι μὲν ἔφη, μισεῖν δ' αὐτὸν κακὰ προφητεύσαντα καὶ προειπόντα ὅτι τεθνήξεται

[1] τοῦ θεοῦ ROS.

[a] This earlier capture of Ramoth by the Syrians is not mentioned in Scripture.

[b] Josephus takes literally Jehoshaphat's expression in

first belonged to his father but had been taken away from him by the Syrian's father.[a] Thereupon Josaphat willingly offered his aid—he too had a force, not smaller than Achab's [b]—and, when he had sent for his force to come from Jerusalem to Samaria,[c] the two kings went out of the city, each sitting upon his throne, and distributed pay to their respective armies.[d] And Josaphat bade him call the prophets, if there were any there, and inquire of them concerning the expedition against the Syrian, whether they advised them to take the field at that time. For there was, indeed, peace and friendship then between Achab and the Syrian, which had lasted three years, from the time when Achab had taken him captive and released him until that very day.

1 Kings xxii. 1.

(4) So Achab called his prophets, who were some four hundred in number, and bade them inquire of God whether, if he marched against Adados, He would grant him victory and the overthrow of the city on which he was about to wage war. And, when the prophets advised him to take the field, saying that he would defeat the Syrian and have him in his power as before, Josaphat, who saw by their words that they were false prophets,[e] asked Achab whether there was some other prophet of God, " in order that we may know more clearly what is going to happen." Achab then said that there was one, but he hated him because he had prophesied evil and had foretold that he

The false prophets foretell victory for Ahab. 1 Kings xxii. 6; 2 Chron. xviii. 5.

1 Kings xxii. 4 = 2 Chron. xviii. 3, " I am as thou art and my people as thy people," which meant that he put his force wholly at Ahab's disposal.

[c] Josephus supplies this information, missing in Scripture.

[d] The payment of the troops is an unscriptural detail.

[e] Scripture does not have this detail, but Targum speaks of them as " false prophets."

νικηθεὶς ὑπὸ τοῦ Σύρων βασιλέως καὶ διὰ ταῦτα
ἐν φυλακῇ[1] νῦν αὐτὸν ἔχειν· καλεῖσθαι δὲ Μιχαίαν,
υἱὸν δ᾿ εἶναι Ἰεμβλαίου[2]· τοῦ δ᾿ Ἰωσαφάτου κελεύσαντος αὐτὸν προαχθῆναι, πέμψας εὐνοῦχον ἄγει
404 τὸν Μιχαίαν. κατὰ δὲ τὴν ὁδὸν ἐδήλωσεν αὐτῷ
ὁ εὐνοῦχος πάντας τοὺς ἄλλους προφήτας νίκην τῷ
βασιλεῖ προειρηκέναι. ὁ δὲ οὐκ ἐξὸν αὐτῷ κατα-
ψεύσασθαι[3] τοῦ θεοῦ φήσας, ἀλλ᾿ ἐρεῖν ὅ τι ἂν αὐτῷ
περὶ τοῦ βασιλέως αὐτὸς εἴπῃ, ὡς ἧκε πρὸς τὸν
Ἄχαβον καὶ λέγειν αὐτῷ τἀληθὲς οὗτος ἐνωρκίσατο,
δεῖξαι τὸν θεὸν αὐτῷ φεύγοντας τοὺς Ἰσραηλίτας
ἔφη καὶ διωκομένους ὑπὸ τῶν Σύρων καὶ διασκορπι-
ζομένους ὑπ᾿ αὐτῶν εἰς τὰ ὄρη, καθάπερ ποιμένων
405 ἠρημωμένα ποίμνια. ἔλεγέ τε σημαίνειν τοὺς μὲν
μετ᾿ εἰρήνης ἀναστρέψειν εἰς τὰ ἴδια, πεσεῖσθαι
δ᾿ αὐτὸν μόνον ἐν τῇ μάχῃ. ταῦτα φήσαντος τοῦ
Μιχαία, πρὸς Ἰωσάφατον ὁ Ἄχαβος "ἀλλ᾿ ἔγωγε
μικρὸν ἔμπροσθεν ἐδήλωσά σοι τὴν τἀνθρώπου,"
φησί,[4] "πρός με διάθεσιν, καὶ ὅτι μοι τὰ χείρω
406 προεφήτευσε." τοῦ δὲ Μιχαία εἰπόντος ὡς προσῆκεν αὐτῷ πάντων ἀκροᾶσθαι τῶν ὑπὸ τοῦ θεοῦ
προλεγομένων, καὶ ὡς παρορμήσειαν αὐτὸν οἱ
ψευδοπροφῆται ποιήσασθαι τὸν πόλεμον ἐλπίδι

[1] Σύρων . . . φυλακῇ] Σύρου ἐν φρουρᾷ δὲ RO.
[2] Ὀμβλαίου R: Ἠμβλαίου O: Ἰεμβλέου MS: Obaei Lat.
[3] καταψεύδεσθαι MSP.
[4] φησί cod. Vat. apud Hudson: om. rell.

[a] The prophecy of Ahab's death is unscriptural.
[b] Unscriptural detail, *cf.* § 392 note.

should be conquered by the Syrian king and meet his death,[a] for which reason he was now keeping him in prison[b]; his name, he added, was Michaias[c] and he was the son of Jemblaios.[d] But, when Josaphat asked that he be produced, Achab sent a eunuch to bring Michaias.[e] On the way the eunuch informed him that all the other prophets had foretold victory to the king. Thereupon the prophet said that it was not possible for him to tell falsehoods in God's name, but he must speak whatever He might tell him about the king. And, when he came to Achab and the king adjured him to speak the truth to him, he said[f] that God had shown him the Israelites in flight, being pursued by the Syrians and dispersed by them upon the mountains like flocks of sheep that are left without their shepherds. He also said that God had revealed that his men should return to their homes in peace, but he alone should fall in battle.[g] When Michaias had spoken these words, Achab said to Josaphat, "Did I not tell you a little while ago how this fellow feels toward me and that he has prophesied evil things for me?" But Michaias answered that it was his duty to listen to all things uttered by God, and that they were false prophets who had led him on to make war in the hope of victory, and that he

Micaiah foretells Ahab's death. 1 Kings xxii. 15; 2 Chron. xviii. 14.

[c] Bibl. Micaiah (*Mîkāyehû*), LXX Μειχαίας.

[d] Bibl. Imlah (*Yimlāh*), LXX Ἰεμλαά (*v.l.* Ἰεμβλαά).

[e] Scripture at this point (1 Kings xxii. 11 = 2 Chron. xviii. 10) introduces the symbolic action of Zedekiah, which Josephus narrates later in § 409.

[f] Josephus omits Micaiah's first ironical reassurance, 1 Kings xxii. 15 = 2 Chron. xviii. 14.

[g] The prophecy of Ahab's death is an amplification of the Scriptural phrase, "And the Lord said, These (Ahab's men) have no master."

νίκης, καὶ ὅτι δεῖ πεσεῖν αὐτὸν μαχόμενον, αὐτὸς μὲν ἦν ἐπ' ἐννοίᾳ, Σεδεκίας δέ τις τῶν ψευδοπροφητῶν προσελθών, τῷ μὲν Μιχαίᾳ μὴ προσέχειν
407 παρῄνει· λέγειν γὰρ αὐτὸν οὐδὲν ἀληθές· τεκμηρίῳ δ' ἐχρήσατο οἷς Ἠλίας προεφήτευσεν ὁ τούτου κρείττων τὰ μέλλοντα συνιδεῖν· καὶ γὰρ τοῦτον ἔλεγε προφητεύσαντα ἐν Ἰεζαρήλᾳ πόλει ἐν τῷ Ναβώθου ἀγρῷ τὸ αἷμα αὐτοῦ κύνας ἀναλιχμήσεσθαι προειπεῖν, καθὼς καὶ Ναβώθου τοῦ δι'
408 αὐτὸν καταλευσθέντος ὑπὸ τοῦ ὄχλου. "δῆλον οὖν ὅτι οὗτος ψεύδεται, τῷ κρείττονι προφήτῃ τἀναντία λέγων, ἀπὸ ἡμερῶν τριῶν φάσκων τεθνήξεσθαι. γνώσεσθε δ' εἴπερ ἐστὶν ἀληθὴς καὶ τοῦ θείου πνεύματος ἔχει τὴν δύναμιν· εὐθὺς γὰρ ῥαπισθεὶς ὑπ' ἐμοῦ βλαψάτω μου τὴν χεῖρα, ὥσπερ Ἰάδαος[1] τὴν Ἱεροβοάμου τοῦ βασιλέως συλλαβεῖν θελήσαντος ἀπεξήρανε δεξιάν· ἀκήκοας γὰρ οἶμαι
409 πάντως τοῦτο γενόμενον." ὡς οὖν πλήξαντος αὐτοῦ τὸν Μιχαίαν μηδὲν συνέβη παθεῖν, Ἄχαβος θαρρήσας ἄγειν τὴν στρατιὰν πρόθυμος ἦν ἐπὶ τὸν Σύρον· ἐνίκα γὰρ οἶμαι τὸ χρεὼν καὶ πιθανωτέρους ἐποίει τοῦ ἀληθοῦς τοὺς ψευδοπροφήτας, ἵνα λάβῃ τὴν ἀφορμὴν τοῦ τέλους. Σεδεκίας δὲ σιδήρεα

[1] Ἴαδος SPE: Iadon Lat.

---

[a] Josephus substitutes this reply of Micaiah for the Scriptural verses (1 Kings xxii. 19-25 = 2 Chron. xviii. 18-22) describing his heavenly vision of the lying spirits put by God into the mouths of the false prophets.

[b] So most MSS. of LXX; bibl. Zedekiah (*Ṣidqîyāhû*).

[c] Zedekiah's allusion to Elijah's prophecy (*cf.* § 361) is unscriptural. It is noteworthy that rabbinic tradition also makes a connexion, though a different one, between the two

alone must fall in battle.[a] So Achab had cause for thought, but a certain Sedekias,[b] one of the false prophets, came to him and urged him not to pay any attention to Michaias, for he did not speak a word of truth. And as proof of this he instanced the prophecies of Elijah, who was better able than Michaias to foresee the future, for, he said, when Elijah had prophesied in the city of Jezarēla in Naboth's field, he had foretold that the dogs would lick up Achab's blood just as they had licked the blood of Naboth who had been stoned to death by the crowd at his bidding. "It is clear, then," said Sedekias, "that this man is lying, since he contradicts a greater prophet in saying that within three days you shall meet death.[c] But you shall know whether he is really a true prophet and has the power of the divine spirit; let him right now, when I strike him, disable my hand as Jadaos caused the right hand of King Jeroboam to wither when he wished to arrest him. For I suppose you must have heard that this thing happened."[d] Accordingly, when he struck Michaias and suffered no harm as a result, Achab took courage and was eager to lead his army against the Syrian. It was Fate, I suppose, that prevailed and made the false prophet seem more convincing than the true one, in order to hasten Achab's end.[e]

incidents by saying that it was Naboth's spirit that had misled Ahab's prophets into foretelling a victory for him, *cf.* Ginzberg iv. 187.

[d] The reference to Jadaos (bibl. Jadon; *cf.* § 231) is not found in Scripture, according to which Zedekiah, after striking Micaiah, asks, "Which way went the spirit of the Lord from me to speak unto thee?", LXX 1 Kings, "What sort of spirit of the Lord speaks in thee?"

[e] These remarks on Ahab's confidence and the working of Fate are additions to Scripture.

ποιήσας κέρατα λέγει πρὸς Ἄχαβον ὡς θεὸν αὐτῷ σημαίνειν τούτοις ἅπασαν καταστρέψεσθαι[1] τὴν
410 Συρίαν.[2] Μιχαίαν δὲ μετ' οὐ πολλὰς ἡμέρας εἰπόντα τὸν Σεδεκίαν ταμιεῖον ἐκ ταμιείου[3] κρυβόμενον ἀμείψειν ζητοῦντα φυγεῖν τῆς ψευδολογίας τὴν δίκην, ἐκέλευσεν ὁ βασιλεὺς ἀπαχθέντα φυλάττεσθαι πρὸς Ἀχάμωνα τὸν τῆς πόλεως ἄρχοντα καὶ χορηγεῖσθαι μηδὲν ἄρτου καὶ ὕδατος αὐτῷ περισσότερον.

411 (5) Καὶ Ἄχαβος μὲν καὶ Ἰωσάφατος ὁ τῶν Ἱεροσολύμων βασιλεὺς ἀναλαβόντες τὰς δυνάμεις ἤλασαν εἰς Ἀραμάθην πόλιν τῆς Γαλαδίτιδος. ὁ δὲ τῶν Σύρων βασιλεὺς ἀκούσας αὐτῶν τὴν στρατείαν[4] ἀντεπήγαγεν αὐτοῖς τὴν αὑτοῦ στρατιὰν καὶ
412 οὐκ ἄπωθεν τῆς Ἀραμάθης στρατοπεδεύεται. συνέθεντο δὲ ὅ τε Ἄχαβος καὶ Ἰωσάφατος ἀποθέσθαι μὲν τὸν Ἄχαβον τὸ βασιλικὸν σχῆμα, τὸν δὲ τῶν Ἱεροσολύμων βασιλέα τὴν αὑτοῦ στολὴν ἔχοντα στῆναι ἐν τῇ παρατάξει, κατασοφιζόμενοι[5] τὰ ὑπὸ τοῦ Μιχαία προειρημένα. εὗρε δ' αὐτὸν τὸ χρεὼν
413 καὶ δίχα τοῦ σχήματος· ὁ μὲν γὰρ Ἄδαδος ὁ τῶν Σύρων βασιλεὺς παρήγγειλε τῇ στρατιᾷ διὰ τῶν ἡγεμόνων μηδένα τῶν ἄλλων ἀναιρεῖν, μόνον δὲ τὸν βασιλέα τῶν Ἰσραηλιτῶν. οἱ δὲ Σύροι τῆς συμβολῆς γενομένης ἰδόντες τὸν Ἰωσάφατον ἑστῶτα πρὸ τῆς τάξεως καὶ τοῦτον εἰκάσαντες εἶναι τὸν

[1] ex Lat. Niese: καταστρέψασθαι RO: καταστρέψαι MSP.
[2] Σεδεκίας . . . Συρίαν spuria esse putat Niese.
[3] ταμιεῖον ἐκ ταμιείου Dindorf: ταμεῖον ἐκ ταμείου codd. E Zonaras.
[4] ed. pr.: στρατιὰν codd.
[5] Niese: κατασοφιζόμενος ROE: κατασοφιζόμενον MSP Lat. (vid.).

Then Sedekias made horns of iron and told Achab that God had revealed to him that with these he should subdue the whole of Syria.[a] But Michaias said that within a few days Sedekias would change his hiding-place from one secret chamber to another[b] in seeking to escape punishment for his lying words. Thereupon the king ordered him to be led away to Achamōn,[c] the governor of the city, for imprisonment and that he should be supplied with nothing but bread and water.

Defeat and death of Ahab. 1 Kings xxii. 29; 2 Chron. xviii. 28.

(5) And so Achab and Josaphat, the king of Jerusalem, marched with their forces to the city of Aramathē[d] in Galaditis. When the Syrian king heard of their march, he, in turn, led his army against them and encamped not far from the city of Aramathē. Now Achab and Josaphat had agreed that Achab should take off his royal garments and that the king of Jerusalem should take his place in the line of battle with the other's robe on[e]; by this trick they thought to escape the fate foretold by Michaias. But Fate found him even though he was without his garments. For Adados, the Syrian king, had given orders that they should slay no one else but only the king of the Israelites. So, when the battle was joined and the Syrians saw Josaphat standing before the lines, they thought that he was Achab, and

[a] *Cf.* § 403 note.

[b] So LXX renders the Heb. idiom "chamber in chamber," *cf.* § 384 note.

[c] Bibl. Amon, LXX Ἀμών (*v.ll.* Σεμήρ, Ἐμμήρ).

[d] *Cf.* § 399 note.

[e] So LXX; according to the Heb. text, Jehoshaphat wears his own robes.

414 Ἄχαβον ὥρμησαν ἐπ' αὐτόν, καὶ περικυκλωσά-
μενοι ὡς ἐγγὺς ὄντες ἔγνωσαν οὐκ ὄντα τοῦτον,
ἀνεχώρησαν ὀπίσω πάντες, ἀρχομένης δ'[1] ἠοῦς
ἄχρι δείλης ὀψίας[2] μαχόμενοι καὶ νικῶντες ἀπέκτειναν οὐδένα κατὰ τὴν τοῦ βασιλέως ἐντολήν,
ζητοῦντες τὸν Ἄχαβον ἀνελεῖν μόνον καὶ εὑρεῖν οὐ
δυνάμενοι. παῖς δέ τις βασιλικὸς τοῦ Ἀδάδου
Ἀμανὸς ὄνομα τοξεύσας εἰς τοὺς πολεμίους τι-
τρώσκει τὸν βασιλέα διὰ τοῦ θώρακος κατὰ τοῦ
415 πνεύμονος. Ἄχαβος δὲ τὸ μὲν συμβεβηκὸς οὐκ
ἔγνω ποιῆσαι τῷ στρατεύματι φανερὸν μὴ τρα-
πείησαν, τὸν δ' ἡνίοχον ἐκέλευσεν ἐκτρέψαντα τὸ
ἅρμα ἐξάγειν[3] τῆς μάχης· χαλεπῶς γὰρ βεβλῆσθαι
καὶ καιρίως. ὀδυνώμενος δὲ ἔστη ἐπὶ τοῦ ἅρματος
ἄχρι δύνοντος ἡλίου καὶ λιφαιμήσας[4] ἀπέθανε.
416 (6) Καὶ τὸ μὲν τῶν Σύρων στράτευμα νυκτὸς
ἤδη γενομένης ἀνεχώρησεν εἰς τὴν παρεμβολήν,
καὶ δηλώσαντος τοῦ στρατοκήρυκος ὅτι τέθνηκεν
Ἄχαβος ἀνέζευξαν εἰς τὰ ἴδια, κομίσαντες δὲ τὸν
417 Ἀχάβου νεκρὸν εἰς Σαμάρειαν ἐκεῖ θάπτουσι. καὶ
τὸ ἅρμα ἀποπλύναντες ἐν τῇ Ἰεζαρήλα κρήνῃ (ἦν
δὲ καθημαγμένον τῷ τοῦ βασιλέως φόνῳ) ἀληθῆ
τὴν Ἠλία προφητείαν ἐπέγνωσαν· οἱ μὲν γὰρ κύνες
ἀνελιχμήσαντο[5] αὐτοῦ τὸ αἷμα, αἱ δὲ ἑταιριζόμεναι
ἐν τῇ κρήνῃ τὸ λοιπὸν λουόμεναι τούτῳ διετέλουν.

[1] πάντες . . . δ'] ἀπό τε ἀρχομένης RO Lat.
[2] ὀψίας om. RO Lat.
[3] ἐκτρέψαντα . . . ἐξάγειν] ἐπιστρέψαι . . . καὶ ἐξαγαγεῖν MSP.
[4] Niese: λειφαιμήσας RO: λιποθυμήσας MSP: λειποθυμήσας E: factus exsanguis Lat.
[5] Hudson: ἀνελικμήσαντο codd.: ἀπελίχμησαν E.

[a] Josephus omits the Scriptural detail that Jehoshaphat was recognized when he cried out.

rushed upon him, but, on surrounding him and coming close, they saw that it was not he,[a] and all of them turned back. From early dawn until late afternoon they fought, and the victorious Syrians, in accordance with the king's command, killed no one, seeking to slay only Achab and not being able to find him. But one of the king's pages, named Amanos,[b] in shooting arrows at the enemy, wounded the king through his breastplate in the lung.[c] Achab, however, decided not to let his army see what had happened lest they should be put to flight,[d] and ordered his driver to turn the chariot and carry him off the field of battle, for he had been gravely and even mortally wounded. But, though he was in great pain, he remained upright in his chariot until the setting of the sun and then, with the blood drained out of him, expired.

(6) And so, as night had now fallen, the Syrian army retired to its camp and, when the herald announced[e] that Achab was dead, they returned to their own country, first carrying the body of Achab to Samaria and burying it there. And when they washed his chariot, which was stained with the king's blood, in the spring of Jezarēl, they acknowledged the truth of Elijah's prophecy, for the dogs licked up his blood; and thereafter the harlots used to bathe

The fulfilment of Elijah's prophecy. 1 Kings xxii. 36.

[b] Targum of 2 Chron. identifies Ahab's slayer, unnamed in Scripture, with Naaman the Syrian (*cf.* 2 Kings ch. v.), to whom Josephus must here be referring.

[c] So LXX; Heb. "through the joints (or "fastenings") of his breastplate."

[d] This explanation of Ahab's reason for withdrawing is unscriptural.

[e] So the LXX; Heb. "and a shout passed through the camp."

ἀπέθανε δ' ἐν Ἀραμάθῃ Μιχαία τοῦτο προειρη-
418 κότος. συμβάντων οὖν Ἀχάβῳ τῶν ὑπὸ τῶν δύο
προφητῶν εἰρημένων μέγα δεῖ τὸ θεῖον ἡγεῖσθαι
καὶ σέβειν καὶ τιμᾶν αὐτὸ πανταχοῦ, καὶ τῆς ἀληθείας μὴ τὰ πρὸς ἡδονὴν καὶ βούλησιν πιθανώτερα
δοκεῖν, ὑπολαμβάνειν δ' ὅτι προφητείας καὶ τῆς
διὰ τῶν τοιούτων προγνώσεως οὐδέν ἐστι συμ-
φορώτερον, παρέχοντος οὕτω τοῦ θεοῦ τί δεῖ φυ-
419 λάξασθαι, λογίζεσθαί τε πάλιν ἐκ τῶν περὶ τὸν
βασιλέα γεγενημένων στοχαζομένους προσῆκε τὴν
τοῦ χρεὼν ἰσχύν, ὅτι μηδὲ προγινωσκόμενον αὐτὸ
διαφυγεῖν ἔστιν, ἀλλ' ὑπέρχεται τὰς ἀνθρωπί-
νας ψυχὰς ἐλπίσι κολακεῦον χρησταῖς, αἷς εἰς τὸ
420 πόθεν αὐτῶν κρατήσει περιάγει. φαίνεται οὖν καὶ
Ἄχαβος ὑπὸ τούτου τὴν διάνοιαν ἀπατηθείς, ὥστε
ἀπιστῆσαι μὲν τοῖς προλέγουσι τὴν ἧτταν, τοῖς δὲ
τὰ πρὸς χάριν προφητεύσασι πεισθεὶς ἀποθανεῖν.
τοῦτον μὲν οὖν ὁ παῖς Ὀχοζίας[a] διεδέξατο.

---

[a] Bibl. Ahaziah (*'Aḥazyāhû*), LXX Ὀχοζείας.

in the pool in this blood. But he died in Aramathē, as Michaias had foretold. Now, since there befell Achab the fate spoken of by the two prophets, we ought to acknowledge the greatness of the Deity and everywhere honour and reverence Him, nor should we think the things which are said to flatter us or please us more worthy of belief than the truth, but should realize that nothing is more beneficial than prophecy and the foreknowledge which it gives, for in this way God enables us to know what to guard against. And further, with the king's history before our eyes, it behoves us to reflect on the power of Fate, and see that not even with foreknowledge is it possible to escape it, for it secretly enters the souls of men and flatters them with fair hopes, and by means of these it leads them on to the point where it can overcome them. It appears, then, that by this power Achab's mind was deceived so that while he disbelieved those who foretold his defeat, he believed those who prophesied things that pleased him, and so lost his life. And so his son Ochozias [a] succeeded him.

AN ANCIENT TABLE OF CONTENTS

ΒΙΒΛΙΟΝ Ε

α′.[1] Ὡς Ἰησοῦς ὁ στρατηγὸς τῶν Ἑβραίων πολεμήσας πρὸς Χαναναίους καὶ κρατήσας αὐτῶν τοὺς μὲν διέφθειρε τὴν δὲ γῆν κατακληρουχήσας διένειμε ταῖς φυλαῖς.

β′. Ὡς ἀποθανόντος τοῦ στρατηγοῦ παραβαίνοντες οἱ Ἰσραηλῖται τοὺς πατρίους νόμους μεγάλων ἐπειράθησαν συμφορῶν, καὶ στασιασάντων ἡ Βενιαμὶς διεφθάρη φυλὴ χωρὶς ἀνδρῶν ἑξακοσίων.

γ′. Πῶς μετὰ ταύτην τὴν κακοπραγίαν ἀσεβήσαντας αὐτοὺς ὁ θεὸς Ἀσσυρίοις ἐδούλωσεν.

δ′. Ἡ διὰ Κενίζου τοῦ Ἀθνιήλου[2] παιδὸς αὐτοῖς ἐλευθερία γενομένη ἄρξαντος ἔτη τεσσαράκοντα λεγομένου δὲ παρά τε Ἕλλησι καὶ Φοίνιξι κριτοῦ.

ε′. Ὅτι πάλιν ὁ λαὸς ἡμῶν ἐδούλευσε Μωαβίταις ὀκτωκαίδεκα ἔτη καὶ ὑπό τινος Ἰούδου[3] τῆς

[1] Numeros om. MSPL.
[2] Bernard: Ἀενιήλου ROML: Ναθαναήλου S: Ναθαήλου P.
[3] Niese: Ἰουδοῦς ROL: Ἠουδοῦς MS: Ἰουδοῦ, ι ex η corr. P: Aod Lat.

[a] Bibl. Othniel, the son of Kenaz; *cf. A.* v. 182 note.

AN ANCIENT TABLE OF CONTENTS

BOOK V

δουλείας ἀπηλλάγη τὴν ἀρχὴν ἐπ' ἔτη κατασχόντος ὀγδοήκοντα.

ϛ'. Ὡς Χαναναίων αὐτοὺς καταδουλωσαμένων ἐπ' ἔτη εἴκοσιν ἠλευθερώθησαν ὑπὸ Βαράκου καὶ Δεβώρας, οἳ ἦρξαν αὐτῶν ἐπ' ἔτη τεσσαράκοντα.

ζ'. Ὅτι πολεμήσαντες Ἀμαληκῖται τοῖς Ἰσραηλίταις ἐνίκησάν τε καὶ τὴν χώραν ἐκάκωσαν ἔτη ἑπτά.

η'. Ὡς Γεδεὼν αὐτοὺς ἠλευθέρωσεν ἀπὸ Ἀμαληκιτῶν καὶ ἦρξε τοῦ πλήθους ἐπὶ ἔτη τεσσαράκοντα.

θ'. Ὅτι μετ' αὐτὸν πολλοὶ γενόμενοι διάδοχοι τοῖς πέριξ ἔθνεσιν ἐπολέμησαν ἱκανῷ χρόνῳ.

ι'. Περὶ τῆς Σαμψῶνος ἀνδρείας καὶ ὅσων κακῶν αἴτιος Παλαιστίνοις ἐγένετο.

ια'. Ὡς οἱ υἱοὶ Ἠλὶ τοῦ ἱερέως ἐσφάγησαν ἐν τῇ πρὸς Παλαιστίνους μάχῃ.

ιβ'. Ὡς ὁ πατὴρ αὐτῶν ἀκούσας τὴν συμφορὰν βαλὼν ἑαυτὸν ἀπὸ τοῦ θρόνου ἀπέθανεν.

ιγ'. Ὡς νικήσαντες ἐν τούτῳ τῷ πολέμῳ τοὺς Ἑβραίους οἱ Παλαιστῖνοι καὶ τὴν κιβωτὸν αὐτῶν αἰχμάλωτον ἔλαβον.

ιδ'. Ὡς οἱ ἀπὸ Κενίζου[1] ἄρξαντες πάντες κριταὶ ἐκλήθησαν.[2]

[1] Κενέζου SP.
[2] Caput XIV om. Lat.

---

[a] The Amalekites are mentioned only incidentally as allies of the Midianites in *A.* v. 210 ff.

[b] These were Abimelech, Jair, Jephthah, Ibzan, Elon and Abdon.

[c] This table omits special mention of the stories of Ruth, §§ 318-337; and Samuel, §§ 341-351.

[d] "Tumbled" in *A.* v. 359.

[e] Section xiii properly belongs before section xii.

[f] Section xiv is obviously out of place; originally it must have belonged to section iv.

Περιέχει ἡ βίβλος χρόνον ἐτῶν τετρακοσίων ἑβδομήκοντα.[1]

ΒΙΒΛΙΟΝ Ϛ

α΄.[2] Φθορὰ Παλαιστίνων καὶ τῆς γῆς αὐτῶν ἐξ ὀργῆς τοῦ θεοῦ διὰ τὴν αἰχμαλωτευθεῖσαν ὑπ' αὐτῶν κιβωτόν, καὶ τίνα τρόπον ἀπέπεμψαν αὐτὴν τοῖς Ἑβραίοις.

β΄. Στρατεία Παλαιστίνων ἐπ' αὐτοὺς καὶ νίκη Ἑβραίων Σαμουήλου στρατηγοῦντος αὐτῶν τοῦ προφήτου.

γ΄. Ὡς Σαμουῆλος διὰ τὸ γῆρας ἀσθενὴς ὢν τὰ πράγματα διοικεῖν τοῖς παισὶν αὐτοῦ ἐνεχείρισεν.

δ΄. Ὡς οὐ καλῶς προϊσταμένων ἐκείνων τῆς ἀρχῆς, τὸ πλῆθος ὑπ' ὀργῆς ᾐτήσατο βασιλεύεσθαι.

ε΄. Σαμουήλου πρὸς τοῦτο ἀγανάκτησις καὶ βασιλέως αὐτοῖς ἀνάδειξις Σαούλου τοὔνομα, κελεύσαντος τοῦ θεοῦ.

ς΄. Σαούλου στρατεία ἐπὶ τὸ Ἀμμανιτῶν ἔθνος καὶ νίκη καὶ διαρπαγὴ τῶν πολεμίων.[3]

ζ΄. Ὡς στρατευσάμενοι πάλιν ἐπὶ τοὺς Ἑβραίους οἱ Παλαιστῖνοι ἡττήθησαν.

η΄. Σαούλου πρὸς Ἀμαληκίτας πόλεμος καὶ νίκη.

[1] + ἕξ (ος′ P) SPEL Lat.

[2] Numeros om. SP.

[3] πολεμίων ἢ (καὶ P) τῶν πόλεων SP.

ANCIENT TABLE OF CONTENTS

This book covers a period of four hundred and seventy[a] years.

BOOK VI

[a] Variant "seventy-six."

θʹ. Ὅτι παραβαίνοντος Σαούλου τὰς ἐντολὰς τοῦ προφήτου Σαμουῆλος ἄλλον ἀπέδειξε βασιλέα κρύφα Δαυίδην[1] ὄνομα κατ' ἐπιτροπὴν τοῦ θεοῦ.

ιʹ. Ὡς καὶ πάλιν ἐπεστράτευσαν τοῖς Ἑβραίοις οἱ Παλαιστῖνοι ἔτι Σαούλου βασιλεύοντος.[2]

ιαʹ.[3] Μονομαχία Δαυίδου τότε[4] πρὸς Γολίαθον τὸν ἄριστον τῶν Παλαιστίνων καὶ ἀναίρεσις τοῦ Γολιάθου καὶ ἧττα τῶν Παλαιστίνων.[5]

ιβʹ. Ὡς θαυμάσας Σαοῦλος[6] τὸν Δαυίδην τῆς ἀνδρείας συνῴκισεν αὐτῷ τὴν θυγατέρα.

ιγʹ. Ὅτι μετὰ ταῦτα ὕποπτον αὐτῷ τὸν Δαυίδην γενόμενον ὁ βασιλεὺς ἐσπούδασεν ἀποκτεῖναι.

ιδʹ. Ὡς πολλάκις καὶ Δαυίδης κινδυνεύσας ἀποθανεῖν ὑπὸ τοῦ Σαούλου διέφυγε καὶ Σαοῦλον δὶς ἐπ' αὐτῷ γενόμενον ὥστε ἀνελεῖν οὐ διεχρήσατο.

ιεʹ. Ὡς στρατευσαμένων Παλαιστίνων πάλιν ἐπὶ τοὺς Ἑβραίους ἡττήθησαν οἱ Ἑβραῖοι τῇ μάχῃ καὶ ὁ βασιλεὺς αὐτῶν Σαοῦλος ἀπέθανε μετὰ τῶν παίδων μαχόμενος.

Περιέχει ἡ βίβλος χρόνον ἐτῶν λβʹ.

[1] Δαυείδην M: Δαβίδην RO: Dauid Lat.
[2] Σαούλου βασιλεύοντος] Σαμουήλου προφητεύοντος P.
[3] Caput XI decimo adiungunt SP.
[4] τότε om. SP.
[5] + κρατερά SP.
[6] Σαοῦλος (Σαούλου RO) post θυγατέρα tr. ROM.

This book covers a period of thirty-two years.

[a] This table omits special mention of the relations of David and Jonathan, the sojourn of David among the Philistines, and Saul's visit to the witch of Endor.

ΒΙΒΛΙΟΝ Ζ

α΄.[1] Ὡς Δαυίδης μὲν τῆς μιᾶς φυλῆς ἐβασίλευσεν ἐν Γιβρῶνι[2] τῇ πόλει, τοῦ δ᾽ ἄλλου πλήθους ὁ Σαούλου παῖς.

β΄. Ὅτι τούτου φονευθέντος ἐξ ἐπιβουλῆς φίλων, ἅπασαν τὴν βασιλείαν Δαυίδης παρέλαβεν.

γ΄. Ὡς πολιορκήσας Ἱεροσόλυμα Δαυίδης καὶ λαβὼν τὴν πόλιν ἐξέβαλε μὲν ἐξ αὐτῆς τοὺς Χαναναίους, ἐνῴκισε δὲ εἰς αὐτὴν Ἰουδαίους.

δ΄. Ὅτι στρατεύσαντας ἐπ᾽ αὐτὸν δὶς Παλαιστίνους ἐν Ἱεροσολύμοις ἐνίκησεν.

ε΄. Ἡ γενομένη πρὸς Εἵρωμον τὸν Τυρίων βασιλέα[3] Δαυίδου φιλία.

ϛ΄. Ὡς τοῖς πέριξ ἔθνεσι στρατεύσας Δαυίδης καὶ χειρωσάμενος, φόρον ἐπέταξεν αὐτῷ[4] τελεῖν.

ζ΄. Ἡ γενομένη πρὸς Δαμασκηνοὺς Δαυίδῃ μάχη καὶ νίκη.

η΄. Πῶς ἐπὶ τοὺς Μεσοποταμίους στρατεύσας ἐκράτησεν αὐτῶν.

θ΄. Ὅτι τῶν περὶ τὴν οἰκίαν αὐτῷ στασιασάντων ὑπὸ τοῦ παιδὸς ἐξεβλήθη τῆς ἀρχῆς εἰς τὴν πέραν τοῦ Ἰορδάνου.

[1] Numeros om. SP.
[2] Χεβρῶνι P: Hebron Lat.
[3] + καὶ codd.
[4] Niese: αὐτῷ codd.: eis Lat.

---

[a] The conspirators were fellow-tribesmen of Saul's son, but were not his "friends," according to Scripture and Josephus.

[b] This section properly belongs before section iv.

[c] The Mesopotamians are only incidentally mentioned as allies of the Ammonites in *A*. vii. 117 ff.

[d] This table omits special mention of the story of David

ANCIENT TABLE OF CONTENTS

BOOK VII

and Bathseba, of Amnon and Tamar, and the exploits of David's warriors.

ι'. Ὡς στρατεύσας Ἀψάλωμος[1] ἐπὶ τὸν πατέρα Δαυίδην ἀπώλετο σὺν τῷ στρατῷ.

ια'. Πῶς εἰς τὴν βασιλείαν πάλιν κατῆλθε καὶ ζήσας[2] εὐδαιμόνως ἔτι[3] περιὼν Σολόμωνα τὸν υἱὸν ἀπέδειξε βασιλέα.

ιβ'. Τελευτὴ Δαυίδου καταλιπόντος τῷ παιδὶ πολλὴν ὕλην ἀργύρου τε καὶ χρυσοῦ καὶ λιθίας εἰς τὴν οἰκοδομὴν τοῦ ναοῦ.

Περιέχει ἡ βίβλος χρόνον ἐτῶν τεσσαράκοντα.

ΒΙΒΛΙΟΝ Η

α'.[4] Ὡς Σολόμων τὴν βασιλείαν παραλαβὼν τοὺς ἐχθροὺς ἀνεῖλε.

β'. Περὶ τῆς σοφίας αὐτοῦ καὶ συνέσεως καὶ τοῦ πλούτου.

γ'. Ὅτι πρῶτος τὸν ἐν Ἱεροσολύμοις ναὸν ᾠκοδόμησεν.

δ'. Ὡς τελευτήσαντος Σολόμωνος ὁ λαὸς ἀποστὰς τοῦ παιδὸς αὐτοῦ Ῥοβοάμου, τῶν δέκα φυλῶν τῶν ὑπηκόων τινὰ Ἱεροβόαμον ἀπέδειξε βασιλέα, τῶν δὲ δύο φυλῶν ὁ υἱὸς αὐτοῦ ἐβασίλευσεν.

1 Ἀβεσάλωμος MS[1]P: Ἀβεσσάλωμος S[2]: Abessalon Lat.

2 ἔζησεν MSP: dum vixisset Lat.

3 ὡς ἔτι MSP novum caput indicantes, cui ιβ' ascribit M.

4 Numeros om. MSP.

BOOK VIII

[a] Lit. "after living happily"; the variant reads "and he lived happily," and begins a new section with the words, "How, while he was still alive, he named, etc."

[b] This table omits special mention of the relations of Solomon and Hiram of Tyre, the visit of the Queen of Sheba, and Solomon's trade and conquests.

ε'. Ὡς Ἴσακος[1] Αἰγυπτίων βασιλεὺς στρατευσάμενος ἐπὶ τὰ Ἱεροσόλυμα καὶ κατασχὼν τὴν πόλιν, τὸν πλοῦτον αὐτῆς εἰς Αἴγυπτον μετήνεγκε.

ϛ'. Στρατεία Ἱεροβοάμου τοῦ τῶν Ἰσραηλιτῶν βασιλέως ἐπὶ τὸν υἱὸν τὸν Ῥοβοάμου καὶ ἧττα.

ζ'.[2] Ὅτι τὴν Ἱεροβοάμου γενεὰν Βασίνης τις ὄνομα διαφθείρας αὐτὸς τὴν βασιλείαν ἔσχεν.

η'. Αἰθιόπων ἐπιστρατεία τοῖς Ἱεροσολύμοις βασιλεύοντος αὐτῶν Ἀσάνου[3] τοῦ Ἀβία παιδός, καὶ διαφθορὰ τοῦ στρατοῦ.

θ'. Ὡς τῆς Ἀβεσσάρου[4] γενεᾶς διαφθαρείσης ἐβασίλευσε τῶν Ἰσραηλιτῶν Ἄμαρις[5] καὶ ὁ υἱὸς αὐτοῦ Ἄχαβος.

ι'. Ὡς Ἄδαδος[6] Δαμασκοῦ καὶ Συρίας βασιλεὺς δὶς ἐπ' Ἄχαβον στρατευσάμενος ἡττήθη.

ια'. Ἀμμανιτῶν καὶ Μωαβιτῶν στρατευσαμένων ἐπ' Ἰωσαφάτην τὸν Ἱεροσολύμων βασιλέα ἧττα.

ιβ'. Ὡς Ἄχαβος ἐπὶ Σύρους στρατευσάμενος ἡττήθη τῇ μάχῃ καὶ αὐτὸς ἀπώλετο.

Περιέχει ἡ βίβλος[7] ἔτη ἑκατὸν ἑξήκοντα καὶ τρία.

[1] Σούσακος ὁ MSP: Sosach Lat.
[2] Caput VII sexto adiungunt MSP.
[3] Σαούλου RO: Ἀσανοῦ SP: Asaph Lat.
[4] Basan Lat.
[5] Ἀμαρεὶς R: Ἀμάρης O: Haber Lat.
[6] Ἄδερ MSP.
[7] + αὕτη RO.

---

[a] This section properly belongs before section vii.

[b] No such form appears either in Josephus or the LXX. Basanēs (Baasha) is meant.

This book covers one hundred and sixty-three years.

[c] The passage in Josephus dealing with Josaphat does not mention this war.

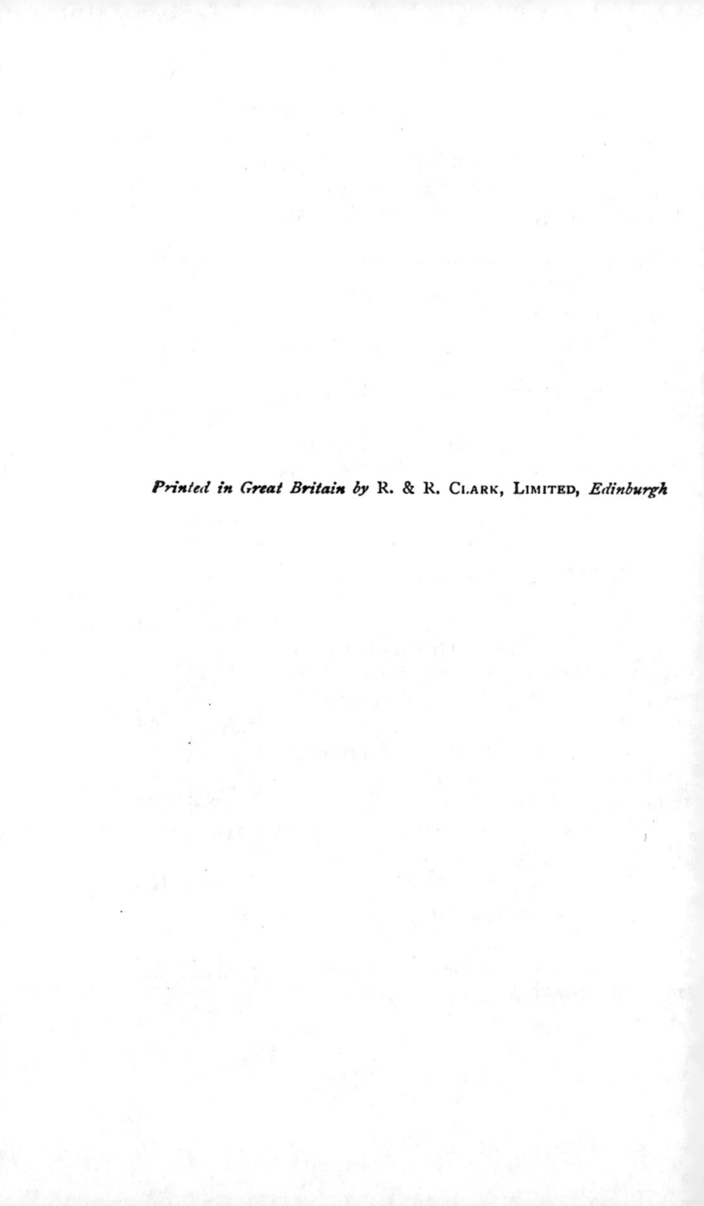

Printed in Great Britain by R. & R. CLARK, LIMITED, *Edinburgh*

THE LOEB CLASSICAL LIBRARY

VOLUMES ALREADY PUBLISHED

LATIN AUTHORS

Ammianus Marcellinus. J. C. Rolfe. 3 Vols.
Apuleius: The Golden Ass (Metamorphoses). W. Adlington (1566). Revised by S. Gaselee.
St. Augustine: City of God. 7 Vols. Vol. I. G. E. McCracken. Vol. II. W. M. Green. Vol. III. D. Wiesen. Vol. IV. P. Levine. Vol. V. E. M. Sanford and W. M. Green. Vol. VI. W. C. Greene. Vol. VII. W. M. Green.
St. Augustine, Confessions of. W. Watts (1631). 2 Vols.
St. Augustine: Select Letters. J. H. Baxter.
Ausonius. H. G. Evelyn White. 2 Vols.
Bede. J. E. King. 2 Vols.
Boethius: Tracts and De Consolatione Philosophiae. Rev. H. F. Stewart and E. K. Rand. Revised by S. J. Tester.
Caesar: Alexandrian, African and Spanish Wars. A. G. Way.
Caesar: Civil Wars. A. G. Peskett.
Caesar: Gallic War. H. J. Edwards.
Cato and Varro: De Re Rustica. H. B. Ash and W. D. Hooper.
Catullus. F. W. Cornish; Tibullus. J. B. Postgate; and Pervigilium Veneris. J. W. Mackail.
Celsus: De Medicina. W. G. Spencer. 3 Vols.
Cicero: Brutus and Orator. G. L. Hendrickson and H. M. Hubbell.
Cicero: De Finibus. H. Rackham.
Cicero: De Inventione, etc. H. M. Hubbell.
Cicero: De Natura Deorum and Academica. H. Rackham.
Cicero: De Officiis. Walter Miller.
Cicero: De Oratore, etc. 2 Vols. Vol. I: De Oratore, Books I and II. E. W. Sutton and H. Rackham. Vol. II: De Oratore, Book III; De Fato; Paradoxa Stoicorum; De Partitione Oratoria. H. Rackham.
Cicero: De Republica, De Legibus. Clinton W. Keyes.

Cicero: De Senectute, De Amicitia, De Divinatione. W. A. Falconer.
Cicero: In Catilinam, Pro Murena, Pro Sulla, Pro Flacco. New version by C. Macdonald.
Cicero: Letters to Atticus. E. O. Winstedt. 3 Vols.
Cicero: Letters to his Friends. W. Glynn Williams, M. Cary, M. Henderson. 4 Vols.
Cicero: Philippics. W. C. A. Ker.
Cicero: Pro Archia, Post Reditum, De Domo, De Haruspicum Responsis, Pro Plancio. N. H. Watts.
Cicero: Pro Caecina, Pro Lege Manilia, Pro Cluentio, Pro Rabirio. H. Grose Hodge.
Cicero: Pro Caelio, De Provinciis Consularibus, Pro Balbo. R. Gardner.
Cicero: Pro Milone, In Pisonem, Pro Scauro, Pro Fonteio, Pro Rabirio Postumo, Pro Marcello, Pro Ligario, Pro Rege Deiotaro. N. H. Watts.
Cicero: Pro Quinctio, Pro Roscio Amerino, Pro Roscio Comoedo, Contra Rullum. J. H. Freese.
Cicero: Pro Sestio, In Vatinium. R. Gardner.
[Cicero]: Rhetorica ad Herennium. H. Caplan.
Cicero: Tusculan Disputations. J. E. King.
Cicero: Verrine Orations. L. H. G. Greenwood. 2 Vols.
Claudian. M. Platnauer. 2 Vols.
Columella: De Re Rustica, De Arboribus. H. B. Ash, E. S. Forster, E. Heffner. 3 Vols.
Curtius, Q.: History of Alexander. J. C. Rolfe. 2 Vols.
Florus. E. S. Forster; and Cornelius Nepos. J. C. Rolfe.
Frontinus: Stratagems and Aqueducts. C. E. Bennett and M. B. McElwain.
Fronto: Correspondence. C. R. Haines. 2 Vols.
Gellius. J. C. Rolfe. 3 Vols.
Horace: Odes and Epodes. C. E. Bennett.
Horace: Satires, Epistles, Ars Poetica. H. R. Fairclough.
Jerome: Select Letters. F. A. Wright.
Juvenal and Persius. G. G. Ramsay.
Livy. B. O. Foster, F. G. Moore, Evan T. Sage, A. C. Schlesinger and R. M. Geer (General Index). 14 Vols.
Lucan. J. D. Duff.
Lucretius. W. H. D. Rouse. Revised by M. F. Smith.
Manilius. G. P. Goold.
Martial. W. C. A. Ker. 2 Vols. Revised by E. H. Warminton.
Minor Latin Poets: from Publilius Syrus to Rutilius Namatianus, including Grattius, Calpurnius Siculus,

NEMESIANUS, AVIANUS, with "Aetna," "Phoenix" and other poems. J. Wight Duff and Arnold M. Duff.
OVID: THE ART OF LOVE AND OTHER POEMS. J. H. Mozley.
OVID: FASTI. Sir James G. Frazer.
OVID: HEROIDES AND AMORES. Grant Showerman. Revised by G. P. Goold.
OVID: METAMORPHOSES. F. J. Miller. 2 Vols.
OVID: TRISTIA AND EX PONTO. A. L. Wheeler.
PETRONIUS. M. Heseltine; SENECA: APOCOLOCYNTOSIS. W. H. D. Rouse. Revised by E. H. Warmington.
PHAEDRUS AND BABRIUS (Greek). B. E. Perry.
PLAUTUS. Paul Nixon. 5 Vols.
PLINY: LETTERS, PANEGYRICUS. B. Radice. 2 Vols.
PLINY: NATURAL HISTORY. 10 Vols. Vols. I-V. H. Rackham. Vols. VI-VIII. W. H. S. Jones. Vol. IX. H. Rackham. Vol. X. D. E. Eichholz.
PROPERTIUS. H. E. Butler.
PRUDENTIUS. H. J. Thomson. 2 Vols.
QUINTILIAN. H. E. Butler. 4 Vols.
REMAINS OF OLD LATIN. E. H. Warmington. 4 Vols. Vol. I (Ennius and Caecilius). Vol. II (Livius, Naevius, Pacuvius, Accius). Vol. III (Lucilius, Laws of the XII Tables). Vol. IV (Archaic Inscriptions).
SALLUST. J. C. Rolfe.
SCRIPTORES HISTORIAE AUGUSTAE. D. Magie. 3 Vols.
SENECA: APOCOLOCYNTOSIS. *Cf.* PETRONIUS.
SENECA: EPISTULAE MORALES. R. M. Gummere. 3 Vols.
SENECA: MORAL ESSAYS. J. W. Basore. 3 Vols.
SENECA: NATURALES QUAESTIONES. T. H. Corcoran. 2 Vols.
SENECA: TRAGEDIES. F. J. Miller. 2 Vols.
SENECA THE ELDER M. Winterbottom. 2 Vols.
SIDONIUS: POEMS AND LETTERS. W. B. Anderson. 2 Vols.
SILIUS ITALICUS. J. D. Duff. 2 Vols.
STATIUS. J. H. Mozley. 2 Vols.
SUETONIUS. J. C. Rolfe. 2 Vols.
TACITUS: AGRICOLA AND GERMANIA. M. Hutton; DIALOGUS. Sir Wm. Peterson. Revised by R. M. Ogilvie, E. H. Warmington, M. Winterbottom.
TACITUS: HISTORIES AND ANNALS. C. H. Moore and J. Jackson. 4 Vols.
TERENCE. John Sargeaunt. 2 Vols.
TERTULLIAN: APOLOGIA AND DE SPECTACULIS. T. R. Glover; MINUCIUS FELIX. G. H. Rendall.
VALERIUS FLACCUS. J. H. Mozley.
VARRO: DE LINGUA LATINA. R. G. Kent. 2 Vols.

VELLEIUS PATERCULUS AND RES GESTAE DIVI AUGUSTI. F. W. Shipley.
VIRGIL. H. R. Fairclough. 2 Vols.
VITRUVIUS: DE ARCHITECTURA. F. Granger. 2 Vols.

GREEK AUTHORS

ACHILLES TATIUS. S. Gaselee.
AELIAN: ON THE NATURE OF ANIMALS. A. F. Scholfield. 3 Vols.
AENEAS TACTICUS, ASCLEPIODOTUS AND ONASANDER. The Illinois Greek Club.
AESCHINES. C. D. Adams.
AESCHYLUS. H. Weir Smyth. 2 Vols.
ALCIPHRON, AELIAN AND PHILOSTRATUS: LETTERS. A. R. Benner and F. H. Fobes.
APOLLODORUS. Sir James G. Frazer. 2 Vols.
APOLLONIUS RHODIUS. R. C. Seaton.
THE APOSTOLIC FATHERS. Kirsopp Lake. 2 Vols.
APPIAN: ROMAN HISTORY. Horace White. 4 Vols.
ARATUS. *Cf.* CALLIMACHUS: HYMNS AND EPIGRAMS.
ARISTIDES. C. A. Behr. 4 Vols. Vol. I.
ARISTOPHANES. Benjamin Bickley Rogers. 3 Vols. Verse trans.
ARISTOTLE: ART OF RHETORIC. J. H. Freese.
ARISTOTLE: ATHENIAN CONSTITUTION, EUDEMIAN ETHICS. VIRTUES AND VICES. H. Rackham.
ARISTOTLE: THE CATEGORIES. ON INTERPRETATION. H. P, Cooke; PRIOR ANALYTICS. H. Tredennick.
ARISTOTLE: GENERATION OF ANIMALS. A. L. Peck.
ARISTOTLE: HISTORIA ANIMALIUM. A. L. Peck. 3 Vols. Vols. I and II.
ARISTOTLE: METAPHYSICS. H. Tredennick. 2 Vols.
ARISTOTLE: METEOROLOGICA. H. D. P. Lee.
ARISTOTLE: MINOR WORKS. W. S. Hett. "On Colours," "On Things Heard," "Physiognomics," "On Plants," "On Marvellous Things Heard," "Mechanical Problems," "On Invisible Lines," "Situations and Names of Winds," "On Melissus, Xenophanes, and Gorgias."
ARISTOTLE: NICOMACHEAN ETHICS. H. Rackham.
ARISTOTLE: OECONOMICA AND MAGNA MORALIA. G. C. Armstrong. (With METAPHYSICS, Vol. II.)
ARISTOTLE: ON THE HEAVENS. W. K. C. Guthrie.

THE LOEB CLASSICAL LIBRARY

ARISTOTLE: ON THE SOUL, PARVA NATURALIA, ON BREATH. W. S. Hett.
ARISTOTLE: PARTS OF ANIMALS. A. L. Peck; MOVEMENT AND PROGRESSION OF ANIMALS. E. S. Forster.
ARISTOTLE: PHYSICS. Rev. P. Wicksteed and F. M. Cornford. 2 Vols.
ARISTOTLE: POETICS; LONGINUS ON THE SUBLIME. W. Hamilton Fyfe; DEMETRIUS ON STYLE. W. Rhys Roberts.
ARISTOTLE: POLITICS. H. Rackham.
ARISTOTLE: POSTERIOR ANALYTICS. H. Tredennick; TOPICS. E. S. Forster.
ARISTOTLE: PROBLEMS. W. S. Hett. 2 Vols.
ARISTOTLE: RHETORICA AD ALEXANDRUM. H. Rackham. (With PROBLEMS, Vol. II.)
ARISTOTLE: SOPHISTICAL REFUTATIONS. COMING-TO-BE AND PASSING-AWAY. E. S. Forster; ON THE COSMOS. D. J. Furley.
ARRIAN: HISTORY OF ALEXANDER AND INDICA. 2 Vols. Vol. I. P. Brunt. Vol. II. Rev. E. Iliffe Robson.
ATHENAEUS: DEIPNOSOPHISTAE. C. B. Gulick. 7 Vols.
BABRIUS AND PHAEDRUS (Latin). B. E. Perry.
ST. BASIL: LETTERS. R. J. Deferrari. 4 Vols.
CALLIMACHUS: FRAGMENTS. C. A. Trypanis; MUSAEUS: HERO AND LEANDER. T. Gelzer and C. Whitman.
CALLIMACHUS: HYMNS AND EPIGRAMS, AND LYCOPHRON. A. W. Mair; ARATUS. G. R. Mair.
CLEMENT OF ALEXANDRIA. Rev. G. W. Butterworth.
COLLUTHUS. *Cf.* OPPIAN.
DAPHNIS AND CHLOE. *Cf.* LONGUS.
DEMOSTHENES I: OLYNTHIACS, PHILIPPICS AND MINOR ORATIONS: I-XVII AND XX. J. H. Vince.
DEMOSTHENES II: DE CORONA AND DE FALSA LEGATIONE. C. A. and J. H. Vince.
DEMOSTHENES III: MEIDIAS, ANDROTION, ARISTOCRATES, TIMOCRATES, ARISTOGEITON. J. H. Vince.
DEMOSTHENES IV-VI: PRIVATE ORATIONS AND IN NEAERAM. A. T. Murray.
DEMOSTHENES VII: FUNERAL SPEECH, EROTIC ESSAY, EXORDIA AND LETTERS. N. W. and N. J. DeWitt.
DIO CASSIUS: ROMAN HISTORY. E. Cary. 9 Vols.
DIO CHRYSOSTOM. 5 Vols. Vols. I and II. J. W. Cohoon. Vol. III. J. W. Cohoon and H. Lamar Crosby. Vols. IV and V. H. Lamar Crosby.
DIODORUS SICULUS. 12 Vols. Vols. I-VI. C. H. Oldfather. Vol. VII. C. L. Sherman. Vol. VIII. C. B. Welles. Vols.

IX and X. Russel M. Geer. Vols. XI and XII. F. R. Walton. General Index. Russel M. Geer.

Diogenes Laertius. R. D. Hicks. 2 Vols. New Introduction by H. S. Long.

Dionysius of Halicarnassus: Critical Essays. S. Usher. 2 Vols.

Dionysius of Halicarnassus: Roman Antiquities. Spelman's translation revised by E. Cary. 7 Vols.

Epictetus. W. A. Oldfather. 2 Vols.

Euripides. A. S. Way. 4 Vols. Verse trans.

Eusebius: Ecclesiastical History. Kirsopp Lake and J. E. L. Oulton. 2 Vols.

Galen: On the Natural Faculties. A. J. Brock.

The Greek Anthology. W. R. Paton. 5 Vols.

The Greek Bucolic Poets (Theocritus, Bion, Moschus). J. M. Edmonds.

Greek Elegy and Iambus with the Anacreontea. J. M. Edmonds. 2 Vols.

Greek Mathematical Works. Ivor Thomas. 2 Vols.

Herodes. *Cf.* Theophrastus: Characters.

Herodian. C. R. Whittaker. 2 Vols.

Herodotus. A. D. Godley. 4 Vols.

Hesiod and the Homeric Hymns. H. G. Evelyn White.

Hippocrates and the Fragments of Heracleitus. W. H. S. Jones and E. T. Withington. 4 Vols.

Homer: Iliad. A. T. Murray. 2 Vols.

Homer: Odyssey. A. T. Murray. 2 Vols.

Isaeus. E. S. Forster.

Isocrates. George Norlin and LaRue Van Hook. 3 Vols.

[St. John Damascene]: Barlaam and Ioasaph. Rev. G. R. Woodward, Harold Mattingly and D. M. Lang.

Josephus. 9 Vols. Vols. I-IV. H. St. J. Thackeray. Vol. V. H. St. J. Thackeray and Ralph Marcus. Vols. VI and VII. Ralph Marcus. Vol. VIII. Ralph Marcus and Allen Wikgren. Vol. IX. L. H. Feldman.

Julian. Wilmer Cave Wright. 3 Vols.

Libanius: Selected Works. A. F. Norman. 3 Vols. Vols. I and II.

Longus: Daphnis and Chloe. Thornley's translation revised by J. M. Edmonds; and Parthenius. S. Gaselee.

Lucian. 8 Vols. Vols. I-V. A. M. Harmon. Vol. VI. K. Kilburn. Vols. VII and VIII. M. D. Macleod.

Lycophron. *Cf.* Callimachus: Hymns and Epigrams.

Lyra Graeca. J. M. Edmonds. 3 Vols.

Lysias. W. R. M. Lamb.

PLUTARCH: MORALIA. 17 Vols. Vols. I-V. F. C. Babbitt. Vol. VI. W. C. Helmbold. Vol. VII. P. H. De Lacy and B. Einarson. Vol. VIII. P. A. Clement, H. B. Hoffleit. Vol. IX. E. L. Minar, Jr., F. H. Sandbach, W. C. Helmbold. Vol. X. H. N. Fowler. Vol. XI. L. Pearson, F. H. Sandbach. Vol. XII. H. Cherniss, W. C. Helmbold. Vol. XIII, Parts 1 and 2. H. Cherniss. Vol. XIV. P. H. De Lacy and B. Einarson. Vol. XV. F. H. Sandbach.
PLUTARCH: THE PARALLEL LIVES. B. Perrin. 11 Vols.
POLYBIUS. W. R. Paton. 6 Vols.
PROCOPIUS: HISTORY OF THE WARS. H. B. Dewing. 7 Vols.
PTOLEMY: TETRABIBLOS. *Cf.* MANETHO.
QUINTUS SMYRNAEUS. A. S. Way. Verse trans.
SEXTUS EMPIRICUS. Rev. R. G. Bury. 4 Vols.
SOPHOCLES. F. Storr. 2 Vols. Verse trans.
STRABO: GEOGRAPHY. Horace L. Jones. 8 Vols.
THEOPHRASTUS: CHARACTERS. J. M. Edmonds; HERODES, etc. A. D. Knox.
THEOPHRASTUS: DE CAUSIS PLANTARUM. G. K. K. Link and B. Einarson. 3 Vols. Vol. I.
THEOPHRASTUS: ENQUIRY INTO PLANTS. Sir Arthur Hort. 2 Vols.
THUCYDIDES. C. F. Smith. 4 Vols.
TRYPHIODORUS. *Cf.* OPPIAN.
XENOPHON: ANABASIS. C. L. Brownson.
XENOPHON: CYROPAEDIA. Walter Miller. 2 Vols.
XENOPHON: HELLENICA. C. L. Brownson.
XENOPHON: MEMORABILIA AND OECONOMICUS. E. C. Marchant; SYMPOSIUM AND APOLOGY. O. J. Todd.
XENOPHON: SCRIPTA MINORA. E. C. Marchant and G. W. Bowersock.

CAMBRIDGE, MASS. HARVARD UNIV. PRESS — LONDON WILLIAM HEINEMANN LTD.